History of the

Mass Media

in the United States

History of the
Mass Media
in the United States

An Encyclopedia

EDITED BY MARGARET A. BLANCHARD

Commissioning Editor
Carol J. Burwash

FITZROY DEARBORN PUBLISHERS
CHICAGO · LONDON

For information write to:

FITZROY DEARBORN PUBLISHERS
70 East Walton Street
Chicago, Illinois 60611
U.S.A.

or

310 Regent Street
London w1r 5aj
England

Cataloging-in-Publication Data is available from the Library of Congress and the
British Library

ISBN 1-57958-012-2

First published in the U.S.A. and U.K. 1998

Typeset by Braun-Brumfield, Inc., Ann Arbor, Michigan
Printed by Edwards Brothers, Inc., Ann Arbor, Michigan
Cover designed by Peter Aristedes, Chicago Advertising and Design, Inc.

CONTENTS

EDITOR'S NOTE
AND GUIDE TO USAGE

The mass media in the United States are arguably one of the most powerful institutions in American society today. As sources of information and entertainment, the mass media often are omnipresent institutions exercising their influence in a variety of ways. Although we tend to group newspapers, magazines, books, motion pictures, television, and radio together under the umbrella of "mass media," we really are talking about many media with many different purposes. One of the simplest divisions to make is between informational and entertainment media.

The information function of the mass media, for example, is performed by journalists. These reporters often call themselves members of the "fourth estate" – placing themselves next to national political leaders in terms of importance to the successful running of American society. As members of this "fourth estate," journalists have long claimed special privilege to gather and disseminate news in the United States and, in their roles as information purveyors, have influenced American political, economic, and social life in many ways. As information media have changed over the years and increased in power and authority, concern over the product they disseminate – its accuracy, its effect on national policy, its intrusion into privacy – has increased as well.

The mass media as an entertainment source also have become increasingly controversial in American society in recent years as concern about the impact that entertainment has on the nation's way of life has heightened. Debates over their role and function in American life have become vociferous as lines are drawn over how influential an entertainment source can be in creating or solving lifestyle problems. Studies of the entertainment media's impact on American society go back at least a century; concern over various entertainment media forms predates our ability to conduct scientific studies on their influence.

When looking at the media as purveyors of information or entertainment, we must look across media forms. Books, magazines, newspapers, radio, and television, for example, all provide information to the American public. That information comes in different forms depending on the medium being used, and, according to some communications scholars, each medium provides information that carries a different impact on its consumer. Books, for instance, might call upon readers to think more about a topic. Televised pictures, on the other hand, might evoke a certain emotional response from their audience. The media of entertainment – books, magazines, motion pictures, radio, and television – also have a different impact on consumers than the media of information. Visual forms of communication – television and motion pictures, for instance – are believed to have a greater impact on their audiences than the more cerebral forms of entertainment such as books and magazines.

Even this breakdown, however, does not provide an adequate framework for investigation of the mass media in the United States. In addition to looking at information and entertainment functions, we must be able to study the media on an individual basis to see how each medium has evolved in the American culture and at how each medium has influenced the American culture. Studying how a particular medium has evolved is far easier than studying its impact on American culture, for the evolution is fairly easily traceable as a historical artifact. Finding how the medium has influenced society is harder because many things influence society, with a mass medium being only one factor. Despite this difficulty, the entries that follow provide readers with both the historical chronology of media growth and development and, where appropriate, with the authors' best estimations of how those media have affected society.

Readers of this encyclopedia will find background on how the media reached their positions of authority, influence, and controversy in American society today. The authors who contributed to this work illustrate the development of media forms and the evolution of their practices; they show how media efforts have succeeded and how they have failed; and they illustrate the manner in which media cope with a changing world and changing demands on them.

The media and their ability to influence American society have become an abiding interest to the nation's people who want to know how the media perform and how they affect society. The media relate news events to American citizens and attempt to influence those events. Because the media are shaped by their own prejudices and help to shape the prejudices of the nation, it is important to know as much about this developmental process as possible.

The time period covered in this encyclopedia begins in 1690, when the first newspaper was founded in Boston, Massachusetts, and generally ends in 1990, a convenient end date that provides three hundred years of media history in the United States. Some entries, however, continue into the 1990s in order to help readers trace the background of more current issues and developments, particularly in connection with electronic media such as the Internet, and to place those developments in context with other media in our past. Because the media are so intertwined and the influence of one medium is hard to separate from another in the more contemporary period, for the purposes of this encyclopedia, the mass media are defined as advertising, books, broadcasting in general, cable, magazines, motion pictures, newspapers, photography or photojournalism, public relations, radio, and television. Because of the wide range of topics to be covered and the substantial time span included, several of these topics (such as public relations, magazines, book publishing, and photography) are covered primarily in long, single entries, with a few of the more pertinent developments pulled out for greater investigation. Entries on the purely entertainment side of the media are fewer than those on the information side, although it certainly is acknowledged that the mass media as entertainers clearly are important in American society. The greatest emphasis, however, is on the traditional media for the communication of ideas that influence the body politic.

Articles look at technological, legal, legislative, economic, and political developments that have affected the media or that were substantially affected by them. Entries look at the way in which various media forms developed and changed owing to technological progress, at major court cases and legislative acts that have influenced the way in which the media function, at economic problems and trends that have influenced media growth, and at the way in which the media have covered and influenced the political scene in the United States. Entries on major industrial organizations and important alternative press institutions will introduce readers to the variety, breadth, and depth of the media industry. Encyclopedia articles also introduce major concepts and theories guiding the understanding of media functioning in American society. For those who wish to focus immediately on specific areas of interest, a special topical list of entries is offered in addition to the traditional alphabetical list of articles.

Readers, however, will not find biographies of most leading figures and institutions in the American media community. Major biographical dictionaries exist to provide this information. Although readers will find a few profiles of individuals who helped shape the media industry, most such biographical material will have to be found elsewhere. The same is true for details on major institutions in the field. This volume looks at trends and issues rather than at individual contributors and allows the names of prominent people and institutions to emerge within the context of other entries.

The authors represented in this volume hope that readers develop interests in reading more about various topics. Consequently, almost every entry carries a brief bibliography with it. The encyclopedia also provides a special general bibliography note that presents the titles of works in the field that should help readers explore topics of interest.

The authors of this volume represent not only outstanding scholars in the field of media history but also leading researchers and writers in many of the fields covered. They are current or former editors of major journals, officers in leading professional organizations, and authors of outstanding books and articles in the field. Their qualifications are listed in the Notes on Contributors section at the end of the volume. Each and every one of them, however, had a single goal in accepting an assignment to write for this volume: to make the history of the media more accessible and understandable for those not expert in this field. Their efforts to that end follow.

Margaret A. Blanchard
Chapel Hill, North Carolina
November 1997

ACKNOWLEDGMENTS

Any work such as this must of necessity be a cooperative effort. First and foremost, of course, I must thank my authors, for without their special knowledge of their subjects, their research, and their writing talents, this book would have not been possible. My advisory board was instrumental in suggesting authors and topics for inclusion. Without the help of these people, this encyclopedia would still be in its formative stages.

Equally important was the work of three doctoral students at the School of Journalism and Mass Communication at the University of North Carolina at Chapel Hill. David Copeland, now an assistant professor at Emory & Henry, was there at the beginning. He helped develop the list of entries, track down authors' addresses, and complete the many tasks necessary to getting this project under way. Mei-ling Yang, who is now finishing her dissertation, was invaluable in the middle stages of the project, as she kept track of entries being submitted and managed piles of correspondence with authors. Robin Gallagher, who is now finishing her Ph.D., was vital at the conclusion of the project. She spent countless hours formatting entries on the computer, tracking down missing facts, proofreading, and finding illustrations for the volume. Without the help of these dedicated historians, the encyclopedia would be far less than it is.

Two master's students provided help of less duration but equally as vital. Lesly Hallman of George Washington University tracked down numerous illustrations in the Library of Congress, which helped to enrich the final product. Holly Hart, a student in the School of Journalism and Mass Communication, helped flesh out the authors' bibliographies and prepared the marvelous graphs that you find in the following pages.

The list of thanks could not be complete without mention of Carol Burwash of Fitzroy Dearborn Publishers, who was a fount of enthusiasm and support in this project. With her help and encouragement, I think we all remained reasonably sane throughout this project and brought it successfully to conclusion.

Others were important in helping this project reach its conclusion as well. Dean Richard R. Cole of the School of Journalism and Mass Communication provided encouragement along the way as did Professor John E. Semonche of the UNC-CH History Department. Barbara Semonche, our School's librarian, was invaluable in finding just the right piece of information necessary to fill pesky holes. Colleagues Cathy Packer and Ruth Walden provided support and knew when to ask questions about the encyclopedia's progress and when not to, which is important in any project of this nature. My parents, Earl and Gladys Blanchard, likewise provided support and much needed respite on occasion.

In the end, the encyclopedia is the project of all these people and more. Without this support, this encyclopedia never would have been completed. With their help, it is in your hands. We all hope that you enjoy what you find.

MARGARET A. BLANCHARD
Chapel Hill, North Carolina
November 1997

ADVISORY BOARD

Perry J. Ashley
Barbara Cloud
Jean Folkerts

Michael D. Murray
Patrick S. Washburn

EDITORIAL ASSISTANTS

David A. Copeland
Robin Gallagher
Mei-ling Yang

CONTRIBUTORS

Trudi Abel
David Abrahamson
Edward E. Adams
Craig Allen
Harry Amana
Edd Applegate
Perry J. Ashley
Roy Alden Atwood
James Aucoin
Bruce A. Austin
Donald R. Avery
Gerald J. Baldasty
R. John Ballotti Jr.
S.M.W. Bass
James L. Baughman
Maurine H. Beasley
Jon Bekken

Robert V. Bellamy Jr.
Louise Benjamin
Marvin R. Bensman
Joseph P. Bernt
Claude-Jean Bertrand
Ronald V. Bettig
Ulf Jonas Bjork
Gregory D. Black
Kenneth R. Blake
Margaret A. Blanchard
Stephen G. Bloom
Thomas L. Bonn
James Bow
Patricia Bradley
Mark J. Braun
Bonnie Brennan
Dwight E. Brooks

James A. Brown
Pamela A. Brown
Donald R. Browne
Bruce G. Bryski
Michael Buchholz
Judith M. Buddenbaum
Douglas S. Campbell
Dom Caristi
Michael L. Carlebach
David Cassady
Lucy Shelton Caswell
Edward Caudill
Jean C. Chance
Marc Charisse
Brad Chisholm
Frank J. Chorba
Patrick J. Clinton
Barbara Cloud
Thomas B. Connery
Russell J. Cook
David A. Copeland
R. Stephen Craig
Rita M. Csapó-Sweet
Douglass K. Daniel
Robert Dardenne
Charles N. Davis
John DeMott
Everette E. Dennis
Corley F. Dennison III
Barbara J. DeSanto
Hazel Dicken-Garcia
Donna L. Dickerson
Joseph R. Dominick
Michael C. Donatello
Pamela K. Doyle
Wallace B. Eberhard
Gary R. Edgerton
Michael Emery
Fred F. Endres
Kathleen L. Endres
Ferrell Ervin
Bruce Evensen
George Everett
Irving Fang
Ronald T. Farrar
Fred Fedler
Frank E. Fee Jr.
John P. Ferré
Raymond Fielding
Kathy R. Fitzpatrick
Dolores Flamiano
Elizabeth Lynne Flocke
Jean Folkerts
Julia R. Fox
Warren T. Francke
Ralph Frasca
John P. Freeman
Robin Gallagher
Ronald Garay
Timothy W. Gleason

Corban Goble
Donald G. Godfrey
Douglas Gomery
David Gordon
Agnes Hooper Gottlieb
Lewis L. Gould
Thomas Gould
Karla K. Gower
Norma Fay Green
David W. Guth
Paul Gutjahr
Bradley J. Hamm
Christopher Hanson
Margot Hardenbergh
Anthony Hatcher
Elsie Hebert
T.J. Hemlinger
Jonathan Y. Hill
Glenn A. Himebaugh
Richard F. Hixson
Laura E. Hlavach
Louis W. Hodges
Jack Hodgson
Carol E. Holstead
Herbert H. Howard
Haney Howell
Kelly W.A. Huff
Thomas A. Hughes
Carol Sue Humphrey
William E. Huntzicker
Frankie Hutton
Matthew F. Jacobs
James Phillip Jeter
Thomas J. Johnson
Anne Johnston
Clifford A. Jones
Donald J. Jung
Lynda Lee Kaid
Samuel V. Kennedy III
Lauren Kessler
Richard B. Kielbowicz
Paulette D. Kilmer
Gorham A. Kindem
Carolyn Kitch
Jerry W. Knudson
Elizabeth M. Koehler
Arati R. Korwar
Peggy J. Kreshel
Philip J. Lane
Gene D. Lanier
Karla M. Larson
Robert H. Lawrence
Linda Lawson
Thomas Letts
Robert W. Leweke
Charles W. Lewis
Regina Louise Lewis
Lawrence W. Lichty
Louis W. Liebovich
Val E. Limburg

Laura R. Linder
William R. Lindley
Greg Lisby
Karen K. List
Steven Livingston
Gary Lovisi
Linda Lumsden
Gregory Makris
Mary S. Mander
Virginia Mansfield-Richardson
Charles H. Marler
Peter E. Mayeux
Jerilyn S. McIntyre
Joseph P. McKerns
Milan D. Meeske
Dan Pyle Millar
Jerry L. Miller
Karen S. Miller
Bruce Mims
Mick Mulcrone
Priscilla Coit Murphy
Sharon M. Murphy
Michael D. Murray
Dean Nelson
John Nerone
Mark Neuzil
David Paul Nord
Amy Kiste Nyberg
Robert M. Ogles
Arlo Oviatt
Cathy Packer
Anna R. Paddon
Darwin Payne
Abe Peck
John C. Peterson
Sarah Wright Plaster
Stephen Ponder
Alf Pratte
Randy Reddick
Barbara Straus Reed
Tom Reilly
Carol Reuss
Jane Rhodes
Sam G. Riley
Ford Risley
Donald A. Ritchie
Milagros Rivera-Sanchez
Brett Robbs
Nancy L. Roberts
Bruce Roche
América Rodriguez
Patricia B. Rose
Susan Dente Ross
Dennis E. Russell

Jeffrey Rutenbeck
Jennifer Scanlon
Richard Scheidenhelm
Michael Schudson
Richard A. Schwarzlose
Barbara P. Semonche
Mary Alice Shaver
Donald L. Shaw
Jon A. Shidler
Todd F. Simon
Wm. David Sloan
Steven Smethers
C. Zoe Smith
Carol Smith
F. Leslie Smith
Kim A. Smith
Penny Pence Smith
Ted Curtis Smythe
James D. Startt
Lowndes F. Stephens
Carl Sessions Stepp
Christopher H. Sterling
Dulcie M. Straughan
Rodger Streitmatter
Herbert Strentz
Teresa Jo Styles
David E. Sumner
Michael S. Sweeney
Sue D. Taylor
John Tebbel
Dwight L. Teeter Jr.
Athan G. Theoharis
Joseph V. Trahan III
Trysh Travis
Debbie Treise
Lucilla Vargas
Stephen Vaughn
Sarah Wadsworth
Ruth Walden
Kay Walsh
Kim Walsh-Childers
Patrick S. Washburn
Janet Wasko
John C. Watson
W. Richard Whitaker
Julie K. Hedgepeth Williams
Michael Williams
Betty Houchin Winfield
Michael Winship
Thomas L. Yancy
Mei-ling Yang
Mark E. Young
Eric J. Zanot
Dhyana Ziegler

ALPHABETICAL LIST
OF ENTRIES

TOPICAL LIST OF ENTRIES

COMMONLY USED TERMS
AND ABBREVIATIONS

AAAA American Association of Advertising Agencies. Formed in 1917 by more than 100 advertising agencies to help standardize agency practices.

ABC American Broadcasting Company. Began as a radio network in 1945. Originally established when the federal judicial system ordered NBC to divest itself of its NBC-Blue network.

ABC Audit Bureau of Circulations. Established in 1914 to review and verify publication circulation figures.

ACT Action for Children's Television. Founded in 1968 by a group of mothers in Boston, Massachusetts, the group has successfully lobbied for major changes in television programming aimed at children.

AFN American Forces Network. Specialized media serving the men and women in the U.S. military dating back at least to 1779.

AIM Accuracy in Media. A conservative media watchdog organization established in 1969.

ALA American Library Association. Formed in 1876 to promote library and librarian interests, it has a substantial program promoting intellectual freedom.

Alien and Sedition Acts of 1798. Legislation enacted to curtail criticism of government, particularly by supporters of Thomas Jefferson.

ANPA American Newspapers Publishers Association. Organization of leaders of the business operations of the daily press established in 1885.

AP Associated Press. The nation's dominant news provider to various media forms, established under that name for the first time in 1860.

APR American Public Radio. Established in 1981 by non-commercial broadcasters who felt that National Public Radio was not permitting enough autonomy. It distributes but does not produce programming.

ASNE American Society of Newspaper Editors. Organization of newspaper editors established in 1922. Group wrote one of the first major codes of ethics for the newspaper profession, the Canons of Journalism.

AT&T American Telephone and Telegraph. Formed in 1885, it has long been a major player in the telecommunication business, especially in the development of radio.

BBB Better Business Bureau. Established in the early twentieth century to promote ethics in the marketplace through voluntary self-regulation.

CBS Columbia Broadcasting System. Established as a radio network in 1927.

CNN Cable News Network. Twenty-four-hour-a-day news service launched by cable entrepreneur Ted Turner in 1980.

Communications Act of 1934. Legislation that generally reenacted the Federal Radio Act of 1927. Serves as basis for regulation of electronic media today.

CPB Corporation for Public Broadcasting. Established by congressional legislation in 1967 to support noncommercial radio and television programming.

CPI Committee on Public Information. World War I agency that combined voluntary censorship, information provider, and propaganda roles. Also known as the Creel Committee after its chairman, former journalist George Creel.

Equal time provision. Part of the Radio Act of 1927 that requires equal opportunities to use the airwaves be offered to all legally qualified candidates for public office if such opportunities are offered to any candidate.

Espionage Act of 1917. World War I legislation designed to catch spies but used more often to punish those who dissented from the war effort.

Fairness Doctrine. A 1949 FCC ruling that allowed broadcast outlets to editorialize, providing they allowed opposing perspectives to be aired. The Fairness Doctrine was dropped by the FCC in 1987 as part of its efforts to deregulate broadcasting.

FCC Federal Communications Commission. Federal agency that regulates electronic communication, established by the Communications Act of 1934.

FDA Food and Drug Administration. Established in 1927 to monitor and ensure safety in food and drugs. Its duties include review of almost all product labeling and some limited supervision of advertising.

FECA Federal Election Campaign Act. A 1972 effort to reform campaigning for federal office. Oft-amended, the act still serves at the primary legislation governing campaign spending.

FOIA Freedom of Information Act. Enacted in 1966 to provide systematized access to federal government records.

FRC Federal Radio Commission. First federal agency regulating broadcasting, established by the Radio Act of 1927.

FTC Federal Trade Commission. Established in 1914 and given a variety of powers relating to unfair methods of competition in interstate commerce, including ability to review advertising alleged to be false and deceptive.

GE General Electric. Long-time participant in the development of broadcasting equipment and programming. A parent of RCA and of NBC.

INS International News Service. Founded in 1910 by William Randolph Hearst to serve his and other newspapers denied service by the Associated Press.

JOA Joint Operating Agreement. Cooperative agreements between competing newspapers that allow the weaker publication to use some of the facilities of the strong newspaper in order to stay alive. Made legal by the Newspaper Preservation Act of 1970.

Mayflower Decision. A 1940 ruling by the Federal Communications Commission that forbade radio stations to broadcast editorials.

NAA Newspaper Association of America. Combination of seven leading newspaper trade associations established in 1992.

NAB National Association of Broadcasters. Organization of broadcasters established in 1923. Presented its first code of ethics regarding programming and advertising practices in 1929.

NARB National Advertising Review Board. Established in 1971 by various constituencies in the advertising industry, its work focuses on self-regulation of national advertising that may be misleading and deceptive.

NBC National Broadcasting Company. First radio network (NBC-Red) aired its first four-hour programming block in 1926. A second NBC network (NBC-Blue) began broadcasting in 1927.

NET National Educational Television. Early programming cooperative for noncommercial programming, operating somewhat like a commercial network in terms of program production and sharing.

NPR National Public Radio. Serves as a program distributor and production service designed to interconnect radio outlets.

OC Office of Censorship. Office established in 1941 to oversee volunteer censorship operation in World War II. Headed by Byron Price, an Associated Press executive.

O&O Owned and Operated. Refers to broadcast outlets owned and operated by one of the major broadcasting networks.

OWI Office of War Information. Office established in 1942 to promote the American war effort at home and abroad. Headed by broadcast commentator Elmer Davis.

PBS Public Broadcast System. Noncommercial broadcast operation that interconnects public television stations.

Radio Act of 1927. Initial legislation governing radio.

Sedition Act of 1918. Further World War I effort to quiet spoken and written criticism of the war and federal military and civilian officers.

UP United Press (1882). Established in 1882 by newspapers outside the Associated Press's membership.

UPA United Press Associations (1907). Established in 1907 by E.W. Scripps to provide his newspaper chain with news because most of his papers did not belong to the Associated Press. Later known as the United Press.

UPI United Press International. Formed by a merger of the United Press and the International News Service in 1958.

GENERAL BIBLIOGRAPHY

A Brief Guide to Reference Sources

Media history studies, long of interest to a few scholars, have increased substantially in number in recent years as curiosity has grown about how the media reached their positions of power in the United States and as the industry itself has become more interested in its past. Courses on the development and influence of media institutions dot college and university curricula across the nation. Elderhostels study the growth and development of the mass media as well. And within the last decade or so, for instance, the American Society of Newspaper Editors has launched a fairly major undertaking to preserve newspapers in various states and to encourage research projects into the newspaper business around the country. More recently, The Freedom Forum has launched its Newseum, a museum of news and newsmaking events, in Arlington, Virginia.

Various members of the scholarly community have been assembling dictionaries and encyclopedias of biographical information about individuals and institutions, such as the Dictionary of Literary Biography studies of newspaper figures edited by Perry J. Ashley and the study of magazines edited by Sam G. Riley, both of whom contributed to this volume. Histories of particular time periods in media history also are appearing with greater frequency, such as the series spanning media history being edited by Wm. David Sloan and James G. Startt, both of whom wrote for this volume.

Biographies of individuals and of institutions abound, and one may read about everyone from John Peter Zenger to Al Neuharth in biographies and autobiographies. Studies of institutions ranging from the *New York Times* to CBS dot library shelves. Any of these books will enrich your study of topics covered less in-depth in the pages that follow.

Listed below are some of the books that you should approach for good overviews of your topics of interest. They appear in this special list because they were cited repeatedly by authors as outstanding books in their fields. Rather then list each volume in numerous entries, they have been grouped for easier access here.

General Media History

Emery, Edwin, and Michael C. Emery, *The Press and America: An Interpretive History of the Mass Media*, 8th ed., Boston: Allyn and Bacon, 1996

Folkerts, Jean, and Dwight L. Teeter, Jr., *Voices of a Nation: A History of Mass Media in the United States*, New York: Macmillan, 1989; 3rd ed., Boston: Allyn and Bacon, 1998

Hudson, Frederic, *Journalism in the United States from 1690 to 1872*, New York: Harper & Brothers, 1873

Kobre, Sidney, *Development of American Journalism*, Dubuque, Iowa: Wm. C. Brown, 1969

Lee, Alfred M., *The Daily Newspaper in America: The Evolution of a Social Instrument*, New York: Macmillan, 1937

Mott, Frank Luther, *American Journalism: A History of Newspapers in the United States Through 250 Years, 1690–1940*, New York: Macmillan, 1941

Sloan, W. David, James G. Stovall, and James D. Startt, *The Media in America: A History*, Worthington, Ohio: Publishing Horizons, 1989; 3rd ed., Northport, Alabama: Vision, 1996

Tebbel, John W., *The Media in America*, New York: Crowell, 1974

Thomas, Isaiah, *The History of Printing in America*, Worcester, Massachusetts, 1810; reprinted, New York: B. Franklin, 1972

Advertising

Fox, Stephen, *The Mirror Makers: A History of American Advertising and Its Creators*, New York: William Morrow, 1984

Marchand, Roland, *Advertising the American Dream: Making Way for Modernity, 1920–1940*, Berkeley: University of California Press, 1985

Pope, Daniel A., *The Making of Modern Advertising*, New York: Basic, 1983

Presbrey, Frank, *The History and Development of Advertising*, Garden City, New York: Doubleday, 1929

Wood, James Playsted, *The Story of Advertising*, New York: Ronald, 1958

Alternative Media

Kessler, Lauren, *The Dissident Press: Alternative Journalism in American History*, Beverly Hills, California: Sage, 1984

Wilson, Clint C., and Félix Gutiérrez, *Race, Multiculturalism, and the Media: From Mass to Class Communication*, 2nd ed., Thousand Oaks, California: Sage, 1995

Books

Tebbel, John W., *Between the Covers: The Rise and Transformation of Book Publishing in America*, New York: Oxford University Press, 1987

_____, *A History of Book Publishing in the United States*, 4 vols., New York: Bowker, 1972–1981

Broadcasting

Barnouw, Erik, *A History of Broadcasting in the United States*, 3 vols., New York: Oxford University Press, 1966–1970

_____, *Tube of Plenty: The Evolution of American Television*, New York: Oxford University Press, 1975; rev. ed., New York and Oxford: Oxford University Press, 1982; 2nd rev. ed., New York: Oxford University Press, 1990

Bittner, John R., *Broadcasting: An Introduction*, Englewood Cliffs, New Jersey: Prentice-Hall, 1980

Chester, Giraud, Garnet R. Garrison, and Edgar E. Willis, *Television and Radio*, 5th ed., Englewood Cliffs, New Jersey: Prentice-Hall, 1978

Gross, Lynne S., *See/Hear: An Introduction to Broadcasting*, Dubuque, Iowa: Wm. C. Brown, 1979

Head, Sydney W., Christopher H. Sterling, and Lemuel B. Schofield, *Broadcasting in America: A Survey of Electronic Media*, 7th ed., Boston: Houghton Mifflin, 1994

Kahn, Frank, ed., *Documents of American Broadcasting*, 3rd ed., Englewood Cliffs, New Jersey: Prentice-Hall, 1978

Sterling, Christopher H., and John M. Kittross, *Stay Tuned: A Concise History of American Broadcasting*, 2nd ed., Belmont, California: Wadsworth, 1990

Magazines

Ford, James L.C., *Magazines for Millions: The Story of Specialized Publications*, Carbondale: Southern Illinois Press, 1969

Mott, Frank Luther, *A History of American Magazines*, 5 vols., Cambridge, Massachusetts: Harvard University Press, 1938

Peterson, Theodore, *Magazines in the Twentieth Century*, Urbana: University of Illinois Press, 1956

Tebbel, John W., *The American Magazine: A Compact History*, New York: Hawthorn, 1969

Tebbel, John W., and Mary Ellen Zuckerman, *The Magazine in America, 1741–1990*, New York: Oxford University Press, 1991

Wood, James Playsted, *Magazines in the United States*, 3rd ed., New York: Ronald, 1971

Media Law

Bezanson, Randall P., Gilbert Cranberg, and John Soloski, *Libel Law and the Press: Myth and Reality*, New York: Free Press, 1987; London: Collier Macmillan, 1987

Bittner, John R., *Law and Regulation of Electronic Media*, 2nd ed., Englewood Cliffs, New Jersey: Prentice-Hall, 1994

Gillmor, Donald M., *Power, Publicity, and the Abuse of Libel Law*, New York: Oxford University Press, 1992

Gillmor, Donald M., Jerome A. Barron, Todd F. Simon, and Herbert A. Terry, *Mass Communication Law: Cases and Comment*, 5th ed., St. Paul, Minnesota: West, 1990

Holsinger, Ralph L., and Jon Dilts, *Media Law*, 3rd ed., New York: McGraw-Hill, 1994

Middleton, Kent R., and Bill F. Chamberlin, *The Law of Public Communication*, 3rd ed., New York: Longman, 1993

Pember, Don R., *Mass Media Law*, 3rd ed., Dubuque, Iowa: Wm. C. Brown, 1984

Sanford, Bruce W., *Libel and Privacy*, 2nd ed., Englewood Cliffs, New Jersey: Prentice Hall Law & Business, 1991

Teeter, Dwight, and Don R. Le Duc, *Law of Mass Communications: Freedom and Control of Print and Broadcast Media*, 7th ed., Westbury, New York: Foundation, 1992

News and Newspapers

Baldasty, Gerald, *The Commercialization of News in the Nineteenth Century*, Madison: University of Wisconsin Press, 1992

Dicken Garcia, Hazel, *Journalistic Standards in Nineteenth-Century America*, Madison: University of Wisconsin Press, 1989

Schiller, Dan, *Objectivity and the News: The Public and the Rise of Commercial Journalism*, Philadelphia: University of Pennsylvania Press, 1981

Schudson, Michael, *Discovering the News: A Social History of American Newspapers*, New York: Basic, 1978

Schwarzlose, Richard A., *The Nation's Newsbrokers*, 2 vols., Evanston, Illinois: Northwestern University Press, 1989–1990

Stephens, Mitchell, *The History of News: From the Drum to the Satellite*, New York: Viking, 1988

Photography

Carlebach, Michael L., *The Origins of Photojournalism in America*, Washington, D.C.: Smithsonian Institution Press, 1992

Newhall, Beaumont, *The History of Photography: From 1839 to the Present Day*, 4th ed., New York: Museum of Modern Art, 1964

Presidents and the Press

Pollard, James E., *The Presidents and the Press*, New York: Macmillan, 1947

Tebbel, John W., and Sarah Miles Watts, *The Press and the Presidency: From George Washington to Ronald Reagan*, New York: Oxford University Press, 1985

A

Abolitionist Press

Antebellum antislavery publications

Abolitionist journalism in the United States can be traced to the seventeenth century with the growth of the Atlantic slave trade. Quakers were in the forefront of publishing tracts and broadsheets denouncing slavery, and antislavery commentary could be found in colonial newspapers. It was not until the nineteenth century, however, that an established press emerged with its stated purpose being the abolition of slavery.

During the antebellum period, upwards of 50 abolitionist periodicals were published by individuals and organizations. Two of the earliest newspapers were the *Manumission Intelligencer,* founded in 1819 by Elihu Embree in Jonesboro, Tennessee, and the *Genius of Universal Emancipation,* founded by Benjamin Lundy in 1821 in Mount Pleasant, Ohio. Lundy, a Quaker, dedicated his life to abolition after witnessing the realities of slavery while living in West Virginia. In 1824, he moved the paper to Baltimore, Maryland, in an attempt to raise circulation. Like other abolitionist journalists who followed him, Lundy struggled to keep the weekly *Genius* afloat; the number of subscribers rose slowly from 50 in 1824 to 350 two years later. The paper was moribund by 1830, and in 1836 Lundy established another publication called the *National Enquirer* in Philadelphia. This newspaper became the official organ of the Pennsylvania Anti-Slavery Society, which ensured it a modicum of financial security.

Originally, abolitionist journalism was the sole province of white Americans who felt a religious, moral, or political obligation to end slavery. This situation changed in 1827 when two African Americans – Samuel E. Cornish and John B. Russwurm – founded the first newspaper that would fight slavery from the perspective of those subjugated by the "peculiar institution." Their newspaper, *Freedom's Journal,* was launched in New York City to give African Americans a vehicle in which to plead their own cause, counteract racist stereotypes prevalent in the press, and disseminate news about their communities. Although *Freedom's Journal* folded within two years, it paved the way for numerous other black-owned abolitionist journals, including the *Colored American* (1837), the *Mirror of Liberty* (1838), the

Mystery (1843), the *North Star* (1847), and the *Weekly Anglo-African* (1859).

Many scholars date the beginnings of widespread abolitionist activism to the founding of William Lloyd Garrison's fiery newspaper, the *Liberator,* in 1831. Garrison had worked with Benjamin Lundy on the *Genius of Universal Emancipation* for two years before launching his own publication in Boston. With little money, Garrison, then 25, relied heavily on the support of Northern free blacks as well as white abolitionists. The *Liberator* cast aside the gradualist, nonconfrontational politics of Lundy's paper to espouse an uncompromising call for immediate abolition. The *Liberator* became the most influential – and controversial – voice of the antislavery movement; it was published continuously until 1865.

The first group to organize under the banner of radical abolition was the New England Anti-Slavery Society, founded in Boston in 1832. Later, as the Massachusetts Anti-Slavery Society, it was a key source of financial and moral support for the *Liberator.* In December 1833, abolitionists across the United States met in Philadelphia to form the American Anti-Slavery Society, spearheaded by Garrison, and the society established its own official organ, the *Emancipator.* When opponents of Garrison and his followers split from the American Anti-Slavery Society in 1840, they took the *Emancipator* with them, and the Garrison camp founded yet another newspaper, the *National Anti-Slavery Standard.* This new publication offered abolitionist women an early opportunity in journalism. Lydia Maria Child, who had been a successful novelist before joining the antislavery movement, edited the *National Anti-Slavery Standard* for two years. The paper's next editor was Maria Weston Chapman, a founding member of the Boston Female Antislavery Society.

Most abolitionist newspapers combined polemics, news, and literature. They were usually four-page broadsheets of six to eight columns, and their front pages frequently were devoted to long letters or editorials on political matters related to slavery or reprints of congressional debates and presidential addresses. They customarily borrowed liberally from other abolitionist sheets, allowing the *Liberator,* for example, to carry stories from the *North Star,* the *Pennsylvania Freeman,* and other relevant journals in each issue. The abolitionist newspapers spurred debate among the

THE LIBERATOR.

VOL. I.] WILLIAM LLOYD GARRISON AND ISAAC KNAPP, PUBLISHERS. [NO. 1.

BOSTON, MASSACHUSETTS.] OUR COUNTRY IS THE WORLD—OUR COUNTRYMEN ARE MANKIND. [SATURDAY, JANUARY 1, 1831.

THE LIBERATOR
IS PUBLISHED WEEKLY
AT NO. 6, MERCHANTS' HALL.

WM. L. GARRISON, EDITOR.

Stephen Foster, Printer.

TERMS.

☞ Two Dollars per annum, payable in advance.

☞ Agents allowed every sixth copy gratis.

☞ No subscription will be received for a shorter period than six months.

☞ All letters and communications must be POST PAID.

THE LIBERATOR.

THE SALUTATION.

To date my being from the opening year,
I come, a stranger in this busy sphere,
Where some I meet perchance may pause and ask,
What is my name, my purpose, or my task?

My name is 'LIBERATOR'! I propose
To hurl my shafts at freedom's deadliest foes!
My task is hard—for I am charged to save
Man from his brother!—to redeem the slave!

Ye who may hear, and yet condemn my cause,
Say, shall the best of Nature's holy laws
Be trodden down? and shall her open veins
Flow but for cement to her offspring's chains?

Art thou a parent? shall thy children be
Rent from thy breast, like branches from the tree,
And doom'd to servitude, in helplessness,
On other shores, and thou ask no redress?

Thou, in whose bosom glows the sacred flame
Of filial love, say, if the tyrant came,
To force thy parent shrieking from thy sight,
Would thy heart bleed—*because thy face is white?*

Art thou a brother? shall thy sister twine
Her feeble arm in agony on thine,
And thou not lift the heel, nor aim the blow
At him who bears her off to life-long wo?

Art thou a sister? will no desp'rate cry
Awake thy sleeping brother, while thine eye
Beholds the fetters locking on the limb
Stretched out in rest, which hence, must end, for him?

Art thou a lover?—no! naught e'er was found
In lover's breast, save cords of love, that bound
Man to his kind! then, thy professions save!
Forswear affection, or release thy slave!

Thou who art kneeling at thy Maker's shrine,
Ask if Heaven takes such offerings as thine!
If in thy bonds the son of Afric sighs,
Far higher than thy prayer his groan will rise!

God is a God of mercy, and would see
The prison-doors unbarr'd—the bondmen free!
He is a God of truth, with purer eyes
Than to behold the oppressor's sacrifice!

Avarice, thy cry and thine insatiate thirst
Make man consent to see his brother cursed!
Tears, sweat and blood thou drink'st, but in their turn,
They shall cry 'more!' while vengeance bids thee burn.

The Lord hath said it!—who shall him gainsay?
He says, 'the wicked, they shall go away'—
Who are the wicked?—Contradict who can,
They are the oppressors of their fellow man!

Aid me, NEW ENGLAND! 'tis my hope in you
Which gives me strength my purpose to pursue!
Do you not hear your sister States resound
With Afric's cries to have her sons unbound?

* * *

TO THE PUBLIC.

In the month of August, I issued proposals for publishing 'THE LIBERATOR' in Washington city; but the enterprise, though hailed in different sections of the country, was palsied by public indifference. Since that time, the removal of the Genius of Universal Emancipation to the Seat of Government has rendered less imperious the establishment of a similar periodical in that quarter.

During my recent tour for the purpose of exciting the minds of the people by a series of discourses on the subject of slavery, every place that I visited gave fresh evidence of the fact, that a greater revolution in public sentiment was to be effected in the free states—*and particularly in New-England*—than at the south. I found contempt more bitter, opposition more active, detraction more relentless, prejudice more stubborn, and apathy more frozen, than among slave owners themselves. Of course, there were individual exceptions to the contrary. This state of things afflicted, but did not dishearten me. I determined, at every hazard, to lift up the standard of emancipation in the eyes of the nation, *within sight of Bunker Hill and in the birth place of liberty.* That standard is now unfurled; and long may it float, unhurt by the spoliations of time or the missiles of a desperate foe—yea, till every chain be broken, and every bondman set free! Let southern oppressors tremble—let their secret abettors tremble—let their northern apologists tremble—let all the enemies of the persecuted blacks tremble.

I deem the publication of my original Prospectus* unnecessary, as it has obtained a wide circulation. The principles therein inculcated will be steadily pursued in this paper, excepting that I shall not array myself as the political partisan of any man. In defending the great cause of human rights, I wish to derive the assistance of all religions and of all parties.

Assenting to the 'self-evident truth' maintained in the American Declaration of Independence, 'that all men are created equal, and endowed by their Creator with certain inalienable rights—among which are life, liberty and the pursuit of happiness,' I shall strenuously contend for the immediate enfranchisement of our slave population. In Park-street Church, on the Fourth of July, 1829, in an address on slavery, I unreflectingly assented to the popular but pernicious doctrine of *gradual* abolition. I seize this opportunity to make a full and unequivocal recantation, and thus publicly to ask pardon of my God, of my country, and of my brethren the poor slaves, for having uttered a sentiment so full of timidity, injustice and absurdity. A similar recantation, from my pen, was published in the Genius of Universal Emancipation at Baltimore, in September, 1829. My conscience is now satisfied.

I am aware, that many object to the severity of my language; but is there not cause for severity? I *will be* as harsh as truth, and as uncompromising as justice. On this subject, I do not wish to think, or speak, or write, with moderation. No! no! Tell a man whose house is on fire, to give a moderate alarm; tell him to moderately rescue his wife from the hands of the ravisher; tell the mother to gradually extricate her babe from the fire into which it has fallen;—but urge me not to use moderation in a cause like the present. I am in earnest—I will not equivocate—I will not excuse—I will not retreat a single inch—AND I WILL BE HEARD. The apathy of the people is enough to make every statue leap from its pedestal, and to hasten the resurrection of the dead.

It is pretended, that I am retarding the cause of emancipation by the coarseness of my invective, and the precipitancy of my measures. *The charge is not true.* On this question my influence,—humble as it is,—is felt at this moment to a considerable extent, and shall be felt in coming years—not perniciously, but beneficially—not as a curse, but as a blessing; and posterity will bear testimony that I was right. I desire to thank God, that he enables me to disregard 'the fear of man which bringeth a snare,' and to speak his truth in its simplicity and power. And here I close with this fresh dedication:

'Oppression! I have seen thee, face to face,
And met thy cruel eye and cloudy brow;
But thy soul-withering glance I fear not now—
For dread to prouder feelings doth give place
Of deep abhorrence! Scorning the disgrace
Of slavish knees that at thy footstool bow,
I also kneel—but with far other vow
Do hail thee and thy herd of hirelings base:—
I swear, while life-blood warms my throbbing veins,
Still to oppose and thwart, with heart and hand,
Thy brutalising sway—till Afric's chains
Are burst, and Freedom rules the rescued land,—
Trampling Oppression and his iron rod:
Such is the vow I take—SO HELP ME GOD!'

WILLIAM LLOYD GARRISON.

BOSTON, January 1, 1831.

*I would here offer my grateful acknowledgments to those editors who so promptly and generously inserted my Proposals. They must give me an available opportunity to repay their liberality.

DISTRICT OF COLUMBIA.

What do many of the professed enemies of slavery mean, by heaping all their reproaches upon the south, and asserting that the crime of oppression is not national? What power but Congress—and Congress by the authority of the American people—has jurisdiction over the District of Columbia? That District is rotten with the plague, and stinks in the nostrils of the world. Though it is the Seat of our National Government,—open to the daily inspection of foreign ambassadors,—and ostensibly opulent with the congregated wisdom, virtue and intelligence of the land,—yet a fouler spot scarcely exists on earth. In it the worst features of slavery are exhibited; and as a mart for slave traders, it is unequalled. These facts are well known to our two or three hundred representatives, but no remedy is proposed; they are known, if not minutely at least generally, to our whole population,—but who calls for redress?

Hitherto, a few straggling petitions, relative to this subject, have gone into Congress; but they have been too few to denote much public anxiety, or to command a deferential notice. It is certainly time that a vigorous and systematic effort should be made, from one end of the country to the other, to pull down that national monument of oppression which towers up in the District. We do hope that the 'earthquake voice' of the people will this session shake the black fabric to its foundation.

The following petition is now circulating in this city, and has obtained several valuable signatures. A copy may be found at the Bookstore of LINCOLN & EDMANDS, No. 59, Washington-street, for a few days longer, where all the friends of the cause are earnestly invited to go and subscribe.

Petition to Congress for the Abolition of Slavery in the District of Columbia.

To the Honorable Senate and House of Representatives of the United States of America in Congress assembled, the petition of the undersigned citizens of Boston in Massachusetts and its vicinity respectfully represents—

That your petitioners are deeply impressed with the evils arising from the existence of slavery in the District of Columbia. While our Declaration of Independence boldly proclaims as self-evident truths, 'that all men are created equal, that they are endowed by their Creator with certain inalienable rights, that among these are life, liberty, and the pursuit of happiness,'—at the very seat of government human beings are born, almost daily, whom the laws pronounce to be from their birth, not *equal* to other men, and who are, for life, deprived of *liberty* and the free *pursuit of happiness.* The inconsistency of the conduct of our nation with its political creed, has brought down upon it the just and severe reprehension of foreign nations.

In addition to the other evils flowing from slavery, both moral and political, which it is needless to specify, circumstances have rendered this District a common resort for traders in human flesh, who bring into it their captives in chains, and lodge them in places of confinement, previously to their being carried to the markets of the south and west.

From the small number of slaves in the District of Columbia, and the moderate proportion which they bear to the free population there, the difficulties, which in most of the slaveholding states oppose the restoration of this degraded class of men to their natural rights, do not exist.

Your petitioners therefore pray that Congress will, without delay, take such measures for the immediate or gradual abolition of Slavery in the District of Columbia, and for preventing the bringing of slaves into that District for purposes of traffic, in such mode, as may be thought advisable; and that suitable provision be made for the education of all free blacks and colored children in the District, thus to preserve them from continuing, even as free men, an unenlightened and degraded caste.

If any individual should be unmoved, either by the petition or the introductory remarks, the following article will startle his apathy, unless he be morally dead—dead—dead. Read it—read it! The language of the editor is remarkable for its energy, considering the quarter whence it emanates. After all, we are not the only fanatics in the land!

[From the Washington Spectator, of Dec. 4.]

THE SLAVE TRADE IN THE CAPITAL.

'The tender ties of father, husband, friend,
All bonds of nature in that moment end,
And each endures, while yet he draws his breath.
A stroke as fatal as the scythe of death;
They lose in tears, the far receding shore,
But not the thought that they must meet no more!'

It is well, perhaps, the American people should know, that while we reiterate our boasts of liberty in the ears of the nations, and send back across the Atlantic our shouts of joy at the triumph of liberty in France, we ourselves are busily engaged in the work of oppression. Yes, let it be known to the citizens of America, that at the very time when the procession which contained the President of the United States and his Cabinet was marching in triumph to the Capitol, to celebrate the victory of the French people over their oppressors, another kind of procession was marching another way, and that consisted of colored human beings, handcuffed in pairs, and driven along by what had the appearance of a man on a horse! A similar scene was repeated on Saturday last; a *drove* consisting of males and females chained in couples, starting from Roby's tavern on foot, for Alexandria, where, with others, they are to embark on board a slave-ship in waiting to convey them to the South. While we are writing, a colored man enters our room, and begs us to inform him if we can point out any person who will redeem his friend now immured in Alexandria jail, in a state of distress amounting almost to distraction.* He has been a faithful servant of a revolutionary officer who recently died—has been sold at auction—parted from affectionate parents—and from decent and mourning friends. Our own servant, with others, of whom we can speak in commendatory terms, went down to Alexandria to bid him farewell, but they were refused admission to his cell, as was said, 'the sight of his friends made him feel so.' He bears the reputation of a pious man. It is but a few weeks since we saw a ship with her cargo of slaves in the port of Norfolk, Va. upon passing up the river, saw another ship off Alexandria, swarming with the victims of human cupidity. Such are the scenes enacting in the heart of the American nation. Oh patriotism! where is thy indignation? Oh philanthropy! where is thy grief? OH SHAME, WHERE IS THY BLUSH? Well may the generous and noble minded O'Connell say of the American citizen, '*I tell him he is a hypocrite. Look at the stain in your star-spangled standard that was never struck down in battle. I turn from the Declaration of American Independence, and I tell him that he has declared to God and man a lie, and before God and man I arraign him as a hypocrite.*' Yes, thou soul of fire, glorious O'Connell, if thou could but witness the spectacles in Washington that make the genius of liberty droop her head in shame, and weep her tears away in deep silence and undissembled sorrow, you would lift your voice even to tones of thunder, but you would make yourself heard. Where is the O'Connell of this republic that will plead for the EMANCIPATION OF THE DISTRICT OF COLUMBIA? These shocking scenes must cease from amongst us, or we must cease to call ourselves free; ay, and we must cease to expect the mercy of God—we must prepare for the coming judgment of Him who, as our charter acknowledges, made all men '*free and equal!*'

* At the same time this man was sold, another—a husband—was knocked off. The tears and agonies of his wife made such an impression on the mind of a generous spectator, that he bought him back.

When a premium of Fifty Dollars is offered for the best theatrical poem, our newspapers advertise the fact with great unanimity. The following is incomparably more important.

PREMIUM.

A Premium of Fifty Dollars, the Donation of a benevolent individual in the State of Maine, and now deposited with the Treasurer of the Pennsylvania Society for promoting the Abolition of Slavery, &c. is offered to the author of the best Treatise on the following subject: 'The Duties of Ministers and Churches of all denominations to avoid the stain of Slavery, and to make the holding of Slaves a barrier to communion and church membership.'

The composition to be directed (post paid) to either of the subscribers—the name of the author in a separate sealed paper, which will be destroyed if his work shall be rejected.

Six months from this date are allowed for the purpose of receiving the Essays.

The publication and circulation of the preferred Tract will be regulated by the Pennsylvania Society above mentioned.

W. RAWLE,
J. PRESTON, } *Committee.*
THOMAS SHIPLEY,

Philadelphia, Oct. 11.

The Liberator served as the leading abolitionist newspaper.

movement's factions by presenting long, impassioned letters that aided in the formation of both ideology and strategy. They also reprinted international news stories, particularly accounts of freedom struggles in Europe and events in Britain's former colonies in the Caribbean. Occasionally these newspapers published eyewitness accounts about slavery and race relations around the nation, although such reporting was not their real purpose.

An important function of the abolitionist press was the dissemination of antislavery literature to a wide audience. For example, Harriet Beecher Stowe's novel *Uncle Tom's Cabin,* considered to be highly influential in galvanizing antislavery sentiment, was excerpted in several publications. Slave narratives written by both prominent blacks like Frederick Douglass and unknown fugitives were often reprinted to provide an "insider's view" of life in slavery. Poetry and short stories by authors like Francis Ellen Watkins Harper designed to inspire concern and outrage among readers also appeared.

Abolitionist editors and publishers were an embattled lot, and many withstood threats to their lives, their families, and their property as proslavery forces sought to silence them. In general, these papers were a minority among America's growing newspaper industry. The editor of the *National Era* estimated that 90 percent of the Northern press opposed the abolitionist cause; in the South, the opposition was virtually unanimous. The First Amendment rights of the abolitionist press were routinely compromised by prejudicial regulations and court rulings, theft, mail censorship, and violence. The most notorious instances of violence targeted at the abolitionist press occurred in the 1830s.

James G. Birney established his antislavery newspaper, the *Philanthropist,* in Danville, Kentucky, in 1835. Local residents quickly attempted to halt publication of the paper, and his printer refused to continue working. Birney relocated to Cincinnati, Ohio, the largest and most prosperous city in the west, where the *Philanthropist* was not welcomed. In July 1836, a group broke into the newspaper's offices and destroyed some equipment; two weeks later, after much public debate, a mob attacked his print shop and descended on Birney's home. A riot ensued, and the mob ransacked Cincinnati's black neighborhoods. When Birney defended the use of arms to protect himself and his family, he became one of the first abolitionists to renounce nonviolence.

A year later, Elijah Lovejoy, a young editor of a Presbyterian abolitionist newspaper in Alton, Illinois, met a worse fate. His newspaper, the *Observer,* was the object of numerous attacks by local mobs. The town's mayor said he could not protect Lovejoy, and Alton's leaders advised Lovejoy to leave. His press was destroyed three times, and his house was invaded repeatedly. Like Birney, Lovejoy felt his nonviolent stance had been a failure, and he vowed to protect his property with force if necessary. In November 1837, Lovejoy's fourth new press arrived, and he stored it for safety in a warehouse near the Mississippi River. An armed mob arrived to seize the press; shooting erupted, and Lovejoy was killed, making him a martyred symbol for the antislavery movement.

Many historians credit the abolitionist press, despite its small size, with rallying public sentiment and influencing public officials who pressed for the end of slavery. The tenacious spirit and commitment of these journalists kept the abolitionist press going until the Civil War, when the fight against slavery was finally won.

JANE RHODES

See also African American Media; Douglass, Frederick

Further Reading

Hersh, Blanche Glassman, *The Slavery of Sex: Feminist-Abolitionists in America,* Urbana: University of Illinois Press, 1978

Kraditor, Aileen S., *Means and Ends in American Abolitionism: Garrison and His Critics on Strategy and Tactics, 1834–1850,* New York: Pantheon, 1969

Mabee, Carleton, *Black Freedom: The Nonviolent Abolitionists from 1830 Through the Civil War,* New York and London: Macmillan, 1970

Nordin, Kenneth D., "In Search of Black Unity: An Interpretation of the Content and Function of 'Freedom's Journal'," *Journalism History* 4 (1977–78)

Pease, Jane H., and William H. Pease, *Bound with Them in Chains: A Biographical History of the Antislavery Movement,* Westport, Connecticut: Greenwood, 1972

Quarles, Benjamin, *Black Abolitionists,* New York: Oxford University Press, 1969

Walters, Ronald G., *The Antislavery Appeal: American Abolitionism After 1830,* Baltimore, Maryland: Johns Hopkins University Press, 1976

Accuracy in Media

Media watchdog organization

Accuracy in Media (AIM), a conservative media watchdog organization, was founded in 1969 by Reed Irvine, who served as chairman of the board and chief executive officer. AIM represented the foremost watchdog of news media, both print and electronic, in the United States. The group published a twice-monthly newsletter, the *AIM Report,* which was sent to members of Congress, media representatives, and AIM members.

Accuracy in Media, through the use of newsletters, radio broadcasts, and television, attacked and criticized the print and broadcast media for what it considered to be biased and slanted coverage of the news. The organization's major goal was to expose and report upon what it perceived as a "liberal bias" and a "consistent pattern of leftist distortion in American news reporting." Accuracy in Media, over the years, attacked such individuals and media organizations as Dan Rather and CBS News, the *Washington (D.C.) Post,* and the Public Broadcasting Service (PBS).

Accuracy in Media, which perhaps experienced the height of its effectiveness during the conservative days of the Reagan administration in the 1980s, was labeled by some as a right-wing advocacy group for conservative causes and politicians, while Reed Irvine was called a "knee-jerk right-wing critic" and a "conservative ideologue." AIM was critical of the *Washington Post* for publishing articles it claimed caused racial animosity in the United States.

Perhaps one of the most publicized and controversial cases involving the media watchdog group took place in 1985 when AIM broadcast an hour-long rebuttal to the 13-part PBS series entitled *Viet Nam: A Television History*. The original PBS documentary, which first aired in the fall of 1983, was widely praised as "a comprehensive and balanced piece of work" and was awarded numerous journalism awards and six Emmy Awards. The AIM rebuttal, entitled *Inside Story*, examined the documentary and claimed that PBS "inaccurately portrayed North Vietnamese leader Ho Chi Minh as a benign nationalist rather than a ruthless Communist; overstated the extent of drug abuse and morale problems among U.S. soldiers in Vietnam; and underplayed the brutality of the Communist regimes that took over in Southeast Asia after the U.S. departure." Aside from any questions of inaccuracy or a liberal slant that PBS may have taken in their own documentary, PBS was criticized by some journalists for setting a "dangerous precedent by broadcasting the reply of an openly partisan group to one of its programs."

Accuracy in Media continued in its watchdog capacity. Among other stories, AIM targeted the *New York Times's* coverage of the death of White House deputy counsel Vincent Foster, questioning whether his death might have been murder rather than suicide.

Irvine was also chairman of Accuracy in Academia (AIA), which he founded in 1985. AIA attempted to build a nationwide network of students and other volunteers to observe and report on college and university professors who were thought to be espousing "liberal" views in the classroom.

BRUCE G. BRYSKI

See also Criticism of Broadcasting; Criticism of Newspapers

Further Reading

D'Souza, Dinesh, "Accuracy in Media," *National Review* 36 (November 2, 1984), pp. 36–37

Irvine, Reed, and Joseph C. Goulden, "Foster Questions," *AIM Report* (January 1995)

Shaw, David, "Of Isms and Prisms," *Columbia Journalism Review* 29:5 (January 1991), pp. 55–57

Zoglin, Richard, "Taking AIM Again at Viet Nam," *Time* 125 (July 1, 1985), p. 47

Adless Newspapers

Experimental newspapers without responsibilities to advertisers

Advertising has appeared in American newspapers since the founding of the country's first continuous paper, the *Boston News-Letter* in 1704, and from the beginning provided an important source of revenue for the news media. A few U.S. publishers, however, have entertained the vision of newspapers unbeholden to advertisers. Yet, no adless paper has ever succeeded financially.

Typical of those who dreamed of an adless paper, Charles Dana, owner and editor of the *New York Sun* in 1868, set a goal of eliminating advertisements from the *Sun* to make room for more news. "Who will start a newspaper from which advertisements are excluded?" Dana asked. "It will come some day . . . and these will probably be esteemed the true models of journalism." He did not hesitate to pull ads from an issue of the *Sun* if news demanded more space, but he also never realized his desired adless newspaper.

Most papers published without ads have been alternative, or underground, publications circulated by special interests to promote political and social causes disliked by advertisers. One of the more successful was the *Appeal to Reason*, a nationally circulated Socialist weekly published by Julius Wayland from 1895 to 1922. At its peak, circulation reached 500,000. For four years, the paper accepted no advertising and after then accepted it only sporadically when finances faltered.

In addition, three commercial, general-interest daily newspapers made notable attempts to survive without advertising: the *Philadelphia News-Post* and the *Chicago Day Book*, both published by the eccentric E.W. Scripps in the early twentieth century, and *PM*, a left-wing daily founded in New York City in 1940 by Ralph Ingersoll.

Scripps built a penny-press empire by championing the rights of the blue-collar working class. He saw advertising as an unnecessary yoke on a free press: it took up space better used for news and often caused editors to censor the news to avoid offending advertisers. Once he became established and wealthy, Scripps pursued his longtime dream of a chain of adless papers. His plan was, first, to establish such a paper in New York City in 1907. Depending upon its success, he planned adless papers in Philadelphia; Boston; Baltimore, Maryland; Chicago; St. Louis, Missouri; and Pittsburgh, Pennsylvania. Plans for the New York paper collapsed, however, when Scripps's chosen editor, John Vandercook, died unexpectedly.

Scripps's next attempt was in Chicago, and on September 28, 1911, the first issue of the *Chicago Day Book* appeared. Edited by Neg Cochran, the *Day Book* was quirky and undistinguished. Rather than looking like a newspaper, it was more like a little book, consisting of 32 eight-inch pages. Scripps's biographer, Vance Trimble, argues that Cochran was incompetent and never succeeded in producing an interesting news product, although one of the paper's reporters was Carl Sandburg, then just beginning his career. While the paper was profitable for only one month of its existence and never achieved the 30,000 subscribers deemed necessary to support publication, its small, regular growth encouraged Scripps, and he looked forward to showing that "the people can have a free press" without advertising subsidization. Scripps published the *Philadelphia News-Post* from 1912 to 1914 without ads and even investigated starting an adless paper in Washington, D.C., before deciding it was financially impossible. In 1917, with World War I driving up the price of newsprint, the money-losing *Chicago Day Book* was closed.

Twenty-two years later, the adless tabloid newspaper *PM* debuted in competitive New York City. Ingersoll, a former editor of Henry Luce's *Fortune* and *Life* magazines, envisioned a paper, managed by writers, that read like a magazine; had superior quality of design, photography, and reproduction; and was uniquely unfettered by the manipulations of advertisers or the traditional journalistic rule of objectivity. Ingersoll's plan was to report merchant news but not accept advertising, relying on subscriptions for revenues. To start the paper, he raised investment funds from business elites and hired an impressive group of writers, including I.F. Stone, Dalton Trumbo, Dorothy Parker, Hodding Carter, and Theodore Seuss Geisel, who later gained fame as Dr. Seuss. Intense publicity resulted in first-day sales of 450,000, but circulation quickly dropped to 31,000.

Within three months, Ingersoll's ideal newspaper had lost so much money that he relinquished management to Chicago's Marshall Field, who bought out the other investors. Eventually, all of Ingersoll's innovations were abandoned or compromised. The paper began accepting advertising in 1946. Two years later, the paper folded.

JAMES AUCOIN

See also Scripps, E.W.

Further Reading

Bass, Paul, "A Vision of the Ideal Newspaper," *Washington Monthly* 17 (June 1985), pp. 54–56

Cochran, Negley D., *E.W. Scripps*, New York: Harcourt, Brace, 1933

Graham, John, ed., *"Yours for the Revolution": The Appeal to Reason, 1895–1922*, Lincoln: University of Nebraska Press, 1990

Hoopes, Roy, *Ralph Ingersoll: A Biography*, New York: Atheneum, 1985

Kessler, Lauren, *The Dissident Press: Alternative Journalism in American History*, Beverly Hills, California: Sage, 1984

Trimble, Vance H., *The Astonishing Mr. Scripps: The Turbulent Life of America's Penny Press Lord*, Ames: Iowa State University Press, 1992

Advertising Agencies

Advertising business development

An advertising agency is an independent business that develops, prepares, and places advertising in media on behalf of companies seeking customers for their goods and services. Traditionally, an agency consists of creative and business people. The creative department has art directors and copywriters; the business side is subdivided into account management, media, and administration. As of January 1995, the Standard Directory of Advertising Agencies reported there were 4,882 agencies in the United States. This figure, however, excluded numerous local advertising agencies.

According to the definition of the American Association of Advertising Agencies, paraphrased from its 1918 statement, a full-service agency provides the following: the study of the client's product or service to determine the advantages and disadvantages inherent in the product itself and in its relation to competition; the analysis of the present and potential market for which the product or service is adapted; the study of the client's distribution and sales operation; familiarity with all media and means by which the message can be conveyed to the consumer and trade; the drafting of an advertising plan; the execution of the plan by preparing the advertisements, contracting the space, and forwarding the advertisements to the media; and the verification of the fulfillment of media contracts, billing, and paying for services. Agencies also offer package design, prepare sales materials and merchandising displays, provide research, and consult on public relations activities.

The advertising agent was the precursor to advertising agencies. Agents brokered advertising space as space sales representatives do in modern times. While postmasters during American colonial times are purported to have served as agents, Volney B. Palmer is the first known advertising agent. He started his business in 1841 in Boston and soon expanded to Philadelphia and New York. Concurrently, John L. Hooper operated in New York. Gradually, both men became independent middle men, or space-jobbers. In 1865, George P. Rowell started an agency in Boston that sold newspaper space wholesale. Rowell bought Hooper's operation in 1867 and moved his headquarters to New York, where he published the first newspaper rate directory in 1869. During this era, J. Walter Thompson went to work with Carlton and Smith to sell space in religious magazines. Ten years later, he bought out Carlton, formed his own agency, and sold space from his "Standard List" of 30 national magazines, most of which were targeted to women. In 1869 the young Francis Ayer formed N.W. Ayer & Son, using his father's name. He bought out Palmer and expanded on the accepted agent pattern by billing advertisers exactly what he paid to publishers plus an agreed-upon commission. This assured advertisers that they were getting a fair price, and advertisers established themselves as Ayer clients. Thus, while J. Walter Thompson had created a powerful, national advertising medium, Ayer had a bevy of established clients.

Creativity, however, was still the province of the advertiser rather than of the agent. The creative aspect of the business began in the 1870s when Charles Austin Bates sold his writing skills to advertisers and agents. Working with a few employees, he provided agents with the ability to offer both creative and business services. In 1875, Ayer incorporated a printing department; in 1879, Ayer conducted the first market survey; and, by 1880, Ayer was writing copy. Other agencies started to do the same. Business in the United States was experiencing increased production, and companies needed to increase demand; advertising was one of its tools. Thus, by 1910, agencies were creating ads, using market research, and conducting research into the psychology of advertising.

With the growth of print media, the size and number of agencies increased; the advent of radio and television created a full-scale industry. The Creative Revolution of the 1960s led to some downsizing as demand increased that ads be created by a copywriter and art director. As many clients wanted to work directly with the creators of their ads, small boutique agencies, consisting solely of creative teams, developed. As these boutiques became successful, however, they reinvested their profits into expanding their businesses, consequently creating larger agencies.

The expansion of the U.S. economy to the global market and the onset of business mergers and acquisitions was also mirrored in the agency milieu. Marion Harper of McCann-Erickson pioneered the era of global mega-agencies. He established Interpublic, a holding company, to acquire other agencies – all of which operated independently. His successor, Phil Geier, acquired SSC&B Lintas in 1978. The age of the mega-agency was dominated, however, by Saatchi and Saatchi, founded in 1970. Although it was a British agency, Saatchi had profound effects on the U.S. agency environment. In 1975 it merged with Compton UK Partners and later acquired all of Compton Communications, adding research firms, management consultant firms, and public relations firms. In 1986, Saatchi bought Dancer Fitzgerald Sample, Backer and Spielvogel, and Ted Bates Worldwide – all New York agencies. These acquisitions enabled Saatchi to remain the largest mega-agency despite the formation of Omnicom by Doyle Dane Bernbach, BBDO International, and Needham Harper Worldwide.

Another Englishman, Martin Sorrell, who had been Saatchi's financial director, continued to affect the U.S. marketplace. Sorrell left Saatchi in 1985 to take over the WPP group. As Saatchi experienced a myriad of client conflicts and lost billings, WPP grew, acquiring JWT and Ogilvy and Mather. In 1990, it was the world's largest agency.

Nonetheless, mega-agencies experienced continuing problems and, in many respects, history was thought to be repeating itself. While some agencies continued to offer full service, many clients unbundled their media buying and creative needs. Coca-Cola shocked the agency world when it continued to use McCann-Erickson – but hired Creative Services, a Hollywood shop, to create its advertisements. To stay competitive, many agencies formed independent media-buying groups; others offered increased services along the lines of integrated marketing communications.

PATRICIA B. ROSE

See also Advertising in the Nineteenth Century; Advertising in the Twentieth Century; *American Newspaper Directory*; Ayer, N.W., & Son; Creative Revolution; Full-Service Advertising Agency; Palmer, Volney B.; Rowell, George P.

Further Reading

Goodrum, Charles, and Helen Dalrymple, *Advertising in America: The First 200 Years,* New York: Harry N. Abrams, 1990

Hower, Ralph M., *The History of an Advertising Agency: N.W. Ayer & Son at Work, 1869–1949,* Cambridge, Massachusetts: Harvard University Press, 1949

Keeler, Floyd Y., and Albert E. Haase, *The Advertising Agency,* New York and London: Garland, 1985

Kleinman, Philip, *Saatchi & Saatchi: The Inside Story,* Lincolnwood, Illinois: NTC Business, 1989

Thorson, Esther, *Advertising Age: The Principles of Advertising at Work,* Lincolnwood, Illinois: NTC Business, 1989

Advertising and Minorities

Advertising business concern

Until the middle of the twentieth century, U.S. advertisers virtually ignored nonwhites as worthy consumers and declined to target them in their advertisements. When racial and ethnic minorities were depicted in advertisements, they usually were presented in offensive, stereotypical ways and as palatable salespersons for the products being advertised. Advertising representations of nonwhites traditionally were produced by the white imagination and appealed primarily to white audiences. These images began to improve as advertisers began to recognize specific minority groups as constituting viable consumer markets, as minorities complained to the advertising industry, and as changes in society included growth in sophistication within the media and advertising industries.

The relationship between racial minorities and advertising underwent significant changes after World War II, with blacks being the primary beneficiaries of the changes. Unfortunately, national advertisers seemed reluctant to learn from the experiences with one group in dealing with others. Consequently, African Americans, Hispanics, Asian Americans, and Native Americans had to mount separate movements to improve their relationships with the advertising industry.

As the smallest and poorest ethnic minority group in the United States, Native Americans were not targeted as a consumer market by most businesses. Like most ethnic groups, Native Americans were portrayed in advertisements in stereotypical fashion. Native Americans, traditionally, appeared frequently in travel-related ads. In the 1920s and 1930s, railway companies incorporated Native American imagery to promote travel. Southern Pacific advertised travel to California through "Apacheland" and depicted a group of ferocious Indians on horses and armed with rifles. The Santa Fe Railroad named one of its passenger lines the Super Chief, and advertisements featured detailed portraits of the "noble Indian warrior." In another Santa Fe advertisement, three white children peer out of a train window above the caption, "Gee! We are going to see real, live Indians." Native American imagery is seldom used in contemporary ads except for automobiles such as Chrysler's Jeep Cherokee and sports teams such as the Atlanta Braves and Washington Redskins. The use of racial team names and images came under protest in the late twentieth century.

Asians are not a single race of people and include Chinese, Japanese, and Koreans, to name a few. Like Native Americans, they were not usually regarded as a separate consumer market. Because of their levels of income and education, however, which were generally considered to be especially high, they have been called a marketer's dream. Even so, Asians continued to be stereotyped in numerous ads. An old television commercial for a laundry product featured a Chinese family that claimed to use an "ancient Chinese secret" to get their customers' clothes clean. Asian women often were placed in exotic, tropical island settings as seductive attractions. They were frequently groomed to present a stereotypical image – darkened eyes, straight hair with bangs, and narrow slit skirts, sarongs, or grass skirts. Another common depiction was that of a submissive female who attentively cared for the needs of white men. One airline promised that those who flew with it would be cared for by a "Singapore Girl."

Advertisements showing Asian men often depicted them as having a proclivity for using cameras and as being possessors of wisdom. In a Colgate toothpaste ad, a wise old Asian man (actor Pat Morita) portrayed the "Colgate Wisdom Tooth" to denote the linkage of wisdom and age in Asian cultures. With the exception of children, Asians were rarely presented in integrated settings. When resentment grew over Japanese trade policies and sales of Japanese products in the United States, advertisements attacking Japan became popular. The lack of a sizable and vocal Asian community and separate consumer market in the United States was a primary reason for the continued offensive images and stereotypes in advertising.

Like Asians, Hispanics include several ethnicities, including Mexicans, Puerto Ricans, and Cubans. As a whole, in the late twentieth century they were the fastest-growing ethnic minority population in the United States. Despite the fact that as early as 1920 Silvestre Terrazas spoke on behalf of Mexican consumers to a group of white advertising men, only recently have U.S. corporations shown serious regard for Hispanic consumers. Terrazas, editor of *La Patria,* a Spanish-language newspaper in El Paso, Texas, discussed issues that, decades later, remained salient for advertisers interested in minority consumers. He pointed to: (1) a growing U.S. population increasing in racial and ethnic differences; (2) the media's role in reaching those audiences; and (3) advertising's influence in using media and other avenues to reach audiences. When businesses began to court Hispanics as consumers in the 1970s, instead of eliminating stereotypes they redefined them using traits useful to advertisers' needs. Hispanic activists claimed that negative stereotypes once reserved for blacks had been transferred to Hispanics.

Perhaps the most prominent Hispanic stereotype in advertising was the Frito Bandito, a six-gun-toting, mustachioed Mexican bandit wearing a broad sombrero. The Frito-Lay Corporation's cartoon salesman stole Fritos corn chips from unsuspecting white mothers. Frito-Lay canceled the highly successful campaign in 1970 following protests by Hispanic groups. Some 10 years later, however, Frito-Lay launched another campaign for its Tostitos product that featured a tall, distinguished-looking man, reminiscent of the Hollywood stereotype of the Latin lover. This time there were no protests against the commercials from Hispanic organizations.

Because of continued population growth and limited competition from English-language media, the Hispanic segment became the advertising industry's new favorite in the 1980s. They presented a difficult marketing challenge, however, requiring narrow and precise market segmentation. Advertisers found that the segment was most receptive to Spanish-language content, and they attempted to package advertisements in settings that reinforced Hispanic cultures and traditions.

Like Hispanics, Asians, and Native Americans, for much of the century, African Americans were defined as outside the intended audience for most advertisements. More than with any other minority group, however, advertising images have appropriated certain aspects of the African American experience. Among the most common negative images are those of African Americans eating watermelons and picking cotton; being submissive servants, domestic workers, and porters; having exaggerated physical and facial gestures; and speaking in dialect or using poor grammar. Many of these images produced advertising symbols that have evolved into icons of U.S. popular culture. The most prominent such advertising symbols are Aunt Jemima, Rastus, Uncle Ben, and the Gold Dust Twins.

In the past, one magazine advertisement for Aunt Jemima Pancake Flour depicted a bandanna-wearing "mammy" caricature serving stacks of pancakes to a crowd of whites. She shouts: "Lawzee! mekkin pancakes is th' mos' impawtines thing ah does, than which dere aint no better, effen ah does say so! . . . Grab em!" A small caption under the product's box depicting the "real" Aunt Jemima reads, "I'se in town, Honey!" Aunt Jemima lost weight and the bandanna, along with other stereotypical accoutrements, over the years, but she remained the prominent spokeswoman for the pancake mix.

Following World War II, U.S. businesses began to allocate resources for new market development. Migration and increasing purchasing power among African Americans led advertisers to initiate aggressive advertising and marketing campaigns to African American consumers. In addition, the civil rights movement of the 1960s saw African Americans use consumer boycotts effectively to end segregation, gain employment, and improve media images. Another aspect of the courtship of black and, later, Hispanic consumers was the creation of persuasive campaigns by advertising agencies and media specializing in African American and Spanish-speaking audiences. Finally, a basic change in thinking among advertising executives that recognized the value of market segmentation compelled advertisers to utilize specialized media to reach these consumers.

Johnson Publishing Company played an important role in breaking barriers of major white businesses toward black consumers and advertising in the African American press. In fact, when *Advertising Age* celebrated its fiftieth anniversary in 1980, Johnson Publishing founder John Johnson was the only African American on the journal's all-time list of the 100 persons who had the most influence on advertising. Johnson's business savvy and string of publishing successes made him one of the first and foremost spokespersons for the African American consumer market.

The shift among advertisers was influenced by Johnson's comprehensive marketing program, which included providing consultants to white businesses and offering films and special literature on marketing to African American consumers. Johnson's personal marketing tips and philosophies on the market appeared in several *Advertising Age* articles. Johnson Publishing claimed to have the most extensive information on that segment of the market and declared *Ebony* magazine the leader in introducing hundreds of advertisers to what was, by the late twentieth century, a multi-billion-dollar market.

Although advertising images of minorities improved considerably over time, strategies for marketing to minority consumers sometimes came under attack. Advertisers frequently used slick advertising to promote prestige-oriented products to low-income consumers. In minority communities, there were many advertisements for alcoholic beverages and cigarettes, most seeming to hold out the promise of power, happiness, and the good life for those who consume. While prestige appeals were used in advertising to all consumers, these ads had a special impact for those who were economically deprived or who lacked opportunity for success. For such people, conspicuous consumption could provide instant gratification and, in some cases, communicate status to those in the same condition.

Unfortunately, beer, liquor, and cigarette companies actively targeted minority groups and their social, political, and economic activities. Although pursuing racial or ethnic groups is not inherently wrong, campaigns that advertise health-threatening products to particularly susceptible populations raise important ethical and policy issues.

DWIGHT E. BROOKS

See also African American Media; Asian American Media; Hispanic Media; Native American Media

Further Reading

Astroff, Roberta J., "Spanish Gold: Stereotypes, Ideology and the Construction of a U.S. Latino Market," *Howard Journal of Communications* 1 (1988–89)
Brooks, Dwight E., "In Their Own Words: Advertisers' Construction of an African American Consumer Market, the World War Era," *Howard Journal of Communications* 6 (1995)
Gutiérrez, Félix F., "Advertising and the Growth of Minority Markets and Media," *Journal of Communication Inquiry* 14 (1990)
Jacobson, Michael F., and Laurie Ann Mazur, *Marketing Madness: A Survival Guide for a Consumer Society,* Boulder, Colorado: Westview, 1995
Johnson, John H., and Lerone Bennett, *Succeeding Against the Odds,* New York: Warner, 1989
O'Barr, William M., *Culture and the Ad: Exploring Otherness in the World of Advertising,* Boulder, Colorado: Westview, 1994
Seiter, Ellen, "Different Children, Different Dreams: Racial Representation in Advertising," in *Gender, Race and Class in Media: A Text-Reader,* edited by Gail Dines and Jean M. Humez, Thousand Oaks, California: Sage, 1995
Woods, Gail Baker, *Advertising and Marketing to the New Majority,* Belmont, California: Wadsworth, 1995

Advertising Appeals

Techniques to sell products

The term advertising appeal refers to the way an ad moves, motivates, or persuades its audience. In the broadest sense, an ad moves consumers by appealing to their emotions or logic. More importantly, ads also motivate their audience through a message that appeals to a human need. Both this message or appeal and the way it is expressed are largely determined by the audience. These three elements – the overall message, its creative expression, and the audience – are critical components of the advertising strategy.

Audience Segmentation

The population of the United States was once small enough, and those able to purchase goods were similar enough, that one advertising appeal could be used for all consumers. Today's market is so diverse, however, that it is practically impossible to design one message that will appeal to everybody. Marketers therefore divide consumers into segments and direct appeals toward particular groups. The audience is frequently segmented by such demographic criteria as age, gender, and income, or by psychographic categories that include lifestyles, values, and attitudes.

Appealing to Human Needs

Some advertising appeals speak to the consumer's need for speed, convenience, or cost savings, but many others focus on needs that are a more integral part of the human personality. These advertising appeals do not vary much from decade to decade because the needs they address are thought to be universal and unchanging.

As described by the psychologist Abraham Maslow, the hierarchy of human needs begins with those most basic to survival and proceed upward to more individualized and personal ones. Maslow's hierarchy is readily adaptable to advertising because consumer goods can often satisfy each of the five need levels. Consequently, the Maslow hierarchy provides a convenient way to consider the range of appeals used by advertisers.

1.) Physical needs for food, shelter, and clothing seem too basic to provide the basis for a strong advertising appeal, especially in a relatively affluent society. Ads for extreme clothing and outdoor gear, however, often appeal to these needs.

2.) Safety and security needs have always been used to motivate the purchase of such items as locks, burglar alarms, insurance, and auto accessories. Modern battery ads, for example, showing cars stalled on dangerous roads play on the same basic fears as a 1925 ad for Philco batteries that showed a stalled car on a railroad track after it had been struck by a train. Ads that depict the problems arising from the failure to use the product are said to use fear appeals.

3.) Love and belonging, not surprisingly, provide the basis for the largest number of appeals. Fragrances and other personal care products generally appeal to these needs. As early as 1911, an ad for Woodbury's soap showed a man caressing a woman's hand with the headline "A Skin You Love to Touch." The ad's sexual appeal is a modest version of the tangled couplings in the ads that appeared during the 1980s for Calvin Klein's Obsession perfume.

Personal care products often play upon the audience's fears by dramatizing the rejection that comes from failure to use the product. As early as 1925, for example, Listerine mouthwash emphasized the dangers of "halitosis" – the term they used in the ad, meaning bad breath – by showing an attractive but unhappy young woman with the headline "Often a Bridesmaid but Never a Bride." The same headline with different copy and illustrations continued to run for more than three decades.

Other advertisers urge the target to buy the product not as a way of receiving love but as a way of expressing it. Such an appeal is at the heart of Hallmark greeting cards' long-running slogan, "When You Care Enough to Send the Very Best," as well as of Pillsbury's "Nothin' Says Lovin' Like Something from the Oven."

4.) Esteem and prestige needs often form the basis of appeals for luxury products that may be used to signal a user's wealth, sophistication, distinctiveness, or superiority. Frequently, the appeal is expressed through ads that depict a way of life to which the consumer aspires. An even more traditional vehicle for such appeals is the celebrity testimonial. The J. Walter Thompson agency was among the first to use this approach. As early as 1920, Thompson's ads for Lux soap proclaimed that "nine out of ten screen stars care for their skin with Lux." The ads featured testimonials by such stars as Joan Crawford and Clara Bow. Celebrity endorsements continue to lend prestige to items ranging from athletic wear to beverages because as Stanley Resor, the president of J. Walter Thompson, wrote in 1927, "we want to copy those whom we deem superior to us in taste, knowledge or experience."

5.) The fulfillment of one's own potential is frequently the focus of ads promoting colleges and careers to young people, as in the U.S. Army's slogan, "Be All that You Can Be." But self-fulfillment is used even more often as the basis of ads aimed at an older audience because members of that target audience have the time and money to devote to such matters.

Finally, a particular product category will almost always satisfy more than one level of need. An automobile, for example, can provide a safe way to transport one's family, or it can lend the driver sex appeal or suggest the owner's prestige, wealth, or intelligence. Determining what appeal the advertising should use depends not only on the product but also on an in-depth understanding of the audience.

Motivational Research

At the end of the Korean War in 1953, manufacturers quickly converted to peacetime production. Ovens, cars, refrigerators, and a host of other products rolled off the assembly lines. For perhaps the first time in U.S. history, supply far exceeded demand. Advertisers felt that if they were to find appeals that would stimulate more demand, they needed to understand consumers better than ever before.

This need coincided nicely with the rise of motivational research that was based on the premise that consumers are not fully aware of the reasons for their actions. Motivational research attempted to uncover the subconscious or hidden needs that motivate purchases. Its leading figure was Ernest Dichter, a Viennese psychoanalyst and strict Freudian. Because the target's underlying feelings about products and services were not easily revealed by direct questioning, Dichter adapted such clinical tools as depth interviews and projective techniques to the study of consumer buying habits.

At its most extreme, motivational research suggested that women baked cakes to satisfy maternal yearnings and that men viewed convertible cars as mistresses and hardtops as wives. Dichter and his associates also helped advertisers begin to understand the complexities of consumer behavior. Motivational research, for example, helped the Leo Burnett agency discover that men viewed tea as a feminine drink. That insight led to ads for the Tea Bureau that featured the theme "Make Mine Hefty, Hale and Hearty."

Gradually, motivational research began to lose its appeal as advertisers came to question its highly subjective and exotic interpretations of rather prosaic behavior. Nonetheless, such research encouraged advertisers to see consumers not as statistics but as people whose behavior is complex, and so it prepared the way for the use of focus groups, lifestyle analysis, and other qualitative methods now employed in consumer research.

Subliminal Appeals

In September 1957, James Vicary, the vice president of the Subliminal Projection Company, announced that his organization had perfected a device that would flash commercial messages on the screen at speeds so rapid they could be perceived only by the subconscious mind. Vicary claimed to have tested his device in a New Jersey movie theater where subliminal messages urging consumers to purchase popcorn and soda had succeeded in increasing their sales.

The suggestion that the public could be manipulated without its knowledge caused both the U.S. Congress and the Federal Communications Commission to investigate. Although Vicary's results could not be replicated and there was little evidence to suggest the widespread use of subliminal advertising, by 1958 all three major networks had prohibited the use of subliminal materials.

The issue quickly faded away but was revived briefly in 1973 when Wilson Bryan Key published *Subliminal Seduction*. Key claimed that advertisers spoke to their target's unconscious mind and caused consumers to purchase products by embedding messages such as sexual images in print advertising. Although Key's book was widely discussed, both leading researchers and top advertising executives have dismissed Key's theories as groundless.

Logical and Emotional Appeals

After the advertiser has analyzed the target and determined the type of overall appeal or message that will be most effective, that message must be translated into an ad. Ads appeal to consumers through the use of logic or emotion.

Initially, logic predominated. Shortly after the turn of the twentieth century, John E. Kennedy told Albert Lasker of Chicago's Lord and Thomas agency that advertising was "salesmanship in print." Lasker and another Chicago copywriter, Claude Hopkins, became the first proponents of what came to be known as "reason why" advertising. In his *Scientific Advertising*, Hopkins argued that good advertising was neither humorous nor charming but was rather a rational, unadorned argument that offered the consumer a concrete reason why the product was worth buying.

"Reason why" advertising found its greatest contemporary advocate in Rosser Reeves, the chairman of the Ted Bates agency, whose approach to advertising dominated the 1950s and early 1960s. Like Hopkins, Reeves believed that a product's advertising must be built around a single overriding selling point that would give consumers a reason to choose it over the competition. Reeves called that point the unique selling proposition and claimed that its logical power was the sole determinant of an ad's effectiveness.

Logical appeals continue to be used, especially in print ads for certain high-end products about which consumers want to be well informed before making a purchase decision. However, with the increasing importance of television, where emotion holds sway, the proliferation of parity products, and the close scrutiny all product claims receive from both consumer groups and federal agencies, advertising has come more and more to rely on emotion.

Emotional appeals have been used by Listerine, for example, since the 1920s to dramatize the dangers of "halitosis" and by AT&T to encourage consumers to "Reach out and touch someone." When advertisers use consistent imagery year after year to generate a single attitude toward a product, that attitude or feeling is known as the brand image. This image endows the product with value above and beyond its specific features and gives consumers an added reason to choose it.

The value of brand image advertising was first suggested by Theodore MacManus in 1910. In describing the advertising he created for Cadillac automobiles and other luxury products, MacManus said he wished to surround the product year after year with an "invisible cloud of favorable, friendly impressions." Such impressions do not produce an immediate sale, but he claimed that they do predispose the target toward the product so that, ultimately, the product will practically sell itself.

Image advertising perhaps found its strongest contemporary advocate in David Ogilvy, the founder of Ogilvy and Mather, who argued that every ad contributes to the complex symbol that is the brand image. Ogilvy's first image campaign, "The man in the Hathaway shirt," was launched in 1951. The advertising gave the shirt an air of prestige through the use of a sophisticated model wearing an eye patch, a symbol Ogilvy continued to use for more than a decade. Among the many agencies to employ brand image advertising was Leo Burnett, which created images for its clients through the continuing use of such figures as the Pillsbury Doughboy, the Jolly Green Giant, and most notably, perhaps, the Marlboro Man. Image advertising, with its heavy reliance on emotional appeals, continues to be used extensively by marketers because as parity products proliferate, the brand image is often the primary basis for the consumer's purchase decision.

Stereotyping

No matter what type of appeal an ad employs, it must communicate quickly and keep attention focused on the product. Consequently, the people featured in ads are placed in easily accepted roles so they will not call attention to themselves and draw attention away from the product. Ads, then, frequently use stereotypes. This practice receives its sharpest scrutiny during periods of social change when traditional roles are called into question.

During the 1960s, as more women entered the workforce and the feminist movement gained power, new attention was focused on the ways in which ads portrayed women. Ads in the 1950s most frequently depicted women as decoration or as sex objects. Although millions of women worked outside the home in the 1960s, ads continued to focus almost exclusively on their role as homemakers. They were also almost never shown making important decisions. Even ads for major household items generally featured both the husband and wife, and the positioning of the woman made it clear that the man was the decision maker.

Whether owing to the feminist movement or to women's increasing economic power, the representation of women changed dramatically after the late 1960s. It became far more common to see women depicted as professionals or shown in offices not only as assistants but as mid-level executives. Where women were once totally excluded from auto ads or relegated to the passenger's seat, they are now shown as the buyers not only of cars but of a wide variety of expensive items. Nonetheless, as numerous scholars have pointed out, women continue to be depicted as sex objects, particularly in fashion ads. Women also have a far more significant presence in the business world than magazine ads and television commercials would suggest.

Thanks in part to the civil rights movement, the 1960s also saw new questions raised about the depiction of African Americans in ads. Prior to 1960, when they were shown at all, it was almost always in the role of cook, servant, porter, or laborer. If they were shown with whites, it was in a subordinate position. By the 1980s, however, African Americans were most often depicted as students, professionals, business people, or occasionally as idle consumers, the role in which whites were most frequently shown. When featured with whites in a business setting, it was generally as an equal. Negative stereotypes persist in advertising, however. African Americans continue to be shown as entertainers, although far less often than in the 1960s. Moreover, they are three times more likely than whites to be shown as athletes. Advertising also continues to underrepresent their presence in business.

As ads have begun to more fully reflect the lives of women and African Americans, increasing attention is being paid to the way in which advertising depicts Hispanics, Asians, gays, and lesbians. Questions also remain about the social impact of negative stereotypes. There is considerable debate over how direct a link there may be between negative stereotypes and the public's attitudes toward the groups represented. Such stereotypes, however, do not exist in a vacuum. They are probably best understood as part of a larger system of cultural assumptions regarding such matters as race, gender, prestige, power relations, and the achievement of social status.

BRETT ROBBS

See also Advertising and Minorities; Hopkins, Claude C.; Lasker, Albert; Resor, Stanley B.; *Scientific Advertising*

Further Reading

Aaker, David A., and Alexander L. Biel, eds., *Brand Equity and Advertising: Advertising's Role in Building Strong Brands,* Hillsdale, New Jersey: Lawrence Erlbaum, 1993

Courtney, Alice E., and Thomas W. Whipple, *Sex Stereotyping in Advertising,* Lexington, Massachusetts: Lexington Books, 1983

Dates, Jannette L., and William Barlow, eds., *Split Image: African Americans in the Mass Media,* Washington, D.C.: Howard University Press, 1993

Goodrum, Charles, and Helen Dalrymple, *Advertising in America: The First 200 Years,* New York: Harry N. Abrams, 1990

Moriarty, Sandra E., *Creative Advertising: Theory and Practice,* 2nd ed., Englewood Cliffs, New Jersey: Prentice-Hall, 1991

Zinkhan, George, Keith K. Cox, and Jae W. Hong, "Changes in Stereotypes: Blacks and Whites in Magazine Advertisements," *Journalism Quarterly* 63:3 (Autumn 1986), pp. 568–572

Advertising Awards

Most important advertising awards are national and international rather than local or regional. Among the national and international awards that are the most prestigious are the Clios for broadcasting advertising, the Andys for all media advertising, the Athenas for newspaper advertising, the Echo Awards for direct marketing, and the National Infomercial Marketing Association Awards.

Without question the best-known and most important award in advertising is the Clio. The name Clio comes from the Greek muse Kleo, the glorifier of history and accomplishments. Like other entertainment awards, such as the Oscars in the motion picture industry and the Emmys in television, the Clios are awarded through a competition among peers. For advertising excellence internationally, the Clios have been awarded in about 25 categories every year since 1960. Also like the Oscars and Emmys, the Clios are judged by a panel of professionals from the field. For Clios, the judges are advertising practitioners from around the world. The winners are judged to be the best in their categories.

Many Clio categories seem somewhat narrow. Among the categories are Best Coffee/Tea, Best Cereal, Best Utilities, and Best Insurance. It is not uncommon for an award in a particular category to go unawarded. Clios are often awarded to the commercials that consumers like most,

demonstrating that some of the commercials admired by the public are liked by industry professionals and are considered innovative and artistic in addition to being effective commercial messages.

Sponsored by the Advertising Club of New York, the Andy Awards are international. In the 1990s, there were 131 categories covering advertising in television, radio, print, posters, and other media such as compact disc covers, billboards, and press releases. Andys have been awarded every year since 1963, and judging is done by a panel of professionals. The purpose of the Andys is to improve the standards of craftsmanship, to provide recognition for those who uphold the standards, and to maintain a unified recognition of excellence in advertising.

The Athenas are to newspapers what the Clio is to television. Sponsored by the Newspaper Advertising Bureau, the award is for excellence in newspaper advertising, and awards are made in 22 categories. All daily newspapers in the United States and Canada are eligible to compete.

The Direct Marketing Association sponsors the Echo Awards, which are given for excellence in direct marketing. The awards are given across media, including television, radio, print, and direct mail.

Another award is that given by the National Infomercial Marketing Association. These awards are given only for lengthy television advertising that sells products and services in 30- and 60-minute formats.

There are several other important advertising awards programs. *Advertising Age* has an annual awards program for best television and radio commercials, best newspaper and magazine advertisements, and best out-of-home advertising. Community Action Network gives media and corporate advertising awards. The New York Chapter of the American Marketing Association awards the Effie for marketing. There is also a range of local awards programs sponsored by advertising groups such as the local American Federation of Advertising Clubs.

DONALD R. AVERY

Advertising Copywriting
Preparing advertising for distribution

The mid-1800s brought the introduction of inventions that increased productivity, and manufacturers were able to achieve uniform quality in mass-produced goods. These manufacturers could survive only if this excess production could be sold to customers living beyond the boundaries of the local market. Since long-distance transportation networks were being transformed by newly built roads and railroads, national media developed as an effective communication system that could reach a broad audience covering a large geographic area.

Early advertising pioneers functioned primarily as media brokers, charging a commission for placing ads in newspapers. The copy for these ads was written almost exclusively by the advertisers themselves and often contained exorbitant and farfetched claims.

John E. Powers is widely considered to have been the first well-known advertising copywriter. Hired in Philadelphia in 1880 by retailer John Wanamaker, Powers wrote a more "journalized" style of advertising copy that contained news value and accurate information. He would update the advertising daily with new copy about the "news" of the store.

In the early years of the twentieth century at the Lord and Thomas agency, John E. Kennedy introduced the "sales" approach to ad copy with his theory that advertising was nothing more than salesmanship in print. His writing style was uncluttered and direct, echoing the same arguments a salesperson might use in a one-on-one selling situation.

Another Lord and Thomas employee of the early 1930s, Claude Hopkins, is often referred to as the greatest copywriter of all time. He was definitely the highest paid, with an uncommon salary of $185,000. Hopkins perfected his writing techniques in direct mail and used that medium to advance his theories and belief in continuous copy testing.

John Caples, a vice president of BBDO in the 1930s, also based his writing techniques on extensive mail-order and inquiry testing. He altered the style of copywriting by replacing wordy and overstated copy with short words, sentences, and paragraphs.

Broadcast advertising became a dominant medium in the 1950s. Increased media vehicle options partially led to the Creative Revolution in advertising in the 1960s.

Adman Leo Burnett was the founder of the Chicago school of advertising. His approach focused on finding the inherent drama in a product and displaying it in its most believable and memorable form. Many ad characters have been created by the Burnett agency, including the Jolly Green Giant, Tony the Tiger, and the Marlboro Man. The strength of Burnett's style was in its ability to reach the average consumer in Middle America.

David Ogilvy founded the Ogilvy and Mather agency. He developed a style of advertising combining the tried-and-true claims of tested copy with a strong sense of story appeal and image.

William Bernbach is considered by many to be the leading innovator of advertising at the height of the creative revolution. He focused on advertising as a combination of persuasion and artistry, and he combined feelings and emotions into memorable imagery that was effective.

The role of the advertising copywriter is constantly evolving. In the 1950s and 1960s, agency copywriters functioned as the sole conceptualists of an ad, often handing a completed advertising idea to the art department for rendering. Later, copywriters and art directors came to be expected to work in teams from the beginning to the end of the creative process.

Advertising copywriters are primarily responsible for the verbal aspect of an advertisement, whether as written copy in a print ad or spoken dialogue in a television or radio commercial. Because advertising needs to be both persuasive and memorable to be effective, the job requires a copywriter to have a delicate balance of abilities as both a salesperson and an artist.

The common personal characteristics of ad copywriters have been described as including intelligence, imagination, highly developed powers of observation, objectivity, determination, persistence, self-discipline, patience, curiosity, interest in human nature, self-confidence, integrity, verbal skills, humility, empathy, capacity for criticism, and mental and physical stamina. Successful copywriters come from a wide variety of academic backgrounds and levels of preparation. The education levels of advertising writers can range from the self-taught to those who have completed traditional university programs through schools of journalism, business, or communication. Increasingly common are credentials earned at advertising portfolio development schools.

Whatever the type of educational preparation, the creative facet of the advertising industry requires a portfolio of sample ads as evidence of a writer's talent in order to acquire the entry-level job. This involves developing speculative advertisements for products and services to showcase a potential writer's ability to create memorable and persuasive work that sells.

Job opportunities for the advertising copywriter are varied. They include employment in the creative department of an advertising agency, in a retail department store, with a catalog retailer, and at in-house advertising departments of corporations both large and small.

ARLO OVIATT

See also Advertising Agencies; Advertising in the Twentieth Century; Creative Revolution; Hopkins, Claude C.; In-House Advertising

Further Reading

Hafer, W. Keith, and Gordon E. White, *Advertising Writing: Putting Creative Strategy to Work*, 3rd ed., St. Paul, Minnesota: West, 1989
Higgins, Denis, *The Art of Writing Advertising: Conversations with Masters of the Craft*, Lincolnwood, Illinois: NTC Business, 1990
Wells, William, John Burnett, Sandra E. Moriarty, and Charles Pearce, *Advertising: Principles and Practice*, 3rd ed., Englewood Cliffs, New Jersey: Prentice-Hall, 1995

Advertising Council

Public service advertising prepared by leading agencies

The Advertising Council is a partnership between media, advertisers, and advertising agencies that creates public service messages addressing a wide range of social issues. A nonprofit organization of volunteers, its work is pro bono, and all media time and space is donated.

The idea for the Advertising Council arose in November 1941 at a meeting of the Association of National Advertisers and the American Association of Advertising Agencies. At that meeting, James Webb Young, a senior consultant to

Smokey Bear is an early public service creation of the Advertising Council.
(Courtesy of The Advertising Council, Inc.)

the J. Walter Thompson agency, suggested that "greater use of advertising for social, political, and philanthropic purposes" would help counter criticism of the advertising profession. Less than a month later, the Japanese attack on Pearl Harbor brought the United States into World War II, and the new Advertising Council was called to Washington, D.C., to discuss how advertising could assist in the war effort at home. On January 5, 1942, the Advertising Council (later renamed the War Advertising Council) was assured funding, and the work of the council began.

During the war, the War Advertising Council planned and executed dozens of campaigns to support the war effort. These campaigns encouraged people to conserve fuel and rubber; to enlist as aviation cadets, cadet nurses, army nurses, WACs, and WAVEs; to plant victory gardens; to buy war bonds; and to make greater use of V-mail. An estimated $1 billion in advertising space and airtime supported War Advertising Council campaigns through 1945. Following the war, the Advertising Council continued its mission to "identify a select number of significant public issues and stimulate action on those issues through communications programs that make a measurable difference in our society." These efforts continue today.

The Advertising Council receives more than 400 campaign-support requests from government agencies and nonprofit organizations each year. Because of limited media availability, many worthwhile causes must be turned down; the Council's board of directors and major committees can accept only three or four new campaigns annually. When a campaign is accepted, a volunteer advertising agency and campaign coordinator oversee its development. The client organization and the Council's Campaign Review Committee monitor the process to ensure that the campaign meets the stated objectives. Once approved, advertisements are produced and distributed to more than 29,000 media outlets that donate time and space to the messages. It is estimated that the Advertising Council generates more than $800 million in media airtime and space each year for public service advertising.

Over the years, many Advertising Council themes have become a part of public conscience – for example, "Keep America Beautiful," "A Mind Is a Terrible Thing to Waste," and "Friends Don't Let Friends Drive Drunk." Advertising Council characters continued to be a part of the popular culture: McGruff, the crime dog, urged people to help "Take a Bite Out of Crime." Vince and Larry, the crash-test dummies, reminded people of the importance of buckling seatbelts. Smokey Bear informed the public for more than 50 years, "Only You Can Prevent Forest Fires."

PEGGY J. KRESHEL

See also War Advertising Council

Further Reading

"Ad Council at 50," *Advertising Age* (November 11, 1991)

Krugman, Dean M., *Advertising: Its Role in Modern Marketing*, 8th ed., Fort Worth, Texas: Dryden, 1994

Museum of Television & Radio, *A Retrospective of Advertising Council Campaigns: A Half Century of Public Service,* New York: Museum of Television & Radio, 1991

Rubicam, Raymond, "Advertising," in *While You Were Gone: A Report on Wartime Life in the United States,* edited by Jack Goodman, New York: Simon & Schuster, 1946

Advertising in the Eighteenth Century

Growing advertising possibilities became impetus of newspaper foundings

Advertising existed almost from the beginning of colonial America, not in newspapers but in their forerunners: pamphlets, bulletins, tavern walls, and even local churches. Advertising did not find its way into newspapers until early in the eighteenth century, and such content became a major impetus for the establishment of newspapers and, to a lesser extent, magazines.

Filling the human need to be informed about events and commerce evolved naturally from the spoken word through handwritten messages to a primitive printed publication. While learning the latest intelligence about events near and far was important, learning about the arrival of goods and the availability of items at retail was of major concern to both merchant and buyer. Before the advent of the newspaper, the clergy often passed along items of interest and advertising tidbits from their pulpits. The colonial equivalent of the English town crier was likely to be found outside church on the Sabbath, passing on snippets of news and advertising. Interestingly, the tavern performed the same functions as the clergy in pre-newspaper days.

Still, the most important medium for advertising in the eighteenth century, as it was to remain until well into the twentieth century, was the newspaper. The colonies' first newspaper, *Publick Occurrences, Both Forreign and Domestick,* carried no advertising in its single issue in 1690. The first continuously operated newspaper in the colonies, the *Boston News-Letter,* however, carried advertising in 1704. The *News-Letter,* like other newspapers of the eighteenth century, was small, gray, and monotonous, but it was an excellent advertising vehicle because it circulated among the elite of society. A typical advertisement looked much like modern classified advertising with lines of small type. Content differed greatly from today's advertising. An eighteenth-century advertisement was likely to seek the return of slaves, animals, or errant wives or to offer for sale real estate or shop goods. Display advertising, however, was unknown in the early years of the eighteenth century.

The earliest advertisements of any size were for the sale of religious books, pamphlets, and copies of sermons by well-known clerics. Much of what passed for news in early newspapers was borrowed from other newspapers – generally English newspapers – and printers often offered copies of foreign newspapers for sale after printers had finished using whatever copy they wanted for their own publications.

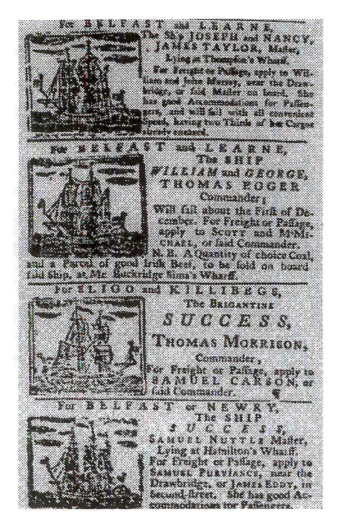

Small ads with rough woodcut illustrations were featured in some eighteenth-century newspapers.

Still, the typical advertisement concerned runaway servants, escaped slaves, and errant wives; goods, houses, and land for sale; and things wanted.

The space devoted to advertising was limited in the *News-Letter* and other early newspapers because each issue was normally only two pages. In fact, John Campbell, Boston's postmaster and the printer of the *News-Letter*, limited advertising to 20 lines, with only a few inches in each issue devoted to advertising. It was not uncommon for early newspapers to have no advertising at all. This state of affairs quickly changed, however, as printers and readers discovered the value of advertising.

The person perhaps most important to the overall health of newspapers and advertising in the eighteenth century was Benjamin Franklin. While still a young man, Franklin bought the *Pennsylvania Gazette* in 1729. Recognizing the value of advertising as a revenue source, Franklin set about turning the *Gazette* into a moneymaker in addition to a vehicle for his creative genius. He increased the size of the newspaper from two to four pages, improved its typography by using large headlines and surrounding the advertise-

ments with white space, and is credited with the first use of illustrations.

Several other printers associated with eighteenth-century advertising are noteworthy. John Peter Zenger, whose trial in 1735 raised important press freedom issues, greatly expanded the space given to advertising in his newspaper, the *New York Weekly Journal*. His newspaper typically carried four or five times as much advertising as other newspapers. He did not restrict the amount of space advertising could use, and he also offered advertisers discounts to entice them to advertise. James Parker, printer of the *New York Weekly Post-Boy*, devoted up to three of his newspaper's four pages to advertising, featured large type for the period, and used display advertisements. John Dunlap's *Pennsylvania Packet and the General Advertiser* used advertising to sell newspapers and featured well-designed advertisements with items separated by column rules and a profusion of illustrations. Dunlap became so successful that by 1784 he was forced to change the weekly to a daily to meet advertisers' demands for space. Francis Childs' New York *Daily Advertiser* began to use labels for advertising that were often as large as 36 points, unheard of in colonial newspapers.

In the decades before the American Revolution, governmental attempts at taxing newspapers, and the shortages of paper those attempts created, began to have an adverse affect on advertising. The effect of taxation itself on newspaper advertising, however, is probably overrated because both New York and Massachusetts enacted so-called stamp acts at least a decade before the British Stamp Act of 1765. The state measures met with only minor opposition and appear to have had little or no effect on advertising.

Although necessary economically, advertising in the eighteenth century was a nuisance to newspaper printers, barely tolerated, ethically immature, and without a sense of direction. There were no advertising agencies or practitioners as they are known today. Even among potential advertisers there was a reluctance to advertise. Unlike modern advertising, advertisements in the eighteenth century were considered to be similar to news, and not all printers even separated their news columns from advertising columns. America would have to wait until the next century for advertising to come of age.

DONALD R. AVERY

See also Campbell, John; Franklin, Benjamin; Newspapers in the Eighteenth Century; *Publick Occurrences, Both Forreign and Domestick*; Stamp Act of 1765; Zenger, John Peter

Further Reading

Applegate, Edd, "The Development of Advertising, 1700–1900," in *The Media in America: A History*, 3rd ed., edited by W. David Sloan and James D. Startt, Northport, Alabama: Vision, 1996

Avery, Donald R., "The Colonial Press, 1690–1765," in *The Media in America: A History*, 3rd ed., edited by W. David Sloan and James D. Startt, Northport, Alabama: Vision, 1996

Brigham, Clarence S., *Journals and Journeymen: A Contribution to the History of Early American*

Newspapers, Philadelphia: University of Pennsylvania Press, 1950

Shaw, Steven J., "Colonial Newspaper Advertising: A Step Toward Freedom of the Press," *Business History Review* 33 (1959)

Advertising in the Nineteenth Century

Some experiments with advertising design conducted during these years

By the early 1800s, the number of newspapers published in the United States had grown to more than 300. Despite the fact that advertising volume was increasing as well, few newspapers depended on advertising revenue. Most newspapers were operated for political purposes and supported by private contributions or subscriptions. Most publishers were satisfied with their advertising, and few worried about how advertisements appeared. Thus, advertising remained constant in appearance for many years. In most cases advertisements carried no more than one illustration each, and the copy was dull and usually small in size. Yet advertising remained popular among businesses. The reason was simple – cities were growing. Proprietors realized that prospective customers were moving close to their enterprises every day, and they had to be informed. This interest was instrumental in the development of advertising in the early nineteenth century; without business interest, advertising might have failed.

When Benjamin Day began the *New York Sun* in 1833, he revolutionized not only journalism but newspaper advertising as well. By its second year, the *Sun* was selling 20,000 copies, more than twice the number of any other newspaper in America. The large circulation made it a popular vehicle for advertisers.

Advertising in the *Sun* cost $30 a year for a "square" of 10 lines a day. This equaled one cent a line. Day wrote most of the copy, which in most cases consisted of 10 lines or less. The advertisements were similar to those in other newspapers, except for their size. Day realized the importance of the want ad, which had been used by advertisers in England. He solicited these small advertisements from businesses and readers and placed them under the heading "Wants." Each entry, two or three lines in length, cost 50 cents. Day also published advertisements for theaters and museums as well as marriage and death notices.

As the number of advertisements increased, Day had to increase the *Sun*'s page dimensions. By 1836, the size was 12 by 19 inches. Advertising accounted for 13 columns a day. In 1839, two years after Day sold the *Sun* to Moses Yale Beach for $40,000, advertisements accounted for 17 columns in the 24-column newspaper.

In 1835, James Gordon Bennett founded the *New York Herald,* which, like the *Sun,* attracted both readers and advertisers. Advertising rates applied to a square of space – from $30 a year to 50 cents a day. These rates changed,

Uneeda Biscuits was one of the first brand names to appear in nineteenth-century advertising.

however, as physical changes occurred in typography and size. Advertisements were separated by lines but contained no boldface headings. Bennett preferred lightface.

Most advertisements carried few, if any, illustrations. A few papers in Boston and Philadelphia were exceptions to the rule, but most advertisements were similar to want ads. They contained small headlines, small amounts of copy, and thumbnail-size cuts of houses, hats, ships, and other illustrations that identified a particular type of business.

In 1836, Bennett's *Herald* published a two-column advertisement for the American Museum that contained a two-column illustration. For several years after that, the *Herald* and other New York newspapers published two-column advertisements, some with illustrations. In the late 1840s, advertisers that placed small advertisements every day complained so much about the few advertisers that placed large display advertisements occasionally that the *Herald* finally banned all display. Consequently, the *Herald*'s advertising columns looked the same, and advertising – at least in the *Herald* and other New York newspapers – seemed to regress.

With the spread of railroads and other forms of transportation and new manufacturing plants, newspaper advertising became important to these industries as well as to new small businesses. These forms of transportation also helped newspapers increase their circulations, thus encouraging an increase in the number of advertising columns.

In 1851, Robert Bonner, who had worked as a compositor on the *Hartford (Connecticut) Courant,* purchased the *Merchants' Ledger,* a business sheet, and changed the name to the *New York Ledger.* At first Bonner refused advertising, but he changed his mind and later made advertising history by publishing stories that appealed to women, which led to more female readers and to an increase in advertisements directed to them. Bonner serviced advertising in another way, too, when he advertised his publication in other newspapers. He broke the barriers against display and soon made publishers of penny papers realize they had made a mistake, monetarily speaking, by restricting advertisers to a certain format. He experimented with copy and typography, which caused other publishers to do the same.

Each of Bonner's advertisements in other newspapers began with the same two lines in capital letters. Copying a style used by auctioneers in England, Bonner wrote his advertisements in the want-ad style and repeated the simple message throughout the available space. One ad promoted a *New York Ledger* story by repeating the same line 93 times in the *New York Herald,* filling a full column. Bonner soon went to two columns with reiteration, then to a full page. Some of his advertisements included one line printed

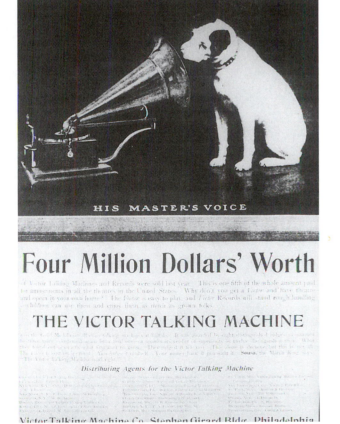

"His master's voice," the dog, and the phonograph became recognizable symbols in the late nineteenth century.

more than 600 times. Bonner was the first advertiser to spend as much as $27,000 a week; only the patent medicine advertisers spent as much as Bonner in a single year.

Bonner's methods had an immediate effect on advertising. Although large, bold display advertisements were not published by most newspapers until the late 1800s, most newspapers experimented with type faces and sizes.

After the Civil War, two large New York department stores – Macy's and Lord and Taylor – moved to two-column advertisements. Lord and Taylor's advertisements contained announcements of specific products or groups of products. The company logo was usually the largest size type – 30-point. The size was increased to 36-point in the 1870s. Lord and Taylor also broke up copy so that three or four advertisements could be printed one under another in one column. Thus the company's logo was seen by the reader more than once. Other advertisers, such as John Wanamaker in Philadelphia, copied this style.

Magazine advertising followed a somewhat different path in the 1800s. Advertising often appeared on the covers, and special sections of four to eight pages catering to advertisers were common. These sections allowed numerous businesses to advertise products and services in copy-filled blocks. Display was seldom used.

In the mid-1800s, several popular magazines, including the *Atlantic Monthly,* the *American Whig Review,* and business reviews, carried advertising for the first time. The *Atlantic Monthly* had 14 pages of advertising in its December 1865 issue. The *American Whig Review,* in order to stay afloat, carried advertising in its last year of publication.

Women's periodicals such as *Godey's, Peterson's,* and *Ladies' Wreath* carried advertising of numerous products and services – from musical instruments, sewing machines, and silverware to schools. These advertisements contained copy and some illustrations. *Leslie's Illustrated,* a weekly periodical, published a full-page advertisement of Mason and Hamlin melodious and other musical instruments on October 20, 1860. The advertisement contained nine illustrations, which was unusual. Most advertisements contained one or two.

Certain periodicals rejected advertising because their publishers believed advertising lowered their magazines' value. The only advertising appearing on the pages of *Harper's Weekly* was for the company's forthcoming books. On the other hand, many magazines depended on patent medicine advertising, leading journalists to criticize the magazine industry.

After the Civil War, advertising in magazines became popular. Circulations increased as more Americans learned to read. *Scribner's,* which enjoyed a large circulation, was one of the first magazines to attract numerous advertisers. *Galaxy* was the first high-toned magazine to run a variety of miscellaneous advertisements in color. From 1868 to 1870, it used colored inserts – one of the main reasons it had at least 24 pages of advertising a month.

Advertising in magazines increased until 1873, when businesses saw profits decrease because of a depressed economy. Consequently, businesses withheld advertisements for the next several years. Publishers of magazines tempted advertisers with various offers. Many of their offers, however, went unnoticed, and many magazines died as a result. Magazine advertisements in this period contained brief but bold captions, bold logos, copy in various sizes and typefaces, and one or more illustrations, depending on the sizes of the advertisements. Advertising rates in the late 1800s were more reflective of circulations. In 1865, the *Saturday Evening Post,* which had a circulation of 20,000, charged 30 cents an agate line. In 1885, it charged 25 cents an agate line, yet it had a circulation of 40,000. The explanation for the apparent paradox is that as circulations increased, the cost of advertising decreased. This was the case for such periodicals as the *Spirit of the Times, Harper's Monthly,* the *Century, Ladies' Home Journal,* and *Godey's.*

By the beginning of the 1890s, new industries had been founded and old industries had grown. Businesses realized that magazines were reaching more consumers, especially in the month of December, and consequently they placed more advertising. As the century ended, magazines accounted for about one-fourth of the dollars businesses spent on advertising. One reason for this growth was national advertising by manufacturers such as W.L. Douglas, Lydia Pinkham, and Royal Baking Powder, which used trade characters that humanized products in their advertisements. Among the firms with large advertising expenditures were Warner's Celebrated Coraline Corsets, Plymouth Rock Three Dollar Pants, and Cluett Shirts and Collars. Agencies for many of these firms used pictures in advertisements to illustrate the benefits of the product.

Other large advertisers included manufacturers of pianos and other instruments, housewares, appliances, bicycles, cameras, breakfast foods, phonographs, soaps, safety razors, and medicines. Some companies became famous as a result of their advertising. Consumers remembered Pears' soap after reading its slogan, "Good Morning, Have You Used Pears' Soap?" Procter & Gamble's Ivory Soap was remembered, too, because it was "99 44/100 per cent pure."

Although many magazines advertised practically everything during the late 1800s, some publishers protected their readers by not running fraudulent advertisements. Fake remedies were especially troublesome. Even the most reputable magazines ignored other complaints, however, including concerns about the use of images of women to sell corsets and underwear, which was considered risqué.

As businesses increased their use of advertising, advertising agencies developed to serve as intermediaries between businesses and media outlets. Initially the agency represented newspaper publishers, serving mostly as wholesalers of newspaper space. Orlando Bourne was doing this as early as 1828. Most agencies worked for one or a few newspapers. Volney B. Palmer, who had offices in Boston, New York, Philadelphia, and Baltimore, Maryland, by 1846, and John L. Hooper, who worked in New York, were the pioneers because they represented several publications. In addition, they promoted advertising as an integral part of marketing and produced as well as delivered advertisements to publishers. Palmer was particularly active in those techniques.

By the 1850s, agents became independent. Space-jobbing, as this stage was called, became popular as agents realized that they could earn more by selling space to advertisers. When advertisers desired space to promote products, the agents would buy it for them in newspapers. During this period, many agents questioned their role. After all, they did not work for publishers, and they did not work for advertisers. Yet they referred to themselves as agents. Where exactly was this business headed?

The direction of advertising changed again somewhat in 1865 when George P. Rowell purchased large amounts of space in newspapers and then resold it in small amounts to advertisers. This stage has been called space-wholesaling. By the late 1860s, Rowell's initial idea had been altered. Advertising concession agencies appeared. This stage occurred when Carlton and Smith (later the J. Walter Thompson Company) purchased most – if not all – of the advertising space in certain publications for a specified period. Consequently, the agency, not the publisher, was responsible for securing advertisers for the entire publication. This practice actually closed the gap between agent and publisher, but the agent worked as an independent middleman nonetheless.

EDD APPLEGATE

See also Bennett, James Gordon Sr.; Brand-Name Advertising; Magazines in the Nineteenth Century; Newspapers in the Nineteenth Century; Palmer, Volney B.; Patent Medicine Advertising; Penny Press

Further Reading
Hower, Ralph M., *The History of an Advertising Agency: N.W. Ayer & Son at Work, 1869–1949,* Cambridge, Massachusetts: Harvard University Press, 1949
Rowell, George, *Forty Years as an Advertising Agent: 1865–1905,* New York: Franklin, 1926; London: Garland, 1985
Rowsome, Frank, *They Laughed When I Sat Down: An Informal History of Advertising in Words and Pictures,* New York: McGraw-Hill, 1959

Advertising in the Twentieth Century

Substantial changes in form, content of ads, structure of advertising business

U.S. advertising at the beginning of the twentieth century was a relatively small, local industry that dealt with a simple mixture of media and experienced significant criticism. The tone of the advertising message was increasingly hard sell. Reflecting business in general, U.S. advertising toward the end of the twentieth century grew massive in size and corporate in nature. It experienced its greatest visibility at the national level, enjoyed an almost overwhelming complex of media through which to reach consumers, and was subject to continuing criticism. The tone of the message could be hard sell or soft sell, depending mostly upon economic conditions.

Somewhere West of Laramie

SOMEWHERE west of Laramie there's a broncho-busting, steer-roping girl who knows what I'm talking about. She can tell what a sassy pony, that's a cross between greased lightning and the place where it hits, can do with eleven hundred pounds of steel and action when he's going high, wide and handsome.

The truth is—the Playboy was built for her.

Built for the lass whose face is brown with the sun when the day is done of revel and romp and race.

She loves the cross of the wild and the tame.

There's a savor of links about that car—of laughter and lilt and light—a hint of old loves—and saddle and quirt. It's a brawny thing—yet a graceful thing for the sweep o' the Avenue.

Step into the Playboy when the hour grows dull with things gone dead and stale.

Then start for the land of real living with the spirit of the lass who rides, lean and rangy, into the red horizon of a Wyoming twilight.

Automobile advertising, circa 1920s

Expenditures on advertising as the nation entered the twentieth century are difficult to determine. After careful analysis, historian Daniel Pope puts them at about $250 million. At the end of the century, expenditures were close to $150 billion.

In the early years of the century, only a handful of relatively small agencies existed, mostly in large cities. The three with largest billings were N.W. Ayer and Son of Philadelphia, Lord and Thomas of Chicago, and J. Walter Thompson of New York. Ayer, the largest, placed $1.6 million in advertising in 1898. At the end of the century, agencies that billed at least $100 million annually were common, and the very largest agencies placed more than a billion dollars of advertising. N.W. Ayer was not among the 10 largest, and Lord and Thomas no longer existed.

In the early years of modern advertising, people such as Albert Lasker, John E. Kennedy, Claude Hopkins, Stanley Resor, Helen Lansdowne Resor, and Theodore MacManus stood as the generals in command of the industry. Later in the twentieth century, probably because of the very size of the advertising business, the generals worked with comparative anonymity within the client and agency armies that plotted the strategies and executed the plans. That said, regarding the later years, the names of William Bernbach, Leo Burnett, David Ogilvy, Rosser Reeves, and Mary Wells stand out from the rest.

One set of numbers suggests that national advertising accounted for only slightly more than one-tenth of all advertising expenditures in 1890. The actual percentage probably was higher. Nonetheless, the advertising industry at that time was mostly local. By the end of the first third of the century, national advertising dollars surged ahead of local, and the rise of large nationwide media made the industry more nationally oriented, a state that became more pronounced as the years went by.

During the first decade of the twentieth century, advertisers had essentially three media available – magazines, newspapers, and signs. While newspaper numbers were declining by the second decade, commercial radio appeared in the 1920s, and television became commercially feasible after World War II. Programming began appealing to more homogeneous audiences, and the proliferation of cable television channels divided the audience even further. Magazines by the thousands became specialized during the last decades of the century.

In terms of message, a pattern began emerging during the 1920s, when soft-sell messages seemed more common and effective. Hard-sell approaches became necessary as economic depression brought difficult times to the nation in the 1930s. This pattern generally held throughout the century, although specific names changed: the hard sell has been called "reason why" advertising or "salesmanship in print," and the soft sell has been known as "prestige," "image," or "emotional," depending upon the era and the speaker.

One of only a few constants in the twentieth-century life of advertising was the abundance of criticism. Advertising had a controversial presence throughout the century. First, muckrakers during the first few years attacked patent medicine advertising and other fraudulent misuse of commercial messages. During the depression-ridden thirties, critics questioned whether advertising was necessary. Later, complaints focused on perceived manipulation by advertisers who, it was charged, used symbols that insidiously prompted people to buy. Some academicians have argued that advertising served U.S. industry, in the words of one critic, as an instrument of social control.

The United States was changing radically as the new century began. The nation was shedding its rural character. Population numbers trended upward sharply, especially in larger cities. Technology was transforming transportation and communication. Business became increasingly industrialized and centralized. Branded products flowing out of large manufacturers encountered resistance among retailers who sold in bulk. The marketers of products such as Campbell's soups, Gillette razor blades, Ivory soap, Quaker Oats, and Postum saw extensive advertising as a means of attracting customers to local stores in search of their brands. A common style of advertising through even the late nineteenth century was that of simply providing information. The would-be national marketers needed something more vigorous than that, and they turned to advertising agencies for help.

One of the owners of Lord and Thomas, Albert Lasker, was searching for an advertising formula beyond pure news, a variant of the information style and a common definition of advertising at the time. He found his answer in the practice of many department stores: what was termed "salesmanship in print." The idea came from John E. Kennedy, who had a variety of copywriting experiences before Lasker hired him. Advertising copy, Kennedy said, must provide reasons people should buy a product, just as a salesman would. Lasker adopted this concept as his agency's basic copy philosophy. Although highly paid, Kennedy left Lord and Thomas after about two years and was replaced by another talented copywriter, Claude Hopkins. Hopkins worked quickly and effectively. He subscribed to the salesmanship-in-print philosophy and added his own ideas. One principle he employed was to establish some characteristic of the product as the property of his client. Thus, Hopkins's copy pointed out that Schlitz beer steam-cleaned its bottles and Quaker puffed wheat was "shot from guns." Competitors, of course, used the same techniques, but Hopkins preempted them for his advertisers.

As Lasker, Kennedy, and Hopkins were developing their hard-sell ideas of advertising in Chicago, Stanley Resor, going to work for Procter & Gamble's advertising agency in his hometown of Cincinnati, Ohio, proved so effective that the J. Walter Thompson agency hired him in 1908 to open its Cincinnati office. In 1912, he moved to New York as vice president and general manager of J. Walter Thompson. Four years later, at the age of 37, he and others purchased the venerable old agency that Resor had begun to revive after years of neglect by its longtime owner, whose name continued to grace the company letterhead. In addition to energy, Resor brought to J. Walter Thompson a respect for the social sciences, research, and psychology. He hired a research director and a psychologist, both of them college professors. To the idea of hard-sell copy Resor wedded the notion of careful research. Under Resor's leadership for 39 years, the agency continued to grow as one of the nation's largest and most respected.

One of the people on the New York staff of J. Walter Thompson was Helen Lansdowne, who had worked for Resor in Cincinnati. She was an inspired copywriter who doubled as the head of the creative department. Her work included advertisements in the Thompson philosophy of thorough research and hard sell, but some of her best-known efforts employed emotions, especially those for Woodbury's Facial Soap. She and Stanley Resor were married in 1917.

During the early years of Lasker's and the Resors' work at their respective agencies, the advertising world was being assaulted by muckrakers, who held patent medicine advertisements in particular scorn. Advertising organizations such as professional clubs and the Associated Advertising Clubs of America (AACA) had been wrestling with the problem of fraudulent advertising for many years, with only moderate success. In 1911, the annual AACA convention established a national vigilance committee to fight false and misleading advertising. The effort led in time to the Better Business Bureaus. Congress, meanwhile, had founded the Federal Trade Commission (FTC) in 1915 with only indirect oversight of advertising.

The year in which the FTC was established also saw the flowering of another school of advertising thought that had been growing parallel with, but slightly behind, the hard-sell philosophy of Lord and Thomas and J. Walter Thompson. While those agencies sought to market inexpensive products, Theodore MacManus had an entirely different task – advertising the Cadillac automobile. He developed a long-term approach with a soft appeal to build credibility toward the day when purchasers made the major investment required by his product. MacManus had been at his task for years when he developed one of the first classic advertisements of the century. It was published in a January 1915 issue of the *Saturday Evening Post*. Entitled "The Penalty of Leadership" and barren of any reference to Cadillac except the corporate symbol at the top, the advertisement sought to establish an image of prestige.

Interestingly, the next step along the path of soft-sell messages, image building, also advertised an automobile, the Jordan. Company owner Ned Jordan developed an advertisement that ran in a 1923 issue of the *Saturday Evening Post*. It, too, became a classic. Under a drawing of a cowboy on a galloping horse and a young woman at the steering wheel of a speeding automobile, the advertisement painted a picture of what life is like when it includes a Jordan. Under the headline "Somewhere West of Laramie," the copy advised the reader to "Step into the [Jordan] Playboy when the hour grows dull with things gone dead and stale. Then start for the land of real living with the spirit of the lass who rides, lean and rangy, into the red horizon of a Wyoming twilight." The advertisement represents a genre that proved effective during the affluent twenties.

The decade also saw the appearance of commercial radio, which grew rapidly from the first stations in 1920. Resistance to advertising on radio was strong initially, from the radio industry itself, from the newspaper industry, and from others who wished to retain the purity of the new medium. But advertisements appeared anyway. Albert Lasker, at first skeptical, became enthusiastic about the new medium after first efforts proved bountifully successful. Soon, Lord and Thomas was doing half of the advertising on radio networks.

As the 1930s began, the United States skidded into a severe economic depression, and advertising reflected the new realities. Advertising expenditures dropped from $3.4 billion in 1929 to $1.3 billion in 1933. Hard-sell copy came back in vogue. Advertisements offered ways to find or keep a job by using the advertised products. Negative appeals were common. Agency billings dropped precipitously, and staff cutbacks followed. Advertising itself was the target of critics, who saw commercial messages as the most visible component of business, the seeming villain of the Great Depression. At the very least, the intent was to impose more restrictions on advertising. Congress and federal agencies were modestly successful at that. The FTC, for example, received broadened powers over false and misleading advertising. Moreover, the Consumers Union was organized in 1936 and began monitoring advertising.

Whatever the criticisms, advertisers also helped bring badly needed entertainment into U.S. homes by sponsoring radio programs. Comedians and singers, soap operas and mystery programs – all allowed listeners relief from the grim economic times. And while most advertising agencies were also suffering from the depression, two agencies actually prospered.

Raymond Rubicam had founded his agency, Young and Rubicam, in 1923 around a soft-sell, highly ethical approach to advertising. Rubicam gave his creative staffs the freedom to develop messages unfettered by management, in contrast with the policies of many agencies. In 1932, he hired George Gallup to run the agency's research program, which the nationally known pollster did for 16 years. The product of Rubicam's philosophy and leadership came in constantly increased billings, even during the depression. A soft-spoken copywriter named Leo Burnett, encouraged by colleagues, established an agency during the middle of the 1930s and watched it prosper. Like Young and Rubicam, its total focus was on the creative product of the agency. Both Young and Rubicam and Burnett enjoyed world-class stature at the end of the twentieth century.

With the rest of the nation, advertising struggled during the 1930s; expenditures climbed to only $2.2 billion in 1941. When the nation entered World War II, conditions changed abruptly. Unemployment dropped from 25 percent to near zero. Suddenly there was an abundance of money but, because most available resources were devoted to war production, limited consumer goods on which to spend it. Encouraged by governmental policy that frowned on excess profits, businesses invested heavily in advertising, reminding consumers that their products would return after the war, talking about their contributions to the war effort, and encouraging patriotic activities. The War Advertising Council was established by the advertising industry to offer professional communication services to help the nation at war.

In the late 1940s, a consumer economy appeared again as peace returned to the nation. During the 1950s, automobile businesses were the big advertisers. In its affluence, this decade was much like the twenties. So, too, was its advertising. The Marlboro man, created by Leo Burnett, appeared. The largest advertising agencies passed the $100-million mark in billings each year, led by J. Walter Thompson. By 1950, annual expenditures on advertising in the nation reached $5.7 billion.

Removed from a freeze imposed by the war, television emerged from the shadow of radio and became a massive advertising medium – from $10 million in the late 1940s to about $1 billion ten years later and $11.4 billion in 1980. Advertisers and agencies evidenced little reluctance to advertise on television, and the rush to the new medium produced embarrassing moments for both television and advertising industries during the middle fifties, when scandals on popular quiz programs were uncovered. Until this time, advertisers commonly sponsored entire programs. Sponsorship costs were so high, however, that advertisers adjusted to less-expensive short commercials to deliver their messages.

During the last decades of the century, major changes occurred in advertising media. Radio adjusted to a mostly local format, and magazines shifted from large, wide readership associated with *Life, Look,* and the *Saturday Evening Post,* to publications for specialized audiences. Cable was added to the television mix, further splintering advertising audiences. Later, computers and the Internet imposed additional pressure toward fragmentation of audiences.

Changing media did not alter Rosser Reeves' view of advertising. Coming from the hard-sell philosophy, Reeves proposed the unique selling proposition in his 1961 book, *Reality in Advertising.* It was a new name for Claude Hopkins' old method of promoting an unusual aspect of the product. In these affluent decades following World War II, soft-sell-oriented, highly creative work became more common. Two new agencies appearing in the late 1940s captured that mood and were destined to exercise signal influence on the advertising industry. David Ogilvy was the dominant force in one and William Bernbach in the other. Ogilvy, a native of Great Britain and author of the popular book *Confessions of an Advertising Man,* seemed drawn to both soft- and hard-sell schools. He also possessed a capacity for developing memorable campaigns such as one for Hathaway shirts using a distinguished-looking gentleman wearing a black eye patch. Bernbach became the creative soul of Doyle Dane Bernbach, which produced campaigns noted for uniqueness and a soft-sell approach. The best example is the one marketing a humble little German car, the Volkswagen, to a public satiated with advertisements for domestic cars trumpeting size and opulence. The Bernbach solution: "Think small."

Perhaps because of the creative and image-oriented advertising associated with this era, two critics attracted attention because of their highly visible charges against advertising. In Vance Packard's 1957 book *The Hidden Persuaders* and Wilson Bryan Key's 1973 *Subliminal Seduction,* the authors sought to show that advertisers employ hidden symbols to manipulate consumers to buy products. Cognizant of criticism, of which Packard and Key represented only the most recent iteration, the American Advertising Federation, the American Association of Advertising Agencies, the Association of National Advertisers, and the Council of Better Business Bureaus (CBBB) established the National Advertising Division (NAD) of the CBBB and the National Advertising Review Board (NARB) in 1971 to hear objections to advertisements at the national level. The steps proved effective.

In spite of the work of the NAD and the NARB, complaints about political advertising grew especially loud during the last decades of the century. At the national level, political advertising on television first appeared during the 1952 presidential campaign. Television asserted an increasing presence with each campaign. In 1964, a Doyle Dane Bernbach television commercial for President Lyndon Johnson showing a small girl picking the petals off a daisy against a background of an atomic explosion brought a protest from Republicans, who argued that the spot had misrepresented their candidate's position on the use of nuclear weapons. Four years later, author Joe McGinniss charged the Republicans with selling their candidate, Richard Nixon, through television advertising. Negative political advertising, employing all media, grew in popularity at all levels.

During the same period, stereotypical images of minorities and women were in decline. Moreover, the industry itself, largely dominated by white males, began diversifying its racial and gender makeup. Mary Wells, a highly respected copywriter and manager, became the first woman to head a major advertising agency, Wells Rich Greene. Women came to occupy numerous positions of leadership at smaller agencies and in professional advertising clubs and associations. At the same time, several waves of agency mergers swept through the industry, producing increasingly larger organizations, though not necessarily better work.

Advertising was the star of the promotion function during most of the century. As the century drew to a close, however, other activities that had been operating quietly in the background for many decades – notably direct marketing, public relations, and sales promotion – began edging onto the promotional stage with advertising. A new concept called integrated marketing communications proposed to merge the four functions into one effort. The question became whether advertising would become submerged in this approach to marketing, and whether integrated marketing communications would move into the position of primacy occupied by advertising during the twentieth century. If so, the new Albert Laskers, Stanley Resors, and Raymond Rubicams could be expected to develop the new concept, even as the pioneers of modern advertising had performed that function during the century that was reaching its end.

BRUCE ROCHE

See also Advertising Agencies; Advertising and Minorities; Advertising Appeals; Ayer, N.W., & Son; Better Business Bureau; Brand-Name Advertising; Broadcast Advertising; Criticism of Advertising; Federal Trade Commission; Hopkins, Claude C.; Muckraking; National Advertising Review Board; Patent Medicine Advertising; Political Advertising; Reeves, Rosser; Resor, Helen Lansdowne; Resor, Stanley B.; War Advertising Council

Further Reading

Diamond, Edwin, and Stephen Bates, *The Spot: The Rise of Political Advertising on Television,* Cambridge, Massachusetts: MIT Press, 1984
Gunther, John, *Taken at the Flood: The Story of Albert D. Lasker,* New York: Harper and Brothers, 1960; London: Hamilton, 1960
Pollay, Richard W., ed., *Information Sources in Advertising History,* Westport, Connecticut: Greenwood, 1979
Strasser, Susan, *Satisfaction Guaranteed: The Making of the American Mass Market,* New York: Pantheon, 1989

Advertising Photography

Developing a tool of persuasion central to advertising's mission

Photography was a tool of persuasion almost from its beginnings, but not until the twentieth century did photography become central to advertising in the United States. From the earliest daguerreotypes in the 1840s to the cartes de visite and stereoscopic views of the latter nineteenth century, photography promoted individuals, businesses, and government policy. Such work was usually done by portrait photographers who produced "travelogue" or "exotica" images, which were photographic prints depicting important public figures, unusual people such as circus performers, scenes of distant lands, or dramatic happenings such as the American Civil War.

As early as the 1850s, photography was used to help sell actual products, particularly exclusive clothing and other elite wares. Such images, however, were painstakingly distributed as genuine prints or replicated through the mass-reproduction processes of engraving or lithography. These exacting techniques often resulted in beautiful images, but they involved the translation of a photographic image onto a plate through the handwork of an artist or engraver. Thus the methods were slow and did not allow for direct reproductions of photographs. Not until the perfection of the halftone processes in the 1880s was the direct reproduction of photographs possible in magazines and newspapers printed by high-speed presses.

Still, most advertisers refused to embrace photography during the late nineteenth century. Hand-drawn illustrations remained prevalent through the turn of the century because they often tended to cost less while having higher quality than photographs reproduced through halftones. The poor quality of the paper used by many mass newspapers, periodicals, and catalogs adversely affected the quality of photographic reproduction.

In addition, advertisers often considered line drawing to be more elegant, meaning that it better conveyed an association between the product and an elite mode of life. Photographs, on the other hand, were often linked with the sensational reporting of yellow journalism. Those few photographs used in advertisements were usually plain images, unadorned and crisp, depicting products or their users.

Often in larger ads, paintings or drawings provided the most attention-getting power through depicting an ad's theme, while a small photograph depicting the product might be inserted into a corner of the ad, thus adding "realism." When a photographic image was used as the main theme-setting illustration in an ad, it was usually because the ad was trying to provoke insecurity or fear in the consumer, such as depicting the consequences of not using mouthwash or not buying life insurance. Advertisers thought photographs best conveyed the hard reality of such situations, as they imagined it.

Advertisers began to use more photographs in the 1920s and finally came to a wide acceptance of photographs during the Great Depression, when such images became cheaper to produce than drawings or paintings. By 1932, photographs accounted for more than 50 percent of advertising illustrations in a typical issue of the *Ladies' Home Journal.* The print media's changing practices in the presentation of news and entertainment also led advertisers to accept more photography. Photographic realism was becoming more acceptable during the 1920s, and with the documentary fervor of the depression years, photographic realism became quite popular. A 1932 Gallup poll indicated most consumers found the photograph to be the most effective advertising illustration.

By the 1920s, photography was no longer considered merely the crude practice of would-be artists or journalists. By then, Alfred Stieglitz's Photo-Secession, the dynamic society of art photographers founded in 1902, had influenced photography not only in the art world but in mass media as well. Edward Steichen, one of the founders of the Photo-Secession, was instrumental in bridging the gap between the aesthetic concerns of art photography and the more practical concerns of advertising, fashion, news, and documentary photography.

Steichen, who during his long photographic career would work for the U.S. Army and Navy, Condé Nast Publications, and New York's Museum of Modern Art, was a pioneer of U.S. advertising photography during the 1920s and 1930s through introducing what he termed "naturalism" in ad images. In compositions for Jergen's Lotion, Kodak, and other firms, Steichen helped advertise a product without actually showing it through an illustration. His Jergen's photographs depicted a woman's hands peeling potatoes, scrubbing a floor, and doing other skin-damaging tasks – all without showing the lotion product. In addition, Steichen and other art photographers, such as Man Ray and Francis Bruguiere, introduced the convention of using an art style for advertising purposes. Steichen stressed art deco in his advertising photography while Ray and Bruguiere helped sell products with surrealist photographs.

The late 1940s and 1950s saw advertising's first widespread use of color photography, which came to prevail in the ad industry. Changes in technology, such as the perfection of large-format transparency films, ensured the success of color, as did the work of pioneer color photographers such as Anton Bruehl.

During the 1950s, photography came to dominate advertising in magazines, newspapers, and catalogs. Realism and the abstractions of artistic approaches were used as part of many advertising strategies. Although art photographers claimed distance from their more market-oriented counterparts, several photographic styles eventually tended to merge in the latter years of the twentieth century – a process that began in the 1920s. Art, advertising, commercial, fashion, and professional portrait photographers often used similar equipment, lighting methods, and composition techniques. Unlike many fashion or art photographers, however, advertising photographers were not well known by the public; they did, however, develop significant reputations within the advertising community.

Starting in the 1980s, changing technologies again began to influence the practices and conventions of advertising photography as electronic imaging started to replace older photographic processes. Computer-based digital imaging systems made it possible to produce an image without traditional equipment, retouching methods, or even chemical-based film and paper. Images could be made, manipulated, and stored through electronic means. Such processes simplified what were formerly cumbersome and time-consuming retouching methods involving airbrushing and other procedures. They also streamlined other aspects of the design and production processes. With major corporations such as Eastman Kodak heavily investing in electronic-imaging research, the new technology was expected to have a continuing effect on all forms of photography in the future.

CHARLES W. LEWIS

See also Documentary Photography; Photojournalism in the Nineteenth Century; Photojournalism in the Twentieth Century

Further Reading

Beaton, Cecil, and Gail Buckland, *The Magic Image: The Genius of Photography from 1839 to the Present Day,* Boston: Little, Brown, 1975; also published as *The Magic Image: The Genius of Photography,* London: Pavilion, 1989

Leiss, William, Stephen Kline, and Sut Jhally, *Social Communication in Advertising: Persons, Products & Images of Well-being,* New York and Toronto, Ontario: Methuen, 1986

Lester, Paul Martin, *Visual Communication: Images With Messages,* Belmont, California: Wadsworth, 1995

Marchand, Roland, *Advertising the American Dream: Making Way for Modernity, 1920–1940,* Berkeley: University of California Press, 1985

Mason, Jerry, ed., *International Center of Photography Encyclopedia of Photography,* New York: Crown, 1984

Newhall, Beaumont, *The History of Photography: From 1839 to the Present,* New York: Museum of Modern Art, 1982; London: Secker & Warburg, 1982

Advertising Strategy

Market segmentation develops as plans evolve to appeal to certain consumers

Advertising strategy, to the marketer, consists of media and creative strategies. To the advertiser, however, advertising strategy is normally thought of as the tool that directs creative development. Advertising strategy identifies the basis upon which customers are expected to buy one set of products or services in preference to the competition.

Media strategy became important with the proliferation of print media in the late nineteenth century. As the variety of magazines increased in the early twentieth century, advertisers began to segment their markets. After the Audit Bureau of Circulation was formed in 1914, circulation in major print vehicles could be tracked. Media underwent a metamorphosis in 1923 with the birth of the first regular radio series to be sponsored by an advertiser, the *Eveready Hour,* and changed forever with the advent of television. During the broadcasting era, mass marketing reached its peak. Even so, the proliferation of cable television and the electronic information highway in the late twentieth century changed the focus of media strategies to narrowcasting and niche marketing.

Generally, however, creative strategy is paramount to advertising strategy. Procter & Gamble's archetypal strategy, for instance, consisted of an objective or benefit, which included target audience identification, a support statement, and a statement of tone or brand character. Agencies have multiple approaches to formulating strategy: McCann used a consumer model, Foote, Cone and Belding used a planning grid, and Young and Rubicam used a five-point creative work plan.

Some prototypical strategies have evolved over the years. The late nineteenth and early twentieth centuries were fueled by the increased supply of goods; thus, early advertising was used to increase consumption. As media options were limited, "salesmanship in print" was the common strategic approach. Copywriters such as John Caples, Claude C. Hopkins, John E. Kennedy, and James Webb Young worked on a direct-response principle – testimonials were used, and ads were credited for sales. Advertising during the Great Depression continued to use a hard sell; promotions were paramount. During World War II, however, goods were scarce and advertising revenues plummeted.

Thus, the postwar production boom allowed for change. Young and Rubicam made research and art direction an integral part of the strategic process; at a minimum, strategic considerations included the product, the target audience, and the competition. Advertising focused primarily on the product and its qualities. The 1950s saw the beginning of multidisciplinary approaches to the study of consumer behavior. Since then, advertisers benefited from a proliferation of consumer motivational and buying studies. In the same era, Rosser Reeves, former chairman of Ted Bates, coined the phrase "Unique Selling Proposition," the embodiment of those qualities that distinguish a brand from its competition and offer the consumer a unique benefit.

In 1961, Russell Colley aided in the specification of communication strategies by introducing his paradigm, "Defining Advertising Goals for Measured Advertising Results," which enumerated four communication objectives: awareness, comprehension, conviction, and action. Aided by the above, the 1960s brought forth a creative revolution. The decade of the image, started by Bill Bernbach, was based on the power of one idea. The original Volkswagen automobile ads embodied this concept. David Ogilvy stressed the need for a consumer benefit, treating the consumer as an intellectual peer, and Leo Burnett believed in inherent drama, as embodied in the Marlboro Man.

As discretionary income increased and product differences narrowed, consumption became more related to the consumer's mode of living. Thus, strategy in the 1970s centered on properly positioning the product or service within the mind of the consumer. It was the era of the Avis rental-car campaign, "We're Number Two." The 1980s brought about greater awareness of psychographics and lifestyle differentials; the communication of what were known as values and lifestyles became an important tool. Additionally, television had matured and strategy was based on simple, visual messages as epitomized by notable ads for Infiniti automobiles. The late 1980s heralded the realization of the value of brand equity to the firm. As products became less differentiated, the brand added to the product and corporate value. In addition, marketing had fully evolved from a production to a consumer mentality, and more strategic emphasis was placed on consumer wants and needs. The eco-

nomic pressures of the 1990s increased competition and led to greater emphasis on bottom-line results. Thus, many advertisers focused on defending brand equity and started using relationship marketing, direct response, and public relations activities. Accordingly, there was a growing tendency for proportionately less money to be spent in advertising media, and hence, advertising strategies became integrated with other communication activities.

Patricia B. Rose

See also Advertising Appeals; Creative Revolution; Hopkins, Claude C.; Niche Theory; Psychology in Advertising; Reeves, Rosser

Further Reading

Bogart, Leo, *Strategy in Advertising: Matching Media and Messages to Markets and Motivations,* 2nd ed., Lincolnwood, Illinois: NTC Business, 1984

Goodrum, Charles, and Helen Dalrymple, *Advertising in America: The First 200 Years,* New York: Harry N. Abrams, 1990

Kotler, Philip, *Marketing Management: Analysis, Planning, and Control,* Englewood Cliffs, New Jersey: Prentice-Hall, 1967

Norins, Hanley, *The Young & Rubicam Traveling Creative Workshop,* Englewood Cliffs, New Jersey: Prentice-Hall, 1990

Schultz, Don E., and Beth E. Barnes, *Strategic Advertising Campaigns,* 4th ed., Lincolnwood, Illinois: NTC Business, 1995

Advertising Trade Associations

Advertising trade associations began appearing about the time that advertising moved into the modern era: the late nineteenth and early twentieth centuries. In the late twentieth century, they could be seen as composing three groups by the breadth of the interests they represented. The broadest, consisting of the American Advertising Federation alone, included in its local and national membership all elements of the advertising business: advertisers, agencies, educators, media, production, and others. A second group, including the American Association of Advertising Agencies and the Association of National Advertisers, was composed of two of the major components of the national advertising industry. Finally, the third group consisted of seven trade associations in the other major component of the national industry, the media. All trade associations functioned similarly in that they labored in the interests of their constituents. The media associations focused on encouraging use of their vehicles in advertisers' promotional programs.

The earliest of the trade associations brought together businesses in what is probably the oldest advertising medium, signs. Those who posted the signs, known as bill posters, organized the International Billposters' Association of North America in 1872 and the Associated Bill Posters' Association in 1891. The latter group had standardized the outdoor industry by 1912 and renamed itself the Outdoor Advertising Association of America in 1925.

The first advertising clubs in the nation began organizing in the early 1890s. The Denver Advertising Federation, probably the oldest, appeared as the Alfalfa Club in 1891 and was followed by similar clubs in other large cities. On the west coast, a regional trade group, the Pacific Coast Advertising Men's Association, was assembled in 1904. Advertising people in the eastern part of the United States established the Associated Advertising Clubs of America in 1906, which proved particularly influential in the development of the better business bureaus in the 1910s. The two regional organizations merged to form the American Advertising Federation in 1967.

Representatives of 12 firms manufacturing items for advertising purposes joined in 1904 to organize the Advertising Novelty Manufacturers Association. With more than 5,000 members, the trade group came to call itself Promotional Products Association International.

Reflecting the growth of advertising aimed at people throughout the United States, the Association of National Advertising Managers was organized in 1910. Four years later it became the Association of National Advertisers.

The Newspaper Advertising Bureau, which later merged with the American Newspaper Publishers Association to form the Newspaper Association of America, began its work in 1913. In 1917, the American Association of Advertising Agencies was organized by 111 agencies. It sought to standardize agency practices and continued to function under its original name in the late 1990s. Another organization formed in 1917 was the Direct Mail Advertising Association. A change of name to the Direct Marketing Association reflected the use of all media in direct promotional efforts. It operated the Mail Preference Service, which removed consumers' names at their request from national mailing lists. In later years, with the appearance of broadcast media, the Radio Advertising Bureau, the Television Bureau of Advertising, and the Cable Television Advertising Bureau were formed.

BRUCE ROCHE

Advertising Trade Press

In the late twentieth century, there were three major publications serving advertising: *Printer's Ink, Advertising Age,* and *ADWEEK,* although other publications, such as *Sales and Marketing Management* and *Direct Marketing,* touched on related topics.

Printer's Ink was the oldest trade journal that consistently covered issues involving the advertising industry from the perspective of the advertiser. Established in 1888 by George Presbury Rowell, the New York City publication cataloged the growth of advertising as a profession from its roots as a space brokerage – when agencies bought large blocks of space and then attempted to resell it in smaller units to various advertisers – to an industry that used much more than advertising to help sell a product.

Printer's Ink did have a predecessor: *Advertiser's Gazette,* also started by Rowell, was founded in 1867. In 1871, the name was changed to *American Newspaper Reporter,* and it was subsequently published privately by the Rowell advertising agency. *Printer's Ink* was in the vanguard of those in the advertising industry fighting for audited circulation and claimed to have been the initiator of the impetus to form the American Association of Advertising Agencies. *Tide,* a Time, Inc., publication that started in 1927, was absorbed by *Printer's Ink* in 1959.

Advertising Age, founded in 1930, was the perceived leader of the advertising trade journals in terms of both circulation and industry recognition. *ADWEEK* hotly competed for this market, but *Advertising Age* was generally perceived as more industry-focused. Perhaps owing to its tabloid size or to its hard-news editorial approach, at the end of the twentieth century, *Advertising Age* was winning the circulation war, having almost double (79,667) *ADWEEK's* circulation of 42,541 as of February 1996.

THOMAS GOULD

Further Reading

Assael, Henry, and C. Samuel Craig, eds., *Printers' Ink: Fifty Years 1888–1938,* New York: Printers' Ink, 1938

Other Advertising Entries: Better

Business Bureau; Brand-Name Advertising; Broadcast Advertising; Bureau of Advertising; Burnett, Leo Noble; Censorship of Advertising; Classified Advertising; Commercial Speech; Counteradvertising; Creative Revolution; Criticism of Advertising; *Crystallizing Public Opinion;* Direct Mail Advertising; Federal Trade Commission; Food and Drug Administration; Full-Service Advertising Agency; In-House Advertising; *Madison Avenue, USA;* Magazine Advertising; Mass Media and Tobacco Products; National Advertising Review Board; Newspaper Advertising; Open Contract; Patent Medicine Advertising; Political Advertising; Program-Length Commercials; Psychology in Advertising; Reeves, Rosser; Resor, Helen Lansdowne; Resor, Stanley B.; Retail Advertising; Rowell, George P.; *Scientific Advertising;* Shoppers; Truth in Advertising Movement; War Advertising Council; Wheeler-Lea Amendments

African American Media

Creates positive images of a racial group

The premise upon which all African American mass media have been based was captured in New York City, March 16, 1827, in the first editorial of the first African American newspaper, *Freedom's Journal:* "We wish to plead our own cause. Too long have others spoken for us. Too long has the publick [sic] been deceived by misrepresentations, in things which concern us dearly."

Ideologically, this was an effort to counter the lies and distortions about African Americans in the mainstream newspapers; to create opposing, positive images of the race; and to fight for the abolition of slavery. Pragmatically, there was also the goal to make enough money to keep the publication afloat. The primary audience was the small community of free African Americans who lived mostly in northern cities, but it also was directed toward interested whites who, it was thought, might be influenced on moral principles to support the "Negro Cause."

The weekly *Freedom's Journal* was founded in 1827 by two African Americans – Samuel E. Cornish, a clergyman, and John Russwurm, a college graduate – in opposition to the anti-black attacks by the *New York Enquirer*. Cornish left the paper six months after it started but returned in 1829 when Russwurm emigrated to Liberia. On May 29, 1829, Cornish renamed the publication *The Rights of All* and published it monthly until its failure October 9, 1829.

Throughout the pre–Civil War period, at least 40 African American newspapers were published in six states. The *New Orleans (Louisiana) Creole*, was the first African American paper published in the South and the first to publish daily. New Orleans also had two bilingual newspapers, *L'Union* and *La Tribune de la Nouvelle-Orleans*. In Canada, expatriates published two weeklies: *The Toronto (Ontario) Provincial Freeman*, the first African American paper published by a woman, Mary Ann Shadd; and the *Windsor (Ontario) Voice of the Fugitive*, edited by Mary Miles Bibb. These early papers supported the abolition of slavery and urged their readers to be moral, educated Christians.

The most prolific of the antebellum papers was the *North Star*, founded in Rochester, New York, by former slave, writer, and orator Frederick Douglass. A superbly written paper that focused almost exclusively on the abolition movement, the *North Star* was widely supported by white abolitionists. It was published continuously from November 1, 1847, until June 1851, when it merged with the *Liberty Party Paper* and was renamed *Frederick Douglass' Paper*. It remained in publication until August 1860. Meanwhile, in 1858, Douglass had founded *Douglass' Monthly*, a magazine directed primarily at British antislavery sympathizers.

After the Civil War and the Reconstruction Act of 1867, 4 million newly freed African Americans quickly created churches, schools, and other institutions that formed the basis for communities that needed newspapers. When the Hayes-Tilden Compromise of 1876 marked the end of Reconstruction, African Americans by the hundreds of thousands left the South for places north and west. By the turn of the century almost 200 African American papers were publishing nationwide. The oldest continuously published paper, the *Star of Zion*, was founded in 1876. The official publication of the African Methodist Episcopal Zion Church, it was still published weekly in the mid-1990s in Charlotte, North Carolina.

Most of the newspapers founded at the end of the nineteenth century did not last into the last quarter of the twentieth. Some, like the *Free Speech* (1889) in Memphis,

Tennessee – edited by the "princess of the black press," Ida B. Wells – lasted two or three years before they were destroyed by angry whites when the editors spoke against segregation and lynchings. Others, like the *New York Age* (1890) – edited by the "dean of black journalism," T. Thomas Fortune – were supported early by leaders like Booker T. Washington and lasted into the middle of the twentieth century.

Those that survived, publishing continuously into the mid-1990s, included the *Philadelphia Tribune*, founded in 1884 by Chris J. Perry Sr.; the *Afro-American* of Baltimore, Maryland, and Washington, D.C., founded in 1892 by John H. Murphy Sr.; the *Houston (Texas) Informer*, founded in 1893; the *Indianapolis (Indiana) Recorder*, founded in 1895; the Los Angeles *Watts Star Review*, founded in 1904; the *Norfolk (Virginia) Journal and Guide*, founded in 1907 by P.B. Young; the New York *Amsterdam News*, founded in 1909; and the *Pittsburgh (Pennsylvania) Courier*, founded in 1910 and operated in the 1990s by the Sengstacke family.

The most influential of these papers was the *Chicago Defender*, established in 1905 by Robert S. Abbott and run in 1995 by his nephew, John H. Sengstacke. The *Defender* was noted for its bold red headlines, sensational crime stories, and fierce editorials. At its peak in the 1920s, it had a circulation of 250,000 and was distributed nationally by the Pullman railroad porters. In 1956, it began daily publication; by the mid-1990s, it was one of only two African American dailies.

Another significant paper of this period was the Richmond, Virginia, *Planet*, edited by John Mitchell. During the Spanish-American War, the *Planet* led the modern African American press into six decades of war-related animosity with the U.S. government as it launched the "no officers, no fight" campaign. This effort to persuade the government to commission black officers to lead its all-black units would be the first of three protests against African Americans fighting foreign wars while serving in segregated units.

The protests continued during World War I. After the war, Marcus Garvey's solution in the pages of his *Negro World* was for African Americans to organize, pool their money, and go "back to Africa." Simultaneously, African American magazines protested Southern lynch laws. This mounting criticism alarmed the U.S. government, and in 1919, Attorney General A. Mitchell Palmer testified before the U.S. Senate on the "Radicalism and Sedition Among the Negroes as Reflected in Their Publications." When the Bureau of Investigation (later the Federal Bureau of Investigation [FBI]) was taken over by J. Edgar Hoover in 1924, the African American press came under continuous scrutiny that lasted into the 1960s.

The third national protest, during World War II, would send the modern African American press to peak circulation figures. This time, the *Pittsburgh Courier* launched the "Double V" campaign – victory against fascism in Europe, and against segregated armed forces and racism at home. The *Courier's* circulation would approach 300,000, the *Defender's* 160,000, and the *Amsterdam News'* 115,000. Meanwhile, the FBI sought unsuccessfully to use sedition statutes to silence the press criticism.

FREEDOM'S JOURNAL.

" RIGHTEOUSNESS EXALTETH A NATION."

CORNISH & RUSSWURM, Editors & Proprietors. } NEW-YORK, FRIDAY, MARCH 16, 1827. VOL. I. NO. 1.

TO OUR PATRONS.

IN presenting our first number to our Patrons, we feel all the diffidence of persons entering upon a new and untried line of business. But a moment's reflection upon the noble objects, which we have in view by the publication of this Journal; the expediency of its appearance at this time, when so many schemes are in action concerning our people—encourage us to come boldly before an enlightened publick. For we believe, that a paper devoted to the dissemination of useful knowledge among our brethren, and to their moral and religious improvement, must meet with the cordial approbation of every friend to humanity.

The peculiarities of this Journal, render it important that we should advertise to the world the motives by which we are actuated, and the objects which we contemplate.

We wish to plead our own cause. Too long have others spoken for us. Too long has the publick been deceived by misrepresentations, in things which concern us dearly, though in the estimation of some mere trifles; for though there are many in society who exercise towards us benevolent feelings; still (with sorrow we confess it) there are others who make it their business to enlarge upon the least trifle, which tends to the discredit of any person of colour; and pronounce anathemas and denounce our whole body for the misconduct of this guilty one. We are aware that there are many instances of vice among us, but we avow that it is because no one has taught its subjects to be virtuous: many instances of poverty, because no sufficient efforts accommodated to minds contracted by slavery, and deprived of early education have been made, to teach them how to husband their hard earnings, and to secure to themselves comforts.

Education being an object of the highest importance to the welfare of society, we shall endeavour to present just and adequate views of it, and to urge upon our brethren the necessity and expediency of training their children, while young, to habits of industry, and thus forming them for becoming useful members of society. It is surely time that we should awake from this lethargy of years, and make a concentrated effort for the education of our youth. We form a spoke in the human wheel, and it is necessary that we should understand our dependence on the different parts, and theirs on us, in order to perform our part with propriety.

Though not desirous of dictating, we shall feel it our incumbent duty to dwell occasionally upon the general principles and rules of economy. The world has grown too enlightened, to estimate any man's character by his personal appearance. Though all men acknowledge the excellency of Franklin's maxims, yet comparatively few practise upon them. We may deplore when it is too late, the neglect of these self-evident truths, but it avails little to mourn. Ours will be the task of admonishing our brethren on these points.

The civil rights of a people being of the greatest value, it shall ever be our duty to vindicate our brethren, when oppressed, and to lay the case before the publick. We shall also urge upon our brethren, (who are qualified by the laws of the different states,) the expediency of using their elective franchise; and of making an independent use of the same. We wish them not to become the tools of party.

And as much time is frequently lost, and wrong principles instilled, by the perusal of works of trivial importance, we shall consider it a part of our duty to recommend to our young readers, such authors as will not only enlarge their stock of useful knowledge, but such as will also serve to stimulate them to higher attainments in science.

We trust also, that through the columns of the FREEDOM'S JOURNAL, many practical pieces, having for their bases, the improvement of our brethren, will be presented to them, from the pens of many of our respected friends, who have kindly promised their assistance.

It is our earnest wish to make our Journal a medium of intercourse between our brethren in the different states of this great confederacy: that through its columns an expression of our sentiments, on many interesting subjects which concern us, may be offered to the publick: that plans which apparently are beneficial may be candidly discussed and properly weighed; if worthy, receive our cordial approbation; if not, our marked disapprobation.

Useful knowledge of every kind, and every thing that relates to Africa, shall find a ready admission into our columns; and as that vast continent becomes daily more known, we trust that many things will come to light, proving that the natives of it are neither so ignorant nor stupid as they have generally been supposed to be.

And while these important subjects shall occupy the columns of the FREEDOM'S JOURNAL, we would not be unmindful of our brethren who are still in the iron fetters of bondage. They are our kindred by all the ties of nature; and though but little can be effected by us, still let our sympathies be poured forth, and our prayers in their behalf, ascend to Him who is able to succour them.

From the press and the pulpit we have suffered much by being incorrectly represented. Men, whom we equally love and admire have not hesitated to represent us disadvantageously, without becoming personally acquainted with the true state of things, nor discerning between virtue and vice among us. The virtuous part of our people feel themselves sorely aggrieved under the existing state of things—they are not appreciated.

Our vices and our degradation are ever arrayed against us, but our virtues are passed by unnoticed. And what is still more lamentable, our friends, to whom we concede all the principles of humanity and religion, from these very causes seem to have fallen into the current of popular feeling and are imperceptibly floating on the stream—actually living in the practice of prejudice, while they abjure it in theory, and feel it not in their hearts. Is it not very desirable that such should know more of our actual condition, and of our efforts and feelings, that in forming or advocating plans for our amelioration, they may do it more understandingly? In the spirit of candor and humility we intend by a simple representation of facts to lay our case before the publick, with a view to arrest the progress of prejudice, and to shield ourselves against the consequent evils. We wish to conciliate all and to irritate none, yet we must be firm and unwavering in our principles, and persevering in our efforts.

If ignorance, poverty and degradation have hitherto been our unhappy lot; has the Eternal decree gone forth, that our race alone, are to remain in this state, while knowledge and civilization are shedding their enlivening rays over the rest of the human family? The recent travels of Denham and Clapperton in the interior of Africa, and the interesting narrative which they have published; the establishment of the republic of Hayti after years of sanguinary warfare; its subsequent progress in all the arts of civilization; and the advancement of liberal ideas in South America, where despotism has given place to free governments, and where many of our brethren now fill important civil and military stations, prove the contrary.

The interesting fact that there are FIVE HUNDRED THOUSAND free persons of colour, one half of whom might peruse, and the whole be benefitted by the publication of the Journal; that no publication, as yet, has been devoted exclusively to their improvement—that many selections from approved standard authors, which are within the reach of few, may occasionally be made—and more important still, that this large body of our citizens have no public channel—all serve to prove the real necessity, at present, for the appearance of the FREEDOM'S JOURNAL.

It shall ever be our desire so to conduct the editorial department of our paper as to give offence to none of our patrons; as nothing is farther from us than to make it the advocate of any partial views, either in politics or religion. What few days we can number, have been devoted to the improvement of our brethren; and it is our earnest wish that the remainder may be spent in the same delightful service.

In conclusion, whatever concerns us as a people, will ever find a ready admission into the FREEDOM'S JOURNAL, interwoven with all the principal news of the day.

And while every thing in our power shall be performed to support the chracter of our Journal, we would respectfully invite our numerous friends to assist by their communications, and our coloured brethren to strengthen our hands by their subscriptions, as our labour is one of common cause, and worthy of their consideration and support. And we do most earnestly solicit the latter, that if at any time we should seem to be zealous, or too pointed in the inculcation of any important lesson, they will remember, that they are equally interested in the cause in which we are engaged, and attribute our zeal to the peculiarities of our situation, and our earnest engagedness in their well-being.

THE EDITORS.

From the Liverpool Mercury.

MEMOIRS OF CAPT. PAUL CUFFEE.

" On the first of the present month of August, 1811, a vessel arrived at Liverpool, with a cargo from Sierra Leone; the owner, master, mate, and whole crew of which are free blacks. The master, who is also owner, is the son of an American slave, and is said to be very well skilled both in trade and navigation, as well as to be of a very pious and moral character. It must have been a strange and an animating spectacle to see this free and enlightened African, entering as an independent trader with his black crew into that port, which was so lately the *nidus* of the slave trade.—*Edinburgh Review for August*, 1811.

We are happy in having an opportunity of confirming the above account, and at the same time of laying before our readers an authentic memoir of Capt. *Paul Cuffee*, the master and owner of the vessel above alluded to, who sailed from this port on the 20th ult. with a licence from the British Government, to prosecute his intended voyage to Sierra Leone.—The father of Paul Cuffee was a native of Africa,—whence he was brought as a slave into Massachusetts. He was there purchased by a person named Slocum, and remained in slavery a very considerable portion of his life. He was named Cuffee, but as it is usual in those parts, took the name of Slocum, as expressing to whom he belonged. Like many of his countrymen he possessed a mind far superior to his condition; although he was diligent in the business of his master, and faithful to his interest, yet by great industry and economy he was enabled to purchase his personal liberty. At the time the remains of several Indian tribes, who originally possessed the right of soil, resided in Massachusetts. Cuffee became acquainted with a woman descended from one of those tribes, named Ruth Moses, and married her. He continued in habits of industry and frugality, and soon afterwards purchased a farm of 100 acres at the point in Massachusetts.

Cuffee and Ruth had a family of ten children. The three eldest sons, David, Jonathan, and John, are farmers in the neighborhood of West Point; filling respectable situations in society, and endowed with good intellectual capacities. They are all married, and have families to whom they are giving good educations. Of six daughters four are respectably married, while two remain single. Paul was born on the Island of Cutterhumpker, one of the Elizabeth Islands, near New-Bedford, in the year 1759—when he was about fourteen years of age, his father died, leaving a considerable property in land, but which being at that time unproductive, afforded but little provision for his numerous family, and thus the care of supporting his mother and sisters devolved upon his brothers and himself. At this time Paul conceived that commerce furnished to industry more ample rewards than agriculture, and he was conscious that he possessed qualities which under proper culture, would enable him to pursue commercial employments with prospects of success—he therefore entered at the age of sixteen, as a common hand on board of a vessel destined to the bay of Mexico, on a whaling voyage. His second voyage was to the West Indies, but on his third he was captured by a British ship during the American war, about the year 1776—after three months detention as a prisoner, at New-York, he was permitted to return home to Westport, where owing to the unfortunate continuance of hostilities he spent about two years in his agricultural pursuits. During this interval Paul and his brother John Cuffee, were called on by the collector of the district, in which they resided, for the payment of a personal tax. It appeared to them, that by the laws and constitution of Massachusetts, taxation and the whole rights of citizenship were united. If the laws demanded of them the payment of the personal taxes, the same laws must necessarily and constitutionally invest them with the right of representing and being represented in the state legislature. But they had never been considered as entitled to the privilege of voting at elections, nor of being elected to places of trust and honor. Under these circumstances they refused payment of the demands. The collector resorted to the force of the laws, and after many delays and detentions, Paul and his brohter deemed it most prudent to silence them by paying the demands; but they resolved, if it were possible to obtain the rights which they believed to be connected with taxation. They presented a respectful petition to the state legislature. From some individuals it met with a warm, and almost indignant opposition. A considerable majority was, however, favorable to their object. They perceived the propriety and justice of the petition, and with an honorable magnanimity, in defiance of the prejudice of the times, they passed a law rendering all free persons of color liable to taxation, according to the established ratio, for white men, and granting them all the privileges, belonging to the other citizens. This was a day equally honorable to the petitioners and the legislature—a day which ought to be gratefully remembered by every person of color, within the boundaries of Massachusetts, and the names of John and Paul Cuffee, should always be united with its recollection.

To be Continued.

COMMON SCHOOLS IN NEW-YORK.—It appears from the report of the Superintendent of Common Schools in the state of New-York, presented last week to the House of Assembly, that of the 723 towns and wards in the State, 721 have made returns according to law: That in these towns there are 811[illegible] school districts, and of course the same number of schools; from 7544 of which returns have been received: That 341 new school dis-

Freedom's Journal was the first U.S. African American newspaper.

After World War II, circulation in the African American press declined dramatically. This was due in part to the development of radio and television. It also is attributed to the fact that the civil rights movement captured the attention of the mainstream electronic and print media, creating daily and hourly competition for the weekly African American press. Finally, with the end of legal discrimination and the integration of newsrooms and television stations, the African American press found itself in the mid-1990s fighting to compete for journalists, advertisers, and readers.

The African American magazine press began in 1838 when the first African American periodicals were founded – the *Mirror of Liberty* in New York City in July, and the *National Reformer* in Philadelphia in September. These were followed in 1841 by the *African Methodist Episcopal Church Magazine* in Brooklyn, New York, and in 1843 by *L'Album Litteraire*, a literary magazine for free men of color in Louisiana. These were short-lived publications that terminated by 1848. Five other magazines were published between 1854 and 1863, but none lasted past the American Civil War.

After the Civil War, more than 80 periodicals were published in 24 states, the Oklahoma Territory, and the District of Columbia through 1909. Several were journals in which women journalists played major roles. They included *Our Women and Children* (1888), in Louisville, Kentucky; the *Musical Messenger* (1886), in Montgomery, Alabama; and the *Woman's Era* (1894), published in Boston by Josephine St. Pierre Ruffin and her daughter, Florida Ruffin Ridley. Women also wrote regularly for newspapers in major cities nationwide.

After World War I and the continuing migration north, the African American magazine found its niche as a truly mass-circulation medium in New York during the Harlem Renaissance in the 1920s. Some of the magazines included the *Crusader*, the *Challenge*, the *New Negro*, and the big three: the *Crisis* (from 1910), the NAACP monthly edited by W.E.B. DuBois; the *Messenger* (1917–28), organ of the Socialist Party and, later, the Brotherhood of Pullman Porters, edited by A. Philip Randolph; and *Opportunity* (1923–49), organ of the Urban League, edited by Charles S. Johnson.

These three well-edited monthlies dominated the period, publishing well-researched articles, poetry, reviews, and politically inspired commentary. Their editors debated the strategies needed to attain equality. Randolph took the Socialist-activist approach, DuBois the academic-legislative approach, and Johnson the social analysis approach. However, the *Messenger* failed before the end of the decade, and the *Crisis* and *Opportunity* dropped drastically in circulation as the Great Depression took its toll. Still, on September 13, 1930, Robert S. Abbott published a 98-page magazine, *Abbott's Monthly*, that might have been the prototype a decade later for the Johnson Publications magazines. The *Monthly* reached a circulation of 50,000 and was published regularly until it folded in 1933.

The next major African American magazine venture came about in 1942. *Negro Digest,* created by John H. Johnson for "the development of interracial understanding and the promotion of national unity," reprinted previously published articles by black and white writers. Modeled after *Readers' Digest,* its tone was moderate and its content eclectic. Published monthly until November 1951, when it had a circulation of 100,000, it was replaced by *Jet,* which had first appeared in October 1951.

Negro Digest returned to publication from June 1961 to April 1970, when it had become a political and literary journal whose writers were part of the Black Nationalism movement. In May 1970, under editor Hoyt Fuller, it was renamed *Black World* and published the major artists and activists of the period. Containing few advertisements, it was supported by the Johnson Publications empire until February 1976, when it stopped publication.

Johnson's second and most successful venture, *Ebony,* was born in November 1945, and by 1980 it had a circulation of 6 million readers. By the mid-1990s, circulation had fallen to 2 million copies. Modeled somewhat after the pictorial magazine *Life, Ebony* was a family-interest publication. Unlike *Abbott's Monthly,* its content was less eclectic and more narrowly geared toward success stories that looked at the bright side of life. During the turbulent years of the civil rights movement, *Ebony* and its sibling weekly, *Jet,* became the national publications to which the African American community turned for inside coverage of its issues. *Jet* was the conversion of *Negro Digest* into a pocket-size news weekly. It published small news items, gossip, briefs, news photos, entertainment features, and a centerfold "bathing beauty."

The next explosion of African American magazines occurred under conditions similar to those that spawned the Harlem Renaissance. During the late 1960s, in the wake of anti-Vietnam War protests and the black arts and student movements, scores of black-oriented publications appeared. They included *Black Theatre, Black Creation, Umoja,* and *Pride.* Although almost all failed to last into the mid-1970s, two of them, first published in 1970, were still successfully publishing in the mid-1990s: *Essence* and *Black Enterprise.*

Essence, "The Magazine for Today's Black Woman," was founded, ironically, on Wall Street by four men who wanted to create a magazine for the newly visible African American woman. Early issues of the magazine featured women with Afro hairdos, focused on activists like Rosa Parks, and featured articles that dealt with such issues as the "double subjugation" of black women. After its first year, its nationalistic tone softened. In the early 1990s it enjoyed a monthly circulation of just under 1 million copies.

The other survivor from 1970 was *Black Enterprise,* a magazine that rode the changing tide toward "black capitalism." Earl G. Graves, its publisher and editor, set out – with the advice of business leaders – to take advantage of the growing number of African Americans who had just completed college and wanted to enter corporate America. The magazine focused on business and career strategies and job opportunities. In the early 1990s, its monthly circulation was 274,000.

The African American experience in broadcasting is not always easy to categorize. It may include partial ownership of stations that do not have black formats or joint ventures where majority ownership is difficult to discern. In 1948, WDIA in Memphis, Tennessee, became the first big-city sta-

The *Chicago Defender* was noted for its bold red headlines, sensational crime stories, and fierce editorials.
(Reproduced from the Collections of the Library of Congress)

tion to air black music played by African American disk jockeys, but it was not a black-owned station. Black ownership occurred October 3, 1949, when certified public accountant Jesse B. Blayton bought WERD, an AM station in Atlanta, Georgia, and with disk jockey Jack Gibson set the tone for black ownership in broadcasting.

The infiltration was slow, however, because of the high cost of station ownership and the reluctance of financial institutions to finance such ownership. Consequently, African Americans did not enter the field in large numbers; they owned only 30 stations by 1976. In 1978, the Federal Communications Commission enacted Section 1071 of its regulations, which allowed tax breaks for firms that sold stations to minority-owned companies. In the next 16 years, 188 stations would be acquired by African Americans. By the mid-1990s, African Americans owned 118 AM stations, 71 FM stations, and 19 television stations – 208 stations among a national total of 11,021. In 1995, Section 1071 was repealed by Congress.

African American broadcast owners included W. Don Cornwell, who founded New York–based Granite Broadcasting Corp., in 1988 and Ragan Henry, the first African American to own a VHF television station in a top-100 urban market (Rochester, New York). In network media, Sydney Small and Ronald R. Davenport formed the American Urban Radio Networks (AURN) with a merger of their radio networks in the early 1990s. As AURN, the two networks had more than 250 affiliates in 31 states, the District of Columbia, and the Virgin Islands.

The largest African American venture into network cable television was Black Entertainment Television, a cable programming company founded in 1980 by Robert L. Johnson. By 1994, BET was a $75-million conglomerate that reached 40 million homes. Its enterprises included the BET 24-hour cable station, a pay-per-view operation, and a publishing house that published *Emerge* and *Young Sisters and Brothers* magazines. In 1991, it became the first black-owned company traded on the New York Stock Exchange.

Other joint ventures include the World African Network, put together in early 1995 by Sydney Small, Percy Sutton, and others as a 24-hour pay-television network targeting African Americans; Blackstar L.L.C, a $20 million black-owned television group proposed and supported by Fox Broadcasting in 1995; BET-Home Shopping Network, home shopping aimed at African Americans; and Jones-Tribune group, called the largest "minority-controlled" U.S. broadcasting company, founded in 1994 by entertainment executive Quincy Jones and others with Tribune Broadcasting.

HARRY AMANA

See also Abolitionist Press; *Chicago Defender;* Douglass, Frederick; Mass Media and Race; Wells-Barnett, Ida B.

Further Reading

Bryan, Carter R., "Negro Journalism in America Before Emancipation," *Journalism Monographs* 12 (September 1969)

Bullock, Penelope L., *The Afro-American Periodical Press, 1838–1909,* Baton Rouge: Louisiana State University Press, 1981

Daniel, Walter C., *Black Journals of the United States,* Westport, Connecticut, and London: Greenwood, 1982

Dann, Martin E., ed., *The Black Press, 1827–1890: The Quest for National Identity,* New York: Putnam's, 1971

Finkle, Lee, *Forum for Protest: The Black Press During World War II,* Rutherford, New Jersey: Fairleigh Dickinson University, 1975

Vincent, Theodore G., ed., *Voices of a Black Nation: Political Journalism in the Harlem Renaissance,* San Francisco: Ramparts, 1973

Washburn, Patrick S., *A Question of Sedition: The Federal Government's Investigation of the Black Press During World War II,* New York: Oxford University Press, 1986

Wolseley, Roland E., *The Black Press, U.S.A.,* 2nd ed., Ames: Iowa State University Press, 1990

Agenda Setting

Shaping the public's thoughts

Cited as a milestone in twentieth-century mass communication research, the original agenda-setting study was based upon a description that is surprisingly simple. The description came from Bernard Cohen in *The Press and Foreign Policy:* the press may not be successful much of the time in telling people what to think, but it is stunningly successful at telling its readers what to think *about.*

This simple declaration sparked decades of research. As media researchers have since learned, the agenda-setting process can be quite complex. The original agenda-setting study, by Maxwell McCombs and Donald L. Shaw, was published in 1972 in *Public Opinion Quarterly.* The study took place in Chapel Hill, North Carolina, in 1968. The researchers, who were both professors at the University of North Carolina (UNC), tried to match what 100 Chapel Hill voters said were key issues in the 1968 presidential campaign against the actual content of the mass media used by the voters.

McCombs and Shaw found that media coverage matched closely what individual voters named as key issues. This shared definition of what were important issues suggested an agenda-setting function of the mass media, they argued.

The idea for the 1968 study began after a discussion in 1966 that McCombs had with a University of California at Los Angeles faculty colleague in a restaurant after work. They talked about how front-page headlines in that day's newspaper affected conversations they heard around them, as if the press set the conversational agenda. McCombs tested his ideas after moving in 1967 to teach at UNC, where his office was near Shaw's.

Since 1972, several hundred studies of agenda setting have been published in efforts to determine such factors as how the agenda is set for specific issues; the power of different media; the role of groups such as politicians and public relations personnel in shading the agenda; the cycles through which items rise and fall on the agenda list for the media and the audience; and the audience's control and involvement in developing agendas. This research has extended beyond mass media departments to political scientists, sociologists, public opinion researchers, and other scholars.

One important scholar in mass media agenda-setting research was David Weaver, a doctoral student under McCombs and Shaw in the 1970s before becoming a professor at Indiana University. In one particularly significant study, Weaver examined audience needs to help explain which groups of people would be most affected by agenda setting and why. Weaver and McCombs developed a model of their concept of "need for orientation," which included two important variables: interest in the message content and uncertainty about the subject of the message. The higher the need for orientation, the more likely that person would increase his or her media use, and the more likely that agenda-setting effects by the media would be increased. This theoretical study suggests that mass media agenda setting is influenced by basic psychological drives to reduce uncertainty in human environments.

BRADLEY J. HAMM

Further Reading

Cohen, Bernard C., *The Press and Foreign Policy,* Princeton, New Jersey: Princeton University Press, 1963

McCombs, Maxwell, and Donald Shaw, "The Agenda-Setting Function of the Mass Media," *Public Opinion Quarterly* 36 (1972)

Protess, David L., and Maxwell McCombs, eds., *Agenda Setting: Readings on Media, Public Opinion, and Policymaking,* Hillsdale, New Jersey: Lawrence Erlbaum, 1991

Agnew, Spiro T., and the Media

Press critic during the Nixon administration

Former U.S. Vice President Alben W. Barkley, commenting on the obscurity of most of the nation's vice presidents, said: "Once upon a time there was a farmer who had two sons. One of them ran off to sea. The other was elected Vice-President of the United States. Nothing more was heard of either of them."

Spiro T. Agnew, vice president under Richard Nixon, escaped the obscurity that befell most occupants of that position for at least three reasons. First, he was the first vice president to be forced to resign after he pleaded no contest in 1973 to tax evasion charges. Second, he introduced several memorable phrases such as "effete corps of impudent snobs" and "nattering nabobs of negativism," which were immortalized by journalists. Third, he launched a series of broadsides against the so-called "Eastern establishment press." Agnew's November 13, 1969, speech in Des Moines, Iowa, which attacked network television news, and one a week later in Montgomery, Alabama, that took on the *Washington Post* and the *New York Times* set off a three-year campaign by the Nixon administration against the press.

While consensus began building during the fall of 1969 among Nixon administration officials on the need to silence

Vice President Agnew repeatedly targeted newspapers like *The Washington Post.* (National Archives)

their critics, the catalyst for Agnew's attacks on the media came on November 3 after Nixon made a nationally televised speech on Vietnam. Nixon's desire to use television to help shape public opinion on the Vietnam War was undercut by network analysis that suggested that the speech broke no new ground.

The opening salvo of Agnew's campaign against the press was a paragraph inserted into a speech to the National Municipal League in Philadelphia on November 11, 1969, in which he called for reporters to abandon sensationalism and to strive for more responsible reporting. He chose a speech before the Midwest Regional Republican Committee two days later in Des Moines to issue his most stinging attack against the press.

Agnew's Des Moines speech was both a response to the instant analysis of the November 3 speech and an attempt to defuse a large and potentially volatile antiwar demonstration scheduled two days later in Washington, D.C. The speech opened with an attack against "instant analysis and querulous criticism" of the president's talk by "a small band of network commentators and self-appointed analysts." Attacking the whole system of network news, Agnew complained that the power of the networks was immense because they were the sole source of news for millions of people in the United States. Their influence could be subtle, he said. "A raised eyebrow, an inflection of the voice, a caustic remark dropped in the middle of a broadcast can raise doubts in a million minds about the veracity of a public official or the wisdom of a government policy." This power was concentrated in the hands of a small group of news anchors, commentators, and executive producers who, because they also shared a similar background, shared a particular (specifically, liberal) view of the world that was out of step with the beliefs of most people in the United States. In addition, Agnew said, the networks portrayed a distorted image of the nation in which bad news drove out good news and in which "a single dramatic piece of the mosaic becomes, in the minds of millions, the entire picture." He argued that the networks constituted a dangerous monopoly that was not responsive to the views of the nation. Claiming not to favor government censorship, Agnew finally called for public pressure for responsible news, noting, "The people can register their complaints on bias through mail to the networks and phone calls to local stations."

Agnew followed up his Des Moines speech with an attack a week later in Montgomery, Alabama, against newspapers, particularly his old nemeses, the *New York Times* and *Washington Post*. Again he decried the concentration of power in the media, in particular the *Washington Post*'s ownership of *Newsweek* magazine, a major Washington television station, and an all-news radio station. He warned against media monopolies that "harken to the same master" and noted that newspaper competition was declining throughout the country, which made the surviving newspapers "fat and irresponsible." To illustrate his point, he incorrectly accused the *Times* of ignoring a letter signed by 359 members of Congress who backed Nixon's Vietnam policy.

The Des Moines and Montgomery speeches were his most famous attacks against the press, but he peppered several later speeches over the next three years with pronouncements against the media. For instance, in 1971 he lambasted CBS for airing documentaries, such as "The Selling of the Pentagon," that criticized Nixon policies.

Agnew's charges, particularly his claims of press bias, were vigorously debated in the weeks after the Des Moines and Montgomery speeches. Scholars, however, have found Agnew's claims of press bias overstated; most coverage, including coverage of Agnew's own speeches, was overwhelmingly neutral. Researchers do suggest, however, that Agnew's complaints of network negativism were on the mark; negative statements outnumbered positive ones.

Even if Agnew's criticisms were not always accurate, they had the desired effect. Both anecdotal evidence and research suggests that the press altered its reporting style in response to Agnew's attacks. For instance, after President Nixon delivered his 1970 State of the Union speech, network commentators summarized rather than analyzed the speech. CBS instituted a policy of no "instant analysis" following presidential speeches, a policy that lasted five months. Studies suggest that after Agnew's Des Moines speech, the networks ran fewer stories that made judgments and a greater percentage of reports were attributed to a source. Newspapers also changed. Large papers such as the *New York Times* and the *Washington Post* made an effort to run more conservative columns on their editorial page to provide editorial balance. The Agnew-led attacks may have also intimidated media coverage for the remainder of Nixon's first term of office. Political observers suggest that the media avoided criticizing Nixon and did not aggressively cover the Watergate scandal during the 1972 presidential campaign. Finally, Agnew's attacks against the press gained unprecedented attention for an office that has traditionally been ignored.

THOMAS J. JOHNSON

See also Nixon, Richard M., and the Media; Watergate Scandal

Further Reading

Albright, Joseph, *What Makes Spiro Run: The Life and Times of Spiro Agnew,* New York: Dodd, Mead, 1972

Bagdikian, Ben H., "Election Coverage '72–1: The Fruits of Agnewism," *Columbia Journalism Review* (January/February 1973)

Coyne, John R., Jr., *The Impudent Snobs: Agnew vs. the Intellectual Establishment,* New Rochelle, New York: Arlington House, 1972

Frye, Jerry K., "American Newspapers vs. Agnew's 1970 Political Campaign," *Journal of Applied Communication Research* 4 (1976)

Lowry, Dennis T., "Agnew and the Network News: A Before/After Content Analysis," *Journalism Quarterly* 48 (1971)

Lucas, Jim G., *Agnew: Profile in Conflict,* New York: Scribner's, 1970; London: Tandem, 1970

Porter, William E., *Assault on the Media: The Nixon Years,* Ann Arbor: University of Michigan Press, 1976

Spear, Joseph C., *Presidents and the Press: The Nixon Legacy,* Cambridge, Massachusetts: MIT Press, 1984

Witcover, Jules, *White Knight: The Rise of Spiro Agnew,* New York: Random House, 1972

Alien and Sedition Acts of 1798

Early American restrictions on freedom of speech and press

The Alien and Sedition Acts of 1798 consisted of four laws designed to restrict internal dissension and national disloyalty during a tense period in the history of the infant United States. Relations between the United States and France had eroded since their cordial collaboration during the American Revolution. By 1798, the French navy regularly raided American ships and French diplomats exhibited disdain for U.S. ambassadors, demanding bribes in exchange for routine courtesies. In response, the United States prepared for war with France, which was already embroiled in its own internal revolution. As American national pride took offense and anti-French sentiment blossomed, the Federalist-dominated Congress passed laws intended to reduce political discord and the divisive influence of nonnaturalized French sympathizers. These laws may have been inspired by similar ones adopted in England.

The first of the four laws was the Naturalization Act, passed on June 18, 1798. This measure extended the period of residence required for citizenship from five to 14 years. A section of the act that failed to pass would have virtually eliminated the naturalization of aliens – most of whom supported the opposition Republican or Jeffersonian party – and barred foreign-born persons from voting or holding public office.

The second of the four laws was the Alien Act, passed seven days later. It gave the president power to deport, without a hearing or specific reason, any non-naturalized foreigner deemed "dangerous to the peace and safety of the United States." President John Adams was uncomfortable with this authority and refused to exercise it. Consequently, no aliens were expelled under this law.

The third of the four laws was the Alien Enemies Act, passed on July 6. In the event of war, it gave the president authority to label as enemies any citizens of the hostile country living in the United States whose actions or presence he regarded as dangerous, and to have them apprehended or deported. This measure was not invoked because war with France was averted, but it became a permanent statute and was used to justify the internment of U.S. citizens of Japanese origin during World War II.

The fourth law, and the one most relevant to journalism history, was the Sedition Act, passed on July 14. This law made it a crime to utter or publish "any false, scandalous, or malicious writing or writings against the Government of the United States, with intent to defame . . . or to bring them . . . into contempt or disrepute." Violations were punishable by a maximum fine of $2,000 and imprisonment of up to two years. This edict had the effect of punishing political opponents of the Federalist-controlled government, including printers who supported the opposition Republican party or favored France.

The Sedition Act represented a progressive reform of the era's common law of seditious libel. The act stipulated that harmful intent had to be proved, truth was a defense, and juries could decide not only the facts but the application of the law. The latter provision meant that juries could return general verdicts of guilty or not guilty, rather than leaving it to judicial pronouncement.

Supporters of these four laws believed that the impending war with France justified strong measures to promote national harmony and remove internal threats to domestic security. Specific to the Sedition Act, they contended the First Amendment guarantee of press freedom meant absence of prior restraint, not unrestrained liberty to falsely and maliciously defame government and cause domestic dissent. Opponents argued that the laws generally, and the Sedition Act in particular, could be used to punish and stifle all criticism of government and its officers.

About two dozen people were charged with violating the Sedition Act, most of whom were Republican printers and writers. They included Benjamin Franklin Bache, publisher of the vituperative *Philadelphia Aurora*, and Matthew Lyon, a Vermont congressman and frequent contributor to the Republican press. The most unusual prosecution was of Luther Baldwin, a Newark, New Jersey, tavern patron, who suggested that cannons firing a salute for President Adams should fire through his rear end. Baldwin was prosecuted and fined $150.

The wisdom of the Alien and Sedition Acts became a major presidential campaign issue as Adams sought reelection in 1800 against Republican opponent Thomas Jefferson. Jefferson prevailed, and both houses of Congress shifted from Federalist to Republican majorities. The Republican triumph signaled the death knell for the Federalist party, which was never able to recapture the executive or legislative branches. Jefferson kept his campaign promise to abolish the Alien and Sedition Acts and allowed them to expire, unenforced, in 1801.

RALPH FRASCA

Further Reading

Elkins, Stanley, and Eric McKitrick, *The Age of Federalism*, New York: Oxford University Press, 1993
Levy, Leonard W., *Emergence of a Free Press*, New York and Oxford: Oxford University Press, 1985
Smith, James Morton, *Freedom's Fetters: The Alien and Sedition Laws and American Civil Liberties*, Ithaca, New York: Cornell University Press, 1956
Tagg, James, *Benjamin Franklin Bache and the Philadelphia Aurora*, Philadelphia: University of Pennsylvania Press, 1991

Almanacs

Favorite early American publications

Almanacs were an American household item beginning when Stephen Daye published the first American almanac in 1639. It was the second publication issued from a colonial printing press.

Most seventeenth-century almanacs were about 16 pages long, including the covers. Offering at least one page for each calendar month, they also carried advertisements, es-

Poor Richard, 1733.

AN

Almanack

For the Year of Chrift

1733,

Being the Firſt after LEAP YEAR:

And makes ſince the Creation	Years
By the Account of the Eaſtern *Greeks*	7241
By the Latih Church, when ☉ ent. ♈	6932
By the Computation of *W. W.*	5742
By the *Roman* Chronology	5682
By the *Jewiſh* Rabbies	5494

Wherein is contained.

The Lunations, Eclipſes, Judgment of the Weather, Spring Tides, Planets Motions & mutual Aſpects, Sun and Moon's Riſing and Setting, Length of Days, Time of High Water, Fairs, Courts, and obſervable Days.

Fitted to the Latitude of Forty Degrees, and a Meridian of Five Hours Weſt from *London*, but may without ſenſible Error, ſerve all the adjacent Places, even from *Newfoundland* to *South-Carolina.*

By RICHARD SAUNDERS, Philom.

PHILADELPHIA:

Printed and fold by *B. FRANKLIN*, at the New Printing-Office near the Market.

Poor Richard's Almanack was a popular favorite in the late colonial period.
(Reproduced from the Collections of the Library of Congress)

says, and other features, such as planting information, moon and tide changes, astrological forecasts, recipes, poems, suggested cures for ailments, pithy sayings, and tidbits of practical information and humor.

Probably the most famous – and profitable – early American almanac was Benjamin Franklin's *Poor Richard's Almanack*, which featured an imaginary astrologer, Richard Saunders (Poor Richard). Started in 1732, it was published for 26 years, with 10,000 copies reputedly sold annually. Other popular early almanacs included the *Astronomical Diary and Almanack*, compiled by Nathaniel Ames, and the *North American Almanack*, issued by Benjamin Edes and John Gill, publishers of the *Boston Gazette*.

As almanacs grew in size, they became more magazine-like, carrying articles and essays that sparked discussions on politics and religion, provided information about American life and thought, and entertained with American folklore. They helped to publicize the provisions of the Constitution, and one is reputed to have helped Abraham Lincoln, the country lawyer, impeach the testimony of a witness.

By the end of the eighteenth century, most of the almanacs were running from 24 pages to almost 200 pages. The larger publications began to be more informational in style, akin to the modern *World Almanac and Book of Facts*.

ELSIE HEBERT

Further Reading

Banks, Noreen, *Peoples Bicentennial Commission Early American Almanac,* New York: Bantam, 1973
Chitwood, Oliver P., *A History of Colonial America,* 2nd ed., New York: Harper & Brothers, 1948
Sagendorph, Robb, *America and Her Almanac: Wit, Wisdom, and Weather, 1639–1970,* Dublin, New Hampshire: Yankee, 1970
Stitt, J. Michael, and Robert K. Dodge, *A Tale Type and Motif Index of Early U.S. Almanacs,* New York: Greenwood, 1991
Thomas, Isaiah, *The History of Printing in America,* 2 vols., 2nd ed., Albany, New York: Joel Munsell, 1874

Alternative Press

Varying publications of dissident groups

The alternative press – the publications of political, social, cultural, and religious dissidents – has existed alongside the conventional or mainstream media throughout the history of the United States. As much a part of the journalistic heritage of the United States as the *New York Times* or *Time* magazine, the alternative press has chronicled the ideas, goals, and actions of those at odds with the norms of their day. Although often tied to particular historical eras (e.g., the fight for women's enfranchisement or the Vietnam War), the alternative press has had a long and unbroken history, from the pamphlets of Thomas Paine to the countercultural zines of the late twentieth century.

U.S. history is rich with the voices of hundreds of groups who created alternative journalism: African Americans seeking first the end to slavery, then enfranchisement and equality; women seeking the vote and full participation in the life of the nation; utopianists working for their vision of a perfect world; religious dissidents interested in gaining followers and spreading their ideas; immigrants wanting to preserve their culture while learning the ways of their adopted land; Socialists, Populists, radical unionists, anarchists, syndicalists, Communists, fascists, survivalists, and any number of left- and right-wing political groups offering their own solutions to the country's problems; pacifists, noninterventionists, isolationists and antiwar advocates striving to keep themselves and their country out of armed conflict; gays, lesbians, and bisexuals promoting self-respect, civil rights, and acceptance in society; counterculturalists in music, art, and literature seeking self-expression and the opportunity to tweak and critique prevailing cultural norms; older and aging citizens fighting for dignity and against the heavy burden of stereotype; prisoners exposing the conditions of their confinement; environmentalists fighting to protect the land. Additionally, countless single-issue groups, from those seeking to protect the right to bear arms, to those insisting on the right to die, to those fighting for the rights of animals, have created their own alternative voices.

While the conventional press has traditionally spoken to and for a relatively homogeneous middle united by its belief (and often personal stake) in the culture and ideology of the day, the diverse alternative press has given voice to "fringe" ideas, from equality for women to freedom for African Americans to acceptance of homosexuals. Over time, many of the fringe ideas first voiced in the alternative media have made their way into the conventional press, the mainstream political system, and finally, the life of the nation. The importance of the alternative press as a marketplace of ideas – some of which enter the mainstream, some of which are forever relegated to the backwaters and eddies – cannot be overstated.

The men and women who devoted their time and energy to publishing alternative newspapers, magazines, and journals were people convinced of both the righteousness of their causes and the power of the press. The motto of an early-twentieth-century newspaper published by the Industrial Workers of the World, a radical unionist group, might stand as the battle cry for alternative journalists across time: "The power to transmit ideas is the power to change the world." Those involved in creating the alternative press were both malcontents who wanted change and idealists who believed that change – explained and promoted by the press – was possible. Many were simultaneously leaders and chroniclers of their cause.

They were both male and female and represented virtually every racial, ethnic, and religious group in the nation. As one U.S. political dissident once put it: "A radical group without a newspaper is a contradiction in terms." Coming from both urban centers and rural outposts, they lived and worked in every state in the Union. Some were native-born; others were immigrants. A few were wealthy, like millionaire Socialist Gaylord Wilshire (who subsidized a 300,000-circulation radical magazine with his personal fortune); many were poor, like Frederick Douglass, who after borrowing money to buy his freedom went on to publish the most important African American newspaper in the pre–Civil War period. These journalists were young, middle aged, and old. Demographically, they were as varied a group as one could imagine, yet they had in common their devotion to a cause and their belief in the power of the press.

For the majority, journalism was not a separate calling or a profession for its own sake. It was a means to reach people with ideas, a way to organize and propagandize for what they believed. Publishing a newspaper or magazine was not the path to wealth; it was the path to a better world. Underlying all of their journalistic activity was the suspicion – and often the concrete evidence – that the mainstream press was ignoring, trivializing, stereotyping, or ridiculing their ideas and actions. Contemporary historical research has for the most part supported these criticisms concerning lack of access.

Some alternative journalists were harassed or ostracized by their communities, as were white antislavery editors, some of whom were literally tarred and feathered, and some of whom had their presses destroyed and buildings burned. Some were harassed by the government, like publishers and distributors of anti–Vietnam War newspapers who were singled out by the Federal Bureau of Investigation and Central Intelligence Agency. Some were jailed for their writings. In fact, two late-nineteenth-century anarchist journalists were convicted, found guilty, and hanged based on supposedly incendiary statements they made in the alternative press. Alternative journalism has never been a safe avocation.

One problem all alternative journalists share for all or most of their careers is the financing of their journalistic efforts. Most publications are started on a shoestring and remain financially unstable throughout their lives. Alternative media, with a few exceptions, have not and do not attract lucrative advertising. The contents of the publications are controversial; their aims are frequently unsettling; their readerships are most often demographically unappealing to big-money advertisers. Instead, the alternative press has often subsisted on subscription revenue and small donations from loyal readers. This accounts for the generally limited life span of alternative newspapers and magazines, although there have been notable exceptions like the long-lived *Chicago Defender*, a voice for African Americans, and *Woman's Journal*, a suffrage newspaper that was published continuously for almost 50 years. The advent of desktop publishing and the Internet allowed individuals with almost no capital to publish and sustain alternative newspapers. Still, these solitary communicators needed to find ways to support themselves as they engaged in their journalistic enterprises.

The need to communicate currently unacceptable ideas coupled with lack of access to the conventional press led to the development of separate news channels for dissident groups. In many cases, it is clear that dissidents would have rather used the conventional press than start their own publications; not only did the conventional press reach vast audiences with whom dissidents wished to communicate, it also involved no extra expense. As long as mainstream media continue to limit their scope to currently acceptable ideas and groups, as long as they define news as action rather than thought, dissident groups will continue to support their own alternative media.

LAUREN KESSLER

See also Abolitionist Press; African American Media; Asian American Media; *Chicago Defender;* Douglass, Frederick; Ethnic Press; Feminist Media; Gay and Lesbian Press; Hispanic Media; Native American Media; Peace/Pacifist Press; Socialist Press; Suffrage Press; Underground Press

Further Reading

Armstrong, David, *A Trumpet to Arms: Alternative Media in America,* Los Angeles: J.P. Tarcher, 1981

Kessler, Lauren, *The Dissident Press: Alternative Journalism in American History,* Beverly Hills, California: Sage, 1984

Leamer, Laurence, *The Paper Revolutionaries: The Rise of the Underground Press,* New York: Simon & Schuster, 1972

AM Radio: *see* Radio Technology

American Library Association and Intellectual Freedom

Aims to safeguard the freedom of inquiry, freedom to read

The American Library Association was organized in 1876 to promote library and librarian interests in the United States. The largest and oldest national library association in the world, it grew from a small organization with a very simple structure to a complex association with more than 55,000 members in 1995. It was the chief advocate for the citizens of the United States in their search for library and information services. It maintained a close relationship with more than 70 other library organizations in the United States and around the world.

Although the ALA had a number of other priorities, intellectual freedom and access to information by all individuals were always top considerations. Its Intellectual Freedom Committee (IFC) was established in 1940 as the Committee on Intellectual Freedom to Safeguard the Rights of Library Users to Freedom of Inquiry. This was in answer to increased fear concerning national security, Communism, and the approaching war. There were many demands for strict control in the dissemination of propaganda and "subversive" literature that might be found in libraries.

Earlier, in 1939, a special committee on censorship formulated the *Library Bill of Rights,* a basic operating document of the ALA, which continues to be one of the guiding policy documents to which professional librarians subscribed in their attempt to ensure freedom of access to information for all citizens. The ALA affirmed that all libraries are forums for information and all points of view regardless of the origin or background of those contributing to their creation. It also believed that the right to use a library by all should not be denied or abridged because of a person's origin, age, background, or views. This is in accordance with the First Amendment to the U.S. Constitution.

Many interpretations of this document, which was officially adopted in 1948 and amended in 1961, 1967, and 1980, were approved to help librarians and library users adhere to the tenets of the *Library Bill of Rights.* Focusing on such issues as confidentiality, labeling, expurgation, diversity, access for minors, economic barriers, and access to electronic resources, the interpretations were adopted by the ALA Council as official policy.

Owing to its firm belief in freedom of speech and access to information, the American Library Association through the years was one of the most vocal and supportive organizations in these areas. It issued statements in opposition to censorship, loyalty oaths, labeling materials, segregation, the war in Vietnam, the Meese Commission report, and the Federal Bureau of Investigation Library Awareness Program.

To further its fight for the freedom to read and to have access to information, the ALA established the Office for Intellectual Freedom in its Chicago headquarters in December 1967. This office was the administrative arm of the IFC and implemented intellectual freedom policies. Recognizing that the most effective safeguards for maintaining these rights for library users and librarians are an informed citizenry and a library profession aware of repressive activities, the office educated on how to combat censorship challenges. Through its services, publications, projects, and workshops, the Office for Intellectual Freedom was extremely successful in combating censorship in the libraries of the United States.

The office coordinated many intellectual freedom programs and events. The annual conference program with noted speakers was always a big draw. It prepared an annual Banned Books Week resource book that provided ideas for displays and events for celebrating the freedom to read. This commemoration called attention to the dangers of censorship and encouraged support of intellectual freedom. Each year this event was cosponsored by the ALA, the American Booksellers Association, the National Association of College Stores, the Association of American Publishers, and the American Society of Journalists and Authors.

All the ALA's intellectual freedom programs were enhanced by its close affiliation with the Freedom to Read Foundation, a separate legal entity with its own membership, income, and funding. The foundation was incorporated in 1969 to promote and protect freedom of speech and other freedoms guaranteed by the Constitution and other laws. One of its goals was to supply legal counsel and support to libraries and librarians suffering legal injustices by reason of their defense of freedom of speech and of the press. It fought repressive legislation and often joined the ALA and other associations as coplaintiffs in challenging state and federal statutes.

GENE D. LANIER

See also Book Publishing in the Twentieth Century; Censorship of Books

Further Reading

Office for Intellectual Freedom, American Library Association, *Intellectual Freedom Manual,* 4th ed., Chicago: American Library Association, 1992

Reichman, Henry, *Censorship and Selection: Issues and Answers for Schools,* Chicago: American Library Association, 1993

Thomison, Dennis, *A History of the American Library Association, 1876–1972,* Chicago: American Library Association, 1978

American Newspaper Directory

Nineteenth-century listing of newspapers

The *American Newspaper Directory* was started by advertising agency pioneer George P. Rowell in New York City in 1869. The *Directory* consisted of several sections, one of which was a listing of newspapers in each state and territory of the United States. These lists were compiled alphabetically by state, city, and town, with each entry noting the name of the newspaper; day of publication; political affiliation; number of pages; size of pages; subscription cost; year of establishment; editor, owner, publisher; circulation; and ethnic affiliation.

Modeled after *Mitchell's Directory of the Newspapers of Great Britain*, Rowell's *American Newspaper Directory* differed from it in one main respect: Rowell inserted estimates of each newspaper's circulation. Rowell was by design an underestimator, choosing to err on the side of safety rather than accord to one newspaper an unfairly positive representation. This practice resulted in several hundred libel suits (none of which made it to court) and, in his own words, "made me no friends."

Established to make a profit, Rowell's directory carried a large amount of advertising. For example, the 1891 issue of the *Directory* contained 1,221 pages of ads. Using the *Directory* as an advertising medium, however, opened the door for accusations that Rowell quoted higher or lower circulation rates for papers that either did or did not advertise in the *Directory*.

The *Directory* was published annually from 1869 to 1877 and then quarterly, with annual compilations, until it merged with *N.W. Ayer and Son's American Newspaper Annual* in 1905.

JEFFREY RUTENBECK

See also Newspaper Circulation

Further Reading

Rowell, George P., *Forty Years as an Advertising Agent: 1865–1905*, New York and London: Garland, 1985
Rutenbeck, Jeffrey B., "Newspaper Trends in the 1870s: Proliferation, Popularization, and Political Independence," *Journalism & Mass Communication Quarterly* 72:2 (Summer 1995), pp. 361–375

American Revolution and the Press

The nation and the press face war for the first time

The media performed an important function during the American Revolution by providing the major source of information concerning the conflicts between the colonies and Great Britain. During both the decade of debate prior to 1775 and the years of fighting that followed, newspapers enabled readers to learn something of what was happening throughout the colonies. Access to news and opinion encouraged unity and bolstered morale as the colonies fought for independence.

The conflict between the colonies and Britain developed out of arguments over taxation. Having finally defeated France in 1763, Britain was deeply in debt. Parliament turned to the colonies to help pay for the war. Beginning in 1764, Britain passed a series of acts designed to raise revenue across the Atlantic. Colonial leaders protested against these taxes, declaring, "no taxation without representation," and complaining that their rights as Englishmen were being denied when they were taxed by legislators whom they did not elect. Basically, the conflict centered around who controlled the colonies – the British Parliament or the local governments. Failure to reach a compromise on this issue finally resulted in the Revolution. As these arguments occurred, both sides used the media to publicize their ideas. The patriots proved more successful, as they capably used the newspapers to convince many Americans that the British government had become tyrannical and must be corrected or eliminated.

The press came into its own in 1765, when the newspapers participated in the Stamp Act controversy. One of Parliament's attempts to raise money, the Stamp Act taxed all printed materials and legal documents produced in the colonies. This legislation affected the most vocal groups in colonial society – lawyers, merchants, and printers. Printers disliked the Stamp Act because it threatened to eliminate their profits and thus make printing a losing proposition. All the publishers opened the pages of their newspapers to authors who wrote to protest the tax. Printers also sought ways to bypass the legislation. Some chose to suspend publication until the act was repealed, while others transformed their newspapers into handbills by dropping the volume numbering from the masthead. Others defied the legislation by continuing to print without any changes. The result was that no newspaper appeared on stamped paper.

The Stamp Act controversy convinced many on both sides of the conflict that the media provided a useful mechanism to communicate ideas to the public. As a result, both Loyalists and Patriots sought to control the content of newspapers in hopes of influencing neutral Americans who had not made up their minds as to which side to join in the

Four coffins illustrated the deaths in the Boston Massacre.

Isaiah Thomas Reports the Battle of Lexington and Concord

They pillaged almost every house they passed by breaking and destroying doors, windows, glass, etc., and carrying off clothing and other valuable effects. It appeared to be their design to burn and destroy all before them, and nothing but our vigorous pursuit prevented their infernal purposes from being put into execution. But the savage barbarity exercised upon the bodies of our unfortunate brethren who fell is almost incredible. Not content with shooting down the unarmed, aged, and infirm, they disregarded the cries of the wounded, killing them without mercy, and mangling their bodies in the most shocking manner.

The Massachusetts Spy, May 3, 1775

---

conflict. The Patriots were so much more successful in achieving this goal that Loyalist papers were limited only to areas under British control by the time independence was declared in 1776.

Prior to 1775, however, a number of newspaper printers tried to remain neutral, presenting both sides of the argument between Great Britain and the colonies. They soon found that neutrality was impossible, and most chose to support the colonial side. Those who continued to support the Crown were few in number, but they proved vocal in defense of the British position. John Mein, publisher of the *Boston Chronicle*, was typical of this group. Mein began his newspaper in 1767, seeking to be nonpartisan. He became more and more pro-British, however, as he increasingly disagreed with the actions of the Sons of Liberty in Boston. When a mob attacked his office in 1769, Mein defended himself and accidentally shot a bystander. He fled to England to avoid prosecution. Other printers who supported the British cause included James Rivington and Hugh Gaine. Both of these men produced newspapers that supported the Crown prior to 1775, but they ceased publication when the war began. After the British occupied New York, both established new papers in that city and continued to trumpet the Royal cause from that safe haven under the protection of the British army.

Patriot printers abounded, as most of the newspaper publishers supported the colonists. The best of the Patriot printers operated in Boston, where the Revolution began. The leading Patriot printers were Benjamin Edes and John Gill, publishers of the *Boston Gazette*. Edes and Gill used the pages of their newspaper to convince readers of British tyranny as Parliament continued to seek ways to raise money in the colonies. Edes and Gill were aided in their efforts by Sam Adams, a leader of the Boston Sons of Liberty and one of the best essay propagandists writing during the Revolutionary era. Edes and Gill had to cease publication following the battles of Lexington and Concord, and they never recovered their position of leadership. The most vocal Patriot printer after Lexington and Concord was Isaiah Thomas, publisher of the *Massachusetts Spy*. Thomas began his newspaper in Boston in 1770 but moved to Worces-

ter in 1775. He spent the rest of the war urging his readers to join together to fight the British threat: "Let us not busy ourselves now about our private internal affairs, but with the utmost care and caution, attend to the grand American controversy, and assist her in her earnest struggle in support of her natural rights and freedom."

Once fighting broke out in 1775, the role of the media changed somewhat. Prior to 1775, the dissemination of ideas constituted the primary goal. Following Lexington and Concord, news and rumors about the fighting became of greater interest. The function of the newspapers during the years of fighting centered around boosting morale by reporting American successes. As a result, the media played an essential role in keeping many Americans convinced that they could win and that the war was still worth fighting. Without such an outlook on the part of Americans, the war would have been lost. By publishing materials from throughout the colonies and keeping readers apprised of events in other places, the newspapers provided a necessary communications link that proved vital for ultimate success and victory.

CAROL SUE HUMPHREY

See also Stamp Act of 1765; Washington, George, and the Press

Further Reading

Bailyn, Bernard, and John B. Hench, eds., *The Press & the American Revolution*, Worcester, Massachusetts: American Antiquarian Society, 1980

Davidson, Philip, *Propaganda and the American Revolution, 1763–1783*, Chapel Hill: University of North Carolina Press, 1941

Humphrey, Carol Sue, *"This Popular Engine": New England Newspapers During the American Revolution, 1775–1789*, Newark: University of Delaware Press, 1992; London: Associated University Presses, 1992

Schlesinger, Arthur M., *Prelude to Independence: The Newspaper War on Britain, 1764–1776*, New York: Knopf, 1958

American Tract Society

Early users of mass media to disseminate ideas

The American Tract Society (ATS), a religious publishing house founded in 1825, was one of the first organizations in U.S. history to imagine and develop genuinely mass media. In its earliest years, the ATS conceived the idea of placing the same printed messages into the hands of everyone. While this millennial goal was never reached, the society by the late 1820s was annually printing and distributing 5 million tracts – at least five pages for every man, woman, and child in America. By 1850, the ATS had published 2.5 billion pages of religious literature. Although the four-to-eight-page gospel tract was the society's trademark medium, the ATS at mid-century was also a major publisher of religious books and periodicals. To realize the dream of religious mass media, the ATS early on became a leading innovator in printing technology and in organizational methods for the national distribution of religious media.

The ATS was born of a merger of regional tract societies in New York and Massachusetts, and one of the main goals of the merger was the consolidation and centralization of stereotyping and printing operations in New York City. The use of stereotype plates for printing tracts and books, a process crucial to ATS operations, was a major step forward in the mass production of standard texts. The ATS stereotyped 155 tracts during its first year and began the stereotyping of books in 1827. The ATS was a leading patron of improvements in printing press technology as well. In 1826, the society installed the first steam-powered Treadwell press in New York. Along with the American Bible Society, the ATS was also a major patron in the 1820s of the growing industry of machine-made paper. By 1827, the ATS managers announced in their annual report that they had the technical capacity to place at least one tract into the hands of every U.S. citizen in a single year: "Twelve millions of inhabitants are indeed a great many; but twelve millions of tracts can be printed and printed in one year, with no essential sacrifice to the community . . . this *can be done.*"

The creation of genuine mass media, however, required organization as well as technology, and the ATS gradually emerged as an innovator in that area as well. In the 1820s and 1830s, despite a growing printing capacity and a national network of auxiliary societies, the ATS was unable to achieve the goal of delivering religious literature to everyone. Therefore, in 1841, the Society launched the first major effort of religious colportage in the United States. Colporteurs were traveling agents employed by the society to deliver tracts and books door to door, especially in the frontier regions of the trans-Appalachian West. By 1850, the society had more than 500 colporteurs in the field. In the first ten years of the colportage enterprise, these men visited more than 2 million families (11 million individuals), nearly half the population of the country. They sold 2.4 million books and gave away 650,000 books and several million tracts.

Through both its printing and its distribution activities, the ATS established the significance of the not-for-profit sector in American mass media. The ATS was keen to foil the commercial marketplace in publishing, which it viewed as Satan's domain. The leaders of the society put the case plainly:

No nation on the globe, perhaps, has so large a reading population; and in none is the press more active, or more influential. What the reading matter prepared for such a nation would be, if left solely to private enterprise, may be inferred from an examination of the catalogues of some of the respectable and even Christian publishing houses. Self-interest would shape the supply to the demand; and the mightiest agent God has given to the world for moulding public opinion and sanctifying the public taste, would be moulded by it, and be made to reflect its character, were there no conservative, redeeming influences.

The ATS aimed to provide those "conservative, redeeming influences." ATS leaders aimed to turn the market on its head, to make demand respond to supply, their supply – the opposite of the marketplace they loathed. In other words, the ATS leadership (along with a growing number of other religious and associational publishers) believed that the invisible hand of the market must be restrained by the visible hand of organization.

From the beginning, the ATS was a "union society," a nondenominational enterprise founded and operated mainly by orthodox Congregationalists and Presbyterians, with support from several other denominations in the Reformed tradition. The rising tide of denominationalism and sectionalism gradually took a toll on the society. By 1860, the business of religious publishing, like much missionary and charitable work, was moving away from union societies and into the denominations. This cost the ATS some support. The society also suffered from its efforts to maintain a presence in both the North and South during the era of intensifying sectional tension in the United States. In 1858, the Boston society seceded over the unwillingness of the ATS to oppose slavery. After the American Civil War, the society was active in evangelical work among freed slaves, but gradually its financial support and its publishing activities declined.

In the late nineteenth century, the ATS abandoned its vision of universal mass religious media in the United States and turned more of its attention to books for sale (rather than for free distribution) and to foreign-language publications (142 languages by 1875) and foreign mission work. In 1947, the society returned to its original enterprise – the publication of small, English-language tracts – and by the mid-1970s was publishing some 30 million tracts per year. In 1962, the society moved from Manhattan to suburban New Jersey. In 1978, it moved once again to Garland, Texas.

DAVID PAUL NORD

Further Reading

Moore, R. Laurence, *Selling God: American Religion in the Marketplace of Culture*, New York: Oxford University Press, 1994

Nord, David Paul, "The Evangelical Origins of Mass Media in America, 1815–1835," *Journalism Monographs* 88 (May 1984)

_____, "Systematic Benevolence: Religious Publishing and the Marketplace in Early Nineteenth-Century America," in *Communication and Change in American Religious History,* edited by Leonard I. Sweet, Grand Rapids, Michigan: Eerdmans, 1993

Twaddell, Elizabeth, "The American Tract Society, 1814–1860," *Church History* 15 (1946)

Animated Motion Pictures

Making drawings or inanimate objects "move"

Animation is a technical and creative process for motion pictures in which drawings or inanimate objects are given the illusion of movement. Typically, the animator places a series of drawings on cels – transparent cellulose acetate

Mickey Mouse tries his hand as the "Sorcerer's Apprentice" in *Fantasia*.
(© Disney Enterprises, Inc.)

sheets – with ink and paint. Each drawing is slightly but progressively different from the last. When the cels are photographed frame by frame, then projected at 24 frames per second, the appearance of fluid movement can be achieved. Most animated films produced in the United States have been short subjects or cartoons, each lasting about eight minutes. Feature films run at least 60 minutes, and the most complex, such as Walt Disney's *Fantasia,* may require the talents of several hundred artists and technicians.

The first animated motion picture appeared in 1906. *The Humorous Phases of Funny Faces* was drawn on a chalkboard by J. Stuart Blackton. In 1914, cartoonist Winsor McCay released *Gertie the Dinosaur,* consisting of 5,000 drawings laboriously outlined on paper. Every background detail that remained the same had to be retraced by hand on each sketch. Within a year, inventor Earl Hurd devised the cel, eliminating the tedious redrawing of backgrounds that remained identical from frame to frame.

During the silent film era, filmmakers began to solve a problem inherent in any animated film: making inanimate characters appear live. Notable achievements were Otto Mesmer's *Felix the Cat* series, which premiered in 1919. One of the most endearing creations was Max and Dave Fleischer's Ko-Ko the Clown, first appearing in *Out of the Inkwell* (1916). These cartoons effectively combined live-action cinematography and the drawn figure of Ko-Ko.

During the same period, Walt Disney started his animation career. His *Alice Comedies* (1924) also combined live action with drawings. In 1928, Disney produced the first sound cartoon fully synchronized with music and sound effects, *Steamboat Willie,* which also introduced Mickey Mouse. Between 1928 and 1941, Disney developed a sophisticated studio organization to develop animation techniques for his innovative stories. In 1932, Disney released *Flowers and Trees,* the first Technicolor cartoon in the *Silly Symphonies* series. *The Three Little Pigs* premiered in 1933, demonstrating Disney's ability to develop personality, or

character, animation. Disney's landmark achievements were his features: *Snow White and the Seven Dwarfs* (1937), *Pinocchio* (1940), *Fantasia* (1940), and *Dumbo* (1941).

During the 1930s and 1940s, other Hollywood studios began to produce animation. Warner Brothers assembled the best talent in the industry to create cartoons, matching Disney's *Silly Symphonies* with *Merry Melodies* (1931) and *Looney Tunes* (1932). The studio created Porky Pig (1935), Daffy Duck (1938), and Bugs Bunny (1940). MGM, Twentieth Century-Fox, Columbia, and Universal Studios also released animated cartoons, introducing such famous characters as Tom and Jerry, Woody Woodpecker, Betty Boop, Superman, Popeye, Mighty Mouse, and Casper, the Friendly Ghost.

During World War II, American animation turned to defeating the Axis powers through training, propaganda, inspirational, and documentary films. *Private Snafu* shorts from Warner Brothers helped train Army recruits. Frank Capra's *Why We Fight* documentaries were animated with Disney Studios' maps. Disney's *Der Fuehrer's Face* (1943) won an Academy award. Such cartoons used racial and ethnic stereotyping of Germans and Japanese to rally American audiences to the cause.

Following the war, United Productions of America (UPA) designed cartoons that disavowed the Disney style of representational animation, the creation of cartoon characters as

Walt Disney and his friend, Mickey Mouse
(Museum of Broadcast Communications)

The three little pigs sing in the color animated short of the same name.
(© Disney Enterprises, Inc.)

lifelike and naturalistic as possible. In such films as *Mr. Magoo* (1949) and *Gerald McBoing Boing* (1951), UPA created a simplified, almost abstract style called limited animation.

As television became the predominant outlet for cartoon animation, the simplicity of the UPA style surpassed the subtle design sophistication of Walt Disney in popularity. Increased cartoon programming after school and on Saturday mornings meant completing approximately 24 minutes of animation a week per show; production speed became much more important than quality, and simplification of style became the rule. Nevertheless, many of these works were creative, among them *Crusader Rabbit, Tom Terrific,* and *Rocky and His Friends.* A three-dimensional, animated character called *Gumby* premiered in 1955.

Hanna-Barbera Studios produced the first prime-time animated series, *The Flintstones* (ABC, 1960–66). Several other series emerged, but animation disappeared from the prime-time weekly schedule in the early 1970s, returning in January 1990 when the Fox Network premiered *The Simpsons.* Animated specials in prime time flourished, however, and became a popular holiday staple. Shows such as *How the Grinch Stole Christmas* (1966), *Frosty the Snowman* (1969), and several "Charlie Brown" specials became classics that were repeated every year.

Several important trends modified American animation

after 1960 as it became necessary to save time and cut costs. For example, Walt Disney adopted Xerography for *101 Dalmatians* (1961) to reduce the toil of transferring an animator's pencil drawings in ink to a cel. Some studios also began to hire animators in Japan to reduce the costs of animation for television. Three-dimensional (3-D) model animation became a common technique by the late 1970s, especially in science fiction films. The special-effects company created by George Lucas, Industrial Light and Magic, perfected 3-D animation for the "Imperial Walker" sequence in *The Empire Strikes Back* (1980).

Animation based on computer programming began in the early 1960s, and over the next 20 years, computer-animated projects multiplied. Many were designed for training purposes such as flight simulation, but numerous projects reached the public eye, such as *Tin Toy* (1988), which won an Oscar. Television commercials animated by computer also achieved wide acceptance, led in popularity by Coca-Cola's Polar Bear campaign for the 1994 Winter Olympics.

The desire to combine live-action cinematography with animation has existed since the birth of the art. Among the most successful features in the sound era were MGM's *Anchors Aweigh* (1945), starring Gene Kelly and Jerry the Mouse, and several Disney features including *Song of the South* (1946). By the 1980s, techniques emerged that allowed virtually perfect integration of cinematography with drawings and computer-generated image animation. *Who Framed Roger Rabbit* (1988) created such a believable cartoon world that the film's live-action characters had to adapt to it rather than the other way around. Computer-generated image animation reached maturity with the 1995 Disney release of *Toy Story*. All of the film's imagery, even backgrounds, was generated by computer.

The animation industry in the United States remained labor intensive, but digital devices removed some of the creative barriers animators face, permitting much more visually sophisticated and complex imagery. As the art of animation reached its centennial, filmmakers were designing animation that literally could not be drawn by human hands.

JOHN P. FREEMAN

See also Motion Picture Technology; Silent Motion
 Pictures; Sound Motion Pictures

Further Reading

Halas, John, and Roger Manvell, *Design in Motion,* New
 York: Hastings, 1962; London: Studio, 1962
Hoffer, Thomas W., *Animation: A Reference Guide,*
 Westport, Connecticut: Greenwood, 1981
Holliss, Richard, and Brian Sibley, *The Disney Studio
 Story,* New York: Crown, 1988; London: Octopus, 1988
Maltin, Leonard, *Of Mice and Magic: A History of
 American Animated Cartoons,* rev. ed., New York: New
 American Library, 1987
Schneider, Steve, *That's all Folks: The Art of Warner Bros.
 Animation,* New York: Holt, 1990; London: Aurum,
 1994
Solomon, Charles, *Enchanted Drawings: The History of
 Animation,* rev. ed., New York: Wings Books, 1994
Thomas, Frank, and Ollie Johnston, *Disney Animation:
 The Illusion of Life,* New York: Abbeville, 1981

Armed Forces Media

Information and entertainment sources for the military

The military forces of the United States have a long tradition of using the print and electronic media for their own information and entertainment. These efforts have ranged from hand-printed newsletters independently produced by one or two soldier-journalists to an international system of newspapers and radio and television stations staffed by hundreds of military and civilian workers.

Troop newspapers have been around since the nation's beginnings, with several known to have been produced specifically by and for American forces during the Revolution. Although little is known about these early editions, evidence indicates that the first to appear was the *South Carolina Gazette,* published in Parker's Ferry in 1779.

During the Civil War, troop-published newspapers were quite common among both Northern and Southern forces. Federal soldiers published as many as 100 different "camp papers"; a few were even produced by sailors aboard naval vessels. Ranging from elaborate multipage dailies to one-time-only single sheets, they were often printed on presses commandeered from local towns. The scarcity of wartime resources in the South meant that the Confederate efforts were necessarily more modest, but even a shortage of press and paper did not stop a few soldiers who used "pen printing" (hand lettering) to produce manuscript editions. Civil War troop newspapers generally contained news and commentary aimed at encouraging the soldier's resolve and boosting his morale. Some were very official in tone, carrying primarily military orders and reports of battles, but others included more lighthearted features such as jokes, stories, and verse. While they were usually financed by per-copy sales, many also sold advertising to the provisioners, photographers, and other camp followers who counted on the soldiers' trade.

With World War I, the troop newspaper entered a new era. Although numerous, small "post newspapers" were still published in individual Army camps, the establishment in Paris of the *Stars and Stripes* to serve American forces serving in Europe marked a new level of journalistic sophistication. With a staff of 300 and a circulation of more than 500,000 at its peak, the World War I *Stripes* (as it became popularly known) rivaled many stateside commercial papers in both readership and journalistic talent. Although it published only 71 weekly issues, it became popular and influential among the soldiers. Established by the U.S. command and headed by an Army officer, its soldier-journalists were given much latitude to write about the vicissitudes of Army life. Like its predecessors, the *Stripes* contained news, poems, drawings, and stories, but it also carried letters from its readers and became a sounding board for doughboy complaints about food, weather, and even the military establishment. The paper's success demonstrated for many in the military the substantial benefits to troop morale of disseminating timely news, information, and entertainment in an easily digestible form.

Between the two world wars, the military press established several important journals. With titles like *Military Review* and *Naval Affairs,* they carried essays on military philosophy and tactics and were aimed at the professional officer corps.

American entry into World War II sparked the resurrection of the *Stars and Stripes* as the soldier's major newspaper. It quickly became a daily with nearly 30 different editions produced and distributed almost everywhere U.S. forces operated. At the same time, many individual units, posts, and ships published their own, more modest, papers. World War II also saw the evolution of radio as a major troop medium, surpassing even the *Stripes* in popularity. Early in the war, the military established a radio network that eventually consisted of both United States–based short-wave transmitters and smaller troop-operated "local" stations around the world. Programming was distributed by the newly organized Armed Forces Radio Service (AFRS). Many radio personalities granted AFRS rebroadcast rights to their shows; one program, "Command Performance," was produced specifically for the troops and regularly featured many big-name Hollywood stars.

PACIFIC EDITION
THE STARS AND STRIPES

U. S. Armed Forces Daily   In The Pacific Ocean Areas

Vol. I, No. 1 | Monday, May 14, 1945 | Two Cents Per Copy

Drive Into Naha's Edge

Kind Hand to Nazis Slapped By Gen. 'Ike'

PARIS (AP)—Gen. Eisenhower said he regrets instances in which senior U. S. Army officers treated captured Nazi and high German officials on a "friendly enemy" basis in direct violation of his orders.

The supreme commander's statement was made following widespread criticism appearing in the British and American press on treatment of Reichsmarshal Hermann Goering by the 7th Army.

General Eisenhower said in a statement:

"My attention has been called to press reports of instances of senior United States officers treating captured Nazi and high German officials on a 'friendly enemy' basis. Any such incident has been in direct violation of my express and long standing orders."

"Drastic measures have been set in motion to assure termination of these errors forthwith.

"Moreover, any past instances of this nature are by no means indicative of the attitude of this army, but are result of faulty judgment of individuals concerned, who will be personally acquainted with expressions of my definite disapproval."

Chinese Drive To Open Port

CHUNGKING (UP)—The possibility of opening a major harbor for seaborne American supplies to reach China was seen with the official announcement that Chinese troops have entered the port city of Foochow.

The Chinese high command war bulletin said Gen. Chiang Kai-shek's troops fought their way into Foochow on Friday night and also captured the Japanese airfield south of the city. Foochow, which has a normal population of about 322,000, lies 540 miles due west across the East China Sea from Okinawa.

The war bulletin said several Chinese columns on Thursday morning launched the attack on Foochow, and by Friday morning Jap positions northwest of the city had been shattered. Friday night the Chinese entered the city and at latest reports were fighting the Jap garrison in the streets of Foochow.

To the north, other Chinese forces seized Sinchang, putting them within 40 miles of the coast at a point 265 miles northeast of Foochow and 130 miles southwest of Shanghai.

Chinese control of a port on the China Sea, coupled with U. S. naval and air superiority in the Pacific, may have a vital effect on the course of war against Japan. War supplies for China are being flown in or carried over the tortuous route through Burma. One useable port—if the Chinese can hold it—would offer a chance to multiply this trickle of supplies many times.

MOURNING ENDS

WASHINGTON, (ANS)—Flags at Army posts will remain at half staff until sundown May 14, end of the period of official mourning set by President Truman for the late President Roosevelt.

HEADQUARTERS UNITED STATES ARMY FORCES,
PACIFIC OCEAN AREAS
OFFICE OF THE COMMANDING GENERAL
APO 958

To The Staff of "THE STARS AND STRIPES":

The first printing of the Pacific Edition of "THE STARS AND STRIPES" marks another stride toward Tokyo. The American fighting man in this Theater now has his own daily newspaper to record his inevitable victory over our country's final enemy.

It is your task to carry on in the great tradition of the Army newspapers which have proudly held aloft the banner of "THE STARS and STRIPES." Make your newspaper accurate, complete and enterprising, distribute it wherever our troops may go, and you will fulfill your mission.

Soon you will be publishing editions of "The STARS AND STRIPES" not only on Oahu but in the forward bases, which will greatly enlarge your opportunity of serving the American soldier. To every member of the staff my best wishes for success.

ROBERT C. RICHARDSON, JR.
Lieutenant General, U. S. Army,
Commanding

Saga Of An Arkansas Coon Hunter

46 Japs, So That's Why They Call Him 'Killer' Freeman

By Pfc. BILL LAND
Stars and Stripes Staff Writer

WITH 10th ARMY, OKINAWA —There is no single Army manual on how to kill the enemy in battle, but if the War Department should decide to publish one, S/Sgt. John Freeman of Lowell, Ark., an infantry rifle platoon sergeant, should be called to Washington to serve as technical advisor.

His technique of digging out and killing Japs is nearly perfect.

During the Leyte campaign he earned the name "Killer" Freeman, because in the first six weeks of fighting, he single-handedly sent 27 Japs to their ancestral home.

No Probables

He takes credit only for single-handed killings, not those scored in a campaign. He particularly delights in sniper hunts or investigating bypassed or burned-out caves. He has been known to wait for hours to get a Jap.

"If he counted all the probables, there'd be thousands of 'em," a member of his platoon said.

Here on Okinawa he has lived up to his title, for to date there are 19 more notches carved on the butt of his M-1. "And we're only startin'," John added, smiling grimly.

A Born "Killer"

Back in Arkansas, "Killer" Freeman was a farmer and he liked to hunt squirrels and coons. On his broad shoulders sits a head with hair as yellow as ripe corn. His features are soft and child-like until he looks at you with steel-blue eyes. Keen and piercing, they are the eyes of a hunter.

John was born with a gun in his hand, and at the age of seven bagged his first rabbit. He claims that his experience as a hunter has kept him alive during nine months of fighting on Leyte and Okinawa.

To him, the Jap is an animal which has to be hunted. Once the nature of the animal is understood, hunting becomes simple.

Didn't Trust Cave

He said, "In Leyte them Japs put me in mind of the coons we hunt down in Arkansas. But here on Okinawa they're like rats . . . . run from one corn shock to another—never can pin 'em down."

This is the story of Jap warfare in Okinawa in a nutshell, and John relates an incident describing the problems doughfeet face.

Our troops had taken "Tombstone Ridge", a heavily fortified row of cliffs, honeycombed with caves and connecting tunnels. The mopping-up had been completed and flamethrowers and demolition platoons had burned out or closed up all visible exits.

Still, there was constant sniper fire from the rear on the advancing troops.

Carefully, John made his way back, trying to trace the direction of fire. Presently he stood before a big cave, its opening seared black by flamethrowers.

Continued on Back Page

Killing Japs Is His Hobby

JAP KILLER—S/Sgt. John Freeman, Lowell, Ark., has been dubbed "Killer" by his fellow infantrymen. In the first six weeks of fighting on Leyte, he singlehandedly wiped out 27 Japs. On Okinawa, to date, he's killed 19. "Shoot him from the belly up" is his advice to would-be Jap killers.
Photo by Pfc. Bill Land

Yanks Battle Heavy Counter-Attacks

OKINAWA— Locked in one of the most savage battles of the Pacific war, American forces on Okinawa reached the outskirts of shell-blasted Naha and brought under siege an important enemy artillery observation hill, front lines dispatches reported.

Holding their ground despite the influx of Japanese reinforcements and a terrific artillery and mortar barrage, Yanks warded off savage action by Japanese carrying satchel charges, mines and anti-tank guns.

Army News Service reported that the Yanks were steadily driving against a house on Shuri, veritable fortress city. The 32rd Regiment of Maj. Gen. James L. Bradley's 96th Division scaled an important conical hill about one mile from Shuri.

Enemy Loses 93 Planes

A few enemy planes approached American shipping off Okinawa but caused no damage, the Associated Press said. A strong Nip air fleet which struck on Friday damaged several U. S. fleet units. In all, 93 attacking planes were shot down.

Seventy-six enemy aircraft were destroyed in other actions for a one-day total of 169.

Japs loosed a variety of weapons including an anti-tank variation of the Molotov cocktail, against the four U. S. divisions attacking along the five mile front, according to the United Press.

6th Cross Flats

The 6th Marine Division is dug in on the northern rim of Naha at the edge of wide mud flats of the Asato River valley. Crossing the coverless flats will take the
Continued on Back Page

First U-Boat Surrendered To U.S. Navy

CAPE MAY, N. J. (UP)—The German submarine U-858, the first enemy warship to surrender to American naval forces since V-E Day, was brought to an anchorage in lower Delaware Bay with the U.S. flag flying over her conning tower.

A second German submarine was expected to arrive off Portsmouth, N. H., tomorrow, Navy announced.

The first U-boat, stripped of her destructive power under terms of the surrender, was turned over to triumphant American bluejackets five days ago, 300 miles south of Cape Race, Newfoundland, some 720 miles off the eastern seaboard.

Sank 16 Ships

Imprisoned crewmen of the raider said the sub sank 16 Allied ships during 30 months of operation. An American crew specially trained to operate German submarines took over for the last stage of the journey.

The sub is 740 tons, 240 feet long with 105 and 37 mm deck guns in addition to an anti-aircraft installation. It has four torpedo tubes forward, two astern and customarily carried 18 torpedoes. 14 unused torpedoes were in tubes and racks.

Russians Bag Million Nazis Since V-E Day

MOSCOW (INS)—Four Soviet armies cleared all but scattered pockets of renegade Nazi resistance from Austria and Czechoslovakia as the Red Army prisoner bag since the German surrender May 8 swelled to 1,000,000.

A total of 92 German generals were listed in the official Soviet communique as among the German troops who surrendered their arms on six Russian fronts.

The Moscow report said the 1st, 2nd, 3rd and 4th Ukrainian armies had eliminated all but scattered pockets of outlaw Nazi forces under the command of Marshal Ferdinand Schoerner and Col. Gen. Hans Whoehler, who ignored orders to lay down their arms.

Neither of these two die-hard Nazi commanders were listed among the generals who surrendered to the Soviets and it was
Continued on Back Page

Wewak Taken By Australians

MANILA (AP)—Wewak, a tough core of Japanese resistance for more than two years, fell to 6th Division Australians in a swift drive from the west, a communique from Gen. MacArthur's headquarters announced.

The Aussies who landed Friday on the northeast New Guinea peninsula under cover of British fleet units, drove to the edge of the westernmost airfield. Field dispatches emphasized the strong military resistance which still remains in the area, but additional
Continued on Back Page

The Stars and Stripes served military personnel in many wars.
(Davis Library, University of North Carolina at Chapel Hill)

Armed Forces Network broadcasts, such as this one from Honduras, provide military personnel with information and entertainment.
(Official U.S. Army Photo [Released])

With the end of the war came a new role for the Allies – that of occupiers. By 1946, the American Forces Network (AFN) in Europe had become military broadcasting's most extensive service, operating a network of stations spread throughout France, Germany, and the Netherlands. AFN's mission continued to be to serve U.S. troops, but it also garnered unexpected popularity among the "shadow audience" of European civilians. Postwar Europeans, bombarded by Cold War propaganda from both East and West, came to consider AFN to be one of the few trustworthy news sources available, the logic being (fairly correctly) that U.S. soldiers would not stand for propaganda on their own network. Although AFN broadcast only in English, it quickly acquired a very large listenership among the civilians, especially in Germany. AFN's music programming for young U.S. soldiers was also immensely popular and has been credited (or blamed) with helping Americanize the music tastes of a whole generation of Europeans.

After World War II, the military's media remained a fix-ture wherever large concentrations of U.S. forces were stationed. *Stars and Stripes* remained in continuous operation, with expanded editions cropping up during the Korean, Vietnam, and Persian Gulf conflicts. Smaller publications, such as post newspapers and professional journals, also thrived. The Armed Forces Radio and Television Service also continued operating and, using newer distribution technologies, steadily expanded the availability of television. Remote military installations and ships at sea received rotating libraries of videotapes containing not only theatrical movies but also news, information, and entertainment programs from the major American networks. Larger television outlets, such as AFN in Europe, received live television feeds via satellite.

The military media have not been without controversy. Although frequently billed as "by soldiers for soldiers," troop broadcasting and newspapers have historically been plagued by charges of censorship from above. Despite a Pentagon policy stating that troop media should be as free and unfettered as their civilian counterparts, conflicts between editorial freedom and local military commanders have not been uncommon. Yet in general, American troops have been well served by their media. Through them, they receive news, information, entertainment – and a touch of home.

R. STEPHEN CRAIG

Further Reading

American Forces Information Service & Armed Forces Radio and Television Service, *History of AFRTS: "The First 50 Years,"* Washington, D.C.: U.S. Government Printing Office, 1993

Cornebise, Alfred E., *Ranks and Columns: Armed Forces Newspapers in American Wars,* Westport, Connecticut: Greenwood, 1993

_____, *The Stars and Stripes: Doughboy Journalism in World War I,* Westport, Connecticut: Greenwood, 1984

Craig, R. Stephen, "The American Forces Network, Europe: A Case Study in Military Broadcasting," *Journal of Broadcasting & Electronic Media* 30:1 (Winter 1986), pp. 33–46

_____, "American Forces Network in the Cold War: Military Broadcasting in Postwar Germany," *Journal of Broadcasting & Electronic Media* 32:3 (Summer 1988), pp. 307–321

Hutton, Oram C., and Andrew A. Rooney, *The Story of The Stars and Stripes,* Westport, Connecticut: Greenwood, 1970

Army-McCarthy Hearings

Early indicator of the power of television to shape public opinion

The Army-McCarthy hearings were one of the earliest indicators of the power of television. The televised hearings went on for 36 days in 1954, and although they were extensively covered by all the media, the broadcast of the

Television cameras and print media representatives crowded the Army-McCarthy hearings in 1954.
(UPI/Corbis Bettmann)

hearings gave Americans their first sustained view of Senator Joseph McCarthy and his staff in action.

Prior to the hearings, McCarthy had become an international figure based on his virulent pursuit of Communists in the U.S. government. McCarthy had first been elected to represent Wisconsin in the U.S. Senate in 1946. Like other Republicans that year, he had charged his opponent with being soft on Communism, but it was certainly not a central issue in his campaign. In January of 1950, facing a tough reelection campaign, McCarthy, at the suggestion of an acquaintance, chose anti-Communism as his central issue.

One month later, McCarthy gave a speech in Wheeling, West Virginia, before a group of Republican women. According to broadcast and print reporters present, McCarthy claimed to possess a list of 205 Communists "working and shaping policy" in the U.S. State Department. The story was carried by the Associated Press, although most major newspapers did not run it immediately. McCarthy was be-

sieged by reporters wanting the list of names. McCarthy claimed to have left it in his luggage. When he was next approached, his story had begun to change. At one point there were 81 Communists, then 57; sometimes they were Communists, other times merely "bad risks." McCarthy's charges brought him continuing media attention, and soon the Communist issue was identified with him.

When the Senate demanded evidence of the 205 (or 81 or 57) Communists in the State Department, McCarthy responded with a lengthy presentation of cases, almost none of which supported his contention. The media, however, reported McCarthy's charges. In this way McCarthy dominated the news for four years, making charges without evidence and then quickly moving on to new charges. Most susceptible to McCarthy's strategy were the wire services, which functioned under intense competition and lacked the time to check out the accusations before reporting them. Later stories rebutting the earlier ones were usually too late

Senator Joseph McCarthy, left, created an indelible impression on American television audiences when the Army-McCarthy hearings were broadcast.
(Museum of Broadcast Communications)

for most media deadlines. McCarthy knew reporters' deadlines and timed his announcements accordingly. He was adept at turning a phrase in a way that made eye-catching headlines.

In 1953, McCarthy became chair of the Senate Committee on Government Operations and its Permanent Subcommittee on Investigations. He used the latter to continue his attack on Communist infiltration of the government, although now he was investigating his own party's administration. One such inquiry, which began in the fall of 1953, concerned civilian scientists employed by the Army Signal Corps at Fort Monmouth, New Jersey.

An Army dentist named Irving Peress, who had a history of membership in left-wing organizations, became a focus of the investigation. As a dentist, Peress had been automatically promoted to major, but during a loyalty investigation he refused to answer several questions and was to be discharged. When McCarthy learned of the Peress case, he

called him before the subcommittee, where the dentist again refused to answer many questions about his political beliefs. McCarthy then demanded that Peress be court-martialed, but he already had been discharged. Angered, McCarthy called before the subcommittee Brigadier General Ralph W. Zwicker, commander of Camp Kilmer, where Peress had been stationed, demanding to know who was responsible for discharging Peress. During the hearing, McCarthy browbeat Zwicker, calling him stupid and unfit to wear his uniform.

McCarthy's treatment of Zwicker was followed the next month by Edward R. Murrow's critical *See It Now* documentary on McCarthy. Murrow and his producer, Fred Friendly, had been collecting footage on McCarthy for more than a year, and they were able to let McCarthy's methods speak for themselves by showing him taunting and intimidating subcommittee witnesses like Zwicker, making reckless accusations, and using inflammatory language. The response to the CBS broadcast was overwhelmingly favorable, perhaps setting the stage for what was to come – the daily television drama of the Army-McCarthy hearings.

The televised hearings came about because McCarthy's subcommittee counsel, Roy Cohn, was charged by the Army with using the loyalty inquiry to bargain for special treatment for Private David Schine, who was also affiliated with the subcommittee. McCarthy countercharged that the Army was holding Schine hostage to force the subcommittee to end its inquiry.

The hearings were a boon for the ABC television network, which lacked daytime programming. ABC broadcast the hearings daily, garnering high ratings. Although McCarthy relinquished his position as chairman, he still dominated the hearings with continual requests to raise a "point of order." The most dramatic moment came when McCarthy launched an attack on a young lawyer who worked for Joseph Welch, attorney for the Army. As the cameras rolled, even Cohn tried to signal McCarthy to stop, but he would not. In response, an emotional Welch berated McCarthy and asked, "At long last have you left no sense of decency?" Welch was met with resounding applause throughout the hearing room.

The subcommittee's verdict was inconclusive in regard to the charges on both sides. The public verdict on McCarthy, however, was clearer. Media criticism of McCarthy was widespread. On television, McCarthy and Cohn had emerged as dark and mean. Polls showed that the major effect was on those who previously had no opinion of McCarthy; many of them saw him in an unfavorable light as a result of the hearings. Moderate Senate Republicans had a similar reaction, thus paving the way for McCarthy's condemnation by the Senate later that year.

The Army-McCarthy hearings were extensively and often critically covered by all the media, but their televised nature had the most impact. McCarthy came to prominence at the same time that television began to boom. By the time of the hearings, television had extended into most areas of the nation. The televised hearings provided a copious helping of McCarthy that left a bad taste in the mouths of both the public and government officials. Most historians therefore attribute McCarthy's downfall to the Army-McCarthy hearings.

PAMELA A. BROWN

See also Cold War and the Media

Further Reading

Bayley, Edwin R., *Joe McCarthy and the Press*, Madison: University of Wisconsin Press, 1981
Belfrage, Cedric, *The American Inquisition, 1945–1960*, Indianapolis, Indiana: Bobbs-Merrill, 1973
Cohn, Roy M., and Sidney Zion, *The Autobiography of Roy Cohn*, Secaucus, New Jersey: Lyle Stuart, 1988
Gabler, Neal, *Winchell: Gossip, Power, and the Culture of Celebrity*, New York: Knopf, 1994; also published as *Walter Winchell: Gossip, Power and the Culture of Celebrity*, London: Parpermac, 1996
Goldston, Robert, *The American Nightmare: Senator Joseph R. McCarthy and the Politics of Hate*, Indianapolis, Indiana: Bobbs-Merrill, 1973
Griffith, Robert, *The Politics of Fear: Joseph R. McCarthy and the Senate*, Amherst: University of Massachusetts Press, 1987; London: Eurospan, 1987
Rovere, Richard H., *Senator Joe McCarthy*, New York: Harper, 1973; London: University of California Press, 1996

Asian American Media
Media for a rapidly growing population segment

Asian Americans were the fastest-growing minority group in the United States according to the 1990 U.S. Census. Asian Americans, who represented 19 ethnic subgroups (including Pacific Islanders), made up nearly 3 percent of the U.S. population; according to the census, that number was expected to continue growing at the same rate or faster into the next decade.

Most of the media catering to the Asian American community came about following the Asian American panethnicity movement of the late 1960s and 1970s. The leading publications from this era were: *AACTION*, published in Philadelphia; *AASA*, California State University at Northridge; *Aion*, Cornell University; *Amerasia Journal*, originally published at Yale University and then at the University of California at Los Angeles (UCLA); *Ameri-Asia News*, Forest City, Florida; *Asian American for Equal Employment Newspaper*, New York City; *Asian Expression*, California State University at Dominguez Hills; *Asian Family Affair*, Seattle, Washington; *Asian Spotlight*, College of San Mateo in California; *Asian Student*, Berkeley, California; *Asian Student Voice*, San Francisco State University; *Bridge: An Asian American Perspective*, New York City; *Crosscurrents*, Los Angeles; *East Wind*, Los Angeles; *Eastern Wind*, Washington, D.C.; *Getting Together*, New York City; *Gidra*, Los Angeles; *Jade: The Asian American Magazine*, Los Angeles; *Pacific Ties*, Los Angeles; *Rice Paper*, Madison, Wisconsin; and *Rodan*, San Francisco.

However, as the focus of the Asian American movement both broadened – to include East Indian Americans and Middle Eastern Americans – and narrowed, as ethnic subgroups gave more attention to their own histories and community issues, many of these publications folded. One of the leading academic journals not only to survive but also to grow in stature was *Amerasia Journal*. It was founded in March 1971 and published by members of the Yale University Asian American Students' Association. The journal later moved to UCLA, where it was published by the Asian American Studies Center there. Leading Asian American academics worldwide contributed to this journal.

In the 1990s, there were several other publications representing the entire Asian American community, as well as publications representing ethnic subgroups. Following is a list of 20 leading publications (not presented in ranked order) of those audiences, based on three criteria – (1) stability of the circulation, (2) representations of the community or communities to which the publication targets, and (3) coverage of issues reflective of the targeted group or groups. The academic journals were *Asian America: Journal of Cul-*

ture and the Arts, English Department at the University of California at Santa Barbara; *The Hawaiian Journal of History,* Hawaiian Historical Society in Honolulu; *Asian Pacific American Journal,* Asian American Writers' Workshop in New York City; *Critical Mass: A Journal of Asian American Criticism,* Asian American Studies program at the University of California at Berkeley; and *Amerasia Journal,* UCLA. Popular magazines were *YOLK,* Los Angeles; *FACE,* Malibu, California; *Transpacific,* Malibu; *A Magazine,* New York City; *Special Edition: Philippine-American Quarterly,* New York City; and *Filipinas Magazine,* San Francisco. Newspapers were *Little India,* Reading, Pennsylvania; *Hawaii Herald,* Honolulu; *Rafu Shimpo,* Los Angeles; *Northwest Asian Weekly,* Seattle; *Hawaii Filipino Chronicle,* Honolulu; *Pacific Citizen,* Monterey Park, California; *Korea Times* (monthly English edition) Los Angeles; *AsianWeek,* San Francisco; *KoreAm Journal,* Gardenia, California; *International Examiner* (the journal of the northwest's Asian American communities), Seattle; and *Asian New Yorker,* New York City.

The number of radio and television programs that catered to Asian Americans, and specifically to ethnic subgroups of Asian Americans, also increased rapidly after about 1985. Many of these programs were in the cities with the largest populations of Asian Americans: San Francisco, Seattle, Los Angeles, and New York. The films of Asian American filmmakers also began to receive wider acceptance within the Asian American community and by movie audiences in general. The movies *The Joy Luck Club, Who Killed Vincent Chin?, Slaying the Dragon,* and *Yellow-Tale Blues: Two American Families* are examples of movies produced or directed, or both, by Asian Americans that received much acclaim.

There were three leading organizations for Asian Americans in the media. The Asian American Journalists Association (AAJA), based in San Francisco, was the largest, with approximately 1,500 members in the 1990s. It helped produce several publications on Asian Americans and the media, including *Asian American Handbook* (a guide to covering Asian Americans and Asian American issues), *Why Asian American Journalists Leave Journalism and Why They Stay* (a report written by Alexis Tan, director of the Edward R. Murrow School of Communication at Washington State University, which was commissioned by AAJA), *A Journalist's Guide to Middle Eastern Americans* (published by the Detroit Chapter of AAJA), *News Watch: A Critical Look at Coverage of People of Color* (published by AAJA, National Association of Black Journalists, National Association of Hispanic Journalists, and the Native American Journalists Association), and *Project Zinger: A Critical Look at News Media Coverage of Asian Pacific Americans.* Asian CineVision Inc., a New York–based organization, served Asian American filmmakers and persons interested in Asian and Asian American films. The National Asian American Telecommunications Association was another nationwide group representing several hundred Asian Americans working in television, radio, and other areas of telecommunications.

Each year the American Society of Newspaper Editors compiles an annual count of minorities who work in newsrooms across the United States. The 1994 survey found a total of 983 Asian Americans working in newsrooms – 412 reporters, 207 copy editors, 195 photographers, and 169 supervisors. A 1992 survey conducted by the Radio Television News Directors Federation (RTNDF) polled 411 television stations and 296 commercial radio stations about employee ethnicity. It found that 18.5 percent of all television news personnel and 11.6 percent of radio news personnel were minorities. Of those percentages, approximately 800 employees were Asian Americans, representing 475 Asian Americans working on television news staffs (215 men and 260 women), and 340 Asian Americans working for radio news staffs (170 men, 170 women). Most surprising was the low number of Asian Americans that the survey found employed in management positions at radio and television news operations. The RTNDF study found 10 Asian Americans working as television news directors and 51 as radio news directors.

VIRGINIA MANSFIELD-RICHARDSON

See also Alternative Press; Ethnic Press; Minority Journalists' Organizations

Associated Press

Dominant domestic wire service

Responding in the 1840s to the promise by telegraphy and transatlantic steamers of more and fresher news, groups of newspaper editors created cooperatives to share the cost of, and to control, their news reports. These cooperatives, at first commonly called associated presses, were the first of several local and regional wires that exchanged news as a national confederation known formally by 1860 as the Associated Press (AP). In the 1990s, AP was the dominant domestic wire service and one of six international wire services.

The first recorded AP cooperative appeared in mid-1846 when newspaper editors, who were located along the first telegraph line between Albany and Buffalo, New York, established an agent in Albany and a telegraph link to New York City and began receiving the same daily telegraph dispatches for use in their papers. Meanwhile, even though New York City was for most of AP's history the site of the wire's headquarters, the precise founding date of the AP in that city is obscured by the sporadic, changing cooperative news gathering arrangements that were formed among the city's leading dailies dating from the mid-1820s.

New York City's AP, however, is believed to have arisen in the spring of 1848 to expedite delivery of news of the extraordinary political revolutions then sweeping Europe. It provided news to a partnership of the city's six most powerful newspapers – the *Courier and Enquirer,* the *Journal of Commerce,* the *Express,* the *Sun,* the *Herald,* and the *Tribune.* When the *New York Times* was founded in 1851, it became the seventh partner in the New York City AP.

AP's first general agent, Alexander Jones, supervised the

partnership's news operations and arranged contracts with various telegraph companies. He stepped down in May 1851, replaced by Daniel H. Craig, who had been AP's foreign news agent in Halifax, Nova Scotia.

Craig organized AP's exclusive contracts with telegraph companies so that most of the foreign and domestic telegraphic news funneled through his New York City AP office to his seven New York City AP newspapers before he relayed the news reports to other newspapers and the various local and regional APs. The daily news report in the 1850s consisted of about three columns of lean, factual dispatches, generally written without partisan bias.

AP's Civil War battlefield dispatches were a series of short bulletins of the latest happenings. President Abraham Lincoln, relying on AP's nonpartisanship to reach many readers, released much of his administration's news exclusively to the AP's Lawrence A. Gobright in Washington, D.C.

By the 1880s, the New York City AP office was delivering its news reports to agents of 13 local and regional news cooperatives in the AP confederation. While the length of AP's news report grew over time and telegraphic innovations moved dispatches into newsrooms more rapidly, the report remained generally factual and impartial.

After three mediocre post–Civil War competitors failed to subdue AP, United Press (UP), a rapidly growing wire financed by two powerful newspapers, challenged AP in 1882. During the next 10 years AP's and UP's national leaders secretly pooled stock and shared news dispatches to avoid competing with each other.

When this collusion was discovered in 1892, AP publishers replaced general manager William Henry Smith with Melville E. Stone, organized AP as a single national wire, and went to war with UP. After a national fight for the allegiance of U.S. dailies, AP forced UP out of business in 1897.

Although another United Press, financed by Scripps newspapers, appeared in 1907, and the Hearst-controlled International News Service appeared in 1909, the Associated Press remained the dominant U.S. wire, its membership growing from 622 U.S. dailies in 1900 (28 percent of all dailies) to 1,542 U.S. dailies (87 percent of all dailies), 6,000 U.S. broadcast stations, and 8,500 foreign news outlets in 1990. For much of the twentieth century the industry regarded AP's news report as accurate and reliable, if stodgy and establishmentarian – a report written foremost for use by newspapers.

Kent Cooper, AP's general manager from 1925 to 1948, successfully freed AP from an international news cartel in 1934 that had restricted AP's international news coverage and distribution since 1870. In 1945, the U.S. Supreme Court declared that AP's bylaws restricting membership violated antitrust laws, leading to a growth in membership and the merger of competitors UP and INS as United Press International (UPI) in 1958. In the 1980s and 1990s, discovering that cable news was usurping its spot news coverage, AP began experimenting with more features and in-depth news coverage, while UPI fell farther behind as a domestic competitor.

RICHARD A. SCHWARZLOSE

See also Cooperative News Gathering; International News Service; United Press (1882); United Press Associations (1907); United Press International

Further Reading
Cooper, Kent, *Kent Cooper and The Associated Press: An Autobiography,* New York: Random House, 1959
Gramling, Oliver, *AP: The Story of News,* Port Washington, New York: Kennikat, 1969
Schwarzlose, Richard A., "The Associated Press and United Press International," in *The Future of News: Television–Newspapers–Wire Services–Newsmagazines,* edited by Philip S. Cook, Douglas Gomery, and Lawrence W. Lichty, Baltimore, Maryland: Johns Hopkins University Press, 1992
_____, *The Nation's Newsbrokers: Vol. 1, The Formative Years: From Pretelegraph to 1865,* Evanston, Illinois: Northwestern University Press, 1989
_____, *The Nation's Newsbrokers: Vol. 2, The Rush to Institution: From 1865 to 1920,* Evanston, Illinois: Northwestern University Press, 1990
Smith, William Henry, "The Press as a News Gatherer," *Century* 42 (August 1891)
Stone, Melville E., *Fifty Years a Journalist,* New York: Greenwood, 1968

Audience Research for Broadcasting

Attempts to measure size of listening audience

As radio gained popularity during the 1920s, broadcasters wanted to discover the dimensions of their listening audience. At first, station owners were curious about how far their stations' signals traveled. Consequently, early announcers asked listeners to write the station indicating that they had heard a particular broadcast and to comment on the strength and clarity of the signal. The need for audience data became more crucial when advertisers discovered that radio was a potent means for distributing their messages. In response to pressure from advertisers, the national networks NBC and CBS and some local stations used some rather crude methods, such as fan mail and requests for prizes, to gauge listenership.

Advertisers, however, particularly those with products marketed on network radio, wanted more accurate data. Consequently, in 1930, the Association of National Advertisers, working with the market research firm of Archibald Crossley, founded the Cooperative Analysis of Broadcasting. The CAB used a data-gathering technique pioneered by Crossley, the telephone recall method. Calls were placed at four different times during the day to homes selected at random from phone directories, and respondents were asked to recall the programs that they had listened to recently.

In 1934, Clark-Hooper, Inc., conducted a survey in 16 cities using the telephone coincidental technique, asking if respondents were then listening to radio. If the answer was yes, they were then asked to what program they were listening and to name the station broadcasting it. The company split up in 1938, with C.E. Hooper, Inc., assuming responsibility for radio audience measurement. The reports produced by this new company, commonly called Hooperatings, were sold to advertisers, advertising agencies, and broadcasters. Hooper's service became so popular that the CAB ceased operations in 1946.

In 1942, the A.C. Nielsen Company started a radio ratings service using a different method of audience measurement: the Audimeter. A mechanical device attached to a radio, the Audimeter consisted of a sharp stylus that moved over a roll of paper tape (later replaced by film) in synchronization with the radio's tuning dial. Careful analysis of this record revealed the stations the set was tuned to and for how long. By 1949, Nielsen had placed Audimeters in more than 1,100 homes. The Nielsen sampling area encompassed more than 97 percent of the United States, making the company's ratings generalizable to virtually the entire nation. Advertisers and broadcasters favored Nielsen's technique, and in 1950 Nielsen bought out most of C.E. Hooper, Inc.

As television supplanted radio as audience favorite, Nielsen adapted the Audimeter to the new medium; by the mid-1950s, approximately 700 television households had Audimeters. This formed the basis for the Nielsen Television Index (NTI), a report of the viewership of network programs. The NTI was followed by the Nielsen Station Index, which reported audience viewing data for selected local markets. Nielsen introduced the Storage Instantaneous Audimeter, an Audimeter connected by phone lines to a central computer, in several markets throughout the 1960s and 1970s. This new device enabled Nielsen to publish overnight ratings.

Nielsen found itself with a competitor in local television ratings when the American Research Bureau (which eventually changed its name to Arbitron) began a local ratings service in 1949 and expanded its coverage during the 1950s and 1960s. Using the diary technique, a sample of viewers was asked to record viewing behavior in specially prepared diaries and to mail the completed documents to Arbitron. Nielsen also adapted the diary technique in its local television market sample. By the end of the 1960s, Arbitron, emulating Nielsen, had developed its own version of a mechanical device to measure television viewing.

During the 1960s, congressional hearings about the accuracy of radio ratings prompted Nielsen to redesign its measurement technique. Clients, however, balked at the increased cost of this new method. Partly because of this and because the company was losing money in radio, Nielsen ended its radio rating service in 1963. Shortly after that, Arbitron began using the diary technique in local radio ratings.

The broadcast audience measurement situation was fairly stable from the late 1960s to the late 1970s. Nielsen's NTI was the only report of network television viewing, while Arbitron and Nielsen offered competing reports for local market television ratings. In radio, Arbitron was the dominant company providing local market radio ratings. After Nielsen's departure from radio, network radio ratings were handled primarily by Radio's All Dimension Audience Report (RADAR), a collaborative effort of the major radio networks.

By the late 1970s, Arbitron was faced with a competitor when Birch Radio went into business in 1978. Using the radio recall method first popularized by the CAB, Birch offered ratings in about 270 local markets. A depressed economy during the early 1990s, however, forced Birch out of business.

The Nielsen company's monopoly in network ratings was also threatened in the late 1980s when an English company, AGB Television Research, introduced a new device, called a Peoplemeter, to measure television viewing. Whereas the Audimeter could only record when and to what channel the set was tuned, the Peoplemeter provided information about the demographics of the viewing audience. Nielsen introduced its own version of the Peoplemeter; AGB was unable to gain enough broadcast and advertising clients to make its service viable and ceased operations in 1988.

Nielsen's other rival in local television market ratings, Arbitron, also introduced its version of the Peoplemeter. The same depressed economy that forced Birch Radio out of business also had an impact on Arbitron's television service. In a cost-cutting move, many stations that had formerly subscribed to both services canceled their contracts with Arbitron. In 1993, Arbitron announced it would concentrate its efforts in radio.

As of 1995, Nielsen's Peoplemeter sample of 4,500 households provided the basis for network and cable ratings. Nielsen also provided reports on local market television based on measurements obtained from diaries and mechanical devices. In radio, network radio listening was measured by RADAR. Arbitron dominated local market radio ratings, although AccuRatings, started in 1992, provided competition in about 50 local markets.

JOSEPH R. DOMINICK

See also Audience Research for Motion Pictures; Audience Research for Newspapers; Broadcast Ratings

Further Reading

Beville, Hugh M., *Audience Ratings: Radio, Television, Cable,* Hillsdale, New Jersey: Lawrence Erlbaum, 1988

Dominick, Joseph, Barry Sherman, and Gary Copeland, *Broadcasting/Cable and Beyond: An Introduction to Modern Electronic Media,* 3rd ed., New York: McGraw-Hill, 1996

Webster, James G., and Lawrence W. Lichty, *Ratings Analysis: Theory and Practice,* Hillsdale, New Jersey: Lawrence Erlbaum, 1991

Audience Research for Motion Pictures

Uncovering the interests of moviegoers

In the context of commercial leisure in the early twentieth century, movies were foremost among other inexpensive amusements in terms of quickly attracting and holding the fascination of a large and diverse audience. Unlike other forms of recreation, movies were especially magnetic because they were so democratic. Playing continuously, silent motion pictures neither presented a language barrier nor discriminated by age or gender, unlike other amusements. They were inexpensive and situated at specialized venues typically located along mass transit lines, thereby making access easy.

Significantly, the film industry early on established a tradition of eschewing scientific research on its audiences in favor of its own idiosyncratic methods. Filmmaker Mack Sennett, for instance, believed his own personal "laughter scale" would predict audience response to his comedies; at Columbia Pictures, studio boss Harry Cohn reputedly used a "seat-of-the-pants" assessment to gauge audience response.

Industry disinterest in audience research was justified in several ways. With no advertising to sell, there was no need for Hollywood to account to anyone for the size or composition of its audience. In addition, the rapid and enormous popularity of the medium acted as a deterrent to research as producers took little interest in why audiences attended, as long as they did attend. The seemingly cold, clinical, and dispassionate methods of scientific research were also viewed as being at odds with the artistic endeavor of filmmaking. Finally, each film was viewed as unique and could not be considered a typical "product," thereby rendering meaningless any generalizations from the results of one audience research study to another.

The industry was prompted to initiate audience research largely as a function of two closely associated events in the 1950s: diminished theatrical attendance as a result of television and Hollywood's need to legitimize itself in the eyes of the Wall Street investment and banking communities. In each instance, bringing to bear the mantle of "science" through audience research was thought to accomplish the goal of returning patrons to the theaters and harvesting investment dollars. Nonetheless, as late as 1978, the "science" of movie marketing was still being described as a technique whose goals and roles were in an evolutionary state.

Leo A. Handel's research for the industry, beginning in the 1940s, ushered in the initial attempts to analyze movie audiences scientifically. Since then, industry audience research has sporadically focused on three dimensions for any given film. Preproduction research, including concept and casting tests, was brought about and popularized especially during the 1970s as a result of former Madison Avenue advertising executives' entry into movie marketing departments. Research conducted while movie production is in progress includes title and trailer tests, awareness studies, and advertising research. Finally, postproduction research has focused primarily on sneak previews, both production and marketing previews.

Despite the medium's 100-year history, scientific research conducted outside Hollywood on the audiences for motion pictures was, even in the 1990s, similarly scattered and scant. For most academics, the study of film has been just that – the study of film without an analysis of the economic and industrial processes that bring motion pictures to audiences. More often than not scholars have investigated what is on the screen without inquiring how what is on the screen got there or who viewed the image.

Independent scholars went along with the industry's argument that each picture represented a unique problem. Additionally, these researchers found it difficult to attract funding for movie audience research. With television's arrival in the 1950s, that medium not only usurped movies' role as popular entertainment, it also attracted researchers' attention.

Although slender, the thread of movie audience research conducted by the scholarly community can nonetheless be traced back to nearly the beginning of the medium. The rapid rise of movies in popularity provoked a backlash from moralists, reformers, vice crusaders, and governmental agencies prompting, perhaps ironically, the earliest audience research. The Payne Fund Studies, initiated by William Short and published in 1933, investigated the movies' influence on a variety of social concerns. Later investigations focused on such issues as people's motivations for moviegoing, the decision process involved in selecting a movie for attendance, different contexts of the moviegoing experience, movies' effect on attitudes and people's attitudes toward movies, and selected policy concerns, including the efficacy of the self-regulatory movie rating system. Such inquiries more often represented isolated investigations than theory-driven research.

BRUCE A. AUSTIN

See also Audience Research for Broadcasting; Audience Research for Newspapers; Motion Picture Ratings

Further Reading

Austin, Bruce A., ed., *Current Research in Film: Audiences, Economics, and Law,* vols. 1–5, Norwood, New Jersey: Ablex, 1985–1991
_____, *The Film Audience: An International Bibliography of Research with Annotations and an Essay,* Metuchen, New Jersey: Scarecrow, 1983
_____, *Immediate Seating: A Look at Movie Audiences,* Belmont, California: Wadsworth, 1989
Handel, Leo A., *Hollywood Looks at Its Audience: A Report of Film Audience Research,* Urbana: University of Illinois Press, 1950
Jowett, Garth, *Film: The Democratic Art,* Boston: Little, Brown, 1976

Audience Research for Newspapers

Newspapers seek to tailor products to audiences

Newspaper audience research seeks to estimate the size of individual publications' audiences, their demographic characteristics, and their product consumption and general media-use habits. Syndicated local newspaper research, which provides standardized data on local audiences, has its roots in the creation of the Audit Bureau of Circulations, the reliance on audience research by competing media (e.g., magazines, radio, and television), and numerous noncomparable audience studies offered by vendors of custom research.

Cutthroat competition between publishers in the late nineteenth and early twentieth centuries fueled the industry's expansion and had an important by-product: the Audit Bureau of Circulations. The ABC, created in 1914 from the merger of the Advertising Audit Association and the Bureau of Verified Circulations, was the successor to a number of efforts by advertisers and their agents to obtain accurate estimates of newspapers' circulations.

The ABC-verified circulation figure stood as the only universally accepted measure of newspaper audience for nearly two decades. As radio matured into a serious competitor for advertising revenue, however, advertisers were introduced to a new way of conceptualizing media audiences; that is, as the number of individuals exposed to the advertising vehicle, rather than the number of paid copies of the vehicle in circulation. Newspapers had to have audience figures similar to those produced for radio. The print media found their equivalent by adopting the tool used by broadcasters: the audience survey.

Such audience surveys concentrated on the number and characteristics of audience members rather than on the number of copies sold. ABC-verified circulation figures left publishers at a competitive disadvantage in their search for advertising revenue precisely when national brand advertising was increasing. Because broadcast audience numbers were not comparable to ABC figures for print media, publishers found it advantageous to adopt their own audience measurement techniques.

Magazines began widespread use of audience surveys in the mid-1930s, but newspapers lagged behind, primarily because newspaper publishers did not see as great a benefit in moving to readership as a measure of audience size.

From the conclusion of World War II through the 1970s, hundreds of studies of newspaper audiences were conducted for individual papers by dozens of companies contracted to provide proprietary research. These individualized data, enumerating size and demographic characteristics of the local audience, often included detailed examinations of newspaper page and section readership, audience use of newspaper advertising, and readers' interest in specific types of content or coverage. While useful at the local level, such studies were vexing for national advertisers, who were often stymied by the dizzying variation in questionnaire construction, interviewing methodologies, and geographic definition of markets. Even the definition of "reader" was subject to debate: Some vendors defined readers via the average-issue operationalization (in which daily newspaper readership is calculated as the number of individuals reporting reading the paper "yesterday," averaged over five days, with interviews conducted Tuesday through Saturday), while others used variations of the "regularly – sometimes – almost never or never" scheme, in which readers categorized themselves into more qualitative groupings.

The 1961 benchmark national readership study, *The Daily Newspaper and Its Reading Public,* not only began the long drive to establish the average-issue formula as the industry-accepted means for calculating newspaper audiences but also was one of the first studies to incorporate

sampling, interviewing, and geographic definition procedures standardized across each of the markets in which the newspaper audience was measured. Without such standardization, subtle variations in interviewer training, respondent selection, and other methodological details prevented the unbiased assessment of differences among markets across the country. With standardization, between-market comparisons became easier.

Despite its benefits, standardization of research methodology was slow throughout the newspaper industry. The resulting lack of uniform estimates of local newspaper audiences lasted well into the 1970s until syndicated research companies began to provide a standard service to advertisers who wanted to compare newspaper audience characteristics with those of other media.

Syndicated research helped raise newspapers' status as a medium for national advertising. Five vendors of syndicated data emerged as major players in the market for local newspaper audience research.

Audits and Surveys. Founded in 1953 as a general marketing and survey research firm providing both custom and syndicated studies, the company was a leader in establishing syndicated studies of product movement data at the retail level. It provided the data for the Bureau of Newspaper Advertising's *The Daily Newspaper and Its Reading Public,* as well as follow-up studies conducted in 1963 and 1971.

Mediamark Research. Founded in 1979, Mediamark Research aimed to fill the national advertisers' need for extensive "single source" data; that is, detailed information on media and product use, audience demographics, activities, and lifestyles collected from individual respondents by the same vendor throughout the markets surveyed. Its newspaper audience estimates were a somewhat secondary product of a broader survey that gathered detailed information on magazine audiences and product usage.

Roper Starch Worldwide. At the end of the twentieth century, the Starch Advertising and Media Research division of Roper Starch Worldwide was the primary vendor worldwide of readership figures for print advertising; its syndication of local newspaper audience estimates was a secondary source of revenue for the company. Founded in 1923, Starch built its reputation on the measurement of print (mainly magazine, but also newspaper) advertising readership, measured as the ads appeared in regular issues of publications.

Scarborough Research Corporation. Founded in 1974, Scarborough initially provided proprietary studies for large newspaper clients in major metropolitan areas, relying on lengthy telephone and personal interviews to determine audience size, demographic characteristics, and product use habits. By 1989, Scarborough was providing media surveys in the eleventh- through thirtieth-ranked markets. By the late 1990s, it conducted annual studies of the top 50 metropolitan markets and was generally acknowledged as the dominant vendor of syndicated research on local newspaper audiences.

Simmons Market Research Bureau. The W.R. Simmons Company, founded in 1963, was by 1965 among the first companies to measure use of all four major media – newspapers, magazines, radio, and television – as well as product use, by individual respondents and within the confines of a single study. In 1978, it merged with Axiom Market Research Bureau to form Simmons Market Research Bureau (SMRB). By 1981, when SMRB acquired the Three Sigma Study of Major Market Newspapers, it offered syndicated data on local newspaper audiences. As the late 1990s, SMRB's *Study of Media and Markets* comprised the largest single syndicated study of media and product use available.

MICHAEL C. DONATELLO

See also Audience Research for Broadcasting; Audience Research for Motion Pictures; Newspaper Circulation

Further Reading

Bennett, Charles O., *Facts Without Opinion: First Fifty Years of the Audit Bureau of Circulations,* Chicago: Audit Bureau of Circulations, 1965

Bogart, Leo, *Preserving the Press: How Daily Newspapers Mobilized to Keep Their Readers,* New York: Columbia University Press, 1991

_____, *Press and Public: Who Reads What, When, Where, and Why in American Newspapers,* 2nd ed., Hillsdale, New Jersey: Lawrence Erlbaum, 1989

Bureau of Newspaper Advertising, *The Daily Newspaper and Its Reading Public,* New York: Audits & Surveys, Inc., for the Bureau of Advertising of the American Newspaper Publishers Association, 1961

Fletcher, Alan D., and Thomas A. Bowers, *Fundamentals of Advertising Research*, 4th ed., Belmont, California: Wadsworth, 1991

Smythe, Ted Curtis, "The Advertisers' War to Verify Newspaper Circulation, 1870–1914," *American Journalism* 3 (1986)

Thorn, William J., and Mary Pat Pfeil, *Newspaper Circulation: Marketing the News,* New York: Longman, 1987

Ayer, N.W., & Son

Advertising agency

In 1869, Francis Wayland Ayer bought out the business of Volney B. Palmer, the first known advertising agent. He persuaded his father, Nathan Wheeler Ayer, to work with him in forming an advertising agency, and the duo opened N.W. Ayer & Son. The agency bore the name of his father because the younger Ayer not only admired his father but believed the combined name sounded more impressive.

The Ayer agency began by soliciting advertisements from merchants and placing them in the 11 religious newspapers listed with the agency. Functioning as did other advertising agents of his time, Francis also purchased the total advertising space in certain publications and resold it in parcels to advertisers, also placing advertisements in publications that were not on his list. By the end of its first year, the agency represented several additional newspapers and had to move to a larger office.

Within two years, the agency was handling more than 300 publications. When his father died in 1873, Francis purchased his share of the business and took on a partner. An in-house printing department, added in 1875, allowed Ayer to place advertisements in any newspaper published in the United States or Canada while most other agencies still hired outside printers.

After investigating other agencies' techniques, Ayer decided to represent the advertiser by revealing the cost of space purchased and the agency's commission. Ayer's agency was now a space-buyer paid by the client and soon earned a profit from its open-contract-plus-commission system. This system allowed Ayer to buy advertising space wisely as well as to consider the advertiser's needs – hallmarks of modern agencies.

In 1879, Ayer conducted a national market survey to win a new client, and by 1880, the agency was writing advertising copy. In that same year the agency issued the *American Newspaper Annual,* which listed every newspaper and magazine published in the United States and Canada. This annual later became the *N.W. Ayer & Son's Directory of Newspapers and Periodicals,* which was still published at the end of the twentieth century.

Ayer's business policy changed in the 1880s when the agency began to refuse certain kinds of advertising. From 1894 to 1898, its clients were affected by the economic recession and consequently reduced their advertising budgets, but when businesses expanded in the late 1890s, so did Ayer. One of its major campaigns launched Uneeda Biscuit, the first such product to be mass marketed in individual airtight packages, in 1899. The campaign, which was for the National Biscuit Company and was the largest up to that time, included newspaper, magazine, and outdoor advertisements.

Such success stories allowed Ayer to stop handling beer and whiskey accounts completely as well as to curtail its patent medicine accounts. These successes also led him to realize before 1900 that advertising specific brands was just as important as advertising new products, principles he introduced to the business community by way of a massive campaign for the agency. By 1900 Ayer saw his agency, which was based on his character and innovative ideas, grow into the largest in the nation, with more than 160 employees.

EDD APPLEGATE

See also Advertising Agencies; Advertising in the Nineteenth Century; Brand-Name Advertising; Open Contract

Further Reading

Cahn, William, *Out of the Cracker Barrel: The Nabisco Story, from Animal Crackers to Zuzus,* New York: Simon & Schuster, 1969

Hower, Ralph M., *The History of an Advertising Agency: N.W. Ayer & Son at Work, 1869–1949,* New York: Arno, 1978

B

Barnum, P.T.

Helped develop public relations techniques

Most people remember Phineas Taylor Barnum for his circus, but far more significant was his role in the development of advertising and public relations. Born in 1810 in Bethel, Connecticut, Barnum attended school for at least six years; his father died when Barnum was 15, and he became a clerk to help his impoverished mother. In 1835, he met Joice Heth, an elderly African American woman whose sponsors claimed she was the 160-year-old former nursemaid to George Washington. Barnum purchased the right to exhibit Heth, who became an instant celebrity. Soon Barnum bought the American Museum, where he profitably displayed everything from whales to the midget Tom Thumb.

In many cases – for example, with Heth, the "Fejee Mermaid" (actually a monkey and a fish ingeniously sewn together), and the opera singer Jenny Lind – Barnum was not the first to "discover" his exhibits, but he was undeniably their best promoter. He recognized an exhibit's potential, bought the right to display it, and then used advertising and publicity to capture public interest. He sponsored contests, crafted well-written and humorous advertisements and press notices, and distributed brochures. He even planted rumors suggesting that attractions like Heth or the Mermaid were fakes, which he vigorously denied – thus stirring desire for people to see and decide for themselves. He was an overwhelming success.

Advertising and publicity cannot account for all of Barnum's achievements, however. As Barnum himself said, he could not have produced sustained success unless people agreed his attractions were worth the price of admission.

KAREN S. MILLER

See also Media Events; Public Relations

Further Reading
Barnum, P.T., *The Life of P.T. Barnum,* New York: Redfield, 1855; London, Routledge, 1889
Harris, Neil, *Humbug: The Art of P.T. Barnum,* Chicago: University of Chicago Press, 1981
Saxon, A.H., *P.T. Barnum: The Legend and the Man,* New York: Columbia University Press, 1989

Barton, Bruce

Advertising pioneer

Bruce Barton joined Roy Durstine and Alex Osborn in 1918 to start the Barton, Durstine and Osborn advertising agency. In 1928, Barton, Durstine and Osborn merged with the George Batten Company to form Batten, Barton, Durstine and Osborn, later known as BBDO.

Barton has been recognized as the most famous advertising executive of the 1920s. He was visible to the public and served as spokesman for the advertising business. Under Barton's creative direction, his agency became the fourth largest agency in the country by 1924. His achievements included the creation of successful corporate images for General Motors Corporation and General Electric Company.

After graduating from Amherst College in 1907, Barton supervised book sales for P.F. Collier and wrote inspirational editorials for *Every Week* and *Redbook* magazines. During World War I, he chaired the United War Work Campaign publicity committee.

Much of Barton's fame stemmed from his popular writing. His major work was *The Man Nobody Knows,* a controversial best-seller in which Barton portrayed Jesus Christ as a talented salesman and advertising executive. *The Man Nobody Knows* sold 250,000 copies in the 18 months following its publication in 1924.

Barton was politically active. In the 1920s, he wrote articles supporting Calvin Coolidge and wrote part of Herbert Hoover's acceptance speech at the Republican National Convention. In the 1930s, he represented New York's Seventeenth District in the U.S. Congress. In 1940, Barton ran for the Senate. After losing that election, he returned to Batten, Barton, Durstine and Osborn.

REGINA LOUISE LEWIS

Further Reading
Marchand, Roland, "The Corporation Nobody Knew: Bruce Barton, Alfred Sloan, and the Founding of the General Motors 'Family'," *Business History Review* 65:4 (1991), pp. 825–875
Pollay, Richard W., ed., *Information Sources in Advertising History,* Westport, Connecticut: Greenwood, 1979

Winski, Joseph M., "BBDO at 100: On the Right Track Again," *Advertising Age* 62:41 (September 30, 1991), pp. S4–S17

Bell System

Telephone operating system

Until 1984, the Bell System included American Telephone and Telegraph (AT&T), formed in 1885; its 23 local Bell Operating Companies; Bell Labs, established in 1925; the Western Electric manufacturing subsidiary; and the Long Lines division. In 1984, after a decade-long legal battle in the courts, AT&T was forced to divest its local operating companies. A dozen years later, facing a more competitive telecommunications market, AT&T broke itself into three separate companies, one each to focus on telephone service, manufacturing, and computer devices. While AT&T was in the 1990s primarily a long-distance and cellular telephone carrier and equipment manufacturer, it played three historically important roles in mass communication.

First, from 1922 to 1926, AT&T operated pioneering New York City radio station WEAF, on which the company experimented with radio programming and created the first broadcast commercials and the idea of program sponsorship. Determining that broadcasting and telephony were substantially different businesses, AT&T sold WEAF to the Radio Corporation of America, which based its new National Broadcasting Company on what became WNBC.

Second, AT&T was the sole provider of wired radio network links from 1926 and, later, coaxial cable and microwave-based television network interconnections from 1946. Initial television links connected Boston to Washington, D.C., while the first coast-to-coast relay began service in 1951. By the mid-1980s, domestic communications satellite relays provided by other carriers replaced AT&T's terrestrial links.

Third, AT&T's Bell Labs introduced various high-quality sound devices, early mechanical television systems, microwave and coaxial cable transmission systems, the landmark transistor (1948), and, later, multimedia and interactive telecommunications systems. To varying degrees, all of these have become a part of mass communications.

CHRISTOPHER H. STERLING

Further Reading

Banning, William Peck, *Commercial Broadcasting Pioneer: The WEAF Experiment, 1922–1926*, Cambridge, Massachusetts: Harvard University Press, 1946
Brooks, John, *Telephone: The First Hundred Years*, New York: Harper & Row, 1976

Bennett, James Gordon Sr.

Transformed newspaper content

James Gordon Bennett, founder of the *New York Herald* in 1835, was first and foremost an editor and a reporter. Under his direction, this entry into the Penny Press became a pioneer in "reporting" the news. One long-running story that he himself wrote focused on a verbatim account of the trial of a man charged with murdering a prostitute.

In addition to establishing the courts as a source for news, Bennett, a former economics teacher, assigned reporters to cover Wall Street. *Herald* reporters also told of society, sports, and church news and reviewed the arts. He stationed correspondents in U.S. state and national capitals as well in important capitals of Europe.

He and his readers valued news published soon after its occurrence; consequently, he experimented with various ways to obtain news quickly: pigeons, pony express, boats,

James Gordon Bennett Sr.
(Reproduced from the Collections of the Library of Congress)

trains, and telegraph. The costs of rapid news gathering led Bennett and his colleagues at other New York newspapers to band together in 1849 to establish the Harbor News Association, a forerunner of the Associated Press.

In the business field, he made advertisers pay for newspaper space as they contracted for it, and he made readers pay in advance for long-term subscriptions. He also experimented with advertising and newspaper design.

An aggressive journalist, Bennett combined with other papers to bring news of the Mexican and American Civil Wars to his readers as rapidly as possible. He encountered problems with President James K. Polk and President Abraham Lincoln over his energetic reporting of war news.

MARGARET A. BLANCHARD

See also Associated Press; Cooperative News Gathering; Penny Press

Further Reading
Carlson, Oliver, *The Man Who Made News*, New York: Duell, Sloan & Pearce, 1942
Crouthamel, James L., *Bennett's 'New York Herald' and the Rise of the Popular Press*, Syracuse, New York: Syracuse University Press, 1989

Bernays, Edward L.
Public relations pioneer

Although he was not the "father of public relations," as some have called him, Edward L. Bernays did much to develop both public understanding of the role of public relations in modern society and the occupation itself. Born in 1891 in Vienna, Austria, Bernays was the nephew of psychoanalyst Sigmund Freud, whose ideas became integral to Bernays' practice of public relations.

Bernays, whose family emigrated to New York City in 1892, began his career as a publicist for stage and film stars, as well as ballet and opera luminaries like Nijinsky and Caruso. In 1917 he joined the Committee on Public Information, where he worked to promote the ideals of the United States during World War I. The committee's work was thought wildly successful, and his experience led Bernays to believe that the public was easily influenced. Because Freud suggested that people were driven by irrational desires, Bernays saw a connection between his publicity work and his uncle's psychoanalysis. If people were subject to irrational convictions, then a public relations practitioner must learn to appeal to these impulses in order to influence public opinion.

After the war Bernays returned to New York City, married Doris Fleischman, who was his partner at work as well, and coined a term with his new title, "counsel on public relations." Like his predecessor, Ivy Lee, Bernays insisted on access to top management. Unlike Lee, Bernays used research – relying, not surprisingly, on psychology – rather than intuition to develop public relations campaigns for

many famous clients, ranging from Ivory soap to the electrical industry and the Red Cross.

Perhaps the best example of Bernays' use of psychology occurred during a 1920s cigarette promotion. Hired by the American Tobacco Company to persuade women to smoke in public, Bernays had to break the smoking taboo for women. He consulted a psychologist, who told him that cigarettes were like "torches of freedom" for women, whose battle for equality had only recently earned them the right to vote. Bernays convinced 10 debutantes to light their "torches" while strolling down Fifth Avenue on Easter Sunday, generating both press coverage and public discussion. Although no cigarette brand was mentioned, Bernays had managed to attract publicity with an angle carefully calculated to appeal to his target audience.

Just as important was Bernays' work to educate the public and increase acceptance of public relations. He wrote numerous books, beginning in 1923 with *Crystallizing Public Opinion*, often considered the first book on public relations. He taught the first college course with the title "Public Relations," at New York University, also in 1923 (although other universities had courses in publicity that were similar). Throughout his long life he campaigned for licensing for public relations practitioners because he hoped to screen out the "charlatans and incompetents" who sullied the field's name. Although many practitioners disdained Bernays as too self-promotional, his crusade to improve public understanding of his field ultimately resulted in accolades from many, such as the Public Relations Society of America, which gave him its prestigious Gold Anvil award in 1976.

KAREN S. MILLER

See also Committee on Public Information; *Crystallizing Public Opinion*; Lee, Ivy Ledbetter; Public Relations

Further Reading
Bernays, Edward L., *Biography of an Idea: Memoirs of Public Relations Counsel Edward L. Bernays*, New York: Simon & Schuster, 1965
_____, "Emergence of the Public Relations Counsel: Principles and Recollections," *Business History Review* 45 (1971)
Cutlip, Scott M., *The Unseen Power: Public Relations, A History*, Hillsdale, New Jersey: Lawrence Erlbaum, 1994
Tedlow, Richard S., *Keeping the Corporate Image: Public Relations and Business, 1900–1950*, Greenwich, Connecticut: JAI, 1979

Best-Sellers
Measurement of book sales

As a measurement of sales, the term "best-seller" was not established until the end of the nineteenth century, but the idea it embodies was well understood from the beginning of American publishing. Until 1720, religious books were the

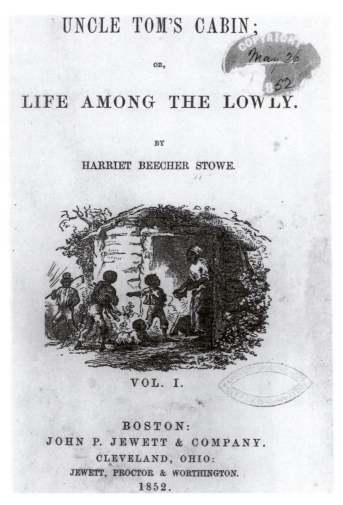

Uncle Tom's Cabin was a best-seller for years and helped to promote Northern outrage over the issue of slavery.
(Reproduced from the Collections of the Library of Congress)

only best-sellers. Aside from that perennial best-seller – the Bible – the first leader was John Bunyan's *Pilgrim's Progress,* first issued in 1681 with 120 editions following in the next 50 years.

Among purely secular titles in early publishing, tales of Indian captivity led the list, beginning with Mrs. Mary Rowlandson's *Captivity and Restoration.* Both children and adults made *Aesop's Fables* popular, while Samuel Richardson's novels *Pamela* and *Clarissa* were leading works of adult fiction. Presaging the modern romance novel as a best-seller was Susanna Haswell Rawson's *Charlotte Temple,* published in 1793. Appearing in more than 200 editions in its century-long life, it surpassed all its contemporaries, even steady-selling behavior books. The American Revolution made a best-seller of Thomas Paine's *Common Sense,* rivaled later by Benjamin Franklin's *Autobiography* and Parson Weems's largely imaginary biography of George Washington.

In the early nineteenth century, the development of the cylinder press created a mass market that was soon dominat-

ed by fiction. With this development, the meaning of "best-seller" had to be reevaluated. From 1800 to 1809, a sale of 50,000 was the minimum to warrant the designation, according to the modern scale devised by the historian Frank Luther Mott. By 1869, the figure had risen to 300,000.

One nineteenth-century novel was an all-time best-seller. Harriet Beecher Stowe's classic *Uncle Tom's Cabin,* published in 1852, was a best-seller in its own time, and by the late twentieth century, it had sold more than 7 million copies and was still in print. In the new climate of best-selling fiction, women writers were dominant. There had been only four women fiction writers in American before 1800, but in 1872 they produced nearly three-fourths of fiction titles, many of them best-sellers. Prominent male writers on the list were Sir Walter Scott, especially in the South, Charles Dickens, and James Fenimore Cooper.

Between 1890 and 1918, fiction became a national craze, deplored from the pulpit and the political platform, and completely dominating best-seller lists, where such writers as Harold Bell Wright and Gene Stratton-Porter recorded sales of more than a million copies of their novels. However, an earlier writer of cheap popular fiction, Mrs. E.D.E.N. Southworth, who began writing in the mid–nineteenth century, was still selling (although in paperback) into the 1930s.

The fiction boom inspired the first best-seller lists, beginning in 1895, when a new magazine, *The Bookman,* polled bookstores in 16 cities to produce a list of titles "in order of demand." Nearly all these titles were fiction. In 1911, the trade journal *Publishers Weekly* established its own best-seller consensus.

Although fiction dominated the market, best-seller lists reflected more and more the moods and new interests of the nation. Mary Baker Eddy's *Science and Health,* the keystone of Christian Science, signaled the advent of a new religious denomination, while the works of Horatio Alger Jr. celebrated the "American dream" credo. Period sentimentality appeared on the lists with classic stories like Margaret Saunders' *Beautiful Joe* and Frances Hodgson Burnett's *Little Lord Fauntleroy.* The romantic novel continued to flourish in George Barr McCurtheon's *Graustark* novels, but the new realism was apparent in the work of Bret Harte, Jack London, and Frank Norris, now appearing on the lists. That still left enough room for Edgar Rice Burroughs' *Tarzan* series and the Western novels of Zane Grey.

The best-seller lists reflected another major change in American tastes during the 1920s. Nonfiction rose steadily in popularity as the dominance of fiction came to an end in the grim climate of the 1930s, when the new realism of Erich Maria Remarque's novel *All Quiet on the Western Front* and of the works of Sinclair Lewis appeared.

As the twentieth century drew to a close, the new age of technology and the ascendancy of marketing in the publishing industry made mass market fiction dominant on one side of the best-seller lists, and culture-based and self-help books the most prevalent on the nonfiction side. Mass distribution in various media meant that sales in the hundreds of thousands, or in some cases millions, were required to achieve the best-seller lists.

JOHN TEBBEL

See also Book Publishing in the Eighteenth Century; Book Publishing in the Nineteenth Century; Book Publishing in the Twentieth Century; Trade Book Publishing

Further Reading
Tebbel, John, *Between Covers: The Rise and Transformation of Book Publishing in America,* New York: Oxford University Press, 1987
_____, *A History of Book Publishing in the United States,* 4 vols., New York: Bowker, 1972–81

Better Business Bureau

Developed from Truth in Advertising movement

The Better Business Bureau, a system of local organizations promoting ethics in the marketplace through voluntary self-regulation, has many bureaus throughout the United States and Canada. These are linked by a national organization, the Council of Better Business Bureaus (CBBB), located in Arlington, Virginia.

The Better Business Bureau had its origins in the Truth in Advertising movement initiated in the early years of the twentieth century by the Associated Advertising Clubs of America. In 1911, that organization drafted a model statute proposing that dishonest advertising become a misdemeanor. Local advertising clubs worked for enactment of this *Printers' Ink* statute. The clubs also formed vigilance committees to investigate alleged advertising offenses in their cities and to otherwise enforce the statute through moral suasion. In 1912, the Associated Advertising Clubs of America appointed a National Vigilance Committee to handle alleged misrepresentations in national advertising.

The activities of the vigilance committees quickly expanded beyond advertising to include other business practices. In 1916, the advertising clubs sought a name that would more accurately describe their activities and eliminate the negative connotations associated with the term "vigilance." The name Better Business Bureau was suggested, and soon the more representative name was in use throughout the country. In the late 1990s, there were more than 150 local bureaus funded by more than 230,000 member businesses.

Local bureaus were responsible for responding to consumers' prepurchase inquiries and to complaints regarding advertising and business practices from consumers and other businesses. The CBBB encouraged truth and accuracy in national advertising through its involvement in the National Advertising Review Council. The NARC, founded in 1971, included representatives from the CBBB as well as from the American Advertising Federation, the American Association of Advertising Agencies, and the Association of National Advertisers.

The NARC was the governing body of the National Advertising Review Board (NARB), a "court of appeals" made up of national advertisers, advertising agency representatives, and individuals from the public sector. The NARB

and the National Advertising Division (NAD) of the CBBB provided the advertising industry with a self-regulatory mechanism. Cases were initiated with the NAD, which investigated allegations and might ask advertisers to substantiate claims. If claims were found to be unsubstantiated, the NAD asked the advertiser to voluntarily modify or discontinue the advertising. If either party involved were unsatisfied with the NAD resolution, it could appeal the NAD decision to a five-person panel from the National Advertising Review Board. If the NARB panel agreed with the NAD decision, the advertiser would be asked to modify or discontinue the advertising claim or claims. Should the advertiser refuse to comply, the case could be referred to the appropriate government agency – in most instances, the Federal Trade Commission.

This two-tier NAD/NARB self-regulatory process was very effective. While the NARB could impose no sanctions and had no power to force advertisers to stop running an ad, as of the late 1990s there had been only two instances in which cases remained unresolved following NARB action and were referred to the FTC for noncompliance.

PEGGY J. KRESHEL

See also National Advertising Review Board; Truth in Advertising Movement

Further Reading
Kenner, H.J., *The Fight for Truth in Advertising,* New York and London: Garland, 1985
Krugman, Dean M., *Advertising: Its Role in Modern Marketing,* 8th ed., Fort Worth, Texas: Dryden, 1994
Pease, Otis, *The Responsibilities of American Advertising: Private Control and Public Influence, 1920–1940,* New Haven, Connecticut: Yale University Press, 1958

Birth of a Nation, The

Possibly the most controversial motion picture ever made

The Birth of a Nation is arguably the most significant and controversial motion picture ever made. Following its debut in 1915, it established new precedents in film aesthetics, box-office popularity, public controversy, and free speech standards for the movies. The film was produced and directed by David Wark Griffith, widely considered to be the seminal figure in early cinema. The nearly three-hour epic premiered as *The Clansman*, named after the best-selling 1905 novel and the subsequent stage rendition by Thomas Dixon on which it is based. By the time it opened in New York, Griffith had retitled the film *The Birth of a Nation* to better reflect its scope and outlook.

Born in Kentucky, the son of a one-time Confederate colonel and slaveowner, Griffith was reared in the traditions of the old South. He had already produced an estimated 450 one- and two-reel shorts for the Biograph studios between 1908 and 1913 before leaving to work on longer and more ambitious projects elsewhere. He made several quick features in 1914 before starting work on *The Clansman,* an ode to the Ku Klux Klan and a bitter condemnation of African Americans. Griffith actually softened the rabid racism of Dixon's book and play in his filmed adaptation, although its status as a deeply flawed masterpiece is ensured by the many bigoted distortions that still remain.

The Birth of a Nation was immediately hailed as a landmark in screen storytelling and film form. Griffith had expertly knitted an intimate family narrative into the broader historical panorama of the Civil War and Reconstruction. He also perfected most of the principles of film technique, including camera placement and movement, shot selection in building scenes, dramatic lighting strategies, various editing styles, and choreographing large crowd and battle scenes, among many other innovations.

More than 10 percent of the U.S. population attended its original release, making it the preeminent box-office success in silent film history. *The Birth of a Nation* cost $100,000 to produce – five times the amount of any other motion picture up to that point. In turn, the picture grossed approximately $48 million, with worldwide viewership estimated at 200 million by 1946.

The inflammatory nature of the film also resulted in scores of organized protests, many of which were spearheaded by the National Association for the Advancement of Colored People, with civil rights activists and proponents of free speech clashing over whether it should be shown in a given community. The motion picture was eventually banned in five states and nineteen cities. Griffith, shocked and dismayed by the many claims that he had made a malicious and racist film, responded by producing a fictional apologia in 1916, *Intolerance,* which likewise is considered a masterpiece in cinema history.

GARY R. EDGERTON

See also Censorship of Motion Pictures; Silent Motion Pictures

Further Reading
Barry, Iris, *D. W. Griffith: The American Film Master,* New York and London: Garland, 1985

Racial issues made *The Birth of a Nation* very controversial.
(Wisconsin Center for Film and Theater Research)

D.W. Griffith wrote this pamphlet to protest censorship of his masterpiece.

Brownlow, Kevin, *The Parade's Gone By . . .*, Berkeley: University of California Press, 1968; London: Secker & Warburg, 1968

Carter, Everett, "Cultural History Written with Lightning: The Significance of *The Birth of a Nation*," *American Quarterly* XII (1960)

Geduld, Harry M., ed., *Focus on D.W. Griffith*, Englewood Cliffs, New Jersey: Prentice-Hall, 1971

Griffith, David Wark, "The Rise and Fall of Free Speech in America," in *The Movies in Our Midst: Documents in the Cultural History of Film in America*, edited by Gerald Mast, Chicago: University of Chicago Press, 1982

Henderson, Robert M., *D.W. Griffith: His Life and Work*, New York: Oxford University Press, 1972; London: Garland, 1985

Merritt, Russell, "Dixon, Griffith, and the Southern Legend: A Cultural Analysis of *The Birth of a Nation*," in *Cinema Examined: Selections from Cinema Journal*, edited by Richard Dyer MacCann and Jack C. Ellis, New York: Dutton, 1982

Black, Hugo Lafayette

First Amendment supporter

Justice Hugo Lafayette Black, a largely self-taught Alabaman who once belonged to the Ku Klux Klan, had ended a two-term stint as a U.S. senator when President Franklin D. Roosevelt made Black his first appointee to the U.S. Supreme Court. For 34 years, Black stood as one of the Court's two absolutists with regard to the First Amendment. Black, joined frequently in opinions by Justice William O. Douglas, formed a core of support for First Amendment rights on the Supreme Court by arguing that the phrase "Congress shall make no law" abridging the freedoms granted in the amendment should be interpreted literally. Black's absolutism never enjoyed the support of even a significant minority of justices, but commentators credit Black with upholding the First Amendment in some of the most important free speech cases in U.S. history.

In dozens of critical First Amendment decisions, he opposed governmental controls over obscenity, libel, and "subversive" speech. He also fought against the clear and present danger test, judicial balancing, and other nonabsolutist First Amendment tests. Justice Black's legacy is one of undying judicial consistency, plain logic, and drawing lines between speech and action. Although he never was able to champion a majority of absolutists on even a single case, his impact on the bench could never be ignored.

CHARLES N. DAVIS

See also Douglas, William O.; First Amendment in the Twentieth Century

Further Reading
Barnett, Vincent M., "Mr. Justice Black and the Supreme Court," *University of Chicago Law Review* 8 (1940)

Black, Hugo L., *A Constitutional Faith,* New York: Knopf, 1968

Dennis, Everette E., Donald M. Gillmor, and David L. Grey, eds., *Justice Hugo Black and the First Amendment*, Ames: Iowa State University Press, 1978

Dilliard, Irving, ed., *One Man's Stand for Freedom: Mr. Justice Black and the Bill of Rights*, New York: Knopf, 1963

Kalven, Harry, Jr., "Upon Rereading Mr. Justice Black on the First Amendment," *UCLA Law Review* 14 (1966–67)

Snowiss, Sylvia, "The Legacy of Justice Black," *1973 Supreme Court Review*

Black Star Picture Agency

Flight from Hitler leads to growth in U.S. photography

Hitler's rise to power in Germany influenced journalism in the United States in various ways, most notably through the number of Europeans who emigrated to the United States in the 1930s. Three such émigrés, Ernest Mayer, Kurt S. Safranski, and Kurt Kornfeld, came to New York City and together founded Black Star Picture Agency early in 1936.

The three men had valuable training in Germany that enabled them to start this new venture in the United States. In 1929, Mayer had founded Mauritius, a Berlin picture agency that dealt with the growing interest in picture stories on the part of many German picture magazines, including the *Berliner Illustrierte Zeitung* (*BIZ*) and *Münchner Illustrierte Presse* (*MIP*). Although there were news agencies in Germany, very few journalistically oriented picture agencies existed then.

Safranski had business dealings with Mayer at *BIZ* when he was an influential editor there, and Kornfeld was a scientific book publisher in Germany. Kornfeld suggested that the new U.S. company be called Black Star Publishing Company because he wanted a book publishing component, which appeared three decades later.

In the early 1930s, picture agencies became fairly common in Europe because magazines hired few staff photographers, working instead with middlemen who had photographers in their employ willing to shoot on speculation or on assignment. These agency photographers not only worked in Europe but traveled to Africa and the United States as well, giving the picture magazines broader coverage than they could have had with just staff photographers.

Changes in photographic technology, especially the release of the German-made 35mm Leica camera in 1925, allowed photographers and picture magazine editors a new opportunity to tell stories candidly and through a new format called the photo essay.

The idea of a privately owned picture agency was quite new to the United States when the three started their business. Black Star became a conduit through which U.S. publishers and editors in need of talented, trained European photographers could hire those émigrés who were forced to leave their jobs and their homeland because of the Nazis. Agencies such as Black Star not only maintained large photographic collections but also matched photographers with proposed stories and took care of direction and billing.

When starting up *Life*, Henry Luce and his staff turned to Black Star. Eight months before *Life* began publishing, Black Star signed a yearlong contract to supply single photographs and photo essays for Time, Inc. Beginning with the second issue (December 7, 1936), the Black Star credit line appeared regularly in *Life*.

Although the agency serviced a variety of newspapers, book publishers, and advertisers, *Life* and Time, Inc., were its most high-profile clients. Many of the agency's émigré photographers went on to become *Life* staff members, and others were under contract to the magazine for decades.

C. ZOE SMITH

See also Documentary Photography; Photojournalism in the Twentieth Century

Further Reading
Allen, Casey, "Behind the Scenes: An Interview with Howard Chapnick," *Camera 35* (December 1979)

Chapnick, Howard, "The Free-Lancer and the Picture Syndicate," in *Photojournalism: Principles and Practices*, edited by Clifton C. Edom, Dubuque, Iowa: William C. Brown, 1976
_____, *Truth Needs No Ally: Inside Photojournalism*, Columbia: University of Missouri Press, 1994
Gidal, Tim, *Modern Photojournalism: Origin and Evolution, 1910–1933*, New York: Macmillan, 1973
Smith, C. Zoe, "Black Star Picture Agency: *Life's* European Connection," *Journalism History* 13 (Spring 1986)
_____, *Émigré Photography in America: Contributions of German Photojournalism from Black Star Picture Agency to 'Life' Magazine, 1933–1938* (Ph.D. diss., University of Iowa), 1983

Blue Book
Public service responsibility of broadcast licensees

The Blue Book was a document put forth by the Federal Communications Commission (FCC) in 1946 to give programming direction to broadcasters in their obligation to operate in the public interest, convenience, and necessity. Since the passage of the Communication Act of 1934, broadcasters had been expected to render public service through the airwaves in exchange for the use of the frequencies. Just how much public service was required, however, and in what form seemed unclear. FCC hearings on station renewal suggested an increasing problem with stations' "progressive relaxation of standards" that had once been held to be important by the industry itself. Commission hearings had begun to compare broadcasters' promises contained in their station license applications with their current programming practices. Yet, other than guessing on the outcomes of such hearings, there were no definitive means of determining just what licensees' obligations to the public were. Evidence gathered from the hearings led the FCC to articulate its expectations.

In 1945, writers developed the information and recommendations that became known as the Blue Book, so called because (1) its cover was blue; (2) it was seen as a "blue pencil" kind of censoring; and (3) it was connected to the concept of authoritarianism that was often associated with elitist "blue-blooded" character. The content included a history of some stations' breaches of promise in failing to live up to all they had promised to do. The FCC then went on to establish its own authority with respect to program service. Few quarreled with the commission's right to control the frequency allocation as a kind of technical "traffic cop." The government agency's move to have a say in controlling program content at a time when radio was becoming recognized as a part of the nation's "press," however, raised questions in the minds of many regarding the First Amendment and freedom of the press.

The Blue Book went on to outline "Some Aspects of 'Public Interest' in Program Service." These aspects included the following:

1.) The need to carry sustaining programming. Well-balanced programs that included entertainment; educational, religious, agricultural, civic, and governmental shows; and news were not always paid for by advertising – the stations or networks had to sustain, or carry, them, without pay, and this was their obligation.

2.) The need to carry local live programs. The FCC recognized "adequate reflection in programs of local interests, activities, and talent." This definition of public interest emphasized local public interest for stations licensed to a specific locale.

3.) The need to discuss public issues. Radio was cited as an unequaled medium for the dissemination of news, information, and opinion, and for the discussion of public issues. As such its promise ought to be fulfilled, according to the Blue Book.

4.) The need to curb advertising excesses. While the economic base of radio was acknowledged, abuses and excesses in advertising were the very activities that could jeopardize a station's license renewal. Various kinds of problems were specifically identified, revolving around the length of time devoted to commercials and the piling up of commercials in one time slot.

Basically, the clash between making high profits from radio and obligations to serve the public interest created many of the problems that generated this 1946 FCC policy statement. For example, it was the need for higher profits that caused stations such as WBAL or WCAU (both cited in the Blue Book) to air commercial entertainment programs rather than sustained public service programs.

The commission concluded its report by outlining some procedural proposals – using uniform definitions and program logs, recognizing segments of the broadcast day, requiring annual reports and statistics, and revising application forms. The bottom line was the threat of not renewing station licenses. Reaction to the Blue Book reflected sharp criticism, especially from broadcasters.

While much of the general tone of the Blue Book became a part of the way the FCC operated, the specific procedures such as the requirement for sustaining programming were not all kept. Many of the good intentions behind the Blue Book dissipated over the years. In a few years, with the advent of television and amid concern about payola and quiz show scandals, the FCC issued its 1960 *Programming Policy Statement,* replacing much of what was in the Blue Book. The need for local programming, program balance, and elimination of advertising excesses were still there, but the mandate of sustaining programming was omitted. Still later, during the 1980s, programming regulation all but disappeared, making the Blue Book an interesting relic of a past era.

VAL E. LIMBURG

See also Broadcast Regulation; Federal Communications Commission; Payola; Quiz Show Scandals

Further Reading

Federal Communications Commission, *Public Service Responsibility of Broadcast Licensees,* Washington: Government Printing Office, 1946

Meyer, Richard J., "Reaction to the 'Blue Book'," *Journal of Broadcasting* VI:4 (1962)

Bok, Edward W.

'Ladies' Home Journal' editor

Edward Bok was editor of the *Ladies' Home Journal* from 1889 to 1919, the period of its ascendancy to becoming the nation's most influential women's magazine. Under Bok, the *Journal* was unequivocal in establishing a blueprint for a middle-class life in the areas of house architecture, home furnishings, and social mores, and in establishing an agenda of reform issues that did not include votes for women. Bok's editorial leadership was so successful that by the time he retired, the *Journal* had a million subscribers, making it the first magazine to reach that mark.

Bok was born in The Netherlands in 1863 to a well-known family. In New York, however, where his immediate

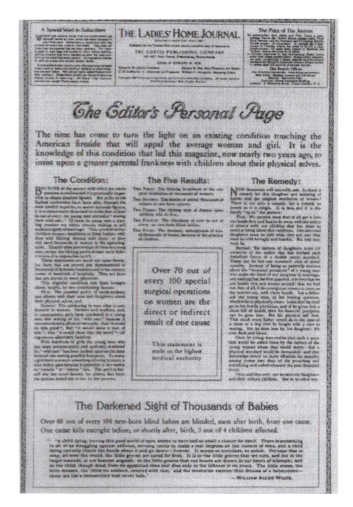

The Ladies' Home Journal editor took his charge seriously.

family settled upon arrival in the United States, Bok left school early to help out at home. Bok's devotion to his mother was central to his life, and it played a substantial role in his views of the importance of domesticity. But, as he said of himself, he was an unlikely choice for the *Journal* position: "He did not dislike women, but it could not be said that he liked them. They had never interested him."

From its Philadelphia base in the "city of homes," the *Journal* was already a successful women's service magazine when Bok took over the editorial duties from Louisa Knapp, wife of the magazine's publisher, Cyrus H.K. Curtis. Curtis gave Bok wide latitude in developing the magazine. Bok early initiated a column, "Side Talks with Girls," that included queries of a sexual nature, unusual for the time. He also led various reform campaigns, including a drive for food and drug legislation and a campaign for the beautification of U.S. cities. The magazine was heavily criticized, however, and lost subscribers when Bok attempted to promote an open discussion about the then-forbidden subject of venereal disease.

In addition to reform issues, Bok emphasized publication of fiction by well-known writers of the day and articles that drew attention to the roles of the wives and daughters of successful men. The magazine also contained many service departments aimed at assisting women in what were regarded as their domestic duties.

Prompted by his ongoing fascination with fame and his belief that the editor of a magazine should be known to readers, Bok courted fame and lived like a celebrity. He was a world traveler, owned a large suburban estate, and moved in a wealthy and famous circle, which included Theodore Roosevelt. His own wealth came from ownership of Curtis stock. He married the Curtises' only daughter. Bok published two autobiographies, a biography of Curtis, and other writings that urged thrift, honesty, and hard work as the recipe for success.

PATRICIA BRADLEY

See also Magazines for Women; Magazines in the Nineteenth Century; Magazines in the Twentieth Century; Muckraking; Patent Medicine Advertising

Further Reading

Bok, Edward W., *The Americanization of Edward Bok: The Autobiography of a Dutch Boy Fifty Years After. . .*, New York: Scribner's, 1920

_____, *A Man from Maine*, New York, Scribner's, 1923

_____, *Twice Thirty: Some Short and Simple Annals of the Road*, New York: Scribner's, 1925; London: Scribner's, 1927

Hummel, Michael D., *The Attitudes of Edward Bok and the 'Ladies' Home Journal' Toward Woman's Role in Society, 1889–1919* (Ph.D. diss., University of North Texas), 1982

Kaul, A.J., "Edward W. Bok," in *Dictionary of Literary Biography: American Magazine Journalists, 1900–1960*, vol. 91, edited by Sam G. Riley, Detroit, Michigan: Gale, 1990

Steinberg, Salme Harju, *Reformer in the Marketplace: Edward W. Bok and the 'Ladies' Home Journal'*, Baton Rouge: Louisiana State University Press, 1979

Book Clubs

Making purchasing books easier for readers

Perhaps more than any other media delivery system, book clubs embody the tensions between culture and commerce, uplift and economics, that characterized the twentieth-century culture industry. To their founders and supporters, the clubs were efficient and economical means to solve the industry's chronic problems of promotion and distribution. To their critics, however, book clubs interfered with the free exercise of taste, judgment, and intellect, and as such signaled the deterioration of reading culture.

The earliest and largest clubs were both founded in 1926; the Book-of-the-Month Club (BOMC) was the brainchild of advertising executive Henry Scherman, while the Literary Guild was started by publisher Harold Guinzberg and entrepreneur Samuel Craig. Imitators, ranging from the Crime Club to the Free Thought Book of the Month Club, followed throughout the 1920s.

Operating on similar principles, the clubs sought to expand the market for good books by making purchasing simpler and more convenient for readers. Members received a monthly newsletter from the club's panel of expert judges describing forthcoming titles. They paid full price for one

Book clubs worked to promote book sales and reading.

book a month; if they did not like the selection, they could exchange it for an alternate title from an approved list. Later, clubs added additional features, such as specially priced editions and book-dividend plans, which gave members additional books as bonuses. The clubs promised to solve many of the industry's most pressing problems: in an era without many bookstores, mail-order books would reach underserved potential buyers in a regular and timely fashion. In addition, the subscriber base would guarantee a large market for each title selected. This economy of scale would hold down production costs, so the book could be priced lower for sale in stores. The lower price, along with the favorable word of mouth generated by the clubs' adoption of a title, would create larger overall sales. Finally, the subscription feature, which bound readers to purchase a set number of books each year, would overcome the central problem in modern book marketing: how to guarantee repeat customers when each commodity is unique.

Initially, both clubs met with heated opposition, especially from booksellers, who were angered by the implication that they had failed to meet readers' needs. Complaints died down, however, in the face of the clubs' enormous successes. The BOMC's membership increased 10-fold within 1926 alone and spawned numerous imitations. During the Great Depression, even as they irritated vendors by issuing cheap reprints, the clubs ingratiated themselves with publishers by buying up backstock to give away as bonuses. Their growth continued throughout World War II and exploded in the decade following it.

Capitalizing on direct mail's ability to reach specialized audiences, many highly targeted clubs appeared. Some of these, like the Marboro Book Club, were general interest clubs that addressed specific demographic groups, while others were subject-specific, like the Travelers Book Club, the Classics Club, and the Playboy Book Club. During the postwar period, levels of education and earning power increased among the buying public, and reading was marketed as an ideal leisure pursuit. This marketing strategy, combined with an enormous proliferation of titles during the publishing boom, ensured the popularity of the clubs' selection, recommendation, and delivery services. In 1980, 2.5 million books, valued at approximately $503 million, were sold through more than 200 clubs.

Most publishers and even some bookstore owners agreed that, in the long run, clubs benefited the industry by expanding the market and developing the reading habits of potential customers. Beginning in the 1920s, however, the clubs came under fire for diluting many of the values traditionally associated with book culture, even as they seemed to bring that culture to a wider public.

Critics have traditionally denigrated book clubs as instruments of "middlebrow" culture. The middlebrow is usually seen as a watered-down version of an elite intellectual and aesthetic community that trades on its participants' anxieties about social status; the stereotypical middlebrow individual wants to seem smart without exerting much effort. Accordingly, critics believed book club members were less interested in reading books than in merely knowing about them. Advertising copy that emphasized how books could help members' social status – like the Literary Guild's "The Hallmark of Literary Distinction: The Guild Book on Your Table" or the BOMC's "What a deprivation it is to miss reading an important new book at a time everyone else is reading and discussing it!" – seems to support these criticisms. Thus it could be argued that the convenience factors that club founders so proudly advertised also encouraged a shallow relationship to books. In addition, by inviting readers to rely on "experts," the club model encouraged passivity and conformity rather than the exercise of individual critical judgment. Finally, critics questioned whether the clubs actually defined and recommended quality literature. The BOMC's selections, for instance, were characterized by Dwight Macdonald as "reading matter of which the best that can be said is that it could be worse."

In the late twentieth century, scholarship on the clubs' literary selection and evaluation processes and on the way members use the recommended books began to question the validity of some of these criticisms. Studies suggested that selection committees, and, by extension, readers, were involved in a complex process of judgment and evaluation with its own logic and meaning. Literary critic Janice Radway suggested that BOMC judges and readers valued literature containing lessons that they could apply to their own lives. She argued that, while this was very different from both the formal and the political criteria by which many academic and intellectual critics judged literature, it was no less valid a way to measure the way books mean and matter.

Even as scholarship suggested that critics might have misunderstood the role played by book clubs in readers' lives, industry trends continued to complicate what book clubs mean. During the 1980s, the expansion of chain bookstores offering heavy discounts threatened the clubs' financial security. After a wave of buyouts and mergers, the 200 clubs of the early 1980s stabilized at about 150 in 1995. Their profit margins dwindled, however, and many of them became (like much of the rest of the book industry) subsidiaries of multimedia conglomerates. Within this business structure, the principle the clubs were founded on – efficient distribution of good literature – was subsumed by the larger goal of total corporate profit. For instance, the BOMC, owned in the 1990s by Time Warner, made little money for its parent company. Instead, its value came from its subscription list, which provided an enormous database of potential customers for other, more profitable Time Warner products.

In this instance, at least, books and reading may have become only incidental to the continued operation of the book club. While some would argue that this was the logical outcome of the club structure, it is perhaps more accurate to say that it was a result of economic changes that made the book trade just one of many cultural industries competing for consumer attention and dollars. How these developments in the distribution of books would change the actual reading of books – for better or for worse – remained to be seen.

TRYSH TRAVIS

See also Best-Sellers; Book Publishing in the Twentieth Century; Trade Book Publishing

Further Reading

Carvajal, Doreen, "Triumph of the Bottom Line," *New York Times* (April 1, 1996)

Macdonald, Dwight, "Masscult and Midcult," in *Against the American Grain*, New York: Random House, 1962

Radway, Janice, "The Book-of-the-Month Club and the General Reader," in *Reading in America: Literature and Social History*, edited by Cathy N. Davidson, Baltimore, Maryland: Johns Hopkins University Press, 1989

_____, "The Scandal of the Middlebrow: The Book-of-the-Month Club, Class Fracture, and Cultural Authority," *South Atlantic Quarterly* 89:4 (Fall 1990), pp. 703–736

Book Publishing Awards

Following the establishment of the Nobel Prize for literature in 1901, the number of book awards in the United States multiplied through the twentieth century (as it did abroad), as organizations at all levels and in all regions of the country chose to honor specific books, authors, or illustrators. Bowker, publisher of information about the publishing community, in the late 1990s listed more than 100 named national awards, many of which listed prizes in several categories, such as fiction, nonfiction, biography, criticism, poetry, or history. Other than the Nobel Prize, one of many international prizes sometimes awarded to U.S. writers, there were several national awards of particular prestige in U.S. publishing. While some monetary reward was occasionally included, the value of these awards was most often in their recognition of merit and, when given to books or authors not already well known, the accompanying publicity.

In 1918, a prize for literature was included in the establishment of the annual Pulitzer Prizes, following the terms of Joseph Pulitzer's will. Offered each year by the Columbia University Graduate School of Journalism, the Pulitzer Prizes in Letters honor distinguished work by U.S. authors in fiction "preferably dealing with American life," U.S. history, biography or autobiography, drama (a play), verse, or any other area not eligible for the other categories.

The National Book Awards were created by participants in publishing and education in 1950 to honor distinguished works written or translated by U.S. writers. Awarded each November – in the 1990s, by the nonprofit National Book Committee – they have been sponsored by various committees of publishers, librarians, scholars, and booksellers, with membership drawn from such organizations as the American Academy of Arts and Letters, the American Association of Publishers, the Book Publishers Council, the American Booksellers Association, and the Book Manufacturers Institute. The three original categories of awards – fiction, poetry, and nonfiction – were expanded into ten, including translations and children's books.

The National Book Critics Circle Awards were established in 1975 by the National Book Critics Circle. Announced each January by this group of U.S. book reviewers and critics, they honored works of fiction, general nonfiction, biography or autobiography, poetry, and criticism by U.S. writers.

In children's literature, the two most prestigious national awards were awarded under the sponsorship of the American Library Association. The John Newbery Medal, established in 1922 and the first such award in the world, was given to the author of the most distinguished work in children's literature in the United States. The Randolph Caldecott Medal, established in 1937, was given to the illustrator of the "most distinguished American Picture Book for Children."

Among the many other U.S. book awards are those given for work in specific academic disciplines (e.g., Bancroft and American Historical Association awards for history), genres (the Poe awards in mystery and the Dick awards in science fiction), subject themes (Coretta Scott King awards for peace and brotherhood), regions (Commonwealth Club of California awards to Californians), craftsmanship (to illustrators, photographers, designers, binders, or other participating artists), and professional status (awards for first novels or lifetime achievement).

PRISCILLA COIT MURPHY

Further Reading

Association for Library Service to Children, *The Newbery and Caldecott Awards: A Guide to the Medal and Honor Books, Chicago*: American Library Association, 1995

Ink, Gary, "Literary Prizes, 1994," in *The Bowker Annual Library and Book Trade Almanac, 1995,* New Providence, New Jersey: Bowker, 1995

The National Book Awards: Forty-one Years of Literary Excellence: Winners and Finalists, 1950–1991, New York: National Book Foundation, 1992

Weber, Olga S., ed., *Literary and Library Prizes,* 6th ed., New York: Bowker, 1967

Book Publishing in the Eighteenth Century
Period of rapid growth for U.S. publishers

The eighteenth century was a period of transition and rapid growth in book publishing. While only a handful of U.S. cities had printing offices at the start of the century, by midcentury all of the 13 colonies had presses, and by the turn of the nineteenth century there were presses in such remote locations as Louisiana, Florida, Maine, Ohio, and Michigan. Not all of these presses were used to produce books, though. In fact, until the American Revolution most of the books sold in the colonies were imported from England. By the end of the century, however, with increases in population, literacy, and leisure time; changes in reading tastes; the extension of printing technology and transportation; and organizational changes within the business; book publishing was on its way to becoming a well-developed industry in the United States.

The three major publishing centers in eighteenth-century America were New England, Philadelphia, and New York. New England had the longest history of printing activity: Jose Glover brought the first press to Cambridge, Massachusetts, in 1638, and *The Whole Booke of Psalmes* (the *Bay Psalm Book*) was published two years later. Until the middle of the eighteenth century, Boston was the most active publishing center in the colonies, thanks to the efforts of bookseller-publishers like Daniel Henchman, Samuel Gerrish, and Isaiah Thomas.

After the Revolution, Philadelphia became the country's primary publishing center. Like Massachusetts, Pennsylvania had a long tradition of printing (beginning with William Bradford in 1685), and during the colonial period the output of Philadelphia's presses was more varied than that of any other city. Mathew Carey, who became the most successful and important publisher of the early national period, established his business in Philadelphia in 1785. Most of the books he published were reprints of British works, although he also encouraged U.S. authors. In 1794, he published Susanna Rowson's *Charlotte Temple,* a sentimental novel that proved so popular that Carey reprinted it 200 times.

The German-language press further contributed to the diversity of book publishing in Pennsylvania. Andrew Bradford began to print German books in Philadelphia in the late 1720s, and by the mid-1740s books of theology and German choral music were issued from the press of the Ephrata Monastery. Indeed, the largest book produced in the colonies, the 756-page Mennonite book of martyrs, *Der Blutige Schau-Platz,* emanated from the Ephrata press in 1748 in an edition of 1,300 copies.

By the end of the eighteenth century, New York City, already the largest city in the country, surpassed Philadelphia in book production. With its location on the Atlantic seaboard and its access to navigable rivers, New York had geographic advantages that were favorable to the importing and exporting of books as well as to the distribution of books in the interior of the continent. There, eighteenth-century entrepreneurs like Hugh Gaine and James Rivington helped to establish New York as the publishing capital of the United States.

The role of the publisher, as distinct from that of the printer, was not clearly defined in the colonial period. Printers typically supported themselves through a combination of newspaper publishing, job printing (forms, advertisements, government publications, etc.), book production, and retailing. Most authors published their works at their own risk; only fairly established authors had the option of sharing publication costs with the printer and bookseller. After the Revolution and the legislation of copyright laws, printers and booksellers began to lease publication rights from authors for designated periods of time. The books would then be offered for sale to the general public, and it was up to the booksellers to market them. The separation of the functions of printer and publisher occurred in Massachusetts earlier than in the other states. In the 1780s, Isaiah Thomas became one of the preeminent book publishers in the United States while continuing his printing and newspaper businesses as sidelines.

Lacking anything more than a rudimentary system of distribution, eighteenth-century printers tended to produce material that was largely for local consumption. According to William Charvat and others, this continued to be the case until well into the nineteenth century. Nevertheless, eighteenth-century printer-publishers were very much concerned with the problem of getting their books to potential customers. As Hellmut Lehmann-Haupt explains, four methods of book distribution came into use in the colonial period, and these laid the foundations for the national distribution channels that would be in place by the middle of the nineteenth century. The most common method was retailing through printers' bookshops. These shops were frequently attached to the printing office and offered items printed by the proprietor, along with notions, books imported from England – a mainstay of the business – and books purchased on consignment from other printers. A distribution method that became very important in the eighteenth century was sales by subscription. In this arrangement, patrons agreed to purchase a book upon publication at a set price; thus, the buyers of a book collectively financed its production. A third method involved itinerant booksellers who would hawk their wares, primarily in rural areas. (Some of the colonies passed anti-peddling laws in the eighteenth century, prohibiting hawkers, restricting the types of literature they sold, or requiring them to become licensed.) The best-known of these traveling agents was Parson Mason Locke Weems, who began working for Mathew Carey in 1792. During his 33 years as Carey's chief salesman, Weems helped to expand Carey's distribution far beyond the boundaries of the Philadelphia area, with routes extending from New York, New Jersey, and Pennsylvania in the north to Virginia, the Carolinas, and Georgia in the south. The fourth method of book distribution was selling in public auctions. The first known use of this mode of distribution in America was in 1713 in Boston. The practice soon came into general use in New York and Philadelphia as well. Although auctions were not a frequent occurrence (Lehmann-Haupt counts about four each year between 1713 and 1800), they were an accepted means of selling new books as well as used books and remainders.

The book output of eighteenth-century presses tended to be highly practical, consisting largely of educational and religious books, legal handbooks, cookbooks, conduct books, mercantile guides, and medical texts. It was not uncommon for printers to run off editions of these types of books in the thousands. Works of theology were particularly abundant in this period, although their numbers declined progressively throughout the century. Almanacs, another staple, sold in enormous quantities. Between 1725 and 1764 Nathaniel Ames's *Almanack* reportedly sold an average of 60,000 per year, and Benjamin Franklin's *Poor Richard Improved* sold about 10,000 annually. Still another popular genre was the Indian captivity narrative.

A typical print run for new literary or political works in the mid–eighteenth century was 300 to 500, although both of these genres increased in popularity as the century advanced. Samuel Richardson's *Pamela* went through three

American editions in 1744 alone (with additional copies sold as imports), and Laurence Sterne's *A Sentimental Journey* had seven editions between 1768 and 1795. The audience for fiction became increasingly female, and although British works were favored by U.S. readers and publishers (the lack of an international copyright facilitated book piracy), the eighteenth century witnessed the rise of the U.S. novel with entries such as William Hill Brown's *The Power of Sympathy* (1789), Hugh Henry Brackenridge's *Modern Chivalry* (the first volume of which appeared in 1792), *Charlotte Temple*, Hannah W. Foster's *The Coquette* (1797), Royall Tyler's *The Algerine Captive* (1797), and Charles Brockden Brown's *Wieland* (1798) and *Arthur Mervyn* (1799). The eighteenth century also saw the first illustrated books produced by American printers: the earliest American books featuring copperplate engravings were Increase Mather's *Blessed Hope* (1701) and *Ichabod* (1702). In the latter half of the century, woodcut and copperplate engravings were used increasingly as embellishments in books.

The development of the book publishing industry in eighteenth-century America would have been seriously hindered without parallel developments in the manufacturing of printing materials and equipment. Prior to 1769 when Isaac Doolittle of Connecticut built a press for Philadelphia printer William Goddard, American printers had to obtain their presses from manufacturers in England. Similarly, type was generally imported from England until after the Revolution, when type-founding became a viable industry in the United States. And, although U.S. book publishers continued to import paper (and ink) from England for some time, Pennsylvania became a leading paper producer in the eighteenth century. While the most significant innovations – stereotyping, electrotyping, machine-made paper, paper made from wood pulp, lithography, composing machines, and steam-powered presses – did not emerge until the nineteenth century, the rise of these supporting industries eventually released American printers from dependence on British manufactured goods and gave them more control over vital technologies. Thus, by the end of the eighteenth century, the publishing business in the United States was poised to take advantage of the coming technological and social changes that together made possible the growth of the U.S. book trade in the nineteenth century.

SARAH WADSWORTH

Further Reading

Charvat, William, *Literary Publishing in America, 1790–1850,* Philadelphia: University of Pennsylvania Press, 1959

Joyce, William L., ed., *Printing and Society in Early America,* Worcester, Massachusetts: American Antiquarian Society, 1983

Lehmann-Haupt, Hellmut, Ruth Shepard Granniss, and Lawrence C. Wroth, *The Book in America: A History of the Making, the Selling, and the Collecting of Books in the United States,* New York: Bowker, 1939

Madison, Charles A., *Book Publishing in America,* New York: McGraw-Hill, 1966

Wolf, Edwin, *The Book Culture of a Colonial American City: Philadelphia Books, Bookmen, and Booksellers,* Lyell Lectures in Bibliography, 1985–6, New York: Oxford University Press, 1988; Oxford: Clarendon, 1988

Wroth, Lawrence C., *The Colonial Printer,* New York: Dover, 1994; London, Constable, 1994

Book Publishing in the Nineteenth Century

Period of growth and consolidation

As it was for the nation as a whole, the nineteenth century was a period of growth and consolidation for book publishing in the United States. In 1800, the U.S. book trade was disorganized and chiefly a local affair, still largely dependent on the British book trade centered in London. Book production remained a craft activity, based in small printing shops that could rely only partially on native materials and texts.

Distribution was also a problem. Not only were there difficulties with transportation, but the lack of efficient systems for the exchange of information as to what was available and what was wanted, and for the exchange of credit, meant that few books were able to find markets beyond the immediate site of production. Furthermore, publishing had yet to establish itself as a specialized activity within the book trade: few entrepreneurs had the capital or desire to venture their livelihoods in these primitive conditions. Book publishing was a part-time and risky activity, undertaken by printers and others who generally insisted that the author or another sponsor – often a religious, social, or governmental organization – underwrite the costs and hazards involved in the publication of their texts.

By century's end, all this had changed. A national book trade system had emerged, increasingly dominated by New York even while secondary centers such as Philadelphia, Boston, and Chicago continued to play an important role. Book production had become industrialized and now took place in large plants filled with newly invented machinery that required new patterns of labor and manufacture. An efficient national distribution system had also been developed, relying on the railroad, the postal system, and banking and credit networks to reach a national market of bookstores and book buyers. Large publishing houses (e.g., Harper, Scribner, Lippincott, and Houghton Mifflin) had now emerged to dominate trade publishing. Founded earlier in the century as simple partnerships or sole proprietorships, these publishing firms were fast becoming the complex corporate organizations that would continue to shape trade publishing well into the next century.

The technological revolutions of the industrial era altered the production of books in many ways. Although the large, steam-driven Hoe rotary press became the most public symbol of the increasing power and importance of print, its role in book manufacture was minor; most books were in fact produced on much smaller flatbed presses. But these were a far cry from the wooden hand presses of 1800. The complex, power-driven machines could print much larger sheets at much greater speeds. Most books were printed from stereotype or electrotype plates. Introduced in the 1810s and 1840s respectively, these printing plates stored a text set in type, page by page, and provided a means for incorporating relief illustrations and diagrams within the text. As a result, publishers were able better to control patterns of publication: books could be printed and reprinted over many years in small or large runs to meet demand, avoiding the expense and risk of storing printed sheets.

Paper represented a considerable expense of book manufacture (equaling roughly from one-quarter to one-third of the total cost) and was subject to fluctuating prices and limits of supply. The fourdrinier and cylinder papermaking machines, introduced in the 1820s, increased output and enabled the production of larger and larger sheets. This in turn required new sources of fiber; increasingly, waste from cotton mills and, later, mechanically or chemically treated wood pulp was used in place of rags. Lithography and photography provided new means for reproducing images, supplementing the traditional use of relief wood engravings, and by century's end, illustrations reproduced cheaply by photogravure and other means became a common feature of many books.

From the customer's perspective, the development of the publisher's cloth-covered, cased binding was the most visible and remarkable feature of the nineteenth-century book. Perfected during the 1820s and 1830s, publisher's bindings employed a new material – a specially prepared and patterned binding cloth – that could carry gold- and blind-stamped decoration applied by means of large cast-iron stamping presses on mass-produced binding cases that were attached to the printed sheets of a book cheaply and firmly. Books could now be offered to consumers in a standard package that reflected their contents and displayed the publisher's style and taste. Although publisher's bindings were expensive to produce (roughly equivalent to paper as part of the total cost), purchasers and readers of books came more and more to appreciate, choose, and judge books by their covers.

Because of its geographic size, the United States posed a considerable challenge to the distribution of books in the nineteenth century. As book publishing and manufacture became concentrated in a few urban centers, the problem of getting books out into the market had to be met. Trade publishers relied chiefly on retail bookstores in cities and towns across the nation, which supplied a local clientele but presumably also supplied customers in the surrounding countryside. Proprietary circulating and, later, publicly funded libraries provided an alternative means of distribution, reaching especially readers without the means to purchase new publications. Those without easy access to a retail bookstore or library could order books directly through the mail but probably also found some books in local general stores and through an informal network of friends and neighbors.

Retail bookstores received their stock at a discount (ranging typically from 20 to 40 percent off the retail price), from which they paid shipping and overhead expenses before taking any profit. Most shipments were sent via the express companies, which organized the business of transporting goods on the growing and complex rail network, and were received on credit of anywhere from one to 12 months. Returns of unsold stock were often accepted, although they were discouraged and often a source of contention. Book orders were placed based on information in a steady stream of publisher's catalogs and trade publications such as *Publishers Weekly*. Further information on new publications for booksellers and customers alike was provided by the notices, reviews, and advertisements carried in most magazines and newspapers.

Two institutions supported this system of retail bookstores: jobbing and trade sales. Jobbers were wholesaling middlemen who offered the publications of numerous publishers, thus simplifying the process of creating a diverse stock, and who managed the task of offering and collecting credit. Jobbing played a vital role in book distribution, and many publishers (e.g., Appleton and Lippincott) were also important jobbers. Trade sales were specially organized auction sales, strictly limited to members of the book trade and regularly scheduled in New York, Philadelphia, Boston, and Cincinnati, Ohio. At trade sales publishers offered both their new publications and their backlist, and retailers and jobbers, gathered together for the event, could purchase stock. First held in 1825, trade sales were a constant feature of the nineteenth-century book trade, although they became less important after the Civil War when publishers and jobbers relied increasingly on book travelers (traveling salesmen) to manage their accounts with retailers.

The industrialization and organization of book publishing did not result simply in the increased production of cheap books for a growing mass market but rather in the diversification of product aimed at many niche markets. The clothbound trade book was only one possible manifestation of nineteenth-century book publishing; other forms included subscription publishing of elaborate and often expensive books sold door-to-door by agents, and the publication of cheap, paper-covered books in libraries or series marketed through the mails or newsdealers. Regional and specialized publishers continued to target books for specific or immigrant populations; many publications continued to be subsidized by their authors or an institutional sponsor. Even the large east coast publishing houses included a variety of books on their lists, although their trade publications – novels, poetry, biography, history, essays, and other literary prose – came to represent and symbolize the triumphant role of book publishing in the nineteenth century. Authors of these works became national figures, widely read and able to support themselves with their writings.

To some extent, trade publishing defined a national literary culture that represented and was supported by the ideology and values of the emerging middle class. Books found their place within the home as an agent of domesticity, prominently displayed in the parlor and serving as the locus of the family reading circle. Children and adults both found in books a source of personal consequence around which they could shape and establish their own sense of identity. Even more, within nineteenth-century American life books

Book publishing became more diverse in the nineteenth century.
(Davis Library, University of North Carolina at Chapel Hill)

came to take on an authority of their own: one could now speak of "book learning" or insist that things be done "by the book." But the apparent triumph of the book was in many ways illusory. Books had always existed side by side with other cultural forms produced in a variety of media, and as the nineteenth century came to a close, their central place in the cultural life of the United States would be further challenged by the emergence of film and, later, by radio and television.

MICHAEL WINSHIP

See also Best-Sellers; Newspaper Technology

Further Reading

Charvat, William, *Literary Publishing in America, 1790–1850,* Amherst: University of Massachusetts Press, 1993

Hall, David D., and John B. Hench, eds., *Needs and Opportunities in the History of the Book: America, 1639–1876,* Worcester, Massachusetts: American Antiquarian Society, 1987

Lehmann-Haupt, Hellmut, Lawrence C. Wroth, and Rollo G. Silver, *The Book in America: A History of the Making and Selling of Books in the United States,* 2nd ed., New York: Bowker, 1951

Sheehan, Donald, *This Was Publishing: A Chronicle of the Book Trade in the Gilded Age,* Bloomington: Indiana University Press, 1952

Tanselle, G. Thomas, *Guide to the Study of United States Imprints,* 2 vols., Cambridge, Massachusetts: Belknap Press of Harvard University Press, 1971

Winship, Michael, *American Literary Publishing in the Mid-Nineteenth Century: The Business of Ticknor and Fields,* New York and Cambridge: Cambridge University Press, 1995

Book Publishing in the Twentieth Century

The industry faces new challenges, new possibilities

Twentieth-century book publishing began in an era of reading frenzy unequaled before or since in the United States. In later decades, publishers worked hard to promote literacy amid changing consumer tastes, competing media, shifting economies, and revolutionizing technologies.

The small, independent family-run printing and bookselling enterprises that moved into the 1900s carried with them a legacy of distribution, discounting, and copyright woes. Those that survived, as well as those that started in the century, emerged with new solutions to old problems. As early as 1914, anxious publishers organized "Revival of Readers," the largest cooperative advertising campaign to date. Running in newspapers across the country, it sought customers for their burgeoning book inventory.

Nonfiction books displaced the fiction craze that had

highlighted the first few years of the new century. Magazine articles on the corporate world helped spur an interest in business books. By the 1920s, readers wanted technical books on the new medium of radio. In the late 1930s, books on the social sciences and humanities thrived with the formation of the American Association of University Presses. The international book trade grew between the world wars when tariff restrictions were eased. Academic publishing grew again in the 1960s when scholars and scientific communities abroad adapted English as their international information exchange language.

Fiction never died out, however. With increased urbanization and industrialization, detective stories set in big, crime-ridden cities became a popular category in the 1920s. Around World War II, U.S. historical fiction was popular, and by the 1980s, horror, romance, and technological thriller novels topped the million-copy best-seller lists.

While tastes in various literary genres shifted with the decades, overall production of books steadily increased from some 7,000 new titles in 1900 to 50,000 by the 1990s. The industry doubled its book output from the turn of the century to 1913. As did other media, book publishing suffered through wartime restrictions and economic depressions, but despite national manufacturing hardships, it seemed to emerge virtually unscathed. In 1944, for example, short-staffed publishers managed to produce more books than in any previous year while using less paper, which was in short supply. Along with more books, more sales outlets appeared. Four times as many places to buy books emerged between 1950 and 1991, as 8,000 bookstores increased to 25,000.

As more personal bookshops dispersed throughout the country, book publishers concentrated their activities in New York. While Boston, Philadelphia, and Chicago had regional concentrations of publishers, new publishers Simon and Schuster, McGraw-Hill, Prentice-Hall, and Random House joined nineteenth-century carryovers in New York. By the World War II era, a few innovative publishers like Pocket Books, Bantam Books, New American Library, and Fawcett World Library had revived the paperback tradition of the previous century and joined hardcover companies in Manhattan.

Robert Fair de Graff was the twentieth-century pioneer of paperbacks with his Pocket Books, which were unabridged reprints of hardcover best-sellers and sold for 25 cents. The affordable books, printed on inexpensive paper, attracted a new wave of readers starting in 1939. Paperback books were displayed at newsstands, drugstores, variety stores, railroad terminals, and cigar shops, just like magazines. Fawcett, a pulp magazine publisher, became known for the sizable sums it paid for paperback reprinting of hardcover books as well as for rights it negotiated for original works. Along with paperbacks, the 1930s and 1940s saw a boom in pamphlets, a convenient book form harking back to the days of Thomas Paine's *Common Sense.*

Unlike the political nature of earlier pamphlets, the twentieth-century versions dealt with practical matters and topical interests. Simon and Schuster began its series with *The Coming of the American Boom,* which sold 30,000

New Books and New Editions Published
1880–1990

Year	Total Books Published	Year	Total Books Published
1880	2,076	1940	11,328
1885	4,030	1945	6,548
1890	4,559	1950	11,022
1895	5,469	1955	12,589
1900	6,356	1960	15,012
1905	8,112	1965	28,595
1910	13,470	1970	36,071
1915	9,734	1975	39,372
1920	8,422	1980	42,377
1925	9,574	1985	50,070
1930	10,027	1990	46,738
1935	8,766		

Notes: Beginning 1959, data not strictly comparable with previous years because of change in definition of "book"; prior to 1961, number includes military; beginning in 1967, counting methods were revised – prior years not strictly comparable with subsequent years; 1880–1919 includes pamphlets; 1920–1928 pamphlets included in total only, thereafter, pamphlets excluded entirely.

Source: Datapedia of the United States 1790–2000: America Year by Year. George Thomas Kurian (Bernan Press: Lanham, Maryland, 1994).

copies in 10 days. This was followed by a pamphlet about highway fatalities, which sold 25,000 copies, and J.K. Lasser's *Your Income Tax.*

After World War II, trade paperbacks, or so-called quality reprints available at bookstores rather than mass outlets, became popular. Doubleday's Anchor Books and Knopf's Vintage Books were leaders in college bookstores, which enjoyed remarkable growth thanks to the G.I. Bill of Rights, the general trend to higher education, and the baby boom generation. Avon Books became a paperback leader of romance novels in the seventies but was soon outpaced by Harlequin Romances, which in 1990 sold more than 200 million books, or about 40 percent of all mass-market paperbacks

Impressed with the important influence of magazines' covers on their newsstand sales, paperback publishers spent much time and money on book covers to attract impulse buyers. Although Simon and Schuster was among the first of the new century's publishers to use artwork and promotional copy on book jackets as a sales tool for hardcover books, the paperback covers came routinely to feature embossed or die-cut illustrations with metallic ink and even holography to attract attention. The cover trend even included experiments with differently colored versions or illustrations for the same book or slightly varied covers that fit together in a bookshelf display.

Reversing a nineteenth-century book publishing trend of creating magazines such as *Harper's* and *Atlantic* to promote books, several twentieth-century magazine publishers built book subsidiaries from material first printed in their periodicals. Meredith Corporation, *American Heritage,*

Reader's Digest, and Time-Life were examples of such enterprises; William Randolph Hearst's Internal Library Company was established in 1914 to use his magazines to secure book rights for the mass market. Even so, the *New Yorker,* which had no links with particular book publishers, nevertheless managed to procure book contracts for many of its article writers.

Other media made similar connections with book publishers. Motion picture companies were always looking for good sources of material and adapted many books into successful screenplays. Mark Twain's *Huckleberry Finn* was the first advertised tie-in between book publishers and film producers. By 1922, 110 novels became screenplays, and between 1933 and 1944 some 200 books, especially mysteries and classics, were translated to the silver screen.

Wars have always spurred great surges in reading, and World War II was certainly no exception. Grosset and Dunlap promoted books to soldiers, and publishers of maps and atlases scurried to meet the overwhelming demand from U.S. citizens after the Japanese attack on Pearl Harbor. As in previous times of conflict, the Bible became the most widely distributed book to both civilians and soldiers. The U.S. military issued Protestant, Roman Catholic, and Jewish versions to every serviceperson, marking the first time in American history that a book had become part of government general issue. During the conflict, more than a million copies of a thousand paperback secular titles were distributed.

While books grew in popularity, the U.S. post office continued indirectly impeding their distribution. Beginning in colonial times, the post office had imposed a postal surtax on books to subsidize the distribution of newspapers and magazines. Not until the twentieth century did book publishers, who had long lobbied for the same postal rates that newspapers and magazines enjoyed, receive some attention. In 1914, after lawsuits and pleas to Congress, a new postmaster general reclassified books as fourth-class, parcel post, which allowed them to be delivered via rural free delivery. President Franklin Roosevelt lowered the book rate, and Congress approved a new postal rate structure for books in 1942. Meanwhile, the first decrease in postal rates for books paved the way for the formation of book clubs in the 1920s.

Modeled after book guilds from post–World War I Germany, U.S. book clubs adapted magazine methods of subscription and mail order. The Book-of-the-Month Club and the Literary Guild started within months of each other in 1926. They advertised their books with direct mail promotions, which overcame distribution problems that had plagued publishers for centuries. The book clubs reached out to readers who had no access to most retail outlets.

As book production increased, publishers looked for ways to keep demand high. Their resources, however, were often limited by the high inventories of books they carried. Their relationship with booksellers, established through business policies set early in the century, allowed bookstores to return any books they had not sold for credit with publishers. In addition, publishers negotiated list-price discounts of nearly 50 percent for booksellers. Postwar changes in tax law led many family-owned publishing companies to issue public stock or merge with larger corporations in order to grow. The mergers, which brought new management styles and less antiquated business practices, may also have compromised the original intent of the publishers. Between 1958 and 1970, some 500 such mergers occurred, many of them with larger companies unfamiliar with book publishing. Deregulation and a weak U.S. dollar encouraged international investors from Europe and Asia to buy U.S. book companies, and some of the larger multinational, multimedia corporations saw the publishing enterprises as sources for investment growth and tax loss write-offs. By the 1980s, the book publishing industry had consolidated, with fewer than a dozen publishers responsible for two-thirds of all U.S. book sales.

During the 1970s, literary agents gained more power as brokers between authors and publishers for lucrative million-dollar contracts. The line editors who actually edited manuscripts were subsumed or eliminated in favor of acquisitions editors who negotiated with agents and developed book divisions under their own names within larger companies. The century-old struggle between publishers and consumers over copyright was addressed during this period as well. Teachers had been copying paragraphs, pages, and chapters of textbooks for their students since 1924. This early form of multigraphing foreshadowed the widespread use of photographic copying and the lawsuits brought by publishers against professors and duplicating companies. In 1976, the copyright law of 1891 was finally revised, but it continued to be discussed in light of new and unforeseen ramifications of electronic publishing.

The multimedia publishing of the late twentieth century began after World War II. McGraw-Hill saw the possibility of audiovisual tie-ins with printed training materials for business. Books had been recorded on audio tape for the visually impaired since the 1950s, but beginning in the 1970s, when portable cassette players for pedestrians were introduced and cassette systems became common in automobiles, audiobooks became popular as orally transmitted versions of the printed text on tape. In addition, computers assumed a bigger role in the publishing industry, from the transmission of the author's manuscript, through printing, to the electronic cash registers in bookstores that track inventory and sales. The biggest retail trend of the 1990s was chain book superstores, 40,000-square-foot spaces that accommodated many thousands of books along with cafes and rooms for readings and performances. The national chain bookstores such as Barnes and Noble and Borders often drove out local, independently owned stores. Accounting for nearly half of all book sales, the chains could determine how many copies of a book a publisher would print.

The technological revolution of the late twentieth century allowed books to be digitized onto a chip or disc that anyone with a computer modem could access. This system of book delivery eliminated most of the transportation problems that had plagued publishers for centuries. Solving the storage problem for unsold inventory, computer discs also reduced the time involved in getting books from authors through publishers. The next step occurred in 1986 when author Rob Swigart wrote the first novel specifically designed to be read on a computer. He took advantage of the hypertext concept that structures written passages to allow the reader to take different paths through the story. Computer users had the opportunity to hear and see various texts. At the end of the century, even such venerable institutions as multivolume encyclopedias were changed by computerization. In the late 1990s, it was suspected that there might soon be no more print revisions, since most encyclopedias had been transformed into CD-ROMs. That trend began and continued as electronic encyclopedias were sold as part of a package of preloaded software with computer purchases.

NORMA FAY GREEN

See also Best-Sellers; Book Clubs; Economics of Book Publishing; Instant Books; Internet; Paperback Books

Further Reading

Bonn, Thomas L., *Under Cover: An Illustrated History of American Mass-Market Paperbacks,* New York and Harmondsworth, Middlesex, England: Penguin, 1982
Compaine, Benjamin M., *The Book Industry in Transition: An Economic Study of Book Distribution and Marketing,* White Plains, New York: Knowledge Industry, 1978
Davis, Kenneth C., *Two-Bit Culture: The Paperbacking of America,* Boston: Houghton Mifflin, 1984
Lehmann-Haupt, Hellmut, Lawrence C. Wroth, and Rollo G. Silver, *The Book in America: A History of the Making and Selling of Books in the United States,* 2nd ed., New York: Bowker, 1951
Madison, Charles A., *Book Publishing in America,* New York: McGraw-Hill, 1966
Max, D.T., "The End of the Book?," *Atlantic Monthly* 274:3 (September 1994)
"Publishing Books," *Media Studies Journal* 6:3 (Summer 1992)

Book Publishing Trade Organizations

From the early twentieth century, many different professional organizations served the members of the book trade. Their functions were several: to share information about the state of the industry; to preserve the history of book culture and advocate its continued importance; and to unite the diverse workers involved in the production, promotion, and sale of books into national, professional networks.

Two of the largest organizations in the 1990s were the American Booksellers Association (founded in 1900) and the Association of American Publishers (founded in 1945 as the American Book Publishers Council). A professional information-sharing and promotional organization, the American Booksellers Association's purpose was "to define and strengthen the position of the book retailer in the book distribution chain." The Association of American Publishers worked to expand the market for books and, as a lobbying group, kept "member publishers informed about legislative, regulatory, and policy issues that affect[ed]" them. Both organizations disseminated information within the book community about new goods and services, technological change, and trade economics. Simultaneously, both went outside the profession to promote a set of cultural ideals to the government and the public at large. Both the Association of American Publishers and the American Booksellers Association sponsored publications, conferences, and press campaigns to promote literacy and reading and to advocate publicly the intellectual freedom of all members of the book community – writers, producers, vendors, and readers.

While all book trade organizations were interested at some level in expanding the literary marketplace, some focused more exclusively on the politics and culture of books. For example, the Freedom to Read Foundation (1969) and the National Coalition for Literacy (1981) united many different book professionals – writers, publishers, librarians, teachers – who were concerned with how social and political issues like censorship and education affect the fate of book culture. Similarly, organizations like the Women's National Book Association (1917), the Before Columbus Foundation (1976), and the Multicultural Publisher's Exchange (1989) crossed the lines of production and sales to unite practitioners across the nation who have common interests underserved by the larger organizations.

Many national organizations for book writers, promoters, and readers reflected and reinforced the book industry's conflicted relationship with the worlds of culture and of commerce. The organizations specifically for book manufacturers, however, showed a different two-way pull – between the industry's origins in early modern craftsmanship and its investment in state-of-the-art information technology. Organizations like the Guild of Bookworkers (1906) and the Center for Book Arts (1974) were dedicated to preserving the centuries-old crafts of papermaking, hand binding, calligraphy, and engraving through classes and exhibitions. On the other hand, groups like the Book Manufacturer's Institute (1933) and the National Association of Desktop Publishers (1987) disseminated information to their members about the newest technological innovations in conventional and computer-assisted production.

Throughout its history, the book trade has been diffuse and divided. Its highly differentiated business structure has contributed to this, as has the trade's need to serve both commerce and culture. Economic and technological developments in the late twentieth century exacerbated these conditions.

TRYSH TRAVIS

Further Reading

Coser, Lewis A., Charles Kadushin, and Walter Powell, *Books: The Culture and Commerce of Publishing*, New York: Basic, 1982

Williams, Maurvene D., *The Community of the Book: A Directory of Organizations and Programs*, 3rd ed., Washington, D.C.: Library of Congress, 1993

Book Publishing Trade Publications

At the end of the twentieth century, more than 100 trade publications in the book industry were produced for the people who wrote, published, promoted, and sold books. The sheer number reflected the industry's long history, diverse interests, and highly differentiated business structure.

The most important general interest journal was *Publishers Weekly (PW),* which began publication in 1871. Its original title, *The Publisher's and Stationer's Weekly Trade Circular,* reveals the close ties between nineteenth-century book publishing and selling and the related crafts of papermaking, printing, and engraving. By the 1990s, *PW* not only advertised the appearance of new titles but also reported on sales figures, changes in personnel, and contemporary attitudes toward books and reading.

In 1983, the editors of *Publishers Weekly* issued the first *Publishers Weekly Yearbook* (later called *Book Publishing Annual*). The *Annual* reviewed the year's developments through subject-based chapters on the economy of publishing, books and the law, retail issues, technological advances, and educational opportunities. Beginning in 1976, the Book Industry Study Group, a nonprofit research consortium, published *Book Industry Trends,* a statistical survey of the business aspects of book production used for forecasting production and sales. From 1940, *Literary Marketplace* indexed publishers, press agents, distributors, manufacturers, and artists. The *American Book Trade Directory,* from 1915, compared the number of independently-owned bookstores to the number of chain and mail-order outlets and listed vendors by state and subject specialty, including private dealers, auction houses, and appraisers.

Many smaller publications catered to the specialized needs of different sectors of the book trade. Some covered aspects of book acquisition, display, and sales; others dealt with the economy, aesthetics, and technology of book production; and still others addressed both producers and vendors sharing an interest in specific subjects and markets.

TRYSH TRAVIS

Further Reading

Literary Marketplace, New Providence, New Jersey: Bowker, 1994

Other Book Entries: Censorship of Books; Dime Novels; Economics of Book Publishing; Instant Books; Mass Culture; Mass Market Book Publishing; Paperback Books; Textbook Publishing; Trade Book Publishing; University Presses

Boosterism

Newspapers helping to build their communities

The success of small-town newspapers depended upon the survival of towns in which their subscribers and advertisers lived. As town builders moved west in the nineteenth century, they attracted newspaper editors to promote town settlement.

Some town boosters hired editors; some lent them money to start their businesses, and others gave them town lots to increase the newspaper's stake in town prosperity. Independent editors moved to towns in which they hoped to prosper without subsidies.

Editors depended on optimism to assure the stability of their towns and on exaggeration to attract new settlers. Booster publishers asked their readers to buy copies for friends and relatives who might move there. "The purpose of a booster newspaper," according to journalism historian Barbara Cloud, "was to print stories about the town and to distribute copies around the country, both to other newspapers that might reprint the stories and to friends and relatives who might be interested in moving west." Cloud said that newspapers stimulated growth, but she found no correlation between the town's size and the number of its newspapers.

In a study of Wisconsin newspapers, A.L. Lorenz found a tenuous relationship between editors and their sponsors. "But as soon as the boosters lost their vision or their money or simply left to find new challenges in the land farther west, the newspapers they had supported failed, and the printers had to seek new sources of support."

Despite the odds against town survival, town promoters displayed incredible optimism about each town's prospects. They talked about the future, ignoring the dismal present. Essays in local papers and advertisements in neighboring towns and eastern cities extolled town potential.

Boosters depended upon adjectives, especially superlatives. Each new valley became "happy valley," a Garden of Eden, or the promised land. Newspapers promised the most productive soil, water supply, climate, or people. Looking at the *Eagle* of Wichita, Kansas, Julie Dagenais found language describing its locale as "the broadest, deepest and richest valley in Kansas, the fairest prospect, the fastest growth, the most flourishing town" in an area with "the best climate, the most productive soil, the handsomest women, and the smartest children on God's green earth."

Boosterism became such a basic part of westward expansion early in the nineteenth century that some papers spoofed it. In 1819, the *Augusta Chronicle* ran a widely reprinted advertisement from "Andrew Air Castle, Theory M'Vision, and L. Moonlight Jr., & Co.," described as proprietors of Skunksburgh. A folksy town description touted its potential on the middle ground between all major North American cities. "A line of Velocipede stages will be immediately established from Skunksburgh straight through the O-ke-fin-o-cau Swamp, to the southernmost point of the Florida peninsula; and, as soon as a canal shall be cut through the rocky mountains, there will be direct communication with the Columbia river, and thence to the Pacific Ocean. Then opens a theatre of trade bounded only by the Universe!"

Boosters stretched credibility. In Wichita, the *Eagle* wrote: "Much complaint is heard from physicians who in vain endeavor to eke out an existence here. Sickness is almost unknown hence the necessity of importing centenarians from Missouri to lay the nucleus of a grave yard." Farther west, editors ignored gunfights to promote their towns as peaceful places appropriate to family life. In dry farming areas, some even promised that plowing the soil would increase the amount of rainfall, hence the slogan that "rain follows the plow."

Newspapers carried the banner of regional pride in competition with other western towns and eastern cities. Early in the nineteenth century, Pittsburgh, Pennsylvania, newspapers worried that the completion of the Erie Canal and the National Road could turn Philadelphia and Pittsburgh into deserted villages. The *Gazette* charged that the "canal scheme" by New York and Baltimore, Maryland, would steal business from western Pennsylvania. Later in the century, Kansas cattle towns competed to attract the herds with their cowboys bearing spending money. The completion of transcontinental railroads brought a boom in boosterism. Railroads attracted settlers to assure ridership and to help sell their huge land grants.

Boosterism continued well into the twentieth century. Developers of the southwest United States continued to tout the region as a land of promise, especially for retirees seeking worry-free leisure and good health. Businesses were promised suburban services and freedom from government regulation.

WILLIAM E. HUNTZICKER

See also Frontier Press; Newspapers in the Nineteenth Century; Reporters and Reporting in the Nineteenth Century

Further Reading

Blodgett, Jan, *Land of Bright Promise: Advertising the Texas Panhandle and South Plains, 1870–1917,* Austin: University of Texas Press, 1988

Cloud, Barbara Lee, *The Business of Newspapers on the Western Frontier,* Reno: University of Nevada Press, 1992

_____, "Establishing the Frontier Newspaper: A Study of Eight Western Territories," *Journalism Quarterly* 61:4 (1984)

Dagenais, Julie, "Newspaper Language as an Active Agent in the Building of a Frontier Town," *American Speech* XLII:2 (1967)

Hage, George S., *Newspapers on the Minnesota Frontier, 1849–1860,* St. Paul: Minnesota Historical Society, 1967

Halaas, David Fridtjof, *Boom Town Newspapers: Journalism on the Rocky Mountain Mining Frontier, 1859–1881,* Albuquerque: University of New Mexico Press, 1981

Katz, William A., "The Western Printer and His Publications, 1850–90," *Journalism Quarterly* 44:4 (1967)

Lorenz, A.L., "'Out of Sorts and Out of Cash': Problems of Publishing in Wisconsin Territory, 1833–1848," *Journalism History* 3:2 (1976)

Lyon, William H., *The Pioneer Editor in Missouri, 1808–1860,* Columbia: University of Missouri Press, 1965

Brady, Mathew

Photographer of the American Civil War

Mathew Brady, a world-renowned portrait photographer before the Civil War, brought the reality of war to the public and politicians. Born in New York, Brady began as a portrait artist, which allowed him to develop sensitivity and artistry that he used as a photographer. In 1860, he photographed Abraham Lincoln, who was campaigning in New York. Lincoln credited that photograph, which showed him as "Honest Abe" instead of a country bumpkin, with helping make him president. Brady took numer-

ous photographs of Lincoln, including those used on the Lincoln penny and the $5 bill. By 1861 Brady had photographed nearly every famous American, including presidents from Andrew Jackson to William McKinley.

Brady sensed immediately the importance of becoming the curator of the Civil War. He was at the first battle of Bull Run and soon had photographers in almost every theater. Brady's failing eyesight precluded him from taking many of the photographs himself, but he organized and financed the expedition. In all, he and his men made more than 7,000 exposures, usually under uncomfortable conditions and occasionally under fire. The *New York Times* credited Brady with bringing home "the terrible reality and earnestness of war."

Brady was neither the best nor the most prolific photographer of the Civil War, but he was the most important and the most famous. After the war, Brady was bankrupt from financing the photography expedition. He lost his preeminence as a photographer and died destitute in New York City in 1896.

T.J. HEMLINGER

See also Civil War Photography; Civil War Press (North); War Photography

Further Reading

Hobart, George, *Masters of Photography: Mathew Brady,* London: Macdonald, 1984

Horan, James D., *Mathew Brady, Historian with a Camera,* New York: Crown, 1955

Kunhardt, Dorothy M., and Philip B. Kunhardt, *Mathew Brady and His World,* Alexandria, Virginia: Time-Life, 1977

Meredith, Roy, *Mr. Lincoln's Camera Man: Mathew B. Brady,* New York: Dover, 1974

Moeller, Susan D., *Shooting War: Photography and the American Experience of Combat,* New York: Basic, 1989

Photographer Mathew Brady after the Battle of Bull Run
(Reproduced from the Collections of the Library of Congress)

Brandeis, Louis Dembitz

Supporter of First Amendment rights

Louis D. Brandeis, the son of Bohemian immigrants, took his seat on the U.S. Supreme Court in 1916 and over the years became a strong proponent of popular democracy and free speech. He firmly believed that more speech was the answer to speech that advocated potential evils, and that to justify suppression of free speech, the danger must be imminent and the evil to be prevented serious. Some of his most famous language on these points can be found in the 1927 decisions in *Ruthenberg* v. *Michigan* and *Whitney* v. *California.*

Brandeis, whom President Woodrow Wilson appointed to the Court, frequently joined Oliver Wendell Holmes Jr. in dissent on matters of the First Amendment that came before the conservative courts of Chief Justices William Howard Taft and Charles Evans Hughes. Their most famous dissents were in response to a string of cases provoked by the Espionage Act of 1917 as well as state sedition laws. Brandeis also fought for what he and his Boston law partner, Samuel Warren, pioneered as "the right to privacy." It was the theme, as well as the title, of their *Harvard Law Review* article in 1890 and the focus of Brandeis's dissent in *Olmstead v. United States* (1928), in which the Court held that wiretapping did not violate the Fourth Amendment.

In 23 years on the Court, Brandeis advocated freedom of speech, the right to privacy, judicial self-restraint, deference to legislation, and "sociological jurisprudence," the use of nonlegal materials to understand the impact of law upon society and economics. This approach is also known as the "Brandeis brief."

RICHARD F. HIXSON

See also First Amendment in the Twentieth Century; Holmes, Oliver Wendell Jr.; Privacy

Further Reading

Baskerville, Stephen W., *Of Laws and Limitations: An Intellectual Portrait of Louis Dembitz Brandeis,* Rutherford, New Jersey: Fairleigh Dickinson University Press, 1994; London: Associated University Presses, 1994
Mason, Alpheus T., *Brandeis: A Free Man's Life,* New York: Viking, 1946
Urofsky, Melvin I., *Louis D. Brandeis and the Progressive Tradition,* Boston: Little, Brown, 1981
Warren, Samuel D., and Louis D. Brandeis, "The Right to Privacy," *Harvard Law Review* 4 (1890)

Brand-Name Advertising

A new way to sell products appears

Brand names in advertising are the road signs along the shelves of products and services that distinguish one product or service from its competitors. Coca-Cola's simple red-and-white swirl is recognized around the world as representing refreshment with a distinctive taste; the elegant script used by Cadillac on its automobiles suggests a certain type of luxury and quality; and the name Levi's is synonymous with blue jeans.

Distinguishing one product or service from another was not necessary until the mass production of the Industrial Revolution in the late 1800s replaced the agrarian way of life, with each family producing what it needed for itself. As more products were made in factories instead of at home, manufacturers had to separate their often similar products from others to capture their share of the market.

From the early 1900s, brand names seemed to serve the utilitarian, somewhat generic, function of providing the product with a name. It was not until the 1950s that brand names became recognized as entities that could evoke in consumers emotions and feelings about products that in turn would create relationships between consumers and brand-name products and services. Burleigh Gardner of Social Research Incorporated and Sidney Levy explored the concept of brand images, defining brand image as a symbol that incorporated physical characteristics and ideas. The new notion of brand advertising seemed to be that the idea or emotions associated with a product or service could be more powerful than the actual physical characteristics of the product.

While Gardner and Levy contributed to the academic understanding of brand-name advertising, and Gardner is generally credited with coining the term "brand advertising," advertising giant David Ogilvy was busy contributing to the actual use of brand advertising. His well-known 1950s Hathaway shirt campaign is generally recognized as one of the first modern-day brand-name campaigns.

Advertisers create brand names by selecting words that not only physically describe a product or service but also set it apart in consumers' minds from sometimes hundreds of other similar products or services available. Research plays a critical part in carefully selecting words, distinctive graphics, appealing typestyles, and symbols or characters that all play a part in creating a brand image or personality.

In other cases, product personalities created specifically for advertising campaigns are linked to brand names and become icons in their own right. The Snuggle Bear for a leading fabric softener, the Jolly Green Giant and Sprout for Minnesota Valley vegetables, the California Raisins, and the Keebler Elves are widely known characters that almost all consumers can associate with a brand product. The characters also emphasize the feelings and emotions the advertisers want consumers to associate with their products.

Consumers' responses are not just logically based reactions to the physical characteristics of a product or service; emotions and feelings also influence their choices, creating a relationship between the product and the consumer. Brand names are usually associated with products that have little physical difference among them, such as laundry soap, macaroni, or shampoo. But brand names often evoke in consumers' minds brand image perceptions such as quality, color, or price.

As consumers become accustomed to using one brand-name product or service over another, they develop brand loyalty. The promise is that every time customers purchase brand-name products, they are getting the same quality. The result is an ongoing relationship in which it is expected that that quality will be maintained because a brand name says so. Brand loyalty is the ultimate relationship between a manufacturer's product or service and its consumers, who, based on previous use, unquestionably choose one product over another without considering any alternatives.

Once a brand name has established itself, advertisers can build on the name's reputation to enhance and expand their product lines. For example, a well-established name-brand potato company can expand its line of products to include fresh and frozen potatoes of different types, knowing that consumers will equate the name with a quality product.

In the 1970s and 1980s, generic products were introduced into the marketplace based on the assumption that consumers would trade more expensive brands for economy. Although generic products had limited success, the predominance of brand-name products and service served as

Eastman Kodak was an early beneficiary of brand-name advertising.

testimony to the strength of the relationships based on brand-name recognition. Transformational advertising, a 1990s version of brand-name advertising that relied heavily on brand-name recognition, concentrated even less on the physical attributes of a product and more on the experience of using that product.

BARBARA J. DeSANTO

See also Advertising in the Nineteenth Century; Advertising in the Twentieth Century; Creative Revolution

Further Reading

Melanson, Wayne W., "The Value of Understanding the Evolution of Advertising Ideas," in *Proceedings of the 1986 Conference of the American Academy of Advertising,* edited by Ernest F. Larkin, Washington, D.C.: American Academy of Advertising, 1986

Russell, Thomas, and W. Ronald Lane, *Kleppner's Advertising Procedure,* 12th ed., Englewood Cliffs, New Jersey: Prentice-Hall, 1993

Wells, William, John Burnett, Sandra E. Moriarty, and Charles Pearce, *Advertising: Principles and Practice,* 3rd ed., Englewood Cliffs, New Jersey: Prentice-Hall, 1995

British Antecedents of the American Press

Major emphases mirror those in British newspapers

From its inception, journalism in the United States mirrored its British counterpart. The writings of English essayists like Daniel Defoe, Samuel Johnson, Alexander Pope, and Jonathan Swift were emulated in the colonial press in both substance and style. This is best exemplified by Benjamin Franklin, who confessed in his autobiography that his writing style was borrowed from a London magazine, *The Spectator:* "I thought the writing excellent and wish'd if possible to imitate it," Franklin wrote. He did, endeavoring to become "a tolerable English Writer, of which I was extreamly ambitious." Other colonists followed Franklin's mode of expression, solidifying the British influence on writing in its colonies.

In addition to the writing, the vehicles of its expression were transplanted across the Atlantic Ocean. Colonial newspapers, pamphlets, and almanacs were patterned after the products of the London press. Many colonial publishers had trained and worked in English printing houses and sought to produce as master printers the type of publications with which they were familiar as apprentices and journeymen.

One of the most influential British antecedents was reliance upon and submission to government. Just as in England, many American colonial printers depended on financial support in the form of government printing contracts. According to Arthur Schlesinger, "the ruling group possessed an effective financial leash on newspaper proprietors insofar as they executed or desired to execute government printing." This reliance on political patronage, Daniel Boorstin noted, meant that the printer "had to be a 'government man,' acceptable to the ruling group in his colony." Historians have debated the degree of editorial control government subsidy represented, but it derived from the English press system.

Laws restricting free expression were equally important press restraints. Licensing practices prohibiting criticism of government or its officers as "seditious libel" developed in England and were exported across the Atlantic. As a vehicle for news and ideas, the early American press got off to a discouraging start, chiefly due to anxiety in seventeenth-century England that it would serve as a means of relaxing colonial subservience to British rule. In 1662, two years after the restoration of the monarchy, Parliament passed a series of licensing acts limiting the number of printers throughout the British Empire and restricting their ability to print. Intent on controlling free expression specifically in the colonies, King Charles II sent commissioners to Massachusetts in 1664 to impose strict restraints on printing and free speech. Forty years earlier, the House of Commons had expressed similar concern over the corrupting influence of published opinion.

Prosecutions for seditious libel also continued to restrain the English and American press. In several extreme examples, writings perceived to advocate the death of the king were found treasonable, and their authors were punished accordingly. For printing a 1663 tract contending that people possessed the natural right of revolution against bad rulers, William Twyn was sentenced to be hanged, cut down while still alive, and then castrated, disemboweled, quartered, and finally beheaded.

Punishments in America were not so drastic but were nonetheless extant. For accusing a monarch of marital infidelity and charging allied Native Americans with savagery, Boston publisher Benjamin Harris' *Publick Occurrences* newspaper was suppressed in 1690 by Massachusetts authorities after only one issue for violating licensing laws. Colonial governors received instructions from London "to provide by all necessary orders that no person KEEP any press for printing, NOR that any book, pamphlet, or other matters whatsoever be printed without your especial leave and license first obtained."

These British licensing mandates were partly responsible for the tardy development of the American press and thus served to reinforce government authority against the dangers the press represented. "I thank God, there are no free-schools, nor printing; and I hope we shall not have, these hundred years," Virginia governor William Berkeley gleefully observed of colonial America, in a 1671 letter to his London superiors. "For learning has brought disobedience and heresy, and sects into the world, and printing has divulged them and libels against the best government: God keep us from both!"

Colonial America did not have a continuously published newspaper until 1704, and even that was produced by a government official. As the American press grew more assertive and independent, however, colonial printers criticized British government and proclaimed the notion of press freedom as a basic human right. Borrowing from British libertarian thought, notably by Thomas Hobbes, John Locke, and the team of John Trenchard and Thomas Gordon, American writers argued that government should not exercise arbitrary power. Their persuasive force accelerated during the 1760s and 1770s, fomenting the American Revolution.

RALPH FRASCA

See also Colonial Press; *Publick Occurrences, Both Forreign and Domestick*

Further Reading

Boorstin, Daniel, *The Americans, The Colonial Experience*, New York: Random House, 1958; London: Cardinal, 1988

Hudson, Robert V., "The English Roots of Benjamin Franklin's Journalism," *Journalism History* 3 (1976)

Schlesinger, Arthur M., *Prelude to Independence: The Newspaper War on Britain, 1764–1776*, New York: Knopf, 1958

Broadcast Advertising

Financial roots of broadcasting developed in radio

Broadcast advertising is naturally rooted in the history of radio. Along with the popular acceptance of radio, advertising was developed as an industry-wide operational support. The alternative support systems included a tax on receiving sets and a government-owned system, which were not popular options. Radio station WEAF, which was owned and operated by American Telephone and Telegraph (AT&T), set the most important advertising precedent when it started to sell advertising. WEAF was the first station licensed to operate a toll station. In 1922 it became available for hire by those wishing to reach the public by radio telephony. On August 18, WEAF broadcast the first commercial program – it was a 10-minute message from a real-estate company and promoted the sale of apartments. This broadcast gave the fledgling radio industry a reason to improve that was based on dollars and cents. There were earlier commercial sales experiments, but it was the WEAF broadcast that created the optimistic catalyst for a growing industry.

Optimism was high during the early commercial years of radio, but advertising revenues were not substantial. The $61.9 million in radio advertising revenue reported for 1932 represented only 5 percent of the advertising occurring in the media overall. The print media took the larger portion of the advertising dollar in the early years. The major stations received the heavy support of parent corporations.

There were also restrictions on early radio advertising. Most advertisers and stations felt that the value of radio advertising was one of time, good will, and having a product associated with an entertainment commodity – a radio program. As a result, there were brand-name programs, orchestras, and, some said, even stations. The commercial

messages were confined to the mention of the brand name and the product. No direct-sales prices were ever quoted. Personal and intimate products, such as toothpaste, were not mentioned over the air.

The growth of commercial radio programs and network audiences created the realization within advertising agencies that radio was a viable medium, and radio advertising increased. The Great Depression eliminated all the barriers to direct advertising and single-voice announcements at the introduction and conclusion. Radio became the theater of the mind, in terms of both programming and advertising. The commercials were dramatized, and with advanced technology, the electrical transcription, they could now be controlled by the advertising agency. With this, national spot radio advertising began. In other words, the advertising agency could create one commercial, duplicate it via electrical transcription, and ship it to stations in different markets to facilitate the sale of national spots. In effect, the advertiser had three methods of communication to reach the larger radio audience: individual stations, the networks,

Early television advertising featured people, such as Betty Furness, showing the finer points of products.
(Courtesy of Westinghouse Electric Corporation)

Animated characters, such as Tony the Tiger, became popular in later television advertising.
(Museum of Broadcast Communications)

and the national spot radio; these remained the primary methods of broadcast advertising.

The processes in selling radio advertising have been generally superimposed over other electronic media. The need begins with the advertiser, who has some message to communicate to a broader audience. The advertiser can contact the media outlet directly or work with an advertising agency. Small and rural businesses often go directly to the station, working with an account executive at the station. In this process, the messages and the buying of time are often simple and direct – the station and the business work together closely to assure success and a continued relationship. Larger advertising enterprises require the services of an advertising agency. The agency provides research, creative, and buying services for the larger business clients. The usual agency commission for these services is 15 percent of the gross budget. The agency then works with the advertising client to research the market. Such research can include audience research, market research, product research, product testing, and general audience rating information. With this research knowledge, the agency's creative department works to develop a commercial that will communicate to, and affect, the targeted audience. The agency buys the most effective combination of network, national, or station time for the campaign.

The 1994 *Broadcasting and Cable Yearbook* reported more than 11,500 radio stations, 1,500 television stations, 11,600 cable systems, and 6 television networks operating in the United States. These statistics represented an astounding electronic media advertising opportunity as well as a challenge. According to the Television and Radio Bureaus of Advertising, revenues for 1992 were reported at $35.9 billion, with 75 percent of that figure going to television. An average network television spot ranged in cost

Radio Advertising Expenditures 1935–1990 (per million dollars)

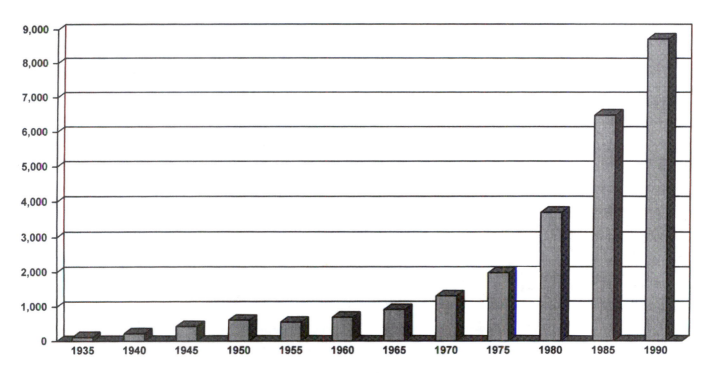

Source: Datapedia of the United States 1790–2000: America Year by Year. George Thomas Kurian (Bernan Press: Lanham, Maryland, 1994).

from $100,000 to $300,000, and a network Super Bowl spot running 30 seconds could reach $1 million.

DONALD G. GODFREY

See also Commercialization of Broadcasting; Economics of Broadcasting; Radio Networks

Further Reading

Bergendorff, Fred L., Charles H. Smith, and Lance Webster, *Broadcast Advertising and Promotion: A Handbook for Students and Professionals,* New York: Hastings House, 1983
Heighton, Elizabeth J., and Don R. Cunningham, *Advertising in the Broadcast and Cable Media,* Belmont, California: Wadsworth, 1984
Sherman, Barry, *Telecommunications Management: Broadcasting/Cable and the New Technologies,* New York: McGraw-Hill, 1995

Broadcast Awards

One of television's most recognizable symbols in the late twentieth century was the Emmy Award. It was so well known that two televised Emmy ceremonies were held each year – one each for prime-time and daytime programs. Yet the Emmys were by no means the only broadcasting awards; in some respects, they were not even the most important. Broadcasters were honored each year for accomplishments in journalism (news, documentary, educational, and sports), technical excellence (lighting, camera work, graphics, etc.), writing, and even promotions. The awards numbered in the dozens each year.

The Emmys covered many of those areas. The National Academy of Television Arts and Sciences and its younger relative, the Academy of Television Arts and Sciences, divided responsibility for oversight. Nominations were made by members of the two organizations, and a panel of experts in each field chose the winners. There were also regional Emmys in several major markets.

The award itself was created in 1948, a statuette of a woman with long, sharp wings, wearing a flowing dress and holding up a sphere. Designer Louis McManus used his wife, Dorothy, as the model. The Emmy was named after the "immy," jargon for the image orthicon camera tube.

The National Association of Broadcasters (NAB), the Radio Television News Directors Association (RTNDA), and the Associated Press (AP) Broadcasters also gave coveted awards. The NAB honored public service, contributions to the industry, and other achievements in a total of nine categories. The RTNDA recognized broadcast journalists for outstanding service and major contributions to their profession. The RTNDA's Edward R. Murrow Awards for excellence in broadcast journalism were among the industry's most prestigious. The AP Broadcasters honored journalistic excellence and the cooperation of stations that supplied the AP with news for distribution to other stations.

What were sometimes called the Pulitzer Prizes of broadcasting came from the University of Georgia's Henry W.

Television's Emmy
(Courtesy of Academy of Television Arts and Sciences)

Grady School of Journalism. The Peabody Awards were established in 1940 and named after George Foster Peabody, a Georgia banker and philanthropist. Stations and networks submitted entries, and a national advisory board selected the winners in up to six categories: news, entertainment, education, programs for children, documentaries, and public service. There was no required number of winners per category.

Outstanding college broadcasters were recognized with several national and regional awards. The most prestigious of these were presented by the William Randolph Hearst Foundation, which honored top achievements in radio and television reporting, as well as in print categories, in an annual nationwide competition.

Many other organizations, though not confined to broadcasting themselves, honored excellence in television or radio. Some were professional groups, such as the Society of Motion Picture and Television Engineers, the National Association of Black Journalists, and the National Press Photographers Association. Others groups consisted of specialists, such as aviation writers and education writers. Some awards were given not by the journalists but by groups representing those they cover; for example, the American Bar Association recognized outstanding broadcast reporting that exposed problems or helped the public understand the legal system.

THOMAS LETTS

Further Reading
O' Neil, Thomas, *The Emmys: Star Wars, Showdowns, and the Supreme Test of TV's Best,* New York: Penguin, 1992
Steinberg, Cobbett S., *TV Facts,* New York: Facts on File, 1980

Broadcast Blacklisting

Attempts to purge Communists from radio and television

Although rumors of blacklists had circulated in the television industry after World War II, formalized blacklisting began with the June 1950 publication of *Red Channels, the Report of Communist Influence in Radio and Television.* Issued by American Business Consultants, who also pub-

Red Channels was a primary vehicle for naming alleged Communists.

lished *Counterattack, the Newsletter of Facts on Communism,* the special report listed 151 prominent individuals whom the editors claimed had past or present ties to "Communist causes."

The premise underlying *Red Channels* was that Communists were infiltrating entertainment industries and must be removed. Beneath a front-cover illustration of a microphone entrapped by a red hand, each name was followed by a professional description and the person's suspected links to Communist activities. Organizations were deemed subversive based on the judgment of the U.S. Attorney General, the U.S. House Un-American Activities Committee, and other sources, including the editors of *Red Channels* themselves. Persons listed included actors José Ferrer, Judy Holliday, Henry Morgan, and Edward G. Robinson; commentators William Shirer and Howard K. Smith; musicians Leonard Bernstein, Burl Ives, and Lena Horne; and writers Lillian Hellman, Arthur Miller, and Dorothy Parker.

The editors of *Red Channels* were participants in the Red Scare, a war against dissent and nonconformity. They did not claim that everyone listed in the pamphlet was a Communist. They believed, however, that each person whose name appeared in *Red Channels* had done something questionable and should be required to prove their anti-Communism if they wanted to continue working in the industry. To clarify its position, *Red Channels* appropriated a quote from *Broadcasting Magazine:* "Where there's red smoke there's usually Communist fire."

Red Channels soon became known as the "Bible of Madison Avenue." Network executives, radio and television packagers, sponsors, and advertising agencies relied on the report and accepted *Counterattack*'s standards of employability. Each feared the effects of an economic boycott of advertisers' products by people who disapproved of certain individuals affiliated with broadcast programs. It was not important that no boycotts actually occurred; the mere possibility was enough to warrant economic exile of those listed.

The first firing directly linked with the publication of *Red Channels* was that of actress Jean Muir. In August 1950, Young and Rubicam advertising agency announced that Muir would join the cast of the popular television show, *The Aldrich Family.* Shortly after the announcement, *Counterattack* editor and former Federal Bureau of Investigation (FBI) agent Theodore C. Kirkpatrick organized a protest against sponsor General Mills' product Jell-O, for the hiring of Muir, who was listed in *Red Channels.* As a result of efforts by his right-wing pressure group, General Mills fired the actress from her television role.

When the firing became public, General Mills received complaints from all sides. In hundreds of editorials and at many group meetings, the Muir case and political screening were discussed. General Foods received thousands of letters, both supporting and opposing the firing; the company decided that public debate on the Muir issue was bad for business. In an effort to silence liberal concerns, placate right-wing critics, and retain their customers, General Mills began checks into the backgrounds of employees before they were hired. Soon, all networks, sponsors, and advertising agencies were secretly investigating the political beliefs of their potential employees, and blacklisting became institutionalized.

At the CBS network, policy was implemented by a vice president. Each of the network's 2,500 employees was also required to sign a loyalty oath testifying to his or her anti-Communism. Executives at advertising agencies such as Batten, Barton, Durstine and Osborn served as "security officers." At NBC, the legal department became responsible for security checks. Independent consultants made considerable money from servicing sponsors and agencies that lacked a full-time investigator.

Vincent Hartnett, who wrote the introduction to *Red Channels,* offered political background checks and kept an updated mimeographed list of blacklisted individuals, titled *Confidential Notebook,* which he sold for $5 a copy. Launching his own "talent consultant" business, Aware, Inc., Hartnett charged his clients about $20 for each thorough background check. Hartnett used protection-racket tactics against the Borden Milk Company. In an article for *American Legion Magazine,* Hartnett criticized Borden for their sponsorship of Communist sympathizers. Before the article was printed, however, Borden hired Hartnett, at a fee of more than $6,000 for the year. The article that then resulted was a testimonial to the company's commitment to anti-Communism.

Despite efforts by the American Civil Liberties Union and others to protect the guarantees of free speech and thought, by 1952 political screening was almost universally practiced in the television industry, and an elaborate blacklisting machinery was in order. Right-wing groups including the American Legion and the Veterans Action Committee of Syracuse Supermarkets, run by Laurence Johnson, compiled their own lists. Many people who had not previously been listed in *Red Channels* now found that they were "in trouble." Johnson repeatedly threatened to remove manufacturers' products from his stores if they sponsored entertainers he considered pro-Communist.

Newspaper columnists including Walter Winchell, Jimmy Fidler, and Westbrook Pegler encouraged the blacklisting frenzy as they vied to expose "Commies" and "Pinkos." Pegler agreed with Pennsylvania governor James H. Duff that all Communists should be hanged. Actors, commentators, directors, producers, singers, and writers who had been listed in *Red Channels,* cited in *Counterattack,* or otherwise charged with Communist sympathies soon found it virtually impossible to get work in broadcasting without prior clearance.

Clearance involved a lengthy and difficult process of convincing those responsible for an individual's blacklisting that the person had been wrongly listed. A person charged was required to clear him or herself in such a way as to reassure employers that the employer would not run into difficulty if that individual was hired. A worker who wished to be cleared had to provide evidence that he or she was not a Communist or a Communist sympathizer, and in many cases, the person had to show that he or she was "actively" anti-Communist.

For a fee, "public-relations experts" helped with the clearance process. They arranged an FBI interview in which the blacklistee answered questions and declared his or her patriotism. The clearance expert helped to determine where his or her client was blacklisted and who outside the industry was damaging the client's reputation. The process often involved multiple confessions during emotional meetings, after which, if successful, the individual was then considered employable. Some blacklisted writers attempted to sell their scripts under false names. Even when they succeeded, however, they paid out most of their earnings to fronts who represented themselves as the authors.

Blacklisting shattered thousands of lives and destroyed hundreds of careers. For more than 10 years writers, singers, producers, directors, commentators, and actors were denied a right to earn a living. Broadcaster John Henry Faulk's libel suit against Aware, Hartnett, and Johnson, helped end blacklisting in the television industry. In 1957 Faulk was fired by WCBS after he was accused of being a Communist. Following a lengthy court battle, in 1962 Faulk was awarded more than $1 million in damages. Although on appeal the award was reduced to $550,000, the judgment exposed the blacklisting system and began to vindicate those individuals ruined by it.

BONNIE BRENNAN

See also Cold War and the Media; Motion Picture Blacklisting; Sound Motion Pictures

Further Reading
Belfrage, Cedric, *The American Inquisition, 1945–1960,* Indianapolis, Indiana: Bobbs-Merrill, 1973
Caute, David, *The Great Fear: The Anti-Communist Purge Under Truman and Eisenhower,* New York: Simon & Schuster, 1978; London: Secker and Warburg, 1978
Cogley, John, *Report on Blacklisting: Radio-Television,* New York: Fund for the Republic, 1956
Faulk, John Henry, *Fear on Trial,* New York: Simon & Schuster, 1964
Kanfer, Stefan, *A Journal of the Plague Years,* New York: Atheneum, 1973
Miller, Merle, *The Judges and the Judged,* Garden City, New York: Doubleday, 1952; London: Odhams, 1961

Broadcast Competition

Seeking the advantage in the development of new media

Technological innovations that culminated in the phenomenon known as broadcasting date back to the nineteenth century. Broadcasting was not the invention of any one person. A myriad of inventions and their ownership had to be harnessed before broadcasting could develop. At the end of World War I, President Woodrow Wilson identified three industries vital to the American national interest: shipping, petroleum, and communications. However, the Marconi Company, owned chiefly by British citizen and "wireless" innovator Guglielmo Marconi, was in the best position to capture control of this important industry.

To prevent this, three major U.S. corporations – American Telephone and Telegraph (AT&T), General Electric (GE), and Westinghouse – encouraged by the federal government, forced the Marconi company to sell its American interests to them. In 1919, AT&T, GE, and Westinghouse became major stockholders in the newly formed Radio Corporation of America (RCA). With Marconi's interests reduced to minority status, AT&T, GE, and Westinghouse agreed to pool a series of diverse patents that each controlled, and radio was allowed to grow.

Each of the three major corporations operated experimental stations on the AM band. Prior to transmissions of the sort carried out by KDKA, the Westinghouse station in Pittsburgh, Pennsylvania, the practical use of wireless, as radio was first called, was for point-to-point communication. The identity of the first actual broadcast station is a matter on which historians cannot agree. However, many consider KDKA's transmittal of the 1920 election returns, combined with music and other programming intended for anyone interested in listening, to have been the first concerted, continuous attempt at reaching a mass audience simultaneously.

AM Radio Stations and Households with Radio Sets
1921–1990

Year	Radio Stations	Households with Radio Sets	Year	Radio Stations	Households with Radio Sets
1921	1	–	1956	2,896	46,800
1922	30	60	1957	3,079	47,600
1923	556	446	1958	3,253	48,500
1924	530	1,250	1959	3,377	49,450
1925	571	2,750	1960	3,483	50,193
1926	528	4,500	1961	3,602	50,695
1927	681	6,750	1962	3,745	51,305
1928	677	8,000	1963	3,860	52,300
1929	606	10,250	1964	3,976	54,000
1930	618	13,750	1965	4,025	55,200
1931	612	16,700	1966	4,075	57,000
1932	604	18,450	1967	4,135	57,500
1933	598	19,250	1968	4,203	58,500
1934	593	20,400	1969	4,254	60,600
1935	623	21,456	1970	4,288	62,000
1936	656	22,869	1971	4,250	
1937	704	24,500	1972	4,273	
1938	743	26,667	1973	4,295	
1939	778	27,500	1974	4,305	
1940	847	28,500	1975	4,463	71,400
1941	897	29,300	1976		
1942	925	30,600	1977	4,474	
1943	912	30,800	1978	4,459	
1944	924	32,500	1979	4,511	
1945	955	33,100	1980	4,589	78,600
1946	1,215	33,998	1981	4,634	
1947	1,795	35,900	1982	4,668	
1948	2,034	37,623	1983	4,733	
1949	2,066	39,300	1984	4,754	86,700
1950	2,144	40,700	1985	4,718	87,100
1951	2,281	41,900	1986	4,863	88,100
1952	2,355	42,800	1987	4,902	89,900
1953	2,458	44,800	1988	4,932	91,100
1954	2,583	45,100	1989	4,975	92,800
1955	2,732	45,900	1990	4,987	94,400

Notes: Authorization of new radio stations and production of radio receivers for commercial use halted from April 1942 until October 1945 during World War II. Table includes Alaska, Hawaii, Puerto Rico, Guam, and Virgin Islands for all years. Prior to 1948, the FCC did not keep records on the number of stations on the air. Therefore, data for 1933–1948 are for authorized stations and may include a number that were not actually on the air. Figures for Alaska and Hawaii included beginning 1959. In the 1970 census of housing, only battery-operated radios were counted.

Source: Datapedia of the United States 1790–2000: America Year by Year. George Thomas Kurian (Bernan Press: Lanham, Maryland, 1994).

KDKA's success started other stations "broadcasting," and the popularity of this service spread. Nearly 600 radio stations were on the air by 1923. WEAF, the AT&T experimental station, aired the first radio commercial in 1922.

Competition almost proved the downfall of broadcasting. For most of the 1920s, anyone who had the technical and financial resources to build and operate a radio station could do so. Many people did. That all the stations initially had to use the same frequency did not make the budding service any less attractive. Although additional frequencies became available, there were not enough of them to match demand. With new stations added at will, the airwaves degenerated into a cacophony of sound and chaos as station operators changed frequencies and power at will to make themselves heard over the din. Congress finally solved the situation when it passed the Radio Act of 1927. This legislation created the Federal Radio Commission, a federal regulatory agency that was the forerunner of the Federal Communications Commission (FCC), which had the right to assign stations licenses, designate frequencies, and assign power. Federal control over broadcast licensing provided the environment and framework for the service to be able to grow.

In 1926, AT&T withdrew from the broadcasting business. GE, Westinghouse, and RCA formed the National Broadcasting Company to operate the first radio network, the NBC Red Network. It started the NBC Blue Network in 1927.

The NBC monopoly on network broadcasting lasted less than one year. A disagreement over access to the NBC networks led to the creation of the United Independent Broadcasters (UIB) in 1927. UIB was in danger of folding before William S. Paley, the heir to a Chicago cigar fortune, stepped in to buy the company. By then, the company was known as the Columbia Broadcasting System (CBS). Faced with federal government concern about a monopoly on the radio network broadcasting business, GE and Westinghouse sold their NBC interest to RCA in 1932. A fourth radio network appeared in 1934 with the debut of the Mutual Broadcasting Company. Additional government concern over NBC's operation of two networks surfaced in the 1940s. NBC sold its Blue Network, the weaker of the two. The Blue Network became the American Broadcasting Company (ABC) in 1945.

Newspapers envisioned radio as a threat because of radio's ability to be first with the news. In the early 1930s, newspapers attempted to restrict radio's access to news from the wire services the newspapers controlled. By the mid-1930s, however, it was clear that news could not be kept off the radio. As the world moved toward war, radio's ability to provide immediate and often live coverage of events led to increased demand for news and, ironically, more demand for newspapers.

Although there was a quartet of networks, CBS and NBC became chief and bitter rivals for supremacy. After years of trying to beat NBC, CBS succeeded in achieving parity with its rival by offering most of the NBC radio stars lucrative contracts to come to work at CBS. The FCC authorized FM radio service in 1941, the same year it authorized very high frequency (VHF; channels 2 through 13) television service.

Radio became the number-one national entertainment and news medium in the 1930s and enjoyed this status until television claimed that position in the 1950s. Television forced radio to become a local medium with stations fighting for supremacy on a market-by-market basis. The development of domestic satellites led to the development of scores of radio networks capitalizing on the specialized nature of radio. Westwood One bought the Mutual Radio network in 1985 and two years later acquired the NBC radio network. ABC and CBS remained involved in the network radio business into the 1990s.

AM broadcasters, hard put in the 1990s to match the technical superiority of FM radio for delivering music, the staple of radio programming, frequently used news and talk programming to differentiate themselves. Overall, AM radio listening accounted for about 30 percent of the U.S. listening audience; FM services claimed the remaining 70 percent of the audience. This was a virtual reversal of listening data from the early 1970s.

Because of the economics of the radio segment of the broadcast industry, many radio stations turned to satellite-delivered formats for program content. The effect was a more professional sound than a local announcer might provide. The ultimate result was that more and more stations sounded alike because more and more stations were getting their total programming, not just music, from the same sources. In 1995, there were more than 11,000 commercial and noncommercial radio stations on the air.

Over-the-air radio broadcasters faced the possibility of competition from a new service called digital audio broadcasting. This service would use communications satellites to deliver compact disc–quality sound directly to individual radio receivers in homes and cars, eliminating the need for local radio stations, the heart of the radio industry structure in the late twentieth century.

The major radio networks established the business and programming practices for broadcasting. Since the same companies pioneered television broadcasting, they used the radio model of broadcasting supported by the sale of time to advertisers interested in showcasing their goods and services to consumers. RCA maintained its technical research and development interests in broadcasting and was instrumental in developing television as well. RCA demonstrated its version of television at the 1939 World's Fair in New York. AM radio continued to enjoy popularity because television was on hold during World War II while the electronics industry supplied materials for the war effort. Only six television stations operated in the entire country during the war. After the war, Mutual did not attempt to operate a television network. The Dumont Network joined ABC, CBS, and NBC as early television networks; Dumont ceased operation in 1955.

After World War II, demands for television stations inundated the FCC. Faced with a repeat of the 1920s radio fiasco, the FCC instituted a freeze on station applications and licenses in 1948. When the FCC lifted the freeze in 1952, the FCC had established a national television policy that allocated television channels to local communities, authorized broadcasting on the ultrahigh frequency (UHF) band, and designated some channels for educational use. The

Commercial and Non-Commercial Television Stations
1941–1970

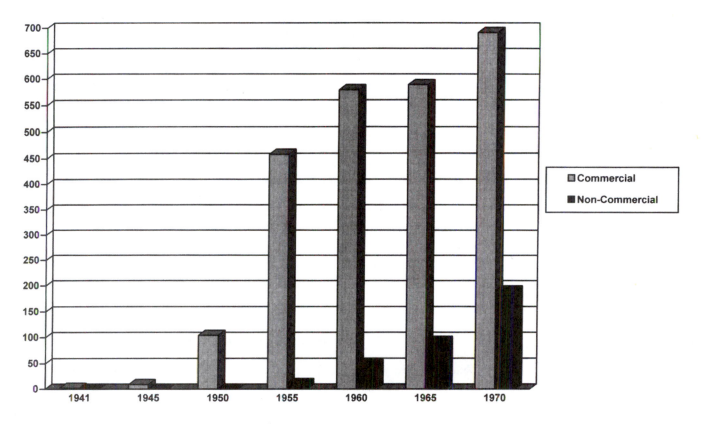

Note: Figures include Alaska, Hawaii, Puerto Rico, Guam, and the Virgin Islands for all years. Prior to 1948, the FCC did not keep records on the number of stations on the air. Therefore, data for 1941–1948 are for authorized stations and may include a number that were not actually on the air.

Source: U.S. Bureau of the Census, *Historical Statistics of the United States: Colonial Times to 1970* (Washington, D.C.: GPO, 1960).

channels reserved for educational use evolved into the Public Broadcasting Service in the late 1960s. The diffusion of television was one of the most remarkable phenomena of the twentieth century. By the mid-1950s, it was clear that television would become a more central force of life in the United States than radio.

In the history of prime-time television, ABC, CBS, and NBC (called the Big Three) took turns being the most-watched network as determined by the ratings, with CBS finishing on top more years than the others. The Big Three had the national television audience to themselves for more than 20 years before cable television began to become a serious competitor. Since its inception during the television freeze, cable television had merely retransmitted existing over-the-air television station signals. In the 1970s, cable television started offering new, unique, or original programming. As a result of this and other competition, the Big Three's share of the prime-time television audience dropped from routinely more than 90 percent in the 1970s to less than 60 percent in the 1994–95 season. In addition to cable

television, an increase in the amount of television programming led to the start of many UHF stations that had been dormant since the FCC freeze was lifted in 1952.

The rise of cable television's popularity began when Home Box Office (HBO) began to distribute programming to cable systems in 1972 by microwave relay. In 1975, however, domestic satellites allowed HBO access to a method of distribution that was more efficient than microwave and could cover a larger area. Later that year, WTBS, a UHF television station owned by Ted Turner, became the first superstation. Turner used satellites to relay his station signal initially intended for the Atlanta, Georgia, market to any cable system operator that needed programming to fill up available channels. Both services filled the need to provide programming that was not available from network affiliates. The HBO and WTBS success stories launched numerous imitators. A series of court rulings gave cable access to the largest markets out of which broadcasters had successfully kept them out for years. Cable penetration increased from less than one-half of 1 percent of U.S. homes in the early 1950s to nearly 68 percent in 1995.

As competition from cable increased, ABC, CBS, and NBC faced another competitor. In 1985, Australian media baron Rupert Murdoch became a naturalized U.S. citizen and bought the Twentieth Century-Fox television and motion production company and six television stations. He proceeded to build a fourth network, the Fox network, and started affiliating other independent stations. In 1995, two additional broadcast networks were started. Warner Communications and Paramount, two major television and production companies, started their own television networks, the WB Network and the United Paramount Network (UPN), respectively. It remained to be seen how many of these six networks would survive.

In addition to competition from cable, television broadcasters faced competition from a series of other media vehicles that were or could be alternative delivery systems. In the 1980s, the FCC established low power television stations and multichannel multipoint distribution service (also called wireless cable). In 1994, two direct broadcast satellite services launched and offered up to 150 channels of programming available directly to homes from satellite. Demand for one of the services was so great during the 1994 Christmas shopping season that there was a backlog on receiver orders.

The telephone companies would also have liked to enter the home video delivery business. From 1984, however, the law barred them from the business, although the telephone companies were vigorously lobbying Congress to change the law at the end of the century. The development of the electronic superhighway, a two-way interactive voice, audio, and data delivery mechanism, attracted the interest of the telephone companies.

In the late-twentieth-century information age, broadcasting was no longer the sole delivery system for audio and video material. Its future would depend on how well it adapted to a significantly more competitive environment than it knew for most of its existence.

JAMES PHILLIP JETER

See also Broadcast Talk Shows; Cable Networks; Radio Act of 1927; Radio Networks; Radio News; Radio Technology; Television Networks; Television Technology

Further Reading
Gross, Lynne, *Telecommunications: An Introduction to Electronic Media,* 4th ed., Dubuque, Iowa: Wm. C. Brown, 1992

Broadcast Documentaries
Presenting factual material over broadcast media

The television documentary has roots in documentary photography and movies, newsreels, factual drama on radio, and documentary phonograph recordings. It also borrowed heavily from other motion picture forms, including feature films and travelogues. By the 1990s, the documentary film on a single topic was rare on the four major entertainment networks, having been replaced by magazine-style documentaries that presented several shorter stories. The documentary, based on radio traditions of the 1940s and early 1950s, began on television in the early 1950s, exploded in number, and then declined during the 1960s. The factual form on television evolved because of regulatory pressure for public affairs programming and in response to criticism of the networks after the quiz show scandals of 1958.

Despite controversies and threats to cut federal financing in the 1980s and 1990s, the Public Broadcasting Service continued several excellent anthology series covering public affairs (*Frontline*), science (*Nova* and *Nature*), and history (*American Experience*). Each week most noncommercial television stations also carried several one-time-only documentaries covering a wide variety of subjects. Several cable channels (Discovery, Arts and Entertainment, and its spin-off, the History Channel) devoted a large part of their programming to documentaries of many different styles. Other cable services also used the documentary format for occasional programs – often historical compilations about celebrities, sports, and popular culture or "hidden camera" exposés (usually salacious) such as *Real Sex* on HBO. The format and style of the documentary was also carefully imitated to sell products (so-called infomercials) and to promote new feature films ("The Making of" . . . a particular film title).

Television documentaries brought much glory and respect to the original three networks. They continued to produce traditional documentaries on topics of great importance (e.g., AIDS, the Persian Gulf War, and Bosnia) or of particular interest or when news executives could persuade the network to carry them.

The broadcast documentary dates to the first seasons of radio, when "informative dramas" such as *Biblical Dramas* and *Great Moments in History* appeared. The *March of Time,* which dramatized several important news stories each week with actors imitating known people, began on CBS in 1931. *March of Time* lasted for 13 seasons on radio, was partly responsible for the development of the *March of Time* newsreel series, and was a precursor to the later form of the docudrama television movie.

Numerous dramatized news and historical dramas (many produced by, or in cooperation with, the government for propaganda purposes) appeared on the radio networks during and just after World War II. *You Are There,* a series with real CBS reporters covering dramatized historical events, began on radio in 1947 and moved to television in 1953. Just after the 1950 general elections, Edward R. Murrow, who had gained fame as a war correspondent, tried a new radio format the announcer introduced as "a document for ear." *Hear It Now* was partly based on an earlier phonograph documentary series (*I Can Hear It Now,* 1949), was produced with Fred Friendly, and used the new technology of audiotape to capture the news sounds of the week. After one season Murrow and Friendly took the format to television, using film for reportage.

Film shot by military and newsreel cameramen during the war, combined with that taken from the Germans and

An American Family, a portrayal of real-life people, was produced for public television by Thirteen/WNET in 1973.
(Courtesy of Thirteen/WNET)

Japanese, contributed to the first wave of compilation documentaries. *Crusade in Europe* – produced by the *March of Time* team and based on General Dwight D. Eisenhower's memoir – and *Victory at Sea* were pioneering series. They earned accolades for their networks and revealed a significant audience for such programming. Often less expensive to produce than original drama programs, they have been repeated on their original networks, in syndication, and by cable services.

Although television provided live coverage of many important events – political conventions, elections, tragedies, and congressional hearings – it was not until the Murrow-Friendly collaboration moved to television that the traditional public affairs and issue documentary series was born. On November 18, 1951, soon after AT&T completed a television connection between the east and west coasts, *See It Now* began with the announcement that it was "a documentary for television" – apparently the first use of the word. *See It Now* began as a magazine-style program with several topics or stories in a half hour, but soon it often did just one "documentary" investigation each week. The most controversial of these was about Senator Joseph McCarthy, an assemblage mostly of his own speeches and interviews, broadcast on March 9, 1954.

This and other controversial programs, low ratings, and the lack of a sponsor caused CBS to cancel *See It Now* after the 1958 season. In November 1959, however, the network began a new series, *CBS Reports,* with Friendly as producer. This program, and the incredible explosion of documentary programming in general, was attributed to the quiz show scandals of 1958, in which it was revealed that the producers of a number of big-money quiz programs had rigged the games' outcome. After the cancellation of *See It Now*, Murrow described a week of television as "evidence of decadence, escapism and insulation from the realities of the world in which we live." A year later, in a speech referring to the quiz show scandals, CBS President Frank Stanton noted that broadcasting had lost "the public trust and confidence," and he announced that his network would schedule "regular hour-long informational broadcasts once a month in prime evening time."

In January 1960, FCC chairman John Doerfer proposed that each network devote at least one evening hour a week to informational, educational, or cultural programming. The networks quickly agreed. As a result of this promise, *CBS Reports* became a weekly program in January 1961. (In later years, the title was used for occasional, prestigious documentaries.) On NBC, new documentary series included *White Paper* and weekly programs hosted by Chet Huntley and David Brinkley.

The total amount of prime-time documentary programming declined steadily and steeply after its peak in the early 1960s from more than 200 hours to about 150 hours a year. From the late 1970s through the 1980s, it averaged about 50 hours per year.

A small but important subgenre of documentary programs also started in the early 1960s. NBC and CBS, with more popular programming, better affiliates, and greater revenues than ABC, produced about twice as many documentary hours through the 1980s. This led to ABC's development of cinema verité, or direct cinema, television documentaries. Robert Drew, experienced as a photojournalist, experimented with motion picture film to record events as they happened – as if the camera were just an observant fly on the wall. Drew and Associates produced a fascinating series of documentaries. After beginning with "Primary," which documented the contest between John Kennedy and Hubert Humphrey in the spring 1960 Wisconsin primary, they provided an inside look at auto racing, school integration, President Kennedy's first months in office, capital punishment, and the first black students at the University of Alabama.

Cinema verité became the form for many rock concert and celebrity profile documentaries in the 1960s. More importantly, it contributed a new style for some network documentaries; for example, *Berkeley Rebels, Ku Klux Klan,* and *Sixteen in Webster Groves* on CBS in 1965 and 1966. The style was developed further by independent filmmakers whose work was often seen on PBS. Cinema verité style also was adapted by movies and television as a way of indicating candid or seemingly truthful storytelling.

While NBC and CBS had done a few "instant documentaries" – a middle ground between live coverage and the long-in-production documentary – in the 1950s, early in the 1960s both created special units and programs to produce very fast, detailed coverage of important events. Often, these were broadcast just after local stations' late-night news broadcasts. In the fall of 1979, ABC began doing just such an instant documentary soon after the taking of U.S. hostages in Iran. By March 21, 1980, that program had evolved into *Nightline.*

As the documentary developed, a number of critics and broadcasters noted that not all topics were important or interesting enough for full-hour treatment, and the television magazine was reinvented. With Ford Foundation financing, the *Public Broadcasting Laboratory* began in the fall of 1967. Usually running two hours, it offered several significant documentary segments as well as interviews, debate, commentary, and sometimes comedy or entertainment features.

In the fall of 1968, *60 Minutes* began alternating on Tuesday nights with the *CBS News Hour,* the generic title for traditional documentaries. Usually offering three documentary segments per episode, after three seasons *60 Minutes* became a weekly series and eventually became one of CBS' most highly rated programs. NBC and ABC copied the format in *First Tuesday* and *20/20.*

Quality fare continued to be offered by public broadcasting. Funded by federal, state, and local contributions, viewer donations, and corporate underwriting, public television presented the most important, elaborate, revealing, and controversial documentaries. PBS generally offered a long (usually at least 13 hours, and often a compilation form) documentary series each season. *Vietnam: A Television History* (1983); *Heart of the Dragon,* about China (1985); *The Story of English* (1986); *Eyes on the Prize,* about the civil rights movement (1987); *War and Peace in the Nuclear Age* (1989); *The Civil War* (1990); and *Baseball* (1994) are examples.

LAWRENCE W. LICHTY

See also Broadcast Newsmagazines; Docudramas; Motion Picture Documentaries; Noncommercial Television; Quiz Show Scandals

Further Reading

Barnouw, Erik, *Documentary: A History of the Non-Fiction Film,* rev. ed., Oxford: Oxford University Press, 1983; 2nd rev. ed., New York: Oxford University Press, 1993

Bluem, A. William, *Documentary in American Television: Form, Function [and] Method,* New York: Hastings House, 1965

Campbell, Richard, *'60 Minutes' and the News: A Mythology for Middle America,* Urbana: University of Illinois Press, 1991

Friendly, Fred W., *Due To Circumstances Beyond Our*

Control . . ., New York: Random House, 1967; London: MacGibbon & Kee, 1967

Hewitt, Don, *Minute by Minute,* New York: Random House, 1985

Lichty, Lawrence W., and Thomas W. Bohn, "Radio's *March of Time*: Dramatized News," *Journalism Quarterly* 51:3 (1974)

Rosteck, Thomas, *'See It Now' Confronts McCarthyism: Television Documentary and the Politics of Representation,* Tuscaloosa: University of Alabama Press, 1994

Yellin, David G., *Special: Fred Freed and the Television Documentary,* New York: Macmillan, 1973

Broadcast Editorials

Taking a public stand on the air

Although Congress began regulating radio broadcasting in 1927, it took several decades to finally determine whether station operators could use their facilities to editorialize – that is, to take a public stand on the air. The print media had long published editorials about public concerns, and some broadcast licensees felt they should have the same rights under the First Amendment. In 1941, the Federal Communications Commission (FCC) made its first definitive ruling on the issue. The case involved a Boston station, WAAB, which was seeking renewal of its license. The station had been airing broadcasts in which it supported various candidates for political office and took stands on public issues.

The FCC told WAAB that its license would be renewed only if it stopped editorializing. This ruling became known as the Mayflower Decision, a name derived from the Mayflower Broadcasting Corporation, which had applied for the frequency used by WAAB. The commission said:

> A truly free radio cannot be used to advocate the causes of a licensee. It cannot be used to support the candidacies of his friends. It cannot be devoted to the support of principles he happens to regard most favorably. In brief, the broadcaster cannot be an advocate.

Individual citizens, broadcasters, and the National Association of Broadcasters objected to the FCC position, and in 1949, the FCC reversed itself by enacting the Fairness Doctrine. The doctrine gave stations the right to editorialize. Stations were not obligated to do so but, if they did, they had an affirmative duty to seek out contrasting viewpoints. In a 1960 policy statement, the FCC more directly endorsed editorializing, identifying it as one of 14 program elements stations could use to serve the public interest.

Several individual provisions of the Fairness Doctrine have spelled out specific rules regarding editorials. One provision, the personal attack rule, was added in 1967. It says that if a station broadcasts an attack on the honesty, character, integrity, or like personal qualities of an identified person or group during an editorial or similar presentation, then the station is obligated to provide a right of reply to the person or group.

A similar provision applies to political endorsements. If a station editorializes for or against a candidate for office, a right of reply is required. If a candidate is endorsed in an editorial, all other legally qualified candidates for that office must be offered reply time. If a station's editorial opposes a candidate, the station must notify the candidate and offer reply time.

Studies of editorial practices show that the opportunity to editorialize has not been universally embraced by broadcast stations and has declined since the mid-1980s. Figures on the number of stations editorializing vary from 56 percent of stations in 1967 to a high of 78 percent of top-50 market television stations in 1972.

Broadcast stations never have widely employed personal attacks or political endorsements. The 1967 study reported that only 9 percent of stations said they endorsed political candidates, a figure that grew slightly to 11 percent in 1976.

The decline in editorializing in the mid-1980s came from a change in business conditions. Many broadcast stations were faced with heavy debt payments and a soft advertising market that affected certain programming practices including editorializing. Industry support for editorializing eroded, and in the early 1990s, the National Broadcast Editorial Association, which had 100 members in 1986, disbanded.

A 1991 study of editorial practices at television stations reflected the decrease in editorializing, with just 30 percent of stations saying they editorialized. Of those that did editorialize, however, 11 percent said their station endorsed political candidates, the same as in 1977, and 27 percent of the stations reported broadcasting personal attacks, up from 11 percent in 1977.

The respondents to the 1991 survey also reported some differences in the presentations of editorials they broadcast. While the most popular length for an editorial in 1977 was two minutes, one minute was the most popular length in 1991. A third of the 1991 sample also said they shot some of their editorials on location, an apparent desire to add visual variety to the editorials. The 1991 respondents who did not editorialize cited two reasons for not doing so. One was a lack of budget, and the other was a lack of time and staff to prepare the editorials.

MILAN D. MEESKE

See also Fairness Doctrine; Mayflower Decision; Personal Attack Rule

Further Reading

Fang, Irving E., and John W. Whelan, Jr., "Survey of Television Editorials and Ombudsman Segments," *Journal of Broadcasting* 17 (1973)

Meeske, Milan, "Editorial Practices of Television Stations," *Journalism Quarterly* 55 (1978)

Smith, Dillon, "Budget Ax Hits Television Editorials," *Washington Journalism Review* 13:3 (April 1991), p. 46

Spiceland, Roy David, Jr., *The Fairness Doctrine, the Chilling Effect, and Television Editorials* (Ph.D. diss., University of Tennessee), 1992

Broadcast Interview Shows

Winning listeners and viewers by asking guests questions

Interview shows have been a staple of both radio and television programming because they are relatively simple and easy to produce yet retain the interest of listeners and viewers through the continual introduction of new guests and topics. Like discussion and talk programs, interview shows generally adopt a simple, direct presentation style, and the difference among the forms is more a matter of degree than an opposition of value or style. All these forms emphasize verbal exchanges over action or visual effects, but discussion shows generally have multiple guests offering opinions on a topic, making the topic rather than the identities of the participants central to the program. The strategies employed by talk shows run the gamut from discussion and interview episodes to confrontations between estranged lovers or feuding neighbors. Talk shows may have episodes featuring matchmaking, makeup and fashion, or audience participation.

The narrower focus of interview shows makes the guests themselves the primary topic of the program. The efforts of the host are devoted to interrogation of the guest, and the relationship between interviewer and subject is of primary importance. Although the interviewer may refer to the fact that he or she is serving as a representative of the audience, interview shows rarely accommodate direct participation from audience members. Whether the style of the interviewer is sympathetic, inquisitive, or confrontational, the focus remains on the words and views of the interview subject.

During the 1920s, simple interview segments were included in the earliest commercial radio programming, with variety show hosts carrying on short chat segments with their performer-guests. As radio programming – particularly news programming – matured in the 1930s, interviewing evolved from an adjunct to performance to a distinct programming element. Both entertainment and information programs began to include longer interview segments. The practice of on-air interviewing became an art in itself as hosts and commentators competed to coax interesting and informative material from their guests. However, interview segments generally remained one portion of longer shows.

Dave Garroway, seated, ran an informal interview format program on the early *Today Show.*
(Museum of Broadcast Communications)

Lawrence E. Spivak, left, was host of the Sunday morning standard, *Meet the Press*.
(Museum of Broadcast Communications)

A notable step in the development of the interview show as a freestanding program came with the 1945 appearance of *Meet the Press* in the wake of World War II. It was created by Martha Rountree and Lawrence Spivak in conjunction with the *American Mercury* magazine. The durable *Meet the Press* featured noted journalists interviewing public figures, and the program not only made a successful transition to television but marked its fiftieth year in 1995. Moderators of the program over the years included Rountree, Spivak, Ned Brooks, Bill Monroe, Marvin Kalb, and Chris Wallace.

In 1953, Edward R. Murrow's *Person to Person* became a landmark program in the development of the celebrity interview. In those very early days of network television, the *Person to Person* crews undertook the difficult and time-consuming task of broadcasting live from the celebrity's home. Murrow, from his studio vantage point, received the same tour that the at-home viewer was getting. Guests ranged from scientists to politicians, from entertainers to clerics. Murrow hosted the program until 1959 when Charles Collingwood assumed the role of interviewer.

In the developmental years of network television broadcasting, magazine shows assumed an important role in the development of broadcast program formats – including the interview. NBC's *Today Show, Tonight Show,* and *Omnibus* all contributed to broadening the range of interview topics and approaches to the broadcast interview. In its many incarnations, the *Tonight Show* acquired a large following and exposed viewers to numerous interview styles. With Steve Allen at the helm from 1954 through 1956, the interviews were chatty and casual, more a conversation than a question-and-answer session. When Allen began to rotate hosting responsibilities with a series of guest hosts, the interview strategies varied according to the host. In 1957, the emotionally intense Jack Paar assumed hosting responsibilities, and his interviews become the primary strength of the program. Paar became involved with his guests' stories and was passionate in the discussion of many topics. His volatility and his well-publicized feuds with other celebrities and his network employers sparked a good deal of viewer interest in the program. When Paar left the program in 1962, a six-month series of guest hosts ended with the appointment of Johnny Carson. With Carson, the interview portion of the program returned to a more conversational approach, and the importance of sketches and guest performances increased. The mix seemed successful, and various late-night competitors over the next decades, including Merv Griffin, Joey Bishop, Joan Rivers, and Alan Thicke, failed to present a serious challenge to Carson's late-night ratings supremacy.

In 1969, competition among the interview shows flared briefly in prime time. ABC tried out a prime-time interview show with Dick Cavett at the helm. Although some musical and dramatic interludes were incorporated into the program, it was – at the heart – an interview show. Cavett spiced the usual menu of movie stars and sports figures with the addition of philosophers, political analysts, and artists, but the mass audiences simply did not respond. Cavett's fans were enthusiastic and loyal, but there simply were not enough of them to keep the show on the air after 1972. Cavett enjoyed a very brief return to the air in 1986, but this show, too, suffered from low ratings and was canceled after just three months. British satirist David Frost appeared in a syndicated offering from 1969 to 1972 that presented a more conventional choice of guests than Cavett's program and generally treated those guests with the greatest courtesy, if not reverence.

The next notable change in the status and style of the interview program came in 1980 with the conversion of ABC's Monday-through-Thursday reports on the Iranian hostage crisis to a regularly scheduled news program called *Nightline*. As anchor of the nightly program, Ted Koppel proved to be a skilled interviewer, handling difficult interview subjects and difficult topics with aplomb. Koppel's treatment of serious information built a loyal audience for a form that had not previously been successful in the late-night time period.

Another ABC news anchor possessing noteworthy interviewing skills was Barbara Walters. After an unsuccessful trial in the anchor's chair, Walters launched an irregular series of celebrity interview specials that earned her Emmy awards for best interviewer in 1982 and 1983. The interview specials were a combination of Murrow's sociable tours of the celebrity's property and a more serious one-on-one session that covered private and sensitive topics. In 1995, the entire series was repackaged and aired as *Barbara Walters – Interviews of a Lifetime*.

In 1986, Robin Leach translated the public hunger for inside information on the stars into a successful, if superficial, series called *Lifestyles of the Rich and Famous*. The most successful of numerous series focusing on the minutiae of celebrity style, *Lifestyles* offered attractive production venues to offset the rather insipid nature of its interviews. In network radio in the 1990s, most of the substantive interviewing was conducted under the auspices of National Public Radio.

KAY WALSH

See also Broadcast Newsmagazines; Broadcast Talk Shows; Commercialization of Broadcasting; Noncommercial Radio; Radio News

Further Reading

Brooks, Tim, *The Complete Directory to Prime Time TV Stars, 1946 to Present*, New York: Ballantine, 1987
_____, and Earle Marsh, *The Complete Directory to Prime Time Network TV Shows, 1946 to Present*, 4th ed., New York: Ballantine, 1988
MacDonald, J. Fred, *Don't Touch That Dial!: Radio Programming in American Life, 1920–1960*, Chicago: Nelson-Hall, 1979

Broadcast Journalism: *see* Cable News; Radio News; Television News

Broadcast Labor Organizations

Numerous organizations represent broadcast employees

As in other businesses, employees in electronic mass communication may organize in trade unions and use collective bargaining to improve wages, conditions, and other elements of work. Larger outlets (e.g., stations or cable systems) in larger cities may have at least two unions, one for creative personnel and another for technicians. Broadcast television networks each work with numerous unions; however, the smaller the outlet, the less likely employees are to be unionized.

Organizations representing creative employees are usually called guilds, while those representing technicians are termed unions. Both are structured similarly. Employees – for example, a station's engineering staff – form a local union, which is chartered by a national union, such as the National Association of Broadcast Employees and Technicians (NABET). National unions that are similar may form a federation. At the top, the American Federation of Labor–Congress of Industrial Workers came to speak for all labor in dealing with government and the public.

The first union to affect broadcasting was the American Federation of Musicians (AFM). When radio began, musicians and performers broadcast free for the sake of novelty. In 1922, though, James C. Petrillo, president of the AFM's Chicago local, demanded that musicians be paid to broadcast. Most stations produced no revenue; the licensee paid for station operation out of pocket. The AFM's demand helped raised the issue of how broadcasting would be financed.

Broadcast employees began unionizing in 1926. That year the International Brotherhood of Electrical Workers (IBEW), primarily an electricians' group, organized engineers at KMOX in St. Louis, Missouri. The station refused to negotiate, so KMOX's engineers went on strike. After a week, KMOX agreed to recognize the IBEW as the bargaining agent for its technical staff, and the strike ended. The IBEW eventually enrolled all St. Louis broadcasting technicians, then went on to other cities. CBS purchased KMOX in 1931, and the IBEW organized the network's technical staff.

The first union just for broadcasting employees formed in 1933. A group of NBC technicians and engineers organized as the Association of Technical Employees (ATE) and successfully negotiated a network contract.

In April 1935, Congress passed the National Labor Relations Act (NLRA), the federal government's first comprehensive support of collective bargaining; organized labor thrived. Encouraged by NLRA and the rapid development of network radio, broadcasting employees accelerated unionizing activities. The Radio Directors Guild (RDG) formed in 1935, and the Radio Writers Guild (RWG) began in the late 1930s. In 1954, the RWG merged with the Screen Writers Guild, Dramatist Guild, and other groups to form the Writers Guild of America, West, and the Writers Guild of America, East. The RDG changed its name to the Radio and Television Directors Guild and in 1958 merged with the

Screen Directors Guild to become the Directors Guild of America.

At KMOX in 1937, performers first organized as the American Federation of Radio Artists (AFRA). In New York, the AFRA won contract acceptance by the networks and the right to represent radio actors who worked directly for advertising agencies and sponsors. It then organized stations and regional networks.

The ATE (the NBC technicians' union) began expanding. By 1940, it was renamed National Association of Broadcast Engineers and Technicians. The IBEW was also expanding, and the two technical unions had frequent jurisdictional disputes during the 1940s. The NABET enlarged its scope and, when nontechnical personnel joined, changed the word Engineers in its name to Employees. In 1943, the U.S. Supreme Court's *National Broadcasting Co. v. United States* ruling forced divestiture of NBC's Blue Network (later the American Broadcasting Company), and the NABET went along as the union with jurisdictional influence.

In 1940, a federal court ruled that musicians' rights to compensation for music performed on a recording ended with the sale of the record. The AFM's Petrillo, then the national president, demanded that broadcasters pay a fee whenever they used recorded music more than once. Talks with the networks broke down; in 1942, the AFM voted to stop making recordings. Petrillo refused to lift the ban, even for the national effort in World War II. He finally settled in 1943 and 1944 when broadcasters and record companies agreed to a trust fund and royalties for recordings.

In 1943, Petrillo banned NBC broadcasts from the Interlochen, Michigan, music camp because the student musicians were not union members. In 1944, he demanded that platter turners, technicians who handled recordings during broadcast, be AFM members. The NABET challenged this and won, except in Petrillo's Chicago.

Petrillo also felt that the practice of FM stations duplicating programming of co-owned AM stations cheated musicians out of jobs. He demanded that networks and co-owned AM-FM stations hire duplicate orchestras. Not sure how television might fit in, he forbade musicians to play for that medium. In 1946, Congress nullified Petrillo's duplicate orchestra demand. Under the Lea Act, forcing stations to featherbed (i.e., to hire unneeded personnel) was unlawful. In 1947, the U.S. Supreme Court upheld the Lea Act, and Congress passed the Labor-Management Relations Act. Dubbed the Taft-Hartley Act for its chief sponsors, this law aimed to reduce the power of unions. Petrillo finally dropped his duplicate orchestra demand for AM-FM simulcasts.

When television began to grow, unions already in broadcasting viewed it as an extension of radio and worked to expand jurisdiction to this new medium. But television programs required elements unknown in radio – settings, makeup, wardrobe, graphics, lighting, and cameras. A further complication involved the production medium. Many early programs used electronic cameras and transmitted live, as they were performed. Some, however, were produced on film and could be aired repeatedly; in this respect, television was an extension of theater and movies, so unions from those areas moved in. The International Al-liance of Theatrical Stage Employees and Moving Picture Machine Operators, for example – a union for theatrical and movie craft and technical personnel – felt it had a stake in television. During the 1950s, the National Labor Relations Board had to resolve jurisdictional battles among the IATSE, the NABET, the IBEW, and other unions attempting to organize television employees.

In 1950, the Television Authority, formed years earlier by performers' groups, negotiated the first television network performers contract. Shortly after, the Television Authority merged with the AFRA, and in 1952 the merged organization became the American Federation of Television and Radio Artists (AFTRA). Screen Actors Guild (SAG), the movie performers' group, challenged the AFTRA's jurisdictional claim over both electronic and film television. The National Labor Relations Board agreed with the SAG. This meant that the SAG would represent performers in television film production while the AFTRA would in live (and, later, videotaped) production. Most television actors joined both. Eventually the two guilds began working together to standardize contract terms. In 1958, they started joint bargaining for television commercials. Merger discussions begun in 1980 were still under way in early 1995.

In 1952, SAG negotiations established the concept of residuals – payment for working on a program during production and for each time that program was rerun. Other creative guilds expanded the concept to cover work by writers and directors and to include other types of productions, most notably commercials.

During the early 1950s, the AFTRA became involved in blacklisting. A group of AFTRA members who supported Aware, Inc., a blacklisting agency, sought and won election to the union's board of directors. The implicit threat of Aware's witch-hunting tactics scared off challengers, so the pro-Aware majority was reelected until 1955, when an anti-Communist and anti-Aware slate won 27 of the 35 board seats.

Unions representing broadcast employees have used strikes over the years at both local and network levels. The NABET, for example, struck NBC in 1942 and 1959 and ABC in 1958 and 1967. The IBEW struck CBS in 1958. The Writers Guild staged a summer 1988 strike that delayed the start of the television season that fall.

One memorable strike took place in 1967. The networks balked at accepting an AFTRA wage proposal for news personnel at network-owned stations, and in March, the union called its first national walkout. On-camera network employees, in both news and entertainment, did no broadcast work and took turns on the picket line. Sixteen other unions joined the AFTRA. The 13-week strike prevented broadcast of any live network programs except news, for which supervisors and other nonunion personnel handled operational and talent duties. Some news staffers, however, felt that the AFTRA was an entertainer's union and not appropriate to represent journalists. A few did not honor the strike. When the NABET struck ABC later that year, the AFTRA supported the strike, but many news staffers still felt dissatisfied with the AFTRA and refused to honor the NABET picket lines.

Strikes by unions outside electronic media have affected

programming. A professional baseball players' strike, for example, canceled games and telecasts at the end of the 1994 season and threatened the opening of the 1995 season. Hockey players struck in the fall of 1994, canceling televised matches until the strike was settled later in the season.

Cable television's growth during the 1970s and 1980s attracted both the IBEW and the Communication Workers of America (CWA), a telephone workers' union. The CWA pushed particularly hard to organize cable employees. Overall, however, electronic media unions lost membership and influence during the 1980s and early 1990s, victims of automation and corporate downsizing.

Among other unions active in electronic media were the American Guild of Variety Artists, the International Brotherhood of Teamsters, and many specialized locals, such as the Motion Picture and Videotape Editors Guild Local 776 (IATSE).

F. LESLIE SMITH

See also Broadcast Blacklisting

Further Reading

Austin, Henry R., "The Maddy-Petrillo Controversy," *Journal of Broadcasting* 14:3 (1970)
Brody, David, *In Labor's Cause: Main Themes on the History of the American Worker,* New York: Oxford University Press, 1993
Filippelli, Ronald L., *Labor in the USA : A History,* New York: Knopf, 1984
Koenig, Allen E., "AFTRA and Contract Negotiations," *Journal of Broadcasting* 7 (1962–63)
_____, "AFTRA Decision Making," *Journal of Broadcasting* 9 (1965)
_____, ed., *Broadcasting and Bargaining: Labor Relations in Radio and Television,* Madison: University of Wisconsin Press, 1970
_____, "Labor Relations in the Broadcasting Industry: Periodical Literature 1937–1964," *Journal of Broadcasting* 9 (1965)
Leiter, Robert David, *The Musicians and Petrillo,* New York: Bookman, 1953

Broadcast Licensing

Government supervision of the broadcast media

As wireless transmission stations sprang up early in the twentieth century, Congress passed the Radio Act of 1912, giving the secretary of commerce the task of issuing licenses to radiotelephone operators but without providing any power of sanctions. In the following decade stations proliferated, causing havoc with listeners' reception as they arbitrarily shifted their transmitting frequencies and power. Broadcasters urged Congress to rescue senders and receivers. It responded with the Radio Act of 1927, creating the Federal Radio Commission (FRC) to license stations and to penalize them, even to the point of revoking licenses, if they failed to serve the general "public interest, convenience, and necessity." The basic rationale lay in the nature

of the electromagnetic spectrum of frequencies as a limited natural resource; the government was to oversee its best use on behalf of the citizenry. Congress created the FRC as a "traffic cop" of technical engineering, mandating it to ensure that the airwaves were used to serve the public. Courts through the decades interpreted that to imply some oversight of program content as well as radiated signals. The Communications Act of 1934 forwarded those principles, reconstituting the regulatory agency as the Federal Communications Commission (FCC), which continued to issue, monitor, renew, and revoke broadcast licenses as the twentieth century drew to a close.

The FCC granted licenses based on data submitted by applicants about themselves, their finances, related business involvement, and program plans. Into the 1970s, detailed outlines of program types and percentages of airtime were submitted at triennial renewals, so the commission could compare applicants' initial promise to their performance over the three years – or to compare with counter-applicants seeking their spectrum frequency. Consumer activism that challenged licenses at renewal times in the 1960s and 1970s faded in the 1980s, partly because the multiplicity of radio, television, and cable services undercut the argument of scarcity. The heavy underbrush of paperwork and procedures that accrued had become less purposeful in ensuring substantive program service, so successive Democratic- and Republican-affiliated FCC chairmen sought to reduce regulations imposed on licensees. The trustee model on behalf of the public interest yielded to the marketplace model responding to popular support of program service (this was mostly a marketplace of economic forces rather than of ideas). Congressional reaction to the FCC's widespread reduction of its rules prompted a return to modest regulation in the 1990s, especially regarding alleged indecency and violations of equal employment guidelines.

The commission expanded limits on terms of license (from three years, to seven for radio and five for television stations) and on the numbers of stations a single licensee could own (from seven each for AM, FM, and television up to 12 each; then to 18, 18, and 12, respectively; and then to 20, 20, and 12), with further extensions planned. The agency deleted from application forms most details about program categories or formats; it reduced voluminous license renewal applications to postcard-size forms. The FCC levied forfeitures (fines) infrequently and rarely issued short-term renewals or revocations. The circumstances under which the FCC might take those actions included licensees' lack of candor (lying) in responding to the commission or "repeated and willful" violations of technical matters; alleged indecency; equal employment opportunity shortcomings; excessive commercial time in children's programming; and public inspection file lapses. Over the decades, licensees felt penalized more by the extensive time and enormous legal fees required to respond to even routine FCC inquiries.

JAMES A. BROWN

See also Broadcast Regulation; Communications Act of 1934; Federal Communications Commission; Federal Radio Commission; Radio Act of 1912; Radio Act of 1927

Broadcast Newsmagazines

Blending journalism and entertainment to win audiences

The "yardstick for all other news programs" began inauspiciously on a Tuesday night in 1968. CBS's *60 Minutes* was "news of different order, designed to make waves, entertain, and score big in the ratings." It bounced around the schedule for a few years before settling into Sunday nights in 1975. Thereafter, *60 Minutes* became one of the longest-running and most profitable programs in broadcast history.

From the first, it was a blend of journalism and entertainment – high drama and fluff. Two men were most closely associated with the program from its beginning – executive producer and creator Don Hewitt and reporter Mike Wallace. Hewitt said, "It's impossible to describe Mike Wallace's contributions to *60 Minutes* because Mike Wallace is *60 Minutes.*" In a career that started in 1939, Wallace did most everything – acting, hosting game shows and talk shows, and reporting. He developed his adversarial style on *Night Beat,* a late-night interview series he hosted on the Dumont Network in New York in 1956. Wallace's role on *60 Minutes* was to be the "guy in the black hat" to counter coanchor Harry Reasoner's kindly demeanor.

Don Hewitt was the first permanent director of CBS's evening news program in the 1950s. The term "producer" became part of broadcasting's dictionary when Hewitt combined the responsibilities for the look and editorial content of the program into one job that he called "producer." He was not in the scholar-journalist mold of Edward R. Murrow, Charles Collingwood, or Eric Severeid, but more of Hollywood and the show business aspects of television. Despite Hewitt's success with the evening news, he was fired as producer in 1964. Hewitt came close to leaving CBS but then created *60 Minutes,* changing television news forever.

The popularity and financial success of *60 Minutes* spawned a host of imitators, the most successful of which was ABC's *20/20.* It debuted in June 1978, almost 10 years after *60 Minutes.* Like *60 Minutes,* it took time to find an audience, but ABC's patience was rewarded. The program did well for many years in its Friday night time period, proving the point made by Edward Fouhy, a former news executive for all three networks, who said, "Once established, news shows last forever."

Another of the longer-running newsmagazines was ABC's *Nightline.* The late-night program was the result of a news event – the taking of U.S. hostages by Iran for more than a year beginning in 1980. ABC aired a nightly update called *America Held Hostage,* hosted by Frank Reynolds. The program was so successful that when the hostage crisis ended, ABC retained the program, renaming it *Nightline* and giving the host duties to Ted Koppel. Unlike most of the newsmagazine programs, *Nightline* was put together just hours before it aired, giving it immediacy and the advantage of providing expanded coverage of breaking news stories.

Journalist Leonard Zeidenberg observed that television newsmagazines "provide a gloss of respectability and credibility for the network and its affiliates." Zeidenberg had several lessons for those who would do a prime-time news-magazine show: they should "focus on journalism, keep frills under control, and have patience."

After failing with more than a dozen news programs since 1969, NBC finally succeeded with *Dateline,* although it, too, had its problems. Just when it looked like NBC would finally have a successful newsmagazine, the producers of a 1992 *Dateline* story used incendiary devices to make sure that a vehicle's gas tank would explode. NBC was forced to make a public apology. The program eventually regained its credibility. The 1992 incident demonstrated, said Everette Dennis, executive director for the Freedom Forum Media Studies Center, that "the constant race for ideas leads to a tendency to sensationalize and blow things out of proportion." Jane Pauley, cohost of *Dateline,* said that she tried to keep sensationalism out of her stories. She also said, however, that extravagant publicity was "not so much theater as marketing." Pauley added, "It's business."

The real race, however, was usually for the "get" – the big interview all the newsmagazines sought. Some magazine show anchors and producers sent gifts, flowers, or even a birthday cake to someone they were trying to "get." Many well-known news anchors also made personal phone calls, relying on their names to get the interview.

One of the influences on the newsmagazines was the television talk shows – shows like *Donahue, Oprah Winfrey, Sally Jessy Raphael, Ricki Lake,* and others that featured live audiences interacting with the show's guests. The producers of these shows, which aired during the daytime or late at night, considered them infotainment – a combination of information and entertainment – but critics often called them trash TV. One of the more outrageous of these shows was Morton Downey Jr.'s in the 1980s. Downey, with his loud and confrontational style, claimed to be "democratizing TV," making more information available to a larger audience. Downey said that the mainstream news media were too elitist, too out of touch with the entertaining way in which the average American liked to be informed. Producers of such shows said that infotainment programs not only attracted viewers but could also perform a community service as well. At least one network news executive, however, considered that making money was the only object of producers of such talk shows.

Broadcast newsmagazines and talk shows had great appeal for both the audience and the networks or syndicators. CBS newswoman Connie Chung quoted her husband, Maury Povich, another of the syndicated daytime talk show hosts in the 1990s, as saying that his ratings were better than his soap opera competition because "people find the real-life soap-opera story more watchable than the fictional soap-opera stories." Sixty percent of the talk show viewers were women. In addition to the audience attraction, newsmagazines in the late 1990s cost less than $500,000 per program, while an hour of comedy or drama could run more than $2 million, and newsmagazines earned nearly as much in advertising income. According to Andrew Heyward, a CBS executive producer, newsmagazines "have kept the news divisions viable and healthy at a time when economic pressures are enormous."

The broadcast newsmagazines learned from their print predecessors, magazines such as *Life, Look,* and the *Satur-*

60 Minutes correspondent Mike Wallace talks with Coretta Scott King and her children on the first Christmas after the assassination of her husband, Dr. Martin Luther King Jr.
(UPI/Corbis-Bettmann)

day Evening Post, to tell stories through people and with visuals. The broadcast newsmagazines in turn influenced the networks' nightly newscasts to run longer stories. PBS's *Newshour with Jim Lehrer* consisted each day of about five to ten minutes of news, followed by three or four in-depth stories.

While some of the programs initially tried different formats, most settled into the *60 Minutes* practice of presenting three stories of similar length and a light, short piece at the end. Journalist Richard Zoglin said, "Everyone in magazineland seems to agree on what the good stories are: consumer rip-offs, miscarriages of justice, teary tales of people victimized by bad doctors or trampled on by insensitive government agencies." He said, "The magazines serve up morality tales of black hats versus white hats, with the reporter as avenging U.S. marshal." The journalist's weapons, he continued, "are a hidden camera and a handheld mike, thrust at reluctant witnesses before they slam the car door. It's 'Gotcha!' journalism." Such an approach brought up questions as to whether some stories were important enough to justify violating people's privacy or trust. CBS correspondent Bernard Goldberg said, "We wanted to be on every week, seen by millions of people. And Hollywood (the networks' entertainment divisions) said 'Fine.' So now we're playing by entertainment rules. But there's only one rule: ratings."

Over the 1994 and 1995 seasons, the ratings of a number of newsmagazine shows declined, and some were canceled or had their schedules reduced. The vice president in charge of newsmagazines for ABC, Alan Wurtzel, said, "TV imitates success until it overdoses." Television is a cyclical business, however, and it was likely that the popularity of newsmagazine shows would return again in the future.

JACK HODGSON

See also Broadcast Talk Shows

Further Reading

Alter, Jonathan, "*Candid Camera* Gone Berserk?," *Newsweek* 122 (August 30, 1993), p. 36

Boyer, Peter J., *Who Killed CBS? The Undoing of America's Number One News Network,* New York: St. Martin's, 1989

"Fifth Estater: Myron Leon Wallace," *Broadcasting* 122:11 (March 9, 1992), p. 59

Noah, Timothy, "The View from the Tube," *New Republic* 195 (August 4, 1986), pp. 29–33

Range, Peter Ross, "Are TV Magazines Dying?," *TV Guide* 42 (December 10, 1994), pp. 16–20

Smith, Sally Bedell, *In All His Glory: The Life of William S. Paley,* New York: Simon & Schuster, 1990

Zeidenberg, Leonard, "News Magazines: The Prime Time Paradox," *Broadcasting* 117:24 (December 11, 1989), pp. 68–70

Zoglin, Richard, "The Magazining of TV News," *Time* 142 (July 12, 1993), pp. 50–51

Broadcast Pioneers

Contributors to the evolution of U.S. broadcasting

Several individuals contributed significantly to the early technical evolution of broadcasting in the United States. What began as point-to-point message systems eventually evolved into a rich array of electronic media.

The telegraph, the undersea cable, and the telephone were immediate precursors of wireless communications. Federal money helped Samuel F.B. Morse to install the first operational telegraph link between Washington, D.C., and Baltimore, Maryland, in 1844. U.S. businessman Cyrus W. Field successfully laid a transatlantic telegraph cable between Ireland and Newfoundland in 1866. By the 1870s, inventors were working on ways to transmit speech sounds over wires. The process required a transducer, a device that could convert energy from one medium to another. Many inventors were close to a solution when Alexander Graham Bell filed for his key telephone patent in 1876.

In 1873, James Clerk Maxwell argued that electromagnetic waves, or wireless transmissions, existed and that these invisible forms of radiant energy traveled at the speed of light. Fifteen years later, Heinrich Hertz verified Maxwell's theory by creating, detecting, and measuring electromagnetic waves in a laboratory experiment.

Guglielmo Marconi developed wireless telegraphy into a lucrative communications empire in Great Britain as well as in the United States. In 1901, Marconi beamed a signal from Cornwall, England, to St. John's, Newfoundland. Military and business interests found practical applications for the radio waves that Marconi proved could carry messages.

On Christmas Eve, 1906, ship wireless operators along the eastern seaboard heard Reginald Fessenden's faint voice break through the cold night air from Brant Rock, Massachusetts, as he explained his experiment to get voices heard on wireless sets. Fessenden also developed the heterodyne receiver to detect and decode continuous-wave signals.

In 1906, two U.S. inventors, H.H. Dunwoody and Greenleaf Whittier Pickard, almost simultaneously invented the crystal detector receiver that dominated all wireless and early radio receivers. Quartz and galena crystals could detect wireless waves and pass them along to headphones, but incoming signals still needed amplification to be heard by more than one listener.

Lee De Forest solved the amplification problem by inserting a tiny wire grid between the filament and plate in a tube, or valve, developed by John Ambrose Fleming for Marconi in 1904. De Forest's Audion, or triode, was later refined into the vacuum tube and eventually replaced in the 1950s by the transistor and subsequent advances in solid-state electronics.

Cross-licensing agreements between 1919 and 1923 allowed companies such as General Electric, Westinghouse, the Radio Corporation of America (RCA), and American Telephone and Telegraph to share discoveries to develop wireless communications.

In 1933, Edwin Howard Armstrong showed RCA engineers the improved sound quality of his FM (frequency modulation) system. RCA's David Sarnoff, satisfied with AM (amplitude modulation) radio's success, was busy considering the future of television, and he rebuffed Armstrong's discoveries. Although World War II delayed FM's development, Armstrong's achievement eventually would evolve into a commercial success, but not until after his suicide in 1954.

The technological achievements of radio served as the basis for perfecting the American television system. Mechanical systems evolved into electronic television pictures.

George R. Carey in 1875 used banks of selenium cells to reproduce pictures electronically. In 1884, Paul Nipkow, a German scientist, patented a rotating disk that scanned pictures using perforations arranged in a spiral pattern. In 1907, Russian physicist Boris Rosing developed the cathode ray tube that used a stream of electrons steered across a photosensitive screen to create an electronic picture.

The versatile U.S. inventor Charles Francis Jenkins in 1925 developed a mechanical scanning system and transmitted a radio vision signal five miles. In 1927, Herbert E. Ives of Bell Telephone Laboratories transmitted still and moving pictures hundreds of miles over wires; Ives also demonstrated early three-channel color systems. At about the same time, John Logie Baird received financial backing for his experiments after he presented three shows daily for three weeks in a London department store window. Electronics manufacturers started television stations hoping to increase sales of the sets. Despite high hopes, electronic scanning systems would eventually shape television's future.

Vladimir Zworykin and Philo T. Farnsworth were primarily responsible for the development of the U.S. system of electronic television. Zworykin convinced David Sarnoff that the iconoscope electronic television camera would capture the market. Farnsworth's image dissector used a different design but worked essentially like Zworykin's iconoscope. RCA paid $1 million for the rights to use Farnsworth's inventions. Zworykin perfected his all-electronic television system in the 1930s.

PETER E. MAYEUX

See also Broadcast Regulation; Conrad, Frank; De Forest, Lee; Farnsworth, Philo Taylor; Hoover, Herbert, and Radio Regulation; Paley, William S.; Radio Act of 1912; Radio Act of 1927; Radio Entertainment; Radio Networks; Radio News; Radio Technology; Sarnoff, David; Television Entertainment; Television News; Television Technology; Westinghouse; Zworykin, Vladimir

Further Reading

Lewis, Tom, *Empire of the Air: The Men Who Made Radio*, New York: E. Burlingame, 1991
Lichty, Lawrence W., and Malachi C. Topping, comps., *American Broadcasting: A Source Book on the History of Radio and Television*, New York: Hastings, 1975
Shiers, George, and May Shiers, *Bibliography of the History of Electronics*, Metuchen, New Jersey: Scarecrow, 1972

Broadcast Propaganda

Spreading messages to influence public opinion

The term broadcast propaganda refers to the dissemination of messages intended to influence public opinion. Broadcast propaganda between nations has been used as an instrument for both public diplomacy and psychological warfare. Thus, its historical development has been linked to international political and military conditions. While the legality of trans-border propaganda broadcasts is questionable and there is little empirical evidence for the assumed potential of these messages to change political attitudes, many countries have invested considerable resources to spread their ideologies over the airwaves. In addition, nations like the former Soviet Union and other Communist countries have also spent large sums to jam hostile stations.

There are four kinds of broadcast propaganda: factual, which is manifestly political; bureaucratic, which consists of official reports; linguistic, which makes use of legitimizing symbols and other verbal strategies; and sociological, which seeks to transform a society's whole way of life. Because sociological propaganda includes messages without manifest political content, much of the material aired by international stations (e.g., news, music, talk shows, and language lessons) can be considered sociological propaganda.

International stations traditionally have sent their signals over shortwave radio, but in the late twentieth century, many broadcasters also transmitted over medium-wave, FM, and cable radio. In addition, some broadcasters used television. The world broadcasters are in fact large networks involving many stations and transmitting on multiple frequencies. Stations are often classified according to the color code used for propaganda. White stations are legal and open about their purpose, location, and sponsorship; black stations are completely covert operations; and in between there is a large array of gray stations. White stations are government overseas services, and because they are symbols of international involvement, most nations have one. Black stations appear and disappear with political conflict; frequently they are part of a military strategy and are operated either by revolutionaries and exiles or by enemy governments.

In accordance with its Communist theory of the press, which viewed mass media as tools for state propaganda, the former Soviet Union aired the first propaganda broadcast in 1929. With its attacks on Nazi Germany in 1933, the Soviets initiated one of the most active periods of radio propaganda. In the late twentieth century, the world broadcaster enjoying the best reputation for credibility was the British Broadcasting Corporation (BBC), which, despite domestic criticism for including viewpoints opposed to governmental policy, was the paradigm for international radio after World War II.

Because the United States champions freedom of the press, government control of international broadcasting periodically met with opposition. The U.S. government began psychological operations in 1942 through shortwave radio, but after World War II, government-controlled radio faced strong opposition in Congress. Nevertheless, in 1948, Congress approved the Department of State's informational and educational activities abroad, and the U.S. official radio service Voice of America (VOA) was established as the Cold War escalated. In 1953, the Eisenhower administration created the U.S. Information Agency (USIA) to oversee public diplomacy efforts and to separate the VOA from the State department.

In 1994, the VOA transmitted in 47 foreign languages, and its English broadcasts covered Africa, Europe, the Middle East, Asia, and the Pacific, plus the Caribbean and the American republics. (The BBC's World Service transmitted in 39 languages.) Like other major international broadcasters, the VOA had its own reporters and stringers, but it also aired news compiled from wire services and other sources. Fulfilling its mandate to "present a comprehensive picture of life in the United States," the VOA also broadcast popular music and light features about U.S. culture.

The VOA lived with a paradox. On the one hand, it strove to maintain the standards of objectivity set by U.S. journalism, but on the other hand, it was sometimes expected to air anti-Communist, factual propaganda. Apparently this ideological tension resulted in more-objective reporting about domestic affairs (e.g., the Watergate scandal) than about foreign policy (e.g., toward Vietnam).

Despite the uneasiness of U.S. citizens about government control of the media, the U.S. government was heavily involved in broadcast propaganda. In addition to the VOA, various military stations overseas, and a number of Central Intelligence Agency (CIA) black stations, the government sponsored two surrogate services. One of them comprised Radio Free Europe (RFE) and Radio Liberty (RL), which broadcast from Munich, Germany, to eastern Europe and the former Soviet Union from the early 1950s. The second surrogate service was Cuba Broadcasting, and it transmitted from Miami, Florida, to Cuba beginning in 1983. Since exiles from Communist countries were involved in these surrogate stations, their status was ambiguous, and their anti-Communist propaganda was at times heavy-handed.

An earlier U.S. station, Radio in the American Sector of Berlin, had shown that many people living under Communist rule listened to Western-style radio. RFE and RL were set up to provide these people with a surrogate or alternative means for independent journalism. Although they were privately incorporated stations, RFE and RL were financed covertly by the CIA until 1967. The stations were consolidated in 1973 and, after a congressional investigation, began receiving public funds through the Board for International Broadcasting. By 1982, their annual appropriation was roughly equivalent to the VOA's.

During the years of the Reagan and Bush administrations, U.S. international broadcasting grew considerably. The VOA modernized its equipment, the USIA started its Worldnet television system in 1983, and the government renewed its broadcast propaganda against the regime of Fidel Castro in Cuba. Cuba and the United States were involved in an intense radio war from 1961, when Radio Swan was launched to support the Bay of Pigs invasion. Soon after that, Radio Havana Cuba began its powerful international broadcasting. With Radio Martí, the United States inaugurated its second surrogate system in 1983; five years later, the system added television. Although Radio and TV Martí followed the RFE and RL model, like the VOA they were under the USIA. The radio programming aired 24 hours a day, but because of international regulations, the television station only broadcast from 3:45 to 6:45 A.M.

The demise of the Soviet Union, coupled with the large U.S. federal deficit, gave rise to calls for consolidation of U.S. radio services. Nonetheless, in 1993 Congress approved $800 million for radio and $44 million for television. The VOA received $227 million plus $167 million for construction; RFE/RL, $220 million; Worldnet, $23 million; Radio Martí, $19 million; and TV Martí, $21 million.

Critics in the 1990s questioned the need for surrogate services, and the Clinton administration proposed to consolidate RFE and RL with the VOA. In 1994, RFE and RL broadcast in 23 languages to the former Soviet Union, the Baltic countries, Afghanistan, and east-central and southeastern Europe. Since some of these regions' local media used RFE and RL as wire agencies, advocates of the stations insisted that their "home service" (which reported on events happening within targeted countries) contributed in a different way than the VOA to build political democracy and market economies in the former Soviet sphere.

LUCILA VARGAS

See also Motion Picture Propaganda; Propaganda; United States Information Agency; Voice of America

Further Reading

Alexandre, Laurien, *The Voice of America: From Detente to the Reagan Doctrine,* Norwood, New Jersey: Ablex, 1988

Browne, Donald R., *International Radio Broadcasting: The Limits of the Limitless Medium,* New York: Praeger, 1982

Frederick, Howard H., *Cuban-American Radio Wars: Ideology in International Telecommunications,* Norwood, New Jersey: Ablex, 1986

Mickelson, Sig, *America's Other Voice: The Story of Radio Free Europe and Radio Liberty,* New York: Praeger, 1983

Nakamura, Kennon H., and Susan B. Epstein, *International Broadcasting Consolidation of U.S. Radio Services,* Washington, D.C.: Congressional Research Service, Library of Congress, 1994

Wasburn, Philo C., *Broadcasting Propaganda: International Radio Broadcasting and the Construction of Political Reality,* Westport, Connecticut: Praeger, 1992

Broadcast Ratings

Trying to determine audience size

Broadcast stations use ratings as a means of gauging the size of the viewing or listening audience. In turn, audience ratings determine the base dollar amount that broadcast stations can charge advertisers for being seen or heard in a given program. In the late twentieth century, two companies held a practical monopoly on the ratings industry: Arbitron determined ratings for radio stations, and Nielsen conducted surveys for television stations and television networks.

When network radio became the dominant medium of the 1930s a need arose to gauge audience interest in the prime-time programming. Some programs had relied on listener requests for premium gifts – for example, an autographed picture of Kate Smith – as a means of determining the potential audience. Network radio and national advertisers required a more sophisticated means of measuring the listening audience.

Several companies began using statistical methods of measuring audience levels. The Crossley Company and the Hooperatings both began conducting surveys either door-to-door or by telephone, called coincidental surveys. The listener, who by answering the phone or door was picked to represent the household, told the survey taker what program he or she was listening to at the moment. Later telephone survey methods would ask listeners what programs they had listened to during that day, a method called the telephone recall survey.

By the 1990s, radio and television estimating techniques

had improved so that ratings represented individuals and not households. In fact, program directors could obtain some very sophisticated information about the gender, income, education, and age of the audience. These figures represented only an estimate on the part of the survey company and not an actual count of all the homes watching or listening. Nielsen only surveyed 1,200 homes to gauge the overnight success of network television programs. Inferential statistical theory holds that once a base, random sample of the population at large has been taken, then repeating patterns will occur in the numbers. These repeating patterns eliminate the need for larger samples.

A typical Arbitron radio survey would involve the mailing of diaries to a number of households in the listening area. Listeners were asked to write down the radio programs they listened to in a one-week period. Arbitron used the information collected in the diaries to determine the cumulative or total size of the listening audience and to determine the size of the audience for each quarter hour.

For television, Nielsen used a diary system and an electronic method of gathering information called a Peoplemeter. These meters were connected to the television set in the home. A viewer logged onto the Peoplemeter, and viewing information was automatically collected.

Even though Nielsen and Arbitron held virtual monopolies on the rating industries, not all broadcast executives were happy with their collection methods. Dormitories, army barracks, and bars were not counted in surveys. Many advertisers questioned the complete reliability of the diary method of information collection, and they sometimes questioned the reliability of diary placement within a survey area.

CORLEY F. DENNISON III

See also Audience Research for Broadcasting

Further Reading

Eastman, Susan Tyler, *Broadcast/Cable Programming: Strategies and Practices,* 4th ed., Belmont, California: Wadsworth, 1993

Warner, Charles, and Joseph Buchman, *Broadcast and Cable Selling,* 2nd ed., Belmont, California: Wadsworth, 1991

Broadcast Regulation

"Scarce" resource leads to governmental oversight

Generally, broadcasting has enjoyed less First Amendment protection than the print media. The courts have tolerated regulation of the broadcast media based on the notion that the spectrum is a scarce resource and that the government may impose obligations or restrictions on broadcasters in exchange for the privilege of obtaining a license to broadcast. This notion of "scarcity" was challenged in the late twentieth century by critics of government regulation. Nonetheless, the concept of "public interest," which was at

the heart of the regulatory scheme governing broadcasting, remained a strong justification for many of the regulations affecting broadcasting, particularly those that were content-based.

The basis of broadcast regulation into the 1990s was the Radio Act of 1927. The act created a five-member Federal Radio Commission (FRC) that had as its mission solving the station interference problems that existed at the time. Prior to its passage, hundreds of stations broadcast with no regard for power or frequency. The Radio Act of 1912, which was never meant to regulate broadcasting, was inadequate to control the explosive growth of the new medium.

The FRC was supposed to be a temporary body, but it remained in power until 1934, when Congress passed the Communications Act creating the Federal Communications Commission (FCC). The 1927 act gave the FRC the power to license stations and to assign frequencies, power, and times of operation.

The 1927 act included three important content-based clauses that, despite some modifications, remained in effect at the end of the twentieth century. An anticensorship clause prohibited the commission from abridging freedom of speech. There was also a ban on the broadcast of obscene, indecent, or profane language. The act also required that stations giving access to political candidates provide all other candidates running for the same office "equal opportunities," in order to avoid political favoritism. In addition, stations could not censor the content of a candidate's program or commercial in any way.

Since the number of stations was scarce and the FRC was to choose who among the many applicants would receive licenses, Congress established "public interest, convenience, and necessity" as the standard the FRC could use to base its regulatory decisions. Using the public interest as its justification, the FRC removed numerous stations from the air in its first year of existence.

FRC commissioners saw themselves as more than technical regulators. For most of the regulatory history of broadcasting, the FRC, or the FCC, attempted not only to define the public interest but also to give guidance to broadcasters in meeting the standard when they sought to renew their licenses. For instance, in 1928, in its first attempt to explain what the public interest was, the FRC said that the interests of the public should take precedence over those of broadcasters. One year later, the FRC said that broadcasters should carry well-rounded, quality programming that served the "needs, tastes, and desires" of the community. The commission also said that the public interest required "ample play for the free and fair competition of opposing views" in the discussion of issues of public importance. This was the seed of the Fairness Doctrine.

In 1934, Congress passed the Communications Act. The new act incorporated most of the provisions of the Radio Act and regulated not only public, private, and governmental use of radio, and later television, but interstate telegraph and telephone services as well. The new law was based on the same public interest philosophy and emphasized that the electromagnetic spectrum belonged to the public, not to the licensee. The commission could enforce its regulations by either refusing to renew a license or revoking it. Years later, Congress amended the Communications Act to allow the commission to issue short-term renewals, fines, and cease-and-desist orders.

Applicants seeking a license had to be U.S. citizens, have good character, and be financially and technically capable of operating the station. Once candidates met these criteria, the FCC looked at other qualifications – such as programming plans and whether the ownership and management of the station would be local – to decide which station, if two were competing for the same frequency, would better serve the public interest. Licenses lasted three years; this later changed to five years for television and seven for radio.

At renewal time, the incumbent could be challenged by others seeking to obtain the occupied frequency. The FCC had the discretion to renew the license or to give it to a challenger who promised to provide better service than the incumbent, although reassignment seldom happened. If a station was sold, the commission had to approve its sale, and the purchaser had to meet the qualifications of an original licensee.

Following in the footsteps of the FRC, the FCC sought to explain broadcasters' obligations under the public interest doctrine. For instance, in 1960, the FCC told broadcasters that they had to ascertain the needs and interests of the community they served and demonstrate programming to meet those needs and interests. This requirement, known as ascertainment, was part of the FCC formal requirements until it was repealed in the 1980s. In addition, the commission said that to serve the public interest broadcasters should include in their programming the following: opportunity for local self-expression; development and use of local talent; children's, religious, educational, public affairs, news, and agricultural programs; editorializing by licensees; political broadcasts; weather and market reports; sports; service to minority groups; and entertainment programming.

While the broadcast media are the subject of many regulations, the most controversial ones are related to content. In 1949, the commission announced in a policy statement that broadcasters had a twofold obligation under what became known as the Fairness Doctrine. The commission required broadcasters to devote a reasonable amount of airtime to the discussion of issues of public importance, emphasizing that such discussions should include opportunities for the expression of contrasting views. The commission's application of the doctrine evolved through the years to include rules on personal attacks, editorial endorsements of political candidates, and advertising by noncandidates in political campaigns.

Despite the FCC's good intentions in promoting discussion of controversial issues, applying the Fairness Doctrine was a complex proposition. Determining whether an issue was controversial and whether a broadcaster had allowed reasonable opportunity for opposing viewpoints to be expressed were two of the major hurdles in the application of the doctrine. Moreover, while proponents of the Fairness Doctrine believed that frequency scarcity and the public interest justified requiring broadcasters to cover controversial issues in a balanced manner, critics claimed that the doctrine actually chilled discussion of controversial issues. This

latter view prevailed when the Fairness Doctrine was finally abolished by the FCC in 1987.

In an effort to promote an informed electorate, Congress incorporated the equal opportunity provisions, later known as Section 315 of the Communications Act, into the Radio Act of 1927. Section 315 required that if a broadcaster gave one candidate access to the station, all other candidates for the same office should be afforded equal opportunities. If a candidate did not have the money to pay for the commercial time, the broadcaster did not have an obligation to provide free access unless, of course, other candidates for the same office received free time. A candidate's appearance in a bona fide newscast, news interview, documentary, or on-the-spot coverage of a bona fide news event would not trigger Section 315 obligations.

In addition to affording candidates equal opportunities, Section 315 required broadcasters to sell time at the lowest rate available and forbade broadcasters to censor the content of a candidate's program. While the statute did not require that broadcasters give access to political candidates, most broadcasters did it as a way to serve the public interest. The reasonable access rule, or Section 312 (a)(7), however, did require that broadcasters give access to their stations to candidates running for federal office. This right of access applies only to candidates running for federal office; state or local political candidates and the public in general did not have this right of access.

An area of regulation that has been extremely controversial involves indecent speech. While the indecency ban appeared in the Radio Act of 1927, in 1948 the clause was moved to Title 18, Section 1464 of the U.S. Code. In 1978, in *FCC* v. *Pacifica,* the U.S. Supreme Court upheld the commission's right to channel indecent material to times when children were less likely to be in the audience, but not to ban the material altogether. The case involved the afternoon broadcasting of George Carlin's monologue "Filthy Words." The words that the commission found "indecent" were shit, piss, fuck, cunt, cocksucker, motherfucker, and tits. The FCC defined indecency as language that described, in terms patently offensive by contemporary community standards for the broadcast medium, sexual or excretory activities or organs.

As a result of the *Pacifica* case, the FCC established a "safe harbor," or time when the airing of indecent material would be allowed. The commission made clear that only stations airing any of Carlin's "seven dirty words" between 6 A.M. and 10 P.M. – outside the safe harbor – would be penalized. However, in 1987 the FCC began to enforce the indecency regulations more strongly, and instead of using the seven words as the standard to measure indecency, the commission began to use the definition it had developed in the *Pacifica* case. Between 1987 and 1995, the commission was involved in a series of legal challenges to its indecency regulations and levied almost $2 million in fines.

While the FCC was eager to protect children from indecent programming, it was less assertive in its regulation of children's programming. In the 1970s and 1980s, the FCC said that licensees should make an effort to increase programming aimed at educating and entertaining children and that such efforts would be evaluated at license renewal time. Despite this warning, the amount of programming for children did not increase. Instead of using its enforcement powers to encourage broadcasters to improve or increase children's programming, as children's advocates urged, the commission appeared concerned about infringing on the editorial discretion of licensees.

In 1990, Congress passed the Children's Television Act, which required that television stations demonstrate how they were serving the educational and informational needs of children. Stations were required to keep a file detailing their efforts to comply with the law. The act also established limits on the number of commercials aired during children's programs.

Although many children's advocates were not satisfied with the results of the act, the commission at least made an effort to enforce the part of the statute that regulated commercial limits, levying hefty fines against violators. It was not clear how much the act actually improved children's programming, but children's advocates and some FCC commissioners believed that broadcasters were not doing enough.

A series of incidents prompted the FCC to issue a 1992 rule prohibiting and punishing the broadcast of hoaxes that diverted law enforcement resources and posed a threat to public safety. The rule on hoaxes stated that the commission could fine a station up to $25,000 for knowingly broadcasting false information concerning a crime or catastrophe if the broadcaster could have anticipated substantial public harm that in fact occurred. The commission said that a fictitious program accompanied by a disclaimer would not be considered a hoax.

In the 1990s, the latest controversial regulation appeared to be the regulation of violence. Although citizens' groups had been complaining about the amount of violence in television for quite some time, in the early 1990s Congress began to pressure the entertainment industry to curb violent content on television. In fact, by 1995, several bills had been introduced in the House and Senate that attempted to regulate violent programming and establish a "safe harbor" similar to the one for indecency. It was considered possible that Congress might eventually pass a bill regulating broadcast violence despite broadcasters' efforts to reduce violence in their programs and their willingness to issue warnings about violent content.

MILAGROS RIVERA-SANCHEZ

See also Broadcast Editorials; Censorship of Broadcasting; Children's Television Programming; Communications Act of 1934; Decency Issues in Electronic Media; "Equal Time" Provision; Fairness Doctrine; Federal Communications Commission; Federal Radio Commission; Personal Attack Rule; Radio Act of 1912; Radio Act of 1927; Wireless Ship Act of 1910

Further Reading

Cole, Barry, and Mal Oettinger, *Reluctant Regulators: The FCC and the Broadcast Audience,* Reading, Massachusetts, and London: Addison-Wesley, 1978
Powe, L.A. Scot, Jr., *American Broadcasting and the First Amendment,* Berkeley: University of California Press, 1987
Ray, William B., *FCC: The Ups and Downs of Radio-TV Regulation,* Ames: Iowa State University Press, 1990
Smith, F. Leslie, Milan D. Meeske, and John W. Wright, II, *Electronic Media and Government: The Regulation of Wireless and Wired Mass Communication in the United States,* White Plains, New York: Longman, 1995

Broadcast Talk Shows

Programming first appeared on radio in the 1920s

Talk shows existed from the earliest days of broadcasting, beginning with radio in the late 1920s, and with television when it began nationally in 1948. Pioneers were Edward R. Murrow (as early as 1935 on CBS Radio and on *Person to Person* on television in the 1950s) and *The Tonight Show* with Steve Allen (beginning in 1954), with Jack Paar (beginning in 1957), and later with Johnny Carson (beginning in 1962). Daytime television talk shows began with Phil Donahue, who began in 1967 and went national in 1970. On radio, pioneer talk show hosts Long John Nebel (on local New York City radio in the mid-1950s), Joe Pyne (in the 1960s), Bob Grant (from the 1970s), and Rush Limbaugh (nationally beginning in 1988) all had their effect.

Talk shows, by the late twentieth century, had almost taken over daytime television, even pushing out soap operas and game shows as the big ratings grabbers. They began with daytime talk innovator Donahue and were perfected by ratings queen Oprah Winfrey in 1985 when she went national. The success of Winfrey and Donahue opened the door to other television talk show hosts and to lesser-quality shows that broadened the permissible discussion topic to ever-greater extremes. In fierce competition with each other for ratings, daytime talk television and their hosts constantly sought the most sensational and controversial topics.

One extreme example that drew worldwide attention was the 1995 *Jenny Jones* show on the topic of a "Secret Admirer." While the topic seemed relatively harmless, the twist was that one "secret admirer" had a same-sex crush. The show guest did not know the gender of his admirer. Humiliated by the show, the guest went to the home of his neighbor – who was his secret admirer – and killed him.

There were numerous problems with talk shows. One such show resulted in a televised brawl between host Geraldo Rivera and a neo-Nazi group. There were also off-air suicides, suicide attempts, and hospitalizations following revelations made on the shows.

Daytime TV talk shows originally focused on important women's topics and issues, approaching topics in an uplifting, educating, and inclusive manner. These shows, however, grew to have wider appeal but often advocated the worst aspects of society.

The visual aspect of television gave these daytime talk shows immense impact, for the manner and appearance of what is being said was critical. Arguments, conflict, foul language, even fists in some cases, contributed to what some critics called "bread and circus" audiences. These shows earned much criticism in the 1990s, causing the shows in air time was taken up by talk programming of a nonpolitical nature such as general news, gossip, gardening, medical and health shows, advice columns, economic and investment programs, and religious and spiritual shows. Dr. Ruth Westheimer, who became a popular culture figure, began her media career as a radio talk show host discussing sexual questions with callers on *Sexually Speaking* in the early 1980s.

The area of political talk radio (and to a lesser, but growing, degree, political talk on television) was a relatively late-developing phenomenon. Until the late 1980s, editorial comment by a host on radio or television was limited by the Federal Communications Commission through the Fairness Doctrine. The First Amendment right of free speech, which includes editorial comment, criticism, and discussion for print media, was severely restricted for broadcasters. The dropping of the Fairness Doctrine in 1987 made political talk radio possible.

Conservative talk radio became very controversial in the late 1980s and 1990s because it was becoming a potent force in political debate. Talk radio took many media watchers by surprise because of the general assumption that radio was relatively passé and harmless. Political conservatives, who had been somewhat in the cultural shadows for years, thus found the way open to air their grievances. Rush Limbaugh, debuting in 1988, spread the conservative message through serious talk, satire, and ridicule. Limbaugh and his conservative talk radio colleagues throughout the country grew in influence on the political scene, reaching their apex in 1994. They were considered to have been a factor in the congressional elections of that year, in which Republicans took control of Congress for the first time in 40 years.

The ascent of conservative talk radio encouraged the presentation of even more diverse views through the media – and more talk shows. The success of CNBC on cable television with its lineup of "talk all-stars" and the move of many radio talk show hosts to expand into talk television were trends that were expected to continue. All-talk television was growing even as CNN, CNBC, C-SPAN, and the Big Three networks expanded their percentage of on-air time given to talk shows. The number of political talk shows, such as *Crossfire*, *Capitol Gang*, and others, also increased in number.

Part of this growing phenomenon was owing to the fact that as the Baby Boom generation aged, their interests grew and changed. "Entertainment" came to have a broader definition, encompassing news, current events, and various kinds of talk programming – often with a heavy accent on political talk.

GARY LOVISI

See also Decency Issues in Electronic Media; Fairness Doctrine

Further Reading

Barrett, Marvin, ed., *The Politics of Broadcasting,* New York: Crowell, 1973

Heaton, Jeanne Albronda, and Nona Leigh Wilson, *Tuning in Trouble: Talk TV's Destructive Impact on Mental Health,* San Francisco: Jossey-Bass, 1995

Larry King talks to a variety of guests each night on CNN.
(Museum of Broadcast Communications)

general to backpedal from some of the more extreme topics and practices. Oprah Winfrey, while still at number one in the ratings war, decided to swear off sleaze, a stand that worked well for her, keeping her ratings high and gaining her worldwide respect from viewers and critics alike.

Talk radio was a similar but different phenomenon. While it had been around for a long time, in the late 1990s it received a lot of attention because of conservative talk radio and its hosts. When President Bill Clinton's speeches after the 1995 Oklahoma City, Oklahoma, terrorist bombing spoke out against so-called hate radio or hate talk, it seemed to some an almost McCarthyite attempt to link terrorism with conservative radio talk shows or their hosts.

Nevertheless, most material on radio was not political. Even among the so-called all-talk radio stations, most on-

Limbaugh, Rush, *The Way Things Ought To Be,* New York: Pocket Books, 1992

Broadcast Trade Organizations

Broadcasting and cable trade organizations have been a way for electronic media professionals to become familiar with their constantly changing field. The oldest and most inclusive organization to meet this need was the National Association of Broadcasters (NAB), which beginning in 1923 provided leadership for broadcasters. Serving as a watchdog on Capitol Hill and at the Federal Communications Commission, the organization represented the radio and television industries in Washington, D.C., before Congress, federal agencies, the courts, and in the international arena. The participation of broadcasters from all levels through the NAB boards, committees, and task forces made the organization a success.

In the cable industry, the National Cable Television Association (NCTA), founded in 1952, was the equivalent of the NAB. Although it did not have the detailed committee framework, it did supply its members with a strong national presence by providing a voice on issues affecting the cable industry.

The NCTA interrelated with the NAB by lobbying in Washington, D.C., to advance the cable television industry's public policy interests before Congress, the executive branch, the courts, and the U.S. public. Of equal importance was the NCTA's promotion of programming and technological developments.

The Radio Television News Directors Association (RTNDA), formed in 1946, served as the only professional association devoted to serving the needs of the electronic journalism profession. Unlike the NAB and the NCTA, which focused on the business affairs of broadcasters, the RTNDA's primary concern was to ensure a strong code of ethics and to fight to maintain the First Amendment rights of journalists.

The Broadcast Education Association, housed in the NAB's Washington, D.C., headquarters, emerged in 1955 as a professional association whose members were professors who taught and did research relevant to electronic media in colleges and universities in the United States and overseas. Similarly, the National Association of College Broadcasters, founded in 1988, was the trade organization for students in the electronic media. It allowed students the opportunity to exchange ideas, explore news formats, and assist in shaping the future of electronic media. Unlike most broadcasting organizations, which were located in Washington, D.C., the National Association of College Broadcasters was situated in Rhode Island.

These organizations dedicated to the broadcast and cable industry, the professionals involved, and faculty who taught communications held annual conventions and expositions, produced informative publications, and provided innovative research and development programs that enabled broadcasters to stay current with issues, technology, and electronic media trends. The Broadcast Education Association, the NAB, the National Association of College Broadcasters, the NCTA, and the RTNDA all believed that U.S. society was deserving of a broadcasting system providing programming devoid of governmental intervention and reflective of audience interests.

TERESA JO STYLES

Further Reading

Broadcast Education Association Fact Sheet, 1995
Eastman, Susan Tyler, *Broadcast/Cable Programming: Strategies and Practices,* 4th ed., Belmont, California: Wadsworth, 1993
National Association of Broadcasters' User Guide, Washington, D.C.: National Association of Broadcasters, 1995
National Association of College Broadcasters Fact Sheet, 1995
National Cable Television Association Fact Sheet, 1995
Radio-Television News Directors Fact Sheet, 1995

Broadcast Trade Press

Broadcasting and Cable, a weekly news publication reporting in depth on television, cable, radio, satellite, and other new technology in communications, was established in 1931 as *Broadcasting.* Eventually, however, developments in the electronic industry resulted in the need to change the name in 1993 to include cable.

Broadcasting and Cable was not the official journal of any association. It served those involved in the $67-billion television and radio industry. Recognized as the industry authority, every week the publication provided the news that was essential for industry leaders to make informed decisions. *Broadcasting and Cable* focused on news that could affect the industry, programming, the latest trends in radio, cable, the information superhighway, and the business community. The events in Washington, D.C., that could affect media business and the latest appointments and promotions of those in the industry were also included.

Broadcasting and Cable published special reports on programming such as talk shows, children's television, and situation comedies; convention and conference agendas; and the annual ranking of the top radio and television groups of the year. Reaching thousands of subscribers, *Broadcasting and Cable* was read by top industry executives and decision makers, presidents of major corporations, general managers, programming directors, marketing directors, news managers, and journalists in the television, radio and cable industries. It was also of interest to manufacturers of emerging technologies, advertising agents, government regulators, educators, and financial analysts. The publication gave a balance of news from Washington, along with the important developments in the telecommunications industry.

TERESA JO STYLES

Other Broadcast Entries: *see* Audience
Research for Broadcasting; Cable Networks; Cable News; Cable Television; Censorship of Broadcasting; Children's Television Programming; Commercialization of Broadcasting; Communications Satellite Technology; Communications Act of 1934; Community Access Television; Conrad, Frank; Criticism of Broadcasting; Cronkite, Walter; Cross-Media Ownership; De Forest, Lee; Docudramas; Economics of Broadcasting; "Equal Time" Provision; Fairness Doctrine; Farnsworth, Philo Taylor; Federal Communications Commission; Federal Trade Commission; Frederick, Pauline; Golden Age of Radio; Golden Age of Television; Goldenson, Leonard; Gould, Jack; Hoover, Herbert, and Radio Regulation; *Huntley-Brinkley Report, The;* Kaltenborn, H.V.; KDKA; Kennedy Assassination and the Media; Mass Media and Children; Mass Media and Health Issues; Mass Media and the Antiwar Movement; Mass Media and the Civil Rights Movement; Mass Media and Tobacco Products; Mayflower Decision; Media Conglomerates; Media Events; Murrow, Edward R.; Noncommercial Radio; Noncommercial Television; Paley, William S.; Payola; Persian Gulf War; Personal Attack Rule; Political Advertising; Presidential Debates; Presidential News Conferences; Presidential Press Secretaries; Prime-Time Television; Program-Length Commercials; Public Access to the Mass Media; Quiz Show Scandals; Radio Act of 1912; Radio Act of 1927; Radio Commentators; Radio Corporation of America; Radio Entertainment; Radio Networks; Radio News; Radio Syndication; Radio Technology; *Report on Chain Broadcasting;* Sarnoff, David; Sound Bites; Stanton, Frank N.; Television and Violence; Television Entertainment; Television Networks; Television News; Television Program Ratings; Television Syndication; Television Technology; Turner, Ted; United States Information Agency; Vietnam War; Voice of America; "War of the Worlds"; Wireless Ship Act of 1910; Zenith Radio Case; Zworykin, Vladimir

Broadsides

Large sheets of paper designed to spread news

Broadsides, early imprints of the printing press, were large sheets of paper usually printed on one side. Later those printed on both sides were called broadcasts, and both were used to disseminate news of important contemporary events and advertising messages, sometimes illustrated with woodcuts or copperplate engravings. Each dealt with a single major issue, often an official proclamation, and was designed to attract attention of the citizenry – a colonial type of news bulletin.

The first product of a printing press in America was a broadside, "The Oath of a Free-Man," published by Stephen Daye in Cambridge, Massachusetts, in 1639. The development of broadsides was closely related to the estab-

lishment of newspapers, as broadsides began to be issued with greater frequency.

Toward the end of the seventeenth century, troubled economic, political, and religious times in New England's Massachusetts colony stimulated publication of several "near newspapers." One such early American broadside was *Present State of New England Affairs*, printed in 1689 by Samuel Green of Boston, telling of the recall of England's governor to the colonies, Sir Edmund Andros.

Broadsides were distributed by traveling peddlers who sold them for pennies, by ministers who read them to their congregations, by town officials at town meetings, and by people posting them in prominent public places. Even after the establishment of America's first true newspaper, the *Boston News-Letter*, in 1704, broadsides continued to proclaim major news, as "extras." Probably the most historic broadside was printed by the Continental Congress' official printer, John Dunlap, in Philadelphia on July 5, 1776, proclaiming the Declaration of Independence.

ELSIE HEBERT

Further Reading
Barnhill, Georgia Brady, *American Broadsides,* Barre, Massachusetts: Imprint Society, 1971
McMurtrie, Douglas C., *A History of Printing in the United States,* New York: Bowker, 1936
_____, *Massachusetts Broadsides, 1699–1711,* Chicago: Privately printed, 1939
Ritz, Wilfred J., "From the *Here* of Jefferson's Handwritten Rough Draft of the Declaration of Independence to the *There* of the Printed Dunlap Broadside," *The Pennsylvania Magazine of History and Biography* CXVI:4 (October 1992)

Budget (B) Movies

Term applied to films of lower quality

Originally used to denote the less expensive feature film on a double bill, the term B movie became synonymous with any filmed production of low quality. Even after the double bill faded from theaters in the 1950s, the classification remained for cheap, exploitative motion pictures. B movies occasionally have risen above their limited resources. They have provided audiences with unexpected entertainment in the form of a surprising performance, an intriguing story, or a finely crafted film. More often, however, they have been routine and forgettable.

Studios and exhibitors created the double bill to lure the U.S. audience back to theaters during the Great Depression. Weekly attendance had plummeted from 110 million in 1930 to 60 million in 1933, and two-thirds of the nation's 16,000 theaters had closed. Lowe's and RKO, the leading theater owners, adopted the double bill in 1935. Commonly called a double feature, it presented a modest film 60 to

70 minutes long followed by a high-quality production with major stars (known as the A film). With a cartoon and newsreel, the double bill offered more than three hours of entertainment. Within a year, 75 percent of theaters had double-feature programs.

In addition to building attendance, B films offered theaters and film producers another financial reward. Unlike receipts from A pictures, which were divided between the exhibitor and the studio, B films were rented at a flat rate. Thus, studios assumed little risk if a film were efficiently made, nearly guaranteeing a small profit. The studios that owned theaters – Metro-Goldwyn-Mayer, Paramount, RKO, Twentieth Century-Fox, and Warner Bros. – churned out B movies from production units based on speed and economy. With the major studios unable to supply all the B films required, the double bill proved to be a boon for smaller studios and independent producers. Republic, Monogram, Grand National, Producers Releasing Corporation, and other small studios specialized in B production.

B films were photographed in black and white, on cheap or recycled sets, in one to two weeks, and after little preparation. To further save money on budgets usually set from $20,000 to $80,000, filmmakers used stock footage – generic scenes of car chases, crowds, and location shots that may have appeared in other films and could be used again and again. Often, B films were remakes or based on routine plots, such as two men in love with the same woman, in which only the setting and dialogue changed.

Journeyman directors and actors whose careers never reached the top or had slipped remained busy in B films. Leading men in B movies included Rod Cameron, John Carroll, Dane Clark, Tom Conway, Jack Holt, Chester Morris, Sonny Tufts, and Warren William. Among the leading ladies were Evelyn Ankers, Jane Frazee, Gloria Jean, Vera Hruba Ralston, and Ann Savage. Prolific directors included William Beaudine, Lew Landers, Joseph H. Lewis, and Sam Newfield.

Novices learned their craft in the training ground of low-budget productions. Those who stepped up to higher-quality films after stints in the B movies included directors Edward Dmytryk, George Stevens, Robert Wise, William Wyler, and Fred Zinnemann, and actors Lucille Ball, Glenn Ford, Susan Hayward, Robert Mitchum, Anthony Quinn, and John Wayne.

The genres popular in A films – the musical, thriller, mystery, western, and comedy – all had their B entries. Horror and science fiction were nearly the exclusive territory of the lower bill until such films began attracting larger audiences in the 1950s and after. B movies also featured recurring characters in series films, including detectives Sherlock Holmes, Philo Vance, and Boston Blackie; cowboys Hopalong Cassidy and Red Ryder; and the Frankenstein monster, the Wolf Man, and the Mummy. Occasionally, critics would take notice of an exceptionally compelling B, such as *Detour* (1945), *D.O.A.* (1950), and *The Biscuit Eater* (1940). Most often, however, attention was lavished on A pictures rather than what were called programmers.

In 1948, the major studios were ordered by the U.S. Supreme Court to divest themselves of their theaters under a landmark antitrust ruling. With their monopoly on production and exhibition ending and television providing the public with low-budget entertainment, the studios turned all their resources to extravagant productions with wide-screen photography and major stars to attract audiences. The traditional B movie, particularly those in the western and mystery genres, died with the double bill and the rise of the television series. Yet its low-budget, profit-minded spirit lived on with independent producers who recognized untapped markets in the 1950s, chiefly teenagers and fans of the science fiction, horror, and sexploitation genres.

As they had in previous decades, low-budget films after 1960 nurtured new talent (directors Martin Scorsese and Francis Ford Coppola and actor Jack Nicholson, for example). Rising costs, the popularity of the made-for-television movie, and the industry's focus on the profitable youth market appeared to doom the genre by the 1980s. However, video recordings and cable television created new avenues for distributing low-budget films. Those unworthy of a theatrical showing became straight-to-video releases and were fodder for Home Box Office, Showtime, and other pay television networks. With the market for low-budget entertainment alive and well, the venue moved from theater to home in response to economic, social, and technological changes.

DOUGLASS K. DANIEL

Further Reading

Barbour, Alan G., *The Thrill of It All*, New York: Macmillan, 1971; London: Collier-Macmillan, 1971
Cook, David A., *A History of Narrative Film*, New York: Norton, 1981
Cross, Robin, *The Big Book of B Movies: Or, How Low Was My Budget*, New York: St. Martin's, 1981; London: F. Muller, 1981
McClelland, Doug, *The Golden Age of "B" Movies*, New York: Bonanza, 1981
Miller, Don, *"B" Movies: An Informal Survey of the American Low-Budget Film, 1933–1945*, New York: Curtis, 1973

Bureau of Advertising

Newspaper effort to build the medium's advertising

When advertising revenues replaced subscription rates as newspapers' main revenue source in the late 1800s, newspaper publishers and owners recognized two things: the need to create awareness about newspapers as advertising vehicles and the necessity to develop a structure for the new moneymaking arm of their businesses. Before the creation of the American Newspaper Publishers Association (ANPA)'s Bureau of Advertising in 1913, advertising agents handled advertising and often overlooked local newspapers in favor of other communication channels, including magazines, direct mail, and trolley-car cards.

U.S. society at the beginning of the twentieth century was also ripe for a change in the newspaper-advertising relationship. A rapidly growing U.S. consumer market was developing, and waves of immigrants contributed to the growth of newspapers. Sunday papers became a staple product of daily newspaper organizations.

The ANPA established the Bureau of Advertising to develop and distribute information about newspaper advertising and to assist newspapers with using information to capitalize on advertising revenue sources. As early as 1906, a group of major daily newspapers had developed the idea of a newspaper advertising resource, and at a 1913 national conference, the Daily Newspaper Club, the National Newspapers, and the United Newspapers set up the bureau. William A. Thompson, the *New York Globe*'s assistant publisher, was chosen as the bureau's first director; he served for 35 years.

The Advertising Bureau's primary goals included developing working relationships between advertising agents and newspapers, standardizing commission rates, and serving as an information source for all member newspapers. As the bureau grew, the variety of services it performed grew. The bureau collected ads, campaigns, and case histories for member reference; developed the *Blue Book of Newspaper Advertising* (a compilation of successful sales stories); and published *Ad Facts*, a monthly case history sent to members. It provided educational materials on how to localize sales for specific markets and spearheaded the use of consumer surveys to provide information.

Just 10 years after its beginning, the bureau set up its own research department, which conducted research for member use as well as using it to develop marketing strategies. In 1945, a retail division was set up, which led to the establishment of a classified division in 1973. In the 1950s, a national sales department was added to educate large national and international advertisers about the benefits of newspaper advertising. A co-op department and an insert division were added in the 1960s. In 1982, the Advertising Bureau also created the Athena Awards for newspaper ads.

Changing economic conditions resulted in the 1992 merger of six major newspaper associations, including the Bureau of Advertising. By merging, the six agencies combined advertising, marketing, and circulation under the Newspaper Association of America (NAA) umbrella. The merger allowed the new agency to make more-efficient national advertising buys while consolidating materials and information into more centralized, comprehensive publications and offices available to members and nonmembers. The NAA's main office was in Reston, Virginia, with branches in Washington, D.C., New York City, and Chicago.

BARBARA J. DESANTO

Further Reading
75 Years of the Newspaper Advertising Bureau, Reston, Virginia: Newspaper Association of America, 1989

Burnett, Leo Noble

Leader in creative advertising effort

Born in St. Johns, Michigan, on October 21, 1892, Leo Burnett studied journalism at the University of Michigan and worked as a reporter at the *Peoria Journal* before he moved to Detroit, Michigan, in 1917 and began his career in advertising. After holding advertising positions in Indianapolis, Indiana, and Chicago, Burnett moved to New York City and, at the urging of friends, opened his own agency on August 5, 1935. The Leo Burnett Company's philosophy centered on creativity and applying that creativity to the client's products.

The new agency's clients were the Minnesota Valley Canning Company (Green Giant), Realsilk Hosiery, and Hoover. During the late 1930s and early 1940s, the agency captured Pillsbury, the American Meat Institute, Kellogg's, and the Tea Council. As the agency's creative philosophy spread, other clients were drawn to its offices. Before 1950, the agency's billings were $18 million. By the early 1950s, the agency's billings were $22 million.

In the mid-1950s, Leo Burnett changed the audience for Marlboro cigarettes by creating the Marlboro Man cowboy. Until this campaign, the cigarettes were smoked mostly by women, not men. After a successful campaign, the product was preferred by the more numerous male smokers.

Burnett had other successes. In 1961, he was named one of the first inductees into the Copywriters Hall of Fame. Burnett retired as agency president in 1967 when the agency's billings were almost $200 million. Burnett maintained the title of chairman and, from time to time, worked in an office at the agency. He was 78 when he died on June 7, 1971.

EDD APPLEGATE

Further Reading
Broadbent, Simon, ed., *The Leo Burnett Book of Advertising*, London: Business, 1984
Daniels, Draper, *Giants, Pigmies, and Other Advertising People*, Chicago: Crain, 1974

Business Media

Outlets that deal with monetary issues

The public has always shown interest in business and the economy because those matters affect people's money. Magazines geared for specific trades or industries began as early as the 1830s. Several of those magazines still existed in the late twentieth century, such as *American Banker*, which began in 1836, and *The Banker's Magazine*, started in 1846.

News agencies began springing up along Wall Street in the 1870s, with the emphasis on getting financial information out quickly. Charles H. Dow and Edward D. Jones were two pioneers in this field, and they started their service in 1882. In 1889, they renamed it the *Wall Street Journal*.

General interest newspapers did not place high priority on business, financial, or economic news until the 1890s. One turning point was when Adolph Ochs bought a nearly bankrupt *New York Times* in 1896. To increase circulation, he had his reporters cover market and financial reports, real estate transactions, and news of buyers from retail stores across the country coming to shop in the fashion districts. Readers and advertisers flocked back to the paper and even referred to the *Times'* business and financial pages as the business bible.

More business magazines started during the early 1900s. *Forbes* magazine, focusing on economic trends and large corporations, started in 1917. Clarence Walker Barron, who worked for the *Wall Street Journal* and then became its owner, started the weekly newspaper for investors called *Barron's* in 1921. *Business Week* started in 1929 and *Fortune* started in 1930, just as the Great Depression was taking hold.

As important as economic news was, however, most general interest newspapers continued to pay little attention to it, relegating this kind of news to the few pages after sports news. Financial, business, and industry news ranked last in a 1955 readership survey of 130 daily newspapers and last in amount of space given by the papers. Typical coverage included stories on a factory opening or closing, a story from a wire service on the Gross National Product or the money supply, and a profile on a corporate executive, almost always a white male. This was followed by several pages of stock market quotes.

All of this changed in the 1970s with apparent confusion among politicians and economists after the Vietnam War, the Watergate scandal, inflation, and the rapid rise of oil prices that forced long lines at gasoline pumps. The public concluded that the experts did not have the answers, so people were "relying more on their newspapers to help them understand," one editor said.

After 1973, U.S. citizens began naming the economy as the nation's biggest problem. Researchers said that the presidential campaigns of 1976 through 1992 were influenced primarily by economic concerns.

Reader demand for news about the economy went up dramatically during the 1960s and early 1970s, editors said. In 1978, the *New York Times* did what no other general circulation newspaper in the country had done: it created its own separate Monday-through-Friday business and financial section, in the form of a daily business magazine. The new section, called "Business Day," increased the *Times'* business, finance, and economic coverage by about 30 percent. It included emphasis on communication, fashion, the computer and electronics industries, and increased international coverage.

In that same year, the *Chicago Tribune* had a weekly "Midwest Business Report" section, and within the next several months, papers in Washington, D.C., Los Angeles, Philadelphia, and Atlanta, Georgia, had expanded their business coverage, as did papers in smaller cities such as Rockford, Illinois, and Palm Beach, Florida.

The presence of business magazines also expanded, with business journals in most major cities. National magazines focused on more narrowly defined aspects of commerce. Magazines for virtually every kind of occupation and commerce grew through the 1970s, 1980s, and 1990s.

Television made its first serious attempt to present news of business and the economy in 1970 at a Maryland public television station. Called *Wall Street Week*, the show's host, Louis Rukeyser, gave an opening commentary about the past week's stock market activity, interacted with a panel of experts, responded to viewer questions, and interviewed a special guest. The format for the show endured. The show's popularity eventually convinced producers that viewers, not just readers, were also interested in news about business and the economy.

Cable News Network created a nightly business report called *Moneyline* in 1980 that offered business news and feature stories, with an emphasis on stock market reports. A public television program, the *Nightly Business Report*, started in 1981 as a joint venture with the Reuters News Service.

The Financial News Network (FNN) began in 1981, broadcasting commentary and stock market information five hours a day, and in 1983, the cable network ESPN began a two-hour daily business show. By the end of that year there were 25 business and economy programs on cable, public, and independent stations. Five were national dailies, and the rest were weekly. In 1984, public television added a show, called *Adam Smith's Money World*.

By the mid-1980s, many of the shows died out due to saturation of the market, but the Financial News Network remained. It became the country's most-sought medium on October 19, 1987, when the stock market collapsed. Within months of the crash, a new cable television network was started. The Consumer News and Business Channel eventually merged with FNN in 1991.

Radio has experimented with business news formats since the 1960s. Most business and economic news on radio, however, came in defined segments during news broadcasts. *Marketplace,* a 30-minute daily business news program that started in the 1990s, aired on National Public Radio.

DEAN NELSON

See also Wall Street Journal

Further Reading

Berger, Meyer, *The Story of the 'New York Times',
    1851–1951,* New York: Simon & Schuster, 1951
Drew, Dan, and Cleveland Wilhoit, "Newshole Allocation
    Policies of American Daily Newspapers," *Journalism
    Quarterly* 53 (1976)
Hubbard, J.T.W., "Business News in Post-Watergate Era,"
    Journalism Quarterly 53 (1976)
Myers, David S., "Editorials and the Economy in the 1976
    Presidential Campaign," *Journalism Quarterly* 55
    (1978)
_____, "Editorials and the Economy in the 1980
    Presidential Campaign," *Journalism Quarterly* 59
    (1982)
Nelson, Dean, "Business and Economic Reporting," *Ohio
    Journalism Monographs* 2 (1992)

Swanson, Charles E., "What They Read in 130 Daily Newspapers," *Journalism Quarterly* 32 (1955)

Talese, Gay, *The Kingdom and the Power,* New York: World, 1969; London: Calder and Boyars, 1971

Business Regulation of the Press

First Amendment issues develop regularly over such attempts

In theory, news organizations are no different than other companies when it comes to general regulations and policies such as taxes, antitrust law, labor law, or civil rights law. During colonial times, however, business regulation was often used as camouflage for government attempts to punish unpopular expression before the adoption of the First Amendment. The strongest example was the Stamp Act of 1765, which imposed a tax on legal documents, books, and newspapers, but prompted more protest and disobedience than revenue. That act, plus attempted licensing and limits on supplies, were fresh memories to those debating the Bill of Rights.

Ironically, the framers' plain intent that the First Amendment prohibit even indirect attempts to throttle press content was not clearly adopted by the courts until the 1930s and not fully interpreted until the 1990s. In *Grosjean* v. *American Press Co.* in 1936, the U.S. Supreme Court declared that a tax statute that worked to punish specific newspapers violated the First Amendment. Other business-related cases decided in the late 1930s and 1940s, however, found that the press, as a business, was not exempted from business regulations that affected all businesses.

Even so, the general principle from *Grosjean* remained and was extended to any type of business statute or administrative regulation serving as a cover for discriminatory treatment. In *Minneapolis Star and Tribune* v. *Minnesota Commissioner of Revenue* in 1983, the court extended the principle, declaring that any law that "singles out the press" is presumed unconstitutional. The court created a test making it almost impossible for government to prevail. The principle of the *Minneapolis Star* case extended to any statute, ordinance, or regulation that applied specifically to media.

The case prompted unusual lawsuits challenging all types of taxes or regulations when aimed at a specific medium; one of the most unusual was a claim that Chicago's amusement tax violated the First Amendment rights of movie theaters because no comparable tax was assessed against other media. Because of this case and others, the Court modified its rule a bit in 1991. Business regulation would be upheld if there were no evidence of discriminatory intent or unintentional discriminatory effect. If the relative economic burden was the same for all media, a regulation would likely be constitutional.

Every court opinion on business regulation has stressed that "laws of general application" do not violate the First Amendment merely because they are enforced against the news media. The Associated Press (AP) challenged the constitutionality of the National Labor Relations Act in 1937 and the Sherman Antitrust Act in 1945, losing both times. In each case, the Supreme Court seemed piqued at the AP for arguing that the First Amendment guaranteed absolute license. In the first case, the AP was trying to dismiss an employee who tried to unionize workers. In the second, the AP's near monopoly on wire service news based on exclusionary bylaws had been found to violate antitrust law as a restraint of trade.

Always losing has not stopped the media from challenging general laws, however. As late as 1993, a Nevada newspaper tried to claim that the First Amendment immunized it from a sex discrimination claim under federal civil rights statutes. The newspaper lost the case.

Enforcing antitrust law against the press has been the most problematic of the laws of general application. Due to the unusual double – or triple – market nature of newspapers and other news media, the courts have been unable to apply formulas developed in cases involving other industries. Charges of antitrust have usually not stuck. Under the Carter, Reagan, and Bush administrations, the Antitrust Division of the Department of Justice seldom brought cases against media companies, but the Clinton administration did challenge the sale of a daily newspaper to a competitor in an adjacent county in 1995.

The Newspaper Preservation Act was one area of business regulation that many thought violates the First Amendment, but as of the late 1990s, it had not been challenged by the industry. Under the act, when a community is served by two newspapers and one of them is in danger of going out of business, they may combine business operations under a joint operating agreement, a combination which would otherwise be illegal. A paper need not be in imminent danger of closing; it is sufficient to show that losses are likely irreversible. The joint operating agreement must be approved by the U.S. Attorney General to qualify as an exception to the antitrust laws. The act, passed in 1970, however, did not preserve newspaper competition in most cities.

Application of labor law has been relatively straightforward, but as the percentage of unionized workers in news organizations decreased, the importance of labor law also decreased. The major issues in the late twentieth century concerned whether or not editorial employees in print and broadcast were "professional" employees and therefore ineligible for union membership under the National Labor Relations Act and ineligible for overtime pay under the Fair Labor Standards Act. Journalists were forced to argue that their work was done almost by rote in order to fit within the provisions of the statutes. Media companies saved money by excluding them.

Cases involving tax laws and postal regulations have been frequent. Both tax and postal law feature detailed, often industry-specific, provisions. An excellent example was the sales tax exemption for purchases of newspapers, found in most states, and the sort of tax that led to the *Minneapolis Star* case. Another was the provision that books, periodicals, and newspapers could be mailed at reduced rates. In these examples, the government in effect subsidized some groups of taxpayers or ratepayers at the theoretical expense of others, but positive differential treatment was never overturned by the courts. If the government were to classify members of the same group differently, however, by giving a benefit selectively, a challenge would likely succeed.

A relatively new area of business regulation in the late twentieth century was found in mandatory newsprint recycling, required or threatened by many states. It is somewhat surprising, given its history, that on this issue the newspaper industry worked to not only comply with but to exceed government expectations rather than to challenge them. Industry insiders said that complying was good both for business and for public relations.

TODD F. SIMON

See also First Amendment in the Twentieth Century; Newspaper Preservation Act; Stamp Act of 1765

Further Reading

Gerald, J. Edward, *The Press and the Constitution, 1931–1947*, Minneapolis: University of Minnesota Press, 1948

Lacy, Stephen, and Todd F. Simon, *The Economics and Regulation of United States Newspapers*, Norwood, New Jersey: Ablex, 1993

Smith, Jeffery Alan, *Printers and Press Freedom: The Ideology of Early American Journalism*, New York: Oxford University Press, 1988

C

Cable Networks

Began as a service to small, rural areas

The first commercial cable television service was developed in western Pennsylvania in the early 1950s. Community antenna television distributed television signals from a central receiver or antenna to individual home sets in areas where reception was poor or virtually nonexistent. These early systems were restricted to importing television signals from distant stations and were, generally, the only economically feasible delivery system for small, rural, and remote communities. By 1955, these systems had grown to about 400 in number, broadcasting 12 channels to approximately 150,000 subscribers.

This type of delivery system was restricted primarily to nonurban areas because it had little, if anything, to offer the urban television viewer that was not available from standard broadcast facilities. The number of subscribers totaled approximately 12 to 15 percent of the households with televisions in the mid-1970s.

The community antenna television system was the precursor to a communication network set in space. Visionaries had predicted such a development years before it happened. Arthur C. Clarke, for instance, commented on such a worldwide communication network utilizing satellites in space in an article in the October 1945 issue of *Wireless World*. Clarke's dream was partially realized with the launch of the *Telstar* satellite in 1962. *Telstar* was limited because it was not in a geostationary orbit and could only be used for a few hours each day. This problem was solved with the placing of communication satellites in geosynchronous orbit. At the end of the twentieth century, satellites were virtually "parked" in space at an altitude of 22,300 miles above the equator with their orbits precisely matching the rotation of the earth. This development made national and international distribution of programming economically feasible.

The cable converter was introduced in the early 1970s. This device allowed cable systems to increase their channel capacities from 12 to 20, then 36, and then 54. This increased capacity, combined with the satellite distribution system, made the advent of cable networks possible.

The increased programming, beyond that which was available from the traditional broadcasting stations, now made cable attractive to people in the urban viewing areas. This, in turn, attracted the programmers. The result was an expansion of cable subscriptions from under 10 million in 1975 to more than 55 million in 1991. The early cable programmers seemed to stick to a narrowly focused type of programming such as sports and news. Later programmers took a more traditional general audience approach.

In the 1990s, cable services could be divided into two categories, basic and premium. A basic cable service was one offered to the subscriber as part of the subscription package. Some cable systems offered what were known as "tiers" of service so the subscriber was able to select the amount of service or number of channels received. For example, for $19.95, the subscriber might receive 12 channels; for $24.95, the service might include an additional 10 channels, and so on. To receive a premium channel, the subscriber would pay an additional fee each month. Examples of this type of service were Home Box Office, Showtime, Cinemax, The Movie Channel, The Disney Channel, Bravo, and national and regional sports networks such as The Golf Channel, SportsChannel, and Prime Sports. One might pay $9.95 per month for each of these premium channels or be able to buy multiple premium channel packages discounting each individual channel.

In some major metropolitan areas and population centers, such Chicago, New York, Long Island, and New England, cable systems established 24-hour news channels for those areas. When it came to basic service, there was a cable channel for just about everyone. Cable channels ranging from business to cartoons, from education to movie classics, from science fiction to travel, and from comedy to the weather were available.

Madison Square Garden Television (MSG-TV) was an early pioneer in the cable network field. After going on the "air" or satellite in 1969, MSG-TV provided coverage of the sports teams and sports events in the New York area.

Some of the earlier success in the field of cable "networks" came from the superstation concept. These were actual on-the-air television stations broadcasting in their area of license as well as being fed by satellite to cable systems around the country. WTBS, in Atlanta, Georgia (1976), WGN, Chicago (1978), WWOR, New York (1979), and WPIX, New York (1984), were very successful in supplying viewers with syndicated programming, live sports programming, movies, and original programming, and in marketing themselves to the advertisers as a "network."

Ted Turner used his superstation, WTBS in Atlanta, as a stepping-stone to launch the Cable News Network (CNN), a 24-hour all-news network that virtually revolutionized the concept of network news. First came CNN in 1980, then CNN Headline News in 1982. Headline News offered the news in 30-minute packages throughout the 24-hour day. CNN eventually became a worldwide service.

Turner later purchased the Metro-Goldwyn-Mayer studio's movie library, including *Gone with the Wind* and other film properties, to create Turner Network Television (TNT). The Turner cable empire came to include CNN, CNN Headline News, CNN World Wide, TNT (showing old movies and many new properties made for this network), the Cartoon Channel, Turner Classic Movies (a premium service), and WTBS.

The cable networks, including the premium services, moved more and more into the area of original programming. No longer relying on off-network syndicated programming and movies, they attracted big-name talent and major coproduction partners. These productions won awards, and their producing companies began successfully moving into off-cable syndication and worldwide distribution.

Satellite transmission also has allowed the creation of programming services aimed at specific audiences that may not be totally serviced by normal broadcast facilities. In 1979, Galavision began operation with a service of Spanish-language programming that reached 25 percent of the Hispanic households in the United States. Galavision was joined by Telemundo in 1987 and Telenoticias del Mundo in 1994. Telemundo was a general audience Spanish-language service, and Telenoticias de Mundo, patterned after CNN Headline News, was a 24-hour news service. Both these services were delivered to the United States, Mexico, South America, and Spain via satellite.

In 1980, Robert L. Johnson launched Black Entertainment Television (BET) with a format of unique urban contemporary programming. By the late 1990s, BET had more than 41.3 million subscribers and was a basic cable, advertiser-supported service targeted primarily to the African American community.

Also in 1980, The Learning Channel began operation. In the 1990s, this network reached more than 34 million households, offering "people of all ages an enjoyable, entertaining way to learn and satisfy their natural curiosity." Lifetime, which began operation in 1984 as The Woman's Channel, provided programming for the special interests of women.

Religious television was attracted to the cable network idea from the early days of its development. The Christian Broadcasting Network (CBN) began in 1976, followed in 1978 by Trinity Broadcasting Network, The Eternal Word in 1981, and the Faith and Values Channel in 1984. CBN later changed its name to The Family Channel. While retaining some of its religious programming, it diversified its programming to appeal to a wider audience.

The Entertainment and Sports Network (ESPN), founded in 1979, was very successful and was included in most of the multinetwork packages for major professional and collegiate sports broadcasts. ESPN2 was added in 1993. Both offered sports and sports-oriented programming.

Viacom, a major force in program syndication for many years, founded Music Television (MTV) in 1981. MTV was a hit with younger audiences from the very beginning with its fast-moving, visual versions of music featuring the top musical groups of the day. Through its programming, MTV fostered a new art form, the music video. The MTV Networks included Nickelodeon (1985), targeted for children; Nick at Nite (1985), "providing entertainment service for the TV generation"; VH1 (Video Hits One) (1985), programming music for an audience in the age group of 25 to 49; and Comedy Central (1991), the all-comedy network.

There were successes and failures with cable networks. Many times two networks that have been competing for the same audience will merge and become a successful operation. A good example of this was A&E (Arts and Entertainment). A&E was launched on February 1, 1984, the result of the merger of the Alpha Repertory Television Service and The Entertainment Channel. A&E's goals were to provide quality programming to distinctive, better-educated audiences and to present programming not found elsewhere on television. Owned by the Hearst Corporation and the NBC and Capital Cities/ABC television networks, A&E attracted more than 64 million subscribers. On January 1, 1995, A&E Television Networks launched The History Channel, devoted to "All of History. All in One Place."

One of the more interesting developments in the evolution of cable networks was the shopping channels. Home Shopping Network (1985), QVC (1986), and Home Shopping Spree (1986) displayed merchandise on the air, and the items were purchased by the viewers by calling toll-free numbers. Purchasers paid by credit card or personal check, and the items were then shipped to the viewer. These services claimed 40 to 50 million households as subscribers, and many times the services were not duplicated on individual cable systems. QVC's head, Barry Diller, had plans to create "Q2, an upscale derivative of this genre, and Q-line, a modem-based 'smart agent' network that [would] break new media ground."

The cable networks changed the way many of the viewers use television. If viewers wanted news, they turned to CNN or Headline News. If they wanted to know about the weather, they turned to the Weather Channel (established in 1982). If they wanted to find out how the stock market was doing, they could tune to CNBC, formerly Financial News Network (1982). They could also watch actual trials on Court TV (1991).

With the creation of the National Cable Satellite Corporation and C-SPAN (Cable Satellite Public Affairs Network) (1979) and C-SPAN 2 (1986), cable subscribers were offered complete and unedited coverage of the U.S. House of Representatives and Senate proceedings, along with events of interest from Canada, Great Britain, and other countries, including sessions of Parliament.

In 1994, direct-broadcast satellite transmission brought the cable networks directly to the subscriber, bypassing terrestrial cable service. Additionally, program providers, cable system operators, motion picture studios, videotape rental and sales companies, and telephone companies jockeyed for positions on the information highway.

There were still more changes ahead for the cable networks. Kay Koplovitz, president of USA Networks, a general audience cable program service in operation since 1980, and the Sci-Fi Channel (1992), stated that one of the key issues facing the industry in the mid-1990s was how television, telephone, and computer businesses would continue their path of convergence. Joseph Collins, chairman of Time Warner Cable, foresaw the viewers and subscribers getting the kind of video they wanted, when they wanted it – video on demand.

In response to the challenge from these cable networks, the broadcast networks are getting a facelift by corporations active in the cable field. In 1995, for instance, Viacom purchased Paramount Film Studios and Blockbuster Video and Music Stores. It then started the United Paramount Network, a traditional type of network supplying programming to over-the-air broadcast stations. Time Warner (owner of a cable system, a film studio, HBO, and Cinemax, and partial owner of TBS, Inc.) began the WB Network, similar to UPN.

THOMAS L. YANCY

See also Cable News; Cable Television; Communication Satellite Technology; Community Access Television; Television Syndication

Further Reading

Aufderheide, Patricia, "Cable Television and the Public Interest," *Journal of Communication* 42:1 (Winter 1992), pp. 52–65
Baldwin, Thomas F., and D. Stevens McVoy, *Cable Communication,* 2nd ed., Englewood Cliffs, New Jersey: Prentice-Hall, 1988
Brown, Rich, "The Boundless Ted Turner," *Broadcasting & Cable* 124:15 (April 11, 1994), pp. 30–32
_____, "When It Works, It Really Works Well," *Broadcasting & Cable* 124:8 (February 21, 1994), pp. 34–40
Coe, Steve, "Hispanic Broadcasting and Cable," *Broadcasting & Cable* 125:2 (January 9, 1995), pp. 40–45
"Countdown to DBS," *Broadcasting & Cable* 123:49 (December 6, 1993)
Gross, Lynne S., *The New Television Technologies,* 3rd ed., Dubuque, Iowa: Wm. C. Brown, 1990
Hanson, Stephen L., ed., *Complete Cable Book,* Los Angeles: Homily, 1994

Cable News

Services providing 24-hour-a-day access to news

Cable television was first thought useful for improving the sharpness of local signals for homes that had poor reception even with outside antennas. In the mid-1970s, cable began sending movies from Home Box Office and sitcoms and sports programming from the superstation WTBS in Atlanta, Georgia, into the nation's homes. By 1980, Ted Turner, who had launched WTBS, was ready for his next innovation: the Cable News Network (CNN).

Turner, a great believer in the power of technology, argued that eventually 24-hour news channels such as his CNN would become the main source of news for the people of the United States. Not many viewers would have agreed in the first year or so of CNN production, which featured poor video standards and inexperienced correspondents. Many in the audience, however, appreciated the ability to obtain news at any time of the day, and CNN grew.

Financially, CNN encountered enormous problems, running losses of at least $2 million a month early on. Turner kept CNN afloat with earnings from his highly profitable superstation. CNN's first profits came in 1985. CNN also faced competition from Satellite NewsChannel, provided by Group W Westinghouse and ABC. The two battled for audience loyalty through 1983, when Turner purchased Satellite NewsChannel.

CNN's ability to beat other news outlets to the air with major stories and to stay on the air for hours covering breaking news events won and kept more and more viewers. In 1981, for instance, CNN was the first to report that President Ronald Reagan had been wounded in an assassination attempt. When CNN's films of fighting in El Salvador revealed a U.S. military adviser carrying a weapon, which was against regulations, the station rode the controversy it had caused to further national acclaim. Turner demanded a place in the White House press pool for his reporters and eventually won it.

In many instances, CNN's scoops were owed to the fact that it was present at certain sites when other networks were not. It was covering the blastoff of the space shuttle *Challenger* in 1986 when the shuttle blew up, providing CNN with an instant scoop, even though other networks quickly picked up on the event. Key correspondents Peter Arnett and Bernard Shaw were in Baghdad, Iraq, in 1991 when the Persian Gulf War broke out, enabling the correspondents to tell viewers of the U.S. bombing and Iraqi response from a front-row seat. Arnett stayed in Baghdad to report on the war, with his action raising ethical questions of whether the enemy's view of the war should be reported. His reports from the Iraqi capital generally carried notices that they had been cleared by the Iraqi government, as a warning to viewers.

Complaints about CNN focused on the low salaries paid to staffers and the no-name reporters that the network employed. As time passed, however, the reporters grew better recognized and, although the salaries remained lower than those at ABC, CBS, and NBC, the freedom offered by CNN to report on various stories won staff loyalty. Christiane Amonpour, for example, told other networks bidding for her and her expertise in Middle Eastern affairs that she was staying with CNN because of that freedom. In the late 1990s, CNN had a staff of more than 1,800 – about twice the size of those of its competitors.

By the 1990s, Ted Turner's experiment was relied upon as the place for continuing coverage of news events, and viewers became accustomed to changing the channel to CNN to catch breaking news. If its cameras were not on the scene of breaking news, its contractors were there when news broke anywhere in the United States or around the world. CNN's coverage of the bombing of the federal building in Oklahoma City, Oklahoma, in 1995, and of the O.J. Simpson murder trial further cemented that reputation.

Strangely enough, people around the world were developing the same habit of relying on CNN – in English – for their latest news. As CNN became available in a number of countries, people around the world found that they could talk to one another about viewing the same news on television. Even Saddam Hussein and his military leaders were reported as watching the Gulf War on CNN.

CNN was the long version of the news: long reports, long interviews, long sports, and long news shows. CNN Headline News, a second Turner service, began in 1982. It offered a full 30 minutes of news every half hour around the clock. This provided an on-demand news summary for viewers at any time of the day or night.

Changes were in the making, however. In 1995, CNN was part of the package Turner sold to Time Warner. At the time, CNN and its Headline News Channel had access to 62 million U.S. homes through 15,000 cable systems.

Also in 1995, Microsoft and NBC joined forces to form MSNBC to challenge CNN directly. Other 24-hour news services were starting up or planned in 1996, but CNN International was the world's only 24-hour global news network. The service was transmitted to more than 200 nations and territories over a dozen satellites to an estimated 80 million people.

Even with growing competition, the CNN News Groups continued to prosper. In 1997, those groups included CNN, CNN Headline News, CNN International, CNNfn (financial news), CNN/SI (sports news), CNN en Español (news in Spanish for Latin Americans), CNN Radio/CNNRadio Noticias (information for radio and for radio in Spanish), CNN Interactive (sites on the World Wide Web), and CNN Newsource (syndicated news service).

MARGARET A. BLANCHARD

See also Radio News; Television News

Cable Television

A *major telecommunications industry*

Cable television began during the late 1940s as a grassroots endeavor to provide television signals to people in areas where unfavorable terrain or great distance impaired or prevented the viewing of television broadcasts. All of the channels delivered by early systems were from over-the-air broadcast stations whose signals were picked up by a master antenna and fed by feeder lines to homes in the community. Known as community antenna television, cable initially was a loosely organized and unregulated industry composed of small proprietorships formed mainly by appliance dealers to stimulate demand for receiving sets.

Throughout the 1950s and 1960s, cable expanded rapidly in small cities and towns across the United States as a community antenna service. It usually offered subscribers the signals of one or more affiliates of each television network, educational television, and, in some cases, one or more independent stations, depending on the availability of off-air reception or microwave signals. Since those early years, cable has developed into a major telecommunications industry, available to nearly 98 percent of all television households in the country.

Although broadcast programming was still an integral part of its service in the late twentieth century, cable television had become a significant electronic delivery system for a myriad of broadcast and cable-originated program services. Cable systems had capacities of 100 or more channels, and systems of 500 channels were predicted for the twenty-first century. A typical system in the mid-1990s provided programming from local network affiliates and independent stations, a few distant superstations, a vast array of satellite-delivered cable networks, pay television (movie) channels, pay-per-view programming, and audio services.

Two elements made up the modern cable industry in the 1990s: local systems, mostly owned by multiple system operators (MSOs), and cable network companies, many of which provided several satellite-distributed networks or program services. More than 11,000 local systems in the United States ranged in size from less than 25 to more than 1 million subscribers. Ownership of individual systems ranged from small proprietorships to major multinational firms.

Two major developments during the 1970s strongly influenced the future growth and development of cable television. One was the adoption of rules for the cable industry in 1972 by the Federal Communications Commission (FCC). The other was the initial use of communications satellites in 1975 for the distribution of program services to cable systems.

In its Cable Television Report and Order of 1972, the FCC established a framework for the orderly development of the cable industry. Soon after those rules were adopted, large corporations and bankers began to invest in cable television. The industry grew rapidly during the next two decades, which were characterized by both deregulation and reregulation. Although the Cable Communications Policy Act of 1984 eliminated rate regulation, the Cable Television Consumer Protection and Competition Act of 1992 restored rate regulation on basic service but left cable systems free to set prices on premium channels.

Distributing cable television programming via communications satellites was a dramatic development in 1975, when Home Box Office, a unit of Time Warner, leased satellite transponders to feed its premium movie service to cable systems across the nation. The rapid diffusion of satellite-transmitted television programming revolutionized the communications industry. Superstation WTBS in Atlanta, Georgia, and the Christian Broadcasting Network (later called The Family Channel) quickly turned to satellites for national program distribution to cable systems. The technical feasibility and cost-effectiveness of satellite program distribution ultimately led to the development of numerous new program services with which cable operators could fill their channels. Moreover, the public's demand for access to

Cable Television Subscribers 1970–1995
(subscribers in thousands)

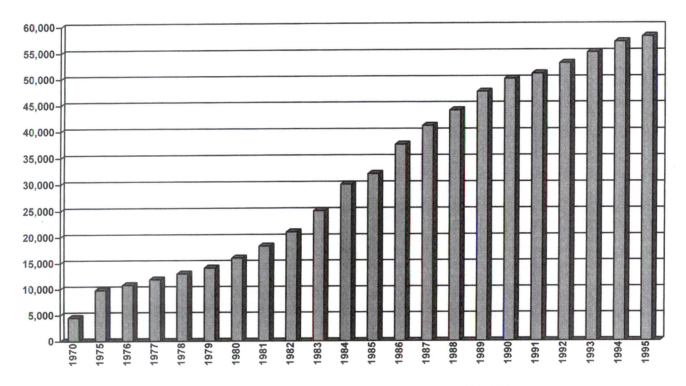

Source: U.S. Bureau of the Census, *Statistical Abstract of the United States* (Washington, D.C.: GPO, 1995).

an ever-growing list of cable networks pressured systems to enlarge channel capacity.

During the period 1975–95, the nature of the cable industry also changed dramatically. No longer merely a basic reception service dependent almost entirely on broadcast television signals and subscriber fees, cable operators came to provide a full range of national and regional programming with a rapidly growing second stream of income from advertising.

Since 1975, cable systems have been built in practically every community across the country. The number of systems has increased from 4,000 in the mid-1970s to more than 11,000 in 1995. In the late 1990s, more than 91,600,000, or 97.1 percent of the nation's 94,300,000 television-owning households, had access to cable. Whereas the number of subscribers was only about 6 million in 1975, an estimated 62,132,000 households (65.9 percent) eventually subscribed to basic cable. Some 28 million also subscribed to additional pay cable services.

Beginning in the mid-1970s, 100 or more satellite-delivered cable networks were established. These varied program services included numerous basic cable networks, superstations, pay channels, regional sports networks, and text and radio services. Popular basic networks included ESPN, USA Network, Cable News Network, Music Television, The Discovery Channel, Black Entertainment Television, The Nashville Network, and The Family Channel.

Various specialty networks served narrower target audiences with niche programming such as Travel, A&E (Arts and Entertainment), Comedy Central, Court TV, The Weather Channel, The Food Channel, Country Music TV, Home and Garden, C-SPAN congressional channels, and many, many more. Even then, new cable networks were launched each year. Many specialized in a single genre, such as comedy, science fiction, courtroom drama, history, quiz shows, cartoons, and classic movies.

Perhaps the most striking trend was the growth of viewership to cable-originated programming. From 1982 until 1994, the share of viewing garnered by basic cable networks in all U.S. television households (all-day basis) rose from 6 percent to 24.6 percent. With such significant audience growth, cable became the nation's fastest-growing advertising medium. Another important growth area was pay-per-view (PPV) programming, in which cable subscribers selected special programs for viewing on a one-time basis.

Although cable system owners held a virtual monopoly in the local marketplace, more than 100 MSOs operated local systems throughout the country. These cable system owners became increasingly concentrated on a national basis through mergers and acquisitions as the industry grew in scope and economic importance. The second segment of the industry, cable networks, consisted of about a dozen companies, several of which were partially owned by cable MSOs. Since these networks provided programming for their affiliated cable systems, this practice constituted a form of vertical integration involving both the production and distribution of programming.

The trend toward greater ownership concentration was driven by the cable industry's pursuit of economies of scale that might have resulted from larger and more cost-efficient operations. For example, the percentage of households served by the 10 largest cable owners increased from 35.7 percent in 1972 to 56 percent in 1994, and the percentage served by the 50 largest MSOs leapt from 60 percent in 1972 to 87 percent in 1994.

Multiple ownership of cable television systems resembles group ownership in broadcasting and newspaper publishing. Unlike radio and television station ownership, however, no limits were placed on the number of cable systems one firm could own or the number or percentage of subscribers that could be served. In 1992, the FCC removed the barriers that previously prohibited telephone companies from cable ownership, allowing them to own systems outside their operating telephone territories. The FCC also amended its rules to allow telephone companies to provide "video dial tone" service, which closely resembles cable, within their franchise areas, a move that was expected to perhaps lead to greater competition within the cable field.

Although no single entity had yet reached 20 percent of the potential market by the late 1990s, the cable industry had become increasingly concentrated and vertically integrated during latter years. Among the largest multiple system operators in 1995 were Tele-Communications, Inc., Time Warner Cable, Continental Cablevision, Comcast, Cablevision Systems, and Cox Cable.

HERBERT H. HOWARD, ROBERT M. OGLES

See also Cable Networks; Cable News; Communication Satellite Technology; Community Access Television

Further Reading
Howard, H.H., "Ownership Trends in Cable Television: 1972–1979," *Journalism Quarterly* 58 (1981)
_____, "An Update on Cable TV Ownership: 1985," *Journalism Quarterly* 63 (1986)
_____, and Robert M. Ogles, "Convergence in Cable Television Ownership: 1972–1994," *Feedback* (Spring 1994)
1994 Cable Facts, New York: Cable Television Advertising Bureau, 1994
Picard, Robert G., ed., *The Cable Networks Handbook*, Riverside, California: Carpelan, 1993

Cameras in the Courtroom

Controversial journalistic practice dates from early 1900s

Journalists have used cameras to record courtroom proceedings since the devices emerged as standard equipment for the newspaper trade at the end of the nineteenth century. Widespread prohibition began in 1938 as a result of overzealous media coverage of the "Lindbergh baby" murder-kidnap trial of Bruno Richard Hauptmann in 1935. Judicial animosity against camera usage in court, however, had surfaced much earlier. In 1917, for example, the Illinois Supreme Court advised its subordinate courts to prohibit photographic and newsreel coverage because cameras undermined the dignity of the judiciary.

Some historians have linked courts' declining tolerance for photography to the rise of tabloid journalism that followed World War I. Newspapers and magazines drew sharp criticism for their sensationalized coverage of the robbery and murder trials of Nicola Sacco and Bartolomeo Vanzetti in 1921, which pandered to anti-immigrant sentiment and a fear of anarchists that led to questionable convictions. Photographers performed no more outrageously than the print journalists in covering the Sacco and Vanzetti trials, but as became increasingly common, they were singled out for sanctions. In 1925, for example, the Chicago Bar Association's Committee on Relations of the Press to Judicial Proceedings recommended banning cameras from state courts. The *Chicago Daily News* endorsed the prohibition, saying that it had assigned photographers to cover trials only because its competitors did.

Restrictions on court photography were still not widespread, however. In fact, when the Scopes "monkey trial" was conducted in Tennessee in 1925, Judge John T. Raulston freely allowed camera and newsreel coverage. John T. Scopes was convicted of violating the state law that forbade teaching that humans evolved from apes. Media coverage of the trial was extensive because of the controversial law and because noted Chicago defense lawyer Clarence Darrow was pitted against a prosecution team led by three-time presidential candidate William Jennings Bryant. That trial is often cited as an example of a media circus, but the coverage was not at issue on appeal of the case.

Two years later, a U.S. court determined for the first time that a judge had the authority to ban cameras from a trial. The Maryland Court of Appeals, in *Ex parte Strum*, upheld a $5,000 fine for contempt levied against two Hearst newspapers and affirmed one-day jail sentences imposed on five editors and reporters for violating the judge's order to refrain from photographing a murder trial.

During the early 1930s, arguments for a ban on courtroom photography focused on the need to preserve the dignity and decorum of trial proceedings. The emphasis gradually shifted until the paramount concerns became due process and preserving the fairness of the proceedings as required by the Sixth, Fourth, and Fourteenth Amendments of the U.S. Constitution. This latter argument claimed that operating cameras in court could affect witnesses and jurors. Journalists argued that in covering trials they were surrogates for the public, and the Constitution guaranteed public trials. Cameras, they said, allowed millions to "attend" trials despite a courtroom's limited size.

In 1931, four years before the Hauptmann trial, the Judicial Section of the American Bar Association (ABA) passed a resolution urging a ban on courtroom photography but made no effort to codify any restrictions. When Hauptmann went to trial for the kidnapping and murder of U.S. aviation hero Charles A. Lindbergh's infant son, there were no standing prohibitions against courtroom photography. More than 130 news photographers flocked to the small Flemington, New Jersey, courtroom where Hauptmann was tried. Some disobeyed Judge Thomas W. Trenchard's explicit instructions not to take pictures while the court was in session. Some used concealed cameras, and a soundless newsreel camera secretly recorded the proceedings from a court balcony. Newspapers published pictures of Lindbergh, his wife, and other witnesses testifying as well as a shot of Hauptmann's reaction as the guilty verdict was announced. One photograph showed Juror No. 11 trying to hide his face with a handkerchief.

Historians claim that only a few journalists using still cameras violated Trenchard's orders. They say the subsequent camera ban was prompted by the newsreel camera operators who recorded several days of testimony shown in more than 70 percent of the country's movie theaters against Trenchard's objections. This led Trenchard to ban all forms of photography from the courtroom.

A circuslike atmosphere pervaded the trial, which had been dubbed the "trial of the century," but photographers were not the sole cause of disruptions. Approximately 500 print journalists and more than 2,000 spectators added to the tumult by talking as witnesses testified and by jockeying for choice positions in a courtroom built to accommodate a fraction of their number. Print journalists kept a steady stream of messengers trooping in and out of the courtroom carrying minute-by-minute accounts of the trial.

The ABA reacted to the Hauptmann trial by closing the courts to cameras nationwide, enacting Canon 35 of the Code of Judicial Conduct in 1938. Despite journalists' claims that the canon violated the First Amendment's free press guarantees, by 1965 every state except Colorado and Texas had adopted some version of the canon to give it the force of law. It was amended in 1952 to include television cameras and was reaffirmed by the ABA in 1963. Canon 35 was superseded by Canon 3A(7) in 1972 but retained its fundamental strictures even as public opinion seemed to be moving toward favoring televised trials.

This change of sentiment became evident in 1955 in Waco, Texas, where a trial was telecast live for the first time and was widely praised by the public, judges, and lawyers for educating the public about the justice system in a nonintrusive manner. In 1956, Colorado became the first state to grant standing permission for journalists to use cameras in court. The ABA did not rework Canon 3A(7) until 1982 to permit the use of cameras and electronic equipment in courts across the country. The delay was at least partially owing to a televised and heavily photographed fraud trial in Texas, which led to a U.S. Supreme Court ruling in 1965 that remained the most potent restriction against photographing or televising criminal trials. The Court ruled in *Estes* v. *Texas* that the use of cameras in court was inherently unconstitutional because the devices were disruptive and affected trial participants, and thereby denied defendants due process. Accordingly, the Court reversed the fraud conviction of Billy Sol Estes, whose trial had attracted intense media attention because he was a friend of Presidents John F. Kennedy and Lyndon B. Johnson.

Cameras remained banned from most courtrooms during the 1960s and into the 1970s, but the prevalence of televisions in U.S. homes, technological advances that made all cameras less obtrusive, the experimental use of cameras in major state trials, and burgeoning support from some quarters of the legal profession caused some state courtroom doors to ease open during the mid-1970s. More opened after 1981 when the U.S. Supreme Court ruled in *Chandler* v. *Florida* that televising or photographing a trial was not per se unconstitutional. The case was an appeal by two Miami, Florida, police officers who claimed the presence of television cameras at their burglary trial had denied them due process. The court did not overrule *Estes* but said that defendants would have to show specifically how the cameras tainted their trials before a conviction would be overturned.

The *Estes* ruling was the last to overturn a conviction based on the presence of cameras, but it continued to be most influential in the federal courts. *Chandler* was most persuasive in the state courts. Cameras were banned from the federal courts and the courts of Washington, D.C., but journalists could secure permission to use them in nearly all of the state trial courts.

U.S. Supreme Court rulings in *Richmond* v. *Virginia* in 1980 and *Globe Newspaper Co.* v. *Superior Court* in 1982 established a constitutional right of the press to attend trials that was rarely curtailed thereafter. That right, however, did not automatically include the right to use cameras or other electronic devices in court. When journalists were allowed to use such equipment in courtroom, they were exercising a revocable privilege. When cameras were banned, journalists usually relied on courtroom sketch artists. Sketching was generally permitted, but individual judges restricted it in isolated instances.

Rule 53 of the Federal Rules of Criminal Procedure forbade the use of any type of camera in federal courts beginning in 1946. The federal court system considered lifting the ban in 1994, but the Judicial Conference rejected the idea by a two-to-one margin. Nonetheless, two of the 13 federal circuit courts of appeal were experimenting with allowing their proceedings to be televised, and a federal district judge allowed a civil trial to be televised in New York City in 1996.

In the late 1990s, only three states – Mississippi, Indiana, and South Dakota – banned televising or photographing any of their court proceedings. The remaining 47 states allowed cameras to be used. In each state, the presiding judge decided case by case whether cameras would be permitted and which restrictions applied. Delaware, Idaho, Illinois, and Louisiana allowed cameras only in their appellate courts.

During the 1990s numerous trials were televised, many through the Court TV cable network founded in 1991, which ignited public discussion and reconsideration of the propriety of allowing television cameras into the courts. In the aftermath of the prolonged televised murder trial of former football player and actor O.J. Simpson, California officials sought to impose a ban. As of January 1, 1997, however, they had succeeded only in revising the camera access rule to prevent television coverage of jury selection and discussions among judges, attorneys, and other trial participants.

JOHN C. WATSON

See also Free Press–Fair Trial Controversy; Photographic
   Technology

Further Reading
Barber, Susanna, *News Cameras in the Courtroom: A Free
   Press-Fair Trial Debate,* Norwood, New Jersey: Ablex,
   1987
Dienes, C. Thomas, Lee Levine, and Robert C. Lind,
   Newsgathering and the Law, Charlottesville, Virginia:
   Michie Law, 1997
Kielbowicz, Richard B., "The Story Behind the Adoption
   of the Ban on Courtroom Cameras," *Judicature*
   63:1(1979)
Thaler, Paul, *The Watchful Eye: American Justice in the
   Age of the Television Trial,* Westport, Connecticut:
   Praeger, 1994

Campaign Financing Reform and the Media

*Attempts to restrict amounts spent on seeking
elective office*

Beginning in the 1960s, the increasing use made by political
campaigns of the mass media, particularly television, was
linked to various proposals for campaign reform in general
and campaign finance reform in particular. The high cost of
television advertising was assigned much of the blame for
increases in the cost of campaigning for office. Candidates
needed to raise so much money to run for office that they
often fell prey to wealthy special interests willing to exchange campaign contributions for influence. The largest
part of campaign expenditures in major electoral contests
went to produce and air political commercials. A high percentage of House and Senate candidates relied on television
more than on any other medium. In the 1992 presidential
election, candidates Bush, Clinton, and Perot and their parties spent more than $120 million on television advertising.

The first major federal campaign reforms enacted in 1907
banned contributions to congressional or presidential campaigns by banks and corporations, and they were still in effect at the end of the century. Further legislation followed in
1911, when limits on candidate spending in House and Senate campaigns were first enacted, along with the first disclo-
sure-of-contribution requirements. In 1925, spending limits
were raised and disclosure requirements reinforced to a degree. Limits on campaign contributions ($5,000 to candi-
dates for Congress or the presidency) were enacted for the
first time. This era of campaign reform was notable for its in-
effectiveness. Until 1971, candidates were required to report
only contributions of which the candidate was aware, resulting in fund-raising being delegated to treasurers, while candidates filed reports showing zero contributions. From the
passage of the 1925 statute until its repeal in 1971, there was
not a single prosecution for violation of the federal campaign law.

The Federal Election Campaign Act (FECA) of 1972 was
the first serious federal campaign statute. It sought to attack
the rising cost of campaigning by limiting spending on
broadcast media advertising, creating a fund for the public
financing of presidential campaigns (which took effect in
1976), and establishing a set of detailed disclosure requirements. In the aftermath of the Watergate break-in, Congress
passed a series of amendments to FECA in 1974 that
amounted to new, comprehensive legislation. The 1974
amendments concentrated responsibility for all contributions and expenditures in one committee, for which the candidate was made responsible. Limits on all contributions
and all spending in the campaign were enacted, disclosure
requirements were strengthened, and, for the first time, an
administrative agency, the Federal Election Commission,
was created to supervise and enforce the regulations.

Under the 1974 FECA amendments, individuals were
limited to contributions of $1,000 per election per candi-
date, so that, including primaries, a contributor could give a
candidate $2,000 per election cycle. Total contributions by
an individual to all candidates, party committees, and political action committees (PACs) were limited to $25,000 per
calendar year, no more than $20,000 of which could go to a
national party committee and no more than $5,000 of
which could go to any PAC or other party committee.

Spending limits contained in the 1974 FECA amendments provided for limits on the amounts that political party committees could spend on behalf of their party's
candidates, limits on the amounts candidates and their families could contribute to their own campaigns, and total
spending limits for House and Senate campaigns. The 1974
amendments also limited independent spending by groups
and individuals supporting or opposing a candidate to
$1,000 per candidate per election. For the presidential elec-
tion, a fund was established that matched individual contributions during the primary campaign and fully funded
major party candidates in the general election. Candidates
who voluntarily agreed to accept FECA spending limits
were eligible for this federal funding.

In 1976, in *Buckley* v. *Valeo,* major provisions of the
1974 amendments came under constitutional challenge,
and a number of them were declared unconstitutional. In
Buckley, the U.S. Supreme Court held that the giving and
spending of money in election campaigns was protected by
the guarantees of freedom of speech and freedom of association contained in the First Amendment to the Constitution. The Court found that political speech in the age of the
mass media requires the expenditure of money and that
making political contributions serves to affiliate the contributor with a candidate and others of like mind, so that
contribution and expenditure limits have an impact on protected associational freedoms. More specifically, the Court
invalidated almost all of the spending limits contained in
the FECA as restrictions on the quantity and quality of political expression, stating, "The First Amendment denies
government the power to determine that spending to promote one's political view is wasteful, excessive, or unwise."

The spending limits associated with the voluntary public
funding scheme for presidential elections were upheld because of their voluntary nature. However, the limits on
spending by candidates, on independent expenditures by

groups and individuals, and on the amounts a candidate could spend in his or her own campaign were declared unconstitutional. The limits on contributions were upheld because of the compelling governmental interest in preventing corruption and the appearance of corruption potentially arising from large or unrestricted campaign donations.

In the 20 years following *Buckley,* there were no major amendments to the FECA. Campaign spending rose sharply between 1976 and 1986, but between then and the late 1990s, expenditures (in constant dollars) actually leveled off or declined. One consequence of *Buckley* was that some PACs engaged in more independent spending, particularly on broadcast advertising, in elections because direct contributions were limited but independent expenditures were not.

The perceived rise in negative campaigning in the 1980s brought with it demands for additional reform to control the contributions and independent expenditures of PACs and individuals. Proposals to regulate the content of broadcast advertising in order to prohibit negative advertising or limit conditions in which it could occur were offered, but none had been adopted by the late 1990s. The principal checks on political advertising style and content (other than state laws) were the voluntary ethics codes of professional organizations such as the American Association of Political Consultants and the American Association of Advertising Agencies.

CLIFFORD A. JONES, LYNDA LEE KAID

See also Mass Media and Politics; Political Advertising

Further Reading

Alexander, Herbert, and Monica Bauer, *Financing the 1988 Election,* Boulder, Colorado: Westview, 1991

Jones, Clifford A., and Lynda Lee Kaid, "Political Campaign Regulation and the Constitution," *Oklahoma Law Review* 29 (1976)

Kaid, Lynda Lee, "Ethical Dimensions of Political Advertising," in *Ethical Dimensions of Political Communication,* edited by Robert E. Denton, Jr., New York: Praeger, 1991

Schotland, Roy A., "Proposals for Campaign Finance Reform: An Article Dedicated to Being Less Dull Than Its Title," *Capital University Law Review* 21 (1992)

Sorauf, Frank J., *Inside Campaign Finance: Myths and Realities,* New Haven, Connecticut: Yale University Press, 1992

Campbell, John

Printed first ongoing newspaper in the American colonies

Begun in 1704 as the first continuous newspaper in the American colonies, John Campbell's *Boston News-Letter* displayed many characteristics that would be prevalent with most early colonial publishers: submission to censorship, association with the post office as a major source of news, and a reliance on political appointments and govern-

mental subsidies as a steady source of income. Aware that Benjamin Harris's ill-fated *Publick Occurrences* had been banned for publishing without a license 14 years earlier, Campbell dutifully had his copy checked in advance by a representative of the royal governor's office. Considered dull even by colonial standards, the *News-Letter* served Boston's needs as a source of news about maritime activities, "intelligence from abroad" gleaned from incoming newspapers, and local political and social affairs.

Campbell knew holding the position of postmaster was desirable, if not crucial, to the success of a newspaper. His post office was the city's center of information, such as exchange newspapers, posted governmental documents, personal correspondence, and local gossip. As postmaster, he was also a political insider and, consequently, trusted with the dissemination of government notices.

Since income from subscriptions and advertisements was not sufficient to cover the cost of his publication, he petitioned the governor's office for political subsidies in return for publishing governmental notices. Little financial help was given, however, forcing Campbell to suspend publication of the *News-Letter* on several occasions.

Campbell lost his postmastership in 1719 but continued to publish the newspaper for two more years before retiring from the business. The *News-Letter* survived under other publishers until 1775.

PERRY J. ASHLEY

See also Publick Occurrences, Both Forreign and Domestick

Further Reading

Cook, Elizabeth Christine, *Literary Influences in Colonial Newspapers, 1704–1750,* New York: Columbia University Press, 1912

Smith, Jo Anne, "John Campbell," in *Dictionary of Literary Biography: American Newspaper Journalists, 1690–1872,* vol. 43, edited by Perry J. Ashley, Detroit, Michigan: Gale, 1985

Thomas, Isaiah, *The History of Printing in America,* Albany, New York: Joel Munsell, 1874

Cartoons and Cartoonists

Drawings designed to make an editorial comment

Political cartoons, the combination of realistic and symbolic images with words to make an editorial comment, are signed statements of the personal opinions of their creators, the cartoonists. They are not illustrations of the news – although cartoons usually, but not always, reinforce the editorial perspective of their publications. The best political cartoonists of any period study current events thoughtfully, are passionate about their subjects, and are capable of expressing their outrage or support through graphic metaphors. The requirements of a good political cartoon have been described as wit, truth (or one side of the truth), and moral purpose.

The use of satirical drawings and caricatures in American mass media predates the Declaration of Independence. "Join, or Die," by Benjamin Franklin, appeared in the *Pennsylvania Gazette* on May 9, 1754, the first cartoon to be published in an American newspaper. The most common outlet for graphic political commentary in the late eighteenth and early nineteenth centuries was separately issued prints (such as Paul Revere's 1770 engraving about the Boston Massacre, "The Bloody Massacre"). The rise of magazines in the United States during the 1800s created another outlet for political graphics, both woodcuts and etchings. In 1870–71, Thomas Nast, cartoonist for *Harper's Weekly*, demonstrated the power of his medium in a vicious and successful campaign against William Marcy "Boss" Tweed, leader of New York City's Tammany Hall. Lithography was introduced in the United States in 1819, and this printing technique made it easier and less expensive to publish cartoons. Joseph Keppler's beautiful chromolithographic cartoons in *Puck* between 1877 and 1918 carried the genre to a new level of excellence.

Because of production costs and time constraints, most newspapers used few cartoons until the 1880s and the invention of photoengraving. The first U.S. newspaper to print political cartoons regularly was the *New York Evening Telegram* (founded in 1867), which ran a large cartoon on the front page each Friday. Joseph Pulitzer and William Randolph Hearst used the popularity of cartoons to sell newspapers to the working class. Political cartoons played a large role in the birth of yellow journalism during the Spanish-American War.

During World War I, virtually all newspaper and magazine political cartoonists supported the Committee on Public Information, the government's propaganda arm. A notable exception to this were the cartoonists for the *Masses*, which the federal government eventually shut down under the Espionage Act of 1917 for its mailing of antiwar materials. The publication of biting political graphics in the

A version of "Join or Die" appeared on the front page of Isaiah Thomas' paper, *The Massachusetts Spy*, in 1775.

mainstream press became less common until World War II. At mid-century, when the McCarthy hearings began, several cartoonists, most notably Herblock (Herbert Block) of the *Washington Post*, sharpened their pens. The best-known and most influential political cartoonists of the last third of the twentieth century were Paul Conrad, Pat Oliphant, and Jeff MacNelly.

In comparison with political cartoonists in many other countries, U.S. cartoonists have enjoyed remarkable freedom under the protection of the First Amendment. As of the late 1990s, no U.S. cartoonist had been successfully sued for libel. The first efforts to restrict cartoonists occurred between 1897 and 1915 when anti-cartoon bills were considered in New York, Indiana, and Alabama, and passed (then later repealed) in Pennsylvania and California. The unanimous 1988 decision of the U.S. Supreme Court in a case involving evangelist Jerry Falwell and magazine publisher Larry Flynt's use of graphic satire in *Hustler* magazine reinforced the legal right of political cartoonists to practice their art.

Women and minorities were usually not well represented in the ranks of U.S. political cartoonists. The first woman to be a full-time political cartoonist was Edwina Dumm, who worked for the *Columbus (Ohio) Monitor* from 1915–17. Since then, only about a dozen women have held similar positions; the first one to win a Pulitzer Prize was Signe Wilkinson, in 1992. The first African American political cartoonist was Henry Jackson Lewis, who drew for several papers including the *Pine Bluff (Arkansas) Commercial* and *Freeman*. Notable twentieth-century political cartoonists in the African American press included Tom Floyd, Oliver Harrington, and Clint Wilson Sr.

A survey in the late twentieth century indicated that cartoons were read by more editorial-page readers than letters to the editor, editorials, or columns. The field was disparaged by some for an increased use of humor at the expense of critical commentary. The number of newspapers having a full-time political cartoonist also declined as management chose to print syndicated cartoons in order to cut costs.

"Join or Die" cartoon first appeared in 1754 but is more associated with the Stamp Act Crisis of 1765 and the coming of Revolution in 1774–75.

This often meant that there was no cartoonist to skewer the local equivalent of Boss Tweed.

LUCY SHELTON CASWELL

See also Committee on Public Information; Espionage and Sedition Acts; Nast, Thomas; Yellow Journalism

Further Reading

Hess, Stephen, and Milton Kaplan, *The Ungentlemanly Art: A History of American Political Cartoons,* rev. ed., New York: Macmillan, 1975

Medhurst, Martin J., and Michael A. Desousa, "Political Cartoons as Rhetorical Form: A Taxonomy of Graphic Discourse," *Communication Monographs* 48:3 (1981)

Mohn, Elsa, and Maxwell McCombs, "Who Reads Us and Why," *The Masthead* 32:4 (1980–81)

Nevins, Allan, and Frank Weitenkampf, *A Century of Political Cartoons: Caricature in the United States from 1800 to 1900,* New York: Scribner's, 1944

Press, Charles, *The Political Cartoon,* Rutherford, New Jersey: Fairleigh Dickinson University Press, 1981; London: Associated University Presses, 1981

West, Richard Samuel, "Selected Bibliography of Political Cartoon Collections," *Inks: Cartoon and Comic Art Studies* 1:3 (1994) and 2:1 (1995)

Censorship of Advertising

Restrictions stem from many groups, for many reasons

Censorship of advertising is any action by which advertising is restricted (i.e., banned, limited, or controlled). Advertising media, retailers, advertising professionals, trade groups, even advertisers themselves have censored advertising; this type of censorship is self-regulation. Censorship has also come from forces external to advertising – consumers, consumer groups, and the media as critics. This is consumerism, or citizen activism. It compels restrictions on advertising through direct pressure (e.g., publicity and boycotts) on advertisers, media, and retailers and through persuasive contact (e.g., lobbying, filings, and complaints) with government regulators.

Government is a primary external force; its restriction of advertising is regulation. On the national level, Congress passes laws and creates agencies that affect advertising. Primary regulatory responsibility is assigned to the Federal Trade Commission (FTC), which issues statements and takes actions that detail what can and cannot be done, said, and depicted in advertising. Other agencies with major influence include the Food and Drug Administration; the U.S. Postal Service; the Federal Communications Commission; the Bureau of Alcohol, Tobacco, and Firearms of the Internal Revenue Service; and the Securities and Exchange Commission. These agencies tend to act against advertising deemed fraudulent, deceptive, or misleading in a material sense; that is unfair in its methods of competition; or that is injurious to public safety or health. They also have sought to protect vulnerable audiences (e.g., children) from advertising.

State and local governments also prohibit deceptive advertising. They control advertising in a myriad of other ways as well, from laws forbidding the advertising of certain goods and services (e.g., alcoholic beverages and casinos) to ordinances restricting signs.

That advertising is subject to so much government control, relative to other types of expression, is a product of action by the federal courts. The courts have labeled advertising "commercial speech" and ruled that, while it does qualify for First Amendment protection, it has less protection than other types of speech, such as political comment. Thus, for example, federal courts have ruled that pharmacists may not be prohibited from advertising prices of prescription drugs, attorneys from advertising prices of routine services, or contraceptives firms from advertising their products – but the courts also have ruled that Puerto Rico may prohibit advertising of its tourist casinos to local residents and a university may prohibit certain sales promotions in its dormitories.

Historically, there were few attempts to restrict advertising until the nineteenth century, when publications began to reach a mass audience. Medical quacks and nostrums advertised heavily in newspapers and magazines; most such advertising was blatantly deceptive. A typical advertisement would tout a supposed cure for problems as diverse as tuberculosis, syphilis, cancer, diabetes, gallstones, impotence, and "female trouble," while in reality the "cure" was useless and sometimes even harmful.

At first, some publications refused certain advertising because of the morally objectionable nature of the copy or the product. In the 1840s, for example, the *New York Tribune* rejected ads from abortionists and "cures" for venereal disease. Some farm publications did tell readers as early as 1860 that they would refuse deceptive advertising. But media concern over advertising claims grew slowly until 1892, when Cyrus Curtis announced that his *Ladies' Home Journal* would no longer accept medical advertising. The *Journal,* with its large circulation, was influential; other magazines and newspapers followed its lead and restricted medical advertising.

Efforts to regulate fraudulent medical advertising intensified during the Progressive Era. Among those working for reform were muckraking journalists, and their efforts helped secure passage of the Pure Food and Drug Act of 1906. That act required that patent medicine labels list certain dangerous ingredients, and the Sherley Amendment of 1912 banned false curative claims from labels.

Meanwhile, advertisers had become concerned over other deceptive advertising. National distribution of mass-produced, brand-name goods had grown, and the process of creating and placing advertising had evolved into a specialized occupation. To Eastman Kodak, Campbell Soup, Procter & Gamble, Nabisco, and other companies who marketed these goods, it was important that consumers believe their national advertisements. Department stores, who depended on local clientele and repeat sales, also campaigned for advertising honesty.

The desire by advertisers and agencies to clean up advertising coalesced at the 1911 convention of the Associated Advertising Clubs of America. Its reform theme touched off the Truth in Advertising movement. Later that year, *Printer's Ink* published a model state statute that would make dishonest advertising illegal; although often weakened in form, the model was enacted into law in 43 states. In 1912, the Associated Advertising Clubs formed a National Vigilance Committee, and local ad clubs subsequently formed local vigilance committees. These groups, which reported fraudulent advertising to government authorities, evolved into Better Business Bureaus.

As the United States moved toward entering World War I, the Truth in Advertising movement lost momentum. The FTC, created in 1914, could prohibit deceptive advertising only if such advertising was also an unfair method of competition. Meanwhile, patent medicine manufacturers took advantage of the fact that no federal law covered non-label advertising. They labeled their concoctions as honestly as the law required but used repetitive, continuous advertising to push the wildest of claims.

Advertising grew rapidly during the 1920s. The advertising business had, through self-regulation, made some headway toward building a good reputation. The American Association of Advertising Agencies, for example, published its *Code of Ethics* in 1924, encouraging member agencies to refuse to produce false advertising. Other organizations, even trade associations for some advertiser industries, adopted codes that discouraged false advertising. Most codes, however, were superficial and had no enforcement provisions, and the volume of fraudulent advertising continued to grow.

A major consumer movement developed in the 1930s. During the economic depression, many people castigated business and advertising for the country's plight. Critics, mainly from consumer organizations and government, looked askance at the very function of advertising itself. Consumers Research and Consumers Union, formed in 1929 and 1936, respectively, assumed that most advertising was fraudulent, tested goods and services, and issued reports and ratings. Books and articles excoriated advertising, supported consumer testing agencies, and called for federal control of advertising. Cynicism concerning advertising spread throughout the country.

Franklin Roosevelt, inaugurated president in 1933, brought into government people who sympathized with advertising's critics. Bills to regulate advertising were introduced in Congress – bills that were supported by citizen groups. Advertisers feared government regulation and fought bitterly against these bills. Finally, in 1938, Congress passed the Wheeler-Lea Act amending the Federal Trade Commission Act to give the FTC power to deal directly with deceptive advertising.

The next major consumer movement that resulted in restrictions on advertising developed in the 1960s. During the prior decade, television had grown into a pervasive and assumedly powerful advertising medium. Advertisers and agencies increasingly used puffery and exaggeration. Although broadcasters adopted tough self-regulatory language, advertisers and other media saw no reason to tighten self-regulation. Consumers, on the other hand, grew in-

creasingly disturbed with advertising. Numerous books criticized business generally and advertising particularly. Consumer activists such as Ralph Nader gained public support. Newspapers, magazines, and broadcasters established consumer advocate features. By the time the advertising community did try to act, public interest groups and the government had begun an effective push for legislation.

During the period 1960–72, Congress passed more than 25 major laws restricting advertising. Among those acts were the following: limitations on drug advertising under certain circumstances; requirements for uniform packaging standards; prohibition of advertising of products that are hazardous to children; requirement that credit and payment advertising reveal terms and finance charges; prohibition of cigarette advertising on broadcast media; and requirement that cigarette packages and advertising carry health warnings.

In an effort to forestall further legislation, the advertising community set up the National Advertising Division/National Advertising Review Board system in 1971. Ten years later, some cities set up a local equivalent, the Local Advertising Review Program. Shortly after, however, one well-known mechanism for media self-regulation was dismantled. The code structure for the National Association of Broadcasters (NAB) had provided specific guidelines for comparative advertising, advertising to children, and the advertising of personal care products, lotteries, alcohol and tobacco, and health issues. Additionally, the NAB Code Authority prescreened commercials dealing with certain controversial areas. That ended with a 1982 federal district court ruling that the NAB code's limitation on advertising time and multiproduct commercials violated antitrust laws. The ruling did not affect the standards and practices divisions of television broadcast networks, and their requirements and prescreening efforts continued to affect what could and could not be depicted in television advertising.

F. LESLIE SMITH

See also Better Business Bureau; Commercial Speech; Federal Trade Commission; Food and Drug Administration; National Advertising Review Board; Patent Medicine Advertising; Truth in Advertising Movement

Further Reading

Beales, J. Howard, *State and Federal Regulation of National Advertising,* Washington, D.C.: AEI, 1993

Boddewyn, Jean J., *Global Perspectives on Advertising Self-Regulation: Principles and Practices in Thirty-Eight Countries,* Westport, Connecticut: Quorum, 1992

Miracle, Gordon E., and Terrence Nevett, *Voluntary Regulation of Advertising: A Comparative Analysis of the United Kingdom and the United States,* Lexington, Massachusetts: Lexington Books, 1987

Preston, Ivan L., *The Great American Blow-up: Puffery in Advertising and Selling,* Madison: University of Wisconsin Press, 1975

Turner, E.S., *The Shocking History of Advertising,* New York: Dutton, 1953; London: Michael Joseph, 1953

Censorship of Books

Suppression of books long practiced in the United States

Censorship should concern all citizens of the United States because it affects their basic rights and freedom as individuals. No consistent philosophy appears to undergird the various interpretations of the First Amendment to the U.S. Constitution. The shield of the First Amendment has been enlarged since it was first conceived and adopted to better protect freedom of speech and of the press.

Early laws such as the Alien and Sedition Acts of 1798 limited free speech by making it illegal to criticize the government. Political reasons and obscenity charges were first used to limit access to information. In the twentieth century, information presented on television or in a book or magazine was selected by someone else. Some people believed that there should be controls on what the people of the United States read or viewed or heard.

Censorship is defined as the suppression of ideas and information that certain persons – individuals, groups, or government officials – find objectionable or dangerous. Censors try to use the power of the state to impose their view of what they consider truthful and appropriate, or offensive and objectionable, on everyone else. In most cases, the censor wants to prejudge materials for everyone in bookstores, libraries, classrooms, art museums, and theaters, and on television and radio.

Fanny Hill, the 1750 English classic by John Cleland, was the first book to be declared obscene in the United States, in Massachusetts in 1821. Other states followed Massachusetts in passing laws to prohibit obscene literature. Problems with antislavery books, French drawings and prints, and Italian art imports resulted in government officials becoming involved and passing tariff acts to prevent the materials from entering the country.

Reasons for challenging materials, in addition to political content and sexual expression, were that the language and writings were offensive to someone's racial, cultural, or ethnic background; gender or sexuality; or religious beliefs. In 1865, the U.S. Congress made it illegal to mail obscene materials. After the American Civil War ended, groups such as Boston's Watch and Ward Society and New York's Society for the Suppression of Vice were organized to suppress certain books, magazines, and newspapers.

One of the most vocal vice fighters of the time was Anthony Comstock, who lobbied Congress to pass a strong law prohibiting obscenity in 1873. He was appointed a special agent of the Post Office Department, and he reportedly seized many thousands of books, pictures, decks of playing cards, and rubber articles. He also raided bookstores and had their owners brought to trial.

Objectionable books, such as Mark Twain's *Tom Sawyer* and *The Adventures of Huckleberry Finn,* were removed from libraries. Titles by Walt Whitman, Nathaniel Hawthorne, George Sand, Leo Tolstoy, and George Bernard Shaw were banned. Authors were intimidated to the point that many fled to Europe to write freely. Some publishers would not accept works from some authors because the publishers felt the authors' books might be considered controversial.

Another sedition act was passed in 1918, outlawing the publication of any materials that condemned World War I or U.S. involvement in it. Librarians were forced to make certain that their collections contained no materials that appeared to speak unfavorably about the war. For the first time, the U.S. Supreme Court ruled that certain narrow categories of speech were not protected by the First Amendment. In later years, the Court would add obscenity, child pornography, and defamation to the list of unprotected speech. The government also was allowed to enforce secrecy of some information to ensure national security.

After the war, works by Upton Sinclair, Theodore Dreiser, Ernest Hemingway, and Aldous Huxley were among those banned along with titles by Jean-Jacques Rousseau, Aristophanes, François Rabelais, and Daniel Defoe. James Joyce's *Ulysses* was confiscated in 1933. In this case, the judge used new criteria in deciding obscenity by looking at the book as a whole rather than at isolated passages; he asked whether it would stir the sexual impulses of normal citizens rather than those of the weakest members of society. This opened the door to many works of literature that previously had been banned.

The censors found a new area to suppress in the 1940s because of the threat of Communism, and many states tried to pass laws restricting the mention of anything Russian. Many vigilante groups were formed and libraries were told to remove such titles as *Moby Dick, Joseph in Egypt,* and *Robin Hood* because they supposedly taught Communist doctrine. Civil rights, sex, and offensive language were not forgotten by the censors, with the works of Sigmund Freud, the *Kinsey Reports, The Grapes of Wrath,* and the Tarzan series among the books attacked.

In 1957 and 1973, the Supreme Court revised its definition of obscenity to include a consideration of the work as a whole, the application of contemporary community standards, and a consideration of its appeal to the prurient interest in sex, along with whether it had any serious literary, artistic, political, or scientific value. President Lyndon Johnson in 1967 set up a commission to study scientifically the effects of pornography on society. After several years of study, the commission found no evidence that there was a connection between pornography and crime. The Nixon administration, however, rejected the report.

Later, under the Reagan administration, the Attorney General's Commission on Pornography was appointed. Its 1986 report was reviewed as an unsatisfying analysis since the commission had no funds to authorize original scientific research, no subpoena authority, and little interest in probing beneath the surface of most witnesses' claims. The report often relied on the unquestioned testimony of a single witness for its conclusions. Many people felt that rather than clarifying the issues, the report largely polluted the debate over sexually explicit materials and censorship and that causation was not proved. Many groups felt the chilling effect of the report on the free flow of information and ideas.

Organizations such as the American Library Association and People for the American Way began keeping statistics on attempts by individuals and groups to limit access to certain library and classroom materials. They promoted the belief in intellectual freedom as the right of every individual to both seek and receive information from all points of view without restriction. The groups argued that this was the basis of the nation's democratic system of government and that it promoted well-informed citizens.

Beginning in about 1980, censors justified their attempts to limit or remove materials from libraries and classrooms by saying that the materials were offensive or destructive and should not be made available. They subscribed to the idea that certain individuals or institutions would be endangered if some ideas were disseminated without restriction. Many groups seeking restrictions on material saw themselves acting as concerned parents rather than censors.

More than 1,000 attempts at censorship were reported by librarians and educators each year in the United States in the late twentieth century. The numbers tended to increase with each new report. These included only reported challenges, and intellectual freedom groups believed that many more challenges remained unreported.

Book-banning and book-burning incidents have arisen in all parts of the country. This phenomenon is not exclusively urban or rural, northern or southern, liberal or conservative. Reports indicate that censorship is a nationwide activity played out in many settings – legislative hearings, school board proceedings, public library board of trustee meetings, governmental committees, parent group meetings, pressure group conferences, publishing decisions, and court proceedings.

Keeping watch over what citizens read – as well as what they write and view – became for many a national pastime. The 1990s revealed many attempts to remove, alter, or restrict library users' access to a wide variety of materials. The attempts were initiated by a variety of sources: parents, teachers, school officials, board of trustee members, members of city or county boards, librarians, civic groups, publishers, organized pressure groups, local clergy, television pastorates, and other church-related groups.

Intellectual freedom supporters argue that decisions as to selection, an inclusive process, must be made by librarians and educators. These professionals affirmatively seek out materials that serve the mission of the institution by providing a broad diversity of points of view and subject matter. By contrast, censorship is an exclusive process, by which individuals and institutions seek to deny access to or otherwise suppress ideas and information because they find those ideas offensive and do not want others to have access to them. Librarians, for example, select materials using written criteria approved by the governing board of the institution. The library, as an example, is a neutral provider of information from all points of view and does not necessarily endorse the ideas expressed in the materials.

Although a large percentage of reported censorship incidents appear to have been initiated by isolated individuals, the reasons cited for these attempts consistently followed the philosophy of some nationally organized pressure groups. The latest statistics in the 1990s indicated that more than 40 percent of the challenges succeeded in having the materials removed or restricted. Some organizations most vocal in attacking library and classroom materials were Donald E. Wildmon's American Family Association, Pat Robertson's and Ralph Reed's Christian Coalition, Phyllis Schlafly's Eagle Forum, Robert L. Simonds' Citizens for Excellence in Education, Beverly LaHaye's Concerned Women for America, and James C. Dobson's Focus on the Family. Most of these organizations were well funded and used electronic mail, the Internet, and the other media to spread the word.

GENE D. LANIER

See also Alien and Sedition Acts of 1798; American Library Association and Intellectual Freedom; Espionage and Sedition Acts; Obscenity and Pornography

Further Reading

DelFattore, Joan, *What Johnny Shouldn't Read: Textbook Censorship in America,* New Haven, Connecticut: Yale University Press, 1992

Foerstel, Herbert N., *Banned in the U.S.A.: A Reference Guide to Book Censorship in Schools and Public Libraries,* Westport, Connecticut: Greenwood, 1994

Hurwitz, Leon, *Historical Dictionary of Censorship in the United States,* Westport, Connecticut: Greenwood, 1985

Noble, William, *Bookbanning in America: Who Bans Books? – And Why?,* Middlebury, Vermont: Paul S. Eriksson, 1990

Simmons, John S., ed., *Censorship: A Threat to Reading, Learning, and Thinking,* Newark, Delaware: International Reading Association, 1994

Censorship of Broadcasting

Attempts to limit the nature and amount of material presented

Censorship generally is thought of as government control of information. Some may consider as censorship any kind of control, such as a news director's decision not to use a reporter's story, a program director's choice not to carry a program, or a station not playing the music of certain artists on the air. This discussion of censorship, however, examines only formal government or regulatory control.

Censorship by government usually is considered antithetical to democratic government, which is based in the power of its citizens. Thus, an informed citizenry is critical, and that status is achieved by a free flow of information. The belief in an informed citizenry has been enshrined in the First Amendment of the Constitution since the earliest days of the republic. That amendment indicates that "Congress shall make no law . . . abridging the freedom of speech, or of the press." Although numerous cases defining this idea have verified that "press" includes broadcasting, laws have frequently been interpreted by the courts to favor information control.

Society, in fact, has usually consented to some form of

control of information that may be destructive to basic freedoms. As First Amendment scholar Zechariah Chafee once wrote,

> The very utterance of . . . words (with destructive effect) is considered to inflict a present injury upon listeners, readers, or those defamed, or else to render highly probable an immediate breach of the peace. This is a very different matter from punishing words because they express ideas which are thought to cause a future danger to the State.

Broadcasting, with its perceived limited frequencies, became regulated by Congress mostly for the sake of directing the use of the electromagnetic spectrum. Over the years, the demand for licenses has exceeded the number of frequencies available. Thus, the government agency responsible for regulating broadcasting, the Federal Communications Commission (FCC), has given preference to stations that promised the best programming performance. For some observers, this control constituted a kind of censorship because of the rejection of programming that some government official deemed less important than other kinds. The FCC's right to give selective preference has been upheld by federal courts.

Discussions of censorship also must take into account whether the concern is prior restraint, which prevents something from being published or released, or after-the-fact punishment, where the desire to avoid known consequences prevents disclosure. Dislike for prior restraint is long-standing among the people of the United States. Even before the colonies had formulated their constitutional foundations, British jurist William Blackstone wrote, "The liberty of the press is indeed essential to the nature of a free state: but this consists in laying no *previous* restraints upon publications, and not in freedom from censure for criminal matter when published."

Licensing, whether of a journalist, a newspaper, or a broadcast station, might be considered prior restraint because it requires government sanction or approval before the information is published or aired. Most print journalists would not think of tolerating such controls. Yet broadcasters must obtain a station license in order to operate, and this is considered by some as a kind of prior restraint.

Prior restraint need not always be actual physical restraint; it may also be in the form of threatened penalties if specific information is aired or published. This may manifest itself by laws that carry penalties. The FCC enforces federal laws relating to broadcasting, but that agency occupies itself more with its own policies and guidelines. FCC enforcement of federal laws would include attention to such statutes as that which prohibits the utterance of "any obscene, indecent, or profane language by means of radio communication."

Another such law enforced by the FCC is the Communications Act of 1934, the federal legislation that created the FCC, directs its powers, and created laws governing broadcasting. Section 315 of that act, the "Equal Opportunities" provision, ordered a station that allowed one candidate for political office to use the airwaves to allow equal time to all other candidates for the same office. Some may consider such legal directives as a kind of censorship, since it is a government influence in the communication process that is constitutionally protected from such interference.

Censorship happening after the fact may include those occurrences where a broadcaster is punished (and discouraged from any further similar activity) for information aired or published. What may be aired or what is "censored" has been shaped over the years by FCC hearings and court cases, the outcome of which has molded law and policy controlling free expression in broadcasting. Such shaping has taken many forms in the history of broadcasting. Some instances are listed here:

1.) When CBS broadcast a radio adaptation of H.G. Wells's "War of the Worlds" in 1938, the FCC issued some strongly worded statements warning of the dangers of a program that "caused widespread excitement, terror and fright." Radio networks later understood that a covert censorship prevented them from airing such dramatizations again.

2.) In a 1940 decision, the FCC, in ruling on strong editorial stances taken by a station licensee in Boston, ordered a complete ban on editorializing by a station. Radio, it was thought, had such a compelling power over listeners' access to information that it was much too ominous for the licensee or its staff to take strong positions of advocacy. This Mayflower Doctrine was perhaps one of the most blatant forms of censorship practiced in broadcasting. It was in effect until 1949, when the FCC issued the Fairness Doctrine.

3.) The Mayflower Doctrine was softened somewhat by the Fairness Doctrine, but a more benign censorship was put in its place. The Fairness Doctrine allowed stations to take an editorial stance, but only if other viewpoints were allowed "equal opportunities." In other words, stations still were censored from advocating a controversial point of view unless they aired other perspectives, sometimes unwillingly. For many journalists, forcing coverage of the subjects of their stories was almost as bad as the outright prior restraint. When a station licensee challenged this Fairness Doctrine, the U.S. Supreme Court allowed the FCC to keep and enforce it. It stood until 1987, when the FCC, in its efforts to deregulate broadcasting, dropped the controversial policy.

4.) Regarding obscenity and indecency, because so much of society disapproves of explicit sexual references in broadcasting and because there are federal laws against such broadcasting, few observers have viewed the muzzling of indecent language as a form of censorship or control over broadcasts. In the early 1970s, "topless radio" would discuss sexual matters in a frank and candid manner. When complaints arrived at the FCC, the commission announced that there would be inquiries into whether federal anti-obscenity statutes had been violated. Such threats of inquiries at once created a cooling down of such programming.

5.) In the matter of strong language, it was not until WBAI radio in New York broadcast comedian George Carlin's "seven dirty words" that a full examination of appropriateness of language on radio and television was examined by both the FCC and the courts. In its ruling, the U.S. Supreme Court upheld the FCC's power to censor the station for using indecent programming materials, writing, "The concept of 'indecent' is intimately connected with the exposure of children to language that describes, in terms patently offensive as measured by contemporary community standards for the broadcast medium, sexual or excretory activities and organs, at times of the day when there is a reasonable risk that children may be in the audience." The commission then went on to suggest that at times of the day when children were less likely to be listening, such as late-night hours, "a different standard might conceivably be used."

In the 1990s, the FCC fined Infinity Broadcasting, the licensee that aired the Howard Stern Show. Stern's frank, explicit language and off-color humor led to the FCC's fining Infinity more than $600,000 for repeated "indecent" broadcasts of the show on its stations in New York, Philadelphia, and Manassas, Virginia.

VAL E. LIMBURG

See also Broadcast Licensing; Broadcast Regulation; Censorship of Advertising; Censorship of Motion Pictures; Criticism of Broadcasting; "Equal Time" Provision; Fairness Doctrine

Further Reading

Chafee, Zechariah, Jr., *Free Speech in the United States,* New York: Atheneum, 1941
Friendly, Fred W., *The Good Guys, the Bad Guys, and the First Amendment: Free Speech vs. Fairness in Broadcasting,* New York: Random House, 1976
National Association of Broadcasters, *Broadcast Regulation,* Washington, D.C.: NAB, 1993
Powe, Lucas A., Jr., *American Broadcasting and the First Amendment,* Berkeley: University of California Press, 1987

Censorship of Motion Pictures

Content-related censorship began with early motion pictures

The history of film in the United States is the history of censorship. It is a complex story of bigotry, greed, political intrigue, and most fundamentally, conflicting visions of the American dream, art, and liberty. From Edison's *The Kiss* (1895) to Kubrick's *Lolita* (1962), every film made or shown in the United States was subject to formal governmental censorship. It is impossible to understand U.S. film without understanding the climate of control that shadowed the medium from its outset.

First displayed in the 1890s, films were originally a novelty, presented at penny arcades and traveling shows. Early films appealed largely to the working classes, and the civic-minded guardians of tradition and social norms feared the "dark theaters with bright screens." The medium's unusual blend of technology, spectacle, and entertainment, with "origins deep in the gritty cauldron of urban amusements"

and vaudeville, "set it off as something quite unfamiliar and threatening." Beyond moral concerns, civic leaders worried that movies would "introduce [viewers] to social standards far beyond their reach." As early as 1897, "censorship stripes" were superimposed over what were deemed the more suggestive parts of a dancer's body in the film *Fatima*. *The Great Train Robbery* (1903) was criticized for fear its theme would lead young people, especially, to a life of crime.

By 1907, the call for tighter film restrictions had grown so loud that many locales, such as New York and Chicago, began to set up licensing boards on their own, establishing arbitrary rules for determining the appropriateness of films for their communities. Not surprisingly, these differing and inconsistent standards quickly threatened industry profits. Still, censorship remained largely informal until 1910, when a film of a prizefight prompted laws and boards of censorship across the nation. The fight was the Jack Johnson–Jim Jeffries bout, in which the black boxing champion Johnson knocked out Jeffries, the "Great White Hope," calling into question the prevailing social Darwinist view of racial superiority. The civil unrest that followed and the desire to stop film footage from being exhibited in other cities created an atmosphere of repression and fear that helped spawn so-called reforms like film censorship. Progressive, upper-class groups, such as local women's clubs, campaigned in the name of civic improvement to raise the moral standards of their communities. Film censorship was considered a fashionable and acceptable form of public service.

Although it might be expected that censorship of films dealt primarily with obscenity, censors generally did not confine themselves to areas of public decency; they also included social and racial concerns. For film censors as a whole, there was no clear line between public morals and public mores. Through the years, censors attempted to prevent distribution of three basic types of films: films that were deemed to be obscene or indecent, films that condoned criminal behavior or explained how crimes were committed, and films that undermined racial or social norms. Film censorship in the United States became a means of maintaining and promoting the status quo. In Atlanta, Georgia, for example, the film reviewer – she abhorred the label "censor" – not only assessed the suitability of films for local audiences but also was heavily involved in efforts to influence the content of films before they were made, including *Gone with the Wind* (1939).

By 1914, there were some 18,000 theaters in the United States, making about $300 million by admitting 7 million customers daily. This boom in film attendance roused strong opposition from traditionalists who feared that dark theaters and bright screens "filled with the glamour of love making" would undermine public decency.

Thus, when the U.S. Supreme Court denied films the protection of the First Amendment in *Mutual Film Corp.* v. *Industrial Commission of Ohio* (1915), the reasons the Court offered were not surprising. First, films were entertainment, not political discourse or debate – the type of expression most fully protected in the United States. Second, films were "a business, pure and simple, originated and conducted for profit . . . not to be regarded . . . as part of

In the early 1900s, *The Great Train Robbery* was seen as inspiring viewers to lead a life of crime.
(Wisconsin Center for Film and Theater Research)

the press of the country." Finally, the Court worried that the audiences films attracted – men, women, and children together in the dark – made "them the more insidious in corruption."

With the rising wealth and prominence of Hollywood in the silent era of the 1920s, sex and drug scandals, coupled with the new "suggestiveness" on display in films, intensified the clamor for governmental control of films. Local censorship boards responded angrily to these scandals, and an unprecedented number of state legislatures introduced censorship bills. To forestall impending state censorship efforts, the film industry established its own censorship office, headed by Will H. Hays. As the new president of the Motion Picture Producers and Distributors of America, Hays soon claimed to be reviewing "95 percent of the total film output." During the "golden age" of censorship, the Hays office expanded its powers and contacts with local censorship boards until it influenced all areas of production and exhibition, including what film projects were allowed to be developed. To help quell further pressure, the Hollywood studios created the Hollywood Production Code in 1930.

Despite this script-to-screen oversight, local censorship efforts were not slowed; communities continued to censor films based on local perceptions of lewdness. In New York, for example, this authority was given to the Department of Education, which censored even newsreels until stopped by the state legislature. In Memphis, Tennessee, the result was that Lena Horne was cut from every film because there were "plenty of good, white singers." In addition, *The Outlaw* (1947) was banned there because it had "too much shootin'." In Chicago, where censorship powers were vested in the police force, Charlie Chaplin's *The Great Dictator* (1940) was banned to avoid offending German Americans. In Atlanta, the film censor prohibited the subsequent showings of D.W. Griffith's *Birth of a Nation* (1915) because of "instinctive fear of Negro men," the result of the "vivid memory" of a scene from the film "in which an impressionable girl jumps from a cliff to avoid the caresses of an ex-slave." In Birmingham, Alabama, an elected inspector of public amusements was part of a de facto regional network that monitored the "special concerns" of the South. In all parts of the country, film censorship became an obsession, marked by revivals, clubs, and annual conventions.

From the 1930s through the 1950s, the Catholic Legion of Decency wielded an unprecedented amount of control over the film industry through threats of economic boycotts, ensuring that films adhered to its moral standards. Other groups – including the Protestant Motion Picture Council, the General Federation of Women's Clubs, Daughters of the American Revolution, and the American Library Association – adopted less coercive measures and produced a weekly newsletter for filmgoers, *Joint Estimates of Current Motion Pictures*. (Many in the industry referred to this as the "democratic answer to censorship.") On the other hand, formal film censorship nationwide was often less concerned with moral issues than with sectional prejudice. Thus, increasingly, film censors throughout the nation came under scrutiny and criticism. Bold foreign and domestic filmmakers challenged the ethical and legal authority of censorship.

The U.S. Supreme Court began to cut away at the social justifications for film censorship in *Burstyn* v. *Wilson* (1952). In that case, it decided films were indeed "a significant medium for the communication of ideas" and thus were entitled to the protection of the First Amendment. This ruling left censorship boards in the precarious position of having to justify their rulings and made it more difficult for them to prevent the distribution of increasingly salacious films. Finally, in *Freedman* v. *Maryland* (1965), the Court – while not completely throwing out the entire legal foundation of film censorship – set up three principles for film review. First, film review could not be overly burdensome on the theater owner. From that time, the legal presumption was that any given film was suitable to be shown unless proven otherwise, not the other way around. Second, filmmakers and theater owners had to be guaranteed due process of law. Provisions for the appeal of any censor's decision to the courts had to be readily available. Third, films had to be reviewed in a timely manner. This, over time, proved particularly difficult for censors, given the growing numbers of films released and the limited local funding available to review them.

Although formal film censorship around the country ended for the most part soon thereafter, de facto attempts to censor or regulate films still continued unabated, framed as controversies over the growing availability of and interest in pornography and as the industry's film rating system, which was instituted in 1968 as an informational system to forestall future censorship efforts. Although filmmakers in the late twentieth century were not required to submit their movies for rating review, the system had become so well entrenched that it was often difficult for producers to get their films distributed to theaters without an official rating. In addition, an NC-17 rating by the Motion Picture Association of America could mean the death of a film's commercial prospects and could be used as a means of forcing a producer to alter style, artistic expression, and content.

GREG LISBY

See also Motion Picture Ratings; Sound Motion Pictures

Further Reading

Black, Gregory D., *Hollywood Censored: Morality Codes, Catholics, and the Movies*, New York and Cambridge: Cambridge University Press, 1994
Carmen, Ira H., *Movies, Censorship, and the Law*, Ann Arbor: University of Michigan Press, 1966
Czitrom, Daniel J., *Media and the American Mind: From Morse to McLuhan*, Chapel Hill: University of North Carolina Press, 1982
De Grazia, Edward, and Roger K. Newman, *Banned Films: Movies, Censors and the First Amendment*, New York: Bowker, 1982
Randall, Richard S., *Censorship of the Movies: The Social and Political Control of a Mass Medium*, Madison: University of Wisconsin Press, 1968

Checkbook Journalism

Paying sources for providing information to journalists

Checkbook journalism involves paying informants for information used in the production of news reports, especially those featured on television news programs and in news-oriented magazines. Newspapers exploring sensational aspects of mainstream news events or the personal lives of those involved in such events also have practiced checkbook journalism from time to time. Celebrities of all kinds, particularly political insiders, have been targets of journalists seeking to buy their exclusive stories. Although most checkbook journalism has involved paying informants for information about other persons, in the late twentieth century it increasingly involved payment to someone for his or her own story. As a result, the perceived undesirable features of the practice became more highly visible from the 1960s, and criticism more frequent. Inspired by attempts by convicted criminals to profit from books or articles ghostwritten for them, various efforts to outlaw checkbook journalism occurred in state legislatures. Often these were called Son of Sam laws, after the New York serial killer who tried to sell his story to a book publisher.

Because the competition for sensational material among bigger and bigger media corporations became more intense every year, persons involved in news events of every kind were increasingly aware of the commercial value of their information. Consequently, they were in a position to solicit bids for such information. That situation, critics of the practice argued, tended to compound the advantages that exceptionally wealthy news organizations enjoyed over their competitors, encouraging the trend toward greater concentration of society's system of mass communication and its power into fewer and fewer hands. In addition, critics pointed out, the greedy anticipation of monetary reward for their information encouraged some persons to exaggerate, magnify, embellish, and otherwise distort their stories, thus compromising journalistic integrity. Critics also argued that the media's payment for scandalous or titillating material concerning the sexual, financial, or bizarre behavior of famous people could inspire more frequent invasions of privacy. Whatever its other problems, critics sometimes charged that the practice of checkbook journalism was an offense against the democratic principle of the public's right to know and the free flow of information in a society. News of legitimate public interest should not, they argued, be treated as a commodity.

In response to their critics, practitioners of checkbook journalism argued that many news sources in possession of information crucial to the resolution of important public issues might not offer it otherwise. The fear of reprisal that they might experience in disclosing their information might be overcome by anticipation of the reward. Under such circumstances checkbook journalism added to, rather than subtracted from, the free flow of information and empowered the public's right to know. Since media outlets profited – immensely, in some cases – from information obtained from news sources, should not those sources share in that profit?

On the issue of privacy invasion, newspeople practicing checkbook journalism pointed out that such consideration had to be subordinated to that of newsworthiness. Moreover, they asserted, no information need be released just because some medium paid the provider for it. Concerning checkbook journalism's tendency to compound the advantages that comparatively wealthy outlets enjoyed, its practitioners pointed out that such is the nature of free market enterprise.

JOHN DeMOTT

See also Codes of Ethics; Country Club Journalism; Criticism of Newspapers

Chicago Defender

Longtime leader in African American press ranks

Founded on borrowed money and resources on May 15, 1905, by Robert Sengstacke Abbott, the *Chicago Defender* is noted as the paper that most exemplifies the coming-of-age of the modern African American newspaper. During the first quarter of the twentieth century, Abbott's weekly *Defender* led the fight against lynchings, racial segregation, and race prejudice in the United States. During its peak between the world wars, it was distributed nationally by African American railroad porters and had an estimated paid circulation of 250,000. Its "pass around" rate was estimated at two to five times that number.

During the 1920s, the *Defender's* relationship to the African American press was often compared to the Hearst papers' relationship to the mainstream press of that time. It was noted for sensationalized crime stories, bold red headlines, stinging editorials against racial discrimination, and innovations in creating, among other things, a children's section and an annual parade named after Bud Billiken, said by Abbott to be a mythical Chinese character who watched over children.

The history of the *Defender* is synonymous with the reputation of Abbott, who was born on St. Simons Island,

Georgia, on November 28, 1868, to former slaves, and that of his nephew, John H. Sengstacke, who was born November 25, 1912, in Savannah, Georgia. Abbott graduated from Hampton Institute (later Hampton University) in Virginia in 1896 and trained as a printer. In 1899 he graduated from Kent College of Law in Chicago with an LL.B. degree but was discouraged from practicing when he was told he was "a little too dark" to succeed. The unionized print industry had been closed to him also, so he decided to create his own newspaper dedicated to uplifting his race.

The *Defender* is credited with fueling the movement of tens of thousands of African Americans from the nation's south to Chicago, part of the so-called Great Migration of African Americans to northern cities that began at the turn of the century. Gradually, the *Defender's* national circulation and influence declined in the 1930s as Abbott experienced health and personal problems. His death in 1940 put the paper completely in the hands of his nephew, who had been vice president and general manager of the publishing company since earning a bachelor's degree in business administration from Hampton Institute in 1934.

Sengstacke also helped found the Negro Newspaper Publishers Association (now the National Newspaper Publishers Association) in 1940. Meanwhile, the *Defender,* un-

Robert S. Abbott
(*Chicago Daily Defender* Photo)

der his leadership, maintained its regional influence as it became a daily newspaper in 1956. In 1995, it was one of only two African American dailies and had an estimated circulation of 28,000.

Sengstacke established 16 other newspapers during his career. In 1995, he was president of Sengstacke Enterprises, which included the *New Pittsburgh Courier* in Pennsylvania, the *Tri-State Defender* in Memphis, Tennessee, and the *Michigan Chronicle* in Detroit.

HARRY AMANA

See also African American Media

Further Reading

Amana, Harry, "Robert S. Abbott," in *Dictionary of Literary Biography: American Magazine Journalists, 1900–1960*, First Series, vol. 91, edited by Sam G. Riley, Detroit, Michigan: Gale, 1990
Folkerts, Jean Lange, "Robert S. Abbott," in *Dictionary of Literary Biography: American Newspaper Journalists, 1926–1950*, vol. 29, edited by Perry J. Ashley, Detroit, Michigan: Gale, 1984
Lochard, Metz T.P., "Robert S. Abbott – 'Race Leader'," *Phylon* 8:2 (1947)
Ottley, Roi, *The Lonely Warrior: The Life and Times of Robert S. Abbott,* Chicago: Henry Regnery, 1955

Chicago Newspaper Trust

Chicago's way of coping with intense competition among newspapers

Chicago was long an intensely competitive newspaper market, with up to a dozen English-language dailies competing for readers alongside dozens of specialized and foreign-language titles. By the 1880s, newspapers had become big business, and the leading publishers determined that their competition needed to be kept within bounds in order to maintain profitability.

In 1884, morning publishers developed a system whereby one carrier delivered all morning papers in each territory, thus saving on distribution costs and eliminating the battle to deliver morning editions first or entice readers and distributors with more attractive terms. Publishers later expanded this cooperation to newsgathering, advertising policies, promotions, press times, labor relations, and political action. A dense network of cooperative relations united the leading publishers in what became widely known as the Chicago Newspaper Trust. While the newspaper trust saw its heyday in the 1890s, it remained a significant force in the Chicago newspaper market for decades. In the 1990s, it survived primarily as a mutual-assistance pact whereby the *Tribune* and *Sun-Times* were pledged to help each other maintain publication in the event of strikes, fire, or other disaster.

Before the organization of the newspaper trust, competitive pressures enabled advertisers, newsboys, and newspaper unions to play publishers off against each other to extract better terms. Costs soared as newspapers added reporters, pages, and editions to meet the competition while simultaneously cutting their cover prices.

After the organization of the trust, publishers presented a common front to unions, negotiating joint contracts, assisting each other during strikes and lockouts, blacklisting union militants, and ensuring that no publisher would take advantage of a rival's labor troubles to advance his own position. The trust-owned City Press Association, which continued to survive in the late twentieth century, enabled publishers to slash the costs of newsgathering by jointly hiring reporters to handle routine coverage (police court, meetings, gathering election returns, etc.). Publishers set common retail and wholesale prices, agreed to restrictions on promotional expenditures, and established detailed rules governing advertising policies and display. Publishers even agreed, for a time, not to lure each other's workers away for higher wages, recognizing that such behavior would ultimately result in higher wages all around.

The trust resulted from a simple calculation of self-interest. While the *Tribune* generally dominated the morning field and the *Daily News* the evening, their positions were by no means secure. Competitors could quickly gain short-term circulation through promotion campaigns, lower cover prices, or more favorable terms to newsboys and distributors. But these advantages were only momentary, as other newspapers soon responded in kind, leading to what *Daily News* publisher Victor Lawson termed "an annoying and profitless competition" that led to "extravagant wages," "union rule," and lower profits. Publishers saved hundreds of thousands of dollars a year by eliminating free marriage, death, and birth notices; limiting advertising commissions and discounts; restricting extra editions; setting joint release times for regular editions; limiting returns; and adopting a common labor policy.

The trust was at the peak of its power in 1898. The next year, the *Inter Ocean* withdrew from the group, and in 1900, Hearst's *Chicago American* entered the market, touching off a full-scale newspaper war. In order to build circulation, Hearst offered newsboys larger discounts and unlimited returns. Trust publishers responded by trying to force the *American* off newsstands. Some 27 newsdealers were killed and scores injured in fighting that stemmed from a bloody newspaper strike in which the trust publishers (now including Hearst) banded together to crush the unions and drive rival newspapers off the streets.

The trust was less active in later years, temporarily retreating from agreements on press times, promotional schemes, and advertising rates while continuing to cooperate in distribution, newsgathering, and the compilation of statistical information for advertisers. Publishers attempted, however, to return to their earlier arrangements. Evening newspapers reached a series of agreements in the 1930s and 1940s on press times, returns, and promotional expenditures, while morning and evening publishers negotiated regarding how newspapers should be displayed on downtown newsstands and refused to supply papers to newsboys who violated their agreement. In 1942, publishers agreed to raise their cover prices, although one publisher feared this might violate the Sherman Anti-Trust Act.

The newspaper trust helped to strengthen trust publishers, enabling them to develop an all-but-unassailable market position, to gain the upper hand over the workforce, and to control a wide range of costs in newsgathering, advertising sales, production and distribution. The trust discouraged effective competition both through these economies and by its efforts to exclude nontrust newspapers from newsstands and busy street corners.

JON BEKKEN

See also Newsboys

Further Reading
Abramoske, Donald Joseph, *The 'Chicago Daily News': A Business History, 1875–1901* (Ph.D. diss., University of Chicago), 1964
Bekken, Jon, "'The Most Vindictive and Most Vengeful Power': Labor Confronts the Chicago Newspaper Trust," *Journalism History* 18 (1992)

Chicago Tribune

"World's Greatest Newspaper"

Chicago's dominant newspaper in the late twentieth century, the *Chicago Tribune*, was founded in 1847. The paper was taken over by Joseph Medill and his partners in 1855; in 1861, the paper absorbed another Chicago paper, the *Democrat*.

Medill's support of Lincoln's presidential candidacy gave the paper a decidedly Republican party slant in a series of editorials backing the future president. The paper became known for its strong pro-Union and antislavery position. Following the American Civil War, Horace White gained editorial control of the paper, redirecting the editorials to liberal, rather than radical, Republicanism. Following the Panic of 1873, when the paper lost money, Medill resumed editorial control.

The paper became known as a conservative one when, in 1910, Robert Rutherford McCormick and his copublisher and cousin, Joseph Patterson, took over. McCormick's editorials were extremely opinionated and nationalistic, always advocating an isolationist's view of the future of the United States. McCormick maintained his isolationist position throughout his career. Indeed, three days before Pearl Harbor was bombed, the *Tribune*'s anti-Roosevelt position was manifested in a front-page story announcing that Roosevelt had plans of going to war. Following McCormick's death in 1955, editorial control of the paper was assumed by J. Howard Wood. In the late 1990s, the paper published continuous editions throughout the day and had a total daily circulation of about 760,000.

ROBIN GALLAGHER

Further Reading
Squires, James D., *Read All About It!: The Corporate Takeover of America's Newspapers,* New York: Times, 1993

Children's Television Programming

Television viewing by children steadily increasing in time, influence

Television played a dominant role in the lives of children in the United States at the end of the twentieth century. With at least one television set in almost every home, viewing by children steadily increased from an average of two and one-half hours during the preschool years to almost four hours in early adolescence. Put another way, most children in the United States spent more time watching television than in any other activity except sleep.

Television entered U.S. homes after World War II at a significantly faster rate than had radio a generation earlier. Fewer than 10 percent of homes had a television in 1950, but a decade later penetration was almost 90 percent. Early studies indicated that television viewing quickly changed children's lives, reducing the amount of time they spent playing, helping with household chores, going to movies, talking with their parents, and reading.

Questions were quickly raised about the power of this new medium to harm younger viewers. Because few programs were broadcast specifically for them, children in the early days of television spent considerable time viewing the fare intended for the adult audience, which attracted advertising revenue. Largely adapted from network radio, television programming in the 1950s was remarkably similar to that available to viewers 40 years later, consisting of soap operas and game shows during the day and situation comedies, westerns, police dramas, mysteries, and variety programs during prime-time hours.

A series of studies conducted between 1958 and 1960 by Wilbur Schramm and his colleagues in the United States and Canada demonstrated the major influence that television had become in the lives of children only a decade after it had become commercially available. Their research indicated that children were affected by television in a variety of ways, including being frightened, learning about public affairs, mimicking fads, and increasing passivity, delinquency, and violent behavior. These effects, however, were contingent on the child's age, gender, intellectual ability, and social relations with parents and peers, among other factors.

Based on these results, Schramm, Lyle, and Parker concluded: "For some children, under some conditions, some television is harmful. For other children under the same conditions, or for the same children under other conditions, it may be beneficial. For most children, under most conditions, most television is probably neither harmful nor particularly beneficial."

Such equivocal statements did not assuage the fears of those who believed that there was a connection between the growing dominance of television in the lives of children and the dramatic rise in violence in U.S. society during the 1950s, particularly among young people. The possible connection between the two phenomena was the subject of several congressional hearings during the 1950s and 1960s. Despite pledges by industry representatives to conduct their own investigations of the effects of televised violence, only one study, sponsored by CBS, was conducted. This study

Howdy Doody, left, and his friend "Buffalo Bob" Smith hosted an early children's television program.
(Museum of Broadcast Communications)

surveyed the attitudes of parents about television programming, but it did not directly assess effects.

After several years of violent social disruptions, President Lyndon Johnson appointed the National Commission on the Causes and Prevention of Violence, which held hearings in 1968 that targeted television programming as a factor causing the rise in violence. Reported the commission:

> We believe it is reasonable to conclude that a constant diet of violent behavior on television has an adverse effect on human character and attitudes. Violence on television encourages violent forms of behavior, and fosters moral and social values about violence in daily life which are unacceptable in a civilized society.

By the late 1960s, a number of citizens' groups had also begun to exert pressure on the broadcast networks to reduce content harmful to children, the most effective of which was Action for Children's Television (ACT), founded in 1968 by a group of concerned mothers from Boston, Massachusetts. ACT initially devoted its efforts to petitioning the Federal Communications Commission and the Federal Trade Commission, as well as lobbying Congress, to ban advertising of cereal and toy products on children's programs. Led by its president, Peggy Charron, ACT pursued a number of issues concerning children and television, including reducing violence in the programming they watched.

Responding to the growing public concern about televised violence, U.S. Surgeon General William H. Stewart announced in March 1969 that his agency would sponsor a major study to determine if there was a direct causal relationship between televised violence and antisocial behavior. To this end, 23 new studies were commissioned, the results of which were published in 1972 in a five-volume report, *Television and Social Behavior*. The Surgeon General's Scientific Advisory Committee summarized the results of these studies this way:

> Thus the two sets of findings (laboratory and survey) converge in three respects: a preliminary and tentative conclusion of a causal relation between viewing violence on television and aggressive behavior; an indication that any such causal operation operates only on some children (who are predisposed to be aggressive); and an indication that it operates only on some environmental contexts. Such tentative and limited conclusions are not very satisfying. But they represent substantially more knowledge than we had two years ago.

These conclusions produced considerable controversy, leading to hearings conducted by Senator John Pastore in 1972. Critics of the report charged that the Surgeon General's Scientific Advisory Committee was packed with pro–broadcast industry members. Researchers who had conducted the studies argued that the evidence was strong enough to warrant a less equivocal statement about the causal relationship between viewing televised violence and aggressive behavior. Broadcast industry representatives disagreed with them. As a result, perhaps the most important effect of the 1972 *Surgeon General's Report* was to promote funding for further research on television effects during the 1970s. In fact, 90 percent of all published reports on the effects of television on children appeared in the 10 years after the 1972 *Surgeon General's Report*. In 1982, the National Institutes of Mental Health issued an extensive report summarizing this new evidence, *Television and Social Behavior: Ten Years of Scientific Progress and Implications for the Eighties*. On the issue of effects of televised violence, the report concluded: "The convergence of most of the findings about televised violence and later aggressive behavior by the viewer supports the positive conclusion of a causal relationship."

The report also summarized evidence on the wide range of effects television has on children and their families. Evidence was described in the report, for example, that television can promote altruism, friendliness, self-control, and fear-coping skills in children. Other studies indicated that considerable racial, ethnic, and gender stereotyping existed in the television programming that children commonly viewed.

Backed by this evidence, Congress in 1990 passed the Television Violence Act, sponsored by Senator Paul Simon and Representative Paul Markey, which provided the networks a three-year exemption from antitrust legislation so that they could jointly develop standards for reducing violence on television. Implied in this legislation was the threat that if televised violence were not voluntarily reduced by

Bob Keeshan's *Captain Kangaroo* provided learning within the children's show.
(Museum of Broadcast Communications)

Big Bird teaches children about letters and numbers on *Sesame Street.*
(Courtesy of the Children's Television Workshop)

the broadcast industry, Congress would enact legislation to do so. As a result of this legislation, the networks and cable television agreed to label violent television programs, and violence in them was reduced in 1994 for the first time.

KIM A. SMITH

See also Mass Media and Children; Television and Violence

Further Reading

Dorr, Aimée, *Television and Children: A Special Medium for a Special Audience,* Beverly Hills, California: Sage, 1986

Liebert, Robert M., Joyce N. Sprafkin, and Emily S. Davidson, *The Early Window: Effects of Television on Children and Youth,* 2nd ed., New York: Pergamon, 1982

Lyness, Paul I., "The Place of the Mass Media in the Lives of Boys and Girls," *Journalism Quarterly* 29 (1952)

Maccoby, Eleanor E., "Why Do Children Watch Television," *Public Opinion Quarterly* 18 (1954)

Schramm, Wilbur Lang, *Television in the Lives of Our Children,* Stanford, California: Stanford University Press, 1961

Steiner, Gary A., *The People Look at Television: A Study of Audience Attitudes,* New York: Knopf, 1963

Civil War Photography

Images bring the reality of war home for the first time

The American Civil War marked the first time in history that photography played a significant part in warfare. It was the first war that received extensive photographic coverage, due in large part to one man, Mathew Brady, who saw himself as a pictorial historian. Brady's early participation inspired others; by the war's end, some 2,000 photographers had taken perhaps 1 million exposures. Those photographs changed the face of war for the people of the United States, many of whom had had a romantic or idealized notion of battle. It also produced other innovations still practiced at the end of the twentieth century, including the beginnings of photojournalism and the use of photography by the military.

Brady and many of the other men who photographed the Civil War, including Alexander Gardner (whom Brady had brought to the United States from Scotland), Timothy H. O'Sullivan, T.C. Roche, George N. Barnard, and John F. Gibson, were portrait photographers before the war began. Brady had been a portrait artist until he was introduced to the daguerreotype after he moved to New York City. He immediately switched media, and by 1851, he showed such talent in the new field that he won an award for overall mastery of the medium at London's Great Exhibition. By 1861, he was wealthy, the owner of a thriving business with studios in New York and Washington, D.C., and world famous. This financial and professional background allowed him access to top military and government officials in Washington at the beginning of the Civil War. He received permission from General Irwin McDowell and, later, from President Lincoln, whom he had photographed in 1860 during Lincoln's presidential campaign, to gain access to military facilities and battlefields.

Brady took photographs of the first major campaign of the Civil War, the Army of the Potomac's ill-fated attempt to take Richmond, Virginia. The defeat at the first battle of Bull Run showed a surprised North a side of the war it had not anticipated, and subsequent photographs of the carnage of the four-year war put a different face on the "glory" of war. Photographers would display pictures in their galleries or sell them from catalogues, and for the first time civilians saw men lying as they had fallen, some in the agonies of death. The grim, shocking pictures repelled some, fascinated others.

The photographs transmitted the stark fact that men died in war. The picture by O'Sullivan of a dead Confederate sharpshooter behind a stone wall in a crevice at Gettysburg was more than a simple war photograph. It was a portrait. It showed a dead human being; it was a picture of a man who had lived and of where he had fallen. It was a quality that sketches or words could not communicate. Evidence suggests, however, that O'Sullivan composed the photograph after hauling the dead man some 20 yards to the site. It would not have been unusual; Civil War photographers were not above rearranging men and other objects to suit their tastes and their cameras, nor were they shy about using live human props as the "dead" for greater impact.

Photographers also took portraits of individuals and groups both before they left for war and once they were in camp. These mementos became treasured in the case of the death of the soldier. Also, men carried photographs of their loved ones with them as they left home, giving an economic boost to the burgeoning business of photography.

It was the cruelty of war, however, that was driven home to civilians. It no longer was heroic or for a "cause"; the view arose that war was something to avoid. Photography has been said to have changed the basis for the war; the Civil War participants were fighting to prevent another war.

That impact was the unexpected genesis of photojournalism. One of the early goals of photography was to record and report on current events. Brady's motivation for going into the field was to become the curator of the war and to satisfy his sense of historical mission (he also envisioned a commercial demand for war photographs). Even though Civil War photographers were limited by technology to taking pictures of static or staged scenes – there are perhaps only three or four action shots from the Civil War – the subjects they recorded, such as soldiers, camps, battlefields, and the dead, are the same subjects recorded by photographers in subsequent wars.

Perhaps more importantly, the military also was quick to recognize the importance of photography. General Winfield Scott was one of the first to realize how valuable pictures would be for topographers. Also, Brady's record of the rout at Bull Run showed how inexperienced and ill-prepared the Army of the Potomac was. Following that, military leaders saw the importance of records, and they began ordering photographs of the engineering works. These photographs of bridges, forts, and other construction achievements were circulated throughout the army for other engineers to study. In addition, maps, plans, and other documents were photographed for distribution and to make permanent records,

A photography wagon is stationed with the Union Army at Cold Harbor, Virginia.
(Reproduced from the Collections of the Library of Congress)

The Civil War dead of Gettysburg, Pennsylvania
(Reproduced from the Collections of the Library of Congress)

and the Quartermaster Department would have potential battle areas photographed to show the lay of the land and existing facilities, including buildings that could be used as hospitals.

Another military use was espionage. Gardner was employed to take photographs for the purpose of detecting Confederate spies. Groups or units would be photographed, and the pictures would be studied by Union spies or the new Secret Service to ferret out spies, who generally were unaware that they had been compromised.

Despite the contributions, war photography was difficult. The cameras were large and bulky; photographers had to work close to the front; the plates had to be developed immediately in portable darkrooms that were cramped, hot, and suffused with the odor of chemicals. But Civil War photographers left a record of part of the nation's history. Brady's exposures are housed in the Library of Congress, and his fame endures because he originated and sustained

the idea of recording the Civil War. Others received less recognition, but Civil War photography left a legacy that exists today.

T.J. HEMLINGER

See also Brady, Mathew; Civil War Press (North); Photographic Technology; Photojournalism in the Nineteenth Century; War Photography

Further Reading

Henisch, Heinz K., and Bridget A. Henisch, *The Photographic Experience 1839–1914: Images and Attitudes,* University Park: Pennsylvania State University Press, 1994
Lewinski, Jorge, *The Camera at War: A History of War Photography from 1848 to the Present Day,* London: W.H. Allen, 1978; New York: Simon & Schuster, 1980

Miller, Francis Trevelyan, ed., *The Photographic History of the Civil War*, New York: Thomas Yoseloff, 1957

Sweet, Timothy, *Traces of War: Poetry, Photography, and the Crisis of the Union*, Baltimore, Maryland: Johns Hopkins University Press, 1990

Thompson, William Fletcher, *The Image of War: The Pictorial Reporting of the American Civil War*, New York: Thomas Yoseloff, 1960

Civil War Press (North)

Changing the face of war reporting

In 1861, the Union was better prepared to wage – and win – any war with the Confederacy. All the statistics were tipped in the North's favor. The North had a much larger pool from which to draw an army: the more than twice the free male population of the South. The region could draw on its industrial might to produce the weapons of war: the North had many times the number of factories as the South and almost all the capacity to manufacture armaments. The North also stood to benefit from its modern transportation and communication systems. Canals, railroads, and turnpikes crisscrossed the North. These enhanced the Union's modern communication system that included not only the mails but the telegraph. At the start of the war, the North had a considerable lead over the South in the amount of telegraph wire strung across the region. At the beginning of the Civil War, the Union was a modern industrial society compared with the Confederacy's agricultural economic system.

This had ramifications for the press system of each region. As a product of a modern industrial society, the Northern press was prepared financially and technologically to cover any war with the Confederacy. Financially, Northern periodicals – especially urban daily newspapers – enjoyed the climbing circulations and increased advertising revenues that urbanization and industrialization had generated. Thus, these periodicals had the financial resources to hire additional reporters and invest in the extra expenses associated with wartime coverage. Technologically, the Northern press had many advantages – from the steam-powered printing presses within production to the telegraph that sped the transmission of news.

By the eve of the Civil War, the Northern press had experienced enormous growth. The 1860 census reported that 276 dailies were published in the Union states (compared to 69 in the Confederacy). These represented some of the best-known newspapers of the day. The *New York Herald,* with its circulation of 77,000 daily, was probably the largest, but the *New York Tribune*'s weekly edition reached 200,000 throughout the North, making it the closest thing that the Union had to a national newspaper. New York City was a center for newspapers and reporting. Besides the *Herald* and the *Tribune,* the *Times,* the *Evening Post,* and the *World* sent reporters into the field during the Civil War. The *Herald* sent the most, more than 60; the others could not afford to send as many, but competition among these newspapers remained strong. New York City newspapers led the way in the amount of war coverage, the number of reporters in the field, the amount of money spent on covering the battles, and the problems they caused Union generals.

Although New York City had the largest number of dailies in the United States, newspapers in other cities reached regional and national importance and even managed to scoop the bigger New York papers. The Chicago papers were at an advantage in their coverage of the western war theater; the *Chicago Tribune* once boasted that it spent more money on war coverage than any paper outside of New York. The Cincinnati, Ohio, papers were close enough to the battlefields to send reporters out who could return to the office to file their stories covering the action.

The telegraph created problems for daily newspapers, reporters, and the military. Representing a fast, virtually instantaneous, form of communication between reporter and editor, it remained an expensive alternative. Although 50,000 miles of telegraph wire crisscrossed the nation, prices for transmitting were high. Companies charged one set fee for the first 10 words and more for each additional word. Because reporters tended to be verbose and stories on battles were long and detailed, transmitting a story via telegraph could mean prohibitively high charges. Some newspapers spent a large part of their budgets on news. For example, the *New York Herald* – far removed from much of the battle action – spent huge amounts on telegraphed news; a reporter's account of the capture of New Orleans alone cost $1,000, a substantial amount for the period.

But there was another dimension that newspapers editors and reporters had to be concerned about – military censorship. The telegraph office was the ideal location for censorship.

Because of this censorship and the high charges, the telegraph was not always the method of transmission. Some newspapers hired special couriers, who rushed dispatches back to the newspaper office via train, boat, horseback, or the mails. Sometimes the reporter even hand-delivered stories.

Almost from the start of the war, the military assumed

The Disaster at Bull Run

WASHINGTON, July 22, 1861—Our troops, after taking three batteries and gaining a great victory at Bull's Run, were eventually repulsed and commenced a retreat on Washington.

Our Union forces were advancing upon the enemy and taking his masked batteries gradually but surely, by driving the rebels towards Manassas Junction, when they seem to have been reinforced by twenty thousand men under General Johnston, who, it is understood, then took command and immediately commenced driving us back. We were retreating in good order, the rear well covered with a solid column, when a panic among our troops suddenly occurred, and a regular stampede took place.

New York Herald, July 23, 1861

some degree of control over news dispatches over the wire. In July 1861, General Winfield Scott, then the supreme commander of the Union forces, tried his hand at censorship by placing restrictions on news transmitted on the telegraph: no reports on army movements, mutinies, or expected military actions. The Union's devastating losses at Bull Run caused Scott to rethink his censorship policies. By 1861, Secretary of War Simon Cameron established more specific guidelines with regard to reporters' use of the telegraph. Under the new order, no news of army movements could be telegraphed "without the authority and sanction of the major general in command." Violators could be executed. Initial censorship under the Department of State was uneven; the War Department took the job over in 1862.

Newspapers often published stories that included information about troop movements and army strength that clearly breached guidelines to protect national security. In addition, dailies, especially the *New York Herald,* carried maps that showed the location of troops. Neither the editor nor the reporter seemed concerned about publishing information that might be helpful to the enemy. Individual generals attempted to control these abuses by controlling reporters. Thomas W. Knox of the *New York Herald,* for example, faced execution if convicted of the charges of giving intelligence to the enemy, being a spy, and disobeying orders. Knox was found guilty of only disobeying orders and was expelled from the Army of Tennessee.

Government officials controlled the press during the war

150   HARPER'S NEW MONTHLY MAGAZINE.

HEROIC DEEDS OF HEROIC MEN.

BY JOHN S. C. ABBOTT.

DICTATING DISPATCHES BY MOONLIGHT.

Illustrated magazines depicted the way Civil War correspondents worked.
(Davis Library, University of North Carolina at Chapel Hill)

through suspension, arrest of the editor, and revocation of mail privileges. In almost every Northern military department, at least one newspaper was suppressed or its editor arrested. In Iowa, three papers were suppressed or their editors arrested.

The situation was especially acute in the border states; Maryland and Missouri found many of their newspapers suppressed and their editors arrested. The newspapers most likely to suffer such actions were the Copperheads, those Northern (or border) newspapers that supported the South. Newspapers, large and small, were targets. In 1863, General Ambrose E. Burnside, commander of the Department of the Northwest, even closed down the powerful *Chicago Times* for two days for its "disloyal and incendiary sentiments."

Civil War reporters did not have the training, education, or ethics to adequately and thoughtfully cover the war. Most were young, inexperienced, and underpaid. Some 500 print reporters from the North covered the war at some point. The majority were "occasionals," who floated into the war, were paid at space rates, covered one or two battles, and then disappeared; some were soldiers, who doubled as reporters. Probably only 200 were full-time reporters who spent any length of time in the field. Little is known about these individuals. Bylines were not always given, and even if they were, reporters often used pseudonyms, a common practice in nineteenth-century newspapering. Biographical information is available only for the best-known reporters who worked for the bigger papers or wire services. A sketchy profile reveals a young, white male – in his twenties in 1863 – who had some journalism experience before the war; the largest number of them were associated with New York City newspapers.

As a class, Northern reporters were neither well regarded nor well paid. The average pay was between $15 and $35 a week, plus expenses. The occasionals and soldier-reporters were paid less, by the column inch. As a group, they were not well regarded by the general public or the generals. That perception had much to do with reality. War reporting did not attract the best quality of individual. Henry Villard, a reporter during the Civil War, was especially critical of many of his compatriots: "Men turned up in the army as correspondents more fit to drive cattle than to write for newspapers. With a dull or slow perception, incapable of logical arrangements of facts, innocent of grammatical English, they were altogether out of place in the positions they tried to fill."

These reporters worked under enormous pressure. They had to get the story – and get it first. A circular issued by the *New York Herald* illustrates the point: "In no instance, and under no circumstances, must you be beaten." Accuracy was not necessarily a consideration. Newspaper reporters made up eyewitness accounts (Junius Brown's fabricated account of the battle of Pea Ridge that appeared in the *New York Tribune* was reprinted in England as an example of the finest war reporting), made deals with generals for favorable treatment (two *Herald* reporters promised General Benjamin F. Butler that no derogatory comments would appear in that newspaper's editorial columns), and eavesdropped on private meetings (one *New York Times*

correspondent was discovered lying on his belly in the bushes frantically taking notes as Generals Ulysses S. Grant and George G. Meade planned strategy for the Army of the Potomac).

Little wonder that generals were skeptical of reporters, "intolerable and unavoidable nuisances," as one general called them. Nor was it surprising that commanding officers would try to keep reporters under control – one way or another. General William T. Sherman was so disgusted with reporters that he threatened to bar all of them from his department. Other generals cultivated special relationships with specific reporters. Grant retained a fond friendship with Sylvanus Cadwallader of the *Chicago Times* after the reporter saved the inebriated general from certain embarrassment after he was thrown from his horse. These friendships represented symbiotic relationships. Generals got favorable treatments in newspapers, and reporters, in turn, got scoops.

This does not mean that the only good reporting was the result of special relationships between generals and reporters. Many reporters risked their lives and health covering this war. Newspapers and wire services did not require their reporters to put themselves in danger, but given the competitive nature of reporting during this war, many reporters took chances – and a number died. A Chicago reporter, for example, became one of the casualties during the fierce fighting at Shiloh; another died at Fort Henry. Camp diseases claimed the lives of at least eight other reporters. Other Northern reporters were captured. Most were released quickly, but others, like the *New York Tribune*'s Junius Browne and Albert D. Richardson, languished in Confederate prisons for more than a year.

The reporters risked their lives, their health, and their freedom to cover a war that was marked by fierce hand-to-hand combat and more casualties than any war before or since. The best reporters were as accurate as any war allows; they captured not only the facts of the war but the essence as well. News stories were not in the classic news-reporting inverted pyramid style – that type of writing would be developed later. Civil War reporters were not dispassionate observers; they were involved. As Ned Spencer of the *Cincinnati Times* recounted at the battle of Shiloh:

> As I sit tonight, writing this epistle, the dead and wounded are all around. The knife of the Surgeon is busy at work, and amputated legs and arms lie scattered in every direction. The cries of the suffering victim, and the groans of those who patiently await for medical attendance, are most distressing to any one who has any sympathy with his fellow man. All day long they are coming in. . . . I hope my eyes may never again look upon such sights.

War reporting was never the same after the Civil War. The conflict had introduced too many innovations. The telegraph had introduced an immediacy that remained an important news value even some 150 years later. The questions of national security that were raised in that war have never been satisfactorily answered. Yet it would be misleading to think that the Civil War was a modern one journalistically. The writing style, the standards of reporter behavior, and the lack of concern about national security all illustrate Civil War journalism's immaturity.

KATHLEEN L. ENDRES

See also Civil War Photography; Civil War Press (South); Telegraph; War Correspondents; War Photography

Further Reading

Andrews, J. Cutler, *The North Reports the Civil War,* Pittsburgh, Pennsylvania: University of Pittsburgh Press, 1955
Blondheim, Menahem, *News over the Wires: The Telegraph and the Flow of Public Information in America, 1844–1897,* Cambridge, Massachusetts: Harvard University Press, 1994
Hughes, Thomas Andrew, "Historiographical Essay: The Civil War Press: Promoter of Unity or Neutral Reporter?," *American Journalism* 6 (1989)
Mindich, David T.Z., "Edwin M. Stanton, the Inverted Pyramid, and Information Control," *Journalism Monographs* 140 (August 1993), pp. 1–28
Starr, Louis Morris, *Bohemian Brigade: Civil War Newsmen in Action,* New York: Knopf, 1954
Weisberger, Bernard A., *Reporters for the Union,* Boston: Little, Brown, 1953

Civil War Press (South)

Reporting the news and upholding morale

The Southern newspapers had a tremendous responsibility to Southerners during the bloody American Civil War that they met in varying degrees. They were important to the morale of Confederate soldiers and citizens by providing a credible information source for all Southerners and being a Confederate government watchdog.

To its credit, Jefferson Davis's Confederate government administration never suppressed or destroyed a single Southern newspaper during the war. However, the Confederate government also decided not to use the press to propagandize its war efforts, which some historians believe was a serious shortcoming for the Confederacy. It was not until World War I that the U.S. government finally decided to officially propagandize war efforts by forming the Committee on Public Information, headed by George Creel.

Henry Hotze, a Confederate propagandist in England during the American Civil War, provided a superb analysis of the Confederate press in 1862 in his publication *The Index.* Hotze wrote, "The *Richmond [Virginia] Enquirer* is the leading journal, the oldest in the Confederate state, Democratic in background, careful in its statements, and like the *London Times,* supporting the government. Its chief rival, the *Whig,* formerly leaning to centralization, now watches with utmost jealousy the powers and conduct of the Confederate government and advocates restrictions that would make the executive powerless and useless but adopts a fair and patriotic course on all great questions. The *Rich-*

> **Southern Account of Pickett's Charge**
>
> The sun rises, clouds obscure its brightness as if loath to look upon the scene to witness such inhumanity, but from which no people are exempt who ever left a history or benefited the human race. . . . But where is that division which is to play so conspicuous a part in this day's tragedy? They are in line of battle, from which heavy batteries are belching forth shell and shrapnel with fatal accuracy. Hours pass, and the deadly missiles come thick and fast on their mission to death. See that shattered arm; that leg shot off; that headless body, and here the mangled form of a young and gallant lieutenant.
>
> *Richmond Enquirer,* July 12, 1863

mond Examiner is described as the Ishmael of the Southern press. So far as it is against everybody, written with wit and smartness, but in nine cases out of ten offering virulent censure that is undeserved. The *Richmond Despatch* is described as a cheap paper selling for two cents a copy, printed in small type, professing no political creed, catering to the taste of the masses, and enjoying a large circulation."

Hotze described the Southern newspapers outside Richmond in his *Index* publication on November 27, 1862, in this manner:

> The *Charleston [South Carolina] Mercury* was "almost rabid" on states rights, the *Mobile [Alabama] Register* is one of the most frequently quoted papers of the Confederacy, noted for its eminent literary quality, the extent and reliability of its news, its exceeding frankness, and its political moderation, and thorough independence. It supported the policies of the Davis administration, but not so closely as did the *Richmond Enquirer* or the *Charleston Courier.*

The American Civil War greatly affected the Southern editors' ability to cover and publish the war's news, in large part because so many journalists enlisted in the South's armies. Confederate journalism efforts also were greatly hampered by other factors: a lack of paper, the decrease of paid advertisements, unpaid subscriptions, incompetent postal service, rising newspaper operation costs, and, finally, the occupying Union armies. A number of Southern papers, however, continued to persevere against all odds.

Even though Southern editors were cut off from their original information source – the North – they devised other ways to gather their news. Three Southern news agencies were founded in New Orleans, Louisiana; Nashville, Tennessee; and Montgomery, Alabama. The Montgomery news agency transferred to Richmond when the Confederate government moved. This news agency was controlled by William H. Pritchard, a South Carolinian, former editor of the *Augusta (Georgia) Constitutionalist,* and Southern representative for the New York Associated Press.

After Pritchard's death in 1863, the Press Association (PA) of the Confederate states began work. This associa-

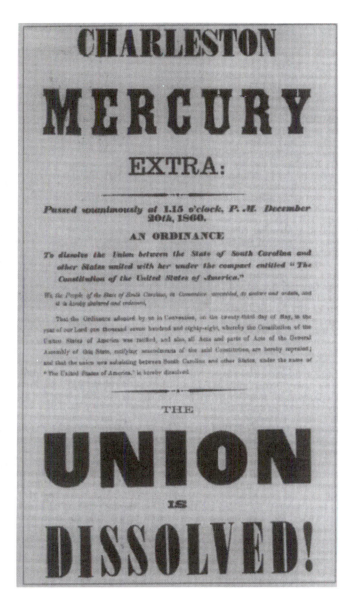

Secession begins; civil war follows.

tion, the Confederacy's version of the modern Associated Press, served all dailies east of the Mississippi River and some triweeklies. Dr. R.W. Gibbs of Columbia, South Carolina, was elected president and J.S. Thrasher of Atlanta, Georgia, general manager. The PA scattered its reporters throughout the South to cover the war and report back to the association via telegraph. The Atlanta editor of the *Southern Confederacy* newspaper wrote on April 23, 1863, that, "the association's efficient news reporting was a thing unprecedented in the history of our Western Telegraph." However, some Southern editors complained that the association's code procedure, which led to their reporters omitting certain implied words in transmission in order to save telegraph costs, made it very difficult, if not impossible, for editors to make sense out of the dispatches. Another Atlanta *Southern Confederacy* editor wrote on May 7, 1863, "The Superintendent of the Press Association was not employed to educate editors or supply them with brains, but to send dispatches in a shape that would be intelligible to men who are capable of conducting a daily paper."

Working for $25 a week, the Southern field reporters found it difficult to exist in Confederate Army camps and primary news centers throughout the war. Thrasher, the PA's general manager, was unable to obtain food and horses for his reporters from the Confederate Army supply system, which made their daily lives a true challenge.

The protection of Confederate national security was the paramount concern of the Confederate Congress and its generals throughout the war. Therefore, in January 1862, the Confederate Congress enacted a law that made it a crime for anyone to publish any information on military strength, numbers, movements of military forces, and disposition of any military unit's morale and physical condition. The Confederacy's generals reacted with vigor to this new law, with the Army of Northern Virginia banishing all newspaper correspondents. General Robert E. Lee exclaimed, "We put all our worst generals to commanding our armies, and all our best generals to editing newspapers . . . . If some of these better generals will come and take my place, I am willing to do my best to serve my country editing a newspaper." Generals Earl Van Dorn and Braxton Bragg threatened to suspend the publication of any Southern newspaper that published anything derogatory concerning their individual leadership, and Provost Marshal John H. Winder went after the *Richmond Whig* with a vengeance, threatening to shut it down if it did not "abandon its vicious habit of uttering unpalatable truths."

The Confederate government, however, did not suppress any newspapers during the war. The Union government suppressed, restricted, or destroyed at least two dozen of their newspapers by governmental or mob action. Southern restraint held despite the fact that Southern newspapers freely criticized Confederate generals for their shortcomings and failures, which provided Northern generals critical and valuable intelligence to defeat them.

In the final analysis, the Southern papers supported their government during the war by, for the most part, not publishing military security secrets and by attempting to improve Southern morale by downplaying their armies' failures and enthusiastically proclaiming their victories.

JOSEPH V. TRAHAN III

See also Civil War Press (North); Civil War Public Relations; Davis, Jefferson, and the Press

Further Reading
Andrews, J. Cutler, *The South Reports the Civil War*, Princeton, New Jersey: Princeton University Press, 1970

Randall, James G., "The Newspaper Problem and Its Bearing upon Military Secrecy During the Civil War," *American Historical Review* 23 (1918)

Reynolds, Donald E., *Editors Make War: Southern Newspapers in the Secession Crisis*, Nashville, Tennessee: Vanderbilt University Press, 1970

Wilson, Quintus C., "The Confederate Press Association: A Pioneer News Agency," *Journalism Quarterly* 26 (1949)

Civil War Public Relations

Early effort to mold public opinion in wartime

The Confederate States of America's master propagandist was a nineteenth-century public relations professional who was far ahead of his time because of his understanding and use of modern public relations strategies and tactics from 1861 to 1865. Henry Hotze's campaign to change European public opinion from pro-Union to pro-Confederate was a forerunner to the four-step public relations of the twentieth century. Although he did not fully accomplish his ultimate goal of obtaining European recognition for the Confederacy, Hotze definitely changed European public opinion from anti- to pro-Confederate during his five years of hard and dedicated propaganda efforts.

More importantly, Hotze understood and employed modern public relations techniques: the four-step public relations process of research/fact-finding, planning, communication/action, and evaluation. He also understood the importance of getting credible experts to speak during attempts to change public opinion. Additionally, he published 172 issues of a Confederate propaganda newspaper, *The Index*. With limited funds and English writers and editors, he attempted to publish a classified list of English products that the Confederacy consumed and their cost; published numerous propaganda pamphlets that were written by French and German writers; wrote speeches for English opinion leaders; utilized symbols to keep the Confederacy's cause in the forefront of all of England's masses; analyzed issues and tried to turn them to the Confederacy's cause; and finally, evaluated his activities. In the end, Hotze failed in his ultimate quest for European recognition because the Confederacy was defeated on the battlefield.

In evaluating Hotze's work, Civil War historian Burton J. Hendrick wrote in *Statesman of the Lost Cause* that "Hotze possessed a suavity, a subtlety, and silence in method that would have distinguished an experienced diplomat." Frank L. Owsley, in his book *King Cotton Diplomacy,* praised Hotze as "a very able man, as able as any agent who went abroad during the Civil War. He showed more insight into public opinion and tendencies than did either [James M.] Mason or [John] Slidell, and his lightness of touch in a delicate situation was remarkable. His resourcefulness had a masterly finesse that would have done honor to Cavour or Bismarck. Finally he was intellectually honest and unafraid to face the facts." And Douglas S. Freeman, in *The South to Posterity*, labeled *The Index* "a unique Confederate publication . . . one of the most effective of all organs of propaganda before the period of the [First] World War."

JOSEPH V. TRAHAN III

See also Civil War Press (South); Committee on Public Information; Public Relations

Further Reading

Freeman, Douglas Southall, *The South to Posterity,* New York: Scribner's, 1939
Hendrick, Burton J., *Statesmen of the Lost Cause: Jefferson Davis and His Cabinet,* Boston: Little, Brown, 1939
Owsley, Frank L., *King Cotton Diplomacy: Foreign Relations of the Confederate States of America,* 2nd ed., Chicago: University of Chicago Press, 1959

Classified Advertising

Longtime form of advertising

Advertisements of a few lines with no illustration have been a part of newspapers since colonial days. The first newspaper ads were in the format that in the twentieth century was considered classified, although there was no categorization to the listings. Ads were small and typically mentioned goods for sale, an upcoming speech or event, or a ship's arrival or departure. These notices were often on the front page, as they were considered important commercial news. As ads became more numerous, the "line" ads were placed at the back of the paper and put into subject and type categories to enable readers to sort through them more easily.

Advances in technology and the emergence of the department store in the latter half of the nineteenth century resulted in retail advertising assuming more importance than line ads. Beginning in the late 1980s, however, classified advertising continually increased in its share of revenue contributions, and in the late 1990s, the classified section delivered up to 40 percent of ad revenue at many large papers. Many classified sections offered telephone call-in service for users to place ads. These services might be for the personal ads, employment, real estate, or any category where additional information might be sought by the prospective buyer.

Payment may be by the word or by the line; weeklong packages and contracts were common. Attention-getting illustrations and white space were used to attract readers. A subcategory, classified display, featured ads that were often quite large with some kind of graphics. These were generally used by car dealers, employment agencies, and real estate firms.

MARY ALICE SHAVER

Codes of Ethics

Efforts to promote image of professionalism

Throughout the twentieth century, U.S. media associations and businesses adopted codes of ethics to soften public criticism and the threat of government regulation. Even before the big-government era that followed the stock market crash in 1929, the media were vulnerable to interference from diverse quarters – from states, which had begun to regulate movies; from courts, which continued to judge news; and from new federal agencies, which had been designed to oversee advertising and broadcasting. So one after another, the media created their codes, defining their industry standards in hopes of protecting their autonomy. The exact purpose of the codes varied among the media and their professional associations, but all of them sought to project an image of professionalism that would make additional regulation by outsiders appear to be unnecessary.

The first to develop media codes were journalists, whose trustworthiness had been undermined not only by government propaganda and public relations but also by their own sensationalism and the mercenary dimensions of the institutions for which they worked. Numerous state press associations followed the lead of the Kansas Editorial Association, which had adopted a code of ethics in 1910: Missouri and Texas in 1921, South Dakota and Oregon in 1922, and Washington in 1923. In that year, the American Society of Newspaper Editors adopted the Canons of Journalism, which heralded responsibility, freedom, independence, honesty, accuracy, impartiality, fair play, and decency as virtues of news reporting. The Society of Professional Journalists adopted the canons in 1926.

Journalism codes received little attention again until the 1970s, by which time U.S. journalism had entered a state of flux. Television news had become a primary source of income for networks and their affiliates alike, and the number of daily newspapers had begun a steady decline. Any news at all seemed fit to print when one's livelihood or very existence was at stake, and the more lurid or titillating the better. The saucier the news became in its relentless search for audiences, the more the public began to doubt the methods and the sincerity of journalists.

Finding themselves in a crisis of credibility, individual news organizations by the dozen wrote new codes of ethics, and the national associations of reporters, photographers, editors, and publishers revised their old ones. ABC, CBS, and NBC; the *Chicago Sun-Times;* the *Courier-Journal* of Louisville, Kentucky; the *Des Moines (Iowa) Register;* the *Milwaukee (Wisconsin) Journal;* the *Philadelphia Inquirer;* and the *Washington (D.C.) Post* were among the prestige news organizations that wrote detailed and enforceable codes of ethics. By contrast, the codes of the national associations were hortatory and entirely voluntary, and cries of press freedom would arise to silence the issue of code enforcement whenever it was voiced. It became clear that individual company codes, unlike those of national associations, were designed with actual implementation in mind.

By the mid-1980s, news organizations began to fear that written codes of ethics could be used against them by libel plaintiffs trying to prove that reporters recklessly disregarded journalistic standards. This fear had a chilling effect on journalistic codes of ethics. After 1987, when the Society of Professional Journalists stopped asking its members to censure reporters who violated the discipline of the code, most code activity in journalism moved quietly to the privacy of individual newsrooms.

The history of journalistic codes bears some resemblance to the code activity of the National Association of Broadcasters (NAB). Written in 1928, the Radio Code was a direct response to the Federal Radio Commission, established by Congress the year before to clear "the confusion in the ether." The code consisted of eight guidelines that encouraged broadcasting in the public interest. Originally consisting of unenforceable platitudes, the Radio Code grew more specific with every revision, so that the twenty-second edition in 1980 was a booklet 31 pages long.

The Radio Code and the Television Code were specific, but adherence was voluntary and noncompliance went unpunished. In 1963, for instance, the Federal Communications Commission discovered that 40 percent of television stations exceeded the time limits for advertising set forth in the Television Code. The codes did have some impact, though, because the advertisements that television and radio stations broadcast were usually designed with NAB code standards in mind.

In 1979, the U.S. Justice Department surprised broadcasters by asserting that the Television Code violated antitrust laws. The Justice Department attacked the code's limits on the amount of time for commercials per hour, on the number of commercial interruptions per hour, and on the number of products per commercial, saying that these restrictions harmed both advertisers and consumers by raising the price of broadcasting time unnecessarily. The NAB signed a consent decree and eliminated its codes, presenting another example of ethics codes succumbing to legal pressure.

Unlike the NAB codes, the Code of Professional Standards of the Public Relations Society of America (PRSA) was not designed to reduce government regulation. Instead, it was designed to serve as a signpost that PRSA members were true professionals, and as such deserved full recognition and status. PRSA's code, which appeared in 1950 and was revised and expanded several times since, was largely hortatory, exhorting members to be honest, discreet, fair, democratic, and honorable. It also was specific in places, condemning the use of false fronts, for instance, and forbidding PRSA members from intentionally damaging the professional reputation or practice of other practitioners. To clarify its intentions, the code came with an official interpretation covering issues in financial and political public relations.

One central criticism of the PRSA code was that few public relations practitioners were bound by it. The PRSA might be the largest public relations organization in the United States, but most practitioners did not belong to it and thus were not obligated to follow the association's code. Furthermore, the businesses for which public relations practitioners work were not bound by the code either, which meant that the code's jurisdiction was small.

Enforcing the PRSA code was consequently ticklish because not only were PRSA members loath to criticize one another, but the ultimate punishment was only expulsion from the organization, to which most practitioners did not belong in the first place. It is therefore no surprise that in the 35 years between 1950 and 1985, only 10 persons were expelled, suspended, censured, or reprimanded for violating the code. Although PRSA interpreted this minimal enforcement to mean that its members were following the code, it is more likely that there was so little trust in the code and its enforcement mechanisms that they were seldom applied.

This limp enforcement was well illustrated in the case of Anthony M. Franco. Months before he became president of the PRSA in 1986, Franco's client, the Crowley, Milner, and Company Department Store, decided to put itself on the market for $50 a share. With this confidential information, Franco ordered 3,000 shares of Crowley stock at $41 each two days before the sale was to be announced, which would yield a $27,000 profit. He rescinded the order later the same day after learning that the Securities and Exchange Commission (SEC) had inquired into his unusually large purchase. The SEC continued to investigate Franco's attempted insider trading until he signed an out-of-court agreement that was made public.

It was this publicity that led Franco to relinquish the presidency of the PRSA and to leave the organization altogether. As president he had declared his personal goal of making PRSA members more cognizant of the society's ethics code. But he stopped the PRSA's investigation into charges of his dishonesty and conflict of interest by quitting. Because the PRSA was able to investigate ethics violations only of current members, its impotence was only a resignation away.

Not all communication codes can be eluded as easily as the PRSA's, and not all have vanished due to legal pressure. Indeed, as a rule, the more local the code, the more closely it is followed. Journalists are more likely to follow their employer's code of ethics than that of an association to which they may or may not belong. Even on the national level, the very process of writing codes may stimulate reflection and discussion that can make individuals more sensitive to the moral dimensions of their chosen work. The process may even produce a map of the occupation's moral waters.

Whatever their role in curbing the power and self-indulgence of the media, however, codes are incapable of providing concrete moral guidance to nebulous or dispersed groups such as aspiring professional and national associations. By necessity, codes are ambiguous, and they tend to lack enforcement. The history of codes suggests that self-regulation is manifestly self-serving, that codes are capable of public service only if their design and enforcement involve more than just those persons who are privileged with access to the media.

JOHN P. FERRÉ

See also Criticism of Advertising; Criticism of Broadcasting; Criticism of Newspapers; Journalism Reviews

Further Reading

Hulteng, John L., *Playing It Straight: A Practical Discussion of the Ethical Principles of the American Society of Newspaper Editors*, Chester, Connecticut: Globe Pequot, 1981
Johannesen, Richard L., *Ethics in Human Communication*, 3rd ed., Prospect Heights, Illinois: Waveland, 1990
Saalberg, Harvey, "The Canons of Journalism: A 50-Year Perspective," *Journalism Quarterly* 50 (1973)

Cold War and the Media

U.S. media support government efforts to contain Communism

The Cold War that followed World War II was a new kind of war for the people of the United States and quite different from the "hot" one in which their nation had just achieved victory. It was a war in which the weapons were mainly words and symbols and, thus, one in which the role of the media was key. On a daily basis, the U.S. public read in their newspapers, heard on their radios, and saw on their televisions a clash between the Communist Soviet Union and the United States that always seemed to threaten to erupt into hot war but mainly consisted of ongoing mutual hostility in the form of threats and posturing.

The term "Cold War" was introduced publicly by President Truman's appointee Bernard Baruch in 1947 and was popularized by journalist Walter Lippmann in his columns and in a 1947 book. By mid-1947, most of the U.S. media had embraced this term and used it to communicate to their audiences that the United States was engaged in a great battle between good ("us") and evil ("them"). Given the long history of distrust and fear of Communism in the United States, the idea that the Soviet Union was a mortal enemy was not difficult for most citizens to accept. The end of World War II had left these two nations as the most visible actors on the world stage. Most of the Allies from World War II were economically, militarily, or psychologically exhausted, leaving the United States alone to take the role of protector of the so-called free world. Furthermore, the United States was glorying in postwar prosperity and the possession of the atomic bomb. The nation also wanted to ensure open doors for expanding foreign markets to allow for the growth of U.S. capitalism.

President Truman essentially declared the cold war on March 12, 1947, in a speech to Congress in which he established the need to wage a "global battle against Communism." In so doing, he created a conundrum for the U.S. media. In a state of hot war, the media historically had considered it a patriotic duty to accept government propaganda and help mold public opinion to support the cause. A cold war was something different; behavior was not so easily prescribed, yet most of the media slipped back into their World War II posture. They supported the Truman Doctrine editorially and in news stories that almost never allowed for the possibility of another way of looking at the world.

Further, this world view was supported by events: the collapse of Nationalist China in 1949; the explosion of an atomic bomb by the Soviet Union in that same year; the espionage trial of Alger Hiss in 1949 and his conviction in 1950; Senator Joseph McCarthy's famous 1950 Wheeling, West Virginia, speech (claiming he had the names of 205 Communists in the State department); the outbreak of the

Korean War; and the arrest of alleged Communist spies Julius and Ethel Rosenberg. In the media, these emerged as common threads in the international tapestry of the Communist menace and the imperative to support presidential policy and maintain a united front. It was not seen as a time for dissident ideas to be expressed; if there were problems in the American way of life, discussing them would be divisive, and the nation could not afford to be divided when facing a great enemy.

In this way, the media participated in the forging of a national consensus around the ideas that war with the Communists was imminent, that there were spies and saboteurs among "us" who had made and were continuing to make the nation vulnerable to attack, and that it was necessary to root them out and protect "our way of life." Even off of the editorial pages, the editorial "we" lurked behind stories. Much of this can be seen in the media through the formation of a cold war lexicon in which the terms "red," "Communist front," "Communist-dominated," and "fellow traveler" were used to describe those groups or individuals who objected to the consensus; the terms "subversion," "disloyalty, "crisis," "fear," "threat," "danger," and "menace" were used in discussion of the U.S. climate. In the post-Sputnik years, the idea of a competitive race with the Soviet Union was linked to all aspects of life, including armaments, education, hydrogen bombs, knowledge, missiles, production, and space exploration.

The efforts of the media to line up clearly on the "we" side of the dichotomy certainly helped the domestic corollary of containing Communism abroad – the campaign to cleanse the nation of disloyalty. This began in 1947 with Truman's government loyalty program but invaded all aspects of life in the 1950s. Both the newspaper and broadcast industries themselves underwent scrutiny for signs of disloyalty. The newspaper industry was the subject of inquiries by both the House Committee on Un-American Activities and the Senate Internal Security Subcommittee, and most of those found to have past connections to Communist or "Communist front" organizations lost their jobs. Organized blacklisting became the norm in broadcasting as those with suspect pasts were only able to work in the industry if cleared of any Communist taint. The word that is most often used to identify this Cold War compulsion is "McCarthyism." Senator Joseph McCarthy was able to grab headlines with accusations that were seldom proven, and the denials that followed were seldom given the attention of the original accusations. Although McCarthy and his methods fell from grace in 1954, the assumptions upon which those methods sat continued to shape media content. Rather than defend First Amendment freedoms, the mainstream media cooperated with and openly supported the effort to enforce loyalty as it was being defined in the Cold War climate.

Overall, the media performance during the Cold War was marked by its tendency to be a participant in the creation and maintenance of the national consciousness in terms of the Cold War. Only in the mid-1960s, after the resolution of the Cuban missile crisis left the people of the United States feeling confident again, did the media begin to emerge from this way of defining life in the United States

and begin to address both foreign and domestic policy more critically.

PAMELA A. BROWN

See also Army-McCarthy Hearings; Broadcast Blacklisting; Motion Picture Blacklisting

Further Reading

Aronson, James, *The Press and the Cold War,* Indianapolis, Indiana: Bobbs-Merrill, 1970
Bayley, Edwin R., *Joe McCarthy and the Press,* Madison: University of Wisconsin Press, 1981
Belfrage, Cedric, *The American Inquisition, 1945–1960,* Indianapolis, Indiana: Bobbs-Merrill, 1973
Caute, David, *The Great Fear: The Anti-Communist Purge Under Truman and Eisenhower,* New York: Simon & Schuster, 1978; London, Secker and Warburg, 1978
Goldman, Eric F., *The Crucial Decade – And After: America, 1945–1960,* New York: Knopf, 1966
Halberstam, David, *The Fifties,* New York: Villard, 1993
Hodgson, Godfrey, *America in Our Time,* New York: Vintage, 1978

Colonial Press
Newspapers slow to appear during these years

The colonial press began in Boston on September 25, 1690, when Benjamin Harris printed *Publick Occurrences, Both Forreign and Domestick.* The newspaper, which was three pages long, promised to provide citizens of Massachusetts with accounts of "considerable things" each month. This first experiment with newspapers in the American colonies ended after one issue, however, because of governmental objections. No other newspaper appeared in the colonies until John Campbell started the *Boston News-Letter* in 1704.

The colonial press grew out of London newsletters and newspapers and developed slowly. After the *Boston News-Letter,* no other newspapers appeared in America until December 1719, when the *Boston Gazette* and *American Weekly Mercury* started in Boston and Philadelphia, respectively. Within a decade, printers began another five newspapers – one in New York, another in Philadelphia, and three in Boston. The number of newspapers expanded to 12 by 1750 with papers printed in Maryland, Virginia, and South Carolina as well as Massachusetts, New York, and Pennsylvania. By 1775 and the end of the colonial period, 40 papers appeared in weekly, biweekly, or triweekly form in all colonies except New Jersey and Delaware. Most newspapers were weeklies, but printers tried biweeklies in the 1720s and triweeklies in the 1770s. More than 25 other newspapers lived and died during the period.

Governmental support was important to the first newspapers. The nameplate of the *Boston News-Letter* declared that it was "Printed by Authority." Colonial governments supported the first newspapers begun in most colonies – or suppressed them, as in the case of *Publick Occurrences*. Other factors fostered the development of newspapers, too. These included a population adequate to support newspapers and the existence of causes to advocate in a newspaper. Both outweighed governmental support by 1740 throughout the colonies and as early as the mid-1720s in Boston.

The colonial press employed essentially the same printing process as that developed by Johannes Gutenberg in 1455. Printers, along with their families or their apprentices, set type by hand with each individual letter held in place on a piece of metal called a stick. Printers transferred the type to an iron frame and placed it on the press. The lead letters were then inked and transferred to the paper. Printers produced approximately 250 sheets per hour, and each required drying time before the second side of the sheet could be printed.

Newspapers appeared on single two-sided sheets or folded four-page editions. Most printers produced newspapers of four pages, but as the period progressed, newspapers of six or more pages were not uncommon. Printers used no headlines on stories but occasionally grouped news under generic titles such as "News from London." Only paragraph indentations separated stories.

The colonial press depended on Europe for presses, paper, and type for most of the period. Soft lead type deteriorated after use, and paper, which was made from cloth, was not always readily available to printers. Newspapers sometimes became difficult to read, and printers requested that readers donate rags in order to produce newsprint.

Newspapers cost between 10 and 12 shillings per year for a subscription, and circulation before 1765 ran from a few hundred to approximately 1,000 issues per year, the average circulation for American papers being 600 in 1750. In 1765, after the Stamp Act crisis, newspapers developed into strong political organs, and circulation increased. By 1774, some newspapers in Boston and New York sold in excess of 3,500 subscriptions per year. Circulation figures do not accurately represent the impact of the colonial press. Subscribers passed along papers to non-subscribers. Papers were available in public places such as taverns. The accessibility of papers increased their penetration and their effect upon society.

Newspaper circulation depended upon carriers, the colonial postal system, and waterways for distribution. Carriers distributed newspapers to a central location within a town where they were picked up by subscribers. The postal system carried newspapers to nearby areas. Printers considered the post critical to the survival of newspapers in the 1720s and 1730s. Printers attempted to become postmasters so that they could send newspapers without charge to subscribers. Postmasters often blocked the use of the mails by competitors. Water access was required for newspapers to be transported to other regions of the colonies. All newspapers of the colonial period were located in towns with water access.

The placement of news in the paper's layout represented a different outlook in the colonial press than obtained in later years. Printers placed the most recent news on the inside of the paper rather than on page one. The colonial press did not consider page one the place of the most significant news, although the most significant news did sometimes find its way onto the front page of newspapers. Printers considered page-one news more stately or worthy of extended discussion by readers. Newspapers often ran essays and political news from Europe and the colonies there. News on page one represented information that printers had available to set before press day. They saved late-breaking news and new advertisements for the last when setting type. The last news to appear was almost always news from the town in which a paper was printed. Whenever there was more news than an edition would hold or vital news arrived between press days, printers issued supplements or extras with this news.

The subjects of news in the colonial press varied as much as news in modern newspapers. In fact, every aspect of modern newspapers, with the exception of photographs, comics, and color printing, could be found in newspapers of the colonial period. While speeches, essays, legislative action, and politics represented more than half of the news content of newspapers, the colonial press kept readers apprised of shipping and trade, Native American activity, pirates and privateers, religion, disease outbreaks and medical cures, slave activity, sports, and weather. The colonial press often described events in very graphic detail, and sensationalism was a regular feature of news, especially in the period before 1750.

Most printers claimed objectivity for their newspapers, but objectivity was not a major facet of writing during the period. Few editorials appeared, but editorial comment accompanied many stories. Because letters and essays submitted to printers discussed the controversial issues of the day, articles rarely maintained neutrality. Early in the period, the press did avoid controversial subjects when those subjects posed a threat to the life of a newspaper. No colonial newspapers outside of New York City mentioned the 1735 trial of John Peter Zenger – a libel trial in which the printer and publisher was acquitted, establishing the first important victory for freedom of the press in the colonies – except to state that his lawyers were disbarred until 1738.

This tendency to avoid issues that threatened the life of a newspaper disappeared as the power of the colonial press grew in the 1760s. By 1765 and the Stamp Act crisis, the number of newspapers in America climbed to 26. The unity of the press on this issue allowed the press to avoid repercussions from its refusal to use stamped paper. Even though the press continued to grow in size and strength after 1765, the press never again attained complete unity. From 1765 to 1775, the colonial press splintered into factions, some supporting nonimportation and other Patriot causes. Other printers adopted a more Tory, or pro-England, stance. The press ended the colonial period divided, with many Patriot presses shut down or destroyed by invading British troops.

DAVID A. COPELAND

See also: Advertising in the Eighteenth Century; Newspapers in the Eighteenth Century; *Publick Occurrences, Both Forreign and Domestick*; Reporters and Reporting in the Eighteenth Century; Stamp Act of 1765; Zenger, John Peter

Further Reading

Botein, Stephen, "'Meer Mechanics' and an Open Press: The Business and Political Strategies of Colonial American Printers," in *Perspectives in American History,* edited by Donald Fleming and Bernard Bailyn, Cambridge, Massachusetts: Harvard University Press, 1975

Brigham, Clarence S., *History and Bibliography of American Newspapers, 1690–1820,* Worcester, Massachusetts: American Antiquarian Society, 1947

Cook, Elizabeth Christine, *Literary Influences in Colonial Newspapers, 1704–1750,* New York: Columbia University Press, 1912

Copeland, David A., *Colonial American Newspapers: Character and Content,* Newark: University of Delaware Press, 1997

Kobre, Sidney, *The Development of the Colonial Newspaper,* Gloucester, Massachusetts: Peter Smith, 1960

Sloan, W. David, and Julie Hedgepeth Williams, *The Early American Press, 1690–1783*, Westport, Connecticut: Greenwood, 1994

Thomas, Isaiah, *The History of Printing in America,* New York: Weathervane, 1970

Wroth, Lawrence, *The Colonial Printer,* Portland, Maine: Southworth-Anthoensen, 1938

Comic Books

Originally served as premium for buying grocery items

The modern comic book in the United States originated in the early 1930s as an experimental giveaway premium to spur the sales of everything from soap to cereal. The colorful magazines, printed in a distinctive half-tabloid size, proved so popular that some publishers decided to try issuing comic books on a monthly basis and selling them for a dime, beginning with *Famous Funnies* in 1934. Although popular comic strips had been reprinted before, the idea of publishing regular monthly titles and selling the magazines on the newsstand was a new one. The early comic books reprinted comic strips, but publishers soon began offering readers original characters and stories as well.

The tremendous success of Superman, introduced in mid-1938 in *Action Comics,* and of Batman a year later, spawned a series of costumed heroes with special powers who collectively became known as superheroes. Publishers also offered other types of comics, including funny animal comics, featuring Disney and other cartoon characters, and teen comics, such as Archie. Superheroes dominated sales, however. By 1945, nearly 160 comic books were published each month, and surveys indicated that 90 percent of U.S. children read comic books, along with a substantial number of adults. The comic book had become the country's newest "mass" medium. The period from 1938 to the end of World War II is known as the Golden Age of comic books.

After the war, the popularity of the superheroes waned. In an effort to boost lagging sales, publishers turned to other genres such as crime, horror, romance, and westerns. The transplanting of violence and sex from the superhero fantasy world to a more realistic setting, coupled with a growing concern in postwar society about media effects and juvenile delinquency, led parents and various experts to question the suitability of comic books for children. Some suggested that comic books had a negative impact on youngsters, and a national campaign to clean up comics, led by psychiatrist Fredric Wertham, culminated in a U.S. Senate investigation into comics in 1954. The results were inconclusive, but the industry, worried about negative publicity and fears of government censorship, adopted the Comics Code that year. Publishers modeled their industry self-regulatory code on the one adopted by the film industry in the 1930s. A version of that code was still in effect in the late 1990s.

With sales once again slumping, partly due to the controversy and partly to the competition for children's leisure time from television, the industry resurrected the superhero. The Flash, a popular character in the early days, reappeared in 1956, followed by other Golden Age superheroes updated for a new audience. This marked the beginning of the Silver Age of comics. During this period, creators introduced teams of superheroes in titles such as *Justice League of America,* published by DC Comics, and *Fantastic Four,* published by Marvel Comics. One team, the X-Men, was introduced in the 1960s but did not become enormously popular until its reintroduction in 1975. The "new" X-Men would become the most popular Marvel comic book series ever. The superhero craze was boosted by the popularity of the campy "Batman" television show that premiered in 1966.

The 1960s marked another important historical moment, the birth of underground comics (or, as was often preferred, comix). These comic books, far outside the mainstream of comic book publishing, had close ties to the counterculture and explored taboo subjects associated with that movement, primarily sex and drugs. While the underground comic book as such had virtually disappeared by the late 1990s, several talented underground artists made the transition to more mainstream titles. The Silver Age ended with the 1960s, but not before it helped to establish Marvel Comics as a major publisher (in the 1980s and 1990s, titles published by Marvel and DC Comics accounted for more than 80 percent of all comic books sold).

In the 1970s, comic book publishing entered a new phase with the rise of smaller companies known as independents. Early leaders in the independent movement were Aardvark-Vanaheim, established in 1977; Eclipse in 1978; and First Comics in 1983. Some of these companies permitted creators to retain the rights to their characters, allowing for more artistic control and freedom to experiment.

Also in the 1970s, there was a change in the way comic books were distributed. Until the late 1970s, comic books were distributed by magazine distributors. However, as specialty stores that carried only comic books and related merchandise sprang up, these retailers began to purchase comic books through an alternative distribution system, rather than from newsstand distributors. This new system, direct distribution, or direct market, sales, contributed to the growth of comic book collecting. Specialty stores did not return unsold copies of the comic books, keeping back issues available for collectors seeking to own all the issues of a particular title.

Another innovation of the period was the graphic novel. Some debate exists over exactly how to define a graphic novel and which title constitutes the appearance of the first one. But many fans and creators welcomed the longer, larger format as a way to change the public's perception of the comic book and establish comics as a serious art form. The publication of Art Spiegelman's *Maus* in 1987 (it was first serialized in the magazine *Raw*), which presented his father's experiences at the hands of the Nazis and depicted the characters as cats and mice, is often cited as an example of the maturation of the comic book form. That graphic novel won a Pulitzer Prize. Other notable graphic novels were *Batman: The Dark Knight Returns,* published in 1986, and *Watchmen,* published in 1987.

The success of the Superman and Batman movies and sequels, however, along with the popularity of such newer characters as the Teenage Mutant Ninja Turtles, ended speculation that comic books entered a "new age" in the 1980s. Most of the independent companies folded by the end of the century, the graphic novel had not replaced the comic book, and the superhero was still the dominant comic book genre.

AMY KISTE NYBERG

See also Mass Media and Children; Mass Media and Self-Regulation

Further Reading

Benton, Mike, *The Comic Book in America: An Illustrated History,* Dallas, Texas: Taylor, 1989

Estren, Mark James, *A History of Underground Comics,* 2nd ed., London: Airlift, 1987; 3rd ed., Berkeley, California: Ronin, 1993

Gilbert, James Burkhart, *A Cycle of Outrage: America's Reaction to the Juvenile Delinquent in the 1950s,* New York: Oxford University Press, 1986

Jacobs, Will, and Gerard Jones, *The Comic Book Heroes: From the Silver Age to the Present,* New York: Crown, 1985

Sabin, Roger, *Adult Comics: An Introduction,* New York and London: Routledge, 1993

Savage, William W., *Comic Books and America, 1945–1954,* Norman, Oklahoma, and London: University of Oklahoma Press, 1990

Wertham, Fredric, *Seduction of the Innocent,* New York: Rinehart, 1954; London: Museum, 1955

Comic Strips

First appeared in newspapers in 1895

The term "comic strip" is, in some respects, a misnomer, since comic strips are not required to be humorous, and they may have only one panel. Usually, however, comic strips have pictures in narrative sequence; text as part of the illustrations; interrelated text and pictures (meaning that neither can be completely understood without the other); a preponderance of image over text; continuing characters; and they are created for regular publication in a mass medium. The use of sequential combinations of words and pictures to communicate was common by the Renaissance. What made the newspaper comic strip different was its publication in a mass medium.

The immediate precursors of newspaper comic strips were the cartoons in nineteenth-century humor magazines. Virtually all early comic strip cartoonists began their careers as magazine cartoonists. The first newspaper appearance on February 17, 1895, of Richard Felton Outcault's character Mickey Dugan (who later became known as the Yellow Kid) was in a cartoon reprinted from *Truth* magazine.

Comic strips did not originate as children's entertainment. They were directed toward adult readers with enough disposable income to buy newspapers. The most common type of comic strip, social humor based on ordinary daily life, has its origins in the Yellow Kid and other early features such as *The Katzenjammer Kids,* by Rudolph Dirks, and Bud Fisher's *Mutt and Jeff.* Following World War I, Joseph Patterson, publisher of the *New York Daily News* and co-owner of the Chicago Tribune–New York News Syndicate, adapted the idea of serialized stories into comic strips with features like *The Gumps,* by Sidney Smith, and *Gasoline Alley,* by Frank King. In the early 1930s, strips about family life were overshadowed by adventure comic strips in exotic settings. Milton Caniff's *Terry and the Pirates,* Alex Raymond's *Flash Gordon,* and Hal Foster's *Prince Valiant* are the most outstanding examples of this genre that was established by Roy Crane's *Wash Tubbs.*

Although political commentary had occasionally been part of comic strips from the beginning, it became more overt in the 1930s with Harold Gray's conservative stance in *Little Orphan Annie* and in Al Capp's lampoons of the establishment during the 1940s in *Li'l Abner.* Satire in the funnies reached a new level in *Pogo* by Walt Kelly, who is best known for the famous phrase, "We have met the enemy and he is us." Political commentary in comic strips won two Pulitzer Prizes in the first decades after the Vietnam War: the first in 1975 for Garry Trudeau's *Doonesbury* and the second in 1987 for Berkeley Breathed's *Bloom County.*

The contemporary comic strip began with the appearance of *Peanuts* by Charles Schulz and *Beetle Bailey* by Mort Walker in the fall of 1950. Simply drawn strips that related a stand-alone joke each day, they set a new fashion for the funnies that eventually replaced story strips. In the 1980s, two comic strips based on family experiences, *For Better or for Worse,* by Lynn Johnston, and *Calvin and Hobbes,* by Bill Watterson, reasserted the importance of artistic technique and character development.

Few women and minorities have had successful careers as comic strip cartoonists. The best-known early female cartoonists were Grace Drayton Weiderseim, creator of *Toodles,* and Edwina Dumm, who drew *Cap Stubbs and Tippie.* Lynn Johnston and Cathy Guisewite were the most successful women cartoonists of the late twentieth century.

Hogan's Alley, featuring the Yellow Kid, was a precursor of modern comic strips.
(Reproduced from the Collections of the Library of Congress)

Barbara Brandon's feature, *Where I'm Coming From,* was the only syndicated comic strip by an African American woman in the late 1990s. George Herriman, creator of the critically acclaimed *Krazy Kat,* was of African American heritage, although he passed as white. African American men who have had syndicated comic strips include Robb Armstrong, Steve Bentley, Ray Billingsley, Brumsic Brandon Jr., E. Sims Campbell, Ted Shearer, and Morrie Turner.

An ongoing problem for comic strip cartoonists over the decades was the shrinking publication size of their features. Early Sunday comics often ran as full pages, but gradually half pages became more common as editors attempted to run more comic strips in the same space. Increasing newsprint costs and the adoption of standard advertising units imposed further size restrictions.

Virtually all comic strips were distributed by syndicates, many of which were established in the early 1900s by newspaper magnates who saw opportunities for profits in re-selling to other papers features originally produced for their own papers. In the early days, cartoonists were considered to be producing work for hire, and they usually received half of the revenue derived from the syndication of their work. Bud Fisher of *Mutt and Jeff* was the first cartoonist to copyright his feature in his own name, and over the years, ownership of comic strips was the basis of several lawsuits.

Comic strips are complex and efficient means of communication. A system of symbols (such as drawing a light bulb above a character's head to mean that he or she has an idea, or using large, boldface letters for loud sounds) has evolved, and this visual shorthand is clearly understood by readers. In spite of size reductions that limit the space available for speech balloons, cartoonists continue to entertain readers and to depict serious issues such as divorce, AIDS, and death. According to a study commissioned in 1993, 113 million people read Sunday comic strips. Of this total, 76 percent were adults and 24 percent were children under 18. A development in the 1990s was the application of computer technology to comic strips. Several cartoonists used computer-generated lettering; a few regularly published their E-mail addresses; and some syndicates offered on-line versions of their comic strips.

LUCY SHELTON CASWELL

See also Feature Syndicates

Further Reading
Astor, David, "Study Finds Comics Read by 113 Million," *Editor & Publisher* 126:5 (January 30, 1993), p. 34
Harvey, Robert C., *The Art of the Funnies: An Aesthetic History,* Jackson: University Press of Mississippi, 1994
Kunzle, David, *The History of the Comic Strip,* 2 vols., Berkeley, California, and Oxford: University of California Press, 1990
McCloud, Scott, *Understanding Comics: The Invisible Art,* Northampton, Massachusetts: Tundra, 1993
Turner, Kathleen J., "Comic Strips: A Rhetorical Perspective," *Central States Speech Journal* 28 (1977)
Walker, Mort, *Lexicon of Comicana,* Port Chester, New York: Museum of Cartoon Art, 1980
Waugh, Coulton, *The Comics,* New York: Macmillan, 1947

Commercialization of Broadcasting

Advertising quickly became the chosen way to finance new medium in the United States

When the first words and music wafted out from experimental radio stations, the question of how to finance this new enterprise was in the back of the minds of many people in and out of the industry. The earliest radios, however, were family operations, with crystals and tubes and wires stringing through garages, basements, or spare rooms. When the radio gained a wood casing and found its way into the family living room, listeners demanded more and more programming; how to finance that programming was a leading question.

Early on, radio operators and radio manufacturers worked closely together. The notion was that set sales would finance radio programming, to the benefit of both the burgeoning number of stations and the manufacturers. Soon, however, programming demand outpaced the ability of sales to support it. The audience was demanding more programming and higher quality, professional programming, which would cost a great deal of money to produce.

Advertising was, of course, a possibility. One problem, however, was the kind of advertising that would occur on the airwaves. WEAF in New York City took one approach when Hawthorne Courts, a real-estate development, purchased 10 minutes of time – for one commercial. The speaker avoided mention of the apartments' owner, the Queensboro Corporation, giving its name just once. Most of the 10 minutes was devoted to discussing how wonderful it was to live in the suburbs. Referring to Nathaniel Hawthorne the writer more than he did Hawthorne the apartment development, the speaker concluded by saying, "Let me close by urging you to hurry to the apartment house near the green fields . . . the community life and friendly development that Hawthorne advocated." The sponsoring company paid $50 for the spot.

As it became clearer that advertising could be a source of financing, stations refused to sell time for direct sales pitches. Instead, they wanted businesses to buy programming and to reap goodwill by offering the audience outstanding drama or music or variety shows. Thus the programming often became known by the sponsor's name. Listeners heard from the Cliquot Club Eskimos, the A&P Gypsies, and the Ipana Troubadours, as well as other entertainers offering the Palmolive Hour and the Maxwell House Hour. The goodwill came from introductions and conclusions to various programs. One such introduction said:

> Relax and smile, for Goldy and Dusty, the Gold Dust Twins are here to send their songs there, and "brighten the corner where you are." The Gold Dust Corporation, manufacturer of Gold Powder engages the facilities of [station call letters] so that the listeners in may have the opportunity to chuckle and laugh with Goldy and Dusty. Let those Gold Dust Twins into your hearts and homes tonight, and you'll never regret it, for they do brighten the dull spots.

Characters took on the names of their sponsors as well. Frank Munn, for instance, played "Paul Oliver" and Virginia Rhea played "Olive Palmer" on a show sponsored by Palmolive Soap. Even so, radio equipment producers remained the largest group of advertisers, and in the 1920s, no station earned enough from advertisers to completely finance programming.

This low level of advertising created quite a furor, however. Herbert Hoover, then secretary of commerce and labor, denounced advertising as a way to finance radio even as he sought a sound footing for the medium's development. "The quickest way to kill broadcasting would be to use it for direct advertising," he told one of his national radio conferences.

For the United States, financial support for broadcasting opportunities seemed limited to advertising. Some countries, such as Great Britain, decided on a system of government control – funded by a license fee on receivers, and other countries picked outright government ownership, but private ownership supported by advertising became the way to develop the system in the United States.

Radio very quickly caught on with the advertisers, who were anxious to see what this new medium could offer them. Newspapers protested, and battles between the media over who won the greater share of the advertising dollar became a common occurrence.

By the 1930s, the ban on direct advertising had been abandoned, and commercials hawked products to listeners. Advertising historian Bruce Roche notes that from no advertising money spent on radio to 1920, by 1927, advertisers paid for network advertising to the tune of $4 million a year. In 1928, $10.5 million went into network programming.

The quality of programming increased with the influx of money as many vaudeville stars made the transition to radio programs. Jack Benny, Bing Crosby, and Bob Hope were among those who moved to radio. In addition, programming was developed especially for radio – soap operas for soap manufacturers, for instance.

Historian Robert McChesney argued that the U.S. radio system did not have to develop along these commercial lines. He suggested that with proper regulatory encouragement, an educational system could have grown up beside (or in place of) the commercial-dominated system so well known today. Both the Federal Radio Commission and the Federal Communication Commission conducted research and hearings on how radio was developing, but, said McChesney, the types of questions asked and persons to whom they were directed prejudiced the answers. The studies concluded that the developing advertising-based radio system was ideal for U.S. society.

Over the years, various groups tried to rein in commercialism on radio. Suggestions came from radio professional groups, governmental bodies, and civic groups. Discussions focused on when the commercials were broadcast, what the commercials contained, and at whom the commercials were aimed. Despite long-term concern about the impact of radio advertising on the medium, the product, and society, financial support through advertising continued almost unchanged over time from the early days of radio into television and cablecasting.

Margaret A. Blanchard

See also Advertising in the Twentieth Century; Broadcast Advertising; Radio Entertainment

Further Reading

Czitrom, Daniel J., *Media and the American Mind: From Morse to McLuhan,* Chapel Hill: University of North Carolina Press, 1982

McChesney, Robert Waterman, *Telecommunications, Mass Media, and Democracy: The Battle for the Control of U.S. Broadcasting, 1928–1935,* New York: Oxford University Press, 1993

Roche, Bruce, "The Development of Modern Advertising, 1900–Present," in *The Media in America: A History,* 2nd ed., edited by W. David Sloan, James G. Stovall, and James D. Startt, Scottsdale, Arizona: Publishing Horizons, 1993

Spalding, John W., "1928: Radio Becomes a Mass Advertising Medium," *Journal of Broadcasting* 8 (1963–1964)

Commercial Speech

Debate over protecting speech on economic issues

Commercial speech is a category of expression, including advertising, that receives a lower level of protection under the First Amendment than political or other "core" speech. After 1980, when the U.S. Supreme Court restated its commercial speech doctrine in *Central Hudson Gas & Electric Corp.* v. *Public Service Commission,* restrictions on truthful, non-misleading advertising were constitutionally permissible where the government could establish a substantial interest, so long as the regulation directly advanced that interest and the restriction on speech was no more extensive

than necessary. However, the exact status of commercial speech under this test remained uncertain and even confusing, with the U.S. Supreme Court continuing to decide individual cases each term. For example, in *Rubin* v. *Coors Brewing Company,* decided in 1995, the Court struck down federal regulations prohibiting the inclusion of alcohol content on beer labels. Although widely viewed as victory for advertising rights, the Court held only that a labeling restriction did not directly advance the government's admittedly substantial interest in discouraging "content wars" among beer distributors. Thus, the Court indicated it might uphold extensive restrictions aimed directly at alcohol advertising rather than labeling.

This continuing uncertainty reflected historical reversals in constitutional doctrine. Originally, the term "commercial speech" referred to economic expression thought to be completely outside the protection of the First Amendment. Following the New Deal's repudiation of economic due process, a doctrine that held that economic rights were guaranteed by the Constitution, the Supreme Court had to decide whether advertising regulation should be presumed constitutional or held to the higher "strict scrutiny" standard used in speech cases. In its first commercial speech case, *Valentine* v. *Chrestensen,* decided in 1942, the Court viewed advertising as an extension of economic activity subject to reasonable state regulation. "Whether, and to what extent, one may promote or pursue a gainful occupation in the streets . . . are matters for legislative judgment," Justice Owen Roberts wrote for the unanimous Court. The Court, however, soon began granting exceptions to advertising of constitutionally protected activity, including religion (*Jamison* v. *Texas,* 1943), political advertising (*New York Times* v. *Sullivan,* 1964), and abortion (*Bigelow* v. *Virginia,* 1975), holding that the First Amendment protected advertising on matters of public interest. Finally, in 1976, the Court ruled that the Constitution protected pure product advertising in *Virginia Board of Pharmacy* v. *Virginia Consumer Council,* explicitly rejecting a public interest test. Justice Harry Blackmun's 7–2 majority opinion recognized the rights of consumers to receive economic information, holding that advertising itself was in the public interest in a free enterprise economy.

However, the Court quickly began retreating from this expansive doctrine in dicta, even while extending constitutional protection to advertising in individual cases. In *Ohralik* v. *Ohio State Bar,* for example, the Court in 1978 struck down regulation of attorney advertising while recognizing that advertising enjoyed "a limited measure of protection, commensurate with its subordinate position in the scale of First Amendment values." While the Court had not, by the late 1990s, carefully defined commercial speech, it recognized commonsense differences between advertising and other forms of expression that justified a lower level of protection. Since it is economically motivated, advertising was thought to be "hardier" than other forms of more fully protected expression. Also, commercial speech was considered more "verifiable," since advertisers are in an excellent position to determine the truth of their claims. Since protection stems at least in part from consumer interest in commercial speech, the First Amendment was not seen to be a bar to false or misleading advertising or the advertising of illegal activities.

There was also continuing ideological opposition to the idea that the First Amendment was intended to protect advertising. Conservatives, notably Chief Justice William Rehnquist, who dissented in *Virginia Board of Pharmacy*, remained sympathetic to government regulation, viewing advertising as an extension of economic activity rather than protected expression. In *Posadas de Puerto Rico v. Tourism Company*, Rehnquist's 1986 majority opinion held that the greater power to regulate casino gambling included the lesser power to regulate advertising of gaming. Similarly, in *State University of New York v. Fox*, Justice Antonin Scalia's 1989 opinion held that reasonable restrictions on commercial speech would be upheld as no more extensive than necessary.

The ultimate decision in individual commercial speech cases has apparently depended upon the perceived public interest in the advertising the government seeks to regulate as well as the ideological predisposition of individual justices writing majority opinions. Those seeking consistency in the commercial speech doctrine may be disappointed until the ideological tensions underlying decisions are more fully settled.

MARC CHARISSE

See also Business Regulation of the Press; Corporate Speech; First Amendment in the Twentieth Century

Further Reading

Baker, C. Edwin, "Commercial Speech: A Problem in the Theory of Freedom," *Iowa Law Review* 62 (1976)
Jackson, Thomas H., and John Calvin Jeffries, Jr., "Commercial Speech: Economic Due Process and the First Amendment," *Virginia Law Review* 65 (1979)
Redish, Martin H., "The First Amendment in the Marketplace," *George Washington Law Review* 39 (1971)
Rome, Edwin P., and William H. Roberts, *Corporate and Commercial Free Speech: First Amendment Protection of Expression in Business,* Westport, Connecticut: Quorum, 1985
Shiffrin, Steven, "The First Amendment and Economic Regulation: Away from a General Theory of the First Amendment," *Northwestern University Law Review* 78 (1984)

Commission on Freedom of the Press

Non-media–based attempt to evaluate press performance

The Commission on Freedom of the Press (often called the Hutchins Commission, after its chair, Robert Maynard Hutchins) was an assemblage of distinguished intellectuals whose deliberations from 1943 to 1947 resulted in several books exploring various aspects of freedom of the press. The idea for a commission originated with Hutchins, then president of the University of Chicago, and his longtime friend, Henry Robinson Luce, head of Time, Inc. Funding came largely from Luce, supplemented by a grant from the *Encyclopaedia Britannica*.

While no professional representatives of the media were included among the commissioners, many testified before the commission. Seventeen two-day or three-day meetings were held approximately every six weeks from December 1943 to September 1946. The commission's work was augmented by staff research, regional meetings, and subcommittee reports. All became the grist for lengthy and thoughtful discussions at formal commission meetings.

Several books drawing on the commission's deliberations were subsequently published. The two works for which the commission is perhaps best known are its general report, *A Free and Responsible Press*, and William Hocking's *Freedom of the Press: A Framework of Principle*.

The commission defined "the press" broadly to include all media of mass communication, including such new technologies as television. The primary issues with which commissioners grappled were the nature of freedom and its relationship to freedom of expression. Building on ideas fundamental to political liberalism in the 1930s and 1940s, the commission developed a concept of media responsibility it called accountability.

Most commissioners agreed with Hocking's argument that freedom of the press was both "freedom from" government interference with the right of individuals to express themselves and "freedom for" access to a wide variety of ideas and opinions. In the commission's judgment, the moral obligations inherent in "freedom for" had become difficult to exercise in modern society because the agencies of mass communication had become large, commercialized, and interconnected. Members of the commission therefore rejected a laissez-faire approach to the exercise of freedom of the press because they did not believe that the abuses of the media could be corrected through a self-righting process. Most members also rejected government intervention or regulation. They recommended instead that a continuing commission, composed of private citizens representing a wide variety of ideas and opinions, be established to enforce accountability by monitoring the performance of the media and exposing abuses.

Written in a simple and direct style, the general report was intended for widespread public discussion. It was received unfavorably, however, by some major publishers and publications. Hocking's volume and other reports issued by the commission were better regarded as scholarly studies.

In the 1950s, the "accountability" concept was reformulated by Theodore Peterson into the "social responsibility theory of the press" in *Four Theories of the Press*, a book widely read by journalism educators and professionals. Press councils established in that era and later were inspired in part by the idea of a continuing citizens' commission.

JERILYN S. MCINTYRE

See also Mass Media and Self-Regulation; National News Council; News Councils; Ombudsman

Further Reading
Blanchard, Margaret A., "The Hutchins Commission: The Press and the Responsibility Concept," *Journalism Monographs* 49 (May 1977)
Chafee, Zechariah, Jr., *Government and Mass Communications,* 2 vols., Chicago: University of Chicago Press, 1947
Commission on Freedom of the Press, *A Free and Responsible Press,* Chicago: University of Chicago Press, 1947
Hocking, William E., *Freedom of the Press: A Framework of Principle,* Chicago: University of Chicago Press, 1947
Inglis, Ruth A., *Freedom of the Movies: A Report on Self-Regulation from the Commission on Freedom of the Press,* Chicago: University of Chicago Press, 1947
McIntyre, Jerilyn S., "Repositioning a Landmark: The Hutchins Commission and Freedom of the Press," *Critical Studies in Mass Communication* (June 1987)
White, Llewellyn, *The American Radio: A Report on the Broadcasting Industry in the United States from the Commission on Freedom of the Press,* Chicago: University of Chicago Press, 1947
_____, and Robert D. Leigh, *Peoples Speaking to Peoples: A Report on International Mass Communication from the Commission on Freedom of the Press,* Chicago: University of Chicago Press, 1946

Committee on Public Information

Government propaganda agency in World War I

President Woodrow Wilson established the Committee on Public Information (CPI), the first large-scale U.S. government propaganda agency, by Executive Order 2594 on April 13, 1917. The CPI expanded rapidly under the leadership of its chairman, George Creel. By the end of the war in November 1918, the Creel committee, as it also was known, had both a Domestic Section that dealt with propaganda in the United States and a Foreign Section that had offices in more than 30 countries abroad. Although the CPI work was curtailed after the armistice, it did not cease operation until June 1919.

The CPI came into existence for several reasons. Because President Wilson was uncertain about public support for the United States' entry into the war, he wanted an agency to mobilize opinion. Moreover, in early 1917, citizens received a great deal of confusing or contradictory information; several branches of the U.S. government as well as numerous groups not connected with the government put out material on the war. The CPI served as the authoritative voice of the Wilson administration. In addition, liberals such as Creel and journalist Arthur Bullard (whose ideas may have helped convince Wilson to establish the CPI) opposed the strict wartime censorship practiced by the British, French, and Germans. They hoped that the CPI would provide as much news about the war as possible.

Creel, who was a muckraking journalist, came to lead the CPI because of his friendship with Wilson. Creel viewed

A Howard Chandler Christy poster promotes recruiting during World War I.

progressivism as a moral crusade and a "spiritual revolt," and he brought a crusading mentality to his wartime work. He enlisted the support of many other liberal, reform-minded journalists and intellectuals such as Ida Tarbell, Jane Addams, Charles Edward Russell, Carl Becker, Josephine A. Roche, Will Irwin, and Ernest Poole, as well as Socialists such as Algie Martin Simons and John Spargo.

Believing that every man, woman, and child had a role to play in winning the war against Germany, Creel built an organization that used virtually every form of communication then available. The Domestic Section had several subdivisions, each specializing in a particular type of propaganda.

From the outset, the CPI emphasized the news. Creel set up a Division of News, which churned out more than 6,000 news releases during the war. The CPI published the nation's first daily government newspaper, the *Official Bulletin.* A Division of Syndicated Features aimed for the readers of Sunday papers. The Foreign Language Newspaper Division monitored virtually all such publications in the United States.

The CPI published a wide range of pamphlet literature under the leadership of historian Guy Stanton Ford. Ford, who headed the Division of Civic and Educational Publications, turned to university professors and other intellectuals, who contributed to the *Red, White and Blue Series,* the *War Information Series,* and the *War Cyclopedia.* Ford's division had several objectives. First, because it was a war "to make the world safe for democracy," many writers speculated about the meaning of modern democracy. Second, several contributors portrayed Germany as a militaristic, authoritarian state. Third, some pamphlets, such as John S.P. Tatlock's *Why America Fights Germany* and Evarts B. Greene's *American Interest in Popular Government Abroad,* argued against U.S. isolationism and justified intervention. Finally, the division gave citizens practical suggestions to aid the war effort.

In a time before voice transmission over radio was common, the CPI organized speakers to deliver the government's message. One ingenious method was the Four Minute Men. The CPI issued a *Four Minute Man Bulletin* with a weekly topic and a sample message from President Wilson. Local orators, usually respected members of their communities, then gave a four-minute talk, often in movie houses or at other popular gathering places. A Speaking Division also arranged engagements for well-known orators who gave longer addresses.

The CPI targeted specific groups. A Division of Industrial Labor spoke to workers. A Division of Women's War Work mobilized women. To reach schoolchildren, the committee published a weekly bulletin, the *National School Service,* which continued after the war under the auspices of the Department of the Interior. The CPI set up a Division of Work with the Foreign Born in 1918.

Former newspaperman George Creel headed the Committee on Public Information.
(National Archives)

The committee exploited visual media. The Bureau of Cartoons offered commentaries on events. The Division of Film, with its subsidiary departments, captured the war with photography and moving pictures and produced newsreels. The Bureau of War Expositions and the Bureau of State Fair Exhibits created numerous displays seen by an estimated 7 million people at 60 sixty state fairs.

Posters, some of the most striking and controversial propaganda of the war, originated in the Division of Pictorial Publicity, which worked closely with the CPI's Division of Advertising. The Division of Pictorial Publicity, headed by Charles Dana Gibson, enlisted some of the best-known artists in the country. The Division of Advertising, which was not established until early in 1918, attracted such advertising leaders as Herbert Houston, William H. Johns, and Lewis B. Jones. The work of the advertising division convinced skeptics that ads could be powerful instruments of persuasion. But many of the posters – especially for the Fourth Liberty Loan campaign in 1918 – used scare tactics that undoubtedly fueled anti-German hysteria.

By generating pressure for conformity, the CPI contributed to the repressive atmosphere of 1917–18. The committee publicized the idea that restrictions on speech were justified during the war emergency. In his capacity as chairman of the CPI, Creel sat on the Censorship Board created under the Trading-with-the-Enemy Act in 1917. Still, the CPI was not the most extreme organization that promoted patriotism during the war, and contemporary critics sometimes accused it of "treasonable moderation." The state councils of defense, along with such extra-governmental organizations as the National Security League and the American Defense Society, bear even more responsibility for the anti-German sentiment of this time.

Abroad, the CPI sought to spread the "gospel of Americanism to every corner of the globe." The Foreign Section had three main branches – a Wireless-Cable Service, a Foreign Press Bureau, and a Foreign Film Division. An interesting array of people worked for this section. Edward L. Bernays, for example, who later helped pioneer the field of public relations in the United States, was in charge of news in Latin America. The CPI worked closely with the Military Intelligence Branch to coordinate propaganda. It attempted to destroy civilian morale and foster separatist movements in Germany and Austria-Hungary. It occasionally resorted to bribery and illegal activity to prevent neutral countries from siding with the Central Powers. In Britain and France, it sought support for Wilson's peace program and surely contributed to the president's tumultuous reception at the Paris Peace Conference.

Although many of the people who contributed to the CPI had a genuine commitment to democracy, the excessive ideological fervor that Creel and others brought to their work left an unfortunate legacy. The CPI encouraged a type of nationalism that too often endangered democracy. It was too ready to suspend free speech. It stereotyped women and blacks. It publicized Wilson and his ideas in such a way as to encourage an imperial presidency. It assumed too readily that the U.S. system could be exported abroad. Too many of its posters and other forms of propaganda appealed to fear and other emotions, and the apparent success of such

COMMUNICATION SATELLITE TECHNOLOGY 157

endeavors encouraged postwar cynicism about democratic theory and the rationality of public opinion.

STEPHEN VAUGHN

See also Propaganda; World War I

Further Reading
Mock, James R., and Cedric Larson, *Words that Won the War: The Story of the Committee on Public Information, 1917–1919,* Princeton, New Jersey: Princeton University Press, 1939
Vaughn, Stephen, *Holding Fast the Inner Lines: Democracy, Nationalism, and the Committee on Public Information,* Chapel Hill: University of North Carolina Press, 1980

Communications Act of 1934

Established the Federal Communications Commission

The Federal Communications Commission (FCC) began operating on July 11, 1934, as the successor agency to the five-member Federal Radio Commission, which was created by the 1927 Radio Act to issue station licenses, allocate frequency bands to various services, assign specific frequencies to individual stations, control station power, and assign hours of operation. The same act let the secretary of commerce retain the power to inspect radio stations, to examine and license radio operators, and to grant radio call signs. Much of the early effort of the Federal Radio Commission was to rearrange the allocations for the AM broadcast band and to prevent interference between the 732 radio stations then operating.

In 1933, President Franklin D. Roosevelt requested the secretary of commerce to convene a governmental interdepartmental committee to study both wired and wireless communication regulation. The Radio Act of 1927 was replaced with the Communications Act of 1934, which authorized a single agency to regulate all interstate and foreign communication by wire and radio, including telegraph, telephone, and wireless communication. However, the Communications Act of 1934 incorporated most of the Radio Act of 1927.

The 1934 legislation was to make available to all the people of the United States a rapid and efficient national and worldwide service with adequate facilities at reasonable charges. This service also would aid in national defense and promote safety of life and property.

The act granted the FCC the power to make rules and regulations to implement its functions. By law, all licensees were obliged to sign a statement that they did not have any right to operate the station or use the frequency beyond the term of the license. The maximum term for a radio station was seven years; the maximum term of license for a television station was five years.

Under the Communications Act, applicants were required to be legally, technically, and financially qualified and to show that their proposed operation would be in the "public interest, convenience and necessity." Only citizens of the United States were eligible to apply, and corporations with alien officers or directors or with more than one-fifth of the capital stock controlled by foreign interests might not be licensed.

The Mass Media Bureau of the FCC was charged with regulating AM, FM, television, direct broadcast satellites, Instructional Television Fixed Service, cable, microwave radio, and other mass communication services. The key regulatory areas authorized either directly by the Act of 1934 or incorporated through other legislation or interpreted by the courts as permissible included frequency assignments and licensing, indecency, political broadcasting, monopoly and multiple ownership, station management responsibilities, advertising, payola, lotteries, network relations, national defense, and equal employment opportunity.

MARVIN R. BENSMAN

See also Broadcast Licensing; Broadcast Regulation; Federal Communications Commission; Federal Radio Commission; Radio Act of 1927

Further Reading
Bensman, Marvin R., *Broadcast/Cable Regulation,* Lanham, Maryland: University Press of America, 1990
"Brief History of Broadcasting and Cable," in *Broadcasting and Cable Yearbook,* New Providence, New Jersey: Bowker, 1995
Hilliard, Robert L., *The Federal Communications Commission: A Primer,* Boston: Focal, 1991

Communication Satellite Technology

Creating a worldwide system for radio, television, and telephone

Artificial, or Earth, satellites are launched into a temporary or permanent orbit around the Earth. The first satellite orbited by the United States was *Explorer I,* launched on January 31, 1958. By the late 1990s, more than 5,000 Earth satellites had been orbited by more than 15 different nations. Earth satellites are used to collect scientific information about the Earth's surface, to collect atmospheric and astronomical information, to provide navigational data, and to gather reconnaissance and surveillance intelligence, as well as to relay telecommunications signals. Those satellites relaying telecommunications signals are referred to as communications satellites. Communications satellites provide a worldwide, interconnected system of radio and television transmissions and telephone service.

All communications satellites have five key elements: transponders, antennas, power supplies, telemetric (navigational) devices, and thrusters. Transponders are receive-transmit components that receive, amplify, and transmit signals. Antennas are for receiving uplink and sending downlink signals, as well as for receiving telemetric data. Power supplies provide energy, allowing the components to operate. Telemetric devices provide information on the satellite's operating conditions, and thrusters are used to keep the satellite orientated properly in its assigned position.

The particular path or orbit in which a satellite is placed is largely determined by the function of the particular satellite. Many communications satellites are placed in what is called synchronous or geostationary orbit. The United States launched the first synchronous-orbit satellite (*Syncom 1*) in 1963. By establishing a satellite orbit in an imaginary band extending around the equator approximately 22,300 miles above the Earth and fixing its velocity, the satellite's rotation is synchronized with the Earth's rotation, suspending the satellite in a fixed location above the planet. In this fixed position the satellite provides line-of-sight coverage (footprint) of more than one-third of the Earth's surface. This allows a network of three strategically located satellites to relay signals between Earth stations, or dishes, to provide coverage of the entire planet.

Communications satellites generally have numerous radio repeaters, or transponders. Each of these transponders has a receiver to pick up the uplinked microwave signal and a shifter to move the signal to different frequency so the signal can be downlinked (transmitted) without interfering with the uplink signal. Each transponder also contains an amplifier to boost the downlinked signal. The communications capacity of a particular satellite is determined by the number of transponders. Typically, most C-band satellites carry 24 transponders. The bandwidth of a single transponder is typically 36 megahertz, which allows for a single uncompressed color television signal or approximately 1,200 one-way telephone signals to be transmitted on a single transponder channel.

Relative to terrestrial stations, satellites operate at very low power ranging from 5 to 400 watts. Solar cells are the most common source of electric power in communications satellites. The transmitter power on a satellite is limited by its weight and life. Virtually all electronic functions in satellites are carried out by solid-state devices such as transistors or integrated circuits that are used to generate and amplify signals and to operate various control functions. Increased miniaturization has allowed for the inclusion of more circuits with more power while decreasing weight.

By international agreement, three major bands of frequencies have been assigned for nonmilitary satellite communications. These bands include the C band (5.925 to

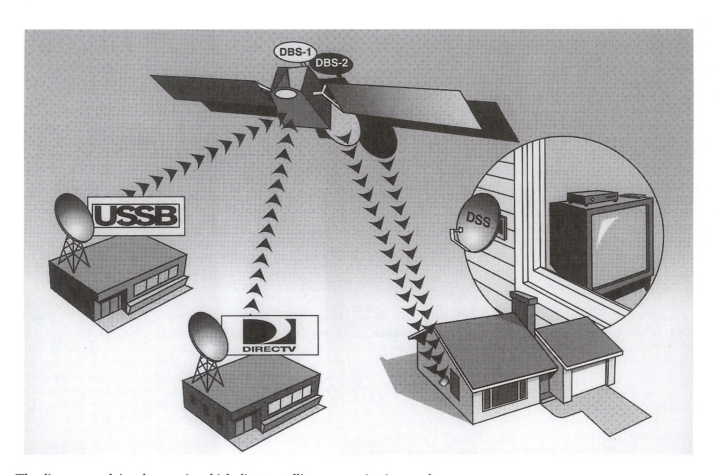

The diagram explains the way in which direct satellite communication works.
(Museum of Broadcast Communications)

6.425 gigahertz for uplink and 3.7 to 4.2 for downlink); K bands (14 to 14.5 and 12.75 to 13.25 gigahertz for uplink and 11.7 to 12.2 and 10.7 to 11.7 gigahertz for downlink); and another assignment of 27.5–30 gigahertz for uplink and 17.7–20.2 gigahertz for downlink.

Satellites in the late 1990s used both wide-deviation frequency modulation (FM) and digital transmission of voice by pulse-code modulation. The trend was increasingly toward digital transmission. Digital transmission is more efficient than FM because it allows multiple signals to be transmitted using a single channel. Digital transmission does this by controlling the division of time when a given signal is sent from one location to another. Combined use of time-division and frequency division multiplexing were increasing the limited channel capacity exponentially. Costs for satellite time, however, rise in response to greater demand, and experts predicted that further advances in compression technology would ease some of the crunch. Digital compression technology was advancing rapidly in the 1990s, and compression ratios of 20:1 were becoming standard. As an example of costs, effective July 1, 1995, Hughes prices for both its C- and K-band satellites were $1,000 an hour. These rates were a doubling – and, in some cases, more – of previous prices.

Communications satellites allowed live television programs to be transmitted between nations and continents. Developments in satellite technologies in the 1970s were instrumental in the development of the U.S. cable television service. They allowed for the relaying of programming, the development of pay-cable services, the growth of superstations such as WTBS and WOR, the creation of satellite-relayed cable networks such as CNN and C-SPAN, and the introduction of pay-per-view programming. Public broadcasting pioneered using satellites for network relays. In the 1970s, the Public Broadcasting Service interconnected its member stations using domestic communications satellites. Satellites are an efficient and cost-effective means of distributing programming and have reduced operating costs of stations, systems, and networks.

Satellites also allowed for international telephone and data services between Earth stations in more than 100 countries. A number of satellite systems provided regional and domestic service as well as maritime service. The international organization responsible for all international non-military satellite communication was the International Telecommunications Satellite Organization (Intelsat). Intelsat was founded by the United States in 1964, and by the end of the twentieth century, more than 100 countries were member-owners. The U.S. signatory to Intelsat was the Communications Satellite Corporation (Comsat).

Satellites can carry television signals between stations where cables or microwave towers cannot be built. Satellites are active relays in space. They receive coded television signals from Earth stations, amplify them, and return them to another Earth station that may be thousands of miles away. Generally, the lower the power of a satellite signal, the larger the receiving Earth station antenna. Most cable television systems and broadcast stations receive their satellite-feed programs with what are called television receive-only (TVRO) antennas. TVROs are 12 to 15 feet in diameter and concentrate weak satellite signals into a narrow beam directed at a second small reflector mounted in the center of the antenna on a tripod. This secondary reflector directs the beam to a low-noise amplifier. By 1994, more than 3 million TVRO dishes were in use by individuals to pick up signals from domestic satellites.

Despite the obvious advantages provided by satellite communications, there are also disadvantages. Satellites cannot provide the separate circuits to individual homes and offices that wires, cables, and optical fibers can; radio waves from one satellite can cause interference with other satellites close by; satellite broadcasts can interfere with communications systems on the ground; and the amount of communications that satellites can provide is limited by the number of orbital positions and frequencies available. Other disadvantages include the high costs of building and launching communications satellites and their limited life spans (seven to ten years). For this reason, most communications satellites in the 1990s were built, launched, and operated by large companies or government agencies.

On December 17, 1993, the first U.S. all-digital high-powered direct broadcast satellite (DBS-1) was successfully deployed. In 1994, DBS service began being offered in the United States. DBS service allowed for relatively small receive-only antennas because DBS employs higher power satellites. For example, Hughes built and launched two K-band satellites each containing 16 transponders of 120 watts. By utilizing digital compression broadcasting, four to eight channels per transponder was possible, allowing a total of about 180 to 200 channels. Hughes programming service was called DIRECTV. DBS was not technically feasible in the 1980s because of the high cost of the satellite, lack of compression technology, and unproved encryption technology. Technical feasibility aside, prior to 1992 there was no guarantee that programming would be available for such a service. But in October 1992, Congress passed a cable act that contained program access provisions assuring that programming would be available.

In the late 1990s, the FCC was considering satellite radio. Unlike locally licensed radio stations, subscribers anywhere in the satellite's footprint could tune in a radio program from a single source. Subscribers would need to buy special radio receivers that could pick up satellite signals and would need to pay a monthly fee.

Donald J. Jung

Community Access Television
Public use of cable operator's facilities

Community access television, or public access television, is comprised of people not affiliated with a cable operator who use their own equipment or equipment provided to them by the cable operator or local government to produce noncommercial television shows that are cablecast over a channel provided solely for that purpose. Community access is generally segmented into three areas: public, educational, and governmental. Public access is programming produced by and for the general public. Educational access is programming produced by an educational institution (i.e., public schools, colleges, or universities). Governmental access is programming produced by a governmental agency (i.e., city councils, police, and health departments).

The first cable channel for community use in the United States appeared in Dale City, Virginia, from 1968 to 1970. Earlier roots of community access can be found in Challenge for Change, a social service organization created by the National Film Board of Canada in 1966. George Stoney, a director of Challenge for Change from 1968 to 1970, helped to found the Alternate Media Center at New York University, which became the hub of community access television activity in the United States. That same year, Sterling Information Services and Teleprompter Corporation (later Group W Cable) agreed to provide two community access channels, studios, and equipment free with the awarding of their cable franchises in New York City.

Other roots of community access television were the radical video collectives of the late 1960s and early 1970s. These groups (including Raindance, Videofreex, People's Communication Network, and Video Free America) were trying to unite the underground press with the new communications technologies to create what was called "guerrilla television." The Alternate Media Center, the video collectives, and others were helping people produce programming for community access in Manhattan in the early 1970s.

In 1972, the Federal Communications Commission (FCC) began to require cable systems with 3,500 or more subscribers to set aside three access channels: public, educational, and governmental. Although these requirements were set aside by the U.S. Supreme Court in FCC v. Midwest Video Corp. (1979), access continued to grow, primarily because growth of the cable industry had created a buyers' market. Communities were able to demand access facilities in exchange for awarding their cable franchises.

With slower growth in the cable industry came a cry for greater governmental regulation, and Congress passed the Cable Communications Act of 1984, amending the Communications Act of 1934. The 1984 act required cable operators to provide channels for community access (along with educational and governmental access).

The Cable Television Consumer Protection and Competition Act of 1992 added language allowing franchisers to require public, educational, and governmental access as part of their negotiated agreements. It did not require the cable operators to provide community access; it only allowed the franchisers, usually local governments, to require community access as part of their franchise agreements.

LAURA R. LINDER

See also Cable Networks; Cable News; Cable Television; Public Access to the Mass Media

Further Reading

Engelman, Ralph, "The Origins of Public Access Television," *Journalism Monographs* 123 (1990)

Gillespie, Gilbert, *Public Access Cable Television in the United States and Canada,* New York: Praeger, 1975

Janes, Barry T., "History and Structure of Public Access Television," *Journal of Film and Video* 39 (1987)

Price, Monroe E., and John Wicklein, *Cable Television: A Guide for Citizen Action,* Philadelphia: Pilgrim, 1972

Sturken, Marita, "An Interview with George Stoney," *Afterimage* (January 1984)

Conrad, Frank

Engineer behind debut of KDKA

The man most responsible for the debut of radio station KDKA laid the groundwork in a small garage workshop at his home near Pittsburgh, Pennsylvania. Frank Conrad was assistant chief engineer for Westinghouse, one of the leading companies in broadcast research, during and after World War I. From his workshop, he conducted amateur radio experiments in his spare time.

After the war, under the call sign 8XK, Conrad broadcast phonograph music to other amateur radio enthusiasts, his only audience in those days when people had to assemble their own sets. Conrad frequently asked listeners to write to tell him how their reception was. He started getting requests for music, and he began airing live musical performances, often by his own family and friends. As word spread and the number of requests grew, Conrad started regular broadcasts for two hours each on Wednesday and Sunday nights, sometimes adding variety with talks or sports scores.

Conrad's work led to KDKA's debut in 1920. A Westinghouse executive wanted to broadcast the results of that year's presidential race and to promote that broadcast as a way of selling the preassembled radio sets Westinghouse was developing. Conrad built a transmitter in a shack on Westinghouse's roof, and KDKA began operating on November 2, 1920, broadcasting music and election returns telephoned in by the *Pittsburgh Post.*

Conrad patented more than 200 inventions. These included broadcasting equipment, electric meters, electric clocks, and electric devices for trains and automobiles.

THOMAS LETTS

See also Broadcast Pioneers; Radio Technology

Further Reading

Douglas, George H., *The Early Days of Radio Broadcasting,* Jefferson, North Carolina: McFarland, 1987

Hilliard, Robert L., and Michael C. Keith, *The Broadcast Century: A Biography of American Broadcasting,* Boston: Focal, 1992

Radio pioneer Frank Conrad works to improve his broadcast operation.
(Library of American Broadcasting)

Contempt

Tool to regulate media comment on court cases

Contempt is a legal remedy that has been applied against mass media in the United States in various ways. Direct contempt refers to the misbehavior of any person in the presence of the court or, to use the language of the federal statute, "so near thereto as to obstruct the administration of justice." A reporter, for example, who is ordered to testify and refuses on the ground that his source is confidential may be cited for contempt.

Indirect, or constructive, contempt applies to misbehavior out of the presence of the court. From colonial days until World War II, newspaper editors and publishers could be prosecuted for "contempt by publication" if they published remarks that had a tendency to prejudice the public with respect to the merits of a case pending in court.

A contempt by publication proceeding generally re-quired an affidavit setting out the nature of the offense, an arrest warrant commanding the arrest of the accused, and the appearance of the accused before the court to answer questions from the bench concerning the publication. If the judge was not satisfied with the answers, he or she could sentence the defendant to a fine and imprisonment. Although most fines were relatively small and most jail terms were limited to 90 days or less, the doctrine of newspaper contempt provided an important vehicle for the discussion of issues of freedom of the press in a legal setting.

Nineteenth-century contempt cases occasionally resulted in attempts to impeach judges who employed the remedy. The best-known of these proceedings was the 1830–31 impeachment trial of James H. Peck, a federal district judge who attempted to discipline a lawyer for criticizing him in print. Although Peck was acquitted by the U.S. Senate, Congress enacted the law prohibiting federal courts from pursuing cases of constructive contempt.

During the 1880s, the remedy was revived by state

courts. After the beginning of the twentieth century, the doctrine of contempt by publication became a widely accepted device used by judges not only to respond to an alleged interference with the judicial process but also to punish words that "scandalized" the court. One case, involving Senator Thomas Patterson of Colorado, owner of the *Rocky Mountain News,* reached the U.S. Supreme Court in 1907. The Court dismissed Patterson's appeal, finding that the imposition of a fine of $1,000 for a series of articles and a cartoon calling the Colorado Supreme Court "The Great Judicial Slaughter House and Mausoleum" was "a matter of local law."

In 1918, the U.S. Supreme Court nationalized the law of contempt when it upheld a $10,000 fine imposed by a federal district judge against the *Toledo (Ohio) News-Bee.* The fine was imposed after a cartoon ridiculed the attempt by a street railway company to seek a federal court injunction against a local ordinance regulating the use of city streets. Writing for the Court, Chief Justice Edward White acknowledged the "reasonable tendency" test – that words were actionable if they possessed a "direct tendency to prevent and obstruct the discharge of judicial duty."

The 1920s represented the high-water mark for the doctrine of newspaper contempt. Judges in Oklahoma and New Mexico issued jail sentences of up to one year in response to offending publications. Academic criticism of the doctrine followed. Sir John Fox published a critical history of the English law of contempt in 1927; the U.S. law of contempt was discussed by Walter Nelles and Carol Weiss King in 1928. A strong dissent by Oliver Wendell Holmes Jr. in the *Toledo News-Bee* case led to increasingly critical comments by federal and state court judges. In the words of Federal District Judge Learned Hand: "It is in small encroachments upon the right of free criticism of all the acts of public officials that the real danger lies."

Bridges v. *California,* announced by the U.S. Supreme Court on the day following the Japanese attack on Pearl Harbor, essentially concluded the debate over newspaper contempt. Reversing a fine against labor leader Harry Bridges for threatening to "tie up" the West Coast in response to a judge's ruling, the Court adopted what became known as the "clear and present danger" test. Under this test, "the substantive evil must be extremely serious and the degree of imminence extremely high before utterances can be punished."

Under the clear and present danger test, most cases of newspaper contempt were thrown out on appeal. The U.S. Supreme Court ended newspaper contempt cases through *Wood* v. *Georgia* in 1962.

RICHARD SCHEIDENHELM

See also Libel

Further Reading

Fox, Sir John Charles, *The History of Contempt of Court: The Form of Trial and the Mode of Punishment,* Oxford: Clarendon, 1927
Gleason, Timothy W., *The Watchdog Concept: The Press and the Courts in Nineteenth-Century America,* Ames: Iowa State University Press, 1990
Goldfarb, Ronald L., *The Contempt Power,* Garden City, New York: Anchor, 1963; London: Columbia University Press, 1963
Lofton, John, *The Press as Guardian of the First Amendment,* Columbia: University of South Carolina Press, 1980
Nelles, Walter, and Carol Weiss King, "Contempt by Publication in the United States," *Columbia Law Review* 28 (1928)

Cooperative News Gathering

Reporters working together to cover important news events

Cooperative news gathering in the mass media refers to a variety of collaborations among individual reporters or news organizations either to cover a specific, often complex, news event or to generate a daily news report for the common use of all collaborators. In difficult reporting situations, such as investigations of corruption or when a deadline is approaching, reporters representing noncompeting news organizations may divide the news-gathering duties and then share their findings for the common use by all participating reporters. Such cooperation among individual reporters is uncommon.

One well-known example of newsgathering cooperation between reporters occurred in the spring of 1961 when, amid persistent rumors that Cuban exiles were being trained in the United States for an invasion of Fidel Castro's Cuba, Tad Szulc of the *New York Times* and Stuart Novins of CBS Radio cooperatively gathered and shared information for simultaneous release in the newspaper and on the network. Their stories on April 6 authoritatively reported that the CIA was training paramilitary forces, an effort that led to the Bay of Pigs invasion fiasco on April 17. Historically, the more common form of cooperative news gathering involves generally noncompetitive news organizations – such as newspapers and broadcast stations, located in different cities or targeting different audiences in the same city – that combine reportorial or financial resources either to cover an important news event or to provide participants with a continuous flow of news dispatches.

During the first two decades of the nineteenth century, as post roads and coastal shipping increased in the United States, editors of east coast metropolitan dailies discovered that horse and ship expresses could hasten the arrival at their newsrooms of such sought-after coverage as that of presidential and gubernatorial addresses, proceedings of legislatures, news from Europe, and the latest market prices. They also realized that such headlines as "Latest Intelligence from Europe" and "Yesterday's Congressional Proceedings" attracted readers and advertisers.

The expense for an individual editor to run overland horse expresses from Washington, D.C., or to patrol the harbor or coastal waters in search of news soon made the practice prohibitive, and by the mid-1820s, newspapers in

A RACE FOR THE WIRES.

Competitive reporting such as the "race for the wires" lessened with the arrival of cooperative news gathering.
(Davis Library, University of North Carolina at Chapel Hill)

eastern cities were cooperating to share the cost of such activities.

The earliest recorded cooperative news-gathering effort among newspapers was the Association of Morning Papers, which, at an annual cost of $2,500, covered harbor and shipping news for three established New York City dailies – the *Gazette,* the *Daily Advertiser,* and the *Mercantile Advertiser.* The subsequent appearance in New York City of four aggressive news-gathering dailies – the *Journal of Commerce* in 1827, the *Courier and Enquirer* in 1829, the *Sun* in 1833, and the *Herald* in 1835 – heightened the competition for news and set off a decade of changing, sporadic cooperative associations among the city's dailies to gather European, harbor, and domestic news.

The introduction of regular transatlantic steamer crossings in 1840 and of the telegraph in 1844 prompted the formation of permanent news-gathering cooperatives. Several groups of local and regional daily newspaper editors formed cooperatives in the mid- or late 1840s to share the expense and control the content of news dispatches amid a rapidly growing telegraph system in the United States. These early cooperatives were commonly known as "asso-

ciated presses," a name that by 1860 was formalized as the Associated Press (AP), referring to each agency and to all of them collectively.

Although metropolitan newspapers had routinely used horses, locomotives, boats, and ships to gather and expedite news by the mid-1840s, telegraphy in its infancy was unfamiliar and economically challenging to newspaper editors. Telegraph's early promoters and builders competed fiercely among themselves for patent rights, rights-of-way, and customers, presenting the public with a bewildering array of claims and rate scales for their lines in the early years. Because telegraphy was still struggling to its feet, its performance in the early years was generally unpredictable and expensive.

Editors became frustrated by the telegraph's early unreliability. Rebelling at the high cost of telegraphing special news dispatches coming to their own papers exclusively and then seeing those news dispatches appear in other newspapers, editors resorted to transmitting their dispatches in code to cut costs and to protect their news from thieving telegraphers and editors along the lines. At the same time, newspapers printed scathing editorial criticisms of the young technology that made the public skeptical and telegraphers furious. Telegraph proprietors retaliated by eliminating special low press rates, refusing to transmit press codes, and attempting to form their own news-gathering agency aimed at monopolizing the intercity gathering and telegraphing of news.

Clearly, a compromise was needed between the telegraphers and the newspaper editors that would blunt the technological stranglehold telegraphers could impose on the news distribution system, reduce the cost to newspapers of telegraphic dispatches, and reduce the volume of dispatches that clogged the wires and gave one newspaper the advantage over all others because of telegraphy's first-come, first-served rule. The compromise that gradually emerged in the 1840s was the cooperative news-gathering agency, in which the news agency and its news reports were controlled by newspaper editors, who formed a not-for-profit partnership or corporation to oversee their agency. The editors were guaranteed daily transmission of their report at a time convenient to their press deadlines and at low press rates.

All newspapers in the cooperative received the same news report, consisting of whatever political, business, crime, weather, and other news that was daily available in the agency headquarters from the agency's correspondents and nonlocal newspapers available when the news report was being assembled for transmission. Since newspapers in the antebellum cooperatives either operated in different towns or addressed different readership audiences in large cities, competition for news "scoops" or "exclusives" was less important than it later became in the twentieth century. The leading New York City dailies that belonged to the AP in that city, for example, carried identical telegraphic reports for many years before, during, and after the Civil War.

As part of the 1840s compromise that created cooperative news gathering, the telegraph companies agreed to transmit the news report exclusively for the cooperative agency in exchange for guaranteed steady revenue from the patron newspapers. Because most antebellum metropolitan dailies were morning papers that went to press in the early-morning hours, the bulk of the news report could be transmitted late in the evening after the day's peak of commercial and public telegraph traffic.

Permanent news-gathering cooperatives first appeared on the east coast along the emerging telegraph system in the 1840s and 1850s. The first cooperatives were in New York City, Boston, Philadelphia, and Baltimore, Maryland, and along the principal early telegraphic trunk lines, such as between Albany and Buffalo, New York, and between Washington, D.C., and New Orleans, Louisiana.

The first recorded AP cooperative appeared in mid-1846 when newspaper editors who were located along the first telegraph line being constructed between Albany and Buffalo established an agent in Albany and a telegraph link to New York City and began receiving a single daily telegraph news report for use in all of their papers. Meanwhile, even though New York City has been for most of AP's history the site of the wire's headquarters, the precise founding date of the AP in that city is obscured by 20 years of sporadic, changing news-gathering coalitions among the city's leading dailies dating from the 1820s, as described earlier.

New York City's AP, however, is believed to have arisen in the spring of 1848 to expedite delivery of the news of extraordinary political revolutions then sweeping Europe for use by a partnership of the city's six most powerful newspapers – the *Courier and Enquirer,* the *Journal of Commerce,* the *Express,* the *Sun,* the *Herald,* and the *Tribune.* When the *Times* was founded in 1851, it became the seventh partner in the New York City AP.

In the early years of operation, the New York City AP dailies divided equally the total annual cost of $25,000 to $30,000, consisting primarily of telegraphic charges, some rentals, and small salaries for about 12 agents in various bureaus. By the 1880s, with telegraph lines crisscrossing the nation and with over 850 dailies publishing in towns and cities from coast to coast, there were 13 regional and local cooperative APs, forming a national confederation that exchanged news dispatches and reports.

The post–Civil War commercialization of the U.S. newspaper turned local niche daily newspapers into cutthroat competitors for the newfound general circulation reading audience and expanded cooperative newsgathering's mission beyond efficiency and economy. Increasingly, AP's exclusive membership structure offered protection from many new local competitors to the AP papers (most of which were older, better established, and conservative).

Between the end of the Civil War and 1900, four privately owned, or commercial, news-gathering agencies arose to serve many of the 1,500 new dailies that appeared in the United States during those 35 years. While delivering a constantly enlarging and improving news report, by the 1880s, AP became an exclusive club, membership in which, while sought by many, was offered only to those dailies that were not competitors of existing AP members. AP's older partnership cooperative structure gave way in the 1870s and 1880s to a membership cooperative, which gave each member not only the news report and a voice in the running of the news-gathering agency but also the chance to decide whether any local competitors could become members of the cooperative.

After it was discovered in 1892 that for six years the officers of AP and its only serious commercial competitor, the United Press (UP), founded in 1882, had secretly formed a stock pool trust and were sharing news dispatches to avoid competition with each other, AP editors in the midwest reorganized AP, removed AP's old officers, and replaced the confederation of regional and local cooperatives with a national AP that was a not-for-profit stock company, incorporated in Illinois.

Still competing with UP and needing to bring UP to its knees, AP opened its membership in the 1890s to accept all newspapers not prohibited by local AP competitors from gaining membership. AP's membership grew from 207 members in 1893 to 637 in 1897 when the first UP went out of business. Even so, AP's membership included only 30 percent of all U.S. dailies when UP died in 1897.

What began as a cooperative arrangement to share expenses and to control dispatches in the 1840s had in 50 years become a powerful force in U.S. journalism, delivering the most authoritative and comprehensive news report in the United States while allowing long-standing AP members to prohibit delivery of that news report to local newspaper competitors. The vast majority of U.S. newspapers were outside of AP, and the cooperative emerged from combat in the 1890s appearing to be a dangerous collusion seeking to monopolize national news gathering.

All members of the AP of Illinois received the news report, but those dailies that paid more for a higher class of membership or purchased stock in AP had more voting power in AP and could sit on the local AP boards that determined whether a local daily would be accepted or rejected for membership. When AP received an adverse ruling from the Illinois Supreme Court in 1900 that threatened its independence, the cooperative moved to New York, where it was incorporated as a not-for-profit membership news-gathering cooperative. In the transition, as a protection for the existing AP members, stock holding (which was forbidden under the New York membership law) was converted into bond holding. The cooperative had thus preserved its protectionism of powerful members.

From the time he took office in 1925, AP general manager Kent Cooper lobbied members to relinquish their right to refuse admission of local competitors to AP (at that time called the franchise right). When an AP member exercised the right, AP lost assessments payments, Cooper argued.

Cooper had made modest headway in convincing members to give up their AP protection when the U.S. Supreme Court in June of 1945 declared unconstitutional AP's bylaws that permitted members to bar their competitors from AP. This decision opened AP's doors to all and began the slow but steady decline in the client totals of commercial competitors, leading the second UP and the International News Service (INS) to a merger as United Press International in 1958.

AP officers, aware that cooperative news-gathering was an unusual approach, traditionally emphasized that AP's structure made the wire a servant and a clearinghouse of its members' news, supplying to all what each member covered and supplementing that with staff reports from major news centers. Being not-for-profit, they argued, AP was free of corporate bias. Defending his wire's cooperative structure in 1913, AP president Frank B. Noyes said that "a powerful, privately owned and controlled newsgathering agency is a menace to the press and people."

Calling AP's cooperative structure "a socialist experiment," Karl A. Bickel, the United Press Associations' president, however, observed in 1927 that like the goal of "every great and enduring privately owned American newspaper, to render a service and to make a profit, (his privately owned United Press) was organized upon the same firm and sound business principles that have made the great business institutions of the United States the marvel of the world."

The cooperative not-for-profit nature of AP continued to be reflected in the wire's use of such terminology as "members," "assessments," "annual meeting," and a "board of directors" to oversee AP's operations. Membership could not be denied, however, to applicants that could pay the assessment, and most of the news in the daily report was supplied by AP's own reporters and correspondents, not by member dailies.

Whether an anachronism or an efficient way of doing business, modern cooperative news gathering as practiced by AP in the late twentieth century consisted primarily of an assessment structure that covered annual expenses and provided support for significant research and development. The AP did not make a profit as such, but it was able, by means of a relatively steadily increasing assessments of members, to assemble and maintain one of the largest staffs of reporters and editors in international journalism and to develop and introduce many of the most significant technological innovations in journalism during the last 25 years of the century. (AP's modern commercial competitors ordinarily made profits by relying on either revenues from features or subsidies from their parent companies.)

Although a few news-gathering agencies abroad were cooperative (some of which were established by AP in Europe after World War II), most of them were conducted either as private companies or departments of governments. The continuing appeal of cooperative news gathering, however, could be seen in the U.S. national election arena, where soaring costs forced the television networks and the wire services in the 1960s to form the News Election Service to report the raw vote totals for the use of all participating national news organizations. In 1992, after the expense to television news departments of attempting to determine winners in national elections based on exit polls became excessive, the networks agreed to share one exit poll and one analysis.

RICHARD A. SCHWARZLOSE

See also Associated Press; International News Service; United Press (1882); United Press Associations (1907); United Press International

Further Reading

Rosewater, Victor, *History of Coöperative News-gathering in the United States*, New York and London: D. Appleton, 1930

Schwarzlose, Richard A., *The Nation's Newsbrokers: Vol. 1, The Formative Years: From Pretelegraph to 1865*, Evanston, Illinois: Northwestern University Press, 1989

———, *The Nation's Newsbrokers: Vol. 2, The Rush to Institution: From 1865 to 1920*, Evanston, Illinois: Northwestern University Press, 1990

Copyright

Protection of rights in intellectual property

The origins of U.S. copyright law can be traced back to political, economic, and technological developments that occurred in early modern Europe. The dawn of capitalism, the emergence of centralized city-states, and the deployment of the printing press were the key factors fostering the emergence of property rights in literary works. From the outset, copyright served as an economic right granted by the state to protect publishers and printers from competition by bestowing on them the exclusive rights to publish certain categories or titles of literary works. The state granted these rights in an effort to encourage the growth of a domestic publishing industry and as a means of controlling what was published.

Britain established the first modern copyright statute in 1709, which gave authors and their assignees (mainly publishers) the exclusive right to publish a work for a period of 14 years. The preamble of the act justified it as a means of encouraging learning by increasing competition in the book trade. The statute explicitly recognized authors as owners of their intellectual labor, following the labor theory of property put forward by John Locke, but only protected that property right when the work was published. U.S. copyright law generally followed in the Anglo-Saxon tradition. Although in the late 1990s U.S. copyright law covered unpublished works, it served primarily as a statutory right protecting a work from infringement upon publication. Since few authors have had the capital means to publish their own works, copyright has tended to favor the economic rights of publishers.

Copyright laws developed during the colonial period reflected their British antecedents. Twelve of the original 13 states passed copyright laws between 1783 and 1786. Publishers and certain of the literary elite soon realized the inefficiency of state-level copyrights and lobbied for a unified federal copyright system in order to facilitate the growth of a national literary industry and culture. Their efforts came to fruition with the inclusion of a clause in the U.S. Constitution (Article 1, Section 8) empowering Congress to establish copyright and patent systems in order to "Promote the Progress of Science and useful Arts, by securing for limited Times to Authors and Inventors the exclusive Right to their respective Writings and Discoveries." Congress acted upon this mandate by passing the first federal copyright law in 1790, which conferred statutory protection to authors and publishers of books, maps, and charts for a period of 14 years. Anyone who made copies of a work without the copyright owner's authorization was subject to criminal penalties. The act denied copyright protection to nonresident authors, however, underscoring the fact that copyright in the United States was designed to promote the economic interests of U.S. publishers rather than to protect the moral rights of authors.

Subsequent federal legislation led to the revision and extension of copyright law to take into account new media of artistic and literary expression, such as photography, motion pictures, and musical recordings, and derivative uses of copyrighted works, such as translations and public performances. With the advent of electronic media, such as radio and television broadcasting, Congress further expanded the scope of copyright to grant copyright owners the right to authorize the distribution of their works over the airwaves.

The rather simple arrangements between authors and publishers that prevailed during the first hundred years of U.S. print culture became increasingly complex. The growth of large-scale culture industries and the continuing introduction of new communications media produced significant tensions within the copyright system among actual creators of artistic and intellectual works, the owners of communications media, and the public. For example, beginning in the mid-1960s, copyright owners of filmed entertainment and cable system operators engaged in a decade-long judicial and legislative battle over whether retransmission of broadcasts by cable constituted a public performance that required cable companies to obtain copyright clearances. Book and journal publishers sought to control the reproduction of their copyrighted works by individuals and organizations using photocopiers. In the late 1970s, the filmed-entertainment industry tried to stop the sale of videocassette recorders, arguing that their primary use, to record copyrighted programming, constituted an infringement.

These examples reflect the inherent tension within the copyright system between protecting the property rights of copyright owners and encouraging the dissemination of knowledge and information. This tension was exacerbated with the concentration of the most valuable copyrighted works in the hands of transnational media corporations.

RONALD V. BETTIG

Further Reading

Bettig, Ronald, *Copyrighting Culture: The Political Economy of Intellectual Property,* Boulder, Colorado, and Oxford: Westview, 1996

Bugbee, Bruce, *Genesis of American Patent and Copyright Law,* Washington, D.C.: Public Affairs, 1967

Edelman, Bernard, *Ownership of the Image: Elements for a Marxist Theory of Law,* London: Routledge & Kegan Paul, 1979

Kaplan, Benjamin, *An Unhurried View of Copyright,* New York: Columbia University Press, 1967

Patterson, Lyman Ray, *Copyright in Historical Perspective,* Nashville, Tennessee: Vanderbilt University Press, 1968

Plant, Arnold, "The Economic Aspects of Copyright in Books," *Economica* 1 (1934)

Ploman, Edward W., and L. Clark Hamilton, *Copyright: Intellectual Property in the Information Age,* Boston and London: Routledge & Kegan Paul, 1980

Whale, Royce F., *Copyright: Evolution, Theory and Practice,* London: Longman, 1971

Corporate Speech

Effort to protect free speech rights of non-media corporations

Corporate speech is a legal concept that was first elucidated by the U.S. Supreme Court in the late 1970s. It provides non-media corporations with limited First Amendment rights. Historically, non-media corporations did not enjoy First Amendment rights. The reasoning was that these corporations were engaged in the economic marketplace, not the marketplace of ideas.

The U.S. Supreme Court modified this view in three key cases during the late 1970s and mid-1980s. The first case, in 1978, was *First National Bank of Boston v. Bellotti.* In it, the Court struck down a Massachusetts law that prohibited corporations from publicizing their views on political issues, particularly those subject to the ballot box. The corporation had stated its views on an upcoming state referendum involving taxation in an advertisement. The Court said this kind of speech was political and therefore "at the heart" of the First Amendment. The Court said that citizens had the right to receive such information, which could assist them in making a decision about the issue in question.

In 1980, the Supreme Court expanded its concept of First Amendment protection for corporate speech in *Consolidated Edison Co. of New York* v. *Public Service Commission of New York*. The Court ruled that a state statute that prohibited public utilities from making statements on matters of public policy or controversy was unconstitutional. Consolidated Edison had sent brochures that supported nuclear power along with its monthly bills to customers. The Court said that the corporation's customers had the right to "discussion, debate and the dissemination of information and ideas." Furthermore, the Court said that First Amendment protection could not be denied Consolidated Edison just because it was a corporation. The Court stated, "the First Amendment means that the government has no power to restrict expression because of its message, its ideas, its subject matter or its content."

In a case heard six years later, *Pacific Gas & Electric Co.* v. *Public Utilities Commission of California,* the Supreme Court struck down a California public utilities commission regulation that had required utility companies to include with their mailings to customers information put out by an environmental group that was critical of the company's rate-making procedures, among other issues. The Court said that a public utility company had the same rights as a newspaper in deciding what material to present in its newsletter. The Court added that because the company's newsletter, which was distributed to customers with their monthly bills, contained energy-saving tips, recipes, and stories, it "extends well beyond speech that proposes a business transaction and includes the kind of discussion of 'matters of public concern that the First Amendment both fully protects and implicitly encourages.'"

In 1990, however, the Supreme Court narrowed the limited First Amendment protection it had provided to non-media corporations in its decision in *Austin* v. *Michigan State Chamber of Commerce*. The Court upheld a Michigan state statute prohibiting corporations from using treasury funds to buy advertising in support of political candidates during an election. The state statute was part of the state's campaign finance law. The Court said in the majority opinion that the corporation had other means of advocacy for a political candidate, such as political action committees. The state statute, said the Court, helped protect the public from real or threatened corruption that could result from large political expenditures by wealthy corporations. Some members of the Court dissented from the majority opinion, saying that the *Austin* ruling would, in effect, serve as a censor.

DULCIE M. STRAUGHAN

See also Commercial Speech

Further Reading
Pratt, Catherine A., "First Amendment Protection for Public Relations Expression: The Applicability and

Limitations of the Commercial and Corporate Speech Models," *Public Relations Research Annual* 2 (1990)
Wilcox, Dennis L., Phillip H. Ault, and Warren K. Agee, *Public Relations: Strategies and Tactics*, 4th ed., New York: HarperCollins, 1995

Counteradvertising
Encourages the voices of opponents of certain products or services

"Counteradvertising" refers to unpaid broadcast advertising that voices a critical or counter opinion of a commercial product or service. A direct reply to a paid advertisement that has raised an issue of public importance, counteradvertising has been most closely associated with the debate between smoking and anti-smoking factions. It evolved from an interpretation of the Fairness Doctrine of the Federal Communications Commission (FCC).

The Fairness Doctrine required all broadcast licensees to provide sufficient time for the free and fair competition of opposing views that included all discussions of issues of public importance. The Equal Time Provision of the Fairness Doctrine, instituted in 1959, allowed equal time to the other side of an issue: stations were required to provide a full spectrum of viewpoints.

In 1960, after years of research found a link between smoking and the incidence of lung cancer, the American Cancer Society produced its first antismoking commercial. After trying unsuccessfully to place the spots with the three dominant networks – ABC, CBS, and NBC – it petitioned the FCC to require the networks to air the commercials under the Equal Time Provision of the Fairness Doctrine. In the absence of government-produced statistics on the effects of cigarette smoking, the FCC denied its request.

In 1966, however, the FCC received a complaint backed by the Surgeon General's report of 1964 that concluded cigarette smoking was harmful to one's health. In *Banzhaf* v. *FCC,* the commission ruled unanimously that denying airing of anti-tobacco ads was a violation of the Fairness Doctrine. The U.S. Supreme Court upheld the FCC's ruling, saying there must be advertising to counter the cigarette commercials because they implied the desirability and safety of smoking. Such an assertion by the tobacco industry created a fairness obligation to broadcast counter information. The first time the Fairness Doctrine was applied to commercial advertising, this interpretation called only for reasonable access for the differing sides on the cigarette debate. Indeed, for every 4.4 cigarette commercials that ran between the FCC ruling and the 1971 federal law banning cigarette broadcast ads, one antismoking commercial ran.

The FCC then attempted to restrict the application of the *Banzhaf* decision to cigarettes, citing them as a unique case. It feared that extending counteradvertising to other product advertising would lead to a unmanageable situation. Several challenges to the FCC's assertion that cigarette advertising was unique ensued. The Court of Appeals of the District of Columbia found that if a product had an effect on public health, then such advertising raised an issue of public importance and was subject to the Fairness Doctrine. More importantly, the court rejected outright the assertion of the FCC that the *Banzhaf* case and cigarette advertising were unique. Conceding the point, the FCC went on to assert that if an ad implicitly or explicitly debated a controversial issue of public importance, fairness obligations were applicable.

Many believed the FCC assertion that commercials engaging in controversial debate would be subject to the Fairness Doctrine and would lead to more counteradvertising claims. The FCC sidestepped much of the issue by allowing the Federal Trade Commission (FTC) to deal with most controversial ads. The FCC would deem the ad in question to be deceptive advertising, which was the domain of the FTC. The FTC did require counterads when product ads raised implicit or explicit controversial issues, but the FTC restricted those issues to ones in which there were debatable scientific claims. False or misleading claims were subject to other actions by the FTC such as the removal of the ad from the airwaves or broadcasting corrective ads. Counteradvertising should not be confused with corrective advertising, which does not present another side of a controversial issue; it only seeks to correct specific deceptive claims made in previous ads.

Because the FCC routinely took responsibility for interpreting advertising complaints as false or misleading and directed them to the FTC, counteradvertising was not prevalent by the 1990s. Occasional discussion about counteradvertising was met with strong opposition from advertisers and broadcasters alike. In the late 1980s, there was a movement to curb or restrict alcohol advertising, and one of the measures being discussed was counteradvertising. By 1989, Surgeon General Everett Koop proposed a requirement of a one-to-one matching of alcohol ads with pro-health and safety messages. The National Association of Broadcasters and the Association of National Advertisers publicly opposed the recommendations, and the requirement was never established.

SARAH WRIGHT PLASTER

See also Advertising in the Twentieth Century; Mass Media and Tobacco Products; Public Access to the Mass Media

Further Reading

Andrews, J. Craig, "The Effectiveness of Alcohol Warning Labels: A Review and Extension," *American Behavioral Scientist* 38:4 (1995), pp. 622–632

Glatzer, Robert, *The New Advertising: The Great Campaigns From Avis to Volkswagen,* New York: Citadel, 1970

Schuster, Camille P., and Christine Pacelli Powell, "Comparison of Cigarette and Alcohol Advertising Controversies," *Journal of Advertising* 16 (1987)

"Television Counteradvertising: 'And Now A Word Against Our Sponsor'," in *Advertising Law Anthology,* edited by Philip A Garon, Washington, D.C.: International Library, 1973

Vestal, David, "The Tobacco Advertising Debate: A First Amendment Perspective," in *Advertising and Commercial Speech*, edited by Theodore R. Kupferman, Westport, Connecticut: Meckler, 1990

Country Club Journalism

Criticism of press connections with upper-class society

An aspect of U.S. mass communication brought to public attention by William Allen White and others, country club journalism is the reflection in news reportage of attitudes, beliefs, values, and sentiments associated mostly with society's upper class. The term came into common use during the 1920s, when more and more comparatively wealthy Americans became engaged in building exclusive private clubs in rural or suburban areas.

Because many U.S. journalists came from families of modest means, they were resentful toward such ostentatious displays of fortune and tended to identify with society's underprivileged. Other journalists, however, coveted the privileges of the rich and courted their favor by adopting antilabor policies and lauding the achievements of big business leaders. Since business leaders and others of extraordinary wealth have always sat astride the media's access to information concerning many areas of public interest, journalists have always found it necessary to cultivate them as sources. Such association has tended, the critics point out, to influence many newspeople to adopt a "country club" mentality. Although many U.S. newspeople resisted that tendency and some became identified closely with liberal interests during the period of the Great Depression and its political aftermath, the Republican party's success in the presidential elections of the 1980s and congressional campaigns of 1994 brought about a new wave of complaints that newspaper companies rapidly were becoming bigger and bigger businesses and therefore instruments of the economically well-positioned in U.S. society.

JOHN DEMOTT

See also Checkbook Journalism; Codes of Ethics; Criticism of Newspapers; Journalism Reviews

Creative Revolution

Change in approach to advertising products

The Creative Revolution was a shift in advertising from ads that primarily promoted a product to ads that differentiate a product from competing brands. The revolution reached its peak in the 1960s. The industry shifted away from puffery and began to deal with the strengths and weaknesses of products directly. Often the perception of product differentiation was created through the advertising itself. The industry began to understand and exploit the intrinsic value of a product's advertising. It recognized that great and memorable advertising cannot help an inferior product but that good advertising could help an average product or a product that was very similar to its competitors by setting it apart in some way. Instead of talking down to the intended consumer, ads began to speak to them more intelligently, more honestly, and more humorously.

The birth of the Creative Revolution has been dated from 1949, when David Ogilvy and Bill Bernbach established advertising agencies. Leo Burnett, who had set up his own shop in 1935, also had a role in the Creative Revolution.

All of these men were talented copywriters, but their approaches to selling a product were markedly different. Ogilvy believed that research was the fundamental building block of good advertising and that advertising was good only if it increased sales of the product. Bernbach believed that good advertising was persuasion and that persuasion was an art, not a science based on research. Burnett believed that there was "inherent drama" in every product and that good advertising capitalized on it. Although Ogilvy embraced maxims developed through research, Bernbach hated rules and relied heavily on intuition. Ogilvy worked primarily alone, whereas Bernbach was known for being a great teacher and for letting many of the ads he conceived be written and produced by others. All of these men, however, understood the power of an ad that could set the product apart from its competition, or, in advertising terms, an ad that found the "big idea."

Ogilvy often established a "personality," or brand image, for his products. This personality was embodied in his ads through the use of story appeal or by creating interest in what was happening in the ad. In a series of ads for Hathaway shirts, the model was wearing an eye patch, which increased not only the curiosity inspired by the ad but also its memorability. The advertising succeeded in setting the product apart by the use of the unforgettable model and by the suggestion in the copy that Hathaway shirts were not "ordinary" or "mass-produced." The model reinforced the idea visually that he was not ordinary. The ads talked of fine cloths from around the world for the shirts made in the little town of Waterville, Maine. And although Hathaway shirts were not produced more remarkably than were their competitors, the perception that they were was created, and the ads succeeded in selling more shirts.

In Ogilvy's famous Rolls-Royce ad whose headline read, "At 60 miles an hour the loudest noise in this new Rolls-Royce comes from the electric clock," the ad asked what made the Rolls-Royce the best car in the world. Such a question placed the car in the undisputed position as the best in the world, and the ad explained why. All of the reasons appeared to be unique to the car – none were comparative. Other luxury cars might have had the same features, but because of positioning, the impression was given that the Rolls-Royce was the best in the world.

Bill Bernbach was a genius at taking what appeared to be an undesirable attribute of a product and using it to benefit the product. In one of his most famous campaigns, he turned being the number-two position in an industry into a positive. He posited that because Avis was number two in the rental car business, it tried harder. The ads boasted of shorter lines and counters that were not jammed with people. The simple slogan, "We're Number Two. We Try Harder," was persuasive in convincing people the company would put forth more effort. People bought the idea that Avis tried harder despite there being no tangible evidence that Avis's effort was greater than that of its main competitor, Hertz.

Bernbach's Volkswagen ads focused on the virtues of the cars without ignoring how the cars were different from what Detroit was producing. At the time these ads began, the U.S. automobile industry had yet to seriously produce any fuel-efficient or small cars. A billboard showing just a Beetle and three effective words, "Relieves Gas Pains," promoted the car's fuel efficiency. A print ad urged readers to "Think Small," extolling the glories of smaller parking spaces, smaller insurance premiums, and smaller repair bills. What were attributes that were originally seen as negative, Bernbach used in the product's favor.

Leo Burnett, in his search for the inherent drama in each product, created the Green Giant and the Marlboro Man. His agency created Charlie the Tuna, Morris the Cat, the Pillsbury Doughboy, and Tony the Tiger. Burnett did not merely create clever characters to pitch a product, however; he used characters to give a brand a unique personality and to position the product. The Green Giant was created for a Minnesota vegetable packer to make the ads memorable and to communicate the watchfulness of the Green Giant in ensuring that only the finest ingredients went into its products.

Burnett's greatest coup was when he took a fledgling brand of filtered cigarettes and moved them to "Marlboro Country." Filtered cigarettes were thought to be effeminate by 1950s standards, and men stayed away from them. Women, almost exclusively, smoked them until Burnett started using a ruggedly handsome cowhand in the ads in 1954. The "Marlboro Man" was born, propelling the brand out of obscurity and into the position it still held in the late 1990s as one of the best-selling cigarettes. The Creative Revolution succeeded in making advertisements more sophisticated, more intelligent, more clever, and more effective.

SARAH WRIGHT PLASTER

See also Advertising in the Twentieth Century; Burnett, Leo Noble

Further Reading

Bendinger, Bruce, *The Copy Workshop Workbook,* Chicago: Copy Workshop, 1993

Glatzer, Robert, *The New Advertising: The Great Campaigns from Avis to Volkswagen,* New York: Citadel, 1970

Ogilvy, David, *Ogilvy on Advertising,* London: Pan, 1983; New York: Vintage, 1985

Credibility Gap

Government secrecy during Vietnam era led to mistrust

"Credibility gap" is a term that was used to describe the U.S. public's distrust of President Lyndon Johnson and his policies during the 1960s. It made its first appearance on May 24, 1965, when a headline writer for the *New York Herald Tribune* took the words "credibility" and "gap" from a story the *Tribune*'s David Wise had written about the federal government and put them together in quotes in the story's headline. Seven months later, Murray Marder of the *Washington (D.C.) Post* used the term to describe the growing sentiment among Washington reporters that President Johnson's words did not always match his actions. The press was beginning to contrast Johnson's 1964 presidential campaign promises of peace with his increasingly military stance in Vietnam. The phrase caught the imagination of the U.S. public, and "Ambushed at Credibility Gap" was soon appearing on buttons. Although public mistrust of government officials had started before Johnson, the times and the man came together to produce the credibility gap. Johnson was a consummate politician given to secrecy in a decade in which youth decreed that no one over the age of 30 was to be trusted.

Johnson believed that the president had the right to weigh all of the options before a final decision was made on either foreign or domestic matters. Speculation on the part of the press as to what the president might do infringed, according to Johnson, on the president's ability to make decisions. This view, combined with his deep suspicion of the press, whom he considered the enemy, led Johnson to demand secrecy from those who worked for him. But the more he attempted to keep things from the press, the more reporters started to examine his statements. By the spring of 1964, the press was growing suspicious of what it was told by Johnson and his staff. Too often, Johnson either made statements that did not check out, or he denied rumors that ended up to be true.

The press's concern over Johnson's desire for secrecy was compounded by his tendency to play fast and loose with the truth, especially when he had a sympathetic audience. His World War II service, for example, consisted of one flight as an observer, but with each retelling, his role grew more heroic, until the experience bore little resemblance to reality. And, during a speech in Seoul, Korea, in 1966, he told his audience that his great-great-grandfather had died at the Alamo, even though there was no evidence that any of Johnson's relatives died at the Alamo or were even present at the time.

Johnson's most serious deceptions, however, came in the area of foreign policy. On April 28, 1965, Johnson went on the air to announce that U.S. troops were on their way to the Dominican Republic, where rebels were engaged in an uprising. Although Johnson's actions appear to have been triggered by fear that the rebel movement was led by Communists, Johnson did not tell the public of his concerns. Instead, he justified sending in the Marines on the basis that the blood of U.S. citizens would be shed if he did not. John-son later told the press that 1,500 innocent people had been murdered on the island, some by decapitation. That information turned out not to be true.

It was Johnson's decision in 1965 to commit U.S. troops to the conflict in Vietnam without advising the nation, however, that particularly outraged the press. When the decision was finally leaked two months later, Johnson told his aides to deny the story. Television made the deception all the more evident to the U.S. public. The nightly news footage of the fighting in Vietnam stood in stark contrast to the 1964 campaign promises made by Johnson that he would end the conflict.

The public's distrust continued to haunt President Johnson after 1965. In March 1967, Walter Lippmann wrote a series of articles on the subject, and in February 1968, a White House staff member even presented a position paper that attempted to explain the psychology of the credibility gap. Acknowledging the general feeling of disillusionment and frustration that had settled over the United States, President Johnson in 1968 announced that he would not seek reelection.

Prior to Johnson's administration, presidents had been viewed with some reverence and respect. The press tended to be patriotic, especially in the area of foreign affairs. Criticism of presidential policy was kept to a minimum in the mainstream press. But Lyndon Johnson's deceptions tarnished the image of the president, and his credibility gap paved the way for the Watergate scandal and the fall of Richard Nixon.

KARLA K. GOWER

See also Johnson, Lyndon B., and the Media; Nixon, Richard M., and the Media; Watergate Scandal

Further Reading

Caro, Robert A., *The Years of Lyndon Johnson: Means of Ascent,* New York: Knopf, 1990
Culbert, David, "Johnson and the Media," in *Exploring the Johnson Years,* edited by Robert A. Divine, Austin: University of Texas Press, 1981
Deakin, James, *Lyndon Johnson's Credibility Gap,* Washington, D.C.: Public Affairs, 1968
Goldman, Eric F., *The Tragedy of Lyndon Johnson,* New York: Knopf, 1969; London: Macdonald, 1969
Steinberg, Alfred, *Sam Johnson's Boy: A Close-up of the President from Texas,* New York: Macmillan, 1968
Wise, David, *The Politics of Lying: Government Deception, Secrecy, and Power,* New York: Vintage, 1973

Crisis Management

Specialty area within public relations

Generally viewed as a specialty practice area within public relations, crisis management refers to the process of anticipating and preparing for unexpected occurrences that have the potential to damage an organization's reputation with important constituents and thereby influence the organiza-

Public relations experts point to the *Exxon Valdez* disaster as a reason for developing crisis management plans.
(Photo courtesy of AP/World Wide Photos)

tion's survival. Natural disasters, product recalls, environmental pollution, legal disputes, white-collar crime, striking employees, and human errors all signal potentially devastating consequences for an institution.

The development of crisis management as a discipline reflects both the recognition of the influence of public opinion on an organization's ability to operate successfully and the increasing number of crises occurring in U.S. institutions. Crisis management became particularly trendy in the business world during the 1980s following the Union Carbide disaster in Bhopal, India, the Tylenol product tampering case, the Exxon Valdez oil spill, and numerous other crises and business scandals. The Institute for Crisis Management reported that the frequency of crises in U.S. businesses more than doubled between 1985 and 1990.

As organizations began to take seriously the risk that disaster could strike close to home, crisis management became part of the strategic planning process. While much attention is focused on ways to reduce the risk of crises occurring, of even greater concern is how to mitigate the effects of external forces that cannot be controlled. Thus, crisis management primarily involves the management of an organization's response to an existing crisis.

Vital to that response is an institution's willingness and ability to communicate effectively with internal and external audiences. Of particular importance is an organization's communication with the mass media, which interpret crises for news consumers and determine continuing coverage of crisis events. Because the media define the significance of crises for readers and viewers and, to a great extent, determine public response to crisis situations, an organization's relationship with the media is critical to its success in surviving a crisis with its credibility intact.

Modern technology provides for instantaneous, worldwide media coverage of crises as they happen, including the immediate response of the institutions involved. While ineffective communication can turn a manageable situation into a full-blown disaster, a well-managed crisis response can turn a potentially devastating situation into an upside-down opportunity. By handling a crisis in a responsible manner, organizations can take advantage of heightened media interest and actually enhance their reputations.

According to crisis management experts, the key to successful crisis management is preparation – anticipating the worst and planning for it. A plan of action that can be implemented when crisis does strike is crucial. Appointing and training employees who will serve as spokespersons during crisis situations is also important. A proactive – rather than reactive – approach to crisis management allows an institution to control the flow of information about the crisis event. Strategic communication with the media and other affected audiences is vital. An open and candid approach to communication is advised, with consideration of both the public relations and legal implications of the organizational response.

KATHY R. FITZPATRICK

See also Public Relations

Further Reading

Barton, Laurence, *Crisis in Organizations: Managing and Communicating in the Heat of Chaos*, Cincinnati, Ohio: South-Western, 1993

Center, Allen H., and Patrick Jackson, "Crisis Management," in *Public Relations Practices: Managerial Case Studies and Problems*, 4th ed., Englewood Cliffs, New Jersey: Prentice-Hall, 1990

Lesly, Philip, "Policy, Issues, Crises, and Opportunities," in *Lesly's Handbook of Public Relations and Communications*, 4th ed., Chicago: Probus, 1991

Newsom, Doug, Alan Scott, and Judy VanSlyke Turk, *This Is PR: The Realities of Public Relations*, 5th ed., Belmont, California: Wadsworth, 1993

Criticism of Advertising

Focuses on how advertisements shape society

Advertising has attracted criticism since its earliest days, and the industry has responded to such criticisms in a variety of ways. As an integral part of doing business in the United States, advertising communicates about products, services, and ideas in order to inform and persuade. In serving its economic role, however, advertising creates a reality of its own, transmitting social cues about life in the United States. Much of the criticism of advertising is directed toward its role as a vehicle of social communication. Most social criticisms of advertising fall into one of four categories: the products advertised, the nature of advertising exposure,

the content of advertising, and advertising's influence on behavior and cultural norms.

Consumers object to advertising for particular products and services for a variety of reasons. Some argue that advertising for alcohol and tobacco harms public health. Advertising for professional services such as those offered by the medical and legal communities are often viewed as unethical both by consumers and by some professional organizations. Certain products are seen to be inappropriate for child audiences. Many feel that advertising for feminine hygiene and other extremely personal products, like condoms, is in bad taste.

No product has stirred more debate than tobacco. Cigarettes are an excellent example of a product that successfully used advertising to reach a mass market. Efforts to regulate communication about the product, however, began soon after connections between smoking and cancer emerged in the 1950s. Over the next two decades, evidence of detrimental effects of smoking on health mounted, and manufacturers were forced to put warning labels on packages, and later, in ads. The Public Health Cigarette Smoking Act passed by Congress in 1970 banned all cigarette advertising on television and radio as of January 1, 1971. Despite the fact that the impact of regulatory efforts was uncertain, calls for a ban on all cigarette advertising continued.

Advocates of a ban pointed to increases in smoking-related diseases. A ban, they said, would decrease consumption and improve public health. Advocates of a ban believed that much of the tobacco industry's advertising was targeted to teens; they also were vocally opposed to advertising targeted to minority and low-income groups that had a higher incidence of smoking-related illnesses. Tobacco companies denied targeting youth; their advertising efforts, they said, were directed toward creating brand loyalty and brand switching rather than encouraging people to start smoking. Further, tobacco companies claimed a First Amendment right to truthfully advertise a legal product. Critics argued that images of health and vigor in tobacco advertising misrepresented the reality of smoking-related illness; these ads, they said, were deceptive and had no First Amendment protection.

Criticisms related to advertising exposure typically revolve around its intrusiveness and pervasiveness. For example, suggesting that outdoor advertising ruined the landscape, the Highway Beautification Act of 1965 restricted the placement of signs along interstate highways. In the 1990s, numerous local jurisdictions continued to limit the number of billboards despite claims that such a limitation infringed upon an advertiser's freedom of speech. Zapping (changing the channel when a commercial comes on), zipping (fast-forwarding past commercials on prerecorded videotapes), and the popularity of cable movie channels that played no advertising during films provided evidence that audiences seek to avoid advertising intrusion into their television and movie viewing. Similarly, advertiser attempts to place ads on videocassettes and in movie theaters also met with considerable consumer resistance. Many objected to the sheer pervasiveness of advertising and to the universal institutional message of the imperative to consume.

Criticism related to advertising content has been wide-ranging. Critics often charge that ads are silly, patronizing, or in poor taste; that claims are exaggerated; that ads are uninformative; that advertising images are too sexually explicit; and that ads create and perpetuate stereotypical portrayals, particularly of women, racial and ethnic groups, and the elderly.

Finally, a number of criticisms of advertising are based upon advertising's perceived influence upon human behavior and cultural norms. These critiques are directed to advertising's institutional impact – that is, to advertising in the aggregate, rather than to individual advertising campaigns. Advertising, for example, is said to cause people to buy things they do not need and to promote a lifestyle based upon consumption and materialistic values. Defenders of advertising charge that critics actually are questioning the values of a capitalist system. Advertising, they say, provides consumers with information about choices and with incentives toward which to strive. Critics also contend that advertising lowers values and moral standards, not only through advertising content, but also through advertiser control of media content. Arguments have often been reduced to the question of whether advertising is a mirror or a shaper. Critics contend that advertising is a shaper, influencing society in primarily negative ways – encouraging greed and selfishness, cynicism, irrationality, and indulgence. Defenders of advertising view it as merely a reflection of society.

Most criticism of advertising has focused on its social effects. Defenders are more likely to turn attention to its economic function. Yet, while advertising clearly has economic impact, there is little consensus on the nature of that impact. Questions raised about advertising's economic role center upon advertising's effect on corporate profits, competition, innovation, consumer prices, and aggregate consumption. Views on economic impact hinge on whether advertising is seen as information that enhances the efficient functioning of the market or as a form of persuasion that creates market power and inhibits the function of the market.

Advertising is an inescapable part of life in the United States. In the 1990s, advertisers spent more than $130 billion on commercial messages annually. Given advertising's pervasiveness, the institution naturally attracts vocal, persistent critics and defenders. Advertising's success as a business tool hinges upon its ability to adapt and to operate in the context of these persistent criticisms.

PEGGY J. KRESHEL

See also Advertising and Minorities; Advertising Appeals; Advertising in the Twentieth Century; Counteradvertising

Further Reading

Caifee, John E., "Cigarette Advertising Regulation Today: Unintended Consequences and Missed Opportunities," in Advances in Consumer Research, vol. XIV, edited by Melanie Wallendorf and Paul Anderson, Provo, Utah: Association for Consumer Research, 1987
Courtney, Alice, and Thomas Whipple, Sex Stereotyping in Advertising, Lexington, Massachusetts: Lexington Books, 1983
Gostin, Lawrence O., and Allan M. Brandt, "Criteria for Evaluating a Ban on the Advertisement of Cigarettes: Balancing Public Health Benefits with Constitutional Burdens," Journal of the American Medical Association 269:7 (February 17, 1993), pp. 904–909
Holbrook, Morris B., "Mirror, Mirror, on the Wall, What's Unfair in the Reflections on Advertising?," Journal of Marketing 51:3 (July 1987), pp. 95–103
Krugman, Dean M., Advertising: Its Role in Modern Marketing, 8th ed., Fort Worth, Texas: Dryden, 1994
Leiss, William, Stephen Kline, and Sut Jhally, Social Communication in Advertising: Persons, Products and Images of Well-Being, 2nd ed., New York and London: Routledge, 1990
Norris, Vincent P., "The Economic Effects of Advertising: A Review of the Literature," Current Issues and Research in Advertising (1984)
Pollay, Richard W., "The Distorted Mirror: Reflections on the Unintended Consequences of Advertising," Journal of Marketing 50 (April 1986)
Schudson, Michael, Advertising, the Uneasy Persuasion: Its Dubious Impact on American Society, New York: Basic, 1984

Criticism of Broadcasting

Consumers, media practitioners concerned about what is seen

In the late twentieth century, criticism of broadcasting was heard daily from the "television newspaper" critics and dissatisfied viewers. It was of growing concern not only to consumers but to media practitioners as well. This popular criticism traditionally stemmed from six broad topics: 1) the effect on audiences of violent content; 2) mediated and perceived reality versus social reality; 3) sex and stereotyping; 4) the effect of television on politics and the political process; 5) the effect on children and education; and 6) the overall impact of advertising.

Violent Content

Was the rampant violence portrayed on television affecting audience behavior? The research findings were generally inconclusive. There were studies that indicated that television is a cause for social violence and others that indicated it is not. Social scientists too seemed to agree that it is *a* cause, but they also agreed that it is not *the* cause of aggressive behavior and social unrest. The direct effect of violence on the screen is affected by demographics and family intervention as well as the way the violence is presented on the screen. The debate continued over the years and led to the V-chip provision of the Telecommunications Act of 1996. The addition of this chip to a television set allowed parents to monitor the violent content of programs viewed in the home.

Reality Content

The real world varies significantly from what is portrayed on television. It takes people a lot longer to walk from the house to work in real life than it does on television, for example. Television seems to have the capacity of compressing reality and time into a capsule. People in television commit more crimes, they have more children out of wedlock, and they settle more trials by jury than in real life. In other words, television exaggerates life. Social science research seemed to indicate that the amount of experience a viewer has with the reality affects the perception of that reality as depicted on television. For example, people who live in a high-crime area are more likely to believe they live in a scary world, and this worldview is reinforced in television viewing. Thus, their viewing cultivates a perception of reality.

Sex and Sex-Role Stereotyping

The depiction of sex on television was on the increase throughout the 1980s and 1990s. Questions arose: Does the depiction of recreational sex erode traditional family values? Is it denigrating to women? The issues here were not unlike those regarding violence. Again there was no overall consensus. There was an increasing concern over the characterization of women on television. In television's early years, women were cast as housewives, secretaries, and in the more emotional roles; men were the more dominant and powerful. Modern television became somewhat sensitive to such stereotyping and began portraying women in a broader range of occupations and status positions.

Television and Politics

Do the media influence voting behavior? What impact do the electronic media have on our political institutions? These were key questions concerning political scientists in the late twentieth century. There was agreement that television had had an effect on the U.S. political system. It shaped how the voting electorate perceives a candidate's image. People rely heavily on the media for information about their political process. Further, there was some evidence that television influences electoral choices. In terms of television's impact on the political system, it affects the political agenda and thus helps to set that agenda. It affects people's knowledge of the political system and how it operates. Despite this consensus, the study of media effects on politics remained a complex one. There was little evidence to show that media affects such things as voter turnout or a voter's choice in the ballot box. These decisions work along with other factors that affect political decision making.

Children and the Electronic Media

This topic was one of primary concern to lawmakers, regulators, and parents alike. The Telecommunications Act of 1996 introduced not only the V-chip but also provided tougher penalties for exposing of children to pornography. Although the U.S. Supreme Court considered the regulations on pornography a violation of the First Amendment, the FCC continued to consider special rules related to children's television. The possibility that children might be in the audience and the concern over the issues of sex and violence continued to foster debate related to the impact the portrayal of these activities had on children. Unfortunately, there was little consensus among social scientists. There

was evidence that television has decreased the attention span of children, thus affecting teaching and the classroom. However, there was little evidence to support conclusively that television enhances aggression or a child's scholastic aptitude.

Advertising

There is probably no other topic in media as well researched as that of advertising. People in advertising obviously believe that they can deliver a message that motivates the audience. Such companies as Procter & Gamble spend hundreds of millions of dollars to sell products to the U.S. homemaker. Often, every frame of a television commercial is analyzed to determine whether or not it is having its intended impact. The commercial advertising unit is the most highly researched unit of televised communication. The impact this produces is often an emotional one. Television is a portrayer of emotions. Commercials, that is, "sell comfort, not shoes; or luxury, not the automobile." Studies have pointed to a consideration in advertising for children. Regulations in the late twentieth century worked to separate program and commercial content, and reality versus perceived reality, in children's commercial products. Research also pointed out that as children grow, they develop increasing skepticism for commercials.

The amount of research on the impact of television on daily lives, already an important field for researchers, was likely to increase as the criticism of television content continued to increase.

DONALD G. GODFREY

See also Advertising and Minorities; Children's Television Programming; Mass Media and Children; Mass Media and Politics; Mass Media and Race; Mass Media and the Sexual Revolution; Television and Violence

Further Reading

Esslin, Martin, *The Age of Television,* San Francisco: W.H. Freeman, 1982

Newcomb, Horace, ed., *Television: The Critical View,* 3rd ed., New York: Oxford University Press, 1982

Orlik, Peter B., *Critiquing Radio and Television Content,* Boston: Allyn and Bacon, 1988

Primeau, Ronald, *The Rhetoric of Television,* New York: Longman, 1979

Criticism of Newspapers

Press long held responsible for its real or perceived behaviorial errors

Throughout its history, the press in the United States has been subjected to criticism of many kinds. Responding to one of that criticism's earliest expressions, Benjamin Franklin penned his perceptive "Apology for Printers." During the colonial period and prelude to the American Revolution, newspapers encountered frequent criticism for expressing partisan attitudes toward the British government's administration; charges of political partisanship continued through the nation-building period and beyond, far into the twentieth century. As the press grew and became a more complex and influential institution, its increasingly diverse readership acquired more and more sophisticated expectations that inspired performance evaluation of greater and greater diversity. Over the many years during which early America's press proliferated itself into the modern world's high-technology industry, the following themes of criticism have surfaced:

1.) Inaccuracy, a basic and simple theme that has pervaded every era. Basic to any news enterprise, of course, is a commitment to present the facts accurately. Upon that premise U.S. journalists and their critics have always generally agreed. They have disagreed from time to time, however, upon whether the reported facts communicate the essential truth of the event or development being reported.

2.) Bias, at times resulting in outright partisanship, but at other times the result of unconscious predisposition. Much has been made in criticism of U.S. newspapers of their conservative bias in politics, although in the 1990s, some described the press as liberal. Except for rare newspapers of the left, however, the U.S. press has never been seen as anti-capitalistic or Socialist. In the field of religion, critics cite U.S. journalism's strong Judeo-Christian bias, about which Muslims complain frequently. Other controversies involving press bias revolve around charges of sexism, white racism, discrimination against the elderly, and increasing gentrification of newspaper staffing, which compounds the press's empathy with society's affluent. Consequently, the press is seen as reflecting an upper-middle-class, white, male, Judeo-Christian economic conservative perspective on the news and its interpretation. That pattern of biases creates, critics allege, a press of strong pro-establishment character that is strengthened by a need for journalists to obtain and cultivate reliable news sources in high places.

3.) Suppression of news for one reason or another. Computer technology and public information law continue to create an information overload that makes editorial judgment more and more discriminating. Consequently, the media have been accused of suppressing stories that lack universal appeal – or are offensive, perhaps, to common myths in U.S. culture.

4.) Invasion of privacy. Although it surfaced in the nineteenth century, this criticism became more common in the late twentieth century as eavesdropping and photographic and computer-assisted probe technology became more sophisticated.

5.) Abrogation of leadership. Despite its status as the "fourth branch of government," critics have alleged that the press frequently neglects in-depth coverage and interpretation of public affairs.

6.) Obsession with novelty at the expense of importance.

7.) Profiteering. Impelled by venal greed, critics claim, U.S. journalists accept misleading or harmful advertising, slant news coverage, nourish sacred cows, and otherwise compromise professional standards.

8.) Overzealous competition, resulting in numerous failures to cover the news adequately. Journalism's "scoop mentality," it is argued, leads to "herd" news coverage that squanders reportorial talent.

9.) Abuse of power. Although many appraisals of its power have been challenged in research, the press has been accused of using its power to manipulate readers through selective reporting and propaganda.

10.) Professional arrogance. In many ways, critics allege, journalists display disrespect for others and see themselves entitled to special privileges.

11.) Irresponsibility. Newspapers refuse to accept appropriate responsibility, critics assert, for the impact that their behavior has upon others.

12.) Distortion of social reality. Although a news report may be absolutely accurate, critics point out, it can misrepresent the situation.

13.) Pandering to the baser appetites of readers. In their exercise of such license, hyper-competitive journalists sometimes argue that if they are not satisfying the public's craving for scandal, violence, and sleaze, their competitors surely will.

14.) Fixation on political candidates while neglecting the exploration of issues involved in campaigns. Such fixation results, critics allege, in "horse-race" coverage of the electoral process.

15.) Sensationalism – over-dramatization of conflict, tragedy, and the misfortunes of other people.

16.) Over-emphasis on bad news. To counter this criticism, the press argues that concerned readers suffer from a "kill-the-messenger" complex.

17.) Glorification or glamorization of antisocial conduct, which critics charge influences readers – especially adolescents – to copy it, or to tolerate rather than condemn it.

18.) Preoccupation with the behavior of celebrities, while neglecting figures devoted to unglamorous pursuits.

19.) Frustration of the criminal justice system through prejudicial publicity.

20.) Cynical attitudes toward newsmakers or sources and their credibility, which often leads to "ambush" or "gotcha" journalism – or, at the extreme, to "wolf-pack" journalism.

21.) Hostility toward government. In a mistaken belief that journalists should play an adversarial or watchdog role toward officialdom, many have adopted a "kill the king" approach to government news.

22.) Superficiality in news coverage.

23.) Unjustified assault on the reputation of others – character assassination and McCarthyism.

24.) Trivialization of the news. In order to be more entertaining and exciting, critics allege, newspapers concentrate on material that requires little education to understand and that features unimportant aspects of the news.

25.) Exploitation of figures in the news. This comparatively new complaint alleges that the press treats other persons callously, as raw material out of which to manufacture stories for the entertainment of others.

Prominent in criticism of the media have been persons as different in their insights as Spiro Agnew, Reed Alvine, Ben Bagdikian, Noam Chomsky, Jeff Cohen, Jeff Greenfield, Richard Harwood, Robert Hutchins, Will Irwin, Maggie Kuhn, Anthony Lewis, A.J. Liebling, Walter Lippmann, Edward Said, Herbert Schiller, Charles Seib, Upton Sinclair, and Norman Solomon. The media they have used, in their criticism, includes every kind. Especially important, however, have been journalism reviews such as *MORE*, the *Columbia Journalism Review*, the *American Journalism Review* (formerly the *Washington Journalism Review*), the *Nieman Reports, Lies of Our Times,* and *Extra;* critiques by newspaper ombudsmen; broadcast commentaries; the reports of press councils; and the report of the national Commission on Freedom of the Press.

JOHN DEMOTT

See also Commission on Freedom of the Press; Free
    Press–Fair Trial Controversy; National News Council;
    News Councils; Ombudsman; Pack Journalism; Privacy;
    Sensationalism

Further Reading
Bagdikian, Ben H., *The Effete Conspiracy, and Other
    Crimes by the Press,* New York: Harper & Row, 1972
Brown, Les, *The Reluctant Revolution,* New York: David
    McKay, 1974
Crouse, Timothy, *The Boys on the Bus,* New York:
    Random House, 1973
Liebling, A.J., *The Press,* New York: Pantheon, 1981
Lippmann, Walter, *Public Opinion,* New York: Macmillan,
    1922; London: Allen and Unwin, 1922
Marzolf, Marion, *Civilizing Voices: American Press
    Criticism, 1880–1950,* New York: Longman, 1991
Seldes, George, *Lords of the Press,* 2nd ed., New York: J.
    Messner, 1938
Sinclair, Upton, *The Brass Check: A Study of American
    Journalism,* New York: Arno, 1970

Cronkite, Walter

CBS News correspondent and anchor

Walter Leland Cronkite was born in Kansas City, Missouri, the son of a professor of dental medicine who later moved his family to Texas. Cronkite attended the University of Texas for two years while working as a stringer for the *Houston Post* and as a state capital reporter for the International News Service. He left the university to work full-time at the *Post* and then for Scripps-Howard and the United Press (UP). One of the first U.S. reporters accredited to cover World War II, he reported the campaign in North Africa, the D-Day landing, and the Nuremberg trials. After the war, he also helped to establish UP bureaus throughout Europe and was assigned to Moscow. He returned to the United States, worked briefly in radio, and then joined CBS-TV in Washington, D.C., in 1950.

Cronkite began covering national political conventions in 1952 and was invited to New York to host the network news and documentaries. Later selected to serve as anchor of the "CBS Evening News," he eventually assumed the title of managing editor. He was at the helm when CBS television shifted to a half-hour evening news format, the first national network to do so. Cronkite had a special interest in Vietnam and eventually took an editorial position against

Walter Cronkite
(Museum of Broadcast Communications)

U.S. involvement in southeast Asia. He is also credited with providing careful coverage of the space race and for following up and reporting on the Watergate crisis. His daily sign-off, "And that's the way it is," became well known, a familiar part of U.S. popular culture. He retired in 1981 but continued serving on the CBS board of directors.

MICHAEL D. MURRAY

Further Reading
Gates, Gary Paul, *Air Time: The Inside Story of CBS
    News,* New York: Harper & Row, 1978
Matusow, Barbara, *The Evening Stars: The Making of the
    Network News Anchor,* Boston: Houghton Mifflin, 1983
Slater, Robert, *This . . . is CBS: A Chronicle of 60 Years,*
    Englewood Cliffs, New Jersey: Prentice-Hall, 1988

Cross-Media Ownership

Ownership of outlets in two or more media fields

Cross-media ownership exists whenever an organization owns outlets in two or more media fields, either within a single local market or on a national basis. Specific media fields include radio, television, cable, newspaper, and, increasingly in the 1990s, telephone operation. The Federal

Communications Commission (FCC) imposed certain limits on both multiple station ownership and cross-media ownership on a local and national basis. The FCC was particularly concerned with combinations of daily newspapers and broadcast stations within a given market area.

Two significant concerns underlay the government's interest in cross-media combinations. First was the concern that the common ownership of two or more media properties might restrict the diversity of viewpoints presented in those media. A second concern, expressed by the Justice Department, was that a media combination could exercise too much economic power in comparison with competitors.

The issue of cross-media ownership has been debated by Congress, the Justice Department, and the FCC ever since radio first achieved popularity. After decades of study, in 1974, the FCC adopted rules that prohibited the formation of any new combination of television stations, radio stations, and daily newspapers in the same market. Other local cross-media rules adopted by the FCC prohibited combinations of television stations and cable systems and telephone companies and cable systems. No restrictions applied to the establishment of newspaper and cable combinations in the same local marketplace. Although the FCC's 1974 action prevented the formation of new media combinations, most existing ones were left intact, or grandfathered. Firms with such media combinations were encouraged to break up their holdings through the sale of their broadcast and newspaper properties to different buyers.

By 1995, local cross-media ownership of newspapers and television stations had become rare, with only 19 of the 734 stations (2.6 percent) in the top 100 markets being commonly owned with local daily newspapers. This contrasted with 60 stations (16.1 percent) at the beginning of 1973. Thus, with the exception of 19 grandfathered stations, the FCC's goal of eliminating local cross-media ownership had largely been achieved. Cities in which grandfathered newspaper-television combinations still existed in the 1990s included Chicago; San Francisco; Atlanta, Georgia; Dallas, Texas; and Cincinnati, Columbus, and Dayton, Ohio.

The FCC's cross-media rules only affected individual markets, leaving media companies free to acquire both broadcast and newspaper properties in different market areas. Consequently, the total number of newspaper-affiliated television stations in the top 100 markets increased from 104 in 1973 to 165 in 1995. This trend reflected the diversification of media companies into both broadcast and publishing enterprises and the FCC's tolerance of newspaper-related ownership of television stations where it did not conflict with local cross-media ownership rules.

The FCC, which adopted its long-standing rules governing cross-media ownership when media voices were scarce, began relaxing those rules in the late twentieth century as the media environment changed to one of plentiful competitive voices in the electronic media field. For example, in 1993, the FCC allowed commonly owned radio duopolies (consisting of two AM and two FM stations) in local market areas. The agency also was considering allowing radio-television station combinations in a given market area. Furthermore, telephone companies won the right to offer "video dial tone," a cablelike service, within their operating territories, as well as to own and operate cable systems outside franchised areas. In an environment of declining numbers of newspapers, less restrictive policies regarding newspaper-television ownership were thought to be useful in bolstering weaker newspapers in their efforts to survive.

HERBERT H. HOWARD

Further Reading

Howard, Herbert H., "Group and Cross-Media Ownership of TV Stations: A 1989 Update," *Journalism Quarterly* 66:4 (Winter 1989), pp. 785–792

Smith, F. Leslie, Milan D. Meeske, and John W. Wright II, *Electronic Media and Government: The Regulation of Wireless and Wired Mass Communication in the United States*, White Plains, New York: Longman, 1995

Waterman, David, "A New Look at Media Chains and Groups: 1977–1989," *Journal of Broadcasting & Electronic Media* 35:2 (Spring 1991), pp. 167–177

Crystallizing Public Opinion
Written by Edward Bernays

With his book *Crystallizing Public Opinion*, Edward Bernays began his crusade for public relations to be accepted as a profession. According to Bernays, public relations had been transformed from press agentry and publicity into an essential, complex, and ethical profession much like the practice of law. Indeed, a public relations practitioner was a counselor who advised clients and argued on their behalf before the court of public opinion. As an intermediary between an organization and its public, the public relations counselor applied communications and psychology to align the client's policies and public opinion.

Because the ability to articulate public opinion can be used for good or for evil, Bernays warned public relations counselors to diligently avoid propagating movements or ideas that were harmful. Choosing clients responsibly would allow public relations to fulfill its social value, "bring[ing] to the public facts and ideas of social utility which would not so readily gain acceptance otherwise."

Crystallizing Public Opinion was published in 1923 and reissued on Bernays's seventieth birthday in 1961. It was the first book that defined public relations as an occupation worthy of professional status and the first book that highlighted the two-way character of public relations. This book also introduced the term public relations counselor, which quickly became part and parcel of the industry's self-definition.

JOHN P. FERRÉ

See also Bernays, Edward L.; Public Relations

Further Reading

Bernays, Edward L., *Crystallizing Public Opinion*, New York: Boni and Liveright, 1923

Cutlip, Scott M., *The Unseen Power: Public Relations, a History*, Hillsdale, New Jersey: Lawrence Erlbaum, 1994

D

Davis, Jefferson, and the Press

Confederate president had rocky relationship with press

Jefferson Davis, the only president of the Confederate States of America, was not immune to vicious press attacks on his administration's performance during his tenure between 1861 and 1865. Throughout the four bloody years of the American Civil War, Davis clung vehemently to the concept of freedom of the press for the young, struggling Confederacy. Davis believed that nothing would be gained by suppressing the newspapers' rights to publish whatever they wanted to, but he also could not praise press behavior. As he wrote to General Robert E. Lee in 1863, Davis said, "I wish I could feel that the public journals were not generally partisan nor venal."

Newspaper criticism of President Davis did not surface until the late winter of 1861–62, when the Confederacy's armies suffered defeats at Fort Donelson and Roanoke Island. The anti-Davis press attacked him for sins of omission and of commission. Davis was criticized for being a despot, for disregarding public opinion, for being incompetent, for allowing barefoot Confederate soldiers to march, for favoring unpopular and ineffective generals, and for suspending the writ of habeas corpus and enforcing the Impressment Act. President Davis's newspaper enemies and supporters were fairly evenly divided, with the great majority of the antagonists being geographically located in the capital of the Confederacy, Richmond, Virginia. Of the five Richmond newspapers, three were anti-Davis: The *Richmond Examiner,* the *Enquirer,* and the *Whig.* The *Richmond Examiner* hated Jefferson Davis so much that when the president addressed the Confederate Congress in 1863, it criticized Davis's remarks harshly and published President Abraham Lincoln's message to the U.S. Congress in detail.

The *Dispatch* and the *Sentinel* were pro-Davis, and Davis's critics charged both publications with being nothing more than extensions of President Davis's propaganda machinery. Some support was given to that charge by an August 1862 announcement by Confederate Adjutant General Samuel Cooper that the *Enquirer* and the *Sentinel* would be the Confederacy's official information organs because, according to Cooper, "they sometimes came to the defense of Davis." Outside of Richmond, the *Charleston (South Car-*

olina) Daily Courier was one paper that remained loyal to Davis and his administration, commenting about Davis's opponents on November 23, 1864, to the effect that "the freedom of press was really threatened more by the reckless abuse and excessive license practiced by some of its advocates and expounders than by anything Davis could do." The pro-Davis papers probably believed that by supporting President Davis's governmental policies and supporting the Confederate cause that the government would succeed for all Southerners.

Davis's opponents extended throughout the Confederacy. The *Lynchburg Virginian,* the *Memphis (Tennessee) Appeal,* the *Atlanta and Macon (Georgia) Southern Confederacy,* the *Macon Intelligencer,* the *Macon Telegraph,* the *Columbus (Georgia) Sun,* the *Augusta (Georgia) Chronicle and Sentinel,* the *Savannah (Georgia) Republican,* the *Charleston Mercury*, and the *Raleigh (North Carolina) Standard* all attacked Jefferson Davis during the Confederacy's lifetime. The *Standard,* edited by William A. Holden, came the closest of all Southern newspapers to committing outright treason against the Confederacy by writing that Davis was a tyrant and that the Confederacy's cause was doomed to failure.

Amazingly, Davis did not suppress a single Southern newspaper during four years of vicious attacks on his administration, his generals, and his person by these anti-Davis publications. Of these experiences, British Colonel Arthur Fremantle reported that he "constantly saw in the Confederate press the most violent attacks upon the President, [and] upon the different generals and their measures, and that the liberty of the press was carried to its fullest extent." In spite of this excess of liberty, Secretary of War George W. Randolph wrote in 1862 that he hoped "this revolution may be successfully closed without suppression of one single newspaper in the Confederate States, and that our experience may be able to challenge comparison with our enemy." Oddly enough, it was the winning side that suppressed, restricted, or destroyed at least two dozen of their newspapers by official governmental or mob actions.

Perhaps, in the final analysis, President Jefferson Davis understood that the Confederate States of America could only exist if it had strong public support and that a free, uncensored press was the key to winning Southern hearts and minds. More practically, however, Davis probably understood and practiced the tried and true theory that it is best not to argue with a person who buys ink by the barrel.

JOSEPH V. TRAHAN III

See also Civil War Press (North); Civil War Press (South); Lincoln, Abraham, and the Press

Decency Issues in Electronic Media

Problems arise of disseminating certain kinds of programming

When the U.S. Congress passed the Communication Act of 1934 – a law that gave the Federal Communications Commission (FCC) the authority to penalize and forbid the broadcast of obscene and indecent speech – it may have been thinking about the Parent Teachers Association, women's civic groups, and others who loudly protested that many radio programs tended to have an immoral influence on children. The practice of agitating for greater control of broadcast content in the interest of protecting children from indecent or obscene speech – be it on the radio, the television or on the Internet – is a long-standing custom in the United States, one that was alive and well at the end of the twentieth century.

First Amendment protection of broadcast speech has been interpreted as much more limited than the protection of printed speech. Whereas pornographic and indecent speech are protected in published form, the same type of speech would not be protected in a broadcast medium. In 1934, Congress considered the airwaves to be a public resource and subject to scarce supply. The scarcity of frequencies requires that some body – that is, the government – allocate broadcast rights, and the government grants them to those who agree to provide programming in the "public interest, convenience, or necessity." Broadcast content, therefore, may not include indecent or obscene speech.

Although many U.S. citizens have long protested certain speech in the interest of protecting children, it was not until the 1970s that the FCC began to exert its belief that a growing number of programs contained speech unsuitable for minors. As broadcast historians have established, the Nixon administration took an active interest in the FCC in the late 1960s, appointing members who would not only attempt to curtail political criticism but also would vigorously enforce penalties on broadcasters whose programs seemed to violate the common sense of decency. Following a dramatic increase in the number of complaints the FCC received about "topless radio" programs – shows that often discussed sexual issues in explicit terms – in 1973 the commission received a complaint from a father who protested a monologue by comedian George Carlin. The comedian's routine focused on four-letters words, and he listed seven of them that "one cannot say on the public airwaves." The complaint ultimately resulted in a 1978 U.S. Supreme Court case in which the Court upheld the FCC's right to restrict the broadcasting of indecent speech to a "safe harbor" period between the hours of midnight and 6 A.M., when chil-

dren would unlikely be in the audience. Following the decision in *FCC* v. *Pacifica Foundation*, the general definition of indecent speech rested largely upon the broadcast of any one of Carlin's seven words.

The new restrictions, however, did not satisfy many concerned citizens who believed that the FCC failed to enforce the safe harbor period and that broadcast speech was becoming more, rather than less, indecent. In the 1980s, the National Federation of Decency, the American Family Association, and Morality in Media struck an agreement with the FCC in which the commission agreed to investigate broadcast complaints that the various groups agreed to produce. Responding to the subsequent complaints about programs that focused on homosexual and heterosexual relations, the FCC issued a new decency standard in 1987. The new and broader definition, which combined parts of the U.S. Supreme Court's test for printed obscenity and the essence of Carlin's monologue, said that "language or material that depicts or describes, in terms patently offensive as measured by contemporary community standards for the broadcast medium, sexual or excretory activities or organs" could not be broadcast. The new standard also broadened the safe harbor period to between 10 P.M. and 6 A.M., and it expanded the definition of children from those 12 years of age and under to those 17 and younger. Although the broader definition of indecency was upheld by the U.S. Circuit Court 1988 (*Action for Children's Television* v. *FCC*), the expanded safe harbor period was not.

Near the end of the 1980s, the fight to curb so-called indecent speech over the airwaves intensified. In 1988, Republican Senator Jesse Helms of North Carolina proposed an amendment to the FCC's budget that called for a 24-hour ban on the broadcast of indecent speech. In 1991, a U.S. circuit court found the Helms Amendment an unconstitutional restriction on the listening rights of adults (*Action for Children's Television* v. *FCC*). The U.S. Supreme Court refused to hear the case. Following defeat of the 24-hour ban, Congress passed the Public Telecommunications Act of 1992, which required that the FCC effect regulations that would prohibit the broadcasting of indecent speech between 6 A.M. and 10 P.M. on any publicly supported radio or television station that ceased broadcasting before midnight. For other stations, the safe harbor was to be from midnight to 12 noon. In 1995, the U.S. Circuit Court of Appeals subsequently (in *Action for Children's Television* v. *FCC*) ruled these restrictions unconstitutional violations on the First Amendment rights of those broadcasters not supported by public funds. The U.S. Supreme Court refused to hear the case.

Also in 1992, Congress attempted to control indecent broadcast speech in its new Cable Act. This law permitted a cable operator to deny leased access programming to parties the operator believed would broadcast programming that "describe[d] or depict[ed] sexual or excretory activities or organs in a patently offensive manner." The law also allowed operators to prohibit such content on public, educational, and governmental access channels. Finally, the law required that cable operators, if they did carry indecent leased access programming, to segregate it on a separate channel, scramble that channel, and unscramble it only upon a subscriber's written request. Although the U.S. Supreme Court found that the statute had a very important justification – protecting children from "harmful" indecent speech – the Court overturned two of the law's three clauses in 1996 (in *Denver Area Educational Telecommunications Consortium* v. *FCC*). The Court found constitutional that part of the law that gave a cable operator the right to deny a lease to an individual the operator believed would broadcast indecent speech.

In the continuing effort to control broadcast content in the interest of safeguarding children, Congress passed the Communications Decency Act in 1996. As part of the Telecommunications Act of 1996, the law sought to criminalize the transmission over the Internet of obscene or indecent messages to any recipient under 18 years of age. The Telecommunications Act also said that the television industry would have to establish a "voluntary" rating system so that parents could shield their children from violent, sexually explicit, or indecent programming.

On June 26, 1997, in *Reno* v. *ACLU*, the U.S. Supreme Court ruled two sections of the Communications Decency Act to be unconstitutional violations of the First Amendment; one section prohibited the transmission to those under 18 of "any comment, request, suggestion, proposal, image, or other communication which is obscene or indecent"; another section prohibited the display of speech that "in context, depicts or describes, in terms patently offensive as measured by contemporary community standards, sexual or excretory activities or organs, regardless of whether the user of such service placed the call or initiated the communication."

The Telecommunication Act's mandate that the television industry "voluntarily" rate its programs according to its violent, sexually explicit or indecent programming content, however, remained unchallenged legally in its first years. The industry presented a rating system in February 1997 that was modeled after Hollywood's movie rating system. The system was met with great disapproval from certain legislators and citizen action groups. They charged that the guidelines failed to tell parents if a program's content included indecent language or themes. Steps were taken to try to force the industry to include additional ratings that would tell parents if a program contained violence (V), sexual topics (S), "bad" language (L), or "suggestive" dialogue (D). The "D" rating was supposed to indicate that a program contained sexual innuendo. The messages would be added to the already proposed ratings of PG (parental guidance suggested); TV-14, for children younger than 14; and TV-MA, for mature audiences only. Such a rating system began to be put into practice in 1997.

Some legislators felt that even these steps were insufficient to protect children from indecent speech on television. Several members of the U.S. Senate threatened to bring a "Sense of the Senate" to essentially shame broadcasters into creating a "family viewing hour." This plan would mean that television broadcasters would have to commit the first hour of prime-time broadcast to programming appropriate for people of all ages.

Although the courts often overturned legislative efforts to curb so-called indecent speech on the airwaves, it would be a misunderstanding of the overall success of groups such as Morality in Media to say that their concerns were not met in large part. Although the Communication Act of 1934 was enacted at a time when radio programming was roundly criticized for its "harmful" effect on children, the law did not proscribe the broadcast of indecent and obscene speech *because* it might have a detrimental effect on children. By 1978, however, the U.S. Supreme Court agreed with those who argued that such speech was harmful to children, ruling that the FCC could channel indecent speech to a safe harbor period. Furthermore, the continued outcry of the various citizens' groups resulted in a definition of "indecent" speech that was significantly broader than it was in the *Pacifica* decision.

Some critics of increased broadcast restrictions argued that, although there were numerous studies of the effect that obscene speech might have on children, there had been no significant study of the possible harmful effects of indecent speech. Thus, they said, the First Amendment rights of broadcasters were restricted largely because of agitation by certain concerned groups. Other scholars suggested that the motivations of those individuals arguing for broader definitions of indecent speech should be examined.

ROBIN GALLAGHER

See also Broadcast Regulation; Community Access Television; Internet; Obscenity and Pornography; Television Program Ratings

Further Reading

Blanchard, Margaret A., *Revolutionary Sparks: Freedom of Expression in Modern America,* New York: Oxford University Press, 1992
Powe, L.A. Scot, Jr., *American Broadcasting and the First Amendment,* Berkeley: University of California Press, 1987
Spring, Joel H., *Images of American Life: A History of Ideological Management in Schools, Movies, Radio, and Television,* Albany: State University of New York Press, 1992

De Forest, Lee

Developer of radio's audio tube

A giant in the development of broadcast technology and the promotion of the new medium to the public, Lee De Forest is probably best known for one of his early inventions: the audion tube, which made radio a long-distance-broadcast, not just point-to-point, medium. De Forest also used the audion to develop technology for sound in movies.

After earning a doctorate at Yale in 1899, De Forest experimented with early wireless communications to ships at sea and to moving passenger trains. He eventually earned more than 300 U.S. and foreign patents in fields such as broadcasting, wire communications, sound on film, and high-speed facsimile.

De Forest was one of radio's most energetic and imaginative early promoters. On his honeymoon in Paris in 1908, he hung an aerial from the Eiffel Tower, set up a transmitter at the tower's base, and broadcast a program of gramophone records heard up to 500 miles away. In early 1910, he broadcast two operas from New York's Metropolitan Opera House. He also demonstrated radio at the 1915 San Francisco World's Fair.

De Forest began experimental broadcasting in 1907 and got his own station in New York in 1916. In addition to music, he broadcast news of the 1916 presidential election. Those reports, however, were taken straight out of the newspapers – and relayed the papers' mistaken reports that Charles Evans Hughes had defeated Woodrow Wilson. De Forest went on to form several companies, including one of the nation's leading vacuum-tube makers.

THOMAS LETTS

See also Broadcast Pioneers; Radio Technology

Further Reading

De Forest, Lee, *Father of Radio: The Autobiography of Lee De Forest,* Chicago: Wilcox & Follett, 1950
Douglas, George H., *The Early Days of Radio Broadcasting,* Jefferson, North Carolina: McFarland, 1987
Hilliard, Robert L., and Michael C. Keith, *The Broadcast Century: A Biography of American Broadcasting,* Boston: Focal, 1992

Design Trade Organizations and Trade Press

With the advancement of printing technologies in the early 1900s, the increasing use of visuals in print media created a growing marketplace for the work of illustrators, photographers, and designers. Like most professionals, these visual communicators formed groups to further their personal development and to speak collectively for improvement in their working environments.

By the early 1990s, there were nearly 200 groups serving publication design professionals. Of this very large collection, three are especially noteworthy for their breadth of membership or significance to the profession as a whole.

The American Institute of Graphic Arts (AIGA), a national organization formed in 1914 and continuing into the late 1990s, promoted excellence in the graphic design profession. Based on the strength of its network of local chapters throughout the country, the AIGA annually sponsored several hundred programs and events focusing on developments in design, technology, and business.

The AIGA promoted the graphic design profession through competitions, publications, educational activities, and projects in the public interest. *Graphic Design USA* was the organization's annual collection of works from national AIGA competitions and portfolios of artists awarded special honor by the AIGA.

In 1978, journalists involved with the first seminar on newspaper design held at the American Press Institute agreed to produce a newsletter to keep each other informed about design trends. Within the year, interest in the group had grown dramatically, and by January 1979, the structure of a new professional organization called the Society of Newspaper Designers was in place.

In the society's first year, members held a newspaper design workshop attended by more than 150 people, produced programs for the American Society of Newspaper Editors and the Associated Press Managing Editors, and created a videotape, *News by Design,* that became a focal point of change in the newspaper industry. When the first edition of *DESIGN: The Journal of the Society of Newspaper Designers* was published in March 1980, membership had grown to nearly 200 professionals without any organized membership drive.

At the 1981 annual workshop, the organization changed its name to the Society of Newspaper Design (SND) to more appropriately reflect its members' interest in the profession and not themselves. That year, the SND also began publication of *The Best of Newspaper Design,* a collection of winning entries from its annual design competition. The book quickly became a window on the changing landscape of publication design and an idea sourcebook for visual communication techniques.

Incorporated as a union, the Graphic Artists Guild was the largest advocacy association for professional graphic designers in the United States. Organized by geographic chapters, the guild provided educational programs and professional business guidance for its members.

The guild established ethical and business standards for its membership and annually produced *Pricing and Ethical Guidelines,* a handbook that served as the "bible" of the graphics design profession. The Joint Ethics Committee of the Guild served as a mediation and arbitration forum for the resolution of business disputes. Unlike other professional organizations, the guild did not conduct any competitions. Membership was open to all disciplines of the graphic arts and was available to freelance and staff artists.

MICHAEL WILLIAMS

Further Reading

Matlock, C. Marshall, *The Best of Newspaper Design,* 15th ed., Rockport, Massachusetts: Rockport, 1994
Meggs, Philip B., *A History of Graphic Design,* New York: Van Nostrand Reinhold, 1983; London: Allen Lane, 1983

Development Communication

Use of media to improve living conditions around the world

Development communication concerns the use of the media to improve living and human conditions. Much of the work in this interdisciplinary field has studied the planning, implementation, and evaluation of projects that promote development.

Media forms, such as radio, help countries solve their problems.
(Courtesy of Lucila Vargas)

Although most development communicators have applied their ideas and expertise in third world settings, this field emerged in the United States. It thus was shaped largely by U.S. scholarship and foreign aid policies. It originated during the growth of agricultural extension efforts of the 1940s and came of age in the 1960s, as the United States increased its foreign aid to the developing world.

Working within a liberal-capitalist framework, the field's pioneers (e.g., Daniel Lerner, Wilbur Schramm, David McClelland, and Everett Rogers) equated development with economic growth, individual freedom, literacy, and Western-style democracy. For them, history was a unilinear process whose most advanced state was the industrialized West. The poverty-stricken countries were "underdeveloped" because of their traditional practices, beliefs, and attitudes. Since these pioneers also understood communication as the transfer of information, what came to be known as the "modernization paradigm" stressed mass media's power to persuade traditional societies to adopt innovative (mainly Western) ideas, practices, and technologies.

In addition to their marked optimism regarding the media's potential to effect social change, modernization theorists viewed the use of mass media itself as an indicator of development. Consequently, in the 1960s, development experts thought that nations needed at least five radios, two televisions, 10 newspapers, and two cinema seats per 100 people to be considered modern. One could see the global impact of modernization theory in many developing countries' national policies that, in the 1990s, still strongly favored investment in modern communication technologies.

When it became evident in the 1970s that this modernization approach had failed to yield the expected results, the entire field of development studies entered into a period of self-examination and profound criticism. In development communication, dissenting third world, European, and U.S. scholars (mostly Marxists or neo-Marxists) called for a par-

adigm shift. They criticized the modernization school for its ethnocentrism, its emphasis on the individual, and its neglect of issues of political economy. Many of these critical scholars stressed the social structural causes of underdevelopment. For example, the advocates of dependency theory focused on neocolonialism and the evolution of world markets. They argued that the wealth and industrialization of the core (Europe and North America) was intrinsically linked to the poverty of the periphery (Third World).

Concurrently, many communication researchers questioned the hypodermic needle, or bullet, theory of the media and its view of the audience as passive receivers of media messages. Media studies became infused with concepts from semiotics and with other theories of the generation of meaning that emphasized the active role of the audience. Because most media projects before the 1980s lacked a minimal understanding of their audiences, these concepts had far-reaching consequences for development communication.

The theoretical reshaping of the field's parent disciplines gave rise to several approaches that are often grouped under the term "another development." These approaches underlined the social, ethical, cultural, and spiritual dimensions of development. "Another development" means not just economic growth but also social justice and the empowerment of disenfranchised people. While the modernization school viewed non-Western indigenous cultures as obstacles to development, these alternative approaches understood local cultural practices and institutions as a resource base upon which development should be constructed. As a consequence, the field came to include folk media and indigenous communication practices.

Since these approaches assumed that the success of development efforts depends largely on grassroots participation, the media's role shifted from being a multiplier of top-down, persuasive messages to becoming a facilitator of horizontal communication. Improving the local communication of impoverished communities became the principal goal of many contemporary projects. Participatory communication is a catalyst for development, but it also confers a significant benefit in itself, because, as these alternative models assume, access to media is a necessary precondition for the basic human right to communicate.

Finally, one needs to distinguish development communication from the development (or developmental) theory of the press, which states that in newly independent countries all media resources must be enlisted in the service of nation building, thus giving control of the press to the government. While numerous projects have been linked to local governments, many others have been sponsored by international aid agencies and nongovernmental organizations, such as churches. Typical projects have used media to support health campaigns, to boost ethnic pride, or to disseminate agricultural knowledge.

LUCILA VARGAS

Further Reading

Hornik, Robert C., *Development Communication: Information, Agriculture, and Nutrition in the Third World,* New York: Longman, 1988

Melkote, Srinivas R., *Communication for Development in the Third World*, Newbury Park, California, and New Delhi, India: Sage, 1991

Moemeka, Andrew A., ed., *Communicating for Development: A New Pan-Disciplinary Perspective*, Albany: State University of New York Press, 1994

Mowlana, Hamid, and Laurie J. Wilson, *The Passing of Modernity: Communication and the Transformation of Society*, White Plains, New York: Longman, 1990

Dime Novels

Form of nineteenth-century popular literature

In 1946, the Grolier Club in New York exhibited "one hundred influential American books printed before 1900." One of these *Maleska, the Indian Wife of the White Hunter*, was a tale of western adventure by Ann Sophia Stephens that had been published in 1860. Exhibit organizers included the 10-cent, paper-covered novel "not for what it is, but for what it started." *Maleska* was the first in a series of books called "Beadle Dime Novels," and as such, it inaugurated a form of popular literature – mass market fiction – that continues to influence our culture today. Although they were called novels, *Maleska* and the other works issued by Erastus Beadle, his brother Irwin, and partner Robert Adams were fairly short; they were generally 4-by-6-inch, paper-covered pamphlets of about 100 pages. Most of these early dime novels chronicled the adventures of pioneer heroes such as Daniel Boone, Kit Carson, Davy Crockett, and Sam Houston, and the more mythical Buffalo Bill and Deadwood Dick.

The Beadle brothers invented the dime novel in 1860 after they had experimented with other inexpensive books. Erastus Flavel Beadle began his publishing career by issuing "Dime Song Books," cheap, paper-covered books filled with popular songs and ballads. Next, he created an inexpensive series of handbooks on riding, cricket, football, and letter writing. In the summer of 1860, Beadle, together with his partners, issued the first dime novel, *Maleska*. As a pioneer in the field of cheap publishing for a mass audience, Beadle developed new strategies to ensure the regular sale of books produced on a large scale. He employed a system of uniform packaging and adopted formulas that could be used by any number of writers to create stories for a readership that had changing tastes. These strategies brought tremendous success. In 1864, a writer in the *North American Review* reported that Beadle's Dime Books had sold "in aggregate" 5 million copies. These phenomenal sale figures garnered Beadle and his partners a great deal of attention; they also encouraged other enterprising publishers to seek a share of the market.

In the 1860s, rival publishing houses such as Norman L. Munro, Dick and Fitzgerald, George Munro, and Chaney and Williams issued sea stories, romances, and frontier tales to compete with Beadle's offerings. In the 1880s, firms like

Beadle's dime novels were very popular with youths of the 1890s.
(Reproduced from the Collections of the Library of Congress)

Street and Smith and Frank Tousey came to dominate the field of inexpensive fiction. Although production was centered in New York City, the novels were not confined to this particular region. Dime novels traversed great distances to reach their readers. Beadle and Adams, as well as its competitors, relied on the U.S. Post Office and the American News Company to convey literary wares to newsstands across the country. Publishers shipped their publications in bulk to newsstands, whose agents sold the individual novels to the public. Some members of the reading public may have paid publishers a subscription fee to receive a particular dime novel series through the mail.

Because dime novels attracted many children as readers, they inevitably also attracted the attention of Anthony Comstock and other purity crusaders of the late nineteenth century who worried that the books' themes – detective stories and tales of the Old West – would lead the youth astray. One response to this threat to the market came from Beadle, who drafted a list of suggestions that he passed on to his authors that pointed out ways to make the volumes morally uplifting.

By the close of the nineteenth century, observers commented on the disappearance of the dime novel. One Harvard student began his commencement speech in 1899 with a query on the theme, "How are we to account for the decline of the dime novel?" Various scholars have puzzled over this same question. Observers in the late nineteenth and early twentieth century attributed the extinction of the dime novel to a decrease in the quality of dime novel fiction, increased competition in the market from other leisure forms, and outright sensationalism that made other forms of literature more alluring. Michael Denning, whose work *Mechanic Accents* examines the dime novel's place in nineteenth-century working-class culture, suggests that factors contributing to its demise may have been competition from the Sunday newspapers; "the emergence of inexpensive slick and pulp magazines in the 1890s"; "the International Copyright Agreement of 1891, which ended the pirating of British and European fiction that had generated much of the profit of the cheap books and series"; and "John Lovell's attempt to create a cheap book trust," which failed in the Panic of 1893.

Nostalgia for the dime novel grew as the U.S. public witnessed its extinction. Various book collectors turned their attention to this once-popular literature. They created clubs in which they exchanged knowledge about the history and development of these early mass-market books. One club, the Happy Hour Brotherhood, left as its legacy the *Dime Novel Round-Up*, a periodical providing a forum for new scholarship on this extremely popular and ephemeral form of nineteenth-century literature.

TRUDI ABEL

See also Book Publishing in the Nineteenth Century; Mass Market Book Publishing, Mass Media and Self-Regulation

Further Reading

"Beadle's Dime Books," *North American Review* (July 1864)

Bellows, Robert Peabody, "The Degeneration of the Dime Novel," *The Writer* 12 (July 1899)

Denning, Michael, *Mechanic Accents: Dime Novels and Working-Class Culture in America,* New York and London: Verso, 1987

Johannsen, Albert, *The House of Beadle and Adams and Its Dime and Nickel Novels: The Story of a Vanished Literature,* 2 vols., Norman: University of Oklahoma Press, 1950

Robinson, Henry Morton, "The Dime Novel is Dead, but the Same Old Hungers are Still Fed," *The Century Magazine* 116 (May 1928)

Shove, Raymond Howard, *Cheap Book Production in the United States, 1870 to 1891,* Urbana: University of Illinois Library, 1937

Stern, Madeleine B., ed., *Publishers for Mass Entertainment in Nineteenth Century America,* Boston: G.K. Hall, 1980

Direct Mail Advertising

Mail-order shopping dates from late 1800s

Direct mail is an advertising medium in which a printed message requesting a response is addressed to a specific person or jobholder and delivered by mail to a home or business. Direct mail traditionally has taken the form of postcards, letters, folders, circulars, catalogs, invitations, samples, or research. Ward's 1995 Business Directory reported 136 direct mail advertising services and 251 catalog and mail-order houses; the combined dollar value of the business was estimated to be $27.5 billion.

The Business Address Company of New York, established in 1880, is considered the first mailing house in the United States, although the New York Life Insurance Company was using mail promotions as early as 1872. Buckley-Dement, founded in Chicago in 1905, was the first direct mail agency. The first direct mail trade publication was distributed in 1916; the Direct Mail Advertising Association (DMAA) was founded in 1917, and 528 people attended the DMAA 1918 convention. Other agencies were established in the 1920s, but the majority of agencies still in existence at the end of the century were founded in the 1950s.

The early field of direct mail encompassed lettershop users and a few catalog publishers. The first mailed catalogs featured fishing and camping gear. In 1872, Montgomery Ward mailed its catalog; Sears, Roebuck and Company followed in 1886. When Richard Sears launched the Sears credit card in 1910, he facilitated the long-term use of mail order, but decades passed before the catalog business came into its own.

Retail stores and industrial advertisers fueled the direct mail industry during the early twentieth century. In 1926, the launch of the Book-of-the-Month Club spearheaded continuity programs. While occasional political notices were mailed during this period, it was the founding of the March of Dimes in 1930 that propagated the use of direct mail for fund-raising purposes.

Starting in the 1970s, the mail-order business came into its own. With the increased number of women in the workplace and the new premium put on time, the number of catalogs surged. Companies such as L.L. Bean, Land's End, Lillian Vernon, and Spiegel became household names. Roger Horchow started a groundswell for upscale catalogues in 1972. Purveyors of luxury goods, such as Neiman Marcus, Steuben, and Tiffany, continued to direct their offerings to niche markets. By the late twentieth century, many of the more general catalogs, geared to lower-middle-class families, started to disappear; Montgomery Ward, for example, withdrew its catalog in 1985.

Technology advanced the status of direct mail. Computers allowed for merge/purge programs – enabling the elimination of duplicate mailings and, more importantly, the establishment of databases. This allowed advertisers to create promotions designed to prompt specific responses; for example, product re-trials. Niches became even more specialized, and relationship marketing was established. The electronic information highway began to broaden the definition of direct mail. Subscriber services, such as CompuServe and America Online, offered consumers and small businesses direct access to promotional offers via electronic mail.

PATRICIA B. ROSE

See also Niche Theory

Further Reading

Hoke, Henry R., Jr., "At 75, DMA is Poised for Growth," *Direct Marketing* 55:6 (October 1992), pp. 62 ff

Russell, Thomas, and W. Ronald Lane, *Kleppner's Advertising Procedure*, 12th ed., Englewood Cliffs, New Jersey: Prentice-Hall, 1993

Sackheim, Maxwell, *My First 65 Years in Advertising*, Blue Ridge Summit, Pennsylvania: Tab, 1975

Stone, Bob, "Direct Marketing: Then and Now," *Direct Marketing* (May 1988)

Docudramas

Dramatic recreation of actual historical events

The docudrama form traces its history to literature, theater, film, radio, and even a few "live" television anthology dramas from the 1950s and early 1960s in such series as *Hallmark Hall of Fame, Armstrong Circle Theater,* and *Profiles in Courage.* Distinctive for the dramatic recreation of actual events from the lives of real people, both famous and unrenowned, docudramas spur debate over the tension between fact and fiction that is embodied in its name. The charge is often lodged that reality is too easily distorted in this form under the guise of poetic license. The resulting controversies that arise around specific docudramas, moreover, are typically heightened by the power and influence of television in general.

The docudrama enjoyed an extraordinary level of success on prime-time television during the last quarter of the twentieth century. Fewer than 100 television programs could have qualified as bona fide docudramas prior to 1970. In the 1971–72 season, however, ABC initiated the explosive rise of the fact-based drama, in part to boost its share of the young adult, urban audience. ABC probed headlines for television movie topics that were high-concept, relevant, and attention-grabbing, topics well suited to the docudrama.

The television movie form was ideally geared to the currency of most docudramatic ideas because of its gestation period of only six months to a year; a telefeature could be produced and telecast while the newsworthiness of the subject was still fresh. The first case to actually beat the half-year threshold was the July 4, 1976, Israeli raid on the airport at Entebbe, Uganda, in order to rescue a planeload of hostages. On December 13, 1976, ABC premiered *Victory at Entebbe,* a big-budget docudrama starring Kirk Douglas, Richard Dreyfuss, Burt Lancaster, and Elizabeth Taylor.

Most importantly, the production of made-for-television movies skyrocketed in the 1970s, leaving all three networks desperate for 30 to 50 workable television movie ideas a year. The *ABC Movie of the Week,* in particular, produced a movie a week for 39 weeks over six straight seasons. The docudrama resulted in large part from this relentless demand for more producible and easily accessible television movie concepts.

ABC first started its experiments in feature-length reality programming when it premiered *Brian's Song* on November 30, 1971. Attracting 44 million viewers, this real life melodrama chronicled the interracial friendship between two professional football players, Brian Piccolo (played by James Caan) and Gayle Sayers (Billy Dee Williams), and the slow cancerous deterioration and death of Piccolo. Piccolo's illness was presented in what became the typical "disease-of-the-week" fashion, complete with bedside goodbyes and a profusion of sentiment and tears. *Brian's Song* showed, therefore, how the made-for-television docudrama could blend aspects of the documentary and narrative modes, with the demands of fiction usually taking precedence on prime time.

The docudrama genre actually flourished so rapidly that it accounted for one-third of all television movies by 1975–76. That season was the verifiable turning point on which the notion of fact-inspired recreations was broadened to include celebrated events and figures from history. ABC led the way again with *Eleanor and Franklin,* which dramatized the early years and beginning political career of Franklin (Edward Herrmann) and Eleanor (Jane Alexander) Roosevelt. Winning nine Emmy Awards, this historical approach raised the profile of the docudrama and brought increased complaints from historians and journalists over fabrications in plot and distortions in dialogue.

Helter Skelter became the most-watched docudrama in television history when more than 60 million people tuned in on April 1 and 2, 1976. This CBS presentation, based on the Charles Manson "family" and the trial involving the Tate-Labianca murders in the 1960s, pulled a consecutive 57 and 60 share of the prime-time audience. After the success of *Helter Skelter,* the docudrama was firmly entrenched as a prime-time staple on network television.

ABC, CBS, and NBC together averaged more than 50 docudramas annually during the 1980s, and this output continued into the 1990s. Newsworthy events, national issues and controversies, and bits of historical lore and legend were still the genre's forte. The docudrama came to be identified with a small-screen, televisual style and, in the 1980s and 1990s, also became linked to a rising interest in television news and infotainment, especially of the tabloid variety.

Headline-hunting excesses became a spiraling ethical dilemma for the docudrama over the last decades of the twentieth century. Part of a wider surge in so-called trash-television programming, "fact-based" dramatizations from history and "real life" included numerous examples that aggressively exploited existing media scandals, such as the cases of Amy Fisher, Heidi Fleiss (the "Hollywood madam"), and O.J. Simpson. As a result, the need to act responsibly, recreate events faithfully, and protect the rights and reputations of the people being represented, created greater challenges for docudrama producers.

GARY R. EDGERTON

See also Broadcast Documentaries; Documentary Photography; Motion Picture Documentaries

Further Reading

Brode, Douglas, "Video Verite: Defining the Docudrama," *Television Quarterly* 20:1 (1984)

Carveth, Rod, "Amy Fisher and the Ethics of 'Headline' Docudramas," *Journal of Popular Film and Television* 21:3 (Fall 1993), pp. 121–127

Davidson, Bill, "Fact or Fiction: Television Docudramas," in *Understanding Television: Essays on Television as a Social and Cultural Force,* edited by Richard P. Adler, New York: Praeger, 1981

Edgerton, Gary, "High Concept, Small Screen: Reperceiving the Industrial and Stylistic Origins of the American Made-for-TV Movie," *Journal of Popular Film and Television* 19:3 (Fall 1991), pp. 114–127

Hoffer, Thomas W., and Richard Alan Nelson, "Evolution of Docudrama on American Television Networks: Content Analysis, 1966–1978," *Southern Speech Communication Journal* 4:1 (1980)

Marill, Alvin H., *Movies Made for Television: The Telefeature and the Mini-Series, 1964–1986,* New York: Zoetrope, 1987

Musburger, Robert S., "Setting the Stage for the Television Docudrama," *Journal of Popular Film and Television* 13:2 (1985)

Rose, Brian G., ed., *TV Genres: A Handbook and Reference Guide,* Westport, Connecticut: Greenwood, 1985

Schneider, Alfred, "Preserving the Integrity of the Docudrama," *Television Quarterly* 26:2 (1992), pp. 75–81

Documentary Photography

Attempts to present the subject candidly, without manipulation

Nearly all photographs can be considered documents in the broadest sense of the word because of their ability to show evidence or proof about the subject depicted. However, not all photographers produce work that can be described as documentary.

Attempting to define documentary photography brings varied responses, but most would agree that to produce it, photographers use a straightforward approach, attempting to candidly capture the subject while influencing the situation as little as possible. In other words, the subject normally is not manipulated or controlled by the photographer in the genre known as documentary.

Much of what is considered documentary photography would more accurately be described as social documentary. The distinction between the two primarily involves the photographer's intention. Social documentarians usually have a perspective they are trying to convey about difficult social issues, so sometimes they are known as social reformers, which acknowledges their attempt to influence current conditions.

One of the best-known social reformers in the United States was Jacob A. Riis, whose writing and photography about New York City's tenements was published in *How the Other Half Lives* (1890). Born in Denmark in 1849, Riis immigrated in 1870 to the United States, where for three years he lived in poverty before joining the staff of a news bureau as a reporter. In 1878, he became a reporter for the Associated Press and the *New York Tribune,* assigned to police headquarters on Mulberry Street, which was surrounded by slums packed with immigrants.

In the late 1880s, seeking graphic illustrations for articles for his new employer, the *New York Sun,* Riis employed two amateur photographers whose work has mistakenly been credited to him. Soon thereafter, Riis began using large, cumbersome camera equipment to show the human misery and degradation he found inside the tenements and police lodging houses, which he documented for a 10-year period. In addition to publishing a dozen books, Riis also gave countless lectures using lantern slides, which were popular with middle-class audiences.

At the turn of the century, Riis was known as the "Emancipator of the Slums." He since has been credited by some as the founding father of documentary photography, although there were other forerunners to this genre of photography, including John Thompson's depiction of London's street merchants and working class in the late 1870s.

Wisconsin native Lewis Hine followed in Riis's footsteps by using the camera to document the lives of immigrants, especially those Europeans who arrived at Ellis Island shortly after the turn of the twentieth century. This five-year project, published in 1908 in *Charity and the Commons* (later called *Survey Graphic*), was among the earliest works to combine photographs and text.

Trained as a sociologist, Hine masterfully turned his camera on a variety of ills in U.S. life, calling his approach "social photography." In 1911, he was appointed the official photographer for the National Child Labor Committee to explore child labor conditions in U.S. factories, mines, textile mills, fields, and canneries. Hine's photographs were credited with providing shocking evidence of the need for legislative changes to protect children, encouraging them to receive an education before going to work.

His attitude toward his work changed around the time of World War I; rather than concentrating on what needed to be corrected, Hine turned his view camera on what had to be appreciated. The relief activities of the American Red Cross in Europe at the end of the war was the first example of his new approach to documentary work. In the early 1930s, Hine captured the construction of the Empire State Building in New York, which he combined with other life-affirming images of laborers in his book *Men at Work* (1932).

Bandit's Roost, 39¹/₂ Mulberry Street, **was part of Jacob Riis' documentary effort in the 1880s.**
(The Jacob A. Riis Collection #101, Museum of the City of New York)

Despite his success, Hine found it hard to make a living as a photographer by the late 1930s. Roy Stryker of the photographic section of the Resettlement Administration, later known as the Farm Security Administration (FSA), refused to hire Hine; numerous other, younger photographers went on to work for what became the best-known social documentary project in U.S. history.

Beginning in 1935, the federal government employed photographers to document the results of the Great Depression, especially its impact on the rural poor. During its seven-year existence, more than a dozen different FSA photographers created over 270,000 negatives and extensive captions, both of which received permanent housing in the Library of Congress. Some of the FSA photographers went on to have successful careers in magazines, including Dorothea Lange, Carl Mydans, Russell Lee, Arthur Rothstein, and Walker Evans.

Probably no other period in U.S. history has been covered as extensively as aspects of the depression. The view of the nation presented by FSA photographers, however, was from a decidedly New Deal perspective. "The fact that the FSA efforts were used for propagandistic purposes was not offensive, because this was dissemination of the 'truth,'" according to one author. FSA photographs and captions appeared in numerous publications throughout the country at the time, and in several exhibitions as well. Numerous photographic books on the FSA have since been published, including those of a general nature and those about how the FSA documented particular states.

During the depression, socially concerned photographers also found an outlet through the Photo League of New York. Nearly all prominent social documentarians of the day were associated with the League during its 15-year existence (1936–51), including Hine, Lange, and W. Eugene Smith. The society, known early in its existence for some of its radical, leftist photographers, appeared on the U.S. Attorney General's December 1947 list of "Totalitarian, Fascist, Communist and Subversive Organizations."

The social documentary tradition found its way into the work of several photojournalists after World War II. Smith, as well as some European-born photographers like Robert Capa, Henri Cartier-Bresson, Werner Bischof, and David Seymour ("Chim"), became known as concerned photographers, thanks to the humanistic concerns upon which they trained their cameras.

During the civil rights movement, various social documentarians, including Moneta Sleet Jr., Danny Lyons, Bruce Davidson, Charles Moore, and Leonard Freed, captured on film the struggle of black Americans. The pictures appeared in magazines ranging from *Ebony* and *Jet* to *Life*.

The tradition of exposing social ills continued at the end of the twentieth century with such concerned photographers as Donna Ferrato, who documented domestic violence; Eugene Richards, who documented drug abuse and the poor; and Sabastiao Salgado, who documented manual laborers. Many concerned photographers routinely published their work in single-subject books in addition to publishing in magazines and participating in exhibitions.

Countless other documentary photographers work in much the same way their predecessors did – by showing things that need to be corrected as well as things that need to be appreciated.

C. ZOE SMITH

See also Broadcast Documentaries; Motion Picture Documentaries; Photojournalism in the Twentieth Century; Riis, Jacob A.

Further Reading

Doherty, Robert J., *Social-Documentary Photography in the USA*, Garden City, New York: Amphoto, 1976
Featherstone, David, ed., *Observations*, Carmel, California: Friends of Photography, 1984
Goldberg, Vicki, *The Power of Photography: How Photographs Changed Our Lives,* New York: Abbeville, 1993
Newhall, Beaumont, *The History of Photography: From 1839 to the Present Day,* London: Secker and Warburg, 1972; New York: Museum of Modern Art, 1982
Rothstein, Arthur, *Documentary Photography*, Boston: Focal, 1986
Stange, Maren, *Symbols of Ideal Life: Social Documentary Photography in America, 1890–1950*, New York and Cambridge: Cambridge University Press, 1989
Stott, William, *Documentary Expression and Thirties America*, New York: Oxford University Press, 1973; London: Oxford University Press, 1976
Stryker, Roy E., "Documentary Photography," in *The Complete Photographer*, edited by Willard D. Morgan, New York: National Educational Alliance, 1942–43
Trachtenberg, Alan, *Reading American Photographs: Images as History, Mathew Brady to Walker Evans,* New York: Hill and Wang, 1989

Douglas, William O.

Supreme Court justice and free-speech advocate

William O. Douglas was appointed to the U.S. Supreme Court by President Franklin D. Roosevelt in 1939. The foundations of freedom were soon to be shaken by war, and freedom of expression became the most vulnerable of all freedoms.

Douglas made important rulings on basic freedoms, especially freedom of the press and of free speech during World War II and subsequent wars. Always, he felt that the statement of the First Amendment was absolute. He and a few others, such as fellow justice Hugo L. Black, became identified as absolutists.

For Douglas, however, war was not the only threat to the freedom of expression. The dramatic shifts in the moral climate during the 1950s and 1960s were of great concern to conservatives, who moved to stifle sexual explicitness. During Douglas's years on the Court, several obscenity cases came to test how the Bill of Rights was to interpret such language. In one 1957 case, *Roth* v. *United States*, Douglas gave uncompromising allegiance to the absoluteness of First Amendment expression and to the rational nature of the human mind. He wrote, "I have the same confidence in the ability of our people to reject noxious literature as I have in their capacity to sort out the true from the false in theology, economics, politics, or any other field."

When he retired from the Court in 1975, Douglas had served longer than any other justice – 36 years – offering opinions in more than 1,200 cases. He died in 1980 at the age of 84.

VAL E. LIMBURG

See also Black, Hugo Lafayette

Further Reading:
Countryman, Vern, ed., *The Douglas Opinions,* New York: Random House, 1977

Douglass, Frederick

Influential nineteenth-century African American journalist

Frederick Douglass was one of the most influential journalists, orators, and statesmen of the nineteenth century. The fact that he was an African American man born into slavery shaped every aspect of his long social and political life. He played a highly visible and influential role in the abolitionist movement, during the Civil War, and in Reconstruction and its aftermath. During the antebellum years, he published a version of his newspaper for 16 years, making him the most successful African American publisher of the era. He continued his journalistic activities well into the Reconstruction years.

Douglass was born a slave on the eastern shore of Maryland in 1817. Separated from his parents, he witnessed the daily horrors of the slave existence. At the age of eight, he was sent to Baltimore to work as a houseboy for a relative of his owner. During his teenage years, he learned the rudiments of reading from the master's wife and studied borrowed or stolen books and newspapers on the Baltimore docks, where he labored for his owner. He made a daring escape from slavery at the age of 21, when he fled to New York City and then to New Bedford, Massachusetts.

In New England, he was drawn into abolitionist activities and began a career as a lecturer after giving a riveting speech to an antislavery gathering in Nantucket, Massachusetts. He became a close associate of William Lloyd Garrison and began writing for the *Liberator* to gain a wider audience for his views. In 1845, he wrote his memoirs in the *Narrative of the Life of Frederick Douglass,* which presented an eloquent dramatization of his life in slavery. The *Narrative* and a subsequent autobiography, *My Bondage and My Freedom* (1855), were valuable and widely read texts for the abolitionist cause.

In 1847, Douglass launched his newspaper, the *North Star,* from his home in Rochester, New York, despite Garrison's discouragement. Armed with funds from British abolitionists, Douglass announced in the prospectus that the

Frederick Douglass
(Reproduced from the Collections of the Library of Congress)

North Star would "Attack Slavery in all its forms and aspects" and "promote the Moral and Intellectual improvement of the Colored People." Douglass's newspapers lived up to this motto and became a principal forum for the debate on slavery and race relations. In 1851, he changed the journal's name to *Frederick Douglass' Paper.* When funding became scarce in 1859, Douglass had to suspended publication of the newspaper, but he quickly returned with *Douglass' Monthly,* which continued until 1863. After the Civil War, Douglass moved to Washington, D.C., and founded the *New National Era* (1870–74), which chronicled the excitement and progress of Reconstruction. He died in 1895.

JANE RHODES

See also Abolitionist Press; African American Media

Further Reading

Blight, David W., *Frederick Douglass' Civil War: Keeping Faith in Jubilee,* Baton Rouge: Louisiana State University Press, 1989

Fishkin, Shelley Fisher, and Carla L. Peterson, "'We Hold These Truths to be Self-Evident': The Rhetoric of Frederick Douglass's Journalism," in *Frederick Douglass; New Literary and Historical Essays,* edited by Eric J. Sundquist, New York and Cambridge: Cambridge University Press, 1990

McFeely, William S., *Frederick Douglass,* New York: Norton, 1991

Quarles, Benjamin, *Frederick Douglass,* Washington, D.C.: Associated, 1948

E

Economics of Book Publishing

Products that fill a direct audience need

With the creation of the United States came a book industry. Then, as always, three components defined this industry:

1.) Publication: Publishers contract with authors to create a manuscript and then turn that single copy into thousands of finished books. Hardcovers were the rule until the mid-twentieth century; paperbacks dominated after that.

2.) Distribution: The publisher (or a subcontracted party) ships books to stores – originally by wagon, then by rail, and, during the late twentieth century, almost exclusively by truck and air. (As the telephone became more common in the twentieth century, book publishers also sold more and more titles directly to the public.)

3.) Bookselling: The public generally purchases books at specialized bookshops but also acquires titles at various emporia and through mail-order book clubs, as well as borrowing from public and university libraries. (Until the 1950s, it was also possible to rent best-sellers for a few cents a day.)

From its beginnings, the book industry in the United States provided a product filling a direct need, be it religious training, pursuing interests during leisure time, or simply learning something new. Unlike newspapers, magazines, radio, and television, books generally carry no advertising. Success in the book industry is measured by titles sold, not ratings and rates charged to advertisers.

By the late eighteenth century, printers began publishing books, importing the necessary technology, and adapting means of distribution from experienced European publishers. For 100 years thereafter, books were expensive to produce and so remained the province of the well-to-do. Still, the nineteenth century was not without change in the book industry. More and more people in the United States learned to read, thus expanding the potential audience. Better printing techniques lowered the cost of production. The advent of the railroad enabled books to be shipped to all parts of the growing nation. Slowly, the book industry increased in size, and as the strictly elite audience gave way to a mass market, a handful of titles became best-sellers. Less renowned were the hundreds of publishers acquiring and manufacturing thousands of textbooks and specialized tomes.

A revolutionary transformation in the book industry – the coming of low-cost paperbacks – began with the introduction of the dime novel during the latter part of the nineteenth century. Yet change took time, and so as late as the Great Depression of the 1930s, buying a book still meant a costly hardcover. A true mass market developed only during the 1940s and 1950s, with the large-scale printing and distribution of low-priced paperback editions, costing just 25 cents a copy to own. One could buy handy works such as Benjamin Spock's *Pocket Book of Baby and Child Care* and such scandalous reads as J.D. Salinger's *The Catcher in the Rye* in bus stations, from newsstands, and in department stores, as well as at traditional bookstores. As late as 1949, hardcover trade books and paperbacks sold in equal proportions; 50 years later, paperbacks dominated sales of books produced and sold.

Mass sellers, called trade books, dominated the headlines and topped the best-seller lists. Each year, however, millions of textbooks – aimed at college, high school, and elementary school students – were written and sold. Textbooks could be purchased in the nation's thousands of college and university bookstores or were provided directly to secondary and elementary school students. The key economic difference is that, in the textbook market, those who selected the books (the instructor or a committee) and those who bought them (the student or the taxpayer) were not the same individuals. Specialized books, aimed at small, specific audiences such as scholars, members of religious organizations, or enthusiasts of all stripes, rarely made a best-seller list or made an author rich, but they did contribute to the diversity and range of ideas and beliefs in the United States.

Since 1950, with the rise of the mass paperback seller, a vast expansion of public education, and a growing audience of educated readers, the book industry in the United States saw sales increase annually by double-digit percentages. By the close of the 1980s, the book industry was properly labeled a big business, with total sales well in excess of $10 billion a year, a listing of publishers topping 30,000, and bookstores found in every mall and shopping center.

This growth led to mergers and acquisitions in the book industry. During the 1960s, for example, Random House was purchased by RCA (then owner of NBC), and Holt, Rinehart, and Winston, itself the product of two mergers, became part of CBS. That the two leading television networks would purchase important book companies underlined that television did not destroy the book industry in the United States (as some doomsayers had predicted) but that it instead fueled interest in reading and book purchase. During the 1980s, a second wave of mergers took place. So, for example, industry leader Simon and Schuster became even bigger by taking over textbook giant Prentice Hall.

Like most industries in the United States, the book publishing industry had become more and more a part of a conglomerate structure. Diversified publishers functioned as part of massive diversified business organizations such as Time Warner, the world's largest media corporation, and Rupert Murdoch's News, Inc., one of the most ruthless. The largest publisher of books based in the United States as the twentieth century ended was Simon and Schuster, owned by conglomerate Viacom, which was more noted for its Paramount Hollywood studio than as a publisher of hundreds of trade and textbook titles each year.

Often, book publishers were located in conglomerates more famous for other mass media products. The Newhouse newspaper chain owned the Random House and Knopf imprints. Magazine publisher Reader's Digest ranked high in book publishing. McGraw-Hill, best known for its business information services and magazine *Business Week,* was a powerhouse in the book industry.

These mega-publishers created trade, religious, and reference books, as well as textbooks and sometimes even scholarly books. Before World War II, book publishers were typically small enterprises, a family partnership only operating in the United States. By the 1990s, more than half of all book publishers in the United States were controlled by vast multinational corporations with billions of dollars of assets, involved in many forms of media production and distribution, international in scope, and with shares of stock listed on major stock exchanges.

Still, the book industry remained one of the more open and least concentrated of the mass media industries, particularly at the level of specialized book publishing. It remained an economic fact of life that many of the 60,000 works published each year sold but a few thousand copies and were issued by small regional publishing houses.

Yet like Hollywood stars, best-selling authors could and did become very rich and famous. The works of Harold Robbins, Irving Wallace, Louis L'Amour, Janet Dailey, and Barbara Cartland, by the close of the twentieth century, had sold hundreds of millions of copies and made these authors millionaires many times over. Only industry outsiders were shocked when author Tom Clancy, master of the so-called techno-thriller, was reported to earn $15 million a year or when Pope John Paul II received an advance in excess of $5 million from Random House for his *Crossing the Threshold of Hope.*

This continued growth and prosperity led to greater and greater integration of book publishing with other mass media industries. Trade books were regularly previewed through magazine and newspaper excerpts, and aspiring author-superstars hawked their latest works on television talk shows. Best-sellers were regularly turned into feature films and television movies and miniseries. Indeed, by the close of the twentieth century, authors were beginning to write books aimed not at millions of readers but at those handful of Hollywood executives who could turn them into blockbusters and make the author-turned-screenwriter a multimillionaire through participation in a blockbuster and its sequels.

Readers came to expect authors to have their books read on tape as "audio editions" pitched at the growing numbers listening on home cassette players and car stereos. The book industry in the twenty-first century promised even more technological experimentation, principally through electronic publishing on floppy disks, CD-ROMs, and the Internet.

Yet, even with the imposition of Hollywood and all possible innovations, the printed word survived, even thrived. Bookstores constituted one of the fastest-growing segments in retailing in the United States. Both discount stores (such as Crown Books, which sold even current best-sellers at 25 percent off) and the so-called superstores (such as Borders, which stocked well in excess of 100,000 books including trade, textbooks, and specialized titles) could be found in cities of all sizes across the United States. As the book industry in the United States turned into the twenty-first century, it was prospering as never before in its history.

DOUGLAS GOMERY

See also Best-Sellers; Book Clubs; Book Publishing in the Eighteenth Century; Book Publishing in the Nineteenth Century; Book Publishing in the Twentieth Century; Dime Novels; Mass Market Book Publishing; Paperback Books; Textbook Publishing; Trade Book Publishing

Further Reading

Alexander, Alison, James Owers, and Rod Carveth, eds., *Media Economics: Theory and Practice,* Hillsdale, New Jersey: Lawrence Erlbaum, 1993

Compaine, Benjamin M., *The Book Industry in Transition: An Economic Study of Book Distribution and Marketing,* White Plains, New York: Knowledge Industry, 1978

Coser, Lewis A., Charles Kadushin, and Walter W. Powell, *Books: The Culture and Commerce of Publishing,* New York: Basic, 1982

Davis, Kenneth C., *Two-Bit Culture: The Paperbacking of America,* Boston: Houghton Mifflin, 1984

Dessauer, John P., *Book Publishing: The Basic Introduction,* New York: Continuum, 1989

Madison, Charles A., *Book Publishing in America,* New York: McGraw-Hill, 1966

Miller, William, *The Book Industry,* New York: Columbia University Press, 1949

Smith, Datus Clifford, Jr., *A Guide to Book Publishing,* rev. ed., Seattle: University of Washington Press, 1989

Economics of Broadcasting

Spectrum scarcity, government regulation shaped economics

Often overlooked in studies of radio and television content, social impact, and regulation and policy is an understanding of broadcasting as an economic entity. This is an unfortunate oversight, as economic issues have always been a factor in regulatory policy and, by extension, in determining the type of programming made available to an audience.

Historically, scarcity has been the most salient economic factor in broadcasting. The scarcity of spectrum space led the government to institute a system of licensing broadcasters in the 1920s based on an ill-defined "public interest" standard borrowed from transportation regulation. Beyond the physical limitations of the spectrum, the government's allocation and assignment policies institutionalized scarcity by setting standards on to whom, where, and under what conditions a license to broadcast would be granted.

The physical limit to the electromagnetic spectrum and the government's response to it led to and continued to support specific market structures in electronic media. Telephone and cable television, for example, have long operated as monopolies in their service areas. Deemed to be "natural" monopolies due to the large cost of physical construction and the disruptions caused to public rights-of-way by this construction, these services were historically given monopoly rights in their service areas in exchange for governmental oversight of rates and levels of service. By contrast, the radio broadcasting industry is considered by some observers to have a monopolistic competition market structure. Here, while a large group of stations compete for listener attention, only a limited number in any given mar-

ket compete for a specific audience. For example, while a large market may have dozens of radio signals, a small number (or in many cases, only one) would serve the audience interested in rap or country music.

Oligopoly is the term that best describes an economic structure in which a limited number of entities compete for the business of a specific audience. In an oligopoly, each of the small number of competitors in a given market has considerable knowledge of what other competitors are doing. This knowledge is a key component of an industry "culture" that leads each company to behave in ways remarkably similar to the other companies. The best example of the oligopolistic market structure in broadcasting is the Big Three networks (ABC, CBS, and NBC) and their affiliates in the various local markets. The Big Three traditionally shared a common set of operational norms on scheduling practices, program selection, relationship to regulatory bodies, and integration with advertisers. The oligopolistic market structure best describes the historical economic structure of the broadcast industry and still best describes the structure of the television segment of the industry.

After World War I and the U.S. government's decision to privatize the embryonic radio industry, two major, and problematic, results were soon evident. First, without coherent guidelines for spectrum use, so many companies and individuals desired access to the spectrum that interference soon became epidemic in larger cities, while many smaller

Television Advertising Expenditures 1949–1990 (per million dollars)

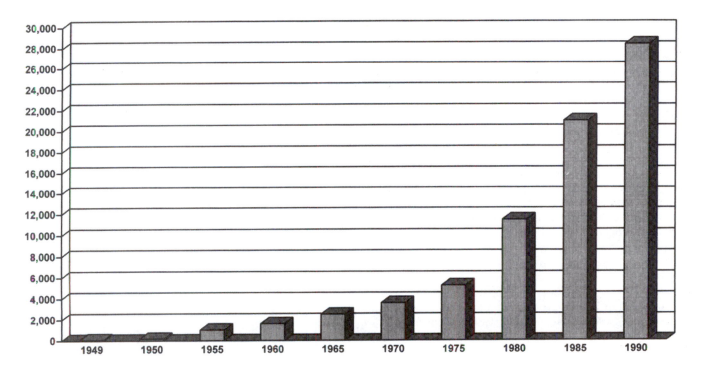

Source: *Datapedia of the United States 1790–2000: America Year by Year.* George Thomas Kurian (Bernan Press: Lanham, Maryland, 1994).

communities were left with little, if any, service. Second, a method of funding was needed to support the new industry. When American Telephone and Telegraph's WEAF in New York began to accept and promote "toll broadcasting" in 1922, it set in motion the idea that advertising would become the main source of economic support for the medium.

The commercialization of radio was nationalized with the founding of the major networks in the late 1920s and the passage of the Radio Act of 1927. The networks brought stability to the previously haphazard radio "industry" through their ability to offer advertisers access to a mass national audience attracted to the high-priced talent that only the networks could afford. The Radio Act established a licensing system that encouraged the growth of networks by strictly limiting the number of broadcast licenses and rejecting public subsidy of the broadcast industry. The system also required financial commitments from prospective licensees, which generally limited licenses to larger entities that tended to be co-owned or affiliated with a network. The general belief of the day was that the requirement that broadcast licensees operate in the "public interest, convenience, and necessity" would temper the worst excesses of commercialization.

As radio rapidly diffused to U.S. households in the 1930s, the Big Three networks developed a business policy that featured (1) a reliance on advertising to pay for programming; (2) increased power over the local stations, including such (later banned) requirements as affiliates must "option" time to the networks; and (3) the near-total abrogation of program scheduling to advertisers. The advertiser generally was the owner and packager of entertainment programming and simply purchased time from the networks to reach the national audience. The relatively minimal role played by the networks in designing program schedules was a remnant of the common carrier model, whereby the conduit owner (as in telegraphy and telephony) played no role in the content. The networks were in essence the classic "middle" of the distribution system – the essential link between advertisers and listeners. A mass audience was firmly established as the product of commercial broadcasting.

The television industry was in most respects an outgrowth of the well-established radio industry, as the major radio networks became the major television networks. As had been the case with radio, the federal government's television allocation policies favored the existing industry powers and further strengthened the Big Three oligopoly. The networks and their affiliates dominated the television industry from the beginning and, unlike radio, exerted control over program scheduling. This was the result of the much greater cost of television, which kept many advertisers from sponsoring entire programs; the recognition that the spreading of advertisements over several programs was a more effective technique in reaching a target audience than the sponsoring of a single program; and the government's pressure on networks to pay more attention to content that was deemed objectionable (such as violence) or fraudulent (as with quiz shows). While television by the late 1950s and early 1960s was *the* mass medium for most of the U.S. audience and the networks shifted most of their resources to

television, radio became a more localized medium tied increasingly to the recorded music industry.

The power of the Big Three in their relationships with local television and the program production industry was such that the federal government, as had been the case with radio in the early 1940s, began to place restrictions on network behavior with the prime-time access and financial interest and syndication rules in the early 1970s. At approximately the same time, the power of the networks and the advertising industry was further limited by the congressionally mandated ban on cigarette advertising, by federal restrictions on the amount and presentation of advertising aimed at children, and by limits on the number of stations that one owner could have and on cross-media ownership in a given market. Despite these restrictions on economic behavior, the networks and their affiliates continued to thrive as the access point for reaching the mass television audience.

The 1980s, with the rapid diffusion of cable television, were a time of uncertainty and concern in the broadcast television industry, with many observers claiming that cable television's multiple channels and ability to target specific niche audiences represented the future of the television medium. The dual revenue stream of cable, whereby revenue is collected from both advertisers and viewers, was regarded as another major advantage over broadcast television.

Despite the diffusion of cable to approximately two-thirds of U.S. households, the broadcast industry as a whole was thriving economically in the mid-1990s as it became apparent that broadcasting remained the only reliable means of reaching a mass, undifferentiated audience, a quality highly desired by most national advertisers. In addition, the doomsday arguments led the government in the 1990s to rescind or modify many restrictions on the broadcast industry, making the industry even more attractive to advertisers and investors. The inherent worth of broadcast delivery was further demonstrated by the success of Rupert Murdoch's Fox Broadcasting Company, which proved that a broadcast network could succeed in delivering specific demographics with a much greater reach than cable. Another important lesson of Fox's success was an increased recognition on the part of program producers of the importance of the guaranteed access to a mass audience that networks could provide in an increasingly fragmented television universe. This was considered to be the key factor in the establishment of Viacom's United Paramount Network and Time Warner's WB networks in January 1995.

Despite the seeming resurgence of broadcasting, the underlying economic base of the broadcast television industry had to be considered problematic. The audience shares of the traditional Big Three continued to decline in the 1990s, and the broadcast audience in general was older and less desirable to the advertiser. The advent of alternative delivery systems such as cable, VCRs, satellites, and (in all likelihood) the telephone, offered viewers and advertisers many new opportunities and outlets. The result was that broadcasting increasingly had to be seen as just one element (albeit a very important one) in the delivery of video programming to an audience, an element of a more encompassing media industry that had as its hallmarks consolidation and convergence. The merger-acquisitions of Time, Inc., and Warner Communications, Viacom and Paramount, Sony and Columbia, and others were all indicators that the Big Three networks were no longer the only, or even the dominant, players in the television business.

While some saw the proliferation of video channels as evidence of a more competitive market in television, the continuing period of economic consolidation could be regarded as evidence that the television industry of the future, while using various means to manufacture audiences (broadcast, videotape, pay-per-view, interactive services, etc.), would itself be controlled by a limited number of large multinational firms. Although a large number of channels would be available to viewers with the economic means to afford access, a limited number of product providers would exist in a given programming niche. The economic model of the television and video industry was expected to continue to be oligopolistic, with a small number of firms providing the programming to the viewer and the viewers to the advertising industry.

ROBERT V. BELLAMY JR.

See also Broadcast Advertising; Broadcast Licensing; Broadcast Regulation; Cable Networks; Cross-Media Ownership; Mass Media and Children; Media Conglomerates; Quiz Show Scandals; Radio Act of 1927; Radio Networks; Television and Violence; Television Networks

Further Reading

Alexander, Alison, James Owers, and Rod Carveth, eds., *Media Economics: Theory and Practice,* Hillsdale, New Jersey: Lawrence Erlbaum, 1993

McChesney, Robert W., *Telecommunications, Mass Media, and Democracy: The Battle for the Control of U.S. Broadcasting, 1928–1935,* New York: Oxford University Press, 1993; Oxford: Oxford University Press, 1994

Owen, Bruce M., and Steven S. Wildman, *Video Economics,* Cambridge, Massachusetts: Harvard University Press, 1992

Picard, Robert G., *Media Economics: Concepts and Issues,* Newbury Park, California: Sage, 1989

Economics of Magazine Publishing

Advertising, circulation pay the bills

Publishing, for most magazines, is a business for profit. Magazines earn money from various sources, in varying percentages. Some magazines derive all their revenue from advertising. Others – fewer – derive all revenues from the readers; that is, from circulation. Such publications carry no advertising. Many publications fall somewhere in the middle, with revenue coming from both advertising and circulation. In 1991, the Magazine Publishers of America reported an industry average for consumer magazines of 47 percent of revenues received from advertising and 53 percent from circulation.

In the United States in the 1990s, more than 20,000 publications could be classified as magazines, depending on the definition used. Generally, these fell into two major categories: consumer magazines and specialized business magazines (formerly called trade magazines).

Consumer magazines, for the most part, can be purchased on the newsstand. Some of these magazines, such as *Reader's Digest,* contain general interest editorial content. From the mid-1970s, consumer magazines became increasingly specialized, with publications on automobiles, crafts, and hair styling, as well as political commentary, business and money making, and environmental concerns. No hobby or collectible is neglected. Magazines focus on cities and regions; they provide humor and self-improvement, gossip and intellectual fare. Some magazines are lavishly produced with sophisticated art direction and graphics. Others reach and serve their audiences with less glitz and sheen.

Most consumer magazines make their money from circulation and advertising. The circulation revenue comes through subscription sales and single-copy sales (newsstand sales). Single-copy sales account for only 10 to 20 percent of most consumer magazines' circulation income. There were exceptions, however. For years, *Cosmopolitan* magazine was sold only on the newsstand. Many of what are called men's sophisticated magazines sell heavily on the newsstand, with few subscription sales. *Family Circle* and *Woman's Day* are staples at the grocery store checkout lanes. Most consumer magazines, however, depend heavily on subscription sales for circulation revenue.

Specialized business publications are also in the business to make a profit. These magazines are closely associated with a specific industry or business and are not usually available to anyone outside the industry. The circulation for these magazines is said to be controlled. This means circulation is limited to those who qualify according to the publication's listed criteria. Generally, those who qualify receive the magazine at no cost. *Supermarket Floral,* for example, serves individuals operating floral departments in supermarkets. Such publications serve entire industries, providing information about the people, goods, services, and developments in that particular business.

Revenue for such magazines comes almost entirely from advertising. These magazines create an ideal marketplace, bringing together the suppliers for an industry with the users of specific goods and services. Advertising in specialized business publications often sells at higher rates, even though the publications deliver a lower total circulation than the consumer magazines. The reason for this is that magazine advertising is sold on the basis of numbers as well as the quality of that number. Specialized business publications deliver a select audience, readers tied closely to a business or industry who need up-to-date information about the business and the suppliers to that business.

Other kinds of publications include newsletters, literary journals, and association and corporate publications. Newsletters might be small – two-to-four-page formats – or larger with eight, 12, 16, or more pages. Some of them cost subscribers more than $1,000 a year.

Scholarly or literary journals, called little magazines because of their smaller format, are almost totally driven by circulation, although a few may carry a small amount of advertising. The editorial material in such publications comes from submissions that are refereed by a panel of experts or scholars. They often are produced by university presses, and many of them are not in business to make money. Such publications are more like association magazines, provided as a benefit of membership. One of the most famous association publications is *National Geographic,* whose revenues in excess of expenses are put back into the work of the National Geographic Society.

The corporate or public relations magazines generally produce no revenue, and their expenses are paid as part of the institutional budget. These publications educate, inform, and foster relations among important constituent groups: employees, retirees, management, stockholders, and influential leaders.

Magazine publishers work alone or in partnership. Many started as small-scale, home enterprises. In 1948, Ed Self and his wife, Gloria, started *San Diego Magazine.* They continued as publishers until 1994, when they sold the magazine. Other magazines are part of larger enterprises or publishing groups. Meredith, of Des Moines, Iowa, published eight titles in the 1990s, including *Midwest Living, Ladies' Home Journal, Traditional Home,* and *Better Homes and Gardens.* The Reader's Digest Association, in Pleasantville, New York, published its flagship magazine as well as four other publications, including *American Health* and *Family Handyman.* Intertec Publishing in Kansas City, Kansas, produced more than 30 magazines for the specialized business press, covering industries as diverse as agriculture and electronics. Time, Inc., produced six titles in addition to its flagship magazine, *Time.* In addition, Time worked in partnership with eight other magazines, including *Cooking Light, Health, Martha Stewart Living,* and *Parenting.*

Magazine publishing presents major problems with cash flow. Most expenses have to be paid up front before much, or any, income arrives. The printers want their money before the magazine goes to press. The postage and delivery costs have to be paid up front. And the most expensive cost of all – building circulation – is an enormous up-front cost. Income, on the other hand, comes slowly, taking up to 90 days to collect fully on single sales or on subscriptions. The industry average for nonpayment of subscriptions runs 30 percent. Advertisers pay only after receiving a tearsheet (their ad in print) and a bill. The payment rate for advertisers is better than for readers, but it still takes up to 90 days to collect on all the ads for one issue.

Regular expenses include manufacturing and production (printing and paper); distribution (freight, postage); circulation costs (promotion and sales of subscriptions and single-copy sales, fulfillment costs to cover the computer and label production); advertising (market research, sales materials, sales commissions and expenses); administrative and operations (overhead, insurance, accounting and legal fees, audit costs); and editorial (manuscripts, art, editors, and graphic designers).

Over a 10-year period ending in the mid-1990s, only small fluctuations occurred in the consumer industry expense averages. One-third went to circulation and distribution. Production cost approximately 33 percent, although the price of paper created some volatility. Advertising averaged 14 percent, and editorial costs hovered around 11 percent of total costs. Administrative costs ranged from 5 percent to 13 percent, often depending on the location of the publishing enterprise.

Circulation and advertising are the two important legs of the business. Each brings in about 50 percent of the revenue. Editorial is the third leg – the product upon which circulation and advertising depend. Without strong, well-focused editorial content, there will be no readers; without readers, there can be no market; without a market, there will be no advertising.

Throughout most of the twentieth century, magazine economics were driven by advertising – more of it meant higher page rates. The publication goal was to appeal to as many people as possible, and before television, reaching this goal was possible. Magazines delivered the best visual media – great moments of writing, photography, analysis, fiction, humor, and illustration.

By the 1970s, many magazines had artificially propped the circulation, giving away the product at prices lower than the cost of production and distribution. Publications driven to this tactic hoped to hold a declining mass market and keep the ad rates going up and up. *Life,* the *Saturday Evening Post, Look,* and *Collier's* faltered, fell, and died. By the 1980s, there were no large-circulation general interest magazines.

The economic strategy changed from depending on advertising to putting greater obligation on circulation. In the 1990s, many city and regional magazine publishers reported that their important revenues came from products ancillary to the parent publication. As CD-ROMS and other publishing opportunities worked out a way to make money, there promised to be even more shifting.

Past economic problems came from dependence on advertising, volatility in the cost of paper, and increases in postal costs. Tomorrow's problems were expected to be more of the same, only with a new spin. Environmental issues were expected to affect paper use, availability, and cost. Postal costs had already driven some publishers to experiment with alternative delivery systems. The major concerns for many publishers would likely revolve around developing and paying for new electronic products that had not yet proven themselves moneymakers. Linked to these problems were those concerning costs of intellectual property and the rights to those properties. Lurking on the edge was apprehension as to the future of print – and even, for some, the future of literacy.

SHARON BASS

See also Magazine Circulation; Magazine Competition; Specialized Business Publications

Further Reading

Click, J. William, and Russell N. Baird, *Magazine Editing and Production,* 6th ed., Madison, Wisconsin: Brown & Benchmark, 1994

Folio: The Magazine for Magazine Management, Stamford, Connecticut: Cowles Business Media

Magazine Publishers of America, *MPA Handbook: A Comprehensive Guide for Advertisers, Ad Agencies and Magazine Marketers*, No. 64, 1992–93, New York: Magazine Publishers of America, 1993

Mogel, Leonard, *The Magazine: Everything You Need to Know to Make It in the Magazine Business*, 2nd ed., Chester, Connecticut: Globe Pequot, 1988

_____, *Making It in the Media Professions: A Realistic Guide to Career Opportunities in Newspapers, Magazines, Books, Television, Radio, the Movies, and Advertising*, Chester, Connecticut: Globe Pequot, 1988

Economics of Motion Pictures

Film production, distribution, and presentation are key elements

In the more than 100 years that motion pictures have been made, the industry in the United States – Hollywood – has been the largest and most influential. Hollywood films, since the early 1920s, have set the standard for mass entertainment storytelling.

Any motion picture industry includes three fundamental components:

1.) Production: In the United States, Hollywood-based studios coordinated filmmaking. Since 1950, most films have been shot on location and then assembled – with special effects added – in a Hollywood studio.

2.) Distribution: Motion picture companies make additional copies from the original negative and deliver these to theaters, television outlets, and video stores.

3.) Presentation: Finally, audiences watch movies in the theaters and on television.

During the second decade of the twentieth century, film company executives discovered that southern California, with its reliably sunny weather, offered an advantage in making movies. By 1920, Hollywood had become the nation's film production center, defining the motion picture business as Detroit, Michigan, did for the manufacture of automobiles.

Through the year-round creation of feature films, the promotion of stars, and the utilization of vast studio complexes for filming, Adolph Zukor of Famous Players–Lasky Corporation taught the world how to make and market profitable movies. Wanting his films to play in the best theaters, Zukor bought the Chicago-based Balaban and Katz in 1925 and renamed his new colossus Paramount.

Other entrepreneurs followed Zukor's lead and created the six other major Hollywood studio corporations. Moviemaking, worldwide distribution, and chains of studio-owned theaters, all under one corporate banner, defined the studio era of the 1930s and 1940s.

Paramount led the way. Its two biggest stars by the measure of box-office receipts – Bing Crosby and Bob Hope – represented the height of Paramount profitmaking. Their five "Road" pictures of the 1940s all raked in millions. Individually, Crosby also did *Holiday Inn* (1942) and *Going My Way* (1944); Hope starred in *My Favorite Blonde* (1942), *Monsieur Beaucaire* (1946), and *Paleface* (1948). From 1944 to 1949, either Crosby or Hope, working for Paramount, ranked as Hollywood's top male star.

Metro-Goldwyn-Mayer (MGM), with its internationally famous symbol of the roaring Leo the Lion, functioned as a successful unit within the larger enterprise, Loew's, Inc. In Culver City, California, a suburb of Los Angeles, MGM had a complete movie factory with 27 soundstages, supplied by a property department with more than 15,000 items to be used in movie after movie, whether they starred Clark Gable, Mickey Rooney, or Judy Garland.

Through the 1930s and 1940s, Twentieth Century-Fox ranked behind Paramount and MGM. By 1931, founder William Fox was out, replaced by new managers Darryl F. Zanuck and Joseph M. Schenck. Zanuck and Schenck brought Twentieth Century-Fox its greatest prosperity during the 1940s with Technicolor musicals starring Betty Grable, including *Moon Over Miami* (1941), *Song of the Islands* (1942), *Coney Island* (1943), and *The Dolly Sisters* (1946).

Warner Brothers was the only true family-run studio operation of the 1930s and 1940s. Eldest brother Harry was the president and had the final word on everything; middle brother Abe supervised world distribution; "baby" brother Jack headed film production in the studio in California. The Warners pioneered motion pictures with sound and are celebrated for their controversial social exposé films, including *I Am a Fugitive from a Chain Gang* (1932) and *Wild Boys of the Road* (1933), and for flashy backstage musicals typified by *The Gold Diggers of 1933* and *Footlight Parade* (1933).

RKO (Radio-Keith-Orpheum) had the shortest, least profitable life of any major Hollywood studio and was out of business by 1955. Studio executives at RKO came and went with regularity. For example, David O. Selznick's tenure at the helm lasted but a year and is remembered best for the creation of *King Kong* (1933). When George Schafer came on as head of production six years later, he hired Orson Welles to direct *Citizen Kane* (1941) and *The Magnificent Ambersons* (1942).

Universal owned no theaters and so never could match the economic muscle of the aforementioned Big Five (Paramount, MGM, Twentieth Century-Fox, Warner, and RKO). It only prospered when it produced low-budget comedies from Abbott and Costello and weekly serials such as *Flash Gordon* and *Jungle Jim*.

Columbia was Universal's low-budget rival. Brothers Harry and Jack Cohn relied on its low-budget B westerns to generate the bulk of corporate profits, but occasionally they produced a high-cost production such as *Lost Horizon* (1937) or *The Jolson Story* (1946).

The studio era reached its apex in 1946, as weekly movie attendance in theaters crested. Theater attendance then began to fall steadily, and by the early 1950s, Hollywood was focusing on drive-ins to revive attendance. A longer-term solution to the suburbanization of the nation came with the shopping-mall theater. By the late 1960s, the locus of movie attendance shifted to the mall and remained there through the remainder of the century.

In the 1950s, Hollywood looked to new motion picture

Motion Pictures in the United States: Average Number of Tickets Sold per Week, 1922–85
(in thousands)

Year	Tickets Sold per Week	Weekly Tickets Sold per Household	Year	Tickets Sold per Week	Weekly Tickets Sold per Household
1922	40,000	1.56	1946	90,000	2.37
1924	46,000	1.71	1948	90,000	2.22
1926	50,000	1.78	1950	60,000	1.38
1928	65,000	2.23	1954	49,000	1.04
1930	90,000	3.00	1958	40,000	0.79
1932	60,000	1.97	1960	28,000	0.53
1934	70,000	2.24	1965	21,000	0.37
1936	88,000	2.71	1970	15,000	0.24
1938	85,000	2.52	1975	20,000	0.28
1940	80,000	2.29	1980	19,600	0.25
1942	85,000	2.33	1985	20,300	0.23
1944	85,000	2.29			

Sources: U.S. Bureau of the Census, *Historical Statistics of the United States: Colonial Times to 1957* (Washington, D.C.: GPO, 1960; *Continuation to 1962 and Revisions* (1965).

U.S. Bureau of the Census, *Statistical Abstract of the United States* (Washington, D.C.: GPO, 1968).

U.S. Bureau of the Census, *Current Population Reports: Population Characteristics* (Washington, D.C.: GPO, 1964).

Notes: Figures after 1980s are from the Motion Picture Association of America.

Figures do not include Alaska and Hawaii. Drop in 1932 due to the influence of the Great Depression.

technologies to tempt patrons. Technicolor differentiated Hollywood's offerings from grainy black-and-white television. CinemaScope projected vast new spectacles. To produce these wide-screen color epics, new studio bosses contracted out to independents who developed a package (a story plus stars) and then agreed to distribute the film through that studio. The job of the head of the studio from the 1950s was to find and "green-light" (approve) 15 to 25 independently made feature films each year.

Through all this change, the major studios of the 1930s and 1940s, save RKO, survived and even thrived. MGM declined and was replaced by Disney. From the late 1970s, six major studios defined Hollywood.

Control of Warner Brothers passed from the founding brothers, who sold out in 1956, to Kinney National by 1969. Steven J. Ross, son-in-law of Kinney's founder, then successfully began to rebuild Warner's and did so well that in 1989 he merged Warner with Time, Inc., to create what was then the largest media company in the world, Time Warner.

Paramount followed an equally rocky transition until 1966, when Charles Bluhdorn of Gulf + Western Industries purchased it. Bluhdorn found only modest success until the mid-1970s, when he installed former ABC-TV executive Barry Diller as studio head. For a decade thereafter, Paramount prospered, until Diller left to become head of the new Fox Television network. Charles Bluhdorn died, and in 1993, Viacom took over Paramount.

Twentieth Century-Fox surged during the 1950s on the strength of CinemaScope and Marilyn Monroe. It then floundered, with few exceptions, until the early 1970s, when Dennis Stanfill took charge and green-lighted such blockbusters as *The French Connection* (1971), *The Posei-*

don Adventure (1972), and *The Towering Inferno* (1973). *Star Wars* (1977) saw Fox become Hollywood's leading studio, and in 1986, Australian Rupert Murdoch purchased Fox and folded it into his worldwide media empire.

Columbia Pictures helped pioneer television production in Hollywood and in the process became a major studio. During the late 1950s, Abe Schneider and Leo Jaffe succeeded the founding Cohn brothers and found success with *Funny Girl* (1968) and *Easy Rider* (1969). The 1970s and 1980s were not kind to Columbia, however, and in 1980, it was sold to Coca-Cola. The soft-drink giant spent millions trying to remake Columbia into an efficient marketing apparatus but gave up after a decade. Columbia became Sony Studios, in the hands of the giant Japanese electronics manufacturer.

Universal studio struggled in the 1950s until former MCA talent agent Lew Wasserman took charge. Under Wasserman, Universal became a powerhouse of television production and home to such filmmaking talents as Alfred Hitchcock and Steven Spielberg. Spielberg's *E.T.* (1981) seemed to be the beginning of another profitable decade for the studio, but success proved illusory. Universal languished, and Wasserman, nearing 80, sold MCA to Japan's Matsushita Electric Company in 1989. In turn, six years later, Matsushita peddled Universal to the Seagrams Corporation of Canada.

The Disney studio had existed on the fringes of the U.S. film industry since the 1920s, specializing with great success in animation. With the transition to television and independent film production, however, Disney moved into these new arenas and began to produce live-action features such as the wildly successful *Mary Poppins* (1965). Still, by the 1970s, Walt Disney's successors were floundering. In 1984, new management, led by Michael Eisner, began to build the modern Disney colossus. Most notably, Eisner revitalized the feature-length animated motion picture with hits such as *Aladdin* (1993) and *The Lion King* (1994) and acquired the ABC television network.

As the twentieth century ended, these six major studios – Warner Brothers, Paramount, Twentieth Century-Fox, Sony-Columbia, Seagrams-Universal, and Disney – defined the motion picture business in the United States and much of the world. Films like *Forrest Gump* (1994) and *Jurassic Park* (1994) not only took in millions of dollars at the theatrical box office but sold as home videos and inspired toys, books, clothing, and popular music. The economics of the Hollywood motion picture studios prospered as never before.

DOUGLAS GOMERY

See also Audience Research for Motion Pictures; Budget (B) Movies; Hollywood Studio System; Motion Picture Competition

Further Reading

Alexander, Alison, James Owers, and Rod Carveth, eds., *Media Economics: Theory and Practice,* Hillsdale, New Jersey: Lawrence Erlbaum, 1993

Balio, Tino, ed., *The American Film Industry,* rev. ed., Madison: University of Wisconsin Press, 1985

Bordwell, David, Janet Staiger, and Kristin Thompson, *The Classical Hollywood Cinema: Film Style and Mode of Production to 1960,* New York: Columbia University Press, 1985; London: Routledge & Kegan Paul, 1985

Conant, Michael, *Antitrust in the Motion Picture Industry,* Berkeley: University of California Press, 1960

Gomery, Douglas, *The Hollywood Studio System,* New York: St. Martin's, 1986; Basingstoke, England: Macmillan, 1986

_____, *Shared Pleasures: A History of Movie Presentation in the United States,* Madison: University of Wisconsin Press, 1992; London: BFI, 1992

Economics of Newspapers

Developed, changed over 300-year history

As the newspaper evolved over more than three centuries from craft to political practice to business, so did its economics. The sources of demand, patterns in revenues, and nature of competition are considerably different depending on the historical moment examined.

During the colonial and American Revolution eras, a printer was a combination of tradesman and merchant, engaging in job printing for business, religious, and governmental customers; bookselling; and such miscellaneous tasks as being postmaster or managing an auction house. Far from every printer was involved in newspaper printing, although more of them were after the Revolution. The technology of eighteenth-century printers, not much different from that of Gutenberg's days, was on a very small scale. However, three conditions suggest that entry into the field

was not easy for those who possessed knowledge of the "Art Preservative": Many wealthy printers had interests in more than one shop; there was a relatively small number of colonial newspapers; and, after the Revolution, there was a boom in the number of newspapers after capital was infused by those with political aims.

There is disagreement about whether the newspapers of this period made business sense. Due to the connection of the colonies with Britain, the newspaper as a product found markets for advertising and circulation. But a newspaper required a considerable amount of labor to produce and involved some hard-to-procure raw materials.

Except in the very largest cities where, by the later colonial period, perhaps three or four papers would be printed each week, many printers' newspapers seem to have enjoyed "monopolies." Not much can be said about the nature of competition that existed in the cities such as Boston and Philadelphia where the public enjoyed the newspaper offerings of more than one printer. While the newspapers were differentiated by content, by the politics and personality of the printer, and by the neatness of the printing, it is not known how the papers competed in the narrow newspaper reading market. One might assume scrappy competition for readers and advertising considering the small size of the market, but the price-fixing that economist Adam Smith detested was known to occur among printers.

The newspaper industry entered an astounding and highly complex growth stage from the 1790s to the 1860s. The growth came in three ways. First, political parties underwrote additional newspaper enterprises in country markets. Second, large urban markets experienced growth through politicization, increased demand for commercial information, and a proliferation of journals oriented to special tastes. Third, there was growth as newspapers became institutionalized on the frontier. The fuel of the growth was successive sources of new demand (political parties, readers, businesses) and greatly enabling technological change. Each of these types of newspaper enterprises – country, urban, and frontier – had its distinctive economics.

The increasing politicization of the press with the onset of the Revolutionary War evolved into a union of the press with political factions and parties in the antebellum period. The rise of numerous parties and voluntary associations in the 1820s and 1830s was accompanied by the establishing and subsidizing of party and reform organs, and investors expected the return on their money to come through political success or social change. The politicization of newspapers brought additional newspapers to many towns and counties that previously would have had only one. Although some political papers had regional and national leadership roles and circulated widely in the mails, and some associational papers were national in focus, most papers were of small circulation and little influence.

That readers' subscriptions and advertising did not provide nearly enough money to support papers seems evident from the general impoverishment of editors and from the practice of political patronage. Patronage ranged from commissioning job printing during a campaign to giving an editor a job at the statehouse if the campaign were won.

In the larger urban areas of the same period can be observed the same process of politicization. The demand for partisan organs, however, was coupled with a rise in demand by the mercantile class for commercial and trade news that was met by advertising-based journals that often bore the word "advertiser" in their names. Other niches in the advertising and reading market were exploited as well: papers devoted to the concerns of the "middling," the artisan and mechanic classes, immigrants who read foreign languages, and readers with interests in literary and cultural matters. Newspapers in these markets were highly differentiated and had small audiences, and most offices derived a significant portion of their revenue from job printing.

A typical impulse for the establishment of an early frontier newspaper was to create a boom in a newly established town by marketing to potential immigrants. Besides the invitation of a developer, what brought a printer to a town was demand for printing services, especially by the government, and the availability of revenue from advertisements of land purchases and claims. The pattern of the industry on the frontier was less than one newspaper per town or county, circulation averaging 600–1,000. With the development of political ambitions for the territory, however, the frontier press quickly joined the politicization trend, and even small towns and counties got more than one paper. This resulted in too many newspapers, making what was already a hardscrabble existence for printers (owing to difficulties in obtaining raw materials and to readers' and advertisers' abuse of credit from publishers) even more so. As the frontier developed, its newspapers became indistinguishable in their economics from their "country" and "urban" counterparts in the east.

The modern economics of the newspaper emerged after 1870, enabled by technological change (especially high-speed presses, processes that significantly cheapened the cost of paper, the railroad, and the telegraph), the drying up of party money for newspaper publishing, and the rise of advertising to stimulate a consumer-oriented economy. The modern economics of the newspaper were characterized by locally bound markets, a heavy reliance on advertising revenue, and the predominance of local, and fewer, less partisan papers of larger circulation in each market.

Technological developments in the 1870s first seemed to be leading to a nationally oriented press. Newspapers in the large urban markets increasingly began to penetrate country markets with daily, semiweekly, and weekly editions pumped out on power presses and sped to readers by railroad express. Many journalists speculated in the 1870s that a London *Times* model of newspapering would develop, in which one New York paper would dominate the newspaper industry nationwide. Strengthened local newspapers stemmed the tide of a nationally oriented press by the 1880s and 1890s. Some country papers fended off urban competition through intensive local news coverage. Others benefited from the extension of the telegraph across the country beginning in the 1850s, which allowed access to the same news available to metropolitan papers, stimulating the rise of small-city daily papers. Many large urban newspapers replaced the revenue streams of their country editions with those from auxiliary businesses that supplied country papers with editorial matter: telegraph news associations, patent-inside syndicates, plate services, and feature syndicates.

Although still often sympathetic with some political faction or party, urban newspapers began moving to a business basis after the Civil War, with local advertising replacing party printing as the major source of revenue. This change in strategy was for many papers a necessity as party support became less available, and it was facilitated by a change in thinking that becoming commercialized was more dignified than being the cat's paw of politicians. Political affiliation persisted longer in the country markets than in the urban markets, as the government printing contract continued to be a critical source of revenue.

In the transition from a party-funded press to an advertising-funded press, the purpose of the newspaper crystallized as being the purveyor of news and entertainment and a medium of advertising. Criticism of commercialism and profit orientation figured prominently in press discussions of the day. As advertising became the name of the game, substitutes for newspaper advertising space, such as streetcar advertising, were being fended off and invested in by newspapers.

Moving to a commercial basis involved in many markets (first in the medium-size markets, and then in the country and urban markets) the rise of "independents," unaffiliated papers seeking broad market appeal. Another aspect of the move to a business basis was the determined pursuit of profits, and this stimulated publishers' desire for mergers, the erection of high barriers to entry (accomplished by locking up news sources, advertisers, or distribution channels), and the shutting down of those who were not in the business "legitimately" – for example, amateur printers, churches doing "fake" advertising, "Bohemian" papers set up to reap revenue from tax lists, or papers started up by disgruntled merchants.

Editors and publishers at the end of the 1800s were sometimes giddy and often uneasy about the implications of the modern newspaper economics. While an advertising basis had made the newspaper a profitable and respectable business enterprise, at the same time the newspaper was increasingly becoming the object of financial speculation by capitalists who saw the potential of even more profits through modern management techniques such as chain ownership.

CAROL SMITH

See also Cooperative News Gathering; Criticism of Newspapers; Cross-Media Ownership; Feature Syndicates; Frontier Press; Government Printing and Patronage; Media Conglomerates; Newspaper Chains, or Groups; Party Press; Telegraph

Further Reading

Baldasty, Gerald J., *The Commercialization of News in the Nineteenth Century,* Madison: University of Wisconsin Press, 1992
Cloud, Barbara Lee, *The Business of Newspapers on the Western Frontier,* Reno: University of Nevada Press, 1992
Dyer, Carolyn Stewart, "Political Patronage of the

Wisconsin Press, 1849–1860: New Perspectives on the Economics of Patronage," *Journalism Monographs* 109 (February 1989)

Sloan, Wm. David, "'Purse and Pen': Party-Press Relationship, 1789–1816," *American Journalism* 6 (1989)

Smith, Carol, and Carolyn Stewart Dyer, "Taking Stock, Placing Orders: A Historiographic Essay on the Business History of the Newspaper," *Journalism Monographs* 132 (April 1992), pp. 1–56

Yodelis, Mary Ann, "Who Paid the Piper? Publishing Economics in Boston, 1763–1775," *Journalism Monographs* 38 (February 1975)

Edison, Thomas Alva

Inventions helped make motion pictures possible

Thomas Alva Edison, inventor of the incandescent lamp, considered the phonograph his most important invention. Among his 1,093 patents (more than anyone in history) were improvements to the telephone, telegraph, typewriter, microphone, motion picture camera and film, storage battery, and electric railway.

Born in Milan, Ohio, the youngest of seven children, Edison received little formal schooling and began working at the age of 12. Edison was known to work around the clock, taking only short naps when necessary.

By the time he was 27, Edison had built a home and laboratory complex in Menlo Park, New Jersey, where he invented the phonograph, electric light, and electricity delivery system and came to be known as the "Wizard of Menlo Park." Early Edison phonographs, manufactured by the Edison Phonograph Company, had to be cranked by hand and used cylinders rather than discs. In 1887, the Edi-

Thomas A. Edison, left, tries broadcasting.
(Library of American Broadcasting)

son General Electric Company was founded to unite the seven Edison electric companies. The name was shortened to General Electric in 1892.

In 1887, Edison moved to a new laboratory in West Orange, New Jersey, where he and W.K.L. Dickson worked on the motion picture camera and built the first motion picture studio in the United States, a Kinetographic studio, in 1893. This tar-paper structure, commonly known as "Black Maria," had a roof that could be opened and was built upon a circular track in order to follow the sun's path, assuring the filmmakers of sufficient light.

LAURA R. LINDER

See also Motion Picture Technology

Further Reading
Baldwin, Neil, *Edison, Inventing the Century,* New York: Hyperion, 1995
Clark, Ronald W., *Edison: The Man Who Made the Future,* New York: Putnam, 1977; London: Macdonald and Jane's, 1977
Conot, Robert, *A Streak of Luck,* New York: Seaview, 1979
Millard, A.J., *Edison and the Business of Innovation,* Baltimore, Maryland: Johns Hopkins University Press, 1990; London: Johns Hopkins University Press, 1993
Wachhorst, Wyn, *Thomas Alva Edison: An American Myth,* Cambridge, Massachusetts: MIT Press, 1981

Eisenhower, Dwight D., and the Media

The nation's first "television president"

Although it is his successor, John F. Kennedy, who is most often credited with the title, Dwight D. Eisenhower was the nation's first "television president." That Eisenhower embraced the new medium is not in dispute.

Public communications were at the heart of his administration's strategy. As historian Stephen Ambrose noted, Eisenhower believed that "a man cannot lead without communicating with the people." In one White House staff meeting, Eisenhower defined public relations as "getting ideas put out in such a way that your purpose is actually understood."

From the aggressive use of campaign spot advertising to frequent television "talks," Eisenhower saw television as a means of bypassing reporters and going directly to the electorate. While his television appearances did not achieve the same stature as Franklin Roosevelt's "fireside chats," Eisenhower left an indelible imprint upon the way his successors would use the medium.

Eisenhower changed the presidential news conference from an exclusive gathering of reporters into a national town meeting. Prior to 1953, broadcast cameras and microphones were barred. Reporters were also prohibited from quoting the president directly. On December 16, 1953,

James Hagerty, holding paper, was the trusted press secretary for Dwight D. Eisenhower.
(Courtesy of Dwight D. Eisenhower Library)

Eisenhower became the first president to release edited recordings of his entire news conference for radio broadcast. One year later, Eisenhower permitted direct attribution. On January 19, 1955, Eisenhower conducted the first televised news conference, albeit on a film-delayed basis.

Eisenhower surrounded himself with people who understood the media. One of the president's close advisers was C.D. Jackson, a Time, Inc., editor who had been a member of General Eisenhower's staff during the war. His press secretary was James Hagerty, who had been a reporter for the *New York Times* and had served New York governor Thomas E. Dewey in several capacities. Actor Robert

Montgomery joined the administration in 1954 to become the first full-time White House television consultant. The administration also assembled some of the nation's best advertising and public relations talent.

However, Eisenhower had a much different relationship with working journalists. In one memo to his cabinet, Eisenhower complained, "While key and top echelon figures in the fields of Journalism, Publications and Public Relations are pro Administration, yet the so important lower echelons have not been too successfully wooed." In his diary, Eisenhower described the press corps as a group with "little sense of humor" and as people who "deal in negative criticism rather than in any attempt toward constructive helpfulness." Although Eisenhower characterized most reporting as "distortion and gross error," he did not criticize reporters openly. The president wanted to avoid personality conflicts with reporters. On those rare occasions on which he chose to express his disapproval, he did so through intermediaries.

By most accounts, the administration successfully practiced the art of news management. News releases were timed to gain maximum exposure on slow news days – such as the announcement of three ambassadorial appointments on a day on which the president was playing golf. To give an appearance of high activity, executive branch information was funneled through the White House, a practice that became known as "woodworking." Press Secretary Hagerty also approached journalists before news conferences and suggested topics for reporters' questions. According to historian Craig Allen, this manipulation was most in evidence when Eisenhower was stricken with a heart attack on September 24, 1955. Allen said that the administration carefully orchestrated the image of a president in charge of the nation's affairs when, actually, Eisenhower was not.

There were some rough spots in the administration's relationship with the media. They included a November 1953 political firestorm that followed Attorney General Herbert Brownell's charge that Harry Truman, while president, had knowingly appointed a Communist spy to a high government post. Another was the administration's bungled attempt to cover up the downing of Francis Gary Powers' spy plane over the Soviet Union in May 1960. The president was often frustrated by criticism of his administration's behind-the-scenes efforts to deal with the nagging problems of McCarthyism and civil rights. Eisenhower also privately bristled over jokes about his often-mangled syntax, which Ambrose said the president occasionally did on purpose to obfuscate.

Despite these and other bumps, contemporary journalists gave Eisenhower's administration generally good reviews on its dealings with reporters. Eisenhower's disdain of journalism, however, outlasted his term of office. When asked during his one hundred ninety-third and last news conference whether reporters had treated him fairly, Eisenhower said, "When you come down to it, I don't see that a reporter could do much to a president, do you?"

DAVID W. GUTH

See also Presidential News Conferences; Presidential Press
   Secretaries

Further Reading
Allen, Craig, *Eisenhower and the Mass Media: Peace, Prosperity, and Prime-Time TV,* Chapel Hill: University of North Carolina Press, 1993
Ambrose, Stephen E., *Eisenhower, Volume Two: The President and Elder Statesman, 1952–1969,* New York: Simon & Schuster, 1984
Eisenhower, Dwight D., *The White House Years,* 2 vols., Garden City, New York: Doubleday, 1963–1965
Ferrell, Robert H., ed., *The Eisenhower Diaries,* New York: Norton, 1981
French, Blaire Atherton, *The Presidential Press Conference: Its History and Role in the American Political System,* Washington, D.C.: University Press of America, 1982

"Equal Time" Provision
Provides equal opportunities to competing political candidates

The Radio Act of 1927 sought to prevent undue influence of elections by broadcasting stations favoring of one political candidate over others. The statute, codified as Section 315 of the Communications Act of 1934, mandated "equal opportunities" (not "equal time") for competing candidates to have access to public airwaves: "If any licensee shall permit any person who is a legally qualified candidate for any public office to use a broadcasting station, he shall afford equal opportunities to all other such candidates for that office in the use of such broadcasting station."

Applications of the statute have vexed the industry. Mere equality of time does not ensure equitable access to potential voters through media (30 seconds in the morning has far less impact than 30 seconds in prime time). A station offering time free to one candidate must offer similar opportunity to all opponents for that position; if it sells time to one, it must let opponents buy time (but if opponents lack adequate funds, the station is not required to donate time). Stations need not seek out opponents to inform them that a candidate used their air; they need only respond if opponents make a request within seven days.

The rule applies only to those formally announced and qualified for the ballot, not to officeholders still undeclared as candidates. A station airing candidates for one position need not provide airtime to those running for other offices. To preclude local stations from simply ignoring all political candidates, Section 312 requires they offer "reasonable access" for those seeking federal office. The Federal Communications Commission (FCC) extended that to state candidates generally, under the "public interest" standard of Section 307. Because they are not common carriers, stations need not give access to candidates for every office. Rather than sell or give time to individuals, some stations choose to present forums or discussion programs offering a single joint appearance of major candidates for selected offices.

Announcements supporting but not featuring a candidate do not require "equal opportunities" for opponents. Yet a representative speaking formally on behalf of a candidate prompts "quasi-equal opportunities" for opponents' spokespersons. A mere appearance by a political candidate – despite his or her not speaking about the election (such as when appearing in a movie scene) – who can be identified by audiences constitutes a "use" and makes opponents eligible for response opportunity. Congress sought to make broadcast airtime affordable by requiring stations to charge no more than the lowest time charges afforded their most favorable volume-purchasing clients.

Historical anomalies, notably perennial candidate Lar Daly in Chicago in the late 1950s, prompted Congress to amend the law to exempt "bona fide" newscasts, news interviews, and special-event coverage of incumbents or opponents, lest legitimately newsworthy items automatically trigger response time for those campaigning against them. To prevent broadcasters' influencing political speech, the law forbids interfering with candidates' text by editing, modifying, or otherwise censoring their material. Therefore, courts have ruled broadcasters not liable for politicians' defamation or other excesses (except obscenity) because they cannot edit political communication.

JAMES A. BROWN

Espionage and Sedition Acts

World War I attempts to quiet criticism and dissent

The Espionage Act of 1917 and the Sedition Act of 1918 were the first wartime sedition laws enacted in the United States. They were applied vigorously on a large scale by the government during World War I, and the principal law, the Espionage Act, was still in force in World War II. However, in the latter war, the Espionage Act was used very little.

When the United States entered World War I on April 6, 1917, sedition legislation was viewed as a necessity. Many regarded the existing statutes as inadequate for punishing those who encouraged draft evasion. Such concerns were heightened by recollections of Civil War opposition being handled entirely, but not well, by martial law, and by a pervasive fear of German propaganda. This already had caused Great Britain and Canada to guard against it legislatively and administratively.

The result was the Espionage Act, which became law on June 15, 1917. Title I, section 3, limited freedom of expression during wartime by declaring it unlawful to do the following: to make false statements that interfered with the military; to attempt to cause "insubordination, disloyalty, mutiny, or refusal of duty" in the military; or to obstruct the military recruiting or enlistment services. Anyone found guilty could be fined up to $10,000 or jailed for up to 20 years, or both.

Of at least equal, if not more, importance to the press was Title XII, which allowed the postmaster general to declare unmailable any printed material that might violate the law. Under the Classification Act of 1879, newspapers and periodicals had to appear at regularly stated intervals to qualify for a second-class mailing permit allowing them reduced postal rates. If the postmaster general withheld just one issue from the mail, a second-class permit could be revoked indefinitely because the publication no longer appeared regularly. Such a revocation frequently made it unprofitable to publish because both first-class and third-class postal rates were substantially higher.

The Espionage Act did not stem the nation's hysteria,

Masses' cartoons, such as this one, led to trouble under World War I legislation.
(Davis Library, University of North Carolina at Chapel Hill)

however, and Attorney General Thomas W. Gregory pushed for an even stricter federal law. The result was the most severe legal limitation in U.S. history on freedom of expression and the press. The Sedition Act of May 16, 1918, amended the Espionage Act by adding nine new offenses. They included speaking, writing, or publishing any "disloyal, profane, scurrilous, or abusive language" about topics ranging from the government to the flag to the armed forces. Also prohibited were writings or statements intended to result in "contempt, scorn, contumely, or disrepute" of the government, the Constitution, the flag, and even the armed forces' uniforms. Penalties for those convicted were identical to those under the Espionage Act.

The Justice Department applied its new legal weapons vigorously. Between 1917 and 1921, it launched 2,168 prosecutions under the Espionage and Sedition acts and secured 1,055 convictions. At least 11 persons received 10-year prison terms, 6 were sentenced to 15 years, and 24 were given 20 years.

No one was more zealous in applying the laws than Postmaster General Albert S. Burleson. On June 16, 1917, only one day after the Espionage Act took effect, he secretly ordered postmasters to forward immediately to him any magazines or newspapers that possibly contained illegal material. He was inundated with material and moved quickly. In the first month, Burleson and Post Office Solicitor William H. Lamar declared unmailable at least one issue of each of about 15 publications. The greater part of the suppressions occurred by November 1917, when Burleson had either declared nonmailable or revoked the second-class permits of 44 publications, and 30 more were allowed to continue using the mail only by promising to not write anything else about the war. The U.S. Court of Appeals upheld the government suppressions in a case brought by the *Masses*. By the time the war ended, the Post Office had taken action against about 100 newspapers and periodicals.

About 60 percent of the suppressions were directed at the Socialist press. The next largest segment affected by the Espionage and Sedition acts was the German-language press. As a result of prosecutions and loss of second-class mailing permits, it declined by about one-half during the war and lost about 50 percent of its circulation.

In 1921, following a two-year "Red Scare" period in which 70 peacetime sedition bills were unsuccessfully introduced in Congress, the Sedition Act was repealed. However, the Espionage Act was left in place for future wars.

The legislation was again in force in World War II, but it was applied by the government on a far smaller scale than in the previous war. Despite massive, generally secret investigations of newspapers and magazines by a number of federal agencies, only six radical publications had their second-class permits revoked by the Post Office, and two of them had their permits restored before the war ended. Furthermore, only 33 persons had Espionage Act convictions sustained during the war for federal prosecutions involving speech and publications.

The decline of Espionage Act press indictments in World War II, and the lesser number of second-class postal permits that were rescinded, can be attributed to several factors. One was the overall tone of the press; it was far more supportive of the war effort than in World War I, and fewer radical publications existed. Another important factor was the presence of Francis Biddle as attorney general. He believed strongly in the First Amendment and felt that there should be no sedition laws. As a result, the Justice Department took to court only a handful of journalists from small, radical publications, and it generally refused to support the Post Office in its desire to take away a large number of second-class mailing permits. Federal Bureau of Investigation Director J. Edgar Hoover also wanted to bring a number of Espionage Act indictments against the press, but the Justice Department refused to sanction most of them.

PATRICK S. WASHBURN

See also Ethnic Press; Socialist Press; World War I

Further Reading

Chafee, Zechariah, Jr., *Free Speech in the United States,* New York: Atheneum, 1969

Fowler, Dorothy Ganfield, *Unmailable: Congress and the Post Office,* Athens: University of Georgia Press, 1977

Johnson, Donald, *The Challenge to American Freedoms: World War I and the Rise of the American Civil Liberties Union,* Lexington: University of Kentucky Press, 1963

Peterson, H.C., and Gilbert C. Fite, *Opponents of War, 1917–1918,* Madison: University of Wisconsin Press, 1957

Washburn, Patrick S., *A Question of Sedition: The Federal Government's Investigation of the Black Press During World War II,* New York: Oxford University Press, 1986

Ethnic Press

Newspapers for non-English speakers have long history

Newspapers intended for non-English speakers are almost as old as the press itself in the present-day United States. Less than three decades after the first regular newspaper in English appeared in the British North American colonies, Benjamin Franklin published a short-lived paper for the German immigrants in and around Philadelphia in 1732. Seven years later, German immigrant printer Christopher Sauer brought out the first German-language newspaper of any duration, *Der Hoch-Deutsch Pennsylvanische Geschichts-Schreiber* (*High German Pennsylvania Annalist*). In the 1780s, a second group of immigrants, those from France and Quebec, established their first newspapers on U.S. soil.

Although some 300 foreign-language publications – mainly in German and French – had appeared by 1860, the U.S. ethnic press was primarily a phenomenon of the era of mass migration from Europe to the United States between the 1880s and the 1920s, when more than 20 million immigrants arrived. As these newcomers sought to establish themselves in new surroundings, the ethnic newspaper became an important part of communities whose other institutions included organizations such as churches and mutual-aid societies. These, like the press, were formed to help the immigrants cope with life in the United States and had no real counterparts in the countries they had left.

The number of ethnic publications peaked at more than 1,300 in the mid-1910s, and the 1915 *Ayer's Newspaper Annual and Directory* revealed their diversity. Some 30 languages were represented, mostly European, but also Chinese, Japanese, Arabic, and Hebrew. By far the largest group of papers, more than 500, were German, followed by Italian, with almost 100, and Swedish and Spanish, both with close to 75. Close to 150 papers were listed as dailies, with a estimated total circulation of 2.6 million.

Although the frequency of publication and the traits of each immigrant group produced some variation in what newspapers offered readers, the basic content of the ethnic press remained remarkably similar across groups and over time. From the first German-language publications in Pennsylvania in the 1700s to the Asian immigrant newspapers in the west coast cities of the late 1900s, one of the most important parts of the ethnic press has been news from the countries that the immigrants left, often broken down to the level of province or city. That kind of news helped immigrant papers retain readers who had acquired proficiency in English, since it was not really offered by the mainstream English-language press. Both for newcomers and for longtime residents in the United States, news from the old country served to maintain a sense of ethnic identity.

Equally important was a secondary content category, news and information about U.S. life, conditions, and institutions. A great deal of this information was given in editorials, where readers were provided with information about such things as the U.S. political and educational system and were urged to become citizens, exercise their right to vote, and send their children to public school, to give a few examples. Rendered in a language that the immigrants understood and tailored to reach people unfamiliar with the United States and, often, with newspaper reading itself, these articles were one of the few ways to reach this segment of the population with information vital to survival in a new country.

A third type of content fell somewhere between the two and was concerned with the immigrants themselves. It told readers about compatriots not only in the city or town where the newspaper was published but across the United States. News in this category could center on the activities of immigrant institutions such as churches and mutual-benefit societies, but it frequently dealt with personal events such as marriages, births, and visits; its purpose was to make the immigrants visible to one another and create a sense of community. An important part of the press' work in this area were editorials that spoke on behalf of the immigrant group to the larger society and defended it from attacks from "Americans" and from other ethnic groups.

Side by side with the content produced by the journalists themselves, most ethnic newspapers also ran advertising, which was a vital source of revenue but also tied in with the different content categories discussed above. The assimilation information given in editorials and news about U.S. matters was supplemented by large and numerous advertisements for department stores and national product brands, which introduced readers to patterns of consumption in the United States. The visibility of the ethnic community was made clearer by a large number of ads from grocery-store owners, physicians, lawyers, and craftsmen of the readers' own nationality. Other types of advertising were less beneficial: patent medicines and other forms of dubious health cures were promoted in the ethnic press early on, and they remained there for some time after they had become disreputable in English-language newspapers.

A few journalists of the foreign-language press were hugely successful, the best example being Joseph Pulitzer, who went on to national prominence as a New York publisher after starting as a reporter for the German-language *Westliche Post* in St. Louis, Missouri, and Herman Ridder, whose New York *Staats-Zeitung,* which, with its circulation of 250,000, was the largest foreign-language daily. The majority of immigrant journalists were far less successful, however, and a great many of them were characterized as foreign-educated intellectuals who had turned to newspaper work because they considered themselves above the manual labor offered to newly arrived immigrants. Most of the papers they published or worked for had circulations below 10,000 and frequently failed to turn a profit. As a consequence, a large number failed after only a few years.

Regardless of the difficult conditions facing individual

newspapers, the first decade and a half of the twentieth century was a prosperous period for the ethnic press as an institution, as the large number of publications indicates. With entry of the United States into World War I in 1917, the favorable climate changed overnight. Among calls for an end to loyalty to countries other than the United States, Postmaster General Albert S. Burleson began using the powers given to him under the Espionage, Trading-with-the-Enemy, and Sedition acts to deny second-class mailing privileges to some foreign-language papers and require that others supply English-language translations of their content. His target was mainly German-language publications, but mailing privileges were also denied to other foreign-language papers because they were Socialist in orientation.

In addition to such direct government action, the generally hostile attitude of the U.S. public toward the ethnic press during the war made many of its readers apprehensive about taking foreign-language newspapers, and circulations fell. Moreover, the war drove up the cost of newsprint and production in general, which spelled the demise of many papers whose finances were already problematic before 1917. As a result, the number of ethnic papers began to decline, due mainly to the many casualties in the German American press, which shrank from 522 publications in 1917 to 278 three years later.

The end of unrestricted immigration through the establishment of quotas in the early 1920s was in all likelihood even more significant than World War I in the decline of the press of many ethnic groups. Publishers and editors repeatedly tried to entice the U.S.-born children of the immigrants into reading foreign-language papers, but such attempts met with little success. Soon it was generally recognized that the ethnic press depended on a steady stream of newly arrived immigrants for its survival. As that stream slowed to a trickle in the late 1920s, many papers, particularly German and Scandinavian, were faced with a readership that was aging and would eventually die off.

As European immigration fell off after 1920, the makeup of the ethnic press changed to reflect new patterns of international migration. The 1994 counterpart to the 1915 *Ayer's* directory, the *Gale Directory of Publications and Broadcast Media,* listed 294 publications in foreign languages across the United States, representing 35 different languages. The largest group, 146, was in Spanish, evidence of the growing Hispanic minority in the United States. The second largest group, the 12 publications in Polish, was an indication that the United States kept receiving a large number of immigrants from countries of the former Soviet bloc throughout the Cold War era. Finally, in reflection of the growing number of immigrants from Asia, were three languages not represented in 1915: Gujarati, Korean, and Vietnamese. For those arriving to establish a new life in the United States, the ethnic newspaper, published in their native languages, continued to serve a vital function.

ULF JONAS BJORK

See also Alternative Press; Espionage and Sedition Acts; Socialist Press; World War I

Further Reading

Brye, David L., ed., *European Immigration and Ethnicity in the United States and Canada: A Historical Bibliography,* Santa Barbara, California: ABC-Clio Information Services, 1983

Geitz, Henry, ed., *The German-American Press,* Madison: Max Kade Institute for German-American Studies, University of Wisconsin, 1992

Kessler, Lauren, *The Dissident Press: Alternative Journalism in American History,* Beverly Hills, California: Sage, 1984

Miller, Sally M., ed., *The Ethnic Press in the United States: A Historical Analysis and Handbook,* New York: Greenwood, 1987

Park, Robert E., *The Immigrant Press and Its Control,* St. Clair Shores, Michigan: Scholarly, 1970

Pozzetta, George, ed., *American Immigration & Ethnicity: Immigrant Institutions: The Organization of Immigrant Life,* vol. 5, New York: Garland, 1991

Zubrycki, Jerzy, "The Role of the Foreign-Language Press in Migrant Integration," in *Media Voices: An Historical Perspective: An Anthology,* edited by Jean Folkerts, New York: Macmillan, 1992; Toronto, Ontario: Maxwell Macmillan Canada, 1992

Exchanges

Earlier editors' method of swapping information

For newspapers in the first 200 years of U.S. journalism, the exchange of newspapers from one newspaper office to another provided the major source of nonlocal news that appeared in publications across the continent. Congress considered the exchanges so important to the nation in its early days that it provided for postage-free delivery of newspapers between offices.

Editors drew freely on the contents of other newspapers and were known as much for their skill with scissors as with pen, the selection of stories from the exchanges being as important a reader service as editorial comment and local news coverage. Stories were reprinted, often verbatim, but not necessarily with credit. The exchanges were the basis for the booster press that printed favorable information about an area with the hope and expectation that it would be reprinted elsewhere and would encourage prospective settlers to move west.

Using exchanges to transmit news was a slow process; sometimes it took months for information to get from the east coast to the west coast. As a result, the telegraph was eagerly received by newspapers in larger centers. Because of the high cost of telegraphed information, however, small papers continued to rely on exchanges for their national and international news until late in the nineteenth century. Many twentieth-century editors continued the tradition by excerpting editorials from other newspapers.

BARBARA CLOUD

See also Cooperative News Gathering; Post Office and the Media; Telegraph

Further Reading

Cloud, Barbara Lee, *The Business of Newspapers on the Western Frontier,* Reno: University of Nevada Press, 1992

Kielbowicz, Richard B., *News in the Mail: The Press, Post Office, and Public Information, 1700–1860s,* New York: Greenwood, 1989

F

Fairness Doctrine

FCC policy on broadcast editorials

Premised on scarcity of the natural resource of frequencies available in the electromagnetic spectrum, the Federal Communications Commission (FCC) forbade broadcasters from using their stations to promote one-sided viewpoints about controversial issues of public importance. This was to ensure that the public had access to varying, contrasting views for the purpose of informing themselves.

As early as 1929, the Federal Radio Commission (FRC) ruled that radio should present contrasting views about public issues. The Communications Act of 1934 confirmed the 1927 act's philosophy of obligating licensees to serve "public interest, convenience, and necessity"; it codified in Section 315 that broadcasters must provide "equal opportunities" to opposing candidates for public office. In 1959, Congress added to Section 315(a) that broadcasters should "afford reasonable opportunity for the discussion of conflicting views on issues of public importance."

Initially, the FCC had prohibited editorializing; it forbade stations from being advocates for a political candidate or for one side of a debated issue (in the Mayflower decision, 1941). In 1949, it relented, permitting station editorials as long as licensees offered reasonable opportunity for contrasting viewpoints; this was the genesis of the "fairness doctrine." Stations licensed to serve the public interest were to offer balanced, fair treatment of debated topics. A decade later, the FCC positively encouraged editorializing as a public service.

But the radio-television industry resisted a federal agency's applying the policy of "fair" treatment to specific issues, claiming that this countered the First Amendment's freedom of the press and also Section 326 of the Communications Act of 1934, which forbade FCC censoring of broadcast content. Respected CBS President Frank Stanton formally objected for decades before congressional committees, calling it the "unfairness doctrine" because it "chilled" broadcasters' airing of robust debate; they feared running afoul of the regulatory agency's interpretation of whether they provided adequate access to varying views on controversial subjects. Broadcasters generally claimed their concern for not offending large segments of their audiences or the advertisers acted as a self-interested check on unbalanced presentations; government after-the-fact sanctions amounted to ex post facto censorship because broadcasters avoided topics in order to preclude complaints to the FCC. (Even if the FCC rarely penalized stations for violating the "fairness doctrine," the extensive time and legal expenses to respond to complainants and federal inquiries was deterrent enough.) Critics and public interest groups, however, judged broadcasters unfair regarding the treatment of some topics or speakers in programs; they supported federal oversight of licensees' stewardship.

Application of the doctrine seriously altered network and station practices in the mid-1960s; the appellate court supported the FCC's requirement that broadcasters offer reply time to counter commercial advertising for cigarettes because whether they were a threat to health was a controversial issue (*Banzhaf* v. *FCC*). This became moot when Congress banned all cigarette ads from electronic media after January 1, 1971.

In 1969, the U.S. Supreme Court supported special requirements for broadcast media because under the First Amendment "it is the right of viewers and listeners, not the right of the broadcasters, which is paramount" (*Red Lion Broadcasting* v. *FCC*). But in 1973, the Supreme Court affirmed broadcasters' rights as "editors to edit" in determining what advertisements they would or would not carry – even when the ads treated controversial issues such as the Vietnam War (*CBS* v. *Democratic National Committee*).

The heated controversy found major corporations, broadcasters, interest groups, and federal officials either supporting the doctrine (such as Mobil Oil, Westinghouse Group W stations, Accuracy in Media, some U.S. senators and representatives) or opposing it (networks, most local stations, the Radio-Television News Directors Association, the American Civil Liberties Union, most U.S. senators and representatives).

As radio and television stations proliferated even in smaller markets, concern diminished about one or another station's alleged unbalanced coverage of controversial issues. The range of licensees, types of program formats, and listening and viewing patterns offered a wide field of "voices" in local markets. (The impact of national networks' news and entertainment programs also diminished as cable program services multiplied, adding to the multiplicity of voices.) In later decades, members of Congress differed in their stances for and against the fairness doctrine. Meanwhile, successive Democratic and Republican FCC chairmen sought to resolve the debate over the doctrine in waves of what was variously termed in the 1970s re-regulation (Republican Richard Wiley) and deregulation (Democrat Charles Ferris), and in the 1980s, un-regulation (Republicans Mark Fowler and Dennis Patrick). Congressional reaction to massive reduction of FCC rules prompted a swing back to modest regulation in the 1990s (Republican Alfred Sikes and Democrat Reede Hundt).

As deregulation advanced under FCC Chairman Mark Fowler in the mid-1980s, a study reported that up until then the commission had revoked only one station license (that of Reverend Carl McIntyre's WXUR in Media, Pennsylvania, 1972) for violating the rule. Of 6,787 complaints to the FCC in 1984 (one in 10 by letter, the rest by telephone), the FCC sent official inquiries to only six stations; just one prompted a judgment that the station acted "unreasonably" – the first negative finding in half a decade. The commission was hardly overbearing, but some questioned whether the FCC by then was simply ignoring most complaints or was ineffectual.

The FCC jettisoned the doctrine in 1987 as not only tortuous to apply and often unworkable but also unconstitutional. Congress objected to the agency's unilaterally abandoning the matter, claiming it was embedded in federal law, not merely in the agency's regulations pursuant to the law. The courts, however, supported the FCC's position that it had crafted the doctrine and that the procedure amounted to intruding into media content contrary to constitutional provisions. Nevertheless, Congress repeatedly reintroduced bills to reinstate the doctrine, including efforts to write an entirely new communications law supplanting that enacted in 1934. Both houses passed a bill codifying the doctrine in 1987 that President Reagan vetoed.

Related topics, in addition to that of "equal time" (equal opportunities) for opposing political candidates, are government regulations on personal attack, political editorializing or endorsements, and the Cullman Doctrine regarding paid advertisements dealing with controversial issues that trigger the requirement of providing time for opposing views even if not paid by sponsors.

JAMES A. BROWN

See also Broadcast Regulation, Communication Act of 1934; "Equal Time" Provision; Personal Attack Rule; Radio Act of 1927

Further Reading
Friendly, Fred W., *The Good Guys, the Bad Guys, and the First Amendment: Free Speech vs. Fairness in Broadcasting,* New York: Random House, 1976

Farnsworth, Philo Taylor

Inventor of key television components

Philo Taylor Farnsworth has been called the forgotten father of television. Although he was raised on a farm, his ap-

titudes were in music, science, and learning. While still in high school, he diagrammed for his teacher, Justin Tolman, a pattern for television. This diagram was later developed through his experimentation into the Farnsworth television system and was instrumental in his winning a patent interference case against the Radio Corporation of America, his fierce competitor throughout the development of the television system.

Farnsworth's first formal laboratories were in San Francisco, where the first single dimension lines were transmitted and a crude television image was created from the Farnsworth system in September 1927. Farnsworth successfully developed a television system and organized Farnsworth Television Incorporated and the Farnsworth Radio and Television Corporation to manufacture and sell radios and televisions. Following World War II, Farnsworth sold his businesses and patents to the International Telephone and Telegraph Corporation (ITT), where he worked on space science technology and nuclear fusion. In 1968, Farnsworth retired from ITT to establish Philo T. Farnsworth and Associates to continue his work on fusion.

His corporate prospectus claimed that ideas from Farnsworth resulted in "every television set sold utilizing at least six of his basic patents." His personal papers listed more than 150 U.S. patents.

Farnsworth's work received numerous scientific honors, and in 1990, a statue was dedicated in Washington, D.C.'s, Statuary Hall. The inscription reads, "Philo Taylor Farnsworth: Inventor of Television."

DONALD G. GODFREY

Further Reading
Everson, George, *The Story of Television: The Life of Philo T. Farnsworth,* New York: Norton, 1949
Farnsworth, Elma G., *Distant Vision: Romance and Discovery on an Invisible Frontier,* Salt Lake City, Utah: PemberlyKent, 1990
Hofer, Stephen F., "Philo Farnsworth: Television's Pioneer," *Journal of Broadcasting* 23 (1979)

Philo T. Farnsworth with his 1929 television receiver
(Museum of Broadcast Communications)

Godfrey, Donald G., and Alf Pratte, "Elma 'Pem' Gardner Farnsworth: The Pioneering of Television," *Journalism History* 20:2 (Summer 1994), pp. 74–79

Feature Syndicates

Providing similar contents to numerous newspapers around the country

Newspaper mail exchanges encouraged editors to borrow poems, short stories, ironic paragraphs, columns, unusual items, and moral anecdotes from each other. During the American Civil War, full pages of human-interest material were offered for the first time. Although the popularity of feature syndicates peaked in 1900 when 14,717 weeklies kept hamlets informed, in 1995 modern syndicates still sold stories, comics, and columns to big and small newspapers all over the country.

The first feature syndicate arose in Wisconsin. When his backshop employees enlisted in the Union army in 1861, Ansel N. Kellogg, the editor of the *Baraboo (Wisconsin) Republic,* ordered preprinted war news. These readyprints saved Kellogg hours of hand-setting type. Initially, he bought half sheets from the *Wisconsin State Journal* to fold around his local half pages. Later, he purchased the first and fourth pages from the *Journal* and ran local copy inside them.

As the war progressed, many editors of small papers needed help filling their pages. The *Evening Wisconsin* of Milwaukee began distributing readyprints with patent medicine ads on the back, which lowered the cost and, thus, appealed to editors. Soon people called the readyprints patents. Some dailies criticized weeklies for using patents, but in 1865, Kellogg, who had moved to Chicago to found a feature service with Andrew W. Aikens, sold his patent insides to 53 clients.

Kellogg's readyprint pages – full of letters from New York, from Washington, D.C., and from foreign correspondents as well as children's reading, agricultural information, serials, women's features, poetry, and miscellaneous material – flourished. When Kellogg died in 1886, the publishers subscribing to his syndicate numbered 1,398. Of course, competitors entered the market, including the Chicago Newspaper Union. In 1880, the Western Newspaper Union was founded. This monopoly swallowed the A.N. Kellogg Company in 1906, the readyprint and mat service of the American Press Association in 1917, and many other syndicates.

The American Press Association changed the readyprint business by developing stereotyped plates in 1875. Instead of sending printed pages, the company shipped plates the editors could cut to fit their column needs. Wags referred to this process as "editing with a saw." Soon, Kellogg and other patent-inside producers also offered the plates. The readyprint business boomed, spreading throughout the east and south.

In the early 1880s, visionaries like Irving Bacheller courted dailies with boilerplate syndicated features. He sup-

plied many Sunday supplements with engaging articles. By 1886, seven large syndicates competed for space in dailies. One served 140 customers, including the *Milwaukee (Wisconsin) Sentinel,* the *Philadelphia Press,* and the *Chicago Tribune.* The stable of authors that syndicates employed helped dailies grow. The American Press Association hired Jack London and Eugene Field. S.S. McClure founded his feature syndicate on October 4, 1884, and charged papers a small fee, which added up as subscribers increased. Helen Hunt Jackson, W.D. Howells, Arthur Conan Doyle, Rudyard Kipling, and Robert Louis Stevenson worked for McClure, who later became a famous magazine publisher. Mark Twain, Bret Harte, Joel Chandler Harris, and Bill Nye also wrote for syndicates.

The syndicates sought stories and articles of particular interest to women and children, the audiences that newspapers courted to secure advertisements from the department stores. In 1891, the United Press (UP) launched a literary bureau to produce 10,000 words of "Sunday miscellany" weekly.

In 1895, William Randolph Hearst launched the King Features Syndicate, and the Scripps-Howard chain started its United Feature Syndicate in 1919. By World War I, the feature syndicates began "budget services" so that customers could select features from a pool of options instead of ordering a fixed package. Publishers then gave the term syndicate to organizations that sold features separately, and the term services to businesses offering packages of features, comics, and news photos. As the twentieth century advanced, technology made obsolete the same readyprints that once had enhanced more than 7,000 papers.

The publisher of the *New York Globe,* Jason Rogers, united 28 newspapers, including the *Chicago Daily News* and the *Boston Globe,* to form the feature syndicate Associated News in 1911. It attracted such stars as R.L. Ripley of "Believe It or Not" fame. J.M. Patterson, the publisher of the *Chicago Tribune,* expanded his paper's nearly decade-old feature service by forming a syndicate with the *New York Daily News.* The *New York Tribune* offered its features to other papers in 1914 and merged with the *New York Herald* to form the Herald Tribune Syndicate in 1924. Walter Lippmann and Mark Sullivan lead their cavalcade of talent. C.H.K. Curtis, the publisher of the *Philadelphia Ledger,* started the Ledger Syndicate in 1915 and culled features from his magazines, the *Saturday Evening Post,* the *Ladies' Home Journal,* and *Country Gentleman,* as well as from the *Ledger.*

The Association of Newspaper Syndicates began with 33 companies in 1925, and in 1926 united 100 affiliates employing 750 writers and artists who generated 2,000 features. A decade later, trunk services like the Associated Press (AP), the United Press, and the International News Service absorbed many separate feature agencies. By 1934, Hearst's King Features Syndicate was called "the greatest circulation combination on earth." It offered the gamut of materials: fiction, nonfiction, short items, picture spreads, inspirational pieces, columns, and sports articles.

In 1936, the Newspaper Enterprise Association (NEA) astounded its competition by delivering 40 to 50 inches of features, photos, and comics via the "aeroplane." A quarter century before the Associated Press entered the feature syndicate field, the United Press launched the NEA in the Scripps empire in 1902. The UP started Acme Newspictures two years before AP launched a comparable service. The giant wire service became UPI after merging with the International News Service in 1958.

Since then, syndicates have remained a vital source of lively copy for newspapers. The 1996 *Writer's Market* listed 49 syndicates to which authors could send a variety of material, including puzzles, comics, columns, fillers, and, of course, features. The *Editor and Publisher Syndicate Directory* contained the contact persons, addresses, and phone numbers for the array of syndicates that battled for newspaper space in the late 1990s.

PAULETTE D. KILMER

See also Exchanges; Readyprint

Further Reading
Watson, Elmo Scott, *A History of Newspaper Syndicates in the United States: 1865–1935,* Chicago: 1936

Federal Communications Commission

Regulator of electronic communication

The Communications Act of 1934 created the Federal Communications Commission (FCC) as an independent federal agency responsible directly to Congress. A regulatory, rather than executive, agency, the FCC was charged with regulating interstate and international communications by radio, television, wire, satellite, and cable. The FCC was empowered to make rules and regulations, hold hearings, and fine those entities it licensed or revoke their licenses. The FCC made frequency assignments and licensed users of those frequencies, who were required to be citizens of the United States.

Initially, the FCC consisted of seven presidentially appointed commissioners who served staggered terms. The FCC was cut back to five commissioners in June 1983. A majority of the appointees could be of the same political affiliation. The commissioners could have no financial interest in the industries they regulated. Most of the people appointed in the initial years of the FCC were lawyers with experience in public utility regulation or governmental service.

When the Communications Act of 1934 was adopted, there were some 623 radio stations licensed or under construction. By 1940, there were 1,465 stations, and until that year, only AM stations existed as authorized broadcast services other than short-wave. The main concerns of the early FCC were to improve program and advertising policies of broadcasters. The Communications Act specifically prohibited the FCC from censoring broadcasting. It was deter-

mined by the courts that the FCC could decide if a station's policies or programs were "in the public interest, convenience and necessity" when the commission was considering approving a license or license renewal. The FCC also was initially concerned over the potential for monopoly in the telephone and broadcast industries. This led to rate regulation of the telephone industry and regulations controlling some of the business relationships between networks and their affiliates. The commission also made rules limiting the number and type of services that could be owned by one person or corporation in each market and restricting the co-ownership of newspapers and broadcast stations in the same market. While the FCC did not license networks as such, station licensees were subject to network regulations to foster competition in broadcasting. Many of those regulations intended to prevent monopoly were allowed to expire in 1995 on the grounds that technology had increased the number of services available and thereby provided diversity.

The FCC set technical standards of operation for broadcasting. After hearings, the FCC approved commercial FM radio operation and commercial television operations to begin in 1941. Television signals were to be transmitted in accordance with FCC regulations regarding the signal format, radiated power, modulation depth, and a variety of other parameters that adhered to the rules of good practice. These standards assured that the viewer would receive a stable, high-quality image and clear sound. In 1942, only 10 television stations were authorized to be on the air, and World War II froze any further licensing. In 1945, the commission allocated 13 channels for commercial television. More than 3,000 new radio stations came into being after the end of World War II with the approval of daytime-only radio stations. From 1948 to 1952, the FCC froze all television licensing after approving only 108 television licenses because of problems with reception and allocation. The television licensing freeze allowed time for the Radio Corporation of American (RCA) and the CBS network to further develop color television and permitted the opening of frequencies in the ultrahigh frequency (UHF) range. The freeze also gave time for public groups to develop support for the idea of reserving channels solely for educational, noncommercial use. In 1953, the FCC approved the industry-endorsed compatible NTSC (National Television System Committee) color television system (developed by RCA and the NBC network), reversing their 1950 decision that had authorized a noncompatible field-sequential system developed by CBS. The FCC also in 1953 approved more UHF television channels and reserved channel space for educational, noncommercial television stations.

The FCC exerted a substantial degree of control over the operations of stations through the dispensing of licenses, reprimands, and short-term license renewals; the denying of license renewals; and the revocation of licenses with fines or forfeitures. The commission could also issue cease-and-desist orders.

When cable television began in 1949, only cities and states seemed interested in regulating this new service. In 1962, after broadcast stations began to argue that cable was introducing competitive services to the communities they served, the FCC asserted limited regulatory control over cable television systems that used microwave relays to bring distant signals into broadcasters' local markets. The FCC began actively to regulate cable in 1965. In 1968, the Supreme Court upheld the FCC's authority to regulate cable television as ancillary to their control over broadcast licenses. The commission required cable operators to carry the signals of local stations; they also were to refrain from duplicating programs broadcast by local stations by carrying other, distant stations showing the same programs within two weeks of the local broadcasts. In 1966, the nonduplication rule was changed to same-day protection. However, the FCC did not preempt localities and states from all regulation of cable. Restrictions were placed on the ownership of cable systems by broadcasters and on broadcasting by cable in the same markets.

In 1972, the FCC began deregulating cable and eliminated the distant-signal and syndicated-exclusivity rules. By 1984, Congress had removed most of the FCC's regulatory power over cable through its passage of the Cable Communications Policy Act of 1984. It restricted how municipalities awarded, administered, and enforced cable television franchises, including rate regulation. It also banned the cross-ownership of cable television systems and cable programming networks by telephone companies in their local telephone service areas.

After some eight years of experience with these policies, Congress reacted to pressure and enacted the 1992 Cable Consumer Protection and Competition Act. This reinstated local government regulation of basic rates, required cable companies to make the same programming available to their competitors, and granted local broadcasters the right to channel space on the cable system or the right to charge for their carriage. The FCC also was ordered to adopt rate regulations to attempt to control the rates subscribers were charged. However, the FCC's rules permitted systems to increase rates as long as the "average" monthly rate did not increase. Many subscribers rates went up rather than down. In March 1994, the FCC was furthered directed by Congress to obtain lower rates, and when these new rules came into effect, most subscribers saw their rates decrease.

In addition to the five commissioners, the FCC employed about 2,200 lawyers, engineers, hearing examiners, administrators, and secretarial employees. These employees were civil servants.

MARVIN R. BENSMAN

See also Broadcast Licensing; Broadcast Regulation; Cable Television; Communications Act of 1934; Cross-Media Ownership; Federal Radio Commission; Noncommercial Television; Radio Act of 1927; Radio Technology; Television Technology

Further Reading

Bensman, Marvin R., *Broadcast/Cable Regulation,* Lanham, Maryland: University Press of America, 1990
Hilliard, Robert L., *The Federal Communications Commission: A Primer,* Boston: Focal, 1991

Federal Radio Commission

First federal attempt at regulating electronic communication

The Radio Act of 1927 created the Federal Radio Commission (FRC), a five-member board, to regulate broadcasting when regulations Secretary of Commerce Herbert Hoover imposed upon radio during the 1920s broke down. Late in 1926, the U.S. House and Senate passed radio bills, but major differences existed between them. The Senate bill designated a new commission as licensing authority, while the House gave the commerce secretary strong licensing authority. In conference, the commission became a temporary agency to straighten out interference, with powers reverting to the commerce secretary after one year. The commission was then to become an appellate body. Commissioners represented different regions of the country and served six-year terms. In 1929, Congress made the commission permanent.

The Radio Commission used the criterion of "public interest, convenience and/or necessity" to set regulations for radio and began to clean up the airwaves in March 1927. Before Congress adjourned, it confirmed only three of the five commissioners nominated by President Calvin Coolidge. Two, including the chairman, died before year's end, and Congress failed to appropriate funds for the commission's operation. Further complicating the FRC's duties was the expiration of all radio licenses two months after the Radio Act became law. The FRC immediately closed 40 stations operating on Canadian frequencies and extended most broadcast stations' licenses for up to 90 days. In addition, the FRC specified frequency, transmitter power, and time of operation for each station. To further eliminate interference, stations in the same city were separated by a minimum of 50 kilohertz (kHz).

While these actions cut interference, they were not a permanent solution. In a series of general orders through 1929, the commission set the broadcast band between 550 and 1,500 kHz, eliminated portable radio stations, placed stiffer rules and penalties on deviation from assigned frequency, removed 109 stations from the air, and set a system of station classification. This system assigned 40 of the 96 frequencies to "clear channels." Only one station was allowed on these high-power frequencies, and eight clear channels were assigned to each of five geographic zones covering the United States. At night, these channels provided better service to rural areas through their singular classifications and grants of power up to 50,000 watts. An additional seven channels per zone, or 35 channels in total, provided regional service. Only two or three stations were assigned to these channels. The balance of 21 channels were assigned to low-power local stations or reserved for Canada or Mexico.

After dealing with these interference problems, the FRC tackled programming issues. Under the Radio Act, it could not censor programming, but it could decide whether a station operated in the public interest or in the private interest of the station's owner. In the early 1930s, the FRC refused license renewal in four noted programming cases: John Brinkley's KFKB in Milford, Kansas; Norman Baker's

KTNT in Muscatine, Iowa; Reverend Robert Shuler's KGEF in Los Angeles and William Schaeffer's KVEP in Portland, Oregon. Brinkley used his station to prescribe his own patent medicines over the air, while Baker attacked individuals and organizations he disliked as well as promoted his own hospital and "cancer cures." Shuler attacked other religious organizations, city and state officials, and law enforcement agencies and courts in southern California. Schaeffer allowed his station to be used by a former political candidate, Robert Duncan, who attacked his former opponent with what the courts termed indecent language.

Of course, these cases and the FRC's overall ability to set regulations for broadcasting under the Constitution were challenged in court. In general, the courts upheld the FRC's right to regulate the medium and upheld the constitutionality of the Radio Act of 1927. In each of the above cases, the courts stated that the FRC had applied the "public interest" standard appropriately, while they confirmed Congress' ability to set up the FRC to regulate radio as a medium of interstate commerce.

By 1932, the commission had established important technical and legal precedents that still stood at the end of the century. In June 1934, under the newly passed Communications Act, the FRC was replaced by the Federal Communications Commission. In its seven-year existence, the Federal Radio Commission had cut station interference, established technical standards for stations, and instituted regulations affecting programming offered in the public interest. In all, under its leadership, broadcasting became a stable medium of information and entertainment.

LOUISE BENJAMIN

See also Broadcast Licensing; Broadcast Regulation; Communications Act of 1934; Federal Communications Commission; Hoover, Herbert, and Radio Regulation; Radio Act of 1927

Further Reading
Rosen, Philip, *The Modern Stentors: Radio Broadcasters and the Federal Government, 1920–1934*, Westport, Connecticut: Greenwood, 1980

Federal Trade Commission

Empowered to regulate deceptive advertising

The Federal Trade Commission Act of 1914 set up the Federal Trade Commission (FTC) with the very broad mandate of preventing unfair methods of competition in interstate commerce. Much of the law's wording was taken from the Sherman Act of 1890, which was enforceable only through the U.S. Department of Justice. Originally, most of the commission's work was presumed to be devoted to trust-busting and such related activities as investigating price-fixing. Indeed, the FTC did function in these areas. However, the broad mandate gave the commission wide latitude in activities as long as the courts agreed these were within its

purview. False and deceptive advertising serves as one example. Although the enabling legislation gave no specific mandate to the FTC to investigate advertising, false and deceptive advertising was seen as an unfair method of competition, and the commission began investigating cases involving the practice as early as 1915.

Successful prosecution of deceptive advertising was hampered because the commission had a difficult burden of proof: not only did it have to prove the ad deceptive, it also had to prove that competitors had been harmed. The passage of the Wheeler-Lea amendments in 1938 eased this burden of proof by no longer requiring that there was injury to competitors. More importantly, it required the commission only to show that the ad had a tendency or capacity to deceive. The intent of the original FTC act was to foster honest competition among businesses. The Wheeler-Lea amendments provided for manifest protection of the consumer as well.

The FTC's powers were enlarged or modified over time through subsequent legislation, such as the FTC Trade Improvements Act of 1975 and the FTC Improvement Act of 1980. The courts, through their power to uphold or overturn FTC decisions, also enlarged or limited the commission's scope and powers.

The Federal Trade Commission was composed of five commissioners, one of whom served as chairperson. Organizationally, the FTC was broken down into the Bureaus of Competition, Economics, and Consumer Protection. Deceptive advertising was the province of a unit within the Bureau of Consumer Protection. Some staff were stationed in regional offices. The 1995 budget of the FTC was approximately $103 million. In 1995, the permanent FTC staff consisted of 911 persons, with 203 in the Bureau of Consumer Protection. About $5,400,000 of the FTC budget went to the Advertising Practices Program.

The FTC had no punitive powers. Its charge was to stop or redress unfair practices. The primary weapons against deceptive advertising were consent orders and cease-and-desist orders. In both cases, advertisers signed agreements not to engage in the deceptive practice again. Consent orders were analogous to plea bargaining, in which the nature and wording of the order is worked out and agreed to by both parties. Cease-and-desist orders were issued as the result of the adversarial process involved in formal litigation. The courts were empowered to fine advertisers who subsequently violated either type of order.

ERIC J. ZANOT

See also Wheeler-Lea Amendments

Further Reading
Krugman, Dean, *Advertising: Its Role in Modern Marketing*, 8th ed., Fort Worth, Texas: Dryden, 1994
Mercer, Dick, "Tempest in a Soup Can," *Advertising Age* 65:44 (October 17, 1994), pp. 25–29
Preston, Ivan, *The Tangled Web They Weave: Truth, Falsity & Advertisers,* Madison: University of Wisconsin Press, 1994
Stern, Louis W., and Thomas L. Eovaldi, *Legal Aspects of*

Marketing Strategy: Antitrust and Consumer Protection Issues, Englewood Cliffs, New Jersey, and London: Prentice-Hall, 1984

Wagner, Susan, *The Federal Trade Commission,* New York: Praeger, 1971

Feminist Media

Communication avenues for feminist movement

Newsletters dominated as feminists' principal communication link during the heyday of the second wave of feminism, which spawned at least 560 newsletters, newspapers, magazines, and journals between 1968 and 1973. Female activists' ties to the New Left spearheaded this broad grassroots communications network in two ways. First, leftist women learned how to write, produce, and distribute publications. Second, they created their own media partly in rebellion against pervasive sexism in underground publications. Women at New York City's *Rat,* for instance, seized the male-run newspaper and transformed it into a feminist paper called *LibeRATion.*

The movement's first national newsletter was a nameless, mimeographed sheet published in Chicago in March 1968 that carried the tagline "Voice of the Women's Liberation Movement." That phrase gained national currency when it was elevated to the masthead in the next issue, one of six that appeared over 16 months. Other influential but short-lived women's liberation publications surfaced in 1968: *Notes from the First Year,* the New York Radical Women journal that created a stir with "The Myth of the Vaginal Orgasm"; and *No More Fun and Games,* published by Cell 16 in Boston. The publication *off our backs,* based in Washington, D.C., and launched in 1970, enjoyed greater longevity along with a reputation for quality production and distinctive humor. It parodied *Playboy* centerfolds with a nude photo spread of a potbellied man in coy poses.

Women's liberation publications were more militant and flamboyant than liberal feminist publications that focused on legal reform. *NOW Acts,* the National Organization for Women newsletter created in 1968, for example, lobbied for the equal rights amendment and women's legislation. Other publications catered to specialized audiences such as Chicanas (*CFM Report*) or gay women (*Killer Dyke*) and reflected the movement's ideological diversity. Newspapers that sprang up nationwide – *Ain't I a Woman* in Iowa City, Iowa; *Bitch* in Milwaukee, Wisconsin; *Women's Press* in Oregon – helped the women's movement gain critical mass.

Far-flung women's liberation publications shared several characteristics. All-female staffs abhorred hierarchy and wrote collective editorials. They banned sexist advertising, and editorial content covered issues ignored or ridiculed by mainstream media, such as violence against women and pornography. Self-help columns ranged from changing a flat tire to do-it-yourself abortions. Poignant, often angry, personal journalism recounted individuals' experience with rape, domestic abuse, or job discrimination. Extended letters columns emphasized reader participation. Poetry, original artwork, and feminist cartoons became staples.

Ms. magazine adopted many of these techniques in 1972, when its preview issue of 300,000 copies sold out in days. Feminism also expanded in the 1970s to include feminist book publishers, music labels, film societies, and radio shows.

Feminist media were not unknown before the 1963 appearance of Betty Friedan's *The Feminine Mystique,* widely credited with sparking the women's liberation movement. Several small publications shouldered the feminist flag prior to the 1960s. *Equal Rights* (1923–54) spearheaded the call for an equal rights amendment originated by the National Woman's Party; the *Independent Woman* (1920–56) championed professionals and businesswomen; and the *Ladder* (1957–62) offered information and community to lesbians.

LINDA LUMSDEN

See also Suffrage Press; Underground Press

Further Reading

Beasley, Maurine Hoffman, and Sheila Silver, *Women in Media: A Documentary Source Book,* Washington, D.C.: Women's Institute for Freedom of the Press, 1977

Evans, Sara M., *Personal Politics: The Roots of Women's Liberation in the Civil Rights Movement and the New Left,* New York: Vintage, 1980

Mather, Anne, "A History of Feminist Periodicals, Part II," *Journalism History* 1 (1974–75)

_____, "A History of Feminist Periodicals, Part III," *Journalism History* 1 (1975)

Morgan, Robin, *Sisterhood is Powerful: An Anthology of Writings from the Women's Liberation Movement,* New York: Random House, 1970

_____, *The Word of a Woman: Feminist Dispatches 1968–1992,* New York: Norton, 1992

First Amendment in the Eighteenth Century

Protection grew from practical political needs

Well into their third century, the free speech and free press provisions of the First Amendment to the U.S. Constitution were treated reverentially. There was general support for the First Amendment even as there was substantial disagreement over the proper meanings of and boundaries for those freedoms. In the United States of the late eighteenth century, however, the speech and press freedoms "guaranteed" in the Bill of Rights were symbols of practical politics far more than evidence of high values placed on expression.

The speech and press clauses of the First Amendment, like other portions of the Bill of Rights, were offered as a compromise, a tactic to quiet opposition to the draft Constitution of 1787. But words are weapons, and the language agreed to by Federalists in order to defuse anti-federalist arguments against ratification of the Constitution survived and gained substance.

The First Amendment's speech and press provisions resonated in the eighteenth century with hundreds of years of Anglo-American struggles for freedom to criticize government, evoking memories of John Milton, John Peter Zenger, and John Wilkes. Even if the speech and press language of the First Amendment began as words used in a largely ceremonial fashion, those words were given lives of their own by court interpretations in the twentieth century.

The First Amendment, it has been said, became both a sword and a shield defending utterance or publication of unpopular ideas. In the pivotal U.S. Supreme Court decision in *Near* v. *Minnesota* (1931), the First Amendment finally attained truly national impact, for it was invoked to prevent prepublication censorship by states as well as by the federal government. The Court held that prior restraint could occur only in time of war, in cases of incitement to violence or overthrow of government, and in cases of obscenity, a term the 1931 Court did not bother to define.

One key to understanding the First Amendment in an eighteenth century context is its first word (italics added): "*Congress* shall make no Law respecting an establishment of religion, or prohibiting the free exercise thereof; or abridging the freedom of speech, or of the press; or the right of the people peaceably to assemble, and to petition the Government for a redress of grievances." Note that the First Amendment enunciated protections for expression and association against national, not state, power. Nine of the original states already had constitutional press clauses, but only one – Pennsylvania – mentioned both speech and press.

James Madison of Virginia, a leading force in the 1787 Constitutional Convention in Philadelphia, in 1789 drafted the amendments that became the federal Bill of Rights. He led the way in keeping the Federalist pledge to submit amendments to Congress. Without those promised amendments, the Constitution could not have been adopted in Virginia and New York, states crucial to organizing a truly national government.

As historian Merrill Jensen emphasized, the Constitution of 1787 was the product of a revolution in 1787. In that "revolution," men he termed extreme nationalists set about replacing the nation's first constitution, the Articles of Confederation, with a document that would move power from the states to the national government.

For the most part, history is taught from the winning side. That explains, in part, why writings of Federalists Alexander Hamilton, James Madison, and John Jay – the "Publius" essays now commonly known as *The Federalist* or *The Federalist Papers* – are so often taught in high school and college history courses.

Often, little or no reference is made to anti-federalist arguments opposing "Publius," arguments expressed in the writings of "Centinel" – George or Samuel Bryan of Pennsylvania. The anti-federalists have not received sufficient credit for providing the opposition that made the Bill of Rights a political necessity for the Federalists.

Even though the newspapers supporting the Constitution were greatly outnumbered and often were slow getting through the Federalist-controlled mails, a skimming of the Bill of Rights will summarize many of the anti-federalist arguments against the Constitution. These rights had to be spelled out to deflect and dilute anti-federalist charges that freedoms of speech, press, assembly, and religion would be taken away under a centralized new government designed by the Philadelphia Constitutional Convention.

However disingenuous some of their protestations, the Antifederalists won the battle of the Bill of Rights but lost what they regarded as the war when a stronger, more centralized government was adopted under the Constitution. One explanation for the bitter opposition to the Constitution is that the popular leaders who brought about the Declaration of Independence in 1776 were not the same men who made the Constitution. As Merrill Jensen noted, only four signers of the Constitution in 1787 had willingly supported independence in 1776: Elbridge Gerry of Massachusetts, Roger Sherman of Connecticut, Benjamin Franklin of Pennsylvania, and George Wythe of Virginia.

Although the new national government first met under the Constitution in 1788, the amendments making up the Bill of Rights were accepted by Congress and were not adopted by the states until December 15, 1791. Thus, the First Amendment – once termed a "chance product of political expediency" by Leonard W. Levy – became a part of the Constitution. Its words and fundamental worth have expanded and contracted but endured.

Throughout much of the twentieth century, lawyers, judges, and politicians frequently tried to read "the original intent," claiming to know the motivations and essential meanings within the First Amendment and the Bill of Rights. There is, however, little legislative history from the first Congress meeting under the Constitution to help divine what the First Amendment's 45 words are supposed to mean; records of votes in ratifying conventions also are lost to history.

Despite the unequivocal command of the First Amendment protecting speech and press – "Congress shall make no law," Congress did pass the Alien and Sedition Acts of 1798, only seven years after the adoption of the Bill of Rights. Driven by hysteria fueled by Federalist fears of an approaching war with France, the Alien Act extended the time to become a naturalized citizen from seven to 14 years. It was hardly coincidental that some of the more troublesome writers and printers did not have their citizenship papers.

Federalist indictments proceeded against opposition Republican journalists and writers. In all, 14 indictments were brought, and all resulted in convictions. In perhaps the most famous prosecution, a member of Congress – the tempestuous Matthew Lyon of Vermont – was jailed for four months and fined $1,000. Matthew Lyon's crime: he had written that President Adams and the executive branch showed "an unbounded thirst for ridiculous pomp, foolish adulation, and selfish continual grasp for power." When Republican editor Anthony Haswell of the *Vermont Gazette* defended Lyon as a victim of "the oppressive hand of usurped power," Haswell was fined $200 (perhaps two years' wages for an average worker) and sentenced to two months in federal prison.

The Bill of Rights
(Reproduced from the Collections of the Library of Congress)

With the Kentucky and Virginia Resolutions of 1798, Thomas Jefferson and James Madison fought strenuously against the Alien and Sedition Acts, beginning to provide a working definition of what the First Amendment ought to mean. The Kentucky Resolutions – written by Jefferson but submitted to the Kentucky legislature by John Breckenridge – were offered late in 1798, before the Supreme Court's 1803 decision in *Marbury* v. *Madison* that the Court had the power to declare acts of Congress unconstitutional.

The Kentucky Resolutions declared that the Alien and Sedition Acts encroached on powers reserved to the states by the Tenth Amendment, including "the right of judging how far the licentiousness of speech and press may be abridged without lessening their useful freedom." In the Virginia Resolutions of 1798, Madison's language was more strident: Despite the First Amendment's prohibitions, the Alien and Sedition Acts were "leveled against the right of freely examining public characters and measures, and of free communication among the people thereon, which has ever been justly deemed the only effectual guardian of every other right."

The Alien and Sedition Acts were allowed to expire in 1801 when Jefferson became the new nation's third president. Although seditious libel was removed from the national scene, other weapons were found to be used against the expression of unpopular views: state prosecutions for sedition or criminal libel, or civil libel suits designed to sue anti-establishment speakers or writers into submission.

No libertarian, Alexander Hamilton argued against bills of rights and a constitutional guarantee for freedom of the press in Number 84 of *The Federalist*. Whatever his motives, one of his conclusions about the security of "the liberty of the press" echoes whenever a national crisis leads to calls for controlling expression. "Its security," Hamilton wrote, "whatever fine declarations may be inserted in any constitution . . . must altogether depend on public opinion, and on the general spirit of the people and of the government."

DWIGHT L. TEETER JR.

See also Alien and Sedition Acts of 1798; American Revolution and the Press; Jefferson, Thomas, and the Press; Libel; Prior Restraint; Washington, George, and the Press; Zenger, John Peter

Further Reading
Anderson, David A., "The Origins of the Press Clause," *UCLA Law Review* 30:3 (1983)
Jensen, Merrill, *The American Revolution Within America*, New York: New York University Press, 1974
_____, *The New Nation: A History of the United States During the Confederation, 1781–1789*, New York: Knopf, 1950
Levy, Leonard Williams, *Emergence of a Free Press*, New York and Oxford: Oxford University Press, 1985
Main, Jackson Turner, *The Antifederalists: Critics of the Constitution, 1781–1788*, Chapel Hill: University of North Carolina Press, 1961
Rosenberg, Norman L., *Protecting the Best Men: An Interpretive History of the Law of Libel*, Chapel Hill: University of North Carolina Press, 1986
Smith, James Morton, *Freedom's Fetters: The Alien and Sedition Laws and American Civil Liberties*, Ithaca, New York: Cornell University Press, 1956

First Amendment in the Nineteenth Century

Laying the groundwork for late First Amendment interpretation

Although the First Amendment was attached to the U.S. Constitution in 1791, the nation knew little of its potential meaning throughout much of the nineteenth century. Few courts addressed free speech issues, and decisions handed down provided almost no guidance in the interpretation of constitutional guarantees. On the federal level, the U.S. Supreme Court sidestepped an opportunity to apply the Bill of Rights to the states in 1833, when Chief Justice John Marshall ruled that citizens had no recourse to the federal Bill of Rights because each state had its own bill of rights that imposed restrictions on its activities.

Regardless of Marshall's language, individual U.S. citizens and groups thought that the Bill of Rights meant something. During the American Antislavery Society's campaign to send abolitionist mail to the South, for instance, the group published a pamphlet defending its access to the mail by saying, "We never intend to surrender the liberty of speech, or of the press, or of conscience–blessings we have inherited from our fathers, and which we mean, so far as we are able, to transmit unimpaired to our children." And when Clement L. Vallandigham, a Southern sympathizer living in the North during the Civil War, was arrested for speaking against the war, he claimed to be incarcerated "for no other offense than my political opinions, and the defense of them and the rights of the people, and of your constitutional liberties." Although there may have been moral support for such claims, judicial backing did not exist.

The Civil War Amendments to the Constitution may have provided some support for interpreting the Bill of Rights more broadly. The Fourteenth Amendment, ratification of which was required for Southern states to rejoin the Union, read in part,

> No State shall make or enforce any law which shall abridge the privileges or immunities of citizens of the United States; nor shall any State deprive any person of life, liberty, or property, without due process of law; nor deny to any person within its jurisdiction the equal protection of the laws.

Such language might have made the Bill of Rights applicable to the state action. The Supreme Court ruled in 1873, however, that the "Privileges and Immunities" clause of the Fourteenth Amendment, under which the case was brought, applied solely to rights accruing to national citizenship.

The issue then became whether the First Amendment provided any protection where laws of the United States were involved. In 1876, a group of free blacks in Louisiana attempted to assemble to plan political action, and a group of whites launched a campaign of intimidation to bar such activity. The Supreme Court ruled that the Fourteenth Amendment did not protect individuals seeking to exercise their rights to associate from private individuals seeking to halt such activities. Constitutional guarantees applied only to official actions by the government against individuals.

Where questions of federal governmental power were properly presented, the Supreme Court upheld the right of Congress to exclude lottery materials from the mails, to impose a variety of restrictions on members of the Church of Jesus Christ of Latter-day Saints (Mormons) in an effort to stamp out polygamy, and to bar most federal workers from participating in political activities, thus denying them their rights of political speech, as part of civil service reform.

The lack of federal action led to an absence of precedent for the use of state courts forced them to deal with free expression matters on their own. State court judges relied on decisions from other jurisdictions, on the few legal treatises in existence that touched on free speech issues, on history, and often on what they perceived to be common sense. In many instances, when U.S. precedents were absent, the judges searched for guidance from more restrictive British interpretations. In the area of freedom of the press, many of their decisions were governed by what they determined to be the "good motives" and "justifiable ends" of the publication involved, terms introduced into the law of libel by Alexander Hamilton in 1805 that had become popular yardsticks over the years. Unfortunately, these terms protected only a narrow range of expression from legal action.

In other areas of expressive activities, state court judges were guided by the prevailing attitude that majority interests should prevail over individual or minority interests. This, too, led to a restrictive interpretation of permissible activities when minorities sought protection. Another dominant rationale in their decisions was their interpretations of the freedom-and-responsibility concept governing freedom of speech included in many state constitutional provisions, which held individuals and newspapers responsible for the abuse of freedom of speech and of the press.

The majority of the court decisions reached during the nineteenth century rejected the free speech claim, no matter how it was presented. In many cases, judges refused even to comment on the argument. Even so, these state court opinions made several common points:

1.) Free speech provisions of state and national constitutions did not protect the abusive use of speech. Courts, for example, restricted obnoxious speech in public places and allowed labor injunctions to stop threats to business well-being. Judges also were willing to hold newspapers responsible for libel and contempt of court with little regard to the impact such decisions had on freedom of the press.

2.) Infringements of expressive activities based upon the police power of state and local governments were permissible. This police power allowed governmental authorities to limit activities deemed to be harmful to a citizen's health, safety, and moral well-being. Under the police power, governments were permitted to engage in a wide range of repressive functions, including forbidding speakers from addressing audiences in public places and banning unautho-

rized parades and picketing. The police power also was used to pursue some objectionable publications in an effort to close them down.

3.) Public property was for the use of the entire public and not for the use of disgruntled minorities. Public streets, however, were important to minorities who could not afford to hire a hall to present their message. Out of these decisions denying access to public places came repeated calls from religious and political minorities, attorneys, and some judges for the development of a doctrine to allow use of public highways, parks, and other facilities for the communication of ideas. Slowly, the idea developed that the outdoors could serve as a public forum.

4.) The social acceptability of the group seeking permission to communicate in unusual ways greatly influenced judicial decision making. The greatest strides at the end of the nineteenth century were made by the Salvation Army, which at first was considered a fringe religious group. Initially, the Army was barred from parading and playing music in the streets because people and horses were upset by the sounds. Slowly, however, the Salvation Army began to gain acceptance and, in turn, to win permission to hold functions on the city streets. Success for the Salvation Army, however, did not lead to success for anarchists or union members to parade; the latter groups were still socially unacceptable. As the public forum notion gained supporters, advocates suggested that demonstrations could be limited solely by reasonable and nondiscriminatory restrictions on their time, place, and manner. Slowly, courts began to listen to such arguments.

5.) Individuals and firms had the right to conduct business unencumbered by outsiders. Many actions in this area focused on the activities of labor unions that were striving for recognition and reform in the workplace. Courts repeatedly decided that the rights of business owners to enjoy the fruits of their property – past, present, or future profits, for instance, or community goodwill – outweighed the rights of workers to inform the public about work-related grievances.

6.) Dangerous speech, such as that by anarchists, could be suppressed. The doctrine used here looked at whether the words used had the tendency to bring about unacceptable behavior, with "bad tendency" being defined as the possibility, however remote, that something unacceptable might happen as a result of the speech.

The nineteenth century also saw the appearance of a number of press-related issues that would remain at the forefront of legal disputation in the twentieth century. These included the following:

1.) The right of privacy. Brought to the nation's conscience by a pair of Boston lawyers, the right of privacy marked a concerted effort to restrict the press from "overstepping . . . the obvious bounds of propriety and decency."

2.) The development of the watchdog concept of the press. This came in part from an increasing number of libel suits. Newspapers argued that they should be immune from libel prosecutions (or face lower judgments) because they were acting in the public interest when they presented the information challenged in court.

3.) The appearance of journalist's privilege. The argument that journalists should be allowed to keep sources confidential appeared as reporters moved aggressively into reporting information at one time considered to be outside a publication's purview.

4.) The evolution of contempt of court. Following the federal government's lead, most state courts outlawed indirect contempt in the first half of the nineteenth century. Direct contempt, actions that occurred "in the presence of the said courts, or so near thereto as to obstruct the administration of justice," remained a problem well into the twentieth century.

MARGARET A. BLANCHARD

See also Contempt; Journalists' Privilege; Libel; Privacy; Watchdog Concept

Further Reading

Abraham, Henry J., *Freedom and the Court: Civil Rights and Liberties in the United States,* 4th ed., New York: Oxford University Press, 1982

Anderson, Alexis J., "The Formative Period of First Amendment Theory," *American Journal of Legal History* 24 (1980)

Blanchard, Margaret A., "Filling in the Void: Speech and Press in State Courts Prior to *Gitlow*," in *The First Amendment Reconsidered: New Perspectives on the Meaning of Freedom of Speech and Press,* edited by Bill F. Chamberlin and Charlene Brown, New York: Longman, 1982

Gibson, Michael T., "The Supreme Court and Freedom of Expression from 1791 to 1917," *Fordham Law Review* 55 (1986)

Gleason, Timothy W., "19th-Century Legal Practice and Freedom of the Press: An Introduction to an Unfamiliar Terrain," *Journalism History* 14 (1987)

_____, *The Watchdog Concept: The Press and the Courts in Nineteenth-Century America,* Ames: Iowa State University Press, 1990

Rabban, David M., "The First Amendment in Its Forgotten Years," *Yale Law Journal* 90 (1981)

Warren, Samuel D., and Louis D. Brandeis, "The Right to Privacy," *Harvard Law Review* 4 (1890)

First Amendment in the Twentieth Century

U.S. Supreme Court begins to define freedoms of speech and press

The First Amendment played a little role in protecting press freedom during the 1700s and 1800s. Only in the twentieth century did it become the primary weapon in the mass media's campaign against government interference. The amendment was interpreted and its scope expanded repeatedly from the 1930s into the 1990s, as the U.S. Supreme Court appeared to take special interest in First Amendment cases. The press obliged by putting a First Amendment gloss

on almost every legal issue. Together, the Court and the press, with some help from legal scholars and theorists, extended constitutional press and media freedoms to most legal issues affecting the media. By the mid-1990s, however, the Court's fascination with First Amendment cases had weakened, and it was inclined to hear fewer cases and expand the scope of the amendment only if necessary.

Momentum for recognition of strong protection for freedom of the press came in part from the unexpected confluence of arguments presented in four cases decided from 1907 to 1936. Only in 1925, in *Gitlow v. New York,* did the Court accept the argument that the Fourteenth Amendment incorporated the protections of the First Amendment against state and local governments. Previously, the First Amendment had been repeatedly held to apply only against the federal government.

The 1907 case, *Patterson v. Colorado,* involved a newspaper publisher's challenge of a contempt of court citation imposed for cartoons and articles that lambasted members of the state supreme court in a pending case. Despite holding that the First Amendment did not apply against state restrictions, the opinion by Justice Oliver Wendell Holmes Jr. used a prior restraint analysis based on his reading of the purpose and intent of the framers. Since the newspaper had not been prevented from publishing, there would have been no First Amendment violation in any event, Holmes said.

The last two cases came after *Gitlow* had opened the gates. *Near v. Minnesota,* decided in 1931, is considered the pivotal case on press freedom. Jay Near, the publisher of the *Saturday Press* in Minneapolis–St. Paul, was charged with violating a public nuisance statute by having persistently published broad, undocumented charges, many of them racist and anti-Semitic, against public officials. State courts declared the newspaper a nuisance and enjoined future publication. When the case reached the Supreme Court, the 5–4 majority opinion by Chief Justice Charles Evans Hughes looked back to Holmes's analysis from the *Patterson* case, concluding that the primary purpose of the First Amendment was to prevent censorship by prior restraints – direct orders from government not to publish – but that subsequent punishment was allowed. The key thing was to assure the right of initial publication, giving an idea entry into the marketplace of ideas.

The fourth case, *Grosjean v. American Press,* decided in 1936 by a unanimous Court, involved a challenge to a Louisiana tax on advertising. The tax exempted newspapers with a circulation of less than 20,000, leaving only 13 of the state's 163 newspapers taxed. Of those, 12 were regular critics of Governor Huey Long, whose administration introduced the statute. The Court turned to history, as Holmes and Hughes had, and easily concluded that preventing "taxes on knowledge," such as that imposed by the Stamp Act during the colonial period, was a primary purpose of the First Amendment. Since the evidence plainly showed the state's intent to punish selected publications, the case was deceptively easy to decide. The newspapers also argued that the law should be declared unconstitutional because it discriminated in favor of some newspapers. The Court said it was unnecessary to decide this "First

Amendment equal protection" argument, but even so, it became a staple of First Amendment law.

In each case, general principles were accepted by a Court majority, principles that resourceful lawyers and judges would extend to other issues during the rest of the century. Perhaps the most important extension was recognition that government restrictions based on content short of prior restraint, even if indirect, were as effective at squelching the press as a direct order. The threat of subsequent punishment can cause a "chilling effect," intimidating the press enough that it might choose not to publish something even though the material might be true and important to public debate.

The key press case addressing chilling effect is *New York Times* v. *Sullivan* from 1964, which partially constitutionalized libel law. Emphasizing that the press must be given "breathing space" to avoid a chilling effect, Justice William Brennan's opinion elevated the burden of proof on public officials when they sued for libel. Again drawing on history, the Court felt that libel suits by public officials were akin to sedition charges, a form of regulation familiar to and disapproved of by the drafters of the Constitution and the First Amendment. Brennan argued for drawing the line of protection so that some erroneous material damaging to reputation would nonetheless be protected; it was better, he said, to let some harmful speech go unpunished than to risk chilling valuable speech by drawing the line too narrowly.

The *Sullivan* opinion also addressed the role of the press in U.S. society, an issue raised in both the *Near* and *Grosjean* cases. It was not enough that ideas might enter the marketplace, Brennan noted. The First Amendment should be interpreted so that expression on public issues would be "uninhibited, robust, and wide-open." The analysis had shifted. *Near* disallowed a government attempt at silencing critics, while *Sullivan* concluded that government, at least the judicial branch, must actively encourage critics.

From the *Sullivan* case in 1964 through *Gertz* v. *Robert Welch, Inc.*, in 1974, the Court expanded and clarified a new area of constitutional libel that provided extraordinary protection, but only to the news media and only because of their special social and political role. The libel cases were in turn a major influence in developing an interpretation of the First Amendment granting special protections and benefits to the press that might not be available to the general public. Again, history was important. Several Court opinions and dozens of scholarly articles broadened the focus. What emerged was a dialogue on whether the press clause of the First Amendment created a "special status" for the press, which in turn justified protection different from, and perhaps stronger than, that provided under the speech clause of the amendment.

By 1980, in *Richmond Newspapers* v. *Virginia,* a case guaranteeing access to criminal trials under the First Amendment, Chief Justice Warren Burger's plurality opinion relied upon the argument that the press acts as the agent of the public when covering judicial proceedings. The Court seemed willing to view denial of access to trials as functionally equivalent to a prior restraint. The analysis was later extended to all types of judicial actions and to court records.

Although the Court, by the end of the twentieth century, had never formally recognized a First Amendment–based confidential source privilege, it also had refused challenges to the constitutional privilege as it had been established in all but one of the federal circuit courts of appeal. The 1971 *Branzburg* v. *Hayes* case, the Court's only case on the issue, refused to create a privilege for reporters called before grand juries. It did, however, leave the door open for the creation of a privilege, which most lower courts and a majority of state legislatures did do. Courts adopting the privilege usually relied upon the agent of the public rationale.

The Court also extended analysis from the *Grosjean* case in unexpected ways. In *Minneapolis Star and Tribune* v. *Minnesota Commissioner of Revenue,* a 1983 case in which newspapers challenged the constitutionality of a sales and use tax statute affecting only newspapers, the Court concluded that any law that "singles out the press" was presumptively unconstitutional and required special judicial scrutiny. The majority said that content-neutral statutes aimed at the press could be assumed to target content as well. Although government might overcome the presumption by showing there was no discriminatory intent or effect, the rule shifted the burden of justification and should make government think twice before passing laws that target the media. The rationale was extended to safeguard the right of newspapers to place vending boxes on public sidewalks. In *City of Lakewood* v. *Plain Dealer* in 1988, the majority opinion by Justice Brennan compared vague, discretionary rules for placing newsracks with prior restraints, arguing that the right to publish without interference implies a constitutional right to distribute without interference.

Media other than newspapers shared in the expansion of First Amendment protection, primarily when engaged in journalistic functions. When journalism is at issue, the Court provides strong protection by using strict tests, tests that government almost always fails to pass. The First Amendment status of advertising, public relations, and broadcasting has been weaker, with the Court opting for a "substantial interest" test that more readily allows government intervention but still places the burden of proof on government.

TODD F. SIMON

See also Business Regulation of the Press; Commercial Speech; Contempt; Corporate Speech; Journalists' Privilege; Libel; Prior Restraint; Stamp Act of 1765

Further Reading

Bollinger, Lee C., *Images of a Free Press,* Chicago: University of Chicago Press, 1991
Friendly, Fred W., *Minnesota Rag: The Dramatic Story of the Landmark Supreme Court Case that Gave New Meaning to Freedom of the Press,* New York: Random House, 1981
Haiman, Franklyn Saul, *Speech and Law in a Free Society,* Chicago: University of Chicago Press, 1981
Helle, Steven, "Prior Restraints by the Backdoor: Conditional Rights," *Villanova Law Review* 39 (1994)
Powe, L.A. Scott, *The Fourth Estate and the Constitution: Freedom of the Press in America,* Berkeley: University of

California Press, 1991; London: University of California Press, 1992

Smith, Jeffery A., "Prior Restraint: Original Intentions and Modern Interpretations," *William & Mary Law Review* 28 (1987)

Smolla, Rodney A., *Free Speech in an Open Society,* New York: Knopf, 1992

Teeter, Dwight L., "The First Amendment at Its Bicentennial: Necessary But Not Sufficient?," *Journalism Quarterly* 69:1 (Spring 1992), pp. 18–27

First Amendment Theory

Scholars work to create framework for understanding freedom of expression

First Amendment theory generally is designed to achieve two goals: 1.) to explain why freedom of expression is important and must be protected; and 2.) to provide a framework for interpreting and applying the First Amendment's guarantees of freedom of speech and press. Most First Amendment theorists take a positive, value-based approach, justifying freedom of expression as serving important societal or personal values. This approach often results in theories that distinguish among categories of speech, such as public and private or commercial and noncommercial, and argue that certain types of speech are entitled to heightened or even absolute constitutional protection because of the values they serve.

The beginnings of modern free expression theory can be traced to the mid-seventeenth century, a time when political and religious tumult in England resulted in a new literature of liberty – thoughtful and often passionate arguments for freedom of conscience and, ultimately, freedom of expression. The seventeenth-century writer whose work had the greatest impact on modern First Amendment theory was poet John Milton. In November 1644, Milton, seeking a divorce and in trouble with the authorities for publishing unlicensed pamphlets calling for divorce reform, released *Areopagitica: A Speech for the Liberty of Unlicensed Printing to the Parliament of England.* Milton planted the seed for what has become known as the marketplace of ideas theory, which holds that if information, beliefs, and opinions are allowed to flow freely in the marketplace of ideas, without government regulation, truth will ultimately emerge. In the most frequently quoted passage of *Areopagitica,* Milton used battle imagery to describe the process:

> And though all the winds of doctrin [*sic*] were let loose to play upon the earth, so Truth be in the field, we do injuriously by licencing and prohibiting to misdoubt her strength. Let her and Falsehood grapple; who ever knew Truth put to the wors [*sic*] in a free and open encounter.

While his prose was eloquent and his reasoning eventually became very influential, Milton offered a limited plea for freedom. For Milton, the ultimate value served by free expression was the discovery of truth. Therefore, beliefs that Milton considered false – "Popery [Roman Catholicism] and open superstition" and "that also which is impious or evil absolutely" – were not entitled to protection.

Writing two centuries after Milton, John Stuart Mill in his book *On Liberty* elaborated on the concept of a marketplace of ideas. Unlike Milton, Mill did not contend that truth would inevitably prevail in its battle with falsehood, but he argued that freedom of expression was essential if truth were to have even a chance. Mill illustrated three dangers of censorship: 1.) If the censored expression is correct, humanity is "deprived of the opportunity of exchanging error for truth"; 2.) even if the suppressed expression is totally false, censorship prevents "the clearer perception and livelier impression of truth, produced by its collision with error"; and 3.) (which Mill considered the most likely situation) if both the accepted and censored ideas contain part of the truth, censorship prevents discovery of the whole truth.

While Milton and Mill used the search for truth as a basis for general arguments in support of free speech, Zechariah Chafee, in his 1941 landmark study, *Free Speech in the United States,* became the first to translate the general philosophy into a theory for interpreting and applying the speech and press clauses of the First Amendment. Chafee said that the First Amendment protected both "an individual interest, the need of many men to express their opinions on matters vital to them if life is to be worth living, and a social interest in the attainment of truth, so that the country may not only adopt the wisest course of action but carry it out in the wisest way." Focusing on the social interest, Chafee saw the First Amendment as requiring a balancing of the interest in the search for truth and public safety. For Chafee, the clear and present danger test, articulated by Justice Oliver Wendell Holmes in *Schenck v. United States,* correctly struck the balance between the two interests by drawing the line between protected and unprotected speech "close to the point where words will give rise to unlawful acts." According to Chafee, though, there were some types of speech, such as profanity and indecency, of such "slight social value as a step toward truth" that balancing was not even necessary. Such worthless speech could be prohibited to protect "order, morality, the training of the young, and the peace of mind of those who hear and see." Thus, Chafee became the first theorist to propose a two-tiered approach to First Amendment interpretation, with one tier occupied by socially valuable expression protected by the First Amendment unless it presented a real threat to public safety, and the other tier occupied by unprotected, socially worthless speech.

Chafee's balancing approach and enthusiastic support for the clear and present danger test came under vigorous attack from his former teacher, Alexander Meiklejohn. For philosopher Meiklejohn, Chafee's fundamental error was in assigning the public and private interests in speech the same constitutional protection. Tying his self-government theory of the First Amendment to social compact theory, Meiklejohn contended that freedom of expression derived from the basic agreement contained in the Declaration of Independence and the Preamble to the Constitution that "We, the People" are sovereigns constituting a self-governing society. The First Amendment, according to Meiklejohn, was intended solely to protect citizens when they participate in the self-governing process. Therefore, public speech, or speech related to self-government, is absolutely – not conditionally, as posited by Chafee – protected under the First Amendment. In contrast, private speech is not protected by the First Amendment but rather is part of the liberty protected by the Fifth Amendment and can be abridged with "due process of law." The First Amendment, in Meiklejohn's view, was enacted to protect the democratic process, not the individual's right to speak.

While early development of free expression theory was slow and sporadic, the latter part of the twentieth century witnessed an explosion of theoretical writings on the First Amendment, spawned by the U.S. Supreme Court's increased activity in the area; social and political phenomena such as the civil rights and feminist movements, anti–Vietnam War protests, and Watergate; and conflicts between the media and government over such issues as government secrecy, journalistic privilege, and public access to the mass media. Perhaps the most influential of the late-twentieth-century theorists was Thomas I. Emerson. While earlier scholars had tended to focus on a single value or function of free expression, such as the discovery of truth or self-government, Emerson saw free expression as fulfilling four broad functions: "assuring individual self-fulfillment," "advancing knowledge and discovering truth," providing for "participation in decision making by all members of society," and "achieving a more adaptable and hence a more stable community" by "maintaining the balance between stability and change."

Emerson sought to devise a comprehensive theory of the First Amendment based on an action-expression dichotomy. "The central idea of a system of freedom of expression is that a fundamental distinction must be drawn between conduct which consists of 'expression' and conduct which consists of 'action.' 'Expression' must be freely allowed and encouraged. 'Action' can be controlled, subject to other constitutional requirements." The bulk of Emerson's work is devoted to explicating the action-expression distinction by exploring a variety of First Amendment issues, such as defamation, privacy, obscenity, sedition and government speech, and determining when words can be deemed actions because of their effects. For example, while Emerson would categorize most obscenity as protected expression, he would define an obscene communication forced upon an unwilling recipient as action because of its shock effect.

Closely related to, yet distinct from, Meiklejohn's self-government theory is the checking value theory developed by Vincent Blasi in 1977. This theory is based on the assumption that "freedom of expression is valuable in part because of the function it performs in checking the abuse of official power." Unlike Meiklejohn, who saw self-government as the sole value underlying the First Amendment, Blasi proposed his checking value as a significant, but not the sole, component of a general First Amendment theory. Also unlike earlier theorists, Blasi envisioned a special role for the institutional media, which, because of their size and wealth, could act as a countervailing force to big government, fulfilling the traditional watchdog role of unearthing and publicizing corruption, wrongdoing, or ineptitude.

In the 1980s, Lee Bollinger constructed a theory based on the premise that free speech is provided special protection not merely because of the functions served by speech itself but more importantly because protecting speech helps "shape the intellectual character of the society." Bollinger saw free speech as a mechanism for combating the natural human tendency toward intolerance, which manifests itself not only in the suppression of speech but also in efforts to prevent or punish a variety of behaviors society finds offensive or threatening. Under Bollinger's general tolerance theory, protecting freedom of speech helps develop a way of thinking that is "important to the operation of a variety of social institutions – the spirit of compromise basic to our politics and the capacity to distance ourselves from our beliefs, which is so important to various disciplines and professional roles."

Like Blasi and Bollinger, Steven Shiffrin recognized the various values identified by earlier theorists but suggested that another value, the dissent value, ought to play a key role in First Amendment theory. The First Amendment, according to Shiffrin, "speaks to the kind of people we are and the kind of people we desire to be, . . . a nation that respects, tolerates, and even sponsors dissent." Contending that abstract theory could not generate satisfactory First Amendment doctrine, Shiffrin proposed what he termed an eclectic, romantic approach. Because First Amendment values "conflict in complicated ways with numerous other values in complicated contexts," Shiffrin recommended a balancing approach that recognizes that First Amendment decisions "have important human consequences" and focuses on the concrete rather than abstract.

While most theorists have focused on the value of free expression to society, a few have developed theories based on the value of speech to the individual. Notable among these is C. Edwin Baker, who espoused a "liberty model" of the First Amendment, under which "speech is protected not as a means to collective good" but because it "fosters individual self-realization and self-determination without improperly interfering with the legitimate claims of others." Under Baker's theory, the First Amendment protects individual – but not commercial – nonviolent, noncoercive speech and expressive conduct.

Although he disagreed with Baker over protection for commercial speech, Martin Redish also focused on the value of expression to the individual. For Redish the "guarantee of free speech ultimately serves only one true value," which he called "individual self-realization," a term he used to refer to both the development of the individual's powers and abilities and "the individual's control over his or her destiny through making life-affecting decisions." Redish contended that regulation of expression was permitted "only in the presence of a significant danger to a truly compelling societal interest," and courts were prohibited from making judgments about the moral, social, literary, or political value of expression.

While the majority of First Amendment theorists have premised their theories on the functions served by freedom of expression, a few writers in the late twentieth century took what might be termed a negative approach, focusing on freedom of speech as a restraint on governmental action rather than an effort to achieve certain individual or social values. For example, Frederick Schauer acknowledged the positive values but concluded that freedom of speech was best characterized as "the absence of governmental interference." Schauer, who described his work as one of political philosophy rather than theory, was concerned with explicating what he termed a free speech principle. For Schauer, the most persuasive argument for a free speech principle was "governmental incompetence" to regulate speech. Governments, according to Schauer, are "particularly bad at censorship . . . and are less capable of regulating speech than they are of regulating other forms of conduct." In evaluating the legitimacy of governmental action that infringes on free speech, the focus should be on the government's motive or purpose, not on the object of the regulation, Schauer contended.

RUTH WALDEN

See also Government Secrecy; Journalists' Privilege; Libel; Mass Media and the Antiwar Movement; Mass Media and the Civil Rights Movement; Obscenity and Pornography; Watergate Scandal

Further Reading

Baker, C. Edwin, "Scope of the First Amendment Freedom of Speech," *UCLA Law Review* 25 (1978)

Blasi, Vincent, "The Checking Value in First Amendment Theory," *American Bar Foundation Research Journal* (1977)

Bollinger, Lee, *The Tolerant Society: Freedom of Speech and Extremist Speech in America,* New York: Oxford University Press, 1986; Oxford: Clarendon, 1986

Emerson, Thomas I., *The System of Freedom of Expression,* New York: Random House, 1970

Meiklejohn, Alexander, "The First Amendment Is an Absolute," *Supreme Court Review* (1961)

_____, *Free Speech and Its Relation to Self-Government,* New York: Harper, 1948

Redish, Martin, *Freedom of Expression: A Critical Analysis,* Charlottesville, Virginia: Michie, 1984

Schauer, Frederick, *Free Speech: A Philosophical Enquiry,* New York and Cambridge: Cambridge University Press, 1982

Shiffrin, Steven H., *The First Amendment, Democracy, and Romance,* Cambridge, Massachusetts: Harvard University Press, 1990

FM Radio: *see* Radio Technology

Food and Drug Administration

Regulating most labeling and some advertising

The first significant regulation of adulterated and mislabeled food and drugs occurred during the muckraking era of the early 1900s. The horrors of the meatpacking industry described in Upton Sinclair's *The Jungle* and the strong support of President Theodore Roosevelt led to the passage of the Meat Inspection Act and the Pure Food and Drug Act in 1906. Enforcement of these statutes was entrusted to the Bureau of Chemistry in the Department of Agriculture.

In 1927, Congress authorized the creation of a specific regulatory agency, the Food and Drug Administration (FDA), to monitor and assure safety in food and drugs. The FDA's powers were greatly strengthened with the passage of the Food and Drug and Cosmetics Act of 1938. Companion legislation strengthened the Federal Trade Commission (FTC) in the same year. The new laws also delineated jurisdictional areas for both agencies. Basically, the FDA initiates actions involving the products themselves and additional violations regarding labeling. The FTC's domain involved false and deceptive advertising of the products. Because labeling and advertising are closely related, the two agencies initiated joint actions in some cases. The FDA's powers were increased with the passage of the Drug amendments in 1962 and the Fair Packaging and Labeling Act in 1967. The FDA was part of the Department of Health and Human Services in the late twentieth century.

The mission of the modern Food and Drug Administration included testing pharmaceuticals and medical devices for safety and efficacy, monitoring the nation's blood supply, and inspecting and protecting the safety and wholesomeness of foods and cosmetics. Almost all labeling and some limited advertising regulation fell within its purview. In 1994, the FDA had approximately 9,300 full-time employees and a budget of more than $870 million.

Although the FDA was much larger than the FTC, it had a much smaller jurisdiction in relation to the regulation of advertising. It enforced all labeling laws concerning foods, drugs, cosmetics, and medical devices. Accurate ingredient and nutritional statements on food products were examples of FDA work in this area.

The FDA had true regulatory powers over deceptive advertising in only the very narrow area of prescription drugs, medical devices, and animal drugs. The FTC had jurisdiction in the related area of nonprescription, over-the-counter drugs. The FDA required that all labeling and advertising for prescription drugs include balanced statements of all relevant facts about the product. Manufacturers also were required to reveal all material facts concerning consequences of usage of the drug. This included information concerning effectiveness, side effects, and contraindications. Omission of relevant information constituted deception. This is why prescription drugs included pamphlets and medical journal ads had extensive disclosure statements.

The FDA could impose a range of sanctions: letters to ensure compliance, injunctions, seizures of product, and criminal prosecution. These last two were especially severe, and the FDA only employed them in the most egregious cases. One of the rare seizure actions was in 1975. The agency had 18 people who monitored and handled matters relating to misleading promotion of prescription drugs, animal drugs, and medical devices.

ERIC J. ZANOT

See also Federal Trade Commission

Further Reading

Fueroghne, Dean K., *Law and Advertising: Current Legal Issues for Agencies, Advertisers, and Attorneys,* Chicago: Copy Workshop, 1995

McCall, James R., *Consumer Protection: Cases, Notes, and Materials,* St. Paul, Minnesota: West, 1977

Foreign Correspondents

Reporting specialty began in the 1830s

There was concern in the 1990s about both the quality and the quantity of foreign news being published and broadcast for the U.S. audience. A number of major news organizations cut back on resources overseas, leaving about 1,000 U.S. journalists and technicians responsible for the reporting, writing, editing, and transmission of print and broadcast materials. Perhaps half of these worked for a press association. The managers of overseas U.S. news offices augmented their staffs with local personnel.

The decline in overseas personnel led to greater consumer dependence on sketchy television reports. Major sections of the world, such as China, were covered by a handful of reporters, as they had been at the start of the century. The challenge to major news organizations remained to offer a comprehensive, unbiased, and timely foreign news report. Throughout the years foreign correspondents had battled against censorship, mechanical problems, language barriers, and sometimes a provincialism found at their U.S. home office. Those struggles continued in the 1990s.

Foreign news had been part of the U.S. newspaper since the colonial period, when printers eagerly republished items from foreign newspapers arriving by ship. The concept of having foreign correspondents reporting from overseas can be traced to 1838, when James Gordon Bennett Sr., the publisher of the *New York Herald,* reported from London on Queen Victoria's coronation and recruited six reporters in Europe to provide a regular flow of stories. A rapid series of mechanical developments enhanced the quantity and quality of foreign news: the telegraph (1844), the transatlantic cable (1866), and a transpacific cable (1903).

The first U.S. foreign correspondents were active during the war with Mexico (1846–48) when Bennett, Horace Greeley of the *New York Tribune,* and other penny press leaders used the telegraph and pony express to bring news from the Mexican battlefields through New Orleans, Louisiana, to the eastern cities. Greeley sent Margaret Fuller to Europe in 1846 to report for the *Tribune.* She is credited with being the first U.S. woman foreign corespondent. Shortly after the American Civil War, Greeley sent George W. Smalley to London, where he established what is considered the first U.S. foreign newspaper bureau.

U.S. coverage of foreign events remained largely dependent on foreign agencies until the World War I period. France (Agence Havas, 1835), Germany (Wolff, 1849), and Great Britain (Reuters, 1851) developed news agencies, and in 1870, they created a news monopoly by designating zones for each agency's exclusive reporting. In the late 1800s, large U.S. papers frequently used stories from British newspapers. Few U.S. correspondents reported from overseas, and the Associated Press was not ready to compete worldwide with the foreign agencies until 1900.

U.S. readers got a large amount of foreign news during the Spanish-American War (1898–99), the Boer War in South Africa (1899–1902), the Boxer Rebellion in China (1900), the Philippine insurrection against U.S. occupation (1899–1901), and the Russo-Japanese War (1904–05). Writers like Frederick Palmer, Richard Harding Davis, Jack London, and James Creelman competed strongly with their British counterparts, while publishers like William Randolph Hearst and Joseph Pulitzer splashed foreign news onto their pages with sensational headlines.

The U.S. foreign correspondent corps matured during World War I as the nation grew as a world power. Daily reports of the Associated Press and the newly established United Press (1907) carried the bulk of the war news, while correspondents for major papers like Paul Scott Mowrer of the *Chicago Daily News,* Floyd Gibbons of the *Chicago Tribune,* and Wythe Williams of the *New York Times* gained fame. Women began playing a more important part in foreign correspondence. Two of the more prominent by-liners were Andrea Beaumont of Hearst's *New York American* and Sigrid Schultz of the *Chicago Tribune.*

The press associations and newspapers trimmed their staffs between the wars, but in the 1930s, foreign news remained popular. The coverage of the 1938 Munich Crisis by radio reporters led by CBS's Edward R. Murrow awakened many in the United States to the dangers of German Fascism.

Foreign news remained a high priority in the post–World War II period, mainly because of the role of the United States as a superpower in the arms race with the Soviet Union. The press associations further developed their worldwide coverage. Over the years, U.S. reporters concentrated in western European capitals, with smaller numbers living in eastern Europe, Asia, Africa, and Latin America.

Reporters flocked to those other regions during times of war, political elections, coups, and natural disasters. Some became household names – for example, Homer Bigart and Marguerite Higgins of the *New York Herald Tribune* during the Korean War; David Halberstam, Neil Sheehan, Malcolm Browne, and Peter Arnett in Vietnam; Arnett again during the Gulf War; and Christiane Amanpour, reporting for CNN from Bosnia in the 1990s.

MICHAEL EMERY

See also Associated Press; Cooperative News Gathering; Penny Press; Telegraph; Transatlantic Cable

Further Reading

Arnett, Peter, *Live from the Battlefield: From Vietnam to Baghdad: 35 Years in the World's War Zones,* New York: Simon & Schuster, 1994; London: Bloomsbury, 1994

Beasley, Maurine Hoffman, and Sheila Silver, *Taking Their Place: A Documentary History of Women and*

Journalism, Washington, D.C.: American University
Press, 1993

Cooper, Kent, *Kent Cooper and the Associated Press,* New
York: Random House, 1959

Desmond, Robert W., *The Information Process: World
News Reporting to the Twentieth Century,* Iowa City:
University of Iowa Press, 1978

Emery, Michael C., *On the Front Lines: Following
America's Foreign Correspondents Across the Twentieth
Century,* Washington, D.C.: American University Press,
1995

Hohenberg, John, *Foreign Correspondence: The Great
Reporters and Their Times,* New York: Columbia
University Press, 1964

Knightley, Philip, *The First Casualty: From the Crimea to
Vietnam: The War Correspondent as Hero,
Propagandist, and Myth Maker,* New York: Harcourt
Brace Jovanovich, 1975; London: Deutsch, 1975

Marzolf, Marion, *Up from the Footnote: A History of
Women Journalists,* New York: Hastings House, 1977

Mills, Kay, *A Place in the News: From the Women's Pages
to the Front Page,* New York: Dodd, Mead, 1988

Rosenblum, Mort, *Coups and Earthquakes: Reporting the
World for America,* New York: Harper & Row, 1979

Salisbury, Harrison E., *Heroes of My Time,* New York:
Walker, 1993

Franklin, Benjamin

Father of American journalism

Benjamin Franklin personifies the spirit of American
independence and enterprise. The "father of American journalism," he had a career that progressed from an appren-
ticeship at the age of 12 in the print shop of his brother
James in Boston to editor and publisher of the most successful and prosperous newspaper and publishing operation
in the colonies.

An avid reader, Franklin had an irrepressible quest for
knowledge, creative genius, organizational ability, and versatile writing talent that made him an invaluable colonial
leader. He was an editor and publisher, statesman, diplomat,
and scientist. He was a member of the Second Continental
Congress, the first postmaster general, signer of the Declaration of Independence (which he helped to draft), and an influential member of the Constitutional Convention.

In 1722, he was made editor of his brother's influential
newspaper, the *New England Courant,* after exhibiting skill
for satirical writing with a series of "Silence Dogood" articles. In 1729, he established his own widely circulated
Pennsylvania Gazette and in 1732, the first foreign-language newspaper, the *Philadelphia Zeitung;* in 1741, he
founded the *General Magazine,* one of the first magazines
in the colonies.

Early in his publishing career, Franklin espoused press
freedom and balanced news coverage. In 1731, he wrote in
his "Apology for Printers" that printers had a special re-

sponsibility to print both sides of a controversy. One of
Franklin's best-known publications was *Poor Richard's Almanack,* launched in 1732.

ELSIE HEBERT

See also Almanacs; Colonial Press; Printers' Networks

Further Reading

Barck, Oscar T., and Hugh T. Lefler, *Colonial America,*
New York: Macmillan, 1958

Cook, Elizabeth C., *Literary Influences in Colonial
Newspapers, 1704–1750,* New York: Columbia
University Press, 1912

Kirkhorn, Michael, "Benjamin Franklin," in *Dictionary of
Literary Biography: American Newspaper Journalists,
1690–1872,* vol. 43, edited by Perry Ashley, Detroit,
Michigan: Gale, 1985

Frederick, Pauline

First female network news correspondent

Pauline Frederick, the first female network news correspondent and the only woman in network news for more than a
decade, was noted especially for her coverage of the United
Nations. Born in Gallitzin, Pennsylvania, she began reporting as a high school student and went on to receive both
B.A. and M.A. degrees from American University in Washington, D.C. Upon graduation she became a feature writer
for both daily and weekly publications, covering the U.S.
Department of State. She began working part-time for NBC
Radio and joined the North American Newspaper Alliance,
which made her a war correspondent. She covered the
Nuremberg trials and won acclaim for her special reports
for the *New York Times* on postwar Red Army suppression
of freedom in Poland.

Returning to the United States, she went to work for
ABC in 1946 and began her familiar political convention
coverage, sometimes focusing on candidates' wives. Starting
special reports from the United Nations the following year,
she wrote and produced the nonnews program "Pauline
Frederick's Guest Books," which aired once a week over
ABC. She covered the trial of Alger Hiss in the Unites States
and reported from the scene of the lifting of the Berlin
blockade. Rejoining NBC as a news analyst in 1953, she
hosted both weekday commentary and interview programs
for radio. She was an occasional panel member on NBC-TV
public affairs programs and continued, until 1974, reporting on the United Nations. In 1976, she moderated a debate
between presidential candidates Jimmy Carter and Gerald
Ford for PBS.

MICHAEL D. MURRAY

Further Reading

Hosley, David H., and Gayle K. Yamada, *Hard News:
Women in Broadcast Journalism,* New York:
Greenwood, 1987

Freedom of Information Act

Institutionalized right of public access to federal information

Enacted in 1966, the federal Freedom of Information Act (FOIA) significantly enhanced the public's ability to receive information about government. Enacted as part of a bipartisan effort to increase access to federal documents, the FOIA replaced a 1946 act that symbolically opened federal records but failed to mandate disclosure. Unlike its predecessor, the law required release of all federal records unless covered by an exemption.

The act applied to "agency records," a term which was interpreted as including the independent regulatory agencies such as the Federal Communication Commission and the Federal Trade Commission, while excluding the president, the president's advisers, Congress, and the federal judiciary.

The central distinction of the FOIA, however, lies in the term "records." The term was left undefined in the act but has been interpreted to mean tangible records and not information that does not exist in physical form. The move toward computerized records created new problems for the act, which was written for paper records. A 1987 law required federal agencies to release computerized information to the public if the information would be available under the FOIA as paper documents, but issues of pricing and format continued to confound journalists and other requesters.

Regardless of the physical form or format of a record, an agency had to maintain possession and control of a record for it to be subject to disclosure. An agency was required to disclose any record that did not fall within one of the nine categories of material that could be exempt from disclosure under the FOIA: national security; agency rules and practices; statutory exemptions; confidential business information; agency memorandum; personnel, medical, and similar files; law enforcement investigations; banking reports; and information about oil wells.

Certain exemptions created more controversy – and litigation – than others. Exemption 6, which protected "personnel and medical files, the disclosure of which would constitute an invasion of privacy," fostered many lawsuits, as did Exemption 7, the law enforcement exemption.

At issue in Exemption 6 cases was whether certain records fall within the definition of "personnel," "medical," or "similar" files. The courts tended to interpret the terms broadly, resulting in protection of a broad range of information. Many of these decision followed *Department of State* v. *Washington Post Co.*, in which the U.S. Supreme Court said that the term "similar" files applied to any information about a specific individual held by the federal government, intimate or not. In a 1989 case, *Department of Justice* v. *Reporters Committee for the Freedom of the Press*, the Court said that the release of such files was "clearly unwarranted" unless the information "sheds light" on the performance of government. A federal court in 1991 cited the *Reporters Committee* case in denying access to an audiotape of the astronauts aboard the space shuttle *Chal-*lenger, concluding that the voices of the astronauts shortly before the space shuttle exploded would provide no insight on the workings of the space program.

Exemption 7 protected information "compiled" for law enforcement purposes. For a law enforcement agency to withhold records, it had to show that the record invaded personal privacy, disclosed the identity of a confidential source, or endangered someone's life.

When deciding an Exemption 7 case, the courts applied a two-part test: first, a government agency demonstrated that the information was compiled specifically for law enforcement purposes; and second, it had to show that the records fell within one of six categories of protected documents.

Much of the controversy over Exemption 7 stemmed from Section 7(c) of the statute, which stated that law enforcement officials could withhold information that might reasonably be expected to constitute an unwarranted invasion of privacy. Much like Exemption 6, Section 7(c) required balancing the privacy right against the public interest in disclosure. However, the courts ruled that Exemption 7(c) gave law enforcement officers much more flexibility by removing the single word "clearly" from the language of the exemption.

Despite these vagaries, the act enabled journalists, scholars, and citizens to investigate a variety of news stories and historical events. Reporters, for example, used the act to tell the public about harassment of civil rights leaders by the Federal Bureau of Investigation, environmental impact studies, cost overruns of defense contractors, and the salaries of public employees.

Nevertheless, many journalists complained that the act was ineffective and that agencies often interpreted exemptions broadly and delayed release until the information was no longer newsworthy. Government officials, on the other hand, contended that the act overwhelmed their offices with mountains of paperwork and that few requesters defined their searches narrowly enough to satisfy clerks searching through millions of pages of documents.

CHARLES N. DAVIS

See also Government Secrecy

Further Reading
O'Reilly, James T., *Federal Information Disclosure: Procedures, Forms, and the Law*, 2nd ed., Colorado Springs, Colorado: Shepard's/McGraw Hill, 1990
Weinburg, Steve, "Trashing the FOIA," *Columbia Journalism Review* (January/February 1985)

Free Press–Fair Trial Controversy

Conflict between two important constitutional guarantees

The free press–fair trial controversy is generally perceived as a conflict between two amendments to the U.S. Constitution – the First Amendment, guaranteeing freedom of the press, and the Sixth Amendment, guaranteeing a criminal defendant the right to a trial by an impartial jury. The conflict can occur in three ways: prejudicial pretrial publicity can make it difficult to find impartial jurors; publicity during a trial can influence a sitting jury, leading to a verdict based on media reports rather than evidence presented at trial; and the presence of journalists and cameras may interfere with the fair administration of justice physically or psychologically, or both.

While concern about the impact of media coverage on trial fairness dates back to at least the early nineteenth century, not until 1961 did the U.S. Supreme Court reverse a state conviction solely on the basis of prejudicial publicity. In *Irvin v. Dowd*, the Court found "the build-up of prejudice . . . clear and convincing," and therefore sufficient to deprive Leslie Irvin of his right to a fair trial. Two years later in *Rideau v. Louisiana*, the Court reversed the murder conviction of Wilbert Rideau, whose filmed confession was broadcast three times by a local television station.

The next Supreme Court free press–fair trial case, *Estes v. Texas*, dealt with the impact of cameras in the courtroom. Opposition to cameras in the courts can be traced to the extensive and sensational coverage of the 1935 trial of Bruno Hauptmann, accused of kidnapping and murdering the child of Charles Lindbergh and his wife. In response to the Hauptmann trial, the American Bar Association (ABA) in 1937 recommended that cameras be banned from courtrooms. Texas was one of the few states that did not follow the ABA recommendation but instead gave judges the option of allowing cameras in their courts. Billie Sol Estes, convicted of swindling in a Texas trial court, contended that the presence of cameras violated his right to a fair trial. The Supreme Court agreed and reversed Estes's conviction, saying that cameras could distract judges and jurors, impair the testimony of witnesses, tempt attorneys to "play to the public audience," and subject defendants to "a form of mental – if not physical – harassment."

In 1966, concern over the free press–fair trial conflict peaked when the Supreme Court reversed the conviction of Sam Sheppard, who had been found guilty of murdering his wife in a trial that combined massive, prejudicial pretrial publicity, sensational during-trial coverage, and disruptive behavior by the scores of journalists covering the trial in Cuyahoga County, Ohio. Various courts described the Sheppard trial as a "media circus," "carnival," and "'Roman holiday' for the news media." Unlike Dowd, Rideau, and Estes, Sheppard was acquitted on retrial.

In all the 1960s cases, the Supreme Court expressed disapproval of the journalists' behavior, but it placed the blame for violations of Sixth Amendment rights squarely on the courts and law enforcement officials, who often instigated, or at least allowed, the violations. It is the judge's responsibility to ensure a defendant is tried by an impartial jury, the Court emphasized. In *Sheppard v. Maxwell*, the Court suggested ways in which the judge could fulfill that responsibility: controlling the number, location, and behavior of journalists in the courtroom; insulating witnesses from the press to prevent premature disclosure of testimony; and proscribing prejudicial, extrajudicial statements by

lawyers, police, witnesses, and court officials. The Court also reminded judges of the traditional remedies used to compensate for prejudicial publicity: continuance, change of venue, voir dire, admonitions to the jury, sequestration, and, as a last resort, ordering a new trial.

The Court never suggested that judges impose gag orders on the press or close courtrooms. Nonetheless, that is what some judges did in an effort to prevent reversals of convictions. A Reporters Committee for Freedom of the Press study, covering 1967–75, identified 39 gag orders directed at the media, 63 gag orders aimed at trial participants, 61 closures of court proceedings or records, and 11 restraints on photography.

In 1976, the Supreme Court began putting a halt to such restrictions on trial coverage. In *Nebraska Press Association v. Stuart*, the Court declared a gag order on the press an unconstitutional prior restraint. While not imposing an absolute ban on gag orders aimed at the media, the Court said judges would bear a "heavy burden" of proving that a fair trial would be impossible without such restraints. To justify a gag order, a judge must find that pervasive publicity is likely to interfere with a fair trial, that no other remedies can mitigate the effects of the publicity, and that a gag order will be effective in preventing prejudicial publicity.

While the Supreme Court made it extremely difficult for a judge to gag the media, it was not as antagonistic toward another remedy that indirectly affects trial coverage by reducing the flow of information to the press – gag orders aimed at attorneys. The ABA's Model Rules of Professional Conduct provided that an attorney should not make extrajudicial statements that "have a substantial likelihood of prejudicing" a pending case. In *Gentile v. State Bar of Nevada*, the Supreme Court held that the ABA's "substantial likelihood" standard, adopted by 32 states, did not violate the First Amendment rights of attorneys, even though that standard allowed judges to gag attorneys more readily than the press.

After severely restricting gag orders on the media in 1976, four years later the Supreme Court began limiting judges' ability to close courtrooms. In *Richmond Newspapers v. Virginia*, the Court held that the First Amendment encompassed a right of the public and press to attend criminal trials. In *Globe Newspaper Co. v. Superior Court*, the Court struck down a blanket rule requiring closure during the testimony of minors in sex crime cases. In *Press-Enterprise v. Riverside County Superior Court*, the Court held that voir dire was an integral part of the trial and, therefore, subject to the constitutional presumption of openness. Finally, in 1986, the Court extended the right of access to pretrial proceedings, ruling in another case titled *Press-Enterprise v. Riverside County Superior Court* that closure of a preliminary hearing was unconstitutional. As it had in the previous cases, the Court said closure had to be necessitated by a compelling or overriding interest and be narrowly tailored. If the overriding interest justifying closure was the defendant's right to a fair trial, a judge had to find that there was "a substantial probability" of prejudice resulting from an open proceeding, that closure would prevent the harm, and that reasonable alternatives to closure would not protect the defendant's rights.

In the 1980s, the Court also altered its stance on cameras in the court, holding in *Chandler* v. *Florida* that the mere presence of cameras did not automatically deny a defendant a fair trial. While there was no constitutional right to bring cameras into courts, states were free to experiment with camera coverage, the Supreme Court declared. As of 1995, 47 states allowed some form of camera coverage of courts.

RUTH WALDEN

See also Cameras in the Courtroom

Further Reading

American Bar Association Advisory Committee on Fair Trial and Free Press, *Standards Relating to Fair Trial and Free Press* (Reardon Report), New York: Institute of Judicial Administration, 1968

Association of the Bar of the City of New York, Special Committee on Radio, Television, and the Administration of Justice, *Freedom of the Press and Fair Trial* (Medina Report), New York: Columbia University Press, 1967

Campbell, Douglas S., *Free Press v. Fair Trial: Supreme Court Decisions Since 1807,* Westport, Connecticut: Praeger, 1994

Friendly, Alfred, and Ronald L. Goldfarb, *Crime and Publicity,* New York: Twentieth Century Fund, 1967

Kane, Peter E., *Murder, Courts, and the Press: Issues in Free Press/Fair Trial,* rev. ed., Carbondale: Southern Illinois University Press, 1992

Siebert, Fred S., Walter Wilcox, and George A. Hough, *Free Press and Fair Trial: Some Dimensions of the Problem,* Athens: University of Georgia Press, 1970

Sullivan, Harold W., *Trial by Newspaper,* Hyannis, Massachusetts: Patriot, 1961

Twentieth Century Fund Task Force on Justice, Publicity, and the First Amendment, *Rights in Conflict,* New York: McGraw-Hill, 1976

French and Indian War

Principal news story in the American colonies for a decade

The French and Indian War (1754–63) was the fourth war fought between Great Britain and France in North America, but it was the first war between the two colonial powers that involved all of the colonies of each country in the New World. Because of the significance of the war for all American colonists, it became the most significant story of the colonial era prior to the revolutionary period and the principal news in America's newspapers for more than a decade.

In 1754, France controlled most of the territory in North America, and French claims beyond the Appalachian Mountains curtailed British expansion westward just as French control of Canada halted northern migration. Even though European treaties gave the land in the Ohio Valley to France, English colonists disputed these claims, and colonists began moving into the region. At the same time, the French built forts and positioned troops in the Ohio Valley and Canada to stop English settlement. Directly involved in the French efforts to stop the English were Native Americans from the St. Lawrence River to the Mississippi River delta, nations with whom the French had cultivated relationships since French colonization began in 1608.

The danger of the French and Indian alliance for English colonists was brought into focus by the newspaper publication of George Washington's journal. Newspapers published the first-person account of confrontations with the French in the Ohio Valley in serial form beginning in March 1754. The news of Washington's activities culminated with reports of his defeat at Fort Necessity in July.

News of French and Indian attacks on English settlements from Maine to New York soon followed. This news led to a call for unity of America's colonies. The *Pennsylvania Gazette* publisher Benjamin Franklin initiated the newspaper call for colonial unity with the publication of the May 9, 1754 woodcut, "Join, or Die," the first use of political cartooning in American newspapers. Other newspaper printers created their own disjointed snakes, which represented the English colonies, and joined Franklin in proposing a meeting of colonial leaders and Native Americans friendly to the English. The newspaper proposals produced the Albany Congress and the Albany Plan of Union, which suggested a council to deal collectively for all English colonies in matters of defense, expansion, land purchases, and Native American relations. Although newspapers supported the plan, colonial legislatures rejected it.

Following the Albany Congress, war news in newspapers increased in proportion to hostilities and by the middle of 1755 captured almost all news space. Following Britain's declaration of war on France in 1756, newspapers began reporting on a global war with news of British and French fighting in Europe, the East Indies, India, and the Caribbean, and on the oceans. The most important news to British colonists explained plans to attack Canada and drive the French from North America. The key to capturing Canada, newspapers reported, was reducing Louisbourg, the French fortress at the mouth of the St. Lawrence River on the island of Cape Breton. Newspapers described the plans for capturing the fort in detail early in 1758.

Louisbourg fell in July 1758, and the newspaper reports of the siege produced two informational firsts – the detailed war map and a hero for the American press, James Wolfe. Newspapers in New York and Boston produced extensive woodcut maps of the harbor of Louisbourg that explained the siege, while the heroics of Wolfe gave newspapers an individual about whom they could report for months after the battle. In fact, news accounts of Wolfe's military bravery remained a fixture in papers for years, especially after the 32-year-old general died leading troops in the successful siege of Quebec in 1759.

Following the fall of Louisbourg and Quebec, newspaper accounts described the surrender of Montreal, followed by the capitulation of Canada. News of the invasion of

Canada came to American papers weekly, and in the process, another new concept for newspapers developed – that of the reporter. As a writer to the *Boston Gazette* said of reports on the advancing English forces in the August 6, 1759, edition, "It will be very difficult for a weekly news writer to keep pace."

The surrender of Canada, as newspapers pointed out, meant that England had successfully removed France from North America. The Ohio Valley quickly opened for colonial settlement. News of fighting with France diminished and was replaced by news of Indian wars in the southern colonies, principally in South Carolina with the Cherokee. Newspaper reports still insinuated that the French were at the root of the fighting. American newspapers reported the official end of British and French hostilities worldwide in May 1763.

Because the French and Indian War threatened the very existence of the British colonies, newspaper coverage of the war stimulated newspaper growth in America. From 1754 to 1760, the number of newspapers in America increased 73 percent, from 11 English-language papers to 19. Newspapers grew at twice the rate of the colonial population, which increased by 36 percent during the same period, from slightly more than 1.17 million inhabitants to 1.59 million.

The French and Indian War helped forge an informational network among colonial printers. The united presentation of news and the sharing of that news by printers became mandatory for colonial survival, and it provided a ready source for common resistance during the Stamp Act crisis of 1764–65. Because newspapers had reported on a universal enemy for the decade before the Stamp Act, uniting to fight the Stamp Act – a common enemy to printers – was a logical step.

Newspapers during the French and Indian War exhibited all forms of war news with letters from the front, firsthand battle descriptions, official releases, accounts of enemy atrocities, letters of troop support, praise of soldiers fallen in battle, and denunciations of the enemy. Even though newspapers played an important role in American society prior to the French and Indian War, the way in which America's press joined together to serve the public with accurate, complete, and up-to-date news during this period ensured newspapers a place of importance and permanence in American society.

DAVID A. COPELAND

See also Stamp Act of 1765

Further Reading
Copeland, David A., *Colonial American Newspapers: Character and Content*, Newark: University of Delaware Press, 1997
Shields, David S., *Oracles of Empire: Poetry, Politics, and Commerce in British America, 1690–1750*, Chicago and London: University of Chicago Press, 1990
Tindall, George Brown, *America: A Narrative History*, New York: Norton, 1984; London: Norton, 1992

Frontier Press
Newspapers moved west with settlers

As the United States expanded westward to fill the continent between the Atlantic and Pacific Oceans, settlers took their institutions with them. Although often modified to meet the conditions of pioneer life, governments, churches, schools, and the press helped maintain the continuity between old lives and new. To many settlers, having a local newspaper represented stability and legitimacy. A town with a newspaper was a real town, not merely a settlement; but, of course, the newspaper was more than symbolic.

On the western frontier, whether Kentucky or Idaho, Connecticut or California, the press served several functions – social, political, and economic – in addition to providing settlers with links to the life they had left behind in the east. Westerners were, by and large, a literate population, and frontier newspapers filled a need for reading matter where books and libraries were rare. Newspapers provided news and information and confirmed the word-of-mouth communications of a small town.

In the political realm, much as they had in the early days of the United States, newspapers facilitated dialogue as political parties and institutions took shape. Many frontier publishers recognized a responsibility to produce a newspaper that would serve a great variety of interests and political persuasions, but they also acknowledged their role in the political process. Although their initial issues might eschew partisanship, at the first election publishers invariably took a political position, which in turn often prompted the opposition party to establish its own newspaper to ensure an outlet for its ideology.

The frontier press participated in economic life in a number of ways. Newspapers gave businesses a means to reach customers through advertising, and, in their role as town boosters, newspapers promoted their communities with a view to growth and prosperity. The "booster press" relied on the custom of exchanging newspapers between editors who clipped freely from one another's publications articles they thought would interest their readers. Frontier editors described their communities in extravagant terms, hoping to catch the eye of an editor in an eastern newspaper office who would reprint their stories.

And it worked. Towns with newspapers attracted settlers and development such as railroads and mills. The settlers in turn attracted more publications, including social, cultural, religious, and educational publications.

Political and economic/booster functions of the frontier press overlapped when a newspaper became an important tool in obtaining status as a county seat or as a territorial or state capital. Such decisions usually favored towns with newspapers because, in addition to the political influence a newspaper might represent, it gave the government and its citizens a place to publish public notices and to get forms, laws, and other materials printed. Frontier newspapers commonly did commercial (job) printing, and government printing contracts usually went to the newspaper that supported the political party in power, thereby enhancing the newspaper's chances of survival. For a time, serving as public printer for a western state or territory was lucrative, and newspapers competed vigorously for the political plum.

Although virtually every state claimed a "frontier" at some point in its development, and therefore a "frontier press," the terms are most often applied to the trans-Mississippi region and to newspapers such as those in the Sierra and Rocky Mountain mining camps, the valleys of the Willamette River and the Great Salt Lake, and along the Pacific Coast.

Spanish-language newspapers were attempted in New Mexico as early as 1834; English-language newspapers began in 1846 on the Pacific coast. In 1850, the census counted 11 newspapers in the 11 states and territories of the far west. Ten years later, the number of newspapers had increased to 285, a 1,135 percent increase; meanwhile, the population increased 248 percent. By 1890, the region had more than 1,000 newspapers for its 3 million people.

The expansive geography of the west both helped and hindered frontier newspaper development. On the one hand, isolated communities craved the connections the newspaper provided and the stability it represented; on the other, difficulty in maintaining a steady supply of paper, ink, labor, and news of the outside world handicapped the frontier publisher.

When rain washed out roads or snow blocked mountain passes, editors of newspapers with names like *Calico Print, Hydraulic Press, Valley Tan, Free Lance,* and *Owyhee Avalanche,* as well as *Leader, Democrat, Republican, Times,* and *News,* printed on wallpaper or wrapping paper. When money was in short supply, they accepted chickens, firewood, and pianos in lieu of cash for subscriptions and advertising. They often printed their first issues in canvas-covered shacks but, if they were successful in town building, went on to occupy fine buildings.

The completion of the transcontinental telegraph reduced the delay in getting news from months and weeks to minutes and hours, but only successful newspapers could afford to purchase telegraph service. Marginal enterprises freely took stories from their wealthier neighbors, but as a rule, even theft of news was not enough to keep the weaker newspapers alive.

Frontier newspapers had a low survival rate. Shifting mining fortunes, fire, flood, poor management, and personal or political misfortune put newspapers out of business almost as quickly as they started; perhaps 10 newspapers were started for every one that survived more than two or three years.

Nevertheless, several newspapers early on carved places for themselves in the history of the west. The *Oregonian* in Portland (1850), the *Deseret News* in Salt Lake City, Utah (1850), the *Rocky Mountain News* in Denver, Colorado (1859), the *San Francisco Chronicle* (1865), and the *Seattle (Washington) Intelligencer* (1865), later the *Post-Intelligencer,* were among the newspapers that survived the frontier to play leadership roles in the region in the twentieth century.

Other newspapers – like the *Territorial Enterprise,* a publication that thrived during the height of the Comstock silver fever in Nevada in the 1860s and 1870s and was best known for hiring Mark Twain, and the *Epitaph,* down the street from the OK Corral in Tombstone, Arizona – had briefer periods of distinction, but all contributed to the eventual eradication of the frontier.

BARBARA CLOUD

See also Boosterism; Exchanges

Further Reading
Cloud, Barbara Lee, *The Business of Newspapers on the Western Frontier,* Reno: University of Nevada Press, 1992
Halaas, David Fridtjof, *Boom Town Newspapers: Journalism on the Rocky Mountain Mining Frontier, 1859–1881,* Albuquerque: University of New Mexico Press, 1981
Huntzicker, William E., "Historians and the American Frontier," *American Journalism* 5 (1988)
Karolevitz, Robert F., *Newspapering in the Old West,* New York: Bonanza, 1965
Lyon, William H., *The Pioneer Editor in Missouri, 1808–1860,* Columbia: University of Missouri Press, 1965
Myers, John Myers, *Print in a Wild Land,* Garden City, New York: Doubleday, 1967
Stratton, Porter A., *The Territorial Press of New Mexico, 1834–1912,* Albuquerque: University of New Mexico Press, 1969

Full-Service Advertising Agency
Provides all a client's advertising needs

In its narrowest definition, a full-service advertising agency should provide all the services necessary to handle a client's advertising needs. Traditionally, this included account services, creative services, media planning and buying, and research. The primary function of advertising agencies has been the selection of media and the creation and placement of advertising messages in mass media. As members of a service industry, advertising agencies have often adapted to meet the needs of their clients. Many agencies, particularly smaller ones, have expanded their services, adding staff or contracting with specialists in closely related communications areas such as sales promotion, direct marketing, or public relations for many years.

In the 1990s, the principal topic of debate in the advertising and marketing arenas was redefining advertising. John O'Toole, American Association of Advertising Agencies president, called on the agency world in 1990 to embrace "The New Advertising," which he defined as the integration of media advertising with such specialties as sales promotion, direct marketing, package design, and public relations. "We think," he said, "that advertising will indeed, must be, redefined to comprise all marketing communication directed to the consumer of the product or service." Others thought that there was nothing new about the idea or the definition.

It was simply integrating communications to properly service clients and effectively reach their consumers, something smaller agencies had been doing for years.

This concept, known as integrated marketing communication, was also more in line with the consumer interpretation of advertising. Readers, listeners, and viewers do not distinguish between various communications elements and tend to identify all persuasive or sales messages as "advertising."

One of the problems facing advertisers and agencies in the 1990s was the fragmentation of traditional mass media. In the 1960s and 1970s, the three television networks – ABC, CBS, and NBC – accounted for 93 percent of the television audience. In the 1990s, even with the addition of another network, Fox, the four networks combined reached only about 60 percent of the audience. Consumers had more and more choices of media. Technology, including computer database management, interactive communication, CD-ROM, and the Internet, were redefining both media and communications. While media alternatives were increasing, what used to be mass market consumers were being segmented into smaller and smaller markets by lifestyle, ethnic background, income, gender, and a variety of other factors. In an effort to reach these diverse consumers, clients were utilizing all the communications elements and calling on agencies for help.

Under integrated marketing communications, or IMC, a full-service agency would offer not only all the traditional advertising services but any and all communications-related services requested by a client. The American Association of Advertising Agencies' definition of a full-service agency stated: "In the simplest terms, a full-service advertising agency is one that is capable of providing all the services necessary to handle your total advertising and marketing program." By including the reference to marketing programs in its definition, the association recognized the ex-panding needs of advertisers in marketing and marketing communications and acknowledged the advertising agencies' desire to meet these needs.

Many advertising agencies moved to increase their services to include strategic market planning, direct marketing, sales promotion, publicity, public relations, event marketing, and package design under a unified strategy from a single source. Fully implementing the IMC concept created some problems for advertising agencies – restructuring management systems, reorganizing and adding staff, and finding acceptable alternatives to the traditional compensation system of media commissions.

Major agencies approached diversification into other communications areas by creating separate agencies and by purchasing or merging with specialty agencies in an effort to provide a full range of services to existing clients. Major agencies Fallon McElliot and Leo Burnett restructured their management and support teams to offer a full range of services to their clients.

While there would always be room for specialty agencies and boutiques, the trend in the 1990s seemed to be toward the offering of a wider variety of communications services by both small and large agencies. As the definition of advertising changes, so will the definition of full-service advertising agencies.

JON A. SHIDLER

Further Reading

Belch, George E., and Michael A. Belch, *Introduction to Advertising and Promotion: An Integrated Marketing Communications Perspective*, 3rd ed., Chicago: Richard D. Irwin, 1995

Schultz, Don E., Stanley I. Tannenbaum, and Robert F. Lauterborn, *Integrated Marketing Communications*, Lincolnwood, Illinois: NTC Business, 1993

G

Gatekeeping

Choosing materials to provide the public

The term "gatekeeping" refers to the mechanisms by which individuals or organizations who professionally process news or other cultural products select what to pass on from the sum of material available. Teachers, librarians, disc jockeys, movie reviewers, public relations professionals, and journalists are all gatekeepers for cultural goods. The gatekeeper makes decisions about what to withhold and what to pass along to audiences.

The concept of gatekeeping, coined by social psychologist Kurt Lewin in the 1940s, came into use in research on journalism through David Manning White's 1950 study of how a wire editor at a small midwestern newspaper decided what wire service stories to run. White concluded that the editor made "highly subjective" decisions.

Walter Gieber in 1964 challenged this conclusion in his study of 16 Wisconsin wire editors, finding choices to be dictated by the demands of bureaucratic routines rather than by individual subjective preferences. Much research has examined how the economy and social organization of news production determines news content.

The gatekeeper metaphor has helpfully drawn attention to the power of cultural mediators. In one respect, however, it is a misleading metaphor. News items are not simply selected but are preselected. Gatekeeper research does not ask how and why one set of items and not another arrives at the editor's desk in the first place, a topic researched by Oscar Gandy in 1982. Gandy drew attention to the "information subsidies" that make it possible for well-endowed organizations to place their preferred items before the journalist while resource-poor organizations have difficulty gaining a journalist's attention.

MICHAEL SCHUDSON

Further Reading

Gandy, Oscar H., Jr., *Beyond Agenda Setting: Information Subsidies and Public Policy,* Norwood, New Jersey: Ablex, 1982

Shoemaker, Pamela J., *Gatekeeping,* Newbury Park, California: Sage, 1991

White, David Manning, "The 'Gate Keeper': A Case Study in the Selection of News," *Journalism Quarterly* 287 (1950)

Gay and Lesbian Press

Genre of alternative journalism

As a gay and lesbian community began to emerge in the United States after World War II, it spawned a new genre of alternative journalism to create a forum for issues that the establishment press was not covering. This specialized press committed itself to advocating gay rights while reporting on events, issues, and cultural trends of interest to gay people. Its history has been a convulsive one, partly because of society's hostility toward homosexuality and partly because of other external forces.

The genre was founded in 1924 when Henry Gerber, a Chicago postal worker, founded the Society for Human Rights and produced two issues of a publication titled *Friendship and Freedom.* When police learned of the activities, they arrested Gerber, who was immediately fired from his job, and destroyed all copies of *Friendship and Freedom.*

The earliest publication of which any copies have survived was *Vice Versa,* a lesbian magazine founded in Los Angeles in 1947. The editor was a woman using the pseudonym Lisa Ben, an anagram for "lesbian." Ben produced 12 copies of *Vice Versa* on a typewriter and distributed them to patrons of lesbian bars. She published nine issues, which consisted mainly of her own short stories, poems, and personal essays.

The first widely distributed gay and lesbian publication was *One,* founded in Los Angeles in 1953. The second and third were the San Francisco–based *Mattachine Review,* founded in 1955 for gay men, and the *Ladder,* founded in 1956 for lesbians. The three monthly magazines consisted largely of personal essays. Their editorial stances differed dramatically. *One* provoked lively debates about gay rights; *Mattachine Review* and the *Ladder* advocated accommodating to the norms of heterosexual society. The magazines had a total circulation of 7,000 but a readership of many

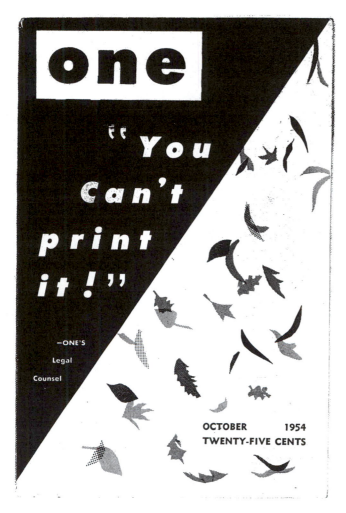

An early newspaper serving the gay community

times that number. All three achieved longevity by surviving more than a dozen years. *One* fought federal censors, and in a 1958 U.S. Supreme Court case (*One, Inc.* v. *Olesen*) won the right for homosexual-oriented materials to be sent through the mail.

During the 1960s, the lesbian and gay press shifted toward militancy. The same women and men editing the magazines also organized the first demonstrations for gay rights at the White House and Independence Hall. Toward the end of the decade, many of the dozen publications that had emerged had adopted the values of the counterculture movement by incorporating explicit language and homoerotic images into their editorial mix and by advocating sexual promiscuity, liberal drug use, and opposition to the Vietnam War. The 1960s publications also increased their news content, and in 1967 the first true newspaper for gays appeared when the *Los Angeles Advocate* was founded with an all-news format.

After the Stonewall Rebellion in June 1969 in New York City ignited the modern phase of the gay and lesbian liberation movement, the number and circulation of this alternative press exploded. By 1972, some 150 publications

boasted an aggregate circulation of 250,000. The most visible publications were sensational tabloids defined by screaming headlines, titillating images, and language designed as much to shock as to illuminate. Titles of the revolutionary journals communicated a sense of what they stood for: *Gay Flames* and *Come Out!* in New York; *Gay Sunshine* in San Francisco; *Gay Liberator* in Detroit, Michigan; and *Killer Dyke* in Chicago. Many of the tabloids were short-lived.

Later in the 1970s, the genre entered a less political phase by exploring the dimensions of the rapidly developing culture. Publications plumbed the breadth and depth of topics ranging from the lesbian and gay sensibility in art and literature to sex, spirituality, personal appearance, "dyke" separatism, lesbian mothers, drag queens, leather men, and gay bathhouses. The most prominent of the decade's publications was the *Advocate,* an upscale lifestyle magazine for gay men that Wall Street multimillionaire David B. Goodstein created by revamping the *Los Angeles Advocate.*

At the end of the decade, this alternative press again shifted focus, this time in response to an antihomosexual campaign led by conservative political and religious forces. Former beauty queen Anita Bryant launched the attack in 1977; antigay violence crested a year later when the only member of the San Francisco Board of Supervisors opposed to the city's gay rights law assassinated Harvey Milk, the first openly gay member of the board. In an effort to convince the mainstream United States that gay people deserved civil rights, publications adopted professional standards. *Big Apple Dyke News* in New York began publishing Associated Press articles; the *Philadelphia Gay News* initiated a standing feature listing how state legislators had voted on issues of particular concern to gay people.

In the early 1980s, the gay and lesbian press confronted its most formidable enemy when AIDS, one of the most devastating diseases in the history of medicine, began killing gay men at an alarming rate. Publications such as the *New York Native* and the *Washington Blade* distinguished themselves by relentlessly reporting on the disease, often breaking important developments before mainstream news organizations with far more resources. Gay newspapers such as the *San Francisco Sentinel* and the *Bay Area Reporter,* on the other hand, opted not to sound the alarm, partly because they feared losing the substantial advertising revenue they received from the gay bathhouses where the disease was being spread.

AIDS and the AIDS hysteria that it spawned continued to dominate the gay press during the late 1980s, propelling the genre into a new phase of radicalism. The leader was *OutWeek,* a New York weekly that burst into the national spotlight when it "outed" (exposed the sexual orientation of) "closeted" men and women such as millionaire publishing tycoon Malcolm Forbes. Other gay publications joined the insolent *OutWeek* to create a press that paralleled radical organizations such as ACT UP and Queer Nation and their demands for more money for AIDS research and treatment, as well as an end to second-class citizenship for lesbians and gay men.

During the early 1990s, another chapter in the life of the genre unfolded as the increased visibility of gay people, primarily because of AIDS and the debate over whether the ban on gays in the military should be lifted, resulted in the emergence of a spate of glossy lifestyle magazines. *Out*, which was based in New York but circulated nationally, led the new phase. *Out*'s upscale design helped attract mainstream advertisers. The magazine, which devalued news in favor of stories on entertainment and fashion trends, became the first gay and lesbian publication sold in mainstream bookstores and featured on the front page of the *New York Times*.

By the mid-1990s, the gay and lesbian press had evolved into a journalistic institution with a history that resembled a roller coaster in its succession of distinct chapters. In the context of alternative media, the genre was impressive. In the mid-1990s, the publications numbered 900 titles with a total circulation of 2 million. Virtually every large and mid-sized city in the country had at least one gay publication, and many cities had several. Most of the publications were weekly newspapers. From 1947, when the first lesbian magazine was founded, more than 2,600 lesbian and gay publications were produced in the United States.

RODGER STREITMATTER

See also Alternative Press

Further Reading

Miller, Alan V., comp., *Our Own Voices: A Directory of Lesbian and Gay Periodicals, 1890–1990*, Toronto, Ontario: Canadian Gay Archives, 1991

Streitmatter, Rodger, "The *Advocate*: Setting the Standard for the Gay Liberation Press," *Journalism History* 19:3 (Autumn 1993), pp. 93–102

_____, "Creating a Venue for the 'Love That Dare Not Speak Its Name': Origins of the Gay and Lesbian Press," *Journalism and Mass Communication Quarterly* 72:2 (Summer 1995), pp. 436–447

_____, "Lesbian and Gay Press: Raising a Militant Voice in the 1960s," *American Journalism* (in press)

_____, *Unspeakable: The Rise of the Gay and Lesbian Press in America*, Boston: Faber and Faber, 1995

General Electric

Important player in development of radio, television

General Electric (GE), one of the world's largest corporations, long played an important role in radio and then television. Indeed, GE helped create commercial radio after World War I by forming (with Westinghouse Electric) the Radio Corporation of America (RCA). In the 1920s, David Sarnoff, longtime head of RCA, developed the first radio network – the National Broadcasting Company (NBC). In 1930, GE sold its stake in RCA but retained ownership of radio and then television stations.

With the coming of television in the 1950s, GE sponsored important prime-time television series, principally *General Electric Theater*, an anthology series on CBS from 1953 to 1962. *General Electric Theater* was a fixture on Sundays at 9 P.M., with Ronald Reagan as its host. During the 1956–57 television season, *General Electric Theater* finished behind only *I Love Lucy* and Ed Sullivan's variety show in the ratings race.

In 1986, GE reentered the television business in a significant way by repurchasing RCA (for $6 billion) and thus acquiring NBC. GE sold NBC's radio network and radio stations, as well as spun off RCA manufacturing. By 1990, GE continued to own and operate the television network and stations only in major cities across the United States. Simultaneously, GE expanded NBC into cable television, most exemplified by its business network, CNBC. But NBC was a small part of GE. From corporate headquarters in Fairfield, Connecticut, GE generated $60 billion in revenue per year, of which NBC made up just 5 percent.

DOUGLAS GOMERY

See also Radio Networks; Radio Technology; Television Networks; Television Technology

Further Reading

Alexander, Alison, James Owers, and Rod Carveth, eds., *Media Economics: Theory and Practice*, Hillsdale, New Jersey: Lawrence Erlbaum, 1993

Bilby, Kenneth W., *The General: David Sarnoff and the Rise of the Communications Industry*, New York: Harper & Row, 1986

MacDonald, J. Fred, *One Nation Under Television: The Rise and Decline of Network TV*, New York: Pantheon, 1990

Tichy, Noel M., and Stratford Sherman, *Control Your Destiny or Someone Else Will: How Jack Welch Is Making General Electric the World's Most Competitive Corporation*, New York: Doubleday, 1993

Global Village

Development of the media-made world community

The world used to be a very big place, with distant lands seeming inaccessible. Distances were measured by the time it took to communicate with those places, and messages would take great lengths of time to travel across the sea or over miles of land. Messages between the North American continent and Europe during the American Revolution, for example, were so slow that the British did not know about the turning tide of the war until several weeks after it had happened. During the Civil War, news correspondents encountered three- or four-day delays in relaying battle information, but several days of delay seemed better to them than eight or 10.

Much of this distance disappeared with the telegraph. Over the next century, other electronic media made some forms of communication instantaneous, and information about other parts of the world became accessible immediately.

This immediate knowledge of other countries, other people, and events from obscure places of the world brought a new world neighborhood, or a kind of "tribalization," creating what scholar Marshall McLuhan called a global village. The world became smaller by means of people knowing about each other without the need to have direct sensory contact, and it was happening with a kind of "all-at-onceness."

The implication of all this, according to McLuhan, was a kind of new world class. "Electric circuitry . . . has constituted dialogue on a global scale," he wrote. "Its message is Total Change, ending psychic, social, economic, and political parochialism. The old civic, state and national groupings have become unworkable. Nothing can be further from the spirit of the new technology than 'a place for everything and everything in its place.' You can't go home again."

Information from every corner of the Earth promised to inform the ordinary citizen and enable intelligent participation in the voting process. The war in Vietnam, for example, has been called the "Living Room War." During the late 1960 and early 1970s, it was watched regularly on the evening news, often over the dinner table, by most of the households in the United States. Regardless of political policy, the public saw from across the world the ravages of war, the napalmed villages, and the U.S. military casualties; equally visible were the antiwar protests at home. Many observers think that these scenes, mainly from television, caused members of the U.S. "village" to rethink war. The tide of public opinion turned, and U.S. troops withdrew. Knowing so intimately about their fellow "villagers" in Vietnam made many people in the United States think differently about the war.

Other developments, such as the ecology movement, probably would have been impossible without an awareness of the parts of the world and its species being dramatically enlarged. For example, why would a New York City resident care about the rain forests of South America? According to McLuhan and others who argued the global village perspective, such a place or event was no longer an abstraction. It was part of an all-involving sensory experience, thanks to the electronic media. People saw, heard, and sensed situations in a strikingly personal way.

McLuhan would argue that the media are extensions of the senses, that electrical circuitry is an extension of the central nervous system: "Media, by altering the environment, evoke in us unique ratios of sense perceptions. The extension of any one sense alters the way we think and act – the way we perceive the world. When these ratios change, men change."

This explanation of how the media have evolved and in turn have changed life is not without its critics. McLuhan's description of the role of the media is an overstatement, according to some scholars, such as Sidney Finkelstein. But then, McLuhan himself would have argued the efficacy of

overstatement. In an all-at-once environment of electronic media, it is difficult to always put things into a logical, linear sequence to explain things, McLuhan would argue.

The fact remains that whether one accepts the arguments or reasoning of McLuhan, the world has become smaller. Hundreds of millions of people or more may watch an event live, as has been asserted about the Persian Gulf War, the Olympic Games, or Super Bowls. Logically, the drawing together of the citizens of the world to the common ground of that event makes a difference in the way people think politically, socially, economically, or perhaps even psychologically. People may never know to what extent this occurs. Perhaps trying to understand the role of the media in the global village is, as McLuhan stated, a little like fish examining the water in which they swim.

VAL E. LIMBURG

Further Reading

Finkelstein, Sidney Walter, *Sense and Nonsense of McLuhan*, New York: International, 1968

Limburg, Val E., *Mass Media Literacy: An Introduction to Mass Communications*, Dubuque, Iowa: Kendall/Hunt, 1988

McLuhan, Marshall, *Understanding Media: The Extensions of Man*, New York: McGraw-Hill, 1964; London: Sphere, 1967

McLuhan, Marshall, and Quentin Fiore, *The Medium is the Massage*, New York: Random House, 1967; London: A. Lane, 1967

_____, *War and Peace in the Global Village*, New York: McGraw-Hill, 1968; London: Bantan, 1968

Godkin, E.L.

Leading newspaper and magazine editor

Edwin Lawrence Godkin was the founder and editor of the *Nation* from 1865 to 1899 and editor-in-chief of the *New York Evening Post* from 1883 to 1899. Under Godkin, the *Nation* was an influential journal of commentary and criticism. Godkin, a reform-minded and contentious editor, was sued several times for libel as he clamored for political and social reform.

Born near Mayne, Ireland, Godkin emigrated to the United States in 1856. He studied law in New York and was admitted to the bar, but he put his energy into writing for newspapers. Godkin, Frederick Law Olmsted, and Frederick McKim established the *Nation* in 1865 as a joint stock company, with Godkin as editor.

In 1881, when the *Nation* was merged with the *New York Evening Post*, Godkin assumed the role of associate editor of the *Evening Post*, becoming its editor in chief in 1883. When the merger took place, the *Nation* became a weekly supplement of the *Evening Post*. Relieved of editorial duties in September 1899, he retained his title until January 1, 1900.

The *Nation* had a modest circulation of about 10,000, but it had an upscale readership of leaders in business, politics, and academia. William James said that the *Nation* was a "towering influence" for a generation's thinking about politics. Woodrow Wilson, while a student at Princeton University, kept notations from Godkin's editorials, and one of William Allen White's professors called the *Nation* a model of literary and political writing. Godkin, who made regular journeys to Europe throughout his life, died in England in 1902.

EDWARD CAUDILL

Further Reading

Armstrong, William M., *E.L. Godkin and American Foreign Policy, 1865–1900,* New York: Bookman, 1957
____, *E.L. Godkin: A Biography,* Albany: State University of New York Press, 1978
Grimes, Alan Pendleton, *The Political Liberalism of the New York 'Nation', 1865–1932,* Chapel Hill: University of North Carolina Press, 1953
Ogden, Rollo, ed., *Life and Letters of Edwin Lawrence Godkin,* New York and London: Macmillan, 1907

Golden Age of Radio

Radio serves as primary source of family entertainment

The 1930s and 1940s were characterized by radio's position as the major source for family entertainment in the United States. The key events that ushered in radio's golden age began as networks developed in the late 1920s.

Radio's popularity skyrocketed as national broadcasting became a reality. During the decade between 1930 and 1940, homes with radios rose from 12 to 30 million and advertising revenues from $40 to $155 million. To attract national sponsors, programming strategies targeted large audiences by catering to the lowest common denominator.

In October 1929, the bottom fell out of the stock market, ushering in the Great Depression. Although radio was briefly jolted, it soon recovered while other entertainment industries suffered and collapsed. Talents, especially from vaudeville and the theater, flocked to radio for jobs. In the process, the quality of radio was greatly enhanced.

During this time of poverty, historian Erik Barnouw recalled, destitute families, forced to give up an icebox or bedding, clung to the radio as if it were the last link to humanity. Radio became the one widely available distraction from the awful daily struggle. By 1932, listeners could identify with nationally known radio personalities.

During the same period, virtually all of the important types of radio programming, including situation comedy, children's programs, adventure and action shows, daytime soap operas, crime shows, adventure stories, westerns, and prestige dramas, were being aired. These shows shared the airwaves with musical programs, news, and quiz shows.

Many new stars were former vaudevillians like Fred Allen and Eddie Cantor. They presented new forms of radio comedy. In contrast to easygoing rural American humor, the "new comedy" was aggressive, ethnic, and rooted in common people faced with the problems of city life.

Every night, families gathered in their living rooms to listen to famous comedians such as Jack Benny, Bob Hope, Fibber McGee and Molly, ventriloquist Edgar Bergen and his dummy Charlie McCarthy, The Great Gildersleeve, and George Burns and Gracie Allen. The popularity of *Amos and Andy* became legendary. The program captured as many as 40 million listeners, nearly 60 percent of the radio audience. Public response was so overwhelming that movie theaters interrupted their screenings so that people could listen to the show over radio sets.

Children's programs included *The Lone Ranger, The Green Hornet, Sergeant Preston of the Yukon, Little Orphan Annie,* and *Jack Armstrong.* Adventure and action shows such as *Dragnet, Gangbusters, Yours Truly Johnny Dollar,* and the most memorable show of them all – *The Shadow* – attracted huge audiences.

Daytime radio serials, which became known as "soap operas" because many of the sponsors were soap companies, were also successful. One of the most listened to was *One Man's Family,* which remained on the air for 28 years. Others were *The Romance of Helen Trent* and *Ma Perkins.*

Less sensational, but significant from an artistic view, was the *Columbia Workshop* (1937–42). This CBS program was an experimental drama series that attracted many innovative writers, notably Arch Oboler and Norman Corwin. CBS later commissioned Corwin to write "On a Note of Triumph," a radio play celebrating the Allied victory in Europe. Also attracted to the *Columbia Workshop* was Orson Welles, who developed a first-person-singular narrative dramatic technique that facilitated the adaptation of full-length novels into radio plays.

In 1938, more U.S. homes were supplied with radios than with indoor plumbing, automobiles, or telephones. In the same year, on Halloween eve, a program titled "The War of the Worlds," directed by Orson Welles, demonstrated the enormous power of radio. What 6 million listeners heard was an adaptation of H.G. Wells's science fiction masterpiece, *War of the Worlds.* However, because the dramatization was presented in such a clever manner, many listeners panicked, believing that Martians had really landed. On October 31, the *New York Times* reported, "A wave of mass hysteria seized thousands of radio listeners throughout the nation."

The 1930s also experienced a rise in radio news. From 1933 to 1934, a brief rivalry occurred between the print media and radio, the "press-radio war," in which news services limited feeds to radio stations. Several independent radio news services began operating in 1934, and shortly afterward, the Associated Press and the International News Service began selling full service to radio.

As radio news programs attracted national audiences, news personalities became as popular as entertainers. Among the most famous reporters were H.V. Kaltenborn, Fulton Lewis Jr., Gabriel Heatter, Elmer Davis, Walter

Winchell, Lowell Thomas, and Edward R. Murrow. Thomas became the longest continually operating newscaster in radio history, acting as a commentator over a 45-year period. News columnist Winchell always worked with his hat on in the studio and began his programs, "Good evening, Mr. and Mrs. North and South America and all ships at sea. Let's go to press."

As World War II began, newscasts gained enormous importance. Beginning in 1937, CBS sent foreign correspondents such as Kaltenborn and Murrow to Europe. Kaltenborn presented live commentary from the battlefields in Spain, and Murrow's *London After Dark* offered nightly reports of the Battle of Britain from London rooftops as German bombers blitzed the city.

On December 8, 1941, the networks covered President Franklin D. Roosevelt's declaration of war as millions heard his historic words, "Yesterday, December 7, 1941, a date that will live in infamy, the United States of America was suddenly and deliberately attacked." There were many other memorable broadcasts: Cecil Brown of CBS reporting the fall of Singapore; George Hicks of ABC recording a D-Day report from a landing barge under German fire; and Murrow's broadcast upon seeing the concentration camp at Buchenwald.

To combat enemy propaganda and coordinate radio services for the war effort, President Roosevelt appointed Elmer Davis to head the Office of War Information in 1942. In the same year, the Armed Forces Radio Service was created to entertain U.S. personnel overseas. The Axis nations had already established similar services. Attempting to undermine the morale of Allied soldiers in the South Pacific, the Japanese aired a program called *Zero Hour,* featuring Tokyo Rose.

Roosevelt was the first president to recognize the mass appeal of radio. In 1933, he reached listeners through his fireside chats. During his career, he made an estimated 300 radio broadcasts. His address to the nation on December 9, a day after war was declared, reached the largest audience in radio history, 90 million. When on April 22, 1945, radio networks reported the president's death from a cerebral hemorrhage, all commercial broadcasting was canceled for three days. Announcer Arthur Godfrey made a memorable broadcast of the funeral procession.

Late in August, Max Jordan of NBC reported on-the-spot coverage of the Japanese surrender on the U.S.S. *Missouri* in Tokyo Bay. The war ended as it began, on radio.

Following the war, radio's prosperity continued until the rapid expansion of television late in the 1940s. The extent of television's growth became evident in 1949. In that year, television sets in homes were estimated to number about 1 million. Only 100,000 sets had existed a year earlier. Television began to replace radio as the dominant medium in the United States.

FRANK J. CHORBA

See also New Deal and the Media; Office of War Information; Radio Entertainment; Radio Networks; Radio News; Roosevelt, Franklin D., and the Media; "War of the Worlds"

Further Reading

Chester, Giraud, Garnet R. Garrison, and Edgar E. Willis, *Television and Radio*, 5th ed., Englewood Cliffs, New Jersey: Prentice-Hall, 1978
Schiffer, Michael B., *The Portable Radio in American Life,* Tucson: University of Arizona Press, 1991
Settel, Irving, *A Pictorial History of Radio,* New York: Grosset & Dunlap, 1967

Golden Age of Television

Time of great creativity and innovation in television

The 1950s represent the golden age of television, a period of unequaled greatness in the medium. Programs were presented live. Creativity and innovation dominated. Television was evolving just as the United States itself was experiencing many changes and challenges in the post–World War II age. It was a time of prosperity, progress, and hope, but it was also a dark time when people lived under the threat of nuclear holocaust. Television helped viewers celebrate good times and escape from bad times.

People in the United States, regardless of their demographics, originally purchased television sets for entertainment, but television programming spanned a wide range of news, sporting events, music, drama, games, quizzes, humor, religion, and variety. A primary influence on radio and television was vaudeville. Many routines were adapted to radio, and the further transition to television was natural. Vaudeville stars such as Jack Benny and the Burns and Allen comedy team were huge successes on radio and then on television. Others were not as fortunate, as their radio routines left much to be desired on the visual medium. Radio also influenced television's penchant for shows featuring a particular star, such as Bob Hope, Lucille Ball, Jackie Gleason, Milton Berle, or Jack Benny. Some shows featured ensembles, such as *Your Show of Shows,* with Sid Caesar, Imogene Coca, Carl Reiner, Howard Morris, and Mel Brooks. Radio shows, such as *The Lone Ranger, Dragnet,* and *Gunsmoke,* were adapted to television. Radio's influence on television was also evident in soap operas and other daytime programs.

The concept of the broadcast network originated on radio and established not only a model for television but a foundation. NBC and CBS, the leading radio networks, made smooth transitions to television. Boasting stars such as Sid Caesar, Milton Berle, Bob Hope, and Groucho Marx, NBC was the foremost network early in the decade. Chairman David Sarnoff was the driving force for the television network as he was with radio.

Sarnoff's principal rival was the formidable William S. Paley of CBS, who had lured many NBC radio stars to CBS in the 1940s. Those same entertainers advanced the charge for Paley's television network. By the end of the 1950s, Paley's direction helped CBS surpass NBC in advertising revenue. Among the legendary CBS entertainers were Jack Benny, George Burns and Gracie Allen, Red Skelton, Edgar

I Love Lucy was a staple of television's golden years.
(Museum of Broadcast Communications)

Bergen, and the creators of *Amos and Andy,* Freeman Gosden and Charles Correll.

Third-place ABC had its own notable stars and programs, including *The Adventures of Ozzie and Harriet,* Danny Thomas's *Make Room for Daddy, The Mickey Mouse Club, Maverick,* and *American Bandstand.* Dumont was the smallest of the original four networks, and the others often lured away its stars. The most notable defection was "The Great One," Jackie Gleason, to CBS.

Many of television's early innovations have endured. Desi Arnaz' multi-camera production approach was employed by most of the situation comedies of the next four or

Jackie Gleason and *The Honeymooners* appeared regularly during television's golden years.
(Museum of Broadcast Communications)

five decades. Arnaz also created the filmed, or "canned," show because he and wife Lucille Ball wanted to live in Hollywood. They filmed *I Love Lucy* episodes and shipped them back to New York for airing, thus enabling the pregnant Lucy to have her real-life baby on the same night as the television birth. Incidentally, since golden age programs reflected conservative family values, the word "pregnant" could not be uttered on *I Love Lucy* or any other television show of the era. The family show also emerged in the golden age. *Leave it to Beaver,* which presented the perspective of a child living in an adult world, is a primary example.

Rod Serling and Paddy Chayefsky led a host of excellent writers whose theatrical adaptations were presented on showcases such as *Playhouse 90, Kraft Television Theater,* and *Studio One.* The 1950s also introduced the United States to the spectacular. An innovation of NBC's Sylvester "Pat" Weaver, spectaculars were specials of various kinds, and the most watched was Broadway's *Peter Pan,* which attracted 65 million viewers to NBC in 1955.

Television of the 1950s also had its bombs and failures. Some shows were just plain bad, and others now would be considered offensive. *Beulah* and *The Amos and Andy Show* were creative and well done for their time but are now considered offensive for their racial stereotyping.

The earliest television news shows appeared on CBS and NBC in 1948, and each was 15 minutes in length. Television news amounted to little more than an announcer reading copy with some film footage added. Unlike radio news and its analysis, television news was superficial and leaned more to entertainment than to information. CBS's entry was *Television News with Douglas Edwards.* NBC's *Camel News Caravan* was hosted by John Cameron Swayze. Swayze eventually was replaced by the Chet Huntley–David Brinkley news team, and Edwards was unseated by Walter Cronkite. NBC also debuted the *Today* morning show with host David Garroway and his gimmicky chimpanzee assistant, J. Fred Muggs.

An important, groundbreaking moment for television news pitted Edward R. Murrow of CBS against Senator Joseph McCarthy of Wisconsin. Murrow was not enamored with television but understood its power. As host of *See It Now,* Murrow and producer Fred Friendly reluctantly decided to take the Communist-hating McCarthy to task in a story dubbed "The Case Against Milo Radulovich, A0589839." McCarthy built his political career by exploiting the Communist phobia in the United States. He turned his powerful attention to Air Force Reservist Milo Radulovich. Radulovich's father had Communist party connections, and although Milo Radulovich himself had not, McCarthy wanted the son expelled from duty. Realizing that McCarthy would demand equal time if *See It Now* profiled the Radulovich case from the defendant's point of view, the show focused almost exclusively on the senator's own words. McCarthy could not legitimately ask for equal time when he was the entire show. Murrow's *See It Now* exposed McCarthy, and the climate of opinion turned against him forever. Radulovich remained in the military after Murrow's intervention.

In the 1950s, color television broadcasting was approved by the Federal Communications Commission. This innovation made the popular medium even more desirable among consumers. Many shows were shot in color, but it was comparatively expensive. Black-and-white programs were in evidence into the late 1960s.

By the end of the 1950s, television was changing quickly and dramatically. Much ado was given to the two-week U.S. visit of Soviet premier Nikita Khrushchev in 1959. Khrushchev loved his dominance of U.S. prime-time television; he was a stark contrast both to his reclusive predecessors and to McCarthyism. In 1958, westerns became the most prevalent fixture on television, with 33 of them on the networks.

Quiz shows peaked in the 1950s, but scandals killed their popularity. The most notable was *The $64,000 Question,* in which various contestants were given the answers to questions in advance. Revlon, the show's sponsor, made the decision on which contestants would be aided. Congress intervened, and many contestants filed lawsuits against the programs.

For the most part, live television ended with the 1950s, and television would never be the same. Despite the frequent accidents, flubbed lines, anxieties, and other problems during television's golden age, there was a magic that has never been recaptured. As television matured, technology improved, but creativity suffered in the process. The golden age of television was fostered during a simpler time for the United States, and, some would argue, the era of innocence and the golden age officially ended with the assassination of President Kennedy in 1963.

KELLY W.A. HUFF

See also Army-McCarthy Hearings; Cold War and the Media; Quiz Show Scandals; Television Entertainment; Television Networks; Television News

Further Reading

Javna, John, *The Best of TV Sitcoms,* New York: Harmony, 1988
MacDonald, J. Fred, *Blacks and White TV: African Americans in Television Since 1948,* 2nd ed., Chicago: Nelson-Hall, 1992
_____, *One Nation Under Television: The Rise and Decline of Network TV,* New York: Pantheon, 1990
Spigel, Lynn, *Make Room for TV: Television and the Family Ideal in Postwar America,* Chicago: University of Chicago Press, 1992
Winship, Michael, *Television,* New York: Random House, 1988

Goldenson, Leonard

Helped make ABC-TV successful

Leonard Goldenson, chairman and chief executive officer of the American Broadcasting Company (ABC), was born in Scottsdale, Pennsylvania, 40 miles from Pittsburgh. He attended Harvard University, graduated from Harvard Law School, joined Paramount Pictures, and took over management of all theater subsidiaries by the age of 32. Goldenson is credited with leading the merger of ABC with United Paramount Theatres, then persuading Hollywood film leaders, especially Jack Warner, into merging program interests with his new network. He diversified the company and fought takeover bids in an era in which ABC was regarded as an also-ran network.

Because of its preoccupation with building an audience

Leonard Goldenson
(Library of American Broadcasting)

and attracting affiliates, news took a back seat at ABC. Goldenson formed an alliance with Disney Studios, and he invested in news by recruiting Elmer Lower from NBC, which began to build an ABC editorial staff. The successful anchor team of Howard K. Smith and Harry Reasoner emerged. By the 1970s, ABC came close to achieving parity in news. One of his accomplishments was the signing of Barbara Walters to a multiyear contract.

Goldenson became chairman of ABC's parent company in 1972. In later years, he became an advocate for broadcast access to courts. Unpretentious and accessible in his private life, Goldenson was totally devoted to the cause of fighting cerebral palsy, which took the life of one of his three daughters.

MICHAEL D. MURRAY

See also Television Entertainment; Television Networks

Further Reading

Brown, Les, *Television: The Business Behind the Box,* New York: Harcourt Brace Jovanovich, 1971
Goldenson, Leonard, *Beating the Odds: The Untold Story Behind the Rise of ABC: The Stars, Struggles, and Egos that Transformed Network Television by the Man Who Made It Happen,* New York: Scribner's, 1991; Toronto, Ontario: Collier Macmillan Canada, 1991
Quinlan, Sterling, *Inside ABC: American Broadcasting Company's Rise to Power,* New York: Hastings House, 1979

Gould, Jack

'New York Times' television critic

John Ludlow "Jack" Gould, television critic, was born in New York City and in 1932 went to work as a copyboy at the *New York Herald Tribune,* where he was a protégé of Stanley Walker. In 1937, he joined the *New York Times* to cover entertainment news. His lifelong interest in the technology of radio led to coverage of that industry and then to appointment as radio critic in 1944. He began to follow the development of television after World War II. In 1947, he was named radio and television editor, a post he held until 1970. He retired from the *Times* in February 1972.

In the 1950s, Gould advocated live television drama and was skeptical about the medium's drive to attain high audience ratings at the expense of cultural standards. He also spoke out against blacklisting of performers during the anti-Communist fervor of the 1950s. The high point of his years as a critic came in 1956 when he assailed the refusal of the networks to air meetings of the United Nations Security Council during the Suez Crisis. The networks relented, and Gould received a Peabody Award in 1957 for his "fairness, objectivity and authority." Along with his criticism, Gould emphasized his role as a television reporter. He broke numerous important stories relating to the evolution of color television, the Nielsen ratings, the career of Edward R. Murrow, and the effects of television on the general public. Although he disliked the term, he was accurately known as "the conscience of the industry."

LEWIS L. GOULD

Further Reading

Friendly, Fred, "Dear Jack Gould, They Say You've Retired," *New York Times* (February 27, 1972)
"Jack Gould, Critic, is Dead at 79; Covered Television for the *Times*," *New York Times* (May 25, 1993)
Saalbach, Louis Carl, *Jack Gould: Social Critic of the Television Medium, 1947–1972* (Ph.D. diss., University of Michigan), 1980

Government Printing and Patronage

Financed numerous newspapers in the early years of nationhood

During the first century of the United States, newspapers were active partners in governing the new nation. The country's leaders recognized early the importance of keeping the citizenry informed. One of the duties of the secretary of state's office, created by Congress in 1789, was to select newspapers in which to publish copies of the laws and resolutions passed by Congress. Thomas Jefferson, the first secretary of state, implemented the legislation, selecting one paper from each of five major cities.

Pressure grew to expand the circulation, so in 1799, Congress passed a new law requiring the secretary of state to select at least one newspaper, and as many as three, in each state to receive printing contracts. Leaders of the country's growing political parties quickly recognized the considerable patronage such legislation provided them. James Madison, secretary of state under Jefferson, selected papers friendly to the administration. He was aided in the process by congressmen eager to build constituencies. By 1824, 76 papers had printing contracts, more than double the number in 1801.

The growing partnership between the government and newspapers was evident in the presidential campaigns of 1824 and 1828. Candidates needed papers to get their messages across, and editors wanted the prestige and money that went with backing successful politicians. President Andrew Jackson rewarded editors who supported him with printing contracts as well as political offices. In all, more than 50 journalists were appointed to national office during the Jackson administration.

By the time Jackson took office, the tradition of Congress having its own newspaper to print documents besides laws and resolutions also had become well established. Not surprisingly, the dominant party in Congress selected the publisher that would handle congressional printing.

In 1842, Congress changed the law giving the secretary of state authority to select newspapers as official printers and instead gave the printing to only four publishers, all in the District of Columbia. Four years later, Congress went back to the old system but reduced the number of papers from three to two for each state. Presidential administrations continued to use the patronage to strengthen themselves and their parties.

During the same period, concerns about the cost and effectiveness of the congressional printing system grew. In 1860, Congress, responding to charges of scandal, created the Government Printing Office (GPO). At about the same time, President James Buchanan withdrew the subsidy of the administration's newspaper after repeated differences with the publisher. The institution of a newspaper as the official presidential organ was over. After much debate, Congress in 1875 also decided to no longer use newspapers to publish the laws. All proceedings were to be published by the GPO in the *Congressional Record*.

The patronage system had played an important role in keeping the electorate informed of the workings of the government. Although the system prevented those papers with government contracts from being truly independent, it helped many gain a financial foothold in their communities. By the time patronage of the press ended, newspapers had become firmly established as important institutions in the United States.

FORD RISLEY

See also Jackson, Andrew, and the Press; Party Press; Penny Press

Further Reading

Ames, William E., "Federal Patronage and the Washington D.C. Press," *Journalism Quarterly* 9 (1972)
Kielbowicz, Richard B., *News in the Mail: The Press, Post Office and Public Information, 1700–1860s*, New York: Greenwood, 1989
Marbut, Frederick B., "Decline of the Official Press in Washington," *Journalism Quarterly* 33 (1965)
Smith, Culver H., *The Press, Politics, and Patronage: The American Government's Use of Newspapers, 1789–1875*, Athens: University of Georgia Press, 1977

Government Secrecy

Long tradition of maintaining government confidentiality

A fundamental principle of democracy in the United States calls for informed participation in government. Undergirding that principle is the idea that citizens must have access to information about government activities in order to play their roles satisfactorily. A national history of government secrecy, however, caused problems for the fulfilling of that responsibility.

As early as the colonial period, government officials sought to keep their proceedings concealed from the public. Philadelphia printer William Bradford was one of the first to run afoul of colonial authorities when he printed a copy of the Pennsylvania charter without permission. Other colonial printers tried presenting readers with laws and legislative proceedings without permission and likewise ran into difficulties. Hugh Gaine, printer of the *New York Mercury*, for instance, was made to apologize to the government for printing the king's instructions to a new governor and the governor's speech to the state assembly without permission in 1753.

When the founding fathers met to write the new Constitution in 1787, their sessions were held in secret, and the press of the day found nothing wrong with that decision. Indeed, journalists tended to praise the decision because of the quality of men gathered for the discussions. Closed meetings were also the hallmark of the newly formed Senate, whose members protested that the Senate chamber lacked appropriate facilities for the press until 1795. The House opened its sessions to the press beginning April 8, 1789, two days after it convened.

The early years of the republic also witnessed the start of executive privilege when George Washington withheld information about an Indian massacre of federal troops from a congressional investigating committee. And the Senate, invoking constitutional privilege, began meeting in secret to discuss foreign policy. Such sessions over the Jay Treaty, which tried to settle outstanding differences with England in 1795, led to news leaks that made such secrecy futile. A similar situation faced President James K. Polk in negotiations over the Treaty of Guadalupe Hidalgo at the end of the Mexican War. Problems over secrecy in diplomatic negotiations continued into the twentieth century, with President Woodrow Wilson, for one, concerned about the coverage of the Paris Peace Conference at the end of World War I.

Government secrecy in wartime almost was to be expected in the United States. Secrecy in peacetime as well became institutionalized during the Cold War under President Harry S. Truman. The classification system, as it later became known, was first established in 1951, ostensibly to help free up executive branch information for distribution to the press and public. Truman said that his rationale was to clearly identify information that must be kept away from the "irresponsible press" in order to promote distribution of other data. The original classification categories were top secret, secret, confidential, and restricted. Classification procedures were defined in terms of the danger release of the information would pose to national security. Unauthorized release of top secret information, for instance, "would or could cause exceptionally grave damage to the national security." The press protested unsuccessfully.

Succeeding presidents issued their own executive orders pertaining to classified documents. Some, such as Richard Nixon and Ronald Reagan, took steps to make the release of information more difficult. Other presidents, such as John F. Kennedy and Jimmy Carter, moved toward greater disclosure.

Congress quickly became involved in the classification process, not because it was allowed a role in the categorizing of documents but because documents were denied to it as well as to the press. By the late 1950s, the House of Representatives set up a special subcommittee under John E. Moss Jr., Democrat of California, to hear complaints about denied access to government information from journalists, researchers, and members of Congress.

Although the Moss committee was by most accounts a successful mediator between those seeking information and those denying it, Congress sought to regularize the process of gaining access to executive branch information by enacting legislation. The Freedom of Information Act (FOIA) was signed into law by Lyndon B. Johnson in 1966. It placed an affirmative responsibility on executive agencies to make information available to the press and public, but it also provided a number of rationales that could be used to deny access. The process for obtaining access was also cumbersome, making evasion of the law's intent possible by cutting back the staff available to process FOIA requests and by increasing the cost of obtaining desired documents. The time lag involved in using the FOIA made the law less than viable for journalists on a deadline. More than 200 years after the ratification of the Constitution, then, the battle over obtaining the information necessary to participate in the administration of the government that document created continued.

MARGARET A. BLANCHARD

See also Freedom of Information Act; Mass Media and Foreign Policy; News Leaks; Truman, Harry S., and the Media

Further Reading

Blanchard, Margaret A., *Revolutionary Sparks: Freedom of Expression in Modern America,* New York: Oxford University Press, 1992

Dennis, Everette E., "Stolen Peace Treaties and the Press: Two Case Studies," *Journalism History* 2 (1975)

Endres, Kathleen L., "National Security Benchmark: Truman, Executive Order 10290, and the Press," *Journalism Quarterly* 67:4 (Winter 1990), pp. 1071–1077

Grotta, Gerald L., "Philip Freneau's Crusade for Open Sessions of the U.S. Senate," *Journalism Quarterly* 48 (1971)

Hoffman, Daniel N., *Governmental Secrecy and the Founding Fathers: A Study in Constitutional Controls,* Westport, Connecticut: Greenwood, 1981

Levy, Leonard, *Emergence of a Free Press,* New York and Oxford: Oxford University Press, 1985

Greeley, Horace

Editor of the 'New York Tribune'

Horace Greeley, founder of the *New York Tribune,* was the most popular and influential newspaper editor of his era. Greeley was born in Amherst, New Hampshire. Raised by poor parents and largely self-educated, he began working for newspapers as a teenager.

Greeley held a variety of printing positions in New York before helping to start the *Morning Post,* a penny paper. The paper failed, and in 1834, Greeley and another partner purchased the *New Yorker,* a weekly literary and political

Horace Greeley
(Reproduced from the Collections of the Library of Congress)

publication. On April 10, 1841, he launched the *New York Tribune,* the first penny paper with Whig loyalties.

The *Tribune* was recognized for its intellectual appeal, high moral standards, and outstanding news-gathering facilities. He attracted an outstanding staff including Charles Dana, Margaret Fuller, and Henry Raymond. On the *Tribune*'s editorial pages, Greeley put forth his own well-intentioned, but often erratic, views on such subjects as agrarianism, worker exploitation, and abstinence from alcohol. On the eve of the American Civil War, the *Tribune*'s circulation far surpassed those of its rivals that were being distributed throughout most of the country.

Greeley was an outspoken opponent of slavery, and the culmination of the campaign was his most famous editorial, "The Prayer of Twenty Millions." After the war, he became active in the Liberal Republican movement and in 1872 accepted its nomination for the presidency. Losing the election just days after his wife's death, he learned that he had lost virtually all control of the *Tribune*. Heartbroken, he died on November 29, 1872.

FORD RISLEY

See also Civil War Press (North); Penny Press

Further Reading

Parton, James, *The Life of Horace Greeley,* New York: Mason Brothers, 1855

Seitz, Don C., *Horace Greeley: Founder of the 'New York Tribune',* Indianapolis, Indiana: Bobbs-Merrill, 1926

Van Deusen, Glyndon G., *Horace Greeley: Nineteenth Century Crusader,* New York: Hill and Wang, 1953

Grenada Invasion

Brief military encounter caused problems for journalists

On October 25, 1983, U.S. troops landed on the small Caribbean island of Grenada. Earlier that month, leftist rebels had overthrown Grenada's Marxist government. Some other Caribbean nations had expressed fears that the island might become a base for Cuban operations. President Ronald Reagan, also citing danger to some 600 U.S. students at a medical school on the island, ordered troops to Grenada, along with smaller forces from six Caribbean nations. It took only a few days for the occupying force to overcome the local militia and some Cuban workers and to control the island, and the U.S. combat troops left Grenada by the end of 1983. However, the invasion also gave rise to a conflict between the military and the press that continued well into the next year and eventually resulted in new procedures for media coverage of combat operations.

In contrast with previous landings (including D-Day during World War II, Inchon during the Korean War, and the Dominican Republic during President Lyndon B. Johnson's term), President Reagan's administration restricted live coverage of the Grenada invasion. No U.S. reporters accompanied troops on the unannounced landing; the military removed journalists who made private arrangements to reach the island; and others who attempted to travel there by sea were intercepted and turned back. Only on the third day of fighting did the military allow a pool of reporters onto the island. On October 30, free access was permitted.

Government officials offered several defenses for their

Students from Saint George's University School of Medicine in Grenada conduct a press conference upon arriving at Charleston Air Force Base, South Carolina.

(Official U.S. Air Force Photo [Released])

policy, including the need for surprise, the wishes of the operation commander, and the potential risks to journalists. Media organizations protested immediately through public editorials and commentaries as well as formal complaints to the Department of Defense.

Jack Landau, then the executive director of the Reporters Committee for Freedom of the Press, called the Reagan administration's action an "unprecedented legal position." Landau wrote, "The American press has had immediate access to observe (although not to immediately report) every previous extended (non-covert) military engagement since the American Revolution."

Several major journalistic organizations (including the Society for Professional Journalists, the American Society of Newspaper Editors, and the American Newspaper Publishers Association) produced a "statement of principle" that included the following section:

Mission security and troop safety interests have been protected – when essential – by limiting the number of journalists accompanying the troops, by voluntary reporting restraints, by limited censorship of information that might aid the enemy, or by delay in the filing of dispatches; but not by the exclusion of all journalists.

In addition, the public expressed itself on the issue, often critically of the press. *Time* magazine, for example, reported that its letters ran eight to one against the media. In a "press alert," the American Society of Newspaper Editors reported what it called the "shocking" conclusion that "the public doesn't seem to give a damn." Other indicators suggested the press might have underestimated public support. A Washington Post/ABC News poll in November 1983 found that 48 percent of respondents felt the government had tried too much to control the news from Grenada, while 38 percent felt it had not.

In response to the furor, the Joint Chiefs of Staff appointed a 14-member panel to recommend guidelines for coverage of future surprise missions. The panel consisted of military officers, journalism professors, and former journalists. Its chair was retired general Winant Sidle. The panel received two dozen written statements and in February 1984 held three days of hearings with military and media representatives.

In its report, made public in August 1984, the Sidle Commission concluded that "it is essential that the U.S. news media cover U.S. military operations to the maximum degree possible consistent with mission security and the safety of U.S. forces." In particular, the commission recommended a press pool system:

When it becomes apparent during military operational planning that news media pooling provides the only feasible means of furnishing the media with early access to an operation, planning should provide for the largest possible press pool that is practical and minimize the length of time the pool will be necessary before "full coverage" is feasible.

The Department of Defense accepted the recommendations and began a lengthy process of instituting them. During the ensuing months, the media and the Defense department negotiated, sometimes contentiously, the size, composition, and procedures for the new pool system and conducted trial runs. The first major use of the pool system occurred during the Persian Gulf War in 1991, but press complaints about the system continued and the rules of operation remained under periodic review.

CARL SESSIONS STEPP

See also Mass Media and the Military; Persian Gulf War

Further Reading

Braestrup, Peter, *Battle Lines: Report of the Twentieth Century Fund Task Force on the Military and the Media*, 2nd ed., New York: Priority, 1985

Report by CJCS Media-Military Relations Panel (Sidle Panel), Washington D.C.: U.S. Department of Defense, Office of Assistant Secretary of Defense, 1984

Gulf War: *see* Persian Gulf War

H

Handwritten Newspapers

Publications date from the colonial period

Newspapers written by hand in pen and ink or pencil have been published in all regions of the United States since the colonial period. Although they ranged from children's school news sheets to hard-hitting community journals of news and opinion, handwritten papers generally possessed the content, style, and tone commonly associated with newspapers of their day. The papers were typically two- or three-column spreads with bold headlines and graphics. Most contained a mixture of news, poetry, editorials, and humor. Some papers, such as *The Flumgudgeon Gazette and Bumble Bee Budget* (Oregon, 1845), were devoted to political satire.

One of America's earliest printed newspapers, the *Boston News-Letter,* a journal for commercial and governmental news, was first handwritten from 1700 to 1704. Other early handwritten news sheets were published in the eastern colonies and states by religious groups, reading clubs, and schools. With the nation's western expansion in the nineteenth century, handwritten papers proliferated in the isolated settlements of the Mississippi Valley and Great Plains and in the mining and logging camps and trading posts of the far west.

Soldiers published handwritten papers throughout the western states and territories in the mid- to late 1800s. Prisoners of Texas's ill-fated Santa Fe Expedition published the *True Blue* in Castle Santiago Prison, in Mexico City, in 1842. Both Union and Confederate soldiers wrote newspapers by hand in the field and in prison camps during the American Civil War. And during World War II, Japanese Americans produced some handwritten, mimeographed papers in their internment camps.

Most handwritten papers were weeklies, but their frequency was often irregular. Hand-lettered news sheets typically had limited numbers of copies in circulation. Some single-copy papers were posted in prominent locations, such as stores, churches, or saloons. The *Bum Hill Gazette,* for example, was posted at a local church kitchen that fed victims of the 1906 San Francisco earthquake. Other papers circulated like chain letters among their audiences, like the *Old Flag* (Texas, 1864), published by Union prisoners at Camp Ford, Texas. Many handwritten papers were "published" by being read aloud.

Some publishers produced multiple copies of handwritten originals using common duplicating methods. Students

Bum-Hill Gazette was published after the great San Francisco earthquake of 1906.

(The Bancroft Library/University of California at Berkeley)

249

often served as scribal copyists for papers published at schools and Indian mission stations. The hectograph, a duplicating device using purple aniline dyes, made multiple copies of the Alaska Forum (Alaska, 1900–06). Some linguistic communities, notably some Native Americans who had no typewriters or type fonts available in their native languages, duplicated their hand-lettered newspapers by mimeograph well into the twentieth century.

Handwritten newspapers were an important medium of communication for many people isolated geographically, socially, and linguistically, especially during periods of national growth and conflict. Manuscript news sheets were a primary means for many amateur journalists to stimulate public discourse in communities without printed newspapers or printing businesses. Hand-lettered papers provided an alternative means of publication for disfranchised and marginalized groups, such as women, children, minorities, political prisoners, and religious sects. They preserved an element of the manuscript tradition in the United States long after the advent of printing technology.

ROY ALDEN ATWOOD

Further Reading

Alter, J. Cecil, *Early Utah Journalism,* Salt Lake City: Utah State Historical Society, 1938

Atwood, Roy Alden, "Handwritten Newspapers of the Canadian-American West, 1842–1910," paper delivered at the Association for Education in Journalism and Mass Communication annual meeting, Kansas City, Missouri, August 1993

_____, "Handwritten Newspapers on the Iowa Frontier, 1844–1854," *Journalism History* 7 (1980)

Brier, Warren J., "The 'Flumgudgeon Gazette and Bumble Bee Budget'," *Journalism Quarterly* 36 (1959)

Earl, Phillip I., and Eric Moody, "Type, Tripe and the Granite Times," *Nevada Magazine* (May/June 1982)

Karolevitz, Robert F., "Pen and Ink Newspapers of the Old West," *Frontier Times* 44 (1970)

Working, D.W., "Some Forgotten Pioneer Newspapers," *Colorado Magazine* 4 (1927)

Harding, Warren G., and the Press

Newspaper publisher served as president

President Warren G. Harding, the nation's first publisher-president, said he always considered himself more of a newspaper man than chief executive. While Presidents Theodore Roosevelt and Woodrow Wilson occasionally held news conferences or met with reporters, Harding set the pattern for the modern relationship between presidents and the media.

Publisher of the *Marion (Ohio) Star,* he understood reporters' deadlines and production schedules and tried to accommodate them. Shortly after Harding's inauguration, regular twice-weekly presidential news conferences were established, and photographers were given a daily schedule of White House events.

Newspaper reporters considered the president to be one of them, and Harding reciprocated with openness and candor. He met with reporters after cabinet meetings and discussed what was said and decided; Harding also directed that sessions of the 1921 Washington Disarmament Conference be conducted openly, with news correspondents in attendance. During the summer of 1922, while mediating nationwide coal and rail strikes at the White House, the president would at times come outside in shirtsleeves after midnight to brief reporters on progress. Harding was also the first president to use radio.

W. RICHARD WHITAKER

Further Reading

Downes, Randolph C., *The Rise of Warren Gamaliel Harding, 1865–1920,* Columbus: Ohio State University Press, 1970

Essary, Jesse Frederick, *Covering Washington,* New York: Houghton Mifflin, 1927

Murray, Robert K., *The Harding Era: Warren G. Harding and His Administration,* Minneapolis: University of Minnesota Press, 1969

Sullivan, Mark, *Our Times; The United States, 1900–1925,* New York and London: Scribner's, 1928

Whitaker, Wayne Richard, *Warren G. Harding and the Press* (Ph.D. diss., Ohio University), 1972

Hearst, William Randolph

Influential figure in publishing and politics

For more than half a century William Randolph Hearst was a powerful player in U.S. media and politics. From 1887, when he persuaded his father, Senator George Hearst of California, to let him run the *San Francisco Examiner,* until his death in 1951, Hearst built and managed a media empire with global influence.

His personal political ambitions were frustrated in the early 1900s when he barely missed being nominated for president, and Hearst concentrated his energies and fortune on establishing and acquiring newspapers in major U.S. cities. His holdings also included magazines, news and feature syndicates, newsreel and motion picture companies, and broadcast properties. Few U.S. homes were untouched by the Hearst influence.

Often criticized for exploiting sensationalism – the term "yellow journalism" comes from the competition between Hearst and Joseph Pulitzer in the 1890s – Hearst also improved the readability of his newspapers by hiring good writers and editors and installing good printing equipment. He conducted a number of flamboyant crusades aimed at reforms ranging from tenements to the U.S. Senate.

When not writing front-page editorials for his various newspapers to publish, he collected art and antiques, buying them by the castleful. He owned a number of homes, the most famous of which is the castle at San Simeon on the California coast.

Hearst's marriage to Millicent Willson in 1903 produced five sons, several of whom were prominent in the Hearst Corporation. However, Hearst and his wife separated, and he had a longtime romance with actress Marion Davies.

BARBARA CLOUD

See also Pulitzer, Joseph; Yellow Journalism

Further Reading
Swanberg, W.A., *Citizen Hearst: A Biography of William Randolph Hearst*, New York: Scribner's, 1961; London: Longmans, 1962

Hidden Persuaders, The

Explored social and ethical consequences of advertising methods

The Hidden Persuaders, written by Vance Packard in 1957, was one of the first works to explore the social and ethical consequences of the psychological tools used by advertising to sell goods and ideas to the consumer target audience. The book examined motivational research and the power and influence it can have in delivering messages and creating desires in the areas of politics and government as well as in selling consumer goods.

Written in a popular style, *The Hidden Persuaders* claimed that advertisers had figured out how to reach into the subconscious mind and deliver a message directed at deeply hidden needs and wants. Packard gave concrete examples of campaigns that he claimed worked because advertisers used this type of manipulation.

With chapters titled "Back to the Breast and Beyond," "The Engineered Yes," and "The Packaged Soul," Packard outlined an industry-controlled selling system. Chapters were short and easy to read. The message was clear: advertisers knew how to reach the public at an emotional level that made messages more powerful than ever. Hucksterism, said Packard, had entered a new era.

The book was a best-seller that alarmed the U.S. public and ushered in a new era of consumerism. It, along with others such as Ralph Nader's *Unsafe at Any Speed,* John Kenneth Galbraith's *The Affluent Society,* and Rachel Carson's *Silent Spring,* exhorted the public to take charge and examine every claim made by manufacturers and advertisers.

MARY ALICE SHAVER

Hispanic Media

Media enterprises serve people of Latin American descent

Hispanic media – media that are produced for people of Latin American descent in the United States – are nurtured by strong ties to Latin America. The first Spanish-language newspaper in the United States, *El Misisipí* (1808), was published in New Orleans, Louisiana, in a bilingual format, Spanish and English, for both news and advertising. This four-page publication catered to the needs of merchants and traders with commercial ties to the Caribbean, Mexico, and South America. Another Spanish-language newspaper of the era, the *Diario de Nueva York,* was also bilingual, "in both languages, or in the one wanted," translating news articles from English-language newspapers about the Napoleonic Wars as well as disturbances in Latin America.

After the U.S. conquest of half of Mexico in 1848, the southwestern territories of the United States were home to dozens of Spanish-language newspapers. Publications such as *El Grito* (The Shout) maintained ties with Mexico, in both advertising and editorial content. In California, the state government subsidized the printing of Spanish-language newspapers, publishing the state's laws in Spanish for its new citizens. Throughout the nineteenth century in Arizona, New Mexico, Texas, and California, many newspapers retained a close relationship to city and state governments, as well as a bilingual format, attempting to reach both longtime Mexican residents and relatively new Anglo settlers.

Other Spanish-language nineteenth-century newspapers in the United States prided themselves on their independence from government and took on the role of defenders of Mexicans in the United States. *El Labrador* (The Laborer) of Las Cruces, New Mexico, *El Sol* (The Sun) of Santa Rosa, California, and *El Clamor Público* (The Public Clamor) of Los Angeles took partisan positions in Mexican politics and published hard-hitting attacks on the "Yankee conquerors" as well as articles detailing the rights of Mexican workers in the United States. These newspapers often were published by fraternal and union organizations, had little advertising, and thus were short-lived.

Two U.S. Spanish-language newspapers founded early in the twentieth century still were published at the end of the century. *La Opinión* of Los Angeles and *La Prensa* of San Antonio, Texas, were first published in 1914 and 1917, respectively, by Ignacio Lozano, a Mexican businessman who made the cultural education of Mexican Americans his life's work. Lozano's newspapers published – in addition to regional, national, and international news – poetry, and essays by Mexican, Spanish, and French authors. The newspapers stressed Mexican American cultural ties to elite Mexican society. While not ignoring the plight of working-class Mexican Americans, the editorial policy of *La Opinión* and *La Prensa* urged Mexican Americans to help themselves.

Historically, Mexican American literacy and educational achievement have been low relative to that of the general U.S. population. Consequently, U.S. Hispanic-oriented newspapers and magazines have often not had the necessary financial support for survival, while Hispanic radio and television have thrived comparatively.

There were no Spanish-language radio stations in the 1930s at the beginning of U.S. Spanish-language broadcasting – only immigrant-brokered Spanish-language radio programs. In the first decades of the broadcasting industry, radio station owners found that some hours of the day were not commercially viable. Owners sold these off-hours for nominal fees, to radio programmers in the Spanish (and in other parts of the country, other non-English) language, and such programmers were responsible for acquiring their own sponsors.

The economic and cultural marginality of this programming created an opportunity for the U.S. Hispanic community; with ownership functionally absent, and airtime restricted to off-hours, members of the immigrant community were largely left alone to produce radio programs as they saw fit. For example, in Los Angeles, broker and programmer Rodolfo Hoyos spent much of his day walking through the commercial district of the barrio, making personal calls on potential sponsors of his one-hour daily music and talk program. During these sales calls on bakeries and bodegas, he would discuss that day's musical selections or a recent community event that might be mentioned on the air.

During the 1920s and early 1930s, a period that preceded that of widely available recordings, Spanish-language radio programmers in the southwest, expressing the seamless binationality of their communities, prided themselves on sounding as if they were still in Mexico, featuring performances by Mexican musicians and actors performing *novelas* (soap operas) and music. They did not, however, limit themselves to entertainment programming. Responding to the perceived needs of their audiences, these producers often assumed the informational and political advocacy roles more commonly associated with immigrant print journalists of the period.

Perhaps the most emblematic of these was Mexican musician and radio producer Pedro González. His radio program, *Los Madrugadores* (The Early Risers), began broadcasting from KELW in Burbank, California (just north of Los Angeles), in 1927. The program mixed performances with information about jobs and community services and was extremely popular with the city's Mexican immigrant community. His response to social and political circumstances of the late 1920s and 1930s transformed him into one of the best known Mexican American political figures of his generation, a man the *New York Times* described in its 1995 obituary as a "folk hero and social advocate."

Until González took on the role of defender and advocate for his listeners, many of whom were being deported by the federal government's Operation Wetback, the owners of the radio station that broadcast *Los Madrugadores* had been pleased with the program's ability to fill the 4 A.M. to 6 A.M. slot. González brought in new advertising dollars from the immigrant business community, as well as general market advertisers. Nonetheless, under political pressure after González's arrest on trumped-up rape charges, the radio station discontinued all Spanish-language programming.

During the early 1930s, other U.S. broadcasters curtailed their foreign-language programming in response to harassment directed at ethnic broadcasters and the imposition of more stringent radio licensing rules. Although some U.S. stations continued to program Spanish-language blocks, others wishing to reach Mexican Americans moved their operations to the Mexican side of the border, out of the reach of U.S. authorities.

Meanwhile, Emilio Azcárraga founded his broadcasting empire with radio stations in Mexico in the 1930s. Through adroit negotiations with the Mexican government and the National Broadcasting Company, then the preeminent U.S. broadcasting company, he created the first and, for decades, the dominant Mexican radio network. These early strategic alliances helped define the conservative, nationalistic character of the entertainment conglomerate known in the late twentieth century as Televisa.

In the 1930s, Azcárraga, who *Time* magazine described as combining "John L. Lewis's burliness and the late Wendell L. Wilkie's charm," was also a theater owner and the sole Mexican agent for RCA Victor Records. He began transmitting music from his Mexico City station XEW, La Voz de América Latina (The Voice of Latin America), to a radio station in Los Angeles, which then relayed it to other U.S. stations. In addition, Azcárraga owned five radio stations along the border with Mexico that transmitted directly into the United States. Mexican artists under contract to Azcárraga would perform in Azcárraga-owned theaters and broadcast stations in Mexico, and subsequently on radio stations in the United States. His export of these commercial formulas to the U.S. borderlands helped shape a U.S. Spanish-speaking mass audience. Azcárraga became the largest and most influential producer of U.S. Spanish-language radio programming.

During this period some general market advertisers began noticing the efficacy of Spanish-language advertising. Whether infusing advertising with a sense of linguistic solidarity did in fact increase ethnic sales seemed immaterial; what mattered is that the station owners and advertisers believed it to be so. Once radio station owners could profitably sell advertising on Spanish-language programs, they dedicated more airtime to it.

During the 1950s, the number of weekly hours of U.S. Spanish-language radio doubled. Two-thirds originated in the southwest, the region most heavily populated with Spanish speakers. By 1960, Spanish-language radio accounted for more than 60 percent of all U.S. foreign-language radio. Spanish was the only foreign language to command entire stations and entire broadcast days. Radio station owners and their advertisers were among the first to notice (in commercial terms) that the Latin American paradigm of immigration to the United States was not identical to that of European immigration.

Most European immigrants, within a generation or two of their arrival, were socially and economically integrated into the majority culture, losing their European mother tongue in favor of English monolingualism. In addition, European immigration to the United States was discontinuous, disrupted by both political events (the world wars) and the vastness of the Atlantic Ocean. In contrast, immigrants from Latin American countries, primarily Mexico, arrived in a steady stream (of varying size) to the United States for most of the twentieth century. Monolingual Spanish speakers settling in the U.S. renewed the life of the language and provided a core audience for Hispanic media.

In the period following World War II, when Emilio Azcárraga might have been expected to be satisfied with his commanding presence in Mexican entertainment industries and his defining role in U.S. Spanish-language radio programming, he instead was considering new challenges. In 1946, he formed an association with other Latin American broadcasters to pressure their respective governments to adopt the U.S. model for television licensing and regulation and not the European noncommercial model. He succeeded and in so doing planted the seed – in Mexico – for U.S. Spanish-language television.

From its inception in 1961, U.S. Spanish-language television was dominated by one monopolistic Mexican broadcasting company, Televisa. For the first 25 years of its existence, U.S. Spanish-language television was owned, financed, and operated by Televisa; U.S. Spanish-language television was the U.S. subsidiary of the largest Spanish-language media conglomerate in the world.

From the point of view of a U.S. entrepreneur in the late 1950s, the U.S. Spanish-speaking market was so small and so poor a community that it was not considered a market at all. The 1960 U.S. Census counted 3.5 million Spanish-surnamed residents. U.S. Spanish-language advertising came to only $5 million annually, or less than one-tenth of 1 percent of all U.S. advertising at that time. From the perspective of a Latin American entrepreneur, in contrast, the millions of Mexican immigrants and Mexican Americans living in the United States were one of the largest and wealthiest Spanish-language markets in the world.

Televisa first approached the three established U.S. television networks, offering them broadcast rights to *telenovelas* (soap operas) and movies, and was rebuffed. Televisa executives were told by U.S. network executives in the late 1950s that they saw no reason to spend any money on "ghetto time" programming. In 1961 Azcárraga bought two U.S. television stations: KMEX in Los Angeles and KWEX in San Antonio, creating SIN, the Spanish International Network. While not holding any broadcast licenses, SIN would become the power center of U.S. Spanish-language television by controlling the supply of programming (exclusively produced by Televisa) and its financial base, the sale of U.S. national advertising. In the following decade, the fledgling Spanish International Network grew to encompass nine U.S. television stations, including four Mexican border stations that broadcast into the United States. During its first two decades, SIN was an extension of Mexico's Televisa north of the border.

Emilio Azcárraga and, after 1972, Emilio Azcárraga Milmo, the Televisa founder's son and heir, exported their Mexican television monopoly to the United States – or, perhaps more precisely, expanded their monopoly of Spanish-language television north of the Mexican border. By the late 1990s, the largest U.S. Spanish-language television network, with more than 600 affiliates, SIN's successor was called Univisión. The process of institutionalizing U.S. Spanish-language television led to the conceptualization by national advertisers of the Hispanic market. At the end of the century, Univisión, the emblem of the Hispanic market, while U.S.-owned, was still dominated by Televisa programming.

AMÉRICA RODRIGUEZ

Further Reading

Fowler, Gene, and Bill Crawford, *Border Radio*, Austin: Texas Monthly, 1987

Gutiérrez, Félix, "Spanish Language Media in America: Background, Resources, History," *Journalism History* 4 (1977)

_____, and Jorge Reina Schement, *Spanish-Language Radio in the Southwestern United States*, Austin: University of Texas, Center for Mexican American Studies, 1979

Hayes, Joy Elizabeth, "Early American Radio Broadcasting: Media Imperialism, State Paternalism, or Mexican Nationalism?," *Studies in Latin American Popular Culture* 12 (1993)

Noriega, Luis Antonio de, and Frances Leach, *Broadcasting in Mexico,* Boston and London: Routledge and Kegan Paul in association with International Institute of Communications, 1979

Rodriguez, América, "Creating an Audience and Remapping a Nation: A Brief History of U.S. Spanish Language Broadcasting, 1930–1980," *Quarterly Journal of Film and Video* (forthcoming)

Sánchez, George, *Becoming Mexican American: Ethnicity, Culture, and Identity in Chicano Los Angeles, 1900–1945,* New York: Oxford University Press, 1993

Sinclair, John, "Spanish Language Television in the United States: Televisa Surrenders Its Domain," *Studies in Latin American Popular Culture* 9 (1991)

Hoaxes

Filling newspaper pages with practical jokes rather than fact

During the 1800s, editors without enough news to fill their pages sometimes created a story: an essay, tall tale, or hoax. The hoaxes entertained newspaper readers. At the time, no one saw anything wrong with them. Rather, hoaxes were a form of practical joking on a grand scale, and readers seemed to enjoy them.

As part of the fun, journalists often included clues that revealed that their stories were fictitious. Typically, however, readers excited by the hoaxes' more sensational details failed to notice the clues. As a result, some readers believed almost every hoax, even the silliest and most obviously implausible.

Editors worked hard to succeed, making their hoaxes as interesting and realistic as possible. Many selected topics that readers were familiar with – ones that had recently appeared in the news. Editors mixed real details with their fictitious ones, quoted familiar sources, and reported that everything had occurred in a distant area (or years earlier), so that no one could easily prove that any of the details were fictitious.

Journalism's first hoaxes also succeeded because many readers were poorly educated, yet they lived in an era of exploration and invention. Newspapers regularly reported on the latest discoveries, and readers were used to believing every detail.

No one knows who published America's first hoax, but

Moon Hoax included drawings of creatures "seen" on the moon.
(Reproduced from the Collections of the Library of Congress)

Benjamin Franklin published some of the best. Some of Franklin's most entertaining hoaxes appeared in his newspaper, the *Pennsylvania Gazette*. Franklin later created other hoaxes as propaganda against the British and to ridicule people who believed in witchcraft, discriminated against women, and favored slavery.

Edgar Allan Poe wrote at least six hoaxes; his most famous described a Dutchman who flew to the moon in a balloon. Similarly, Mark Twain created several hoaxes while writing for a newspaper in Nevada.

The *New York Sun* published journalism's most successful hoax. In 1835, the *Sun* reported that a famous English astronomer had sailed to South Africa to study the Southern Hemisphere. Later stories described the astronomer's telescope, then his discoveries – the moon's landscape and animals. The final and most sensational installments described the moon's inhabitants: winged creatures that resembled angels. The series helped the *Sun* become the

largest newspaper in the world. Typically, other publications reprinted the series, so people all over the world marveled at the astronomer's extraordinary discoveries.

On November 9, 1874, another major hoax filled the entire front page of the *New York Herald*. The hoax reported that dozens of wild animals had escaped from the Central Park Zoo on Sunday afternoon. Some of the animals had become involved in bloody battles with one another. Others had attacked zookeepers and spectators. Families fled in every direction, with animals chasing after them. Police armed with revolvers, and citizens armed with rifles, tried but failed to stop them. Because of the danger, the mayor ordered everyone except members of the National Guard to remain in their homes. The story's final paragraph admitted that it was all a hoax, but thousands of readers panicked before getting that far.

The editors of other papers and some readers later criticized the *Herald*'s "cruel hoax," yet it did not seem to hurt the paper. Rather, it apparently increased the *Herald*'s circulation. The journalists who created the hoax explained that they were trying to warn people about dangerous conditions at the zoo. Moreover, they expected people to be amused, not frightened, by their story.

An even more terrifying hoax appeared in Wilbur Storey's *Chicago Times*. On February 13, 1875, Storey reported that a fire had roasted the audience in a local theater. Eleven headlines appeared above the story, and the eleventh admitted it was a hoax, declaring: "Description of a Supposititious Holocaust Likely to Occur Any Night."

Readers failed to notice, or perhaps understand, the *Times*'s headline. Flames supposedly swept across the theater, killing 150. The *Times* listed the victims, thus adding to readers' horror, since many of the names seemed to be those of friends, relatives, and celebrities. Storey later explained that he hoped the hoax would have a beneficial effect, warning people of the dangers in Chicago theaters, which Storey called "tinder-boxes" and "human fire traps."

A few newspapers, mostly weeklies, continued to publish hoaxes on April Fool's Day, but most dailies had abandoned them by the 1990s. The corporate owners of the late twentieth century were more conservative than their predecessors, and the public was harder to fool. Also, editors feared that hoaxes would harm newspapers' credibility and frighten, inconvenience, or anger today's readers. Journalism, in essence, became more respectable, and editors worried more about their need to be fair, accurate, and responsible.

A few hoaxes continued to appear, but most were the work of a single individual, often a part-time employee, freelancer, or ambitious young reporter anxious to get a major story into print. One of those young reporters, Janet Cooke of *The Washington Post*, wrote about an eight-year-old black child addicted to heroin. Cooke won a Pulitzer Prize for her story, then was fired when her editors learned the details were fictitious.

Other hoaxes were created by outsiders trying to fool everyone, including the media. Some perpetrated the hoaxes for fun; others sought publicity. Still others were seeking revenge by trying to embarrass the media. Many succeeded, because journalists are always looking for good stories and rarely have enough time to verify every detail.

During the Persian Gulf War, for instance, a girl posing as a refugee claimed that Iraqi soldiers had stormed into Kuwaiti hospitals, tearing babies from incubators and leaving them to die. Her testimony apparently was staged by a public relations agency trying to help rally support for U.S. participation in a war against Iraq.

FRED FEDLER

Further Reading

Abel, Alan, *The Great American Hoax,* New York: Trident, 1966

Fedler, Fred, *Media Hoaxes,* Ames: Iowa State University Press, 1989

Hall, Max, *Benjamin Franklin and Polly Baker,* Chapel Hill: University of North Carolina Press, 1960

Koch, Howard, *The Panic Broadcast,* Boston: Little, Brown, 1970

MacDougall, Curtis D., *Hoaxes,* rev. ed., New York: Dover, 1958

Mencken, H.L., *The Bathtub Hoax, and Other Blasts and Bravos from the 'Chicago Tribune',* New York: Knopf, 1958

Hollywood in World War II

Entertainment industry cooperation marked war era

After Japan's attack on Pearl Harbor on December 7, 1941, thrust the United States into World War II, President Franklin D. Roosevelt called upon Hollywood to go all-out in the anti-Axis crusade. Movie studios were quick to comply. The result was unprecedented cooperation between the entertainment industry and the government.

Monitored by the federal propaganda machine – including the newly created Office of War Information (OWI), whose officials sat in on story conferences, reviewed scripts, and suggested changes – Hollywood let fly a barrage of films between 1942 and 1945 that made the case for war. These films vilified Japanese militarists and German Nazis, as in *The Purple Heart* (1944), which portrayed the torture and execution of downed U.S. pilots by sadistic Japanese. The films promoted national unity, downplaying racial and ethnic divisions, as in *Bataan* (1943), about a melting-pot platoon of 13 doomed U.S. soldiers, including a Pole, an Irishman, a Hispanic, and a black (poetic license because the Army was not yet integrated). They attempted to boost home-front morale with patriotic song-and-dance revues like *This Is the Army* (1943), and, in *Mission to Moscow* (1943), to promote wartime allies with heavily airbrushed portrayals that downplayed political repression by the Soviet Union. They tried to inspire wartime sacrifice, as in *Casablanca* (1942), in which Humphrey Bogart put aside selfish personal interests to aid the fight against Germany,

---

The Great Moon Hoax

The specimen of lunar vegetation, however, which they had already seen (through a giant telescope), had decided a question of too exciting an interest to induce them to retard its exit. It had demonstrated that the moon has an atmosphere constituted similarly to our own, and capable of sustaining organized and, therefore, most probably, animal life.

"The trees," says Dr. Grant, "for a period of ten minutes were of one unvaried kind, and unlike any I have seen except the largest class of yews in the English churchyards. They were followed by a level green plain, which, as measured by the painted circle on our canvas of forty-nine feet, must have been more than a half mile in breadth."

New York Sun, August 25, 1835

declaring, "The problems of three little people don't amount to a hill of beans in this crazy world."

Some of these messages were not new to U.S. moviegoers. Even before Pearl Harbor, a few filmmakers were promoting military preparedness and attacking Fascism. In 1940, the armed services shifted from standoffishness to enthusiastic courting of Hollywood, making it known that they would provide military hardware and uniformed extras if movie companies would make preparedness films. Thus were born such join-the-service extravaganzas as *I Wanted Wings* and *Dive Bomber* (1940). Meanwhile, Warner Brothers released *Confessions of a Nazi Spy* (1939), inspired by a real federal investigation of German espionage in the United States. Metro-Goldwyn-Mayer produced two films – *The Mortal Storm* and *Escape* (both 1940) – depicting repression and anti-Semitism under the Nazi jackboot. In that same year, Charlie Chaplin skewered German dictator Adolf Hitler in *The Great Dictator* and Alfred Hitchcock weighed in with *Foreign Correspondent,* in which a reporter uncovers a Nazi plot and warns the United States to gird for battle.

At a time when many in the United States were desperate to keep the country out of a foreign war, these films were controversial. They worried isolationist members of Congress, including Senator Gerald Nye of North Dakota, who warned that Hollywood was inciting anti-German, interventionist sentiment. Nye and Senator D. Worth Clark of Idaho chaired hearings in late 1941 in which they accused anti-Fascist filmmakers, among them studio mogul Harry M. Warner, of spewing incendiary propaganda. The Japanese attack on Pearl Harbor occurred in the middle of the hearings, however, and stopped the inquisition dead in its tracks. Overnight, criticism of the film industry for anti-Fascist agitation was replaced by calls from Congress and the administration for Hollywood's mobilization in the war effort.

This was an era when propaganda, particularly film, was viewed as a political "magic bullet" that could sway the highly malleable mass audience. This position (inspired by the apparent effectiveness of propaganda in World War I) was shared by officials of the United States and of the Third Reich. Not surprisingly, however, the United States, with its democratic traditions, was less heavy-handed than Germany, where Minister for Public Enlightenment and Propaganda Joseph Goebbels had total control over the content of German films (and all other mass communication media). In the United States, film studios remained private and the official propaganda apparatus disjointed. In order to point films in the directions they wanted, an array of federal agencies – the OWI, the Army, Navy, Marines, Department of State, War Production Board, and Office of Censorship – used moral suasion and bureaucratic leverage rather than dictatorial commands. For instance, the OWI could threaten to recommend that a studio be denied a highly lucrative export license for a film unless the script were changed. In one case, the OWI successfully pressed filmmaker King Vidor to change his script for *An American Romance* (1943). It began as an anti-labor portrait of a steel entrepreneur, but the OWI objected that release of a film about labor strife might be exploited by the enemy. Vidor yielded, converting the film into an inspiring saga of co-operation between labor and management.

Still, the studios retained considerable discretion to go their own way. The OWI urged Hollywood not to make spy films about fifth columnists in the United States because the subject might sow panic. Yet in 1942, nearly 60 percent of the war films were about espionage (including *Black Dragon,* in which Bela Lugosi performs plastic surgery on a Japanese infiltrator to let him pass as an American).

Hollywood's propaganda value did not end with what appeared on the screen. Stars were powerful exemplars of patriotic sacrifice and heroism. Jimmy Stewart won medals flying bombing missions over Germany. Tyrone Power became an aviator in the Pacific. Clark Gable joined a bomber crew after his wife, Carole Lombard, died in a plane crash during a war bond drive. All told, about 25 percent of the men working in Hollywood joined the armed services during the war, including directors such as John Ford, George Stevens, and John Huston, who made combat documentaries. Director Frank Capra, commissioned as a colonel in the U.S. Army, produced the acclaimed *Why We Fight* documentary film series, used to indoctrinate troops. Film star "pinup girls" Veronica Lake, Betty Grable, and others toured USO (United Service Organizations) centers and combat zones to entertain troops and boost morale.

The films of World War II projected an image of an idealistic country fighting a necessary war for the good of the world. It is far from clear, however, whether the huge effort the federal government put into its Hollywood operation was effective or necessary. Given the anti-Fascist movies studios were making before the United States entered the war, one can argue that Hollywood would very likely have put its shoulder behind the war effort even if Uncle Sam had not been prodding it to do so. Much of Hollywood's success, then as now, relied on movies with high drama and lots of action. World War II was nothing if not that.

CHRISTOPHER HANSON

See also Committee on Public Information; Office of Censorship; Office of War Information; Sound Motion Pictures; World War II

Further Reading
Hyams, Jay, *War Movies,* New York: Gallery, 1984
Koppes, Clayton R., and Gregory D. Black, *Hollywood Goes to War: How Politics, Profits, and Propaganda Shaped World War II Movies,* New York: Free Press, 1987; London: Collier Macmillan, 1987
Suid, Lawrence H., *Guts & Glory: Great American War Movies,* Reading, Massachusetts: Addison-Wesley, 1978

Hollywood/Radio Controversy of 1932

Part of the problem of fitting a new medium into the existing scheme

In 1932, a temporary but very dramatic breakdown in the relationship between the motion pictures industry and radio broadcasting occurred. Most of the Hollywood studios banned their contract stars from performing on the radio.

The motion picture industry initially had mixed feelings about radio. Some Hollywood executives realized that radio could provide effective publicity for its films. But others in Hollywood believed that stars' radio appearances would cheapen the stars' box-office appeal or that the radio industry was the competitive enemy of the movie industry.

Early cooperative efforts between Hollywood and radio broadcasters met with success. For example, in March 1928, the Dodge Brothers of Detroit, Michigan, sponsored a star-studded live radio show to promote the latest Dodge car. NBC set up a link between Hollywood and Detroit and between Detroit and New York, where Paul Whiteman and his orchestra played music during the show. NBC radio stations switched back and forth among locations during the broadcast. The star lineup, performing from the Hollywood home of Douglas Fairbanks, included some of the biggest Hollywood figures of the day – such as John Barrymore, D.W. Griffith, Charlie Chaplin, and Norma Talmadge. Fairbanks opened with a discussion on "Keeping Fit." Talmadge gave fashion advice to women, and Chaplin told stories. Barrymore performed a soliloquy from Shakespeare's *Hamlet,* and Griffith read an essay about love. A record number of listeners throughout the country tuned in to the show.

Following the successful Dodge Brothers show, some of the Hollywood studios became increasingly enthusiastic about radio's potential to publicize their stars and films. For example, in January 1929, RKO studios, owned by RCA, started *The RKO Hour,* a weekly program that at first primarily featured vaudeville performers but soon began focusing on movies and movie stars. When it was promoting a film, *The RKO Hour* usually consisted of music used in the film, a partial plot summary, performance of a few scenes from the movie, interviews with stars, and gossip from Hollywood. In addition to the RKO show, Paramount Studios began broadcasting the *Paramount Picture Hour* from a radio station located on its lot. Also in 1929, Fox Studios obtained a radio frequency to transmit sound from daily shoots on location in the Fiji Islands to Hollywood.

Movie exhibitors started noticing competition from radio programs. For example, in 1930, some movie theater owners stopped showing films when *Amos and Andy* was broadcast and turned on the popular radio comedy inside their theaters instead. Fearing that audiences would stay home and be entertained for free by their radios, exhibitors began complaining about the performances movie stars were giving on radio during hours of theater operation. Reports in *Variety* and *Motion Picture World* chronicled theater owners' feelings of anger and betrayal toward movie producers for promoting movies and stars on the radio.

While radio remained relatively unharmed by the economic hard times of the early 1930s, the Depression began to hit Hollywood in 1931. By the summer of 1932, Roxy's theater, which was known as the "largest theater in the world" and the "Cathedral of the motion picture," was in receivership. Other large theaters in cities throughout the country reportedly had closed.

In addition to the economic pressures, exhibitors learned that audiences were being treated to free nightly performances by stars in radio recording studios. For example, Warner Brothers broadcast shows from its own Los Angeles theater and admitted studio audiences free of charge. Los Angeles theater owners claimed these free shows cost them about $5,000 a week in box-office revenues.

In 1932, the tension between producers and exhibitors began to intensify as producers increased the use of radio to promote films. That June, NBC began airing a new radio program called *Hollywood on the Air.* The show, created by RKO, promoted films made by all of the Hollywood studios, including Columbia, Universal, and MGM. Exhibitors had been irked by an RKO broadcast a few months earlier. The announcer had ended the broadcast by saying, "Aren't you glad you stayed home this evening to listen to the RKO Theater in the Air? Stay home every Friday night for it." After a celebrity charity broadcast for the unemployed in June 1932, some exhibitors turned to newspapers with their complaints, complaining that despite repeated objections, producers had failed to cut back on star performances on the radio during theater operation hours.

The exhibitors' complaint to the press occurred during the newspapers' war with radio. In response to competition with radio for advertising revenue, the American Newspaper Publishers Association in 1932 decided to deny radio broadcasters access to news wire services. Newspapers wanted the movie industry to join and support their anti-radio campaign and therefore began giving greater publicity to movies and less to radio programming. Many newspapers stopped publishing radio show listings. Other newspapers eliminated the names of advertisers from the listings.

By the end of December 1932, the Hollywood studios appeared to have finally acquiesced to exhibitors' demands and the bad publicity in the newspapers by instituting a ban on contract stars' performances on the radio. All of the major studios except RKO agreed verbally to keep their contract actors and actresses off the air. One scholar, Michele Hilmes, has argued that the ban was a self-serving move by the studios because the studios wanted to be paid for their stars' appearances on radio shows such as *Hollywood on the Air;* advertisers, who were beginning to control radio content, would pay for performances. In addition, the studios would receive favorable publicity in newspaper articles by appearing to stand behind their exhibitors. And finally, the studios for many years had wanted to control their stars' appearances to avoid depleting their box-office appeal.

The ban did not last long. By the summer of 1933, all of the studios except Fox had broken the verbal agreement on the radio ban in favor of exploiting radio's publicity potential. As early as January 17, 1933, just three weeks after the ban was announced, Paramount studios used radio to publicize a new movie.

ARATI R. KORWAR

See also Radio News

Further Reading
Hilmes, Michele, *Hollywood and Broadcasting: From Radio to Cable,* Urbana: University of Illinois Press, 1990

Jewell, Richard B., "Hollywood and Radio: Competition and Partnership in the 1930s," *Historical Journal of Film, Radio and Television* 4 (1984)

Jowett, Garth, *Film: The Democratic Art,* Boston: Little, Brown, 1976

Hollywood Studio System

Major combination of efforts to produce films

Alternatively known as the golden age of Hollywood, the studio system began on the eve of World War I, eight miles from Los Angeles, and successfully combined the production, distribution, and exhibition of motion pictures through a process known as vertical integration for more than four decades. The five major Hollywood studios – Metro-Goldwyn-Mayer, Paramount, Warner Brothers, Twentieth Century-Fox, and RKO – owned theaters and tied up talent – directors, producers, actors, and screenwriters – with long-term contracts that rationalized the business of moviemaking. Along with minor studios, such as Universal, Columbia, and United Artists, the studio system offered moviegoers an entertaining and memorable product that mirrored cultural values and the fantasy life of millions through two world wars and the Great Depression.

The strong-arm tactics of the Motion Picture Patents Trust, composed of 10 production companies based in Fort Lee, New Jersey, forced independent producers to move to Hollywood to make their movies. Ironically, a court suit brought by other independent producers against the major studios led to the historic Paramount Consent Decree of 1948, which ended vertical integration. This court case, combined with the advent of television, helped close an extraordinary chapter in U.S. entertainment history.

As early as 1907, production companies were lured to Hollywood by its favorable weather, varied scenery for on-location shooting, access to theatrical talent, and low tax base. The star system grew up with Hollywood and the development of the feature film, which began to dominate the industry by 1914, thanks in part to the box office success of the silent era's most important director, D.W. Griffith. Star salaries reached $1,000 a week, but the deals worked out by Mary Pickford, Douglas Fairbanks, and Charlie Chaplin, gave them six-figure salaries and a percentage of the film's gross.

Twenty-three million people in the United States went to the movies weekly at the height of the silent era, with Paramount, Universal, and Fox the early leaders in releasing features to the nation's 5,000 theaters. Theater ownership and block booking assured wide and favorable distribution for a studio's films and consolidated the Hollywood studio system. Backed by Wall Street banking houses, MGM and Paramount became the most prosperous of the silent era's studios. Warner Brothers, facing bankruptcy, risked everything on a 1927 Al Jolson "talkie" feature called *The Jazz Singer,* abruptly ushering in Hollywood's sound era.

During the first years of the Great Depression, the novelty of sound, the need for escape, and the cheapness of the entertainment led to a doubling in weekly movie attendance. Five major and three minor studios produced 95 percent of all U.S. films, as well as shorts, cartoons, and newsreels. Seventy-five percent of studio revenues were generated by the major studios' control of 2,600 first-run theaters in major metropolitan areas across the country. At the height of the depression, three-quarters of all the money the U.S. audience spent on amusements went to movies, and the industry accounted for 1.5 percent of the nation's corporate profits.

MGM, thanks to financial backing of Chase National Bank and the deft leadership of studio executive Louis B. Mayer and chief producers Irving Thalberg and David O. Selznick, was the most prolific and prosperous of Hollywood studios in the 1930s and 1940s. The expensive look of MGM's many lavish productions was enhanced by highly literate scripts and an unparalleled stable of contract directors and stars. Directors Victor Fleming, George Cukor, King Vidor, Clarence Brown, Sam Wood, Jack Conway, and W.S. Van Dyke collaborated with actors Clark Gable, Greta Garbo, Spencer Tracy, Joan Crawford, Jean Harlow, Myrna Loy, Judy Garland, Mickey Rooney, Gene Kelly, James Stewart, Robert Taylor, William Powell, and the Barrymores to produce screen classics that included *Grand Hotel, Captains Courageous, David Copperfield, Treasure Island, Anna Karenina, Romeo and Juliet, The Good Earth, A Tale of Two Cities, The Wizard of Oz, Ninotchka, The Great Ziegfeld, Thirty Seconds Over Tokyo, Mrs. Miniver,* and *Goodbye, Mr. Chips.*

Paramount, led by film pioneer Adolph Zukor and Barney Balaban, was next in importance. The spectaculars of director Cecil B. DeMille proved the studio's biggest moneymakers. Ernst Lubitsch gave a European flair to the studio's subtle comedies and musicals. The work of Bing Crosby, Bob Hope, Gary Cooper, Marlene Dietrich, Fredric March, Alan Ladd, Ray Milland, Claudette Colbert, Cary Grant, Fred MacMurray, Paulette Goddard, W.C. Fields, and Mae West assured the studio of profits second only to those of MGM.

The gangster films and musicals of Warner Brothers had a distinct working-class look. Stars James Cagney, Humphrey Bogart, Edward G. Robinson, Paul Muni, and John Garfield took turns rubbing one another out. Backstage musicals like *42nd Street* and the "Gold Diggers" series were staged by Busby Berkeley. The company's leading ladies included Bette Davis and Olivia de Havilland. Michael Curtiz and Raoul Walsh directed Errol Flynn in a series of memorable swashbucklers at Warner Brothers, including *The Adventures of Robin Hood.* Classic World War II productions by Curtiz include *Casablanca* and *Yankee Doodle Dandy.*

Twentieth Century-Fox was best known for its incomparable director John Ford and its child star Shirley Temple. The studio was efficiently run by Darryl F. Zanuck, who had been a producer at Warner Brothers. Its stars included Tyrone Power, Henry Fonda, Loretta Young, Betty Grable, Charles Boyer, Don Ameche, and Alice Faye.

RKO was the smallest of the major studios and the first to suspend operations following the faltering reign of millionaire Howard Hughes. The studio produced eight of the nine Fred Astaire–Ginger Rogers musicals and launched the careers of Katharine Hepburn and King Kong. The studio also produced arguably the greatest motion picture in film history, 1941's *Citizen Kane,* directed by and starring Orson Welles.

Universal Pictures under Carl Laemmle guided the careers of Rudolph Valentino and Lon Chaney during the 1920s and survived the 1930s and 1940s as a minor studio known for its horror classics, including Tod Browning's *Dracula,* James Whales' *Frankenstein, The Mummy, The Invisible Man, Bride of Frankenstein,* and *The Wolf Man.* Stars included Boris Karloff, Bela Lugosi, and Lon Chaney Jr.

Columbia Pictures, begun by Harry Cohn in 1924, released a series of Frank Capra classics during the 1930s These included *It Happened One Night, Mr. Deeds Goes to Town, Lost Horizon, You Can't Take It with You,* and *Mr. Smith Goes to Washington.*

United Artists, founded in 1919 by Chaplin, Pickford, Fairbanks, and Griffith, became the industry's best-known distributor of independent productions. After leaving MGM, Selznick, as well as Samuel Goldwyn, Hal Roach, and Walter Wanger, released films through United Artists.

At the close of World War II, two-thirds of the U.S. population went weekly to the movies, but the collapse of the Hollywood studio system was not far off. By 1949, attendance was off by a quarter, as audiences stayed home to watch television. This coincided with the Paramount consent decree and the loss of studio-owned theaters. The results were immediate and disastrous. Production was halved. Layoffs and salary reductions followed. Stars could no longer be afforded.

Hollywood struck back with sex and wide-screen spectaculars, something that television could not offer. But the postwar competition for the entertainment dollar and the flight of audiences to the suburbs unalterably changed moviegoing. The passing of the Hollywood studio system forever changed the way U.S. films would be made, how many would be made, how they would look, and how they would be seen.

BRUCE EVENSEN

See also Economics of Motion Pictures

Further Reading
Bordwell, David, Janet Staiger, and Kristin Thompson, *The Classical Hollywood Cinema: Film Style & Mode of Production to 1960,* New York: Columbia University Press, 1985; London: Routledge & Kegan Paul, 1985
Cook, David A., *A History of Narrative Film,* 2nd ed., New York: Norton, 1990
Gomery Douglas, *The Hollywood Studio System,* New York: St. Martin's, 1986; Basingstoke, England: Macmillan, 1986
Jacobs, Lewis, *The Rise of the American Film, a Critical History,* New York: Teachers College Press, 1968
Knight, Arthur, *The Liveliest Art: A Panoramic History of the Movies,* New York: Macmillan, 1957
Mast, Gerald, *A Short History of the Movies,* 4th ed., New York: Macmillan, 1986; London: Collier Macmillan, 1986
Mordden, Ethan, *The Hollywood Studios: House Style in the Golden Age of the Movies,* New York: Knopf, 1988
Rhode, Eric, *A History of the Cinema: From Its Origins to 1970,* New York: Hill and Wang, 1976; London: A. Lane, 1976

Holmes, Oliver Wendell Jr.
Developed early theories in defense of free speech

Oliver Wendell Holmes Jr. attended Harvard, fought in the Civil War, was wounded three times, twice almost fatally, and served as an associate justice of the U.S. Supreme Court from 1902 to 1932. He received his legal training at Harvard Law School, but it was his treatise, *The Common Law,* published in 1881, that secured for Holmes his long-lasting scholarly reputation.

Holmes served on the Supreme Judicial Court of Massachusetts for 20 years, becoming chief justice in 1899. President Theodore Roosevelt nominated him to the U.S. Supreme Court in August 1902. He served for 30 years, under four chief justices, during which time he wrote many of the leading opinions on free speech, often in dissent with Justice Louis D. Brandeis. In his first free speech opinion, *Patterson* v. *Colorado* (1907), Holmes upheld the conviction of a newspaper editor for contempt of court on the grounds that, while prior restraints may be unconstitutional, the Fourteenth Amendment did not prevent the subsequent punishment of "such as may be deemed contrary to the public welfare."

He began to change his mind, however, when convinced that the government had increased its actions against political dissidents. In a series of dissents, beginning with *Abrams* v. *United States* (1919), Holmes, joined by Brandeis, explained his famous "marketplace of ideas" concept, that "the best test of truth is the power of the thought to get itself accepted in the competition of the market."

RICHARD F. HIXSON

See also Contempt; Espionage and Sedition Acts

Further Reading
Biddle, Francis, *Justice Holmes, Natural Law and the Supreme Court,* New York: Macmillan, 1961
Novick, Sheldon M., *Honorable Justice: The Life of Oliver Wendell Holmes,* Boston: Little, Brown, 1989
White, G. Edward, *Justice Oliver Wendell Holmes: Law and the Inner Self,* New York: Oxford University Press, 1993

Hoover, Herbert, and Radio Regulation
Developed U.S. government's role in regulation

In 1921, Herbert Hoover became secretary of commerce in President Warren Harding's cabinet, and because the Radio

Act of 1912 gave the commerce secretary power to license all commercial radio stations, he became the "first regulator of broadcasting." After the first broadcast station was licensed in 1920, broadcasting grew rapidly to over 500 stations two years later. Hoover tried to regulate this swiftly developing medium by assigning stations to one of three frequencies allocated for broadcasting, setting station transmitter power, and apportioning time of day and days of week for individual stations. He also called four radio conferences between 1922 and 1925 for the express purpose of getting broadcasters to work with the Commerce Department to set workable regulations for the medium. Hoover's vision called for the Commerce Department to coordinate efforts and work with broadcasters as regulations developed for the mutual benefit of station owners, listeners, and government entities.

The first conference was held in February 1922 with fewer than 30 persons in attendance. The delegates agreed on several recommendations to make to Hoover. Hoover would regulate broadcasting through assigning stations to specific frequencies with set operating power and hours of operation, adding more channels to reduce interference, mandating that radio's operation be in the public interest like other public utilities, and limiting advertising. Bills emphasizing these elements and giving the commerce department regulatory power over radio were introduced into Congress. When

they proved unsuccessful, however, Hoover called the Second Radio Conference in March 1923. This conference recommended that three classes of states be established, that the country be divided into five zones with equal radio service assigned to each area, and that the commerce secretary be given discretionary power to assign stations to applicants. Hoover took these recommendations as a mandate and immediately expanded the broadcast band, with stations assigned to a new system of frequencies as Class A, Class B, and Class C stations.

Congress still did not pass a radio bill, so Hoover called a third conference in October 1924. This conference recommended establishing national broadcasting through station interconnection, increasing power of existing stations to serve rural areas better, extending the broadcast band to increase the number of broadcast channels available, and limiting the power of the Commerce Department to technical areas only. No new bills were introduced into Congress, and in November 1925, the last conference was held. The more than 400 delegates attending supported limiting the number of stations to lessen interference and granting licenses to applicants based on serving listeners in "the public interest." The conferees also recognized that advertising could support broadcasting if it was not "direct," that is, if it did not mention the product or its cost directly. Indirect or institutional advertising was permissible. Delegates urged congressional action, and numerous bills were introduced. But again, none passed, and Hoover continued regulating the medium.

Hoover's regulatory authority was crumbling, however. In 1923, in *Hoover* v. *Intercity,* the Washington, D.C., Court of Appeals held that the commerce secretary had no authority to regulate broadcasting other than assigning frequencies. Hoover had to give an assignment to anyone wanting one, so he began assigning time of day, day of week, and, at times, several stations in the same area to share one channel. While some broadcasters liked this arrangement, others did not, and another challenge to these regulations soon came. In 1924 the Zenith Radio Corporation began broadcasting two hours each week on a channel assigned by the Commerce Department. When its request to increase broadcast time and move to a different channel came in, Hoover denied the application. Zenith defied Hoover and moved its frequency to an assignment reserved for Canadian stations. The Commerce Department had no choice but to take Zenith to court. On April 26, 1926, an Illinois District Court ruled that the Radio Act of 1912 gave the commerce secretary no express power to establish broadcast regulations. When the attorney general was asked by Hoover for an opinion on the situation, he concurred on July 8 that Hoover had no legal power. The resulting chaos, both real and feared, finally forced Congress to act, and the Radio Act of 1927 became law on February 23, 1927. It was built on the regulations Hoover established through the four radio conferences.

During Hoover's presidency, Congress passed several amendments to the Radio Act, including a measure requiring the Federal Radio Commission to equalize the numbers of stations among five geographic zones and among the states. Congress also rewrote the radio act in 1932, and

Herbert Hoover, as secretary of commerce and labor, worked to establish regulation of the airwaves.
(Herbert Hoover Presidential Library-Museum)

among the provisions was one that would have extended the equal opportunities doctrine to all speakers on controversial issues pending before legislative bodies or those to be voted upon during an election. Although it was passed by Congress, the law was pocket vetoed by Hoover in the last days of his administration. A new law, without the equal opportunities doctrine for presentation of ideas, had to wait until 1934 and the passage of the Communications Act under President Franklin Roosevelt.

LOUISE BENJAMIN

See also Communications Act of 1934; Radio Act of 1927

Hoover, Herbert, and the Press

President had difficulties with press relations

Herbert Hoover, the thirty-first U.S. president, was a shy man who sought public office unwillingly and who promoted himself by befriending a select few journalists. Hoover enhanced his pre-presidential image by controlling news flow and managing a variety of difficult public tasks with amazing success. He was an ineffective public speaker and a suspicious man who innately mistrusted journalists. When the stock market crashed in the autumn of 1929, early in Hoover's presidency, he was unable to regain public confidence and support. The ensuing Great Depression greatly tarnished his image and destroyed his career.

Although he had been orphaned at an early age, Hoover was a successful mining engineer and a millionaire before age 40. With the advent of World War I, Hoover helped stranded Americans return home from Europe and then agreed to direct U.S.-sponsored food relief for starving civilians in German-occupied Belgium and France. Later, after Woodrow Wilson declared war, Hoover was appointed U.S. food administrator.

After a halfhearted presidential campaign in 1920, Hoover reluctantly accepted Warren G. Harding's offer to become secretary of commerce. He remained in that post from 1921 to 1928 under both Harding and Calvin Coolidge.

As commerce secretary, Hoover met Washington politicians and reporters regularly for the first time. A few admiring correspondents visited Hoover in his office daily. He spoke with them, offering tips on stories with the understanding that discussions could only be used for background until Hoover gave his approval for publication. Correspondents were grateful for reliable information from the otherwise corrupt and undependable Harding administration and later from the uncooperative Coolidge White House, so they did not object. Consequently, Hoover developed positive relations with a few reporters – on his terms.

In 1928, the much-admired Hoover was the obvious choice for Republicans for the presidential nomination. He easily defeated Governor Alfred E. Smith of New York after personally overseeing a well-managed, well-orchestrated ra-

dio and newspaper public relations blitz. Alfred H. Kirchhofer, managing editor of the *Buffalo Evening News*, directed Hoover's campaign, illustrating how some individuals moved back and forth easily from advocate to journalist in the 1920s.

Radio for the first time served a key role in the campaign. Hoover's acceptance speech, delivered from his home in Palo Alto, California, for instance, was broadcast live to millions of listeners over 84 stations.

Newsreel cameras captured the inauguration on film with sound for the first time. Uncomfortable before cameras because he resented having to "act" a part, he failed to make good use of that new medium during his presidency.

Days after his inauguration, Hoover told reporters that he would allow them occasionally to quote him directly. Preceding presidents had allowed only indirect quotes. On the other hand, Hoover insisted on the traditional policy of all questions being submitted in writing to the president and answers being given days later in writing. Reporters hoped for major changes in White House news flow, based upon Hoover's helpful attitude during his Commerce Department years, but generally they were disappointed. Attendance at press conferences dwindled.

For his part, Hoover never trusted most journalists. Newspapers and reporters, he decided, were all partisan, supporting one party or the other and injecting ideology into all writing, including news stories. In his estimation, journalists either supported him without question or they were his enemies. He had no belief in journalistic objectivity. Worse, he favored certain reporters who had been longtime friends, inviting them to the White House for meals and long chats, while other journalists were shunned until they had proven to be loyal and uncritical.

With the Wall Street crash in October 1929, just 32 weeks after Hoover took office, press relations assumed a new urgency. Business leaders and newly unemployed workers soon turned anxiously to Washington for help. Hoover, however, believed in an unmanaged economy, and his halting steps to stem rising joblessness failed miserably. Anxiousness turned to despair. Shaky press relations and a personality that could not galvanize millions of people added to the president's woes. Reporters stopped trying to gather stories from the White House, and, instead, sought out Hoover's political enemies, who were only too willing to offer quotes about failed Republican policies and an indifferent White House.

Hoover refused to be more amenable toward the press corps, ignoring advice from his most ardent newspaper supporters, including publishers and editors who had enthusiastically endorsed his candidacy in 1928. A sullen silence clouded the White House. Press Secretary George Akerson, a former reporter and editor with the *Minneapolis (Minnesota) Tribune*, proved ineffective and unreliable, and other Hoover aides seemed unable or unwilling to cooperate with the hostile press corps. Theodore Joslin, a Washington reporter with the *Boston Transcript*, replaced Akerson in March 1931, but Joslin held his former colleagues in contempt and only exacerbated tense press relations.

In the spring and summer of 1932, more than 20,000 World War I veterans marched on Washington, D.C., to de-

Although President Herbert Hoover was not at ease with the press, he did meet with them on occasion.
(Herbert Hoover Presidential Library-Museum)

mand from Congress immediate payment of a veterans' bonus. After the marchers had camped for several weeks in and around Washington, a shooting incident led to the routing of the Bonus Marchers from their pitiful makeshift tents. Directing the rout was General Douglas MacArthur, who exceeded Hoover's orders by commanding federal troops to lob tear gas at the ex-soldiers and their families and by chasing them at gunpoint while troops set fire to their makeshift homes. Although newspapers largely hailed the rout and praised Hoover, historians generally regard the federal initiative as a most shameful episode in U.S. history and a symbol of the failure of Hoover's presidency.

Weeks later, the president opened his reelection campaign against the governor of New York, Democrat Franklin D. Roosevelt. Despite the depressed economy, Hoover remained confident, but hostile crowds met the incumbent everywhere he ventured. In Detroit, Michigan, where more than half the workforce was unemployed, crowds of onlookers glared sullenly as the presidential caravan passed from the train station to the convention center. Although more than half the nation's newspapers endorsed the president, there were many fewer endorsements than in 1928, and the editorial boards displayed no particular enthusiasm for Hoover. The president held no press confer-

ences during the campaign, and reporters openly expressed the hope that a new president would bring a more cooperative White House. Roosevelt easily defeated Hoover, sweeping the Democrats into the White House and Congress, initiating a period of Democratic dominance in U.S. politics. Hoover retired from public life and lived quietly away from reporters and publicity. He died in 1964.

Relations between the press and the president had come to a crossroads during the Hoover years. Rarely again would a candidate reach the White House, as Herbert Hoover had, without an effective speaking style and a carefully plotted strategy for interacting with and manipulating the nation's press. The press had changed, and the presidency had to transform with it. Hoover was a small-town entrepreneur who used a superior intellect and amazing organizational skills to reach the White House. Fate, the unwillingness to change government's relationship with the private business sector, and a lack of charisma and personality undercut his failed presidency. He was unable to capture the imagination of the press and the people of the United States during a time of crisis, and he was castigated for his failure for the remainder of his life.

LOUIS W. LIEBOVICH

See also Presidential News Conferences; Presidential Press Secretaries

Further Reading
Burner, David, *Herbert Hoover, a Public Life*, New York: Knopf, 1979
Fausold, Martin L., *The Presidency of Herbert C. Hoover*, Lawrence: University Press of Kansas, 1985
Liebovich, Louis W., *Bylines in Despair: Herbert Hoover, the Great Depression, and the U.S. News Media*, Westport, Connecticut: Praeger, 1994
Lloyd, Craig, *Aggressive Introvert: A Study of Herbert Hoover and Public Relations Management, 1912–1932*, Columbus: Ohio State University Press, 1972

Hoover, J. Edgar, and the Press

Hoover's suspicions affected amount of freedom of the press available

Appointed acting director of the Bureau of Investigation (later the Federal Bureau of Investigation [FBI]) in May 1924, J. Edgar Hoover inherited a difficult public relations problem following a series of revelations between 1920 and 1924 of bureau abuses of power. These included disclosures that bureau agents had monitored political activists, labor union officials, and congressional critics of the Harding administration. Untainted directly by these scandals, the newly appointed director, whose appointment was made permanent that December, succeeded in restoring public confidence in the integrity and value of the bureau. He did so, first, by adopting a low-key public posture, essential given the states' rights and laissez-faire politics of the 1920s. Second, to disarm bureau critics and convey the sense that the recently disclosed abuses had been the product of a lack of professionalism, Hoover announced new hiring policies whereby preference was given to lawyers and accountants. Tight rules were concurrently instituted governing the deportment and conduct of agents in order to promote an image of bureau agents as "gentlemen" of high moral and professional stature.

Franklin Roosevelt's election to the presidency in 1932 and the subsequent institution of the New Deal altered Hoover's press strategy. Committed to a war not only on the economic crisis of the Great Depression but on criminals (in the latter case, symbolized by the recent upsurge of bank robberies and kidnappings and the seeming inability of local and state police to confront this crime problem), Roosevelt lobbied to make bank robberies, kidnapping, and extortion federal offenses. To achieve this legislative objective, Justice Department officials publicized the FBI's importance, personified in the mythical G-man who through skill and diligence "always got his man." Attorney General Homer Cummings and his recently hired press aide, former *Brooklyn Eagle* reporter Henry Suydam, initially orchestrated this public relations effort. Not content to rely on the department's initiatives, Hoover instituted his own press operation, hiring Louis Nichols to handle the Bureau's press liaison. To ensure a favorable press, FBI officials leaked fa-

vorable information to selected reporters, most notably during the 1930s to *American Magazine* writer Courtney Ryley Cooper.

Thereafter, Hoover ordered FBI officials at the bureau's Washington, D.C., headquarters and nationwide field offices to monitor all press stories relating to the FBI, whether commendatory or critical. Based on this intelligence, sympathetic reporters and editors were purposefully cultivated through generous letters of thanks and other quiet assistance; conversely, any negative stories were vigorously rebutted. Hoover had FBI officials compile separate lists, refined over time, of those reporters "not to contact" and those to be considered "special correspondents." Concurrently, Nichols (and his successors Cartha DeLoach and Thomas Bishop) worked closely with movie and television producers to ensure that the mass public received a favorable image of the FBI – insisting, in return, for FBI assistance on the right to review proposed scripts and proffer needed corrections.

There was another dimension to Hoover's media strategy. During World War I, bureau agents monitored critical newspaper and periodical coverage of the Wilson administration's foreign and internal security policies. This monitoring was not confined to radical publications but included such critics of the administration's pro-British, anti-Irish foreign policy as the *Chicago Tribune* and the Hearst newspapers. Bureau agents continued to monitor press reporting in the immediate postwar years, focusing then on radical and black nationalist publications, notably Marcus Garvey's *The Messenger*.

The FBI did not cease its monitoring of radical publications (during the 1930s focusing on Fascist and Communist papers) and then, during the Cold War years, given Hoover's broad definition of "subversive activities," moved beyond the Communist *Daily Worker* to include non-Communist radical and civil libertarian publications such as the *Nation, New Republic, Progressive, American Socialist, I.F. Stone's Weekly, Consumer Reports,* and the American Civil Liberties Union's *Feature Press Service* and *Civil Liberties*. For the most part, Hoover's interest was to uncover information about radical political activities as reported in these publications and about critics of FBI activities and influence. The FBI director, however, had an additional objection: to contain radical influence and dissent over U.S. foreign and internal security policy.

During World War II, FBI agents closely monitored pro-Fascist periodicals and such conservative, isolationist, mainstream newspapers as the *Chicago Tribune,* the *Washington Times-Herald,* and the *New York Daily News*. In this case, Hoover sought to promote President Roosevelt's interest in prosecuting the "seditious" press. Attorney General Francis Biddle's insistence of evidence of criminal conduct, however, frustrated this objective.

In contrast, during the Cold War years, FBI press monitoring focused primarily on the U.S. political left. In February 1946, the FBI director abandoned any interest in prosecution for a strategy of containment, launching an "educational" campaign to "influence public opinion" about the Communist menace by leaking derogatory personal and political information through "available channels." The resulting multifaceted campaign involved carefully orchestrated leaks to congressional committees such as the House Un-American Activities Committee and the Senate Internal Security Subcommittee, to members of Congress including Senators Joseph McCarthy and Karl Mundt, and sympathetic reporters and editors like Don Whitehead, George Sokolsky, and Walter Trohan.

At first instituted on an ad hoc basis, by the 1950s this campaign was formalized in a mass media program. Then, beginning in 1956, Hoover secretly authorized a series of code-named COINTELPROs involving, among other methods, leaks to the media. The leaks were meant to discredit and disrupt targeted organizations and their leaders ranging from the Communist Party, the Ku Klux Klan, and the Black Panthers to the New Left. During the 1960s, Hoover's harassment campaign was extended to the so-called underground press. FBI agents also closely monitored those reporters, entertainers, writers, and prominent personalities who could, in Hoover's view, influence public opinion contrary to the national interest. These included Martin Luther King Jr., William Kuntsler, Leonard Bernstein, Pete Seeger, Ernest Hemingway, Harrison Salisbury, and Peter Lisagor. Hoover insisted on confidentiality as a condition for FBI assistance to favored reporters, members of Congress, and governors – and any violation of this condition resulted in discontinuance of FBI assistance.

Hoover's death in May 1972 was soon followed by highly publicized congressional revelations of the presidential uses of the intelligence agencies for political reasons – first, during the Senate's 1973 investigations of the Watergate affair, and then during 1975 Senate and House investigations of "intelligence activities and the rights of Americans." These disclosures, combined with new opportunities for people to obtain FBI records following the enactment in 1974 of key amendments to the Freedom of Information Act, publicly exposed for the first time the scope of Hoover's abuses of power, and by ensuring public access to FBI records, fundamentally altered future relations between the FBI and the media.

ATHAN G. THEOHARIS

See also Cold War and the Media; Freedom of Information Act; Underground Press; Watergate Scandal

Further Reading

Clancy, Paul, "The Bureau and the Bureaus, Part I," *Quill* (February 1976)
Donner, Frank J., *The Age of Surveillance: The Aims and Methods of America's Political Intelligence System*, New York: Knopf, 1980
MacKenzie, Angus, "Sabotaging the Dissident Press," *Columbia Journalism Review* (March/April 1981)
Peck, Abe, *Uncovering the Sixties: The Life and Times of the Underground Press*, New York: Pantheon, 1985
Powers, Richard Gid, *G-Men, Hoover's FBI in American Popular Culture*, Carbondale: Southern Illinois University Press, 1983
Theoharis, Athan G., "The FBI, the Roosevelt Administration, and the 'Subversive' Press," *Journalism History* 19:1 (Spring 1993), pp. 3–10

_____, and John Stuart Cox, *The Boss: J. Edgar Hoover and the Great American Inquisition*, Philadelphia: Temple University Press, 1988; London: Harrap, 1989

Hopkins, Claude C.
Developed "reason-why" advertising approach

Claude C. Hopkins was born on August 27, 1866, in Spring Lake, Michigan. A minister in his early years, he studied business and then worked for the Grand Rapids Felt Boot Company. Before 1900, he worked for the Bissell Carpet Sweeper Company, where he developed strategies and wrote advertising and sales promotion copy.

He worked as an advertising manager for the Swift Meat Packing Company before he was hired by the J.L. Stack advertising agency. Hopkins wrote advertising copy for Dr. Shoop's Restorative patent medicine, Schlitz beer, and Montgomery Ward. For Schlitz, he learned how beer was made and incorporated this knowledge in a "reason-why" campaign that claimed Schlitz cleaned its bottles with "live steam," a process that, as it happened, every brewing company used. He also wrote the slogan, "The beer that made Milwaukee famous." The campaign moved the product from fifth place to first place.

Hired by Albert Lasker, owner of Lord and Thomas, Hopkins continued employing the "reason-why" style of copy, using sampling techniques, including the use of coupons and taste demonstrations. For Quaker Oats, he created the slogan "The Cereal Shot from Guns." For Pepsodent, he created a campaign that was based on beauty.

Hopkins, a very fast copywriter, worked from 12 to 16 hours a day, almost every day of the week. His ideas concerning creative strategy appeared in the book *Scientific Advertising,* which was published in 1923. Before he retired in 1924, he had been promoted to president of the company. He died in 1932.

EDD APPLEGATE

Further Reading

Hopkins, Claude C., *My Life in Advertising*, London: Harper, 1927; Lincolnwood, Illinois: NTC Business, 1986
Lasker, Albert D., *The Lasker Story, as He Told It*, Chicago: Advertising, 1963
Reeves, Rosser, *Reality in Advertising*, New York: Knopf, 1961

Huntley-Brinkley Report, The
NBC-TV news anchors began team effort in 1956

Beginning in 1956 on NBC, the nation's leading television newscast featured Chet Huntley and David Brinkley. The two had earlier teamed up for political convention coverage and did surprisingly well in the ratings. As a result, a news

David Brinkley, left, and Chet Huntley combined for one of the most popular of the 1960s network news shows.
(Library of American Broadcasting)

format was devised to take full advantage of the differences between the two anchormen, with cross-cutting between Brinkley in Washington, D.C., and Huntley in New York City. Their nightly newscast – ending with "Goodnight, Chet . . . Goodnight, David . . . and Goodnight for NBC

News" – took over as ratings leader, replacing CBS, long regarded as the premier broadcast news organization.

The two anchormen were a study in contrast. Huntley, born in 1911 in Cardwell, Montana, grew up on a ranch and graduated from the University of Seattle (Washington)

in 1934. He began his career at a Seattle radio station and held various reporting assignments at both CBS and ABC affiliate stations on the west coast before joining NBC News in New York in 1955. David Brinkley was a southerner, born in Wilmington, North Carolina, in 1920. He worked at the *Wilmington Star-News* while in high school and took writing courses at the University of North Carolina. Brinkley served briefly in the U.S. Army before joining the United Press. He volunteered to write for the agency's radio wire, graduating in 1943 to NBC Radio in the nation's capital.

Huntley and Brinkley started the transition in television news from the purely news film approach of John Cameron Swayze to a more wide-ranging effort. They were complementary and covered the turbulent 1960s, their work incurring the wrath of certain groups. At the 1964 Republican National Convention, for example, Goldwater followers wore "Stamp Out Huntley-Brinkley" badges.

Brinkley came across as a witty but urbane southerner. His approach was often light-hearted, and his style of delivery emphasized key words – underlined on each page of copy. He covered Congress, the State Department, and the Supreme Court through the use of a staff of specialists who evolved into full-fledged correspondents. Brinkley's senior partner from the west was, by contrast, sober in manner, very deliberate, but with a broader range of responsibility.

When Huntley retired in 1970, John Chancellor replaced him as coanchor, and the network series title was changed to *The NBC Nightly News*. Huntley died four years later at his home in Montana. Brinkley moved into documentaries and *David Brinkley's Journal*, a popular public affairs series. He later joined ABC-TV and hosted *This Week with David Brinkley*. The *Huntley-Brinkley Report* team placed NBC at the forefront when television news changed from purely newsreading to information gathering, a development that was widely copied at the local level.

MICHAEL D. MURRAY

Further Reading

Evans, Katherine W., "A Conversation with David Brinkley," *Washington Journalism Review* (November 1981)

Ewald, B., "The First Team," *Newsweek* (March 13, 1961)

Frank, Reuven, *Out of Thin Air: The Brief Wonderful Life of Network News,* New York: Simon & Schuster, 1991

Huntley, Chet, *The Generous Years,* New York: Random House, 1968

Lissit, Robert, "Huntley and Brinkley, Plus Four," *Quill* (November 1968)

Matusow, Barbara, *The Evening Stars: The Making of the Network News Anchor,* Boston: Houghton Mifflin, 1983

Murray, Michael D., "Creating a Tradition in Broadcast News: A Conversation with David Brinkley," *Journalism History* 21:4 (Winter 1995), pp. 164–169

I

Illustrated Newspapers

Woodcuts brought visual information to readers

A new kind of journal arrived in the United States in the 1850s, just in time to provide pictorial coverage of the country's biggest story – the Civil War. Catapulted to prominence by the demand for war news, the illustrated newspaper remained popular for half a century before the halftone-filled Sunday newspaper supplements crowded it aside in the 1900s.

The first successful example was the *Illustrated London News,* founded in 1842 by English journalist Herbert Ingram. Successful starts the next year included *L'Illustration,* in Paris, and the *Illustrierte Zeitung,* in Leipzig, Germany.

Henry Carter, a 21-year-old illustrator at the London paper, signed his work "Frank Leslie" so that his disapproving father would not know he had gone into the arts. Young Leslie advanced rapidly, but when he learned that engravers were scarce in the United States, he emigrated with his family and set up shop on Broadway in New York City.

U.S. magazines were recognizing the strong public demand for illustration, and in the 1840s and 1850s, some of them began to switch from expensive metal engravings to woodcuts and to call themselves "pictorials." After producing some engravings for promotional materials for P.T. Barnum, Leslie joined one of the pictorials for its 1851 startup – *Gleason's Pictorial Drawing Room Companion,* published in Boston. There he employed a technique he had learned in London: he sawed about a square foot of Turkish boxwood into small pieces, bolted them together, made a skeletal drawing and a few connecting lines of backgrounds on them, then assigned the pieces to a crew of engravers so that they could work on various parts of the woodcut simultaneously, bolt them back together, and finish a large illustration in record time. It was a practice better suited to a newspaper than to the leisurely pace of a literary pictorial like *Gleason's* and probably indicated Leslie's interest in establishing a newsweekly in the United States.

Leslie went to New York and interrupted P.T. Barnum's Thanksgiving dinner in 1852 to make a proposition, from which came the *Illustrated News,* the first successful self-designated news pictorial in America. Leslie was chief engraver. This newspaper was published throughout 1853, approaching 50,000 circulation, but at year's end, Barnum's partners pulled out and it was merged with *Gleason's.* Leslie stayed in New York, laying plans for his own newspaper, which he launched in late 1855 as *Frank Leslie's Illustrated Newspaper.* It bore strong resemblance to the *Illustrated London News* and *Gleason's* – a 16-page folio, with pages 1, 4, 5, 8, 9, 12, 13, and 16 dominated by illustrations, and the other eight pages (the back of the sheet before folding) consisting entirely of text. The first year's coverage included news of U.S. adventurer William Walker's soldiering in Nicaragua, the three-way presidential race of 1856, floods in France, the end of the Crimean War, the coronation of Alexander II of Russia, and caustic reports of Mormon polygamy. The paper sold for 10 cents, with the price reduced to six cents by late 1856.

Leslie employed more than 100 artists, engravers, and printers, and the expense of such an enterprise led him to reduce news coverage and devote more space to fiction and travel features. The price reduction helped circulation, but Leslie's apparent success inevitably led others into the field, most notably *Harper's Weekly,* the project of Fletcher Harper of the large Harper Brothers publishing house. Harper used woodcuts primarily to illustrate fiction at first, but by late 1857 was covering news events as actively as Leslie. The two weeklies competed vigorously for decades.

In 1859, the *New York Illustrated News* joined the fray, and as the Civil War broke out, it joined its two healthier competitors in sending dozens of artists into the field. Leslie would have up to 12 correspondents in the field at a time, and over the four-year span of the war, his 80 artists sent in some 3,000 scenes for the engravers. Of these, only one or two a week would be based on photographs; the rest were sketched from direct observation or, in a pinch, from newspaper reports. It was demanding work, like soldiering without a gun – which would have been lighter to carry than the many supplies required for sketching in the field. Many artists, exhausted, abandoned the work, and a few were killed or captured. Thomas Nast, who worked for all three weeklies at various times during the conflict, was destined to be the most successful of the group as a newspaper artist; Winslow Homer, employed by Harper, was the one to make the biggest name in a postwar artistic career.

Pictorial journalism matured greatly in the 1860s. Before the war, illustrations were so ragged or inaccurate that it became fashionable for literary figures to scoff at the picture weeklies, and this derision continued long after the

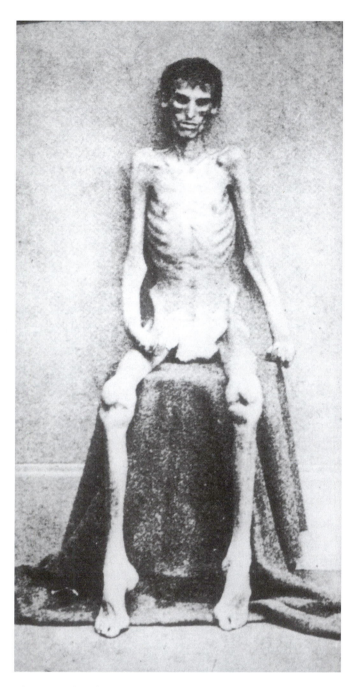

Photographs of liberated Andersonville prisoners showed the horrors of the Civil War Southern prison camp.

artists had proven themselves under fire. (Mark Twain and William Wordsworth were among the critics.) But as the war progressed, the artists learned how to cultivate generals, how to make the battle lines ragged enough that the soldiers would not laugh at them, how to make the war more personal and vivid by portraying individuals instead of battalions.

The circulation of the illustrated weeklies fluctuated in keeping with the importance of the news. These weeklies became a major part of the typical newsstand, grouped apart from the tamer-looking literary journals, and typical-

ly selling for 10 cents (the vendor kept about three cents for himself). They also were sold widely on trains and are sometimes considered by popular historians to be a part of what they call "railroad literature." They often reached six-figure circulations when the news was big enough.

The success of these pioneers led to expansion of the industry. Some publications were begun or were converted to pictorials, which looked similar but seemed more magazine than newspaper because of specialized content. Examples of this type are *Harper's Bazar, Scientific American,* and the *Illustrated Christian Weekly.* Others posed as newspapers but actually relied almost entirely on stories, poems, and humor – for example, the *Illustrated American News* (born and died in 1851, actually predating Barnum's paper), *Once a Week,* and *Every Saturday.* A third type of offshoot was the highly sensational ancestor of modern tabloids. These were often printed on pink paper, and featured a provocative action picture dominating page one – for example, a gunfight in a gambling den, a bloody boxing scene, or an umbrella-wielding matron retrieving her son from a bordello. Such scenes drew the curious irresistibly to the *National Police Gazette,* the *Illustrated Police News,* and Frank Leslie's own *Day's Doings.*

All this competition for the newspaper buyer's coin greatly diluted the revenue of the three war papers, and, indeed, the *New York Illustrated News* did not live to report the end of the war. After Appomattox, *Harper's Weekly* usually led the field in circulation, becoming a powerful journal of political reporting as Thomas Nast aimed his deadly pen at the bosses of Tammany Hall. It is true that the Harper Brothers spun off some circulation by starting *Harper's Bazar* (renamed *Harper's Bazaar* in 1929), but Frank Leslie was starting new publications almost annually in the postwar years. By the 1880s, *Harper's Weekly* had a circulation around 100,000 and *Frank Leslie's Illustrated Newspaper* only about half that. Frank Leslie died in 1880, and his wife established herself as a journalist to be reckoned with as she parlayed President James Garfield's lingering death in the 1881 assassination into a circulation gain of 100,000. The gain was temporary, and she sold the weekly in 1889.

Census taker S.N.D. North reported that he counted 481 illustrated periodicals in the United States in 1880. That was the year that Stephen Horgan at the *New York Daily Graphic* succeeded in converting a photograph into the patterns of dots seen today as the halftone screen. The *Daily Graphic* had been started in 1873 expressly to utilize the new technologies of photography and photoengraving. Its founding was the beginning of the end of the woodcut's usefulness in newspaper journalism.

The *Daily Graphic,* the first daily illustrated newspaper in the United States, itself survived only 16 years, as the Horgan process was too difficult for practical use at that time. Halftone engraving would not be introduced successfully into the mainstream newspaper press until the late 1890s. Another industry development, however, was displacing the illustrated newspaper. The last third of the nineteenth century was the era of greatest expansion in U.S. daily newspapers and particularly for Sunday papers. The number more than doubled in the 1880s, and redoubled in

Americans saw pictures as line drawings in illustrated newspapers.

An artist would perform the transformation from photograph to line drawing.

The line drawing then would be carved on small woodblocks by another craftsman.

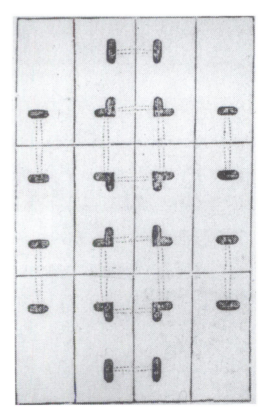

The small blocks then were joined together for the press run.

the 1890s, totaling 567 in 1899. Early in the twentieth century these large Sunday editions began to include Sunday magazines and rotogravure sections. Furthermore, the 1890s are notable as the time when the country's top magazines cut prices and reached mass audiences for the first time. The once-a-week illustrated newspaper, with its mix of artwork, news, features and fiction, had become an anachronism.

Frank Leslie's Illustrated Newspaper was continued by other publishers until 1922. *Harper's Weekly* was merged into other publications in 1916, then revived for the nostalgia market in 1974.

George Everett

See also Magazine Illustrations; Magazines in the Nineteenth Century; Magazines in the Twentieth Century; Photojournalism in the Nineteenth Century; Photojournalism in the Twentieth Century

Further Reading
Exman, Eugene, *The House of Harper: One Hundred and Fifty Years of Publishing,* New York: Harper & Row, 1967
Gambee, Budd Leslie, *Frank Leslie and His Illustrated Newspaper, 1855–1860,* Ann Arbor: University of Michigan, Department of Library Science, 1964
North, S.N.D., *History and Present Condition of the Newspaper and Periodical Press of the United States,* Washington, D.C.: Government Printing Office, 1884
Stern, Madeleine B., ed., *Publishers for Mass Entertainment in Nineteenth Century America,* Boston: Hall, 1980
_____, *Purple Passage: The Life of Mrs. Frank Leslie,* Norman: University of Oklahoma Press, 1953
Taft, Robert, *Photography and the American Scene,* New York: Dover, 1964
Thompson, William Fletcher, *The Image of War,* New York: Thomas Yoseloff, 1960

Image, The
Early exploration of the media event phenomenon

First published in 1961, *The Image: or What Happened to the American Dream?,* by Daniel J. Boorstin, explored the illusory nature of life in the twentieth-century United States. It introduced the notion of the "pseudo-event," something covered by the news media not because it is a spontaneous happening but because someone planned it primarily with a view to getting news coverage. A "pseudo-event," a term that became a staple phrase in the language, has no reality of its own.

Kin to "pseudo-events" were twentieth-century celebrities who were celebrities because they were well known; packaged tours that gave the traveler the flavor of a foreign location without requiring him or her actually to share in the experience of the locals; and digests that allowed the reader to believe that everything worth knowing is at one's fingertips. The pseudo-event flourishes, Boorstin argued, because people in the United States think in terms of images rather than ideals, invention rather than discovery, and prestige rather than honor, and he called for the people to awaken and recognize the difference between dreams and illusions.

His call struck a responsive chord in U.S. readers. The book, retitled *The Image: A Guide to Pseudo-Events in America,* continued to provoke discussion into the late twentieth century.

Barbara Cloud

See also Media Events; Staged News

Further Reading
Boorstin, Daniel J., *The Image, or, What Happened to the American Dream,* London: Weidenfeld and Nicolson, 1961; New York: Atheneum, 1962; also published as *The Image: A Guide to Pseudo-Events in America,* New York: Atheneum, 1971

Indian Wars
Misreporting often a characteristic of battle news

From about 1860 through the 1890s, the U.S. Army waged a battle against the Native Americans, at first believing that the various tribes should be assimilated into the white culture, and finally believing that the country's first settlers should be exterminated in the interest of the westward expansion of the United States. Throughout the Indian Wars, the press ultimately played a critical role in stirring public sentiment against the Indians. Its role has been described by historians of the era as a shameful chapter in press history during which untrained and trained reporters often wrote fictitious stories about Indian atrocities, relied on reports from clearly biased U.S. soldiers, did not understand the political and social differences between the various tribes, and generally displayed an ignorance of the type of military strategy used in classic warfare – that of the American Civil War, for example – and the strategy relevant to fighting Indians.

The Indian Wars spanned the post–Civil War period, during which "war correspondence . . . bloomed into a specialized journalistic function . . . and thereafter the war correspondent took his place as a singular figure in both journalism and adventure." Indeed, there was much adventure for the young reporter anxious to prove himself a part of the country's westward destiny. The reporter who was assigned or who volunteered to cover the Indian Wars was expected to travel and fight with the various military units. There were approximately 1,065 engagements between the U.S. Army and the Indians between 1866 and 1891, averaging about 37 fights a year. One scholar estimated that the peak of fighting occurred between 1867 and 1869. Although the wars were fought in three areas – the plains, the mountains, and the desert – the most vicious fighting occurred on the plains where the first transcontinental railroad was laid across the Indians' hunting grounds. The first

The Battle at Little Big Horn

. . . a party was sent on Custer's trail to look for traces of his command. They found awaiting them a sight fit to appall the stoutest heart. At a point about three miles down the right bank of the stream, Custer had evidently attempt to ford and attack the village from the ford. The trail was found to lead back up the bluff and to the northward, as if the troops had been repulsed and compelled to treat. . . . All along the slopes and ridges, and in the ravines, lay the dead, arranged in order of battle, lying as they had fought, line behind line, showing where the defensive positions had been successfully taken up, and held till none were left to fight. There, huddled in a narrow compass, horses and men were piled promiscuously. At the highest point of the ridge lay Custer, surrounded by a chosen band. . . . Not a man had escaped to tell the tale, but it was inscribed on the surface of these barren hills in a language more eloquent than words.

St. Paul-Minneapolis Pioneer-Press and Tribune, July 1–6, 1876

cluded that the change in coverage could be explained by the need to justify U.S. territorial expansion, by the public's expectation following the Civil War that the papers report war stories, and finally, by the need of the United States, after a war that nearly destroyed the nation's unity, for a new focus that would unify the country behind new heroes.

ROBIN GALLAGHER

See also Native American Media

Further Reading

Curtin, Patricia A., "From Pity to Necessity: How National Events Shaped Coverage of the Plains Indian War," *American Journalism* 12:1 (Winter 1995)
Knight, Oliver, *Following the Indian Wars,* Norman: University of Oklahoma Press, 1960
Watson, Elmo Scott, "The Indian Wars and the Press, 1866–1867," *Journalism Quarterly* 17 (1940)
_____, "The Last Indian War, 1890–91: A Study of Newspaper Jingoism," *Journalism Quarterly* 20 (1943)

Indian war began in 1866; it was sparked when the United States attempted to open the Bozeman Trail to the Montana mining region. The story was reported by untrained and volunteer men who distorted and exaggerated the story. The last Indian war was covered by reporters who were "just plain faking" their stories, according to one historian, who wrote that the 1890–91 battle at Wounded Knee was enflamed by "propaganda disguised as news, to influence the federal government into sending more troops to the 'threatened' areas, thereby adding to the profits of tradesmen in the frontier towns."

While expecting reporters to fight and write objective war stories was in itself problematic, those reporters who abstained from fighting often violated other journalistic practices when they elected to remain in the comfort of the officers' tents writing stories based on soldiers' reports. The stories thus written often coincided with the editorial position of such eastern papers as the *New York Herald* or the *New York Times.* However, one study has shown that the men who covered the Indian Wars later went on to become successful publishers, editors, and businessmen. One of them, Henry Morton Stanley, a reporter for the *New York Herald,* became famous during an expedition to Africa in 1871, one of the goals of which was to relieve the Scottish explorer David Livingstone, who was missing and feared lost. When Stanley came across the explorer, he uttered the now-famous understated words, "Dr. Livingstone, I presume?" Stanley ultimately was elected to the British Parliament.

Several historians have shown that before the end of the Civil War the press did report that the U.S. military had engaged in unjustified massacres of defenseless Indians, and some editorial reports were critical of the reporters' tendency to groundlessly flame hostilities. By the end of the period, however, the coverage changed to that of reporting Indian "atrocities" against the white settlers. One researcher con-

Informational Graphics

Development of visual means to share information

Beginning as the first method of recording human history, illustrated communication evolved from crude drawings on cave walls to informational graphics, or infographics, produced by the highest technology and presented in every form of media published in the modern world. Despite this long history of visual information sharing, the use of infographics as a dominant visual reporting tool of the modern media become commonplace only from the early 1980s.

By definition, an infographic is any presentation of data that allows the reader to analyze the data using visual comparison. The generally accepted forms of infographics include charts (line, or fever; pie; bar, or column; table); diagrams; and maps. Each form has its specific use: line charts compare quantity changes over time; bar charts visualize and compare specific quantities; pie charts divide a whole quantity into its parts; and tables compare statistical or verbal information in columns.

Maps are the simplest method a journalist has for describing places and things within those places. Maps are also the oldest of the standard forms of infographics, with the oldest known map dated to approximately 3800 B.C.

The earliest use of a truly informational graphic is thought to be a map by Edmond Halley published in the 1686 book *An Historical Account of the Trade Winds, and Monsoons, Observable in the Seas Between and Near the Tropicks: With an Attempt to Assign the Phisical Cause of Said Winds.* This map used symbols to represent the known trade winds in sailing channels around the world.

Other early infographic pioneers included William Playfair, Charles Joseph Minard, and Robert Snow. Playfair, an English political economist, was one of the first to use a line, or fever, chart to plot changes in economic data. In 1786, he published 43 of these charts in his book *The Commercial*

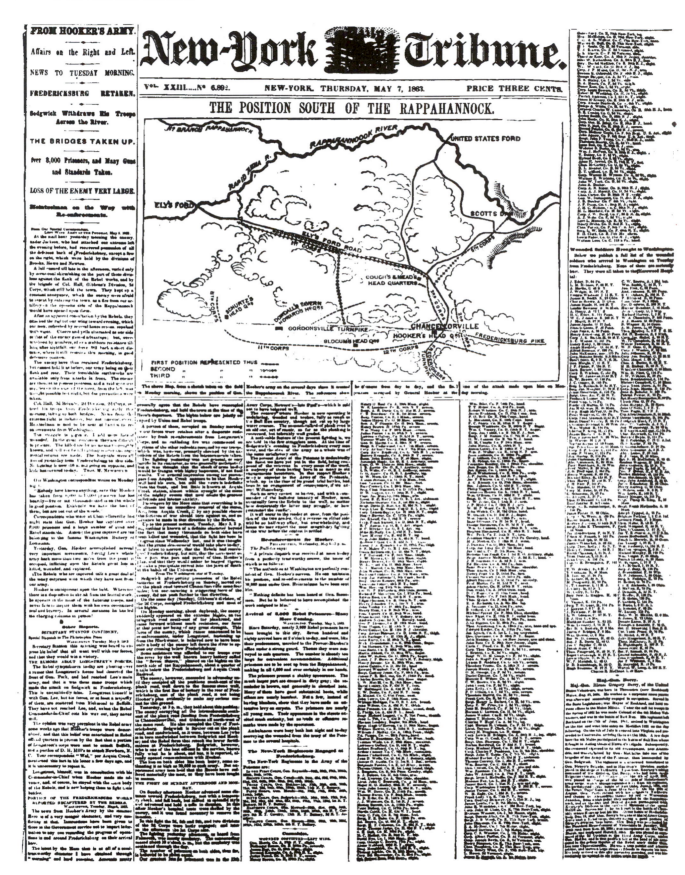

Maps of battlefields often accompanied newspaper stories during the Civil War.
(Davis Library, University of North Carolina at Chapel Hill)

and Political Atlas. During the London cholera epidemic in 1854, Snow used a map plotting the location of cholera deaths to help locate the source of water contamination.

Minard's graphical depiction of the French march on Russia in 1812 is considered one of the best statistical graphics ever produced. Using five different sets of statistical data, Minard illustrated – by date – troop strength, force location, direction of movement, and weather conditions.

When the national newspaper *USA Today* was launched in 1982, it also launched a revolution in the presentation of information. Editors at the newspaper considered the use of infographics a primary form of information presentation and required discussions of graphic potential for nearly every story assigned. Infographics were often used as the lead visual element on many pages and were used daily as stand-alone elements, with no story text beyond what was found within the infographic itself.

While the *USA Today* approach to information presentation had a large impact on the industry-wide recognition of infographics as a reporting tool, the explosive growth of desktop computer technology and telecommunications also played an important role in the widespread application of infographics by the media. The 1984 development of the desktop Apple Macintosh computer and its graphics user interface, and comparable systems on other computer platforms, gave media graphic artists the ability to create statistically accurate, illustrated infographics quickly.

Associated with the development of the desktop computer was the expansion of digital transmission of information over telephone lines. Newsroom access to infographics was increased dramatically as numerous infographic services (Chicago Tribune, Knight-Ridder, Gannett News Service), as well as traditional wire services such as the Associated Press, began providing infographic coverage of regional, national, and international stories.

Early newspaper use of infographics was limited by the printing technology available and the time needed to produce the woodcuts or engravings used to print the infographic. Newspaper use of infographics in the United States began with hand-drawn maps of Civil War battles. These diagrams of the battlefields, although many weeks late in publication, provided clarification of the actual progress of battle for readers in both the North and South.

U.S. newspapers began more frequent use of infographics as printing technology improved around the turn of the twentieth century. During the first decade of the century, large-city newspapers used infographics more regularly to help illustrate major stories. In the 1901 coverage of the assassination of President William McKinley, the *Chicago Record-Herald* diagrammed the location of the fatal bullet wounds. Similar illustrative diagrams would provide 1981 readers with information about the attempt on the life of President Ronald Reagan.

As during the Civil War, readers' need for information about battles during both world wars greatly increased demand on the media to produce concise explanation. Maps again carried the infographic load for most U.S. newspapers, but the regular use of annotated photographs and illustrations also began. These diagrams helped answer the "how" questions readers always asked and reporters often struggled to answer within the finite constraints of the typeset news column.

Modern use of informational graphics began to reach its fullest potential as magazines and newspapers began to use various forms. *Fortune* magazine began using illustrated charts in the 1930s to help clarify the business statistics so important to their readers. Following the crash of the stock market in 1929, the U.S. media and its audience began to recognize the news importance of statistical data.

During this period of growth in the use of statistical charting, many media artists adopted a stark illustrative style that used a new picture language called Isotype (for International System of Typographic Picture Education). Developed by Austrian Otto Neurath, isotypes were simple illustrative representations (icons) of common objects. By using specific quantities of similarly or proportionally sized isotype characters, graphic artists could apply the important principle of visual validity associated with the so-called Vienna Method of representation. It was thought this method of elimination of perceptual distortion and removal of unnecessary decoration from the infographics would allow the graphic to most accurately convey data to the reader. Although not all use of graphics in the media of the late twentieth century would meet the definition of simplicity, the use of this form of information presentation was accepted as a reliable and effective form of communication.

MICHAEL WILLIAMS

See also Illustrated Newspapers; Magazine Illustrations; Newspaper Design

Further Reading
Conover, Theodore E., *Graphic Communications Today*, 2nd ed., St. Paul, Minnesota: West, 1990
Finberg, Howard I., and Bruce D. Itule, *Visual Editing, A Graphic Guide for Journalists,* Belmont, California: Wadsworth, 1990
Holmes, Nigel, *Designer's Guide to Creating Charts & Diagrams*, New York: Watson-Guptill, 1984
_____, *Designing Pictorial Symbols*, New York: Watson-Guptill, 1985
Lester, Paul M., *Visual Communication: Images with Messages,* Belmont, California: Wadsworth, 1995
Tufte, Edward R., *Envisioning Information*, Cheshire, Connecticut: Graphics, 1990
_____, *The Visual Display of Quantitative Information,* Cheshire, Connecticut: Graphics, 1983

Infomercials: *see* Program-Length Commercials

In-House Advertising
On site sales promotion technique

In-house advertising is only one component of the marketing package that is often termed sales promotion. The term usually includes displays placed in retail stores to identify, advertise, or merchandise a product. Although the most important display piece in the store always has been the actual product, other items may be used to draw the attention of interested shoppers. The creation of self-service shopping in retail stores was followed quickly by this point-of-purchase advertising, traditionally offered to retailers with little or no restrictions as to its use.

These advertiser-developed, point-of-purchase materials cost billions of dollars annually in the late twentieth century and made it a major category of advertising. In-house advertising materials often go beyond banners, displays, shelf-talkers, and shelf signs to more elaborate materials, including electronic video terminals mounted on shopping carts, kiosks that provide coupons and recipes at the end-caps of shelves, in-house television monitors that target shoppers in cash register or checkout lines, LED (light-emitting diode) boards, and coupon dispensers mounted to shelf channels. Although offered to retailers for displays and planned for use over a very short duration, the clock, wall ornaments, and product divider point-of-purchase pieces often become permanent store fixtures.

The use of in-house advertising is based on a thorough understanding of most consumer buying practices that suggests that consumers make unplanned shopping decisions. Statistical information gathered by the Point of Purchase Advertising Institute, a trade organization, revealed that nearly two-thirds of consumers' purchase decisions were made in the store, with some impulse categories demonstrating an 80 percent rate.

This type of advertising, which can take advantage of movement, sound, and new production techniques, is plagued by the failure of retailers to make proper use of the materials submitted to them; in fact, some advertising scholars believe that only half of all point-of-purchase materials in the late twentieth century ever were used. This might have been caused by too many advertisers sending too much material to a limited number of retailers. This type of advertising works best when tied to a total advertising program.

The challenge is to reduce the campaign's selling idea or current theme to its simplest elements in a three-dimensional format. This theme often has tie-ins with other related products, storewide promotions based on thematic emphasis, or tie-ins with special events.

Advertisers in the 1990s spent almost as much time planning how to get the displays used as in creating the message. Based on this plan, store managers authorized the use of display materials that usually arrived with product shipments and were set up by store personnel. Because individual stores might have individual promotion and merchandising policies, tailor-made materials were often required to fit the store's policy.

FERRELL ERVIN

Instant Books
Publications report quickly on current events

Instant books historically have been defined as books produced much more quickly than is the norm under prevailing publishing technology. They have usually been published in response to an emergent event, such as a war, a natural disaster or other catastrophe, a court case, or a similarly newsworthy event. As such, they often take the form of expanded news reporting rather than complex analysis of the event. In some cases, however, an instant book is actually the rapid release of material that has been in preparation in anticipation of a probable event, such as a national political convention or the death of a celebrity.

According to Kenneth Davis, who called them the product of a marriage between journalism and publishing, the earliest instant books appeared in Europe with the onset of World War II. Penguin Specials, rapidly produced British publications, dealt with rising issues in the European crisis and the early stages of the war. Davis identified the first instant books in the United States as Pocket Books' editions on Franklin Delano Roosevelt, which appeared within six days of his death, and on the atomic bomb, on sale three weeks after the bombing of Hiroshima. Later, Bantam's Extra editions came to typify the phenomenon. Bantam's publication of the Warren Commission Report on the assassination of John F. Kennedy was accomplished within three days of the release of the report in 1964. Many other particularly timely documents were produced by Bantam through herculean, nonstop editorial and printing efforts. The rapid release of Bantam's edition of the *Pentagon Papers* in 1973 became a significant issue in Supreme Court deliberations about the constitutionality of immediate publication of government documents without prior government review.

Other publishers, including Dell, New American Library, Avon, and even noncommercial houses, have produced their own versions of instant books. The Republican National Committee produced two books listing Richard Nixon as author within a week of his nomination at the 1968 Republican National Convention. The 1995 O.J. Simpson trial spawned an unprecedented number of books identified by the industry as "instant" publications. Another development at about the same time was the rapid distribution of book versions, or novelizations, of films, which seemed to be instant books but which were in fact part of well-planned publicity campaigns.

Traditionally, the difference in production time for a normal book and an instant book has been substantial – the difference between several months and a matter of days or even hours. However, the advent of electronic publishing began to blur the distinction between instant books and standard publication schedules, as authors were able to produce their own camera-ready editions through desktop publishing and editors could perform editorial tasks online. Moreover, the term "instant books" came to refer to books downloaded from CD-ROMS, from on-line services, or even from cyber-bookstores providing on-site printing of texts from electronically stored inventory.

PRISCILLA COIT MURPHY

See also Book Publishing in the Twentieth Century

Further Reading
Davis, Kenneth C., *Two-Bit Culture: The Paperbacking of America,* Boston: Houghton Mifflin, 1984

International News Service

William Randolph Hearst's wire service

After publisher William Randolph Hearst spent 10 years attempting to gain Associated Press (AP) memberships for his New York City and Chicago newspapers, even seeking relief in the Illinois courts, he had AP service for only some of his papers. Realizing that some of the papers that he expect to open in the future might be barred from AP service by local AP competitors, by 1903 Hearst set up a modest news service connecting the papers of his growing newspaper chain.

In May 1909, he expanded this personal service into a national wire, serving his papers and other newspaper clients. Named American News Service, this wire served morning newspapers. The wire was renamed International News Service (INS) in January 1910, reflecting the addition of foreign news to its report the previous August. National News Association, a Hearst wire for evening papers, operated for one year before it and INS were permanently merged in 1911 as International News Service, serving both morning and evening papers.

From the start, the INS report commingled news and features, the latter at times dominating the former. Hearst occasionally inserted stories supporting his political views or interests. To many in U.S. journalism, INS was simply another vehicle for Hearst's sensationalism and political views. INS conducted its world news coverage, especially coverage of World War I, on a shoestring, leading AP at one point to charge INS with having copied AP news bulletins without crediting AP. The 1918 U.S. Supreme Court decision in the matter said that INS had taken something of commercial value by transmitting AP stories verbatim and without credit (*International News Service* v. *Associated Press*).

Curtis J. Mar was the Hearst wires' first president. He was followed by Richard A. Farrelly in 1909, Fred. J. Wilson, Moses Koenigsberg in 1919, Frank Mason in 1928, Joseph V. Connolly in 1931, and Seymour Berkson in 1945.

Barry Faris, named INS's editor in 1916, was still in that post when INS and United Press (UP) merged in 1958. Over the years, Faris shaped INS's news report into a broad and iconoclastic mix of spot news coverage, sensational and dramatic news features, and big-name columnists. Never a wire on which to depend for complete daily news coverage, INS's strength was in giving clients an edge over local competitors with feature columns and news features by such popular writers as Arthur "Bugs" Baer, James L. Kilgallen, Bob Considine, Louella Parsons, Pierre J. Huss, Phyllis Battelle, and Kingsbury Smith.

Sketchy records show that INS's clients totaled 400 in 1918, 600 in 1930, 900 in 1936, and 1,100 in 1948 (compared with AP's 4,274 and UP's 4,327 in 1948). By the early 1950s, however, INS and UP were steadily losing clients to AP as a result of a 1945 Supreme Court decision that opened AP membership to all who could afford its service. Dating from the 1920s, discussions of a merger between INS and UP came to fruition on May 24, 1958, when UP absorbed INS, forming United Press International.

RICHARD A. SCHWARZLOSE

See also Associated Press; Cooperative News Gathering; United Press (1882); United Press Associations (1907); United Press International

Further Reading

International News Service, *INS: The Story of International News Service,* privately published, 1955

Koenigsberg, Moses, *King News, an Autobiography,* Philadelphia: F.A. Stokes, 1941

Schwarzlose, Richard A., *The Nation's Newsbrokers: Vol. 2, The Rush to Institution: From 1865 to 1920,* Evanston, Illinois: Northwestern University Press, 1990

Internet

Vision and imagination necessary to develop new technology

The development of the Internet is a story about people with intelligence, vision, and imagination – engineers, scholars, and scientists, for the most part – who interacted with events and challenges to effect revolutionary changes in technology and world culture. U.S. government agencies, specifically the Advanced Research Project Agency (ARPA) played an early and long-term leadership role. From the Internet's recognized beginning in 1961, its development and support represented a collaborative undertaking among the best and brightest thinkers and researchers in the United States.

The Internet has more than a few definitions. It is at once a worldwide broadcasting capability, a mechanism for information dissemination, and a medium for collaboration and interaction between individuals and their computers without regard for geographic location. The Internet has also been referred to as a vast frontier of information resources, ripe for exploring and plundering, and as a "network of networks," or "metanetwork." The "official" definition, unanimously passed by the Federal Networking Council (FNC) in October 1995, stated:

> Internet refers to the global information system that is logically linked together by a globally unique address space based on the Internet Protocol (IP) or its subsequent extensions/follow-ons; is able to support communications using the Transmission Control Protocol/Internet Protocol (TCP/IP) suite or its subsequent extensions/follow-ons, and/or other IP-compatible protocols; and provides, uses or makes accessible, either publicly or privately, high level services layers on the communications and related infrastructure described herein.

The first recorded description of the social interactions that could be enabled through networking was a series of memos written by J.C.R. Licklider of the Massachusetts Institute of Technology (MIT) in August 1962, discussing his "galactic network" concept. This early concept was very much like the Internet at the end of the twentieth century.

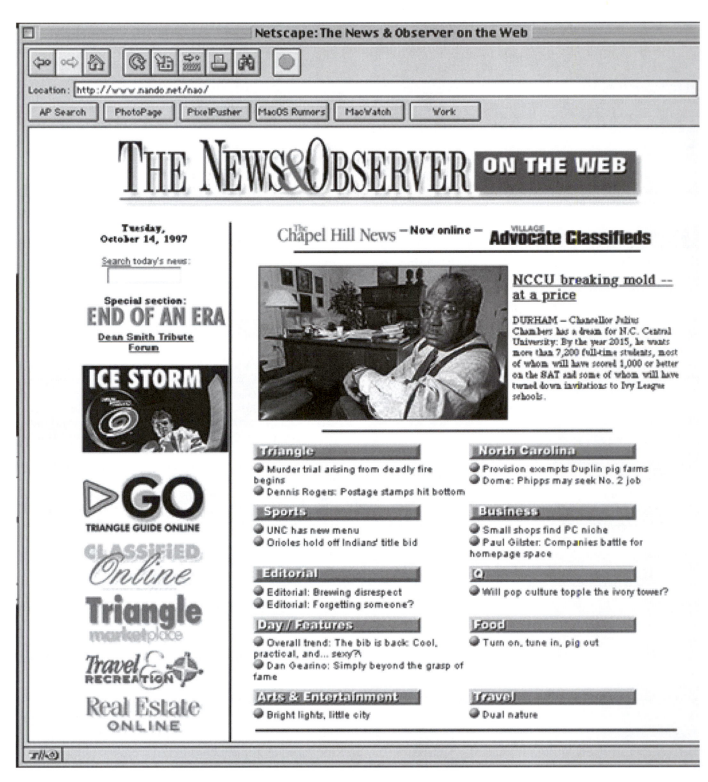

The Raleigh, North Carolina, *News & Observer* was one of the first U.S. newspapers to offer its news electronically. (Courtesy of *The News & Observer*)

Leonard Kleinrock at MIT published the first paper on packet switching theory in July 1961. His 1964 book, *Communication Nets: Stochastic Message Flow and Delay,* was the first on the topic. Kleinrock was convinced of the theoretical feasibility of communication using packets rather than circuits (associated with telephones) as a major step toward computer networking.

In 1966, Lawrence G. Roberts went to ARPA (which later became DARPA, the Defense Advanced Research Projects Agency) to develop the computer network concept, publishing his plan for the "ARPANET" in 1967. Curiously, researchers at MIT (1961–67), at the Rand Corporation (1962–65), and at the National Physics Laboratory (1964–67) had proceeded along similar investigative paths, unaware of each others' efforts. This separate approach was not to continue.

In October 1969, the first host-to-host computer message on the ARPANET was sent by Kleinrock's Network Measurement Center at the University of California at Los Angeles to the Stanford Research Institute. Other computers were added quickly to the ARPANET during the following years, and work proceeded on completing the host-to-host protocol and other network software.

In October 1972, Robert E. Kahn organized a large, public, successful demonstration of the ARPANET at the International Computer Communication Conference (ICCC). Also in 1972, the initial "hot" application, electronic mail, or E-mail, was introduced. Once the basic E-mail message send-and-read software was enhanced by an E-mail utility program to list, selectively read, file, forward, and respond to messages, E-mail took off as the largest network application. Twenty-five years later, worldwide E-mail users numbered in the tens of millions.

ARPANET grew into the Internet. The original concept of multiple independent networks yielded to a new technological idea introduced by Kahn, that of open-architecture networking. In such a concept, individual networks may be separately designed and developed and each may have its own unique interface, yet, enabled with a new, reliable communications protocol, they would still be able to share communications.

Another vital key to developing a reliable delivery communication system was something called network control protocol (NCP). But even this protocol lacked the error control required in the reassembly of packets at the targeted E-mail address site. If any of the packets were lost, the system would not function. Kahn developed a new version of the NCP that could meet the needs of an open-architecture network. This protocol would eventually be called the transmission control protocol/Internet protocol (TCP/IP). Vinton Cerf's collaboration with Kahn in the spring of 1973 on TCP/IP gave rise to the development in the mid-1970s of related Internet protocols. It was not until January 1, 1983, that the transition of the ARPANET host protocol from NCP to TCP/IP could be made. All Internet hosts were required to convert simultaneously or be left behind.

A major motivation for the Internet was resource sharing. File transfer protocol (FTP) and remote log-on (Telnet) became very important applications along with E-mail. These concepts of resource sharing and "electronic communities" gave rise to Free-Nets. Case Western Reserve University started the Cleveland (Ohio) Free-Net, the original Free-Net, in the mid-1980s. The university provided the infrastructure of an electronic town – the administration building, the post office, and the teleport. Other town departments or organizations without their own networks could join the Free-Net and offer their information and data. Local public libraries were the earliest to participate by providing the Free-Net with their on-line catalogs.

During the mid-1980s, mountains of information and data – largely in text format but some offered statistics and graphical files as well – were being digitally stored on the Internet in FTP sites, FAQ (frequently asked questions) files, and RFC (request for comments) documents. Soon, search engines were needed to aid search and retrieval through these enormous files. Gophers, Jugheads, Archies, and Veronicas came to the rescue.

Gopher originated as a browser, a campuswide information search-and-retrieval system created at the University of Minnesota by Mark P. McCahill. A Gopher is one type of client-server software server that enables one's computer and modem to connect with host computers storing information. Once desired information (text, data, and executable files) is found, it is typically downloaded to discs. After its original release, Gopher grew rapidly until the advance of graphical browsers such as Netscape and Internet Explorer in the early 1990s. These World Wide Web sites evolved their own search engines and indexes such as Yahoo!, Infoseek, WebCrawler, Excite, and AltaVista. Even so, Gopher gained in popularity, and by May 1994, traffic volume indicated that Gophers were the sixth most popular protocol.

Archie, a type of search-and-retrieve software developed at McGill University, searched Archie servers identifying the names of FTP sites that stored desired files or archives. Thus alerted to where to find the needed files, a searcher could retrieve them more efficiently. Veronica (which stands for Very Easy Rodent-Oriented Net-wide Index to Computerized Archives), a software program developed by Steven Foster and Fred Barrie at the University of Nevada at Reno's System Computing Department in November 1992, allowed users to search Gopher menus for particular keywords. Jughead was a compatriot of Archie and Veronica. Created in 1993 by Rhett Jones at the University of Utah Computer Center, Jughead (Jonzy's Universal Gopher Hierarchy Excavation and Display) was designed to make restricted searches (on particular servers) of gopherspace possible.

Still other applications emerged in the 1980s, some good and some not so good: packet-based voice communication (the precursor of Internet telephony), various models of file and disc sharing, early "worm" programs that showed the concept of agents and, of course, viruses. One of the earliest and most destructive worms debuted on November 2, 1988. A graduate student let loose a computer worm on the Internet. This worm quickly copied itself to computers all over North America and soon clogged the bandwidth of Internet networks, slowing all infected machines to a crawl. The student did not design the worm to cause harm, but he did not understand what the program would do to the Internet. A key concept of the Internet is that it was not designed for just one application but as a general infrastructure on which new applications could be conceived, as subsequently illustrated by the emergence of the World Wide Web in 1990.

Widespread development of local area networks (LANS), PCs, and workstations in the 1980s allowed the Internet to flourish. Ethernet technology, developed by Bob Metcalfe at Xerox PARC in 1973, was in the late 1990s probably the dominant network technology in the Internet.

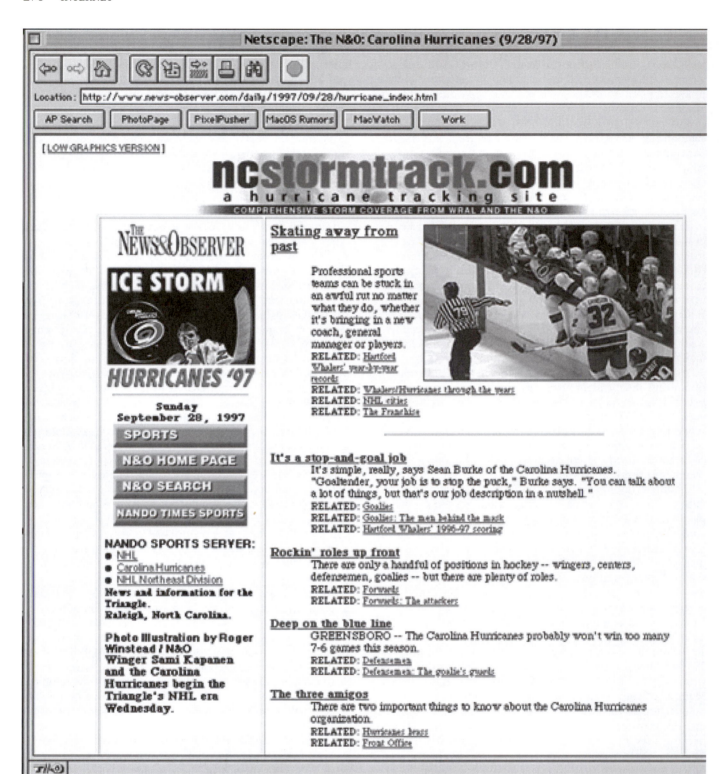

Hockey fans can find more information about their local team online than in the newspaper, which serves a more diverse audience.

(Courtesy of *The News & Observer*)

The next step was to classify these growing numbers of networks by size and geography into national, regional, and local networks. That development meant that having a single table of hosts designated by numerical addresses was no longer feasible. That change gave rise to the invention of the domain name system (DNS), which had the added flexibility of permitting a mechanism for resolving hierarchical host names (e.g., www.freedomforum.**org**) into an Internet address. The range of domain names expanded; in the late 1990s, they included **.com, .edu, .gov, .mil,** and **.net.**

This burgeoning growth led to necessity of increased communication. The Internet organizers launched the first Network Working Group in the late 1970s. That group evolved into the Internet Working Group that later led to the formation of an Internet Configuration Control Board. The subsequent Internet Activities Board was later reorganized into the Internet Engineering Task Force.

Around this time – 1985 – DARPA was no longer the only major player in the funding of the Internet. In addition to NSFNet (National Science Foundation Network) and various U.S. and international government-funded activities, interest in the commercial sector was growing.

The growth in the commercial sector emphasized the importance of establishing Internet standards. The Internet grew beyond its primarily research roots to include a broad user community and increased commercial activity, creating the need for fair standards of access.

In the early 1980s, dozens of vendors were incorporating TCP/IP into their products, but without good effect. Lack of information and appropriate training for vendors needed to be addressed. By 1985, a three-day workshop brought 250 vendors to listen to 50 inventors and experimenters. A two-way interchange of information (conferences, tutorials, design meetings) continued over the decade. In 1988, the first Internet trade show, Interop, occurred. It continued annually in locations around the world, with more than 250,000 people participating. Thus, the reason that the Internet was so useful is that it involved all of the stakeholders, researchers and developers, end users, and vendors in Internet development, training, and promotion.

The Internet, at the end of the twentieth century, was emerging into a commodity service designed to support a global information infrastructure leading toward the adoption of graphicalbrowsers and World Wide Web technology. The overwhelming success of the Internet resulted in some less-than-desirable aftereffects, such as overloaded networks, brownouts, too-rapid hardware obsolescence, under-supported Internet service providers, security problems, and copyright and censorship issues. The reaction from academics and researchers in 22 U.S. universities was to start the groundwork for the development of Internet II. To cope with expanding security challenges to the Internet, computer emergency response teams formed.

By 1997, a FIND/SVP survey of on-line usage reported that on-line advertising banners were being seen and acted upon. The study reported that 36 percent of those interviewed stated that they had clicked on an on-line ad; 11 percent reported making a purchase after clicking on the ad.

Not all industries were equally at home with the Internet. Some of the leading industries using World Wide Web and Internet technologies successfully in 1997 included computer and information technology, hospitality, manufacturing, travel, retail, publishing, and banking and finance. Available research reported that, generally, these industries used the Internet for marketing and advertising, customer service and support, information gathering, and, to a lesser degree, electronic transactions.

The World Wide Web (WWW, or the Web) is not a tool like Telnet, FTP, and Gopher. It has been compared to an invisible network within the larger network of the Internet. Several WWW browsers, such as Netscape or Internet Explorer, were invented to navigate the Web. Using one of these browsers, one can access FTP, Gopher, or Usenet (another worldwide network of newsgroups on tens of thousands of subjects that can be accessed by newsreader software programs). Essentially, the Web links all the resources on the Internet together into an interconnected net of information.

WWW files are encoded with HyperText Mark-up Language (HTML), which creates "links" to different parts of the same document or to other documents. Links transform HTML files into three-dimensional documents, with threads leading to other resources at the same site and to other sites.

The WWW project first was proposed by the European Particle Physics Laboratory (CERN) in Switzerland. CERN developed the first WWW prototype in 1990. The developers initially envisioned the Web as a means of sharing papers and data between physicists internationally.

The developers of the WWW, chief among whom was Tim Berners-Lee, had several goals in mind. The most important was to create a seamless network in which information from any source could be accessed in a simple and consistent way. Before the WWW was developed, researchers had to use many different computer programs to access all the information they needed. To overcome problems of incompatibility between different sorts of computers, the WWW introduced the principle of universal readership, which stated that networked information should be accessible from any type of computer in any country with one easy-to-use program.

As conceived by the developers at CERN, the WWW would embrace most previously networked information systems, including FTP, Gopher, and Usenet. An addressing system called Uniform Resource Locators (URLs) could reference any type of document on the Internet, including text, graphics, and video. This setup permitted the WWW to extend into multimedia.

Other goals of the Web's developers included flexibility, capacity, and ease of use. Because of its user-friendly nature and its ability to encompass all sorts of information on the Internet, the WWW grew dramatically following its initial development. Web traffic rose 2,500 percent between June 1993 and June 1994. Since then, the number of Web pages exploded into the millions, with the U.S. government hosting 4,300 Web sites by mid-1997. Besides research laboratories, many other organizations began providing information over the WWW, including universities; elementary schools; city, state, and national governments; libraries; museums; corporations; and businesses of all sizes.

On-line usage of the Web was reported in a number of surveys. One of the most relevant for the media industry was the 1996 Pew Research Center for the People and the Press. This survey revealed that news was what attracted most Internet users. Georgia Tech provided data from seven surveys covering advertising, security, political opinions, purchasing behavior, data privacy, information gathering, content authoring, and service providers.

A 1997 survey by FIND/SVP indicated that there were 31.3 million adults in the United States accessing on-line services, with another 14 million predicted to join by the following year. Further, an additional 9.8 million persons under the age of 18 were linking computers to telephone lines to access digital news, information, entertainment, and personal communications. This particular survey reported that most people went on-line for news (66 percent), followed by hobby information (62 percent), travel information (56 percent), entertainment (50 percent), government and community information (46 percent), health and medical information (45 percent), sports news (41 percent), and music (41 percent).

Among the subsequent and continuing challenges to effective Web use are reliable search engines and evaluation methods. Determining the value, reliability, currency, and accuracy of the information and data retrieved remained a serious challenge to all World Wide Web users and developers.

Added to the increasing concerns about the Internet and the World Wide Web in the late 1990s were methods of preserving Web sites. Could these relatively ephemeral methods of archiving become a vital record for future historians, scholars, and governments? Further, how could the electronic records be altered when necessary to reflect important corrections and additions? How could older technologies be preserved to retrieve and display these archives? Long-term questions and effects of this very dynamic medium were just being discovered at century's end. The Internet and the World Wide Web were much more than technologies; they were rapidly becoming an integral part of the global community.

Referred to by some observers as more a global yarn ball than a data highway, the information superhighway faced criticism since its debut. In 1991, Senator Al Gore proposed the High Performance Computing Act. That bill, which proposed the establishment of a National Information Highway, passed amid much fanfare from the media and from Congress. The problem of how much the highway would cost and who would pay for it was still under debate at the end of the decade. It was hoped that big business would provide the infrastructure in order to tap into potential markets. Large communications companies, regional and long-distance telephone companies, and cable television companies were all jockeying for position, merging, and setting up new divisions to help build this infrastructure. While large metropolitan areas made progress, smaller communities in rural areas found it difficult to get direct links to the Internet without incurring expenses from Internet service providers and phone companies for long-distance charges.

Internet Talk Radio (ITR), patterned after National Public Radio (NPR), was the first regularly scheduled radio station on the Internet. ITR initially offered programming that reached more than 100,000 people in 30 countries. The first program was *Geek of the Week*, a weekly interview with an Internet expert. ITR also broadcast public affairs programs and specials.

While transmitting video over the Internet eventually became more common, in the early 1990s video broadcasts were limited to experimental broadcasts of special Internet events, conferences, or shows. Video requires expensive equipment, sophisticated and large-capacity computers, but uses the same theory as audio. Expansion of the World Wide Web gave impetus to the increase of audio and video features. Mbone, a multimedia backbone that bypassed Internet backbones (major networks), carried video traffic, and Internet television was not far behind.

Virtual Reality (VR) uses a computer to simulate an interactive environment that appears to the observer as another reality. A VR system uses special hardware and software to give a participant enough information to allow the user to imagine being present in another world. VR allows large amounts of data to be sent back and forth quickly between many sites, permitting groups of people to enter the same virtual world. By 1994, this technology was being used in education, health sciences, business, games, and libraries.

The Internet has changed considerably since its inception. Conceived in the era of time-sharing, it survived into the era of personal computers, client-server and peer-to-peer computing, and the network computer. Designed before LANs existed, it accommodated that new network technology as well as other later services. Envisioned as supporting a range of functions from file sharing and remote log-on to resource sharing and collaboration, it spawned electronic mail between tens of millions of users and the colorful, graphical, audio World Wide Web. Started as the creation of a small band of dedicated researchers, it grew to be a commercial enterprise with billions of dollars of annual investment.

BARBARA P. SEMONCHE

See also Decency Issues in Electronic Media; Global Village; Technology

Further Reading

Cerf, Vinton, "How the Internet Came to Be," 1993, <http://www.geocites.com/SilconValley/2360_cert1.html>; this article originally appeared in *The Online User's Encyclopedia: Bulletin Boards and Beyond*, edited by Bernard Aboba, Reading, Massachusetts: Addison-Wesley, 1993

Georgia Tech Research Corporation, "GVU's 7th WWW User Survey," 1997, <http://www.gvu.gatech.edu/user_surveys/survey-1997-04/>

Hafner, Katie, and Matthew Lyon, *Where Wizards Stay up Late: The Origins of the Internet*, New York: Simon & Schuster, 1996

Internet Literacy Consultants, "ILC Glossary of Internet Terms," 1994–1997, <http://www.matisse.net/files/glossary.html>

Leiner, Barry M., et al., "A Brief History of the Internet," 1997, <http://www.isoc.org/internet-history/>

Outing, Steve, "Join the Party! 300-plus Newspapers Are Online," 1995, <http://www.mediainfo.com/ephome/news/newshtm/stop/stop2/htm>

Interpretative Reporting

World events cause change in journalistic approach

The idea that the news should constitute more than an objective recitation of facts was first considered in the 1930s when, for a number of reasons, people began viewing the world as a much more complex place that necessitated more in-depth explanation. By the 1950s, and on the heels of McCarthyism, interpretative reporting had gained a strong foothold in U.S. newsrooms and journalism schools.

Following a long period in which journalists were trained to be objective – to divide opinion from fact in their news reports – the advent of World War I, the Great Depression, and the New Deal led the public and the press to believe that world and national events needed to be analyzed, or interpreted, such that people might understand where they stood in the global perspective. Readers and reporters wanted news stories that had meaning. In response, the *New York Sun* began a Saturday review of the news in 1931; in 1935, the weekly news summaries of the *New York Times* and the *Washington (D.C.) Post* came to include an interpretative vein. In 1933, the American Society of Newspaper Editors resolved that more attention would be given to the "explanatory and interpretive news . . . [and to] background information"; in 1938, journalism textbook author Curtis MacDougall wrote that the journalist was becoming one who "combin[ed] the function of interpreter with that of reporter."

The evolving belief in interpretative, or interpretive, reporting gained momentum in the 1950s after journalists assessed the damage that objective, or purely factual, reporting could cause. Senator Joseph McCarthy, relying heavily on the fact that reporters would dutifully report his (unsubstantiated) accusations about Communist infiltration in the U.S. government, successfully effected a reign of terror in which the reputations of many innocent people were irreparably harmed. Condemning the "deadpan objectivity" of the press at the time, journalist Elmer Davis said:

> The good newspaper . . . must walk a tightrope between two great gulfs – on one side the false objectivity that takes everything at face value and lets the public be imposed on by the charlatan with the most brazen front; on the other, the "interpretive" reporting which fails to draw the line between objective and subjective, between a reasonably well established fact and what the reporter or editor wishes were the fact.

In the effort to bridge that chasm, two developments in news content evolved. In one area, the press simply extended its old practice of editorial comment to include a growing roster of "analysts." Radio and television broadcasts came to include commentators; newsmagazines and newspapers published the insights of syndicated columnists, and senior reporters wrote bylined analyses of their news beats. In a second development, interpretative reporting was included in objective news stories by reporters who sought the opinions of "experts" – from physicians to economists to physicists – who lent a context or a meaning to the factual story.

In the struggle to divide opinion from fact but still give the reader a meaningful context in its coverage of the news, journalists came to be expected to adhere to professional obligations not dissimilar to those of the scientific researcher. A reporter was responsible for the validity of the data reported and the accuracy of the story's attributions, and was expected to compare a source's assertions to those of other expert sources. So defined, interpretative reporting is more like objective research as conducted by scientists than the objective reports written prior to the 1930s.

ROBIN GALLAGHER

See also Investigative Reporting; News Concepts; Objective Reporting; Reporters and Reporting in the Twentieth Century

Further Reading
Roshco, Bernard, *Newsmaking*, Chicago: University of Chicago Press, 1975
Schudson, Michael, *Discovering the News: A Social History of American Newspapers*, New York: Basic, 1978

Investigative Reporting

Reporting tradition developed during the American Revolution

The emergence of investigative reporting as a separate practice within journalism in the United States is usually associated with Watergate, the exposure of misdeeds within the Nixon administration during the early to mid-1970s. The exploits of the young reporters for the *Washington (D.C.) Post*, Bob Woodward and Carl Bernstein, and the subsequent resignation of President Nixon combined to create a myth about the romance and importance of reporting that digs beneath the surface.

Investigative journalism, however, has a tradition in American journalism dating to the colonial era, when government corruption was exposed by feisty newspapers to fuel the fire of revolution. The prominence of the tradition, however, has been cyclical.

Nineteenth-century investigative reporters included Jacob Riis, who used photographs to document the squalid living conditions of immigrants in New York City tenements, and Nellie Bly, who went undercover into an insane asylum to expose mistreatment of patients. Journalists during the latter part of the nineteenth century and the early twentieth century, adopting the Progressive Party's zeal for reform, published an unprecedented quantity of exposé reporting and became known as muckrakers. With the coming of World War I, however, the tradition subsided and appeared infrequently during the next 40 years.

St. Louis (Missouri) Post-Dispatch reporter Paul Y. Anderson's exposure of the Teapot Dome scandal during the Harding administration in the mid-1920s and *Des Moines (Iowa) Register* reporter Clark Mollenhoff's exposés of Teamster Union corruption in the 1950s prove that the tradition remained alive, but it was not widely practiced by the nation's press. During the 1940s and 1950s, local crusading by some newspapers exposed corruption and pushed for reforms, but on the national level such reporting was limited to small-circulation political magazines, such as the *Nation*, and alternative publications like I.F. Stone's weekly newsletter.

Investigative journalism once again gained a substantial foothold in the turbulent 1960s, showing up in local newspapers, on local and national television news programs, and in magazines such as *Look, Argosy*, the *Saturday Evening Post*, and *Ramparts*. Muckraking fueled the growth of the nation's underground and alternative media as well.

Investigative reporting has altered the course of cities, counties, and the nation through its exposure of corruption and bad government policies. In 1975, a group of reporters, editors, and columnists founded Investigative Reporters and Editors (IRE), a national service organization devoted to creating a network for investigative journalists, offering training in investigative reporting and editing skills, and maintaining high standards for the practice.

IRE defined investigative journalism as reporting that exposes information about an important public issue that someone or some organization had been keeping secret. In addition, it said, the reporting must be the original, time-consuming "digging" of the reporters themselves, rather than the revelation of information compiled and analyzed by a government agency or another entity. Although not written into IRE's official definition, investigative journalism also tends to be reformist in nature.

In the 1980s, the definition broadened to include extensive analyses of social issues and institutions that may not necessarily involve specific corruption or other wrong-doing. One example of this latter type of investigative project was the exhaustive 1991 study of the nation's tax laws and their effects on the nation's economy, "America: What Went Wrong," by Donald Barlett and James Steele of the *Philadelphia Inquirer.*

Broadcast news pioneers such as Edward R. Murrow carried the investigative tradition to radio and television in the late 1950s. CBS's *60 Minutes* and local station investigative teams proved popular beginning in the late 1960s.

The skills mastered by investigative journalists include conceptualization of news stories at the systemic level; exhaustive searches and analyses of public records and other documents, often through the use of computers; extensive interviews with dozens, if not hundreds, of sources; presentation that allows for easy comprehension of complex issues and backed up with overwhelming evidence of the charges being made; and surveillance techniques that may include hidden cameras, undercover infiltration of organizations or groups, and surreptitious observations.

Investigative reporters often work in teams, such as the Pulitzer prizewinning *Newsday* team headed by Bob Greene that investigated the trafficking of heroin in 1974. The team traced the drug trail from the poppy fields of Turkey, through clandestine processing factories in France, and into the arms of New York City addicts.

JAMES AUCOIN

See also Interpretative Reporting; Muckraking; News Concepts; Objective Reporting; Reporters and Reporting in the Twentieth Century

Further Reading

Downie, Leonard, *The New Muckrakers*, Washington, D.C.: New Republic, 1976

Dygert, James H., *The Investigative Journalist: Folk Heroes of a New Era*, Englewood Cliffs, New Jersey: Prentice-Hall, 1976

Mitford, Jessica, *Poison Penmanship: The Gentle Art of Muckraking*, New York: Knopf, 1979

Schudson, Michael, *Discovering the News: A Social History of American Newspapers*, New York: Basic, 1978

Weinberg, Steve, *Telling the Untold Story: How Investigative Reporters Are Changing the Craft of Biography*, Columbia: University of Missouri Press, 1992

J

Jackson, Andrew, and the Press

Press played important role in his presidency

The 1830s were a dynamic period in U.S. newspaper history, with the press operating at a frenetic pace. The traditional, expensive commercial and mercantile papers were joined by the new, innovative, urban, sensational one-cent dailies and the reform publications, dealing with women's rights, temperance, and abolition.

Into all that activity came the political press, those partisan, vitriolic, colorful sheets that thumped the drum for a given candidate, cause, or party, and without which the U.S. political party system could not have survived and flourished. The politically partisan press had its roots in the pre-Revolutionary period. By the late 1820s and early 1830s, it was at its apex, spurred on by the friends, supporters, and enemies of Andrew Jackson – Indian fighter and military savior of New Orleans, Louisiana. According to at least one historian, Jackson was the first president to rule the country by the newspaper press.

Following the supposed "bargain and corruption" election of John Quincy Adams in the House of Representatives in 1824, supporters of Henry Clay, John C. Calhoun, and Jackson quickly started organizing political parties to support their candidacies. Because it was thought ungentlemanly and downright unseemly for candidates to boost their own availability for the White House, parties and party newspapers did the dirty work for them.

Political parties in the Jacksonian era used newspapers in a "flagship" system. Usually one newspaper spoke for the candidate or party at the national level, and the political gospel included therein was picked up by a chain of statewide newspapers across the country, and then by small weekly papers at the local level.

The importance of these papers in unifying often fragmented party elements and in advancing the political fortunes of disparate candidates cannot be overlooked. The rise of the new political press of the 1830s and the emergence of local, state, and national political parties were inextricably intertwined. The new electorate of 1828, including most free white males, looked to the newspapers for political guidance and inspiration, both during a campaign and once a candidate was in office.

Political editors, theretofore relegated to second-class status by the governing bodies, enjoyed new political and social status. They served as members, if not leaders, of local, state, and national party central committees.

Certainly, the candidates-in-waiting took the papers and their editors seriously. In Jackson's successful bid for election in 1828, "Old Hickory" newspapers quickly appeared in hundreds of villages and hamlets. Jackson, once elected, owed so many political debts to editors who had supported him that at one time or another he had some 57 editors placed in federal patronage jobs, many of them sinecures.

Two editors who rose above the mundane level of editor-turned-government-appointee were Amos Kendall and Francis P. Blair. Along with Isaac Hill, editor of the *New Hampshire Patriot,* Kendall and Blair were members of Jackson's unofficial, but exceedingly influential, Kitchen Cabinet. Kendall became a Jackson supporter while editor of the *Argus of Western America* in Frankfort, Kentucky; Blair succeeded him as editor of the *Argus* when Kendall moved to Washington, D.C., and followed him to the capital in late 1830 to start a new, national Jackson paper, the *Washington Globe.* It supplanted the *United States Telegraph,* the former flagship paper whose editor, Duff Green, let his warm feelings for the candidacy of John C. Calhoun be too widely known.

Political patronage supported the partisan press network. Party loyalists were expected to subscribe to the papers at the national, state, or local level. Political advertising was to be placed in the "proper" journal. Government printing contracts were to be awarded to the "politically correct" newspapers. Indeed, Jackson is supposed to have told all federal appointees making more than $1,000 a year to subscribe to Blair's *Globe* or find work elsewhere.

In addition, party newspapers were awarded government printing contracts, at the national level earning the editors a substantial amount of income and at the local level, a more modest amount. Green's *United States Telegraph,* for example, during one session of Congress, received more than $34,000 from the Senate, $108,000 from the House, and $6,000 for Supreme Court printing jobs. Blair's *Globe* got about $47,000 for printing government bills, reports, and journals. One historian estimated that during the 1830s, Blair averaged about $25,000 annually in income from executive branch printing jobs alone.

Opposition editors also were supported financially. A House of Representatives investigation, for example, found an interesting corollary between the switch of the *New York Courier and Enquirer* from anti-bank to pro-bank and a "loan" of $15,000 to the paper from Nicholas Biddle, head of the Bank of the United States.

Jackson's use of partisan newspapers was unparalleled to that point in U.S. history. Kendall and Blair, in return for their political appointments and access to Jackson, provided superb political and journalistic advice and service. Using the *Globe* and, through it, the state and local Jackson papers, the three men sought to circulate Jackson's stand on domestic and foreign issues and to build and reinforce his image among the electorate, protecting it from the virulent charges and accusations thrown his way by editors of opposition party newspapers.

The *Globe* became so important to Jackson, and his friendship with Blair so trusting, that whenever a problem arose that needed to be addressed in the press, Jackson supposedly declared, "Give it to Bla'r!" The *Globe* (and, later, the *Extra Globe*, introduced during the 1832 reelection campaign) published the gospel according to Jackson.

The manner in which Blair and Kendall defended Jackson – the language they employed to advance his name and programs – was pure propaganda, based largely on military metaphor. Blair, for example, trumpeted in the *Globe*: "Andrew Jackson will march on, conquering and to conquer. Heaven raised him up to great ends. He will see justice done."

Kendall, in a reelection pamphlet, the *Review*, reprinted in the *Globe*, declared that a political party, like a nation, must

> sustain its true men. When the attack is most fierce upon them, the more firmly must we rally to their support. When each man confides in those to his right and left, and when he knows that if the enemy's columns be concentrated upon him, thousands will instantly rush to his rescue, he marches on, regardless of consequences to himself.

And, from Kendall again, in the *Extra Globe*:

> Here stands Andrew Jackson, the Hero of New Orleans, at the head of the American people grasping the glorious standard of "E Pluribus Unum," protecting our rights abroad, fostering our interests at home and viewing with an eye as unbleaching as his country's eagle's, the gathering array of hostile forces.

Jackson's use of the partisan press was copied by others, but none succeeded as did he and his journalistic duo of Kendall and Blair.

Earlier journalism historians called this partisan press the "dark days" of U.S. journalism. Yet it is clear from both contemporary and modern viewpoints that this type of press activity was logical and necessary from a cultural, social, and political standpoint. Jackson and his partisans grasped that point and, in doing so, used the press to advance his image, to promote his political agenda, and to develop and strengthen the political party system of the United States of the 1830s and 1840s.

FRED F. ENDRES

See also Government Printing and Patronage

Further Reading

Baldasty, Gerald J., "The Press and Politics in the Age of Jackson," *Journalism Monographs* 89 (August 1984)

Endres, Fred F., "Public Relations in the Jackson White House," *Public Relations Journal* 2 (1976)

James, Marquis, *Andrew Jackson: Portrait of a President*, New York: Grosset and Dunlap, 1937

Remini, Robert V., *The Election of Andrew Jackson*, Philadelphia: Lippincott, 1963

Schlesinger, Arthur Meier, Jr., *The Age of Jackson*, Boston: Little, Brown, 1945; London: Eyre & Spottiswoode, 1946

Van Deusen, Glyndon G., *The Jacksonian Era, 1828–1848*, New York: Harper & Row, 1959; London: H. Hamilton, 1959

Ward, John William, *Andrew Jackson, Symbol for an Age*, New York: Oxford University Press, 1955; London: Oxford University Press, 1962

Jazz Journalism: *see* Tabloids

Jefferson, Thomas, and the Press

Supporter of a free press in the growing republic

No public figure in U.S. history was reviled more by the press than Thomas Jefferson, third president (1801–09), which made his steadfast adherence – with rare exceptions – to freedom of the press all the more remarkable. One of the foremost civil libertarians, Jefferson realized the need for an enlightened citizenry to make democracy work, and newspapers were the mechanism to thrash out the issues of the day. As Jefferson wrote to Edward Carrington in 1787,

> The basis of our government being the opinion of the people, the first object should be to keep that right; and were it left to me to decide whether we should have a government without newspapers, or newspapers without a government, I should not hesitate a moment to prefer the latter.

Jefferson was not indulging in hyperbole – he firmly believed this in a simpler society, but he added that everyone should receive those papers and be capable of reading them. Illiteracy was high in the former colonies, and circulation barely exceeded the numbers of the affluent few as newspapers emerged from the mercantile into the political phase, where comment and invective were mixed with "news" throughout the papers. Jefferson also wrote Charles Yancey in 1816, "Where the press is free, and every man able to read, all is safe." Throughout a long and stormy public life, Jefferson's faith in the wisdom of the people never wavered, although at times he was disappointed in the performance of the press.

THE PROVIDENTIAL DETECTION

An editorial cartoon criticizes Thomas Jefferson's political views during his term as vice president.
(Library Company of Philadelphia)

Jefferson was elected president in 1801 after 35 ballots in the House of Representatives – the first transfer of political power in U.S. history, ending 12 years of uninterrupted Federalist rule. At the time, four-fifths of the young nation's 235 newspapers were Federalist, bitterly opposed to Jeffersonian Republican rule.

Not as active in the journalistic arena as Alexander Hamilton for the Federalists, Jefferson never wrote for the "bear-garden scene" of the public prints. Nevertheless, as secretary of state under George Washington, he had nurtured Philip Freneau's *National Gazette* (1791–93), and in 1801, he asked Samuel Harrison Smith to move his *National Intelligencer* from Philadelphia to the new capital in Washington, D.C., as the semiofficial organ of his administration. Smith was so moderate, however, that Federalists dubbed his newspaper, "MISS Silky-Milky Smith's National Smoothing Plane," and Jefferson continued to rely on William Duane's combative *Aurora* in Philadelphia as the leading party newspaper.

Editorial comment separate from news columns first tentatively appeared after 1800, and some printers became aware of their roles as editors. By 1812, Jeffersonian Republican newspapers equaled those of Federalists, who faded away. But most of the press of this period was still blatantly politically partisan. Printer-editors confused comment with abuse, measures with men, liberty with license. As the venerable *Gazette of the United States* declared in 1801, Republican newspapers "must have been written by mad-men for the use of fools." The *Gazette* printed that Duane of the opposition *Aurora* "hurries back to lying like an old bawd not three weeks out of service." Republican papers were equally virulent in denouncing their Federalist opponents.

Jefferson was the butt of much of this vituperation. When he was a candidate for the presidency in 1800, for example, the Federalist *New-England Palladium* protested, "Should the infidel Jefferson be elected to the Presidency, the *seal of death* is that moment set on our holy religion, our churches will be prostrated, and some infamous prostitute, under the title of the Goddess of Reason, will preside in the Sanctuaries now devoted to the worship of the Most High." Even the Declaration of Independence, which Jefferson had largely drafted in 1776, was denounced years later by Joseph Dennie of the Philadelphia *Port Folio* as "that false, and flatulent, and foolish paper."

James Thomson Callender, an immigrant printer from Scotland whom Jefferson had befriended and who later turned against his benefactor, added to the furor by printing stories in 1802 in his *Richmond (Virginia) Recorder* that Jefferson had fathered five children by his slave Sally Hemings. There is no credible evidence that this was so. Callender was embittered because of a delay in repaying his fine under the Alien and Sedition Acts (1798–1801), refusal of money from Jefferson to start a new press, and denial of the postmastership in Richmond. Callender's motives became clear when he repeatedly taunted Jefferson, printing such statements as, "How stands the great accompt [*sic*] 'twixt me and vengeance? Much has been done, but much does still remain. And I will not forgive 1 SINGLE GROAN."

Such tirades momentarily shook Jefferson's confidence in a free press. He later advocated a few salutary state criminal libel actions on behalf of public figures, notably an action brought at common law in 1804 against Harry Croswell, editor of the *Wasp*, a satirical Federalist newspaper published in Hudson, New York. Croswell lost and an appeal failed, but his attorney Alexander Hamilton made a brilliant argument that truth be allowed as a defense in such cases.

Later, in 1809, Jefferson discouraged 17-year-old John Norvell, who had written him for advice, from going into journalism. The president wrote, "Nothing can now be believed which is seen in a newspaper. Truth itself becomes suspicious by being put into that polluted vehicle." The man who had drawn on John Locke and John Milton for his intellectual wellsprings seemed broken and despairing.

Yet in later life, with some distance between himself and the presidency, Jefferson recovered his equilibrium. Three years before his death in 1826 he wrote his old friend, the Marquis de Lafayette: "But the only security of all, is in a free press. The force of public opinion cannot be resisted, when permitted freely to be expressed. The agitation it produces must be submitted to. It is necessary, to keep the waters pure."

JERRY W. KNUDSON

See also Alien and Sedition Acts of 1798; First Amendment in the Eighteenth Century; Party Press

Further Reading

Knudson, Jerry W., "Political Journalism in the Age of Jefferson," *Journalism History* 1:1 (1974)

_____, "The Rage Around Tom Paine, Newspaper Reaction to His Homecoming in 1802," *New York Historical Society Quarterly* 53:1 (1969)

Levy, Leonard Williams, *Jefferson and Civil Liberties: The Darker Side,* Cambridge, Massachusetts: Belknap Press of Harvard University, 1963

Malone, Dumas, *Jefferson and His Time,* 6 vols., Boston: Little, Brown, 1948–1981

Mott, Frank L., *Jefferson and the Press,* Baton Rouge: Louisiana State University Press, 1943

Johnson, Lyndon B., and the Media

Changes in mass media substantially influenced his presidency

In 1971, when a CBS news team took a break in filming the televised memoirs of former President Lyndon B. Johnson, one of the producers casually asked the former president what had changed the most in his years in Washington, D.C. Johnson, who first went to Washington as a legislative assistant in 1931 and stayed until he left the White House in 1969, responded vigorously and forcefully, "All you guys in the media. All of politics has changed because of you." For Lyndon Johnson, the changes that occurred in the world of mass media during his lifetime also reflected the changes in the industry from print media to radio and to television.

Born on August 27, 1908, near Stonewall, Texas, Johnson's childhood and teenage years were spent in the rugged, rural, poor, and isolated section of central Texas known as the Hill Country. For years, the only means of information was the local weekly newspapers. As late as the early 1930s, radio made few, if any, inroads into the Hill Country. In Johnson's youth, the newspapers were the sole source of information from the world outside the Hill Country.

When Johnson's father served in the Texas State Legislature, Johnson watched in fascination at the world of politics and at the nearby reporters and lobbyists always mingling with the legislative members. Johnson's first introduction to the world of the media occurred in Austin during the second and third decades of the twentieth century. While in the capital city with his father, Johnson watched the reporters work at their craft and then learned how different newspapers covered the events of the day, ranging from sedition laws concerned with World War I to funding for state road construction.

When Johnson attended Southwest Texas State Teachers College (later Southwest Texas State University), he served first as an editorial writer for the student newspaper, the *College Star,* and later as editor during the summer of 1928. Johnson's college foray into journalism, however, was determined by economic necessity more than by the pursuit of journalism as a profession.

After college, Johnson initially worked as a school-teacher, but, through intermediaries, he became the congressional secretary to Texas congressman Richard Kleberg. While working for the congressman, Johnson rekindled his fascination with the influence of newspapers and radio. Kleberg left the administration of the office to his secretary, and, as a result, Johnson soon gained a close working relationship with the small-town newspaper publishers in south Texas. Some of them, like Sam Fore of the *Floresville Chronicle-Journal,* became supporters of Johnson throughout his political career. Furthermore, Johnson's roommate in his early days in Washington was Robert Jackson, who eventually became editor of the *Corpus Christi Caller-Times.*

In 1937, Johnson ran for Congress in the Tenth District of Texas. This special election attracted seven other candidates. Johnson campaigned that he alone was for "Roosevelt 100 percent" and spread this message through the district newspapers, dailies, and weeklies. Johnson did not rely on the newspaper alone. He also gave speeches on the radio in the larger cities in the district. Johnson soon earned the endorsement of the district's largest newspaper, in the district's largest town – Austin, the state capital. Johnson courted and won the affection of Charles E. Marsh, the owner of the Austin paper as well as other newspapers in Texas and across the southern United States.

Because of the amicable relationship between Johnson and Marsh and the favorable publicity that Johnson received from the Marsh-owned Austin papers, a pattern soon developed that repeated itself throughout Johnson's political career. Johnson developed the belief that those who owned the media outlets also controlled the thoughts and actions of their employees. Throughout his career, Johnson established contact with the owners or executives of newspapers, newsmagazines, and television and radio networks in an effort to court favorable press. To Johnson, a close friendship with the publisher or network executive enabled him a certain power and influence over reporters and correspondents.

In 1942, Johnson's wife, Claudia "Lady Bird" Johnson, purchased an Austin radio station that became the foundation for the family media and corporate empire, including the dominant Austin television station and other radio and television stations. Throughout his political career, the Johnson media properties flourished. When the Johnsons bought the radio station in Austin (and renamed it KTBC), Johnson arranged for his station's affiliation with the Columbia Broadcasting System (CBS) by personally going to New York and meeting with William S. Paley, president of CBS, and Frank Stanton, manager of CBS network affiliations and a future CBS president. In this manner, Johnson assured the success and profitability of his wife's radio station.

As a congressman and an owner of a government-regulated industry, Johnson took an active role in securing the success of the family media business. Ethically, Johnson's involvement in securing favorable rulings from the Federal Communications Commission (FCC) was questionable; however, no laws were broken. When questions arose about his role in securing favorable FCC treatment toward the family stations, Johnson always pleaded ignorance. He

President Lyndon B. Johnson, his dogs, and the press go for a walk.
(Cecil Stoughton, Lyndon B. Johnson Library Collection)

claimed that the stations were Lady Bird's property, and he knew nothing of their activities. When Johnson became president, he implemented an official hands-off approach to station management.

Typical of Johnson's style, he worked both ends of the media – management and reporter – to assure himself as much good press coverage as he could manage. While still a congressman, Johnson courted the favor of influential publishers from Texas cities outside his own congressional district. Conservative publishers Amon Carter of the *Fort Worth Star-Telegram,* the Dealy family of the *Dallas Morning News,* and William P. and Oveta Culp Hobby of the *Houston Post* were all impressed with the Texas congressman. Johnson worked hard for pet projects located in the districts of these and other publishers in his effort to court Texas newspaper endorsements. Houston Harte, co-owner of the Harte-Hanks chain of newspapers that served mid- and small-size Texas cities, recalled that Johnson "knew how to advise us as to what we should do" for our communities. Furthermore, Johnson sought out the Washington correspondents for Texas newspapers. Bascom Timmons,

Sarah McClendon, Leslie and Elizabeth Carpenter, and Allen Duckworth wrote about Texans in Washington. Johnson cultivated these correspondents. Although he was not always successful, he recognized that good relations with these corespondents enhanced his reputation with their editors and publishers and produced favorable publicity in the papers back home.

When Johnson entered the Senate, he went from representing a district with 10 counties to representing the entire state with 254 counties. Thus, he increased his courtship of Texas newspapers and other media outlets. Moreover, his Senate staff also became intimates of the correspondents in Washington as well as the newspaper staff back in Texas. Johnson increased his recognition back home by using radio and, later, television reports to his Texas constituents. In most years, these reports were sent to stations free of charge because a Johnson supporter picked up the cost of recording and production. In election years, when stations were reluctant to play the reports for fear of election violations, these reports became paid advertisements with local Johnson supporters covering the charges.

When Johnson became Senate majority leader, his press coverage increased. Johnson became more sensitive to press reports about himself, yet he still courted favor among the reporters and their superiors. One reporter described him as a "whiner." Like any politician, Johnson coveted favorable press that would draw a "smile and a comment." On the other hand, a critical report would put him in a bad mood for several days. When an article appeared in the *Saturday Evening Post* describing in complimentary tones the amount of work and pace that Johnson set for himself and his office, he was unhappy. Because the word "frantic" appeared in the title, Johnson saw the reference as an uncomplimentary description of himself and ignored the positive aspects of the article. George Reedy, a Johnson Senate aide and presidential press secretary, wrote that Johnson saw journalists as "critics not as purveyors of information." To Johnson, the press was an arena where politicians fought for good publicity rather than part of the "governing process." Johnson saw the press as either on his side (whatever the issue may have been) or on the opposing side, not as chroniclers of the current events in U.S. society.

When Johnson entered the White House following John F. Kennedy's assassination, he carried the hopes of the nation, including those of the media. Johnson's legislative program as well as his press relations prospered early in his White House tenure. His success in the legislative arena captured the imagination of the news media. The media, energized by his legislative prowess, praised Johnson's early actions as president. Johnson, though, believed that the office he held entitled him to favorable press. Furthermore, he believed his own solicitations toward the fourth estate should benefit his public image.

Johnson saw the media only in terms of good and bad. Scholars have argued that Johnson's purpose in providing new levels of access to the media included making reporters beholden to him. He rewarded favorable reports on his policies with direct attention or lavish praise but never realized that his extravagant praise made journalists bridle at his approach. A bad report often resulted in the president thinking it a personal attack, and such interpretations guided his behavior. Johnson attempted to cultivate the reporter, lodged threats at the reporter, or telephoned the news agency director and complained to the reporter's boss. If that failed, he froze the reporter out of any discussions and ignored any questions the reporter asked until a suitable time had elapsed or he had forgotten about the issue.

In his tenure in the White House, Johnson went through four presidential press secretaries. Pierre Salinger, who was Kennedy's press secretary, left in 1964. George Reedy, a longtime member of his staff, eventually retired due to a combination of health problems and Johnson's desire to replace him with Bill Moyers. Growing national disillusionment with domestic affairs and Vietnam marked Moyers' tenure. After 18 months on the job, Moyers left the position because of disenchantment with the job and with Johnson. George Christian was the final, and by most accounts, most successful of Johnson's press secretaries. Christian used his job to present presidential statements and opinions with accuracy and clarity. Part of his success stemmed from excess confidence in his abilities.

When his presidency began to sour over the failures in Vietnam, Johnson defined the negative press reports as a personal betrayal. With the phrase "credibility gap," the press introduced a new term to the national lexicon to describe the lack of faith people held in the president. First with the press and then with the general public, Johnson unwittingly developed a reputation for duplicity. Thus the press struggled to avoid what they termed "presidential manipulation" when Johnson sought the public dissemination of his views. James Reston recalled how Johnson "devoured newspapers every morning," checking to see if his views were getting coverage. Yet by the mid-1960s, Johnson feared that the members of the press had plotted against him and the goals of his administration. He believed that the media campaign against him relied on character assassination and the slander of his family.

Television for Johnson was a disaster. Whereas his predecessor appeared smooth, articulate, and handsome, television only made Johnson appear flat, unappealing, and, worst of all, unconvincing. All through his presidency, Johnson tried to master television, seeking help from people within the television and movie industries. But the man who could be so persuasive in small groups never mastered the medium. Network television news, which came of age simultaneously with Johnson's presidency, brought the Vietnam war home to the living rooms of the United States. The daily reporting of the death, destruction, and misery in a far away country succeeded in turning citizens against the war. When Walter Cronkite, the most trusted television anchorman of the decade, reported that the war had reached a stalemate, Johnson reflected that, without Cronkite, he had no hope of retaining support from average citizens for continuation of the war.

Further complicating his presidency was the appearance of an increasingly adversarial press that used more aggressive tactics in ferreting out stories. A veteran White House reporter affirmed the adversarial relationship in reporting on the president. "A reporter must go in there every day with the attitude that I am going to knock on doors and keep knocking on doors until somebody opens the door and lets me know what is going on in there." This approach to news gathering, new in its intensity, conflicted directly with Johnson's view of reporters.

Johnson's relationship with the media throughout his political career was moderately successful until he entered the national spotlight. President Johnson's skill in legislation did not transfer to successful manipulation of the media. One media critic described the Johnson presidency as fighting two wars, in Vietnam and against the press. Yet scholars recognize that Johnson and the media also found occasion to cooperate as each sought control over the journalist's end product. Other critics of Johnson and the media are more harsh, arguing that Johnson in the White House used the worst traits he had developed in his previous political career, which resulted in the tumultuous battles with the media that marked his presidency. Johnson's lack of media success resulted from his lack of understanding of what a free press is all about. When he entered the White House, press scrutiny only intensified his lack of understanding. Coupled with unpopular administration policies, particularly the war in Vietnam, the increase of television coverage, and a new style of journalism, the Johnson presidency had a failed relationship with the media.

MARK E. YOUNG

See also Credibility Gap; Kennedy Assassination and the Media; Kennedy, John F., and the Media; Mass Media and the Antiwar Movement; Vietnam War

Further Reading

Bell, Jack, *The Johnson Treatment: How Lyndon B. Johnson Took Over the Presidency and Made It His Own,* New York: Harper & Row, 1965

Cormier, Frank, *LBJ the Way He Was,* Garden City, New York: Doubleday, 1977

Dallek, Robert, *Lone Star Rising: Lyndon Johnson and His Times, 1908–1960,* New York: Oxford University Press, 1991

Halberstam, David, *The Powers That Be,* New York: Knopf, 1979; London: Chatto and Windus, 1979

Purvis, Hoyt, ed., *The Presidency and the Press,* Austin: University of Texas, Lyndon B. Johnson School of Public Affairs, 1976

Reedy, George, *Lyndon B. Johnson, a Memoir,* New York: Andrews and McMeel, 1982

Reston, James, *Deadline: A Memoir,* New York: Random House, 1991

Turner, Kathleen J., *Lyndon Johnson's Dual War: Vietnam and the Press,* Chicago: University of Chicago Press, 1985

Joint Operating Agreements: *see*
Newspaper Preservation Act

Journalism Education

Robert E. Lee instrumental in starting college curriculum

Beginning as instruction in printing in 1869, journalism education by the late twentieth century prepared thousands of students for careers in mass communications. Robert E. Lee, president of Washington College (later Washington and Lee University), recommended a program to train young men in printing and journalism in 1868. It opened in 1869 with six students but was dropped in 1878. Printing instruction began at Kansas State in 1873, and the University of Missouri listed courses in the history and materials of journalism between 1878 and 1884. Cornell University offered journalism courses through its English department from 1888 to 1890. The nation's first organized curriculum in journalism was offered at the University of Pennsylvania between 1893 and 1901. Other universities offering journalism courses before 1900 were those of Indiana, Iowa, Kansas, Michigan, Nebraska, and Ohio State.

Joseph Pulitzer offered to fund an undergraduate school of journalism at Columbia University in 1892 but was rejected. When Pulitzer offered $2 million in 1903, Columbia accepted, and the Pulitzer School of Journalism opened there in 1912. The University of Missouri established the first autonomous "School of Journalism" in 1908. Its genesis was a 1896 Missouri Press Association resolution to establish a university program to train journalists for the state's newspapers. A chair of journalism was established in 1898, and in 1908, the state legislature appropriated funds to construct the school.

The Missouri and Columbia programs became models for future curriculum development, but they differed in philosophy and objectives. Columbia emphasized the intellectual development of a journalist, while Missouri stressed occupational training.

The University of Illinois combined journalism classes offered since 1901 into a four-year program in 1904. At Wisconsin, Willard Bleyer started teaching journalism classes in 1904, then organized them into a two-year curriculum in 1906. Bleyer believed students should study journalism's role in society, and he placed liberal arts education foremost in a journalist's training.

Most journalism academic associations began before 1920. In 1909, Sigma Delta Chi, later the Society of Professional Journalists, began for male students at DePauw University in Indiana, and Theta Sigma Phi, later called Women in Communication, opened for females at the University of Washington. Kappa Tau Alpha, a national honorary fraternity, started in 1910 at the University of Missouri. Teachers organized the American Association of Teachers of Journalism (AATJ) in 1912 in Chicago. It reorganized as the Association for Education in Journalism (AEJ) in 1950, and again in 1982 as the Association for Education in Journalism and Mass Communication.

Ten journalism program administrators created the American Association of Schools and Departments of Journalism (AASDJ) in 1917. Member programs were known as Class A schools, implying that others were inferior. Its capricious application of membership criteria drew criticism from those who were excluded. The AASDJ disproportionately favored programs at the large, public institutions in the midwest and west. In 1923, it rejected the application of the Baylor College for Women's school of journalism, the first at a women's college. When West Virginia University's school of journalism was rejected, its director, Perley Reed, founded the American Society of Journalism School Administrators in 1944. The two rivals merged in 1984 as the Association of Schools of Journalism and Mass Communication.

A 1912 report to the AATJ identified 31 colleges offering instruction in journalism, including three professional schools (Columbia, Marquette, and Missouri) and seven departments (Iowa State, Kansas, Kansas State, Notre Dame, Oregon, Washington, and Wisconsin). By 1930, more than 300 colleges offered journalism courses, with 56 programs recognized as separate departments or schools.

The credibility of journalism education has been questioned by academics and media professionals. Unlike law or medical schools, journalism programs are criticized by a profession that values actual newsroom experience above college-based training. In response, programs began in the 1930s to stress occupational training for undergraduate students. Accreditation of journalism programs began in 1939 with the National Council on Professional Education for Journalism. The council was renamed the American Council on Education for Journalism in 1945. In 1982, it added Mass Communication to its name. Accreditation was intended to promote quality journalism education, but it also encouraged curriculum development that reinforced, rather than challenged, professional journalism.

In response to academics who criticized journalism as too technical, programs emphasized their interdisciplinary nature and initiated research-based graduate programs in the 1930s. Willard Bleyer organized a doctoral program in political science, with a double minor in journalism, at Wisconsin in the 1920s. The first doctorate in journalism was awarded by Missouri in 1934. By the late 1940s, there were other doctoral programs at Wisconsin, Illinois, Iowa, and Minnesota. The field's oldest research journal, *Journalism Quarterly*, dated to 1921, but it was not until 1930 that it emphasized research.

Beginning in the 1960s, enrollment growth; expansion to include broadcasting, advertising, and public relations; and affirmative action altered the predominantly white, male, middle-class composition of journalism education. Women had been present from the early years, but in small numbers. The 1916 AATJ directory listed four female faculty members. In the 1920s, Helen O. Mahin headed journalism programs at Mercer University and Wesleyan College in Georgia, and Helen Zene Wortman organized the program at Baylor College for Women. In 1946, Helen Hostetter became the first female full professor of journalism at a major university, Kansas State.

As enrollments swelled from 11,000 in 1960 to more than 140,000 by 1990, women supplanted men as the majority of journalism undergraduates. The number of female faculty also grew along with increases in graduate student enrollments in the 1970s. In 1974, only 8.4 percent of journalism and mass communication doctoral students were women. By 1986, 44 percent were women. Recruitment of minorities was less successful. In 1968, the AEJ initiated a program to attract minorities. The percentage of minority students majoring in journalism, however, remained low into the 1990s.

As universities faced shrinking resources in the 1990s, some programs reduced enrollments when faculty positions were eliminated. Other programs merged with speech communication departments to consolidate resources, and some even faced extinction. Existing programs strove to keep pace with rapid advances in communication technology.

JOSEPH P. MCKERNS

Further Reading

Asher, Brad, "The Professional Vision: Conflicts over Journalism Education, 1900–1955," *American Journalism* 11 (1994)

Emery, Edwin, and Joseph P. McKerns, "AEJMC: 75 Years in the Making: A History of Organizing for Journalism and Mass Communication in the United States," *Journalism Monographs* 104 (1987)

Hochberger, Simon, "Fifty Years of Journalism Education," *Journalism Educator* 35 (1958)

Lasswell, Harold D., "Communications as an Emerging Discipline," *Audio-Visual Communication Review* 6 (1958)

O'Dell, De Forest, *The History of Journalism Education in the United States*, New York: Teachers College, Columbia University, 1935

Sloan, W. David, ed., *Makers of the Media Mind: Journalism Educators and Their Ideas*, Hillsdale, New Jersey: Lawrence Erlbaum, 1990

Sutton, Albert Alton, *Education for Journalism in the United States from Its Beginning to 1940*, Evanston, Illinois: Northwestern University, 1945

Journalism History

Developing a way to analyze historical work

When Isaiah Thomas published *The History of Printing in America* in 1810, he initiated an enduring form of study. If book sales and popular articles in the late twentieth century were any indication, history held more interest than any other area of the mass media except, perhaps, entertainment.

The writing of journalism history has gone through several periods and perspectives. The most conspicuous are the nationalist, romantic, developmental, progressive, consensus, and cultural schools.

The earliest writing, including Thomas' seminal history, was done by nationalist historians of the early nineteenth century. They believed that the story of journalism history was the progress of freedom within an overall story of the developing liberty of the people of the United States.

The romantic historians shared the view of history as the story of the progress of liberty, civilization, and, especially, the United States. However, whereas nationalist historians told journalism history within the bigger picture of U.S. history, romantic historians usually placed their studies within the framework of narrative biographies. The premier romantic historian was James Parton, author of such works as *Life of Horace Greeley* (1855) and *Life and Times of Benjamin Franklin* (1864).

In the 1870s, history began to be taught in universities, ushering in the period of the professional historian. The increased emphasis on history resulted in the appearance of several publications, such as the *Magazine of American History*, devoted exclusively to the field. Yet a change had taken place in journalism even before then, and it was to alter the study of history. In 1833, Benjamin Day had begun publication of the *New York Sun*, the first successful "penny" newspaper. Many people came to think of the popular newspapers that followed as representing the proper sort of journalism. Some journalists began to think of history as the story of how journalism had originated and progressed to reach the successful, proper stage that the penny press had inaugurated.

The first and, in many ways, most important of these developmental historians was Frederic Hudson, author of

Journalism in the United States (1873), which covered the period from 1690 to 1872. Many historians since Hudson have drawn on his interpretation. With his news-oriented background, he viewed the history of journalism as the origin and evolution of journalistic techniques. He emphasized episodes and journalists that had contributed to progress.

As the field of journalism expanded in the late 1800s, historical studies increased in number. They largely echoed Hudson's themes. In the twentieth century, historians, most of whom had a background in the profession, began to apply the concept of professional development even more widely, and the developmental interpretation pervaded most historical studies. It has accounted for approximately half of all works.

In the early 1900s, the appearance of journalism education at the college level led not only to greater reliance on the developmental interpretation but to a surge in publishing. Most professor-historians approached history with the perspective of professional journalism. With early textbooks such as Willard Bleyer's *Main Currents in the History of American Journalism* (1927), the developmental interpretation became entrenched. In the 1940s, Frank Luther Mott's *American Journalism* continued the developmental influence.

After World War II, many developmental historians – influenced by such episodes as the civil rights movement, the Vietnam war, and the Watergate political scandal – viewed history as a clash between the press and institutions such as government and big business. Thus, the later developmental historians emphasized such historical topics as press freedom in which the press confronted other units of society. The devotion of the press, they argued, should be to journalistic ideals rather than to a nation.

The rise of journalism education resulted in one other fundamental change. In 1924, the American Association of Teachers of Journalism (later renamed the Association for Education in Journalism and Mass Communication) began publishing *Journalism Bulletin* (later *Journalism and Mass Communication Quarterly*). It was the first journal to provide a specific outlet for works devoted to journalism history, and it therefore encouraged a number of professors to do historical study. In 1974, *Journalism History* began publication. It was followed in 1983 by a second history journal, *American Journalism*.

Next to the developmental interpretation, the progressive school has been most important. Beginning in the early 1900s, reform-oriented historians began to view the past in terms of conflict between social classes. They told history as the story of a struggle in which journalists were pitted on the side of freedom, reform, democracy, and equality against the powerful forces of wealth, class, and conservatism. They believed that the press should crusade for liberal causes and fight on the side of the masses against entrenched interests. The progressive approach continued to influence writing at the end of the century.

The progressives' emphasis on class differences and economic motivations was challenged by consensus historians beginning in the late 1930s. They argued that even though the people of the United States historically may have disagreed on isolated issues, their differences took place within a broader agreement on underlying principles. They also assumed that the nation as a whole was more important than a single institution, the press. They therefore favored journalistic philosophies that worked for the good of the nation.

Beginning in the 1930s, cultural historians, like consensus historians, looked at the press as an integral part of society and were therefore influenced by it. They were concerned with how such forces as economics, technology, and culture acted on the press. The most prolific cultural historian was Sidney Kobre, who attempted to explain journalism as a product of environment.

In 1974, James Carey proposed that history be approached from a "symbolic-meaning" perspective, and a number of theory-oriented historians attempted to apply the concept. Carey argued that mass communication plays an essential part in people's understanding of the world about them. Historians, he said, should be concerned about what communication means to the audience.

At the same time that some historians took the philosophical approach that Carey encouraged, others emphasized the need for rigorous research along the lines of traditional historical scholarship. They encouraged historians to avoid ideology and broad philosophy and instead to search for explanations of history through attention to historically accurate sources and the broad context of the society within which journalism was operating.

WM. DAVID SLOAN

Further Reading

Emery, Michael, "The Writing of American Journalism History," *Journalism History* 10 (1983)
Nevins, Allan, "American Journalism and Its Historical Treatment," *Journalism Quarterly* 36 (1959)
Schwarzlose, Richard A., *Newspapers, a Reference Guide*, New York: Greenwood, 1987
Sloan, W. David, *Perspectives on Mass Communication History*, Hillsdale, New Jersey: Lawrence Erlbaum, 1991

Journalism Professional Organizations

While there were a number of professional organizations in the newspaper field in the late twentieth century, one of the longest standing was the Society of Professional Journalists (SPJ). Founded in 1909, the organization in the late 1990s included 13,500 members in 300 chapters throughout the country. In 1974, it became known as the Society of Professional Journalists/Sigma Delta Chi; in 1988, it became simply the Society of Professional Journalists.

The organization was dedicated to the promotion of a free and unfettered press, high professional standards and ethical behavior, and journalism as a career. The SPJ conducted lobbying activities and maintained a legal defense fund. It sponsored Barney Kilgore Freedom of Information Internships in Washington, D.C., and offered distinguished service awards in journalism, distinguished teaching in journalism awards, and outstanding graduate student citations, among others. The SPJ published *The Quill;* a magazine, *SPJ Leader;* and *SPJ Freedom of Information Report. Talent, Truth and Energy* was a history of the society.

Another well-known and long-standing professional organization, Women in Communications, Inc. (WICI), was also founded in 1909, in part because Sigma Delta Chi was established as a male-only organization. Both organizations later admitted men and women. WICI had 12,000 members in the 1990s and was dedicated to the various interests of women in communication. Before 1972, the organization was known as Theta Sigma Phi. The organization offered a placement service for its members as well as an annual recognition for excellence in the promotion of female communicators. The Vanguard Award was offered to those companies exhibiting positive action in the hiring and promotion of women to positions of equality in communication fields. WICI also published several periodicals, including *Careers in Communications* and the *Professional Communicator.*

ROBIN GALLAGHER

Journalism Reviews

Periodicals devoted to criticism of the news media

Journalism reviews generally are periodicals devoted primarily to the criticism of news media. This uniquely American phenomenon experienced a golden age between 1968, at the apex of the protest movement, and 1975, after the U.S. withdrawal from Vietnam and the Watergate and oil crises. Journalism reviews, however, existed before and after those years.

From 1940 to 1950, veteran newsman George Seldes put out *In Fact,* the first review to pick as its only target the sins of the press. The biweekly established a circulation record for journalism reviews – 176,000 copies, distributed with the help of the Congress of Industrial Organizations. And, with one exception, it was the longest-lived of the journalism reviews made by working journalists.

The first campus-based journalism review appeared when the School of Journalism at Columbia University launched the *Columbia Journalism Review* in 1961. It was preceded in 1947 by *Nieman Reports,* a critical review put out five times a year by newspeople enjoying a fellowship at Harvard University.

Local journalism reviews developed by reporters were based in their discontent with press operations. One triggering event was police violence against the press during the 1968 Democratic Convention in Chicago, which journalists contended had been distorted in local media. In response, journalists started the *Chicago Journalism Review.*

Over the next five years, 25 such publications were launched. Eight of the nation's 10 largest cities had reviews, as did half the states. They were national (*Washington [D.C.] Journalism Review*), local (*Philadelphia Journalism Review*), militant (the *Unsatisfied Man,* in Denver, Colorado, 1970–75), and commercial (*[MORE]* in New York, 1971–78).

They were produced by newspeople (*Hawaii Journalism Review*), journalism students (*feed/back* at San Francisco State University), minorities (*Ball and Chain Review,* by African Americans), women (*Media Report to Women,* 1972), outsiders (*Media and Consumer* by the Consumers Union) – or even by a single individual (*Overset*).

Some looked like magazines (especially *[MORE]* in 1976–78), others like newsletters (e.g., the mimeographed *AP Review*). Some were slick, others amateurish. Most were autonomous; some, like the one-shot *Atlanta (Georgia) Journalism Review,* were inserted into other publications. Most were full-time journalism reviews, a few only part-time (like Roldo Bartimole's *Point of View* in Cleveland, Ohio, 1968). A few journalism reviews went on the air, from *CBS Meets the Press* on radio in the post–World War II period to *On the Media,* a weekly call-in program produced in 1995 by WNYC, a public radio station in New York.

Contents ranged from documented denunciations of particular misdeeds, discussion of general media issues, publication of "censored" material, news of interest to professionals, profiles of practitioners and organs, brief items of praise or blame, and, for comic relief, lists of typos and goofs. Themes included the dissatisfaction of newspeople; the mediocrity of the news; the conservatism and greed of media barons; clashes between the press and government, police, or the courts; and sexism and racism in the news and newsrooms.

A journalism review was a watchdog, of course, but it also served as a consciousness raiser and a forum. Many reviews organized get-togethers, from dinner parties to the famous Liebling Conventions called by *[MORE]* from 1972 to 1976.

The average life span of journalism reviews between 1968 and 1975 was less than 18 months. Only a third of them endured for more than 10 issues. Some, like *Inside Media* (1970), were only able to put out one issue.

Journalism reviews received little or no support from press-related institutions such as press clubs, professional associations, unions (although the Newspaper Guild provided protection), foundations, journalism schools, or the Association for Education in Journalism. Journalism reviews faced the hostility of most publishers and editors – and, curiously, that of many reporters. More importantly, local journalism reviews lacked enough muck to rake and had small potential audiences. Moreover, they had to decide whether to function as anti–house organs or as critical newsletters for a wider public.

Besides, most reviews suffered from major flaws. Campus journalism reviews (like the annual *Pretentious Idea* in Tucson, Arizona) were scorned by the profession as being out of touch with journalistic reality. Reporter-based journalism reviews were said to lack a philosophical undergirding; they criticized, but without a vision. They were said to be superficial, blinkered, and myopic. They tended to accuse all but journalists and to ignore media other than newspapers.

Since the reviews could not pay for material, rhetoric, gossip, and vendettas often replaced serious reporting. Actually, considering the circumstances, many journalism reviews were strikingly good. Because a journalism review was a labor of love by a few, however, it died when their enthusiasm burnt out.

Journalism reviews probably were indicators rather than factors of change. Their function was taken over partly by professional reviews (e.g., the *ASNE Bulletin,* the Society of Professional Journalists' *Quill*) and by the regular media. Journalism reviews made media criticism respectable – to the extent that it was granted a Pulitzer Prize for the first time in 1991.

In the two decades after 1975, more than fifteen print journalism reviews appeared. In 1995, 20 or so survived. These included the nonpartisan reviews, like *Forbes Media Guide;* the college campus-based *Columbia Journalism Review* and *American Journalism Review;* and the only local journalism review in the tradition of the 1960s, the *St. Louis (Missouri) Journalism Review.* Other survivors in the late 1990s included more partisan journalism reviews such as mainly right-wing watchdogs (like *Media Monitor,* 1986, or *Media Watch,* 1987), which imitated the bimonthly *AIM Report* published from 1972 by Accuracy in Media. On the left wing, FAIR started *Extra* in 1986. Journalism reviews started using the new technology, including cable (like *Paper Tiger TV,* started in 1987 on a New York public access channel) and the Internet (*BONG!* [1988] was delivered by electronic mail).

In the media boom of the 1990s, journalism review seemed a necessary part of the informal network of non-governmental "media accountability systems" needed to preserve the public interest – including newspaper ombudsmen, media reporters, consumer associations, and press councils.

CLAUDE-JEAN BERTRAND

See also Accuracy in Media; Mass Media and Self-Regulation; Ombudsman

Further Reading

Bertrand, Claude-Jean, "A Look at Journalism Reviews," *Freedom of Information Center Report 0019* (September 1978)
Block, Eleanor S., "A Survey of Media Criticism: National Rather than Local Reviews," *St. Louis Journalism Review* 22:158 (July 1993), p. 14

Journalistic Interview

Journalistic technique developed in the late nineteenth century

The term "journalistic interview" refers to a social interaction between a person of public interest, or a person with information relevant to a topic of public interest, and a professional writer who gathers information from that person. It refers equally to the literary product of such an interaction. The term "interview" was widely used in the nineteenth century, much more broadly, to refer to any kind of meeting and conversation between two people. It took on its more precise meaning in the late nineteenth century as interviewing came to be common journalistic practice.

Reporters in the late twentieth century relied overwhelmingly on interviews in their news gathering, but this was not always so. In U.S. journalism, historians trace the first newspaper interview variously to James Gordon Bennett (in the *New York Herald* in 1836) or to Horace Greeley (in the *New York Tribune* in 1859) or to Cincinnati, Ohio, journalist Joseph McCullagh soon after the Civil War. Whoever the first interviewer was, it is clear that in the antebellum years, reporters talked with public officials but did not refer to these conversations in print. Politicians and diplomats dropped by the newspaper offices but could feel secure, as one reporter recalled, that their confidences "were regarded as inviolate." President Lincoln often spoke with reporters informally, but no reporter ever quoted him directly.

After the Civil War, interviewing became much more widely practiced; by 1871, a *New York World* correspondent referred to the interview as "this modern and American Inquisition." European observers also recognized that the practice of interviewing was a distinctly U.S. invention. It was at first regarded as rather unsavory. *Nation* editor E.L. Godkin in 1869 called it "the joint production of some humbug of a hack politician and another humbug of a newspaper reporter." But the idea "took like wildfire," wrote Atlanta, Georgia, reporter Henry Grady in 1879.

After 1900, English journalists also began to accept the interview, often through the tutelage of U.S. correspondents, who, by their example, taught Europeans that their own elites would submit to interviews. This education was accelerated during World War I. One U.S. reporter recalled that his assignment to interview European heads of state in 1909 seemed "ridiculous and impossible" (and he failed at it) but that 20 years later it was easy, the interview no longer "a shocking innovation to the rulers of Europe." Interviewing was regarded early on as the basis for feature articles; the integration of direct quotation into straight news stories did not become common practice in the United States until the 1920s.

In the late nineteenth century and into the twentieth century, leading journalists counseled against note taking, and journalists were encouraged to rely upon their own memories. By the 1920s, however, journalism textbooks dared to recommend "the discriminate and intelligent use of notes." The growing acceptance of note taking suggests the acceptance and naturalization of interviewing. This is not to say that the interview was no longer controversial. Questions about the authenticity of news from interviews continued to crop up. Journalists' memoirs make clear that there was good reason for skepticism; reporters frequently protected their subjects from exposure by advising them that certain statements would make them look bad and urging them to retract them. There was still a sense that an interview was a contrived event in which the journalist, in collusion with a person seeking publicity, invented rather than reported news. The Associated Press prohibited its reporters from writing interviews as late as 1926.

"MACK" INTERVIEWING ANDREW JOHNSON.

Interviewing presidents has long been a tradition for reporters, as a journalist here talks to President Andrew Johnson.
(Davis Library, University of North Carolina at Chapel Hill)

Interviews also were attacked as invasions of privacy; the distinguished U.S. editor Henry Watterson complained in 1908 of importunate interviewers at railway stations and hotel lobbies who gave "an added terror to modern travel." The English writer G.K. Chesterton reported in 1922 that even before his ship touched land in New York, interviewers had "boarded the ship like pirates."

By the late twentieth century, interviewing had become a well-established journalistic practice in both print and broadcasting. The live broadcast interview became a familiar cultural form internationally and one that operated by strict rules. A broadcast interview is not at all like normal conversation. The interviewer's utterances are almost all questions, while what linguists call continuers – "mm-hm" or "yes" or "I see" – are frequent in ordinary conversation but almost entirely absent in broadcast interviews. This absence serves two purposes. First, it helps establish that the news audience, rather than the interviewer, is the audience for the interviewee's talk. Second, it helps the interviewer adhere to a visibly neutral stance. Whether by law, as in Great Britain, or by journalistic custom, as in the United States, the interviewer is required to display a scrupulous neutrality toward the interviewee and to stick to the role of mediator through whom important public figures can relay their opinions to a general audience.

Interviewing continued to raise uncomfortable issues of whether an interviewer makes news or reports it. In the 1980s and 1990s, particular styles of questioning – as whether Dan Rather of CBS News overstepped his legitimate neutral role in asking vice president and presidential candidate George Bush about the Iran-contra affair in 1988 – became controversial. So did particular questions – for example, should Paul Taylor of the *Washington Post* have asked presidential candidate Gary Hart whether he had ever committed adultery, or did this violate unspoken rules separating private from public behavior? Familiar as interviewing was in the late twentieth century, it had not altogether lost its aura of transgression.

MICHAEL SCHUDSON

Further Reading

Clayman, Steven, David Greatbatch, and John Heritage, *The News Interview: Studies in the History and Dynamics of a Social Form,* Beverly Hills, California: Sage, forthcoming

Schudson, Michael, *The Power of News,* Cambridge, Massachusetts: Harvard University Press, 1995; London: Harvard University Press, 1996

Journalists' Privilege

Efforts to protect the confidentiality of sources

Legal battles in the United States over confidentiality of journalists' sources go back at least to 1848, when a *New York Herald* reporter refused to tell a U.S. Senate committee how he obtained a copy of a proposed treaty under Senate consideration in executive session. The reporter was jailed briefly for contempt of Congress. Several similar nineteenth-century cases stemmed from refusals to testify before Congress; seven state cases dealt with journalists' confidentiality as well. An 1886 Maryland case led 10 years later to the passage of the first state "shield" law, granting journalists a statutory right to refuse to testify about the identity of confidential sources.

New Jersey passed the second shield statute in 1933, and eight other states had followed suit by 1950. By the mid-1990s, slightly more than half the states and the District of Columbia had enacted versions of these laws. Efforts to pass a federal shield law went back to 1929 but had not succeeded by the late 1990s. Some state shield laws protected both the identity of confidential sources and the information obtained by promising confidentiality. However, they varied considerably in qualifying the circumstances under which journalists were privileged to withhold testimony.

Supporters of legal protection for journalistic confidentiality have drawn parallels to the societal benefit rationale underlying similar evidentiary privileges for doctor-patient, lawyer-client, clergy-congregant, and spousal relationships. They argue that the benefits of preserving confidential journalist-source relationships outweigh the loss of evidence that would otherwise be available because of all citizens' normal duty to testify. Journalists, however, were largely unsuccessful through the early 1970s in persuading judges to grant an exception to the general duty to provide evidence, in the absence of specific shield laws.

Starting in 1958, journalists also argued for judicial recognition of First Amendment protection for their confidential sources. *Garland* v. *Torre* (1958), the first reported case where this claim was asserted, was a civil proceeding in which the claim was denied because the information was deemed essential to the plaintiff's case. In *Torre,* as in most journalistic confidentiality cases, the news medium was not directly involved. Rather, the journalist was asked the identity of sources who might be useful witnesses but who had provided information under a promise that their identities would not be revealed.

The first Supreme Court consideration of First Amendment protection for confidentiality came in *Branzburg* v. *Hayes* (1972). Although the Court ruled 5–4 that reporters could not assert First Amendment rights to protect confidential material before grand juries, it was a dissent by Justice Potter Stewart that had the greatest impact on subsequent cases. Stewart, who had written the Torre opinion while still on the Circuit Court of Appeals, said that the First Amendment should protect confidential journalist-source relationships unless a three-part test were met by the party seeking disclosure. Stewart's qualified First Amendment protection would compel disclosure only if it were clearly established that the information sought was relevant to the proceeding; that no alternative sources less damaging to First Amendment rights were available; and that there was a compelling need for disclosure that outweighed First Amendment values.

Because the fifth and concurring vote in *Branzburg* indicated that under other circumstances First Amendment protection might well be granted, Stewart's dissent has been followed by many lower courts. This has been true especially in civil cases, starting with *Baker* v. *F&F Investment* (1972). The Supreme Court declined to review this case, thus giving tacit approval to the use of Stewart's dissenting test as a precedent. Later, in occasional criminal proceedings, courts applied Stewart's test to protect journalist-source confidentiality. Libel cases against the media, though, usually have produced far less protection for journalists' confidential sources than in proceedings in which journalists are third parties.

The only other Supreme Court case involving journalists' privilege as of the late 1990s was *Cohen* v. *Cowles Media* (1991). Here, the Court held that an editor's decision – on the grounds of newsworthiness – to identify a source despite reporters' pledges of confidentiality breached an oral contract between reporters and the source. The 5–4 decision sent the case back to the Minnesota courts, where the plaintiff was eventually awarded $200,000. The majority opinion largely ignored First Amendment issues and left state law to determine whether broken promises of confidentiality merited monetary damages.

Journalistic confidentiality has also been protected in other ways, especially since the *Branzburg* decision. Some states recognized a qualified privilege based on their own constitution, and more than a dozen others approved limited common-law privileges, as did a few federal courts.

Arguments favoring protection of journalists' confidential sources and information center on the need to promise confidentiality in order to obtain information that is important or interesting to the public. Privilege proponents also have argued that in many cases, the confidential material could be obtained by other means during legal proceedings or that it was not needed to ensure due process of law.

Opponents of journalists' confidentiality stress the need for every person's evidence to assure due process, the need to treat journalists like other citizens, and the possibilities of abusing such protection. Some supporters of confidentiality have argued against the statutory approach, on the grounds that what a legislature confers, it can also take away, and that exceptions written into shield laws can erode any real protection.

Courts sometimes have ruled against journalists' privilege claims even when a state shield law exists. For example, this happened three times between 1943 and 1964 and again in 1978 in New Jersey. A 1970s study indicated that more journalists had been jailed for refusing to testify in states with shield laws than in states without them.

Protecting confidential sources is an ethical as well as a legal issue for journalists, and in only a handful of situations have journalists broken promises of confidentiality, even when faced with jail terms for contempt of court. On the other side of the ethics coin is the concern that some journalists may be promising confidentiality when that step is inappropriate or unnecessary, thus setting up needless opportunities for conflict between journalists and the courts.

DAVID GORDON

Further Reading

Allen, David Stanley, *Professionalization and the Narrative of Shield Laws: Defining Journalism and the Public Sphere* (Ph.D. diss., University of Minnesota), 1992

Dennis, Everette E., "Stolen Peace Treaties and the Press: Two Case Studies," *Journalism History* 2 (1975)

Gordon, Aaron David, "The 1896 Maryland Shield Law," *Journalism Monographs* 22 (February 1972)

_____, *Protection of News Sources: The History and Legal Status of the Newsman's Privilege* (Ph.D. diss., University of Wisconsin), 1971

Kaminski, Thomas H., "Congress, Correspondents and Confidentiality in the 19th Century: A Preliminary Study," *Journalism History* 4:3 (1977)

Van Gerpen, Maurice, *Privileged Communication and the Press: The Citizen's Right to Know Versus the Law's Right to Confidential News Source Evidence*, Westport, Connecticut: Greenwood, 1979

K

Kaltenborn, H.V.

Prominent radio commentator

In the midst of a long newspaper career, H.V. Kaltenborn in 1922 began delivering daily radio editorials over station WEAF in New York City. He was one of the first persons to broadcast news and commentary to U.S. listening audiences. Kaltenborn joined CBS in 1929 and switched to NBC in 1940, where he remained until his retirement. His crisp, incisive words brought him a large, faithful audience. His news and commentary every weekday evening drew millions of loyal listeners. Presidents and world leaders granted him special interviews.

Born in Milwaukee, Wisconsin, in 1878, he lived most of his younger years in Merrill, Wisconsin. Kaltenborn joined the Brooklyn Daily Eagle staff in 1902 and worked as an editor and reporter there for most of 28 years, with time out to earn a degree at Harvard University. Once he began broadcasting, he was both newspaper journalist and radio personality for eight years. In 1930, he switched to broadcasting only.

He was most popular during World War II, when audiences at home listened eagerly to his reports about action at overseas battlefronts. Election night in 1948 provided perhaps his most famous moment, when he predicted erroneously throughout the evening that late vote counts would give Thomas Dewey a victory over Harry S. Truman. The president took his good-natured revenge a few months later, when he mimicked Kaltenborn's election-night commentary as the audience at a Democratic banquet roared its approval. Kaltenborn died in 1965.

Louis W. Liebovich

See also Radio Commentators

Further Reading

Culbert, David Holbrook, *News for Everyman: Radio and Foreign Affairs in Thirties America,* Westport, Connecticut: Greenwood, 1976

Kaltenborn, H.V., *Fifty Fabulous Years, 1900–1950,* New York: Putnam's, 1950

_____, *It Seems Like Yesterday,* New York: Putnam's, 1956

KDKA

Pioneer radio station

To most scholars, KDKA in Pittsburgh, Pennsylvania, the first to broadcast with a federal license as more than an experimental station, was the first radio station in the United States. It debuted on November 2, 1920, election night, from a shack on the roof of a Westinghouse building in East Pittsburgh.

The inspiration for KDKA came from Westinghouse researcher Frank Conrad and vice president Harry P. Davis. Davis became interested in September 1920, when a newspaper advertisement mentioned the amateur experimental broadcasts Conrad had been making from his garage. The ad indicated a potential market for broadcasting and the fully assembled radio sets Westinghouse was developing.

At Davis's request, Conrad built a transmitter in the rooftop shack. KDKA broadcast most of the evening, reporting election news telephoned in by the *Pittsburgh Post* and playing music from a hand-wound phonograph. Conrad was not present; he stayed in his garage, ready to broadcast from his experimental station if KDKA failed. It did not.

Nightly broadcasts, chiefly of music, ensued. At first, KDKA was on the air from 8:30 to 9:30 P.M., but it soon expanded its schedule. Westinghouse boosted the station's power, and with no competition for the airwaves except for amateur radio buffs, KDKA could be picked up as far away as Illinois and Washington, D.C.

At least three other stations began regular experimental broadcasts before KDKA. They were KQW in San Jose, California (later KCBS in San Francisco); WHA, Madison, Wisconsin; and WWJ, Detroit, Michigan. KDKA, however, was the first to go beyond experimental status.

Thomas Letts

See also Conrad, Frank; Radio Technology

Further Reading

Douglas, George H., *The Early Days of Radio Broadcasting,* Jefferson, North Carolina: McFarland, 1987

Kennedy, John F., and the Media

Television played a key part in Kennedy's presidential administration

The relationship between television and the U.S. presidency reached a new level in the presidency of John Fitzgerald Kennedy. The thirty-fifth president of the United States was young, good-looking, dynamic, energetic, and most of all, photogenic. He had the physical qualities necessary to maximize results from the close scrutiny of television cameras. His physical qualities notwithstanding, his Harvard education, quick wit, and willingness to engage the press made him uniquely qualified to become the first president to use television to educate the public and pass along public affairs information.

Kennedy was the first president to allow live televised press conferences. Many factors contributed to this decision. The president felt it was his responsibility to educate the public and keep it informed; live broadcasts of press conferences were the best way to ensure that none of his remarks would be edited and rebroadcast or printed. He liked journalists but had a disdain for publishers and therefore did not trust the print media. However, he was not above using the printed word when it fit his needs.

Shortly after his election, Kennedy went to Florida. The purpose of this trip was for him to organize and select his cabinet; at this time, the Kennedy wit and purpose was exposed. During the Florida trip, in the second week of December 1960, the *Washington (D.C.) Post* received an anonymous call reporting that a deal had been made that would allow Dean Rusk to leave his post as director of the Rockefeller Foundation, a position that paid $60,000 annually, and accept the cabinet position of secretary of state, a

position that paid only $25,000 annually. The Rockefeller Foundation had agreed to make up the difference in salary so Rusk could accept the appointment. During the same visit, the *New York Times* was advised by an anonymous caller that Franklin Delano Roosevelt Jr. was to be appointed secretary of the Navy. Roosevelt never got the position, but in both cases the anonymous caller was Kennedy himself. He may not have liked the press, but his imprimatur proved he knew how to use it. Kennedy would later leak other information to the press during his term in office as the event warranted.

Often, when Kennedy and the mass media are mentioned, so are his live televised press conferences. But Kennedy and the television eye had been no strangers before the press conferences. Kennedy received national television exposure in 1956 when he made the nominating speech for Adlai Stevenson at the Democratic National Convention. He also used television and television commercials during the primary campaign to swing support for his nomination from the older, more hard-line Democratic machinery. Then, of course, came the famous Kennedy-Nixon debates during the 1960 general election campaign. Perhaps here, more than anywhere else, the nation was exposed and transfixed by the Kennedy mystique. His rested, tanned, well-coiffed physical appearance added to his youthful charm and was in striking contrast to Nixon, who had recently been discharged from a hospital and was visibly pale by comparison during the first debate. These debates, devoid of commercial and press editing, showcased Kennedy to the entire nation. By the time Kennedy took the oath of office, he knew the best way to reach the masses and disseminate his message was by means of the enormous power of television and live televised and radio broadcasts of his press conferences. Once again, he was inviting the press to do the work.

Presidents have had differing opinions as to their like or dislike of press conferences, but all seem to agree that press conferences are used to help shape public opinion. Franklin Roosevelt allowed spontaneous questions, but many were planted with receptive newsmen by his staff. Harry Truman did not seem to mind having to conduct press conferences but did not always perform well. Eisenhower used television to record his conferences, but they were edited before rebroadcast. Kennedy liked television, permitted live coverage, and used the press conference to demonstrate his humor, intellect, and ability to joust verbally with the press.

From January 1961 to November 1963, Kennedy conducted 21 press conferences. His preparation for the event would begin the day before, when his press secretary, Pierre Salinger, provided him information concerning current affairs; other major White House departments prepared briefing books with possible questions and answers. Kennedy studied this data, and on the morning of the conference he would have breakfast with various cabinet secretaries and other aides and rehearse for the conference by answering possible press questions submitted by his guests.

His preparation for the conferences not only assisted him for the actual event but resulted in his staff remaining current on world and national events. The Kennedy cool was evident in the conferences as the president listened to

Walter Cronkite conducts a televised interview with President John F. Kennedy.

(John F. Kennedy Library)

questions, many with long preambles, without losing his temper or his control of the situation. He did not enter into polemics during conferences, but he used the opportunity to engage reporters and answered their questions with a response that often sounded extemporaneous.

The Kennedy administration was not perfect in its relationship with the media, however. One of the biggest blunders to befall the Kennedy administration involved the military-like Bay of Pigs invasion of Cuba. The attempt failed, and the administration was severely embarrassed. Instead of denying that he knew anything, Kennedy went before the United States on live television and accepted full responsibility for the debacle. The public let it pass.

R. JOHN BALLOTTI JR.

See also Kennedy Assassination and the Media; News Leaks; News Management; Presidential Debates; Presidential News Conferences; Presidential Press Secretaries

Further Reading

Denton, Robert E., Jr., and Dan F. Hahn, *Presidential Communication: Description and Analysis,* New York and London: Praeger, 1986

Kennedy, John F., *The Kennedy Presidential Press Conferences,* New York: Earl M. Coleman, 1978

Reeves, Richard, *President Kennedy: Profile of Power,* New York: Simon & Schuster, 1993; London: Papermac, 1994

Sorensen, Theodore C., *Kennedy,* New York: Harper & Row, 1965; London: Hodder and Stoughton, 1965

Kennedy Assassination and the Media

Challenged the press's news-gathering capabilities

The assassination of President John F. Kennedy on November 22, 1963, on the downtown streets of Dallas, Texas, not only represented a turning point in U.S. history but was also a watershed event in the history of news reporting. For a single event, it placed probably the heaviest burden in modern times on the press's news-gathering capabilities. The shocking news caused a traumatized nation to turn quickly to television, still in its relative infancy, for immediate information. Television viewing reached the highest level in its history during the fateful days following the assassination. Millions of Americans were watching television on Sunday, November 24, when the alleged assassin, Lee Harvey Oswald, then in police custody, was gunned down in the police station basement by nightclub owner Jack Ruby. It was the first murder to be shown live on television.

When President Kennedy arrived in Dallas by airplane on the morning of November 22, he was accompanied by 58 journalists from Washington, D.C., and 10 Texas journalists. Most of these individuals – newspaper, magazine, and television reporters, photographers, and camera crews – ac-

Dallas police bring Lee Harvey Oswald through a crowded hall where Jack Ruby, the man in the hat at the far right, waits to shoot him.
(UPI/Corbis-Bettmann)

companied the presidential motorcade by bus as it traveled through Dallas amid cheering crowds; a few had space in designated press cars. The local press had stationed personnel at strategic points in the city from Love Field airport to downtown Dallas to the Trade Mart, where the president was to give a noon address to a group of local dignitaries.

Many of the journalists in the motorcade could hear the shots that rang out at Dealey Plaza. Merriman Smith, of United Press International, traveling in a press car, grabbed a radiophone and dictated a bulletin to his office: "Three shots were fired at President Kennedy's motorcade today in downtown Dallas." Without knowing for certain what had happened, he relayed as many details as he could muster while physically holding off his Associated Press competitor. Smith won a Pulitzer Prize for his coverage that day. A few journalists managed to dismount from their vehicles at the place where the shots had been fired. Local reporters quickly descended on the area, too, as a manhunt began for the assassin. A handful of journalists managed to get inside the Texas School Book Depository, from where the fatal shots allegedly were fired. Press buses in the motorcade continued to the Trade Mart; from there, many reporters made their way to nearby Parkland Hospital, where the stricken president had been taken.

Lee Harvey Oswald, 24, an employee of the depository and former U.S. Marine who had earlier defected to the Soviet Union as a self-declared Marxist, fled the building immediately after the shooting. In the nearby Oak Cliff section of town he allegedly shot to death a Dallas police officer, then found his way to a movie theater. Two Dallas newspaper reporters were inside the theater as eyewitnesses when officers arrested Oswald after a brief struggle.

With the announced death of the president at Parkland and with the apprehension of the suspected assassin, the news media focused their attention on the Dallas police station. Law enforcement officials there held periodic news

The world attended the funeral of President John F. Kennedy via nonstop television programming.
(Museum of Broadcast Communications)

conferences over the weekend for the growing numbers of journalists who congregated in the hallway outside the homicide office. These news conferences, broadcast live, were dominated not by print journalists but by television reporters, whose microphones, lights, and national audiences commanded the attention of the officials.

On Friday evening, police accommodated press demands to talk to the suspect by bringing Oswald out for a midnight press conference in a basement assembly room. As many as 100 journalists attended the event, which ended prematurely after about five minutes when officers feared the press was becoming too disruptive.

Journalists from throughout the nation and the world descended on the police department over the weekend, and the nation saw via live television broadcasts the police hallways that were congested, noisy, and seemingly chaotic. The suspect himself was brought through the hallway from the jail elevator to the homicide offices a total of 16 times over the three days he was in custody, and each time he was besieged with questions that he answered hurriedly while moving between officers. Estimates of the journalists in the hallway ranged up to 300, but the investigating Warren Commission later calculated that "upwards of 100" were present.

On Saturday evening, the journalists' attention began to focus on the imminent transfer of the suspect from the city jail, a temporary holding facility, to the county jail. Police Chief Jesse Curry assured the now-exhausted news representatives that they would not "miss anything" if they returned by 10 A.M. Sunday. Some of the journalists in Dallas – including all three networks – gathered in the police basement parking area to see Oswald led to a car for his transfer. Many others gathered at the county jail to witness his arrival. When Oswald, handcuffed to an officer, appeared after 11 A.M., a crowd of 110 persons had gathered in the police basement. At this moment Jack Ruby, who had been standing adjacent to a Dallas detective whom he knew, fired a fatal shot at Oswald. *Dallas Times Herald* photographer Bob Jackson recorded the event in a dramatic photograph for which he won the Pulitzer Prize.

In recounting this moment, the Warren Commission described Ruby as lunging from a "crowd of newsmen" whose numbers had effectively concealed him from officers. However, a Dallas Police Department investigation revealed that of 110 persons present in the basement, only 46 were journalists. Others were officers, many of them wearing plain clothes. The charge that the news media's presence in large numbers had permitted Ruby to conceal himself was unfair and inaccurate.

How well the press served the U.S. public during this critical weekend in Dallas has been a subject of debate. The Warren Commission, appointed by President Lyndon B. Johnson to examine the assassination and events surrounding it, blamed the press not only for its unwitting role in permitting Ruby to slip into the police basement but for hindering the official investigation because of their numbers and the chaotic conditions created in the police hallway. Others, including the American Bar Association, expressed concern that the press had publicized information about Oswald that would have made it difficult, if not impossible, for him to receive a fair trial.

> **Kennedy Assassination**
>
> Washington, Nov. 23 (UPI) – It was a balmy, sunny noon as we motored through downtown Dallas behind President Kennedy. The procession cleared the center of the business district and turned into a handsome highway that wound through what appeared to be a park. . . . Suddenly we heard three loud, almost painfully loud cracks. The first sounded as if it might have been a large firecracker. But the second and third blasts were unmistakable. Gunfire. . . . the Secret Service agent was leaning over into the rear of the car. "He's dead," he said curtly. I recall a babble of anxious voices, tense voices – "Where in hell are the stretchers. . . . Get a doctor out here. . . ." And from somewhere, nervous sobbing.
>
> UPI account, November 23, 1963

Most observers, however, praised the press – both broadcast and print representatives – for rapidly disseminating news of the assassination and its related developments, for maintaining a high degree of accuracy in a stressful and difficult situation, and for abstaining from harmful speculation and the spreading of rumors. It is generally acknowledged that the press provided a calming influence to an anxious nation that desperately wanted and needed information about the assassination of its president.

DARWIN PAYNE

See also Kennedy, John F., and the Media; Television News

Further Reading
Mayo, John B., *Bulletin from Dallas: The President is Dead,* New York: Exposition, 1967
Payne, Darwin, "The Press Corps and the Kennedy Assassination," *Journalism Monographs* 15 (February 1970)
Warren Commission, *Report of the President's Commission on the Assassination of President John F. Kennedy,* Washington, D.C.: U.S. Government Printing Office, 1964
Zelizer, Barbie, *Covering the Body: The Kennedy Assassination, the Media, and the Shaping of Collective Memory,* Chicago: University of Chicago Press, 1992

Kerner Commission Report

Investigation of civil unrest in 1967 discussed press performance

The Kerner Commission bore witness to the urban poverty, violence, riots, conflagration, and death that highlighted the long, hot spring and summer of 1967. As the first federally funded official inquiry into civil disorders, the commission was assembled on July 28, 1967, by President Lyndon B. Johnson, who directed the illustrious group to produce a "profile of the riots – of the rioters, of their environment, of their victims, of their causes and effects." The commissioners visited riot cities and heard from witnesses and expert counsel during their investigation. They also directed surveys by field teams in 23 cities, with further, intensive investigations in 10 of those cities. Approximately 1,200 persons were interviewed, including a cross section of city officials as well as observers of and participants in the riots. At the time the commission was appointed, President Johnson also ordered Secretary of Defense Robert S. McNamara to begin new riot-control training standards for the National Guard to help it prepare for future riots.

The commission's major work was completed in March 1968 with the issuance of the *Report of the National Advisory Commission on Civil Disorders*, often called the Kerner Report after the group's head, Otto Kerner, who was then governor of Illinois. Kerner's vice chairman was John V. Lindsay, mayor of New York City. Other commissioners were Fred R. Harris, U.S. senator from Oklahoma; Edward W. Brooke, U.S. senator from Massachusetts; James C. Corman, U.S. representative from Ohio; I.W. Abel, president of the United Steelworkers of America; Charles B. Thornton, chairman of the board of Litton Industries, Inc.; Roy Wilkins, executive director, National Association for the Advancement of Colored People; Katherine Graham Peden, commissioner of commerce, state of Kentucky; and Herbert Jenkins, chief of police, Atlanta, Georgia. Only two African Americans and one female were named as commissioners. More than 130 business leaders, public servants, professionals, and students aided the commission in an advisory or research capacity.

The product of their work was issued in 17 chapters and more than 400 pages of discussion and analysis, including initial chapters that presented an overview of the characteristics and pattern of the disorders. The Kerner Report provided profiles of incidents leading to destruction in various riot-torn urban areas including Tampa, Florida; Cincinnati, Ohio; Atlanta, Georgia; Newark, Plainfield, New Brunswick, and northern New Jersey; and Detroit, Michigan. In Detroit riots, 38 people were killed and 700 others were arrested as federal troops intervened. The death toll in four days of rioting in Newark in July 1967 was 26, and 1,000 were arrested. Less-publicized riots took place in other cities such as Buffalo, New York, where 14 people were shot.

While the Kerner Report ameliorated none of the social problems that led to the civil disorders, Chapter 15, titled, "The Mass Media and the Disorders," has been of enduring academic interest. Focused on President Johnson's query, "What effect does the mass media have on the riots?," this chapter continues to be a pivotal topic of research and discussion in undergraduate and graduate programs in journalism and mass communication. In an effort to answer President Johnson's question, the commission took several courses of action, including a quantitative analysis of the content of television programs and newspaper reporting in 15 riot cities in the periods just before, during, and after the disorders. The commission also held a conference for media representatives at all levels and conducted special interviews with ghetto residents about their response to the coverage. Overall, the commission found an exaggeration in the scope and magnitude of the riots as well as an imbalance between what actually happened in riot cities and what newspapers, radio, and television coverage reported as occurring. The mass media failed to analyze and report adequately on racial problems in the United States because it reported and wrote from the perspective of a white man's world.

Mass communication scholar David Sachsman has found that even in the 1990s, "deeply held traditions and procedures in mass communication education create barriers to diversity and restrict the ability of the field to recruit minority students and female faculty members." Training and education in mass communication continued to be a white-dominated endeavor that promoted the status quo with few changes in basic approaches over the years. This fact may be a root cause for the failure of mass media professionals to adequately cover civil disturbances and other major race-sensitive stories. While efforts have been made to increase the numbers of women and minorities in mass communication education, the membership breakdown for the major mass media academic group, the Association for Education in Journalism and Mass Communication, was 92 percent white and 72 percent male in 1993. Nonwhites were projected to constitute a majority in the United States before the year 2100 if population trends of the late twentieth century continued. Even in the 1990s, so-called minority groups constituted a larger percentage of the population than in the past.

While the Kerner Report is the most widely known and widely consulted of official reports on collective black violence in the United States, it was preceded by a number of other such inquiries, including the *Report of the Special Committee by Congress to Investigate the East St. Louis Riots* (1917), *The Negro in Chicago: A Study of Race Relations and a Race Riot* (1919), the *Final Report of the Governor's Committee to Investigate the Riot Occurring in Detroit June 21, 1943*, and the *Governor's Commission on the Los Angeles Riots* (1965). There were no "typical" riots during the summer of 1967, when U.S. cities were rudely shaken by destruction, violence, and death. The Kerner Commission concluded that the discrimination and segregation that had permeated life for African Americans had begun to threaten the future of all citizens. The nation was moving toward two societies, one black and one white, separate and unequal. Not surprisingly, this tale of two societies was just as much a reality in the late 1990s as it was in 1967, as millions of African Americans were joined by growing numbers of Hispanics, Native Americans, and other minorities in an unaccepting and unaccepted violence-prone underclass.

Echoing the magnitude of the socioeconomic problems that led to the civil disorders of 1967, former Kerner Commissioners Fred Harris and Roy Wilkins published *Quiet Riots: Race and Poverty in the United States* in 1988 to show that segregation was worse, poverty was deeper, and unemployment had doubled by then. They stressed that these problems were even more destructive of human life than the violent riots of the 1960s. Harris and Wilkins pointed to a growing ghetto underclass while noting that no significant new social welfare or job programs had been launched since the 1967 riots. Owing to a series of economic recessions, little progress had been made toward better housing for those who lived in the ghetto between 1970 and 1980, although some gains had been made in the years just before and just after the riots. When they focused on the period 1970–80, Harris and Wilkins found that "segregation remained extremely high . . . and progress was least in the kind of metropolitan communities that were of greatest interest to the Kerner Commission: the older urban centers with the largest number and highest percentage of blacks." In addition, educational segregation continued to exist, perpetuating inequality by providing weaker and less effective training for young blacks and Hispanics than for whites. The intractability of these problems continued to pose problems for the news media charged with relaying information about the entire nation to their audiences.

FRANKIE HUTTON

See also Advertising and Minorities; Mass Media and Race; Mass Media and the Civil Rights Movement

Further Reading

Harris, Fred R., and Roger W. Wilkins, eds., *Quiet Riots: Race and Poverty in the United States,* New York: Pantheon, 1988
Platt, Anthony M., comp., *The Politics of Riot Commissions, 1917–1970: A Collection of Official Reports and Critical Essays,* New York: Macmillan, 1971
Wilson, Clint C., II, and Félix Gutiérrez, *Minorities and Media: Diversity and the End of Mass Communication,* Beverly Hills, California: Sage, 1985

Korean War

U.S. media react quickly to cover the conflict

The Korean War erupted on Sunday, June 25, 1950 – Saturday night, June 24, in the United States. The people of the United States learned of the assault on the radio, much as they had heard of the Pearl Harbor attack less than a decade before. Sunday morning newspapers carried terse dispatches from the wire services.

The world was surprised by the attack, although some cross-border skirmishes had occurred earlier. Otherwise, the lightning attack by two divisions across the thirty-eighth parallel that had divided North and South Korea since the end of World War II caught the world, military forces, and the journalistic establishment off guard.

Only five U.S. correspondents formed the Seoul press corps when the war started. U.S. media organizations reacted swiftly, however, sending veteran journalists to report the initial clashes. By the end of the year, 270 journalists had been accredited by the U.S. Far East Command, with perhaps 60 on the battlefield on any given day. Ten journalists were killed during the war, and an Associated Press photographer, Frank Noel, spent two and a half years as a prisoner of war. The war marked the last major conflict dominated by print and radio journalism. During the war, the emerging medium of television continued to develop its own audience and overcame barriers of time differences, distance, and cumbersome equipment to include visual accounts of the bloody campaigns on the Korean peninsula. Television newscasts overlapped the newsreels, which still were being shown regularly in motion picture theaters across the country.

Although by its very nature war reporting is difficult and dangerous, the Korean War produced its own special heritage: renewed censorship of the press, largely at the request of the press corps, and renewed animosity toward female journalists by a few in and out of the military. It also produced its share of dramatic stories, pictures, and broadcasts.

The first six months or so of the war produced a campaign of invasions, withdrawals, dogged last-ditch stands, retreats, and seaborne invasions that taxed reporters as much as the military. Reuters journalist Roy McCartney summarized it best in one of his early dispatches:

> The Korean campaign is one of the toughest, most frustrating and mentally worrying that any correspondent was ever called upon to cover. . . . In addition to the physical difficulties of covering the campaign and the filth and disease abounding in the country, there is a responsibility resting almost on the correspondents alone to see that nothing is published which might cost American soldiers their lives.

Walter Simmons of the *Chicago Tribune* was the lone newspaper correspondent in Seoul when the attack came. There to cover a speech by a U.S. official and the opening of the South Korean National Assembly, Simmons had stayed on for a few days and had become caught in the war. Soon other print and broadcast journalists, many well known to the U.S. reading public, joined the press corps covering the war. These included Keyes Beech of the *Chicago Daily News,* Homer Bigart and Marguerite Higgins of the *New York Herald-Tribune,* Frank Gibney of *Time,* and Burton Crane of the *New York Times.*

Filing stories in the early weeks of the war was difficult. Communication lines were in tatters, and the military claimed priority to use the available telephone and radio links as more forces were committed after President Harry Truman and the United Nations pledged to defend South Korea. Reporters accompanied forces that retreated to an 80- by 50-mile defensive perimeter around Pusan at the southern tip of the Korean Peninsula. Ray Richards of International News Service and Corporal Ernie Peeler of *Pacific Stars and Stripes* became the first media casualties on July 10, 1950, when the unit they accompanied was overrun. Because of the imminent danger, most correspondents carried weapons and sometimes used them.

The UN's supreme commander, General Douglas MacArthur, who as a major had served as the Army's first official press officer, was authorized to impose censorship early in the war. MacArthur announced his abhorrence of censorship and told journalists to write what they wished, adding they would be held accountable for breaches in mil-

Korean War correspondents used a railroad car as a newsroom.
(National Archives)

itary security or "unwarranted criticisms." In time, this voluntary arrangement satisfied no one, including reporters who were often uncertain about the risks to units in publishing certain information. On December 20, 1950, the Far East Command imposed censorship. Most journalists favored the World War II–type arrangements established, although uniform application never was achieved and a few journalists bypassed the system when it suited their competitive needs. Censorship did not extend beyond the war zone, and although both military and political leaders fumed at stories critical of military operations and political decisions, publication of such material was never challenged legally.

The war and the politics surrounding it provided raw material for gripping reports and pictures. The defense of the Pusan perimeter, the Inchon invasion, MacArthur's march to the Yalu River, the Marines' retreat from the Chosin Reservoir to Hungnam Harbor, Truman's sacking of MacArthur in early 1951, the static warfare of the war's last two years, and the peace talks leading to a cease-fire in July 1953 all presented the press corps with compelling and important story opportunities.

The best-known radio commentator of the time, Edward R. Murrow, wasted little time in getting to Korea, as did many other broadcasters. By August, he was touring the front lines, building a base of material for his popular *Hear It Now* program on CBS radio. In November 1951, he created a television version of the show, *See It Now,* and later returned to Korea to shoot film for a special, "Christmas in Korea," which in 1952 became the first hour-long television news documentary. The film was a success with the U.S. audience, by then rapidly tiring of the drawn-out war.

Mass magazines like *Life, Collier's,* and the *Saturday Evening Post* promoted their own brand of coverage, calling on such veterans as photographers David Douglas Duncan and Carl Mydans, Bill Mauldin, and Harold Martin to put their own imprint on Korean War coverage. Finally, Marguerite Higgins, who had proved her talent as a World War II war correspondent in the European theater, became the focus of a struggle to stay in Korea, fighting off the animosity of a *Herald-Tribune* colleague, Homer Bigart, and the opposition of some military commanders to having female journalists in combat areas. She prevailed in both struggles, eventually appealing a military expulsion edict to MacArthur himself.

WALLACE B. EBERHARD

See also War Correspondents

Further Reading

Braestrup, Peter, *Battle Lines: Report of the Twentieth Century Fund Task Force on the Military and the Media,* New York: Priority, 1985

Brodie, Howard, *War Drawings: World War II, Korea,* Palo Alto, California: National, 1963

Duncan, David Douglas, *This is War!,* New York: Harper and Brothers, 1951

Dvorchak, Robert J., *Battle for Korea: The Associated Press History of the Korean Conflict,* Conshohocken, Pennsylvania: Combined, 1993

Emery, Michael, *On the Front Lines: Following America's Foreign Correspondents Across the Twentieth Century,* Washington, D.C.: American University Press, 1995

Higgins, Marguerite, *War in Korea,* Garden City, New York: Doubleday, 1951

Knightley, Phillip, *The First Casualty: From the Crimea to Vietnam: The War Correspondent as Hero, Propagandist, and Myth Maker,* New York: Harcourt Brace Jovanovich, 1975; London: Pan, 1989

McFarland, Keith D., *The Korean War, an Annotated Bibliography,* New York: Garland, 1986

Toland, John, *In Mortal Combat: Korea, 1950–1953,* New York: Morrow, 1991

Voorhees, Melvin B., *Korean Tales,* New York: Simon & Schuster, 1952; London: Secker & Warburg, 1953

L

Labor Media

Early form of alternative media serving specialized audience

The labor press has been part of the U.S. scene since workers first began to coalesce around common interests in the early nineteenth century. The first newspaper devoted to the needs of workers appeared in Philadelphia in 1827. Although the *Journeymen's Mechanic's Journal* survived only a few months, it marked the beginning of an expanding labor press.

The labor press blossomed during the years of the Jacksonian democratic revolution as emerging labor parties started newspapers to give voice to working-class concerns and to rail against the social and economic inequities wrought by the Industrial Revolution. Between 1828 and 1834, 68 labor newspapers – including several dailies – appeared in print. Most were short-lived, but many outlived the parties that gave them birth.

The *Working Man's Advocate* (1829–49) was a successful representative of the early labor press. Published weekly in New York City, the *Advocate* called for public education, universal suffrage, and a 10-hour working day. Like other labor newspapers of the period, the *Advocate* promoted working-class unity as a means of achieving social change.

The labor press continued to expand in the 1860s and 1870s, although the level of activity ebbed and flowed with the general health of the labor movement and the degree of governmental and employer repression. The 1886 Haymarket bombing cast a pall of suspicion on the workers' movement, and the labor press entered a period of decline.

By the turn of the twentieth century, however, the labor press had reemerged as a vital force. Fueled by immigration, urbanization, and explosive industrial growth, labor newspapers burst forth in a rich profusion of ideological perspectives and tongues. The labor press had entered its golden age.

Three types of labor publications competed for attention. Trade union periodicals, published with union funds for union members, tended to be inward looking and conservative. They provided members with information about union policies and served as mouthpieces for union officials. Party papers supported by party funds tried to mobilize workers in support of political and economic change.

The independent Socialist/labor press also appealed to a broad working-class readership on behalf of social transformation. Most were funded by subscriptions and contributions; some had loose affiliations to radical industrial unions or Socialist parties.

Socialists and labor activists were driven by a compulsion to publish newspapers. Between 1905 and 1919, the Industrial Workers of the World (IWW) published upward of 70 newspapers and periodicals. In 1912, more than 300 Socialist newspapers and magazines were in print, including five English-language dailies and eight foreign-language dailies.

Many independent Socialist/labor newspapers followed high journalistic standards and gained large readerships. The *Masses,* which flourished between 1910 and 1920, attracted some of the finest writers of the era. *Appeal to Reason,* an independent Socialist weekly, had a circulation of 760,000 in 1913. Daily newspapers such as the *New York Call,* the *Milwaukee (Wisconsin) Leader,* and the *Cleveland (Ohio) Citizen* possessed qualities equal or superior to those of the mainstream commercial press. They were, according to one assessment, "excellent newspapers of record . . . possessing what seems in retrospect to have been the highest ethics in the business."

The labor press reached a high-water mark in the years prior to World War I. By 1917, the wave had crested and began to recede. The inexorable decline of the labor press was a consequence of three factors: market forces, governmental hostility, and the anti-labor attitudes of the mainstream press.

Empowered by the Espionage Act and urged on by mainstream newspapers, the federal government harassed and killed off scores of IWW and Socialist periodicals in 1917 and 1918. Some survived the war years intact. The *Milwaukee Leader* continued to publish as a collectively owned, independent daily until 1942. But the war and the postwar Red Scare forced alternative periodicals – including labor – onto the defensive.

The labor press also found it increasingly difficult to compete with the mass circulation commercial press. Some daily newspapers – especially those owned by Scripps and Hearst – appealed to working-class readers as a marketing strategy. Independent labor newspapers were motivated by ideology rather than profit, and most depended on subscriptions and contributions for survival. Readers were often poor. Without advertising revenue or financial support from unions or political parties, independent labor papers eventually went under.

Organized labor tried to gain a foothold in broadcasting during the early days of radio. Efforts to establish independent labor radio stations in the 1920s and 1930s were defeated by commercial interests, union indifference, and a hostile regulatory climate. Of 732 licensed broadcast stations in 1927, only one was labor-owned and -operated – the Chicago Federation of Labor continued to operate WCLF AM until 1979. In the 1940s and 1950s, both the American Federation of Labor (AFL) and the Congress of Industrial Organizations (CIO) sponsored evening newscasts and used free airtime provided under Federal Communications Commission (FCC) regulations for public service announcements.

The AFL and the CIO (after 1955, the AFL-CIO) also made some short-lived attempts to produce labor programming during the early days of television. These efforts were thwarted by high production costs.

By the 1990s, the independent labor press had all but disappeared, harried to near extinction by market forces and a changing culture. A handful of publications such as *Labor Notes* and the *Union Democracy Review* still struggled at the margins to promote a progressive labor agenda.

Most union periodicals in the late twentieth century were little more than vehicles of self-promotion. A few, such as *Solidarity,* the national magazine of the United Auto Workers, and *UMW Journal,* published by the United Mine Workers, continued to provide important information to working people and serve as vigorous vehicles for discussion.

Labor also maintained a tenuous presence on public television. *Labor Beat* was produced in Chicago from 1983. *We Do the Work,* a labor affairs program based on the west coast, was syndicated across the country.

The vitality of the labor press has paralleled the fortunes of the labor movement. The labor media served as critical forums for working-class concerns marginalized or ignored by the mainstream press. Many of the reforms first promoted in the early labor press – universal suffrage, tax-supported public education, child labor laws – became part of the fabric of life in the United States.

Labor reporting had all but disappeared from the mainstream press in the 1990s. In an era of increasing corporate ownership of the channels of mass communication, however, a vigorous labor press was all the more important if the marketplace of ideas were to have any meaning.

MICK MULCRONE

See also Alternative Press; Espionage and Sedition Acts; Socialist Press

Further Reading

Beck, Elmer A., "Autopsy of a Labor Daily: 'The Milwaukee Leader'," *Journalism Monographs* 16 (August 1970)
Bekken, John, "'The Most Vindictive and Most Vengeful Power': Labor Confronts the Chicago Newspaper Trust," *Journalism History* 18 (1992)
Conlin, Joseph R., ed., *The American Radical Press, 1880–1960,* Westport, Connecticut: Greenwood, 1974
Douglas, Sara U., *Labor's New Voice: Unions and the Mass Media,* Norwood, New Jersey: Ablex, 1986
McChesney, Robert W., "Labor and the Marketplace of Ideas: WCFL and the Battle for Labor Broadcasting, 1927–34," *Journalism Monographs* 134 (August 1992), pp. 1–40
McFarland, C.K., and Robert L. Thistlewaite, "Twenty Years of a Successful Labor Paper: The Working Man's Advocate, 1829–49," *Journalism Quarterly* 60:1 (1983)
Pizzigati, Sam, and Fred J. Solowey, eds., *The New Labor Press: Journalism for a Changing Union Movement,* Ithaca, New York: ILR, 1992
Puette, William, *Through Jaundiced Eyes: How the Media View Organized Labor,* Ithaca, New York: ILR, 1992

Lasker, Albert

Advertising industry innovator

Albert Lasker helped shape the advertising industry during the first 40 years of the twentieth century. Beginning as an office boy with the Lord and Thomas advertising agency in 1898, Lasker owned the agency by 1912.

Among those who worked for Lasker were advertising pioneers John E. Kennedy and Claude C. Hopkins. Lasker was partly responsible for the "salesmanship in print" and "reason-why" styles of copy and for "scientific" advertising. He promoted ethical principles and opposed questionable or dishonest advertising.

Under his leadership, agency billings rose from $3 million in 1906 to $6 million in 1912. Offices were opened in New York; Toronto, Ontario; Paris; London; San Francisco; and Los Angeles.

After a brief time in partisan politics, Lasker returned to a troubled agency in 1923. After Hopkins left the agency in 1924, Lasker attracted new clients, including Kleenex, which he promoted as "the handkerchief you can throw away," and Lucky Strike cigarettes, which he promoted by changing the public's perception toward women smoking in public.

The agency merged with the Logan Agency and acquired the Radio Corporation of America account, which led to ties with the National Broadcasting Company (NBC). By 1928, Lord and Thomas was responsible for about 50 percent of the advertising placed with NBC. With the help of radio, Lasker's Lord and Thomas agency became the largest in the world in the 1930s.

Retiring in 1938, Lasker, returned to advertising briefly during World War II. In 1942, Lasker again retired, selling the agency to his senior executives; it then became known as Foote, Cone, and Belding.

EDD APPLEGATE

Further Reading

Belding, Don, "End of an Era in Advertising," *Advertising Agency and Advertising & Selling* (July 1952)

Cone, Fairfax M., *With All Its Faults,* Boston: Little, Brown, 1969

Gunther, John, *Taken at the Flood: The Story of Albert D. Lasker,* New York: Harper and Brothers, 1960; London: Hamilton, 1960

Hopkins, Claude C., *My Life in Advertising,* London: Harper, 1927; Lincolnwood, Illinois: NTC Business, 1986

Lee, Ivy Ledbetter

"Father figure" of public relations

Public relations historian Scott M. Cutlip called Ivy Ledbetter Lee the "father figure" of contemporary public relations. The reason was that Lee was the first to move beyond press agentry and to articulate public relations precepts that organizations and individuals still follow as they attempt to garner public understanding and support.

Ivy Lee was born in rural Cedartown, Georgia, on July 16, 1877. His father was a minister whose assignments took the family to St. Louis, Missouri, then Atlanta, Georgia, where some of the South's leading intellectuals, including Henry W. Grady, influential managing editor of the *Atlanta Constitution,* gathered regularly in the Lee home to debate social and political issues. These discussions helped teach the young man how to interact in complex business and cultural settings. They also piqued Lee's interest in news reporting, which became the springboard to his career as a pioneer and leading public relations counselor.

Throughout his life, Lee was energetic, inquisitive, and articulate. While a student at Emory College, he worked part-time as editor of the college department of the *Constitution.* After he transferred to Princeton University, he was editor of the *Daily Princetonian* and an enterprising stringer for the Associated Press, the *Philadelphia Press,* and the *Chicago Record,* as well as active in many campus organizations. He graduated in 1898, and his allegiance to Princeton continued through his life. His papers were given to the university after his death.

From Princeton, Lee moved to New York, where he was a police reporter for the *New York Journal,* then finance and Wall Street reporter for the *New York Times* and *New York World.* By 1903, he was married to Cornelia Bigelow, he was the father of the first of their three children, and he was tired of newspaper work schedules. He also was beginning to understand how the news media helped shape public opinion, a concept that became increasingly important to him as he moved from reporting to press agentry, then public relations counseling.

Lee worked for two years as a political publicist, first for a local candidate, then for the Democratic National Committee, before joining press agent George F. Parker in 1904 as a partner in a publicity agency, Parker and Lee. Press agentry was a young field then. The Publicity Bureau had been operating in Boston in 1900, but it left few records of its 12 years of operations. This was not so with Lee, who protected the confidentiality of his clients while seeking opportunities to articulate why and how businesses should seek public acceptance and respond to public criticism.

He began to counsel clients to be proactive, especially when they were attacked by adversaries and the media. He was comfortable in the offices of millionaire businessmen, and they accepted his advice, even his admonition that words – publicity – had to be backed by deeds.

Before long, Lee sought opportunities to show why and how businesses should seek acceptance from the public. He gave speeches, some of which he printed and distributed, and he sat for interviews to explain his ideas, which were revolutionary at the time because the prevailing sentiment among industrialists had been "the public be damned." He told his audiences that Parker and Lee was not a secret operation and that it worked openly on behalf of clients to supply information, even verify queries. Its purpose was to respond to the press and the public with prompt and accurate information about subjects of value and interest to the public.

The Anthracite Coal Operators and the Pennsylvania Railroad were among Parker and Lee's early clients. Lee helped the coal operators tell their side of a bitter strike by coal miners, and he counseled the railroad about ways to help the press cover accidents, as well as ways to oppose pending regulatory legislation being promoted by President Theodore Roosevelt and others.

Parker and Lee closed in 1908, and Ivy Lee became director of publicity for the Pennsylvania Railroad. Both the title and the concept of having an in-house publicity operation were new at the time. Before long, however, other opportunities beckoned Lee. He went to England to manage the European office of Harris, Winthrop and Co., then returned to become public relations counsel to the Standard Oil Company and the Rockefellers, Bethlehem Steel Company, Chrysler Corporation, and many other major clients. During World War I, Lee served in several offices in Washington, D.C., including the American Red Cross War Council and the War Council.

Lee set the foundation for the contemporary practice of public relations. His advice was to be open, honest, and authoritative, and to interpret decisions to whomever would listen. He insisted on developing relationships of trust and confidence with clients and with the press. He counseled clients to keep the media informed and not to play favorites or give exclusives. He recommended that clients give reasonable cooperation to help the press get stories and photographs and that clients, especially millionaire industrialists like John D. Rockefeller, occasionally meet personally with members of the press. Lee counseled clients to willingly supply information to the press – and he wrote much of it – but left it to the editors to decide what to do with it and explained to clients why this was important. He knew how to hobnob with the elite giants of the industry. He also knew how to speak the language of the people, and he helped his clients do likewise because he knew the public could affect how clients were perceived and how legislation often resulted from negative perceptions. Above all, Lee realized that good public relations is based not on saying but on doing, and he convinced many clients to change their ways. Not everyone appreciated Lee's activities, however, and opponents sometimes called him "Poison Ivy" because he advised the barons of industry.

That sobriquet was a minor discomfort compared to the problem that haunted Ivy Lee from the 1920s until his death. A success in the United States and Great Britain, Lee became interested in taking on more international work. He became counsel to I.B. Farben, parent company of the German Dye Trust. In time, he realized that the company planned to support Hitler and the Nazi party. He advised Farben to sever those ties, but his advice was ignored. Even though Lee quit the account, he was vilified in the United States, and he was called before the House Un-American Activities Committee, accused of being a Nazi propagandist. Lee testified and was exonerated.

In late October 1934, months after he testified and was exonerated, Lee was hospitalized in New York with a brain tumor. He died on November 9, 1934. Hiebert wrote that Lee's positive influence in opening business to public scrutiny far outweighed the criticism of him that accompanied the controversies he dealt with during his life.

Lee's counseling firm operated under various names over the years. In 1961, his sons were no longer associated with Ivy Lee and T.J. Ross and Associates, so Ivy Lee's widow requested that the Lee name be removed from the firm. That action had no effect on Ivy Lee's legacy as "father figure" and his reputation for having established the foundation of contemporary public relations.

CAROL REUSS

See also Public Relations

Further Reading

Cutlip, Scott M., *The Unseen Power: Public Relations, a History*, Hillsdale, New Jersey: Lawrence Erlbaum, 1994

Hainsworth, Brad E., "Retrospective: Ivy Lee and the German Dye Trust," *Public Relations Review* (Spring 1987)

Hiebert, Ray E., *Courtier to the Crowd: The Story of Ivy Lee and the Development of Public Relations*, Ames: Iowa State University Press, 1966

Lee, Ivy, *Publicity: Some of the Things It Is and Is Not*, New York: Industries, 1925

Libel

Long-time threat to press activities

In the common law, libel is an unprivileged, false, and malicious published communication that injures a person's reputation. Because of varying interpretations of the common law and differences among state statutes, uniformity does not exist across the United States.

The law distinguishes libel, or published defamatory communication, from slander, or verbal defamation. After some confusion following the introduction of broadcasting technology, published communication has been interpreted to include spoken communication disseminated by mass media; the status of communication over the Internet and other new technologies in the late twentieth century, however, remained unclear.

Following *New York Times* v. *Sullivan* (1964), in which the U.S. Supreme Court held that the First Amendment applied to libel law, all plaintiffs in libel actions brought against mass media defendants were required to prove at least negligence (i.e., failure to exercise reasonable care), and plaintiffs found to be "public figures" or "public officials" were required to show actual malice (i.e., knowledge of falsity or reckless disregard for the truth of the defamatory statements).

A libel may be prosecuted under criminal statutes or as a civil lawsuit. Criminal libel prosecutions were common in the United States into the twentieth century, but thereafter were rare occurrences.

Libel has been an important battleground in the history of press freedom in the United States. From the colonial period to modern times, courts and legislatures have balanced the interests of a free press against the individual's right to a good reputation. The common-law doctrines of the late twentieth century remained closely linked to their English roots.

The origins of the modern law of libel can be traced to the medieval categories of private libel and seditious libel – that is, speech critical of the government or public officials. In early English law, libel existed to prevent disturbance of the civil order, to protect the authority of the government, and to protect the reputations of private individuals. The history of the Crown's aggressive use of libel accusations in England and in the American colonies to punish seditious speech was a primary influence on the early history of libel law in the United States and on the interpretation of freedom of the press.

The common law seditious libel trial of John Peter Zenger in 1735 was a landmark in the history of freedom of the press and libel because the jury rejected the existing common-law standard that truth was not a defense. The trial marked the end of common-law prosecution for seditious libel in the colonies. While the Zenger trial set no new legal precedent, it is an important example of the dichotomy between the practice and the theory of freedom of the press.

In the period leading up to and including the drafting and adoption of the First Amendment, two conditions existed that continue to puzzle historians: the law of libel was extremely unfavorable to publishers, yet newspaper publishers and pamphleteers routinely published libelous material, and few were prosecuted for doing so. These conflicting conditions contribute to the difficulty in establishing the original intent of the framers of the First Amendment.

The First Amendment, some have argued, superseded the common law of libel and was intended to end the category of seditious libel in the United States; late-twentieth-century scholarship, however, showed that the understanding of freedom of the press when the Bill of Rights was adopted did not preclude seditious libel prosecutions. This interpretation is supported by the passage of the Alien and Sedition Acts of 1798, which resulted in a number of trials for seditious libel.

Following the expiration of the Alien and Sedition Acts in

1801, the question of seditious libel faded with the increase in the use of both criminal and civil libel to protect private reputation, especially among government officials and businessmen. For most of the century, efforts were made in both the courts and state legislatures to expand the protection of free speech by shifting the balance in the law of libel in favor of newspaper publishers. While publishers realized modest success in several states – for example, New York and Massachusetts – libel law at the end of the nineteenth century continued to be a significant burden on newspaper publishers.

Throughout the 1800s, with the greatest activity during the first and last 30 years of the century, criminal and civil libel (and, to a lesser extent, contempt by publication) were viewed by public men as the primary tools for combating the excesses of the press and by journalists and publishers as the primary threats to the freedom of the press. From the 1870s on, significant debate over the protection of freedom of the press in libel law occurred in courtrooms and legislative chambers across the United States.

By the end of the century, a few states had minimally expanded the narrow common-law privileges, but for the most part the libel doctrine advocated by Alexander Hamilton in the landmark case of *People* v. *Croswell* (1804) remained intact: "The right to publish, with impunity, truth, with good motives, for justifiable ends, though reflecting on government, magistracy, or individuals." Truth was not an absolute defense claim, and the determination of good motives and justifiable ends remained at the discretion of the court. With the rise of mass market newspapers and yellow journalism, the newspaper industry's efforts to reform libel law fell on deaf ears in state courts and legislatures.

Libel was not at center stage in free speech debate for much of the first half of the twentieth century; however, the foundation for *New York Times* v. *Sullivan* developed in state courts early in the century. In *Coleman* v. *MacLennan* (1908), the Kansas Supreme Court held that material proved to be false was privileged if the newspaper believed it to be true and publishes it for the benefit of the electorate. This position remained a minority position adopted by as many as 16 states in the 1940s.

In *Sullivan*, the U.S. Supreme Court adopted a similar "fault" requirement for libel plaintiffs in all libel suits filed against mass media defendants. L.B. Sullivan, a law officer in Alabama, brought a libel suit in the state of Alabama against the *New York Times* and four ministers based on an advertisement about a civil rights demonstration. The jury awarded the public official $500,000. The Alabama Supreme Court upheld the judgment. On appeal to the Supreme Court of the United States, the *Times* argued that the common law of libel placed an impermissible burden on the people's right to criticize government and government officials. The effect, the paper argued, was no different than a prosecution for seditious libel.

The Supreme Court accepted the *Times*'s argument and, in a decision that free press advocates said was cause for "dancing in the streets," overturned the lower court decisions. The promise of *Sullivan*, however, had not been realized by the end of the twentieth century. Rather than creating a safe harbor for reporting about public affairs, libel law in the post-*Sullivan* era was an expensive, time-con-

suming legal endurance test that adequately protected neither the free press interests of media defendants nor the interests or the reputations of plaintiffs.

Over the last 30 years of the twentieth century, the Supreme Court expanded the category of plaintiffs who must prove actual malice to include individuals who were not government officials but who took a prominent role in a public controversy. Also, the Court attempted to define more clearly the meaning of "actual malice" and the standards used to prove that it existed. Further, the Court established constitutional standards concerning the awarding of damages and the protection of statements of opinion.

In the 1970s and 1980s, media advocates and legal observers argued that the problems in libel law had reached a crisis. They cited several high-profile libel trials, such as *Sharon* v. *Time* (1984) and *Westmoreland* v. *CBS* (1984), as examples of the failure of *Times* v. *Sullivan* to protect adequately either reputation or freedom of the press. The Libel Resource Defense Center, a legal advocacy group, reported that both damage awards in libel judgments against media defendants and the cost of defending the average libel suit had reached record dollar amounts. Advocates for libel plaintiffs argued that plaintiffs were ill-served by the complexity and the cost of the law. As a result, the question of truth – the central issue for most plaintiffs – was lost in the legal process.

There were several proposals for libel law reform. In 1995, the Uniform Clarification Act, a model law proposed by the National Conference of Commissioners on Uniform State Laws and approved by the American Bar Association, was being proposed in a number of state legislatures. The law would limit potential damages for libelous statements if a potential plaintiff requested a clarification and it was published. The potential for success was uncertain.

TIMOTHY W. GLEASON

See also Alien and Sedition Acts of 1798; First Amendment in the Eighteenth Century; Zenger, John Peter

Further Reading
Gleason, Timothy W., "The Libel Climate of the Late Nineteenth Century: A Survey of Libel Litigation, 1884–1899," *Journalism Quarterly* 70:4 (1993), pp. 893–906
_____, *The Watchdog Concept: The Press and the Courts in Nineteenth-Century America*, Ames: Iowa State University Press, 1990
Levy, Leonard W., *Emergence of a Free Press*, New York and Oxford: Oxford University Press, 1985
Lewis, Anthony, *Make No Law: The Sullivan Case and the First Amendment*, New York: Random House, 1991
Rosenberg, Norman L., *Protecting the Best Men: An Interpretive History of the Law of Libel*, Chapel Hill: University of North Carolina Press, 1986
Smith, Jeffery A., *Printers and Press Freedom: The Ideology of Early American Journalism*, New York: Oxford University Press, 1988
Soloski, John, and Randall P. Bezanson, eds., *Reforming Libel Law*, New York: Guilford, 1992

Lincoln, Abraham, and the Press

President needed to rely on the press to rally public support

As president, Abraham Lincoln had one of the first modern working relationships with the nation's press. On balance, his public statements and actions indicate that he understood and respected the press and its complexities. As a national leader, Lincoln needed the press to rally public support for his wartime decisions, but he also had occasional problems tolerating it when it appeared to threaten the security of the government or the armed forces.

Lincoln learned the value of the political press early in his career. Joseph Medill and Charles H. Ray of the *Chicago Tribune* were early and zealous advocates of his presidential prospects. The intense press coverage of Lincoln's unsuccessful 1858 campaign against Illinois Senator Stephen A. Douglas helped provide a record of their famous debates that the Republicans used to advantage in the 1860 presidential campaign. Lincoln became the first president-elect to receive regular coverage when the *New York Herald* sent correspondent Henry Villard to Springfield, Illinois, to record Lincoln's daily political and presidential activities.

Lincoln and many of his wartime policies and decisions were vilified in the press in both the north and the south. Leading editors of the day – Horace Greeley of the *New York Tribune*, James Gordon Bennett of the *New York Herald*, William Cullen Bryant of the *New York Post*, Samuel Bowles of the *Springfield Republican*, and Henry J. Raymond of the *New York Times* – alternately supported and criticized the administration's wartime decisions. The well-known Greeley was cut off from influence in the administration when Lincoln appointed the editor's political enemy, William Seward, as secretary of state. Thereafter, Greeley at times supported Lincoln and at times bitterly opposed the president and his policies.

Bennett supported the war in his high-circulation *Herald*, but his editorial criticism was a continual annoyance to

Lincoln. The independent Raymond generally was supportive in the pages of the *Times*, and he headed the national Republican campaign that reelected Lincoln in 1864. As late as the summer of 1864, key Northern editors were expressing doubt about Lincoln's reelection, but many finally rallied to his support after the Union's battlefield successes that fall.

On a personal level, Lincoln had considerable contact with Washington, D.C., correspondents and encouraged them to share their war news and views. His frequent contact led one member of his cabinet to complain that "he permits the little newsmongers to come around him and be intimate." From his pre-Washington days, Lincoln had a habit of visiting newspaper and telegraph offices, benefiting from the flow of information and opinion. At one point during the war the president observed, "The press has no better friend than I am – no one who is more ready to acknowledge its tremendous power for both good and evil."

From his vantage point in the wartime White House, Lincoln had many occasions to reflect on good and evil in the press. Working through army generals and Secretary of War Edwin M. Stanton, the administration's wartime record included suspending dissident newspapers, arresting journalists, denying them access, and censoring reports. Stanton, in particular, tightly controlled telegraph access, denied battlefield passes to correspondents, and supported military commanders when they hampered press coverage. Lincoln's statements and actions toward journalists indicate that he generally opposed punishing the many judicious editors and army correspondents for the sins of an occasional indiscreet individual.

In one of the Civil War's most famous press cases, Lincoln did not overturn the decisions of his generals, U.S. Grant and W.T. Sherman, after the latter arrested *New York Herald* reporter Thomas W. Knox on allegations of being a spy because he wrote about troop movements. The president often showed restraint, however, regarding the nettlesome Copperhead press (Northern newspapers that supported the Southern cause), even when some commanders sought to arrest prominent editors and to suspend specific publications.

In the final analysis, Lincoln's relationship with the press was somewhat bittersweet. As a political leader, he often was publicly supportive, but as a wartime president, he occasionally made difficult decisions that showed less tolerance for a free press.

TOM REILLY

See also Bennett, James Gordon Sr.; Civil War Press (North); Davis, Jefferson, and the Press; Greeley, Horace; Raymond, Henry J.

Further Reading

Andrews, J. Cutler, *The North Reports the Civil War*, Pittsburgh, Pennsylvania: University of Pittsburgh Press, 1955

Harper, Robert S., *Lincoln and the Press*, New York: McGraw-Hill, 1951

Horner, Harlan H., *Lincoln and Greeley*, Urbana: University of Illinois Press, 1953

Lincoln's Assassination

Special Dispatch

WASHINGTON, Friday, April 14, 1865, 1 1/4 A.M. – The President is slowly dying. The brain is slowly oozing through the ball hole in his forehead. He is of course insensible. There is an occasional lifting of his hand, and heavy stertorous breathing; that's all. . . . A large number of surgeons, generals, and personal family friends of Mr. Lincoln fill the house. All are in tears. Andy Johnson is here. He was in bed in his room at the Kirkwood when the assassination was committed. He was immediately apprised of the event, and got up. . . . Later – The accounts are confused and contradictory. We go to press without knowing the exact truth, but presume there is not the slightest ground for hope.

Associated Press dispatch

A Mathew Brady photograph of Abraham Lincoln
(Reproduced from the Collections of the Library of Congress)

Monaghan, Jay, *The Man Who Elected Lincoln,* Indianapolis, Indiana: Bobbs-Merrill, 1956

Neely, Mark E., Jr., *The Fate of Liberty: Abraham Lincoln and Civil Liberties,* New York: Oxford University Press, 1991

Lippmann, Walter

Influential twentieth-century journalist

Considered one of the most influential journalists of the twentieth century, Walter Lippmann won international recognition as an author, editor, and columnist. He wrote more than 25 books, including the much-acclaimed *Public Opinion* in 1922, and was a founder of the *New Republic* magazine.

In *Public Opinion,* Lippmann argued that complex political issues of the nation and world were beyond the average citizen's understanding. Thus, he argued, society needed to be managed by a specialized class. His book questioned central theories about democracy and the press, and it provided insight into the formation of public opinion. His 1955 best-seller, *The Public Philosophy,* argued that uninformed mass opinion was limiting governments from making difficult but necessary decisions.

Lippmann became editorial page editor of the *New York World* in 1924 and later was its last editor in 1931. In September 1931, he began writing a column, "Today and Tomorrow," for the *New York Herald-Tribune.* Over the next four decades, his column was syndicated to nearly 300 newspapers. His work influenced U.S. presidents from Woodrow Wilson to Lyndon Johnson. Despite the early closeness between Lippmann and Johnson, they engaged in a bitter public feud about the Vietnam War. Lippmann's feeling of being misled by the administration about war policy helped lead to his retirement in 1967.

Lippmann was awarded two Pulitzer Prizes, a special citation in 1957 for editorial comment and a prize in 1962 for distinguished reporting of international affairs. He received the Medal of Freedom in 1964.

BRADLEY J. HAMM

See also Johnson, Lyndon B., and the Media; Newspaper Columnists

Further Reading

Childs, Marquis, and James Reston, eds., *Walter Lippmann and His Times,* New York: Harcourt, Brace, 1959

Riccio, Barry D., *Walter Lippmann: Odyssey of a Liberal,* New Brunswick, New Jersey: Transaction, 1994

Steel, Ronald, *Walter Lippmann and the American Century,* Boston: Little, Brown, 1980; London: Bodley Head, 1980

Literacy and the Mass Media

High literacy rates contribute to growth and success of media forms

Dating back to the seventeenth century, the people of the United States have long enjoyed the nickname "the people of the Book." Although this book was the Bible, such a nickname underlines the fact that for centuries Americans have been characterized by their ability to read. Although U.S. literacy rates have differed over the past 400 years according to gender, ethnicity, and economic status, the consistently large percentage of people who have been able to read and write has always ranked the United States among the world's most literate countries. Such high literacy rates have had much to do with the emergence and perseverance of various forms of U.S. mass media.

A diverse array of factors have fostered the desire to read in the United States. Originally, literacy was motivated by religious belief; early Protestants in the colonies wanted everyone to be able to read the Bible. Later, literacy became subject to other motivations, including political ideologies that proclaimed that the very existence of a democratic society depended on an informed citizenry; industrialization that increasingly demanded greater literacy for obtaining lucrative jobs; and recreation, where reading simply provided an entertaining diversion.

Tied to literacy rates that reached well over 80 percent of the nation's white men and women by the Civil War was the emergence of huge printing enterprises in the nineteenth century. The story of literacy and mass media in the United States is inextricably bound to the story of publishing in the country. Changes in printing technology in the early 1800s revolutionized the publishing industry; the circulation of newspapers, pamphlets, magazines, and books all experienced exponential growth. With the possible exception of sermons by enormously popular preachers like George Whitefield in the First Great Awakening, the growing ability of printed material to be produced and distributed to large reading audiences became the first example of mass media in the United States.

Not surprisingly, the first items produced on a mass scale were Bibles and religious tracts. Beginning in the second decade of the nineteenth century, the American Bible Society and American Tract Society produced thousands of Bibles, sermons, and religious pamphlets that were distributed in all parts of the United States. It is important to note that literacy often served, in the midst of this mass production of religious material, as a means of conservative ideological control rather than something that automatically led to liberating modern thought. Literacy does not exist in a vacuum. It is subject to the institutions that help employ it. In the case of mass-produced religious material, Sunday schools, churches, and even the common school structures used literacy to reinforce more conservative religious cultural norms rather than encourage unchecked, liberated thinking.

While mass production of printed texts was largely monopolized by religious societies through the 1820s, in 1833 the penny press emerged, in large part fueled by a belief that a well-informed citizenry constituted the foundation upon which a democracy was built. Newspapers were the principal vehicle of information dispersal. "Good" citizens would read them to figure out how they might vote, as well as simply to gather local, national, and international news. In 1830, the nation had approximately 65 daily and 650 weekly papers. Circulation of such papers averaged 2,000 copies per edition. The first penny paper – named after its cost, a mere fraction of that of the usual daily or weekly paper – was the *New York Sun*, which claimed a circulation of 15,000 copies a day just two years after its birth in 1833. The *Sun* caused a revolution in the newspaper business as imitators multiplied throughout the country in the 1830s and 1840s attempting to recreate its unprecedented success. The enormous popularity of these penny papers allowed for the dispersal of information to a hitherto unknown degree.

Newspapers were not the only growth industry in early U.S. publishing. Book publishers also were discovering the phenomenon of the best-seller at about the same time. By 1850, publishers found it not only economically viable but often economically essential to produce books in 100,000 copy press runs. Two of the most famous mass-produced books in the nineteenth century were Harriet Beecher Stowe's *Uncle Tom's Cabin* (1852) and Lew Wallace's *Ben-Hur* (1880). The popularity of these stories allowed them to bleed into other forms of mass media such as touring theatrical companies and motion pictures. A dramatic version of Wallace's Ben-Hur traveled the country for 30 years and sold 6 million tickets, making it a mass media spectacle that would be echoed three times in different twentieth-century movie versions.

Other notable examples of printed mass media in the nineteenth century were schoolbooks, magazines, and chapbooks. Webster's blue-black speller and McGuffey readers were printed in the millions of copies, giving two generations of eighteenth- and nineteenth-century U.S. schoolchildren a common childhood text. Magazines such as *Godey's Lady's Book* and *Harper's Weekly* helped establish fashion trends and national codes of genteel thought and behavior. These magazines, among others, also contributed to the development of various senses of regional and national identity. The cheaply produced paperback books known as chapbooks provided entertainment – and, as some scholars have argued, new ways of interpreting one's own life experience – for the millions of readers who devoured these works on trains, in their homes, or on work breaks.

Entering the twentieth century, mass-produced newspapers, magazines, and books met new competition in the forms of moving pictures and radio broadcasts. Later joined by television in the 1950s, radio and film stood as new mass media forms that provided the printed word with significant competition for public attention. Even though these new media were able to reach huge audiences in a way that once only printed material enjoyed, they did not prove to be the death knell of either literacy or publishing in the United States. They did, however, exert pressures that changed U.S. reading and printing practices.

While the emergence of films, radio, and television is often blamed for a decrease in U.S. literacy rates, such a causal relationship is difficult to prove. Literacy rates are tied not only to other forms of mass media; they are influenced by factors as diverse as educational structures, immigration, government policy, and how well members of one's own family are able to read. The roles of reading and printed material simply have changed in the presence of other mass media forms. For example, as the twentieth century progressed, radio, newsreels, and television news programs usurped much of the newspaper's role as informant of the people. People in the United States still read newspapers, but the availability of multiple news sources certainly contributed to the national decline in newspaper circulation.

Another popular belief is that the newer forms of mass media created a society that read less and less. Again, it would be more accurate to say that the U.S. public read some forms of material less and other forms of material more. For instance, various forms of advanced technology have done much to create a society in which jobs are increasingly tied to institutional networks and training that demand ever higher levels of education. The case can be made that on-the-job reading was more critical in the late twentieth century than at any time in U.S. history.

Film, radio, and television have, however, exerted pressures that forced U.S. literacy and printing to change. Perhaps the most notable area in terms of printed material was in the area of recreational reading. While people in the United States in the late twentieth century did more reading on the job than ever before, one also can argue that they did far less nonwork-related reading. Although publishers still had a huge readers' market in genres such as romance, mystery, and horror, competition for people's free time was at a premium as computer games, television, and movies all vied for limited recreational time.

The coexistence of mass media forms such as printed books and television has caused scholars to ponder how U.S. culture has changed in a world where verbal and visual texts circulate coterminously. Although empirical studies are in short supply, some trends have been documented concerning how the people of the United States have changed with a society moving away from strictly printed forms of mass media. These trends included shorter attention spans, the inability to think in the abstract terms fostered by reading text rather than viewing images, and a growing lack of analytical reasoning abilities. Despite these trends, the United States in the late 1990s was not in a postliterate era regarding the mass media. The huge number of schoolbooks, paperback novels, and magazines sold each year pointed out the fallacy of such a belief. At the same time, however, visually oriented mass media brought changes in U.S. literacy that were only beginning to be identified at the end of the century.

PAUL GUTJAHR

See also American Tract Society; Best-Sellers; Book Publishing in the Nineteenth Century; Magazines in the Nineteenth Century; Penny Press

Further Reading

Davidson, Cathy N., ed., *Reading in America: Literature & Social History,* Baltimore, Maryland: Johns Hopkins University Press, 1989

Kaestle, Carl F., *Literacy in the United States: Readers and Reading Since 1880,* New Haven, Connecticut: Yale University Press, 1991

Kintgen, Eugene R., Barry M. Kroll, and Mike Rose, eds., *Perspectives on Literacy,* Carbondale: Southern Illinois University Press, 1988

Nord, David Paul, "The Evangelical Origins of Mass Media in America, 1815–1835," *Journalism Monographs* 88 (May 1984)

Literary Aspects of Journalism

Journalistic writing that breaks traditional boundaries

U.S. journalism always has had its writers, its literary stylists whose writing has had voice and flair and whose work has had life beyond the immediate and influence beyond the often narrow journalistic purpose. The literary form of U.S. journalism, however, has been determined by its role within society, by cultural expectations, and by those owning or operating newspapers and magazines. For instance, from the colonial days of the country through the 1840s, journalistic writing was dominated by a prose style primarily designed to convince and persuade a public rather than inform. It might best be described as informed argument, and much of it would today be called propaganda or adversarial writing.

U.S. newspapers and magazines have generally always contained at least small amounts of dramatic narrative – what might be called traditional storytelling. Accounts of certain major events, such as battles and natural disasters, often were written with a mixture of dramatic detail and rhetorical outrage, astonishment, or pleading, not unlike Isaiah Thomas's account of the battle of Lexington, which ran in a number of colonial newspapers. Otherwise, before the mid-nineteenth century, most newspaper content that did not consist of declarations – announcements, listings, notices – and magazine content that was not fictional, tended to be broadly expository or argumentative in style and structure.

This writing often was thoughtful, reasonable, and influential in America and abroad, consisting of clear arguments for or against British colonial rule or, later, dealing with the nature and structure of the country's constitution and first government. Much of it was fiery and passionate, appealing to the emotions of its readers and serving as a call to arms.

Some of the eighteenth-century writing – for instance that by James Rivington, a colonial printer, bookseller, and loyalist, or by Joseph Dennie, the founding editor of *Port Folio* magazine and the writer of the "Lay Preacher" essays – was witty, satirical, and polished. But Dennie's work, like that of Benjamin Franklin before him, also was intended to speak from the voice of knowledge and experience, often through a fictional character who would instruct readers on morals, manners, and behavior, just as Franklin's "Silence Dogood" had.

It also was not uncommon through the mid-nineteenth century to treat journalism as one of literature's streams. Thus, a significant early U.S. poet, Philip Freneau, wrote travel accounts for the *United States Magazine* in the style common to literate people, saw his poetry published in the newspapers he edited, and wrote scathing attacks on President George Washington. Dennie, meanwhile, wrote biting criticism of Thomas Jefferson but also was known as the "American Addison" and the premier cultural critic of the late 1700s. In the 1800s, William Cullen Bryant was a well-known poet and literary critic before becoming a journalist and eventually editor of the New York *Post,* where he worked from 1829 to 1878.

As the nineteenth century proceeded, literary aspects of U.S. journalism style tended to follow a path similar to that of U.S. fiction. Two emerging printed prose forms – news writing and novel writing – both sought to capture contemporary reality by actually depicting peoples' lives and behavior. Fiction, through the local color and realism movements, started to capture the common and ordinary through the use of local and regional dialect and vivid, specific description. Use of dialect, dialogue, scene setting, and vignettes that revealed distinctly "American" behavior became common to fiction and to journalism.

Not only did the newspaper become a vehicle for realism and local color, but the magazine did as well, especially *Harper's Monthly.* Longtime *Harper's* editor Henry Mills Alden demanded writing that presented life as a "living, moving drama," writing that contained faithful portrayals of human nature. By the 1880s and 1890s, newspaper reporters such as Julian Ralph or Richard Harding Davis saw material from their reporters' notebooks that did not get in the newspaper get printed in magazines such as *Harper's,* where descriptive narrative or literary journalism was welcomed.

Nevertheless, newspapers also contained their share of human drama, descriptive narrative, and storytelling. Prominent examples can be found in Mark Twain's work for newspapers in Nevada and San Francisco, including his dispatches to the Alta, California, newspaper that later became the book *The Innocents Abroad,* or in Lafcadio Hearn's gruesome and poignant accounts of Cincinnati, Ohio, street life for the *Cincinnati Enquirer.*

By the 1890s, led to a degree by Charles Dana's *New York Sun* in the 1870s and 1880s, stories of a city's people, its crimes, its neighborhoods, and its rising immigrant population were a major ingredient of any metropolitan newspaper. A French observer noticing this trend declared in *Scribner's Magazine* in 1906 that the U.S. newspaper was "a huge collection of short stories."

Nevertheless, that was already in the process of changing. By the turn of the twentieth century, poets were no longer editing newspapers, and perhaps the epitome of the new editor was Carr Van Anda of the *New York Times,* with his education in science, his devotion to factual thoroughness, and his many years diligently putting out newspapers in Ohio, New York, and Baltimore, Maryland.

Newspapers had become businesses run by businessmen, while newspaper content tended to be shaped by reporters and editors who were increasingly treated as professional journalists.

As the twentieth century progressed, the information model of news writing, exemplified by the *New York Times* and the Associated Press, soon came to dominate newspaper style. Magazines, on the other hand, tended to use descriptive narrative only as one technique of many in the investigative reporting and exposé writing that was known as muckraking.

When *Time* magazine was founded in 1923, its emphasis on colorful details and chronological narration stood in direct contrast to the established newspaper style that placed the most important facts – the who, what, and where – in the first paragraph. The rest of the article was filled with information and official literary aspects of journalism quotes, presented in descending order of importance.

By the 1930s, most non-advertising newspaper content consisted of informational news reports, formulaic features, and columns by commentators who mostly tried to provide context and perspective to the news. The newspaper industry sold its journalism not as a literary form or a cultural form of expression, although it was that, but as a neutral disseminator of facts and information, with commentary designed to enlighten or illuminate. Readers were no longer to treat the newspaper's content as writing, subjective depiction, or interpretation (unless so designated by the editor), but as science and truth.

Journalism as literature, or journalism with a literary purpose rather than an informational purpose – nonfiction writing that focused not on facts but on the themes and ideas suggested by the facts – came to be found primarily in magazines, including the *New Yorker, Life,* occasionally *Fortune,* and eventually *The Saturday Evening Post.* Some publications, such as *Harper's* or the *Atlantic,* remained journals of literary and cultural criticism but devoted much space to in-depth articles on public policy and social issues.

As publications changed their editorial mix, the one magazine that consistently published high-quality literary journalism was the *New Yorker,* whose outstanding writers of nonfiction that tended to inform at a level common to fiction included Joseph Mitchell, A.J. Liebling, John Hersey, Lillian Ross, and Truman Capote. By the 1970s, Jane Kramer, Calvin Trillin, Tracy Kidder, and John McPhee could be added to the list of *New Yorker* writers serving a journalistic tradition that was more than 100 years old. One critic's comment regarding McPhee – that he had "a journalist's reverence for facts" but "a novelist's propensity for symbols" – might be said about any of these writers and literary journalists generally.

The so-called new journalism of the 1960s and 1970s marked a major rediscovery of literary journalism. This would be the third time that literary journalism became so visible and important culturally, the first time being in the 1890s and the second in the 1930s and 1940s. In addition to the *New Yorker, Esquire* and two new magazines, *Rolling Stone* and *New York,* became prominent sources of literary journalism, a term that came into favor in the 1980s.

There also arose a fresh interest in style and literary technique at newspapers as well. Not only did many newspapers place new emphasis on improving and encouraging strong writing, but some newspapers demanded more imaginative approaches to writing the news, in effect returning journalism to its more literary roots.

THOMAS B. CONNERY

See also Magazines in the Eighteenth Century; Magazines in the Nineteenth Century; Magazines in the Twentieth Century; New Journalism (1880s); New Journalism (1960s – 1970s)

Further Reading

Berner, R. Thomas, "Literary Newswriting: The Death of an Oxymoron," *Journalism Monographs* 99 (October 1986)

Connery, Thomas B., ed., *A Sourcebook of American Literary Journalism: Representative Writers in an Emerging Genre,* New York: Greenwood, 1992

Fishkin, Shelley Fisher, *From Fact to Fiction: Journalism and Imaginative Writing in America,* Baltimore, Maryland: Johns Hopkins University Press, 1985; Oxford: Oxford University Press, 1988

Hughes, Helen M., *News and the Human Interest Story,* Chicago: University of Chicago Press, 1940

Pickett, Calder M., *Voices of the Past: Key Documents in the History of American Journalism,* Columbus, Ohio: Grid, 1977; London: Collier Macmillan, 1977

Sims, Norman, ed., *Literary Journalism in the Twentieth Century,* New York: Oxford University Press, 1990

Snyder, Louis L., and Richard B. Morris, eds., *A Treasury of Great Reporting,* 2nd ed., New York: Simon and Schuster, 1962

Los Angeles Times

Founding of a powerful voice in journalism

When Harrison Gray Otis became editor of the year-old *Los Angeles Times* in 1882, the town of about 5,000 was a poor cousin to San Francisco. Thanks in no small part to the newspaper dynasty Otis subsequently founded and to the family's use of the *Times* to promote southern California, both the region and the newspaper prospered mightily.

Otis became sole owner of the *Times,* as well as its companion publication, the *Mirror,* in 1886, about the same time he was joined in the business by Harry Chandler, a younger man who had moved to California for his health. Chandler subsequently married Otis's daughter Marion.

Otis and Chandler were antiunion and pro-development, and politically conservative. Chandler became a major landholder in southern California and was instrumental in bringing Owens River water to the region, making his own fortune in the bargain. Harry and Marion Chandler's son, Norman, continued the family's conservative management of the newspaper.

The ascension of Norman's son, Otis, to *Times* executive

ranks in 1960 brought a commitment to quality journalism. In the second half of the twentieth century, the newspaper that at one time had been little more than a parochial California organ became one of the most respected daily newspapers in the world.

BARBARA CLOUD

Further Reading

Gottlieb, Robert, and Irene Wolfe, *Thinking Big: The Story of the 'Los Angeles Times', Its Publishers, and Their Influence on Southern California,* New York: Putnam's, 1977

Halberstam, David, *The Powers That Be,* New York: Knopf, 1979; London: Chatto and Windus, 1979

Luce, Henry R.

Founder of 'Time' magazine

The son of Presbyterian missionaries, Henry R. Luce graduated from Yale University in 1920. Luce and college classmate Briton Hadden founded *Time,* a newsmagazine, three years later. *Time* presented weekly news summaries assembled in a sometimes irreverent, always omniscient fashion. *Time*'s circulation expanded greatly in the 1930s and 1940s, especially among the country's opinion leadership.

A year after Hadden's death in 1929, Luce started *Fortune,* a business monthly. Relying on innovative photojournalists and talented young writers, *Fortune* proved a success financially and journalistically. Luce oversaw two more popular ventures: the *March of Time* radio programs, weekly news summaries modeled after *Time* that first aired in 1931, and a newsreel version that debuted in 1935.

In 1936, Luce established *Life,* the country's first inex-pensively priced "picture weekly." *Life* benefited from the public's long-unmet preference for visual communication of news, in addition to technical advances in photography; it quickly became one of the most popular magazines in the United States.

Luce began to involve himself in politics in 1940–41, when he joined other prominent journalists and publishers supporting U.S. involvement in World War II. In a February 1941 *Life* essay, "The American Century," Luce admonished the people of the United States to end their historic affinity for isolationism and assume global leadership. Soon after the war's end, Luce urged a hard-line against the Soviet Union and the Communist Chinese.

As editor-in-chief of Time, Inc., Luce supervised the start of *Sports Illustrated* in 1954. *Time* and *Life* continued to flourish, although their political biases, in favor of the Republican party and U.S. globalism, increasingly annoyed critics. Luce retired in 1964 and died three years later.

JAMES L. BAUGHMAN

See also Magazines in the Twentieth Century; Newsmagazines; Pictorial Magazines; Time Warner

Further Reading

Baughman, James L., *Henry R. Luce and the Rise of the American News Media,* Boston: Twayne, 1987

Elson, Robert T., *Time, Inc.,* 3 vols., New York: Atheneum, 1968–1986

Herzstein, Robert E., *Henry R. Luce: A Political Portrait of the Man Who Created the American Century,* New York: Scribner's, 1994; Don Hills, Ontario: Maxwell Macmillan Canada, 1994

Kobler, John, *Luce: His Time, Life, and Fortune,* Garden City, New York: Doubleday, 1968; London: Macdonald, 1968

Swanberg, W.A., *Luce and His Empire,* New York: Scribner's, 1972

M

Madison Avenue, USA

Study of cultural and social aspects of the advertising industry

When it was published in 1958, *Madison Avenue, USA,* by Martin Mayer, was unlike any previous volume on advertising. Most advertising works before Mayer's book either were unabashed promotions of advertising or concluded that virtually every ill in the United States could be laid at advertising's doorstep. *Madison Avenue, USA,* was a generally accurate and insightful look at all aspects of advertising, including personalities, agencies, media, campaigns, research, and advertising industry problems.

While something of an apology for advertising, the book still managed to penetrate to the heart of the craft as it was practiced in the middle of the twentieth century. Mayer went into all aspects of advertising by talking to about 400 practitioners. This resulted in an emphasis on the cultural and social aspects of advertising. The book was a story about people rather than the business and economics of advertising.

Beyond dealing with the craft in all its day-to-day manifestations, one of Mayer's most important discussions looked at how advertising represented political entities in the United States. While still written from the perspective of big names, the book looked at the role of advertising practitioners in the political campaigns of the 1940s and 1950s in a way that still has application for today. There is still much that is accurate in *Madison Avenue, USA,* but the years also have bypassed some of what the author had to say.

DONALD R. AVERY

Further Reading

Mayer, Martin, *Madison Avenue, USA,* New York: Harper, 1958; London: Bodley Head, 1958

Magazine Advertising

As magazines grew in number and importance, advertising in them increased

For centuries, advertising was concentrated in handbills and circulars, outdoor signs, and newspapers. Once considered an embarrassment for which few took responsibility, in the late 1800s, the industry began to reform itself by obtaining trustworthy circulation statements from publishers, developing contracts for proper associations between agents and advertisers, establishing successful campaigns by national advertisers other than patent medicines, and implementing legitimate copywriting and advertising styles.

Another factor in the reformation of advertising was the national magazine. Changes in advertising helped create a new medium that successfully combined information, entertainment, and selling. The evolution of the magazine into a respectable advertising medium included changes in magazine publishing and coincided with other transformations in U.S. society.

Magazines proliferated in the nineteenth-century United States to include special interest magazines and strong editorial figures such as Sara Hale, publisher of *Godey's Ladies' Book.* Magazine content included political news, essays on society, short fiction, poetry, and polemics. For much of the century, magazines contained little, if any, advertising other than a few classified notices. Separated from the editorial and textual content, advertisements were restricted to a page or two per issue. *Godey's* promoted the Great American Tea Company on its back cover while the more popular monthly magazines such as the *Atlantic, Harper's,* and *Scribner's* were financed by publishing houses that ran advertisements on the back pages for their own books. The more successful magazines aimed their considerable reading material at a more affluent, literate readership and derived their revenue mainly from subscription fees.

One exception to this trend in magazine publishing was achieved by E.C. Allen, who recognized the potential of magazines as an advertising medium. Allen's *People's Literary Companion* was launched to advertise his soap powder formula. Unlike other magazines of the era, Allen's lived by advertising and attracted readers to its short stories and household hints with an inexpensive price of 50 cents or less. When circulation jumped to more than 500,000, Allen expanded his publishing empire to a dozen magazines for home and farm readerships – or "mail-order journals," as they were called. The "polite" magazines with their "gentle readers," however, took pride in not emulating Allen's methods, at least for a while.

National advertising was central to the so-called maga-

Nineteenth-century advertising dealt mainly with words.

(Davis Library, University of North Carolina at Chapel Hill)

zine revolution of the late nineteenth century. Like E.C. Allen, advertising agency pioneer J. Walter Thompson realized that magazines were prominent advertising vehicles because they remained on reading tables in people's homes for a month and were read repeatedly, often by women, who usually were responsible for household purchases. Thompson explored the advertising potential of magazines by placing an advertisement for asbestos roofing in *Godey's* and *Peterson's*. Despite being placed in women's journals, the ads sold more roofing than any promotion in the company's history. Thompson repeated the demonstration with another product and, based on these successes, was able to convince the leading monthlies to run advertisements for such products as Pabst beer, Mennen talcum powder, Kodak cameras, Prudential insurance, and Durkee's salad dressing. By 1876, *Scribner's* was carrying 20 pages of ads per issue with no apparent loss in literary integrity. Thompson attracted advertisers by brandishing a list of 25 to 30 magazines that were under his exclusive contract. This "Standard List" included virtually all of the leading U.S. magazines such as the *Atlantic, Harper's, Godey's, Peterson's,* and *Century* (the successor to *Scribner's*).

Magazine publishers began to capitalize on a formula that identified a mass audience and gave it what it wanted to read, reduced the price of magazines to below the cost of production, and sold advertising space at rates based on (large) circulation figures. Profits were made on advertising revenues instead of on subscriptions. Two of the first publishers to employ consciously this new formula were Frank Munsey and Cyrus Curtis. After two years of moderate success, Munsey reduced the price of his *Munsey's Journal* in October 1893 from a quarter to a dime. The circulation of *Munsey's Journal*, which featured light topical stories and pictures of scantily dressed women, rose from 40,000 in October 1893 to 200,000 the following February, and to 500,000 in April. In 1895, two other general monthlies, *McClure's* and *Cosmopolitan*, also dropped their prices to 10 cents.

Cyrus Curtis spun off the *Ladies' Home Journal* in 1883 from his farmer's weekly, the *Tribune and Farmer*. The *Journal* started with a circulation of 50,000, and after a major advertising campaign on its behalf by the Wayland Ayer agency, circulation rose to 750,000. Unlike his colleagues, Curtis doubled the subscription cost and launched a campaign that saw the magazine's ad columns filled with Ayer clients. Curtis spent $150,000 on advertising in 1890 and eventually hired a sales force just for the *Journal*. Curtis paid close attention to the format and presentation of ads and initiated the process of actually designing ads and selling them to advertisers. In 1896, editor Edward Bok began the practice of ad-stripping, or tailing, whereby fiction and other features were interrupted and continued into columns in the back pages, thus drawing readers' attention back to advertisements otherwise ignored.

By the beginning of the twentieth century, magazines contributed to a revitalized advertising industry and provided a foundation for subsequent developments in the commercialization of mass media. Not only were print media and advertising altered by magazine publishing's innovations in photographic and color reproduction techniques, but magazines established many of the marketing and distribution methods that would come to be used by most commercial media institutions. Magazines eventually provided services desired by advertisers such as consumer panels and research services. The use of audience research instead of circulation data became the standard response to broadcasting's competitive challenge as an advertising medium. Magazines' practice of selling target audiences to advertisers became the dominant media marketing strategy in the twentieth century.

DWIGHT E. BROOKS

See also Advertising in the Nineteenth Century; Advertising in the Twentieth Century; Magazines in the Nineteenth Century; Magazines in the Twentieth Century

Further Reading

Leiss, William, Stephen Kline, and Sut Jhally, *Social Communication in Advertising: Persons, Products and Images of Well-Being,* 2nd ed., New York and London: Routledge, 1990; Scarborough, Ontario: Nelson Canada, 1990
Ohmann, Richard, "Where Did Mass Culture Come

Twentieth-century magazine advertising contained illustrations and fewer words.

(Davis Library, University of North Carolina at Chapel Hill)

From? The Case of Magazines," *Berkshire Review* 16 (1981)

Schmidt, Dorothy, "Magazines," in *American Popular Culture: A Historical Bibliography,* edited by Arthur F. Wertheim, Santa Barbara, California: ABC-Clio Information Services, 1984

Wilson, Christopher P., "The Rhetoric of Consumption: Mass Market Magazines and the Demise of the Gentle Reader, 1880–1920," in *The Culture of Consumption: Critical Essays in American History, 1880–1980,* edited by Richard Wightman Fox and T.J. Jackson Lears, New York: Pantheon, 1983

Magazine Awards

The most prestigious magazine awards in the United States at the end of the twentieth century were the National Magazine Awards, sponsored by the American Society of Magazine Editors (ASME) and administered by the Columbia University Graduate School of Journalism. The awards were given annually from 1970 and were awarded in 11 categories: general excellence (with four subcategories by circulation); personal service; special interests; reporting; feature writing; public interest; design; photography; fiction; essays and criticism; and single-topic issue. In each category, the award – represented by an Alexander Calder sculpture known as an Ellie (for its resemblance to an elephant) – was given to the magazine itself, rather than to the individual writer, editor, photographer, or designer of the winning entry. As of the late 1990s, the *New Yorker* had won the most National Magazine Awards, most of them in the reporting and fiction categories. This highly competitive competition drew 1,310 entries from 323 magazines in 1995.

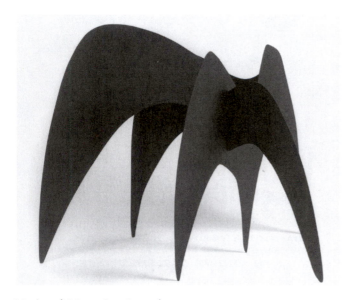

National Magazine Award
(Courtesy of the American Society of Magazine Editors)

The Magazine Publishers of America (MPA), which included the ASME, gave two other annual awards. One was the Henry Johnson Fisher Award, a tribute to magazine executives who made significant contributions to the business. The other was the Kelly Award, named for former MPA president Stephen E. Kelly and given from 1981 to recognize outstanding magazine advertising. Awards were made in several categories; the general excellence prize of $100,000 went to the advertising agency creative team judged to have produced the year's best magazine ad campaign. Other advertising competitions recognizing magazine work included the American Advertising Federation's Addy Awards and the American Marketing Association's Effie Awards.

The business-press counterpart of the National Magazine Awards were the Jesse H. Neal Awards, awarded annually by the American Business Press (ABP) and named for the organization's first managing director. In 1995, the awards' fortieth year, a national group of judges considered nearly 700 entries in six categories. The ABP also gave the Crain Award to recognize individuals' career contributions to business publishing. The American Society of Business Press Editors Awards honored trade publications as well.

Other awards for magazine journalism were the John Bartlow Martin Awards for Public Service Magazine Journalism, sponsored by the Medill School of Journalism at Northwestern University; the magazine categories of the George Polk Journalism Awards, administered by Long Island University; the Computer Press Awards; and the Gerald R. Loeb Awards for Distinguished Business and Financial Journalism. In addition, magazine editorial content was considered for annual awards given by national media organizations including the following: the Society of Professional Journalists (Sigma Delta Chi Awards); Investigative Reporters and Editors (based at the University of Missouri); the Overseas Press Club of America; the National Press Photographers Association (Pictures of the Year Awards); and Women in Communication (Clarion Awards). Finally, magazine entries were eligible for awards made by several groups representing minorities and other special interests, including the National Association of Black Journalists; the Gay and Lesbian Press Association; the Amy Foundation (awards for religious and inspirational writing in secular media); the National Easter Seal Society (EDI Awards for coverage of disability issues); and the Casey Journalism Center for Children and Families (Casey Medals for coverage of disadvantaged children).

CAROLYN KITCH

Magazine Circulation

Evaluating how magazines get into the hands of readers

Magazine circulation governs how magazines get into the hands of the publications' readers. For consumer magazines (those generally available to the public), circulation is a major source of revenue, providing an industry average of 53 percent of the publication's revenue in 1991.

Magazines operate as paid-circulation publications, controlled-circulation publications, or some combination of the two. Operating under a paid-circulation policy means that readers pay for the magazine, either by subscription or single-copy sales. A controlled-circulation policy means that readers are limited (or controlled) to those who meet specific criteria or qualifications set by the publication; such readers usually receive the magazine free.

Since advertising prices, or rates, and sales are determined by the audience number and its quality, publications must be able to prove just how many readers, paid or qualified, the magazine has. Advertisers expect magazines to deliver the stated minimum number of readers. For example, if a magazine sells advertisements based on a total paid circulation of 100,000, its circulation must have been at least 100,000 during the previous six months. If not, the publisher owes the advertiser a refund.

One way in which magazines and advertisers provide such proof is by means of an audit. In the late 1990s, there were two major auditing groups. Both groups set uniform practices and standards by which circulation was defined and reported. Audits make meaningful comparisons among publications possible. Audits provide a thorough breakdown of the average circulation by issue, identifying circulation, subscriptions, single-copy sales, association sales, duration and price of subscriptions sold, whether or not the sale involved a premium, and the channel of sale.

The Audit Bureau of Circulations and the Business Publications Audit of Circulation, Inc., were membership groups made up of publishers, ad agencies, and advertisers. Dues were based on circulation for the publishers and on annual print media billings for the advertisers. When a publication was audited, the member paid the cost of the audit. Auditors examined postal receipts, printers' bills, paper inventories and usage, data from national distributors, circulation records, and income receipts. They also sampled mailing lists and examined the request lists of controlled magazines. Some magazines offered a sworn statement while others used an independent verification service or simply postal receipts.

A paid-circulation magazine has the obvious advantage of generating revenue through subscriptions and single-copy sales. Paid-circulation publications also qualify for lower second-class postage rates. Paid circulation usually means cleaner mail lists, and cleaner lists mean that a publication might be able to rent that list for a higher fee. Clean lists also mean less waste. Publications may continue sending issues to subscribers after the expiration of the subscription for up to three months. This is called gracing the subscription. After that time, however, the name may no longer be counted toward the circulation total. Since it is expensive to send publications to those who do not pay and cannot be counted in the circulation number for generating advertising dollars, good circulation practice purges them from the active mail list. In addition, paid-circulation subscribers renew, usually annually. This renewal process provides an ongoing report on the organization's vitality, direction, service, and editorial content.

The major disadvantage of paid circulation is the expense of generating new subscriptions and maintaining that subscriber base. Publications generate some circulation through single-copy sales, but there is also a cost involved in this line of sales. The average industry return on the cover price is approximately 50 percent, the rest being taken by national distributors, wholesalers, and retailers. In addition, single-copy sales simply do not generate high circulation numbers. In 1980, single-copy sales accounted for an average 16 percent of the circulation revenues. By 1991, the percentage of single-copy revenue had dropped to 14 percent.

Consequently, subscriptions become crucial. Sales often are generated through expensive, direct-mail campaigns. These campaigns put thousands, even millions, of promotions in the mail, and only 2 to 5 percent of the recipients respond. Of those who do, an average of 30 percent of them never pay the subscription rate. These direct-mail packages cost more than $300 for every 1,000 packages. Launching a new publication by direct mail might easily cost $500,000 to more than $1 million; each new subscriber may cost publishers from $10 to $40. The industry average annual subscription rate in 1990 was $27.11.

Controlled circulation avoids this major expense, since the publisher determines who qualifies for the magazine. The advantages show up in greatly reduced promotional costs and the ability to build circulation quickly. In addition, controlled publications reach all significant persons in a particular field and therefore have an interested audience. Such publications can be structured horizontally, going to specific personnel regardless of industry – for example, purchasing officers, or even purchasing officers who manage $10 million in annual expenditures. Publications also can operate vertically, top to bottom, in one industry – from the chief executive officer to the producer and all the middlemen in between.

Magazines may have both paid and controlled circulation. Most magazines, however, have a predominance of one or the other. Some publications may begin life in one form and gradually convert as business strategy determines. *Folio*, the publication for the magazine industry, began as a controlled-circulation publication. After a few years it began to qualify fewer readers and converted some of them to subscribers. By 1994, *Folio*'s circulation was 71 percent paid.

Once subscribers are on board, the circulation department has to get the magazine into their hands. This service is referred to as fulfillment. The preparation of mailing lists, purging of names, and addition of new names can be done in-house or contracted to others. Fulfillment houses process data for hundreds of magazines and charge a fee (75 cents to more than a dollar per name per year). Given the specialized nature of fulfillment, it may make sense to farm that operation out. On the other hand, each circulation department provides its own customer service to deal with complaints and queries.

S.M.W. BASS

See also Specialized Business Publications

Further Reading

Click, J. William, and Russell N. Baird, *Magazine Editing and Production,* Dubuque, Iowa: W.C. Brown, 1974

Magazine Publishers of America, *MPA Handbook: A Comprehensive Guide for Advertisers, Ad Agencies and Magazine Marketers,* No. 64, 1992–1993, New York: Magazine Publishers of America, 1993

Mogel, Leonard, *The Magazine: Everything You Need to Know to Make It in the Magazine Business,* 2nd ed., Chester, Connecticut: Globe Pequot, 1988

_____, *Making It in the Media Professions: A Realistic Guide to Career Opportunities in Newspapers, Magazines, Books, Television, Radio, the Movies, and Advertising,* Chester, Connecticut: Globe Pequot, 1988

Magazine Competition

Publications vie for readers, advertisers

Magazines have long held positions of influence and impact on U.S. journalism. Like newspapers, they have evolved in size, circulation, price, typography, market, and means of distribution, as well as in editorial and advertising content. The one constant in the world of magazines has been intense, even fierce, competition. Virtually every successful magazine has spawned similar publications that sought to further segment the market. Since the late 1800s, the center of the U.S. magazine industry has been located, with few exceptions, in New York City.

Benjamin Franklin and Andrew Bradford are generally credited with starting in 1741 the first magazines in the United States. Franklin's *General Magazine and Historical Chronicle* lasted six issues before folding; Bradford's *American Magazine* lasted three. Since the founding of the *Saturday Evening Post* in 1821, magazines in the United States truly have become a national institution. *Harper's New Monthly* was started in 1850, followed by *Harper's Weekly,* which during the Civil War boasted a circulation of more than 100,000. The *Atlantic Monthly* was founded in 1857, and two years later, *Vanity Fair* was launched. *Harper's Bazaar,* begun in 1867, became the precursor to the high-fashion monthly magazines of the twentieth century. The Postal Act in 1879 pioneered relatively inexpensive mass mailing rates that eventually allowed mass circulation of thousands of start-up magazines. The inaugural issue of the *Ladies' Home Journal* came out in 1883, and by 1903, it was the first magazine to boast 1 million subscribers. The high-end women's fashion magazine *Vogue,* originally a weekly, started in 1892.

The magazine industry is studded with milestones. *McClure's,* published in 1893, published strong political exposés, a type of journalism labeled "muckraking" by President Theodore Roosevelt. In 1896, the National Geographic Society launched a monthly that carried as its title the society's name. In 1919, Bernarr Macfadden started *True Story,* triggering the entry into the marketplace of scores of detective and confession magazines, known as "pulps." Named because originally they were printed on rough, wood-pulp stock, the magazines carried fiction and ran little advertising. Popular titles included *Argosy, Detective Story,* and *Amazing Stories.*

DeWitt Wallace in 1922 introduced *Reader's Digest,* an advertisement-free compendium of reprinted articles. To accommodate the post–World War I boom years, Meredith Corporation launched *Better Homes and Gardens* in 1922, which followed the earlier entries on domesticity, *Town and Country,* originally launched in 1846, *House Beautiful* in 1896, and *House and Garden* in 1901.

In 1923, Henry Luce and Briton Hadden began the publishing concept of the newsweekly with *Time,* followed a decade later by *Newsweek,* which was started by Thomas J.C. Martyn, and *United States News,* begun by syndicated columnist David Lawrence. Legendary editor Harold Ross in 1925 first published a sophisticated literary magazine,

Periodicals Published
1935–1990

Year	Total	Weekly	Semi-Weekly	Monthly	Bi-Monthly	Quarterly
1935	6,546	1,484	203	3,608	196	493
1940	6,432	1,399	427	4.466	241	538
1945	6,569	1,359	246	3,503	309	578
1950	6,960	1.443	416	3,694	436	604
1955	7,648	1,602	503	3,78	2608	674
1960	8,422	1,580	527	4,113	743	895
1965	8,990	1,716	550	4,195	876	1,030
1970	9,573	1,856	589	4,314	957	1,108
1975	9,657	1,918	537	4,807	1,009	1,093
1980	10,236	1,716	645	3,985	1,114	1,444
1985	11,090	1,367	801	4,088	1,361	1,759
1990	11,092	553	435	4,239	2,087	2,758

Notes: Totals for Alaska and Hawaii included as of 1960.

Source: Datapedia of the United States 1790–2000: America Year by Year. George Thomas Kurian (Bernan Press: Lanham, Maryland, 1994).

the *New Yorker*. Large-format magazines *Esquire* and *Life* came on the market in 1933 and 1936, respectively, followed by another similar general-circulation publication, *Look*. To compete with business magazine *Forbes,* started in 1917, two influential titles were launched, ironically, just before or during the Great Depression: McGraw-Hill in 1929 started *Business Week,* followed five months later by Time, Inc.'s, *Fortune.*

In 1950, Hugh Hefner launched *Playboy;* in 1953, Walter Annenberg started *TV Guide;* and in 1954, Time, Inc., inaugurated *Sports Illustrated.* Jann Wenner started *Rolling Stone* in 1967 to cover the world of rock music and the youth subculture. In 1972, a collective group of women led by Gloria Steinem published the first issue of *Ms.,* a monthly largely devoted to issues raised for the women's movement. Time, Inc., in 1974 entered the gossip magazine market by introducing *People.* In the late 1990s, magazines numbered more than 11,150; the average cover price was $4.15.

Throughout the rise of such consumer magazines, there was a similar increase in launches of trade, technical, and professional magazines. At the end of the twentieth century, every conceivable profession and hobby had its own specialty magazine. Titles included *Pizza Today, Cigar Aficionado, Bowling Proprietor,* and *Mortuary Management.*

The rapid rise of specialized, so-called niche magazines in the early 1970s was destined by the popularity of general circulation publications, which had fallen victim to their own success. *Life,* for example, had a circulation of 8.6 million readers in 1970, but with such a large circulation, production and distribution costs outpaced advertising dollars. A prevailing sentiment among advertisers was that such mass audience subscribers could be reached more economically through television advertising. Such views, coupled with a dramatic increase in postal rates in 1972, spurred many advertisers to opt for other, more cost-efficient ways to reach consumers.

While specialty magazines were not new – niche publications targeted for women had been around for almost 100 years – during the early and mid-1970s, economic factors pushed publishers to invent magazines designed to appeal to increasingly narrow segments of the reading public. Such magazines focused on issues such as sports, food, exercise, computers, and health. Many were not pitched solely to the subscribers but to casual newsstand buyers. The change prompted publishers to carefully consider magazine covers as inducements for impulse buying.

As cable television boasted increasing numbers of subscribers in the 1980s, a further erosion occurred. Declining advertising revenue and a drop in circulation in the 1990s plagued the magazine industry and further forced publishers to target even greater specialized markets. Controlled-circulation publications (magazines distributed free to demographically select audiences) flourished. With few exceptions, magazines that increased advertising pages included those that could pinpoint-deliver a specific market that could not be reached as effectively by any other medium. Magazines that flourished targeted very selective niche markets (i.e., specific geographic regions, lifestyles, age-groups, and avocations). Desktop publishing made small-circulation start-ups as easy as owning or borrowing a computer

and software. As the cost of postage increased, magazines also moved to smaller sizes and lighter paper stock, which reduced mailing costs.

To further customize content to niche readers, publishers in the early 1990s began using a technique known as selective edit, in which special editorial sections could be inserted into magazines and sent to targeted readers. Such sections differed from advertorials, which combine editorial and advertising content to provide special themed sections. Selective edit called for specialized information the subscriber wanted, and often paid for, about specific sports teams, players, businesses, and mortgage rates in subscribers' regions. Another practice, selective binding, in which different ads were inserted in the same issue of a magazine based on the issue's zip code destination, also flourished.

A final entry to the world of magazines in the late twentieth century included multimedia development, such as niche cable markets of the content of magazines as well as CD-ROM versions, and on-line electronic versions of magazines. Subscribers accessed these last two variations electronically, by computer. The profitability of these entries, which remained to be seen in the late 1990s, was eagerly watched, as traditional magazines' circulation and ad revenues were not seen as increasing dramatically.

STEPHEN G. BLOOM

See also Muckraking; Post Office and the Media; Specialized Business Publications

Further Reading

Carmody, Deirdre, "Magazines Go Niche-Hunting with Custom-Made Sections," *New York Times* (June 26, 1995)
Ford, James L.C., *Magazines for Millions,* Carbondale: Southern Illinois University Press, 1969
Holm, Kirsten, "Current Trends in Publishing," in *Writer's Market, 1995,* edited by Mark Garvey, Cincinnati, Ohio: Writer's Digest, 1994
Kummerfeld, Donald D., "New Media and Magazines: Where Do We Go from Here?," *Folio: Special Sourcebook 1995*
Noack, David, "Cyberspace in Print; Magazines for the On-line Industry," *Quill* (June 1994)
Wolseley, Roland E., *The Changing Magazine: Trends in Readership and Management,* New York: Hastings House, 1973

Magazine Design

Technology and art combine in creating overall impression

To the layperson, magazine design may seem little more than the arrangement of type and images on the printed page. In fact, magazine design embodies a rich history, one that reflects technology, art, and shifting social values, as well as the sensibilities of the people who have practiced it.

What historians consider modern magazine design – design that weaves together art, type, and space – is largely a product of the twentieth century. In the 1800s, magazine formats were smaller than today, which allowed for little flexibility in design. Most magazines featured one- or two-column layouts with titles centered on the pages. Illustrations were made from woodcuts – illustrations engraved on wood and impressed onto paper. The limitations of technology and space dictated the design of magazines.

Printing technologies developed at the turn of the twentieth century made it easier and less expensive to reproduce color and black-and-white art. The new technology also opened the way to two design movements that were taking shape in Europe: modernism and dadaism.

The modernists are credited with creating the cohesive look of the contemporary magazine. Modernists looked at magazine stories as packages inside the larger package of the magazine. They emphasized designing stories across several pages rather than on individual pages. Type and art reinforced the theme of a story, and by setting type in varying sizes on a page, they created a hierarchy to lead readers through a story.

Modernism's predecessor, and its opposite, was dadaism, which advocated expressing ideas through flexible, even chaotic, treatments of type and art. Dadaist designers were the first to use collage and photomontage in magazine design. They also were the first to place photos in storytelling sequence, the genesis of photojournalism in magazines.

Modernism's home was the Bauhaus design school in Germany. Founded in 1919, the school preached that "form follows function." It promoted utilitarian, geometric layouts that contained only the elements necessary to tell a story. Adolf Hitler shut down the school in 1933, but not before its influence had spread far beyond Germany's borders.

Modernism came across the ocean in the late 1920s with the Parisian designer M.F. Agha, whom Condé Nast hired to reinvent the formats of his flagship magazines, *Vogue* and *Vanity Fair.* Agha was more than a page designer; he exercised artistic as well as editorial judgment, which, in ef-

fect, made him the first art director in the United States. As a result, he was able to weave art, type, space, and editorial content into a whole. Agha simplified the design of *Vogue* and *Vanity Fair* to give emphasis to the photos. He got rid of all decorative elements: lines, borders, column rules. After *Vanity Fair* became a victim of the Great Depression, Agha continued to direct the design of *Vogue,* as well as *House and Garden,* until 1942.

Agha's work at Condé Nast heralded a new era in U.S. magazine publishing, one in which the art director played a key role. Other than Agha, the two most prominent art directors to emerge in the 1930s were T.M. Cleland at Time, Inc., and Alexey Brodovitch at Hearst Magazines. The trio formed a design triumvirate that permanently influenced U.S. magazine design.

Cleland was hired to devise a format for *Fortune,* which debuted in 1930. Cleland's spartan style – big, dramatic photos and clean, unornamented layouts – suited the magazine's focus on business and industry. *Fortune* became a favored venue for the photographs of Margaret Bourke-White, and its covers attracted the work of the best European and U.S. illustrators.

Brodovitch was, arguably, the most influential art director in U.S. history. A Russian-born Parisian designer, he went to the United States in 1934 after Hearst hired him to serve as art director of *Harper's Bazaar,* where he worked for 24 years. Brodovitch pioneered the use of bleed photographs in magazines. He encouraged his photographers, among them Richard Avedon and Irving Penn, to design the page through the camera lens and to use plain backgrounds so that headings and stories could be superimposed on photos, creating a seamless whole. His use of type, photography, and space had a musical feel to it.

Through teaching in classrooms and on the job, both Brodovitch and Agha had a far-reaching influence on magazine design. In fact, by 1964, their students, and their students' students, accounted for the art directors at most of the prominent U.S. magazines. Through Agha's influence, Cipe Pineles served as art director at *Glamour* and *Seventeen,* and Bradbury Thompson became art director at *Mademoiselle.* Henry Wolf, who trained with Brodovitch, took *Esquire* in a bold new direction when he became the magazine's art director in 1952, and he later replaced Brodovitch at *Harper's Bazaar.* Another of Brodovitch's protégés, Otto Storch, virtually saved *McCall's* in 1958 with his inspired redesign.

In the late 1960s, magazine design seemed to split in two directions. At one extreme were the corporate magazines, which adopted the uncluttered and orderly "Swiss Gothic" look. At the other extreme were the magazines influenced by the politics and social unrest of the late 1960s, which gravitated toward the chaotic influences of the dadaists.

One of the most influential magazine designers to emerge during the 1960s and 1970s was Herb Lubalin. Lubalin was known for his inventive use of type, but he was a stickler for details, especially when it came to setting type and making it readable. He designed or redesigned the *Saturday Evening Post, Eros, Fact, Reader's Digest,* and *Avant Garde.* He also was editor of *U&lc,* a magazine about typography.

An example of bleed photographs in magazine design – where subjects are set up in the picture to allow space for type on them.
(Courtesy *Harper's Bazaar*)

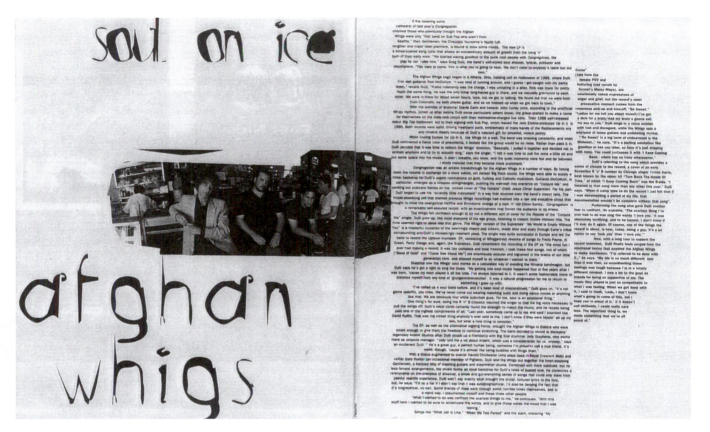

A photomontage from the October 1993 edition of *Ray Gun* shows the influence of dadaism, arbitrarily shaped columns of type, and custom-designed type faces.
(Courtesy David Carson Design)

Milton Glaser and Walter Bernard also set design standards in the late 1960s and 1970s with their design of *New York,* a regional magazine that combined activist journalism with a strong visual style. They created the magazine for readers with short attention spans and for easy reading. There were lots of lines, boxes, headlines, and subheads, devices that attracted legions of imitators.

At about the same time, *Rolling Stone,* a music and counterculture magazine, was making waves in California. Editorially, *Rolling Stone* was distantly related to the underground magazines, but its design was a clear departure from their psychedelic style. The magazine's art directors emphasized type design over art to convey the theme of an article. Typically, they picked a new typeface for the title of every story.

Several other magazines made significant contributions during the 1970s, including *Psychology Today,* a slick, well-designed magazine addressing the behavioral sciences; *Ms.,* which served the women's movement; *West,* a *Los Angeles Times* supplement; and *Texas Monthly,* which was designed by Fred Woodward, who later became art director of *Rolling Stone.*

But despite the exceptional work produced by a few magazines, the 1970s was a decade remembered more for mediocrity in design than excellence. In 1972 and 1974, the economy turned downward, and the magazine industry suffered. Advertising and readership of magazines declined

and paper costs skyrocketed. To attract newsstand buyers, some magazines abandoned sophistication for commercialism. They adopted gaudy covers with multiple sell lines and clashing colors. The introduction of computers into magazine design also opened the way for inexperienced designers to abuse and distort type.

In the 1980s, the magazine industry began to recover some of its equilibrium, and good taste and imagination were revived in the design of many magazines. One of the most successful magazines introduced in 1980s was the U.S. edition of the fashion magazine *Elle. Elle* took a direct, modernist approach to its design. It relied on primary colors, full-bleed photography, and the consistent use of Futura type to create a strong, elegant graphic statement. *Elle* provided a stark contrast to the overwrought design of other women's magazines published at the time.

During the last half of the 1980s, most magazines anchored their design to postmodernism, rebelling against the rule-bound modern movement established in the 1920s. Postmodernism meant a revival of colorful, decorative, and multilayered experimental design. Examples of postmodern magazines from the 1980s included *Spy, Esquire, Wigwam, Metropolitan Home, New York,* and *Egg.*

In the 1990s, elements of modernism and postmodernism were still at work in many magazines. At the postmodern extreme was the wildly experimental music magazine *Ray Gun.* Some credited the art director at *Ray*

Gun, David Carson, with creating a new graphic style, albeit a highly controversial one. Geared to the video-game generation, *Ray Gun*'s design was more concerned with visual stimulation than readability.

Although *Ray Gun* had its detractors, its willingness to experiment was applauded at a time when many consumer magazines sacrificed good design as they competed for advertising and readers. Critics of contemporary design also attributed declining standards to magazines' dependence on computers, which so easily facilitated excess.

Among the best-designed magazines of the 1990s were the fashion and culture books, as well as many specialized publications, which were geared to audiences with specific interests. The design of such magazines as *Health, Outside, Interview, Men's Journal, Harper's Bazaar,* and *Zone* was both imaginative and historically inspired. What is more, these magazines used computer technology as a tool – as a means to an end, not as the end itself.

CAROL E. HOLSTEAD

See also Magazines in the Twentieth Century; Newspaper Design; Photographic Technology

Further Reading
Hurlburt, Allen, *Publication Design: A Guide to Page Layout, Typography, Format, and Style*, rev. ed., New York: Van Nostrand Reinhold, 1976
Nelson, Roy Paul, *Publication Design*, 5th ed., Dubuque, Iowa: Wm. C. Brown, 1991
Owen, William, *Modern Magazine Design*, New York: Rizzoli, 1991; also published as *Magazine Design*, London: L. King, 1991

Magazine Freelancing

Writers provide growing magazine industry with fresh copy

The turning point for freelances in magazine work came in 1840, when George Graham merged the *Casket* and *Gentleman*'s magazines. Calling the new magazine *Graham's,* he initiated a sliding fee for writers and cultivated talented writers, paying them liberally. One of the first freelances, Nathaniel Willis, became a wealthy man, earning more than $1,500 a year writing for *Graham's* and other magazines. Graham was the first to spend money on talented writers. He also began copyrighting the work he commissioned. Years later, in the 1920s under Harold Ross and his *New Yorker* roundtable of writers, and then in the 1930s with Arnold Gingrich's *Esquire,* freelance writers found equally nourishing spirits. In the 1980s, Tina Brown resurrected *Vanity Fair* by discovering new writers, encouraging them, and paying them well. In the 1990s, most magazines depended on freelance writers.

Editors assign articles to freelances or agree to buy proposed articles. Called queries, these proposals can result in an assignment or in an agreement to take the article on speculation, which means the editor will purchase the idea if it is submitted on time and follows the proposal's general outline. An assignment from an editor is commissioned work, with specifications as to delivery time, expenses covered, kill fees, and terms of purchase.

Most magazines continue to pay on publication, which means the writer does not receive payment until the piece is in print. There may be a loose agreement about publication date, but usually an article is in the publishing process for weeks. At any time, an article can be shelved by editors. In some instances, publications will pay a kill fee to a freelance when the story is not published through no fault of the writer's. Considerably less than the purchase price, a kill fee sometimes is a percentage specified in the contract.

Freelance articles in George Graham's days paid between $4 and $60 a page. The freelance of the 1990s could earn as little as $75 or as much as $10,000 for an article. The average freelance price for an average-length piece (1,000 to 2,000 words) requiring normal levels of reporting would fall between $500 and $900.

Magazines paying upon acceptance develop loyal writers. These magazines pay either upon receipt of the assigned article (given that it fulfills the assignment) or upon a positive editorial decision after taking a piece on speculation, or even upon taking it from the slush pile.

The term "slush pile" refers to unsolicited manuscripts and queries. Sometimes called "over the transom" material, the term dates from a period when magazine offices had a window over the door that opened for ventilation and writers would slip unbidden manuscripts over the transom, through the opened window. In many places, such material is screened first by editorial assistants; if it seems promising, the work moves on to review by a more senior editor and possible acceptance.

The editorial process takes what is considered publishable freelance work and prepares it for the publication's audience. Editors work with freelances (as deadlines permit) on revisions of any part of the manuscript, check the facts, and perform a line-by-line editing job to bring it into house style and catch any error of substance or style.

S.M.W. BASS

Further Reading
Janello, Amy, and Brennon Jones, *The American Magazine,* New York: Harry N. Abrams, 1991
Land, Myrick E., *Writing for Magazines*, 2nd ed., Englewood Cliffs, New Jersey: Prentice-Hall, 1993
Rivers, William L., *Free-lancer and Staff Writer – Newspaper Features and Magazine Articles*, 5th ed., Belmont, California: Wadsworth, 1992

Magazine Illustrations

Changing the face of pictorial content

Early illustrations, appearing in nineteenth-century periodicals, were produced by engravers who first traced an artist's sketch on a block of wood (sometimes copper or steel) and then cut around it, so that only the lines of the drawing

Painting by N. C. Wyeth   Illustration for "The Mysterious Stranger"

ESELDORF   WAS   A   PARADISE   FOR   US   BOYS

A painting by N.C. Wyeth illustrated Mark Twain's "Mysterious Stranger" in a 1916 issue of *Harper's Magazine*.
(Davis Library, University of North Carolina at Chapel Hill)

would come into contact with the printer's ink. The resulting artwork often was signed by the artist and the engraver, since both contributed to the creation of the image. *Godey's Ladies' Book* printed relatively high-quality fashion illustrations as early as the 1840s, and weekly illustrated newspapers published by Frank Leslie and the Harper brothers contained detailed drawings of Civil War scenes. Even so, few magazines used illustrations extensively until the early 1880s, when the more sophisticated technique of halftone photoengraving produced clearer images and faster reproduction of artwork; the new process also minimized the role of the engraver. In the following decade, the advent of color lithography – a technology co-pioneered by the booming sheet-music industry of the day – further improved the quality of the artwork and enabled magazines to put color art on their covers.

Early twentieth-century magazines famous for their illustrations included *McClure's, Harper's Monthly, Century, Collier's, Scribner's, Life,* the *American Magazine,* the *Saturday Evening Post, Good Housekeeping,* the *Ladies' Home Journal, McCall's, Redbook,* and *St. Nicholas,* a children's magazine. Among the artists regularly published in these periodicals during the golden age of magazine illustration, roughly 1890 to 1930, were Winslow Homer, Frederic Remington, Edwin Austin Abbey, Howard Pyle, N.C. Wyeth, Maxfield Parrish, Arthur B. Frost, James Montgomery Flagg, Jessie Willcox Smith, Charles Dana Gibson, Elizabeth Shippen Green, John Sloan, and John Held Jr.

Most illustrators of the day were trained in the fine arts and had simultaneous careers as painters; they also illustrated books as well as journalistic media. Their magazine work often was commissioned to illustrate fiction, but some early artists worked as journalists whose job was to report news. Henry Farny was sent west during the 1880s by *Century,* which printed his drawings of the frontier landscape and its people, both white settlers and Native Americans (including Sitting Bull). *McClure's* assigned Joseph Pennell to sketch the building of the Panama Canal and William Glackens to reproduce scenes of the Spanish-American War, a conflict also depicted by Howard Chandler Christy for *Scribner's.* Reform journalism included not just muckraking prose but also political illustrations – from Thomas Nast's illustrated criticism of New York's Tammany Hall political machine in the various *Harper's* periodicals of the early 1870s, to John Sloan's drawings of immigrant slum life in the *Masses* of the 1910s.

Certain illustrators became associated with particular magazines. Charles Dana Gibson, whose drawings of beautiful, healthy, young women created the "Gibson Girl" ideal of the turn of the twentieth century, made 100 drawings for *Collier's* between 1904 and 1908 (under a contract that paid him $100,000 over those years). Between 1917 and 1933, Jessie Willcox Smith drew more than 200 covers of charming children for *Good Housekeeping.* Neysa McMein produced the majority of *McCall's* covers between 1923 and 1937, many of them sleek drawings of the sophisticated "New Woman." Alfred Parker sketched some 50 mother-daughter covers for the *Ladies' Home Journal* during the 1930s and 1940s. J.C. Leyendecker and Norman Rockwell each produced more than 300 covers for the

Magazine covers often were works of art.

Saturday Evening Post. Garrett Price created more than 50 covers, most of them humorous slice-of-life sketches, for the *New Yorker* over 25 years. The work of illustrators also was found in the advertisements contained in consumer magazines: Henry Patrick Raleigh's stylish drawings of high-society life for Maxwell House coffee, Haddon Sundblom's Coca-Cola Santa Claus, Leyendecker's Arrow Collar Man, and Maxfield Parrish's beautiful drawings for General Electric (which he republished as art prints during the 1920s).

After World War II, although many magazines still featured drawings on their covers – and the *New Yorker,* founded in 1925, never stopped doing so – the pages inside national magazines were more likely to carry photography rather than illustration, which largely was confined to fiction and fashion pages. (The field of fashion illustration was dominated from the 1920s to the 1950s by Carl Erickson, better known simply as "Eric.") During the 1950s, when the new medium of television began to compete successfully for magazines' mass audiences, one of the editorial consequences was the decline of magazine fiction, further shrinking the market for illustrators' work. Notable artists who continued to do magazine editorial work after the century's midpoint included Jon Whitcomb, James Avati,

Robert Weaver, Milton Glaser, Murray Tinkelman, Bernard Fuchs, and David Levine.

CAROLYN KITCH

See also Illustrated Newspapers

Further Reading
Best, James J., *American Popular Illustration: A Reference Guide,* Westport, Connecticut: Greenwood, 1984
Bogart, Michele H., "Artistic Ideals and Commercial Practices: The Problem of Status for American Illustrators," *Prospects: An Annual of American Cultural Studies* 15 (1990)
Janello, Amy, and Brennon Jones, *The American Magazine,* New York: Harry N. Abrams, 1991
Reed, Walt, and Roger Reed, *The Illustrator in America, 1880–1980: A Century of Illustration,* New York: Society of Illustrators/Madison Square Press, 1984

Magazines for Children

Early publications looked at what adults thought children liked

The first children's magazine appeared on February 2, 1779, when the publishers of the newspaper the *Connecticut Courant* produced the *Children's Magazine* for young readers from 7 to 12 years old. Historian Lyon Richardson wrote that the magazine's contents were aimed more at what late-eighteenth-century adult readers thought suitable reading material for children than at what might interest children, because the magazine bore "unmistakably the aura of editorial minds well-intentioned and age-hardened, unable or unwilling to appreciate childhood's urges and desires." An advertisement for the magazine said that the serial would include a variety of lessons on various subjects written in easy-to-understand language. While the advertisement promised the magazine would act as a supplement to schoolroom lessons, the publishers quit the magazine after four issues – no doubt disappointing the likes of Noah Webster, who had enthusiastically endorsed the idea of a children's magazines in correspondence with the Connecticut publishers.

Capturing what it was that satisfied a child's "urges and desires" in a magazine proved difficult in the early part of the nineteenth century – even for a fourteen-year-old publisher. In 1812, Thomas G. Condie Jr. began a weekly publication, the *Juvenile Port-Folio*. While the age of the publisher was remarkable, so, too, was the magazine's longevity; the *Juvenile Port-Folio* was published weekly – except for a three-week break at the end of each year – from October 30, 1812, through December 7, 1816. Exceptional as the magazine's existence was, according to historian Frank Luther Mott, the magazine's content likely did not trigger a child's interest because the writing was as "stilted as most of the adult writing of the time."

Early periodicals aimed at juvenile audiences tended to be "wooden and unnatural" before the Civil War, according to Mott. In the postbellum era, however, more and more publications were aimed at children's interests rather than at their education or morality. This is not to say, however, that magazines designed to aid in a child's moral upbringing did not exist. Indeed, half the juvenile periodicals after the Civil War were essentially Sunday school tracts. But, as Mott notes, the circulation of secular periodicals geared to excitement and extravagant adventure exceeded the others, in spite of the fact that most of the Sunday school publications were distributed without cost. One of the oldest of the religious magazines still in print in the 1990s was *Wee Wisdom,* published since 1893.

Although a number of children's magazines appeared in the second half of the nineteenth century, *Youth's Companion,* which first appeared in 1827, enjoyed a surge in subscriptions in the 1870s owing to writers such as C.A. Stephens, who wrote to engage the interest and imagination of younger readers. By 1879, a publication designed to appeal to the intellectual and emotional interest of older children – *Harper's Young People* – debuted. Well illustrated, the magazine survived until 1899. The bent toward intellectual publications was checked, however, by the "blood-and-thunder, bang-bang-bang type" of the serial. Between 1875 and 1894, the *Boys of New York,* an eight-page weekly, capitalized on the excitement and sensationalism created by the publishers of the dime novels so popular during the era. The pages of the *Boys of New York* were full of daring hero stories and illustrated by big action pictures on the front page. As the Industrial Revolution came into full swing, the stories came to focus on exciting mechanical inventions.

Among twentieth-century magazines for children, *Cricket,* published beginning in 1973, remained a popular general interest magazine for 6- to 12-year olds. Imaginative writing dominated this well-illustrated, 80-page monthly serial. *Highlights for Children,* published beginning at the middle of the century, included fiction, poetry, nature stories, and contributions from readers. It was intended for children of all ages. *Junior Scholastic,* published continuously from 1937, was a popular biweekly classroom periodical for sixth- to eighth-graders. Much as the *Children's Magazine* of 1779 was designed as a schoolroom supplement, the *Junior Scholastic* was likewise designed to enhance social studies and current events curriculum presented in the classroom.

Clearly, children's magazines have played a significant role in the history of U.S. magazines. While many early publications capitalized on the eighteenth- and nineteenth-century push for public education, other, more popular, magazines sought to engage the interest of children with thrilling action stories. In the late twentieth century, the American Library Association listed more than 100 magazines published for children.

ROBIN GALLAGHER

See also Dime Novels; Mass Media and Self-Regulation

Further Reading
Richardson, Lyon, *A History of Early American Magazines, 1741–1789,* New York: Thomas Nelson and Sons, 1931

Richardson, Selma K., *Magazines for Children: A Guide for Parents, Teachers, and Librarians*, 2nd ed., Chicago: American Library Association, 1991

Magazines for Men

Publications for this specialized audience appeared in the 1820s

Men's magazines first appeared in the second quarter of the nineteenth century; at that time, such publications carried news and information about crime and criminals, sporting events, outdoor recreation, adventure, and hunting and fishing. By the middle of the twentieth century, the definition of men's magazines was broadened to include, and to be dominated by, publications that emphasized urban life, with an emphasis on sexual liberation.

Probably the first of the sports publications was the *Turf Register* (1829–44), published in Baltimore, Maryland, and devoted to horse racing. Longer lived and better known was William T. Porter's *Spirit of the Times,* founded in 1831 as the nation's first all-around sporting journal and enduring in one form or another until 1912. As the nineteenth century matured and the nation began to devote energy to participatory sports, new publications arose. Baseball was covered notably in a weekly, the *Sporting News,* that would become the "bible" for the national pastime. The publication, still in existence in the 1990s, was founded in St. Louis, Missouri, in 1886 by Albert H. Spink. The bicycling craze brought about *Bicycling World, Outing,* and *American Cyclist.* Golf was represented by the *Golfer.* As early as 1856, the *Billiard Cue* appeared to give a voice to that predominantly male activity, and bowling had a voice in *Bowlers' Journal* (1893–1934). Prizefighting, however, was more important as a topic than any other sport, and it was a subject covered notably for many years by the *National Police Gazette.*

The *Police Gazette,* one of the longest-lived and best-known of the men's magazines, was founded in 1845 by George Wilkes and Enoch Camp to inform and alert readers about crimes and criminals, often using specific names. On occasion, those identified assaulted the publication's editorial offices, with serious consequences; six deaths occurred in an 1850 incident. The publication moved on to stories with sexual slants and to an emphasis on prizefighting and other sports. By the 1880s, the *Police Gazette* was a powerful voice in the sporting world. The publication lasted far into the twentieth century, becoming noted primarily for its prizefighting coverage, tawdry pinups, and cheap sensationalism.

In the latter decades of the nineteenth century, many U.S. men turned their attention to the vanishing great outdoors. This gave rise to a long-lasting new genre of outdoors publications that emphasized hunting and fishing, such as *Sportsmen's Review* (1890), *Field and Stream* (1896), and *Sports Afield* (1887).

Later magazines offered a more general adventure content. Their material was largely factual, but some fiction was included. *Argosy, True,* and *Saga* were examples of these publications that peaked in popularity by mid-century. Other men's magazines that emphasized the mechanical arts included *Popular Science* (from 1872), *Popular Mechanics* (from 1902), and *Home Mechanix* (from 1928).

As early as 1837, *Burton's Gentleman's Magazine* in Philadelphia recognized men's interests in art and literature, but the magazine lasted only three years. This broader, more sophisticated genre found an audience in 1933 with the arrival of *Esquire: The Magazine for Men,* founded by Arnold Gingrich as an oversize, lavishly illustrated, and well-designed publication with an emphasis on quality. Gingrich's initial issue carried pieces by Ernest Hemingway, John Dos Passos, and Erskine Caldwell. *Esquire's* general content included a preoccupation with sex, as indicated by the drawings of seductive women by George Petty and Alberto Vargas. These pinups and accompanying cartoons were sufficiently explicit – by the standards of the day – to cause the postmaster general in 1943 to attempt in vain to deprive the magazine of the right to use second-class postage (*Hannegan* v. *Esquire*).

In 1953, the basic formula established by *Esquire* was picked up by Hugh Hefner, a former employee of that magazine, and carried considerably further in its sexual content by *Playboy.* The first issue of *Playboy* carried a nude calendar photograph of the reigning U.S. movie sex goddess, Marilyn Monroe. The magazine's emphasis on the urbane, sophisticated, sexually liberated male found a ready audience in an age noted for its permissiveness. *Playboy* thrived as a magazine and spawned an empire of clubs, books, videos, and even a television show. Its circulation reached a high in 1972 of 71.2 million, a figure that later would decline as the "*Playboy* philosophy" came under attack for being exploitative of women.

So many imitators appeared on the newsstands – with some marked successes, such as *Penthouse* – that in the second half of the century the general term "men's magazines" was understood to refer to those in this category. *Esquire,* with some bumps and adjustments over the years, survived the challenge of these more daring publications. However, the new era was accompanied by a decline in the fortunes of older men's magazines such as *True* and *Argosy.*

DARWIN PAYNE

Further Reading

Nourie, Alan, and Barbara Nourie, eds., *American Mass-Market Magazines,* New York: Greenwood, 1990

Magazines for Women

Specialized publications long available for female readers

Women's magazines historically have been a profitable business investment and have had a tremendous influence on U.S. life. Competition exists for the title of first women's

Godey's Lady's Book featured ornate illustrations to attract women readers.
(Davis Library, University of North Carolina at Chapel Hill)

magazine published. Historian Frank Luther Mott listed *Lady's Magazine,* published from 1792 to 1793, as the first. Others list *Ladies' Magazine,* started by Sarah Josepha Hale in Boston in 1828, the first women's magazine to publish for more than five years.

Louis Godey started his magazine in Philadelphia in 1830. In 1837, he bought Hale's magazine, combined it with his, and hired Hale as editor. *Godey's Lady's Book* became the prominent women's magazine of the antebellum period, imitated by both women's and general interest magazines. *Godey's* departments – beauty, cooking, health, interior decorating, gardening – were still, in the late twentieth century, the backbone of women's magazines. Although Hale advocated education for women, *Godey's* published little on politics but still greatly influenced the manners, morals, homes, and diet of people in the United States.

Godey's first focus was fashion, lavishly illustrated by hand-colored fashion plates and copper engravings. Contributing authors included Ralph Waldo Emerson, Henry Wadsworth Longfellow, and Edgar Allan Poe. More often, *Godey's* relied on popular female writers, including Lydia Sigourney, Ann Stephens, and Harriet Beecher Stowe, whose work Hale introduced.

Competition eventually defeated *Godey's* and its rival, *Peterson's Ladies' National Magazine,* which, in 1866, claimed to have the largest circulation of any women's periodical in the world. *Godey's* and *Peterson's* were faltering when the *Ladies' Home Journal* appeared in 1883, and both of the older magazines died in 1898.

In 1879, Cyrus Curtis's new farm paper featured a "Woman and the Home" column. When his wife, Louisa, criticized the column, he turned it over to her. It immediately became so popular that Curtis created a separate supplement, the *Ladies' Home Journal.* When Louisa Curtis resigned in 1889, Cyrus hired self-educated, self-made Edward Bok.

Bok changed magazines' image of women. Hale at *Godey's* wrote for a delicate, genteel "lady." Bok wrote for a "woman" who was as strong, able, and practical as his Dutch mother and grandmother. Bok broadened the magazine's content, adding work by Mark Twain and Arthur Conan Doyle, but still supplied readers with solid information on homemaking, cooking, and fashion.

He led the *Journal* on several crusades. Its refusal to accept patent medicine advertisements helped lead to the Food and Drug Act of 1906. To improve U.S. homes, the magazine in 1895 began publishing plans for houses that cost from $1,000 to $5,000. Not all campaigns were successful. When Bok fought for a ban on aigrettes – feathers "harvested" by killing nesting egrets – some women rushed to buy the feathers while they were still available.

In 1891, Bok announced that the *Journal* had the largest circulation of any magazine in the world. By 1912, it was the most successful monthly magazine in the world.

When World War I started, the leading women's magazines were the *Journal, Good Housekeeping,* the *Woman's Home Companion, McCall's,* the *Pictorial Review,* and the *Delineator.* The contents of all six were quite similar, although *McCall's,* the *Pictorial Review,* and the *Delineator*

In the nineteenth century, *Godey's Lady's Book* strove to keep women up-to-date on the latest fashions.

emphasized fashion and patterns and *Good Housekeeping* emphasized food. Elias Howe's invention of the sewing machine in 1841–46 and Ebenezer Butterick's patented tissue-paper clothing patterns in 1863 helped launch several magazines. The *Delineator,* launched in 1873, promoted Butterick patterns, and *McCall's* (1873) promoted McCall's patterns. *Good Housekeeping,* founded in 1885, became noteworthy in 1911 when William Randolph Hearst bought it and highlighted its food pages.

When Bok retired in 1919, the *Journal* moved away from his idealized view of women. During the Great Depression, circulation slid downward, as it did at most women's magazines. *Good Housekeeping,* however, was extremely successful during this period because of its popular fiction, its strong home features, its food and appliance testing institute, and its seal of approval.

In 1900, *Good Housekeeping* began testing homemaking practices it recommended. In 1909, it created the *Good Housekeeping* Institute and in 1912 hired pure-food advocate Harvey Wiley to work at the institute, which tested food and appliances in proposed advertisements and gave items that passed a seal of approval. The Federal Trade Commission (FTC) in 1939 charged that this seal was misleading. In response, the magazine changed the seal's meaning and use. The FTC's actions did not hurt the magazine, whose circulation reached 2.5 million in 1943 and 3.5 million in the mid-1950s.

By the 1950s, the six leaders of the 1920s had shrunk to three: *Good Housekeeping,* the *Ladies' Home Journal,* and *McCall's.* New women's magazines instead targeted niche audiences. *Mademoiselle* and *Seventeen* appealed to younger women, and *Ms.,* founded in 1972, appealed to "liberated" women.

LAURA E. HLAVACH

Further Reading
Woodward, Helen Rosen, *The Lady Persuaders,* New York: Ivan Oboloensky, 1960

Magazines in the Eighteenth Century

Few publications started in these years; fewer survived

Eighteenth-century magazines can best be described as transitory. Almost 100 were published from 1741 to 1800, half of those starting in the last six years of the century. They lasted an average of 14 months, with only two publishing as long as eight years. Until 1794, no more than three were published in the entire country at any one time, and the average number available was one. As much as 75 to 90 percent of their contents were copied from books, pamphlets, newspapers, and each other. They lacked not only originality but sophistication. Subscribers were few, with circulations averaging about 500, and profits for most, if not all, were nonexistent.

And yet, the impact of eighteenth-century magazines was substantial. They were read and considered by more people than their low circulation figures might indicate, and they were models for more financially successful publications to come.

Historian Frank Luther Mott was amazed that there were any magazines at all in the eighteenth century, considering the problems associated with their publication, including printing, distribution, audience indifference, and nonpayment of subscription costs. Magazines, like newspapers, were printed with paper, ink, and other supplies imported from England on handpresses that had not changed since the fifteenth century. They were distributed generally at the discretion of postmasters. The Postal Act of 1792 was interpreted in some parts of the country as requiring letter postage for magazines, which was prohibitive and caused several to stop publication. The Postal Act of 1794 was considered more favorable. Still, many people in the United States did not have time to read magazines, and even when they did, they often did not pay for them. Nonpayment of subscriptions was particularly significant because magazines carried almost no advertising.

Since conditions for publication of early magazines were less than favorable, other factors motivated publishers to undertake them: a desire to profit financially, an interest in promoting U.S. products and ideas, and a recognition of magazines' potential utility. Mathew Carey's *Columbian Magazine,* for example, saw itself as "a future criterion of the opinions and characters of the age."

Whatever their publishers' motivations, the magazines clearly were miscellanies, similar to those published by Joseph Addison and Richard Steele in England. Their contents resembled those of early newspapers but in different proportions. The magazines carried more essays, fiction, poetry, literary and dramatic criticism, and commentary on manners, morals, religion, education, slavery, and women. They published fewer pieces on politics and economics. Some included engravings, woodcuts, illustrations, and cartoons. Most were five to six by eight to nine inches, printed in six-point type on 34 to 64 sheets of rag paper.

Benjamin Franklin conceived the idea for an American

The General Magazine and Historical Chronicle was an early, and unsuccessful, magazine published in Philadelphia, Pennsylvania, by Benjamin Franklin.

magazine, but his editorial assistant defected with his plans to Andrew Bradford, a rival Philadelphia printer. Bradford got his *American Magazine* out three days before Franklin's *General Magazine.* Both were dated January 1741: Bradford's was published on February 16 and Franklin's on February 19. Franklin's was the more thorough and lively of the two, and it published twice as long, lasting six months. The next magazine was published in Boston, with New York producing the next one.

Events like the American Revolution, the passage of the Constitution, and the formation of the new republican government were discussed in these magazines, making for more content that reflected the country's development. Contributions were made by virtually every eminent writer and statesman of the time. Isaiah Thomas's *Royal American* (1774) printed Patriot propaganda and Paul Revere's engravings. The magazine was the first to last more than a year. Thomas Paine printed much of his revolutionary rhetoric in the *Pennsylvania Magazine* (1775). Hugh Henry Brackenridge's *United States Magazine* (1779) was the first to display primarily U.S. content. Noah Webster continued that pattern, aiming at a national audience with his *American Magazine* (1787). Two of the most successful magazines were those edited by Mathew Carey in Philadelphia: the *Columbian Magazine* (1786) and the *American Museum* (1787).

The elite not only contributed to but read and appreciated these magazines, as indicated by George Washington, who wrote to the *American Museum* in 1788: "I consider such vehicles of knowledge more happily calculated than any other, to preserve the liberty, stimulate the industry and meliorate the morals of an enlightened and free people." The subscription list of *New-York Magazine* in 1790, however, indicates that readership was broadly based: half the subscribers were professionals or merchants, and half were shopkeepers or artisans. Historian David Nord concluded that magazines were a republican literature, stressing themes like public virtue, suspicion of luxury, and the power of knowledge.

Although men, for the most part, wrote for and subscribed to the magazines, women read and occasionally contributed to them as well. But it was men's advice to and commentary on women that increased as the century progressed. The first publication to pay attention to women was the *Gentlemen and Lady's Town and Country Magazine* (1784), and the first devoted to women was the *Lady's Magazine* (1792). Although occasional references to the rights of women were published, the overwhelming message was that women identified themselves through their husbands and children. The magazines assigned them to the "women's sphere," a social construct that such publications worked hard to maintain well into the twentieth century.

Eighteenth-century magazines, although always short-lived and often unoriginal, were improving on both scores as the century came to a close. Thomas's *Massachusetts Magazine* (1789) and the Swords brothers' *New-York Magazine* (1790) each lasted eight years. The more favorable Postal Act of 1794 led to the introduction of more magazines in the last six years of the century than in the first 53 years of their history. By 1794, Philadelphia was home to 15 magazines. Already some were beginning to seek specialized audiences like clergy, doctors, lawyers, teachers, and farmers. Whatever their failings, they had traced the course of popular ideas on all of the topics that mattered to people in the eighteenth-century United States. They reflected U.S. life and helped shape it as well. In doing so, they transmitted the country's heritage to the next century and established the models that would be developed within 25 years into golden age publications.

KAREN K. LIST

Further Reading

Janello, Amy, and Brennon Jones, *The American Magazine,* New York: Harry N. Abrams, 1991

List, Karen K., "Realities and Possibilities: The Lives of Women in Periodicals of the New Republic," *American Journalism* 11 (1994)

Nord, David P., "A Republican Literature: Magazine Reading and Readers in Late-Eighteenth Century New York," in *Reading in America: Literature and Social History,* edited by Cathy N. Davidson, Baltimore, Maryland: Johns Hopkins University Press, 1989

Magazines in the Nineteenth Century

Magazines become a significant factor in the publishing world

Although the nation's first two magazines appeared in 1741, not until the following century would publications defined as magazines become a factor of any significance in U.S. publishing. Several hundred new magazines appeared in the first third of the nineteenth century, but almost without exception they were local in orientation and short-lived. Their content was much like that of their more mature and prolific cousins, the newspapers. There was no special need for magazines that newspapers did not already fulfill. Joseph Dennie, editor of the nation's first significant magazine, the *Port Folio* (1801–25) confessed that his eight-page publication was "not quite a Gazette, nor wholly a Magazine." It contained "something of politics . . . and something of literature." This pithy description rang true for many magazines of the age. As to why a need might exist for a magazine, in 1853 the editor of a new magazine, *Putnam's Monthly Magazine of American Literature, Science and Art,* wrote that "a man buys a Magazine to be amused – to be instructed, if you please, but the lesson must be made amusing."

The introduction of the steam-driven cylinder press in the 1820s, followed by the double-cylinder press in 1832, had a profound impact on newspapers and magazines. The penny press that resulted altered forever the nature of daily journalism; the change for magazines was less dramatic and later in coming. The new cylindrical presses permitted uninterrupted streams of paper to be printed, in contrast to the far more laborious process of one sheet at a time. Printing costs per issue were sharply reduced; a broad new audience of consumers now could be attracted. Coupled with technological advances were improvements in transportation leading to regular and more rapid mail delivery between the states, which benefited publications seeking national circulation.

The first magazine to emerge under these improved circumstances that could attract and hold a national audience was the *Knickerbocker,* published in New York from 1833 to 1865 under the editorship of a man who became the arbiter of U.S. letters, Lewis Gaylord Clark. As would be true

PUTNAM'S MONTHLY.

A Magazine of Literature, Science, and Art.

VOL. X.—AUGUST, 1857.—NO. LVI.

LAKE GEORGE.

THE waters of Lake George are so pure and beautiful, that the Indians called it *Horicon*, or silver water; and, as it stretches away from Lake Champlain, they also named it *Canideri-ott*, or the tail of the lake. But the pious French Jesuits, who had settled upon the shores of Champlain, and used the

VOL. X.—10

silver water in baptism, called it *San Sacrament*, the lake of the holy sacrament. Then came the loyal English, and called it Lake George. It is a sweet Saxon name, and, on the whole, we are fortunate; for another king, with another name, might have sat upon the throne—Jeremiah, or Thaddeus, or Abimelech, for instance, or worse.

Of course you have been, or will go, to Lake George. And of course you will compare it with Como, and the Swiss lakes, and the English and Scotch lakes. But it is not necessary to do so. All sheets of water among mountains have a general resemblance; and when, as in the Tyrol, great glaciers lean down the precipices from off the until the arrival of truly mass magazines in the last decade of the nineteenth century, the *Knickerbocker* was primarily literary in content and – unlike most of its predecessors – a U.S. literary magazine. Among its contributors were Washington Irving, Henry Wadsworth Longfellow, Nathaniel Hawthorne, William Cullen Bryant, John Greenleaf Whittier, James Fenimore Cooper, and Francis Parkman. The *Knickerbocker* carried gossipy columns under wooden titles such as "Literary Notices," "Drama," and "Music," as well as a more general chitchat column reminiscent of the "Talk of the Town" made famous a hundred years later by the *New Yorker.* By the mid-1850s, the *Knickerbocker* had a circulation between 25,000 and 30,000.

Similar to the *Knickerbocker* in format and almost as successful was *Graham's,* which began publication in Philadelphia in 1840 (and ceased publication in 1858) under the name of its editor and publisher, George R. Graham. Circulation peaked in 1842 at about 40,000. The magazine featured the same contributors that graced the pages of the *Knickerbocker.* A familiar writer appearing frequently in both *Graham's* and the *Knickerbocker* was Nathaniel Park Willis, who, because he earned a living with his magazine writing and editing, became known as the nation's first "magazinist."

These early magazines were small in format – usually no bigger than six by nine inches – divided into two columns, printed in small typeface, and illustrated occasionally with wood engravings. There were printed on rough but durable paper that remained in good condition even at the end of the twentieth century.

Other magazines of note to arise in this period, outside the dominant New York – Philadelphia–Boston axis, included the *Southern Literary Messenger,* founded in 1834 in Richmond, Virginia, to give voice to "the pride and genius of the South." (It ceased publication in 1864.) Between 1835 and 1837, its editor was Edgar Allan Poe. In New Orleans, Louisiana, a magazine called *De Bow's Review* (1846–80) emerged to give a commercial slant from a southern perspective. On its masthead was the slogan, "Commerce Is King."

A publication with a specific point of view – that of women – was represented in the highly successful *Godey's Lady's Book,* founded in 1830 in Philadelphia. This magazine, which contained engravings of the fashionable dresses of the day, sentimental stories, and poems, reached a circulation of approximately 150,000 by the late 1850s. One of its editors was Sarah Josepha Hale, who wrote the poem "Mary Had a Little Lamb." *Godey's Lady's Book* endured until 1898, at which time another woman's magazine – *Ladies' Home Journal,* founded in 1883 by Cyrus H.K. Curtis as the cornerstone of a huge publishing empire – was approaching the 1 million mark in circulation. (It would reach that goal in 1903, the first magazine to do so).

By 1860, an estimated 600 magazines were being published in the nation. Most of these publications were creatures of their times, important for a few years or at most a few decades, but unable to transcend generations. In 1850, however, there appeared a magazine that was destined to endure into the next century as a significant publication. Created by Harper and Brothers, a successful book publishing

The Saturday Evening Post was a popular nineteenth-century weekly publication.

house in New York City, *Harper's New Monthly Magazine* was to serve as an accessory to the books they published and "to place within the reach of the great mass of the American people the unbounded treasures of the Periodical Literature of the present day." These works would be "transferred"; that is, material that had appeared elsewhere, particularly in the English magazines, would be reprinted. In a sense, *Harper's* anticipated by some seven decades *Reader's Digest,* with its policy of abridging articles appearing elsewhere. *Harper's* transferred articles on exploration, travel, science, art, social and domestic life, and poetry and fiction. After six months, the magazine's circulation had reached 50,000; by the time of the Civil War it was 200,000, which meant that it had a higher circulation than any other monthly magazine in the world.

Harper's was bigger, better promoted, and enjoyed firmer financial footing than predecessors such as *Knickerbocker* and *Graham's,* but in overall content, it was not that much different. The successful general magazines that followed in the next two decades – the *Atlantic, Scribner's, Lippincott's, Putnam's,* and the *Century* notable among them – also fit into the same general description. They stressed serialized novels, short stories, poetry, travel, biography, and political commentary, and as such were all of a genteel nature. Richard Watson Gilder of the *Century,* the most successful of these publications, observed that he had achieved success in his magazine "without once appealing to vulgar taste or prejudices." Henry Mills Alden, editor of *Harper's*, said that "magazines intended for general circulation must, of course, exclude politics and theology." Nor, he said, should magazines publish the works of authors whose "sole aim is popularity . . . or who have achieved only that."

Working to the advantage of all these publications was the fact that the United States was not a participant in international copyright laws. Thus, the best works of European writers could be used without payment. In addition, advance copies of the magazines and publicity releases about them were sent routinely to newspapers throughout the country, which in turn regularly alerted their readers to each issue's contents and frequently offered critical reviews.

By the time of the Civil War, Harper and Brothers had yet another highly successful entry into the magazine publishing industry. This was *Harper's Weekly* (1857–1916), an oversize publication that featured woodcut illustrations by famous artists reproduced at twice the normal size to illustrate articles on politics, sports, disasters, travel, and – quite notably – the Civil War. A similar publication, founded two years earlier in 1855, was *Frank Leslie's Illustrated Newspaper* (1855–1905), which also achieved great success. These publications were forerunners to the news and picture magazines of the twentieth century.

These two magazines, in their direct coverage of events of the day, broke from the mold of their more genteel sister publications, which appealed to educated, upper-class readers with material that was far removed from the daily concerns of most people of the United States. New magazines soon would be more alert to changing conditions in national life, like the erosion of once-rigid class distinctions. Dress, speech, and manners less and less defined one's station in life; a great middle class was emerging that represented a broader audience for magazines.

Continuing technological advances had dramatic effects on the magazine industry, democratizing their content in much the same way that penny press newspapers of the 1830s had appealed to the masses. New magazines such as *McClure's*, *Munsey's*, and *Cosmopolitan* directed their efforts to the daily, more practical concerns of a less genteel audience. Instead of a travel article about life in Pago Pago, readers could learn what it was like to work in the coal mines of Ohio or about how Standard Oil squeezed out small oil operators. The old wooden engravings, so expensive to produce and practically the private domain of the established publications, now were replaced by actual photographs, which were more immediate and produced at a lower cost. Moreover – and this was a key – magazines could be produced far more cheaply and in greater quantities than before. Huge circulation figures could be obtained through lower newsstand prices and more popular content. While lower newsstand prices could not cover the costs of these high circulations, that could be more than accommodated by advertisers who now needed to reach a national audience and were willing to pay for it. Thus, Frank Munsey and Samuel S. McClure could offer their publications at 15 cents, even 10 cents. A frenzy of competition arose, not just in price but in appeal to readers. All this was linked inseparably to what was occurring in the nation at large – the rise of national industries and mass-produced goods that required widespread advertising.

In 1896, the assistant editor of the *Century*, C.C. Buell, told his editor, Richard Watson Gilder, that he had just returned from the newsstand and that he had counted 35 cheap new magazines. His opinion was that two or three additional new publications would appear each week over the next several years but that their impact would negligible, for they would "reawaken the people to a sense of the value of the serious, 'high-priced' magazines." Buell could not have been more wrong. The *Century* and *Scribner's* would disappear altogether; *Harper's* and the *Atlantic* would survive, but just barely and with greatly altered formats.

Ironically, the new magazines that displaced the genteel giants at center stage themselves would not endure. They would be around beyond the turn of the twentieth century, however, and they would perform vital services through muckraking articles that called attention to national problems and helped to usher in the Progressive Age. Their adoption of more practical, issue-oriented content would be picked up by their successors, however, and endure into the twentieth century.

Also visible long before the dawn of the new century was the development of specialized magazines. As early as the second decade of the nineteenth century, magazines intended especially for educators, lawyers, mathematicians, and scientists had arisen. By the 1890s, the magazine reader could find publications as varied as *Woman's Medical Journal*, *Bernarr Macfadden's Physical Culture*, *National Geographic*, *Christian Century*, the *Ladies' Home Journal*, *Sports Afield*, the *Sporting News*, and *House Beautiful*.

U.S. magazines, in their infancy in 1800 with about a dozen publications in existence, had reached a surprising level of maturity by the end of the century. By 1865, about 700 magazines were being published; by 1885, the number had leaped to 3,500. By the end of the nineteenth century, the industry had experienced almost everything that it would see in the twentieth century – highbrow political and literary publications, oversize illustrated news and picture magazines, specialized publications, circulation wars, publishing empires, reliance upon advertising for profits, appeals to the masses, and the realization that addressing the special interests of readers in specialized magazines could be profitable.

DARWIN PAYNE

See also Copyright; Economics of Magazine Publishing; Magazine Competition; Magazine Illustrations; Magazines for Women; Muckraking; Penny Press

Further Reading

Edgar, Neal L., *A History and Bibliography of American Magazines, 1810–1820,* Metuchen, New Jersey: Scarecrow, 1975

John, Arthur, *The Best Years of the Century: Richard Watson Gilder, 'Scribner's Monthly', and 'The Century' Magazine, 1870–1909,* Urbana: University of Illinois Press, 1981

Nourie, Alan, and Barbara Nourie, eds., *American Mass-Market Magazines,* New York: Greenwood, 1990

Magazines in the Twentieth Century

For a while, the dominant medium of popular culture

The origins of the twentieth-century magazine lie in the extensive economic and social changes of the latter portion of the preceding century. The newly commercialized national periodical that emerged served as the dominant medium of popular culture for 50 years. Further, while the centrality of magazines as shapers and reflectors of the nation's popular discourse began to diminish at mid-century, the form itself continued to prosper as new, more specialized types of magazines arose to serve the specific informational needs of more narrowly defined audiences. This progress of the U.S. magazine through the twentieth century might, for the purposes of historical analysis, be divided into four major eras: the magazine's triumph as a commercial enterprise (1900–20), the golden age of mass magazines (1920–60), the rise of the specialized magazine (1960–90), and magazines as new media (from 1990).

The first 20 years of the twentieth century saw the emergence of modern magazine publishing. Inherent in this triumph of the magazine as a large-scale commercial enterprise was the widespread validation of the advertising-based model of magazine publishing developed during the 1890s. The rise of magazines as a national medium, however, was driven by broader economic and societal factors that gathered increasing force throughout the latter half of the nineteenth century. These included the success of the Industrial Revolution and the attendant urbanization of the nation, the rise of public education and the subsequent spread of literacy, and the emergence of a national consumer market.

More specific technological and commercial developments also played a role in the transformation of the magazine industry. Economies of scale provided by new high-speed printing presses, as well as improvements in photoengraving technology, made both larger press runs and higher-quality reproduction affordable. The prospect of marked increases in readership became a reality once distribution networks could be tied to the newly completed national railroad system. Circulation growth also was encouraged by favorable postal rates. Explicitly intended as a subsidy for magazines, the creation of the second-class mailing permit in 1879 and an additional lowering of its rates six years later, as well as the establishment of rural free delivery in 1897, significantly reduced the cost of delivering magazines to their growing national readerships. The most important factor in shaping both the form and the content of the twentieth-century magazine, however, likely was the advent in about 1900 of national advertising. With the rise of nationally branded consumer goods and a significant shift from retailer advertising, which was largely the province of newspapers, to that placed by manufacturers, national advertising quickly became an essential source of revenue for magazines.

Historical transformations within any industry often can be traced to success of specific individuals, and the journalistic professions certainly have enjoyed a cast of central characters amply blessed with both vision and visibility. Samuel McClure, Cyrus H.K. Curtis, Edward Bok, and George Horace Lorimer all played prominent roles in defining the nature of magazine publishing during the first two decades of the twentieth century.

Possessing both a businessman's acumen and an editor's imagination, Samuel S. McClure had great success with *McClure's Magazine,* founded in 1893, which demonstrated the viability of a lively popular periodical aimed at a mass audience. His secret, quickly imitated by others, was a greatly reduced cover price, and within a decade, the "10-cent" magazines represented 85 percent of the total circulation of magazines in the United States. His second contribution, largely based on the reformist impulses of the Progressive movement, was the advent of muckraking journalism. By publishing such widely read articles as Lincoln Steffens' "Shame of the Cities," Ida Tarbell's exposé of Standard Oil, and Ray Stannard Baker's "Right to Work," McClure led the attack on the prevalent political corruption and business abuses of the day. Other magazines such as *Cosmopolitan* and *Munsey's* soon joined the fray, and, until shortly before World War I, the muckraking magazines set much of the agenda for the nation's political discourse.

Three other individuals, a publisher and the editors-in-chief of two of his magazines, ensured the success of the commercial model that still characterized much magazine publishing 100 years later. Cyrus H.K Curtis, founder in 1890 of the Curtis Publishing Company, understood as no publisher before him the reach and power of mass marketing. His advertising salesmen spread out across the country to promise the nation's largest consumer advertisers a national audience, which his editors duly delivered. Edward William Bok at the *Ladies' Home Journal* created the first modern women's service magazine, and his Curtis colleague George Horace Lorimer turned the previously moribund *Saturday Evening Post* into the largest weekly magazine in the world.

The second major era in the history of twentieth-century magazines, beginning after World War I and ending in the late 1950s, might be termed a golden age. Indeed, the 15 years between 1922 and 1937 saw a large variety of significant magazines established, many of which still flourished at century's end. These included *Reader's Digest* (founded 1922), *Time* (1923), *Liberty* (1924), the *New Yorker* (1925), *Fortune* (1930), *Esquire* (1933), *Newsweek* (1933), *U.S. News* (1933), *Life* (1936), and *Look* (1937).

Most magazine publishers in these years used the commercial model pioneered by Curtis and sought large circulations attractive to national advertisers. Newsstand and subscription prices were kept low, and readers rarely were charged the full cost of producing the publication. Instead, a majority of the revenue came from advertising sources. The reason this was possible was that, despite the Great Depression, the prominence of the consumer economy, fueled by the new willingness of U.S. consumers to buy on credit, increased markedly during the period. Acting as both a cause and an effect of this increase, the importance of national advertising grew exponentially.

As the potential for new audiences expanded, publishers

devised new magazine genres to serve them. The *Reader's Digest* of DeWitt and Lila Wallace spoke to the country's faith in uplift and self-improvement. *Time,* conceived by Briton Hadden and Henry R. Luce, offered busy readers the news in brisk, capsuled form, and before long other newsweeklies were founded on a similar formula. Luce also oversaw the creation of three other important titles. In the depths of the depression, *Fortune* debuted to shore up the nation's shaken faith in the promise of market capitalism. *Life,* with its pioneering photojournalism, celebrated both the power of the visual image and the marvels of modernity – and soon was imitated by *Look*. With the 1954 founding of *Sports Illustrated,* Luce and his colleagues clearly foresaw the heightened role of sports in the national consciousness.

Never intended as a mass magazine, the *New Yorker* of Harold Ross redefined urbane intellectualism, and, in the process, challenged the long-standing dominance of much older elite publications such as the *Atlantic Monthly* and *Harper's*. In the men's magazine field, Arnold Gingrich's *Esquire* offered a new sort of urbanity, concerned with style, fashion, and other matters of the moment, yet also introspective and often certifiably literary. Founded in 1953 by Hugh Hefner, a former *Esquire* staffer, *Playboy* pursued a similar editorial strategy, generously leavened with the mild eroticism of idealized "pictorials." Two other magazines reflected the particular changes reshaping the United States during the era: the 1945 debut of *Ebony,* founded by John H. Johnson, mirrored the nascent prosperity of the emerging African American bourgeoisie, while the first appearance of *TV Guide* in 1953 followed the success of the ubiquitous new broadcast medium.

Magazines also marked the prevailing social realities of this period. The United States emerged from the depression and World War II on the cusp of unparalleled affluence; an unprecedented percentage of the population – more than two-thirds, by most measures – would soon claim membership in an expanding middle class. As both a product of and a catalyst for this sociocultural transformation, magazines, particularly the general interest publications serving mass audiences, enjoyed a special place in U.S. life. By helping to both define and reinforce the communal, consensual, and conformist values of postwar society, magazines became the dominant medium for the popular discourse of the nation.

Beginning shortly before 1960, the third major historical era might be denoted by the rise of the specialized magazine. A number of interrelated factors, larger social forces as well as changes within the media industries, influenced this trend. For example, as the conformist verities of the 1950s gave way to the heightened individualism of the 1960s, a shift from communally defined values to more personal ones took place. Ever-increasing levels of affluence, education, and leisure time both enhanced social mobility and greatly expanded the range of life choices available to many citizens. As a result, a large number of magazines devoted to specific personal interests, particularly those related to leisure pursuits, blossomed. Founded in the late 1950s and early 1960s by less prominent magazine publishers such as Ziff-Davis, Times Mirror, and Hearst, magazines such as *Car and Driver, Road and Track, Boating and Sail,*

Flying and Pilot, Skiing, and *Ski,* all spoke directly to this new, more individually defined view of the "good life" and soon surpassed older, more established rivals.

Another factor in the success of the smaller, more targeted magazines was the changing nature of marketing and advertising during this period. Mass market advertising revenues, long the lifeblood of the large general interest magazines, were being siphoned off by television. First introduced in 1947, commercial television's advertising revenues surpassed those of magazines in 1954; by 1963, its ad income was double that of magazines. Unable to compete, the three flagship mass audience magazines – *Life, Look,* and the *Saturday Evening Post* – all ceased publication between 1969 and 1972. Yet at the same time, computerized techniques for finely focusing marketing efforts at specific groups of prospective customers made the more narrowly defined audiences of specialized magazines particularly attractive to advertisers, and smaller magazines prospered. Moreover, advances in production and printing technology reduced costs, eliminating many economies of scale and improving the profitability of publications with smaller circulations.

In concert with the ascendancy of television in the 1960s, this advent of niche publishing, with its increasing emphasis on the segmentation of audiences, removed magazines from their central place in popular culture. For the next 30 years, however, by explicitly striving to serve the specific informational needs of particular niches, the magazine industry as a whole prospered. Trade magazines, or business-to-business publishing, for example, did notably well during this period, and by the early 1990s, more than 10,000 titles were published regularly. Similarly, consumer magazines flourished. In some cases, established magazine genres benefited; both religious periodicals of all denominations and "handyman" magazines for the do-it-yourselfer proliferated. In others, whole new categories of magazines emerged. These included a new breed of city and regional magazines, largely modeled on *New York,* which was founded in 1967 by Clay Felker and featured a unique combination of investigative journalism and shopping advice; a wide variety of self-awareness and self-improvement magazines ranging from *Ms.* to *Psychology Today* to *Self;* magazines such as *PC* and *PC World* that earned record revenues from the microcomputer craze of the late 1980s; and narrowly focused magazines offering everything from insights into right-wing cultural politics (e.g., *New Criterion*) to relief for baby boomers' parental angst (e.g., *Family Life*). By the early 1990s, more than 2,000 consumer titles were being published.

The final historical era of the twentieth-century progress of the U.S. magazine began in the early 1990s. Tremendous advances in both computer and communications technology suggested that newly efficient ways of distributing greater quantities of needed information to readers would be both possible and profitable. By the mid-1990s, it was clear that much of the innovation in these "new media" areas would be led by magazine firms. With their expertise at editing for and marketing to specific audiences, they were uniquely positioned to explore the potential of electronic publishing. By mid-decade, magazines still were investigating possibilities, since it was not yet certain what technology would prove the most commercially attractive.

DAVID ABRAHAMSON

See also African American Media; Internet; Muckraking; Niche Theory; Post Office and the Media; Specialized Business Publications

Further Reading

Abrahamson, David, *Magazine-Made America: The Cultural Transformation of the Postwar Periodical,* Cresskill, New Jersey: Hampton, 1996
Cohn, Jan, *Creating America: George Horace Lorimer and the 'Saturday Evening Post',* Pittsburgh, Pennsylvania: University of Pittsburgh Press, 1989
Janello, Amy, and Brennon Jones, *The American Magazine,* New York: Harry N. Abrams, 1991
Schacht, John H., *A Bibliography for the Study of Magazines,* Urbana: University of Illinois Press, 1968
Schneirov, Matthew, *The Dream of a New Social Order: Popular Magazines in America, 1893–1914,* New York: Columbia University Press, 1994
Taft, William H., *American Magazines for the 1980s,* New York: Hastings House, 1982

Magazine Technology

Publications adapt as new equipment becomes available

Magazines, like the other print media that preceded them in the United States, have developed as successful products along a time line dictated as much by advances in production technology as by changes in competition. These advancements led the medium and its production processes in an almost complete historical circle.

The first colonial magazines, although different in content and purpose than their newspaper predecessors, also usually were authored, edited, and produced by printers. This unified production process would remain the normal method of publication until changes in technology created greater job specialization in the pre-press production and press operation stages of the process.

By the end of the nineteenth century, mechanization of the typesetting and printing process had created a clear separation between those who created the content of a publication and those who set the type and ran the press. With the rapid advancement of computer technology in the last quarter of the twentieth century, the historical cycle began its return to a more unified publication process.

The technological history of magazine publication easily can be defined by three periods: manual, mechanical, and electronic. In each of these eras, the production of the magazine as well its content and appearance were dictated by the technology available.

The manual age of magazine technology is defined by its reliance on the hand labor of individuals throughout the production process. The basic areas of publishing all required specialized skills, but could be, and often were, completed by the same individual.

The printing process changed little in the 300 years between Gutenberg's development of movable type and the appearance of magazines in the American colonies. Text still was written in longhand and then set, character by character, into a locking form to be used on the press. The type characters often were designed by the printers, who also worked as type founders, individually casting each letter from molten metal. These characters were kept in sorting boxes for easy, if tedious, access as pages were composed for printing. Illustrations, although seldom used in these earliest days of the medium, were painstakingly hand carved from wood or soft metal.

Printing was labor-intensive, as handpresses printed one side of one sheet of paper as it passed through the press. Ink was applied to the type manually, and the impression of ink to paper occurred only as rapidly as the printer could manipulate the press.

Unlike the books used to educate or the newspapers used to inform, magazines did not appear in the colonies until the mid–eighteenth century. The first American periodical was printed in 1741.

Through the remainder of the eighteenth century, magazines continued to come and go. As the editorial content improved, magazines gained enough popularity to sustain regular publication schedules. Despite this growing demand, problems with the high costs of manual printing continued to keep circulations down.

Recognizing the time and printing limitations created by printing from hand-set individual type characters, several attempts were made to improve the process. In the late 1720s, William Ged, an Edinburgh, Scotland, goldsmith, began working with a process of producing a metal plate from a casting of the completed hand-set typographic page form. His first production of a publication using this stereotype plate occurred in 1739. Although initially shunned by most printers, who took great pride in the individualized characteristics of their foundry's hand-cast typography, as demand for magazines increased toward the end of the century, variations of the stereotype plate process began to gain acceptance.

A second, equally important, timesaving development occurred in the 1770s. François Barletti de Saint Paul demonstrated in Paris his idea of casting several characters together as one piece of type, producing logotypes. These typographic combinations were added to the type box, giving the compositor a choice of commonly used letter sets in addition to the individual letter characters. Like the stereotype, logotypes generally were disliked by the type founder-printer. Eventually, the number of logotypes grew so large that setting type by individual character actually became quicker than searching through the vast number of logotypes in the sorting box. Despite these moves toward simplification of the printing process, little overall improvement was seen until the mechanical developments of the nineteenth and early twentieth centuries.

Dramatic changes in publishing technology occurred during the industrial growth of the 1800s. Mechanization of many parts of the printing process gave publishers the ability to produce their magazines more quickly and economically. Typewriters allowed writers to produce more text faster. Mechanical typesetters revolutionized the pre-press preparation of the magazine. Rotary press operations accelerated the printing process to the point where circulation in the millions of copies became a reality. This growth in the variety and complexity of printing equipment also contributed to the specialization of skills that would find the writers and editors of the magazine moving out of the pressroom.

Probably the most significant development of this era was the creation of a mechanical method of setting type. William Church, an American living in England, developed the Church Composing Machine, first used in 1822. Using a system of tracks, gates, and gravity, the individual characters contained in racks or tubes above the machine were selected by means of a keyboard and would then drop through channels into place, in order, for collection and placement on the press form.

This process of moving type was damaging to the individual metal characters, creating a need for frequent replacement. To avoid the expensive and time-consuming practice of using the founder's hand-cast type, Church invented a companion device to recast type characters as needed. The Church Typecaster would melt down the old characters as they became worn and cast new characters mechanically from that molten metal.

Through the combination of his two machines, Church effectively developed both halves of what would become the traditional mechanical typesetter. During the next hundred years, more than 300 variations of a typesetting machine would receive U.S. patents. With each improvement in technology came an improvement in the process. By the early twentieth century, five systems of mechanical typesetting had been developed. Each found extensive use in some area of the publishing trade:

1.) Single typesetters replaced or assisted the hand compositor by mechanically assembling the individual type characters in a line in the same way that a human would manually. This use of the individual raised-surface letter forms still required much hand work before and after the printing job.

2.) Matrix-using machines moved into place the individual character matrices (metal molds of each character with the character shape recessed below the surface) and then cast this line of type into one slug using hot metal. The resulting cast slug produced the raised character surface required for printing. This form of typesetting would become the basis for Ottmar Mergenthaler's Linotype machine in the 1880s.

3.) Direct printers composed large blocks of text to be printed by the lithographic (stone) printing process. Letter forms were cast in such a way as to make an inked impression of the typographic image on a transfer material that then was pressed against the paper, thus printing the image of the original casting. With the development of photographic processes in the late 1800s, the direct method of typesetting gained greater acceptance in non-letterpress or offset press productions.

4.) Stereotyping and electrotyping solved some production problems created by higher speed rotary presses. The individual characters of traditional typesetting methods had a tendency to come loose from the round drums at the operating speeds of the press. Based on William Ged's stereotype principle, these systems used molds for casting complete-page plates. After a column or page was filled with these cast slug lines, the entire group was locked into a box to form the metal stereotype plate. The resulting plates then were used on the press.

5.) Cold impression used matrix (recessed letter form) or patrix (raised letter form) dies to press the character into a soft metal blank. The matrix method produced an embossed letter form slug. The patrix method created an intaglio mold from which the printing slug was cast. Both methods had problems, as the process caused inconsistent character quality.

By the 1920s, the use of steam- and then electric-powered typesetters had long since replaced the treadle-driven Church machine. But the process of setting type character by character and line by line continued to dictate the look and production of most magazines. Limited by the size of the characters and width of each line of type, little variation in design was attempted.

Improvements in press mechanization also played a large role in the growth of the magazine format. In 1811, Friedrich Koenig of Germany developed a mechanical press with a movable type bed that allowed the type to be inked more quickly after each impression. Three years later, Koenig added opposing print cylinders, which permitted printing on both sides of the paper at once. This perfecting press and its variants became the standard for speed through the next several decades. The 1815 patent of William Cowper's press marked the first practical application of curved stereotype plates. In the 1830s, Daniel Treadwell of Boston developed a steam-powered book press, and David Napier of England perfected the Koenig steam press.

While much of the development of powered presses occurred in Europe, the development of the high-speed rotary press in the 1840s proved to be one of the most important steps. Richard Hoe and his press company of New York took the basic principle of Napier's powered press and greatly improved its speed and dependability. The Hoe high-speed rotary press, a lithographic press first used in 1846, was capable of producing 4,000 double-sided page impressions per hour, a quantity sufficient to supply the growing circulation demand.

By the end of the nineteenth century, most letterpresses had been converted to use stereotype plates, allowing much greater speed. Color printing, developed in France in 1890, was used in many U.S. publications. The successful development of chromolithography by English printer William Sharp, and later improved by John H. Buford of the United States, pushed the application of color to new heights.

The invention of mechanical papermaking machines allowed the use of continuous rolls of paper. Primarily a boon for the newspaper industry, where cheap, low-quality paper was acceptable, magazines used "web" press configurations for 10-cent magazines and other inexpensive publications at the end of the century.

The perfection of photoengraving techniques, especially the development of the successful photo halftone by Frederic E. Ives in 1886, allowed photography to become a major part of the print presentation. By the Spanish-American War, photographs were commonplace in most newspapers and would eventually become the hallmark of many twentieth-century magazines.

The etching process, perfected with photoengraving, also allowed the development of the rotogravure method of high-speed printing. In the mid-1890s, Karl Kleitsch of Austria created a rotary press that used a smooth metal cylinder etched with the type characters and images. Ink was applied to the cylinder and scraped from its surface, leaving ink only in the etched areas to be transferred to the paper. Gravure, or intaglio, printing proved to be excellent for high-volume jobs that required speed and economy. Because the plate did not wear as quickly as the raised type surfaces of a letterpress, many thousands of impressions could be made without changing plates.

Rotogravure printing, because of its roots in photoengraving, was obviously an excellent method for photo reproduction. Many of the earliest photo magazines were printed on gravure presses. Most magazines of the twentieth century also used gravure printing for covers and other photo-display pages.

In addition to the use of images, other design changes were becoming evident as the result of technological advancements. The use of mechanical typesetters allowed greater flexibility in typography. Demands for visual variety created a need for new typographic families for use as text and as display or headline faces. The machinery for casting new characters simplified this process.

The use of stereotype plates allowed the width of columns to be varied. Gravure and offset printing further erased the design limitations, allowing color, photography, page makeup, and design to give publishers the opportunity to create a visual identity for their publication.

With the development of the industrialized printing plant came the continued separation of work responsibilities. By 1900, the editorial staff virtually was excluded from the production staff by the specialization of mechanical skills and the work rules of the unions formed during the previous decades.

With the improvement of photographic and electronic technology in the 1950s, magazine publishing took its next major evolutionary step. Of great importance to all the era's advancements was the move from "hot" to "cold" type.

Improvements in photographic processes permitted the move away from the use of "hot" cast-metal typography to "cold" type, set photographically. This process of photo composition allowed the elements of a page to be printed on paper, pasted together on a page, and then photographed to produce a film negative from which any type of press plate could be produced. The elimination of the molten metal typesetting machine and its reliance on skilled tradespeople led to tremendous changes in staffing and production. These changes in work habits led to the return of a more unified production process. Writers and editors once again became typesetters. Improvements in the writer's basic tool, the typewriter, led to its electrification and eventual connection to phototypesetting machines.

With the improvement of computer technology in the late 1960s, the ability to electronically create and store information further changed the publishing industry. The video display terminal (VDT) eventually replaced the typewriter to become the main tool of the writer, the editor, and, eventually, the page compositor. Characters typed from a keyboard would appear on the VDT screen, and the digital information was stored in a central computer. Corrections and rewrites happened instantly with electronic ease. When ready for typesetting, a push of the right keys would send the styled text to the typesetter where it would be printed out for pasteup.

The greatest advantage of the CRT- (cathode-ray tube-) type machine was its ability to manipulate the size and shape of the type characters. With this added tool, the page designer was no longer limited to a small assortment of type sizes and styles. Within the limits of the typesetter and associated photographic methods, any typographic look could be achieved.

Prior to the mid-1980s, pre-press production usually involved the design of pages using hand-drawn dummies, the pasteup of cold type and photo halftones on full-size page grids, and the production of plates from negatives photographed from the pasteups. Early attempts at pagination, or the typesetting of all page elements in position on one output, began with the improvement of computer capacity in the 1960s. Most of these pagination systems used a VDT similar to the writing terminal. Page elements such as stories, headlines, captions, and some digitized art would be positioned within the on-screen page form.

By the early 1980s, the electronic handling of all elements of a page could be done by large, but very expensive, computer-driven systems. The Scitex system became an industry standard for pagination and color manipulation. With its ability to work with large amounts of digital information, it could produce the complete design of full-color magazine spreads without the manual handling of any pasteup.

With the explosive growth of micro-computer technology of the late 1980s, magazine production took another step toward the reunification of production. Led by the power and flexibility of the Apple Macintosh computer and similar microcomputers developed by IBM and others, all pre-press aspects of the publication process became electronic.

With each year, improvements in hardware and software expanded the capability of the micro-systems. Each area of magazine production benefited from the progress. Word processing software included spelling checkers, grammar editors, word counters, and length measurers. Photo and image editing software became so powerful that the resulting manipulation of images became virtually undetectable, raising serious ethical questions. Page design software eliminated most problems associated with pagination.

As early as 1973, Xerox had introduced the first electrostatic, or laser, printing device. In this machine, page information is electrostatically charged to a print drum by a laser. Dry toner is attracted to the charged areas on the drum and is transferred to the page, where it is heat-fused to the paper as it passes. By the time the microcomputers were developed, laser printing had become an economical, high-quality method of print output. When combined with the microcomputer's ability to manipulate the digital data that defines each character, the output of the most basic page element, the type character, was no longer limited to a few standard fonts. Typographic bedlam often resulted, but for skilled designers, type became a new communication tool of the magazine.

With only the actual platemaking and mass printing processes not on their desktop, some publishers soon explored other methods of delivering their now-digital publications. With advancements in the long-distance transmission of digital signals by wire and satellite, several publishers experimented with interactive information systems in the late 1980s.

Videotext, the common name for this method of broadcasting (usually by telephone or cablevision wire) information to an in-home video monitor or television, was met with limited acceptance. Most systems, which usually were text-only, were visually dull by the standards of the television-based society, and much of the public was still not very comfortable with computerized, interactive communication.

By the mid-1990s, however, a new generation of interactive on-line services opened an additional area for the magazine publisher. Many magazines found ways to transfer copy and images from the digital archive of their print publication to a presence on-line. Computer-savvy younger readers quickly adapted to this electronic version of magazine reading, and the number of on-line magazines expanded.

With this step in the evolution of magazine technology, the historical circle of production was complete. Just as the first magazines were written, printed, and distributed by an individual with information to publish, so, too, were the on-line magazines of the end of the twentieth century.

MICHAEL WILLIAMS

See also Newspaper Technology; Photographic Technology

Further Reading

Baird, Russell N., *The Graphics of Communication: Methods, Media, and Technology*, 6th ed., Fort Worth, Texas: Harcourt Brace Jovanovich, 1993

Click, J.W., and Russell N. Baird, *Magazine Editing and Production*, 2nd ed., Dubuque, Iowa: Wm. C. Brown, 1979

Conover, Theodore E., *Graphic Communications Today*, 2nd ed., St. Paul, Minnesota: West, 1990

Huss, Richard E., *The Development of Printers' Mechanical Typesetting Methods, 1822–1925*, Charlottesville: University Press of Virginia, 1973

Meggs, Philip B., *A History of Graphic Design*, New York: Van Nostrand Reinhold, 1983; London: Allen Lane, 1983

Nelson, Roy Paul, *Publication Design*, 5th ed., Dubuque, Iowa: Wm. C. Brown, 1991

White, Jan V., *Designing for Magazines: Common Problems, Realistic Solutions*, 2nd ed., New York and London: Bowker, 1982

_____, *Graphic Design for the Electronic Age*, New York: Watson-Guptill, 1988

Magazine Trade Organizations

Business, creative sides of the industry well represented

The magazine industry in the late twentieth century had two major trade organizations. The Magazine Publishers Association (MPA), established in 1919, brought together members to solve common problems as well as to present a united front to Congress and other legislative and regulatory bodies. Its leaders testified in favor of lower postal rates for magazines. Based in New York, the MPA also had offices in Washington, D.C.

Affiliated with the MPA, the American Society of Magazine Editors, founded in 1963, was composed of a few hundred editors. This group cosponsored the annual National Magazine Awards through Columbia University's Graduate School of Journalism, in addition to a yearly summer internship program.

The second major trade organization, the American Business Press, Inc. (ABP), started as the Federation of Trade Press Association in 1906, which evolved into the Associated Business Publications. In 1940, the National Business Papers Association was established for free-circulation publications, and eight years later, the National Business Association, for free and audited magazines, was founded. In 1965, these became the ABP, with headquarters in New York. In the late 1990s, this association of publishers of trade, business, and technical magazines and journals served businesses, industries, and professions.

Members of the ABP had their circulations audited through independent auditing bureaus, either the Audit Bureau of Circulations or the Business Publications Audit of Circulation. These organizations made comparisons easy for prospective advertisers, putting magazines into recognized categories. The market data these groups gathered served this group.

BARBARA STRAUS REED

See also Magazine Circulation; Magazine Freelancing

Magazine Trade Press

Publishers, writers, and editors served

Trade journals serve the informational needs of publishers, writers, and editors in the magazine publishing industry. Whereas trade journals for those in the newspaper industry first appeared at the turn of the twentieth century, *Folio: The Magazine for Magazine Management* first was published in 1972. In the late 1990s, the semimonthly publication had a circulation of more than 15,000. It was written for executives at the management level in the publishing industry. Readers received information on industry changes, new publications, economic projections, and their effects on future production. *Folio* was published by Cowles Business Media in New York.

Magazine writers and editors were served largely by two

trade publications – *Writer's Digest* and the *Writer*. *Writer's Digest* had a circulation over 250,000 in the late 1990s and was published monthly. The magazine focused on the markets, methods, tools, and personalities involved in writing in the United States. The magazine included information on current story needs of magazine editors and publishers. *Writer's Digest* was founded in 1921.

The *Writer*, with a circulation of about 52,000, was also a monthly publication. The magazine first was published in 1887 in Boston. It was designed to help freelance writers establish contacts with various publications through highlighting how, where, and when to sell a manuscript to a publisher. The magazine, which still was published in Boston in the late twentieth century, also included information on new writing techniques, personnel changes in the magazine industry, and events that were of interest to magazine publishers and contributors.

Both the *Writer* and *Writer's Digest* published numerous self-help books for writers interested in pursuing certain careers. In addition, *Writer's Digest* published an annual guidebook on magazine markets and marketing tips called *Writer's Market*.

ROBIN GALLAGHER

See also Magazine Freelancing; Magazines in the Nineteenth Century; Magazines in the Twentieth Century; Specialized Business Publications

Other Magazine Entries: Economics of Magazine Publishing; Literacy and the Mass Media; Newsmagazines; Opinion Magazines; Pictorial Magazines; Specialized Business Publications

Mass Culture

Development of common experiences nationwide

The development of mass culture in the United States represents a confluence of national forces – extensive transportation and communication networks, the emergence of national manufacturing of brand-name products, the growth of advertising as the foundation of mass media, and the national production of media content.

The tentacles of a national network of transportation and communication began to spread across the vast regions of the United States before the Civil War broke out in 1861. That devastating conflict temporarily halted the network that would bind the nation together as a mass audience. Telegraph lines between North and South were cut. Railroad development temporarily ceased.

The cessation of the war allowed for the resurgence of national development that had shown early promise. National "quality monthly" magazines originated as early as 1850 and gained prominence during the war. *Harper's* began as a stepchild of the Harper brothers' publishing enterprise and

was intended to advertise the publishing company's new releases. After the war, with the expansion of nationally based brand-name products, advertising came from a variety of sources and appealed to a broad section of the upper middle class. An improved and less expensive postal system allowed the quality monthlies and other general interest publications to gain a national audience. The number of magazines published grew from 700 in 1865 to 3,300 in 1885, and to 4,400 in 1890.

From 1870 to 1890, increased consolidation of business contributed to a concept of corporate capitalism in which publishers regarded themselves as an extension of the nation's marketing system, participating in the infancy of consumer culture. Transportation and communication lines were in place. By 1880, 148 telephone companies were operating along 34,305 miles of wire. During the next 30 years, long-distance lines connected New York, Chicago, and San Francisco. By the early twentieth century, the federal government had granted railroads 155,504,994 acres of public land – territory that, if pieced together, would have been almost the size of Texas. Railroads operated in almost all parts of the country. Telegraph lines traversed the land.

The proliferation of department stores in the new manufacturing climate fueled newspapers' consumption of local advertising. Department store advertising remained a mainstay of newspaper revenues until the 1980s. In the 1890s, the department stores not only displayed an exotic array of goods, but they also built their own auditoriums, putting on musical performances and plays. The commercial department store – focused on consumption – became the cultural center of the city, a center in principle accessible to almost all. Department stores contained restaurants, roof gardens, and beauty parlors. William Leach, in an analysis of the emergence of department stores, wrote that the new "abundance of commodities" established the foundation of a capitalist culture, and "advertising gave it shape."

Fueled by advertising, the newspaper industry thrived between 1870 and 1900. The number of dailies grew from 574 in 1870 to 1,536 in 1890, and circulation more than tripled. Weeklies exhibited similar growth.

Newspapers in the nation's rapidly developing urban communities sought a mass audience. No longer was the market segmented along political and mercantile lines. William Randolph Hearst and Joseph Pulitzer crossed class lines in their appeal to potential subscribers in New York City, and they expanded to the nation with editorials and stories that reflected concerns about the consequences of industrialization.

During the latter years of the nineteenth century and the early twentieth century, workers increasingly joined the industrialized and white-collar workforce. Industrialization of the workforce had immense consequences. Artisan culture nearly disappeared. Those who had been accustomed to setting their own work schedules in prior agrarian or artisan work now adhered to policies of employers and time clocks. Further, safety standards and concern for employees was practically nonexistent. Through the 1920s, there was widespread resistance to industrial capitalism.

Employers began to recognize the necessity of neutralizing potential worker unrest, and management experts began to explore the concept of social control. Within this context, wrote Stuart Ewen, "the advertising industry began to assume modern proportions and . . . the institution of a *mass* consumer market began to arise." The goal of advertising, Ewen argued, was to produce new conceptions of individual attainment. Now, whiter teeth and no "halitosis" would help individuals find favor at work, at home, and within their communities. Businessmen, Ewen argued, wanted to move beyond being captains of industry and become "captains of consciousness."

Mass media provided access to the new world of mass consumption, freeing individuals from the influence of home and local community and promoting the concept of individual emancipation and social change. At the same time, it left people in a state of uncertainty about social standing, vulnerable to advertising's promise of a good life founded on consumption of goods.

In the 1920s, radio entered the U.S. household. Some critics argued that it would end cultural disruption, unifying the nation by democratizing society and allowing information to transcend space and time. Others feared that traditional authority would be eroded and that radio would contribute to the continuing decrease in the influence of home and community. The motion pictures of Hollywood presented dazzling images, and advertising promoted a new set of cultural norms.

Advertising agencies flourished in the age of mass consumer culture. Stanley Resor and Helen Lansdowne combined his social science research skills and her talented copywriting to increase the effectiveness of advertising. Resor used demographics to define his audience. In 1917, as part of an attempt to professionalize the advertising industry, the American Association of Advertising Agencies formed. By 1917, agencies handled 95 percent of national advertising.

During the 1920s, businesses turned to public relations departments and agencies to improve their image in society. They had survived resistance to industrialization and had prospered during World War I, but after the war they began to experiment with an information model of public relations designed to convince consumers that business had the nation's best interest at heart.

The activities of advertising and public relations agencies, combined with the development of national radio networks, furthered the concept of a national mass culture. Most radio content was generated at the national, rather than the local, level. Most media relied on national advertising for success. Although newspapers continued to carry significant amounts of local advertising, increasingly they turned to national agencies, which provided more visually sophisticated graphics and made it more difficult for local newspapers to portray the local community as central to its citizens' lives.

Postmodern theorists speculate that the development of satellites and cable, along with computer technologies, would spell the end of mass – although not consumer – culture. The increasing ability to segment the audience, to direct advertising to specific tastes, lifestyles, and demographics, challenged the concept of audience unity best represented by the late 1960s, when three television net-

works could command a large portion of the national audience. At the same time, corporate mergers and consolidation meant that transnational companies controlled much of media content, so that the production of culture would become "disarticulated from existing national societies and polities."

Mass culture defined mass media from the 1880s through the 1970s, and it still dominates the underlying structures of media. As technological capability expands, however, segmentation may bring new forms of dissension, as well as new forms of national identity.

JEAN FOLKERTS

See also Advertising in the Nineteenth Century; Advertising in the Twentieth Century; Brand-Name Advertising; Cable Networks; Communication Satellite Technology; Post Office and the Media; Public Relations; Radio Networks; Silent Motion Pictures; Sound Motion Pictures; Telegraph; Television Networks

Further Reading

Carey, James, "The Press, Public Opinion, and Public Discourse," in *Public Opinion and the Communication of Consent*, edited by Theodore L. Glasser and Charles T. Salmon, New York: Guilford, 1995

Ewen, Stuart, *Captains of Consciousness: Advertising and the Social Roots of Consumer Culture*, New York: McGraw-Hill, 1976

Leach, William R., "Transformations in a Culture of Consumption: Women and Department Stores, 1890–1925," *Journal of American History* 71 (1984)

Schudson, Michael, *Advertising, the Uneasy Persuasion: Its Dubious Impact on American Society*, New York: Basic, 1986

Wilson, Christopher, "The Rhetoric of Consumption: Mass-Market Magazines and the Demise of the Gentle Reader, 1880–1920," in *The Culture of Consumption: Critical Essays in American History, 1880–1980*, edited by Richard Wightman Fox and T.J. Jackson Lears, New York: Pantheon, 1983

Mass Market Book Publishing

Uses specific methods of sale to reach larger audiences

The method of sale, more than any other characteristic, most clearly defines the mass market book. To reach a mass audience, book distribution must extend beyond normal retail bookselling channels. Throughout the history of the book in the United States, innovative marketing methods have combined with existing nonbook distribution conduits for the successful publication of mass market books. Other characteristics that mass market books often have held in common are the popular or sensational nature of the editorial content, publication in series, flashy cover or cover wrapper design, portable size, innovative and economical manufacturing methods, the use of direct mail and mail order solicitation, and cheap unit pricing.

Books have been published in America since 1640. Books aimed at a "mass" audience, however, are harder to identify. The American Library of Useful Knowledge, bound in hardcovers and sold by subscription, began publication in 1831 and is generally considered the first book series appealing to a mass market. Published by the Boston Society for the Diffusion of Knowledge, the self-help volumes echoed a similar series begun four years before in England. Before that time, however, many individual volumes – Bibles, sermons, hymnals, and almanacs – used the emerging postal and transportation systems to reach audiences beyond the larger cities and towns where bookstores, often attached to printing establishments, existed.

The first of the so-called paperback revolutions in the United States was a concerted effort by the U.S. book trade to reach larger numbers of people. Two New York–based weekly periodicals, *Brother Jonathan* and *New World,* brought out supplements, or extras – full-length fictional publications filled with pirated fiction of popular British writers in the early 1840s. Other mass market series, some sponsored by established U.S. book publishers, followed. Distribution was assisted by mushrooming railroad networks that both displayed the books at their stations and freighted the cheap publications. The most notable were the beloved dime novel series of cheap, sensational fiction introduced immediately before the American Civil War. Illustrated soft covers wrapped sensational stories of Indian encounters and the western frontier. Exported to Great Britain and imitated in Europe, dime novels were the campfire literature of the war. By the end of the war, Beadle, the best-known publisher of dime novels, had published more than 4 million books; individual title sales ranged from 30,000 to 80,000.

The 1870s witnessed the rise of the second paperback revolution, inspired by rising literacy rates, cheaper paper, and faster book manufacturing equipment. Editions cost one-fourth to one-eighth the price of hardcover titles and sold for as little as 10 cents. Like the mass volumes published 30 years before, these often were pirated British editions. Sold in series, these "libraries" with imprints like Lakeside Library, Seaside Library, and Fireside Library reflected the growth of leisure time in the United States. Genres included romances, westerns, and thrillers. Some series were trimmed to what roughly corresponded to the size of today's trade paperbacks; some publishers sponsored more portable pocket-size books that resembled modern mass market editions. Overproduction, coupled with the passage of a new copyright law that recognized the rights of foreign writers, killed off most of these series in the early 1890s. The most notable series to continue – selling at 10 and 15 cents – were the Street and Smith paperbacks, which dominated the mass marketplace well into the twentieth century, with stories by Horatio Alger Jr. and those about the long-lived detective Nick Carter.

Before the third paperback revolution, a variety of hardcover and softcover book series reached the U.S. mass market. With more than 300 million sold by mail and sub-

scription, the "Little Blue Books" of Kansas publisher Emanuel Haldeman-Julius represented an odd combination of nonfiction topics including philosophy and Socialism as well as self-help, short stories, and poetry. Often found in the offices of doctors and dentists in the 1920s and 1930s, the imprint ended in the early 1960s.

A more permanent imprint legacy to U.S. book mass marketing was the Modern Library that Horace Liveright and Albert Boni started in 1917. In 1925, Random House founders Bennett Cerf and Donald Klopfer acquired the Modern Library – hardcover reprints of classic world literature. Retail bookstores, department stores, and a variety of mail order techniques were used to sell these attractively dust-jacketed volumes.

At the beginning of the twentieth century, hardcover reprinters began to appear on the book publishing scene. Grosset and Dunlap, soon followed by A.L. Burt, specialized in selling cheap, cloth-covered reprints priced at a dollar or less, usually a year or more after their initial hardcover publication. Hardcover reprints flourished in the 1920s and 1930s. Their title selection and attractive dust jackets had great initial influence on modern mass market paperback editorial selection and cover design. Hardcover reprints gradually died out in the 1940s and 1950s when the third explosion of paperback book publishing in the United States captured and extended their market.

In 1926, the Book-of-the-Month Club and the Literary Guild introduced a new method in the mass distribution of hardcover books – book clubs. They combined display, mail order, and direct mail advertising with subscription selling and discount prices. In their early years, they were both supported and opposed by the regular book trade and by a number of trade book publishers. After World War II, Reader's Digest, Time-Life, American Heritage, and various paperback book and specialty book clubs expanded the range of material offered to mass subscribers. The expansion of retail chain bookstores and superstores in the 1980s and 1990s, however, blunted the growth of general book clubs. Nevertheless, they continued to be an important source of subsidiary rights revenue and advertising for authors and publishers and a significant source of mass book distribution.

Most attempts to reach the U.S. mass market have focused on the selling of adult books; however, the Little Golden Books series, started in 1942 as a joint venture of Simon and Schuster and the Western Printing and Lithographing Company, was aimed at the children's book market. Colorful, cardboard flats, they sold at 25 cents in supermarkets, toy stores, department stores, and retail bookstores. Together with the Giant Golden Books that were priced initially at $1.50, more than 300 million volumes were sold in their first decade of operation.

The most significant development in mass market book publishing in the United States began in 1939 with the introduction of the first Pocket Books paperback titles, also partially housed under Simon and Schuster. Founder and publisher Robert F. de Graff had long experience in hardcover reprint publishing and was inspired by the success of the Penguin softcover reprints in England. De Graff employed careful reprint selection, colorful design formats, and fast and cheap manufacturing methods. The key element to his success in reaching a wide retail mass market for his softcover reprints was the use of the North American wholesaling system. Independent regional wholesalers of slick, pulp, and digest magazines and out-of-town newspapers sold the softcover reprints to mass retail outlets that never before had sold adult books.

Over the 20 or so years it took for mass market paperbacks to become firmly established as a integral part of general book publishing in the United States, Pocket Books was joined by several other significant and successful mass market imprints: Bantam, Dell, Avon, Ballantine, and New American Library. In 1949, Gold Medal Books, an imprint of Fawcett magazines, became the first major mass market publisher to issue original publications rather than reprints. This editorial policy added the final key element of success to mass market paperback publishing.

By the early 1960s, mass market paperbacks had become the dominant category of general book publishing. Throughout the latter half of the twentieth century, mass market imprints were bought by larger media publishers, started their own hardcover series, or merged with hardcover trade book operations. By the end of the century, mass market paperback books' marketing methods – covers, advertising, and promotion – had been wholly incorporated into general hardcover publishing.

THOMAS L. BONN

See also Book Clubs; Book Publishing in the Nineteenth Century; Book Publishing in the Twentieth Century; Dime Novels; Literacy and the Mass Media

Further Reading

Bonn, Thomas L., Under Cover: An Illustrated History of American Mass-Market Paperbacks, New York and Harmondsworth, Middlesex, England: Penguin, 1982

Davis, Kenneth C., Two-Bit Culture: The Paperbacking of America, Boston: Houghton Mifflin, 1984

Schick, Frank L., The Paperbound Book in America: The History of Paperbacks and Their European Background, New York: Bowker, 1958

Schreuders, Piet, Paperbacks, U.S.A.: A Graphic History, 1939–1959, San Diego, California: Blue Dolphin, 1981

Mass Media and Children

Concerns about harmful effects increased with each new medium

The introduction of each new medium of mass communication into the lives of children during the twentieth century raised the concerns of their elders about its harmful effects. These concerns stimulated considerable research about each medium's effects after it was introduced into U.S. homes. In 1985, a comprehensive bibliography compiled by Ellen Wartella and Byron Reeves found 242 studies of media effects on children conducted between 1900 and 1960, a time frame corresponding to the introduction of movies, radio, and television into U.S. society. After 1960, thousands of studies were conducted that examined the effects of television and other communication technologies on children.

By the late 1920s, weekly movie attendance was common for most U.S. children and adults. As Wartella and Reeves pointed out, the earliest research on movies examined children's attendance patterns and the types of movies they preferred. Alice Miller Mitchell, for example, surveyed the moviegoing habits of 10,052 Chicago children, finding that more than 90 percent attended at least once or twice a week. The vast majority of children went to the movies without their parents, and 78 percent of them said they selected the movie without guidance, most often choosing westerns and adventures.

Researchers began to turn their attention to the effects of movies when the industry came under attack from a variety of citizens' groups for having negative influences on children. In 1928, the Motion Picture Research Council invited university researchers from several disciplines to conduct studies to assess the influence of movies on children, which would be financed by the Payne Fund, a private philanthropic foundation.

This research provided an extensive assessment of the cognitive, attitudinal, and behavioral effects of movies on children. The studies demonstrated that children learned and retained for long periods of time a surprisingly high amount of information from the movies they watched. They also indicated that children's attitudes about racial and ethnic groups were influenced by portrayals of them in movies, and the studies also provided the first suggestion that children might become more aggressive as a result of viewing violence in the movies.

The innovative Payne Fund studies only provided evidence about how young people in the 1920s reacted to the movies of that era. The results of this research, however, did raise concerns about the effects of radio, which by the end of 1920s was heard nightly by most young people. In an article in the February 27, 1933, *New York Times,* for example, the chairperson of the Radio Committee of the Parent-Teacher Association in Scarsdale, New York, told of children who had nightmares "directly attributable to lurid radio bedtime stories" and of others who "scream in fright and turn off the radio or stop their ears until reasonably certain that the danger was past."

Early scientific research, however, provided a more balanced picture of radio's effects on children. Ariel L. Eisenberg studied the effects of radio on more than 3,000 children in New York City during the early 1930s. These children stated that they preferred listening to the radio more than listening to a record, reading an adventure book, solving a puzzle, or playing a musical instrument. The children also reported learning a great deal from radio about such subjects as history, geography, music, health, and current events.

Based on his research, Eisenberg concluded that this new invader of the privacy of the home had brought many a disturbing influence in its wake. Parents, he said, had become aware of a puzzling change in the behavior patterns of their children. Parents were bewildered by a host of new programs and found themselves unprepared, frightened, resentful, helpless. They could not lock out this intruder because it had gained an invincible hold over their children.

After World War II, television rapidly replaced radio as the primary source of home entertainment for children. Between 1950 and 1959, the number of U.S. homes with a television set rose from 6 percent to 88 percent. Early studies showed that U.S. families rearranged their homes and schedules when they acquired a television set. Watching television decreased other entertainment activities for children, including listening to the radio, reading comic books, playing with friends, and going to the movies. By the 1960s, the average U.S. child was watching more than 23 hours of television per week, totaling almost one solid year in front of the television by the time a child turned 12 years old.

The extraordinary dominance of television in the lives of children resulted in an unabated outpouring of studies documenting its capacity to both harm and help them. The 1982 report by the National Institutes of Mental Health, *Television and Social Behavior: Ten Years of Scientific Progress and Implications for the Eighties,* summarized the research on television's effects on children in this way: Almost all the evidence testifies to television's role as a formidable educator whose effects are both pervasive and cumulative. Television can no longer be considered as a casual part of daily life, as an electronic toy. Research findings have long since destroyed the illusion that television is merely innocuous entertainment. While the learning it provides is mainly incidental rather than direct and formal, it is a significant part of the total acculturation process.

Not all of television programming has been considered "a vast wasteland," as former Federal Communications Commission head Newton Minow once described it. The Corporation for Public Broadcasting (CPB) was created by Congress in 1967 to provide high-quality entertainment, educational, and informational programming that would not otherwise be seen on commercial broadcast stations. Among the more popular programs broadcast by the CPB since 1969 was *Sesame Street.* Created by the Children's Television Workshop, *Sesame Street* was intended to provide preschool experiences at home, particularly for disadvantaged children, by teaching basic educational skills in an entertaining manner. An immediate hit with children, *Sesame Street* successfully taught such basic skills as the alphabet, counting, and spelling.

When the radio industry began to lose its audience to television in the early 1950s, it adapted by creating specialized formats, most of which were based on music. The most popular of these formats proved to be rock and roll, an electrified combination of country and western and rhythm and blues music. The perceived "antiestablishment" nature of rock and roll, combined with the performances of such stars as Elvis Presley, Little Richard, Chuck Berry, and Buddy Holly, from the beginning raised fears that the values and morals of youth were being corrupted by listening to this music. While research has not supported this conclusion, under pressure from groups such as the Parents' Music Resource Center, the music industry in 1986 began attach-

ing warning labels to albums with sexually explicit or violent content.

As the end of the twentieth century approached, traditional broadcast and print media were being transformed by computer-based production, storage, and distribution of textual, audio, and video information through fiber-optic networks. Typically, parents and teachers expressed concerns about the amount of time children spent on computers, playing violent games, surfing the Internet, and communicating by electronic mail with other users on a vast array of topics.

KIM A. SMITH

See also Children's Television Programming; Decency Issues in Electronic Media; Internet; Mass Media and Self-Regulation; Mass Media and Tobacco Products; Television and Violence

Further Reading
Blumer, Herbert, *The Movies and Conduct,* New York: Macmillan, 1933
Charters, Werrett Wallace, *Motion Pictures and Youth: A Summary,* New York: Macmillan, 1933
Eisenberg, Azriel L., *Children and Radio Programs,* New York: Columbia University Press, 1936
Mitchell, Alice Miller, *Children and Movies,* Chicago: University of Chicago Press, 1929
Pearl, David, Lorraine Bouthilet, and Joyce Lazar, eds., *Television and Behavior: Ten Years of Scientific Progress and Implications for the Eighties,* 2 vols., Rockville, Maryland: U.S. Department of Health and Human Services, 1982
Peterson, Ruth C., and L.L. Thurstone, *Motion Pictures and the Social Attitudes of Children,* New York: Macmillan, 1933
Schramm, Wilbur Lang, *Television in the Lives of Our Children,* Stanford, California: Stanford University Press, 1961
Wartella, Ellen, and Byron Reeves, "Historical Trends in Research on Children and the Media: 1900–1960," *Journal of Communication* 35 (1985)

Mass Media and Foreign Policy

Conflicting theories on how much information the public should have

If there is one area in media-government relations that was destined to cause conflict between the two parties, it is foreign policy. Two diametrically opposed notions of what is right for the nation clash without hope for compromise. The press generally has believed that information on foreign policy should be released to the people on the theory that the people are sovereign and should know what their government is doing in their name internationally. The government generally has felt that foreign policy should be conducted confidentially so that government leaders can have a firm control of the international affairs agenda. The two theories have been in opposition since the founding of the republic.

Throughout U.S. history, the problem has been complicated by a propensity for news leaks by government officials of various ranks and stations. In the late twentieth century, the problem was compromised further by the impact of modern technology, which made the press an influential player in the contest to win public opinion on foreign policy issues.

The conflict between the press and the government over foreign policy began even as the new national government was being established. George Washington was the first president to be caught in this struggle as he sought confirmation of the Jay Treaty, which tried to make Great Britain honor agreements made at the end of the Revolution. The president sent the treaty to the Senate with a copy of Jay's instructions and much of the pertinent correspondence. Senators, disappointed by the limited gains made in the treaty, had to decide whether to debate its approval in public, and thus reveal their concerns, or to keep the debates secret. Much of the treaty's contents had already been made public by the British, but the Senate decided to keep its debate secret. This sent the opposition press into a frenzy, complaining, "The English prints have already announced the prominent characters of the Treaty, and yet the people of the United States are kept in as profound ignorance of it by their administration, as if they were Hottentots or Orangutans!" The editor added, "If . . . the people are the sovereign, how extraordinary that they should be kept in profound ignorance."

The treaty ultimately was ratified by a 20–10 vote, the minimum vote required by the Constitution. Before adjourning in June 1795, the Senate again discussed the secrecy issue, deciding to allow the president to release the treaty at his pleasure. Washington was making arrangements to have the treaty published in the *Philadelphia Gazette*, the usual outlet for official publications, when it suddenly appeared in the pages of Benjamin Franklin Bache's *Aurora*. Senator Stevens T. Mason of Virginia had given a copy of the treaty to Bache for publication. The ardent Republican journalist first printed a summary of the treaty and then the full text, which he also reproduced in a pamphlet that he personally hawked from a stagecoach traveling from Philadelphia to Boston.

President James K. Polk encountered similar difficulties in the Mexican War. A president who had at best rocky relationships with the press, Polk regularly found details of his secret diplomatic plans spread across the front pages of daily newspapers such as the *New York Herald*. The most embarrassing such disclosure centered on his plans to bring Santa Anna back to power based on the pledge from the Mexican general, who had butchered the defenders of the Alamo, that he would negotiate a peace settlement. Other missions were likewise publicized. When Polk sent Nicholas P. Trist, the man who ultimately negotiated the end of the war, to Mexico as peace emissary, details were again front-page news.

"The statement is so accurate and minute that the writer must have obtained information on the subject from some-one who was entrusted with the secret," Polk said of the *New York Herald* story. Unable to believe that a member of his cabinet was the source, the president focused his attentions on a clerk in the Department of State who happened to be a Whig. The president was so concerned that he himself took a hand in the interrogation of the clerk about the leak.

Polk's anger increased when details of the draft treaty sent to the Senate for ratification appeared in the *New York Herald* on March 13, 1848, barely a week after Senate ratification and before Mexican ratification. Publication of the treaty text was followed by details taken from the president's official correspondence sent to the Senate. A *Herald* correspondent was interrogated by the Senate in an effort to discover the government official who had leaked the documents. The effort was unsuccessful.

Woodrow Wilson's major problem with the press and foreign policy came during the Paris Peace Conference that followed the armistice ending World War I. Owing to the president's language in his Fourteen Points address of January 1918, reporters believed that they would be able to witness the peace negotiations firsthand. The first point of the address promised "open covenants of peace, openly arrived at, after which there shall be no private international understandings of any kind but diplomacy shall proceed always frankly and in the public view."

Wilson, however, firmly believed that the press could release too much information to the public before agreements were finally settled; diplomacy was far too delicate to conduct in the spotlight. Rather, Wilson believed that his Point One would be served if the public knew of the general topics of discussion and was told of agreements after they were finished.

U.S. journalists arriving in Paris found themselves barred from all but the most formal occasions and restricted to daily briefings by the press attaché. U.S. journalists tried unsuccessfully to convince reporters from other countries that they jointly should demand greater access to sessions. The U.S. journalists soon discovered that not all reporters throughout the world agreed with the U.S. definition of freedom of the press and of the rights of coverage that such a term encompassed.

To a certain extent, U.S. reporters were responsible for their exclusion from the discussions. Little remained secret once it fell into the hands of U.S. journalists, and the country's allies had more than once complained about the way in which the press released national secrets. As a result, foreign diplomats were more than likely to demand extra secrecy from their U.S. counterparts. In addition, U.S. journalists often were guilty of pursuing special interests in their reporting. Many correspondents attending the Paris Conference, for instance, went prepared to support or oppose President Wilson's plans for peace without even knowing the details of his proposals. Their decisions were based on political alliances that existed back in the United States.

Government officials became more adept at developing what could be called patriotic journalism in the first 50-plus years of the twentieth century. Through expert propaganda efforts in two world wars and superb manipulation of public opinion during the early Cold War, journalists often came to think of themselves as "Americans first, newspapermen second." Such an approach made journalists more willing to take the government's word on how to interpret news events and led to much news being filtered through a patriotic lens.

John F. Kennedy likely was the last president to enjoy such a relationship with the press, in part because of his efforts to promote friendships with journalists. Never before had so many reporters had so much access to a president of the United States. Such closeness, however, led to compromises and accessions to presidential requests that journalists later came to regret. In a variety of international crises, ranging from the Bay of Pigs invasion in 1961 to the Cuban missile crisis of 1962 and the U.S. buildup in South Vietnam, U.S. journalists were besieged by presidential entreaties to release less information than the journalists actually knew.

The first major conflict between the president and the press came early in his administration. Kennedy had inherited a plan from the Eisenhower administration to send Cuban exiles into their homeland to overthrow Fidel Castro. Many members of the press discovered the exiles training for the invasion and uncovered the connection that these individuals had with the Central Intelligence Agency. Stories about these activities dotted the nation's press in late March and early April 1961. A *New York Times* story came perilously close to revealing invasion details, but after consultation within the newspaper, the story was toned down considerably and many specifics were deleted. The attack was a disaster, with most of the invading force either killed or captured. Part of the blame for the failure, Kennedy believed, rested with the U.S. press. Shortly after the abortive effort to overthrow Castro, he said that during a cold war such as existed then, journalists needed to display the same caution they would bring to a declared, shooting war. "Every newspaper now asks itself with respect to every news story, 'Is it news?' All I suggest is that you add the question: 'Is it in the interest of national security?'"

Kennedy, however, was also guilty of sending conflicting messages on press coverage of foreign policy. At a meeting with press leaders, for instance, he criticized various stories about the invasion that had appeared in the *New York Times,* while at the same time telling *Times* executive Turner Catledge, "If you had printed more about the operation you would have saved us from a colossal mistake." More than a year later, the president was still taking the latter approach, telling *Times* publisher Orvil Dryfoos, "I wish you had run everything on Cuba . . . I am just sorry you didn't tell it at the time."

Just how far Kennedy could go in misleading the people of the United States and in seeking journalistic cooperation in that deception was tested in the Cuban missile crisis of 1962. At least initially, Kennedy was able to put off members of the press who had information on the presence of Soviet missiles in Cuba. When he discovered that James Reston, Washington, D.C., bureau chief for the *New York Times,* had the story, Kennedy personally called Reston and his publisher to request that the data not be published until the government announced its plans. The *Times* complied. At about the same time, Arthur Sylvester, assistant secretary of defense for public affairs, was authorizing the release of

the statement that "the Pentagon has no information indicating the presence of offensive weapons in Cuba." The statement was a blatant lie, but Sylvester later justified it by saying, "News generated by actions by the government . . . are part of the arsenal of weaponry that a President has. . . . The results, in my opinion, justify the methods we used."

Press concerns about obtaining accurate information mounted during the missile crisis. No reporters were allowed on the ships that maintained the quarantine of Cuba, making journalists totally reliant on government sources of information. As Sylvester later told the journalists, "It's inherent in [the] government's right, if necessary, to lie to save itself when it's going up into a nuclear war. That seems to me basic – basic."

Despite their concerns about accurate information, journalists, in the main, continued to honor government requests to stay away from stories about the Cuban missile crisis. Indeed, one journalist, John Scali of ABC News, served as a go-between between the United States and the Soviet Union during the negotiations, forgoing his own professional interests for national concerns.

The differences inherent in the two Cuban crises have perplexed journalists. *New York Times* columnist Reston, for example, noted that, in the Bay of Pigs incident, government officials – after the fact – admitted that more publicity would have been helpful. In the Cuban missile crisis, however, news coverage could have plunged the nation into nuclear war. The question then became one of how a journalist could tell the difference. To Reston, "the rising power of the United States in world affairs . . . requires, not a more compliant press, but a relentless barrage of facts and criticism, as noisy but also as accurate as artillery fire." Journalists, he stressed, should not serve as "cheerleaders" but should "help the largest possible number of people to see the realities of the changing and convulsive world in which American policy must operate."

The price of releasing diplomatic information, however, had increased substantially during the Cuban missile crisis. A diplomatic blunder or press leak at that moment could mean national annihilation. At the same time, television news became more omnipresent and more competitive. The first television war, Vietnam, raised substantial concerns among governmental leaders. Journalists in Vietnam discovered increasing discrepancies between what leaders in the United States said was going on in southeast Asia and what they could see for themselves. John F. Kennedy sought to have correspondents who told a different version of the truth removed from Vietnam. Lyndon B. Johnson continued to tell his version of Vietnam occurrences, and journalists developed the term "credibility gap" to characterize the difference between Johnson's truth and reporters' truth. Richard M. Nixon put quieting press coverage of the war at the top of his list of things to accomplish. All three presidents argued that journalistic practices made it harder to conclude a peace treaty. The government's strategies, they said, were revealed through the news, and journalists also gave too great credence to the war's opponents at home, leading the North Vietnamese to continue the war for years.

The problems connected with finding diplomatic solutions to world problems only increased with the develop-

Live telecasts of the student uprising in Beijing, China, in 1989 made it more difficult for the U.S. government to determine its reaction.
(Museum of Broadcast Communications)

ment of new technology that made it possible to transmit news instantaneously from any part of the globe. Dan Rather of CBS News broadcast live from Tiananmen Square in Beijing during the student protests, and Tom Brokaw of NBC News was in Berlin when the wall came down. Pictures flooded the world's homes.

Earlier presidents often had to worry about whether the press was revealing diplomatic information prematurely – telling information that would have become public anyway at a later date. In the late twentieth century, presidents had to be concerned over whether the media were helping to shape foreign policy – taking the final decision making out of the hands of government. According to David Gergen, White House communications director during the Ford and Reagan administrations, such media coverage often made policy decisions turn on "how well the policy will play, how the pictures will look, whether it sends the right signals, and whether the public will be impressed by the swiftness of the government's response—not whether the policy promotes America's long-term interests."

Surely, that was a problem for U.S. interests abroad. Another problem, however, rested in what Marvin Kalb called "patriotic journalism." "Patriotic journalism," Kalb said, "was – and is – dangerous, because it denies the public the information and detached perspective people need to make sound decisions." The problem of adjusting the competing needs of foreign policy and journalism remained more than 200 years after the founding of the republic.

MARGARET A. BLANCHARD

See also Credibility Gap; Mexican War; News Leaks; News Management; Party Press; World War I

Further Reading

Bennett, W. Lance, and David L. Paletz, eds., *Taken by Storm: The Media, Public Opinion, and U.S. Foreign Policy in the Gulf War,* Chicago: University of Chicago Press, 1994
Blanchard, Margaret A., *Americans First, Newspapermen Second? The Conflict Between Patriotism and Freedom*

of the Press During the Cold War, 1946–1952 (Ph.D. diss., University of North Carolina), 1981

Dennis, Everette E., "Stolen Peace Treaties and the Press: Two Case Studies," *Journalism History* 2 (1975)

Nelson, Anna Kasten, "Secret Agents and Security Leaks: President Polk and the Mexican War," *Journalism Quarterly* 52 (1975)

O'Heffernan, Patrick, *Mass Media and American Foreign Policy: Insider Perspectives on Global Journalism and the Foreign Policy Process,* Norwood, New Jersey: Ablex, 1991

Reston, James, *The Artillery of the Press: Its Influence on American Foreign Policy,* New York: Harper & Row, 1967

Seib, Philip, *Headline Diplomacy: How News Coverage Affects Foreign Policy,* Westport, Connecticut: Praeger, 1997

Serfaty, Simon, ed., *The Media and Foreign Policy,* Basingstoke, England: Macmillan, 1990; New York: St. Martin's, 1991

Mass Media and Health Issues

Health information comes increasingly from media sources

In the late twentieth century, the mass media were important sources of health information, cited more often than any other information channel except doctors, dentists, and other health professionals. Given the public's relatively limited access to health professionals, this might seem encouraging. Unfortunately, however, researchers concluded that mass media health messages often were inaccurate, misleading, or both, frequently producing unintended negative consequences.

In her comprehensive review of media health information, Nancy Signorielli concluded that the media's portrayal of health issues was unrealistic. In particular, the media ignored potential social, political, or economic causes of poor health and presented health and medical treatment (rather than preventive behavior) as virtually synonymous. The result appeared to be a reduction in personal health.

A great many researchers have examined various aspects of the health-related content and effects of mass media, and any summary of their findings inevitably must exclude some important results. Nonetheless, the following will attempt to describe the most consistent findings from studies of four types of mass media health content – news coverage, entertainment programming, commercial advertising, and public service campaigns.

Health issues were among the most covered topics in the news media. For instance, researchers noted more than 7,000 health-related items in three consumer magazines between 1959 and 1974. News stories usually presented health problems as resulting from individual behavior and isolated, relatively unpredictable events, and they focused on medical experts and expertise – including drugs and

high-technology treatment – as the solutions. The causes of death most often appearing in news stories frequently bore little resemblance to the top killers in real life. News stories rarely covered preventive medicine or social or environmental changes that might improve public health.

Health-oriented news directed at women focused on appearance, particularly diet and exercise, caring for a family, and reproductive health. For instance, one study of health articles in three popular women's magazines found no articles about lung cancer, the dangers of smoking, heart disease, stroke, suicide, or physical abuse.

When the news media did cover common health risks, the information often was inadequate. Stories about cancer, for instance, tended to focus on cancer in general rather than on specific types and emphasized dying rather than coping. Cancers affecting "unmentionable" organs, such as the colon, rectum, or reproductive organs, received far less coverage than other types of cancer, especially in comparison to their relative incidence.

News coverage also perhaps was influenced by the fear of offending advertisers, especially cigarette manufacturers. Researchers found that even the most respected newsmagazines rarely published comprehensive articles discussing the dangers of smoking, and some reported that news and women's magazines actually deleted negative information about cigarettes from special health supplements.

Perhaps the most heavily studied area of news content other than that related to smoking was the coverage of AIDS. This extensive coverage was linked to increased public awareness and knowledge of AIDS. Critics complained, however, that AIDS stories blamed HIV-infected individuals for their plight if they contracted the disease through "non-normative" risky behaviors such as homosexual sex and IV drug use. Researchers also found that the extent of AIDS coverage in the United States was related to its likelihood of threatening people who were part of the mainstream.

Even topics perceived to affect mainstream audiences, however, often were covered poorly. During 1993 and 1994, health care reform topped the list of health-related media subjects. However, that coverage focused on how reform efforts would affect institutions rather than individuals. One study showed that stories dealing with the political implications of reform were nearly twice as common as stories about how health care reform would affect individuals and families, and the most common subject was the impact on the health care system.

Studies linking news consumption with individual health effects were relatively rare, and most focused on agenda-setting effects on public opinion. For instance, news coverage was linked to public opinion and policy change related to illegal drugs and government-funded catastrophic illness coverage. In fact, some researchers argued, the most important health-related effects of mass media might occur through impact on health policy rather than individual behavior change. Proponents of "media advocacy" argued that using news (and entertainment) media to reframe public discussion about particular health problems could produce policy changes that improved public health without depending on individual behavior change.

Health issues were among the most common topics for

television entertainment programs. For instance, one study showed that nearly half of all daytime drama characters were involved in health-related occurrences, including – in order – psychiatric disorders, heart attacks, pregnancies, car accidents, attempted homicides, attempted suicides, and infectious diseases. Entertainment media virtually never presented illness as chronic, focusing instead on acute, often rare illnesses that were cured by the end of the program through the brilliant, sometimes heroic, efforts of highly skilled doctors. Medical care was presented as necessary, noncontroversial, and freely available; patients sought and obtained the best treatment without concern for costs or access.

Despite the common belief that television characters frequently smoked, researchers found smoking to be relatively rare. Rarer still, however, were instances in which characters refused to smoke, made antismoking statements, or worried about passive smoking. Smoking was more common in theatrical films and actually increased in the early 1990s; negative consequences rarely were shown.

Entertainment programs portrayed drug and alcohol use as equally benign. Alcoholic beverages appeared more frequently than any other kind of drinks, and more than one-third of all major television characters were shown consuming alcohol. References to harmful effects of alcohol, however, were quite uncommon, and drinkers almost never were portrayed as alcoholics.

Studies of the nutrition-related content of entertainment programming suggested that some improvement occurred over the last few decades of the twentieth century. However, most television characters suffered no ill effects from frequent snacking and drinking; overweight or obese television characters were less than half as common as overweight or obese adults in the real world.

Finally, researchers devoted considerable attention to media content related to sexuality and reproductive health. The results were not positive. Although sexual activity in television, movies, and music lyrics was increasingly common and increasingly explicit, discussion of potential sex-related health hazards was rare. For instance, one study of 1987–88 prime-time programs showed that references to sexual intercourse occurred 20 times as often as references to sexually transmitted diseases, and characters' actions to prevent unwanted pregnancy or sexually transmitted diseases were equally scarce.

Despite these findings, relatively little conclusive evidence linked use of entertainment media with health effects. What evidence there was, however, strongly suggested that the effects were negative. For instance, heavy television viewing was related to obesity among all viewers and to poorer eating habits and lower nutrition knowledge among children. Other studies showed that watching sexual content in television programs and movies might increase adolescents' acceptance of premarital sex and promiscuity and that viewing sexually explicit movies increased callousness toward women and the tendency to downplay the harm done to rape victims. Some research revealed a positive association between heavy viewing of "sexy" television shows and sexual intercourse among teenagers.

The legal drugs – alcohol and tobacco – cost the United States more in lost lives and economic losses than all illicit drugs combined, yet advertising for these products was expanding in the late twentieth century, with few counterbalancing messages to promote healthy behavior. Although the alcohol industry spent $1.04 billion promoting beer, wine, and liquor through measured media in 1990 (and staunchly insisted that the goal of alcohol advertising was not to increase consumption but to compete for brand share among competitors), research failed to demonstrate a strong relationship between alcohol advertising and consumption. For example, findings suggested positive relationships between advertising and consumption of wine and distilled spirits but not of beer; positive relationships for repetition of wine commercials to women; and a strong influence of alcohol advertising on drinkers who were not sober. In contrast, however, several studies showed opposite results.

Much of the debate centered around the industry's targeting of minorities and the unintended effects of commercials on susceptible groups such as children. For example, studies suggested that African Americans paid more attention to advertising and responded more readily than the average consumer. Furthermore, research showed that African Americans were targeted disproportionately in certain alcoholic beverage advertising. Researchers found that middle-school children believed the advertising messages that beer drinking would lead to good times, having fun, and being cool, while few of these children held beliefs about the dangers of drinking as portrayed in health promotion advertising. Early results of the few studies of alcohol advertising's effects on problem drinkers and recovering alcoholics suggested that the images in such advertising might trigger the impulse to drink in this vulnerable group.

Cigarettes were one of the most heavily advertised and hotly debated products on the U.S. market. Most of the controversy mirrored the debate in the alcoholic beverage industry and centered primarily on images and targeting practices. For example, cigarette advertising typically employed appeals to sexual attractiveness, beauty, health, nature, and sports – images particularly desirable to adolescents. While tobacco companies insisted that their advertising was intended only to induce smokers to switch to their brands, critics charged that R.J. Reynolds's "Smooth Dude" Joe Camel campaign was a thinly veiled attempt to attract underage smokers.

Additionally, to counter the downturn in smoking among whites, R.J. Reynolds developed a high-tar and -nicotine menthol cigarette targeted specifically to blacks, even though the high incidence of smoking among minorities was thought to have a direct impact on their smoking-related diseases. (Black men developed heart disease 20 percent more often than white men; black women developed heart disease 50 percent more often than white women.)

When faced with the most common health problems reported by adults (weight problems, upset stomach, muscle aches, minor eye problems, fatigue), consumers used nonprescription medicines to treat the symptoms 35 percent of the time. The imagery and symbolism used in advertising for these products could be problematic. Research suggested that many of these ads focused on women's concerns about their appearance and the psychological or social benefit that could be gained from their use. These findings were particularly disturbing in light of the fact that a direct cause-and-effect relationship had been found between television advertising and the use of over-the-counter drugs. Research also showed that younger children exposed to large numbers of nonprescription medicine ads overestimated the frequency of illness in society and therefore the need for medicines.

Researchers in the 1990s expressed concern about the promotion of prescription and formerly prescription drugs for poorly or newly defined health problems (e.g., advertising minoxidil – Rogaine – as a solution to male pattern baldness; these campaigns later often targeted women as well). These ads might lead to misuse of these drugs when patients use them without proper medical advice.

While most literature devoted to mass media health care issues focused on the negative effects of advertising, sensitive, targeted, and well-planned public service advertisements (PSAs) had the potential both to raise awareness and to encourage healthier behavior. However, little research existed to guide PSA planners in developing successful advertisements. Consequently, many PSAs were of low quality. Additionally, because the media traditionally received many more PSAs than they could run, only a small fraction of broadcast-bound PSAs ever reached the air, and gatekeepers traditionally ran PSAs during less desirable times that had not been sold for commercial messages.

Among the numerous success stories in PSA campaigns (i.e., AIDS awareness, breast self-examination), one exemplar bears mentioning. In 1986, the Partnership for a Drug Free America brought together representatives from advertising agencies, television networks, cable companies, trade associations, publishers, and others to develop PSA campaigns to prevent drug abuse. Unlike many public service campaigns, the Partnership conducted needs assessments, continuously monitored the success of its campaign, and produced high-quality, targeted advertising (for example, the famous campaign showing a fried egg, with the voiceover, "This is your brain on drugs"). The Partnership elicited the cooperation of marketing and media executives who obtained unprecedented placement in such highly rated shows as *Beverly Hills 90210*. Results suggested that, in areas of high broadcast frequency, there was an increased awareness of the risks of drugs, a 33 percent decrease in marijuana use, and a 15 percent decrease in cocaine use. During the first two years of the campaign, children from ages 9 to 12 and adults 18 and older showed widespread change in attitudes and beliefs about drugs and users. Teenagers showed more resistance to attitude change, although there was a significant increase in their perception of the dangers of drug use. Adolescents were therefore the target for future Partnership campaigns.

Conversely, another "public service" or institutional effort not only blurred the distinction between commercial and public service advertising but also drew fire from critics. To counter flat sales, potential regulation, and mounting criticism of alcoholic beverage advertising during the mid-1980s, the alcohol industry began using paid advertising to promote responsible drinking. In 1990, Anheuser-Busch alone spent a total of $15 million to promote its

"Know When" programs. Although these campaigns could help educate the public about the dangers of alcohol consumption, critics charged that the themes and images used in these ads were similar to those of the beer companies' normal brand promotions and might serve to increase consumption. For example, the Anheuser-Busch campaign's advice to "Know When to Say When" and the Miller campaign asking consumers to "Think When You Drink" and "Drink Safely" still assumed alcohol consumption; they failed to acknowledge that in some instances, people should not drink at all. A more appropriate slogan, critics said, would be "Know When to Say No" or "Think Before You Drink." Many of the moderation-oriented beer ads seemed to suggest that the problem of alcohol-impaired driving was caused by having one too many, leaving the definition of "too many" vague.

Many of the later responsible drinking commercials devoted less time to discouraging alcohol abuse. For instance, in a Coors campaign, half of each 30-second spot was dedicated to promoting beer consumption through the use of pro-drinking scenes such as male bonding and crowded bars – the same scenes used in their brand advertising. These "responsible" themes neglected many important public health messages: no level of consumption is completely safe, drinking and driving should be depicted as totally separate behaviors at all times, and abstinence is a perfectly acceptable choice. Additionally, through the use of themes consistent with their standard brand promotions, beer companies negated any pro-health messages they may have communicated.

In summary, then, the overall effect of mass media on health appears to be rather negative. Although news coverage, public service advertising, commercial advertising, and even entertainment programming have the potential for providing important and useful health information and encouraging healthier behavior, such content has been the exception rather than the rule. Throughout the mass media, health messages have tended to focus on treatment of health problems after they develop rather than on prevention and wellness. Individuals are blamed for their poor health but are directed to medical experts for the solution; both governments and corporations are "let off the hook" for either causing or preventing health problems.

KIM WALSH-CHILDERS, DEBBIE TREISE

See also Federal Trade Commission; Food and Drug Administration; Mass Media and the Sexual Revolution; Mass Media and Tobacco Products; Patent Medicine Advertising

Further Reading

Atkin, Charles, and Lawrence Wallack, eds., *Mass Communication and Public Health: Complexities and Conflicts*, Newbury Park, California: Sage, 1990
Backer, Thomas E., and Ginna Marston, "Partnership for a Drug-Free America: An Experiment in Social Marketing," in *Organizational Aspects of Health Communication Campaigns: What Works?*, edited by Thomas E. Backer and Everett M. Rogers, Newbury Park, California: Sage, 1993

Brown, Jane D., and Kim Walsh-Childers, "Effects of Media on Personal and Public Health," in *Media Effects: Advances in Theory and Research,* edited by Jennings Bryant and Dolf Zillman, Hillsdale, New Jersey: Lawrence Erlbaum, 1994

Dejong, William, Charles Atkin, and Lawrence Wallack, "A Critical Analysis of 'Moderation' Advertising Sponsored by the Beer Industry: Are 'Responsible Drinking' Commercials Done Responsibly?," *Milbank Quarterly* 70:4 (1992), pp. 661–678

Montagne, Michael, "The Promotion of Medications for Personal and Social Problems," *Journal of Drug Issues* 22:2 (Spring 1992), pp. 389–405

Rice, Ronald, and Charles Atkin, eds., *Public Communication Campaigns,* 2nd ed., Newbury Park, California: Sage, 1989

Signorielli, Nancy, *Mass Media Images and Impact on Health: A Sourcebook,* Westport, Connecticut: Greenwood, 1993

Mass Media and Politics

Government-press relations changed over time

During U.S. history, two general models of government-press relations have existed. The first, a political advocacy model, characterized the period from the American Revolution to the middle of the nineteenth century. During this period, a sense of common purpose between press and politicians was widespread; individual newspapers were highly partisan, containing advocacy for their particular party's issues and leaders. The second, an objectivity or source-based news model, characterized government-press relations since the late nineteenth century. News reporters strove to keep their distance from politicians and government, relying on "balanced" or "objective" news rather than the partisan advocacy of the earlier era.

Political advocacy was born in the press of the Revolutionary era. Threatened by the economic implications of Stamp Act taxes, editors such as Edes and Gill of the *Boston Gazette* and John Holt of the *New York Gazette* joined with Patriot forces to attack British rule and, eventually, to advocate independence. Newspapers were full of partisan essays, written both by editors and by Patriot leaders (such as Boston's Sam Adams). Editors performed a second political function; in addition to editing their partisan papers they also served as political activists. Boston's Edes and Gill, for instance, helped to organize opposition to the East India Company's sale of tea in the New World in 1773. Edes and Philadelphia editor William Bradford also both were active in their city's Sons of Liberty, the vigilante arm of the Patriot cause.

In the new nation, partisan content and political activism continued. In the 1780s, editors made clear their belief that they had not only the right but the obligation to discuss key political issues; partisan advocacy remained the staple of newspaper essays. Newspapers and pamphlets served as an important forum for political debate and dis-

course throughout this period, particularly during the debates over the ratification of the U.S. Constitution of 1787. Early factions in the new federal government relied on newspapers to take their cause to the nation's people. Alexander Hamilton and the Federalists provided financial support to John Fenno's *Gazette of the United States,* and in turn, that paper carried essays defending Federalist policies and assailing the opposing Jeffersonian anti-Federalists – who provided financial support for Philip Freneau's *National Gazette.*

Partisan journalism continued to flourish in the first half of the nineteenth century. An extensive system of political patronage on federal, state, and local levels provided a necessary subsidy for newspapers. Expanding political parties created a greater need for a vehicle to reach potential voters; newspapers served that function well. New political groups such as the Antimasonic party and various states' rights parties of the late 1820s and early 1830s relied extensively on newspapers to attract voters.

Leading state newspapers in the antebellum era included the *Albany (Georgia) Argus,* the *Richmond (Virginia) Enquirer,* the *Frankfort (Kentucky) Argus of the Western World,* and the *Charleston (South Carolina) Mercury.* Like the Patriot editors of the Revolutionary era, antebellum editors not only filled their columns with highly partisan essays but also served as political organizers outside their office. Editors such as Francis Preston Blair of the *Washington (D.C.) Globe* and Duff Green of the Washington *United States Telegraph* were key political organizers in the 1820s, 1830s, and 1840s, organizing meetings and selecting candidates for party tickets. On the state and local levels, editors were usually members of party central committees, charged with the day-to-day operation of their parties.

In the middle decades of the nineteenth century, changes both in the press and in society at large provided the foundation for a new model of government-press relations. Business patronage (advertising) displaced political patronage as a major revenue source, loosening once-strong party-press financial ties. Advertisers wanted to sell their goods to all consumers regardless of individual political predilections; thus, the "ideal" advertising-based paper tended to be more neutral than overtly partisan. Broad philosophical debates about the role of journalism in society – including a sense that the interests of readers were changing – further steered the media away from advocacy for an individual party and toward a notion of news that would be balanced between various points of view.

Part of the redefinition of journalistic norms revolved around the growing sense that many politicians were corrupt; scandals in federal, state, and local governments provided ample evidence that some politicians willingly accepted – or even extorted – bribes and kickbacks. The Grant administration (1869–77) was rife with corruption; the Crédit Mobilier scheme tainted prominent leaders of both major political parties. In New York state, Boss Tweed proved that local politicians also could reap a fortune through greed and payoffs. In such a political world, many came to see that the press could best serve the public at large not by advocacy for an individual party but through careful, skeptical scrutiny of all politicians. St. Clair McKelway, editor of the *Brooklyn (New York) Eagle,* argued that newspapers should act as impartial judges by carefully analyzing all political parties.

By the end of the nineteenth century, the key elements of this new model of journalism were clearly in place. First, the press in general no longer provided automatic and fervent support for politicians and their parties. Just the opposite was often true; reporters tended to view themselves as the representatives not of political parties but of the public. Their articles often focused on governmental fraud or ineptitude. Second, reporters did not inject their own opinions into stories; rather, they presented "facts" about an issue or event. In the early twentieth century, this separation of "fact" and "opinion" became known as objectivity. The need for facts placed particular emphasis on access by the media. Third, the "facts" were the views or statements of key participants in the issues or events of the day; interviews of such sources became a chief characteristic of news gathering in the latter third of the nineteenth century.

In practice, reform-minded journalists in the late nineteenth and early twentieth centuries detailed graft, greed, and corruption in government. Their goal was to present facts, practicing a "journalism of exposure" that ideally would prompt reform. The best-known reform journalists were the so-called muckrakers. Lincoln Steffens, Ray Stannard Baker, and others detailed an extensive and dizzying array of government corruption at the local and state levels. Other progressive journalistic leaders – including Edward W. Scripps, who founded the nation's first newspaper chain – also were dedicated to exposing fraud in government. Throughout the twentieth century, journalists remained dedicated to serving as a watchdog on government, uncovering dishonesty or crime.

This journalism of exposure left politicians and public officials with no easy way to garner sympathetic news or editorial support for their programs. In the late 1890s, however, Gifford Pinchot – head of the U.S. Forest Service – began to adapt to the changing news norms by generating "facts" about the forest service that reflected well on his agency. Pinchot served as a close adviser to President Theodore Roosevelt from 1901 to 1909 and directed early stages of governmental news management. Roosevelt was the youngest person to serve as president to that time, and he kept a frenetic pace in horse riding, bronco busting, and even boxing. He was happy to invite reporters along to record his stamina and competitive abilities. Roosevelt was one of the first presidents to understand that most presidential activities could get news coverage. He and his advisers created news events, such as the first national governors' conference, in part because these events allowed him to focus attention on key issues – and to garner press coverage for them.

Government news management became institutionalized during World War I, when the Committee on Public Information – headed by a former journalist, George Creel – served as a gargantuan public relations agency to gain favorable news coverage for the war effort. According to Creel, the committee's news releases filled more than 20,000 newspaper columns a week during late 1917 and early 1918.

During World War I, the U.S. government attempted to shape public opinion not only by influencing news via public relations work but also by suppressing criticism. The Espionage (1917) and Sedition Acts (1918) led to the suppression of more than 40 newspapers that criticized the war effort, including German-language, Socialist, and Irish American newspapers. In 1919, in *Schenck* v. *United States,* the U.S. Supreme Court upheld these laws, ruling that they posed no substantive challenge to First Amendment rights of speech or press.

The presidency of Franklin Roosevelt (1933–45) represented growing sophistication by government officials in news management strategies. Roosevelt and his advisers had a keen sense of news reporters' needs for access to events and information; in 12 years, Roosevelt held almost 1,000 press conferences. Roosevelt and his advisers – notably Press Secretary Steven Early – also were particularly active in attempting to frame news coverage; they recognized that key sources had a distinct advantage in defining issues and thus in shaping news reporters' articles. Roosevelt's accessibility, coupled with his warm personality, made him popular with the press and successful in framing news coverage of his own administration.

Roosevelt also turned to the relatively new medium of radio to reach the U.S. public. Radio allowed him to create a personal bond with voters; his famous "fireside chats" relayed his warmth and charisma. They also allowed him to reach the people directly, circumventing the news-framing decisions of journalists and their editors.

In the post–World War II era, U.S. presidents increasingly relied on experienced journalists in their efforts to deal with the mass media. James Hagerty, a well-respected news reporter, served as Dwight Eisenhower's press secretary, while Pierre Salinger held that position in John F. Kennedy's administration. Presidential press secretaries represented just part of the institutionalization of efforts to influence the news; other agencies – such as the White House Office of Communications (established in the Eisenhower era and expanded in the Richard M. Nixon and Ronald Reagan eras) – reflected the degree to which successful news management had come to be seen as one of the key ingredients to a successful presidency.

The post–World War II era also witnessed the rise of television as a potent force in national politics. John F. Kennedy was the first president to capitalize on the image-sensitive nature of television. Young, intelligent, and good-looking, Kennedy used television as an effective public relations tool. His televised live press conferences were a tour de force of humor, intelligence, and stage presence. Kennedy also wooed the press corps – and was fairly successful at managing the news – through accessibility, friendliness, and willingness to provide information and news, as well as socializing with reporters.

In the post–World War II era, Kennedy's media skills were matched by only one other president – Reagan (1981–89). As a veteran Hollywood actor, Reagan had finely honed his media image over decades. He was aided by a staff with a sophisticated sense of how sources can influence news. Administration personnel developed a "line of the day," whereby all executive branch members discussed a similar issue with the press, thus ensuring that that issue became a key element of the day's news reports on the administration. In this way, the Reagan White House skillfully dominated the nation's news agenda.

The pivotal role of television in national elections began in 1960, when the presidential debate between Kennedy and his Republican opponent, Nixon, greatly aided Kennedy's campaign against the seasoned vice president. Kennedy aides concluded after the election that they could not have won without television's focus on their candidate. In subsequent elections, candidates focused increasing attention to their television image, and huge sums poured into television political advertising. By the 1980s, the single largest expenditure in a national political campaign (as well as in many state political campaigns) was political advertisements. Candidates and their advisers liked ads because they – and not reporters – controlled their images in ads.

Not all presidents were as successful in managing the news or in controlling their television image as was Kennedy. The post-Kennedy years witnessed fairly heavy-handed – but ultimately unsuccessful – efforts at news management by the Lyndon B. Johnson and Richard M. Nixon administrations. Johnson was undone by Vietnam and protest at home, Nixon by Watergate.

Prior to the Watergate scandal, the Nixon administration (1969–74) was fairly adept at news management. Nixon and others in his administration systematically attempted to intimidate the press; they also attempted to shape the news by controlling news sources. Nixon also relied extensively on live television addresses to take his views to the nation directly rather than through journalists. The break-in at Democratic National Headquarters at the Watergate apartment complex – tied to Nixon's reelection aides and covered up feloniously by the president himself – ultimately destroyed the administration.

GERALD J. BALDASTY

See also Committee on Public Information; Espionage and Sedition Acts; Kennedy, John F., and the Media; Muckraking; News Management; Nixon, Richard M., and the Media; Party Press; Pinchot, Gifford, and Government Public Relations; Presidential Debates; Presidential Press Secretaries; Roosevelt, Franklin D., and the Media; Roosevelt, Theodore, and the Press; Watchdog Concept; Watergate Scandal

Further Reading

Baldasty, Gerald J., *The Commercialization of News in the Nineteenth Century*, Madison: University of Wisconsin Press, 1992

Hertsgaard, Mark, *On Bended Knee: The Press and the Reagan Presidency*, New York: Farrar, Straus, & Giroux, 1988

Leonard, Thomas C., *The Power of the Press: The Birth of American Political Reporting*, New York: Oxford University Press, 1986

Porter, William E., *Assault on the Media: The Nixon Years*, Ann Arbor: University of Michigan Press, 1976

Spear, Joseph, *Presidents and the Press: The Nixon Legacy*, Cambridge, Massachusetts: MIT Press, 1984

Turner, Kathleen J., *Lyndon Johnson's Dual War: Vietnam and the Press*, Chicago: University of Chicago Press: 1985

White, Graham J., *FDR and the Press*, Chicago: University of Chicago Press, 1979

Winfield, Betty Houchin, *FDR and the News Media*, New York: Columbia University Press, 1994

Mass Media and Race

Relationship between press and minority groups has been stormy

African, Native, and Asian Americans are three of the peoples called "minorities" when the term refers to the major U.S. racial and ethnic groups. The fourth major category, Hispanic, is an ethnic, not racial, designation. Race has mattered in the geographic area that became the United States of America since the Europeans arrived in the early seventeenth century and embarked on a course of action that put them on a collision course with Native Americans. In a society where it became important to tell one group from another, race became a major criterion.

Race is one of the great Gordian knots in the United States, and nowhere has this issue been more evident than in the media. The relationship between Asian, African, and Native Americans (who comprise approximately 17 percent of the population of the United States) and the mass media has been a stormy one. Over the years, this relationship most often has focused on three areas: portrayal, employment, and entrepreneurship. At various times, the state either has dispossessed these groups of land and property, exploited their labor, or systematically excluded them from participation in the social and political institutions of America.

The establishment of the Jamestown, Virginia, colony in 1607 marked the beginning of a permanent European presence in the land that became America. However, Native Americans, or Indians, had lived on the land for thousands of years before Europeans arrived. Relations between Native Americans and the colonists were harmonious at first, but the situation changed. Native Americans and the colonists engaged in battles that became wars for possession of the land. The media portrayed Native Americans as a monolithic group of people, even though there were thousands of different Native American cultures east of the Mississippi River at the time.

The black presence in America dates back to 1619, when the captain of a Dutch ship exchanged a group of 20 Africans for supplies from the Jamestown colonists. Initially, blacks were indentured servants and had the same status as whites. By the mid–seventeenth century, however, black equality had disappeared. As a group, blacks were slaves for more than 200 additional years. An Asian presence in the United States can be found as early as the 1820 census. However, the Chinese who came in 1848 to work the California goldfields were the initial large group of Asian immigrants.

In books, newspapers, and colonial theater, Native Americans had to deal with the European-created images of Native Americans as inferior, savage, yet noble, heathens whose presence was preventing the civilization of the New World. The same media depicted blacks as childlike creatures for whom slavery was the best thing that could happen because this group of people was incapable of participating in a "civilized" society. Two articles in the only edition of *Publick Occurrences, Both Forreign and Domestick,* the first colonial newspaper, mentioned Indians. With the existence of slavery and the systematic dispossession of Native Americans, white superiority was the guiding philosophy in the colonies by the mid–seventeenth century. This philosophy was the rationale for the virtual genocide of Native Americans, the enslavement of blacks, the segregation of Asians, and discrimination against all three groups.

Although the American Revolution changed the lives of the Europeans (whites) in America, it did little for Native and African Americans. The initial Constitution of the United States of America did not allow Native Americans to be citizens, and blacks were considered only to be three-fifths of a person. Many of the powerful men who became known as the Founding Fathers (e.g., Thomas Jefferson and George Washington) owned black slaves. Jefferson, for example, used newspapers to offer rewards for the return of slaves who had run away. Newspapers routinely carried advertisements of slaves for sale and notices of slave auctions.

For more than 200 years, the relationship between Native and African Americans and the media was linear. The larger society controlled all forms of the popular media – books, theater, and newspapers. Consequently, Native Americans and blacks had certain stereotypes associated with them as portrayed by the mass media. They were either invisible, or when seen, dismissed as trivial or depicted as a threat. During this period, the issue of portrayals dominated the relationship between Native Americans and blacks and the mass media. Media employment required literacy. Native Americans and blacks, deliberately excluded from educational opportunities, lacked the requisite literacy skills. Entrepreneurship required access to capital and was an even more problematic consideration.

The first minority media vehicles appeared in the nineteenth century. Samuel Cornish and John Russwurm, two free blacks, published the first black newspaper, *Freedom's Journal,* in New York City on March 16, 1827. The paper carried on page one what has been the credo of all racial minority media in the United States: "We wish to plead our own cause. Too often have others spoken for us. Too long has the public been deceived by misrepresentation in things which concern us dearly." At the time, there was serious talk of sending blacks back to Africa.

The *Cherokee Phoenix,* the first Native American newspaper, published its first edition on February 21, 1828, in Georgia. At the time, the U.S. government was attempting to move the Cherokee Nation from lands it occupied in Georgia, North Carolina, and Tennessee. Like *Freedom's Journal,* the *Cherokee Phoenix* attempted to make sure that the marketplace of ideas contained certain views: "Our

views, as a people, on this subject [i.e., relocation] have been most sadly misrepresented. These views we do not wish to conceal, but are willing that the public should know what we think of this policy, which, if carried into effect, will prove pernicious to us."

Although historians do not agree on a date, they consider the *Golden Hills News* the first newspaper published by Asians in America, with a founding date in California sometime between 1851 and 1854. Asians, too, felt a need to establish a publication that would urge better treatment of the members of their group. Subsequent publications by each Asian, African, or Native American group were similar advocates for their concerns.

The Civil War was the defining event of the nineteenth century in the United States. Native Americans lost more land as the country's boundaries expanded; the white press on the frontier crusaded against them. The Union victory in the Civil War, and subsequent reconstruction, gave blacks some hope for change, but societal retrenchment resulted in the institution of the "separate but equal" racial doctrine at the end of the nineteenth century. Several hundred black newspapers started between the founding of *Freedom's Journal* and the end of the nineteenth century; most failed to survive. A low literacy rate among African Americans and few white readers made financial viability always a concern of black newspapers. Native American publications fared no better. Asian, African, and Native American media were usually on the periphery of the marketplace of ideas. Nineteenth-century minstrel and "Wild West" shows entertained audiences by parading the familiar stereotypes of Native Americans and blacks.

Racism remained inured in the major U.S. institutions of politics, economy, and society in the twentieth century; the majority of the media were no exception. The majority of the media, through their commentary and reportage, supported the idea that racial minorities were different from whites along the dimensions of work and industry, intelligence, patriotism, and civility. As new forms of the mass media developed – motion pictures, sound recordings, and later broadcasting – other characteristics continuously associated with Asian, African, and Native Americans were sexual promiscuity, poor speech patterns, involvement in criminal activity, drug and alcohol abuse, and a low regard for human life.

Asian, African, and Native Americans continued to publish newspapers. Black newspapers enjoyed their heyday during the 1940s when five newspapers (the *Pittsburgh [Pennsylvania] Courier,* the *Chicago Defender,* the *Amsterdam News,* the *Journal and Guide,* and the *Afro-American* group) were able to exert national influence on their readers. J. Edgar Hoover, director of the Federal Bureau of Investigation, had these and other black newspapers investigated for possible sedition charges because of the newspapers' campaign to end discrimination during World War II. Blacks attempted to become involved in motion picture production as the medium developed early in the twentieth century, but the economics and consolidation of the film industry in the 1920s and the Great Depression limited these entrepreneurial activities.

The official "separate but equal" era in the United States ended in 1954 when the U.S. Supreme Court ruled the doctrine unconstitutional. Although Congress passed landmark civil rights legislation in the mid-1960s, riots occurred in many major U.S. cities. A commission appointed by President Lyndon Johnson to study the causes concluded in 1967 that one of the causes of the riots was that "the media report and write from the standpoint of the white man's world."

A combination of the effects of civil rights legislation passed in the 1960s, the affirmative action policy, and urban riots in major cities did much to spur a call for sensitivity to Asian, African, and Native American stereotypes and employment. However, the portrayal and employment issues remained alive in the 1990s. A 1991 national public opinion survey found that a majority of whites believed that blacks were lazier, more prone to violence, less intelligent, and less patriotic than whites. The same survey indicated that the between one-third and one-half of the whites polled felt the same way about Asians.

By the late 1990s, racial minority groups formed formidable consumer market segments that made such considerations of portrayal important for owners of media vehicles who hoped for mass market success. The three major racial groups constituted a consumer market of more than $400 billion in 1995 that met the marketing segmentation criteria of identifiability, substantiality, accessibility, and measurability. Taken together, Asian, African, and Native Americans rivaled the wealth of many of the nations of the world.

Subtle stereotypes have replaced gross racial stereotypes. Broadcast, cable television, and newspaper industry employment data indicated that Asian, African, and Native Americans were employed at levels below their presence in the population or the workforce. The arenas that became more contentious related to management-level jobs and entrepreneurial issues. Nearly a generation after the employment breakthroughs made possible by 1960s civil rights legislation and affirmative action efforts, the 1990s saw attention focused on breaking through the "glass ceiling." Critics argued that racial minorities could rise only so high in media organizations because the top, key decision-making jobs seemed reserved for whites, particularly white males. One school of thought argued that racial minorities who hoped to ascend to such positions had to assimilate "white" values and be thought of as "safe" to succeed in major media organizations.

At the end of the twentieth century, anyone with adequate financing could enter many media businesses, such as newspapers, magazines, music recordings, and motion pictures. Broadcasting was not one of those industries, however. Because the federal government licensed broadcast stations to prevent station signal interference, not everyone could have a station. In the 1970s, the government established policies – including tax credits, preferential broadcast sale, and licensing considerations – designed to increase the number of Asian, African, and Native Americans who operate broadcast stations.

Data (which include Hispanics) indicate that in 1994, minorities owned fewer than one-half of 1 percent of the 98,000 telecommunications firms, 3 percent of the over 10,000 commercial radio stations, and 2 percent of approximately 1,000 commercial television stations. Asian, African, and Native Americans were less than one-tenth of 1 percent of the 7,500 cable operators in the United States. Given these meager levels of ownership, Asian, African, and Native Americans were concerned about falling further behind as the United States rushed to build and travel the information superhighway. As new forms of the mass media developed, many of them were more expensive to start, own, and operate than the more widely known media. The historic minority concerns over lack of access to capital and loan discrimination made it necessary for new media vehicles of Asian, African, and Native Americans to have as their primary concern maximizing wealth for investors rather than pleading the "cause" of group members.

The United States turned increasingly conservative in the 1990s, with calls for less government interference, an end to affirmative action, and a move to a "color-blind society." While flagrant racial discrimination by then was illegal, the relationship between Asian, African, and Native Americans and the media remained as contentious as ever over the traditional concerns of portrayals, employment, and entrepreneurship.

JAMES PHILLIP JETER

See also Advertising and Minorities; African American Media; Alternative Press; Asian American Media; Ethnic Press; Hispanic Media; Kerner Commission Report; Minority Journalists' Organizations; Native American Media

Further Reading

Bogle, Donald, *Toms, Coons, Mulattoes, Mammies and Bucks: An Interpretive History of Blacks in American Films,* 3rd ed., New York: Continuum, 1994; Oxford: Roundhouse, 1994

Dates, Jannette Lake, and William Barlow, *Split Image: African Americans in the Mass Media,* 2nd ed., Washington, D.C.: Howard University Press, 1993

MacDonald, J. Fred, *Blacks and White TV: Afro-Americans in Television Since 1948,* Chicago: Nelson-Hall, 1983

Murphy, James E., and Sharon M. Murphy, *Let My People Know: American Indian Journalism, 1828–1978,* Norman: University of Oklahoma Press, 1981

Sampson, Henry T., *The Ghost Walks: A Chronological History of Blacks in Show Business, 1865–1910,* Metuchen, New Jersey: Scarecrow, 1988

Washburn, Patrick S., *A Question of Sedition: The Federal Government's Investigation of the Black Press During World War II,* New York: Oxford University Press, 1986

Wilson, Clint C., II, *Black Journalists in Paradox: Historical Perspectives and Current Dilemmas,* New York and London: Greenwood, 1991

_____, and Félix Gutiérrez, *Minorities and Media: Diversity and the End of Mass Communication,* Beverly Hills, California: Sage, 1985

Wolseley, Roland, *The Black Press, U.S.A.,* 2nd ed., Ames: Iowa State University Press, 1990

Mass Media and Religion

Coverage of religion a long-time media staple

The mass media always have provided news about religion, but the coverage has changed over time in response to changes in U.S. culture and in journalistic practices. First settled by Puritans who came to the New World for religious freedom, colonial New England developed a religious culture that was reflected in the first newspapers. Early American journalism was, in fact, religious journalism. Publishers understood their papers to be performing both informational and religious functions. In 1690, the first American newspaper, *Publick Occurrences, Both Forreign and Domestick,* listed among its stated purposes, "First, That Memorable Occurrents of Divine Providence may not be Neglected or Forgotten, as they too often are." James Franklin's *New England Courant* initially received its financial backing from prominent Anglicans who saw having their own newspaper as a way to destroy Puritan popularity and establish in its place the Church of England as the official church in the British colonies.

The *Courant* began publishing on August 7, 1721, at the height of heated public debate over inoculation as a way to curb smallpox, which had reached epidemic proportions in the Massachusetts Bay Colony. Early issues were filled with articles attacking inoculation and its supporters, including the influential Puritan clergyman Cotton Mather, on both medical and religious grounds. When the smallpox epidemic ended, attacks on Puritanism and Puritan leaders continued. Many were personal and petty, but the paper also published Benjamin Franklin's "Silence Dogood" letters, which sometimes poked gentle fun at religion.

While the circumstances surrounding founding of the *New England Courant* and its religious perspective were unusual, its practice of reporting and commenting from a religious perspective was not. The *Boston News-Letter* and the *Gazette* provided the Puritan viewpoint. Both frequently printed letters and essays by Cotton Mather and other Puritan leaders.

One noteworthy exception to the practice of reporting from a particular religious perspective was Benjamin Franklin's *General Magazine,* which provided a forum for various religious viewpoints. Because of his more neutral approach, Franklin could be considered the father of modern religion journalism, but that honor is generally given to James Gordon Bennett.

During the early nineteenth century, industrialization led to an increasingly urban, immigrant, and religiously diverse population. In this climate of social, economic, and religious change, Bennett began publishing his *New York Herald* in 1836 as a cheap alternative to the party papers. Recognizing that people cared about religion, Bennett provided religion coverage that in many ways foreshadowed modern journalistic practices.

Although Bennett's satires and commentaries were often personal and polemical, they were also quite different from earlier attacks on religion. Before Bennett, most criticism had been done from a religious perspective to defend one's own religion or to correct perceived errors in the religious beliefs of others. That style persists, but after Bennett, it was no longer the norm.

A Scot and a Roman Catholic in the predominantly Protestant United States, Bennett wrote as an outsider. Instead of defending a religion, he defended religious freedom for all at both the individual and social levels. It was this essentially secular and evenhanded approach that made Bennett's religion journalism the new model for religion reporting.

In the *Herald,* virtually every religion received attention, but the coverage ran the gamut. His extensive favorable-to-neutral attention to church histories, worship services, revivals, and other events served as a model for church pages for more than a century. His favorable coverage of individual examples of charitable and moral behavior provided human interest, while his thorough coverage of sexual and fiscal improprieties and of ecclesiastical interference with individual and congregational affairs and politics paved the way for treating religion as hard news.

For the first five years, Bennett wrote most of the religion stories himself. As his paper became financially more secure, however, and as transportation and communication systems improved, he used staff reporters to cover local religion news and correspondents to cover news from around the nation and the world. Thus, he set the pattern for treating religion primarily as local news, while also providing some attention to developments elsewhere as stories presented themselves.

Before the American Civil War, religion stories were scattered through the newspaper, but as newspapers became larger, stories began to be segregated by subject matter. Since about 1900, weekly religion pages, usually on Saturday or Sunday, have been a regular feature of at least four-fifths of all daily newspapers. Until well into the 1970s, most religion pages were devoted primarily to relatively short stories about local people and events. This emphasis fostered the idea of religious pluralism because it depicted people actively involved in the church of their choice, but it was really a very limited kind of pluralism. Because newspapers frequently provided coverage for churches according to their size and influence in the community, most attention went to well-established Protestant or Roman Catholic churches. Coverage of Christian churches serving ethnic or racial minorities was left primarily to the newspapers serving those communities. Except in urban areas with large Jewish populations, there was little mention of non-Christian religions.

Newsmagazines were the first to provide in-depth coverage of religion. From its beginning in 1923, *Time* magazine devoted a regular section to religion and often featured religious subjects on the cover. Other newsmagazines followed that lead.

Conflict and church-state tension were always the dominant themes in newsmagazine stories when religious people or organizations participated in national and international politics or were parties to court cases. After World War II, attention to conflict within and between churches increased, although the magazines continued to provide some favorable stories about church leaders and interchurch cooperation.

At newspapers, initial efforts to broaden religion coverage came from the churches. By the late 1920s, most churches and religious organizations had public relations or public information offices. In 1929, they created a professional organization, the Religious Public Relations Council, to improve church public relations practices and supplement individual efforts to garner favorable publicity. In 1934, the National Conference of Christians and Jews established the Religious News Service to provide the media with an unbiased, alternative source of news about religion.

Both developments led indirectly to more thorough, balanced coverage by increasing the number of available sources and stories from which religion journalists could choose. Those choices were increased further after World War II, when religion news became regularly available through the wire services. In 1950, George Cornell wrote his first bylined religion story for Associated Press; a few years later, Louis Cassels began covering religion for United Press International (UPI).

Religion remained primarily a local beat, however, at all except the elite papers with large national circulations. Newspaper coverage of the kind of national and international religion stories featured in newsmagazines came primarily from reporters working other beats.

That pattern did not begin to change until events in the 1970s forced the media to recognize religion as an important social and political force. In response to the election of the born-again evangelical Christian Jimmy Carter as president, the advent of the electronic church, the increasing political influence of the New Christian Right in the United States, and the rise to power of the Ayatollah Ruhollah Khomeini in Iran, some newspapers abolished religion pages in order to treat religion more like hard news. Others added or expanded them to assure space for stories and satisfy reader interest. Most also redefined religion news.

Routine coverage of meetings decreased, and sermon stories virtually disappeared. Religion stories became longer and more issue-oriented. Attention to mainline Protestant churches decreased. Coverage of conservative Protestantism, non-Christian, and new religions increased as conflict and consequence replaced consensus as the dominant news values and as journalists began to allocate space according to a diversity approach that provided more information about smaller Christian and non-Christian groups.

Religious organizations always had produced some radio and television programs devoted to religion news, but broadcast journalists were much slower to recognize religion as news than were their counterparts in the print media. Radio stations rarely made religion coverage a priority, although some obtained religion news by purchasing special feeds from wire services, such as the UPI Radio Network, which had a religion editor only beginning in the 1980s. *The World of Religion* was available to CBS radio affiliates, but only a few large stations such as WINS in New York ever produced their own religion news.

On national network television newscasts, about 5 percent of all news stories in the 1970s and 1980s mentioned religion, but most were shorter than 20 seconds and were not really about religion. With the exception of holiday features, which often were selected more for their visual appeal

Coverage of the Rev. Billy Graham's crusades has long been popular on radio and television.
(Museum of Broadcast Communications)

than for their news value, mentions of religion occurred primarily in coverage of political conflict. More than half of all mentions were in reports from traditional religious trouble spots such as the Middle East and Northern Ireland. Domestic attention occurred primarily in stories about major court cases or political activities of the New Christian Right.

Although newscasts provided some longer analytical or investigative stories and some features explaining particular religions and religious practices, much of the issue-oriented coverage appeared as occasional segments on magazine-style shows. Examinations of the place of religion in people's lives and in U.S. culture were the province of public television, largely because of the work of journalist Bill Moyers.

In general, the broadcast media did not take religion news coverage seriously until the early 1990s, when *Time* magazine's religion editor, Richard Ostling, began providing occasional religion coverage for public television's *Mac-Neil-Lehrer Newshour*. In 1993, National Public Radio assigned Lynn Neary to a newly created religion beat; in 1994, ABC became the first television network with a religion specialist when it hired Peggy Wehmeyer, who had covered religion news for WFAA in Dallas, Texas. WFAA and KSL in Salt Lake City, Utah, were the only VHF television stations with religion specialists until 1993, when KOTV in Tulsa, Oklahoma, hired Howard Licht.

Mass media attention to religion always has sparked criticism. Puritans, convinced that the *New England Courant*'s attacks presented a danger to true religion, orchestrated James Franklin's arrest on charges of seditious libel. Clergy offended by James Gordon Bennett's approach joined forces with business and political leaders to launch a "moral war" against him.

In the late twentieth century, the change to issue-oriented coverage of religion sparked two kinds of complaints. One group of critics, comprised almost entirely of highly religious people, contended that news coverage was deliberately biased against religion. The other, which also included many religious people, complained primarily about inadequate, shallow, and inaccurate coverage.

Those who saw deliberate bias frequently quoted surveys showing that journalists working for eastern, elite media were less likely to be religious than the general public as evidence both that journalists did not understand religion and that they were biased against it. Surveys based on national samples, however, indicated that journalists were as likely as members of the general public to have been raised in a religious home; religion specialists were actually more likely to identify with a religion and to be active in it. Therefore, perceptions of deliberate bias more likely stemmed from differences in opinion between journalists and critics about the definition and purpose of news.

Most journalists considered the move away from local, feature-oriented coverage appropriate because they had come to see religion news as serving surveillance and watchdog functions. But the resulting coverage of minority religions and of conflict and controversy appeared as anything but fair to those critics who preferred a kind of religious journalism designed to promote and defend religion. From the perspective of those who complained of deliberate bias, stories about religions with which they disagreed promoted false religion; stories with conflict as the news value created a false image of religion that undermined support for it.

Although those who saw deliberate bias usually approved of feature stories allocated among religions according to their strength in the local community, no extant model totally satisfied the other group of critics. They agreed that the hard news emphasis was inadequate because that approach provided too little attention to those churches not caught up in controversy and to the reality of religion as most people experienced it, but they also disliked feature-oriented coverage because it usually provided too little information about substantive issues and minority religions. Backed by surveys showing that public participation in religion and interest in religion news was higher than for sports, they contended that media content should reflect public interest. Because some who were interested in and attended to religion news liked features, and others preferred hard news, these critics wanted the media to report both feature stories and hard news more thoroughly and sensitively than was often the case.

Most mass media, however, always have considered religion an expendable beat. Few newspapers set aside more than two pages a week exclusively for religion. Fewer than a dozen newspapers ever had employed two full-time religion reporters; some had no religion reporter, and many assigned a person only part-time to the beat. The problems were even more severe in broadcasting, where newscasts were very short and specialists were rare.

With few resources allocated to the religion beat, many stories were ignored or badly reported because of time and space limitations. Although surveys indicated that, in the 1990s, full-time religion journalists were more experienced and better educated in both religion and journalism than they once had been, stories reported by those specialists accounted for only a small fraction of the religion news. Most stories were covered by part-time religion journalists or by reporters from other beats. Because both groups often were uninterested in religion and ill equipped to cover it, they accounted for many egregious examples of missed or poorly reported stories that offended both groups of critics.

Serious efforts to improve religion reporting began in 1949, when the Religion Newswriters Association (RNA) held its inaugural meeting at Syracuse University in conjunction with the establishment of that school's program in religious journalism. By 1994, the RNA had grown to include more than 200 religion reporters working for secular media who were devoted to improving religion reporting.

Beginning in 1980, the Rockefeller Foundation, the National Press Foundation, the Lilly Foundation, the Freedom Forum, the Poynter Institute for Media Studies, the Society for Professional Journalists, and the Knight Center for Specialized Journalism at the University of Maryland sponsored research, national symposia, or training events for working journalists. Some church-affiliated colleges had programs in religious journalism; a few nonsectarian schools offered individual courses.

For 25 years, however, the Syracuse master's degree program in religious journalism, started by Roland E. Wolseley and headed by Robert Root, was the only nonsectarian degree program for those interested in covering religion for the mass media. When that program ended in the mid-1970s, no similar program was available until 1994, when Temple University began offering a master's degree through its departments of journalism and religion, and the Medill School of Journalism at Northwestern University created one in cooperation with Garrett Evangelical Theological Seminary.

JUDITH M. BUDDENBAUM

See also Publick Occurrences, Both Forreign and Domestick; Religious Journalism

Further Reading

Bromley, David G., Anson D. Shupe, Jr., and J.C. Ventimiglia, "Atrocity Tales, the Unification Church, and the Social Construction of Evil," *Journal of Communication* 29 (1979)

Buddenbaum, Judith M., "'Judge . . . What Their Acts Will Justify': The Religion Journalism of James Gordon Bennett," *Journalism History* 14 (1987)

_____, "Network News Coverage of Religion," in *Channels of Belief: Religion and American Commercial*

Television, edited by John P. Ferré, Ames: Iowa State University Press, 1990

_____, "News About Religion: A Readership Study," *Newspaper Research Journal* 3 (1982)

_____, "The Religion Beat at Daily Newspapers," *Newspaper Research Journal* 9 (1988)

Dart, John, and Jimmy Allen, *Bridging the Gap: Religion and the News Media,* Nashville, Tennessee: Freedom Forum First Amendment Center of Vanderbilt University, 1994

Hart, Roderick P., Kathleen J. Turner, and Ralph E. Knupp, "Religion and the Rhetoric of the Mass Media," *Review of Religious Research* 21 (1980)

Said, Edward W., *Covering Islam: How the Media and the Experts Determine How We See the Rest of the World,* New York: Pantheon, 1981; London: Routledge & Kegan Paul, 1981

Sloan, W. David, "The *New England Courant*: Voice of Anglicanism," *American Journalism* 8 (1991)

Mass Media and Self-Regulation

Medium tries to avoid outside restrictions by enacting behavior code

Over the course of the nineteenth and twentieth centuries, the mass media came under increasing scrutiny by their growing audiences. Audience concerns largely focused on the corrupting influences that media might have on society in general and the young in particular. The media form under attack has varied over the years, but the issues have remained virtually the same.

Dime novels were the first to feel the impact of community outrage. These inexpensive storybooks for young people in the latter part of the nineteenth century were among those items termed "devil-traps for the young" by purity crusader Anthony Comstock and his followers. Community efforts concentrated on stopping the circulation of these volumes, which featured brash western heroes and hard-boiled big-city detectives. Judges, teachers, church workers, and police officers all labored to show how these tales of Deadwood Dick and other fictional characters could lead young people into lives of crime and degradation.

Erastus Beadle, who headed one of the major dime novel publishing houses, took steps to safeguard his empire. In what likely was the first code of self-regulation imposed on the communication industry because of community protest, Beadle told his authors to obey certain rules in framing their stories. Primary among these rules was the statement that "we prohibit all things offensive to good taste, in expression or incident." At the end of the publisher's instructions was the statement that "we prohibit what cannot be read with satisfaction by every right-minded person – old and young alike."

The Beadle code of self-regulation was like many others that followed in that (1) it came in response to intense community opposition to a media form or practice; (2) it incor-porated many of the opposition's complaints as positive injunctions for the medium in an attempt to forestall further interference; and (3) once formed, it was ignored more often than it was followed, with the public, whose criticism led to the industry statement, frequently paying little attention to actual practice. The motion picture industry, which was just beginning at the turn of the twentieth century, added the remaining major point to the formula for self-regulation: (4) the statement or code also was aimed at preventing governmental intervention with the medium, which often loomed as the ultimate threat over the medium's freedom.

Almost as soon as primitive motion pictures appeared, community criticism likewise appeared. A short 1895 film, *Dolorita in the Passion Dance,* was pulled quickly because her dance was a little too passionate. *The Widow Jones,* a film version of a Broadway play, brought complaints about a prolonged kiss. And *The Great Train Robbery,* released just after the turn of the century, was condemned for promoting crime and violence. Thus, by 1903, sex, crime, and violence – still the big three as far as criticism of media content is concerned – had been joined in a triumvirate of objectionable themes.

Municipal, state, and federal authorities quickly enacted a variety of regulations affecting motion pictures. Films had to be edited substantially to meet the different jurisdictional requirements. In an attempt to fend off so many levels of regulation, representatives of the move industry set up the National Board of Censorship of Motion Pictures, which served as an official clearinghouse for films. Theater owners would agree not to show films without the board's stamp of approval.

Critics of the effects of motion pictures on children and other "susceptible" groups, such as immigrants, however, were less than pleased about this arrangement, charging that the board was not strict enough. Indeed, of 228 films reviewed by both the Pennsylvania State Board of Censorship and the National Board of Censorship in one year, the state censor called for 1,464 deletions while the National Board asked for only 47.

The battle over regulation of films continued until the 1920s, when the industry made another substantive try at regulation. In 1921, the National Association of the Motion Picture Industry issued the Thirteen Points, a statement pledging members to avoid certain controversial topics in their films. The topics included those "which emphasize and exaggerate sex appeal or depict scenes therein exploiting interest in sex in an improper or suggestive form or manner," or those which were "predominantly concerned with the underworld or vice and crime and like scenes, unless the scenes are part of an essential conflict between good and evil."

The film industry kept revising and reissuing codes; the public kept complaining; films skirting the edges of acceptability kept being produced. The most successful efforts at regulating motion pictures came in the 1930s in the wake of the Payne Fund Report about motion pictures and children and its popular rendition, *Our Movie Made Children* by Henry James Forman. This study said that "at their best," movies "carry a high potential of value and quality in entertainment, in instruction, in desirable effects upon mental attitudes and ideals, second, perhaps, to no medium now known to us. That at their worst they carry the opposite possibilities follows as a natural corollary."

The results of this study were joined with the moral concerns of the Roman Catholic Church in the creation of the Legion of Decency in 1933. Members of the Legion pledged not to attend objectionable motion pictures. The movie industry, in response to the Payne Fund studies and the Legion of Decency, set up the Motion Picture Code, which required producers to have their films reviewed before distribution. Distribution without a Code Seal prominently displayed brought a $25,000 fine. "No picture shall be produced which will lower the moral standards of those who see it. Hence the sympathy of the audience will never be thrown to the side of crime, wrong-doing, evil or sin," the code said.

Such regulations posed real threats for the translation of some books to the silver screen. One classic that ran into substantial difficulties was *Gone with the Wind*. Margaret Mitchell's use of the term "nigger," her references to the Ku Klux Klan, her portrayal of a sexual relationship between Belle Watling and Rhett Butler, and her scene of forced intercourse between estranged husband Rhett and wife Scarlett were among the elements that collided with Hollywood's code of screen morality. But when Rhett's actions in sweeping Scarlett off her feet and carrying her up the staircase for what would later in the century be termed "spousal rape" drew cheers from the audience, producer David O. Selznick had won the battle to portray the bestseller on the screen. When Rhett's parting words to Scarlett, "My dear, I don't care," failed to arouse an audience reaction and his "Frankly, my dear, I don't give a damn" won warm audience support, the barrier against certain language forms on the screen had been breached as well.

The motion picture battle continued through the middle of the 1960s when the industry stopped trying to regulate what producers could put on the screen and moved instead into regulating the age of the audience that could attend certain films. Although there were controversies over such age-based ratings, they apparently worked, for motion pictures thereafter were no longer prime targets of parental attacks.

By the early 1950s, another of youth's favorite media forms – comic books – came under the scrutiny of the community at large. The concern now was, at least in part, juvenile delinquency and the impact that comic books might have on susceptible persons. New York City psychiatrist Fredric Wertham was largely responsible for rousing the nation's parents into a state of frenzy over the effects of comic books on their children. Wertham claimed that comic books provided young people with a blueprint for a life of crime and delinquency.

Wertham couched his remarks in scientific terms, and his criticisms of this relatively new medium gained greater credibility than did some comments from early critics of other media. Government officials became interested in the claims made by the critics of comic books, and, as with motion pictures, a formal inquiry into the industry was launched.

Comics of the age indeed were oriented more toward crime and socially unacceptable behavior. Crime and violence played a key role in the story lines, and, often, the "hero" had few redeeming social values. As a result of the congressional inquiry and the pressure from community sources, the Comics Code Authority was formed, and in order to be sold, comic books had to bear the authority's seal.

Code authority members were given the power to inspect story lines, artwork, and advertising to make sure that none of these violated the code, which was geared toward keeping details of crime and violence out of print. One provision of the code, for example, read, "Inclusion of stories dealing with evil shall be published only where the intent is to illustrate a moral issue and in no case shall evil be represented alluringly, nor so as to injure the sensibilities of the reader." Another segment of the code said, "Respect for parents, the moral code, and for honorable behavior shall be fostered."

The comics code may well have been the most successful of those discussed here; 24 of the 29 publishers producing crime- and violence-filled comic books went out of business. Civil libertarians and comic book enthusiasts have claimed that the comic book code of the 1950s stifled the growth of the medium and left it frozen at the superhero stage while comic books in other countries developed into quite sophisticated mediums.

This battle between those who would regulate certain media forms and those who run certain media forms has gone on for generations. Neither side has seemed able to find grounds on which to finally end the struggle. Although the media form under attack changed with the years, one fact remained clear: Self-regulation occurs when critics get too close to success in rousing public and governmental interest. In the 1980s and 1990s, for instance, the critics attacked music lyrics for various reasons, and record producers created a system for rating records according to audience age level. Makers of certain video games followed suit. Television programming was likewise a target, and a new system of rating programs according to age suitability began in 1997. An effort also was begun to regulate Internet content in similar fashion.

Much of this self-regulation was based on age appropriateness, after the pattern of the motion picture ratings. Many of these systems were debated loudly in the mass media, adopted with great fanfare, and ignored.

The above talks mainly of entertainment-oriented media. The information media also have their codes and self-regulation, but in many instances, they are gathered under the title of "ethics." The nation's newspapers, for example, began their ethics code work with the Canons of Journalism in 1923, which came in the wake of substantial criticism of newspaper practices in the Jazz Age. The National Association of Broadcasters developed its first code of ethics in 1929 to address advertising and programming issues.

MARGARET A. BLANCHARD

See also Censorship of Books; Censorship of Motion
　　Pictures; Codes of Ethics; Comic Books; Dime Novels;
　　Internet; Motion Picture Ratings; Sound Motion
　　Pictures; Television and Violence; Television Program
　　Ratings

Further Reading

Black, Gregory D., *Hollywood Censored: Morality Codes, Catholics, and the Movies,* New York and Cambridge: Cambridge University Press, 1996

Blanchard, Margaret A., "The American Urge to Censor: Freedom of Expression Versus the Desire to Sanitize Society – From Anthony Comstock to 2 Live Crew," *William and Mary Law Review* 33 (Spring 1992)

Feldman, Charles, *The National Board of Censorship (Review) of Motion Pictures, 1909–1922,* New York: Arno, 1977

Inglis, Ruth A., *Freedom of the Movies,* Chicago: University of Chicago Press, 1947

Noel, Mary, "Dime Novels," *American Heritage* (February 1956)

Williams, J.P., "Why Superheroes Never Bleed: The Effects of Self-Censorship on the Comic Book Industry," *Free Speech Yearbook* 60 (1987)

Mass Media and Terrorism

Debates continue over role of media in coverage of terrorism

Several dramatic strikes by "terrorists" in the 1980s and 1990s fixed the attention of international audiences and encouraged systematic inquiry by communications scholars and media practitioners on the theater of terror. These events included the assassination of Israeli Prime Minister Yitzhak Rabin in November 1995, the bombing of the Alfred P. Murrah Federal Building in Oklahoma City, Oklahoma, in April 1995, and the terror visited on academics and information technology workers by the so-called Unabomber in the 1980s and 1990s. These were attacks by citizens who violently opposed the policies of their national governments. The World Trade Center bombing in February 1993 was the most dramatic example of international terrorism targeted at (and within) the United States.

Terrorists also often threaten citizens who live or travel outside the country the terrorists seek to victimize. The most dramatic examples involving U.S. citizens were perhaps the Iranian hostage crisis of 1979–81 (and the arms-for-hostages deal that came after a failed attempt to rescue the hostages), the Trans World Airlines hostage incident and the hijacking of the Italian cruise ship *Achille Lauro* in 1985, the bombing of Libya in 1986, the downing of Pan Am Flight 103 in 1988, and the ordeal of several U.S. hostages held in Lebanon in the 1980s and early 1990s.

Although hundreds of definitions of the word "terrorism" exist in the literature, Alex Schmid's 200-word definition of terrorism "as a method of combat in which random or symbolic victims serve as an instrumental target of violence" is a widely accepted definition by scholars in the field, as is Donna Schlagheck's notion that terrorism is "the actual or threatened use of violence against victims of symbolic importance in such a way as to gain psychological impact for the purpose of achieving political objectives."

Critical theorists and neo-Marxist scholars focus on terrorism sponsored by capitalist states, arguing that countries like the United States use their considerable economic and military power to protect their security and economic interests around the world. The central arguments of these scholars, whose most prominent representative is U.S. linguist, educator, and political activist Noam Chomsky, include the belief that state-sponsored terrorism by the United States and its third-world confederates is extensive. Further, these activities are not covered by the mass media as thoroughly as the activities of anti-Western terrorists because the mass media with global reach are owned by media monopolies run by capitalists from Western or social democracies who, along with democratic governments, encourage and fund scholarship that will reinforce a mainstream Western perspective on the terrorism-media nexus.

The mainstream, social science research agenda on media and terrorism has emphasized understanding the symbiotic relationships among the news media and terrorists and how the terrorism-media nexus influence public opinion and policy making. Scholars apply their theories in an attempt to make sense out of a growing list of terrorist acts. Some of the conclusions that these scholars have reached include the following:

Terrorist Acts

The U.S. Central Intelligence Agency, the U.S. Department of State, and the Pentagon maintain datasets on terrorist behavior. The dataset maintained by the RAND Corporation, a think tank in Santa Monica, California, is considered the most reliable by terrorism researchers because RAND uses a more conservative definition of an "event" – for example, counting one mail bombing event by one organization to many targets on a given day as only one event – and more varied sources of information to identify events, including classified government documents, press reports, journal articles, and open sources. Gabriel Weimann and Conrad Winn analyzed the RAND Corporation dataset on terrorist behavior covering 5,589 events from 1968 to 1986. Few high-profile terrorist activities occurred after this period until the World Trade Center bombing in 1993 and the assassination of Rabin and the Oklahoma City bombing in 1995. The number of terrorist events increased threefold from 1968 to 1986, from 135 to 418. The number of injuries increased by a factor of 17, from 53 in 1968 to 868 in 1986, and the number of fatalities increased by a factor of 28, from 7 deaths to 196 deaths. The targets have been diplomats (29 percent), businesspeople (21 percent), airlines (15 percent), and private citizens (9 percent). About 35 percent of these events took place in Europe, 23 percent in Latin America, 23 percent in the Middle East, and 12 percent in North America. U.S. citizens were the targets of 1,790 of these terrorist events, or one-third, compared to 396 attacks against Israeli citizens, 374 attacks against French citizens, and 289 against the British. The Pentagon estimated that there were 52 organized terrorist groups around the world.

Media-Terrorism Nexus

The news media are attracted to spectacular events that are unexpected, violent, intense, abnormal, unambiguous, and visual. Terrorists consider these conventions for defining what is newsworthy in planning their strikes. Sometimes terrorists take advantage of what Dayan and Katz called "high holiday media events," such as coverage of the Olympic Games, to turn a ceremony of human achievement into a pathology, as happened during the 1972 Olympic Games in Munich, West Germany, when Palestinian terrorists took Israeli athletes hostage, ultimately killing them. Television, the medium from which people in the United States get most of their national and international news, depends on video to tell a story, so bombing incidents, for example, are "made for television." Terrorists who target democratic governments, argued Columbia University political scientist Brigitte Nacos, try to exploit the linkages among the news media, public opinion, and presidential decision making.

Media-Government Nexus

A counterweight to the media-terrorism nexus is the symbiotic relationship that exists between journalists and government officials. "Golden triangle" sources, at the White House, the U.S. Department of State, and the Pentagon, are very effective in setting the domestic and foreign policy agenda. The news media, Nacos demonstrated, are likely to tell their (the administration's) side of a story involving terrorist strikes within the United States.

"Offshore" versus "Onshore" Strikes

Terrorists seek attention, recognition, respectability, and legitimacy. Nacos's content analysis of six terrorists events in the 1980s and 1990s supported her hypothesis that terrorists are more successful in achieving these goals when they strike "offshore." The Iranian hostage crisis of the 1970s is an example of an offshore strike that succeeded. The media, including Ted Koppel's *Nightline* program on ABC, which got its start during the crisis, came to rely on sources other than the "golden triangle" administration sources. The failed rescue attempt in 1980 contributed to President Jimmy Carter's defeat by Ronald Reagan. The United States agreed to return to Iran $8 billion in frozen assets, and the 52 U.S. citizens held hostage for 444 days in Iran were released minutes after President Reagan's inauguration on January 20, 1981. Those assets were needed by Iran, which would fight a bloody war with Iraq from 1980 to 1988.

Onshore strikes are less successful, Nacos believed, because terrorists groups must compete with authoritative administration sources that journalists tend to consult in foreign policy matters. Government sources were more like-

The siege of the Olympic Village in Munich, Germany, in 1972 brought coverage of terrorism to American television programming.
(Museum of Broadcast Communications)

ly to be quoted in the aftermath of the World Trade Center bombing in New York City. Nacos argued that government officials within the targeted country have considerable advantages in the battle for media attention, public opinion, and dominance of the policy debate.

Patterns of Media Coverage of Terrorism

Journalism educator Robert Picard concluded, "After five years of study, nearly every member of that group has come to the conclusion that media do not cause terrorism, but they can make it worse by poor reporting practices, by allowing themselves to be manipulated by interested parties, and by not giving audiences a better understanding of the issue."

Weimann and Winn's study of new coverage of terrorist events by leading broadcast and print outlets around the globe from 1968 to 1986 revealed the following:

1.) International terrorists achieved an approximately 50 percent success rate in securing media recognition for their motives. The proclaimed motives of terrorists had a good chance of being mentioned in the first page of a daily newspaper or among the first three stories in a nightly television newscast.

2.) Media coverage was associated strongly with a contagion effect – the tendency of terrorists to copy or model the actions of other terrorists. That is, coverage of terrorists in newspapers and on television shortened the time lag to emulation. The contagion effect was strongest in the case of kidnapping, attacks on installations, hijackings, bombings, and assassinations.

3.) Scarcity, drama, and intensity of human emotion – traditional newsworthiness values – predicted print coverage. Hijackings, for example, were twice as likely to be covered as attacks on installations. The television networks were more likely to cover an event if injuries and fatalities were involved, if the perpetrators were Palestinian, and if a particular group had claimed responsibility for the action.

4.) There was a strong correlation between the emphasis on terrorism stories in the *New York Times* and in other English-language newspapers. The coverage of the *New York Times* and *Yediot* (the Israeli newspaper in the sample) were very similar. The Egyptian and Pakistani newspapers were more independent of the other newspapers in their patterns of coverage.

5.) The three major U.S. television networks gave greater attention to incidents in North America and in the Middle East.

Improving Press Performance in Covering Terrorism

Terrorism scholars and media practitioners by and large do not favor government restraints on media coverage of terrorism. Most agree with publisher Katharine Graham's view that "while publicity may be the oxygen of terrorists . . . news is the lifeblood of liberty." After that basic agreement, scholars and practitioners diverge. Nacos, for instance, led a group of scholars arguing that better information about terrorist events, threats, and demands, not less information, was needed. Weimann and Winn continued that line of argument when they wrote that an "untamed press is indispensable not only for liberal democracy

as a whole but also for effective counterterrorist efforts in particular . . . and to inhibit security forces under siege from lashing out in ways that would debilitate the democratic regime they defend." Picard warned against limiting discourse on terrorism to official government sources, a likely outcome if governments start suing the press for the way it covers terrorism. The other side of the argument was presented by Richard W. Schaffert, who believed that governments should sue the media because research shows that the press has helped terrorists gain concessions from targeted governments. Newspaper columnist David Broder also moved into the more restrictive realm when he argued that terrorists should be denied access to media outlets and that vigorous self-criticism by the press of its coverage of terrorist events would be healthy.

M. Cherif Bassiouni recommended several guidelines for the press to follow in covering terrorists events. The press should delay reporting details that may influence or aggravate the incident, or provide terrorists with intelligence. Coverage should be proportionate to the event's objective news value, and the event should be placed in context (e.g., by means of background on similar incidents, intellectual roots, and consequences to victims and terrorists). Excessive publicity should be avoided, and unverified rumors or deaths should not be reported. The press should be cautious about revealing "how to" strategies that might encourage "copycats" or reveal what law enforcement agencies are doing or planning to do. Journalists should avoid being party to any negotiating process unless agreed upon by senior news executives and law enforcement officials. The media should be willing to cooperate in press pools with other news organizations and with law enforcement agencies. Finally, Bassiouni said that the news media should educate audiences by emphasizing that terrorism is antisocial behavior involving high levels of risks with low probabilities of success and that society can deal with terrorism but must do so within a legal framework.

LOWNDES F. STEPHENS

Further Reading

Bassiouni, M. Cherif, "Media Coverage of Terrorism: The Law and the Public," *Journal of Communication* 32 (1982)

Dobkin, Bethami A., *Tales of Terror: Television News and the Construction of the Terrorist Threat,* New York: Praeger, 1992

Ermlich, Ferdinand A., "Terrorism and the Media: Strategy, Coverage and Responses," *Political Communication and Persuasion* 4 (1987)

Nacos, Brigitte Lebens, *Terrorism and the Media: From the Iran Hostage Crisis to the World Trade Center Bombing,* New York: Columbia University Press, 1994

Paletz, David L., and Alex P. Schmid, eds., *Terrorism and the Media,* Newbury Park, California: Sage, 1992

Picard, Robert G., *Media Portrayals of Terrorism: Functions and Meaning of News Coverage,* Ames: Iowa State University Press, 1993

Schaffert, Richard W., *Media Coverage and Political Terrorists: A Quantitative Analysis,* New York, Praeger, 1992

Weimann, Gabriel, and Conrad Winn, *The Theater of Terror: Mass Media and International Terrorism,* New York: Longman, 1994

Mass Media and the Antiwar Movement

Debates continue over media's role in promoting opposition to the war

The media's interaction with the anti–Vietnam War movement is marked by myth and reality. One perception holds that journalistic coverage of the antiwar protests were responsible for the war's outcome being unfavorable for the United States – that journalists encouraged protesters and led the antiwar campaign. The converse view notes that U.S. journalists were substantially slower than the country's people in coming to oppose the Vietnam War and that journalists joined the antiwar campaign rather late, if they joined at all. Evidence points to the truth of the latter view but also, somewhat contradictorily, notes that the flamboyance of the antiwar movement was largely the media's responsibility.

College students already had been protesting about a number of things when antiwar protests began. In early 1965, the Students for a Democratic Society (SDS) called for the United States to get out of the war and asked those who agreed to join SDS members in Washington, D.C., for a protest march. About 15,000 persons showed up in the spring of 1965 to protest increasing U.S. involvement in the war. The protest, which proceeded without incident, brought the burgeoning New Left and the student movement to the attention of the news media.

Increasing air attacks on North Vietnam and the dispatching of additional troops to South Vietnam brought about small protests, often on college campuses. Orderly picketing and demonstrations and the placement of carefully worded newspaper advertisements against the war were key elements used to combat the war in its early days. Intellectual challenges to U.S. involvement in Vietnam were often the key to such protests. One of the most popular antiwar activities on college campuses, for instance, was the teach-in, which began in March 1965 on the campus of the University of Michigan in Ann Arbor.

Teach-ins spread coast-to-coast as both professors and students sought to obtain information to counter the official administration line on U.S. involvement, a point of view that many believed was being passed on to the people uncritically by the news media. Administration representatives and spokesmen for the South Vietnamese government regularly were invited to present their sides of the issue. When pro-administration speakers did appear, the audience engaged in some heckling, which, of course, made news. Although news coverage was not as substantive as teach-in organizers wanted, the movement did win media attention.

Opponents of the war, however, fairly quickly decided that calm and peaceful activities were not gaining the kind of attention necessary to bring about change. As Bayard Rustin, a longtime pacifist and an organizer of the 1963 civil rights march on Washington, told a New York rally in June 1965,

> We know that the Wagner Act which gave labor the right to organize and bargain collectively was empty until workers went into the streets. The civil rights movement has learned this lesson. This is a lesson that must be applied now to the peace movement as well. We must stop meeting indoors and go into the streets.

In addition, the media, whose attention was vital if the antiwar protest was to win a spot on the national agenda, paid little attention to calm protests and logical discussions. As Todd Gitlin, an SDS activist, noted,

> Everyone in the movement had to acknowledge the rising threshold for [media] coverage. For it was obvious from within the movement that the media were giving lurid prominence to the wildest and most cacophonous rhetoric, and broadcasting the most militant, violent, bizarre, and discordant actions, and, within the boundaries of any action, the most violent segments. . . . Where a picket line might have been news in 1965, it took tear gas and bloodied heads to make headlines in 1968.

By 1965, then, antiwar demonstrations began increasing in size, and opponents of the war began searching for ways to win the nation's attention. Young men publicly burning their draft cards brought the desired media attention. Other participants in antiwar demonstrations carried Vietcong flags; some desecrated U.S. flags. Scenes of war opponents defying the federal government by such actions became commonplace in the nation's media.

Ignoring the growing antiwar movement became increasingly difficult. Protests escalated in 1967, as did news coverage. A major march on the Pentagon in October 1967, showed the media's interests. "With few exceptions," said historian Melvin Small, "the media concentrated on the violent and the sensational, seeking out the most colorful sound bites or photographs, and virtually ignoring the peaceful aspects of the largest Washington antiwar protest to date."

News coverage of the Tet Offensive in early 1968 compounded problems for the media and the antiwar movement as well. From January 30 to 31, 1968, the North Vietnamese and their allies in the South, the National Liberation Front (Vietcong), carried out simultaneous attacks on more than 100 cities and towns throughout South Vietnam. The attack was a complete surprise and led to some of the heaviest fighting of the war. When the battle showed that even the grounds of the U.S. Embassy in Saigon were not safe, reporters began to reevaluate their stances on the war. Back at home, public opinion polls as early as 1967 had begun to show that a plurality of U.S. citizens believed that even entering the war had been a mistake. The information that the press in South Vietnam sent back about Tet further convinced the nation, sweeping journalists along with the flow.

Anti-Vietnam War protesters demonstrate in front of a government building in Washington, D.C.
(National Archives)

Editorializing against the war picked up substantially after Tet, with both print and broadcast journalists participating. The key statement against the war, however, came from one man–*CBS Evening News* anchor Walter Cronkite, who went to South Vietnam in the wake of Tet to evaluate the situation for himself. Upon his return, he used time on his news show to call for an end to the fighting. He said,

It seems now more certain than ever that the bloody experience of Vietnam is to end in a stalemate. To say that we are closer to victory today is to believe, in the face of the evidence, the optimists who have been wrong in the past. To suggest we are on the edge of defeat is to yield to unreasonable pessimism. To say that we are mired in stalemate seems the only realistic, yet unsatisfactory, conclusion.

The solution was clear to Cronkite. "The only rational way out then will be to negotiate, not as victors but as honorable people who lived up to their pledge to defend democracy, and did the best they could." When Lyndon Johnson heard Cronkite's statement, he knew support for the war among the people of the United States was lost. A little more than a month later, the president took to the airwaves to announce his decision not to seek another term and to devote himself, instead, to seeking peace in Vietnam.

After Tet, protest against the war involved more and more mainstream people, even though those gaining the most attention were the radical activists. Journalism reflected the split within the nation. Protest became an increasingly legitimate story to cover, and the government's pronouncements no longer were accepted uncritically. As antiwar forces continued to argue that the Vietnam conflict was a civil war in which the United States should not interfere, as U.S. casualty figures mounted, and as the financial costs of continuing the conflict grew, support for the government dwindled.

As support for its position increased, the antiwar movement sought to force the political conventions of the summer of 1968 to reflect opposition to the war in their platforms and nominations. Most of the attention was focused on the Democratic National Convention in Chicago, where protesters wanted to show Lyndon Johnson the contempt in which he was held for his escalation of the war and to pull Hubert H. Humphrey, the likely presidential nominee, into the antiwar camp if possible.

Protesters in Chicago were a mixed bag – members of the radical fringe, representatives of the counterculture, average college students, and middle-class professionals. Protest organizers had hoped that tens of thousands of activists would show up in Chicago; perhaps ten thousand were present at the peak of the demonstrations on Wednesday, August 28. According to some estimates, police outnumbered the demonstrators by at least three to one.

Encounters between demonstrators and police occurred throughout the convention. The conflicts were exceedingly brutal, with police using clubs and tear gas to subdue demonstrators, who initially were unarmed but later equipped themselves with bricks and stones.

Before long, the nation's attention was turned as much to what was happening outside the convention hall as within it. Television cameras focused on increasingly nasty encounters between police and demonstrators; and the smell of tear gas invaded some of the leading convention hotels. Hippies and clean-cut demonstrators, young and old, black and white, male and female, rich and poor alike were targets of police action.

Suppression of the protests outside of the convention hall became a major news story. Television cameras were trained on those activities almost as much as on the nomination process inside the hall. Journalists also became the targets of police brutality. Even if reporters identified themselves as such, the police were likely to take out their frustrations on the journalists, who, they thought, were spurring the protesters on to greater feats of violence and were giving Chicago a bad name. Correspondents said that police officers had removed their badges, name tags, and other identifying information before they plunged into the melee. Comments such as "Get the cameras," and, "That doesn't mean a damn thing to me," in response to the presentation of news credentials were reported.

Journalists were appalled by what they witnessed in Chicago, and they told their readers and viewers of their concerns. *New York Times* columnist Tom Wicker, for instance, wrote, "These were our children in the streets, and the Chicago police beat them up." Perhaps even more than the Tet offensive, the confrontation in Chicago radicalized the U.S. news media and pushed them into the arms of the antiestablishment demonstrators. Arthur Ochs Sulzberger of the *New York Times,* Katharine Graham of the *Washington Post* and *Newsweek,* Otis Chandler of the *Los Angeles Times,* Bailey Howard of the *Chicago Sun-Times* and *Chicago Daily News,* the heads of the three networks, and Hedley Donovan, editor in chief of Time Inc., collaborated on a telegram to Chicago Mayor Richard Daley. Journalists, the profession's heavyweights declared, "were repeatedly singled out by policemen and deliberately beaten. . . . [T]he obvious purpose was to discourage or prevent reporting of an important confrontation between police and demonstrators which the American public as a whole has a right to know about."

Much to their amazement, however, journalists soon discovered that they were in the minority in their outrage over the way in which the demonstrators had been treated in Chicago. Many people, especially those who wrote or telegraphed or telephoned news outlets, it seems, supported the actions that Mayor Daley had taken to suppress the demonstrations. At CBS affiliates, the mail ran something like 11 to 1 in support of the mayor and his approach to the demonstrators. At NBC, some 8,500 letters were received; only about 1,000 of them supported the protesters.

Analysts saw a substantial change in U.S. society after the Chicago demonstrations as middle America demanded that television reduce its emphasis on protest. As CBS correspondent Eric Sevareid explained,

> Over the years the pressure of public resentment against screaming militants, foul mouthed demonstrators, arsonists and looters had built up in the national boiler. With Chicago it exploded. The feelings that millions of people released were formed long before Chicago. Enough was enough: the police *must* be right. Therefore, the reporting *must* be wrong.

Lyndon Johnson appointed the obligatory presidential commission to investigate the violence in Chicago. Headed by Chicago lawyer Daniel Walker, the commission reported, "the Chicago police were the targets of mounting provocation by both word and act. It took the form of obscene epithets, and of rocks, sticks, bathroom tiles and even human feces hurled at police by demonstrators." Such was the provocation that "the nature of the response was unrestrained and indiscriminate police violence [occurred] on many occasions, particularly at night," the report said. "Newsmen and photographers were singled out for assault, and their equipment deliberately damaged. Fundamental police training was ignored; and officers, when on the scene, were often unable to control their men."

When Richard Nixon came into office, he vowed to end

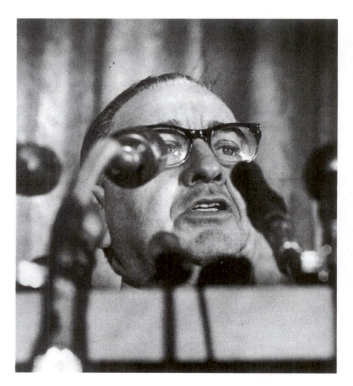

Chicago Mayor Richard J. Daley denounced antiwar protesters at the 1968 Democratic National Convention.
(Museum of Broadcast Communications)

the Vietnam War and protest against it, and to control media coverage of that protest. Through repeated appeals for quiet so that he could pursue his efforts to end the war and through repeated threats against the press, coverage of the antiwar movement decreased. Indeed, the antiwar movement was struggling. Under Nixon's expert guidance, the war was winding down, and through his pressure on the press, it was less an issue in newscasts and newspapers. A miscalculation changed all that.

With the war not ending quickly enough for the president, he ordered U.S. forces to bomb Cambodia, which had been off-limits. When the bombing incursion became known, antiwar protest erupted once more across the country.

On Monday, May 4, 1970, students at Kent State University in Ohio gathered on their campus to continue protesting. When the National Guard started to disperse the students, tear gas canisters were thrown into the crowd, and the students threw them back at the guardsmen. Rocks and other materials also were thrown at the guardsmen, although few found their mark. A number of troops, believing that their tear gas was exhausted and that they were about to be assaulted by the students, dropped to their knees, readied their rifles, and fired. According to an audiotape made at the scene, the shooting lasted for 13 seconds. When it was over, four students lay dead; nine others were severely wounded. The deaths at Kent State set the nation's campuses on fire. In many locations, the school year was abruptly shortened in order to send students home to end the disruptions.

Indeed, the antiwar movement, for all intents and purposes, collapsed in the wake of Kent State. The nation's media did not pursue the issue owing to increasing problems with the Nixon administration on a variety of issues. Even so, public opinion polls indicated that more and more U.S. citizens wanted the war to end.

As the antiwar protests passed into history, the mass media became the primary villain in the story. Journalists still are blamed routinely for the protests escalating and for the United States withdrawal from Vietnam. For protesters, the Vietnam War has provided a textbook of ways to attract media attention, if not win media approval.

MARGARET A. BLANCHARD

See also Vietnam War

Further Reading

Blanchard, Margaret A., *Revolutionary Sparks: Freedom of Expression in Modern America,* New York: Oxford University Press, 1992
Gitlin, Todd, *The Sixties: Years of Hope, Days of Rage,* New York and Toronto, Ontario: Bantam, 1987
_____, *The Whole World Is Watching: Mass Media in the Making & Unmaking of the New Left,* Berkeley: University of California Press, 1980
Miller, Jim, *"Democracy Is in the Streets": From Port Huron to the Siege of Chicago,* New York: Simon & Schuster, 1987
Powers, Thomas, *The War at Home: Vietnam and the American People, 1964–1968,* New York: Grossman, 1973
Small, Melvin, *Covering Dissent: The Media and the Anti-Vietnam War Movement,* New Brunswick, New Jersey: Rutgers University Press, 1994
_____, *Johnson, Nixon, and the Doves,* New Brunswick, New Jersey: Rutgers University Press, 1988
Zaroulis, Nancy L., and Gerald Sullivan, *Who Spoke Up? American Protest Against the War in Vietnam, 1963–1975,* Garden City, New York: Doubleday, 1984

Mass Media and the Civil Rights Movement

Media coverage important to growth, development, success of movement

The civil rights movement in the United States faced three distinct phases, each of which is important in understanding its coverage by the media. The first phase, between 1954 and 1960, followed the 1954 U.S. Supreme Court decision outlawing school segregation. The Montgomery, Alabama, bus boycott in 1955, Martin Luther King's subsequent rise to prominence, and battles over school desegregation were the highlights of these years. The second phase, initiated by the 1960 lunch counter sit-ins, saw mass public demonstrations pushing for integration in public facilities. These demonstrations, highlighted by the 1963 March on Washington, D.C., led to the Civil Rights Act of 1964, which outlawed segregation in public facilities such as restaurants and hotels.

During the third phase, after 1965, civil rights leaders sought economic and political equality for African Americans as the movement went from the south into other parts of the country. Around 1966, the word "black" replaced "Negro," and the movement became known as the Black Power Movement, led by such black leaders such as Malcolm X and Stokely Carmichael.

The media, and especially television, were most effective in covering the civil rights movement during the second phase. During the first phase, the mass media covered the major events, such as the Montgomery bus boycott; Little Rock, Arkansas, school integration; and other public conflicts surrounding public school integration. There is little evidence that they examined the problems and issues that led to these conflicts. During the second phase, journalists were seen as allies and supporters of the civil rights movement by most observers. During the third phase, coverage became problematic, and most black Americans began to view the white-dominated media with distrust, if not antagonism.

The relatively young medium of television in the 1950s and 1960s needed action and tight stories for its 15-minute newscasts, and the civil rights movement needed a national forum. They helped each other. Broadcast journalist Bill Monroe called television the "chosen instrument" of the civil rights movement.

John Lewis, a leader in the 1960 Nashville, Tennessee, sit-in movement and later a member of Congress from Georgia, stressed the importance of media coverage in a

1989 interview: "We felt that the media was necessary to help educate people, to convince people that our cause was right and just. The media became an ally." Lewis said that television was especially important in conveying a movement that focused on nonviolence. When clashes occurred between peaceful demonstrators and police or white observers, television could show that it was usually the police or observers who caused the violence.

The media's role in the civil rights movement has long been examined by journalists themselves. As William Drummond wrote in a 1990 article,

> By bringing the demonstrations to the front pages and onto the television screens, reporters and editors kept the pressure for reform on white leaders. By publicizing the civil rights movement, the media gave its leaders and its rank and file legitimacy within the black community as well as among whites.

Civil rights groups and leaders used the media attention to fullest advantage. For example, one frequently repeated story tells of a group of demonstrators in Alabama praying in the streets. They saw a television newsman beside a camera pointing a microphone at them trying to pick up the sound as well as the picture. Immediately they started praying a little louder.

"Television newsmen, local and national, are accustomed by now to the phone calls from civil rights groups with the details on when and where demonstrations are to be held. The civil rights groups quickly became sensitive to the possibilities of television," Bill Monroe wrote. Other journalists also noticed the way in which the media and the civil rights movement interacted. *Chicago Daily News* executive editor Lawrence Fanning wrote,

> By the early 1960s . . . it was no longer certain whether these demonstrations were protests against injustice or extravaganzas for the mass media. A second consequence was the silent, implicit pressure by the media on the various civil-rights organizations to put on bigger and better shows. Whereas 100 arrests once managed to attract our collective attention, we began to look for 500.

The media cannot, of course, be characterized as uniformly sympathetic to the civil rights movement. Southern newspapers often ignored or criticized civil rights activities and demonstrations. Those editors who supported it paid a price in canceled subscriptions, advertiser boycotts, or threats of violence. Hodding Carter II of the *Greenville (Mississippi) Delta Democrat-Times* and Ralph McGill of the *Atlanta (Georgia) Constitution* were among the best known who outspokenly supported integration.

Southern and northern journalists who covered civil rights activities in the south were often victims of violence. Richard Valeriani of NBC News, for example, was beaten with a wooden club by white segregationists while they sprayed the NBC camera lens with black paint. The modern reporter's notebook was created during the civil rights movement to replace the wider stenographer's notebook. It could be hidden conveniently in a coat pocket to help disguise the reporter's identity.

While the media aggressively covered activities and demonstrations, civil rights leaders faulted the press and television for ignoring the problems facing African Americans that led to the demonstrations. After mounting racial tensions touched off rioting in several major U.S. cities in 1967, President Lyndon Johnson created the National Advisory Commission on Civil Disorders – better known as the Kerner Commission – to look into the root causes of the disturbances.

Its often-quoted *Report of the National Advisory Commission on Civil Disorders* said that, although the press had done a good job of covering the events of the civil rights movement, it had: 1.) failed to cover blacks as a normal part of U.S. society and had instead presented the kinds of coverage that promoted stereotypes and reinforced prejudice; 2.) failed to portray the serious problems facing blacks in the United States; 3.) failed to explain the causes and underlying conditions of black protest and instead focused on the conflict aspects of the civil rights movement; 4.) tended to ignore local racial problems while emphasizing racial unrest in other locations; and 5.) reflected in its coverage indifference and antipathy towards blacks. "They have not communicated to whites a feeling for the difficulties and frustrations of being a Negro in the United States. . . . Our evidence shows that the so-called 'white press' is at best mistrusted and at worst held in contempt by many black Americans," the commission concluded.

In reviewing newspaper coverage of the civil rights movement, Carolyn Martindale echoed the Kerner Commission in her conclusion. Even after the civil rights movement had been a major story for years, she wrote, some African American leaders felt that the press still had failed to explain "the disenfranchisement of black citizens in the South, Jim Crow laws, economic and educational inequality, discrimination in hiring and housing, oppression by law enforcement officers, inadequate city services and schools in black inner city neighborhoods."

The failure to cover the underlying problems is what led to distrust and antagonism toward the media during the third phase, when the civil rights movement moved out of the south. It was easy for the media to cover the "good guys" taking the high moral road against the segregationist, southern "bad guys" in their fight to integrate. When faced with larger problems such as access to housing, jobs, and the economic mainstream, "good guys" and "bad guys" were not so clearly visible. After 1965, the issues became more complex and difficult to cover, as race riots occurred in Newark, New Jersey; Detroit, Michigan; and Los Angeles.

"When Martin Luther King took on the fight against poverty and moved his theater of operations to Chicago, the storyline became more complicated and press coverage became more problematic," William J. Drummond explained. "When the urban riots of the late 1960s struck, the honeymoon between the press and the black community was over." He cited a study of more than 500 black mayors and legislators in which the authors concluded, "From their vantage point, black mayors see a local press that does a

Rev. Dr. Martin Luther King Jr.'s actions always drew substantial media attention.
(Museum of Broadcast Communications)

poor job covering the black community; does not recognize important black-oriented stories; does not understand black issues; and is led by publishers who don't care about black issues."

Scholarly inquiry into media coverage of the civil rights movement has been sporadic and inconclusive, with little done between 1980 and the late 1990s. The scholarly literature falls into two distinct categories: comparison of how a few, easily accessible national newspapers covered specific aspects or episodes in the civil rights movement; and other reports containing "broad stroke" treatments (such as symposia or panel discussions of media and civil rights) that

The world watched when Birmingham, Alabama, firemen turned fire hoses on young demonstrators on the orders of Commissioner of Public Safety "Bull" Connor.
(Museum of Broadcast Communications)

lack analysis with any degree of precision or detail. In a 1986 review of the literature, Martindale summarized the findings of the previous 30 years by saying, "Only a few empirical studies of newspaper coverage of blacks in the years between 1950 and 1970 have been done, and each of them illustrates some inadequacy of coverage."

In 1987, "Covering the South: A National Symposium on the Media and the Civil Rights Movement" was the focus of a reunion held at the University of Mississippi of journalists who had covered the civil rights movement. The only record of its proceedings, however, is a half-hour video, *Dateline Freedom: Civil Rights and the Press,* produced by WETA-TV in Washington, D.C., in conjunction with the Center for the Study of Southern Culture at the university.

DAVID E. SUMNER

See also Kerner Commission Report; Mass Media and Race

Further Reading

Drummond, William J., "About Face: From Alliance to Alienation," *American Enterprise* 1:4 (July 1990), pp. 22–29

Fisher, Paul L., and Ralph L. Lowenstein, eds., *Race and the News Media,* New York: Praeger, 1967

Hill, George H., and Sylvia Hill, *Blacks on Television: A Selectively Annotated Bibliography,* Metuchen, New Jersey: Scarecrow, 1985

Kerner Commission, *Report of the National Advisory Commission on Civil Disorders,* New York: Dutton, 1968; London: Bantam, 1968

Lyle, Jack, ed., *The Black American and the Press,* Los Angeles: Ward Ritchie, 1968

Martindale, Carolyn, *The White Press and Black America,* New York: Greenwood, 1986

Rubin, Bernard, ed., *Small Voices and Great Trumpets: Minorities and the Media,* New York: Praeger, 1980

Mass Media and the Military

Technology one factor determining coverage of the military

Several factors have shaped the nature of news reporting of military operations. Chief among them have been communication technology, perceived levels of public support of operations, and commercialism.

When the American Revolution began with battles in

Lexington and Concord, Massachusetts, on April 19, 1775, the *Boston News-Letter* had news of it that day. Word of these events did not reach newspapers in Philadelphia and New York until April 24, while the *Savannah (Georgia) Gazette* published accounts of the conflict on May 31, more than a month later. Geographic distance was perhaps the principal factor in determining the content of news.

To overcome this impediment, express postal services were developed as early as 1825. The first commercial railroad also opened in 1825. Physical distance, however, still impeded news. Although years apart in their development, electronic communication technologies – telegraph, telephone, radio, television, and computer – shared one feature in common: each freed communication from the confines of time and space. News no longer traveled, fast or otherwise. Instead, it was transmitted. This produced the most radical change to news coverage of war.

The War of 1812 was the last U.S. conflict to be fought entirely in the era of transportation-dependent news, although the Mexican War (1846–48) was nearly so. The remoteness of the southwest put it beyond the reach of telegraph lines.

The American Civil War (1861–65) was one of the bloodiest conflicts of the nineteenth century. The entire society was mobilized, including journalists. The *New York Herald*, for example, spent more than $500,000 in correspondence costs alone. It was also the first war fought in the age of transmitted news. Within four years of Samuel Morse's patenting of the telegraph in September 1837, there were 12,000 miles of wire; that doubled to 23,283 by 1852.

The federal government also undertook an ambitious telegraph construction program. By July 1862, there were 3,571 miles of telegraph line for military use, with another 1,755 added the next year. By the end of 1865, the U.S. Military Telegraph had constructed about 15,000 miles of line; in 1863 alone, approximately 1,200,000 messages were sent.

While the Union armies were eager to take advantage of the new communication technology, they were less willing to allow it to be used for news gathering. On February 2, 1862, President Lincoln was given authority by Congress to seize control of all telegraph lines in regions under military supervision. From that point on, all war-related news carried over the lines was subject to censorship, although no clear standard was established, leaving journalists unsure of what was acceptable to write. At the same time, many Union units and most Confederate units refused to allow journalists in their encampments or to travel with the troops, although this, too, was unevenly applied.

The combined effects of censorship and the control of access to the front led to a reliance on communiqués issued by the War Department, which often distorted information to support its war aims. Secretary of War Edwin M. Stanton also had certain reporters banned from the front, editors arrested, and newspapers suspended.

Journalism took center stage in the Spanish-American War. William Randolph Hearst's *Journal* and Joseph Pulitzer's *World* are often credited with igniting the war. According to the *World* and the *Herald,* the Spanish had committed numerous atrocities while brutally suppressing the Cuban insurrection. When the U.S. battleship *Maine* sank in Havana harbor on February 15, 1898, Hearst's newspaper attributed it without proof to an enemy's secret infernal machine. War fervor swept the country, and Hearst had his war. A halfhearted attempt was made at establishing a military censor, but any censorship was indifferent and in part unnecessary because of the highly positive tone of the news and the war's short duration.

The December 1898 peace treaty gave the United States control of several Spanish colonial holdings, including the Philippines. Not pleased with the replacement of one imperial power for another, Filipino nationalists led a revolt against U.S. control of the islands. By 1902, at least 200,000 Filipinos had died.

U.S. military attempts to crush the insurrection were controversial. Several U.S. newspapers regularly reported U.S. atrocities. In response, General Elwell S. Otis, the U.S. commander in the Philippines, instituted strict press censorship. The only alternative to the telegraph was the mail, which took weeks to reach the United States. After the last of the nationalists' leaders surrendered in the summer of 1902, President Theodore Roosevelt declared the campaign complete.

The scale of the conflict made reporting World War I a huge challenge for even the wealthiest of newspapers. Adding to the difficulties, strict censorship was enforced by all sides, including the United States once it entered the war. To be accredited, a reporter was required to give a loyalty oath, pay a $1,000 fee for expenses, and post a $10,000 bond to be forfeited in the case of bad behavior. Correspondents also were required to submit all dispatches to military authorities for review.

The United States entered the war on April 6, 1917. On April 16, President Woodrow Wilson declared that any aid or comfort to the enemy provided by a publication would be treated as an act of treason. The Espionage Act, passed on June 15, 1917, imposed fines of up to $10,000 and imprisonment up to 20 years for those who were found guilty of promoting disloyalty or insubordination. The Trading with the Enemy Act, passed in October, authorized the censorship of overseas communication. It also established the Censorship Board, responsible for monitoring newspapers and magazines. On May 16, 1918, Congress passed the Sedition Act, amending the Espionage Act. It made it illegal to write or speak language deemed critical of U.S. government, its flag, or its armed forces. Between 1917 and 1921, the Justice Department initiated 2,168 prosecutions under the Espionage and Sedition Acts, with 1,055 resulting in convictions.

The government also established an official propaganda agency to provide news organizations with information it regarded as favorable to the cause. Headed up by George Creel, in two years the Committee on Public Information issued 6,000 news releases, generating about 20,000 columns of newsprint each week.

U.S. involvement in World War II began on December 8, 1941. World War II was the first U.S. war covered by newspapers, radio networks, mass circulation magazines, and newsreel companies. The total number of U.S. correspondents in the field far exceeded those of previous wars, with

Photographers such as these trying to cover an insurrection in the Philippines in the late nineteenth century caused problems for military forces.
(National Archives)

2,600 accredited correspondents active at some point of the war.

Censorship in the United States was carried out by the Office of Censorship, established by the First War Powers Act on December 19, 1941. On January 15, 1942, it published the *Code of Wartime Practices for American Press.* Although compliance with the Code was voluntary, it worked quite well, with few breaches of security. The attitude of military planners toward the press had changed following World War I. Media were understood as crucial to the war effort, rather than as a nuisance as before. If managed well, they could boost morale at home and encourage support for the war. As a result, the reporter's job was made easier. Military authorities often made every effort to provide information. Yet, as one historian noted, there was a quid pro quo: reporters were expected to write positive, supportive stories that would reflect well on the performance of the military and the policies of the government. Reporters in the field were typically willing to comply with the restriction and offer the positive coverage desired by commanders.

This general rule was evident during the Korean War. North Korea invaded the south on June 25, 1950. On June 27, the United Nations issued a resolution calling on the international community to come to the assistance of South Korea. The first U.S. combat troops began fighting on July 5. General Douglas MacArthur initially resisted the use of censorship, relying instead on the sort of voluntary restraint seen during World War II. By December, however, military commanders became convinced that the reporting from the field was hurting the war effort and that voluntary restraints were not working.

Eventually, even the Overseas Press Club asked the Department of Defense to institute censorship guidelines. On December 18, 1950, Secretary of Defense George C. Marshall and media representatives decided that the military would take responsibility for reviewing media reports from the battlefield. On December 23, the Eighth Army headquarters in Korea required journalists to submit all dispatches, photographs, and radio broadcasts for clearance. Shortly thereafter, General MacArthur's headquarters in Tokyo issued a code of conduct for journalists. Both the Eighth Army and MacArthur's headquarters were positioned to review and censor the news. Tensions between journalists and military commanders remained high throughout the war.

In the early 1960s, as the United States built up its commitments in South Vietnam, the only U.S. newspaper to have a full-time correspondent in country was the *New York Times,* along with the major wire services. There was general disinterest in Vietnam. This was what the Kennedy administration wanted. In a February 1962 cable to the U.S. Embassy in Saigon, South Vietnam, the administration made this position clear when it stated it did not want stories written reporting that U.S. troops were leading and directing combat missions against the Vietcong. Journalists were denied access to operations that would reveal the extent of U.S. involvement, and more and more information was classified. This began a long slide into mutual animosity between the military and the media.

Denied access by the senior commanders and diplomatic representatives in Saigon, reporters such as Neil Sheehan and Malcome Browne of the Associated Press and David Halberstam of the *New York Times* began using information obtained from junior field commanders. As the tone of their reporting grew increasingly negative and pessimistic, senior commanders redoubled their efforts to conceal bad news. This, in turn, deepened the mistrust of reporters.

As the U.S. involvement grew, so, too, did the interest of the news media. In mid-1964, there were about 40 U.S. journalists in Vietnam. By mid-1965, there were 400. By 1968, there were more than 600 accredited U.S. and other foreign correspondents in Vietnam, with many more there without accreditation.

In February 1965, General Westmoreland, commander of U.S. forces in Vietnam, proposed the creation of formal censorship. It was concluded, however, that without a formal declaration of war, commanders lacked the legal basis for censorship. Advances in communication technology also had made censorship problematic, and voluntary guidelines were left in place.

Vietnam was the first U.S. war to be covered by television, with effects as profound as any seen since the advent of the telegraph. Television news anchors such as Walter Cronkite were trusted conveyers of the news to many and, soon, for most people in the United States, supplanted newspapers and magazines as primary sources of news. Camera technology also improved over the decade, so that, by 1970, camera crews carried no more than 20 pounds of equipment and used satellite transmission facilities to transmit film shot in Vietnam the same day.

Television coverage, more than print, tended to cover what war correspondents refer to as "bang-bang" – the dramatic visual images of combat, rather than the typically more important, though often less visually compelling, political dimensions of the conflict. Television coverage, therefore, was criticized for its banal qualities and for encouraging strong emotions with little understanding. While correspondents saw military and political leaders as duplicitous, these leaders often saw correspondents as histrionic and with questionable loyalties. This combination of impressions and mutual animosities profoundly affected military-media relations.

After Vietnam, the nature of combat missions and the advances in communication technology created continuing tension between the military and the media. With a few notable exceptions, most of the U.S. military undertakings since Vietnam were limited engagements relying on speed and secrecy. The 1975 rescue operation of the U.S. cargo ship *Mayaguez,* the 1980 Desert One hostage rescue attempt in Iran, and the 1986 bombing raid on Libya were all over in a matter of hours.

The small Caribbean island of Grenada was invaded by the United States on October 25, 1983. U.S. military authorities did not allow journalists on the island during the first 48 hours of fighting. Eventually, only a small number of journalists were allowed in under military escort, although nearly 400 were waiting on the nearby island of Barbados. Restrictions on access were not lifted until October 30, long after most fighting had ended. Lightweight video cameras and satellite communication facilities had made censorship difficult or impossible. Denying journalists access, when and where possible, was the next best alternative.

News organizations criticized the Pentagon for this policy of exclusion. On the other hand, the Pentagon argued that modern communication technology threatened operational security, putting lives of U.S. citizens at risk. To resolve these differences, the chairman of the Joint Chiefs of Staff formed a special commission in November 1983. Major General Winant Sidle headed the commission, which issued its recommendations on August 23, 1984. It suggested that a national media pool should be created and activated during military operations. The pools were to consist of a representative from a news agency, an agency photographer, a television correspondent and two technicians, a radio correspondent, a national magazine correspondent, and three newspaper correspondents. When on December 20, 1989, the United States invaded Panama, the press pool system failed miserably. Hours after the start of the invasion, the 16 journalists flown to Panama spent much of their time in an airport facility under armed U.S. guards.

On August 2, 1992, Iraq invaded the small country of Kuwait. A coalition of countries led by the United States soon deployed a massive military force in Saudi Arabia to block further Iraqi advances. The Pentagon waffled for several days on whether to activate the pool system. The Saudi government was also uncooperative during the initial stages of the conflict, unwilling to allow more than a small handful of reporters in the country. On December 14, 1992, Pete Williams, the assistant secretary of defense for public affairs, issued an internal memorandum that stipulated that combat pool material would be subject to security review at the source, which was to say that all pool reports would be edited by a censor at the source of the news prior to release to news organizations. This was the first official wartime censorship since the Korean War. Once the war was under way, the press pool system, in the view of critics, limited access to the war rather than facilitated it.

STEVEN LIVINGSTON

See also American Revolution and the Press; Civil War Press (North); Civil War Press (South); Committee on Public Information; Grenada Invasion; Korean War; Mexican War; Office of Censorship; Panama Invasion;

Persian Gulf War; Spanish-American War; Vietnam War; War of 1812; World War I; World War II

Further Reading

Bennett, W. Lance, and David L. Paletz, eds., *Taken By Storm: The Media, Public Opinion, and U.S. Foreign Policy in the Gulf War,* Chicago: University of Chicago Press, 1994

Furneaux, Rupert, *News of War: Stories and Adventures of the Great War Correspondents,* London: Max Parrish, 1964

Fussell, Paul, *Wartime: Understanding and Behavior in the Second World War,* New York: Oxford University Press, 1989

Knightley, Phillip, *The First Casualty: From the Crimea to Vietnam: The War Correspondent as Hero, Propagandist, and Myth Maker,* New York: Harcourt Brace Jovanovich, 1975; London: Quartet, 1978

MacArthur, John R., *Second Front: Censorship and Propaganda in the Gulf War,* New York: Hill and Wang, 1992

Mathews, Joseph J., *Reporting the Wars,* Minneapolis: University of Minnesota Press, 1957

Thompson, Loren B., ed., *Defense Beat: The Dilemmas of Defense Coverage,* New York: Lexington, 1991

Wilkerson, Marcus, *Public Opinion and the Spanish-American War,* Baton Rouge: Louisiana State University Press, 1932

Mass Media and the Sexual Revolution

Images and messages of changing roles disseminated by media

Although there had been hints of a loosening of sexual attitudes long before the 1960s, the beginning of the sexual revolution is generally traced to 1961 and the advent of the birth control pill. The impact of the sexual revolution was far reaching. It was related intimately to the women's liberation movement and the gay liberation movement, and it forced society to reconsider the role of sexual identity. It was primarily through the media that the images and messages of the sexual revolution came to the public. The media provided a forum for society to question the nature of relationships between women and men, attitudes toward marriage and divorce, and the belief that sex before marriage was not only morally wrong but was also dangerous for women because of the chance of unwanted pregnancy.

Soon after the U.S. Food and Drug Administration (FDA) approved the public sale of the birth control pill, the media began to report on the changes resulting in society, such as the rise in divorce rates and the growing phenomenon of couples living together before marrying. Newsmagazines and network news programs interviewed teenagers to show how dating was becoming less defined by strict social rules

and how men and women were becoming friends and associating with each other in more casual settings.

In particular, the media in the 1960s focused on how the sexual revolution was affecting college campuses, as this was a place where single young men and women were likely to be in close contact with each other. Calling the birth control pill a declaration of independence for college women, newsmagazines looked at the changing social practices on college campuses. A 1964 *Newsweek* article explored how college women were finding sexual freedom and freedom from pregnancy with the birth control pill. Cultural norms, according to media, were becoming less restrictive on college campuses and had resulted in coed dorms and more liberal visitation policies in all dorms.

As this new freedom was being discussed, the media editorialized somewhat with discussion of what all this sexual freedom meant for the notion of "nice girls," who, before the pill, were more cautious or did not have sex before marriage. The media asked whether the availability of the pill was putting pressure on women to have sex before marriage. College students, however, would have none of this moralizing. In interviews with the media, they ridiculed the double standard and argued that the pill had only freed women from concerns about pregnancy. They applauded the loosening of traditional dating patterns and courtship rules, claiming that men and women could now be on more equal footing as friends and as sexual partners.

In 1962, Helen Gurley Brown's *Sex and the Single Girl* argued that single women were freer than ever before, that this liberation came through sex, and that the double standard was dead. Being single and having a job were things to strive for, not things to wait out until a woman found a man and married. This book became, according to some writers, a bible to young women of the 1960s. Films also were reflecting the changing attitudes about women and their sexual desires and concerns. According to Susan Douglas in her book *Where the Girls Are* (1994), these films (which she called "pregnancy melodramas") featured young females with sexual desires that they acted upon without too much harm coming to them, and made subtle attacks on the double standard about men and women and sexual relationships.

News reports during the advent of the pill suggested that the arrival of the pill was coinciding not only with a sexual revolution but also with general social unrest among groups in U.S. society. In the 1960s and early 1970s, the news also featured a counterculture of sexual freedom. The hippies of the 1960s took the new sexual freedom to extremes, and the media showed those extremes by covering life in communes and at rock music festivals, where free love, nudity, and the use of drugs were part of the experience.

In the early to mid-1960s, the sexual revolution was one of the biggest stories in the media. Sometimes the amount of coverage given to the revolution seemed to exaggerate how fast and far the changes had gone. Although the media were saying that sexual permissiveness was widespread in the early 1960s, researchers generally reported that the sexual permissiveness was not as widespread by the early or mid-1960s as the media contended.

In many cases, some members of the media blamed other members for promoting and glamorizing the sexual revolution. Film, in particular, was seen as being the most liberal in its portrayal of the new ideas and attitudes toward sex. Sometimes, news and general interest magazines accused movies of pandering to youth culture and of spreading the sexual revolution. Music and musical groups also came under scrutiny because of their close association with youth culture and their expressions of sexuality.

Popular culture was one of the places in which the more radical or liberal notions of the sexual revolution were portrayed. Plays such as *Hair* and *Oh! Calcutta* explored sexual freedom, communal living, and drug use while using provocative techniques of theater, such as entire casts in the nude. These plays broke rules and cultural mores about sex, love, nudity, and drugs. Movies such as *Bob and Carol and Ted and Alice* (1969), *Midnight Cowboy* (1969), *Carnal Knowledge* (1971), *The Graduate* (1967), and others explored male prostitution, seduction, drugs, sex, and partner swapping. In 1969, *Midnight Cowboy* became the first X-rated movie to win the Academy Awards for best picture and best director.

In addition to popular culture reflecting the new sexual attitudes, researchers and doctors also began to question past assumptions about human sexuality. In 1966, Masters and Johnson wrote *Human Sexual Response,* which destroyed many of the myths about human sexuality. In particular, their honest treatment of sensitive sexual issues and their open discussions about sexuality helped to change society's perspective on female sexuality. In the past, women had read about their sexuality, psychology, and attitudes through the work of male writers. During the sexual revolution, women began to see themselves and their sexuality very differently.

As a result of the sexual revolution, books such as Masters and Johnson's began to reveal more about female sexuality and provide more information to women about their own bodies. In 1969, a group of mainly female doctors met in Boston to explore women's issues. The discussion group, frustrated by the medical community's treatment of women and by the lack of attention to women's health, wrote a book that was a milestone in the sexual revolution. *Our Bodies, Ourselves* (1971) challenged traditional notions of women's health and sexuality and gave detailed information on contraceptives, sexual relations, pregnancy, and abortion procedures in an attempt to dispel some of the mystery, fear, and misinformation that women had about their bodies.

The sexual revolution also allowed questioning of the roles that sexual identity played in U.S. culture and media. Betty Friedan's *The Feminine Mystique* (1963) argued that magazines had glamorized the role of housewife following World War II in an attempt to get women to return home after their help in industry was no longer needed. Popular magazines told U.S. women that their true fulfillment came through their recognition of their own femininity. Friedan claimed that magazines portrayed housewives and mothers as the models for all women.

As college students had questioned the double standard in sexuality, women pushed the debate on old notions of the inferiority of women and their lack of economic and political abilities. Women began to ask openly, if women were

equal to men sexually, why were they not equal in all aspects of society? In their writings, women in the 1960s and early 1970s explored and sometimes exploded the cultural myths about women and women's bodies. Books such as *Sexual Politics* (1970), *The Female Eunuch* (1971), and *Against Our Will* (1975) explored sexuality, relationships among men and women, and myths of female inferiority in a number of ways. They began to look at society as one in which gender was equal to political power and in which problems such as rape could be seen as a problem with society because of the power men had over women. Writers in the late 1960s and early 1970s began to explore what Kate Millet had first voiced in *Sexual Politics* – that "sex is a status category with political implications."

During the late 1960s, as the sexual revolution merged with the movement for women's rights, news coverage of women's liberation was in many ways contradictory. Most news media covered the economic and equality issues with serious news stories, but the more active and aggressive components of the women's liberation movement were covered with condescension, disbelief, and, in extreme cases, ridicule. In 1968, in one of the first actions of the women's liberation movement, a group of women protested the Miss America pageant in Atlantic City, New Jersey, and claimed that the pageant was no more than a cattle auction at which women were judged and rated. During the protest, the women threw bras, hair rollers, and high heels into a trash can. This was the event that led the media to later describe women's rights marchers as "bra burners."

Most of the pieces presented on television news during the late 1960s and early 1970s were unsympathetic to claims of the sexual objectification women while being sympathetic to the economic issues being discussed by women. In an attempt to find only two sides to every issue, media coverage of the women's liberation movement began to feature the movement as a war between feminists and the average working woman. These media contrasts seemed to suggest that not all women wanted to be liberated.

One outgrowth of the attention in the media to the debate about equal opportunities for women was that more women began to enter the creative and managerial side of media, becoming reporters, broadcasters, editors, producers, and directors. Although women on prime-time television continued to be featured in stereotypical roles in the 1960s and 1970s, there was evidence that room was being made on television for strong women and for women who rejected traditional roles. *The Mary Tyler Moore Show* was heralded as a positive depiction of women because of the main character's single status, her love of her job, and her relationships with her female friends.

As the women's liberation movement and the sexual revolution merged, advertising began to use sex in more obvious ways to sell products. The liberated woman emerged in advertising as someone who could have economic success, take care of a household, and be sexy all at the same time. Part of this superwoman's success, at least according to advertising, was that she remained youthful and attractive to men no matter how "liberated" she was.

In the 1970s, films about women's struggle for independence and their rejection of domestic life and marriage could be seen in theaters. In some films, relationships between women were featured (in so-called female buddy films), and more women began to emerge as directors and producers of films that did well with audiences.

In the 1980s, working, single, or strong women on such programs as *Murphy Brown* and *Roseanne* were coming to television mainly because of the growth of women behind the scenes, including those in the role of director, and the growth of the female prime-time audience. As strong women were making their way onto prime-time television, Hollywood continued to have conflicted feelings about the strong, sexually active woman. *Thelma and Louise* (1991) was hailed as a great female buddy film in which men who sexually abused, harassed, or raped women would be "taken care of" by the women themselves. The movie also was attacked by critics who said it only copied and glorified the violence of male buddy films. In addition, the 1994 movie *Disclosure,* about a strong woman sexually harassing a male colleague, caused one film critic to note that it was "a '90s version of one of Hollywood's oldest and most resonant stereotypes: the idea that there is nothing more dangerous than a successful, sexually active, single woman."

At the same time that strong women were appearing in film and television, Susan Faludi, in *Backlash,* argued that the media began an undeclared war against images of the sexually liberated single woman. Newsmagazines were reporting that feminism was dead and that, in fact, many women had been hurt by the move toward sexual equality. Faludi argued that the news media began to report trends among women and in society that showed that feminism had hurt women. Terms such as "toxic day care," "mommy tracking," "cocooning," "traditionalists," "man shortage," and "biological clock" were used by the news media to indicate the high price women had paid for the new sexual and economic freedom they enjoyed. These backlash images attacking single and sexually active women and praising domestic, traditional women also appeared in film and television during the 1980s.

In the 1980s, the sexual revolution began to change because of several news reports about the negative consequences of increased sexual activity. In the late 1970s and 1980s, singles bars and one-night stands were among the topics discussed by the media in news coverage and popular culture.

In the 1980s, however, the media also began to report on a strange mix of symptoms affecting the gay community on the west coast and in New York. In 1982, a new disease called GRID (gay-related immune disease), according to the media, was affecting the gay community. Later stories reported that the disease, by then more accurately called AIDS (acquired immunodeficiency syndrome), affected all types of people because of how it was transmitted (by means of certain sexual practices, blood transfusions, and use of dirty needles), and not because of people's sexual orientation. In the late 1980s, blood donations decreased because of the fear that AIDS could be contracted while giving blood. The American Red Cross began a series of public service announcements on television with celebrities to set the record straight about how AIDS was transmitted.

In many ways, the media helped disseminate the most timely information about AIDS. Honest and open discussions about AIDS and its relationship to sexual activity became increasingly important. As the sexual revolution had led to discussions of changing lifestyles and attitudes among men and women during the 1960s, the media reported in the 1980s and 1990s that the fear of AIDS was leading to a rejection of one-night stands and multiple sex partners in favor of a belief that monogamy and "safer sex" were imperative among sexually active people. Network executives had been hesitant to use the word condom in any public service announcements about AIDS and safer sex. In the late 1980s, however, the Centers for Disease Control began to advocate the use of condoms in public service announcements as one of the ways to prevent the spread of the AIDS virus.

Some reports during the 1980s and 1990s proclaimed the death of the sexual revolution because of the fear of the AIDS virus. Other reports were more optimistic, saying that the sexual revolution simply was evolving because of the adjustments that young people would once again make in their lifestyles and sexual behavior. People, reports said, again were reevaluating earlier beliefs about sexuality.

ANNE JOHNSTON

Further Reading

Brownmiller, Susan, *Against Our Will: Men, Women, and Rape,* New York: Simon & Schuster, 1975; London: Secker & Warburg, 1975
Douglas, Susan, *Where the Girls Are: Growing up Female with the Mass Media,* New York: Times, 1994; London: Penguin, 1995
Faludi, Susan, *Backlash: The Undeclared War Against American Women,* New York: Crown, 1991; also published as *Backlash: The Undeclared War Against Women,* London: Vintage, 1992
Friedan, Betty, *The Feminine Mystique,* New York: Norton, 1963; London: Gollancz, 1963
Greer, Germaine, *The Female Eunuch,* London: MacGibbon and Kee, 1970; New York: McGraw-Hill, 1971
Millett, Kate, *Sexual Politics,* New York: Doubleday, 1970
"The Morals Revolution on the U.S. Campus," *Newsweek* (April 6, 1964)
Waters, Harry F., and Janet Huck, "Networking Women," *Newsweek* 113:11 (March 13, 1989), pp. 48–54

Mass Media and Tobacco Products

Public concern over tobacco use affects advertising, media presentations

Over the years, one of the most controversial forms of media advertising has been that which attempted to sell tobacco products. Running a close second to the advertising of tobacco products as a basis for public concern was the use of tobacco products by persons depicted in the media. The concern over the impact of media images of tobacco products focused primarily on health problems related to such usage, and by the late 1990s, it appeared that the antitobacco forces were winning.

Historians have different ideas as to when the public concern about use of tobacco products began, but there was a significant surge in apprehension about cigarette smoking in the 1920s. At least two factors affected that concern: an increase in the number of men smoking cigarettes, due at least in part to the U.S. military forces receiving a daily ration of tobacco or tobacco products during World War I, and the growing number of women smoking.

Public relations practitioner Edward R. Bernays took credit for the upswing in smoking among women in the United States because the American Tobacco Company hired him to promote its product among women. Bernays hired 10 debutantes to walk down Broadway in New York City smoking cigarettes in public as part of the Easter Parade. He claimed that the stunt led to an increase in women smoking. That was in 1929, but sociologist Michael Schudson argued that women already were smoking in substantial numbers by then, and advertising already was featuring sales pitches aimed directly at them. The reason for increased smoking, Schudson said, was women's desire to be "modern," rather than the influence of advertising.

Opposition to smoking appeared almost simultaneously, with the Women's Christian Temperance Union leading the way. The era featured essay and art contests designed to discourage smoking and promote laws that would forbid smoking in areas where food was displayed. There were also complaints about cigarette advertising and other forms of promotion. Schudson reported that U.S. Senator Reed Smoot, a Mormon from Utah, complained about the promotion of smoking in 1929, saying,

> Not since the day when public opinion rose in its might and smote the dangerous drug traffic, not since the days when the vendor of harmful nostrums was swept from our streets, has this country witnessed such an orgy of buncombe, quackery and downright falsehood and fraud as now marks the current campaign promoted by certain cigarette manufacturers to create a vast woman and child market for the use of their product.

Advertising historian Stephen Fox noted that the 1920s involved efforts by cigarette manufacturers to distinguish one product from another through advertising. Lucky Strike, the company that hired Bernays, was among the most aggressive in this area, trying to associate itself with high society, Hollywood stars, and current-day heroes.

To fight the apprehension – which was current even then – that cigarettes might be harmful to a smoker's health, Lucky Strike staged a counteroffensive. In 1927, for example, opera star Ernestine Schumann-Heink appeared in a Lucky Strike ad explaining how cigarettes soothed her throat. In 1932, a Lucky Strike ad claimed, "More than 200,000 physicians . . . stated that Luckies are less irritating to the throat than other cigarettes."

By the 1950s, the cigarette filter had been developed, and advertisements fought over which brand had the best filter. Liggett and Myers touted its L&M filter as being "just what the doctor ordered."

The debate over advertising tobacco products continued virtually unabated for years until antitobacco efforts began to bear fruit in the 1960s. In 1964, the U.S. Surgeon General issued his famous report in which, for the first time, cigarette smoking was declared to be dangerous to a person's health. In 1965, Congress enacted legislation requiring that all cigarette packages bear labels warning that smoking was harmful. Still, however, cigarette products continued to supply a substantial portion of broadcasters' income from advertising.

John Banzhaf III, an ardent antismoking enthusiast, felt that such a situation was unfair. Millions of dollars in advertising revenue were involved when Banzhaf asked for free time under the Fairness Doctrine to present information on the air about the health dangers of cigarette smoking to the U.S. people. Antismoking advocates, Banzhaf argued, had little money to present their message to the people, thus the radio and television stations of the nation had the responsibility to relay the other side of this controversial issue over the air.

Broadcasters, aware of the income generated by cigarette advertising, were reluctant to endanger that money. The medical evidence connecting smoking to health problems, they argued, was at best circumstantial. In addition, so long as cigarettes could be purchased legally, the First Amendment would not allow government to restrict their advertising. Banzhaf wrote to WCBS, the television network's flagship station, asking that it provide time for the antismoking campaign. Because smoking now was a controversial issue, Banzhaf said, the Fairness Doctrine required that the station make its facilities available for free to individuals who wished to offer other views. The station refused, arguing that it covered the issue adequately in other forums, a defense that usually was sufficient for the Federal Communications Commission (FCC).

Banzhaf persisted, sending his complaint on to the FCC, where commissioners agreed with much of what Banzhaf had asked. The commission said,

> The advertisements in question clearly promote the use of a particular cigarette as attractive and enjoyable. Indeed, they understandably have no other purpose. We believe that a station which presents such advertisements has the duty of informing its audience of the other side of this controversial issue of public importance – that, however enjoyable, such smoking may be a hazard to the smoker's health.

Although the FCC found that stations had to provide a significant amount of airtime for counterprogramming, commissioners refused to order that the antismoking crusade be given equal time, and commissioners allowed the broadcasters to determine the amount and nature of the programming that would provide the antismoking message.

The ruling was so controversial that broadcasters rushed to appeal it in court. Banzhaf beat them to the appeals court, however, arguing that the court system should require broadcasters to provide the same amount of free time for the antismoking message that cigarette manufacturers purchased for advertising. Broadcasters and tobacco industry attorneys responded that any regulations that would affect cigarette advertising abridged the guarantees of the First Amendment.

Ultimately, the court upheld the FCC's decision to require broadcasters to promote antismoking messages – in advertising or programming. In responding to the argument that the FCC ruling infringed on the First Amendment rights of broadcasters, the U.S. Circuit Court of Appeals was far from sympathetic. Chief Justice David L. Bazelon wrote,

> The First Amendment is unmistakably hostile to governmental controls over the content of the press, but that is not to say that it necessarily bars every regulation which in any way affects what the newspapers publish. Even if it does, there may still be a meaningful distinction between the two media justifying different treatment under the First Amendment. Unlike broadcasting, the written press includes a rich variety of outlets for expression and persuasion, including journals, pamphlets, leaflets, and circular letters, which are available to those without technical skills or deep pockets.

In addition, Bazelon wrote, commercial messages are omnipresent in broadcasting:

> There scarcely breathes a citizen who does not know some part of a leading cigarette jingle by heart. Similarly, an ordinary habitual television watcher can avoid these commercials only by frequently leaving the room, changing the channel, or doing some other such affirmative act. It is difficult to calculate the subliminal impact of this pervasive propaganda, which may be heard even if not listened to, but it may reasonably be thought greater than the printed word.

Although the court upheld the FCC order that broadcasters provide time for the antismoking message, the judges refused to decree that each tobacco commercial should be balanced with an announcement against the use of cigarettes. Licensees, they said, should determine how to present the antismoking message. The Supreme Court refused to review the decision, and the ruling stood.

Broadcasters' problems with cigarette advertising, however, were far from over. In April 1969, Congress enacted legislation that banned all cigarette advertising from radio and television as of January 1, 1971. The issue again was brought to court, with broadcasters seeking to stop the government from discriminating against the broadcast industry in this way. The court ruled against those seeking to maintain tobacco commercials on the airwaves; the commercials were withdrawn.

The issue of promoting tobacco products did not disappear, however. Critics complained that the names of some sporting events – the Virginia Slims tennis tournament, for instance, and many motor sports events – bore the names of tobacco products, thus subliminally keeping the brand name in the public eye. Advertising spots at stadiums and on race cars themselves also bore the logos of tobacco products. Some sports stars continued to smoke and chew tobacco products on the air. In addition, cigar smoking became popular as product placement strategies were successful in having film characters make a point of smoking a cigar as part of a role.

Antismoking advocates also argued that tobacco companies were targeting special audiences with certain products. Charges flew that cigarette companies placed more billboards promoting smoking in poor, African American neighborhoods and more cigarette ads in African American magazines. A controversy over the isolation and targeting of an African American audience as potential purchasers of Uptown cigarettes descended on the heads of R.J. Reynolds, the manufacturers, before the brand could even be launched. Dakota, another R.J. Reynolds brand for "virile females" with high school educations, likewise raised a firestorm of opposition.

Advertising directed at children and young people attracted another wave of anger from the antismoking forces, as research argued that 90 percent of the smokers in the country began smoking before age 20. The tobacco advertising symbol Joe Camel drew the largest protest because, it was charged, the ads were directed primarily to young people. Cigarette ads that depicted what appeared to be underage models engaged in a variety of "sophisticated" behaviors to attract young people also came under attack.

As news about the harmful effects of tobacco products on health increased, efforts to restrict cigarette advertising likewise increased. By June 1997, representatives of the tobacco industry were meeting with state attorneys general to find a way to settle government claims for injuries due to cigarette smoking. When finally accepted by all parties concerned, the settlement was likely to include restrictions on advertising that probably would show up in any future agreement. Among the targets were any vestiges of cigarette advertising still remaining – from the last remaining Joe Camel to a 30-foot cutout of the Marlboro Man that adorned a minor league baseball stadium.

Whether such limits on advertising and promotion would likewise limit smoking was another matter because even as ads disappeared from broadcast outlets in the United States, smoking held steady or increased, giving strength to Michael Schudson's hypothesis that the phenomenon of smoking was unrelated to advertising and other promotional efforts.

MARGARET A. BLANCHARD

See also Advertising Appeals; Advertising in the Twentieth Century; Mass Media and Health Issues

Further Reading

Fox, Stephen, *The Mirror Makers: A History of American Advertising and Its Creators,* New York: William Morrow, 1984
Friendly, Fred W., *The Good Guys, the Bad Guys, and the First Amendment: Free Speech vs. Fairness in Broadcasting,* New York: Random House, 1975

Schudson, Michael, *Advertising, the Uneasy Persuasion: Its Dubious Impact on American Society,* New York: Basic, 1984; London: Routledge, 1993

Mayflower Decision

Early ruling prohibited editorials over the air

As radio grew in popularity, some station operators likened the medium to newspapers, at least insofar as information-related activities were concerned. One of the things that newspapers did regularly was editorialize, and some broadcasters soon attempted to do so as well. The Federal Communications Commission (FCC), however, soon decided that editorializing over the airwaves was inappropriate.

WAAB in Boston editorialized regularly in the name of the station, providing its views on political candidates and on controversial public issues. When an applicant competing for the broadcast frequency challenged WAAB's practice, the FCC decided that such programming was not in the public interest. Its ruling said in part that "a truly free radio cannot be used to advocate the causes of the licensee. It cannot be used to support the candidacies of his friends. It cannot be devoted to the support of principles he happens to regard most favorably. In brief, the broadcaster cannot be an advocate." Because the rival applicant was the Mayflower Broadcasting Corporation, the ruling became known as the Mayflower Decision.

Not many radio stations were editorializing at the time because of concerns about upsetting sponsors and audiences. A few who were editorializing protested the ruling on the grounds that it invaded their freedom of speech. No licensee took the FCC to court to protest the matter, and no station lost its license because of editorializing.

Because the ruling did cause confusion and controversy, the FCC later revisited the issue. By 1949, the commission had "clarified" its decision and called for "a reasonably balanced presentation of all responsible viewpoints on particular issues." This opened the way for broadcasters to air editorials if they wished, although not many took advantage of the opportunity. The 1949 decision became known as the Fairness Doctrine.

MARGARET A. BLANCHARD

See also Broadcast Regulation; Fairness Doctrine

McKinley, William, and the Press

President William McKinley was an important contributor to the evolution of modern White House press relations. Although Theodore Roosevelt is often credited with opening up the presidency to greater news coverage, in fact the process of greater press attention began in 1897. When McKinley took office in March of that year, the presidency's

relations with the press stood at a low point. Under Grover Cleveland, reporters had been discouraged from gathering information about the White House.

In the McKinley administration, the attitude became more open and friendly. The president hosted a reception for the press corps soon after his inauguration. The White House also put a table on the second floor where journalists assigned to the presidency could sit. McKinley had his personal secretary talk to the journalists on a regular basis, and officials held informal briefings at noon and 4 P.M. These practices began a slow evolution toward the presidential press conference under Woodrow Wilson a generation later. When McKinley traveled, he insisted that reporters be allowed to accompany him even onto private estates, a gesture that the press corps much appreciated.

The ground rules for reporters were that the president could not be interviewed or quoted directly. Nonetheless, reporters had much more access to McKinley than often is realized. The president was skilled at the timely leak or trial balloon, and he managed the way in which news emerged from his administration. "While apparently not courting publicity," journalist Francis E. Leupp later recalled, McKinley "contrived to put out, by various shrewd processes of indirection, whatever news would best serve the ends of the administration."

A key element in McKinley's deft handling of the press was his personal secretary, George B. Cortelyou. Originally an aide to the president's first secretary, John Addison Porter, Cortelyou supplanted the talkative and erratic Porter within a few years because of his efficiency and discretion. Cortelyou oversaw the distribution of presidential messages and travel schedules. He arranged for reporters to cover the frequent trips that McKinley made around the country. He and his aides provided the journalists with stenographic reports of what the president had said and his itineraries as well as gave them access to the transmission facilities needed to send the news across the country. Cortelyou became the prototype of the modern White House press secretary, a role he continued to play under McKinley's successor, Theodore Roosevelt.

As a result of these efforts to facilitate the job of the press, the McKinley administration enjoyed a generally pleasant relationship with working reporters. Since the editorial policies of major newspapers still reflected their partisan affiliations, the treatment of the president varied whether a newspaper was Republican or Democratic. Still, few presidents have been more adroit than McKinley in getting favorable news about the White House to the public. Even when he was most under political attack, McKinley refrained from denouncing newspapers as a source of his difficulties.

The most controversial aspect of McKinley's presidency dealt with the coming of the war with Spain in 1898. For years, critics of the president charged that he had yielded to the clamor of the "yellow press" that had stirred up public opinion about the war in Cuba. Modern scholarship, however, came to give less weight to the impact of newspaper publishers Joseph Pulitzer and William Randolph Hearst in fomenting a conflict with the Spanish about the future of Cuba. The administration did not frame its demands on

In the anteroom at the White House, showing a press table and the door into Secretary Porter's office, with the doorkeeper, Simmons, in the background.

Journalists stayed close to the president's office during the Spanish-American War.
(Davis Library, University of North Carolina at Chapel Hill)

Madrid in response to press outcries, and the decision to go to war arose from Spanish intransigence rather than newspaper urgings.

When the United States became involved in a guerrilla war in the Philippines in 1899 after the defeat of Spain, a dispute arose about whether the army was censoring bad military news from reaching the U.S. public. McKinley generally supported the actions of the military in screening news reports but also urged that "all considerations within limits of the good of the service be shown." The reporting about the conduct of the war did, however, contribute to a popular disillusion with further imperialism by 1900.

More than most presidents who followed him, William McKinley achieved positive relations with the press. From his administration date the beginnings of the presidential news conference, regular press briefings for the White House reporters, and systematic management of the release of messages and statements. McKinley and Cortelyou were pioneers in modern presidential relations with the press whose important contribution to this aspect of journalistic history has yet to be fully charted.

LEWIS L. GOULD

See also News Leaks; Presidential Press Secretaries; Roosevelt, Theodore, and the Press; Spanish-American War; Trial Balloons

Further Reading

Barry, David S., "News-Getting at the Capital," *The Chautauquan* (December 1897)

Creelman, James S., "Mr. Cortelyou Explains President McKinley" *Pearson's Magazine* (June 1908)

Gould, Lewis L., *The Presidency of William McKinley,* Lawrence: University Press of Kansas, 1980

Hilderbrand, Robert C., *Power and the People: Executive Management of Public Opinion in Foreign Affairs, 1897–1921,* Chapel Hill: University of North Carolina Press, 1981

Media Conglomerates

Collection of firms under central ownership

A media conglomerate is a collection of firms or operations under a central ownership. Each conglomerate owns one or more media subsidiaries from a range of functions, which may include newspapers, local television or radio stations, magazines, television networks, cable networks and systems, book publishing, and computer-related services. Some media conglomerates include non-media firms; for example, General Electric Company, which manufactures electric appliances, in the late twentieth century included the National Broadcasting Company (NBC) as a subsidiary.

From the early 1980s, media conglomerates became noteworthy in scope and number, although chain ownership in U.S. newspapers and magazines had existed throughout the twentieth century, with acceleration from the World War II period. Some U.S. media conglomerates distributed their products abroad, and other media conglomerates were based in other nations, such as Canada, Italy, France, and the United Kingdom.

General Electric's acquisition of the Radio Corporation of America, with its NBC division, in 1985 was one of the first major media mergers of the late twentieth century. Most of the large, broadcast-originated television networks at the end of the century belonged to media conglomerates: NBC; Fox Broadcasting, owned by Rupert Murdoch's News Corporation; and ABC, purchased in 1986 by Capital Cities Communications, which in 1995 merged with the Walt Disney Company.

Major trends in media conglomerates during that period included acquisition and development of related operations so that media subsidiaries could produce or use each others' media products within the conglomerate. This signified vertical integration, as opposed to horizontal integration, in which subsidiaries represent noncomplementary functions. For example, the electronic media were able to promote Disney theme parks or products simply through the use of the Disney name attached to each function. Films and other media products made by Disney had an outlet in ABC network television and through Capital Cities' Lifetime and A&E (Arts and Entertainment) cable channels.

The growth of the number and size of media conglomerates was aided by federal deregulation policies for business and a lessening of Federal Communications Commission (FCC) limitations on acquisition of broadcast stations. In the last 20 years of the twentieth century, the federal government did not raise any significant questions of monopolistic behaviors in mass media mergers and expansions, despite the federally initiated breakup of a non–mass media firm – AT&T. One interpretation by legal scholars was that the size of a conglomerate is not necessarily a sign of being anticompetitive, and the U.S. Justice Department's Antitrust Division did not pursue antitrust action in the cable and telecommunications industries.

Motivations for media mergers rest on some characteristics of the mass media themselves in reaching large audiences. The possession of more media outlets not only means more profit, chiefly through advertising or cable subscriptions, but also the increase of revenue and corporate support for expanding the media product and its distribution. In a merger, the variety of media outlets usually expands, along with the audiences who use them. Media products can be distributed through a corporation's television network, cable systems, computer on-line services, books, and international media outlets owned by the conglomerate. A copyright for a conglomerate-produced book may be retained by the same corporation for distribution as a television series or movie.

While media conglomerates can provide profitability and efficiency for themselves, the public still has choices in an expanding selection of media, including ventures in computer on-line services. Some critics have charged that choice does not necessarily mean quality in the media message. Others claim that the conglomerate structure itself is a potential threat. Ben Bagdikian wrote that the global media oligopolies of the 1990s "exert a homogenizing power over ideas, culture and commerce that affects populations larger than any in history."

The phenomenon of the media conglomerate, or chain, began before 1900 with publishers William Randolph Hearst and E.W. Scripps, who each owned nationwide newspaper chains and subsidiary communications, including international news wire services and, for Hearst, magazines. U.S. radio broadcast networks began in the 1920s, with affiliated local stations rather than corporate-owned outlets, in most cases.

In 1975, the FCC banned future cross-ownership in the same market or community. At that time, 80 percent of radio stations were owned by companies that also owned other media, either broadcast or print. In 1977, however, the FCC canceled regulations on chain broadcasting for radio as part of federal deregulation policies. Later deregulation proposals increased the number of local television stations that could be owned by a communications company.

JAMES BOW

See also Broadcast Regulation; Newspaper Chains, or Groups

Further Reading

Auletta, Ken, *Three Blind Mice: How the TV Networks Lost Their Way*, New York: Random House, 1991

Bagdikian, Ben H., *The Media Monopoly*, 3rd ed., Boston: Beacon, 1990

Hudson, Robert V., *Mass Media: A Chronological Encyclopedia of Television, Radio, Motion Pictures, Magazines, Newspapers, and Books in the United States*, New York: Garland, 1987

Picard, Robert G., et al., *Press Concentration and Monopoly: New Perspectives on Newspaper Ownership and Operation*, Norwood, New Jersey: Ablex, 1988

Media Events

Events staged for media coverage

Media events are historic occasions that are televised live to a transfixed nation or world. The pejorative term "pseudo-events" describes a related phenomenon – events created by or staged especially for the media. The latter satisfy both the needs of an event's organizers and journalism's insatiable appetite for news.

The coronation of Britain's Queen Elizabeth II in 1952 was perhaps the first great media event. Other notable examples include the funerals of U.S. President John F. Kennedy and British Lord Louis Mountbatten, the wedding of Great Britain's Prince Charles and Lady Diana Spencer, the journeys of Pope Paul II and Egyptian president Anwar al-Sadat, the 1960 presidential debate between Kennedy and Richard Nixon, the U.S. Senate's Watergate hearings, and the Olympic Games. Although media events are dependent on television coverage to command widespread audiences simultaneously, the forms they take – stories of conquests, contests, and coronations – date back to folklore.

Media events interrupt regular television viewing schedules. Members of the viewing public stop what they are doing and gather in holiday-like fashion – sometimes in their best clothes – to watch television with friends and family. These events have attracted some of the largest viewing audiences in history.

Media events are planned, announced, and advertised in advance and broadcast live. Ceremonial in nature, they often portray an idealized version of society. Unlike daily news stories, which focus on conflict, media events cele-

brate reconciliation. Always, they are proclaimed to be historic.

In democracies, the free and independent media decide what events qualify for media-event treatment. Usually such events are organized by some part of the establishment that has the authority to command public attention. (The Woodstock music festival, clearly an antiestablishment event, was made into a film, not broadcast on live television.) The meaning of a media event typically is proposed by the organizers and agreed to by broadcasters. It must then be accepted by the public. For example, all three – organizers, broadcasters, and the public – agreed that Britain's royal wedding was like a fairytale. They also agreed that the first moon landing represented the exploration of a new U.S. frontier.

Journalists cover but rarely intentionally intrude on such events. They explain the meaning of symbols, confer roles on individuals, and supply subtitles, all in an interesting and relevant way. However, they seldom say "no" to an establishment proposal to stage an event, and they generally have a reverential attitude and uphold the definition of the event provided by the event's organizer. They rarely analyze and never criticize.

Still, most events are radically transformed by television to the point of being unrecognizable to those who attend in person. A broadcaster can transform an event rhetorically and politically by adding a voice and technology independent of the organizer.

Media scholars have said that media events have multiple effects on participants, viewers, and others. For example, media events set a public agenda by conferring status on persons and issues. They create high concentrations of power by personalizing power. They create an expectation of openness of political institutions. They create camaraderie, and they allow the principal participants in an event to talk directly to the public over the heads of the middlemen who usually mediate between leaders and the public.

Scholars also have written about the social value of media events as a means of celebrating the central values of a society. However, they worry that the international broadcasting of sporting events and televised fund-raising extravaganzas might destroy the genre because, they say, media events must be occasional and heavily value-laden to have social value.

Critics of the media-event phenomenon complain that staged media events have at least one detrimental effect: they depoliticize society by keeping viewing audiences at home while providing them with a false sense of political involvement. In a related vein, in 1962, historian Daniel J. Boorstin coined the term "pseudo-event" to describe what he said were illusions or synthetic novelty reported as news. He explained that a dramatic increase in the demand for news began to build in the United States in the early nineteenth century. Technological changes first in printing and photography and later in the electronic media eventually created a 24-hour-a-day demand for news. To meet that demand, journalists devised new newsgathering methods to create pseudo-events, which journalists covered as if they were news.

One technique reporters use to create pseudo-events is the interview. When no news is actually occurring, a reporter will pose a provocative question to a source. If the response is interesting, the reporter has a news story. The reporter also might ask others the same questions, until he or she finds someone who disagrees with the first source. That creates an even better story.

Furthermore, some mass communication scholars have observed that the mere presence of a television camera can create news. For example, crowds sometimes appear at political events merely in hopes of appearing on television, not to observe or participate in the event.

Newsmakers have taken advantage of the journalists' constant need for news by creating their own pseudo-events, which they can be confident the media will cover. President Franklin Delano Roosevelt is widely considered to be the first modern politician to master the pseudo-event. His "fireside" radio chats, presidential press conferences, and for-background-only interviews enabled him to help reporters manufacture news at the same time that he was shaping their stories. U.S. Senator Joseph R. McCarthy built a political career on pseudo-events in the 1940s and 1950s. Honest news reports ever in need of a story covered all his news conferences and press releases – even when there was little real news in them.

The number of pseudo-events grew rapidly in the twentieth century. Creating them became big business for public relations practitioners, advertisers, politicians, journalists, book publishers, manufacturers, merchandisers, and entertainers, among others.

CATHY PACKER

See also Army-McCarthy Hearings; *Image, The;* Journalistic Interview; Presidential Debates; Presidential News Conferences; Roosevelt, Franklin D., and the Media; Staged News; Watergate Scandal

Further Reading

Boorstin, Daniel J., *The Image: A Guide to Pseudo-Events in America,* New York: Vintage, 1992
Dayan, Daniel, and Elihu Katz, *Media Events: The Live Broadcasting of History,* Cambridge, Massachusetts: Harvard University Press, 1992; London: Harvard University Press, 1994
Rothenbuhler, Eric W., "The Living Room Celebration of the Olympic Games," *Journal of Communication* 38:4 (Fall 1988), pp. 61–81

Mexican War

First foreign war covered extensively by U.S. press

"There is a great lack of excitement, and a war with Mexico is what might be termed a 'real blessing' to correspondents and editors," a *Charleston (South Carolina) Courier* correspondent observed in February 1846. "I'm ready to shed my last drop of ink in the cause." Within months, the war began, and before it ended in the summer of 1848, the U.S. press had devoted a considerable amount of ink to the cause with a continuing mixture of jingoism, pride, business sense, and Manifest Destiny.

The Mexican War provided the nation's press with an excellent opportunity to demonstrate news enterprise. It became the first foreign war to be covered extensively by U.S. correspondents, and the key penny press newspapers made expensive, elaborate arrangements to have their reports carried back to the United States. By combining the abilities of the pony express, steamships, railroads, and the fledgling telegraph, the press established a 2,000-mile communications link that repeatedly beat military couriers and the U.S. mails with the news from the front lines. So effective was the express system devised by the press that an exasperated President James Polk learned of the U.S. victory at Vera Cruz via a telegram from the *Baltimore (Maryland) Sun.*

The goals of the war, however, left a number of editors perplexed. Even though they reported the U.S. victories with enthusiasm, some worried about the moral consequences of the conflict. To Horace Greeley of the *New York Tribune,* it was a war "in which Heaven must take part against us." James Gordon Bennett of the *New York Herald,* meanwhile, was an adamant supporter, arguing, "We are on the verge of vast and unknown changes in the destiny of nations."

Most penny press leaders threw their editorial support behind the war and at the same time established a New York–to–New Orleans, Louisiana, express system to deliver the news from the battle zones. The express system "is a creature of modern times," Bennett explained to his readers, "and is characteristic of the American people." If not characteristic of the people, the system clearly was characteristic of the U.S. press in the 1840s. Led by the New York morning dailies, a number of papers participated, including the *Philadelphia North American* and *Public Ledger,* the energetic *Baltimore Sun,* the *Charleston Courier,* and the *New Orleans Picayune.* During the final six months of the war, these papers pooled their efforts to operate the delivery system on a daily basis.

War coverage by reporters was supplemented by letters written home by soldiers in the field. Sometimes written di-

Fall of Mexico City

City of Mexico, September 14, 1847 – Another victory, glorious in its results and which has thrown additional luster upon the American arms, has been achieved today by the army under General Scott – the proud capital of Mexico has fallen into the power of a mere handful of men compared with the immense odds arrayed against them, and Santa Anna, instead of shedding his blood as he had promised, is wandering with the remnant of his army no one knows whither. . . . The fugitives were soon in full flight towards the different works which command the entrances to the city, and our men at once were in hot pursuit.

New Orleans Daily Picayune, October 14, 1847

YANKEE DOODLE.

"LATEST FROM THE ARMY."

Soldiers provided information about the Mexican War to newspapers back home.
(Davis Library, University of North Carolina at Chapel Hill)

rectly to the newspapers, sometimes written to family members who shared the letters with the newspapers, these letters provided a soldier's-eye view of the war and often were filled with propaganda for or against certain military leaders and with half-truths. Nevertheless, the letters were published regularly.

The New Orleans press, closest to the war zones, led the coverage of the conflict. Because newspapers of the day depended heavily on news from their "exchanges" – free copies they received of other newspapers – the reporting by the New Orleans correspondents was reprinted widely throughout the United States. One of the innovative New Orleans papers was *La Patria,* the nation's first Spanish-language daily. Many U.S. dailies reprinted the letters from *La Patria*'s correspondents and used its translations of Spanish-language papers in Mexico and Latin America.

The star reporter of the war was George Wilkins Kendall, editor-publisher of the *New Orleans Picayune.* Kendall covered major battles from Monterrey to Chapultepec and Mexico City and gave long accounts of the military strategy involved. At least 10 other "special correspondents" followed Kendall into the field, led by Christopher Mason Haile of the *Picayune,* John People for the New Orleans *Bee, Delta,* and *Crescent,* and James L. Freaner of the New Orleans *Delta.* Haile, a West Point

dropout, matched Kendall's reporting ability and provided readers with detailed lists of battle casualties. Freaner and People, former New Orleans printers, became accomplished writers and gained national reputations under their respective pseudonyms of "Mustang" and "Chaparral." Freaner capped his successful career as an army correspondent by personally delivering the peace treaty from Mexico City to Washington, D.C., in a then-record 17 days. Other U.S. correspondents in Mexico were Francis A. Lumsden, Daniel Scully, Charles Callahan, and John E. Durivage of the *Picayune;* George Tobin of the *Delta;* William C. Tobey ("John of York") of the *Philadelphia North American;* and John Warland of the *Boston Atlas.*

The reports from the correspondents at the front often supported U.S. involvement in the war and the philosophy of Manifest Destiny. The correspondents also empathized with the plight of the invading U.S. forces, which were isolated in the interior of Mexico. They reflected attitudes of distrust and bias against the Mexicans and promoted and reinforced the popular war-hero images of Generals Zachary Taylor and Winfield Scott. Taylor, benefiting from a wave of favorable newspaper publicity resulting from his battlefield exploits, won the U.S. presidency in 1848.

A quixotic chapter in the war was provided by the colorful publisher of the *New York Sun,* Moses Yale Beach. Accompanied by Jane McManus Storms, an editorial writer for the *Sun,* Beach went to Mexico City in 1847 on a secret peace mission from the U.S. government. The effort failed, and Beach, suspected of assisting antiwar forces in Mexico, barely escaped arrest. Storms, a strong advocate of Manifest Destiny, wrote pro-war commentaries to the *Sun* and the *New York Tribune* from Havana, Vera Cruz, and the Mexican capital under her pseudonym, "Montgomery." Storms made one of the war's more memorable observations about the press coverage when she wrote, "Truth always goes home in clothes of American manufacture."

Also important to the war's coverage, a large number of U.S. civilians followed in the wake of the army and established "occupation newspapers" in Mexico. Before the conflict was over, enterprising U.S. printers established 25 such publications in 14 occupied cities. Serving both the troops at the front and the public at home, these papers provided considerable war coverage.

Many of the war papers were encouraged by the U.S. military authorities because they helped the army maintain local control by publishing official decrees and regulations. In a number of instances, these papers were supported by U.S. military patronage. Of the 25 U.S. occupation papers operated by U.S. citizens, 16 eventually closed down because of financial or related problems, five were suppressed by the U.S. military, and four continued to operate even after the war ended.

The newspapers proved valuable for the U.S. military occupation of Mexico. For a considerable time during the war, large areas of Mexico had to be occupied by U.S. troops, many of them poorly trained volunteers. Undermanned and spread thin over hundreds of miles, the rear area troops often were harassed by Mexican guerrilla forces and hostile civilian populations. In many instances, order was maintained only through the strict use of martial law.

One of the most valuable functions of the occupation newspapers was to keep public opinion, at home and in Mexico, aware of conditions and issues in the expeditionary army. The U.S. press often was the channel by which officials in Washington and Mexico City learned of actions in the other capital. For the general public, it was the only communication link. Out of a mixture of motives – adventure, patriotism, politics, professional news sense, and desire of personal gain – the U.S. printers established their papers in the Mexican cities. The occupation newspapers helped the U.S. people of the 1840s to better understand the war, and they allow the history of the war to be better understood by the people of later generations.

TOM REILLY

See also Cooperative News Gathering; Penny Press

Further Reading

Copeland, Fayette, *Kendall of the Picayune,* Norman: University of Oklahoma Press, 1943; London: University of Oklahoma Press, 1997
Eisenhower, John S.D., *So Far from God: The U.S. War with Mexico, 1846–1848,* New York: Random House, 1989
Johannsen, Robert W., *To the Halls of the Montezumas:*
The Mexican War in the American Imagination, New York: Oxford University Press, 1985; Oxford: Oxford University Press, 1987
Reilly, Tom, "The War Press of New Orleans: 1846–1848," *Journalism History* 13 (1986)
Schroeder, John H., *Mr. Polk's War: American Opposition and Dissent, 1846–1848,* Madison: University of Wisconsin Press, 1973

Minority Journalists' Organizations

In the late twentieth century, there were at least four minority journalists' associations in the United States: the Asian American Journalists Association (AAJA), the National Association of Black Journalists (NABJ), the National Association of Hispanic Journalists (NAHJ), and the Native American Journalists Association (NAJA). The Asian American Journalists Association was formed in 1981, had its headquarters in San Francisco, and had about 1,600 members throughout the United States. The organization encouraged fair and accurate news coverage of Asian and Asian Pacific American issues. In an effort to increase employment of Asian and Asian Pacific American journalists, the organization maintained a resource file of résumés for potential employers. The AAJA published the *Handbook on How to Cover Asian Pacific Americans* as well as a quarterly newsletter.

The National Association of Black Journalists was founded in 1975 to expand and balance media coverage of the black community and to recruit black youth into the mass communication field. The association, which had 2,100 members in 10 regions in the 1990s, published the *NABJ Journal* 10 times a year. Members of the NABJ were working black journalists who represented most of the nation's major newspapers, magazines, and radio and television stations and networks. NABJ members attended an annual national convention. The NABJ had its headquarters at the University of Maryland in College Park.

The National Association of Hispanic Journalists was founded in 1984 and included about 2,000 members. The organization's purpose was to support Hispanics involved in news gathering and dissemination; it encouraged journalism and communications study and practice by Hispanics and sought recognition for Hispanic members of the profession. The organization also promoted fair and accurate media treatment of Hispanics and opposed job discrimination and demeaning stereotypes. Finally, the organization provided a united voice for Hispanic journalists with the aim of achieving national visibility. Headquartered in Washington, D.C., the NAHJ published a monthly newsletter and met annually in June.

The Native American Journalists Association was founded in 1984 and included about 500 members. It was headquartered in Minneapolis, Minnesota, and was organized to encourage, inspire, enhance, and empower Native American journalists. The NAJA held a national conference annually and published a bimonthly newspaper, the *NAJA News*. The organization's programs were designed to improve the coverage of Native Americans, to offer training and support to journalists already in the field, and to increase the number and quality of Native American journalists. The NAJA provided a number of programs designed to support its goals: Project Phoenix, for example, was geared toward encouraging high school students to pursue a mass communication career. The NAJA also cosponsored journalism workshops in three locations throughout the United States. It offered scholarship and internship programs with Native American and mainstream media.

ROBIN GALLAGHER

See also African American Media; Asian American Media; Hispanic Media; Mass Media and Race; Native American Media

Motion Picture Awards

The most familiar award for achievement in motion pictures in the late twentieth century was the Academy Award, also known as the Oscar. The Oscar telecast was seen live each year by more than 1 billion viewers in more than 70 countries. The Oscar was an industry award given by the Academy of Motion Picture Arts and Sciences, established in Los Angeles in January 1927 by Louis B. Mayer, head of Metro-Goldwyn-Mayer film studios. Mayer founded the organization after a labor union agreement was signed two months earlier by the workers on the technical and craft side of the movie industry. That agreement sent technical costs spiraling, and Mayer was searching for a way to head off the talent – actors, writers, and directors – before they launched their own movement for standardized contracts, further weakening the studio system. What was needed, Mayer insisted, was a blanket group to unite the various branches of the film industry. Thus, Mayer and 35 other members of the film community established the academy for those who had contributed "in a distinguished way to the arts and sciences of motion picture production." Actress and producer Mary Pickford was the only female founder.

A statement of aims for the new academy was seven items long. The fifth paragraph established "awards of merit for distinctive achievements." From this brief mention grew what was perhaps the best-known award in the world. While the number of nominating categories by the 1990s had grown to more than 30, including memorial and specialty awards not given every year, the original 13 categories included awards for best production, actor, actress, director, writing, and cinematography, awards that continued to exist more than 70 years later. Eligible motion pictures from each preceding year were voted on by the academy's members. The first Academy Awards ceremony was held in Hollywood in 1927. The first winners in the best film, actor, and actress categories were *Wings,* Emil Jannings, and Janet Gaynor, respectively.

The statuette given to each award recipient was designed by MGM art director Cedric Gibbons. The design of the award remained essentially the same over the years, described as "a naked knight plunging a crusader's sword into a reel of film." Gibbons placed five slots in the reel to represent the five branches of the industry: producers, directors, actors, writers, and technicians. There is some dispute as to when the statuette was christened "Oscar," but academy archives credit Hollywood columnist Sidney Skolsky with the first usage of the nickname in a 1933 article.

Other film industry awards came from the National Society of Film Critics and similar critical organizations in both New York and Los Angeles. The National Board of Review, established as a film censorship organization in 1909, later concentrated on film quality. The Hollywood Foreign Press Association presented the Golden Globe Awards beginning in 1943. Two film awards established after the mid-1970s were the People's Choice Awards and the American Movie Awards. These awards were based on selections made by the public rather than critics, reporters, or film industry workers.

ANTHONY HATCHER

Further Reading
Holden, Anthony, *Behind the Oscar: The Secret History of the Academy Awards,* New York: Simon & Schuster, 1993
Levy, Emanuel, *And the Winner Is . . . : The History and Politics of the Oscar Awards,* New York: Continuum, 1990
Wiley, Mason, Damien Bona, and Gail MacColl, *Inside Oscar: The Unofficial History of the Academy Awards,* New York: Ballantine, 1987

Motion Picture Blacklisting
Punishing individuals for their alleged pro-Communist leanings

One of the darkest periods of postwar U.S. history emerged in the late 1940s and 1950s, during which time the loyalty of various members of the motion picture industry was questioned because of their suspected involvement with the Communist party. Within the context of the Cold War in the United States, a number of actors, directors, producers, and screenwriters were blacklisted, or banned, from film work because of the stigma of hiring alleged Communist sympathizers.

A central component of the blacklisting period involved the work of the House Un-American Activities Committee, which was formed in the late 1930s to investigate subversive activities in the United States. As of 1947, when the committee dramatically increased its investigation into Communist activities in Hollywood, the committee's chairperson was J. Parnell Thomas (a Republican from New Jersey), and a prominent member was Richard Nixon (a Republican from California). In the fall of 1947, two groups of witnesses were subpoenaed to appear before the committee in Washington, D.C. The first group, labeled "friendly" by the committee, consisted primarily of staunch anti-Communists in Hollywood who were willing to identify fellow workers they believed to have Communist ties. The second group, labeled "unfriendly" by the committee, consisted of 19 actors, writers, directors, and producers suspected of having Communist associations.

Only 11 of the "unfriendly" witnesses were called to the stand to testify. When playwright Bertolt Brecht returned to East Germany after denying Communist party membership, the remaining 10 witnesses were cited for contempt of Congress when they refused to answer the question, "Are you now or have you ever been a member of the Communist party?" These witnesses, dubbed the Hollywood 10, were imprisoned for up to a year on the contempt charges. They were producer Adrian Scott, directors Edward Dmytryk

and Herbert Biberman, and writers Alvah Bessie, Lester Cole, Ring Lardner Jr., John Howard Lawson, Albert Maltz, Samuel Ornitz, and Dalton Trumbo.

By the spring of 1951, the committee's investigation into subversive activities in the entertainment industry was gaining momentum. On March 21, 1951, actor Larry Parks, who starred in *The Jolson Story* in 1946, freely admitted that he had joined the Communist party in 1941 when he was 25 years old because of its "liberality," but that he had left the party in 1945 because of lack of interest. However, Parks pleaded with the Committee not to force him to name other people involved in Communist activities. The plea was rejected. The Committee went into executive session, and two days later the news was leaked to the press that Parks had provided the names.

In the investigations that followed the Larry Parks appearance before the committee, approximately one-third of

Protesters try to keep members of the Hollywood 10 from going to jail.
(Wisconsin Center for Film and Theater Research)

the witnesses who testified about subversion in the entertainment industry chose to provide names. Scholars differ, however, on the specific numbers. For example, it has been reported that, of the 90 Hollywood witnesses who appeared before the House Un-American Affairs Committee between 1951 and 1953, 30 provided names. It also has been reported that 58 of the 110 witnesses who were subpoenaed in the second set of hearings named names. Some of those who were named avoided subpoenas by leaving the country, including John Bright, Ben Barzman, Joseph Losey, and Donald Ogden Stewart. Because not all of the testimony taken in executive session was released and not all of those who were subpoenaed appeared before the committee, exact figures of witnesses providing names cannot be known. Still, the scholarship consensus indicates that the one-third estimate is the most accurate.

The blacklisting scholarship also indicates that the purpose of the hearings was punitive in nature. After all, the procedural safeguards of an impartial judge and jury, cross-examination, and exclusionary rules about hearsay and other evidence were absent at the hearings.

The long-lasting impact of the hearings and the anti-Communist fervor of the time was that scores of artists in the film industry were banned from work by the Hollywood studios throughout the 1950s, with the ban not easing until the early 1960s. With their reputations tainted and no work available, many of the blacklisted artists went into exile or changed their names to try to secure work. The situation of writers, who could change their names to become employed, proved better than that of actors, directors, and producers, who could not change their faces.

Screenwriter Dalton Trumbo, who is often credited with helping to lead the blacklisted back to major studio work, wrote a number of scripts using pseudonyms. Trumbo accepted every underground assignment he could get, and he passed along script assignments that he did not have time to write himself to other blacklisted writers. In 1956, Trumbo's script for *The Brave One*, which he wrote under the pseudonym Robert Rich, won an Academy Award for Best Motion Picture Story.

In January 1959, blacklisted screenwriter Nedrick Young announced that he wrote the script for *The Defiant Ones* under the pseudonym Nathan E. Douglas. Because the film was expected to win an Academy Award for Best Screenplay, the Motion Picture Academy was compelled to rescind its rule disqualifying House Un-American Affairs Committee witnesses who pleaded the Fifth Amendment from Academy Award consideration. Shortly after Young's announcement, Trumbo publicly acknowledged that he wrote the script for *The Brave One*.

A year later, director Otto Preminger announced that Trumbo wrote the script for *Exodus* and that Trumbo's name would appear on the screen. This paved the way for Kirk Douglas to agree to give Trumbo screen credit for writing the script for *Spartacus*. Because of the underground work of blacklist victims such as Trumbo and Young, the blacklist slowly lifted.

However, only about 10 percent of the blacklisted artists were able to reestablish careers in the film industry. Ironically, it was not political prejudice that kept the blacklisters from returning to the industry by that time; instead, it was that a new crop of talent had moved into industry positions.

DENNIS E. RUSSELL

See also Broadcast Blacklisting; Cold War and the Media

Further Reading

Ceplair, Larry, and Steven Englund, *The Inquisition in Hollywood: Politics in the Film Community, 1930–1960,* Garden City, New York: Anchor/Doubleday, 1980; London: University of California Press, 1983
Dunne, Philip, *Take Two: A Life in Movies and Politics,* New York: McGraw-Hill, 1980
Hellman, Lillian, *Scoundrel Time,* Boston: Little, Brown, 1976; London: Macmillan, 1976
Navasky, Victor S., *Naming Names,* New York: Viking, 1980; London: John Calder, 1982
Schultz, Bud, and Ruth Schultz, eds., *It Did Happen Here: Recollections of Political Repression in America,* Berkeley: University of California Press, 1989
Vaughn, Robert, *Only Victims: A Study of Show Business Blacklisting,* New York: Putnam's, 1972

Motion Picture Competition

Technology an important weapon in struggle for competitive edge

The nature of motion picture competition has been a reflection of the state of the industry since the medium began in 1895. As control gradually shifted from immigrant entrepreneurs to conglomerates by the end of its first century, the focus of competition also changed. What began as a battle over technology turned into a race to build powerful monopolies. After antitrust action helped end the studio era, competition centered on promotion and marketing. Throughout the history of cinema, film producers competed for the services of people who likely would create profitable films.

Technology was a potent weapon for competition from the beginning. The Edison Company had patented camera and projection systems by 1895 but was bedeviled by patent violations. Edison and eight rival companies put their differences aside in 1908 to form the Motion Picture Patents Company (MPPC). In a blatant attempt to control production, distribution, and exhibition, the MPPC denied equipment and patents to nonmembers, thus forcing weaker competitors out of business. Independents, including Carl Laemmle, the father of Universal Studios, and William Fox, the founder of Twentieth Century-Fox, survived by using foreign-made equipment or producing their own films. In 1917, antitrust action ended the MPPC, already crippled by unpopular features, but the desire of businesses to monopolize the industry remained.

As the financial heart of the industry, distribution and exhibition naturally engendered the fiercest competition. Early film exhibitors bought prints from producers until entrepreneurs established film exchanges that leased prints they had purchased, thus becoming film distributors. In 1916, Adolph Zukor, whose company would become Paramount Pictures, created block booking, which forced exhibitors to lease a package of films that contained a few quality productions but many more of dubious worth. In response, two dozen theater chains created First National Exhibitors Circuit to both produce and distribute films. Aided by Wall Street investors, Zukor and other studio chiefs began purchasing theaters to control exhibition, a trend that continued into the 1920s and made cinema a huge industry.

By this time, sound had become the center of the next technological fight. Major studios did not want to promote sound, which would have required an incredibly expensive redesign of their operations. Feisty Warner Brothers, a minor studio at the time, gambled that the Vitagraph sound system would attract huge audiences. Only when its success with the partially sound *The Jazz Singer* (1927) and the all-sound *The Streets of New York* (1928) proved talking pictures to be not simply a novelty, as the majors had hoped, did the retooling of Hollywood begin.

The golden age of Hollywood, roughly the 1930s and 1940s, largely was controlled by major companies that produced, distributed, and exhibited films. For example, Lowe's, a theater chain, owned a studio, Metro-Goldwyn-Mayer; Warner Brothers, a studio, owned a theater chain. Smaller studios without theaters, independent producers without studios to distribute their films, and theaters tied to block booking were at a decided disadvantage. World War II postponed the inevitable court action, which came in 1948 when the U.S. Supreme Court ordered the major studios to sell their theaters. Coming amid a postwar drop in attendance and the growth of television, the order was a major blow to the studio system.

Under the threat of television, the studios turned to technology to compete. Color, which had been used in barely one out of 10 films, eventually dominated production as television slowly converted to color. The government provided a much-needed boost in 1950 by forcing the Technicolor Corporation to surrender its patents for color cinematography, sparking the growth of competitive systems and wider use of color. On another anti-television front, studios invested in widescreen systems such as CinemaScope and VistaVision, and theaters installed stereophonic sound. Giving up the losing struggle against television, studios began selling films for broadcast and supplying original programming, which eventually revitalized studios that were near collapse.

Studio chiefs and other producers valued talent and competed for it. When performers eager for regular salaries were placed under long-term contract, the studios controlled their careers and the money their films generated. Under the star system, studios competed for public attention with nonstop publicity about the stars they "owned" and the films they financed. When the long-term contract died with the studio system in the 1950s – another victim of cost-cutting efforts – stars gradually assumed greater power in the industry and were the targets of heavy bidding. With films forced to stand or fall on their own merit in the wake of the antitrust action, independent producers joined stars as the new Hollywood power brokers. With studio monopolies disappearing, independent producers found expanded opportunities for financing and exhibiting their films.

Competition since the 1960s increasingly turned to securing the raw materials for filmmaking – mainly money, actors, directors, and stories – and to shrewd marketing of the finished product. Successful producers were adept at arranging packages featuring star, director, and script and selling the package to a studio or other investor hoping for a profit. Screenplays and book rights were purchased for as much as $3 million by the 1990s. Bankable actors, those whose films seldom lost money, would be paid $10 million and more for a single film. Hit-making directors like Steven Spielberg gradually assumed control of their productions and shared in the box-office receipts of their films.

Technology still played a key role in competition. Filmmakers in this new era relied on expensive computerized special effects to enhance productions that frugal television producers could not afford. Exhibitors continued to improve sound and projection systems, especially in the boom of videorecording and home theaters, to separate the moviegoing experience from television. After *Star Wars* (1977) became a record-grossing film and spawned a billion dollars in sales of tie-in toys and other products, great attention was paid to marketing films and merchandising related products. Immensely profitable films, such as *Batman* (1989) and *Jurassic Park* (1993), had product tie-ins ranging from books and toys to fast-food meals. In competing for audience dollars, the film industry relied more heavily than ever on market research to determine what would sell.

DOUGLASS K. DANIEL

See also Economics of Motion Pictures; Hollywood Studio System; Motion Picture Technology; Silent Motion Pictures; Sound Motion Pictures

Further Reading

Cook, David A., *A History of Narrative Film*, New York: Norton, 1981

Kindem, Gorham, ed., *The American Movie Industry: The Business of Motion Pictures*, Carbondale: Southern Illinois University Press, 1982

Mast, Gerald, *A Short History of the Movies*, 4th ed., London: Collier Macmillan, 1986; 5th ed., New York: Macmillan, 1992; 5th ed., Toronto, Ontario: Maxwell Macmillan Canada, 1992

Pirie, David, ed., *Anatomy of the Movies*, New York: Macmillan, 1981

Shipman, David, *The Story of Cinema: A Complete Narrative History, from the Beginnings to the Present*, New York: St. Martin's, 1982

Squire, Jason E., ed., *The Movie Business Book,*
Englewood Cliffs, New Jersey: Prentice-Hall, 1983;
London: Columbus, 1986

Motion Picture Documentaries

Growing interest in nonfiction films

Documentary film underwent a number of important changes in the United States between 1896 and 1996. In the 1890s, short nonfiction films, called actualities, dominated film production and exhibition. Actualities captured scenes of everyday life. In 1896, itinerant operators of portable film cameras and projectors representing the Lumière brothers of France began projecting actualities in U.S. vaudeville theaters. U.S. producers of actualities, including inventor Thomas A. Edison, often recorded sporting events, such as boxing matches, in more confined studios. They also transported bulky cameras on location to record news events, such as the inauguration of President William McKinley in 1897. While some actualities were staged or faked, including several films ostensibly depicting images of

the Spanish-American War in 1898, many others documented actual historical events during this period.

Shortly after the turn of the century a major transformation occurred in U.S. cinema. Between 1906 and 1907, the number of fiction films produced in the United States for the first time significantly exceeded the number of nonfiction films. Dramatic fiction films, such as Edwin S. Porter's *The Great Train Robbery* (1903), were extremely popular with audiences. As audience and exhibitor demand for new motion pictures significantly exceeded the supply of films, the added organizational control and predictability of dramatic fiction production offered certain advantages over nonfiction production. When a French firm, Pathé Frères, which was one of the largest distributors of motion pictures in the United States and throughout the world, introduced the newsreel in about 1910, nonfiction film found a legitimate, if secondary, role as the preliminary part of movie programs leading up to the showing of a fiction film. Eventually, all of the major Hollywood studios began producing their own newsreels to accompany longer dramatic feature films.

In 1920, the first successful feature-length nonfiction film, or documentary, appeared, Robert Flaherty's *Nanook of the North*. Flaherty, a U.S. explorer turned filmmaker, told the story of Nanook, an Inuit (Eskimo) hunter and

Frank Capra's U.S. propaganda series *Why We Fight* (1942–45) depicted German officers as despicable.
(Reproduced from the Collections of the Library of Congress)

fisherman, and his family, who struggled for survival in a harsh northern climate. Recorded on location in the Hudson's Bay area of Canada, this popular film established a new nonfiction genre and proved that nonfiction feature films could be commercially successful on their own in motion picture theaters.

During the 1930s, another form of documentary, the government-sponsored social documentary, was established by a U.S. filmmaker, Pare Lorentz, and a British producer, John Grierson, who had studied in the United States and coined the term "documentary" in his review of Robert Flaherty's South Sea Island film, *Moana* (1928). Lorentz promoted President Franklin Delano Roosevelt's New Deal policies and the Tennessee Valley Authority's system of dams and planned communities as a solution to flooding along major tributaries of the Mississippi River in his widely screened film, *The River* (1937). Government-sponsored filmmaking units failed to take root fully in the United States, however, although Grierson was able to establish enduring documentary film production units in Great Britain and later in North America when he headed the National Film Board of Canada. In the United States, private enterprise initiatives, such as Time, Inc.'s *March of Time* newsreels, successfully balanced entertainment with information and promoted somewhat longer and more serious forms of journalism during this period.

The production of effective but disturbing pieces of political propaganda in Nazi Germany, such as Leni Riefenstahl's *Triumph of the Will* (1935), stimulated U.S. filmmakers such as Frank Capra to develop their own forms of documentary propaganda within the U.S. military in an effort to support the fight for democracy during the 1940s. Some episodes of Capra's *Why We Fight* series (1942–45), which were designed to explain and promote U.S. involvement in World War II to virtually every military volunteer and inductee, were widely shown in commercial theaters. Other Hollywood feature film directors, including John Ford, John Huston, and William Wellman, also joined the war effort by making documentary films about important military battles during World War II.

During the 1950s, 1960s, and 1970s, technological developments stimulated the rise of new forms of documentary, including television documentaries and direct cinema, or cinema verité. As television news programs and documentaries increased in popularity, theatrical newsreels declined and eventually died out.

The availability of highly portable sound film recording equipment made it possible to shoot long, continuous coverage of events as they happened in films. Direct cinema and cinema verité techniques were applied to feature films focusing upon well-known performers such as Mick Jagger and the Rolling Stones in the Maysles brothers' *Gimme Shelter* (1970). Direct cinema also played a role in public television documentaries such as *An American Family* (1973) and several films by Frederick Wiseman, including *Welfare* (1975) and *Model* (1980).

Several developments during the 1980s and 1990s began to challenge traditional notions of documentary. Documentaries such as Trinh T. Minh-ha's *Reassemblage* (1982) and *Surname Viet Given Name Nam* (1989) seriously questioned ethnographic researchers' and documentary filmmakers' presumptions of objectivity. Other innovative films, such as Jill Godmilow's *Far from Poland* (1984) and Errol Morris's *The Thin Blue Line* (1987), mixed together dramatic restagings, reenactments, and clips from dramatic feature films with interviews and actuality material in ways that called into question traditional classifications and distinctions such as fiction versus nonfiction. Several female and minority filmmakers, including Trinh Minh-ha, Godmilow, and Marlon Riggs, who produced a controversial public television documentary concerning gay black men called *Tongues Untied* (1989), made innovative films which tested and extended the parameters of documentary during this period. At the same time, several commercially successful documentaries, including Michael Moore's *Roger and Me* (1989) and S. James, R. Marx, and P. Gilbert's *Hoop Dreams* (1994), created controversies when they were rejected for Academy Award consideration but effectively demonstrated the continuing popularity of feature-length documentaries in motion picture theaters and on television.

GORHAM A. KINDEM

American officers were portrayed in a much more beneficent light in *Why We Fight*.
(Reproduced from the Collections of the Library of Congress)

See also Broadcast Documentaries; Docudramas; Motion Picture Newsreels

Further Reading

Ellis, Jack C., *The Documentary Idea: A Critical History of English-Language Documentary Film and Video,* Englewood Cliffs, New Jersey: Prentice-Hall, 1989

Nichols, Bill, *Representing Reality: Issues and Concepts in Documentary,* Bloomington: Indiana University Press, 1991

Motion Picture Labor Organizations

Commercial filmmaking highly unionized in United States

Commercial filmmaking in the United States has been highly unionized. Early in the film industry's history, workers were organized by trade unions from related industries, such as the theater and the electrical industry. Eventually, unions and guilds were formed specifically to organize Hollywood workers, and most of these labor groups were still active in the film and television industries in the late twentieth century.

Similar to other U.S. labor organizations, the Hollywood unions and guilds have been challenged by political and economic developments in society in general and the film industry in particular. Difficult struggles in the past have included union recognition in the 1930s and ideological assaults such as the blacklisting period of the 1940s and 1950s. In the 1990s, they faced further challenges from antiunion sentiments as well as power struggles with diversified corporations actively involved in international markets.

According to data from the Bureau of Labor Statistics, motion picture workers in the United States totaled 404,000 in 1992 and 421,000 in 1993. Film workers are a highly skilled and specialized labor force. Unemployment in the field is always high, and workers often must have some unusual or unique characteristics or talents as well. Some workers, such as writers, directors, and actors, share in the profits of films through profit-participation deals. Others may become employers themselves through their own independent production companies or in projects where they serve as producer or director. There also are differences between "creative" (above-the-line) and "craft" (below-the-line) workers, with consequent differences between the labor organizations that represent these different types of labor. In other words, the organization of entertainment unions along craft lines rather than a vertical, industrial structure, has tended to inhibit labor unity within the industry.

The International Association of Theatrical and Stage Employees (IATSE) was long the most powerful union active in the U.S. film industry. Formed at the end of the nineteenth century, the IATSE organized stage employees in the United States and Canada. As the entertainment industry expanded, the IATSE grew to include motion picture projectionists and technical workers at the Hollywood studios and film exchanges throughout North America. When television was introduced, the IATSE organized technical workers in the new medium.

The IATSE had a tradition of local autonomy, with a variety of craft-based locals involved in collective bargaining agreements. Nationwide agreements for film production personnel, however, were negotiated with the producers' association, the Alliance of Motion Picture and Television Producers. The IATSE's history includes some dismal chapters from the 1930s when racketeers and criminals extorted funds from union members, as well its assistance in the blacklisting activities that tainted Hollywood in the 1940s.

The National Association for Broadcast Employees and Technicians (NABET) grew first out of radio, and then television, broadcasting. The union was organized at NBC as a company union (an industrial, rather than craft-oriented, organization) as an alternative to the larger and more powerful IBEW. NABET's relatively militant history is replete with skirmishes with the IBEW and the IATSE, as well as continuous rumors of a merger with the larger IATSE.

In 1990, NABET's Local 15, which organized 1,500 freelance film and tape technicians in New York, merged with the IATSE. Then, in 1992, most of the remaining NABET locals agreed to join the Communication Workers of America (CWA), effective January 1994. About 9,300 NABET members became a part of the much larger CWA, which represented 600,000 workers in telecommunications, printing, broadcasting, health care, and the public sector. While most of NABET's members were to be moved to an independent broadcasting arm in the CWA, NABET's West Coast Local 531 agreed to merge with the IATSE because of its 500 members' closer affiliation with the film industry. Thus, the IATSE became the only union in the United States to represent behind-the-camera film workers.

The International Brotherhood of Teamsters was the largest and strongest union in the United States and also was active in the motion picture industry, organizing studio transportation workers on the west coast and various other workers. The Teamsters claimed a general membership of more than 2 million in 1986; its Hollywood Local 399 had approximately 2,900 members who worked as truck drivers and security personnel in the film industry.

The Screen Actors Guild (SAG) was organized in 1933 after several other organizations, including the Academy of Motion Picture Arts and Sciences, had attempted to organize film performers. The early history of the SAG is dominated by attempts to establish a guild shop, then to gain compensation for actors in the constantly expanding forms of distribution (television, videocassettes, etc.). In 1992, the 3,600 members of the Screen Extras Guild (SEG) became a part of SAG's union coverage, primarily because the SEG lacked the clout to deal with producers and most extras were working as nonunion.

Serious discussions of a merger between the SAG and the American Federation of Television and Radio Artists (AFTRA) took place over the years. The AFTRA was formed in 1937 to represent radio, and then television, performers. The organization's primary jurisdiction was in live television, but the AFTRA shared jurisdiction with the SAG for taped television productions. The AFTRA's 75,000 members also included some vocalists.

The Writers Guild of America (WGA) represented movie and television writers but was split between WGA East (3,500 members) and WGA West (6,500 members). The organization was founded in 1954, although writers were organized previously by groups such as the Authors League of America and the Screen Writers Guild. The WGA was concerned with appropriate credit for writers, as well as pay rates and compensation for work distributed in media other than film.

The Directors Guild of America (DGA) represented directors, unit production managers, assistant directors, and technical coordinators in television and film. The guild was formed in 1960 from the merger of the Screen Directors Guild and the Radio and Television Directors Guild. The organization's membership was about 9,700 in 1992. Prompted especially by the introduction of colorized films, the DGA lobbied strongly for a moral rights law for creative personnel to prevent changes in their work.

The American Federation of Musicians represented musicians working in the film industry. The trade group, which was formed in the 1890s, negotiated contracts with the industry from 1944 and especially was concerned with new technological developments in sound recording.

International corporate expansion has long been of vital concern to workers' organizations, as indicated by the formation of international trade secretariats at the end of the nineteenth century. Entertainment unions also have formed a number of international organizations, although they have had unstable histories, and any real influence, such as international collective bargaining agreements, has been rare.

JANET WASKO

See also Broadcast Labor Organizations; Motion Picture Blacklisting

Further Reading

Hartsough, D., "Crime Pays: The Studios' Labor Deals in the 1930s," *Velvet Light Trap* (1989)

Koenig, Allen E., ed., *Broadcasting and Bargaining,* Madison: University of Wisconsin Press, 1970

Leiter, Robert David, *The Musicians and Petrillo,* New York: Bookman, 1953

Prindle, David F., *The Politics of Glamour: Ideology and Democracy in the Screen Actors Guild,* Madison: University of Wisconsin Press, 1988

Ross, Murray, *Stars and Strikes: Unionization of Hollywood,* New York: Columbia University Press, 1941

Schwartz, Nancy Lynn, *The Hollywood Writers' Wars,* New York: Knopf, 1982

Wasko, J., "Trade Unions and Broadcasting: A Case Study of the National Association of Broadcast Employees and Technicians," in *The Critical Communications Review,* edited by Vincent Mosco and Janet Wasko, Norwood, New Jersey: Ablex, 1983

Motion Picture Newsreels

Provided pictorial news to movie-goers for years

Motion picture newsreels were eight- to nine-minute short subjects shown regularly in film theaters throughout the world, featuring brief moving-image records of newsworthy events. They first appeared in France and England in 1910 and in the United States in 1911.

Released serially, with changes in subject matter twice a week, the newsreels survived for more than half a century as part of the theater's program of motion picture feature films, often accompanied by other short subjects such as cartoons and travelogues. Following World War II, with the commercial introduction of television, the newsreel's function gradually was replaced by that of the television news services. In the United States, the last of the major motion picture newsreels ceased production in 1967, although others continued to be made and released for a few years in some other countries. At the height of their success, U.S. newsreels dominated world release, seen weekly in the United States in more than 15,000 theaters by an estimated audience of 40 million people and, with its narration translated into several foreign languages, by another 200 million worldwide.

Before there were newsreels, there were news films – short films running anywhere from a few seconds to a few minutes in length. Each of these featured a single event of newsworthy character, released to theaters only as the occurrence of such events justified it. As early as 1900, within six years after the first exhibition of motion pictures by means of Thomas Edison's Kinetoscope and more than a decade before regularly released newsreels were introduced, every type of subject matter that would characterize motion picture and television journalism thereafter already had appeared in short news films. Such subjects included international celebrities, pageantry and ceremony, natural and man-made disasters, political and military events, technology and invention, personalities, spectacle, sports, and novelties. News films such as these pictured sports events in 1894, the Boer War in 1898, the funeral of Britain's Queen Victoria in 1901, and the San Francisco earthquake and fire in 1906.

The newsreel, by contrast, was a regularly released component of all theater programs. Each edition of the newsreel ran approximately nine or 10 minutes in length and was comprised of eight or nine more-or-less newsworthy subjects, each subject separated from the others by a title. The form and style of the reel was patterned after the newspaper, with the most newsworthy story appearing first, followed by subjects of less and less journalistic importance. The newsreels usually ended with sports coverage and sometimes an amusing novelty sequence that was the equivalent of the newspaper's comic strip.

The first U.S. newsreel, *Pathé's Weekly,* was introduced to the public by the French firm of Pathé Frères in 1911. It

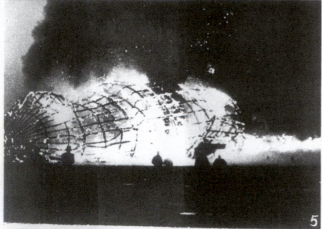

Stills from newsreel footage reveal how film captured the destruction of the German dirigible *Hindenburg* at Lakehurst, New Jersey, in 1937.
(UPI/Corbis-Bettmann)

was followed soon thereafter by competition from other companies on national, regional, and even local levels. Few of these survived for long, however, and with the passing of years, five major newsreels emerged and survived, each produced or released by one of the first major U.S. feature film companies: *Paramount News*, *Universal News*, *Fox Movie-* *tone News*, the *International Newsreel* (*Metrotone News*) produced by the Hearst Company and released by Metro-Goldwyn-Mayer, and *Pathé News* (released first by RKO Radio Pictures and later by Warner Brothers).

As with feature films, sound came to the motion picture newsreels in the late 1920s. The earliest of these had no narration but simply presented the natural sounds and remarks of people and events photographed in the field. Although technically unsophisticated, they were immensely popular with audiences and for a few months, until their novelty wore off, experienced real commercial success.

With the passing of time, technical sophistication in sound recording and reproduction was achieved. A fast-paced music background, sound effect enhancements, and an unseen narrator were added to each of the newsreels, the most famous of the latter being radio news commentator Lowell Thomas for Fox Movietone. Although a popular part of the motion picture program, the newsreels were never financially profitable for their owners, the five major film companies that controlled the production, distribution, and exhibition of films in the United States. Newsreels functioned as a kind of "loss leader" distributed to theaters as a part of a package of shorts intended to support the feature films from which significant revenues were derived. Part journalism, part show business, newsreels never were accorded much respect by their owners and sometimes were criticized by print journalists for their superficial coverage and sophomoric treatment of the news.

"The newsreel," wrote historian Raymond Fielding, "was often shallow, trivial and even fraudulent. But sometimes, it was wonderful – filled with vivid, unforgettable pictures and sound of the people, events, wonders and horrors which the free people of [the twentieth] century did their best to understand and confront."

In 1935, an interpretive quasi-newsreel entitled *The March of Time* was introduced to theater audiences by the publishers of *Time* and *Fortune* magazines. Each issue ran 20 minutes in length and was released once a month to an audience of more than 20 million people in the United States alone, and in foreign-language versions to millions more abroad. High-spirited and iconoclastic in style and content, the series frequently was censored in the United States and banned outright in several nations abroad. If *The March of Time* were to be compared with anything seen later on television, it would be a cross between investigative journalism and a carefully rehearsed, professionally acted docudrama.

Its most unusual feature was the re-creation or staging of news events for the camera, using impersonators in the early years and later the actual celebrities themselves, as actors re-creating their roles in history. The film's founder and producer, Louis DeRochemont, argued that he had the same right to re-create a story with pictures as a newspaper reporter had to do so with words, and that sometimes his re-creation was sharper, truer, and more revealing than authentic footage would have been had it been available. The technique was identical to that used years later in docudramas shown on television, except that *The March of Time* never revealed to its audiences that it was re-creating news events by blending artificially staged scenes with authentic newsreel footage. Sometimes called the editorial page of the newsreel, *The March of Time* survived in U.S. theaters for more than 15 years as the only regularly exhibited motion picture series that consistently presented controversial subject matter of a political, economic, racial, religious, and military kind.

Following the introduction of commercial television in 1945 and the gradual development of its news services, the preeminence of the motion picture newsreel as the world's principal source of moving-image journalism gradually declined. One by one, the five great U.S. newsreels ceased operation, the last of these being *Universal News* in 1967. The motion picture newsreel is one of the few major media of communication ever to have ceased operation and disappeared. In its day, it was considered an essential part of the motion picture theater program and enjoyed considerable popularity with audiences. As a form of journalism, however, it was criticized widely, especially following World War II, as competing television news services offered better coverage, greater sophistication, extended journalistic treatment, and faster speed of delivery.

The newsreel shared the same fundamental limitation as that of the television news services that supplanted it. It was a pictorial medium that depended wholly upon images to tell its story. Without images, there was no story to tell. As a consequence, because of the frequent difficulties encountered in securing such images, many stories never were told. In particular, stories featuring complicated and abstract concepts of a social, political, or economic sort were almost impossible to explore in the newsreel. Only their superficialities could be presented to the extent that they could be visualized. For example, the visible consequences of an economic depression could be illustrated briefly by scenes of soup kitchens, bread lines, labor-management conflict, and violence, but any detailed exploration of the economic dynamics of a depression and its causes was beyond the fast-paced, wholly pictorial capabilities of the newsreel.

The television news services that followed were faced by similar problems, which they addressed first by extending the length of the program, thereby allowing for more journalistic detail. Second, as in radio news broadcasting, they added on-screen field reporters and studio anchor persons who interpreted the news verbally. Third, they extended use of maps, diagrams, charts, animations, and other on-screen graphics.

Although U.S. newsreels no longer were made for exhibition in motion picture theaters after the late 1960s, a good deal of the footage that was photographed by their cameramen during the more than half century of their production still survives in film archives throughout the world. The images recorded in that footage retain both historical and commercial value and are frequently used in the production of so-called compilage films for historical, educational, and informational purposes.

RAYMOND FIELDING

See also Docudramas; Television News

Further Reading

Bächlin, Peter, and Maurice Muller-Strauss, *Newsreels Across the World*, Paris: UNESCO, 1952
Fielding, Raymond, *The American Newsreel, 1911–1967*, Norman: University of Oklahoma Press, 1972
_____, *The March of Time, 1935–1951*, New York: Oxford University Press, 1978
Leyda, Jay, *Films Beget Films*, New York: Hill and Wang, 1964; London: G. Allen & Unwin, 1964
Mould, David, *American Newsfilm, 1914–1919: The Underexposed War*, New York: Garland, 1983

Motion Picture Propaganda

Film considered a good way to manipulate a mass audience

The Russian Communist Party was one of the first political movements to use film-based propaganda, finding the medium's worth during the Revolution of 1917. The founder of Russian Communism, Lenin, termed film "the most important art" and understood its power to move and manipulate a mass audience. The Soviets harnessed the full power of the state, including the film industry and graphic arts, as methods of propaganda. Poster art was a particularly effective means of mass communication at the time. Brightly and elaborately painted "propaganda ships and trains" traveled to the far reaches of the Union of Soviet Socialist Republics. These were mobile theaters and galleries intended to bring culture and propaganda to the average citizen. Some of the Soviet Union's most creative and influential artists – composer Igor Stravinsky, film director Sergei Eisenstein, designer Alexander Rodchenko, painter Kasimir Malevich, and others – helped spread the revolutionary message.

The next peak in mass communication propaganda originated in Nazi Germany, where Adolf Hitler also understood the power of mass communication. One of his first acts as chancellor of Germany was to appoint Joseph Goebbels as minister of propaganda. Under Hitler's Nazis, all means of mass communication in occupied areas were controlled tightly. Books were burned publicly; libraries, newspapers, radio, and film industries were purged of all dissent; only information supporting the Nazis was allowed to be disseminated.

Between World Wars I and II, the German film industry (UFA) was one of most creative in Europe. The UFA trained many prominent film directors who later fled the Nazis and came to the United States, where they helped to build Hollywood during its golden years. The legendary Fritz Lang, Billy Wilder, and Otto Preminger were among them. Under the Nazis, however, Germany produced well over a thousand, mostly sentimental, completely forgettable, escapist films. Also produced were anti-Semitic propaganda films like Fritz Hippler's *The Eternal Jew* and Leni Riefenstahl's *Triumph of the Will*.

The United States, too, generated its share of wartime propaganda. In December 1941, President Franklin D. Roosevelt established a Bureau of Motion Pictures Affairs to bring Hollywood into the Allied war effort. All levels of the film industry were galvanized to create films that glorified World War II and the role of the United States and its

I Was a Communist for the F.B.I. worked to convince viewers of the treachery directed at the United States from the Soviet Union.

allies in that war. Some of the most prominent Hollywood directors – among them Frank Capra, John Huston, and William Wyler – made documentary films that helped to "sell" the war to the U.S. people.

Wartime film propaganda took many forms. Even Hollywood's nonhuman characters helped to promote the war as Disney, Warner Brothers, and other studios put Mickey Mouse, Pluto, Daffy Duck, Porky Pig, Bugs Bunny, and a cast of thousands to work for Uncle Sam. Tex Avery, Chuck Jones, and some of Hollywood's most famous animators created such propaganda films as *In the Fuhrer's Face, Education for Death,* and *Blitz Wolf.*

Cartoon propaganda was designed for adults as well as children, for they helped to simplify concepts like rations, patriotism, buying war bonds, and identifying the country's enemy. Rotoscoping was used to mix live action and animation, thus creating a highly entertaining form of propaganda. In the 1940s, approximately 90 million people in the United States went to the movies each week. Film was the visual mass communication form of the day.

Perhaps the most intense period of propaganda in U.S. history occurred during what is now called the Cold War period. This was the time in the late 1940s and 1950s of the Communist witch hunts led by the House Un-American Activities Committee and Senator Joseph McCarthy. Almost overnight, the Soviet military allies against Nazi Germany became the "evil empire." Hollywood suddenly stopped making films sympathetic to the Soviet Union like *The Battle of Russia* (1942), *Mission to Moscow* (1942), and *The North Star* (1944). Instead, it produced such rabidly anti-Communist films as *Red Menace* (1949) and *I Was a Communist for the F.B.I.* (1951). The methods of using mass communication for demonizing, dehumanizing, and vilifying the Germans and the Japanese during the war now were used against the new enemy – the Communists, both abroad and at home. Film was by no means the only avenue for anti-Communist propaganda. Books, especially mystery novels, comic books, magazines, radio, and, in the 1950s, television, were all creative outlets for America's ultra-patriotic rhetoric in the popular culture.

Television was still experimenting with its new technology in the 1950s, but the new medium was affected by the chill of propaganda. Indeed, the intimacy of television by coming into viewers' living rooms made its influence even more penetrating and potentially dangerous than that of film.

RITA M. CSAPÓ-SWEET

See also Broadcast Propaganda; Propaganda

Further Reading

Altheide, David, and John M. Johnson, *Bureaucratic Propaganda,* Boston: Allyn and Bacon, 1980
Barson, Michael, *"Better Dead than Red!": A Nostalgic Look at the Golden Years of Russiaphobia, Red-Baiting, and Other Commie Madness,* New York: Hyperion, 1992; London: Plexus, 1992
Bojko, Szymon, *New Graphic Design in Revolutionary Russia,* New York: Praeger, 1972; London: Lund Humphries, 1972
Cook, David A., *A History of Narrative Film,* 2nd ed., New York: Norton, 1990
Fraser, Lindley, *Propaganda,* New York and London: Oxford University Press, 1957
Jowett, Garth S., and Victoria O'Donnell, *Propaganda and Persuasion,* Newbury Park, California: Sage, 1986
Larson, Charles, *Persuasion: Reception and Responsibility,*

6th ed., Belmont, California: Wadsworth, 1992;
London: Chapman & Hall, 1992

Lee, Alfred McClung, and Elizabeth Briant Lee, eds., *The Fine Art of Propaganda; A Study of Father Coughlin's Speeches*, New York: Harcourt Brace, 1939

Taylor, Richard, *Film Propaganda: Soviet Russia and Nazi Germany*, New York: Barnes and Noble, 1979; London: Croom Helm, 1979

Motion Picture Ratings

Films evoke efforts to regulate content from earliest days

Attempts to regulate film content in the United States are as old as the movies themselves. Bowing to municipal, state, and federal pressure, the movie industry began self-regulation, with the Motion Picture Production Code, which governed the acceptable boundaries of feature film content in the United States from its introduction in 1930 until its elimination in 1966, being its most successful effort.

A newer era of more explicit sexual and violent portrayals surfaced in the early 1950s and continued throughout the 1960s. A few controversial pictures were released without code approval during this period, while a handful of others were awarded seals even though they contained either strong language or nudity. The code progressively lost its authority with filmmakers, and calls for governmental controls on movie content increased correspondingly.

Hollywood responded by introducing the Code and Rating Administration (CARA) on November 1, 1968, opting for a classification system rather than outright censorship. Representatives from two industry trade organizations – the Motion Picture Association of America, which represented producers and distributors, and the National Association of Theater Owners – drafted a voluntary rating system that provided parents with advance information on sexual, violent, and otherwise taboo depictions.

The number and meanings of the various categories also evolved somewhat. They began in 1968 with G for general audiences, M for mature audiences, R for restricted viewing by children under 17 unless accompanied by a parent or adult guardian, and X for no one under 17 admitted. M was changed to GP and then PG (parental guidance) in 1970 to clarify what was meant by the "mature audiences" designation.

By the early 1980s, however, both industry critics and insiders believed that the PG designation was too lax in its handling of violence. This issue reached a boiling point in 1984 with *Raiders of the Lost Ark*, a movie targeted at children as well as adults. The CARA ruled that this film was "excessively violent" and initiated a fifth category, PG-13 (special parental supervision for children under 13) on July 1, 1984, to further clarify the scope of the PG classification.

Finally, NC-17 (children under 17 not admitted) replaced X in 1990 as a more desirable alternative for the industry, differentiating mainstream productions from hard-core films and videos. X and triple X continued to be self-applied by pornographers.

The CARA's rating board typically was composed of 10 parents from the Los Angeles area with no prior experience in the film industry. This group considered between 400 and 450 movies each year, issuing probable ratings along with suggestions for changes to improve an imminent classification. Appeals were also possible to a wider industry committee if a compromise could not be reached through subsequent negotiations.

A national program for rating movies was a relatively new development in the United States. Most industrialized countries had some system of film classification for most of the twentieth century. At century's end, the United States, Spain, and Japan were the only countries in the world with ratings procedures free of government control or intervention.

GARY R. EDGERTON

See also Broadcast Ratings; Censorship of Motion Pictures; Television Program Ratings

Further Reading
Austin, Bruce A., "G-PG-R-X: The Purpose, Promise and Performance of the Movie Rating System," *Journal of Arts Management and Law* 12 (1982)

_____, Mark J. Nicolich, and Thomas Simonet, "MPAA Ratings and the Box Office: Some Tantalizing Statistics," *Film Quarterly* 35 (1981–1982)

Burroughs, Julian C., "X Plus 2: The MPAA Classification System During Its First Two Years," *Journal of the University Film Association* 23 (1971)

De Grazia, Edward, and Roger K. Newman, *Banned Films: Movies, Censors, and the First Amendment*, New York: Bowker, 1982

Jowett, Garth, *Film: The Democratic Art*, Boston: Little, Brown, 1976

Tusher, Will, "New PG-13 Rating Instituted by MPAA; Will Cover Some Pix That Would've Been R-Rated," *Variety* (July 4, 1984)

Motion Picture Serials

Weekly "chapter play" that ended with a life-threatening cliffhanger

Serials were a staple of motion picture entertainment from 1913 until their production ceased in 1956. Also known as a chapter play, the typical serial told an action-oriented story in 12 or 15 chapters of 20 minutes each, one appearing each week at a theater. Each chapter usually ended with a "cliffhanger" that placed the hero or heroine in peril from which escape seemed impossible. The suspense and promise of more excitement prompted audiences to return for the next installment.

Major and minor studios and a handful of independents produced nearly 500 serials, more than half of them before the sound era. Usually filmed on low budgets as escapist fare, serials did not advance the art of cinema or contribute to its maturation. Few serial stars, directors, or writers went on to major careers in feature films. Thus, serials remain little more than curiosities that reveal more about the cultures that spawned them than the medium itself.

Early serials were tied to articles in newspapers and magazines to promote readership as well as moviegoing. The first serial, *What Happened to Mary* (1912), was a companion to fiction articles in McClure's *Ladies World* magazine about a young woman attempting to claim an inheritance before her twenty-first birthday. Not until *The Perils of Pauline* (1914), by some accounts the fifth serial produced, was the classic formula of action, adventure, and cliffhanger suspense firmly established. The popularity of Pauline's quest for a lost inheritance despite natural and man-made threats spurred more serial production.

Unlike the majority of sound serials, silent chapter plays featured heroines more often than heroes in tales aimed at adults. Serials presented nearly all film genres, from westerns and mysteries to melodramas and romances. Produc-

tion peaked in the mid-1920s but then dwindled as audiences became more sophisticated and demanding. Only about 20 of the nearly 270 silent serials were known to exist by the end of the twentieth century.

The costly transition to sound that began in 1927 and the onset of the Great Depression led most studios and independents to cease serial production entirely. Among the studios, only Universal and Mascot made serials during the early years of sound. Republic, formed in 1935 by a merger that included Mascot, began serial production in 1936, and Columbia followed in 1937.

By then, the serial had become the domain of children, the best source for the suspension of disbelief required to enjoy outlandish adventures and productions of varying quality. For them, a trip to the movies on a Saturday afternoon included a fast-paced chapter in a favorite hero's latest adventure. The serial used comic strips, comic books, radio shows, and pulp magazines for characters and inspiration. Radio programs that made the leap to serials included the *Lone Ranger*, the *Green Hornet*, the *Shadow*, and *Jack Armstrong*. Comics gave the serials *Superman, Bat-*

The Perils of Pauline entertained audiences weekly in the early twentieth century.
(Wisconsin Center for Film and Theater Research)

man, Dick Tracy, Captain Marvel, Captain America, Flash Gordon, and *Buck Rogers.*

An Olympic athlete turned actor, Larry "Buster" Crabbe was the serial king in the sound era. He starred in nine chapter plays, including *Flash Gordon* (1936) and its two sequels. For most players, however, serials were either a career peak or a stop in a career on the way down. One exception, actor John Wayne, appeared in three Mascot serials before finding stardom in feature films, making him the most accomplished serial alumnus.

The decline of the serial has been traced to competition with television, which offered children hours of free adventures. Yet Universal had stopped serial production in 1946, well before the television threat, suggesting that audience interest and financial rewards already had diminished. The studio system itself waned in the face of television and the loss of monopolies in film distribution, forcing cutbacks of salaried crews essential for serial production. Republic halted its serials in 1955, and Columbia produced the last serial, *Blazing the Overland Trail,* in 1956.

Interest in serials has been revived periodically by late-night television airings, revival house screenings, and video-recordings. Their main appeal has been nostalgic and campy. The serial's lasting influence may be seen as the inspiration for the *Star Wars* and *Indiana Jones* film series.

DOUGLASS K. DANIEL

Further Reading
Barbour, Alan G., *Cliffhanger: A Pictorial History of the Motion Picture Serial,* New York: A&W, 1977
_____, *Days of Thrills and Adventure,* New York: Macmillan, 1970; London: Collier, 1970
Kinnard, Roy, *Fifty Years of Serial Thrills,* Metuchen, New Jersey: Scarecrow, 1983
Lahue, Kalton C., *Continued Next Week: A History of the Moving Picture Serial,* Norman: University of Oklahoma Press, 1964
Stedman, Raymond William, *The Serials: Suspense and Drama by Installment,* 2nd ed., Norman: University of Oklahoma Press, 1977

Motion Picture Technology

Development paralleled still photography for years

The art, craft, and technology of the motion picture reached its century mark in the mid-1990s. Film technology includes camera technology or cinematography, devices to project an image to an audience, developments in motion picture film that allow an image to be recorded, the evolution of sound, and the progress in widescreen, special effects, and digital technologies since the 1950s.

The capability of recording an image on photosensitive material was discovered by Joseph-Nicéphore Niepce, a French physicist, in 1827. Further developments over the next 55 years by such experimenters as Louis Daguerre, William Fox Talbot, and James Clerk Maxwell allowed imagery to become more detailed and realistic. During the same period, popular mechanical amusements such as the Zoetrope and Praxinoscope demonstrated that a series of sequential pictures could present the illusion of movement to the viewer.

For motion pictures to become a reality, a strong but flexible film and a mechanism to transport the film through a camera at a constant speed were needed. In 1889, George Eastman, who founded Eastman Kodak, developed such a film on a base of cellulose nitrate. It had sprocket holes down its side to advance the film in the camera, and its width was 35 millimeters. At the same time, Thomas Alva Edison and his assistant, William K.L. Dickson, invented a camera called the Kinetograph that accepted Eastman's film. By 1894, Kinetographs were producing commercially viable films, and Edison opened a "peep show" amusement parlor in New York City filled with Kinetoscopes, small projectors that allowed a single viewer to look at the film through a magnifying glass. By 1895, Edison realized that the future of film exhibition was projection to large audiences, and he left it to others to invent these devices. Despite this fact, Kinetoscopes were a popular peep show amusement throughout the United States until 1900.

Edison's Kinetograph camera employed an intermittent movement, the basis of all subsequent camera design. At the moment the film is exposed – that is, when an image passing through the lens reaches the film to create an image – the film lies perfectly motionless in the camera's aperture. After exposure, a shutter closes, and the camera advances the film one frame. With Edison's Kinetograph, this process was repeated 40 times each second. For other cameras throughout the silent era, the speed was 16 frames per second. With the sound era, the rate increased to 24 frames per second to produce better-quality voices and music. Basically, the system devised by Edison and Dickson more than 100 years before remained in use into the twentieth century.

Cameras have five principal parts: a body that holds the mechanism that advances the film and exposes it to light; a motor; a magazine containing the film; a lens that collects the light and focuses an image on the film; and a viewfinder to allow cinematographers to see what they are photographing. In the silent era of motion pictures in the United States, a highly specialized industry grew in southern California that developed sophisticated techniques of cinematography, lighting, and editing. The Hollywood studio system divided the process of making motion pictures into three stages: preproduction, production, and postproduction. During preproduction, the film was written and planned. The production phase was technology-intensive, with the most important devices being the cameras used to record images and the lights used to illuminate the sound stages. During postproduction, a film was edited and titles were added. A completed film needed additional technology to present an image for audiences: projectors and, in the sound era, loudspeakers.

Early black-and-white films were orthochromatic – that is, the film was sensitive only to blue and violet light. Until the early 1920s, the design of all sets, costumes, and make-up needed to reflect this limitation of the film. In 1921, Ko-

Early model video cinematography camera
(Ikegami Electronics [U.S.A.] Inc.)

dak introduced a panchromatic film that was equally sensi-tive to all the visible colors, producing each as a shade of gray. The quality of panchromatic film was extraordinary even in the silent era, producing luminous white tones and deep, rich blacks.

Nearly from the origins of the cinema in the 1890s, film-makers wanted to produce their films in color. In the early history of motion pictures, this had to be accomplished af-ter cinematography was complete, usually by hand-painting individual frames or by tinting sections of the film. Night-time scenes, for example, could be tinted blue to simulate moonlight. Tinting was popular throughout the silent era. More sophisticated handling of color came with experi-ments started in 1915, when the Technicolor Corporation was formed by Herbert Kalmus and Donald Comstock. By 1932, Technicolor had a fully developed color system using three strips of film running through the camera at the same time. Each strip recorded one of the additive color pri-maries: red, green, and blue. Color cinematography for the

first time had pure hues and intense saturation. Walt Dis-ney's *Flowers and Trees* (1932), *Gone with the Wind* (1939), and *The Wizard of Oz* (1939) are all superb exam-ples of the success of Technicolor's three-strip process. Technicolor was expensive, however, requiring special cam-eras and three times as much film as one shot in black and white. It was largely replaced by Eastman Kodak's East-mancolor in the 1950s. On Eastmancolor, all colors could be faithfully reproduced on one strip of film that had three layers, each sensitive to one of the primary colors.

Edison's Kinetograph camera produced more than 5,000 films, among them the film most historians call the first U.S. film to tell a story, Edwin Porter's *The Great Train Robbery* (1903). By 1910, camera manufacturers such as Pathé and Bell and Howell had invented simpler, more compact and portable cameras that soon eclipsed the Kine-tograph as the choice of cinematographers. Nearly all these cameras were hand-cranked. The operator advanced the mechanism by turning a lever rather than relying on electricity. Operators were amazingly accurate, could maintain the proper speed of 16 frames per second, and could change speed easily. A cinematographer could crank a little faster to produce a slow-motion or lyrical effect, for example. By the mid-1920s, the Mitchell Camera Corporation began manufacturing large, precision cameras that produced steadier images than had been possible previously. These cameras became the industry standard for almost 30 years. From the 1950s, Panavision cameras were preferred by most U.S. cinematographers.

In the first two decades of motion pictures, nearly all films were photographed outdoors, with Edison's Black Maria facility in New Jersey the most famous early site. As the industry moved to California and became larger, and especially as films became longer than the 10 to 20 minutes common before 1913, more control of lighting became necessary. Soundstages were built with suspended ceiling grids to hold hundreds of lights, called luminaires. In the 1920s, the Mole-Richardson Company established itself in Hollywood and became the most well-known supplier of luminaires to the studios – of every conceivable size, from the 50-watt "inky-dink" to the 21,000-watt carbon-arc light aptly called the "Brute." The company still supplied luminaires to the industry, for both studio and location use, in the late twentieth century.

As films became longer and pressures to increase output increased, mechanical devices to help edit film in post-production were needed to improve the productivity of editors. The Moviola editing device became an industry standard and remained so until the 1970s. It sat upright in the editing room, and the editor fed film through one of the picture plates on the machine. It could handle several pieces of film at the same time, and when the sound era came, it could edit a soundtrack in synchronization with the picture. In the 1970s, flatbed editing machines manufactured by such companies as Steenbeck made editing more reliable and faster. Later, editing devices based on videotape technology and computers became the norm. The most prominent "nonlinear" (digital) editing company of the 1990s was AVID.

As early as 1891, William Dickson and Thomas Edison explored ways to add sound to their Kinetograph camera, but they abandoned their efforts because Edison felt that there was no future to sound in the cinema. Although the period until the mid-1920s is considered the "silent" era in U.S. motion pictures, few films in major theaters actually were shown completely without sound. Pianists or organ-

Later model 35 mm film camera for cinematography
(Ikegami Electronics [U.S.A.] Inc.)

ists performed – sometimes full orchestras played in large cities – actors spoke the lines of characters in the films, and even machines and performers created sound effects. What these performances lacked was fully synchronized sound contained within a soundtrack on the film itself.

By 1926–27, experimenters had demonstrated the viability of synchronizing sound with projected film. When Warner Brothers in 1927 released *The Jazz Singer,* containing some synchronized dialog and music using their Vitaphone process, the public and the industry were taken by storm. Sound revolutionized a highly developed and sophisticated system of Hollywood production. Recording voices and sounds became more important than cinematography; theaters had to add sound equipment; distributors had the extra expense of producing soundtracks for their released films. By 1931, however, virtually all films produced in the United States contained synchronized soundtracks. The Vitaphone system was replaced by more reliable sound systems such as Movietone and Western Electric, which reproduced sounds along the edge of the film as an optical track.

Over the next 20 years, sound recording techniques became much more sophisticated, allowing subtleties within soundtracks that few thought possible when the industry made its transition to sound between 1927 and 1931. In the 1950s, stereophonic sound became popular throughout the industry, mostly to accompany wide-screen techniques. Stereophonic sound had been introduced to the viewing public by Walt Disney's *Fantasia* in 1940, but the film's premiere had required the installation of special equipment in selected theaters, the cost of which was high. Stereophonic sound had distinct right and left channels, so sound could be localized and reproduced much as humans hear sound with a right and a left ear. The reproduction of sound became more realistic.

Many developments in sound have occurred since the 1950s. Dolby systems greatly reduced the amount of noise audible on soundtracks. Later, the directionality and intensity of the sound experience in theaters became notable. Surround-sound systems designed by Sony, Dolby, and THX allowed sound to be fully directional within the theater: for example, if a character in a film screamed offscreen behind the viewer, the scream would come from a loudspeaker from the rear of the theater. Improvements in the ability to record and reproduce the dynamic range of sound, the full spectrum of loudness from very soft to very loud, and extremely low frequencies through subwoofers produced sound experiences that audiences not only heard but felt. Many systems in the 1990s were using digital technology such as Sony Dynamic Digital Sound, Dolby Stereo Digital, and Digital Theater Systems.

The shape of the motion picture frame – the image that is recorded and seen by an audience – was set by Edison at an aspect ratio of 4:3. The image, in other words, is 4 units wide by 3 units high, or slighter wider than it is higher. To the eye, this aspect ratio is more pleasing than a box (a ratio of 3:3 or 4:4). It has been a long-lived standard, the most common aspect ratio for most films until the 1960s, and it was still the aspect ratio of broadcast television into the twenty-first century.

By the 1920s, filmmakers were trying novel ways to ex-

pand the frame horizontally, to make it wider, more like the vista one would see with the human eye including its peripheral vision. Twentieth Century-Fox, Warner Brothers, and MGM all brought out movies in that decade on films larger than 35 millimeters, making the image wider, but converting theaters to nonstandard formats was impractical.

The impetus for wide-screen technology to be adopted throughout the industry in the 1950s was television, because films were losing money at the box office. What films could offer that television could not was spectacle and an image much wider than that seen on the home screen. Twentieth Century-Fox's release of *The Robe* in 1953 in the wide-screen Cinemascope process was exactly the sort of spectacular success the industry needed. The film was on 35-millimeter film but with a special anamorphic lens that squeezed the image horizontally. Upon theatrical release, an identical anamorphic lens on the projector unsqueezed the image, producing a horizontal image with a ratio of 2.55:1, almost twice as wide as a standard aspect ratio of 4:3 (or, 1.33:1). Other companies began producing wide-screen films using similar anamorphic processes such as Panascope and Superscope.

Other widescreen systems employed 65-millimeter or 70-millimeter film. One such system was Todd-AO, which was used for several blockbuster movies, the most famous of which were *Oklahoma!* (1955) and *Around the World in 80 Days* (1956). Todd-AO permitted the use of six stereophonic soundtracks, and the visual wide-screen effect was impressive, but the costs of distribution and exhibition were

Proper lighting is important for motion picture production. (Courtesy of Arriflex Corporation)

high. Todd-AO and other formats using film wider than 35 millimeters came to be used little by the industry. In fact, wide-screen formats tended to shrink in the 1960s, and the majority of wide-screen films came out in a modest ratio of 1.85:1.

The idea of using multiple cameras to create a wide-screen effect had occurred to filmmaker Abel Gance in 1927. He created his *Napoleon* on three adjacent screens, called triptychs, sometimes showing entirely separate images, and at other times blending the images together in one sweeping vista. In 1952, Fred Waller introduced *This is Cinerama,* which used the same principle: three cameras side-by-side filming the action; three projectors in the theater beaming the three images to a gracefully curved screen. The effect was majestic, and Cinerama films tended to be travelogues and roller-coaster rides that showed off the technology. Cinerama expired as a three-screen technology in the 1960s, but documentarian Michael Wadleigh used triptychs in his film *Woodstock* (1970). In the 1980s and 1990s, IMAX films appeared on 70-millimeter film for specialized theaters that had an even more spectacular and audience-involving result: the audience was literally surrounded by the imagery and immersed in a multiple-channel surround-sound environment.

Stereoscopy and three-dimensional (3-D) cinematography have been relatively unsuccessful attempts at creating depth in an otherwise flat image. The effect was demonstrated as early as 1922 in a feature film called *The Power of Love.* Most people associate this process with the tinted glasses worn at horror films such as *House of Wax* (1953). 3-D movies were still made decades later for special short films at Disney theme parks, but they were no longer part of the feature-film production process. Cinematographers and directors used special compositional techniques to create the feeling of depth in their imagery rather than relying on costly, artificial means of stereoscopy or 3-D.

The ability to create illusions on the screen has fascinated filmmakers since the 1890s, when it was discovered that running film twice through a camera produced unusual double exposures. Special effects are usually divided into two groups: mechanical and optical. Since the 1980s, computers have added digital options.

Mechanical effects include those devices used to make rain, wind, cobwebs, fog, snow, and explosions. Optical effects allow images to be combined – for example, the animated figure of the ape in *King Kong* (1933) with live-action cinematography. The combination is achieved through creation of traveling mattes run through an optical printer. The matte masks off an area of the film frame during original filming in the camera or optical printing. In subsequent passes through the printer, imagery is inserted into the masked-out areas.

A watershed in special effects was Stanley Kubrick's *2001: A Space Odyssey* (1968). Special effects coordinator Douglas Trumbull used a number of innovative techniques, including front projection, slit-scan cinematography for the "Star Gate" sequence, and sophisticated traveling mattes to combine miniatures of spacecraft with live action. With this film, special effects as well as science fiction was revitalized. In 1977, *Star Wars* had a similar result. Director George

Lucas's special effects team created some brilliant effects. His team, in fact, formed the first company specializing just in special effects, Industrial Light and Magic.

In the 1980s, stunning special effects began to be created on computers, especially animated effects. Examples include Disney's *Tron* (1982) and the imagery of a stained glass man coming alive in *Young Sherlock Holmes* (1985). *Dragonheart* (1996) was a later and more remarkable example of the ability of computer imagery to be combined seamlessly and believably with live-action visuals. Most computer-made films, however, are short subjects.

In the 1980s, a convergence of video technology and cinema technology began. Motion picture camera viewfinders, for example, had video cameras attached to them; this "video assist" allowed cinematographers to record shots on both film and videotape, the latter permitting directors to see each take as it happens or view it back immediately. In postproduction, video equipment and computers created nonlinear environments that allowed editors to edit film much more quickly: film was transferred to videotape, then edited on tape rather than on film. Sound and pictures also could be placed on massive hard drives of computers and edited even more quickly.

Perhaps most importantly, a new field arose: electronic cinematography. High-quality video cameras were used in place of cinema cameras for some projects. Some of these cameras used high-definition television (HDTV) technology. Examples were Ikegami's EC-35 and EC-1135 cameras. Such cameras produced excellent imagery, and they were used for some television commercials and made-for-television movies, but they did not immediately substitute for film cameras for theatrical-release motion pictures. For the cinematographer – and the viewing audience – the look, feel, and quality of motion picture imagery was lost when HDTV was used.

Some observers of the industry felt that motion picture technology would shift entirely to video technology in the future, based primarily on HDTV or some form of advanced television. It was unlikely such a transition would be made for many years, if at all. Motion picture film provides much more detail and image resolution than any video system that was available or in development at the end of the twentieth century. In addition, the film industry was essentially conservative in its adoption of new technology. Video systems would clearly have an increased role in the film production process, however, especially for special effects and postproduction.

JOHN P. FREEMAN

See also Animated Motion Pictures; Photographic Technology; Silent Motion Pictures; Sound Motion Pictures

Further Reading
Brownlow, Kevin, and John Kobal, *Hollywood: The Pioneers,* New York: Knopf, 1979; London: Collins, 1979
Coe, Brian, *The History of Movie Photography,* Westfield, New Jersey: Eastview Editions, 1981; London: Ash and Grant, 1981

"The Expanding Digital Domain: Cinematography, Special Effects, Sound, Editing, Postproduction," *American Cinematographer* special issue 74:4 (1993)

Mathias, Harry, and Richard Patterson, *Electronic Cinematography: Achieving Photographic Control over the Video Image*, Belmont, California: Wadsworth, 1985

Salt, Barry, *Film Style and Technology: History and Analysis*, 2nd ed., London: Starword, 1992

Motion Picture Trade Organizations

While there were numerous trade organizations involved in the motion picture industry by the end of the twentieth century, one of the oldest and best known was the Motion Picture Association of America (MPAA). This organization was originally founded in 1922; it was known then and until 1945 as the Motion Picture Producers and Distributors of America (MPPDA). The MPAA in the 1990s was composed of eight producers and distributors of motion pictures in the United States: Sony Pictures Entertainment; Buena Vista Pictures Distributors; Metro-Goldwyn-Mayer; Paramount Pictures Corporation; Turner Pictures; Twentieth Century-Fox Film Corporation; Universal City Studios; and Warner Brothers. The organization's mission was to establish and maintain high moral and artistic standards in motion picture production by developing the educational as well as entertainment value and general usefulness of the motion picture. The MPAA maintained the Motion Picture Association Political Action Committee and was affiliated with the Alliance of Motion Picture and Television Producers. The MPAA met annually.

The MPPDA grew out of an industry attempt to control the negative image the motion picture industry and its movie stars had made for itself by the early 1920s. The movie moguls, rocked by scandals involving Roscoe "Fatty" Arbuckle and others, established the MPPDA in January 1922. The industry, the moguls believed, needed a clean image to combat the host of censorship bills presented at the state and federal levels.

The organization hired William Harrison (Will) Hays, the postmaster general in President Warren Harding's cabinet and chairman of the Republican National Committee, to reshape Hollywood's image. The Hays Office, as the MPPDA came to be known, was highly successful as a public relations agency, rebuilding the public's perception of the motion picture industry. As Gregory Black wrote, however, Hays was not so successful in getting the industry to change the content of its films. Many civic-minded moralists – Roman Catholics, educators, citizens' groups, to name a few – protested what they considered to be immoral portrayals of loose sexual attitudes and violent behavior. Black wrote that Hays was not successful in controlling the content because movie producers were reluctant to allow him to interfere with film production.

ROBIN GALLAGHER

See also Censorship of Motion Pictures; Motion Picture Ratings

Further Reading

Black, Gregory, *Hollywood Censored: Morality Codes, Catholics, and the Movies,* New York and Cambridge: Cambridge University Press, 1994

Motion Picture Trade Press

In the early years of motion pictures, there were three main sources of entertainment news: the *Hollywood Reporter, Daily Variety,* and the various fan magazines. The first two publications prided themselves on accurate reporting of the film world, with a few puff pieces. The fan magazines, however, more closely resembled tabloid-style journalism.

Variety was founded in 1905 by Sime and Hattie Silverman in New York as an entertainment weekly covering vaudeville and the legitimate theater. By this time, however, nickelodeon movie theaters were becoming popular and giving the stage much competition. *Variety*'s first movie reviews, of a seven-minute comedy and a 13-minute melodrama, appeared on January 19, 1907. Sime Silverman established *Daily Variety* in Hollywood in 1933, continuing his journalistic approach to film reporting.

William R. (Billy) Wilkerson began publishing the first daily independent film trade paper in Hollywood, the *Hollywood Reporter,* on September 3, 1930. Prior to its birth, the major studios carefully controlled and manipulated the news filtering from their lots. Wilkerson changed that by reporting objectively on feuds, delays, financing, marriages, and other sensitive topics. Meeting resistance at first, the paper slowly gained the industry as an ally, enabling it to thrive through cooperation on stories and advertising. Celebrity bylines became commonplace in the paper, including those of Gary Cooper, Mickey Rooney, and John Barrymore.

The fan magazines, more subjective and shallow in content, began with *Photoplay* in 1911. Similar publications with names such as *Silver Screen* and *Modern Screen* flourished until the 1940s.

ANTHONY HATCHER

Further Reading

Levin, Martin, ed., *Hollywood and the Great Fan Magazines,* New York: Arbor House, 1970

Wilkerson, Tichi, and Marcia Borie, *The Hollywood Reporter: The Golden Years,* New York: Coward-McCann, 1984

Other Motion Picture Entries:

Animated Motion Pictures; Audience Research for Motion Pictures; *Birth of a Nation, The;* Budget (B) Movies; Censorship of Motion Pictures; Docudramas; Economics of Motion Pictures; Hollywood in World War II;

Hollywood/Radio Controversy of 1932; Hollywood Studio System; Silent Motion Pictures; Sound Motion Pictures

Muckraking

Investigative reporting pushes various kinds of reform

In the first decade of the twentieth century, a new type of journalism emerged from the demands for political, economic, and social reform to answer the problems accompanying urbanization, immigration, and industrialization. This new journalism, which was tied intrinsically to progressivism, had as its goal searching out and publicly exposing real or apparent misconduct, vice, or corruption. Presenting the facts in a dramatic writing style with critical indignation tempered by optimism, the exposure reporters came to be known as muckrakers.

Many of the writers were college educated and had provincial beginnings tempered by experiences in major cities. Young, urbane, and successful, they believed in morality, Puritan righteousness, and social Darwinism. Most were of the middle class, which was becoming increasingly critical of the concentrations of power. They sought reform of corrupt institutions, attacked the human evildoers who profited by their misdeeds, and exposed the abuses often associated with great wealth. Historian Richard Hofstedter said that muckraking journalists provided the underpinnings for the Progressive movement as they sought to arouse the public to demand the end of abuses and the downfall of the evildoers.

Josiah Flynt (Josiah Frank Willard) has been credited with starting the move toward exposure reporting in 1900 with his "True Stories of the Underworld." He was joined by the premier rank of the muckrakers – Ida Tarbell, Lincoln Steffens, and Ray Stannard Baker. They all worked for *McClure's* magazine, whose mercurial leader, S.S. McClure, provided a major platform for exposure. In one extraordinary issue, January 1903, Tarbell ran the third chapter of her series exposing business abuses by John D. Rockefeller and his company in "The History of the Standard Oil Company"; Steffens wrote "The Shame of Minneapolis," continuing an attack on political corruption in U.S. cities; and Baker discussed right-to-work laws in an effort to expose labor abuses. McClure added an editorial decrying U.S. contempt for the law. With this edition, muckraking became a force.

Other journalists and magazines were attracted to the form. Samuel Hopkins Adams attacked the multimillion-dollar patent medicine business and quack medicine peddlers. William Hard exposed child labor and industry practices. Burton J. Hendrick focused on corruption in New York life insurance companies. Will Irwin concentrated on politics and newspapers. Thomas Lawson, in "Frenzied Finance," sought the reform of the money markets and Wall Street. Alfred Henry Lewis examined the careers of the leading millionaires in the United States. Charles Ed-

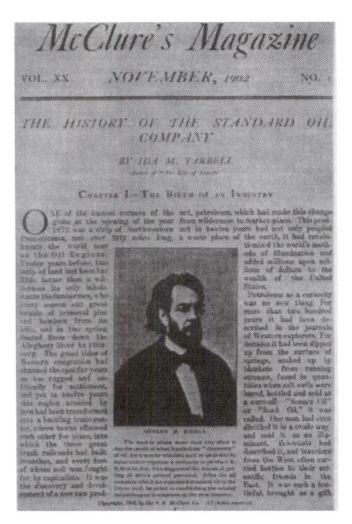

McClure's Magazine led the field in the journalism of exposure.

ward Russell sought the radical reform of Socialism to combat slum landlords, monopolies, legislative graft, and the railroads. William Allen White pushed for political reform.

They and their colleagues wrote at least 2,000 articles in magazines such as *American, Arena, Collier's, Cosmopolitan, Everybody's, Hampton's, Pearson's,* and the short-lived *Ridgway's.* It has been estimated the combined circulation of the magazines reached 3 million a month, but the impact was far greater because of the normal practice of nonmuckraking magazines and many newspapers to copy or print excerpts from the published exposés. The magazines, and some newspapers, made a considerable commitment to muckraking in terms of resources for preparing the articles. Given new freedom with ample space, time, and money, most muckrakers accepted the responsibility of getting the facts, often using new techniques of reporting. They coupled traditional interviews and observation with heavy use of official documents, the advice of experts, and a wide variety of printed materials.

The exposures often were energetic, fueled with indigna-

WOMAN CAN HEALTH OF WOMAN
SYMPATHIZE WITH IS THE HOPE OF
WOMAN. THE RACE

Yours for Health—
Lydia E. Pinkham

LYDIA E. PINKHAM'S
VEGETABLE COMPOUND.

A Sure Cure for all FEMALE WEAK-
NESSES, Including Leucorrhœa, Irregular and Painful Menstruation,
Inflammation and Ulceration of
the Womb, Flooding, PRO-

Lydia Pinkham's patent medicines were a prime target of muckraking journalists.

tion and a varying amount of facts. The use of literary forms such as dialogue and metaphor allowed the muckrakers to highlight drama and excitement in their work without the need for sensationalism or hearsay. One series, David Graham Phillips' "Treason of the Senate," which was stronger on style than facts, so irked President Theodore Roosevelt that the popular president came to the defense of the Senate by attacking the exposure writers and hanging the label of "muckraker" on them.

In a March 1906 dinner speech given in the Gridiron Club off-the-record style, Roosevelt first issued his criticism. Then, prodded by favorable comment on that speech, he repeated his charges in a later well-publicized speech at the dedication of the House Office Building. Quoting from John Bunyan's *Pilgrim's Progress,* the president, who had seen the exposure journalists as supporters and then as

usurpers of his progressivism, attacked them for not knowing when to stop raking the muck. Although some credit Ellery Sedgwick of *McClure's* and later the *Atlantic Monthly* as the originator of the epithet "muckraker," Roosevelt's use of the term made it stick.

Reactions by the muckrakers was mixed, with Phillips and Steffens upset and Adams and Russell proud. Although the Roosevelt criticism did not deflate the muckraking balloon, it did provide a slow leak. The slow descent began as the muckraking, and the progressive energy, waned among the reporters and the middle-class readers. Some writers crossed the line between fact and fiction as Upton Sinclair had in 1906 when his novel, *The Jungle,* had exposed abuses in meatpacking houses. His novel, which raised public ire about food purity, and the series by Adams demanding patent medicine labeling helped gain the 1906 passage of the Pure Food and Drug Act. It became one of the few examples of an attempted legislative remedy to problems exposed by the muckrakers, who usually were content just to bare the evils rather than offer concrete actions to end them.

By World War I, progressivism and muckraking were subsumed into international concerns. Following the war, the public sought normalcy, not reform. Most of the muckraking reporters moved to new topics like biography and new forms like fiction. But the label remained, and many writers since have adopted the term to describe their investigative reporting.

SAMUEL V. KENNEDY III

See also Investigative Reporting

Further Reading
Chalmers, David, *The Social and Political Ideas of the Muckrakers,* New York: Citadel, 1964
Chamberlain, John, *Farewell to Reform,* New York: John Day, 1933
Filler, Louis, *The Muckrakers,* University Park: Pennsylvania State University Press, 1976
Harrison, John M., and Harry H. Stein, eds., *Muckraking: Past, Present, and Future,* University Park: Pennsylvania State University Press, 1973
Miraldi, Robert, *Muckraking and Objectivity; Journalism's Colliding Traditions,* New York and London: Greenwood, 1990
Regier, Cornelius, *The Era of the Muckrakers,* Chapel Hill: University of North Carolina Press, 1932
Shapiro, Herbert, comp., *The Muckrakers and American Society,* Boston: D.C. Heath, 1968
Weinberg, Arthur, and Lila Shaffer Weinberg, eds., *The Muckrakers,* New York: Simon & Schuster, 1961

Munsey, Frank A.

Businessman invades newspapering

Frank A. Munsey towered over U.S. publishing during the decades surrounding the turn of the twentieth century. Ironically for a man who sometimes edited and wrote for his own publications, Munsey left his biggest mark on the media by adopting the profit-maximizing ways of the industrialists he so admired.

Born on a Maine farm, Munsey arrived in New York in 1882 with only $40 and a dream. That same year, he borrowed money to start the weekly *Golden Argosy,* which later became the first pulp magazine. His flagship, *Munsey's Magazine,* begun in 1884, took off in 1893 when he dropped the price from 25 cents to 10 cents and started his own distribution company. This general interest magazine was illustrated liberally but contained writing of uneven quality. It avoided muckraking because Munsey considered that popular movement destructive. Circulation grew to more than 700,000 in 1897 but tailed off by the 1920s, when *Munsey's* merged into a renamed fiction format.

Munsey's attempts to build newspaper chains earned him both political stature and the enduring ire of journalists. Over time, he owned 18 newspapers, among them New York's *Herald* and *Sun.* His actions led to the death of half of them and weakened others. When Munsey died after surgery for appendicitis, Kansas editor William Allen White wrote: "Munsey contributed to the journalism of his day the talent of a meat packer, the morals of a money changer and the manners of an undertaker." Later opinion, however, portrayed Munsey as a typical entrepreneur of the period.

JONATHAN Y. HILL

Further Reading
Britt, George, *Forty Years – Forty Millions: The Career of Frank A. Munsey,* Port Washington, New York: Kennikat, 1972
Munsey, Frank A., *The Founding of the Munsey Publishing-House,* New York: De Vinne, 1907

Murdoch, Rupert

Builder of media empire

Beginning in the 1950s, Australian native Rupert Murdoch built a newspaper, magazine, television, satellite, movie, and book publishing empire on four continents, with a foundation of lively, sensationalistic, and sometimes lurid newspapers. The News International Group Ltd. of London and the News Corporation Ltd. of Sydney, Australia, were the two principal companies that controlled Murdoch's media, including U.S. newspaper and broadcasting outlets, the *Times* of London, HarperCollins books, and Hong Kong's *South China Morning Post.*

Rupert Murdoch's father, Sir Keith Murdoch, was a Melbourne editor with newspaper holdings in Adelaide and Brisbane. A graduate of Oxford University, Rupert Murdoch spent a short internship at Lord Beaverbrook's London *Daily Express* after his father died in 1952 and took over his family's small-circulation Adelaide *News and Sunday Mail.* He added newspapers in Perth and Sydney, with

the Perth paper becoming Murdoch's first opportunity to launch sensationalistic mass appeal.

A U.S. citizen since 1974, Murdoch acknowledged that his worldwide media, especially television, help to homogenize the globe with U.S. culture. He argued, however, that a unified world would be more peaceful.

Murdoch ventured into U.S. journalism in 1973 with the purchase of the *San Antonio (Texas) News* and *Express,* followed by the *New York Post* (1976), *New York Magazine* (1977), and the *Boston Herald* (1982). He formed the Fox television network in 1987 from his Twentieth Century-Fox movie company and his Metromedia broadcasting properties. In 1988, he purchased Triangle Publications, including the high-circulation magazines *TV Guide, Seventeen,* and the *Daily Racing Form.* He also launched the tabloid *National Star* to compete with the *National Enquirer.*

JAMES BOW

Further Reading
Heenan, Patrick, "News Corporation Limited," in *International Directory of Company Histories,* vol. 7, edited by Paula Kepos, Detroit, Michigan, and London: St. James, 1993
Kiernan, Thomas, *Citizen Murdoch,* New York: Dodd, Mead, 1986
Leapman, Michael, *Barefaced Cheek: The Apotheosis of Rupert Murdoch,* London: Hodder and Stoughton, 1983; also published as *Arrogant Aussie: The Rupert Murdoch Story,* Secaucus, New Jersey: L. Stuart, 1985
Shawcross, William, *Rupert Murdoch: Ringmaster of the Information Circus,* London: Chatto and Windus, 1992; also published as *Murdoch,* New York: Simon & Schuster, 1993

Murrow, Edward R.

CBS radio and television news correspondent

Egbert Roscoe Murrow was born in Polecat Creek, North Carolina, and moved with his family to Washington state. A leader at what later became Washington State University, he joined the Institute of International Education after graduation. Hired by CBS Radio on the eve of World War II, he recruited an able staff of foreign correspondents to cover unfolding events. His *This Is London* series brought the Battle of Britain into the living rooms of U.S. listeners.

After the war, he collaborated with Fred Friendly on CBS radio and television documentaries. His *See It Now* program often is cited as representing the best of broadcast news, as the prototype for television documentary programs. His "Report on Senator Joseph R. McCarthy" was perhaps the most controversial broadcast of the early era of television news; using video clips of McCarthy, it included Murrow's strong condemnation of his activity. Critics debate the appropriateness of Murrow's approach to the McCarthy program.

Edward R. Murrow
(Museum of Broadcast Communications)

His other series, *Person to Person,* was regarded as a lightweight celebrity interview series, but it was very popular with television audiences. Murrow shared in the financial success of this series, a fact that became very controversial later in broadcasting circles, especially after Murrow criticized his fellow broadcasters for being too preoccupied with their earnings.

Murrow left CBS just before his death in 1965 to serve in John F. Kennedy's administration as director of the U.S. Information Agency. The U.S. Postal Service issued a Murrow stamp in 1994 – the first broadcaster to be so honored.

MICHAEL D. MURRAY

Further Reading

Kendrick, Alexander, *Prime Time: The Life of Edward R. Murrow,* Boston: Little, Brown, 1969; London: Dent, 1970

Murray, Michael, *The Political Performers: CBS Broadcasts in the Public Interest,* Westport, Connecticut: Praeger, 1994

Murrow, Edward R., *In Search of Light: The Broadcasts of Edward R. Murrow, 1938–1961,* New York: Knopf, 1967; London and Melbourne, Australia: Macmillan, 1968

Sperber, Ann M., *Murrow: His Life and Times,* New York: Freundlich, 1986; London: Joseph, 1987

N

Nast, Thomas

Cartoonist and caricaturist

Perhaps more than any other individual, Thomas Nast proved the power of the pen in the hand of an able cartoonist and caricaturist. His work still lives in such familiar symbols as the Democratic donkey and Republican elephant, patriotic Uncle Sam, and a jolly Santa Claus bearing holiday gifts. But Nast's drawings, most of which appeared in *Harper's Weekly* between 1862 and 1886, also influenced public opinion about the events of his time.

Nast's most important work in *Harper's* focused on the American Civil War and, later, on the Tammany Hall political machine in New York City with telling effectiveness. Noting the recruits lured to the Union army by his patriotic cartoons, President Abraham Lincoln called Nast "our best recruiting sergeant." General Ulysses S. Grant said he "did as much as any one man to preserve the Union and bring the war to an end."

In his crusade against Tammany Hall, featured from 1869 to 1871 in *Harper's*, Nast found himself locked in battle with William Marcy Tweed – "Boss Tweed" – the prototype kingpin of big-city machine politics. Nast and his publishing benefactor, Fletcher Harper, ignored threats of violence and bribes; they discredited Tweed and, with help from the *New York Times*, brought Tammany Hall to its knees. Afterwards, the *Times* claimed that Nast's cartoons had been "the most powerful of all the engines directed against the stronghold of civic shame." Tweed paid Nast the ultimate compliment, saying, "I don't care a straw for your newspaper articles; my constituents don't know how to read, but they can't help seeing them damned pictures."

Nast drew with detail and precision. Authorities who captured Tweed in Vigo, Spain, claimed that they had recognized him from a Nast cartoon. Nast provided continuity to his campaign through repeated use of the Tammany tiger as a visual symbol and by variously illustrating Tweed's favorite utterances: "What are you going to do about it?" and, "It will all blow over."

Born on September 27, 1840, in Landau, Bavaria, Nast immigrated to New York City in 1846. At age 15, he began a three-year stint with *Leslie's Weekly*, followed by assignments in 1859 for *Harper's Weekly* and the *New York Illustrated News*. The *News* sent him abroad to illustrate the Italian nationalist revolutionary Giuseppe Garibaldi's campaign to liberate Italy from the Austrians. Returning to New York, Nast married Sarah Edwards on September 26, 1861. They had five children. His wife provided him with unwavering moral support and ideas and captions for many cartoons. Nast joined *Harper's* as a staff artist in July 1862 and began illustrating the Civil War.

This Thomas Nast drawing of Boss Tweed ultimately led to the politician's arrest.

(Reproduced from the Collections of the Library of Congress)

A TRAITOR'S PEACE

THAT THE

NORTHERN COPPERHEAD LEADERS WOULD FORCE UPON THE COUNTRY.

COMPROMISE *WITH THE SOUTH*

IN MEMORY UNION HEROES IN A USELESS WAR

NORTH

SOUTH

[FROM NASTER'S WEEKLY.]

THE REBEL TERMS OF PEACE!!

Citizens of the United States! The Copperhead Politicians of our country are crying out for "peace on any terms," and they tell you it is a very easy matter to "compromise with our misguided Southern brethren." To clearly understand the position of the enemy, read the following "CONDITIONS OF PEACE" on which the official organ of the rebel government, the Richmond *Enquirer* of October 16, 1863, proposes to *settle and have "peace:"*

"Save on our own terms, we can accept no peace whatever, and must fight till doomsday rather than yield one iota of them; and our terms are:

"Recognition by the enemy of the Independence of the Confederate States.

"Withdrawal of Yankee forces from every foot of Confederate ground, including KENTUCKY and MISSOURI.

"Withdrawal of Yankee soldiers from MARYLAND, until that State shall decide, by a free vote, whether she shall remain in the old Union, or ask admission into the Confederacy.

"Consent on the part of the Federal Government to give up to the Confederacy its proportion of the Navy as it stood at the time of secession, or to pay for the same.

"Yielding up all pretensions on the part of the Federal Government to that portion of the old Territories which lies west of the Confederate States.

"An equitable settlement, on the basis of our absolute independence and equal rights, of all accounts of the Public Debt and Public Lands, and the advantages accruing from foreign treaties.

"These provisions, we apprehend, comprise the minimum of what we must require before we lay down our arms. That is to say, THE NORTH MUST YIELD ALL; WE NOTHING. The whole pretension of that country to prevent by force the separation of the States must be abandoned, which will be equivalent to an avowal that our enemies were wrong from the first; and, of course, as they waged a causeless and wicked war upon us, they, ought, in strict justice, to be required, according to usage in such cases, to reimburse to us the whole of our expenses and losses in the course of that war."

These are the terms of peace, and the "Enquirer" says further—

"As surely as we completely ruin their armies—and without that is no peace nor truce at all—SO SURELY SHALL WE MAKE THEM PAY OUR WAR DEBT, THOUGH WE WRING IT OUT OF THEIR HEARTS."

Citizens of the United States! These are the terms of peace to which you are invited by the Copperhead politicians of the country —the destruction of the Union—the giving up of Maryland, Kentucky, and Missouri, which have all voted by immense majorities for the Union—the surrender of a large part fo our Navy—the loss of more than one half of our territory, *and the payment of the debt of the accursed rebellion of traitors,* by having it "WRUNG OUT OF OUR HEARTS!"

People of the United States! Will you give your assent to such a base surrender of our cause? If not, then repel the "Peace Organizations," and rally only with those who "keep step to the music of the Union," who stand by our brave soldiers in the field, and are for "Liberty and Union, now and forever, one and inseparable."

PRINTED FOR CONGRESSIONAL UNION COMMITTEE, WASHINGTON, D. C.

☞ **Please post this up.**

McGill & Witherow, Printers, Washington, D. C.

Thomas Nast was also the leading Union propagandist during the Civil War, with his illustrations depicting the heartbreak of war.

(Reproduced from the Collections of the Library of Congress)

After Tammany, Nast drew for *Harper's* until December 1886, losing most of his assets through unwise investments. The last of these occurred in 1892, when he obtained the *New York Gazette,* changing its name to *Nast's Weekly* and borrowing funds to keep it alive for just a few months.

Desperate for money, Nast accepted President Theodore Roosevelt's $4,000 appointment as consul general in Guayaquil, Ecuador, in May 1902. He died there of yellow fever on December 7, 1902, at age 62.

GLENN A. HIMEBAUGH

See also Cartoons and Cartoonists; Civil War Press (North); Illustrated Newspapers

Further Reading

Keller, Morton, *The Art and Politics of Thomas Nast,* New York: Oxford University Press, 1968; London: Oxford University Press, 1975

Nast St. Hill, Thomas, "His Grandson Recalls: The Life and Death of Thomas Nast," *American Heritage* 22 (1971)

Paine, Albert Bigelow, *Th. Nast: His Period and His Pictures,* New York and London: Harper, 1904; also published as *Thomas Nast, His Period and His Pictures,* New York: Chelsea House, 1980

Vinson, John Chalmers, *Thomas Nast, Political Cartoonist,* Athens: University of Georgia Press, 1967

National Advertising Review Board

Mechanism designed to promote self-regulation in advertising industry

The National Advertising Review Board (NARB) came into existence in 1971. It was conceived and funded by various constituencies of the advertising trade as a mechanism of self-regulation dealing with misleading and deceptive national advertising. It was housed within the offices of the Council of Better Business Bureaus in New York City.

It was a two-tiered organization. Although the NARB was more widely known, the vast majority of the work was done by a related body, the National Advertising Division (NAD). This body had a staff of 10 people who received and reviewed complaints regarding specific advertisements. These complaints might come from consumers, consumer organizations, or competitors. The NAD also monitored the media and generated complaints internally.

If a complaint disputing the claims made for a specific product was deemed worthy of investigation, the advertiser was contacted and substantiation for the claim in question was requested. Advertising review specialists at the NAD (all lawyers) reviewed materials, and if the advertiser could substantiate the claim made for its product, the case was dismissed. If substantiation was deemed inadequate, the advertiser would be asked to modify the claim or discontinue the advertising. The NAD rendered its decision within 90 days of the receipt of the original complaint. Since it was a self-regulatory body, it avoided many of the legal procedures that encumbered the federal regulatory agencies. Although substantiation materials provided by advertisers were often technical and detailed, the NAD attempted to render decisions on the basis of whether the average consumer would be misled by the advertisement.

Through 1994, the NAD had handled approximately 2,500 cases. The percentage of cases resulting in modified or discontinued advertising as the result of an adverse action by the NAD increased over the years. During the 1970s, approximately 50 to 60 percent of the cases resulted in modification or discontinuance. The percentage increased during the 1980s, and by the 1990s, approximately 70 percent of all cases resulted in modification or discontinuance. The source of the complaints leading to cases also changed over the years. Over its history, the NAD generated approximately 40 percent of all its cases from monitoring. An additional 40 percent came from competitors, and approximately 20 percent came from consumers and consumer organizations.

The NARB served as a court of appeals. An advertiser that had been asked by the NAD to modify or discontinue an ad could request a second hearing of the case from the NARB. The NAD might also request an appeal if the advertiser refused to comply with an adverse verdict. Relatively few cases were appealed to the NARB. Of the 2,500 cases handled by the NAD, only 84 were appealed by the end of 1994.

The NARB had a permanent staff consisting of the chair and one support person. In addition, there were 80 members of the NARB who served two-year appointments and could be elected to serve one additional term. These people were high-ranking individuals from major corporations and advertising agencies or distinguished members of the general public. When an appeal came to the NARB, a five-member panel was selected from the pool to hear the case. As a court of appeals, the NARB panel had the right to confirm or overturn the decision rendered by the NAD. If the advertiser could not substantiate its claims at this level, modification or discontinuance of the ad was requested. Most advertisers complied. If they proved recalcitrant, the NARB forwarded the case file to the appropriate government agency. Historically, this has almost never happened. Between 1991 and 1994, however, the NARB did turn 11 cases over to the government – the most stringent sanction the organization could employ. Antitrust laws make it clear that self-regulatory activities of a trade must be voluntary and that punishment, such as fines or imprisonment, can only be meted out by formal government bodies.

Over its history, the two-tiered organization had both critics and supporters. Early critics charged that such a trade-funded body would be incapable of impartial resolution of claims and would be little more than window dressing for the advertising establishment. However, the large number of cases that resulted in modified or discontinued advertising seemed to blunt that criticism. Another criticism was that advertisers would refuse to abide by decisions because the NAD and NARB had no punitive powers. The vast majority of advertisers accepted the decisions rendered by the NAD and the NARB. Critics also contended that the organization primarily was geared to handling internecine wrangling within the trade and that the general public was largely unaware of its existence. There was substance to this criticism; as noted, a relatively small percentage of the cases came from consumer complaints. Moreover, the organization made no concerted large-scale effort to make itself known to the public. The reason for this lay in funding. If large numbers of the public submitted complaints, the limited staff would be overwhelmed with cases they could not handle. It is clear that if the advertising trade groups that funded the NAD and the NARB significantly increased their support, the organization could raise its profile and thereby be of greater service, not only to the trade, but to the public as well.

The establishment and continued funding of the NAD and the NARB by the advertising community was motivated by enlightened self-interest. This organization was conceived during the period when Federal Trade Commission activity in relation to the prosecution of advertising was at its zenith. From its inception, the avowed purpose of the NAD and the NARB was to curtail misleading and deceptive advertising. Its implicit purpose was to forestall public criticism, dampen efforts at further formal regulation, and legitimize the institution of advertising. The existence of this self-regulatory mechanism had important symbolic value for the advertising establishment. To admit these facts, however, is not to deny that the NAD and the NARB were effective forces in the regulation of advertising.

ERIC J. ZANOT

See also Better Business Bureau; Criticism of Advertising; Federal Trade Commission

Further Reading
Armstrong, Gary M, and Julie L. Ozanne, "An Evaluation of NAD/NARB Purpose and Performance," *Journal of Advertising* 12 (1983)
Boddewyn, J.J., "Advertising Self-Regulation: Private, Government and Agent of Public Policy," *Journal of Public Policy and Marketing* 4 (1985)
LaBarbera, Priscilla A., "The Diffusion of Trade Association Advertising Self-Regulation," *Journal of Marketing* 47 (1983)
Zanot, Eric J., "The Evolution of Advertising Self Regulation at the National Advertising Division and the National Advertising Review Board," in *Proceedings of the 1995 Conference of the American Academy of Advertising*, edited by Charles S. Madden
_____, "The National Advertising Division: Hidden Backbone of the National Advertising Review Board," in *Proceedings of the American Academy of Advertising*, 1979
_____, "The National Advertising Review Board, 1971–76," *Journalism Monographs* 59 (1979)
_____, "A Review of Eight Years of NARB Casework: Guidelines and Parameters of Deceptive Advertising," *Journal of Advertising* 9 (1980)

National News Council

Effort to improve the accountability of the news media

The National News Council, founded in 1973, was an outgrowth of a mood both in the public and among a few journalists that enhanced accountability in the media could be achieved through use of an impartial organization to evaluate press performance. The national council followed in the steps of a number of local, regional, and statewide media councils that had proven successful in promoting greater press accountability and educating the public. The councils had served as a buffer between those who would exploit the media by informing the public about the purposes and achievements of the press in the United States. The goals of the national council were to examine and report on complaints concerning the accuracy and fairness of news reporting in the United States, as well as to initiate studies and report on issues involving the freedom of the press.

The National News Council evolved following a study commissioned by the Twentieth Century Fund that examined councils established in other countries, notably Great Britain, as well as in Minnesota and Hawaii. Started with $100,000 each from the Twentieth Century Fund and the John and Mary R. Markle Foundation, the national council received complaints from a variety of sources concerning "news reporting by the principal national suppliers of news" – the wire services, newsmagazines, syndicates, major broadcasting networks, and any national newspapers. While initially limited to national media in an effort to avoid a deluge of complaints descending upon a small staff, the bylaws were changed in 1976 to include "news reporting in all media, whether local or national in initial circulation, if the matter in question is of national significance as news or of journalism and the council has available to it the necessary resources."

Shunned at first by major media leaders, the council gained support through the credibility of its members, its studies, and its reports on issues, as well as through the fairness of its decisions published first in the *Columbia Journalism Review* and later in *Quill*. The council consisted of 10 public and eight professional members. William B. Arthur, former editor of *Look* magazine and president of Sigma Delta Chi, was executive director. Among the chairpersons were Roger Traynor, former chief justice in California; Stanley H. Fuld, former chief judge of the court of appeals of the state of New York; Richard S. Salant, president of CBS News; and Norman E. Isaacs, former executive editor of the *Louisville (Kentucky) Courier-Journal*.

Among the major principles raised by the young council were the importance of robust opinion, the right to know facts, and the use of unnamed sources. When the Florida Supreme Court upheld a state statute granting political figures the right to equal space to reply to a newspaper editorial, the council commissioned a study of the problem of public access and its implications in a free society. Called *Freedom of the Press* v. *Public Access,* the project developed into a book under joint sponsorship with the Aspen Institute on Communications and Society.

When the debate about the quality of presidential news conferences heightened, the council funded a study on how the White House news conference might be improved. When judicial attempts were made to gag reporters covering some aspects of a trial, the council proposed a forum to study the problem of restrictive orders. The council also questioned the propriety of CBS News paying former White House aide H.R. Haldeman $50,000 for his appearance on a two-hour program, offering guidelines for payments beyond actual expenses so that the public could draw its own conclusions.

The death of the National News Council in 1984 was described by Isaacs in his autobiography. Isaacs claimed that the interplay of personalities, professional rivalries, and the institutions that the organizations served helped kill the national council. Isaacs said that editors of the *New York Times,* as a leading national publication, played a large part in the demise of the national council because of its unwillingness to participate in the council's activities. The council also spent itself out of business, said Isaacs.

ALF PRATTE

See also Commission on Freedom of the Press; Criticism of Newspapers; News Councils; Ombudsman

Further Reading
Balk, Alfred, *A Free and Responsive Press; The Twentieth Century Fund Task Force Report for a National News Council,* New York: Twentieth Century Fund, 1973
Brown, Lee, *The Reluctant Reformation: On Criticizing the Press in America,* New York: David McKay, 1974
Isaacs, Norman E., *Untended Gates: The Mismanaged Press,* New York: Columbia University Press, 1986
National News Council, *In the Public Interest: A Report by the National News Council, 1973–1975,* New York: National News Council, 1975

National Press Club

Social and professional aspects featured in journalism institution

The National Press Club in Washington, D.C., has become a U.S. journalism institution, even a model for Moscow's International Press Center and Club. Ironically, the earliest attempts to establish a Washington-based press club failed repeatedly.

The 1883 Washington Press Club was the first attempt to gather capital reporters fraternally. Primarily a social club, and meeting in the back room of the *Baltimore (Maryland) American,* it disappeared amid its unpaid bar bills and overdue rent notices. Soon after, the Gridiron Club, which still annually roasted the U.S. president in the late twentieth century, was created for elite journalists. Rank-and-file reporters subsequently founded the Capital Press Club in 1891. It, too, quickly succumbed to financial problems.

Finally, in 1908, the enduring National Press Club (NPC)

was created. Supported by local politicians, it adopted a policy still acknowledged as a reason for its longevity: credit was not allowed at the bar. Unfortunately, neither were women, nor were they allowed to participate in any other aspects of the NPC.

In fact, a press club for women arrived in Washington in 1882, one year before the first men's club. The Woman's National Press Association boasted 130 members by 1885. In 1897, the League of American Pen Women (later the National League of American Pen Women) welcomed female writers as well as artists, dramatists, and composers. After World War I, the Woman's National Press Association membership dwindled and by 1922 was replaced by a new Women's National Press Club (WNPC), fueled by the women's suffrage movement. Three of six WNPC founders were National Women's Party publicists.

By the late 1930s, the WNPC welcomed 100 members to noteworthy luncheon programs, such as Lowell Thomas speaking about his experiences with Lawrence of Arabia. Eleanor Roosevelt actively supported the group, believing that in order to keep valuable jobs during the Great Depression, female journalists needed opportunities to write exclusive news stories. The Roosevelt White House held about 350 press conferences for women only.

In 1946, the WNPC invited men to cover its events. Years of vocal conflict with the National Press Club followed. The NPC finally invited women to cover events but restricted them to the upper balconies. In 1959, Dwight Eisenhower's press secretary, James C. Hagerty, tried unsuccessfully to convince the clubs to merge. Later, John F. Kennedy openly supported equal news coverage by both men and women. Militant WNPC members charged the Department of State with booking speakers into locations that discriminated against female reporters, and they wired women Labour Party members of the British Parliament to pressure their leader, Harold Wilson, not to speak at the National Press Club during a planned trip to Washington, D.C. Wilson spoke at the British Embassy.

In 1970, the WNPC voted to admit men into membership and changed its name to the Washington Press Club. In 1971, the NPC opened membership to women, after Lyndon Johnson directed the State Department to avoid scheduling speakers at the National Press Club unless women were allowed to cover the events. Finally, in 1985, the Washington Press Club merged with the National Press Club.

PENNY PENCE SMITH

See also White House Correspondents' Association

Further Reading
Beasley, Maurine, "The Women's National Press Club: Case Study of Professional Aspirations," *Journalism History* 15 (Winter 1988)
Brodell, James, "United States-Style Press Club in Moscow," *Editor & Publisher* 126:32 (August 7, 1993), p. 26
Garneau, George, "National Press Club Is in Its 80th Year," *Editor & Publisher* 121:15 (April 9, 1988), pp. 11–12

Native American Media

Fighters for Indian rights from their inception

Since 1828, when the *Cherokee Phoenix* first appeared in Calhoun County, Georgia, Native American, or Indian, newspapers, magazines, and broadcast media have fought for Indian rights in a world increasingly dominated by non-Indians. To prepare for and survive amid the imminent collision of cultures, their leaders knew that Indians needed to read, write, and converse in the language of non-Indian society. Early newspapers carried news, information, and advertising, and they alerted readers to dangers to their communities. Among non-Indians in the United States and abroad, native newspapers offered alternative views of Indian life and accomplishments.

Like many frontier publications, they often were characterized by infrequency, primitive formats and content, high mortality rates, and minimal staffs and resources. Some offered substantial bilingual or even trilingual content, using English, Choctaw, Cherokee, Chickasaw, and, eventually, Creek.

Unlike many of their contemporaries, these papers faced U.S. government policies and whims able to displace or decimate an entire readership before a paper could establish itself. Back files of many newspapers have not been preserved, and absolutely accurate totals of how many pioneer papers existed are impossible. Carolyn Foreman listed about 250 newspapers established in Indian country before 1900 and about 320 established in the first decade of the twentieth century, some not solely Indian publications because of their religious or agency affiliation.

Native publications were usually official organs of tribal governments. Although they often shaped editorial policy to promote the interest of their tribes, editors were politically outspoken, often inviting dispute and controversy, name-calling and libel suits, physical violence, and in at least one instance, murder.

In the southeastern United States, the so-called Five Civilized Tribes – the Cherokee, Chickasaw, Choctaw, Creek, and Seminole – were at the center of early Native American journalism. Cherokees were the most active journalists. Although many early tribal publications were initiated or at least sponsored by religious missions scattered throughout Indian country, most Indian newspapers began as a result of tribal efforts. Their educational value generally was recognized by both Indian and non-Indian government officials.

Early papers advertised schools and hotels, publicized the settling of estates, announced postal schedules and unclaimed letters, printed steamboat schedules and merchants' sales lists, promoted patent medicine companies, and recorded newly enacted laws. They campaigned for law and order, encouraged temperance, and helped to establish towns by advertising to attract homesteaders.

The first Indian newspapers were 4 to 16 pages in length, about 15 by 24 inches in size, with circulations ranging from 100 to 1,000 readers and subscription prices between $1 and $3 per year, often payable in advance. Their quality was uneven. Often, they criticized one another in their columns.

The *Cherokee Phoenix* (in Cherokee, Tsa-la-ge-tsi-hi-sa-ni-hi), born on February 21, 1828, was printed partly in English and partly in Cherokee, using the 86-character syllabic alphabet developed by Sequoya, a Cherokee silversmith also known as George Guess or Gist. The national newspaper of the Cherokee Nation, the *Phoenix* had religious and political purposes: missionaries recognized the potential of the printed word for "civilizing" and "uplifting" the Cherokee, and the Cherokee National Council wanted an accelerated educational program to further its fight for survival. The council hoped that a newspaper would help unify opinion in the Cherokee nation and gain outside support for Cherokee rights to their homelands. It committed $1,500 to buy a press and type, and sent its editor-select, Elias Boudinot, a Cherokee schoolteacher, council clerk, and New England–educated missionary, to churches and philanthropic groups throughout the eastern United States on a fund-raising tour.

During its early history, the four-page *Phoenix* was both focal point and flash point in the Cherokee nation. Its coverage of politics and, in particular, the early phases of the controversy over government removal of Indians, simultaneously worked for survival and set the stage for political factions, the decline of the newspaper, and the death of Boudinot at Cherokee hands.

On May 31, 1834, publication of the *Cherokee Phoenix* was suspended, ostensibly for financial reasons, but in reality because of Cherokee uncertainty and dissension regarding the threat of removal. In 1835, the Georgia Guard destroyed the press. Following the disastrous Trail of Tears, during which thousands of Cherokee died in a forced march from Georgia to what would later become Oklahoma Territory, another Cherokee national newspaper was established. The *Cherokee-Advocate* began on September 26, 1844, ushering in a fruitful era of pioneer Indian journalism including two Cherokee collegiate newspapers.

Three other tribes, the Choctaw, Chickasaw, and Creek, also figured in frontier press history. The Choctaw, forced from their Mississippi homelands in the early 1830s, established the *Choctaw Telegraph* in 1848; the *Telegraph* and its successor, the *Choctaw Intelligencer,* in 1850; and the *Chickasaw Choctaw Herald* in 1858. Other Choctaw papers soon followed. The *Chickasaw Intelligencer* appeared in 1854 in Tishomingo City, capital of the Chickasaw Nation in Indian Territory (later Oklahoma), ushering in a brief period of journalism interrupted by the outbreak of the American Civil War, which forced southeastern Indians into another losing stance. During the Civil War, Indian publications were suspended, to be reactivated during reconstruction in the South.

Newspapers during this second phase of Native American journalism included the reactivated *Cherokee Advocate,* 1879; the *Choctaw Vindicator,* 1872; the *Atoka Independent,* 1877; the *Caddo Indian Free Press,* 1878; the *Indian Champion,* 1884; and the *Indian Citizen,* 1886. The *Cheyenne Transporter* began in 1878 on the Cheyenne and Arapaho Reservation in Darlington, Indian Territory (later the state of Oklahoma). The *Osage Herald* first appeared in 1875 as a Saturday publication and was followed in 1910 by the *Cheyenne and Arapaho Carrier Pigeon*. General interest publications, they offered community information and advertising, while also bringing Indian affairs into mainstream news and commentary.

After the turn of the century, publications of broader scope appeared. The scholarly *Quarterly Journal,* published by the Society of American Indians, began in 1912 in Washington, D.C. The *American Indian Magazine,* a national magazine focusing on Indians as a race rather than as a mere collection of disparate and competing tribes, followed soon thereafter. About four years later, the newspaper *Wassaja* was established, promoting enfranchisement, greater assimilation into American culture and society, and less emphasis on reservations. A latter-day *Wassaja,* published in San Francisco by the Indian Historical Society, was a major national publication in the 1970s and 1980s. Another Washington, D.C., publication, *NCAI Bulletin,* was the newsletter of the National Congress of American Indians. Established in 1947, it opposed federal government policies aimed at terminating reservations and the reservation rights of Indians.

By the mid–twentieth century, newsletters and newspapers served reservation and urban populations across the country. The *New Cherokee Advocate* was reestablished at the Cherokee national capital in Tahlequah, Oklahoma, in 1950. The Los Angeles–based *Talking Leaf* began in 1935, and *Smoke Signals* began in Sacramento, California, in 1947.

Following World War II, about 400 publications were established, some continuing into the late 1990s. The *Navajo Times,* established in 1959, was a visible leader. In 1983, it became *Navajo Times Today,* the first daily newspaper published for a Navajo readership. Successful Alaska native publications included the *Voice of Brotherhood,* begun in 1954 as an advocate of native rights and well-being, the *Sealaska Shareholder,* the *Tundra Times,* and the *All-Alaska Weekly.* All were generally more sophisticated than their counterparts in the lower 48, owing in part to both historical circumstances and to the fact that in Alaska, native people had not had the same limitations associated with reservation status as Indians in other states. From the late nineteenth century, native people in Alaska attended public schools, competed for political office, and participated in the economic life of the area, giving them advantageous preparation for the business and professional challenges of journalism.

Native newspapers in the late twentieth century published weekly, biweekly, monthly, quarterly, or even irregularly. They were tribal, inter-tribal, urban, regional, or national in scope and affiliation. Although most were printed entirely in English, some editors attempted to include short sections or articles in tribal languages. Few native newspapers were independent commercial ventures. Exceptions included *Qua Toqtii,* an independent and privately owned paper established in 1973 to serve the Hopi people. The South Dakota–based weekly *Indian Country Today* was the leading Native American publication in the United States in the late twentieth century. Begun in the early 1980s, it had bureaus in Phoenix, Arizona; Washington, D.C.; and Seattle, Washington. *News from Indian Country: The Nations Native Journal* was established in 1986 in

Hayward, Wisconsin, and quickly became a nationally recognized resource for news, commentary, and culture.

A popular format for twentieth-century native publications was the tabloid of 12 to 16 pages, closely resembling small-town weeklies found in communities across the country. Desktop technologies made design and publication increasingly attractive. Style and conventions of many native newspapers often differed from news reporting in the established non-Indian press. Stories frequently were written from an Indian viewpoint and revealed the personal opinions of reporters and editors. Editorials, letters to the editor, and political cartoons left no doubt as to where writers and editors stood on various issues. Simultaneously, major Native American newspapers and influential Native American journalists consistently stressed professional reporting and writing. Workshops and seminars, such as those held during yearly meetings of the Native American Journalists Association, included discussion of issues in Indian law and economics as well as the business, design, and editing elements of quality journalism.

Native newspapers had an acknowledged, historical mission: to correct or put into perspective Indian news often misinterpreted or ignored by the majority, non-Indian press. News topics included legal affairs, politics and government, education, health, culture and heritage, language preservation, entertainment, and the interracial situations created by reservation borders that were frequently peripheral zones of conflict. D'Arcy McNickle, the highly respected Flathead Indian and anthropologist, called native newspapers a decisive force in creating an enduring policy of self-determined cultural pluralism. Native American legal publications represented another avenue for self-determination.

In working toward effective communication systems, native editors and tribal leaders explored cooperative efforts including, as early as 1888, the Oklahoma Press Association; the American Indian Press Association, nationally active from 1970 to 1975; a subscription news service called the Northwest Indian News Association, which was begun in 1978; the Southwest Indian Media Collective, which was begun in Albuquerque, New Mexico, in 1977 as a service for subscribers in Arizona and New Mexico; the Southern Plains Indian Media Association; and a cooperative advertising venture called the Indian Newspaper Publishers Association, which originated in the state of Washington in 1977.

In 1980, the Alaska Native Media Association, initially representing 16 native publications and several freelance journalists, was established in Anchorage. Formal planning for the Native American Journalists Association, which facilitated cooperation among Native American journalists, began in 1984 with initial funding from the Gannett Foundation. These associations focused on professional and financial issues. They also addressed continuing tensions between the interests of Indian tribes and the freedom of the press as guaranteed by both the U.S. Constitution and the Indian Civil Rights Act of 1968. The Indian Civil Rights Act contains a fundamental guarantee of freedom of the press for Indian tribes and also emphasizes that freedom of expression within reasonable limits, excepting obscenity, libel, and slander, applies to all Indians.

Native media history includes growing involvement in broadcast, beginning with KTDB-FM, first operated by the Navajo Nation in Ramah, New Mexico, in 1972. The Rosebud Sioux tribe's KINI-FM went on the air in 1977 in St. Francis, South Dakota, followed the next year by KSHI-FM in Zuni, New Mexico.

In the late 1990s, about 25 radio stations, most public and nonprofit, served Native American communities in the United States and Canada. A daily national newscast, *National Native News,* and a national talk-radio program, *Native America Calling,* offered a voice and information.

One of the Native American media's central characteristics has been fluidity of response to changing needs and conditions and to economic, social, and political pressures. While fluidity may endanger growth, it also may guarantee the vitality of response growth. Native American print and broadcast journalism made many important contributions and was expected to be important in the twenty-first century.

SHARON M. MURPHY

See also Advertising and Minorities; Mass Media and Race; Minority Journalists' Organizations

Further Reading

Connelly, William E., *History of Kansas Newspapers. A History of the Newspapers and Magazines Published in Kansas from the Organization of Kansas Territory, 1854, to January 1916; Together with Brief Statistical Information of the Counties, Cities and Towns of the State,* Topeka: Kansas State Printing Plant, W.R. Smith, State Printer, 1916

Foreman, Carolyn Thomas, *Oklahoma Imprints, 1835–1907: A History of Printing in Oklahoma Before Statehood,* Norman: University of Oklahoma Press, 1936

Karolevitz, Robert, *Newspapering in the Old West,* Seattle, Washington: Superior, 1965

McNickle, D'Arcy, *Native American Tribalism: Indian Survivals and Renewals,* New York and London: Oxford University Press, 1973

Murphy, James E., and Sharon M. Murphy, *Let My People Know: American Indian Journalism, 1828–1978,* Norman: University of Oklahoma Press, 1981

Trahant, Mark N., *Pictures of Our Nobler Selves: A History of Native American Contributions to News Media,* Nashville, Tennessee: Freedom Forum First Amendment Center at Vanderbilt University, 1995

Neuharth, Al

Founder of 'USA Today'

Al Neuharth, founder of *USA Today,* was the chairman of the Freedom Forum, formally the Gannett Foundation. As Gannett's chairman (1979–89), he fiercely fought those maligning its credibility. A self-described "s.o.b.," he was called by others an imp, a genius, an entrepreneur, a self-server, and a snake. Neuharth's newspaper vision emerged

in *Florida Today* and matured in *USA Today,* perhaps his most memorable accomplishment. Many found its concise, upbeat news a compelling antidote to traditional journalism. While critics called it "McPaper," implying a resemblance to fast food, few denied its influence on journalism. Neuharth did not originate all of its innovations, but he took risks, nursing it through difficult years.

Neuharth attracted controversy by squabbling with prominent figures, including the *Washington Post*'s Ben Bradlee, and by inelegant comments, once suggesting that airlines hire shapely, attractive "sky girls." He exhibited excess and style (dressing mostly in black, white, and gray) and was the subject of outlandish stories, some apocryphal.

His legacy allowed for few simple conclusions. Accused of shallowness and insensitivity, he nonetheless measured and acted upon the country's tolerance, if not desire, for a concise and ornamental journalism that characterized much modern news, and he led Gannett when it developed policies encouraging the support and promotion of women and minorities. With the Freedom Forum, he vigorously supported First Amendment rights. He was feisty, flamboyant, vengeful, self-promoting, stubborn, thick-skinned, and driven. Those qualities served him well in birthing *USA Today,* perhaps the nation's most imitated, and in that sense, influential, newspaper. If that was true, jokester Neuharth had something else he cherished – the last laugh.

ROBERT DARDENNE

Further Reading

Morton, John, "*USA Today* Product of S.O.B. and Genius," *Washington Journalism Review* 11:9 (November 1989), p. 8

Neuharth, Al, *Confessions of an S.O.B.,* New York: Doubleday, 1989

Prichard, Peter, *The Making of McPaper: The Inside Story of 'USA Today',* Kansas City, Missouri: Andrews, McMeel, & Parker, 1987

Vamos, Mark N., Russell Mitchell, and Pete Engardio, "Al Neuharth Wants It All for Gannett–Even Respect," *Business Week* (September 30, 1985), pp. 112 ff

New Deal and the Media

Massive media operation helped disseminate information

The New Deal, primarily those social programs of the first two Franklin D. Roosevelt presidential terms (1933–41), created a new era for government information and for the Washington, D.C., news media. After a news void during the Herbert Hoover era, the Roosevelt administration's efforts to lessen the impact of the Great Depression were newsworthy. So much was happening with the new agencies that, by 1934, the United Press wires were carrying three times as much Washington news than in 1930. The public's interest was insatiable. The relationship between the agencies, the public, and the news media became symbiotic.

Rather than one coordinated message being released by government through the mass media, differing viewpoints were deliberated in public. New Deal administrators openly debated possible solutions to the depression and continued to do so until World War II. Especially notable were the public feuds between Harold Ickes, secretary of the interior and public works director, and Harry Hopkins, federal relief administrator. The press and the public followed such open decision-making activity.

At the same time, the emergency legislation for the new agencies also had earmarked funds for public information. The Roosevelt administration needed to have an aggressive campaign of public information to advertise the new agencies' services as well as to justify their usefulness and garner congressional and public support.

Overseeing the publicity efforts was the president's secretary for press relations, Stephen T. Early. Early showed the new administrators how to explain their views while at the same time attempting to coordinate the White House information with the executive department and agency publicity for an overall positive effect. He sent memoranda to new administrators on how to call a press conference and urged the officials to explain their efforts. He even edited major speeches and articles of the cabinet and the new agency officials. He also hired as publicity agents experienced journalists who enjoyed the confidence of their colleagues. Many of these new agency information officers had been victims of depression layoffs, newspaper closures, and management changes. Early told them to do their jobs as if they were working on a newspaper.

Individual press agents ran miniature news operations based upon their previous newspaper experience. They attended the president's press conferences to inform their chiefs on the tack the president had taken on various pertinent issues. The press efforts in the National Recovery Administration (NRA) and the Agriculture Adjustment Administration (AAA) employed so many people that they organized their operations like the city room of a metropolitan newspaper. In less than one year, the NRA released 5,200 handouts and the AAA almost 5,000. In addition, complete staffs prepared radio programs and produced motion pictures for the public.

At the same time, the president experimented with different agencies to follow public efforts and collect news clippings as well as to answer the public's questions. In this era before refined public opinion polling, the NRA established a Division of Press Intelligence to compile newspaper and magazine clippings on the national reaction to the government efforts. By 1935, the National Emergency Council had established a U.S. Information Service as an information clearinghouse for answering people's questions on emergency activities. After the council was abolished in 1939, all information functions were transferred to the Office of Government Reports, which, by 1942, was absorbed into the Office of War Information.

There was nothing new about the New Deal informational efforts. Presidents and their secretaries had used various executive branch publicity and information programs for years. The World War I Committee on Public Information only expanded late-nineteenth-century endeavors and combined them with the administration's publicity into a singular all-out war effort. Such official programs did not stop at the war's end. The Hoover administration spent more than $3 million a year on handouts alone. With the Roosevelt system and Steve Early's coordination, the New Deal publicity focus successfully set the New Deal's news agenda. Studies such as those by James L. McCamy in 1939 found similar news styles in the *New York Times* and the *St. Louis (Missouri) Post-Dispatch* and wire services stories.

The over-burdened Washington correspondents welcomed the New Deal information. Many bureaus, already short-handed, did not expand enough to meet the news demands. So much was happening so fast that the reporters could not keep track of it all. Most correspondents covered more than one agency or department and needed those press handouts to explain quickly what was happening, understand the technical information, assemble the news, and find "tips" for news stories.

With the New Deal publicity, the old manner of covering Washington became woefully out of date. Many informal sources were not informative enough or as available. The expanded federal government was so complicated that the average correspondent needed to be able to go to the appropriate official without spending days in aimless inquiry. While the method gave an administrative slant, it was faster and easier to rely upon the designated officers.

At the same time, the reporting style began changing. The previous news emphasis on news events, the "what" of a news story, was not enough. A new reporting style challenged the old-style objectivity – sticking to a factual account of what had been said or done. More and more, the journalists relied upon interpretative journalism to explain "why" and "how" in lay terms. The readers wanted the background and context of the new government agencies. Thus, Washington correspondents created the new form of interpretative journalism as a method of explaining the New Deal's political, social, and economic revolution.

The new reporting style also fit the newspapers' greater reliance on columnists. The depression had caused many cuts in the local news staffs. The news holes began to be filled with syndicated columns on everything from child rearing and Hollywood gossip to the national political news. Many Washington correspondents not only covered the White House and the New Deal but also wrote those syndicated columns to give background and behind-the-scenes information. So, too, did the newsmagazines, such as *Time* and, later, *Newsweek*. By 1938, the major journalism-writing textbook changed its title from *Reporting for Beginners* to *Interpretive Reporting*. The reporting impact was so great that historians Edwin Emery and Michael Emery later called interpretative journalism "the most important press development of the 1930s and 1940s."

The New Deal information system generated a great deal of criticism. Opposition publishers and their organizations labeled such New Deal spot news efforts as "propaganda," especially because the administration successfully had counteracted the publishers' anti-Roosevelt bias. Senators publicly questioned the president's news management and the use of appropriations for publicity. The Senate hired the Brookings Institute to investigate the costs. Its study reported that more printing employees were used for publicity efforts than during the World War I peak. Yet, despite the congressional and press criticism, the New Deal's use of publicity agents and the surfeit of news pumped new life into the Washington press corps and expanded the public's interest in the federal government. With the New Deal and the mass media, there would be an executive branch publicity system in place for the formation of an Office of War Information and an Office of Censorship during World War II. After the war, there would be no going back to the more freewheeling news gathering and administrative open debates that involved the public and the mass media during the New Deal days.

BETTY HOUCHIN WINFIELD

See also Committee on Public Information; Interpretive Reporting; News Concepts; Newspaper Columnists; Office of Censorship; Office of War Information; Roosevelt, Franklin D., and the Media

Further Reading

Clark, Delbert, *Washington Dateline,* New York: Frederick A. Stokes, 1941
Herring, E. Pendleton, "Official Publicity Under the New Deal," *Annals of the American Academy of Political and Social Science* 179 (1935)
McCamy, James L., *Government Publicity: Its Practice in Federal Administration,* Chicago: University of Chicago Press, 1939
Mader, Joseph H., "Government Press Bureaus and Reporting Public Affairs," *Journalism Quarterly* 10 (1942)
Michael, George, *Handout,* New York: Putnam's, 1935
Winfield, Betty Houchin, *FDR and the News Media,* New York: Columbia University Press, 1994
_____, "FDR Wins (and Loses) Journalist Friends in the Rising Age of News Interpretation," *Journalism Quarterly* 64:4 (Winter 1987), pp. 698–706
_____, "New Deal Publicity: The Information Foundation for the Modern Presidency," *Journalism Quarterly* 61 (1984)

New Journalism (1880s)

Carrying a message of social reform to the masses

New Journalism of the 1880s presented a style of sensationalized newspaper journalism that promoted an underlying agenda of social reform. It was popularized by Joseph Pulitzer, who outlined his new philosophy of journalism in the May 11, 1883, edition of his *New York World:*

> There is room in this great and growing city for a journal that is not only cheap but bright, not only bright but large; not only large but truly Democratic – dedicated to the cause of the people rather than that of the purse potentates – devoted more to the news of the New than the Old World – that will expose all fraud and sham, fight all

public evils and abuses – that will serve and battle for the people with earnest sincerity.

Thus, Pulitzer defined his "New Journalism" as a cheap, popular newspaper, which carried a message of social reform that could educate the masses. News stories in Pulitzer's *World* were written for impact and excitement, while his editorial page promoted serious social reforms. Much of the responsibility for this new approach to news has been laid to John A. Cockerill, who worked with Pulitzer at the *St. Louis (Missouri) Post-Dispatch* and became the *World's* managing editor. Pulitzer's style was so successful that the *New York World* was, by 1890, the most profitable newspaper ever published. Its formula was widely imitated.

Specifically, Pulitzer's success can be traced to several publishing strategies. Pulitzer kept his newspaper priced at two cents so that it would be affordable to the masses, especially immigrants like himself, and at the same time increased its size, often publishing up to sixteen pages. He was guilty of tireless self-promotion and was a forerunner in the use of contests to boost circulation. He crammed his newspaper full of all types of news, of both sensational and sobering nature. He promoted a style of journalism that made use of gossip, human interest news, and colorful vignettes – none of which had been defined as news before. At the same time, Pulitzer covered the important news of the day from a serious perspective.

In addition to this, Pulitzer popularized the newspaper crusade. He exposed exploitation of women in sweatshops, mistreatment of immigrants, and the horrific conditions of city tenements. Through publicity in his newspaper, Pulitzer collected enough money from readers to build the pedestal for the Statue of Liberty, and he sponsored Nellie Bly's famous trip around the world. Pulitzer also was a leader in the use of illustrations and realized that, despite his personal distaste for them, photos and illustrations could sell newspapers.

Historian Frank Luther Mott defined the New Journalism of the 1880s as "good news-coverage peppered with sensationalism, stunts and crusades, editorials of high character, size, illustration, and promotion." Headlines underscored this sensationalism: "How Babies Are Baked" described the deaths during a heat wave in July 1883.

When Pulitzer took over the *World* in 1883, the newspaper's circulation hovered at about 10,000. A little more than a year later, the circulation stood at 100,000. Pulitzer himself reflected on his success in a September 29, 1884, editorial: "It is certainly demonstrated that the Eastern public appreciates a style of journalism that is just a bit breezy while at all times honest, earnest and sincere, and a journalism that represents every day a laborious effort to meet the popular demand for news seasoned with just convictions."

Other newspapers incorporated Pulitzer's more successful techniques to meet his challenge. While widely imitated, this fevered approach also attracted much criticism. By the 1890s, when Pulitzer was embroiled in a circulation battle with *New York Journal* owner William Randolph Hearst, competitors labeled the newspapers "yellow journals," a derogatory term aimed at denigrating their sensationalism of the news. In fact, yellow journalism has been defined as "the new journalism without a soul."

The term "New Journalism" was used at the time to describe this new, breezy newspaper style. One early use of the term has been traced to Matthew Arnold, who in 1887 wrote that "a clear and energetic man has lately invented a New Journalism." As Arnold described it, the writing was "full of ability, novelty, variety, sensation, sympathy, generous instincts; its one great fault is that it is featherbrained." Arnold was referring to the writing of British editor W.T. Stead, whose tales of 13-year-olds being sold into brothels by their mothers had been widely reprinted in the United States. Stead relied upon interviews, a new technique at the time, for his reportage. In the United States, the term came to mean the journalism first promoted by Joseph Pulitzer and then imitated by other newspapers.

Agnes Hooper Gottlieb

See also Hearst, William Randolph; Journalistic Interview; Pulitzer, Joseph; Sensationalism; Yellow Journalism

Further Reading

Francke, Warren T., "W.T. Stead: The First New Journalist?," *Journalism History* 1 (1974)
Jones, Robert W., *Journalism in the United States,* New York: Dutton, 1947

New Journalism (1960s–1970s)

In the mid-twentieth century, the term "new journalism" became associated with a type of writing and reporting that first appeared in the 1960s. Initially, however, it referred to several journalistic forms and approaches that appeared rather suddenly and blossomed from the mid-1960s through the mid-1970s.

Although most critics found the term "new journalism" a misnomer and historically inaccurate as a descriptive term, it nevertheless caught on. Among the scholars and critics who attempted to define the term and to make cultural sense of it was Everette E. Dennis. His categories of new journalism, identified in the early 1970s, remain valid descriptions of the various approaches and forms recognized as new journalism. Five of these categories are:

1.) The new nonfiction: This was a subjective and often personal form of reporting that turned away from conventional newspaper and magazine writing formulas, especially the daily newspaper's inverted pyramid style, and used various narrative approaches and structures to tell a story. It tended to be less concerned with the facts of an event, situation, topic, or person, and more concerned with human motivation and behavior, as well as the themes suggested by them – what some would call the "feel" of the facts. The most often cited writers at the time were Tom Wolfe, Gay Talese, Jimmy Breslin, Truman Capote, and Norman Mailer.

2.) Alternative journalism: Sometimes called "modern muckraking," alternative journalism focused on covering the establishment institutions and exposing corruption and wrongdoing. Much of this writing and reporting appeared in alternative papers such as the *San Francisco Bay Guardian* and the *Village Voice.* Soon, alternative weekly newspapers sprang up all over the country.

3.) Advocacy journalism: Writing that appeared in columns in mainstream newspapers, as well as part of the regular article mix and columns that ran in the alternative and counterculture press. Advocacy journalists expressed a specific viewpoint, calling for progressive social change and taking sides in public issues and politics.

4.) Counterculture and underground journalism: These were new publications, many of them short-lived, that contained radical perspectives regarding society, drugs, music, and art. They included the *Berkeley Barb,* the *East Village Other,* and a host of sheets handed out on street corners, at universities and high schools, and on military bases.

5.) Precision reporting: Tied to social science research methods, precision reporting relied on survey and polling techniques to measure and explain public attitudes, opinion, and behavior. Philip Meyer and Ben Wattenberg were two of its biggest advocates and practitioners.

These efforts were connected by a belief that conventional journalism, particularly the daily newspaper, was inadequate in capturing reality and presenting the truth. The temper of the times – with its many subcultures, with the civil rights and antiwar movements, with the broad questioning of authority and traditional values by many – created an atmosphere ripe for journalistic change from the bottom up and for challenges to journalism's claim of authority in depiction and coverage.

Nevertheless, all of these "new" forms and approaches had roots in U.S. journalism history. In a sense, the new journalism was a reminder of U.S. journalism's past, with its early history of powerful writing on the side of causes and movements, from the anti-British press through the abolitionist press through the reform press of the Progressive Era. In addition, personal and subjective reporting that employed various narrative approaches had been a staple of daily journalism well into the twentieth century. Even precision reporting, that odd duck of the bunch, pushed journalism more toward neutral or seemingly scientific depiction or coverage, thereby attempting to make journalism more

---

The Hell's Angels, a Strange and Terrible Saga

Big Frank from Frisco, for instance, is a black belt in karate who goes into any fight with the idea of jerking people's eyeballs out of their sockets. . . . The intent is to demoralize your opponent, not blind him. Red-blooded American boys don't normally fight this way. Nor do they swing heavy chains on people whose backs are turned . . . and when they find themselves in a brawl where things like this are happening, they have good reason to feel at a disadvantage. It is one thing to get punched in the nose, and quite another to have your eyeball sprung or your teeth shattered with a wrench.

Hunter Thompson

truthful by being more objective and scientific, and therefore clearly tied to journalism's decades-old faith in facts.

But the new journalistic forms clearly had an impact. As the counterculture began to either fade or be absorbed into mainstream culture, many of these forms likewise were absorbed by mainstream journalism. Topics covered by the alternative and underground press started to appear regularly in the daily press, and investigative reporting became more common at even small dailies. In addition, newspapers opened their opinion pages to a wider array of viewpoints and to advocates of all sorts of causes; the writing style throughout the newspaper became somewhat looser and more varied; and polls, charts, and public opinion samples became mainstays of daily journalism.

Furthermore, as a number of writers known as new journalists became more popular and successful, new journalism increasingly came to mean the new nonfiction. By the mid-1970s, the writing and reporting associated with Wolfe, Talese, and many lesser-known writers who had abandoned journalism's formulas and turned to traditional literary techniques to cover society became synonymous with the term "new journalism."

Wolfe had been defining and characterizing the new journalism style of writing and reporting in articles in *New York* and *Esquire* magazines. Those pieces and an anthology of articles and book excerpts that Wolfe and E.W. Johnson considered some of the best examples of the form were published as *The New Journalism* in 1973. The success and influence of that book guaranteed that the term "new journalism" would be associated with the type of writing described and documented by Wolfe and Johnson.

Central to Wolfe's conception of new journalism was his belief that it documented reality, that it showed how people behave, depicting the manners and mores of society's classes and subcultures, as social realism in fiction once did. Thus, according to Wolfe, the new journalism was simply accurate reporting that read like fiction. Wolfe said that new journalism was characterized by scene-by-scene construction, complete dialogue, varying narrative point of view, and use of status details, those mannerisms and gestures that distinguish people, classes, and societies, all obtained through what he called intense, "saturation" reporting.

A number of works soon became the most prominent and popular works of new journalism: Wolfe's *The Kandy-Kolored Tangerine-Flake Streamline Baby,* Capote's *In Cold Blood;* Talese's *Fame and Obscurity* collection; Mailer's *Armies of the Night;* Joan Didion's *Slouching Toward Bethlehem;* and Hunter Thompson's *Hell's Angels: A Strange and Terrible Saga* and his *Fear and Loathing in Las Vegas.* Magazines especially accommodating to the new journalism style were *New York, Rolling Stone,* and *Esquire,* although Capote's *In Cold Blood* appeared in the *New Yorker* and much of Didion's work appeared in the *Saturday Evening Post.*

Critics eventually would describe new journalistic writing as everything from "pure transcription" to "new fiction," but Wolfe's definition continued to be influential, even 20 years after it was written. Wolfe's ideas, however, were modified, challenged, revised, and expanded upon by a number of scholars and critics, most significantly by Norman Sims in *The Literary Journalists.*

Through Sims's work, by the mid-1980s, the new journalism was becoming known as literary journalism. The term "new journalism" remained, however, one of those characteristic phrases closely tied to a period of unrest, protest, challenge to authority, and change.

THOMAS B. CONNERY

See also Literary Aspects of Journalism; Precision Journalism

Further Reading

Connery, Thomas B., ed., *A Sourcebook of American Literary Journalism: Representative Writers in an Emerging Genre,* New York: Greenwood, 1992
Dennis, Everette E., and William L. Rivers, *Other Voices: The New Journalism in America,* San Francisco: Canfield, 1974
Hollowell, John, *Fact and Fiction: The New Journalism and the Nonfiction Novel,* Chapel Hill: University of North Carolina Press, 1977
Lounsberry, Barbara, *The Art of Fact: Contemporary Artists of Nonfiction,* New York: Greenwood, 1990
Sims, Norman, ed., *Literary Journalism in the Twentieth Century,* New York: Oxford University Press, 1990
_____, ed., *The Literary Journalists,* New York: Ballantine, 1984
Weber, Ronald, *The Reporter as Artist: A Look at the New Journalism Controversy,* New York: Hastings House, 1974
Wolfe, Tom, *The New Journalism,* New York: Harper & Row, 1973; London: Pan, 1975

Newsboys
Delivering U.S. newspapers daily

Newsboys long made up the bulk of the newspaper workforce, toiling under dangerous conditions for minimal pay. A quarter of a million children in the late twentieth century delivered U.S. newspapers to subscribers every day; nearly as many adults delivered the balance and hawked papers on city streets.

Apprentices distributed newspapers to city subscribers in the 1760s, while carriers covered outlying areas by horseback. The apprentice force became inadequate as newspaper circulation soared in the mid-1800s, necessitating a separate distribution force. As boys could be hired more cheaply than grown men, they quickly became the labor force of choice.

The hordes of ill-clad children selling newspapers on city streets drew the attention of social reformers, inspiring campaigns to limit their working hours, to ensure that underage children (initially, 10 years of age was the cutoff point, but it gradually increased to 14 or 16) did not sell pa-

Children delivered most newspapers through the mid-twentieth century.
(Davis Library, University of North Carolina at Chapel Hill)

pers, and, in some cases, to extend workers' compensation and similar protective legislation to newsboys.

Newsboys often were required to take more newspapers than they needed, "eating" (absorbing the cost of) the extras. In particularly competitive markets, newsboys were victimized by circulation department sluggers seeking to ensure more favorable play for their papers. In 1917, more than half of Cincinnati, Ohio's, circulation men had criminal records, while Chicago publishers hired local gangsters to enforce their interests with knives, clubs, and revolvers. Newsboys also were (and continue to be) frequently injured or killed when struck by cars or attacked by criminals. In Los Angeles alone, 17 newsboys were killed and 283 injured while selling papers between 1940 and 1949.

Newsboys' average daily earnings ranged from 22 cents (in 1902, for a four-hour shift) to 40 cents (1922–26, 2.5 hours). A 1934 government study found newsboys averaging $1.41 per week for 15 hours' work, while a 1970 study found that Utah newsboys earned $42.56 monthly for 50.7 hours work – substantially below the minimum wage.

Relative earnings have fallen sharply. In the 1890s, newsboys typically received 50 percent (and sometimes as much as 60) of papers' cover price and could return unsold papers; in the 1990s, newsboys received 20 to 30 percent on a nonreturnable basis. At the same time, the work in-

volved increased as newspapers grew heavier and added special sections that newsboys were required to insert before delivery.

Newsboys responded to deteriorating conditions with strategies ranging from avoidance (trade journals have long been filled with reports on the difficulties of finding and keeping carriers) to unionization and strikes. Between the 1890s and the early 1940s, newsboys in several cities organized and waged often bitter strikes, ranging from the 1899 New York City strike portrayed in the Disney musical *Newsies* to a 1947 strike in Kansas City. Philadelphia newsboys maintained their union from 1937 until the mid-1950s despite publishers' refusal to recognize or bargain with the union in later years, while the Seattle Newsboys Union survived until 1962.

From the outset, newspaper publishers realized that young children could be induced to work on speculation for wages and under conditions that adult workers generally would refuse. Publishers used the fiction that newsboys were "independent merchants" to exclude them from unemployment, workers' compensation, liability insurance, and health insurance plans. Most newsboys continued to earn less than the minimum wage and ran the risk of having their meager earnings further reduced by nonpaying subscribers. However, the number of children so employed declined sharply in the late twentieth century with the decline in competitive markets and the increased use of motorized carriers.

JON BEKKEN

Further Reading

Ashby, LeRoy, *Saving the Waifs: Reformers and Dependent Children, 1890–1917*, Philadelphia: Temple University Press, 1984

Bekken, Jon, "Newsboys," in *Newsworkers: Toward a History of the Rank and File,* edited by Hanno Hardt and Bonnie Brennen, Minneapolis: University of Minnesota Press, 1995

Linder, Marc, "From Street Urchins to Little Merchants: The Juridical Transvaluation of Child Newspaper Carriers," *Temple Law Review* 63 (Winter 1990), pp. 829–864

Nasaw, David, *Children of the City: At Work and at Play,* Garden City, New York: Anchor, 1985

Postol, Todd, "Hearing the Voices of Working Children: The NRA Newspaperboy Letters," *Labor's Heritage* 1 (1989)

Simpson, Roger, "Seattle Newsboys: How Hustler Democracy Lost to the Power of Property," *Journalism History* 18 (1992), pp. 18–25

Whisnant, David, "Selling the Gospel News, Or: The Strange Career of Jimmy Brown the Newsboy," *Journal of Social History* 5 (1971)

News Concepts

Defining the exact meaning of "news" is difficult

What is news? Few journalists can easily answer that question, and their inability to do so makes it more difficult for them to explain their selection of some stories and rejection of others.

A growing number of people in the United States in the late twentieth century complained that journalists were too critical, sensational, and insensitive. Others worried that some stories embarrassed people involved in the news, invading their privacy and destroying their reputations. Journalists, on the other hand, always want to report stories they consider important and normally do not feel responsible for the consequences of reporting the truth.

Journalists know that the selection of news is a subjective process – an art, not a science – and amazingly complex. Definitions vary from one era to another, one city to another, and one medium to another.

No medium has enough time or space to report every potential story, just as no reader or viewer has enough time to look at every story. Rather, journalists serve as filters, or gatekeepers, who evaluate potential stories and select only the most interesting and important. Journalists rely on their instinct, experience, and professional judgment. The process becomes automatic – they can look at an event and instantly know whether it is news.

Although few journalists can define "news," most agree on its characteristics. News is interesting, timely, and important – and normally emphasizes the unusual or unexpected (problems that require the public's attention, not the normal or routine). In addition, news affects large numbers of people, often occurs close to home, and is likely to involve action, change, conflict, or humor. Journalists also want to beat their rivals – to be the first to report every story. If a rival uncovers a story, other journalists may then downplay or ignore it.

The selection of news also is affected by journalists' habits, traditions, and biases. Historically, most journalists have been white males, and the media have reflected their interests. To correct that problem, editors in the late twentieth century were hiring more women and minorities.

Other biases are more difficult to overcome. Many outlets are owned by big corporations and managed by wealthy business people. As a result, critics often charge that the media reflect a conservative, capitalistic bias. Critics also charge that some outlets

produce the least expensive mix of content likely to attract a large audience, thus maximizing profits, emphasize topics that are interesting, even trivial, rather than important, avoid stories that are difficult (or expensive) to obtain, and avoid stories that are likely to offend powerful interests, especially advertisers.

There is also a shape to the news. Newspaper reporters begin most stories with a brief summary, then present the details in the order of their importance, beginning with the most important. That shape is called the "inverted pyramid."

Other generalizations are difficult because definitions are always changing. The first U.S. newspapers appealed to the wealthy and well educated, emphasizing stories about business, politics, and foreign affairs. When Benjamin Day established the country's first penny paper, the *New York Sun,* in 1833, he redefined news, emphasizing crime, sex, and sports. Day also began to cover local events, to discuss the problems of common man, and to report humorous stories.

During some eras, the media have become more sensational. During others, the media have turned to muckraking, or investigative reporting. Muckraking is especially popular at times when people are troubled by the nation's problems, and journalists help expose those problems. Muckraking is less popular during periods of contentment and prosperity. Renamed investigative reporting, it reemerged during the 1960s, focusing on civil rights, poverty, and the war in Vietnam. Technology contributed to the growth of investigative reporting as print media sought to compete with television by devoting time and space to such reporting. During that time, two of journalism's most famous investigative reporters, Bob Woodward and Carl Bernstein, worked for a newspaper, the *Washington Post.* Together they helped expose the Watergate scandals that led to the resignation of President Richard M. Nixon.

Objectivity, another of journalism's important concepts, also emerged during the twentieth century. Journalists were expected to be neutral, unprejudiced, unopinionated, uninvolved, or unbiased. Journalists might think of these ideals in terms of balance and fairness. Yet the words "objective" and "objectivity" were not used with any regularity until the 1920s and 1930s.

New and more complex issues arose during the Great Depression and World War II, and newspapers began to publish "interpretative stories," which present facts and explain their importance and meaning.

FRED FEDLER

See also Criticism of Newspapers; Gatekeeping; Interpretative Reporting; Investigative Reporting; Muckraking; Objective Reporting; Penny Press

Further Reading

Abel, Elie, ed., *What's News: The Media in American Society,* San Francisco: Institute for Contemporary Studies, 1981
Broder, David S., *Behind the Front Page: A Candid Look at How the News is Made,* New York: Simon & Schuster, 1987
Dunn, Delmer D., *Public Officials and the Press,* Reading, Massachusetts: Addison-Wesley, 1969
Gans, Herbert J., *Deciding What's News,* New York: Vintage, 1980; London: Constable, 1980
Modern Media Institute, *Making Sense of the News,* St. Petersburg, Florida: Modern Media Institute, 1983
Roshco, Bernard, *Newsmaking,* Chicago: University of Chicago Press, 1975
Stephens, Mitchell, *A History of News: From the Drum to the Satellite,* New York: Viking, 1988
Tuchman, Gaye, *Making News: A Study in the Construction of Reality,* New York: Free Press, 1978; London: Collier Macmillan, 1980

News Councils

Local and state efforts to increase media credibility

News councils are the outgrowth of recommendations from the Hutchins Commission as well the example of successful press councils in Great Britain and the ombudsman concept in other European countries and in the United States. Although criticized by many mainstream editors and press trade organizations, a small group of socially conscious editors and communities began to pioneer councils in Colorado and California after World War II. In the 1960s, under the auspices of the Newspaper Guild's Mellett Fund, six other councils were founded as means of public education and enhancing media credibility as well as nudging profit-minded editors and overly aggressive or shoddy reporters to greater social responsibility and professionalism without involving government intervention.

Along with media professionals, a number of academics assisted in the founding of media councils across the country. They included William Rivers and his associates from Stanford University, Kenneth Stark and others from Southern Illinois University, Earl Reeves of the University of Mis-

souri at St. Louis, and David Cassady of Utah State University. Two statewide councils were established in Minnesota (1971) and Hawaii (1969).

Most media councils attempt to reflect the diversity and culture of the communities they represent. This is done by inviting private and public individuals as well as representatives from both the print and broadcast media to receive complaints or congratulations regarding the performance of the media. Concerns are referred to the proper committees that study them, sometimes hearing witnesses before reaching a decision. Their committee recommendation is then forwarded to the entire council for action. Lee Brown said that, in general, all press councils are devised with common features: they are private, disassociated from government at any level; they operate as intermediaries between the press and the public, and in the process educate both; they are composed of executives of the press and prominent persons in the community; they have no coercive or official powers; they draw up rules to govern their own operations; and they often concern themselves with questions of commission and omission in news coverage, ethics, fair play, and balance in news and editorial content.

Despite the fact that some journalists and media organizations fear the councils, most of the complaints made against the media are found to be without merit. Only a handful have substance. The only real power of the council comes in the attention it can generate as a neutral community-observer of the media through publicity in the very media it calls to task. The media have the ultimate veto power in that they do not have to publish or broadcast the media reports.

Criticism of media councils comes from those who see efforts by any outside sources to review media performance as a serious attack on journalistic independence and an infringement of First Amendment rights. Defenders of the councils see the councils simply as an institutionalized extension of editorial interaction with the community. Because news councils are separate from the media, however, they are perceived by the public as being more credible.

ALF PRATTE

See also Commission on Freedom of the Press; Criticism of Newspapers; National News Council; Ombudsman

Further Reading

Brown, Lee, *The Reluctant Reformation: On Criticizing the Press in America,* New York: David McKay, 1974

News Leaks

Publishing information without releasing the name of the source

Although journalism textbooks generally advise against using unnamed or anonymous sources, the tradition of publishing information, especially when dealing with government officials, commonly is practiced from the White House to the county courthouse, often through the informal network of news leaks. The process follows a familiar pattern of obvious calculation by anonymous news sources, generally designated as informed sources or as someone close to the subject at hand. There is generally a frame of reference that clarifies some rationale for the cloak of secrecy. The news leak reporting technique, while perhaps having the appearance of being a contemporary journalistic practice, has colonial roots traceable to the days of Thomas Paine's pamphlets and handbills around 1778 and 1779.

Paine was censured for releasing information about secret French aid to the United States in 1778 and 1779. The information Paine circulated caused a diplomatic scandal of modern proportions, revealing secret deals for weapons, violence, conflict of interest, perjury and espionage, stolen documents, and money laundering. The conflicts involved bore all the familiar ingredients of details secretly provided for contemporary combat coverage – dating from the Mexican War, the Spanish-American War, and the Vietnam War, including Daniel Ellsberg's 1971 *Pentagon Papers* leaks.

Thomas Paine was a dedicated newspaperman in Philadelphia in the late 1770s who used his publications to boost the morale of American troops in the American Revolution and promote public support. He was considered the most popular writer during this period and was most certainly a major opinion leader. The stories that Paine published dealt with secret arms deals between France and the United States, documents to which the revolutionary publisher had special access because of his position as secretary of the Foreign Affairs Committee of the Continental Congress. Paine was censured for his role in what may well have been the country's first newspaper leak, and was certainly not its last.

Because the federal government is the country's most prolific publisher through the Government Printing Office and because of the role government plays in U.S. life, the significance of information from government sources in Washington, D.C., or from government agencies is immense. The dilemma that arises with conflicting social standards comes from the traditions of an unfettered press with First Amendment protections, the need for some government secrecy, and the democratic structure of government interaction.

Although many editors in the late twentieth century decried a growing tendency in modern journalism to rely on information leaked secretly, such as Watergate information delivered to *Washington Post* reporters in a parking garage by an informant nicknamed "Deep Throat," the industry tended to reflect an attitude that there was a certain dynamic force necessitating protection of some sources if the information were to be forthcoming. In 1976, 283 readers were found to be generally suspicious of stories with unnamed sources, but they tended to understand a source's need for secrecy if the news source was considered to be knowledgeable of the subject. Another survey for the American Society of Newspaper Editors in the late 1970s found that larger newspapers relied more than smaller ones on veiled attributions. Reactions to unnamed news sources tended to depend on the readers' knowledge of public affairs.

News leaks, therefore, were crucial for the basic dissemination of details of covert actions by the Central Intelligence Agency in the Bay of Pigs invasion of Cuba, of Oval Office bugging, and of conspiracies by U.S. presidents Lyndon Johnson and Richard Nixon against antiwar activists. They also helped expose military cover-ups, such as the My Lai Massacre, as uncovered by Seymour Hersch, as well as the Watergate scandal that led to Nixon's resignation. The events are not isolated to the types of stories covered only by members of the Washington press corps. In Los Angeles, attorneys in the O.J. Simpson murder case repeatedly were admonished by the presiding judge for unprofessional conduct in their press briefings, including leaking information about whether evidence had been planted by police to frame the defendant. CBS anchorwoman Connie Chung said that she learned of her impending dismissal after sources leaked news of her agent's meeting with network officials.

News leaks infuriate those about whom information, universally unflattering and usually extremely harmful to careers and reputations, is disclosed. Nixon had a passion for secrecy and was known to his close advisers as a contradictory official who hated leaks to the press but also had favored reporters to whom he would leak selected news tidbits. In 1969, when Nixon ordered an unannounced air raid against bases in Cambodia, he was furious over coverage of the raid in the *New York Times*. He conferred with the director of the Federal Bureau of Investigation, J. Edgar Hoover, who advised that the only way to trap leakers within the White House would be to tap phones. Both Nixon and Johnson ordered illegal phone taps during their terms of office to discourage news leaks.

The general perspective in U.S. journalism in the 1990s appeared to reflect a reluctant acceptance of news leaks and unidentified or unattributed sources as a tool of organizational or interorganizational communication, often as a tool used in an attempt to limit unfavorable publicity. Journalists were willing to use such information when it appeared that the information was unlikely to be obtained from conventional sources willing to be named as news sources.

JEAN C. CHANCE

See also Johnson, Lyndon B., and the Media; Mass Media and Foreign Policy; Nixon, Richard M., and the Media; Watergate Scandal

Further Reading
Burriss, Larry Loring, *America's First Newspaper Leak: Tom Paine and the Disclosure of Secret French Aid to the United States* (Ph.D. diss., Ohio University), 1983
Culbertson, Hugh, "Leaks – A Dilemma for Editors as Well as Officials," *Journalism Quarterly* 57 (1980)
_____, and Nancy Somerick, "Variables Affect How Persons View Unnamed News Sources," *Journalism Quarterly* 54 (1977)
Kielbowicz, Richard B., "Leaks to the Press as Communication Within and Between Organizations," *Newspaper Research Journal* 1 (1980)

Nelson, Anna Kasten, "Secret Agents and Security Leaks: President Polk and the Mexican War," *Journalism Quarterly* 52 (1975)

Newsmagazines

Modern publications began in 1923

Every week in the late 1990s, about 10 million people in the United States purchased or received copies of the top-selling three newsweeklies and learned what occurred in the world during the previous week. Pass-along readership added another 40 million readers, and international editions boosted circulation as well. Newsmagazines have influenced newspapers by encouraging analysis stories, backgrounder pieces, opinion writing, and social trends stories.

Newsmagazines had been in existence for some 200 years, but the modern magazines began in 1923 with *Time*. Founded by two young men, Briton Hadden and Henry Luce, *Time* began as a 32-page weekly with 9,000 subscribers and several thousand more readers who purchased the magazine at newsstands. Legend has it that *Time* was written "for the man in a hurry." A parody of its early style went: "Backward ran the sentences until reeled the mind," or "Still never has stood *Time* since it inverted backward sentences." In addition, the magazine's staff coined or popularized unusual words, some of which became accepted in the lexicon – for example, guesstimate, kudos, moppet, pundit, socialite, and tycoon. Moreover, it stretched writers' vocabularies to come up with new words for "say" or "walk." *Time* had 22 departments and was written in brief paragraphs. The magazine cost $5 for an annual subscription.

Because of its high circulation, it became number one in advertising revenue. Luce assumed full control when Hadden died in 1929. Luce saw the publication as one that reflected his Protestant, Republican, capitalist views, and he did not hide his beliefs from readers. Its east coast slant could be interrupted with stories from other areas, if those stories conformed to the editor's stereotypes of those other regions.

In the 1990s, its circulation was more than 4 million. The magazine covered international news, national news, science, religion, and music; it used color photography extensively. Its writing remains colorful. *Time*'s "Man (Person) of the Year" cover, published in late December each year, has included Hitler and Stalin, among others.

A decade after *Time* started, *Newsweek* appeared. Competition between the two was always intense, although *Time* dominated. *Newsweek* began when a former foreign news editor of *Time* became business manager. Samuel T. Williamson was its first editor. Like *Time*, the magazine was departmentalized and carried numerous pictures. *Newsweek*, as it was spelled initially, closely related to newspaper style and organized itself as a newspaper supplement. It adhered to standards eschewing bias, unlike *Time*. After 1935, when it merged with *Today*, it began editorializing or interpreting in news stories. It received financing by the Astor and Harriman families and was acquired by the Washington Post Company in 1961. The magazine began to cover areas not touched by *Time*, such as popular music, and social and political issues like civil rights, gay rights, physical culture, evangelicals, senior citizens, and unwed couples who lived together. In the 1990s, *Newsweek* had a circulation of more than 3 million.

Newsweek was the first of the two to run writers' bylines. Both magazines had many bureaus domestically and overseas. Newsweeklies are produced by a committee process. Reporters and researchers from a particular geographic area send files on particular topics to their editorial office, from where the final story is written. Authors can read proofs but sometimes only find a shred of what they wrote in the final stories.

U.S. News and World Report was the third major newsweekly. It resulted from a merger. In 1926, David Lawrence founded the *United States Daily*, a national newspaper, in Washington, D.C. Seven years later, it became a weekly, designed for readers seeking in-depth news about the government. Another seven years saw it adopt a magazine layout, with patriotic red, white, and blue adorning the cover. In 1940, Lawrence started *World Report*, which covered international affairs. By January 1948, the merger occurred. Lawrence had significant journalism experience, having worked for the Associated Press, having served as Washington correspondent for the *New York Post*, and, in 1919, having established his own news service, Consolidated Press.

U.S. News was always third in circulation, with more than 2 million buyers. It was also slimmer than the other two newsweeklies. Its owner in the 1990s was Mortimer Zuckerman, a New York real estate magnate who also owned the *New York Daily News* and the *Atlantic* magazine. He articulated his views in a last-page editorial, which often continued on preceding pages. James Fallows, formerly editor of the *Atlantic*, was appointed editor of *U.S. News and World Report* in July 1996. The magazine was divided into six sections, ending with the popular "News You Can Use." The magazine had an annual guide on the best ways to stay healthy and another on the best hospitals. Perhaps the most well-known issues were the annual guides to colleges and graduate schools.

BARBARA STRAUS REED

See also Luce, Henry R.; Magazines in the Twentieth Century

News Management

Government attempts to manipulate the public agenda

The U.S. government attempted to guide the public agenda from the time of the Constitutional Convention, when sentries were posted to guard the doors of their litigious debates while press leaks boasted of the "unanimity" present in their discussions. Over the last two decades of the twentieth century, the press and media scholars labeled this practice news management, the credibility gap, or spin control. News management is defined as "widespread government influence in the preparation of news by the American mass media," and the practice spawned conflict between the media and the government due to conflicting views of their roles in interpreting and serving the public interest.

Journalists believe that they serve as a watchdog over the government and that the electorate expects them to act as public guardians, ensuring that elected officials remain accountable to their constituents. Furthermore, reporters cite the First Amendment, which prohibits Congress from "abridging the freedom of speech, or of the press," as their entitlement to political information.

Political officials, however, argue that, in some instances, secrecy is a matter of national security and that effective policy making requires coordination of public information. They also contend that governmental news management provides the media with information access they might not otherwise attain.

Official attempts at news management began with the pressure of legislative and military censorship to preserve public unity and support during times of war. The Sedition Act of 1798 prohibited publication of "any false, scandalous or malicious writing" about the U.S. government and its policies, punishable by imprisonment. Although American Civil War policies were less severe against journalists themselves, at least 28 newspapers were restrained or shut down by the military for supporting the peace movement. The Espionage Act of 1917 provided the basis for punishment of antiwar sentiment during World War I. President Woodrow Wilson commissioned a Committee on Public Information to "coordinate the flow of government news about the war and to rally public support for American intervention in the European conflict." Journalists who failed to comply with the committee's voluntary censorship codes lost second-class mailing privileges.

By World War II, the radio had become a primary source of public information, and with it came opportunities for "going public," a method of circumventing the media to harness or manufacture public opinion by speaking directly to the constituency. President Franklin D. Roosevelt used this tactic, disseminating information consistent with his political agenda through his radio broadcast "fireside chats."

With the rise of media technology and the advent of television came increased opportunities for news management. President Lyndon B. Johnson, for example, found televised press conferences and staged media events useful techniques to distract the public from news and issues unfavorable to White House policies.

Although a common practice from the beginning of U.S. history, news management was not brought to public attention until correspondents first discovered and reported on a credibility gap during the Vietnam War. Presidential concern with threats of public disunity prompted John F. Kennedy, Johnson, and Richard M. Nixon to use the management tactics of pressure, secrecy, distraction, and "going

public" to subdue reports of U.S. military plans. Although reporters had been compliant with the government's desire for "positive, morale-boosting stories" during previous wars, they now strove for accurate reports, however negative and disheartening they might be. The rift between press and government widened, and the press was blamed for instigating fear, disharmony, and public unrest by their mere presence at public demonstrations.

This dangerous political climate prompted President Nixon to once again call for official executive efforts toward news management. In 1969, he established the White House Office of Communications to aid in coordinating media information to fit the executive agenda. This office controlled the "spin" on political news daily by attempting to guide public perceptions of the political landscape by means of "selecting symbols, constructing meaning, and offering a variety of threats and reassurances."

The press and the government remain adversaries, but journalists and government officials still find that it pays to cooperate. The Office of Communications functions to maintain good media relations by providing the press with photo opportunities, press releases, facilities, and access to elected officials.

News management was once characterized only by government secrecy and censorship during times of war, but practices in the 1990s involved not only more sophisticated use of the mass media but also greater efforts at media cooperation. Through balancing these two efforts, political officials attempted to comply with the public's right to know while maintaining public support as well as national security.

KARLA M. LARSON

See also Committee on Public Information; Credibility Gap; Espionage and Sedition Acts; Government Secrecy; Johnson, Lyndon B., and the Media; Kennedy, John F., and the Media; Media Events; Nixon, Richard M., and the Media; Office of Telecommunications Policy; Presidential News Conferences; Roosevelt, Franklin D., and the Media; Spin Doctors; Watchdog Concept

Further Reading

Doig, Ivan, and Carol Doig, *News: A Consumer's Guide,* Englewood Cliffs, New Jersey: Prentice-Hall, 1972
Goldstein, Tom, *The News at Any Cost: How Journalists Compromise Their Ethics to Shape the News,* New York: Simon & Schuster, 1985
Goodwin, H. Eugene, and Ron F. Smith, *Groping for Ethics in Journalism*, 3rd ed., Ames: Iowa State University Press, 1994
Hunter, Julius, and Lynne S. Gross, *Broadcast News: The Inside Out,* St. Louis, Missouri: C.V. Mosby, 1980
Maltese, John A., *Spin Control: The White House Office of Communications and the Management of Presidential News,* Chapel Hill: University of North Carolina Press, 1992
Ponder, Stephen E., *News Management in the Progressive Era, 1898–1909: Gifford Pinchot, Theodore Roosevelt and the Conservation Crusade* (Ph.D. diss., University of Washington), 1985

Sparks, Will, *Who Talked to the President Last?*, New York: Norton, 1971

Newspaper Advertising

Evolved into the major source of newspaper revenue

Newspaper advertising in the United States evolved from announcements of a few lines in eighteenth-century newspapers to the major source of newspaper revenue at the end of the twentieth century. Newspapers as a medium received the highest percentage of advertising dollars spent, although that percentage dropped following the introduction of radio.

The first newspaper advertisement in America appeared in the *Boston News-Letter* and was actually a promotion for the paper itself. As trade grew in the colonies, enterprising merchants competed for customers through many kinds of advertising, and the newspaper became an important outlet. The name *Advertiser* appeared in the title of many early papers. The ads were primarily simple printed notices telling prospective buyers that the goods were available and for sale. Often the ads appeared on the front page. Then, as today, people read the advertisements as a part of the local information carried by the paper. Advertising, however, was only a small part of the content of the early papers, and the revenue from the ads was minor compared to that gained through subscriptions and printing contracts.

It was not until the advent of the penny press that newspaper advertising began to assume its modern form. Attracted by the increasing circulation of these papers, advertisers realized that newspapers were a means of reaching a mass audience on a daily basis.

For the first time, the common worker was able to purchase individual newspapers rather than having to pay for a year's subscription in advance, a practice that had excluded all but the moneyed class. Thus, the advertiser had an entire new audience of prospective customers and soon found that the increased volume of business more than justified the cost of the ads.

Spurred by the growing population of readers, the papers themselves began investing in the newest printing technology. In turn, the quality of the printing and the volume of production increased, further helping the advertiser by making the ads more attractive and by increasing circulation. The introduction of stereotyping – a process of making a mold curved to fit the cylinder of the press – in the mid-nineteenth century made it possible to develop display advertising. Now the advertiser could make use of both larger headlines and illustrations.

With the increased production generated by the Industrial Revolution and the need to move more goods to distant locations, advertising became increasingly important. As national and regional brands began to develop in the 1880s, both newspapers and magazines became natural choices for advertisers, although magazines gained the bulk of the advertising at first. In 1888, *Printer's Ink,* a trade magazine for advertising, began publishing. By the beginning of the twentieth century, several associations worked to promote newspaper advertising. These included the Newspaper Advertiser Executive Association (1900) and the Bureau of Advertising (1913). In the late twentieth century, several advertising organizations operated under the auspices of the Newspaper Association of America.

Early advertising agents prospected for advertising and delivered it to the newspapers, who then paid a fee for the service. Volney Palmer is credited with starting the first agency in 1841 for the purpose of selling newspaper space. Also in the 1840s, George Rowell and John Hooper bought blank space in newspapers at a discounted price and then resold it to advertisers at full price. While the percentage of discount varied at first, a commonly agreed-upon 15 percent was the practice by the end of the century. This was the beginning of agency commissions.

The level of circulation always has been of intense interest to advertisers, not only because it tells them the number of people the ad will reach but also because it is the prime determinant of newspaper rates. Both Rowell and the N.W. Ayer Agency published directories with circulation listings as early as 1869, but their accuracy was doubtful. The Audit Bureau of Circulations, founded in 1914, provided certified circulation thereafter.

By the end of the nineteenth century, the convergence of urban growth, the emergence of the department store, and the circulation surges of the major city papers set the pattern for the development of newspaper advertising as it became known. Retail store advertising contributed heavily to the growth of advertising in both space and dollars from the 1880s on and remained a dominant area into the 1990s. Classified advertising, including both classified display and linage, grew in importance and came to contribute up to 40 percent of the revenue in some markets.

As advertising agencies grew, their newspaper advertising business largely moved to regional and national clients, while most local advertising was sold directly by each paper's own sales force. Because agencies received a commission for their placements, a practice of charging a higher rate for national advertising began. At the same time, a schedule of discounts was developed for local advertisers based upon either volume of advertising placed or frequency of placement. These discounts rewarded greater advertising levels so that the largest advertisers paid less per line or inch.

Advertising originally was sold by the agate line. In the late twentieth century, most advertising was sold by the column inch, which is measured as one column by one inch, or by Standard Advertising Units, a measurement developed in 1980 to standardize ad sizes in response to agency complaints that newspapers used differing column widths, making it impossible to design just one ad for several markets.

The introduction of the offset press and increased color capability during the 1970s and 1980s enabled newspapers to offer ad clients and readers a quality of ads that came close to that of magazines and freestanding inserts. Advertisers also demanded detailed information about readers, and newspapers engaged in more and more reader research, offering zip code and other segmented geographic targeting and developing subsidiary publications to help advertisers reach more narrowly targeted audiences. Customized packages and pricing options offered advertisers a greater choice of products and audience. Customer service was the watchword.

MARY ALICE SHAVER

See also Advertising in the Eighteenth Century; Advertising in the Nineteenth Century; Advertising in the Twentieth Century; Audience Research for Newspapers; Newspaper Circulation; Penny Press

Further Reading

Bogart, Leo, *Press and Public: Who Reads What, When, Where, and Why in American Newspapers*, 2nd ed., Hillsdale, New Jersey: Lawrence Erlbaum, 1989
Chasnoff, Joseph K., *Selling Newspaper Space*, New York: Ronald, 1913

Newspaper Awards

The oldest of newspaper awards – the Pulitzer Prizes – were founded in 1917 by the trustees of Columbia University. Joseph Pulitzer, publisher of the *St. Louis (Missouri) Post-Dispatch* and the *New York World*, had bequeathed $2 million to Columbia to establish prizes for advancement of education, public service, and morals, and for U.S. literature, and to found a school of journalism after his death in 1911.

The Pulitzer Prizes – the most cherished and controversial of newspaper awards in the late twentieth century – were administered by the trustees of Columbia University. Written nominations were processed by the Pulitzer Advisory Board after screening by groups of jurors for each category. The board could accept or reject the recommendations of the juries; the Columbia trustees made the final decision. Categories included prizes for nonjournalistic arts and writing, but newspapers tended to call the most attention to newspaper prizes for beat reporting, criticism, editorial writing, editorial cartooning, explanatory journalism, feature photography, spot news photography, investigative reporting, national reporting, spot news reporting, feature writing, commentary, international reporting, and public service.

Pulitzer controversy peaked in 1981, when Janet Cooke of the *Washington Post* relinquished her feature writing prize after admitting that her story about "Jimmy," an eight-year-old drug addict, was a hoax. Other controversies often have focused upon the prize selection process.

The second oldest of the newspaper awards were the Sigma Delta Chi Awards, founded in 1932 and presented by the Society of Professional Journalism in 27 categories. Other long-time awards, with their establishment dates, awarding institutions, and purposes, were:

National Headliner Awards (1934), National Headliner Awards of Pleasantville, New Jersey, for general, investigative, and public service reporting, columns, features, editorials, photography, and graphics;

Inland News Picture Awards (1940), Inland Daily Press Association, 12 categories of photojournalism;

Pictures of the Year Awards (1943), National Press Photographers Association and the University of Missouri School of Journalism;

The Heywood Broun Awards (1944), the Newspaper Guild, for journalistic performance exemplifying the guild leader's care for the underdog and economically challenged;

George Polk Awards (1946), Long Island University, courage and resourcefulness in reporting and descriptive excellence in story, commentary, and photography;

Inland Local Public Affairs News Awards (1948), University of Wisconsin School of Journalism for Inland Press Association members, local public affairs news, features, and series;

Sidney Hillman Foundation Prizes (1950), journalism focused on humanitarian causes;

Scripps Howard Foundation Ernie Pyle Awards (1954), stories exemplifying the style and craft of the World War II correspondent;

Russell L. Cecil Arthritis/Medical Journalism Awards (1956), Arthritis Foundation, stories about arthritis and other rheumatic diseases;

James T Grady–James H. Stack Awards (1956), American Chemical Society, career accomplishments in interpreting chemistry for the public;

Golden Eye Trophies (1957), World Press Photo Foundation, photos and photo stories by professional photographers;

Gerald R. Loeb Awards (1958), Graduate School of Management of the University of California at Los Angeles, reporting and commentary about business;

Missouri Lifestyles Journalism Awards (1960), JCPenney/University of Missouri, excellence for regularly scheduled feature newspaper supplements.

Hundreds of other annual prizes were awarded to U.S. newspaper journalists by various groups, including journalism associations, foundations, universities, and nonjournalism trade and professional groups.

CHARLES H. MARLER

Newspaper Chains, or Groups

One parent company owns two or more newspapers in different markets

Group ownership became one of the most significant developments of U.S. journalism in the twentieth century. It exists whenever two or more newspapers in different markets are commonly owned and operated as units of the same parent company. In 1994, about 1,550 daily newspapers were being published in the United States. The 20 largest groups, or chains, as they were formerly called, controlled 502 of those newspapers (32 percent) and 35,000,000 subscriptions, or 58 percent of the national daily newspaper circulation. Group ownership was the dominant form of newspaper ownership in the United States in the late twentieth century.

The nation's first great newspaper chain was started in 1878 by Edward W. Scripps, who established the *Cleveland (Ohio) Penny Press* with $10,000 borrowed from his family. By 1880, Scripps controlled five dailies, including papers in St. Louis, Missouri; Detroit, Michigan; and Cincinnati, Ohio. However, the roots of chain journalism preceded Scripps' venture by many years. Cooperation among newspapers of different ownerships on the frontier was common through commercial agreements by which publishers often attempted to control subscription rates and the cost of labor. Even in the colonial era, Benjamin Franklin invested in a number of newspapers to help budding printers become publishers.

Although E.W. Scripps was not the originator of the concept, he was the first press owner to make chain newspaper publishing work. With control of five newspapers, Scripps and his business manager formed the Scripps-McRae League in the mid-1890s, the first of several publishing partnerships that Scripps helped establish. His practice was to loan funds to enterprising young publishers. If they succeeded, Scripps received 51 percent of the profits; if it failed, he took all of the loss. The Scripps-Howard group resulted from one of those partnerships.

As the father of the modern media chain, Scripps left a rich legacy of newspaper groups, consisting mainly of inexpensive, crusading, community newspapers designed for mass readership. At his death in 1926, Scripps left his heirs controlling interests in newspapers in 15 states, plus United Press, United Features Syndicate, and other media properties. The pattern of group newspaper ownership pioneered by Scripps also was quickly adopted by other expansion-minded newspaper publishers.

While Scripps devoted his efforts to business developments and crusades about social and economic conditions, many of the characteristics of the "new journalism" were perfected by another early group publisher, Joseph Pulitzer,

at his *St. Louis (Missouri) Post-Dispatch* and at his *New York World,* acquired in 1878 and 1883, respectively. Pulitzer kept the prices of his newspapers low (two or three cents) while developing strong news-gathering staffs and procedures, expanding advertising, emphasizing objectivity, and promoting civic improvements.

The Hearst family entered the newspaper business in 1880, when George Hearst, a mining millionaire and California politician, bought the *San Francisco Examiner.* His son, William Randolph Hearst, ultimately became Scripps' main rival after adding a newspaper in Boston to those in New York and San Francisco in 1904. Hearst followed the Pulitzer model for his own newspapers, which were typically crusading, enterprising, and sensational. During the World War I era and the 1920s, Hearst acquired and often consolidated newspapers from coast to coast. In all, Hearst owned some 42 newspapers.

With the concept of group publishing firmly established, newspaper chains grew rapidly after 1900. Frank Munsey began such a chain in 1901, when he acquired the *Daily News* in New York. Although Munsey often was criticized for the quality of his papers and for his lack of managerial success, he earned a fortune by buying and selling, merging and consolidating large-city newspapers before and after World War I.

Samuel I. Newhouse, whose company in the 1990s ranked third in daily circulation, became a multimillionaire by acquiring newspapers and making them financially successful in the 1920s and 1930s. His basic technique was to buy ailing newspapers and resuscitate them by modern management methods, including cost-cutting and heavy promotion of advertising and circulation.

The trend toward chain ownership of newspapers accelerated after World War II. By 1960, nearly 30 percent of all daily newspapers in the United States were chain-owned. More than 100 groups existed, but only three were nationally important – Hearst, Scripps Howard, and Newhouse. During the 1970s and 1980s, three other large groups be-

Top 12 Newspaper Companies in the United States
1995

Paper	Daily Circulation	Number of Dailies	Sunday Circulation	Number of Sunday Editions
Gannett	6,109,223	92	6,274,823	73
Knight-Ridder	3,669,580	31	5,157,301	28
Newhouse	2,910,012	26	3,767,941	21
Times Mirror	2,514,298	10	3,217,934	8
Dow Jones	2,334,696	20	536,689	13
N.Y. Times	2,309,94	20	3,238,929	16
Thomson	1,707,449	83	1,625,636	58
Hearst	1,352,594	12	2,609,579	11
Cox	1,325,352	20	1,806,716	19
Tribune	1,297,824	4	1,940,309	4
E.W. Scripps	1,260,610	17	1,323,838	11
Hollinger	1,196.180	108	810,253	27

Source: http://www.naa.org/info/Facts/facts4.html#LUSNPC

came very powerful – Gannett, Knight-Ridder, and Thomson Newspapers, a Canadian company. Other prominent groups included Times Mirror Inc., the New York Times Company, and the Tribune Company.

The Gannett organization, which became the most powerful newspaper company, dates back to 1906, when Frank Gannett, the managing editor of a small upstate New York newspaper, purchased a part interest in the *Elmira Gazette*. However, Gannett's major growth took place in the 1960s, when it purchased nine daily newspapers near New York City. Its early properties were mostly dominant papers in small and medium-size growth markets, while most later acquisitions were in large cities. Gannett also achieved notable success in the mid-1960s with the establishment of *Florida Today*, a new daily publication in the Cape Canaveral area.

Gannett's flamboyant chief executive Alan Neuharth literally transformed the firm from family ownership to corporate dominance. Neuharth led Gannett into public stock ownership, rigorous financial management, market-based decision making, and a bold expansion drive unprecedented in the newspaper business. By 1973, Gannett owned 51 newspapers with 2.2 million daily circulation. At Neuharth's retirement in 1986, Gannett's 93 daily newspapers had a daily circulation of 6 million. In 1995, Gannett owned 82 daily newspapers and led all other groups with 6.3 million daily circulation.

The Knight-Ridder group, second largest in circulation in the 1990s, was developed from a single newspaper owned by its founder, Charles L. Knight. Using the *Akron (Ohio) Beacon-Journal* as a base, his son John Knight led the chain through a period of heavy expansion starting in the 1940s that focused mainly on large-city newspapers. The firm's most significant merger combined 16 Knight newspapers with 19 owned by the Ridder family in 1974.

Prior to the merger, the Knight group earned a reputation for publishing high-quality, well-managed newspapers. It also was known for buying out competing papers to reduce competition. The offering of public stock in 1969 and the merger with Ridder brought financial demands from investors, as well as rigid financial controls and systematic management, to the previously family-owned newspapers. In 1995, Knight-Ridder owned 29 newspapers with about 3.7 million daily circulation.

Although Gannett, Knight-Ridder, and Newhouse led in circulation, Thomson Newspapers, a worldwide company based in Canada, boasted the highest number of daily newspapers in the United States at 109. Thomson's international businesses included newspapers, book publishing, and broadcasting properties in Canada, Scotland, England, Africa, and the United States.

With the shift of newspaper publishing to modern corporate ownerships, the industry's management was transformed from loosely managed, family-controlled organizations to investor-owned, financially sophisticated, market-oriented, and aggressively managed national and regional businesses. Group publishers also derived economic benefits from economies of scale in purchasing newsprint, ink, and syndicated services, as well as sharing corporate expenses among numerous publications. While they often

generated savings by consolidating newspapers within a market, groups also had the resources to restore vitality to ailing newspapers and to successfully establish new publications even when there was great financial risk.

HERBERT H. HOWARD

See also Economics of Newspapers; Hearst, William Randolph; Media Conglomerates; Munsey, Frank A.; Newspaper Competition; Printers' Networks; Pulitzer, Joseph; Scripps, E.W.

Further Reading

Beam, Randal A., "The Impact of Group Ownership Variables on Organizational Professionalism at Daily Newspapers," *Journalism Quarterly* 70:4 (Winter 1993), pp. 907–918
Busterna, John, "Trends in Daily Newspaper Ownership," *Journalism Quarterly* 65:4 (Winter 1988), pp. 831–838
Cose, Ellis, *The Press*, New York: William Morrow, 1989
Facts About Newspapers 1994, Reston, Virginia: Newspaper Association of America, 1994
Picard, Robert G., et al., eds., *Press Concentration and Monopoly: New Perspectives on Newspaper Ownership and Operation*, Norwood, New Jersey: Ablex, 1988
Schwarzlose, Richard A., *Newspapers–A Reference Guide*, New York: Greenwood, 1987
Waterman, David, "A New Look at Media Chains and Groups: 1977–1989," *Journal of Broadcasting & Electronic Media* 35:2 (Spring 1991), pp. 167–177

Newspaper Circulation

Newspaper delivery directly to customers developed in nineteenth century

The development of the penny press in the 1830s and after created a new problem for newspaper publishers, who for the first time needed to get newspapers quickly into the hands of vendors on the street. Previous to this, newspapers had been mailed or picked up in the office.

In the major cities, independent companies quickly arose to handle the distribution of newspapers from all publishers in the city. These agencies kept circulation departments from developing because low-level counters could distribute bundles of papers to independent agents. An exception among eastern cities was Philadelphia, where the press emphasized subscriptions and home delivery. Home delivery required a more complicated organization that taxed the management skills of circulation managers, but eventually, most dailies across the country followed the Philadelphia model.

A newspaper's circulation was, for most publishers, a trade secret from the time of John Campbell's *Boston News-Letter* in 1704 until the 1870s, when enlightened publishers in Detroit, Michigan; Chicago; St. Louis, Missouri; and New York City began to promote circulation figures to advertisers. It took 210 years from Campbell's first issue for the newspaper industry to create and support an

United States Daily Newspapers by Circulation Category
1995

| Year | Total | Number of Daily Newspapers Circulation | | | | Dailies Over 50,000 | |
		Under 50,000	50,000–100,000	100,000–250,000	Over 250,000	Number	Percent of Total
1946	1,763	1,564	91	70	38	199	11.3
1950	1,772	1,571	82	84	35	201	11.3
1955	1,760	1,548	94	82	36	212	12.1
1960	1,763	1,540	96	83	44	223	12.7
1065	1,751	1,510	111	88	42	241	13.8
1970	1,748	1,491	127	92	38	257	14.7
1975	1,756	1,504	135	81	36	252	14.3
1980	1,745	1,479	145	86	35	266	15.2
1985	1,676	1,418	141	82	35	258	15.4
1987	1,645	1,394	137	75	39	251	15.3
1988	1,642	1,377	143	79	43	265	16.1
1989	1,626	1,362	139	81	44	264	16.2
1990	1,611	1,343	143	82	43	268	16.6
1991	1,586	1,336	129	78	43	250	15.8
1992	1,570	1,323	132	72	43	247	15.7
1993	1,552	1,317	125	68	42	235	15.1
1994	1,538	1,303	126	68	41	235	18.0
1995	1,532	1,297	128	67	40	235	15.3

Source: http://www.naa.org/info/Facts/facts4.html#LUSNPC

agency that would verify the circulation of most of the nation's daily newspapers.

Circulation disclosure went through three overlapping stages of development. In the first stage, the question to publishers was, "What is your circulation?" As already mentioned, publishers treated circulation as proprietary information, keeping it secret even from advertising agents who were buying space in the newspaper. As it became more common for some publishers to publicize their circulation, under pressure from advertisers, the question arose, "What do you mean by circulation?" Many publishers publicized the number of copies they printed. Several publishers publicized their record sales, usually earned during the excitement of a major presidential campaign. Still others publicized sales plus all copies that were discounted to hotels or given to advertisers and friends of the publisher. They even included subscriptions that were never paid for.

As the meaning of circulation was being debated in the newspaper business, advertisers wanted to move to the third stage, which was, "How can we know you are telling the truth?" Publishers, after they got used to publicizing circulation, became notorious for lying in those statements.

This third stage culminated in the establishment of the Audit Bureau of Circulations (ABC) in 1914. The ABC was formed from two independent organizations that had been created to verify circulation figures. One agency had been supported by leading publishers, the other by advertisers and agencies. Neither was successful. The publishers lacked credibility, and the advertisers lacked financial support. The ABC brought them together. Publishers even allowed advertisers to control the board of the ABC, a remarkable concession for people who had tried to maintain control of all circulation information. All members, including the advertisers, paid membership fees in order to access ABC audits. All members also had input into determining the auditing process and the meaning of circulation. The ABC was the first successful circulation auditing agency in the country, and it continued at the end of the twentieth century.

George P. Rowell, a New York City advertising agent, was the single most important figure in getting the press to own up to accurate circulation. He had put estimates of circulation with the names of newspapers in his *Directory of American Newspapers* beginning with the second edition in 1870. He would use a publisher's statement, but he estimated circulation for those publishers who refused to make a statement. Of course, Rowell could not know the correct circulation without checking it out himself. His estimates sometimes brought howls of outrage from publishers who thought their figures were unnecessarily low; others accused him of increasing the circulation of publishers who advertised in his *Directory*. Still other publishers lied when they gave him sworn statements, as competitors were able to prove. Nevertheless, he kept up the pressure for accurate circulation figures by publishing estimates in each edition of his *Directory*.

As newspapers grew in size, especially following the Civil War, business managers began to shed the circulation duties they had performed, hiring men – always men – to fold, tie, and distribute the thousands of copies that came from the press each day. Circulation managers became important cogs in newspaper production. They not only distributed papers, they learned to promote them.

United States Weekly Newspapers
Total Number and Circulation 1960–1995

Year	Total Weekly Newspapers	Average Circulation	Total Weekly Circulation
1960	8,174	2,566	20,974.338
1965	8,061	3,106	25,036.031
1970	7,612	3,660	27,857,332
1975	7,612	4,715	35,892.409
1980	7,954	5,324	42,347,512
1985	7,704	6,359	48,988,801
1986	7,711	6,497	50,098,000
1987	7,600	6,262	47,593,000
1988	7,498	6,894	51,691,451
1989	7,606	6,958	52,919,451
1990	7,550	7,309	55,181,047
1991	7,476	7,323	54,746,332
1992	7,417	7,358	54,577,034
1993	7,437	7,629	56,734,526
1994	7,176	10,975	78,763,120
1995	8,453	9,425	79,668,266

Note: Total weekly newspapers figures include paid- and free-circulation newspapers. 1994 and 1995 are not comparable to prior years owing to change in information collection procedures by the National Newspaper Association.

Source: http://www.naa.org/info/Facts/facts4.html#LUSNPC

The field had developed so well by 1898 that 35 publishers and advertising and circulation managers formed the National Association of Newspaper Circulation Managers (NANCM). Even then, at their first convention, some members still managed both advertising and circulation. The NANCM added Canadian newspapers to its roster in 1910, thus becoming the International Circulation Managers Association. The organization began to expand rapidly after that. This expansion took place in large measure because of the need to audit circulation.

The formation of the ABC in 1914 had a dramatic impact on the development of the circulation department. The charter membership of the ABC was 614; one year later, it was 978. Circulation managers needed skill to produce the sophisticated and verifiable data that audits required.

The rise of an association in 1898 to deal specifically with circulation issues gave a patina of respectability to circulation departments that soon received fierce and justifiable criticism. When William Randolph Hearst entered the Chicago market in 1900, he found fiercely aggressive competitors who locked him out of the local distribution trust, so Hearst's lieutenants hired thugs to develop distribution through force and the threat of force. Chicago newspaper publishers retaliated. Several newsdealers were killed, and numerous others were severely injured or maimed before an uneasy peace was declared. Hearst gained access to the market, but the circulation war was too close to a real war for most people.

By 1915, a year after the formation of the ABC, circulation managers played an important role in building circula-

tion through legitimate means. It had been a long, hard struggle for legitimacy.

TED CURTIS SMYTHE

See also American Newspaper Directory; Audience Research for Newspapers; Chicago Newspaper Trust; Newsboys

Further Reading

Bennett, Charles O., *Facts Without Opinion: First Fifty Years of the Audit Bureau of Circulations,* Chicago: Audit Bureau of Circulations, 1965
Boyenton, William H., *Audit Bureau of Circulations,* Chicago: Audit Bureau of Circulations, 1952
Davenport, John Scott, *Newspaper Circulation, Backbone of the Industry,* Dubuque, Iowa: Wm. C. Brown, 1949
Smythe, Ted Curtis, "The Advertisers' War to Verify Newspaper Circulation, 1870–1914," *American Journalism* 3 (1986)
Thorn, William J., and Mary Pat Pfeil, *Newspaper Circulation: Marketing the News,* New York: Longman, 1987

Newspaper Columnists
Writing specialty developed during the Civil War era

A column is an article of modest length that appears on a regular schedule under the byline of its author; a columnist is one who practices this craft. Beyond these simple definitions, however, the world of the columnist is quite diverse.

Some columns are strictly local – written for one paper. Others are self-syndicated – sold to whatever papers will use them. Still others are more widely distributed by conventional syndication agreements or on the wire of a newspaper chain or group. Most columnists write under their own name; a few use pen names (Eppie Lederer as "Ann Landers"), professional names (Larry Zeiger as "Larry King"), or even fictitious names (Otus the Head Cat at the *Arkansas Democrat Gazette*). Some columnists are primarily ruminative; others are more reportorial. Some provide very general reading matter, calling themselves "personal columnists" or "general columnists." Others write almost exclusively about politics or are humorists, writing primarily to provide levity in the midst of the troubled world reflected in the publication. A growing number of syndicated columnists in the late twentieth century specialized by topic: art and antiques, bridge or chess, business and finance, gardening, real estate, sports, travel, and the like.

The work of newspaper columnists has several distinctive characteristics. It is personal; it represents the views of its writer; and it often is about people. Generally written with wit and style and with greater freedom of approach than is encouraged in conventional news reporting, columns can offer opinion, although opinion is not the column's main purpose, as it is for the editorial or the review. The columnist's primary responsibility is to be interesting, a goal often reached by combining the serious with the frivolous.

The first "columnists" appeared in the Civil War era, as did the concept of syndicated copy. The earliest columnists were women, who were given columns to bolster the number of their papers' female readers; men of serious literary bent, who had contributed stories and sketches to newspapers and who eventually adopted a regular schedule for their work in the form of a column; and humorists, who likewise regularized their output by taking on a column with a set schedule. Perhaps the first woman columnist was Sara Parton, whose column dates from 1855. Benjamin Perley Poore's column, "Waifs from Washington," was originated in 1854; Henry Wheeler Shaw, whose literary character was "Josh Billings," started his column in 1867; and satirist Ambrose Bierce began his column in 1868.

These pioneers were followed by a host of other writers, whose entertaining columns appeared both in small U.S. papers and in large-circulation urban dailies. Many of those whose columns ran locally in the smaller papers have been largely forgotten. Chicago was the early leader in the urban centers. Eugene Field launched his column there in 1883, George Ade and Finley Peter Dunne ("Mr. Dooley") in 1893, Bert Leston Taylor in 1899, and Franklin P. Adams in 1903.

As New York City loomed ever larger as the nation's publishing mecca, many of the best columnists migrated there to seek wider fame and greater fortune. Feminist and sentimentalist Sara Lippincott, who wrote as "Grace Greenwood," began her column there in 1892; witty Helen Rowland arrived at about that same time; and Marie Manning, who as "Beatrice Fairfax" was one of the originators of the personal advice column, came in 1898. Two of the greatest of U.S. humor columnists moved to New York in the early 1900s: Irvin S. Cobb in 1905 and Don Marquis in 1909. Franklin Adams and Damon Runyon came in 1914, and in 1917, New York papers began carrying columns by H.L. Mencken and Zöe Beckley, who specialized in writing about interesting people. Society columnist Maury Biddle Paul arrived in New York in 1918, Ring Lardner introduced his mix of humor and sports in 1919, writer Christopher Morley had a column in 1920, Oliver Odd McIntyre began his popular metro column in 1922, and Walter Winchell introduced the Broadway gossip column in the same year. To this point, the job of the columnist was more to entertain than to inform, and many columnists made regular use of light verse in addition to their prose copy.

At about this time, however, the more serious public affairs columnist emerged. One of the early leaders, in 1919, was the *New York Post*'s David Lawrence, who went on to found *U.S. News and World Report*. Others were Walter Lippmann of the *New York Herald-Tribune* in 1931 and Arthur Krock of the *New York Times* in 1932. Also in 1932, Drew Pearson began his investigative column in Washington, D.C. A standout among early female political columnists was Dorothy Thompson of the *New York Herald-Tribune*, whose column began in 1936.

From then to now, thousands of columnists have come and gone. Many began as reporters and eventually were awarded their own columns, the culmination of their careers. Others moved on from column writing to become book authors, screenwriters, broadcasters, or executives. Some newspaper owners – William Randolph Hearst, Dorothy Schiff, and John Knight, for instance – wrote columns of their own, as did some editors in chief. Other columnists deliberately avoided getting into management, preferring to write a column full-time instead.

The field of column writing in the 1990s included "celebrity columnists" who had expertise in some area but lacked a journalistic background – for example, businessman Lee Iacocca and civil rights leader Jesse Jackson – in addition to physicians who wrote medical advice columns and other nonjournalists who wrote topic-specialized columns, many of which were syndicated. In the 1990s, many minority columnists who wrote about the nation's African American, Asian American, Native American, and Hispanic communities emerged. There were, of course, minority columnists early on, such as Gertrude Mossell (1885) and Lillian Lewis (1889), who wrote for the black press, and Delilah Beasley, who in 1923 became the first black columnist at a mainstream U.S. paper. Still, growth in the number of minority columnists was slow until the 1990s.

SAM G. RILEY

Further Reading

Belford, Barbara, *Brilliant Bylines: A Biographical Anthology of Notable Newspaperwomen in America*, New York: Columbia University Press, 1986

Braden, Maria, *She Said What?: Interviews with Women Newspaper Columnists*, Lexington: University Press of Kentucky, 1993

Fisher, Charles, *The Columnists*, New York: Howell, Soskin, 1944

Grauer, Neil A., *Wits and Sages*, Baltimore, Maryland, and London: Johns Hopkins University Press, 1984

Meyer, Karl E., *Pundits, Poets, and Wits: An Omnibus of American Newspaper Columns*, New York: Oxford University Press, 1990

Riley, Sam G., ed., *The Best of the Rest: Non-Syndicated Newspaper Columnists Select Their Best Work*, Westport, Connecticut: Greenwood, 1993

_____, *Biographical Dictionary of American Newspaper Columnists*, Westport, Connecticut: Greenwood, 1995

Weiner, Richard, *Syndicated Columnists*, 3rd ed., New York: Richard Weiner, 1979

Newspaper Competition

Competition caused newspaper deaths, consolidation

Competition claimed the lives of so many daily newspapers in the United States during the twentieth century that companies otherwise competing with one another entered into cooperative business alliances. Hoping to stay ahead of competition, some newspaper companies invested heavily in experiments in electronic publishing. In the hope of preserving newspaper competition, Congress passed legislation permitting practices that in other industries might be seen as anticompetitive.

To understand newspaper competition in the United States, one needs to examine briefly the nature of competition itself. When several persons or companies vie to acquire the same prize or resources, competition exists. Among businesses, competition is commonly viewed as a collection of commercial practices designed to give one company a clear economic advantage over others engaged in the same industry and market as measured by market share and income. The end of such competition is for one company to achieve market dominance and perhaps to eliminate the competition altogether by using practices that may be prohibited by federal antitrust statutes.

Business analysts speak of competitive practices within an industry as well as "environmental" (such as the law) and other forces outside competitors' direct control that have a significant impact on the industry itself. Industry competition, according to Michael E. Porter, is driven by four external forces: buyers, potential entrants, suppliers, and substitutes.

In the newspaper industry at the close of the twentieth century, the buyers included advertisers, subscribers, and, sometimes, purchasers of printing and related publication services. Newspapers within the same market compete for buyers in several ways. To gain readers, they might offer subscription incentives. These incentives could be as simple as offering a week or a month of the newspaper free to people who paid for a number of weeks in advance. They might involve more complex schemes that offered cash or other prizes to people who found clues in each day's paper over a period of several weeks. Newspapers also sought to capture advertisers through incentives as well as through sales pitches meant to place their paper in a better light than the competition. Newspaper publishers who owned presses often sought outside printing jobs to help keep expensive equipment productive when presses were not needed to produce the newspaper. At the close of the century, many newspaper companies also developed on-line news products as a way of reaching new audiences.

The term "potential entrants" refers to companies and individuals in a position to start a new newspaper within a market. In any given industry, there are barriers to overcome in starting a new business. Analysts describe entry barriers as high or low based on how difficult it is to start a new newspaper. In the twentieth century, one of the major barriers to entry was the high cost of printing presses and related equipment.

Suppliers for newspapers include paper mills and ink producers. Paper is by far the most expensive supply. Because there are few suppliers of newsprint, these suppliers may exercise considerable power over newspaper companies with few alternatives from which to choose. This led some newspaper companies – Times-Mirror, for example – to buy paper mills and tracts of paper-producing timber. Newspaper industry organizations like the Newspaper As-sociation of America invested heavily in research into technologies for producing newsprint from alternative sources such as kenaf.

Substitutes are products that fill the same, or similar, needs. Radio and television are seen by some as substitutes for newspapers. If potential newspaper readers satisfy their need for news, for example, by watching television, or if advertisers reach their clientele through radio, these substitutes have entered the newspaper industry's competitive arena.

Intense newspaper industry competition for readers and advertisers in the United States did not develop until the middle of the nineteenth century. Prior to the second quarter of the nineteenth century, the competition among newspapers in the United States was largely a competition for the attention and support of an elite readership rather than a mass audience. Some newspapers were supported by political parties. Others carved out a niche as the "mercantile press" by focusing on the interests of trade and commerce. Commonly, the publisher of a newspaper was a printer first, publishing books, government documents, and other printing. These printers took on newspapers as a secondary endeavor, sometimes to promote their own printing.

In any case, newspapers of the early republic catered to a more or less elite audience who could afford the six cents per day subscription payable in yearly commitments, in advance. Readership, on average was about 2,000 – hardly a mass audience by twentieth-century standards. During the second quarter and into the third quarter of the nineteenth century, emerging technologies and a shift in competitive strategies reshaped the newspaper industry.

First, development of the penny press represented three important shifts in competitive strategy for newspapers. When Benjamin Day launched the first successful penny press in 1833 (the *New York Sun*), he did so as a businessman who saw a chance to make money. He would sell advertising to support his endeavor. His concept was to sell the newspaper at a reduced rate (one cent instead of six) to appeal to a mass audience. A large audience, in turn, would be attractive to advertisers.

The strategy of Day and others who followed his example created a growing class of businessmen who were newspaper publishers first. Development of mass newspaper audiences in the middle of the nineteenth century also was dependent on a few variables in the environment in which the industry operated. Chief among these were development of widespread literacy, faster printing presses, the telegraph (1840s), and improved means of transportation (especially the railroad) to distribute newspapers to wider audiences. By the end of the nineteenth century, newspaper competitive strategy was well on its way to achieving what Kathleen Hall Jamieson and Karlyn Kohrs Campbell called the purpose of all mass media – "to attract and hold a large audience for advertisers."

En route to that competition for a large audience, Joseph Pulitzer and William Randolph Hearst engaged in what has come to be known as "the circulation wars." In these "wars," the two great publishers are alleged to have encouraged ever more sensational reporting in an attempt to win readers and to force the competition out of business.

The Hearst-Pulitzer wars occurred at a time when important forces in the marketplace totally outside the control of either publisher already had begun to reshape the nature of publication. While the circulation wars between Pulitzer and Hearst have attracted much attention, scholarship in the late twentieth century showed that newspaper competition in the late nineteenth century was not limited to flashy headlines and sensational stories designed to capture readers, which in turn attracts the interest of advertisers. In days when several daily newspapers circulated in most cities and new ones might enter a market at any moment, a number of collusive practices became common. Among anticompetitive practices at the time were fixing of advertising rates and circulation prices as well as collusion on printing contracts and the number of pages printed.

Pulitzer's flagship newspaper, the *Post-Dispatch* in St. Louis, Missouri, was engaged in other kinds of competitive practices designed to gain or to preserve advantages over other newspapers. Edward E. Adams found that, in 1894, the *Post-Dispatch,* the *St. Louis Republic,* and the *St. Louis Globe-Democrat* engaged in a price-fixing arrangement aimed at cutting into the advertising base of the *St. Louis Chronicle.* Late in 1894, the *Chronicle* management entered into an agreement with the *Post-Dispatch* to fix rates of rural circulation in order to get the advantage of other papers.

In May 1897, some St. Louis newspapers agreed to fix bidding for lucrative government printing contracts so that the *Republic* would take away the printing from the *Journal.* The arrangement involved fixed bidding by the *Republic,* the *Globe-Democrat,* and the *Post-Dispatch.* Instead of bidding, the *Chronicle* and *Star* ran "news" stories during the week of bidding revealing circulation irregularities by the *Journal.* The stratagem had the desired effect. The county solicitor, fearful of the negative publicity, granted the contract to the *Republic,* and the *Journal* lost its primary source of income.

The practices used by the St. Louis papers were repeated frequently in other cities late in the nineteenth century and into the early twentieth century. Adams described agreements made in Chicago; Los Angeles; Cleveland and Cincinnati, Ohio; Kansas City, Missouri; San Diego, California; and Seattle and Tacoma, Washington.

Some newspapers in the twentieth century engaged in forced combinations for advertising and circulation. Under this practice, buyers (subscribers or advertisers) desiring to purchase one product were compelled to purchase additional products. Acting under the Sherman Act of 1890 and the Clayton Act of 1914, the U.S. Justice Department prosecuted several cases to break up these practices.

In *Associated Press* v. *United States* (1945), the Supreme Court ruled illegal the practice of allowing only one newspaper per market to have access to the Associated Press news wire. The court ruled predatory advertising policies illegal in *Lorain Journal Co.* v. *United States* (1951). The *Journal* had refused to accept advertising from any business who ran commercials on a new radio station in the Lorain, Ohio, market. In *Kansas City Star Co.* v. *United States* (1957), the Supreme Court ruled certain kinds of forced combinations illegal. A ruling in *Citizen Publishing Co.* v.

United States (1969) challenged the legality of some provisions in joint operating agreements, in which two newspapers in the same market share physical facilities and equipment in order to preserve competition. The Tucson, Arizona, agreement ruled illegal in *Citizen Publishing* also involved price fixing and anticompetition clauses. Portions of the ruling in *Citizen Publishing* prompted Congress to pass the Newspaper Preservation Act in an effort to help keep multiple newspapers in some markets.

Technological advances such as the telegraph, high-speed printing presses, and the railroad each in its own time helped one newspaper company gain competitive advantages over others. The telegraph brought dispatches from distant events to newspaper offices at the speed of light. High-speed presses made possible the printing of tens of thousands of copies of a paper in minutes rather than hours, and efficient railroads enabled newspapers to distribute their products in geographic areas outside their primary markets.

Increasing use of computer technology during the last quarter of the twentieth century reduced production costs, improved production quality, affected marketing, and led to experiments in paperless publishing as well as to unique alliances among newspaper companies and between newspapers and other media. Computer technology also opened the door for substitute products, lowered entry-level barriers, and resulted in several companies from outside the newspaper industry positioning themselves as news and information providers – the role traditionally served by newspapers.

Microsoft Corporation, a computer software publisher, hired a number of newspaper and newsmagazine people to develop an "E-zine" (electronic magazine) called *Slate* that appeared on the World Wide Web. AT&T, a telephone service and telecommunications provider, developed a World Wide Web site called "Lead Story," whose purpose was to provide "an exhaustive examination of a timely news subject complete with analysis, opinion, background, and other information."

Newspaper companies, as much out of competitive self-defense as any other reason, banded together to form the New Century Network, conceived as a seamless electronic network of newspaper content including news, advertising, and news background information. By mid-1996, at least 680 U.S. newspapers had developed an on-line presence, among more than 3,000 media organizations accessible through a service called Newslink.

On a more traditional level, computer technologies during the last quarter of the twentieth century offered competitive advantages to companies who computerized their composing room functions. By computerizing news and classified advertising typesetting and other pre-press functions, newspapers eliminated entire levels of production personnel and shortened the length of time required for some aspects of newspaper production. Data management functions of computers enabled larger newspapers to create zoned editions, aimed at specific neighborhoods, thus creating several niche publications out of one larger one.

RANDY REDDICK

See also Business Regulation of the Press; Internet; Media Conglomerates; Newspaper Chains, or Groups; Newspaper Preservation Act; Penny Press

Further Reading

Adams, Edward E., "The Newspaper Business and Anti-Competitive Practices During the Gilded Age: A National Trend," paper delivered at the Southwest Symposium in San Angelo, Texas, October 1, 1995

American Opinion Research, "The State of the Newspaper Industry," 1996, <http://www.facsnet.org/top_issues/state/main.html>

Bagdikian, Ben H., *The Media Monopoly,* 4th ed., Boston: Beacon, 1992

Consoli, John, "NCN Makes Some Strides," *Editor & Publisher* 129:18 (May 4, 1996), pp. 9–10

Jamieson, Kathleen Hall, and Karlyn Kohrs Campbell, *The Interplay of Influence: News, Advertising, Politics, and the Mass Media,* 3rd ed., Belmont, California: Wadsworth, 1992

Porter, Michael E., *Competitive Strategy: Techniques for Analyzing Industries and Competitors,* New York: Free Press, 1980

Thorn, William J., with Mary Pat Pfeil, *Newspaper Circulation: Marketing the News,* New York: Longman, 1987

Newspaper Design

Societal changes among influences on the way newspapers look

In the 300 years since the newspaper emerged in colonial America, its appearance has changed dramatically. In the early days, newspapers resembled the books that were the standard reading material of colonists; in the late twentieth century, colorful newspapers featured text, photos, and graphics not unlike most other print media against which they competed. The design developments along the way followed changes in economics, politics, technology, and the demands of readers seeking information. The evolution of U.S. newspaper design can be generally broken into three periods – preindustrial, traditional, and modern. Each design period was marked by definitive characteristics associated with specific economic and technological changes as well as by changes in the role of newspapers within the larger mass media marketplace.

While some efforts were made to visually differentiate early printed news from the traditional book, the use of the same limited typographic resources and printing presses gave the burgeoning medium few design options. *Publick Occurrences, Both Foreign and Domestick,* published by Benjamin Harris in 1690, stands as a landmark as much for its attempt at a different design as for its content. Patterned after the standard (6 by 9-1/2 inch) book page of the times, this prototypical preindustrial news publication provided three pages of news and a blank fourth page on which the reader could add information before passing the paper to another reader.

Using the book printing press of a Boston colleague, Harris picked a typographic display that gave his pages a visual distinction – choosing to set his text in two columns of equal 17-pica width and unusually large (for this era) 12-point type for the body copy. This text width and size proved to be easier to read than traditional book text, and its all-capital-letter nameplate and initial capital letters provided visual sectioning.

Nearly 14 years later, the *Boston News-Letter* hit the streets in April 1704, the product of postmaster John Campbell and printer Bartholomew Green. Campbell had been using his office and its information resources to produce a report of happenings in other colonies. As demand grew for this handwritten newsletter, he recognized the need for more efficient production and arranged for Green to print the newsletter in his Boston print shop.

Printed on both sides of a page the size of standard writing paper (about 8 by 11 inches), the *News-Letter* attempted to maintain the traditional look of the handwritten dispatches. Using small headlines that were actually only labels for the content of a column, the page size or format and typographic style of the *News-Letter* would become an often repeated standard for the increasingly competitive newspaper marketplace.

Government taxes on printing supplies, especially the Stamp Act and similar taxes on paper, contributed to a change in the format of eighteenth-century newspapers. Because papers were taxed by the number of pages printed and because the increasing quantity of news and advertising demanded more space, page sizes increased dramatically. By the dawn of the nineteenth century, formats were as large as the limits of handmade paper and the capacity of hand-operated presses.

In 1803, mechanized papermaking allowed for substantially larger pages, some reaching more than two feet in page width. Mechanical paper machines also produced greater quantities of paper faster. Despite the size difference, little changed in the way of typography or use of visuals (illustrations) until the mid-1800s.

With Richard Hoe's development of the high-speed rotary press in the 1840s, mechanized production of the newspaper started to play a role in its design. To prevent the individual characters of each row of type from being thrown from the revolving drum, long rules of metal were wedged between each column to lock the type in place. This column rule would print as a hairline between each column of type, visually separating each column and allowing the space between columns to be reduced. From the 1 to 2 picas of space between the columns printed by hand, newspapers now tended to have only about a half pica of space with a hairline rule between columns.

The demand for more news led to text type dropping to as small as 6 points and to column width decreasing to about 13 picas. More characters per line, more lines per column, and more columns per page translated into more news per paper.

While this change to smaller type was dramatic, the increased use of varied typography to create true headlines

An elaborate drawing of former president Andrew Jackson's funeral procession occupied the entire front page of *The New York Herald* in June 1845.

(Perkins Library, Duke University)

for each story is one of the most telling design changes of this era. Although traditionally limited to one-column width, as much by the practice of filling the columns of type from top to bottom as far as the text would flow as by the mechanics of the early rotary press, newspapers found that multiline heads increased paper sales. These lines, or decks, as they were called, allowed the editor to summarize the story and attract readers with different typography.

The increasing use of display typography in advertising also provided the news side the opportunity to use a variety of type families and weights (boldface, italics, etc.) to provide a visual contrast to the overall grayness the reduced text type now produced. The design of the deck headlines also became varied as editors found different ways to display the type. Using short dashes (jim dashes) between each deck and changing the alignment produced additional visual impact. The term "inverted pyramid" originated as a description for a headline style in which decks of decreasing width were centered in a stack above the story. Step headlines were similar in their decreasing width but were even, or flush, with the right edge of the column.

Newspapers also increased their use of visuals. Hand cut from wood, maps and illustrations became informational graphics. With the introduction of photoengraving processes and stereotype plates, photography began to play an important role in the evolution of design, as the one-column format slowly gave way. Multiple-column headlines appeared more frequently, although the traditional stacked, one-column heads held until the end of the century.

Post–Civil War industrial developments improved the mechanics of newspaper production. With the improvement of web perfecting presses and the eventual development of the Linotype mechanical typesetting machine, the capacity of the newspaper industry grew, and its competitive nature caused traditional ideas of makeup to be tossed aside.

Design of the early traditional format closely mirrored the styles and standards of the Victorian era of which it was a part. Although forced into rigid columns by the limitations of the presses, the overall appearance included as many variations of typography and illustration as were mechanically available. The resulting paper was at first visually proper and strict in its narrow columns but featured design flourishes to emphasize the stories of significance.

At the approach of the twentieth century, design was driven by variations in display solely for their ability to attract readers at the newsstand. Label headlines gave way to large, multiple-column banner headlines. Packaging called brace layout, coupled banner heads with long vertical displays, emphasized important stories of the day. Story hierarchy was now a consideration when placing text on the page, and display of the story reflected the importance of the story. The big, black Gothic headlines of the yellow journalism period led the newspaper industry into the era of modern design.

By the end of World War I, the U.S. appetite for visually active newspaper design was as insatiable as its general appetite for news. Competition was at its height, with most cities having many daily newspapers. Design innovation pushed forward with changes in format now accompanying basic typographic revisions.

When Joseph Medill Patterson and Robert McCormick introduced the tabloid format in the *Illustrated Daily News* in June 1919, yet another format greeted readers. Emphasizing the power of photography, flashy design, and what many considered sensationalized reporting, the paper that would become the *New York Daily News* gave the posterized front-page design its truest use.

Other broadsheet and tabloid papers adopted this overall planning approach to the packaging of the news, but the most significant change in newspaper design came from a growing awareness of how readers looked at the printed page. A truly systematic approach to newspaper design began a few years earlier when the *New York Tribune* hired a typographer to redesign the paper.

The typographer, Ben Sherbow, measured the readability of various headline typography and, using his design and typographic skills, radically simplified the look of the *Tribune*. Sherbow's design used only variations of size and weight of only one type family – Bodoni – to give emphasis to headlines. He also changed the paper's headlines from an "up style," in which all words were capitalized, to a "down style," in which only the first word of the headline and proper nouns were capitalized.

John Allen, an employee of the Mergenthaler Linotype company, became one of the most noted advocates of this design style, which he called "streamlining." Throughout the 1930s, Allen used his company publication, the *Linotype News,* to illustrate variations of his streamlining methodology and share with other designers of the day the successes of additional newspapers that were adopting the new modernist approach.

Beyond Allen, others designers such as Allen Hutt, Gilbert Farrar, and Heyworth Campbell strove to bring U.S. newspaper design out of the Victorian era. Edmund C. Arnold, a successor of Allen's at *Linotype News* and an educator at Syracuse University, became an outspoken advocate for the clean, simplified modern design, pushing the use of space as a tool of emphasis within the design.

This increased awareness of the spacing of elements on the page, coupled with a movement away from the vertical makeup so rigidly enforced by the one-column text flow, contributed to a change in who actually created the look of the page display and how they did it. Newspapers were now more likely to be designed or packaged by staff in the newsroom, who understood the importance of story hierarchy and placement.

Soon, many other newspapers were following this modernist design philosophy, bringing to print many of the theories of visual presentation being explored by the modern artists of the time. One of the last significant changes in design evolved through the 1950s and 1960s as newspapers adopted the utilitarian design style noted in the International or Swiss architectural design movement and moved toward precisely formatted page designs.

With the 1970 revision of the *Minneapolis (Minnesota) Tribune,* U.S. newspapers regularly began using a Mondrian-like approach to modular packaging. This late evolution of newspaper design grouped all elements of a story (text, headline, art) into well-defined rectangular spaces.

Changes in technology also helped newspapers move away from the vertical display mode. Phototypesetting (cold type) replaced the metal type cast from hot lead, allowing the unlimited variation of type sizing, both horizontally and vertically, and the electronic processing of type.

New, more legible typefaces were designed for newspapers as the tradition of cramming huge quantities of text onto news pages gave way to a more orderly and readable display. Following the theories of the Bauhaus movement, typographic designers now wanted type stripped of unnecessary embellishment. New sans serif fonts were being drawn and used in the daily paper with the Swiss type family, Helvetica, becoming the standard headline face of most U.S. newspapers that converted to "modular" design.

Improvements in printing presses also allowed newspapers to move toward color reproduction. The traditional letterpress could not produce the quality of color necessary to reproduce photographs adequately. With the acceptance and eventual industry-wide move toward offset presses, the use of full-color photos, graphics, and other design elements became possible.

When *USA Today* first came off the presses in 1982, once again the direction of newspaper design changed. *USA Today* packaged many items onto its colorful, graphics-laden pages. Using a tight writing style that gave only the important details, and complementing these short stories with informational graphics and photos, the newspaper's rigid format maintained the modular ideals but eliminated the spaciousness that had come to be the design standard. *USA Today*'s effective use of color, graphics, varied typography and immediacy soon became much imitated.

MICHAEL WILLIAMS

See also Informational Graphics; Newspaper Technology; *Publick Occurrences, Both Forreign and Domestick;* Stamp Act of 1765; *USA Today*

Further Reading
Allen, John E., *Newspaper Designing,* New York: Harper & Brothers, 1947
Arnold, Edmund C., *Designing the Total Newspaper,* New York: Harper & Row, 1981
Barnhurst, Kevin G., *Seeing the Newspaper,* New York: St. Martin's, 1994
Garcia, Mario, *Contemporary Newspaper Design: A Structural Approach,* 3rd ed., Englewood Cliffs, New Jersey: Prentice-Hall, 1993; London: Prentice-Hall International, 1993
Harrower, Tim, *The Newspaper Designer's Handbook,* 2nd ed., Dubuque, Iowa: Wm. C. Brown, 1992
Lester, Paul M., *Visual Communication: Images with Messages,* Belmont, California: Wadsworth, 1995
Meggs, Philip B., *A History of Graphic Design,* New York: Van Nostrand Reinhold, 1983; London: Allen Lane, 1983
Nelson, Roy Paul, *Publication Design,* 5th ed., Dubuque, Iowa: Wm. C. Brown, 1991

Newspaper Editorials
Opinion essays have long history in newspapers

A newspaper editorial is a piece of opinion writing by a staff member. Containing views on current political or social issues, an editorial may consist of one writer's opinion or the notions of an editorial board, which is made up of several staff members and represents the collective voice of the newspaper. The editorial, usually presented in essay form, is often only 300 to 400 words in length. In most U.S. newspapers, space is reserved in the front section for an editorial page, which also contains editorial cartoons, letters to the editor, and columns of opinion.

Newspapers' conceptions of editorials have changed over time. During the period surrounding the American Revolution, news stories combined narrative with opinion to the extent that it was difficult to distinguish the two, nor was there any attempt made by decidedly partisan writers to differentiate. Early U.S. newspaper journalists were influenced by colonial pamphleteers such as Increase and Cotton Mather, who attempted to influence public opinion by filling handbills and broadsheets with their views on religious and political issues at the turn of the eighteenth century. At about the same time, early English news sheets called corantos and diurnals contained printer's prefaces – long paragraphs of comment – that evolved into "letters introductory," an early example of the separation of news and opinion in print.

An important influence on the opinion writings of the eighteenth century was the work of Joseph Addison and Richard Steele in the British publications *Tatler* (1709–11) and *Spectator* (1711–12, 1714). Their so-called essay papers on important current affairs were reprinted and imitated in the colonies. In addition, colonial newspapers often ran letters to the printer, in the manner of the English papers, which had printed the politically charged "Cato's Letters" and "Letters of Junius." After the Revolution, letter

Is There a Santa Claus?

Yes, Virginia, there is a Santa Claus. He exists as certainly as love and generosity and devotion exist, and you know that they abound and give to our life its highest beauty and joy. Alas! How dreary would be the world if there were no Virginias. There would be no childish faith, then, no poetry, no romance, to make tolerable this existence. We should have no enjoyment, except in sense and sight. The eternal light with which childhood fills the world would be extinguished.

New York Sun, September 21, 1897

writers continued to debate great issues of the day in newspapers, and often publishers and editors joined in the controversies. Among the first editors to publish his own views consistently was James Cheetham, an English radical who edited the *American Citizen* in New York City beginning in 1800.

With the emergence of the populist penny press in the 1830s, newspapers' dependence on political parties weakened; strong, independent-minded editors penned regular columns of opinion. One of the earliest uses of the word "editorial" in this sense was in 1836 by James Gordon Bennett, publisher of the *New York Herald,* who usually printed his opinions on page two or three of his four-page paper. In the August 16, 1836, edition, Bennett described his typical day at the newspaper: "We rise in the morning before 5 o'clock – write our leading editorials." Bennett used what became known as the editorial "we," which strengthened the notion that the editorial was the collective voice of a newspaper.

One of Bennett's rivals, Horace Greeley, founder and editor of the *New York Tribune,* is remembered as one of the great editorial writers in U.S. history. An idealist, Greeley wrote often on the appeal of the American west, agrarian reforms, abolition, labor unions, temperance, and the Whig party from the 1840s until his death in late 1872. It was from Greeley's pen that the famous expression "Go west, young man" sprang, although that phrase first appeared not in a newspaper but in a literary publication he founded in the 1830s. Greeley, who often signed his editorials with his initials, became nationally known because of his writing. Greeley also gave a start to many of the day's most popular editorial writers, including Charles Dana and George Ripley. Dana's paper, the *New York Sun,* printed

one of the most famous editorials in U.S. history, "Is There a Santa Claus?," by Francis P. Church, who answered a letter in 1897 from a little girl named Virginia.

The strong, opinionated editor-publisher archetype declined after the Civil War, but Joseph Pulitzer and William Randolph Hearst revived the genre in the yellow journalism of the 1890s in New York City. Pulitzer, a Hungarian-born immigrant who made his newspaper name in St. Louis, Missouri, had a keen interest in his editorial page at the *New York World.* He often said that he employed a sensational style in the news pages as a means of getting people to read his editorials. Hearst's rival *New York Journal,* under the guidance of Arthur Brisbane, pioneered visual elements that influenced later editorial page editors – wider columns, larger type, editorials on the last page of the paper, and an illustration as the centerpiece of the page.

A noted editorialist of the twentieth century was William Allen White, editor-publisher of the *Emporia (Kansas) Gazette* and a conservative-turned-reformer who was politically active from the presidency of William McKinley to that of Franklin Roosevelt. White, who was seen as a spokesperson for small-town America, rose to national prominence on the strength of an editorial titled "What's the Matter with Kansas?" that was published on August 15, 1896. The editorial railed against the Populists and Democrats running the state, calling them "shabby, wild-eyed, rattle-brain fanatics." Republican newspapers across the country reprinted White's piece during the presidential campaign of Democrat William Jennings Bryan and McKinley.

Much of the personality and vigor was drained from newspaper editorials in the twentieth century as newspapers, purchased by large corporations, became focused on profits. A majority of editorials became unsigned. A few editors, like White and Walter Lippmann of the *New York World* and *Herald-Tribune,* remained national figures, but they were the exception that proved the rule. During the growing civil rights movement after World War II, six southern newspaper writers, including Hodding Carter of the *Delta (Mississippi) Democrat-Times,* won Pulitzer Prizes for speaking on behalf of black citizens. But by 1988, fewer than half the daily newspapers in the United States editorially endorsed a candidate for president, compared to 93 percent in 1932.

MARK NEUZIL

See also Bennett, James Gordon Sr.; Godkin, E.L.; Greeley, Horace; Hearst, William Randolph; Newspaper Columnists; Pulitzer, Joseph; White, William Allen; Yellow Journalism

Further Reading

Babb, Laura Longley, ed., *The Editorial Page,* Boston: Houghton Mifflin, 1977
Ford, Edwin, "Colonial Pamphleteers," *Journalism Quarterly* 13 (1936)
Hart, Jim Allee, *Views on the News: The Developing Editorial Syndrome, 1500–1800,* Carbondale: Southern Illinois University Press, 1970
Nevins, Allan, *American Press Opinion,* Boston: D.C. Heath, 1928

What's the Matter With Kansas?

What's the matter with Kansas?
We all know; yet here they are at it again. We have an old mossback Jacksonian who snorts and howls because there is a bathtub in the statehouse; we are running that old jay for governor. We have another shabby, wild-eyed, rattle-brained fanatic who has said openly in a dozen speeches that "the rights of the user are paramount to the rights of the owners"; we are running him for chief justice, so that capital will come tumbling over itself to get into the state. We have raked the old ash heap of failure in the state and found an old human hoop skirt who has failed as a business man, going to run for congressman-at-large. He will help the looks of the Kansas delegation in Washington. Then we have discovered a kid without a law practice and have decided to run him for attorney-general. Then for fear some hint that the state had become respectable might percolate through the civilized portions of the nation, we have decided to send three or four harpies out lecturing, telling the people that Kansas is raising hell and letting the corn go to weeds.

William Allen White
Emporia Gazette, August 15, 1896

Rystrom, Kenneth, *The Why, Who, and How of the Editorial Page*, 2nd ed., State College, Pennsylvania: Strata, 1994

Sloan, W. David, Cheryl Sloan Wray, and C. Joanne Sloan, *Great Editorials: Masterpieces of Opinion Writing*, Northport, Alabama: Vision, 1997

Newspaper Labor Organizations

Efforts to promote newspaper workers' rights

Newspaper unions were formed to protect and advance the rights of newspaper workers in all aspects of the industry in the same way that unions fought for worker rights in many industries beginning in the early years of the twentieth century. Because newspapers themselves had so many differing and complex functions, many different unions have been associated with the newspaper business. While some were specific to newspapers, others, such as the International Brotherhood of Electrical Workers and the International Brotherhood of Teamsters, served many industries with job-specific membership within newspapers.

While the majority of unions served the traditional blue-collar production and manufacturing workers within a newspaper, the Newspaper Guild, was founded in 1933 as a white-collar union to represent editorial workers. Heywood Broun, a liberal columnist in the 1920s and 1930s, was instrumental in organizing the Guild. Formerly called the American Newspaper Guild (reduced to Newspaper Guild in 1981), this organization began as a loosely organized association of local groups mutually concerned with economic issues. Ultimately, the guild grew to a nationally organized union in its own right and affiliated with the AFL-CIO. In 1996, the 35,000-member Guild voted to merge with the 600,000-member Communication Workers of America, the overall unit that brought together most of the individual blue-collar unions associated with the newspaper industry, to become the Newspaper Guild/Communications Workers of America, AFL-CIO, CLC. In 1997, after a one-year affiliation period, the guild was slated to become a sector of the Communications Workers of America, much as the International Typographic Union did earlier.

Prominent unions within the newspaper business have been the International Typographical Union, which represented composers and typesetters; the Graphic Communication International Union, which represented engravers; the International Brotherhood of Electrical Workers, for those in electrical maintenance; the Machinists, who maintained presses and other equipment; the Newspaper Printing Pressman's Union, for those who operated presses; the Paperhandler's Union, for those who loaded and unloaded the paper rolls onto the printing presses; the Photoengravers and Stereotypers, for those who took pictures of the completed pages and those who used the film to make plates for the press; the International Brotherhood of Teamsters, representing drivers and truckers; and the International Mailer's Union, representing those who worked in the mail room. In a completely unionized newspaper, all functions would fall under the purview of one or the other of the several unions. Editorial workers might be members of the Newspaper Guild, although some unionized newspapers did not have a unit of the guild. In "right to work" states, some employees had the option to choose not to belong to the union representing their particular sphere of activity. While this was legal, union members disliked workers who benefited from union activity without paying union dues.

Common wisdom says that the beginnings of union activity in newspapers began when big-city newspapers, having to solve the problem of an increasing population and geographic distance as cities grew in the late nineteenth century, turned to the fledgling association of draymen who owned horses and carts and entered into an agreement to permit them to control the delivery of the newspapers, thereby relieving the papers of the task of maintaining a fleet of horses and wagons and drivers for the job. For the better part of a century, many big-city papers were delivered by this third-party contractor with the result that the unions, not the newspapers, knew who the subscribers were. Lacking this knowledge, newspapers could not even assure advertisers that the circulation actually was reaching the intended customer. As the demographic profile of the reader became important to advertisers and for marketing purposes, many papers began developing their own customer lists through pay-by-mail procedures and through start and stop lists. Some newspapers, such as the *Los Angeles Times,* purchased the subscription lists from the union; in the case of the *Times,* the price was well over $1 million.

The major function of the unions has been to fight for members' rights and to represent members in contract negotiations. Unions traditionally have fought for better working conditions, for benefits, and for higher pay. Unions collect dues from all members, some part of which is used to pay strikers' benefits during a strike. The goal is to sustain workers at an income at which they can continue to stay out against management until they gain at least some of their points in negotiation.

Management and workers are obliged to continue to attempt to negotiate as long as it is possible that some agreement may be reached. Many long-term negotiations are unsuccessful, in which case the dispute may be brought before the National Labor Relations Board. Should the ruling go against management – as in the *Terre Haute (Indiana) Tribune-Star* strike in the late 1970s, for example – striking workers are owed their back pay.

Under collective bargaining agreements, various unions at newspapers pledge themselves to strike if any other union at that paper goes on strike. In this manner, unions seek to stop the paper from publishing unless concessions are made to the originally striking union. Often, the Newspaper Guild was in the collective bargaining agreement and would walk out with the production and distribution unions, leaving management the choice of writing the stories and producing and distributing the paper or ceasing to publish. Striking workers form picket lines to make it difficult for anyone to come into the newspaper building and facilities during the strike period. Advertisers fear that papers are not being distributed to the full circulation; that concern and the fear that strikers and strike sympathizers may boycott advertising businesses would be enough to cause many advertisement cancellations. Readers who do not receive a paper during a strike may not renew their subscriptions after the strike is over; readership, therefore, may be lost permanently. If the newspaper continues to publish by hiring replacement workers (called "scabs" by the unions), these workers become objects of particular focus by the strikers, who often threaten them. Newspaper strikes have a history of violence.

Union members were threatened particularly by the introduction of new technology during the 1970s. The adoption of cold type, offset presses, and computers made many traditional printing jobs obsolete. During this period, unions fought hard for retraining and for keeping employed workers on the job even though the job no longer existed as it had.

In 1976, a strike at the *Washington (D.C.) Post* heralded a breakthrough in management response. When the pressman's union struck, the other unions followed. A group of pressmen vandalized the presses. Because the *Post* had changed to offset printing, however, it was possible to airlift the plates to many different locations and print the paper for delivery. Once the pressroom was functioning again, publisher Katharine Graham hired replacements for the striking printers; the first group was brought in from Oklahoma and landed on the roof of the *Post* building by helicopter, thereby avoiding the picket line ringing the building.

The advent of technology took away much of the power of unions to actually shut down a newspaper. Before 1975, there might be 30 or 40 newspaper strikes a year of varying duration. Individual strikes might last days, weeks, or even months before an agreement between management and workers was reached. The outcome was a gain in future benefits for the workers, but there were losses in both wages for workers and revenue for owners.

In the late twentieth century, according to John Morton, a newspaper analyst, strikes were fewer – two or three a year – but the result was more likely to be the loss of the newspaper itself, as in the case of the *Pittsburgh (Pennsylvania) Press* in 1992. Under modern financial constraints and competition for advertising, the loss of revenue during a strike period could cause a newspaper to shut down.

Although unions have been a part of newspapers since the beginning of the twentieth century, when many papers entered into an agreement with the Teamsters to deliver papers in large cities, the number of unions has varied among the individual papers. Both membership numbers and collective strength of the unions diminished in the last decades of the twentieth century. Newspapers in the north have a history of unionization, while those in the south do not. In the case of group ownership, some papers may have unions while others do not. In the case of nonunion papers, publishers work hard to keep unions from organizing. However, the decline of unions does not mean a decline in labor problems, according to Robert Ballow, a member of the King and Ballow law firm of Nashville, Tennessee, a firm well-known for its pro-management, union-busting work. The work environment of the 1990s brought new issues such as age discrimination, sexual harassment, downsizing,

and disputes involving the use of independent carriers for delivery.

The move of many unions to merge with the Communications Workers of America created a 635,000-member unit ready to fight management rulings that would have an adverse impact upon them.

MARY ALICE SHAVER

See also Newspaper Technology

Further Reading

Fitzgerald, Mark, "A Warning to Newspaper Managements," *Editor & Publisher* 128:10 (March 11, 1995), p. 14

Garneau, George, "Guild Convention Backs Merger," *Editor & Publisher* 128:27 (July 8, 1995), p. 35

Jaszczak, Sandra, ed., *Encyclopedia of Associations*, Detroit, Michigan: Gale, 1996

Klotzer, Charles L., "Here: What Counts, Words or Deeds?," *St. Louis Journalism Review* 23:163 (February 1994), p. 2

Morton, John, "Just One Strike and You Could Be Out," *American Journalism Review* 17 (January/February 1995), p. 52

Polich, John, "*Daily News*, Its Unions, Newspaper Market Lose in 1990 Strike," *Newspaper Research Journal* 16:1 (Winter 1995), pp. 71–83

Simurda, Stephen J., "Sticking with the Union?," *Columbia Journalism Review* 31:6 (March 1993), pp. 25–30

Newspaper Preservation Act

Legislative protection designed to preserve competition in some areas

The Newspaper Preservation Act of 1970 provided a congressional exemption to the Sherman Antitrust Act of 1890 and was enacted to preserve remaining competitive newspapers in two-newspaper markets. The act came after almost 40 years of cooperation between newspapers to ensure the preservation of competition was declared invalid by a U.S. Supreme Court ruling in 1969. The act created joint operation agreements between competing newspapers in a market as a means of reducing operating costs related to capital-intensive production and distribution equipment and systems.

On February 14, 1933, the first recognized joint operation began when representatives of the *Albuquerque (New Mexico) Tribune,* owned by Scripps-Howard, and the *Albuquerque Journal,* owned by Thomas Pepperday, met at the Scripps Ranch in Miramar, California, and formed a contractual agreement involving both newspapers. While such operations later were challenged, this contract included the consolidation of the business and mechanical departments of both newspapers under a new agency, the Albuquerque Publishing Company. The editorial and news staffs of the two papers shared the Tribune building but were housed on separate floors. Many of the subsequent joint operating agreements would follow this model of arrangement.

After 1933, the following cities created joint operating agreements: El Paso, Texas, in 1936; Nashville, Tennessee, in 1937; Evansville, Indiana, in 1938; Tucson, Arizona, in 1940; Tulsa, Oklahoma, in 1941; Chattanooga, Tennessee, in 1942; Birmingham, Alabama, in 1950; Fort Wayne, Indiana, in 1950; Lincoln, Nebraska, in 1950; Salt Lake City, Utah, in 1952; Shreveport, Louisiana, in 1953; Knoxville, Tennessee, in 1957; Charleston, West Virginia, in 1958; St. Louis, Missouri, in 1959; Pittsburgh, Pennsylvania, in 1961; Honolulu, Hawaii, in 1962; San Francisco, California, in 1965; Columbus, Ohio, in 1965; Miami, Florida, in 1966; Anchorage, Alaska, in 1974; Cincinnati, Ohio, in 1979; Seattle, Washington, in 1982; Detroit, Michigan, in 1988; Las Vegas, Nevada, in 1990; and York, Pennsylvania, in 1990.

The first challenge on the legality of joint operating agreements came in 1969 when the U.S. Department of Justice filed suit against the Tucson joint operating agreement in *Citizen Publishing* v. *United States*. The Justice Department obtained a summary judgment against the Tucson joint operation that was affirmed by the U.S. Supreme Court as being in violation of the Sherman Act.

As a result, newspaper companies around the country petitioned Congress for an antitrust exemption for joint operations. The first legislative effort resulted in the proposed Failing Newspaper Act of 1967, cosponsored by 15 senators. The Justice Department opposed its passage, but senators from 17 states where newspapers participated in existing joint operating agreements – most often in the state capital or a large city in the state – fought back. After three separate series of hearings conducted over a three-year span, the Newspaper Preservation Act was passed in 1970. The underlying philosophy for Congress passing the act was that it was "in the public interest of maintaining a newspaper press editorially and reportorially independent and competitive in all parts of the United States."

The act provided a limited exemption from antitrust laws. Joint operating agreements provide for the arrangement of price fixing, market allocation, and profit pooling. Competing papers desiring a joint operation under the Newspaper Preservation Act had to petition the U.S. Attorney General for an antitrust exemption. One qualifying condition was contingent on one paper failing or being in "probable danger of financial failure." The terms of the contract involved duration of the agreement, profit and loss distribution, and management of joint firms. The duration of the contracts could range from 20 to 100 years. The division of revenue ranged from a 50-50 percentage split to a 90-10 percentage split between the papers contingent on their revenue share at the time of formation. Some contracts had a graduated sliding clause or amendments to reevaluate at timed intervals during the contracts. Two different firms were considered to manage the joint operation; a third company could be established to manage the joint operations. A revenue distribution system then would be appropriately arranged, or one of the newspapers would assume the management of the joint operation.

The act was not without its detractors. The Suburban Newspapers of America, alternative weeklies, and legal and communication scholars created a vast repository of literature reporting on the legal and economic limitations and problems in the marketplace of granting exemption to daily newspapers under the Newspaper Preservation Act.

The act was not entirely successful at preventing closure of newspapers protected by a joint operating agreement. Joint operating agreements ended or continued without a publication partner when one of the papers closed or dissolved the agreement in Anchorage, Alaska, in 1979; Columbus, Ohio, in 1985; Franklin–Oil City, Pennsylvania, in 1985; St. Louis, Missouri, in 1986; Miami, Florida, in 1988; Shreveport, Louisiana, in 1991; Knoxville, Tennessee, in 1991; Tulsa, Oklahoma, in 1992; and Pittsburgh, Pennsylvania, in 1993. Declining revenue share, employee

Newspaper Joint Operating Agreements

Papers	Date Agreement Expires
The Albuquerque Journal Albuquerque Tribune	2022
The Birmingham News Birmingham Post-Herald	2015
The Charleston (W. Va.) Gazette Charleston (W. Va.) Daily Mail	2036
Chattanooga Free Press The Chattanooga Times	2006
Cincinnati Enquirer Cincinnati Post	2007
Detroit Free Press The Detroit News	2086
El Paso Herald-Post El Paso Times	2015
The Evansville (Ind.) Courier The Evansville (Ind.) Press	1998
Journal-Gazette (Fort Wayne, Ind.) Mews-Sentinel (Fort Wayne, Ind.)	2020
The Honolulu Advertiser Honolulu Star-Bulletin	2022
Las Vegas Review-Journal Las Vegas Sun	2049
Nashville Banner The Tennessean, Nashville	2022
Salt Lake City Desert News Salt Lake Tribune	2012
San Francisco Chronicle San Francisco Examiner	2005
Seattle Post-Intelligencer The Seattle Times	2032
The Arizona Star, Tucson Tucson Citizen	2015
The York (Pa.) Dispatch The York (Pa.) Daily Record	2090

Source: http://www.naa.org/info/Facts/facts4.html#LUSNPC

strikes, purchase of competitor, and nonrenewal of the joint operating agreement were contributing factors to the failure of one of the newspapers under the agreement.

The Newspaper Preservation Act was amended in 1987 to accommodate a changing newspaper industry to allow joint operating agreement papers to broaden their permitted publishing activities and to become involved in new technological developments.

EDWARD E. ADAMS

See also Economics of Newspapers; Newspaper Competition; Newspaper Technology

Further Reading
Busterna, John C., and Robert G. Picard, *Joint Operating Agreements: The Newspaper Preservation Act and Its Application,* Norwood, New Jersey: Ablex, 1993
Lacy, Stephen, and Todd Simon, *The Economics and Regulation of United States Newspapers,* Norwood, New Jersey: Ablex, 1993

Newspaper Publicity Act

Calls for identification of owners, investors, circulation statistics

Buried within the 1913 post office appropriations legislation, the Newspaper Publicity Act required commercial newspapers and magazines using the highly subsidized second-class mail privilege to identify their owners and investors and to label advertisements that resembled news stories or editorials. Dailies also were forced to disclose accurate circulation figures with their published ownership statements. Congress enacted these regulations in an attempt to curb some of the common business excesses occurring in the press of the early twentieth century. These abuses included lying about circulation figures, disguising advertisements to appear as news stories or editorials, and concealing the identity of owners and stockholders to hide conflicts of interest.

In order to bypass the First Amendment question, Congress linked the regulations to the press's mail privilege, believing that the courts would uphold congressional authority to set standards for the postal subsidy. In 1913, the U.S. Supreme Court unanimously affirmed the regulations' constitutionality in *Lewis Publishing* v. *Morgan,* after the American Newspaper Publishers Association instigated the court case challenging the law. Soon afterward, the press urged the Post Office Department to enforce the regulations strictly, recognizing the intrinsic business advantages of supporting the Newspaper Publicity Act. In later years, weekly and magazine publishers successfully lobbied Congress to extend the circulation requirement to their publications. The regulations were still in effect at the end of the twentieth century.

LINDA LAWSON

Further Reading
Kielbowicz, Richard B., "Postal Subsidies for the Press and the Business of Mass Culture, 1880–1920," *Business History Review* 64 (1990)
Lawson, Linda, *Truth in Publishing: Federal Regulation of the Press's Business Practices, 1880–1920,* Carbondale: Southern Illinois University Press, 1993
_____, "When Publishers Invited Federal Regulation to Curb Circulation Abuses," *Journalism Quarterly* 71:1 (Spring 1994), pp. 110–120

Newspapers in the Eighteenth Century

Evolved from carrying foreign news to influencing the course of a new nation

The eighteenth century was young when John Campbell published the *Boston News-Letter* in 1704, but news was not a new commodity. As Boston postmaster, Campbell knew and read European periodicals that circulated in the mail. To satisfy people's thirst for news, Campbell had been clipping news from periodicals and letters and then issuing it in handwritten form. The next logical step was to publish a newspaper, and the *News-Letter* became America's first successful one.

As the newspaper industry unfolded, individuals and circumstances shaped it. Newspapers at first depended heavily on foreign news and de-emphasized local news. In Puritan Boston, printer James Franklin proved that local issues would sell newspapers, too. At the request of an Anglican faction, Franklin started the controversial and highly popular *New-England Courant* in 1721. Writers for the *Courant* attacked Puritan minister Cotton Mather for his advocacy of inoculation against smallpox.

Massachusetts was the center of the early American newspaper industry, owing to a relatively dense population and near-universal literacy. However, as other colonial populations grew larger and more educated, newspapers spread. Printers moved into colonies that lacked a press, often at the request of colonial governments that needed printers to issue official documents. Maryland hired experienced English newsman William Parks as its official printer, for example. He established a newspaper there before Virginia hired him away. He opened that colony's first newspaper as well.

Benjamin Franklin spread newspapers in a different way. After achieving success as a printer in Philadelphia, he sponsored promising young printers who set up printshops and newspapers in South Carolina, New York, Connecticut, and Antigua. As part of his influential printing career, Franklin also helped define the character of news. He had purchased a failing newspaper from Samuel Keimer in 1729. Reflecting the public's interest in scientific endeavors, Keimer had been reprinting a scientific encyclopedia, entry by entry, purposely avoiding crime news and nonpolitical events. When Franklin bought the paper, he canceled the

Benjamin Franklin, writing as Silence Dogood, is featured on the front page of his brother James's paper, *The New-England Courant.*

encyclopedia and emphasized stories of news events, including crime and local happenings.

Developing a taste for local news, editors clipped stories from other American newspapers. Colonial news events, such as the travels of evangelist George Whitefield through the colonies, were fully reported in the press and carefully followed by readers. Editors often begged for, and got, submissions from local readers. Some offered essays on topics of general interest, such as the importance of education or the need for steady trade. Others offered how-to articles, discussing agricultural methods or health tips. Still others sent in poems and literary works, turning newspapers into forums for entertainment.

Local items did not eclipse foreign reports, however. Editors continued to emphasize European news, for readers were citizens of European nations and had a vital interest in happenings across the Atlantic. News of American and European shipping was a staple of newspapers, telling readers about ship arrivals, departures, and cargoes.

With such a wide range of reading material available in their newspapers, colonial Americans came to depend on and enjoy their weekly gazettes. In 1725, there were five active newspapers in the colonies. The number rose to 12 by 1740 and to 24 by 1764. By then, colonies from New Hampshire to Georgia had at least one newspaper.

When Britain imposed a stamp tax on American printed goods in 1765, newspaper editors reacted angrily. Every newspaper in the colonies protested the Stamp Act in some fashion and recorded protests in other colonies, allowing readers to see that colonists everywhere disagreed with the tax. Thus, newspapers helped unite the colonies in protest against Britain.

Despite press unity during the Stamp Act, some editors felt that the colonies should work out their differences with Britain. Others disagreed, pushing for a radical break with Britain. When the American Revolution broke out in 1775, the press was fragmented. Some printers were loyal to the crown. Others sided with the Patriots. Pro-American newspapers emphasized American battle victories and painted defeats in the most positive light. Pro-British editors at first tried to print both sides of every story, thinking that they thereby would circulate the British view. However, Patriot groups such as the Sons of Liberty would not allow Loyalist editors to print British views. Mobs roughed up Loyalist

Newspapers had to be printed one page at a time in the eighteenth century.

The Boston News-Letter.

Published by Authority.

From Monday April 17. to Monday April. 24. 1704.

London Flying-Post from *Decemb. 2d to 4th.* 1703.

LEtters from *Scotland* bring us the Copy of a Sheet lately Printed there, Inftituted, *A feafonable Alarm for Scotland. In a Letter from a Gentleman in the City, to his Friend in the Country, concerning the prefent Danger of the Kingdom and of the Proteftant Religion.*

This Letter takes Notice, That Papifts fwarm in that Nation, that they traffick more avowedly than formerly, & that of late many Scores of Priefts and Jefuites are come thither from France, and gone to the North, to the Highlands & other places of the Country. That the Minifters of the Highlands and North gave in large Lifts of them to the Committee of the General Affembly, to be laid before the Privy-Council.

It likewife obferves, that a great Number of other ill affected perfons are come over from *France,* under pretence of accepting her Majefty's Gracious Indemnity; but, in reality, to increafe Divifions in the Nation, and to entertain a Correfpondence with *France:* That their ill Intentions are evident from their talking big, their owning the Intereft of the pretended King *James* VIII. their fecret Cabals, and their buying up of Arms and Ammunition, wherever they can find them.

To this he adds the late Writings and Actings of fome difaffected perfons, many of whom are for that Pretender, that feveral of them have declar'd they had rather embrace Popery than conform to the prefent Government; that they refufe to pray for the Queen, but ufe the ambiguous word Soveraign, and fome of them pray in exprefs Words for the King and Royal Family; and the charitable and generous Prince who has fhew'd them fo much Kindnefs. He likewife takes notice of Letters not long ago found in Cypher, and directed to a Perfon lately come thither from St. *Germains.*

He fays that the greateft Jacobites, who will not qualifie themfelves by taking the Oaths to Her Majefty, do now with the Papifts and their Companions from St. *Germains* fet up for the Liberty of the Subject, contrary to their own Principles, but meerly to keep up a Divifion in the Nation. He adds, that they aggravate thofe things which the People complain of, as to *England's* refufing to allow them a freedom of Trade, &c. and do all they can to foment Divifions betwixt the Nations, and to obftruct a Redrefs of thofe things complain'd of.

The Jacobites, he fays, do all they can to perfwade the Nation that their pretended King is a Proteftant in his Heart, tho' he dares not declare it while under the Power of *France;* that he is acquainted with the Miftakes of his Father's Government, will govern us more according to Law, and endear himfelf to his Subjects.

They magnifie the Strength of their own Party, and the Weaknefs and Divifions of the other, in order to facilitate and haften their Undertaking; they argue themfelves out of their Fears, and into the higheft fffurance of accomplifhing their purpofe.

From all this he infers, That they have hopes of Affiftance from *France,* otherwife they would never be fo impudent; and he gives Reafons for his Apprehenfions that the *French* King may fend Troops thither this Winter, 1. Becaufe the *English & Dutch* will not then be at Sea to oppofe them. 2. He can then beft fpare them, the Seafon of Action beyond Sea being over. 3. The Expectation given him of a confiderable number to joyn them, may incourage him to the undertaking with fewer Men, if he can but fend over a fufficient number of Officers with Arms and Ammunition.

He endeavours, in the reft of his Letters to anfwer the foolifh Pretences of the Pretender's being a Proteftant, and that he will govern us according to Law. He fays, that being bred up in the Religion and Politicks of *France,* he is by Education a ftated Enemy to our Liberty and Religion. That the Obligations which he and his Family owe to the *French* King, muft neceffarily make him to be wholly at his Devotion, and to follow his Example; that if he fit upon the Throne of the three Nations, muft be oblig'd to pay the Debt which he owes the *French* King for the Education of himfelf, and for Entertaining his fuppofed Father and his Family. And fince the King muft reftore him by his Troops, if ever he be reftored, he will fee to fecure his own Debt before thofe Troops leave *Britain.* The Pretender being a good Proficient in the *French* and *Romifh* Schools, he will never think himfelf fufficiently aveng'd, but by the utter Ruine of his Proteftant Subjects, both as Hereticks and Traitors. The late Queen, his pretended Mother, who in cold Blood when fhe was *Queen of Britain,* advifed to turn the Weft of *Scotland* into a hunting Field, will be then for doing fo by the greateft part of the Nation; and, no doubt, is at Pains to have her pretended Son educated to her own Mind: Therefore he fays, it were a great Madnefs in the Nation to take a Prince bred up in the horrid School of Ingratitude, Perfecution and Cruelty, and filled with Rage and Envy. The *Jacobites,* he fays, both in *Scotland* and at St. *Germains,* are impatient under their prefent Straits, and knowing their circumftances cannot be much worfe than they are, at prefent, are the more inclinable to the Undertaking. He adds, That the *French* King knows there cannot be a more effectual way for himfelf to arrive at the Univerfal Monarchy, and to ruine the Proteftant Intereft, than by fetting up the Pretender upon the Throne of Great *Britain,* he will in all probability attempt it; and tho' he fhould be perfwaded that the Defign would mifcarry in the clofe, yet he cannot but reap fome Advantage by imbroiling the three Nations.

From all this, the Author concludes it to be the Intereft of the Nation, to provide for Self defence; and fays, that as many have already taken the Alarm, and are furnifhing themfelves with Arms and Ammunition, he hopes the Government will not only allow it, but encourage it, fince the Nation ought all to appear as one Man in the Defence

The Boston News-Letter was the first successful newspaper in the American colonies, beginning on April 24, 1704.

printers, driving some out of town. Those who survived in British-held territory began printing news slanted toward the British war effort. The press of the American Revolution quickly became highly partisan.

The war was hard on newspapers. Not only did printers have to flee hostile armies or mobs, but they competed for scarce paper and printing equipment. Many papers failed. At the start of the Revolution, 34 newspapers existed in America. During the war, 98 more newspapers were begun, but 78 papers folded.

In 1783, Philadelphia printer Benjamin Towne took the bold step of issuing America's first daily newspaper, the *Pennsylvania Evening Post and Daily Advertiser.* Although most newspapers remained weekly, dailies began to take root. In 1790, there were 91 newspapers in the United States. Eight were dailies. By 1800, the nation had 234 newspapers, 24 of which were dailies.

As the new nation struggled to form a viable government, the press took on great importance. The Bill of Rights to the Constitution guaranteed press freedom. The new president, George Washington, resisted the formation of political parties, but when they did form, the press leaped wholeheartedly into party struggles. Newspapers became mouthpieces for parties such as the Federalists and the Republicans. Editors began stating their political opinions in their newspapers, rather than relying on opinions supplied by readers.

The growing public interest in politics resulted in newspaper coverage of House of Representatives sessions in 1789. When the primarily Federalist Senate refused to open its doors to the press, anti-Federalist *National Gazette* editor Philip Freneau began pressuring for admission. He caused a public outcry, and the Senate reversed its policy in 1794.

By the close of the eighteenth century, newspapers were involved actively in forming the political system of the new United States. Thus, newspapers created a permanent and prominent place for politics as a topic in the U.S. media.

JULIE K. HEDGEPETH WILLIAMS

See also American Revolution and the Press; Colonial Press; Government Secrecy; Newspaper Design; Newspaper Technology; Party Press; Printers' Networks; Reporters and Reporting in the Eighteenth Century; Stamp Act of 1765

Further Reading

Bailyn, Bernard, and John B. Hench, eds., *The Press and the American Revolution,* Worcester, Massachusetts: American Antiquarian Society, 1980
Benjamin, G.G.W., "Notable Editors Between 1776 and 1800. Influence of the Early American Press," *Magazine of American History* 17 (February 1887)
Davidson, Philip Grant, *Propaganda in the American Revolution, 1763–1783,* Chapel Hill: University of North Carolina Press, 1941
Kobre, Sidney, *The Development of the Colonial Newspaper,* Pittsburgh, Pennsylvania: Colonial, 1944
Morgan, Edmund S., and Helen M. Morgan, *The Stamp Act Crisis: Prologue to Revolution,* Chapel Hill: University of North Carolina Press, 1953; London: Collier, 1970
Schlesinger, Arthur M., *Prelude to Independence: The Newspaper War on Britain, 1764–1776,* New York: Knopf, 1958
Sloan, W. David, "'Purse and Pen': Party-Press Relationships, 1789–1816," *American Journalism* 6 (1989)
_____, and Julie Hedgepeth Williams, *The Early American Press, 1690–1783,* Westport, Connecticut: Greenwood, 1994

Newspapers in the Nineteenth Century

Period of great transition and specialization for newspaper publications

U.S. newspapers began the nineteenth century as large, gray pages of solid type set in the same size, broken only by italic or capital letters for emphasis. Illustrations, if used at all, showed a simple pointing finger calling attention to advertisements, the same small house on all real estate ads, a ship on transportation schedules, or a person carrying a bag over his shoulder on ads for runaway children, wives, or slaves. Headings or pictures stayed within one column.

Although newspapers carried political essays, most content was as dull as the newspapers' appearance. Newspapers appealed to elites, mostly white male property owners who read political newspapers for party propaganda and mercantile papers for shipping news and commodity prices. To enliven copy, editors viciously attacked their competitors.

A single printer could assemble a newspaper in 1800. Standing at his type case, he put copy together one letter at a time. An adept editor could write stories while setting type. Out-of-town news came from "exchanges," newspapers with whom editors exchanged copies. Printers set the first story at the top of the first page; they added the latest developments at the end. About 20 of the 200 newspapers were dailies. Each newspaper reached a few hundred to one thousand readers.

By 1900, multicolumn headlines shouted from the tops of pages often dominated by large photographs or drawings. News stories and headlines began with summaries highlighting the latest information from around the world. Name-calling and partisanship moved to special sections called editorial pages, while other sections covered sports, women's issues, and, in some cases, religion, agriculture, or business.

Some of the more than 2,300 dailies in 1900 reached a few hundred small-town residents, while others attracted more than 100,000 readers, including immigrants who barely knew English. Large corporations owned newspapers, even those headed by big names like Joseph Pulitzer or William Randolph Hearst. Dozens of people put out a paper with specialized divisions for news, advertising, circulation, and production.

Historians tend to look for antecedents of modern journalism. Frank Luther Mott, for example, labeled the early nineteenth century "the dark ages of partisan journalism." Editors had a stake in their parties' fortunes. When their candidates won, editors could be rewarded with governmental printing contracts or appointments to political jobs. Defeat, however, could mean bankruptcy.

By the 1830s, President Andrew Jackson had created a mass audience by initiating campaign techniques to reach large numbers of people. Political rallies, conventions, and newspapers broke up old cliques. Several editors started newspapers in 1833 to reach the masses independent from political parties; most failed after a few months.

Editor Benjamin Day succeeded with the *New York Sun,* begun on September 3, 1833. It sold for one cent when other newspapers sold for six cents. Within a week, he hired an unemployed printer, George Wisner, who arose early every morning to put daily police reports into an entertaining column. This emphasis on the cops, crime, and courts became so successful that Wisner quickly became Day's partner. They created the penny newspaper formula: cheap per-copy and subscription prices, advertising rates based on readership, stories written to entertain large numbers of people, and street sales in which newsboys invested 67 cents in 100 papers they had to sell to recoup their money.

Scottish immigrant James Gordon Bennett surpassed the *Sun*'s crime coverage by emphasizing sex and violence. On May 6, 1835, with $500, he opened the four-page *New York Herald* in a Wall Street basement. With the resources he amassed from success, he pioneered the use of telegraphy, financial news, foreign correspondents, and illustrations on news stories. During the Civil War, he sent more than 60 correspondents to the battlefields.

Newspapers remained political advocates. Bennett supported the Democratic Party. New York penny editors Horace Greeley, founder of the *Tribune* in 1841, and Henry J.

Raymond, founder of the *Daily Times* in 1851, helped create the Republican party and promote its candidates.

Editors nationwide discovered a demand for news during the Civil War. Home town people wanted to know the fate of local regiments at distant fronts. Weekly magazines found an eager market for illustrations depicting battle scenes.

Like other corporations, newspapers became capital-intensive. After the penny papers hit the streets, steam power combined with fast rotary presses to replace hand-fed flatbed sheets. Telegraphy, begun with the first wire between Baltimore, Maryland, and Washington, D.C., in 1844, connected much of the nation and increased the competition for timely news when war began in 1861. By 1863, lead stereotype cylinders on a high-speed press could print both sides of a long continuous web of cheap paper. In the 1880s, the Linotype machine allowed printers to set an entire line of type at a keyboard. Although typewriters and telephones were introduced in the 1870s, they were slow to become news-gathering tools.

Hungarian immigrant Joseph Pulitzer became a reporter for a German daily in St. Louis, Missouri, in 1867. Eventually, he bought two St. Louis newspapers which he combined into the *Post-Dispatch*. He added the *New York World* to his company in 1883 and advocated the cause of the poor. The *World* became known for both sensational reporting and thoughtful editorializing.

At Harvard, student William Randolph Hearst read the *World* and thought that journalism would be fun. After being expelled from college, Hearst talked his father into giving him a newspaper. From this base at the *San Francisco Examiner,* Hearst raked in enough money to buy the *New York Journal* in 1896 to challenge Pulitzer. Their competition included raiding each others' staffs and creating a brand of sensationalism known as yellow journalism – allegedly named for the splash of color on a comic character whose creator they fought over. In their frenzy, they sensationalized Spanish conflicts with Cuba and promoted war with Spain.

The Associated Press (AP) grew out of cooperative efforts begun by major New York newspapers seeking efficient ways to cover business news and the Mexican War in the 1840s. Although the AP was a cooperative, it held a monopoly on national news in some major markets.

In the same year as Hearst entered New York, Adolph S. Ochs acquired the *New York Times* to prove that a newspaper did not have to "soil the breakfast cloth" and made his paper a serious alternative to sensationalism. The *Times* became a newspaper of record by reprinting public documents, thoroughly covering major issues, and providing an index.

Looking for precedents and antecedents ignores the rich diversity of nineteenth-century newspapers, especially in the antebellum era, when anyone could start a newspaper with a few hundred dollars and a hand-operated printing press. Small-town promoters, or boosters, started newspapers to attract settlers. Agricultural journalists promoted new farming techniques. Religious and utopian societies formed newspapers to proselytize their ideas. Abolitionists joined associations and hired editors to agitate against slavery. Women's groups organized to promote their right to

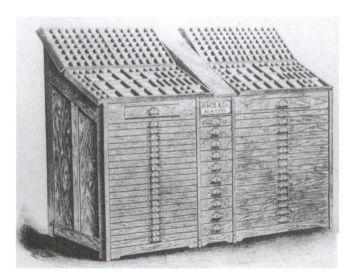

Type was set by hand, one character at a time, on nineteenth-century newspapers.

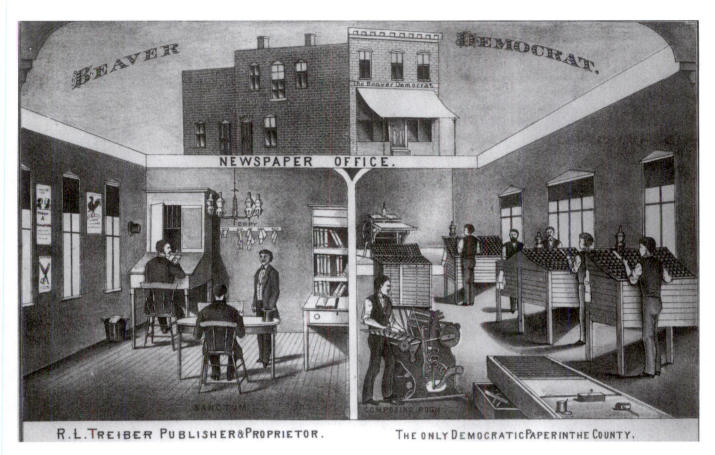

A small newspaper office in the nineteenth century
(Reproduced from the Collections of the Library of Congress)

vote. Ethnic and immigrant communities, like the Germans in St. Louis, published newspapers to build community and attract settlers from abroad. Twenty-seven U.S. daily newspapers published in German in 1860, and *Frank Leslie's Illustrated Newspaper* appeared in a German-language edition. In 1860, New York and San Francisco had daily newspapers in German, French, Spanish, and Italian. African American groups published several papers distributed nationally.

WILLIAM E. HUNTZICKER

See also Boosterism; Cooperative News Gathering; New Journalism (1880s); Newspaper Chains, or Groups; Newspaper Design; Newspaper Technology; Party Press; Penny Press; Photojournalism in the Nineteenth Century; Reporters and Reporting in the Nineteenth Century; Yellow Journalism

Further Reading

Baldasty, Gerald J., *The Commercialization of News in the Nineteenth Century,* Madison: University of Wisconsin Press, 1992
Blondheim, Menahem, *News over the Wires: The Telegraph and the Flow of Public Information in America, 1844–1897,* Cambridge, Massachusetts: Harvard University Press, 1994
Dicken-Garcia, Hazel, *Journalistic Standards in Nineteenth-Century America,* Madison: University of Wisconsin Press, 1989
Lancaster, Paul, *Gentleman of the Press: The Life and Times of an Early Reporter, Julian Ralph, of the 'Sun',* Syracuse, New York: Syracuse University Press, 1992
Smith, Culver, *The Press, Politics, and Patronage: The American Government's Use of Newspapers 1789–1875,* Athens: University of Georgia Press, 1977

Newspapers in the Twentieth Century

Thriving press consolidates, changes technology, encounters problems

In the first part of the twentieth century, newspaper staffs competed actively for stories, which were spread on the pages in black ink. After mid-century, however, the trend to one-paper cities and to computerized production brought sweeping changes, which also were driven by television.

In the history of the U.S. press, few times could compare with this period. Earlier high points included the linkage of newspapers by telegraph in the 1840s and the appearance

Some small newspapers still printed with older presses in the early twentieth century.
(Oregon State Library)

of the Linotype machine in the 1880s, which ended the slow hand-setting of type in many places. By the beginning of the twentieth century, with late and brisk wire news and rapid typesetting, newspapers had reached circulations as high as a million. A format had been established that lasted for decades. The main competition was from other dailies, and competition for scoops – those exclusive big stories – could be heavy.

A high school diploma was sufficient for journalism employment then. It was the writing career that drew reporters, many of whom were advanced to editors; other local reporters worked on newspapers with hopes of writing the Great American Novel someday. The social impact of the news they produced was not of much concern to the reporters.

The big change came at the end of World War II, when veterans enrolled in colleges and universities in great numbers and found that some journalism programs were changing focus from newswriting and typography to communication, with a social science emphasis.

Meanwhile, newspaper mergers gradually left many cities with a single daily, and the political partisanship of competing papers tended to disappear. The print monopolies prospered, but revenue was limited when the new medium of television claimed much of the national advertising and numerous local accounts. Newspapers also had strong competition from direct mail – those leaflets in everybody's mailbox.

Soon, typewriters and paste pots disappeared from newsrooms; by 1976, computer terminals were used widely in writing and editing. Whether they improved content was not certain, but their main advantage to publishers was in saving production costs by "capturing the keystrokes" – meaning the electronic impulses that put words on a screen also were used to set type, a change that displaced great numbers of Linotype operators. Soon, pages were being laid out on screens by editors, and the printers, who had done page makeup, also were gone. The newspaper reader did not necessarily notice much change. The *Wall Street Jour-*

nal, among the most advanced in technology, still had an 1890s kind of format. Soon, however, many papers started to use computers in graphic design.

A major player in this era was Al Neuharth, the chief executive of more than 80 Gannett papers, who launched *USA Today,* a national daily newspaper. Publishers scoffed at the paper's lavish use of color and the brief and peppy stories – just as they had scoffed at television. The paper, begun in 1982, finally reported a profit in 1993. In the meantime, it had made quite an impact. Newspaper staffs had joked about *USA Today* as trivial journalism, but its popularity could not be ignored, and many papers soon copied it.

News stories were changing, too. They frequently were more casual and keyed to social problems. A personalized approach to news, like that of television, often replaced brisk, factual reporting.

Despite all the innovation, newspaper circulations in many cities drifted downward. One reason was the growth of suburban dailies as city people moved to the suburbs. Another trend around mid-century was that the first "television generation" was growing up, and data showed that this generation did not read newspapers as their elders had. Getting youth to read papers was the problem. Overall, the weekday reading audience had dropped from 77.6 percent of the adult population in 1970 to 67.5 percent in 1994.

Other key data showed that the number of daily newspapers had dropped from 1,763 in 1946 to 1,538 in 1994, while Sunday papers, with more casual content, had grown from 497 to 889. Daily circulation grew in the same period from 50.9 million to 59.0 million, a gain but still not equal to population growth. Sunday circulation grew from 43.5 million to 62.4 million.

Newspapers continued to be impressive advertising media and were tied with television in 1993 at 22.5 percent each of all ad expenditures, versus 19.8 percent for direct mail and 7.0 percent for radio. However, many newspapers

In the late twentieth century, newspapers used computers for many facets of production, including page layout.

also owned radio and television stations, as well as other papers.

Direct mail competition proved a problem because it could saturate markets. This led many newspapers to develop advertising sections that were delivered free to nonsubscribers, meeting the goal of "total market coverage," which advertisers began to require. Newspapers also had considerable competition from alternative media, usually weekly tabloids with content closer than the dailies to lifestyles developed in the 1960s. There also were free, competing weekly shoppers, filled with classified ads and widely distributed.

An ongoing problem for newspapers was that print is a physical product that must be moved from pressroom to front porch. This process became increasingly difficult in heavy metropolitan traffic and with the growth of suburbs. Of course, the broadcast media had no such disadvantage. Publishers began looking to electronics, for both better circulation and added markets. By 1994, the total number of full-fledged papers available on-line was expected to reach 90, and more than 600 daily newspapers were providing voice information services, including weather reports and stock quotes; 265 had voice mailboxes for personal ads, according to the Newspaper Association of America.

Except for Neuharth, innovators were rare. The type of strong-minded editor who made the big decisions at mid-century often was succeeded by committees that decided what was news. Many journalism awards still were collected by metropolitan papers, often for investigative reporting. Eastern content weighted the news and the awards, but after all, more than 4,500 correspondents and editors were based in Washington, D.C., the largest collection of journalists in the world.

Two decades after computers arrived, newspapers still were changing, and doing better than skeptics had predicted. As the twentieth century ended, newspapers were thriving, and perhaps that was the most important fact about them.

WILLIAM R. LINDLEY

See also Interpretative Reporting; Investigative Reporting; Media Conglomerates; Neuharth, Al; News Concepts; Newspaper Chains, or Groups; Newspaper Design; Newspaper Labor Organizations; Newspaper Technology; Photojournalism in the Twentieth Century; Reporters and Reporting in the Twentieth Century; *USA Today*

Further Reading

Dertouzos, James N., and Timothy H. Quinn, *Bargaining Responses to the Technology Revolution: The Case of the Newspaper Industry,* Santa Monica, California: Rand, 1985

Lindley, William R., *20th Century American Newspapers in Content and Production,* Manhattan, Kansas: Sunflower University Press, 1993

Zousmer, Steven, *TV News Off-Camera: An Insider's Guide to Newswriting and Newspeople,* Ann Arbor: University of Michigan Press, 1987

Newspaper Technology

Technology changes substantially influence content changes

The nation's first newspaper, *Publick Occurrences, Both Forreign and Domestick,* which appeared on September 25, 1690, had only three pages measuring 6 by 9 1/2 inches, with the fourth page left blank for possible handwritten additions. Circulation was minimal – perhaps 100 or 200 copies. With this paper, however, began America's long and dynamic involvement with the reporting of news, the setting of words into type, and the printing of news on paper.

Although newspapers of the 1990s still reported, set type, and printed on paper, the publications and their millions of copies were produced in different ways. In the course of 300 years, editors and publishers continuously sought new technologies to produce their products – ways that were faster, cheaper, and of better quality. Within the framework of the U.S. mass media, the progress of newspaper technology can be measured and examined in several chronological periods.

Period I, 1690–1800, was marked by little technological change as newspapers began and continued to be printed with type composed by hand. The newspaper's pages were

A 1912 vision of a newspaper composition machine featured a steam-powered robot.

printed on wooden handpresses that came from England. *Publick Occurrence*'s only edition came out nearly 40 years after the first press arrived in colonial America and nearly 250 years after Johannes Gutenberg printed his famous Bible in Mainz, Germany. Printing itself – traditionally defined as the use of a raised surface that is inked and pressed onto paper – seems to have originated with Chinese craftspeople, who used carved wood blocks and even a form of movable earthenware type in the ninth, tenth, and eleventh centuries. Printing from wood blocks with carved illustrations and letters flourished in Europe in the fourteenth century.

The printing press became a highly visible invention and served as an agent of social change. Printing allowed the preparation of materials that could be made available cheaply for a mass audience. These materials encouraged literacy and endeavors associated with the Renaissance and the Protestant Reformation.

The first regularly published English newspaper, the *Oxford Gazette* (later *London Gazette*), was first printed in 1665. The first printing press in the colonies was established in 1638 at Harvard College for producing religious books, broadsides, and sermons.

The technology for printers and newspapers in Period I did not vary greatly from the procedures established by Gutenberg. The large wooden press – known as the English Common press or the Franklin press – was imported from England, along with type, paper, and ink. Compositors stood before their type cases as they picked up the individual characters and placed them in the composing stick. They added spaces between words to justify and fill out the lines. The type, after it was assembled in pages, was locked on the press and inked with handheld, leather-wrapped balls used to transfer ink from a plate to the type. Dampened paper was placed on top of the type form that was then rolled underneath the platen. A stout printer would then pull the lever to make the impression at the rate of about 200 an hour.

Early American newspapers used practically no headlines and sometimes carried editorial cartoons but almost no woodcuts illustrating news events. The papers, however, often created elaborate nameplates, some with large patriotic emblems and other designs. In later years, newspaper advertisements used small woodcuts or designs cut or cast from type metal to depict sailing vessels or various common objects on sale.

About 200 newspapers were being printed in the United States at the end of the 1700s. Generally four pages long, most were weekly publications; the first daily, the *Pennsylvania Evening Post and Daily Advertiser,* appeared in Philadelphia in 1783. Circulation of the larger dailies reached several thousand copies. The first American paper mill was established in 1690. Larger ones were erected by about 1760, at about the same time that the first handpresses were built. The first U.S. type foundries – companies that cast type for the trade – were established several decades later. Ink generally was made by the printers themselves.

In Period II (1801–60), new technology brought vast changes in the presses used for printing newspapers that were enlarging their circulations. The period also saw the

introduction of the telegraph and the development of type-making and papermaking machinery.

The quality and ease of printing newspapers – but not the speed – were enhanced in the early 1800s by the development of handpresses constructed of iron. Patented by Samuel Rust in 1829, the Washington press was manufactured by New York's R. Hoe and Company. Hoe built some 6,000 of these in the nineteenth century. Printers liked them because they were easier to move and operate; the Washington became the staple of the western frontier settlement.

The invention and use of the cylinder press became the first major alteration of the Gutenberg printing style. In these presses, the type was placed on a bed and was alternately inked and printed as the paper passed under the heavy revolving cylinder. Friedrich Koenig, a German, envisioned such a press in about 1803, and its first practical use was at the *Times* of London in 1814. This hand-fed machine increased impression speed from about 200 to about 1,000 per hour. David Napier's speedier version of Koenig's press was first installed in the United States at the *New York Daily Advertiser* in 1825. Although some early cylinder presses were powered by water, horses, and even men, the application of steam power aided their widespread use.

The Hoe company, the principal U.S. press manufacturer in the nineteenth century, built its own cylinder-press models based on Napier's plans. The development of the mass-circulation penny press prompted Hoe to develop the first rotary press, the Hoe "lightning" press of 1847. Here the type itself, held in place by ingenious V-shaped column rules, was locked onto the large cylinder that revolved when the press was operated. Hand feeders fed the sheets from various platforms around the cylinder. The capacity of these presses, which could cost $25,000, could reach 20,000 sheets an hour.

Other aspects of technology affected newspaper procedures. One was the introduction of the telegraph in 1844, which enabled daily newspapers to get reports more quickly and to expand news coverage. As a result, newspapers required more type, more compositors, more paper and ink, and larger press capacities. The need for more type, including a wider selection of type fonts, was answered by the hand-powered casting machine invented by David Bruce Jr. in 1838; later machines were power-driven. Printing ink, a commodity needed at all shops, became an industry after Jacob Johnson developed an ink firm in Philadelphia in 1804. Paper, the other major commodity, continued to be made primarily from rags. The Fourdrinier machine, developed in England, mechanized paper manufacture and was used by U.S. paper mills by 1830.

During Period III (1861–83), paper and press improvements dominated the changing technology. Stereotyping aided progress. Many inventors focused their efforts to devise a successful type-composing machine. Other changes came with the introduction of the telephone, the typewriter, and electricity.

While smaller newspapers continued using handpresses, metropolitan dailies sought even larger presses for growing circulations. The *New York Herald,* for example, claimed a record of 135,600 copies the day after Fort Sumter was shelled at the outset of the Civil War. The adoption of

Five to One

A tale without words for the publisher of a daily paper or for the manager of a job printing plant who in these enlightened days continues to hand-set all of his copy. Figure it out for yourself, or ask the users of

13,000 Linotypes

SEARS, ROEBUCK & CO., Chicago, for instance, have found that

"The Linotype way is the only way"

to set intricate mail-order catalogues.

MERGENTHALER LINOTYPE COMPANY

NEW YORK   CHICAGO   SAN FRANCISCO   NEW ORLEANS   PARIS

SYDNEY, N. S. W.
WELLINGTON, N. Z. } Parsons Trading Co.
MEXICO CITY, MEX.

TORONTO — The Mergenthaler Co., Ltd.
BUENOS AIRES — Louis L. Lomer
CAPE TOWN — John Haddon & Co.
STOCKHOLM — Aktiebolaget Amerikanska Sattmaskiner

HAVANA — Francisco Arredondo
TOKIO — Teijiro Kurosawa
ST. PETERSBURG — Leopold Heller

A 1909 advertisement promotes the efficiency of the Linotype machine over hand-set copy.

stereotyping to newspaper production was accomplished by a Hoe press developed in 1861. The stereotype process involved the making of a papier-mâché flong, or mold, from the type page. A curved lead casting was made from the flong and then mounted on the rotary press. Newspapers now could vary their makeup styles and incorporate multi-column advertisements. Production speeds could be increased because additional stereotypes could be made; the *Herald* used five duplicate presses for some of its Civil War editions.

A second major change came with the development of the web-perfecting press. This machine used stereotype plates and allowed printing on both sides of the paper. This newsprint came from rolls, not sheets as before. The presses also folded the pages and trimmed them as they came off the press. William Bullock's first press of this style was installed at the *Philadelphia Inquirer* in 1863. The Hoe company introduced an improved version in 1871 at the *New York Tribune*. Almost all U.S. newspapers in the 1990s used variations of the web-perfecting rotary press.

Paper costs rose during the Civil War but declined in the 1870s because of the availability of newsprint made in part from ground wood pulp. A German inventor, Friedrich Keller, invented a machine to do the grinding. After it was imported in the late 1870s, newsprint content began to shift to more use of wood pulp and less use of more expensive rags.

Illustrations of products appeared in advertising. Linecuts or engravings depicted war maps of the Civil War, and some newspapers printed woodcut illustrations of Civil War forts and military leaders. Cartoons were used, and a large front-page cartoon became a weekly feature of the *New York Evening Telegram* in the period. Zincographs – linecuts etched by acid on zinc plates – were a French invention used in U.S. newspapers in the early 1870s. Halftone photoengraving, the process by which photographs could be used in newspapers, was pioneered in England. Frederic I. Ives, who worked in the photographic laboratories of Cornell University, made photoengraving practicable by his inventions of 1878 and 1886. The *New York Daily Graphic* and Stephen Horgan were recognized for their experimental halftone engravings appearing in 1880.

Other technological changes affected newspapers in the period. Alexander Graham Bell invented the telephone in 1877. Within several years, the larger newspapers installed them, speeding up the news-gathering process. Typewriters reduced composing costs in the 1880s because compositors no longer had to decipher the handwritten scrawl of reporters and editors. Thomas Edison's invention of the incandescent lamp in 1879 modified newspaper operations wherever electric lights were installed.

In Period IV (1883–1944), the introduction of machine composition was the principal technological change, and at the end, other composition methods were under development. Although letterpress printing from raised surfaces continued to be the almost exclusive process for U.S. newspapers, other printing processes were being tested. The use of photographs in newspapers expanded both in black and white and in color.

Ottmar Mergenthaler's Linotype, first installed at the *New York Tribune* in 1886, became the machine that broke the composition bottleneck. The machine used a keyboard to assemble brass character matrices against which hot lead was poured in a mold. Lines were justified by use of an adjustable spaceband. After casting, the reusable matrices were returned by the machine to their proper magazine channels.

Composing-room procedures changed markedly as the larger newspapers installed Linotypes. Most operators were former hand compositors, a transfer pushed by organized labor in an effort to hold onto as many jobs as possible. Smaller newspapers were slower to change, but by the 1930s, practically all had converted to hot-metal composition on the Linotype or its major competitor, the Intertype, which was introduced after Mergenthaler's patents expired in 1912.

Letterpress printing continued to dominate at newspapers throughout the period. The installation of even larger web-fed rotary presses using stereotyped pages came at a time when two major New York newspapers, Joseph Pulitzer's *World* and William Randolph Hearst's *Journal*, launched a circulation battle during the Spanish-American War. Large newspapers also installed perfecting color presses in the 1890s. Picture supplements that were popular for Sunday newspapers and colored Sunday supplements (magazines) began to be printed on rotogravure presses. Near the end of the period, the *Daily World* of Opelousas, Louisiana, became the first daily to be printed by the offset process (1939).

New distance communication included the teletypewriter (1914), by which wire services could send typewritten articles instead of using the Morse code; the Teletypesetter (1929), by which wire-service articles arrived on perforated tapes used to operate Linotypes; and wirephotos (mid-1930s) sent to wire-service members and clients.

In Period V (1945–95), hot-metal type composition gave way to photocomposition and, ultimately, to computer-generated type and desktop publishing. Traditional letterpress printing gave way to offset and flexographic printing. The marriage of cold type and offset printing, beginning in the late 1950s, produced this second revolution, which continued with multiple satellite applications and the electronic imaging of photographs.

Use of hot-metal composing machines at daily newspapers peaked in 1966, the rise partly aided by development of faster machines as well as the widespread use of Teletypesetters for wire-service news. The use of Linotypes was declining, though, and major dailies ended their hot-type era in the late 1970s. A few small weekly newspapers still set their type on hot-metal machines in the mid-1990s.

The end of World War II, the held-back demands for new equipment and new plants, and labor agitation helped fuel the striving for reduced production costs. In the area of type composition, a few newspapers began using cold-type strike-on typewriters that produced news and ad copy for pasteups and photoengraving; five Chicago newspapers used this process when their typographic union struck in 1947. The Linotype and Intertype companies followed

The Linotype machine made preparation of newspaper copy much faster.

(Reproduced from the Collections of the Library of Congress)

another course by developing composing machines with circulating photographic matrices; one model was Intertype's Fotosetter installed at the *St. Petersburg (Florida) Times* in 1954. The Photon and Linofilm machines of the late 1950s produced photocomposed type used principally for advertisements.

Concurrently, press manufacturers began developing offset presses for newspapers. An offshoot of the lithographic process invented by Aloys Senefelder of Germany in 1796, offset works on the principle that grease (ink) and water do not mix. In the offset newspapers of the twentieth century, pages were photographed and then negatives were exposed onto sensitized aluminum plates. These smooth plates were mounted on the press; ink would stick to the type and illustrations, and water to the rest. The inked image was transferred (or "offset") from the plate cylinder to a rubber-blanketed offset cylinder and then onto the paper web as it rolled between the two offset cylinders of this rotary press.

With offset presses, newspapers bypassed expensive hot-metal composing systems in favor of cold-type equipment. Because of lower conversion costs, weeklies and smaller-city dailies led the transition to cold-type composition and offset printing. VariTypers and Friden Justowriters were among the early devices used to set copy for the pages to be pasted up and photographed. The conversion trend began in the late 1950s and early 1960s. Pasted-up pages of weekly newspapers often were taken for offset printing at the smaller dailies or at central plants. Because of the new technology, Linotype operators at many newspapers had to be retrained as photocompositors, and makeup skills were transferred to pasting up. Letterpress equipment was sold for scrap.

In the 1960s, computers were used for hyphenating and justifying the perforated tape fed to composing machines. Use of optical character readers bypassed further keyboarding by operators. Then came electronic phototypesetting machines that reproduced characters on the face of a cathode-ray tube.

The deathblow to hot type came as major newspapers installed computerized front-end editing systems that provided writers with video display terminals (VDTs) for inputting articles. Editors could call up the stories for editing on their own terminals, and the articles to be pasted up could be produced by high-speed printers. Publishers installed these automated systems in the 1970s, and the *New York Times* in 1978 placed 250 VDTs in service.

Desktop publishing arrived in the mid-1980s with the development of personal computers and laser printers using the xerographic process. Apple Computer's Macintosh, along with Aldus' PageMaker, QuarkXPress, and Adobe Photoshop software, began the trend that enabled smaller newspapers to prepare newspaper pages.

Larger newspapers in the mid-1990s were using various pre-press systems with associated hardware and software as further computerization and digitizing took place. Front-end systems allowed merging of editorial and advertising copy, graphics, and pictures to produce computerized pagination. Electronic scanners converted photos, artwork, and negatives into digital form. Imagesetters produced a high-quality image of the page on either negative film or paper prints. Development continued on computer-to-plate applications that began to eliminate the need for negatives. Pagination and the integration of the various systems required extensive training and retraining for newspaper staffs.

Photography, too, was altered by technology in the late twentieth century. Automatic film processors and the use of scanners for photo negatives eliminated the need to make photo prints. Newspapers in the mid-1990s were beginning to use digital cameras that would eventually make the traditional wet/chemical darkroom obsolete.

U.S. newspapers spent millions of dollars with various manufacturers for new presses in the second half of the twentieth century. The result was that the majority of them were printed by offset in the mid-1990s; this process offered economies in production as well as expanded capacities for color and black-and-white photographs. Additionally, newspapers were installing flexographic presses as replacements or as supplements for existing letterpress units. Flexography is a letterpress process that uses a thin metal plate on which a polymer coating is exposed to a page negative; non-printing areas are removed by a water or air blast, leaving a raised printing surface. Flexographic presses, which use a water-based ink and an anilox inking system, generally provide improved color reproduction. Some daily newspapers continued to print by "letterpress direct" and others by offset on presses converted from letterpress operation, and a few small weeklies continued to print with hot-metal type and older cylinder or rotary presses.

By the late twentieth century, inks were developed to reduce the amount of rub-off, and inks made from soybeans are replacing petroleum-based inks. Recycled newsprint was now included in the paper used by newspapers, sometimes by the mandate of the state government. Experimentation was progressing in the late 1990s on making paper from kenaf, a fast-growing woody plant.

The use of communication satellites also affected newspaper technology. Advertising agencies used them; wire services sent their articles and photographs to clients and members by satellite. Satellites also made it possible for newspapers such as *USA Today,* the *Wall Street Journal,* and the *New York Times* to print copies in distant locations; their pages were sent by satellite to their remote printing plants.

CORBAN GOBLE

See also Newspaper Design; Newspaper Labor Organizations; Newspapers in the Eighteenth Century; Newspapers in the Nineteenth Century; Newspapers in the Twentieth Century; Penny Press; Photojournalism in the Nineteenth Century; Photojournalism in the Twentieth Century; Telegraph; Yellow Journalism

Further Reading

Comparato, Frank E., *Chronicles of Genius and Folly: R. Hoe & Company and the Printing Press as a Service to Democracy,* Culver City, California: Labyrinthos, 1979
Goble, George C., *The Obituary of a Machine: The Rise and Fall of Ottmar Mergenthaler's Linotype at U.S. Newspapers* (Ph.D. diss., Indiana University), 1984

Holtzberg-Call, Maggie, *The Lost World of the Craft Printer,* Urbana: University of Illinois Press, 1992

Huss, Richard E., *The Development of Printers' Mechanical Typesetting Methods, 1822–1925,* Charlottesville: University Press of Virginia, 1973

Karolevitz, Robert F., *From Quill to Computer: The Story of America's Community Newspapers,* Freeman, South Dakota: Pine Hill, 1985

Moran, James, *Printing Presses: History and Development from the Fifteenth Century to Modern Times,* Berkeley: University of California Press, 1973; London: Faber, 1973

Sterne, Harold E., *Catalogue of Nineteenth Century Printing Presses,* Cincinnati, Ohio: Ye Olde Printery, 1978

Strauss, Victor, *The Printing Industry: An Introduction to Its Many Branches, Processes, and Products,* Washington, D.C.: Printing Industries of America, 1967

Newspaper Trade Organizations

Newspaper trade organizations are institutional means by which media groups have advanced their common interests since before the Civil War. With the movement toward professionalization after the Civil War, nearly all the states had their editorial associations, usually dominated by country editors.

The National Editorial Association was founded in 1885. In 1919, the country weekly publisher-editors set up a national headquarters in St. Paul, Minnesota, and in 1932, the headquarters were moved to Chicago.

The largest, most wealthy trade organization, the American Newspaper Publishers Association (ANPA) was founded in 1887 with the goal of establishing a daily newspaper association that would help its members with the problem of obtaining national advertising. Although the ANPA soon became deeply involved in problems of labor relations, newsprint supply, government mail rates, and mechanical developments, it centered much of its attention on the field of advertising.

Sigma Delta Chi, the professional journalism fraternity, was founded at DePauw University in 1909, the same year that Theta Sigma Phi, honorary and professional sorority for women in journalism, was founded at the University of Washington. An example of the fraternity's position on the trade organization pecking order could be seen in its decision to study press coverage of the 1952 election, only to have its recommendations rejected overwhelmingly by the nation's publishers.

The American Society of Newspaper Editors was organized in 1922 to bring together the "directing editors" of the larger daily papers and to improve ethics in the 1920s. Membership was at first limited to editors of papers in cities of 100,000 or more; the limit soon was reduced to 50,000, with the board of directors empowered to elect notable editors from still smaller cities. Annual meetings were devoted to the discussion of professional problems as well as serving

as a platform for distinguished guests, including presidents of the United States.

The Associated Press Managing Editors (APME) was founded in 1931 by news executives who found the annual meetings of the ANPA and the Associated Press (AP) to be too little concerned with improving the news columns' content. Among the APME's major accomplishments were annual reports criticizing AP news coverage and writing style, analyses believed to have improved newswriting techniques.

The last of the major trade organizations or professional groups to be founded was the National Conference of Editorial Writers (NCEW). According to an article in the NCEW's trade publication, the *Masthead,* the group was an outgrowth of discussions at meetings of the American Society of Newspaper Editors and a four-week-long seminar at the American Press Institute.

The NCEW's first meeting in Washington, D.C., was attended by 103 persons. It welcomed all interested editorial writers into membership and by 1994 had grown to nearly 600 members from throughout the United States and Europe. Its annual meetings were known for their hard-hitting critique sessions patterned after their first seminar.

In 1992, seven trade associations serving the newspaper industry merged to form the national Newspaper Association of America (NAA). The NAA's founding members were the American Newspaper Publishers Association, the Newspaper Advertising Bureau, the Association of Newspaper Classified Advertising Managers, the International Circulation Managers Association, the International Newspapers Advertising and Marketing Executives, the Newspaper Advertising Co-op Network, and the Newspaper Research Council. The NAA had its headquarters in Vienna, Virginia.

ALF PRATTE

Further Reading

Emery, Edwin, *History of the American Newspaper Publishers Association,* Minneapolis: University of Minnesota Press, 1950

Fifty and Feisty: APME, 1933 to 1983, St. Paul, Minnesota: North Central, 1983

Pratte, Paul Alfred, *Gods Within the Machine: A History of the American Society of Newspaper Editors, 1923–1993,* Westport, Connecticut: Praeger, 1995

Newspaper Trade Press

Among the best-known of the many professional publications for print journalists in the late twentieth century were *Editor & Publisher,* the *Bulletin of the American Society of Newspaper Editors,* and *Presstime.*

The first in longevity was *Editor & Publisher,* whose progenitor, the *New York Journalist,* was edited for many years by Allan Forman. Begun in 1884, it was consolidated with *Editor & Publisher* in 1907. In addition to its general coverage of current issues in journalism, advertising, publishing, syndicates, and other topics related to the industry, *Editor & Publisher* was known for the publication of its annual *Yearbook,* the best source for information on dailies, weeklies, and other publications in the United States and Canada.

The *Bulletin of the American Society of Newspaper Editors* began in 1925 as a mimeographed sheet before evolving into a glossy printed publication. Its early pages served mostly as a bulletin board for its conservative membership until the 1960s, when it became more involved in the major issues facing journalism and the nation. By the last decade of the twentieth century, the *Bulletin* had become an important vehicle for members looking for news illumination and occasional advocacy.

Presstime, the voice of the Newspaper Association of America, previously served the American Newspaper Publishers Association. Begun in 1979, it came to cover all aspects of the newspaper business, including technology, telecommunications, computers, public policy, news and editorial, research, readership, circulation, advertising, employee relations, diversity, training, and newsprint.

ALF PRATTE

Further Reading
Editor & Publisher 100th Anniversary, 1884–1984 (March 31, 1984)
Pratte, Alf, "We Should Stop Bashing the *Bulletin,*" *ASNE Bulletin* (April 1991)

Other Newspaper Entries: Adless

Newspapers; *American Newspaper Directory;* Associated Press; Audience Research for Newspapers; Bennett, James Gordon Sr.; Broadsides; Business Media; *Chicago Defender;* Chicago Newspaper Trust; *Chicago Tribune;* Classified Advertising; Colonial Press; Contempt; Criticism of Newspapers; Economics of Newspapers; Exchanges; Feature Syndicates; Foreign Correspondents; Free Press–Fair Trial Controversy; Frontier Press; Gatekeeping; Godkin, E.L.; Gould, Jack; Government Printing and Patronage; Government Secrecy; Greeley, Horace; Handwritten Newspapers; Hearst, William Randolph; Illustrated Newspapers; International News Service; Interpretative Reporting; Investigative Reporting; Journalistic Interview; Libel; Lippmann, Walter; Literary Aspects of Journalism; *Los Angeles Times; New York Herald-Tribune; New York Times;* Objective Reporting; Ombudsman; Op-ed Page; Pamphlets; Participatory Journalism; Party Press; Penny Press; Pentagon Papers; Precision Journalism; Printers' Networks; Prior Restraint; Privacy; Professionalism in Journalism; Public Journalism; Raymond, Henry J.; Readyprint; Reconstruction Press in the South; Reporters and Reporting in the Eighteenth Century; Reporters and Reporting in the Nineteenth Century; Reporters and Reporting in the Twentieth Century; Scripps, E.W.; Sensationalism; Shoppers; Society Reporting; Sports Journalism; Stamp Act of 1765; Tabloids; Telegraph; Underground Press; United Press

(1882); United Press Associations (1907); United Press International; *USA Today;* Violence Against Journalists; War Correspondents; *Washington Post;* Watchdog Concept; Watergate Scandal; Women's Pages; Yellow Journalism; Zenger, John Peter

New World Information and Communication Order
Arguments over what countries benefit from the communications revolution

The New World Information and Communication Order (NWICO) has been defined in three ways: 1.) as a philosophical stance regarding the social, economic, and political role of global media and world communications; 2.) as "the great UNESCO (United Nations Educational, Scientific, and Cultural Organization) debate" over international information and communication policies; and 3.) as a political movement led by developing countries, which was itself part of their broader decolonization struggle. The philosophy underlying the NWICO views communication as a basic human right, information as a social good, and modern communication systems as powerful agents for social change. In this philosophy, it is assumed that developing nations need to use modern communications to bolster economic growth and to promote national identity and national integration. Thus, this view justifies state control of the mass media. Also important for this philosophy is the intrinsic link between a nation's economic and social development and its self-reliance in communications.

The great UNESCO debate took place during the 1970s and early 1980s, but its roots reach to the beginnings of the nonaligned movement (NAM) in 1955. The debate ended with the withdrawal of the United States from UNESCO in 1985, followed by the withdrawal of the United Kingdom. However, judging from the number of publications on the topic in the 1990s, the NWICO seemed to be an ongoing controversy in international communications.

UNESCO served as the principal forum for the debate, and the main instigators were the NAM's members, who were joined by the Soviet Union. The West, led by the United States, reacted negatively to the NAM's criticisms of the existing information order and to the NWICO's proposals. The debate started to boil in 1973, and the greatest confrontation occurred in 1976. Looking for a negotiated solution, UNESCO General Director Amadou Mahtar M'Bow established the International Commission for the Study of Communication Problems (also known as the MacBride Commission), which produced one of the most important documents in international communications, *Many Voices, One World.* In 1978, in the same spirit of compromise, UNESCO adopted its Mass Media Declaration; this document provided the first international guidelines for the mass media. Moreover, in 1980, UNESCO established the International Program for Development of

Communications to assist developing countries with their communication infrastructure and human power.

As a political movement, the NWICO was part of the decolonization struggle of developing nations. From the late 1950s, developing countries talked among themselves about the need to redress the inequities of the international economic order and recognized the links between economic relations and modern communications. To lessen their economic dependence on the West and to counteract the growing influence of transnational corporations (especially from the United States), the NAM proposed fundamental changes in the international economic order. Almost concurrently, NAM attempted to restructure global communications. In 1974, the United Nations General Assembly adopted the Declaration on the Establishment of a New International Economic Order. However, the NAM's calls for a New International Information Order (as the NWICO was then called) would never crystallize.

It has been said that the core of the NAM's proposals were decolonization, demonopolization, democratization, and development. Much of the discussion centered on news flow. The NAM argued that the Western agencies controlled the global flow and that North–South news flow contained little, and often negative, information about developing countries. Since NAM members believed that this information flow ill served their development needs and plans, they sought specific changes, such as a more balanced flow and increased South–South, horizontal news exchanges. Two other issues were television flows and advertising. Advertising was considered intrinsic to U.S. capitalism and its ideology and, like U.S. television programming, was seen as a key to spreading cultural imperialism. A further point of contention was the less-industrialized world's increasing dependence on the West for virtually all of its telecommunications knowledge and technology.

In the 1960s, developing countries made several efforts to decolonize their own national communications systems and to participate more fully in global information networks (e.g., in 1963, they created the Organization of Asian News Agencies). By 1970, they concluded that their goals required the enactment of international regulations and the redistribution of global communications resources (such as the geostationary orbit). Hoping to capitalize on their newly emerged international political power, they took their case to UNESCO.

Because the nonaligned movement's struggle took place in the middle of the Cold War, what was essentially a North-South conflict acquired a strong West-East dimension. The Soviet Union was concerned with the detrimental consequences of space communications for both its domestic Communist media policy and its international sphere of influence; it particularly was troubled by the United States' increasing command of trans-border data flow and satellite communications. Consequently, the Soviet Union allied itself with the NAM to advocate a position of information sovereignty. Derived from the principles relating to the sovereign equality of states and to the self-determination of peoples, information sovereignty refers to each state's right to equality in international information relations and to self-regulation regarding its own communications system.

The concept also includes each nation's responsibility for the international communications activities carried out within its borders. These ideas influenced international agreements on global communications, such as the 1971 World Association of Radio Communications' regulations regarding trans-border satellite broadcasting and the 1972 UNESCO Declaration on Space Broadcasting.

The West responded to the NWICO's proposals by defending the free flow of information, a position that was backed by the United Nations' Universal Declaration of Human Rights. Since the United Nations was created by the West, it reflected the Western view of communication – thus, Article 19 of the declaration stated that everyone has the right "to seek, receive, and impart information and ideas through any media and regardless of frontiers." The West opposed all normative measures, arguing that the NWICO would result in government censorship and licensing of journalists. It offered to help redress the inequality by assisting developing countries in improving their communications capabilities. This alternative, known as the "Marshall Plan of communications," inspired UNESCO's International Program for Development of Communications.

The debate reached far beyond the sphere of diplomacy. Some journalists, communications researchers, and, especially, media owners, were among the most active participants. Many of them supported their own governments' official line, but there was also significant opposition within countries. Private interest groups, which played a leading role in the West's counterattack, launched a press campaign that was instrumental in defeating the NAM's initiative. Analysis of this campaign showed that it presented a highly distorted view of the issues involved.

Most criticism of the NWICO in later years came from researchers who sought radical change in world communications but who also thought that the NWICO should be reformulated to include both class and gender analyses. These critics pointed out that the NWICO, formulated by the developing nations' political elites, never became a popular movement. Further, some of the elites backing the NWICO also supported antidemocratic media policies in their own countries. Feminist critics underlined the near invisibility of women in both of the documents resulting from the controversy and the UNESCO debate. In the 1990s, the struggle to decolonize, democratize, and develop Third World communications, which was the essence of the NWICO, found new advocates among nongovernmental organizations.

LUCILA VARGAS

See also Development Communication

Further Reading

Giffard, C. Anthony, *UNESCO and the Media*, New York: Longman, 1989

Harley, William G., *Creative Compromise: The MacBride Commission: A Firsthand Report and Reflection on the Workings of UNESCO's International Commission for the Study of Communication Problems*, Lanham, Maryland: University Press of America, 1993

International Commission for the Study of Communication Problems, *Many Voices, One World,*

New York: Unipub, 1980; London: K. Page, 1980; Paris: UNESCO, 1984

Lee, Philip, ed., *Communication for All: New World Information and Communication Order*, Maryknoll, New York: Orbis, 1986

Nordenstreng, Kaarle, *The Mass Media Declaration of UNESCO*, Norwood, New Jersey: Ablex, 1984

UNESCO Communication Documentation Center, *A New World Information and Communication Order: Towards a Wider and Better Balanced Flow of Information*, Paris: UNESCO, part I, 1979; part II, 1982

New York Herald-Tribune

Literate, in-depth newspaper killed by television, marketing, and strikes

For 42 years, the *Herald-Tribune* distinguished itself as arguably the nation's most literate, most attractive, and most in-depth newspaper before television, misguided marketing, and strikes spelled its demise. The newspaper was the unlikely progeny of the 1924 sale of the *New York Herald,* a scrappy penny press founded in 1835 by James Gordon Bennett, to the conservative *New York Tribune,* unrecognizable as the radical paper Horace Greeley founded in 1841.

The merger proved serendipitous; its contents were intelligent and lively. Walter Lippmann and Joseph Alsop provided commentary. Pulitzer Prizes rewarded the newspaper's national reporting, editorials, cartoons, and international reporting, including Korean War dispatches from Marguerite Higgins. Young writers who graced *Herald-Tribune* pages during its final decade gained names as the best nonfiction writers of their generation: Tom Wolfe, Gloria Steinem, Jimmy Breslin, and sportswriter Walter "Red" Smith. The newspaper excelled in cultural coverage and pioneered a Sunday news-in-review section. Publishers Ogden Reid and Helen Rogers Reid even sponsored a renowned annual forum on current problems.

Quality, however, failed to triumph over quantity in the newspaper's post–World War II circulation battle with the *New York Times,* its only rival in content, but which boasted more ads, subscribers, and pages than the *Herald-Tribune.* Circulation sank steadily from a 1946 Sunday high of 708,754 (348,626 weekdays) before it ceased publication on April 24, 1966. Its name lived on through the Parisian *International Herald-Tribune* and in *New York* magazine, which began life as the *Herald-Tribune*'s Sunday magazine.

LINDA LUMSDEN

See also Bennett, James Gordon Sr.; Greeley, Horace

Further Reading

Benjaminson, Peter, *Death in the Afternoon: America's Newspaper Giants Struggle for Survival,* Kansas City, Missouri: Andrews, McMeel & Parker, 1984

Kluger, Richard, *The Paper: The Life and Death of the 'New York Herald Tribune',* New York: Knopf, 1986

McAuliffe, Kevin Michael, *The Great American Newspaper,* New York: Scribner's, 1978

Villard, Oswald Garrison, *The Disappearing Daily,* New York: Knopf, 1944

New York Times

Considered U.S. newspaper of record

Founded in 1851, the *New York Times* was acquired in 1896 by Adolph S. Ochs, who created the masthead slogan "All the News That's Fit to Print." Managing editor Carr V. Van Anda molded the *Times'* reputation as the world's greatest news-gathering organization by choreographing such masterpieces of reporting as its 15-page deadline coverage of the sinking of the *Titanic.*

Legendary journalists such as reporter Homer Bigart and columnist Tom Wicker influenced its ascendance in national and international news coverage. The theater critic Walter Kerr was just one reason for the newspaper's almost godlike authority in the arts. The *New York Times Book Review* was another. From the 1970s, when the "sectional revolution" led by executive editor A.M. Rosenthal mortified hard-news veterans, the *Times* was a leader in publishing upscale, consumer-oriented sections such as "Home" and "Living."

While sometimes criticized as edited by elites for elites, the *Times* repeatedly challenged government and big business. It fought for the constitutional rights of a free press in such landmark cases as *New York Times* v. *Sullivan* in 1960 and the Pentagon Papers case in 1971.

As the flagship publication of a media conglomerate employing more than 10,000 people worldwide, the *Times* won 73 Pulitzer Prizes through 1995, more than any other newspaper. Ochs's scions continued to guide the newspaper, which had a daily circulation topping 1 million by the 1990s.

LINDA LUMSDEN

See also Libel; Pentagon Papers

Further Reading

Berger, Meyer, *The Story of the 'New York Times', 1851–1951,* New York: Simon & Schuster, 1951

Diamond, Edwin, *Behind the Times: Inside the New 'New York Times',* New York: Villard, 1994

Salisbury, Harrison E., *Without Fear or Favor: The 'New York Times' and Its Times,* New York: Times, 1980

Talese, Gay, *The Kingdom and the Power,* London: Calder & Boyars, 1971; Garden City, New York: Anchor/Doubleday, 1978

Niche Theory

Carefully directed advertising to reach specialized audiences

The niche theory of marketing and advertising offers an alternative to mass communication and mass marketing.

Whereas the mass media attempt to efficiently reach the largest number of potential consumers, niche marketing focuses on selecting smaller segments who are the most likely to buy specific products or services – emphasizing effectiveness rather than efficiency. For example, cornflakes are targeted to a mass audience, while granola cereals are narrowly, or niche, targeted. The concept is not new; many advertisers have marketed selectively for years, with products ranging from doctors' office supplies to big and tall sizes to specialized hobby materials. Typical media used are direct mail, catalogs, and business-to-business publications. The key to successful specialized marketing segments lies with the ability to identify, and reach, the most likely prospects for a given product or service.

Direct marketing flourished in the 1990s, primarily because of new technologies, along with more complete information based on consumer behavior (such as that provided by scanners and access to purchase information, and the use of credit cards and 800 and 900 numbers). These advances made segmentation more accurate, affordable, and accessible through specialty catalogs, cable television, and interactive media.

During the twentieth century, magazines were replaced as the mass media by radio. The magazine industry shifted from mass publications like *Life,* the *Saturday Evening Post,* and *Collier's,* to *Runner's World, MacWeek,* and, later, *Vibe* and *Wired.* When radio was replaced by television, it segmented by format (drama, talk, music) and then further into easy listening, big band, rock and roll, country, alternative, hip hop, and rap. Television is well suited to adapt from mass to niche because of the consumer database provided by cable subscribers and credit card users. Television provides the ability for consumers to see a product demonstrated and then call, order, charge it on a credit card, and have the product delivered without ever leaving home.

One of the problems of the mass media, from an advertiser's standpoint, is that an advertiser pays for the entire audience delivered, many of whom are not potential customers. With the database capabilities of identifying prime prospects and the increasing variety of niche media publications, networks, and services targeted to specific groups and groups of individuals, advertisers can pinpoint their messages to their best prospects.

The concept of integrated marketing communications emphasizes the need for manufacturers to thoroughly study, analyze, and understand their customers in terms of demographics, psychographics, and media habits. The enormous growth and success of niche media offers advertisers more ways to reach smaller and smaller audience segments.

The 1990s offered a seeming paradox in the emphasis on global marketing to reach new markets and a renewed emphasis on niche marketing, focusing on smaller and smaller market segments. However, new technology and the new niche media allowed marketers to identify and reach prospects with common characteristics anywhere in the world, as the Internet demonstrated.

JON A. SHIDLER

Further Reading

Schultz, Don E., and Beth E. Barnes, *Strategic Advertising Campaigns,* 4th ed., Lincolnwood, Illinois: NTC Business, 1995

Schultz, Don E., Stanley I. Tannenbaum, and Robert F. Lauterborn, *Integrated Marketing Communications,* Lincolnwood, Illinois: NTC Business, 1993

Wells, William, John Burnett, and Sandra E. Moriarty, *Advertising: Principles and Practice,* 3rd ed., Englewood Cliffs, New Jersey: Prentice-Hall, 1995

Nixon, Richard M., and the Media

His news manipulation provides a key to both successes and failures

Perhaps no influential person in history found himself more entangled with the U.S. press than Richard Nixon, the thirty-seventh president of the United States. Nixon manipulated the news media successfully throughout most of his amazing and controversial political career, only to be blocked or driven from the Oval Office, once by his inability to control his public image and a second time by newspaper reporters discovering his Watergate connivances. He was a dynamic and contentious politician, serving in the U.S. House, the Senate, the vice presidency, and the presidency. He was thwarted once in a bid for the White House and elected twice, all within 12 years. He led the nation for five years and seven months before becoming the first sitting U.S. president ever to resign. His own tape-recorded conversations proved to be his undoing. At each step, radio, television, newspapers, and magazines recorded his meteoric successes and failures and played decisive roles in his career.

Nixon's political career began in 1946 when he defeated incumbent New Deal Democrat Jerry Voorhis in California's Twelfth District, charging during the campaign that some of Voorhis's labor supporters were Communists. As one of the youngest members of Congress at age 34, Nixon served on the House Un-American Activities Committee, which provided the young congressman with his initial opportunity to manipulate reporters. Whittaker Chambers, one-time foreign editor of *Time* magazine, named Alger Hiss, a former Department of State policy maker, as an active Communist during the 1930s. Nixon's persistent questioning of Hiss eventually led the committee to accept Chambers's version of the investigation. Nixon played to reporters, demanding rhetorically why the Truman administration had not been more vigilant. Hiss was convicted of perjuring himself during his testimony before the House Un-American Activities Committee. The Chambers-Hiss controversy exemplified the fear that swept the nation during the early years of the Cold War. The notoriety allowed Nixon to win the Republican nomination for the Senate in 1950. He then easily defeated Democrat Helen Gahagan Douglas by constantly referring in his campaign speeches to her "Socialist leanings."

President Richard Nixon met with the press when necessary.
(National Archives)

In 1952, Dwight D. Eisenhower selected Nixon as his running mate, but weeks after the Republican convention, it was revealed that Nixon had received large sums of money from political friends during his 1950 Senate race. Nixon arranged for paid national television time to deliver an answer to his critics. Speaking via the new medium to millions of viewers, including Eisenhower, Nixon lashed out at his accusers. He said he never had accepted any political gifts, except a small puppy named Checkers. His children loved the dog, and he was not going to return it, he added. The "Checkers" speech swayed the people of the United States and Eisenhower, who kept Nixon on the ticket. In his first major brush with disaster, Nixon boldly had used television and an emotional outburst to outmaneuver his detractors. Eisenhower and Nixon easily defeated Adlai E. Stevenson and John J. Sparkman.

A former Army general, Eisenhower administered the White House just as he had organized his troops. Responsibilities were delegated. Eisenhower relied upon Nixon to look after political details and to deal with the infighting on Capitol Hill. Nixon remained on the ticket in 1956, and

he and Eisenhower easily defeated Stevenson and Estes Kefauver.

As vice president, Nixon also assumed the duties of foreign goodwill ambassador at large, visiting nations around the world. His most famous foreign trips came in 1958, when he visited Peru and Venezuela, and in 1959, when he went to Moscow. During the 1958 trip, angry leftists attacked the Nixon entourage, nearly injuring Nixon and his wife. In Moscow, Nixon burnished his Cold War credentials by engaging Soviet Premier Nikita Khrushchev in a "kitchen debate." While touring an American National Exhibition in Moscow where a model kitchen had been set up, Nixon and Khrushchev exchanged heated words extemporaneously over the virtues and vices of capitalism and Communism. Eisenhower had allowed Nixon to make the most of a position that traditionally had been a political dead end.

Nixon easily swept to the 1960 Republican nomination for president, while Massachusetts Senator John F. Kennedy, a Roman Catholic, had a much more difficult primary battle. One of Kennedy's strongest primary opponents, Senator Lyndon Johnson of Texas, reluctantly joined Kennedy on the Democratic ticket. Henry Cabot Lodge was named Nixon's running mate.

Kennedy trailed badly. The playboy senator had accrued a modest record on Capitol Hill and limited national notoriety from a failed vice presidential attempt at the 1956 convention. He still generally was known as the son of Joseph Kennedy, the rascal former ambassador to Great Britain under Franklin D. Roosevelt. Nixon, on the other hand, had transformed the vice presidency. His impeccable anti-Communist credentials, as exemplified by the much-discussed confrontation with Khrushchev the year before, seemed to fit the Cold War mood.

Yet all the characteristics that had made Nixon a success during the print media years seemed to work against him in 1960. It was the first television-oriented campaign. Both Eisenhower and Stevenson had eschewed television. Eisenhower's smile came across well, but he disliked answering questions and speaking on television, and the intellectual Stevenson found television a nuisance that only seemed to oversimplify his complex arguments and ideas.

Kennedy, on the other hand, was made for television. His ruddy good looks and glib sense of humor enamored viewers. Nixon was stiff and cold. His smile seemed forced, and his eyes shifted constantly when the camera focused on him. His insight and his ideas far exceeded Kennedy's shallow, ill-formulated campaign platitudes, but this was not a television-age advantage.

Even before the primaries, Republican and Democratic party leaders had agreed to a series of debates between the candidates, so Nixon was faced with a commitment to the first televised presidential debates in history before he even received the nomination. He agreed to honor the commitment, though his large lead in the polls meant he had nothing to gain. Prior to the first debate, Nixon had been hospitalized with a leg infection and looked sallow and downcast at the podium. Kennedy was relaxed, tanned, and buoyant. Surveyed radio listeners thought Nixon had won, while television viewers overwhelmingly felt Kennedy had the upperhand, but most people had watched, not listened. Television delivered a debate victory to Kennedy. Although Nixon fared better in later debates, more enthusiastic crowds followed Kennedy for the rest of the campaign. Television cameras helped him wherever he traveled because he looked the part, while Nixon seemed sullen and angry.

The hard-driving, cynical Nixon engendered mistrust among reporters. The nation's newspapers, particularly in

Richard Nixon preferred not to meet with the press – or to meet with them in more controlled circumstances, such as on *Meet the Press* **with Lawrence Spivak.**
(UPI/Corbis-Bettmann)

the midwest and west, were still dominated by Republican publishers and editors, but Nixon did not fit in well with the national reporters from the east. They related better on a personal level to the gregarious Kennedy, who had graduated from Harvard, not Whittier College, and who provided good quips and quotes.

Nixon's lead in the polls narrowed. Television advocates would argue later that Kennedy won the race because of the first debate, but the election was so close that that assertion seems hardly justified. The debate was a turning point, however. It set the tone for the campaign. Kennedy won by about 100,000 votes of the 68 million cast, one of the narrowest victories in presidential history. Kennedy's electoral count was 303 to Nixon's 219 and independent Harry Byrd's 15.

Nixon had never lost before. What was worse, he had been defeated in an election in which the media had figured heavily for the first time in modern history. Throughout the century, war and economics had decided presidential elections. Now television images did.

Nixon returned to California, away from reporters for the first time in 14 years, and joined a prestigious Los Angeles law firm, but his political abstinence lasted only about a year. He was nominated in 1962 by the Republicans to unseat incumbent governor Edmund G. "Pat" Brown but lost. Nixon told reporters at a nationally televised press conference, "You won't have Nixon to kick around anymore, because, gentlemen, this is my last press conference." The angry and aloof Nixon finally had unburdened his long-nurtured suspicions that reporters had been out to get him. They and he would never forget that exchange.

Nixon moved to New York and joined a Wall Street law firm. He quietly worked on behalf of 1964 Republican standard-bearer Barry Goldwater, who lost badly to Lyndon Johnson. In 1966, Nixon campaigned actively for congressional candidates, winning grassroots political support throughout the country.

When the 1968 Republican front-runner, George Romney, issued some untimely remarks about the Vietnam War in 1967 and New York Governor Nelson Rockefeller waffled, Nixon jumped into a lead for the presidential nomination. Then, astonishingly, he won the nomination easily, only six years after his bitter farewell to reporters in California.

Once again, polls had shown Nixon holding a commanding lead as the campaign opened. This time, he declined to debate and carefully orchestrated all his public appearances and statements. He substituted controlled television interviews with cooperative citizens for close questioning by journalists. Democratic nominee Hubert H. Humphrey, meanwhile, was dogged by anti–Vietnam War demonstrators and the mantle of Lyndon Johnson's unpopular presidential policies.

Still, the Nixon jinx seemed to hold. His lead dwindled throughout the campaign. Despite all the factors in his favor, Nixon won with 301 electoral votes to Humphrey's 191 and segregationist independent candidate George Wallace's 46. Nixon polled 31.7 million votes to Humphrey's 31.2 million, while Wallace drew another 10 million, mostly in the Deep South.

The White House sought immediately to enhance Nixon's image at the expense of the press. Vice President Spiro Agnew attacked the news policies of the networks and major newspapers, in general, as too liberal and too sanctimonious for most people in the United States. He amused and delighted audience with alliterative phrases such as "nattering nabobs of negativism." The assaults seemed to please many, especially conservatives, who were weary and suspicious of the changes of the 1960s and the perceived excessive power of reporters.

Nixon adopted popular domestic and foreign policies, while winding down the war in Southeast Asia. In May 1970, however, he expanded the war into Cambodia, causing violent protests on college campuses around the nation and a clash at Kent State University in Ohio between National Guardsmen and students that left four students dead. In August 1972, he agreed to a surprise visit to the People's Republic of China, a Communist nation that had been quarantined by the United States for 23 years. Newly developed satellite capabilities allowed U.S. citizens to watch Nixon's China visit live on national television, a remarkable media and political event arranged by special adviser Henry Kissinger.

Presidential press conferences were few, and press secretary Ronald Ziegler treated reporters with disdain and indifference, often couching answers to their questions in convoluted language to obscure his meaning. Nixon, meanwhile, plotted against his political enemies and against reporters, keeping dossiers and using the Federal Bureau of Investigation (FBI) to spy on them. The president's aides authorized a break-in at the offices of Daniel Ellsberg's psychiatrist in 1971. Ellsberg, a former U.S. information officer in Vietnam, had leaked documents about policies on the Vietnam War – popularly known as the Pentagon Papers – to reporters.

In 1972, Senator George McGovern of South Dakota stumbled to the Democratic nomination for president. He and Sargent Shriver, a Kennedy in-law who had been director of the Peace Corps, lost badly as Nixon successfully painted them as wild-eyed liberals. The Republicans poured money into a glitzy media campaign complete with television extravaganzas and softball questions asked of Nixon during mock interviews. Nixon scored a landslide victory, polling 47 million votes to McGovern's 29 million and losing only Massachusetts and the District of Columbia.

It was time to pay back those who had opposed him, especially reporters. The Nixon White House aggressively sought to discredit political enemies and journalists who had been critical of Nixon policies. Ziegler's briefings and Nixon's rare press conferences became contentious and combative.

But in June 1972, the White House authorized a break-in at the Democratic National Headquarters in the posh Watergate hotel–office building–apartment complex in Washington. The five burglars were caught, and their court appearance attracted the attention of two young reporters at the *Washington Post*, Carl Bernstein and Bob Woodward. The reporters followed the story and discovered wrongdoings that involved both White House staffers and members of the Committee to Re-elect the President.

At first, the more than 1,100 other reporters in Washington largely ignored the story. A grand jury investigation was launched under the auspices of Federal Judge John Sirica, and in February 1973, the U.S. Senate began its own investigation through the Select Committee on Presidential Campaign Activities, headed by Senator Sam Ervin, a Democrat from North Carolina. A special counsel was appointed. Reporters started paying closer attention. Indictments rained down on the Nixon administration. John Dean, special counsel to the president, testified before the Senate committee in June 1973 that Nixon had known about the break-in a week after it had occurred and had authorized a cover-up. A month later, Alexander Butterfield testified that the president had secret tape recorders in the Oval Office and had taped all conversations during his years in office.

The Watergate investigation shifted its emphasis to attempts to recover the tapes. Nixon had Special Prosecutor Archibald Cox fired in October 1973 to block the probe. Attorney General Elliot Richardson and his assistant William Ruckelshaus quit, refusing to fire Cox. The next month, the Nixon White House released some of the secret tapes, but one tape had an 18½-minute gap. Nixon shamelessly blamed his loyal secretary, Rose Mary Woods, saying that she accidentally had erased the missing conversation.

All legislative activities in Washington ground to a halt. Reporters wrote about nothing but Watergate. Even an oil embargo by Arab nations in the spring of 1973, which left motorists unable to obtain gasoline, could not deter coverage of the Watergate scandal. In the midst of the investigation, Agnew resigned, pleading no contest to charges that he had accepted financial kickbacks while governor of Maryland. He was replaced by House minority leader Gerald R. Ford.

The net tightened around the Watergate figures as more information came to light and more tapes were released. Eventually, 40 persons were convicted and jailed as a result of the investigations, including many influential White House adjutants. Nixon and top aides H.R. Haldeman and John Ehrlichman had not only covered up the break-in but had authorized underhanded activities such as campaign "dirty tricks" to confound the McGovern election effort – illegal wiretaps and surveillances, conveyance of illegal campaign slush fund money, and illegal use of FBI and Central Intelligence Agency records. Aides admitted later that they had committed all these acts because they were devoted to Richard Nixon and his goals.

In the summer of 1974, the House Judiciary Committee voted to recommend articles of impeachment. Nixon resigned weeks later on August 9, 1974, and returned to San Clemente, California. A month later, Ford pardoned Nixon, saying that he wanted to allow the nation to put the Watergate affair behind it. Instead, the pardon created such a furor that Ford's presidency was crippled badly.

Nixon remained away from public scrutiny for years, mostly writing his memoirs. When he finally decided to appear publicly, it was under carefully controlled conditions, such as a series of television discussions with talk show host David Frost, who was not a journalist, and visits to traditionally Republican or conservative communities. Nixon was never again a factor in national politics, nor did he ever concede publicly any criminal or moral culpability in the Watergate affair. He died in 1994.

Print journalism enjoyed a revival as a result of Watergate. Young journalists in the late 1970s sought to emulate Woodward and Bernstein, but the general public had second thoughts. Many were troubled by a media powerful enough to drive a president from office and most of his administrative assistants to jail. Two reporters, young and uninfluential reporters at that, had reversed the wishes of a nation of voters. Nixon's subordinates, even when they conceded that they had committed wrongful acts, argued that they had never done anything that any other modern presidential coterie had not done. They merely had been caught. But they also had been arrogant, careless, and excessively heavy-handed, others noted. The Watergate break-in and the subsequent cover-up were only examples of a long list of deeds that could have subverted the democratic process.

Doubts about Watergate lingered for years. Ben Bradlee, *Washington Post* executive editor, had been a close friend of John F. Kennedy. Many doubted he would have authorized such an aggressive investigation if the target had been Kennedy and not Nixon. In the late 1970s and the 1980s, investigative reporters were portrayed by conservative groups and in television and movie dramas as ruthless, uncaring snoopers who would do anything for stories. Watergate had provided some immediate prestige for print journalism, but in the long run, it provoked grave public doubts.

In Washington, reporters realized that the Nixon White House had perpetrated a great deal of mischief right under their noses. Presidential press conferences became duels in the post-Watergate era, and every aspect of a president's or presidential candidate's life came under scrutiny. No personal matter remained private again, and a general mistrust forced a permanent wedge between the White House and the Washington press corps. Two decades later, Washington still was feeling the fallout from Watergate.

For Nixon's part, Watergate forever overshadowed all the complex and complicated accomplishments he had achieved. A long, illustrious career of successful foreign affairs initiatives and political victories paled beside the revelation that two journalists had driven a sitting president from office, the first time the nation's leader had been forced to step down. Nixon had risen to fame through the media and was driven to disgrace by the same.

LOUIS W. LIEBOVICH

See also Agnew, Spiro T., and the Media; Cold War and the Media; Eisenhower, Dwight D., and the Media; Kennedy, John F., and the Media; Mass Media and the Antiwar Movement; Pentagon Papers; Presidential Debates; Presidential Press Secretaries; Vietnam War; Watergate Scandal

Further Reading

Bernstein, Carl, and Bob Woodward, *All the President's Men*, New York: Simon & Schuster, 1974; London: Quartet, 1974

Ehrlichman, John, *Witness to Power: The Nixon Years,* New York: Simon & Schuster, 1982

Evans, Rowland, Jr., and Robert D. Novak, *Nixon in the White House: The Frustration of Power,* New York: Random House, 1971

Nixon, Richard M., *Beyond Peace,* New York: Random House, 1994

_____, *Six Crises,* Garden City, New York: Doubleday, 1962; London: W.H. Allen, 1962

White, Theodore H., *The Making of the President, 1960,* New York: Atheneum, 1961

Noncommercial Radio

Promotes educational, cultural, and news services

Noncommercial broadcasting seeks to meet needs for education, culture, and news and information that supporters feel cannot be adequately met by commercially driven stations. While in most countries noncommercial or public service broadcasting preceded the formation of commercial broadcasting, in the United States, commercial and noncommercial broadcasting evolved together. During the 1920s, more than 100 colleges and churches were granted licenses, concentrating on home and classroom instruction, civic awareness, religious or institutional promotion, cultural enhancement, and fund raising. The Association of College and University Broadcasting Stations, later known as the National Association of Educational Broadcasters (NAEB), was formed in 1925.

Most early noncommercial stations were underfinanced and were consequently sold to commercial broadcasters desperate for scarce frequencies. The number of noncommercial stations fell to fewer than 50 by 1933 (and to about 25 in 1945), making noncommercial channel reservation an important issue when the Communications Act of 1934 was debated. After an amendment setting aside 25 percent of all frequencies for noncommercial use was defeated in the Senate, a requirement that the Federal Communications Commission (FCC) study noncommercial radio was included in the act. Ultimately, the FCC reserved five channels for noncommercial use in the 1940 FM allocation and, under pressure from the NAEB, increased that number to 20 channels from 88 to 92 megahertz in the 1945 FM reallocation. When demand for these channels proved insubstantial, the FCC created more liberal rules, allowing low-power (10-watt) "Class D" stations that served as "electronic sandboxes" or "starter kit" stations. Thus, noncommercial radio was reborn; the number of stations jumped to about 50 by 1949 and doubled again to 100 in 1952, although many of these stations were used as broadcasting laboratories or run as student activities and failed to grow into full-fledged public stations.

Noncommercial broadcasters in the 1950s focused on establishing public television. Later, the NAEB decided not to pursue federal support for both radio and television, despite the objections of its executive director, who pushed for the inclusion of radio. Consequently, noncommercial radio became known as "the hidden medium" (the name of a 1967 report on public radio). One of the most divisive problems faced by the Carnegie Commission on Educational Television was whether to include radio at all. After some last minute behind-the-scenes negotiating, Congress passed the 1967 Public Broadcasting Act and instructed the new Corporation for Public Broadcasting (CPB) to support both radio and television.

Local facilities and funding at this time were lacking sorely. While there were 412 educational radio stations in 1969 (384 on FM), more than half of the FM stations were still low power. A CPB survey revealed that three-quarters of the noncommercial radio stations had annual budgets of less than $25,000 and that nearly half of the stations had no full-time professional staff. To remedy this situation, the CPB created a six-year plan in 1969 that set minimum levels for facilities, hours, staffing, power, and programming in order for stations to qualify for federal funding. Most importantly, the stations were directed to target the general public instead of more narrow, niche audiences. The CPB increased the standards over the next six years, eventually requiring five full-time staff members and an 18-hour broadcast day. At first, CPB standards were fiercely opposed by many station managers, but clearly these standards helped strengthen U.S. noncommercial radio. While only 73 of approximately 500 noncommercial stations qualified for CPB support in 1970, by 1986 nearly 300 stations qualified. In 1992, about 450 licensees qualified for CPB grants, but this was still only a third of the total number of noncommercial radio stations. In 1978, in order to reduce the number of low-power stations, the FCC required 10-watt stations to either increase power to 100 watts or face sanctions. By 1993, there were just a few low-power stations left on the air.

In terms of programming, active NAEB members met in 1969 in a series of meetings that concluded with the creation of National Public Radio (NPR). Unlike noncommercial television's PBS, NPR was set up specifically as a program distribution and production service. Early NPR programs included a 20-concert series by the Los Angeles Philharmonic, live Senate committee hearings on the Vietnam War, and the news program *All Things Considered.* NPR also vowed to reflect regionalism and provide for member stations to participate in program production, but some stations felt that NPR did not allow them enough autonomy. This resentment paved the way for Minnesota Public Radio to launch an important rival to NPR, American Public Radio (APR) in 1981. APR's flagship program, Garrison Keillor's *A Prairie Home Companion,* became the most listened to program on public radio, and APR (which distributed but did not produce programs) eventually surpassed NPR in programming hours per week.

In the late 1990s, about two-thirds of all NPR-member stations were owned by universities and schools, about 31 percent were owned by community groups, and the remaining 4 percent were owned by states or municipalities. The other 900 noncommercial stations that chose not to join NPR (or did not qualify) were religious stations or community outlets providing more localized, limited, but often highly original, programming.

Financial problems owing to uneven federal funding rocked NPR in the 1970s and early 1980s, and a $7-million loan was secured from the CPB in 1983. This loan was retired in 1986, but not before NPR and the CPB agreed to a new funding mechanism that would appropriate funds directly to the stations, which would, in turn, pay NPR fees based on annual revenue. The plan also called for the CPB to establish a $3-million fund to support "innovative and experimental" national programs as well as independently produced programs and those that would serve minorities and other underrepresented groups. As federal funding for noncommercial radio grew even more uncertain in the 1990s, and as rules for "enhanced underwriting" evolved allowing quasi-commercial announcements, many questioned whether public radio should strive to remain "noncommercial" or whether "nonprofit" radio was more practical.

MARK J. BRAUN

See also Commercialization of Broadcasting; Communications Act of 1934; Noncommercial Television

Further Reading

Looker, Tom, *The Sound and the Story: NPR and the Art of Radio,* Boston: Houghton Mifflin, 1995
Witherspoon, John, and Roselle Kovitz, *The History of Public Broadcasting,* Washington, D.C.: Current, 1987

Noncommercial Television

Independently operated television stations offering diverse programming

There is a good deal of confusion surrounding the meaning of the term "public broadcasting," which actually came into common usage only in about 1967 with the passage of the Public Broadcasting Act. In that statute, "public broadcasting" referred to those noncommercial radio and television stations that were part of the national system coordinated by the Corporation for Public Broadcasting (CPB). This included television stations of the Public Broadcasting Service (PBS) and radio stations that carried National Public Radio and American Public Radio programs.

Many people use the term "public broadcasting" more loosely, however, to mean any noncommercial radio or television station. In fact, many noncommercial stations are independently operated by colleges and universities, religious organizations, community groups, or state and local governments and receive no federal dollars. Moreover, these stations usually operate with goals somewhat different from those of the national system of public stations. Historically, the term "educational broadcasting" has been more broadly used to describe all noncommercial stations, and especially those that existed prior to the 1967 creation of "public broadcasting."

Educational (and later, public) broadcasters in the United States historically have been plagued by several major problems. First, as noncommercial operations, most must rely on public funding. Money is always scarce and frequently comes with strings attached; controversial programming often threatens to undermine financial support. Second, noncommercial broadcasters almost always have relatively small audiences. In trying to offer programming outside the mainstream, these stations give up a broad viewership, limiting their ability to muster both financial and political support. Finally, noncommercial broadcasters frequently have been divided over the exact role their stations should play, resulting in a fragmented voice that undermines what uncertain political support they do have.

In addition, two groups have been the historical adversaries of noncommercial stations – political conservatives and commercial broadcasters. Conservatives often have objected to the use of public funds for broadcasting, and, in different eras, have raised various charges of "Socialism," "elitism," and "liberal bias." Commercial broadcasters frequently have opposed noncommercial stations on the grounds that they attract only small audiences yet occupy scarce frequencies that could be better used (in their view) for additional commercial stations.

Such difficulties faced educational broadcasters almost from the start. As radio developed into a viable medium in the early 1920s, many nonprofit groups such as religious organizations, government agencies, and colleges and universities joined commercial broadcasters in a rush to put new stations on the air. Hundreds of new transmitters were constructed in a very short time; by the end of 1922, there were 576 stations in operation, 72 of them operated by educational institutions. Then, as later, the noncommercial broadcasters' goals were diverse. Some stations were constructed simply as technical exercises carried out by engineering faculty and students, others transmitted weather and agricultural information to farmers, and a few offered extension education – courses taught over the airwaves.

Yet many of these stations were to be short-lived. By the mid 1920s, nearly half of the educational stations had gone off the air, the beginning of a steady decline that was to continue well into the 1940s. There were several reasons for this. First was the funding problem; many simply could not generate the public support necessary to pay the bills. Second, there was little early federal government support for educational broadcasting. The Radio Act of 1927 did not even mention educational radio, and, in the spectrum reallocation that followed, most educational broadcasters were given poor frequency assignments. In addition, new technical requirements imposed by the law made operations even more costly. Compounding these problems were pressures by commercial broadcasters who were demanding new licenses just as available frequencies were becoming more scarce. Several of them purchased educational stations from cash-strapped colleges and universities and converted them to commercial operations.

By the end of the 1920s, many supporters were fearful that educational radio would disappear altogether, but in 1930, the National Committee on Education by Radio was formed and campaigned actively on behalf of educational stations for the next several years. One of their proposals suggested reserving certain frequencies solely for education-

Public Television's *Barney* captivated younger children.
(Museum of Broadcast Communications)

al stations. Predictably, commercial broadcasters were strongly opposed. A competing national group, the National Advisory Council on Radio in Education, was formed and argued that any educational uses the public had for radio could be carried out by commercial broadcasters.

After World War II, when the number of educational stations on the air had fallen to 25, the federal government responded. As part of the general reorganization of FM and television frequency allocations, the Federal Communications Commission (FCC) set aside certain channels in those services specifically for educational broadcasting. The FCC's 1952 *Sixth Report and Order* outlined the plan for all television frequency assignments throughout the country. Rather than setting aside a block of frequencies for educational television, the Commission made 242 separate assignments, one channel for each of 46 educational centers plus one for each large city. In addition, many of these assignments were to be on lower channels located in the more desirable VHF (rather than UHF) band.

From these beginnings, hopes for a national educational television system began to grow, but obtaining funding for new stations was still difficult. A few colleges and universities began to build stations, and the Ford Foundation helped others by providing construction grants. The Foundation also helped fund the creation of National Educational Television (NET), a program cooperative that was the closest thing early educational television (ETV) had to a network. ETV growth was slow but steady; by mid-1955, there were 12 stations on the air, and by 1958, there were 35. By 1961, there were 51, but there were still no stations at all in half of the states. Scarce funds also meant a shortage of programs. Even with sharing among stations through NET, a typical ETV station in 1959 was only on the air 35 hours a week, and stations could not afford to be too discriminating about program quality.

The rising social consciousness of the 1960s sparked a renewed interest in a truly national noncommercial radio and television system; however, educational broadcasters, as always, were divided on precisely what form such a system should take. Some felt that it should focus on instructional programming that could be used in the schools. Others envisioned a national cultural service along the lines of the British Broadcasting Corporation. There were also disputes over whether such a service should be controlled by the local stations or by some new centralized national agency. The question of government funding and control added to the controversy. Although most supporters agreed that public television needed to be free from advertiser influence, it was not clear exactly how the new service also could be isolated from political control by those in government who held the purse strings.

In 1962, Congress took some preliminary steps toward a national service by passing the Educational Television Facilities Act, which provided $32 million to build new stations. This spurred construction, so by the end of 1966, there were 126 ETV stations on the air. In February 1967, a private commission funded by the Carnegie Corporation issued a report outlining plans for a new national system of what they termed "public broadcasting." Among other things, they called for the creation of a private, nonprofit organization to receive and disburse private and government funds for the system. They further proposed that there be a long-term funding source – a tax on the sale of television sets – that would go directly into a trust fund to help insulate the new service from direct government influence.

The Carnegie Commission Report was generally well received, and many of its recommendations were carried out in the landmark Public Broadcasting Act of 1967, which established the Corporation for Public Broadcasting (CPB) generally along the lines of the report's recommendations. Congress, however, pressured by television set manufacturers and other interests, was unwilling to pass the set tax, instead leaving the CPB to receive an annual appropriation from Congress. Further, the law provided that the directing board of the CPB was to be made up entirely of presidential appointees. These two critical changes to the Carnegie recommendations effectively defeated the goal of political insulation and were to have major repercussions for the CPB in the years to come.

Organizing under the new law, the CPB launched the first true national network of noncommercial stations in 1970. The Public Broadcasting Service (PBS) initially interconnected 128 television stations, many of them former NET affiliates. However, disagreements remained over questions of programming choice and funding control. What emerged was a system unlike that of the commercial networks. PBS would, itself, produce no programming. Instead, programs were to be procured from many sources, including member stations, independent producers, and overseas suppliers. The member stations also helped select the programs to be funded and distributed.

Three major types of PBS station operators evolved: community associations, colleges and universities, and state and local government. Station goals were varied, and programming often combined PBS's broad cultural service during prime time with local instructional or minority-oriented programming during daytime hours. Although the CPB used federal dollars to support PBS, the affiliate stations themselves were primarily funded from state and local sources. In fact, during the early 1970s, less than a third of public television's total support came from federal sources – a proportion that declined steadily thereafter.

In 1970, the CPB also created National Public Radio (NPR) to interconnect radio stations. Unlike PBS, NPR both produced and distributed programming. NPR was also selective in choosing its affiliate stations. To be NPR-qualified, stations had to meet minimum criteria for power, facilities, and budget (in the 1990s, only about one-third of noncommercial stations met these standards).

Despite its shortcomings, the Public Television Act helped usher in a new age for noncommercial television. The number of stations on the air grew to 233 in 1972, to 300 in 1983, and, by 1991 – 20 years after the act's passage – to 349, nearly triple the number in 1967. Yet competition for viewers also had increased. The rapid growth of new commercial stations, cable television outlets, and home video rentals gave viewers more choices and, significantly, more narrowly programmed channels. Commercial cable services such as the Discovery Channel, Bravo, Arts and Entertainment, and Cable News Network began to offer programming similar to (and in some cases, identical with) that which had been the traditional PBS fare. By the early 1990s, PBS was doing well to hold its average prime-time audience rating at a fairly steady 2 to 3 percent of U.S. television households.

Other serious challenges to public broadcasting came from political conservatives. In 1972, President Richard Nixon, unhappy with some of PBS's more controversial programming, vetoed the CPB funding bill, arguing that PBS had become too centralized and urging a return to more local program control. Several members of the CPB board resigned and were replaced with Nixon appointees. The move clearly demonstrated the vulnerability of CPB to political pressures and forced public broadcasters to begin seeking increased financial support from nongovernmental sources, such as individual subscribers and commercial underwriters. The Ronald Reagan administration made further cuts in federal support, so by the time of the Republican victories in the congressional elections of 1994, public broadcasting had been under political siege for some time. In 1995, congressional conservatives sponsored hearings on CPB funding, calling for further drastic cuts or even for a total privatization of the system.

In the late 1990s, public broadcasting was the focus of a convergence of political, economic, and technological changes that threatened its very existence. Increased competition for viewers and programming has meant increased financial burdens at the same time that federal, state, and local governments reduced spending. These pressures were compounded by an increased criticism from the political right. It was far from clear that public broadcasting would be able to survive without undergoing some drastic reformations.

R. STEPHEN CRAIG

See also Commercialization of Broadcasting; Noncommercial Radio

Further Reading

Carnegie Commission on the Future of Public Broadcasting, *A Public Trust: The Report of the Carnegie Commission on the Future of Public Broadcasting*, New York: Bantam, 1979

Gibson, George H., *Public Broadcasting: The Role of the Federal Government, 1912–76*, New York: Praeger, 1977

Hoynes, William, *Public Television for Sale: Media, the Market, and the Public Sphere*, Boulder, Colorado: Westview, 1994

Lashley, Marilyn, *Public Television: Panacea, Pork Barrel, or Public Trust?*, New York: Greenwood, 1992

Rowland, Willard D., Jr., "Continuing Crisis in Public Broadcasting: A History of Disenfranchisement," *Journal of Broadcasting and Electronic Media* 30 (1986)

Stone, David M., *Nixon and the Politics of Public Television*, New York: Garland, 1985

Witherspoon, John, and Roselle Kovitz, *The History of Public Broadcasting*, Washington, D.C.: Current, 1987

O

Objective Reporting

Elusive ideal long sought by journalists

Objective reporting, as press scholars are quick to note, is an elusive ideal that journalists variously sought after, embraced, and rejected from the mid-1800s. By the 1960s, whether one regarded objectivity as the "fatal flaw or the supreme virtue of the American press, all agreed that the idea of objectivity was at the heart of what journalism has meant in this country."

As Dan Schiller showed, after the early partisan papers gave way to nonpolitical papers in the mid-1800s, balanced presentation of opposing viewpoints became a media value. Such balancing ultimately became the identifying mark of objective reporting. *New York Times* publisher Adolph S. Ochs, an early advocate of objective reporting, demonstrated the financial value of presenting the news in a truthful, "even-tempered voice" when he reversed the failing paper in the 1890s. But, as critics of the *Times* noted even then, the paper failed to be truly objective because of "the truths it omitted." Journalists subsequently struggled to achieve the illusive ideal of objectivity by avoiding obviously value-laden terms and seeking balance by reporting comments from competing but reliable sources.

As social historians of the press have found, however, the goal of objectivity has proven to be much more unattainable than the U.S. press believed it to be before World War I. Before the 1920s, journalists, along with others, believed in facts – they believed that facts existed apart from their human construction and, as such, they could be objectively reported. They had not yet subscribed to the evolving view of the philosopher and the social scientist who said that "human beings are cultural animals who know and see and hear the world through socially constructed filters." As the view that "facts" were social constructions ultimately became embedded in U.S. thought, many of the nation's cherished ideals – free enterprise and democracy, for example – underwent severe criticism. "Journalists, like others, lost faith in verities a democratic market society had taken for granted. Their experience of propaganda during the war and public relations thereafter convinced them that the world they reported was one that interested parties had constructed for them to report."

Yet the press continued to embrace the idea of objectivity even though many of the so-called truths or facts about the United States, democracy, and the free market revealed themselves to indeed be cultural constructions. As Michael Schudson argued, journalists "came to believe in objectivity . . . because they wanted to, needed to," as a means of escaping "their own deep convictions of doubt and drift." When it became apparent to many that individual enterprise had been replaced by corporate power, that citizens were consumers to be manipulated, that machines, not voters, controlled elections, and that powerful publishers, not the pursuit of truth, governed the press – that, in sum, many of the ideals of the United States were in fact cultural creations – the press upheld objectivity as a means of camouflaging its disappointment.

Although the 1960s saw the resurrection of two reporting traditions – literary, or "new," journalism, and muckraking, or investigative reporting – as efforts to challenge the concept of objectivity, those styles died when the social movements of the period receded. As Schudson noted,

> there is no new ideal in journalism to successfully challenge objectivity, but there is a hope for something new, a simmering disaffection with objective reporting. There has been no magical leap beyond the difficult understanding that human perceptions are subjective and no easy solution to the problem that the events one reports have been prefabricated by powerful institutions, and yet there is more tolerance and encouragement for a variety of ways of knowing and writing.

ROBIN GALLAGHER

See also Interpretative Reporting; Investigative Reporting; Literary Aspects of Journalism; New Journalism (1960s–1970s); News Concepts; Reporters and Reporting in the Twentieth Century

Further Reading

Schiller, Dan, *Objectivity and the News: The Public and the Rise of Commercial Journalism*, Philadelphia: University of Pennsylvania Press, 1981
Schudson, Michael, *Discovering the News: A Social History of American Newspapers*, New York: Basic, 1978
Stephens, Mitchell, *A History of News: From the Drum to the Satellite*, New York: Viking, 1988

Obscenity and Pornography

Varying degrees of sexually explicit speech cause problems for courts

"The subject of obscenity has produced a variety of views among the members of the Court unmatched in any other course of constitutional adjudication," said U.S. Supreme Court Justice John Harlan in 1968. He called it, for short, "the intractable obscenity problem." In 13 obscenity decisions with signed opinions between 1957 – the year of the Court's first major ruling on obscenity – and 1967, arguably the most active period on the topic for the Court, the nine justices filed 55 separate statements of their views. What is even more startling, between 1967 and 1973 the Court put itself at odds with state legislators, local prosecutors, and juries by reversing no less than 31 lower court convictions involving sexual speech.

But the subject of sexually explicit speech, which is called obscenity when proscribed by law, is more than a problem for the courts; it is also a problem for society. Richard S. Randall's observation is a good one: "Whether viewed as a struggle against repression or as a struggle to prevent offending, possibly harmful expression, the pornography issue has an unavoidable and probably permanent place on the public agenda of modern liberal mass democratic society."

The doctrine that obscenity is outside the free speech protection of the First Amendment first was discerned in *Near* v. *Minnesota* (1931), when Chief Justice Charles Evans Hughes, in outlawing prior restraint against the press, qualified his ruling by saying "the primary requirements of decency may be enforced against obscene publications." Such an exclusion continued in *Chaplinsky* v. *New Hampshire* (1942), when Justice Frank Murphy, in dealing with the concept of "fighting words," grouped such language with "the lewd and obscene, [and] the profane" and labeled such words as "no essential part of any exposition of ideas" and thus not protected by the First Amendment. Not until the 1950s did the Supreme Court start applying a speech-protective philosophy to sexual expression – first by scrutinizing censorship of movies by states and municipalities, then by reshaping and reformulating the judicial test for obscenity.

Battles over obscenity in the early twentieth century began with decisions over James Joyce's novel *Ulysses*. Judge John M. Woolsey, author of the 1933 decision in this case, spoke for the judiciary when he said he thought the courts had defined obscene as that speech "tending to stir the sex impulses or to lead to sexually impure and lustful thoughts." The definition the Supreme Court settled on in its *Roth* v. *United States* (1957) ruling included material that treated sex in a manner appealing to the "prurient interest." Judge Woolsey breached conventional morality when he challenged the accepted standard of determining obscenity on the basis of the effect of isolated passages on the most vulnerable members of society. He said that a better test was the impact or dominant effect of the entire work on the average person accompanied by evaluation of the author's intent based on a full reading of the text involved.

In the *Roth* decision, the Court said that obscenity had no social value and therefore did not merit constitutional protection. To protect nonobscene speech, the Court fashioned the first of a series of definitions of obscenity based on a work's dominant theme and on community standards. Obscenity, as defined by Justice William J. Brennan Jr., was "utterly without redeeming social importance." Brennan limited obscenity to "material which deals with sex in a manner appealing to prurient interest," which he described as either "having a tendency to excite lustful thoughts" or a "shameful and morbid interest in sex." A work was obscene, therefore, if, to the average person, applying contemporary community standards, the dominant theme of the material, taken as a whole, appealed to prurient interest. The Brennan test stood until 1973.

With *Jacobellis* v. *Ohio* (1964), the Court reaffirmed its *Roth* position, adding that for a work to be obscene, it had to be "*utterly* without with redeeming social importance [emphasis added]." Brennan, speaking for the Court's majority, also said that national standards should be used in evaluating that social importance. Chief Justice Earl Warren disagreed emphatically. The Court's trend toward minimal regulations culminated in the 1966 "Fanny Hill" case, *A Book Named "John Cleland's Memoirs of a Woman of Pleasure"* v. *Attorney General of Massachusetts*. Here, the attorney tried to convince the Court to substitute "social value" for "social importance" in the obscenity test, believing that it would be easier to convince courts of "value" as opposed to "importance." In his plurality ruling, Brennan declared that material was obscene if its dominant theme was prurient, if it was "patently offensive because it affronts contemporary community standards" and if it was "utterly without redeeming social value." With *Redrup* v. *New York* (1967), the Supreme Court swung the pendulum about as far to the left as it was going to go, establishing a three-part test that had to be met in all particulars before material could be declared obscene. Using this ruling, courts began to overturn just about every obscenity prosecution unless the material involved had been "pandered," or advertised salaciously, or had been sold to minors.

As the U.S. Supreme Court made it more difficult to obtain convictions for the distribution of obscenity, the problem of pornography – or sexually explicit speech not bad enough to be labeled obscene – increased. Some activists believed that the growth in the pornography industry was the direct result of the Court's liberal and "permissive" adjudication and that belief no doubt influenced Congress to create in 1967 the Commission on Obscenity and Pornography, which issued its report in 1970. President Lyndon B. Johnson appointed all but one of the commissioners. President-elect Richard M. Nixon named Charles Keating, a Cincinnati, Ohio, lawyer who headed an organization called Citizens for Decent Literature. The commission, with Keating dissenting, observed early in its report that "much of the 'problem' regarding materials which depict explicit sexual activity stems from the inability or reluctance of people in our society to be open and direct in dealing with sexual matters." Noting the absence of empirical evidence linking explicit sexual materials to criminal behavior, the commission urged that all legislation keeping sexual materials from consenting adults be repealed. "Public opinion in

America does not support the imposition of legal prohibitions upon the right of adults to read or see explicit sexual materials," it said.

By 1973, the Supreme Court, then headed by Nixon appointee Warren Burger, redefined the community standards test to mean "local" rather than "national." The court also replaced the "utterly without redeeming social value" test set in the "Fanny Hill" case with a new test in *Miller* v. *California* (1973). Here, the Court said that sexually explicit material must also have "serious literary, artistic, political or scientific value" before it could escape being condemned as obscene. In an effort to slow down the liberalization of obscenity protection under the Constitution, the Burger majority of five accepted a large number of obscenity cases and handed down seven other decisions with *Miller* and its companion, *Paris Adult Theatre I* v. *Slaton*. Justice Brennan, who had authored many of the Warren Court's obscenity rulings, dissented regularly, arguing that the Constitution prohibited suppression of allegedly obscene matter unless it had been distributed to juveniles or pandered to nonconsenting adults.

Although a majority of the Supreme Court continued to enforce the *Miller* definition of obscenity, six justices during the last quarter of the twentieth century argued that this definition violates free speech principles. In a 1987 dissent, Justice John Paul Stevens, joined by Justices Brennan and Thurgood Marshall, concluded that all criminal obscenity statutes were unconstitutional, at least as applied to consenting adults. Moreover, in that same case, conservative Justice Antonin Scalia urged the Court to reconsider its *Miller* holding: "It is quite impossible to come to an objective assessment of (at least) literary or artistic value, there being many accomplished people who have found literature in Dada, and art in the replication of a soup can. Just as there is no use arguing about taste, there is no use litigating about it" (*Pope* v. *Illinois*).

Meanwhile, two other attacks against sexually explicit speech emerged in the 1980s. First, Susan Brownmiller's *Against Our Will: Men, Women and Rape*, which appeared in 1975, set off a series of events that led to legislative efforts to outlaw pornography on the grounds that it subordinates women. In the early 1980s, Andrea Dworkin, who wrote *Pornography: Men Possessing Women*, worked with law professor Catharine A. MacKinnon in drafting antipornography ordinances for Minneapolis, Minnesota, and Indianapolis, Indiana, both of which failed on constitutional grounds. The foundation of their work was the harm they believed pornography does to women. As MacKinnon once wrote, "Pornography doesn't just drop out of the sky, go into his head and stop there. Specifically, men rape, batter, prostitute, molest, and sexually harass women."

Second, in 1986, the Attorney General's Commission on Pornography, unlike the earlier President's Commission, called for legislation to restrict sexually explicit materials. Yet, even this panel noted that "the bulk of scholarly commentary" has been critical of obscenity rulings for transgressing constitutional values. Harvard law professor Laurence Tribe, for example, said that the Court's treatment of certain sexual expression as constitutionally unprotected was "incompatible with the First Amendment premise that awareness can never be deemed harmful in itself." His explanation, similar to Richard Randall's above, was poignant:

In the last analysis, suppression of the obscene persists because it tells us something about ourselves that some of us . . . would prefer not to know. It threatens to explode our uneasy accommodation between sexual impulse and social custom – to destroy the carefully-spun social web holding sexuality in its place. . . . The desire to preserve that web by shutting out the thoughts and impressions that challenge it cannot be squared with a constitutional commitment to openness of mind.

RICHARD F. HIXSON

Further Reading
Blanchard, Margaret A., *Revolutionary Sparks: Freedom of Expression in Modern America*, New York: Oxford University Press, 1992
Downs, Donald Alexander, *The New Politics of Pornography*, Chicago: University of Chicago Press, 1989
Hixson, Richard F., *Mass Media and the Constitution: An Encyclopedia of Supreme Court Decisions*, New York: Garland, 1989
MacKinnon, Catharine A., *Only Words*, Cambridge, Massachusetts: Harvard University Press, 1993; London: HarperCollins, 1994
_____, "Pornography, Civil Rights, and Speech," *Harvard Civil Rights-Civil Liberties Law Review* 20 (Winter 1985), pp. 1–70
Randall, Richard S., *Freedom and Taboo: Pornography and the Politics of a Self Divided*, Berkeley: University of California Press, 1989
Strossen, Nadine, *Defending Pornography: Free Speech, Sex, and the Fight for Women's Rights*, New York: Scribner's, 1995; London: Abacus, 1996

Ochs, Adolph Simon

Molder of the 'New York Times'

Adolph Ochs bought into the *Chattanooga (Tennessee) Times* at age 20, and by 1882, he had full control. He built the paper into a prominent position in the south, and in the 1890s, his ambition carried him to New York. His earnest, matter-of-fact approach instilled confidence in New York as it had in Chattanooga, helping him find financing to acquire the ailing *New York Times* in 1896.

In the face of sensationalist competition from Joseph Pulitzer and William Randolph Hearst, he positioned his newspaper as the sensible, authoritative, well-mannered alternative, with the slogan "All the News That's Fit to Print." Then, when the sinking of the U.S. battleship *Maine* drew readers back to the yellow sheets in 1898, he cut the price of his paper from three cents to one cent and amazed his fellow publishers by gaining enough circulation to make the daring move pay off. By 1900, he had gained full ownership and control of the *Times*, and the paper's success seemed assured.

He pioneered the use of rotogravure halftones and wireless communications, and the paper excelled in covering business and science. Arranging to share news with the *Times* of London and hiring the matchless Carr Van Anda as managing editor, Ochs was leading the nation in international coverage by World War I. He made steady gains on the mass-audience tabloids of the 1920s without sensationalizing, and in 1931, paid circulation reached 461,000 (755,000 on Sunday). When he died in 1935, the *Times* had become the most prestigious newspaper in the United States.

GEORGE EVERETT

See also New York Times

Further Reading

Berger, Meyer, *The Story of the 'New York Times',* *1851–1951,* New York: Simon & Schuster, 1951

Everett, George, "The Age of New Journalism, 1883–1900," in *The Media in America: A History,* 2nd ed., edited by W. David Sloan, James G. Stovall, and James D. Startt, Scottsdale, Arizona: Publishing Horizons, 1993

Johnson, Gerald W., *An Honorable Titan, a Biographical Study of Adolph S. Ochs,* New York and London: Harper & Brothers, 1946

Office of Censorship

Urged journalists to cooperate voluntarily with World War II restrictions

The Office of Censorship monitored U.S. newspapers, magazines, radio broadcasts, and other means of communication during World War II to prevent the release of information that would hurt the Allied war effort. The office, administered by civilians, urged journalists to cooperate voluntarily with its restrictions on information originating within the United States.

Although President Franklin D. Roosevelt established a censorship system soon after the Japanese attacked Pearl Harbor on December 7, 1941, an atmosphere of self-censorship had existed since war began in Europe. When Germany invaded Poland on September 1, 1939, Roosevelt asked U.S. correspondents to give their full cooperation in "sticking as closely as possible to the facts. . . . I particularly hope that there won't be any unsubstantiated rumors put out." Furthermore, the Navy had made a specific request for censorship in March 1941, when it asked newspapers to withhold information about U.S. shipyard repairs to damaged British ships.

Wartime information control began when Roosevelt ordered Federal Bureau of Investigation Director J. Edgar Hoover to coordinate all censorship about the disaster at Pearl Harbor. Hoover not only suppressed information about the extent of damage to the Pacific fleet, but he also halted all international communications involving Allied forces, shipping, military operations, munitions productions, and the location of war industries, as well as such domestic information as economic news.

Roosevelt outlined the need for long-term censorship on December 16, 1941:

> All Americans abhor censorship, just as they abhor war. But the experience of this and of all other nations has demonstrated that some degree of censorship is essential in war time, and we are at war. . . . It is necessary to the national security that military information which might be of aid to the enemy be scrupulously withheld at the source. . . . It is necessary that prohibitions against the domestic publication of some types of information, contained in long-existing statutes, be rigidly enforced.

By executive order, under the authority of the First War Powers Act, Roosevelt created the Office of Censorship on December 19, 1941, and named Associated Press executive news director Byron Price as director. Price, who had a reputation for integrity and fairness, reported directly to the White House.

Roosevelt empowered Price to censor "in his absolute discretion" all letters, cables, and other private communications between the United States and other countries. He also ordered Price to "coordinate the efforts of the . . . press and radio to withhold voluntarily from publication military and other information which should not be released in the interest of the effective prosecution of the war."

By urging journalists to censor themselves, the president attempted to avoid the World War I excesses of the Committee on Public Information (CPI), whose policing of the press and the mail had led to the suppression of many publications and thousands of arrests. Roosevelt also split the twin CPI functions – censorship and propaganda – by separating the Office of Censorship from the Office of War Information, which distributed government-approved information during World War II.

The Office of Censorship released its voluntary censorship code for the print media on January 14, 1942. The code asked journalists to keep two facts in mind while they decided whether to publish a story. First, the outcome of the war was of vital concern to all U.S. citizens. Second, the security of U.S. armed forces and U.S. civilians would be weakened by disclosures that helped the enemy. Price said that journalists should ask themselves, "Is this information I would like to have if I were the enemy?," and act accordingly.

Specifically, the code urged restrictions on stories about troop size and troop movements; ships and their defenses, routes, and cargoes; planes; fortifications; war production; weather patterns (because North America's weather tends to move toward Europe); and photographs and maps pertaining to these war-related topics. It also urged the press not to publish casualty lists or stories on the movements of the president, damage to military objectives, or the location of national archives and treasures.

Price let military censors make their own censorship decisions in the war zones. He allowed domestic publication of any information released by an appropriate authority, and he urged that all war-related stories be attributed to an authoritative government source. Journalists who had doubts about a story could call his office at any hour, day or night.

Price and his staff settled most censorship issues, but Roosevelt occasionally handed down a decision on whether to censor or release sensitive information. For example, Roosevelt held up publication of atrocity stories about Japanese prisons in 1943 until he had authorized a news release.

The radio code was more far-reaching than its print counterpart because radio posed unique challenges. Unlike newspapers and magazines, radio signals are received the instant they are broadcast and cannot be halted at the nation's borders. Censors feared that spies could exploit these characteristics to send coded messages. Therefore, the Office of Censorship requested an end to radio quiz shows, man-on-the-street interviews, and requests for stations to play specific records. Such programs were popular, however, and broadcasters feared that eliminating them might hurt morale more than defend security. In a compromise, broadcasters agreed to accept written requests for songs but hold them for a while and then read a few at random. Quiz shows also drew contestants at random, and man-on-the-street programs were moved into studios, where broadcasters could exercise more control over who was selected to speak.

The Press Division checked for code compliance by reading newspapers and magazines; citizens also clipped articles and mailed them for review. The Broadcasting Division listened to radio programs at random and conducted spot checks of news scripts that it received in the mail. Most violations involved interviews with returning service personnel or the publication of military addresses, which could identify units overseas. Violators received a warning from the Office of Censorship – which had no legal enforcement powers but could embarrass the offender by naming it as a code violator.

Only one censorship violation was egregious enough to result in prosecution under the Espionage Act of 1917, which established fines or imprisonment for anyone communicating valuable information to an enemy. The *Chicago Tribune* and one of its reporters, Stanley Johnston, were prosecuted briefly in connection with a story on June 7, 1942, that indicated that the Navy had known the Japanese attack plan at the battle of Midway. The government's case collapsed when the Navy refused to tell a grand jury why Johnston's story had compromised military security. To do so would have called attention to the secret that the Navy was reading Japan's coded messages.

Other potentially serious violations of the censorship code occurred during the development of the atomic bomb. On June 28, 1943, Price issued a confidential memo urging editors to avoid all mention of "war experiments" involving atomic energy, related equipment, and radioactive elements. Violations occurred when newspapers began reporting on production facilities in Tennessee, New Mexico, and Washington state. The *Cleveland (Ohio) Press,* for example, printed a story on March 15, 1944, that revealed the existence of a "forbidden city" near Santa Fe, New Mexico, and named J. Robert Oppenheimer as its director. In September 1944, the staff of General Leslie Groves, who was in charge of the atomic bomb project, sent Price's office 104 press clippings that referred to the project or related subjects. However, the Office of Censorship mostly succeeded in limiting news reports on atomic energy as well as speculation about the gigantic explosion in New Mexico on July 16, 1945, that later was revealed to be the first atomic detonation.

The source of greatest friction between censors and the press was the ban on publishing or broadcasting information about the movements of the president. In September 1942, during the congressional campaigns, Roosevelt embarked on a two-week military inspection tour that took him to 20 cities. The Office of Censorship had asked the news media not to mention the trip until Roosevelt was back in the White House.

Reporters kept silent even though thousands of Americans heard and saw the president. It particularly angered the press when Roosevelt told 14,000 shipyard workers in Portland, Oregon, "You know, I'm not supposed to be here today. So you are possessors of a secret – a secret even the newspapers of the United States don't know." At the trip's conclusion, 35 reporters filed a protest, addressed personally to Roosevelt, that said suppressing such news was neither wise nor necessary, since so many people knew his whereabouts. Nevertheless, Roosevelt continued the ban on most presidential travel stories, irritating journalists for the rest of the war.

Yet approval of the Office of Censorship remained high. In July 1945, the American Civil Liberties Union declared, "Censorship arising out of the war has raised almost no issues in the United States." Shortly after the Office of Censorship ended operations on August 15, 1945, a Detroit, Michigan, editor called Price's agency the most efficient and rational of all wartime organizations, and a Pennsylvania editor said Price had the "whole-hearted admiration of every newsman."

MICHAEL S. SWEENEY

See also Committee on Public Information; Office of War Information; Roosevelt, Franklin D., and the Media; World War II

Further Reading

Clough, Frank C., "Operations of the Press Division of the Office of Censorship," *Journalism Quarterly* 20 (1943)

Doan, Edward N., "Organization and Operation of the Office of Censorship," *Journalism Quarterly* 21 (1944)

Koop, Theodore F., *Weapon of Silence,* Chicago: University of Chicago Press, 1946

Price, Byron, "The Censor Defends the Censorship," *New York Times Magazine* (February 11, 1945)

_____, "Governmental Censorship in War-Time," *American Political Science Review* 36 (1942)

Washburn, Patrick S., "The Office of Censorship's Attempt to Control Press Coverage of the Atomic Bomb During World War II," *Journalism Monographs* 120 (April 1990)

Winfield, Betty Houchin, *FDR and the News Media,* Urbana: University of Illinois Press, 1990

Office of Telecommunications Policy

Nixon effort to participate in discussion of telecommunications policy

The Office of Telecommunications Policy (OTP), established in 1970 by President Richard M. Nixon, instantly was embroiled in controversy. The agency's purpose, as stated in the reorganization plan that created it, was to "enable the executive branch to speak with a clearer voice and to act as a more effective partner in the discussions of communications policy with both the Congress and the Federal Communications Commission." The new agency's critics believed it went beyond executive branch authority. The OTP was abolished in 1977 by an executive reorganization plan.

The agency was not unique as an attempt to coordinate communications policy decisions in one office. The need for centralized decision making was a result of increasing conflict between private spectrum users, regulated by the Federal Communications Commission (FCC), and government spectrum users, whose allocations were handled by the Inter-department Radio Advisory Committee. As demands on the electromagnetic spectrum increased dramatically after World War II, a series of studies and executive orders resulted in the establishment of a Telecommunications Coordinating Committee in 1946, a President's Communications Policy Board in 1950, a Telecommunications Adviser to the President in 1951 (whose duties were later shifted to the Assistant Director for Telecommunications in the Office of Defense Mobilization), and an Office of Telecommunications Management in 1962. President Lyndon Johnson created a task force in 1967 to study communications policy, and the resulting Rostow Report was released just as Nixon took office in 1969. The report urged creation of a board to coordinate efficient spectrum use and provide the executive branch with long-range planning.

Two issues made the OTP different from previous telecommunications coordination efforts. First, the agency attempted to affect nongovernmental telecommunication issues. The office played an active role in issues involving cable television, public broadcasting, and satellite communications. Second, and more significant, was the attempt to provide the executive branch with authority in matters that were the responsibility of other government entities. Federal Communications Commissioner Nicholas Johnson said, "The very existence [of the OTP] looms large as a threat to the independence of the FCC as an agency responsible only to Congress."

President Nixon selected Clay T. Whitehead to be the agency's first director. Whitehead previously had served as an adviser to Nixon during the election campaign and had advocated a more active role for the executive branch in telecommunication matters. He adopted a highly visible role, for himself and for the agency. The two subsequent directors, interim director John Eger (who had previously served as an assistant to FCC chairman Dean Burch) and Thomas Houser, did not maintain the visibility that Whitehead had established.

The agency's involvement in public broadcasting demonstrated the extent to which it was used by the executive branch to achieve political objectives. The administration believed that the Public Broadcasting Service exercised too much centralized control over programming on public television stations. After President Nixon vetoed a funding authorization in 1972 for public broadcasting, Whitehead negotiated a compromise whereby more federal dollars would be available for local programs, thus providing less funding for the national programming that so irritated the president.

Some policies proposed by the OTP were not implemented immediately but did occur in some form in later years as the political climate changed. For example, in 1972, the OTP proposed increasing the length of radio and television station licenses from three to five years. Congress lengthened station licenses in 1981, after the agency was defunct.

The OTP was not successful in all of its initiatives. In 1972, the agency began investigating the number of television programs rerun by networks, claiming that the high percentage of reruns meant less original product, resulting in fewer production jobs. The OTP even threatened an antitrust suit but never followed through on its threat. The agency's interest in the issue waned, and the FCC, which had initiated an inquiry into the matter, dropped the subject in 1976 without taking action.

President Jimmy Carter dismantled the OTP. Within six months of taking office in 1977, he submitted his reorganization plan to Congress, which included OTP's elimination in favor of a National Telecommunications and Information Administration. The new agency would be part of the Department of Commerce rather than directly controlled by the president. Assigning the agency to the Commerce department implied that it would continue to examine commercial issues but removed it somewhat from the political process.

DOM CARISTI

See also Nixon, Richard M., and the Media; Noncommercial Television

Further Reading

Lucoff, Manny, "Telecommunications Management and Policy: Who Governs?," *Journalism Monographs* 51 (1977)

Miller, James, "The President's Advocate: OTP and Broadcast Issues," *Journal of Broadcasting* 26 (1982)

Porter, William E., *Assault on the Media: The Nixon Years*, Ann Arbor: University of Michigan Press, 1976

Office of War Information

World War II U.S. propaganda, information agency

The Office of War Information (OWI) was a government agency in World War II that was charged with maintaining confidence in the United States, partly by the use of propaganda. As such, it had a controversial history. Nevertheless, it was ably led by Elmer Davis, who tried to keep the propaganda to a minimum and fought to keep the public as informed as possible.

The OWI had its beginnings in the Office of Facts and Figures (OFF), which was formed by President Franklin D. Roosevelt in July 1941 as part of the Office of Civilian Defense. One of the OFF's main duties was sustaining morale by "collecting and analyzing information and opinion from the news media and, when appropriate, producing corrective material for distribution to the press." In October, Roosevelt made the OFF an independent agency reporting directly to the White House.

Roosevelt apparently gave the OFF an innocuous title to try to hide the fact that it basically was engaged in propaganda. Fiorello La Guardia, the head of the Office of Civilian Defense, claimed jokingly that "the Office of Facts and Figures is not a propaganda agency. There are three reasons why it is not. The first is that we don't believe in this country in artificially stimulated, high pressure, doctored nonsense, and since we don't, the other two reasons are unimportant." Archibald MacLeish, who became the director of the OFF in October 1941, agreed. In a more serious manner than La Guardia, he said both publicly and privately that he did not like "bally-hoo methods" and would con-

Emotional posters were a key element of OWI work during World War II.

fine the OFF to giving out facts and figures that were neither "perverted nor colored." The public was to receive this information from other governmental departments and agencies.

In March 1942, Elmer Davis, a CBS radio news commentator, criticized the government for not providing the press and the public with a truer picture of war events. "The whole government publicity situation has everybody in the news business almost in despair, with half a dozen agencies following different lines," said Davis. He suggested that the answer to what war news was fit to print was the formation of a single agency "under one head." It would decide what news to release and when to release it and would serve as a clearinghouse for this news. Three months later, the OFF, the Office of Government Reports, and two smaller agencies were absorbed by the OWI, which was created by Roosevelt with an executive order. He noted that it was to be a clearinghouse of government war news as well as information on U.S. aims and policies. Davis was named the new agency's director.

In accepting the position, Davis knew there were pitfalls that he wanted to avoid. He particularly did not want the agency to become just a propaganda mill that presented a rosy picture of the war's events. "The American people and . . . all other peoples opposing the Axis aggression," he said, should be "truthfully informed." While he admitted that military security might occasionally be more important than being truthful, he wanted to provide the country with the "fullest and most accurate information possible." Such information, according to Davis, included not only how the war was going "but where it is going and where it came from – its nature and origins, how our government is conducting it, and what (besides national survival) our government hopes to get out of victory."

Over the course of the war, the OWI grew to 9,600 employees and had a three-year budget of $132.5 million. One of its main functions was disseminating the nation's war news. While other government departments and agencies continued to give out publicity, any news that was significant to the war effort or involved more than one agency came from the OWI News Bureau. The armed services had the final authority over withholding military news, however. Eighty-five percent of the agency's budget was for overseas news and propaganda operations, one of the most important of which was the Voice of America on radio.

Davis faced immediate – and long-running – problems with being candid in war news. The military was reluctant to give out information about the front lines or figures on weapons production, even when the news was positive and did not threaten national security. For example, the OWI, in an attempt to bolster domestic morale, wanted to publicize that the U.S. production of warplanes had risen 150 percent from 1941 to 1942. The War Department, however, refused to approve the story, feeling that it would help the enemy more than it would improve morale.

While Davis was not to blame for such news not being disseminated, as the war progressed, critics still charged that he was being less truthful than he had promised. Such accusations were given credence by internal problems in the OWI. These came to a head in the spring of 1943 when

Elmer Davis headed OWI efforts from 1942 to 1945.
(National Archives)

some of the staff writers accused colleagues of deliberately being cheery in giving out information.

Members of Congress, particularly those who did not care for Roosevelt, eventually became some of the harshest critics. Among the charges was that some of OWI's publications were designed simply to promote the president. One particularly troublesome project resulted in *Negroes and the War*. The 1943 publication was designed to inform the black community of what African Americans were doing in the war, but many southern congressmen felt that it presented too positive a view of the possibility of greater racial equality. Such projects resulted in Davis being labeled a "propaganda minister for the New Deal" and being compared with Joseph Goebbels, Germany's main propagandist. Thus, Congress cut funding for OWI's domestic news operation in June 1943.

Nevertheless, Davis had his successes. In September 1943, he complained to Roosevelt that the public was being shielded for no apparent reason from some of the war's harsher realities, which he warned could lead to cynicism. In particular, he mentioned the fact that the government had been withholding all photographs that showed dead U.S. soldiers because it feared that they would make those at home want to stop the war. Shortly after their talk, *Life* published a picture of three dead U.S. soldiers on a Pacific island beach, and such photographs appeared for the remainder of the war as government officials now argued that this would motivate the country to continue to seek a final

victory. At the same time, the government refused throughout the war to allow photographs to be run that were deemed "horrific" or showed mentally ill soldiers.

Davis's continual prodding also led to more thorough coverage of D-Day than the military preferred. It was another example of his impact. In fact, by the time the war ended in August 1945, both the Army and the Navy had come to appreciate his views on the openness of as much war information as possible and had become far more liberal on what they felt the public could and should be told.

When President Harry S. Truman abolished the OWI on August 31, 1945, with an executive order, he praised its "outstanding contribution to victory." Perhaps more important, however, was that it proved to the country's top leaders the contribution that propaganda could make in wartime when it was used in a practical manner rather than as a heavy-handed tool of the government.

PATRICK S. WASHBURN

See also Committee on Public Information; Office of Censorship; Roosevelt, Franklin D., and the Media; War Photography; World War II

Further Reading

Bishop, Robert L., and LaMar S. Mackay, "Mysterious Silence, Lyrical Scream: Government Information in World War II," *Journalism Monographs* 19 (1971)
Roeder, George H., Jr., *The Censored War: American Visual Experience During World War II*, New Haven, Connecticut: Yale University Press, 1993
Voss, Frederick, *Reporting the War: The Journalistic Coverage of World War II*, Washington, D.C.: Smithsonian Institution Press, 1994
Washburn, Patrick S., *A Question of Sedition: The Federal Government's Investigation of the Black Press During World War II*, New York: Oxford University Press, 1986
Winkler, Allan M., *The Politics of Propaganda: The Office of War Information, 1942–1945*, New Haven, Connecticut: Yale University Press, 1978

Ombudsman

Effort to promote press accountability

The term "ombudsman" comes from an office in the Swedish government designed to function as intermediary between government and the citizenry, with the purpose of helping citizens gain effective access to government, especially to air grievances. News ombudsmen function chiefly as intermediaries between news organizations and their audiences. Their purpose is to assure press accountability.

The office of news ombudsman has a short history. John Herchenroeder, the first ombudsman in the United States, was appointed in June 1967 by Norman Isaacs, executive editor of the *Louisville (Kentucky) Times* and the *Courier-Journal*. Very few news organizations adopted the idea, and by the late 1990s, there were only 35 in the United States, almost all of them in newspapers.

Other countries, especially some in which there was an emergent free press, were beginning to recognize the office, and a few news organizations outside the United States appointed ombudsmen. An international network of news ombudsmen in Canada and the United States was created in 1980 with the birth of the Organization of News Ombudsmen. The ONO in the 1990s had approximately 50 members from 11 nations: Brazil, Canada, Columbia, Israel, Italy, Japan, Paraguay, South Africa, Spain, the United Kingdom, and the United States.

Ben Bagdikian, distinguished journalism scholar and former ombudsman at the *Washington Post,* was the first to suggest the idea of ombudsmen for U.S. journalism. Writing in *Esquire* (March 1967), Bagdikian expressed concern about newspaper chains buying family newspapers, a trend he thought would threaten journalistic accountability to the public.

Not all who perform the function of ombudsman have "ombudsman" as title, though that is the most common one. Other titles include "reader advocate," "reader's representative," "public editor," and "special assistant to the editor."

Although ombudsmen are assigned different roles in their respective news organizations, their essential function as intermediary is common to all. Their regular tasks on the job vary, but their several modes of operation fall into three categories: reader representative, internal critic, and columnist.

As reader representative, ombudsmen hear and respond to reader grievances (occasionally compliments) and report reader concerns to appropriate editors or reporters. In the role of in-house critic, ombudsmen offer their own critiques of the paper's performance through internal memoranda (sometimes for general circulation to staff and at other times to individuals) or newsroom conferences (occasionally including complainants).

As columnist, ombudsmen typically seek to explain the inner workings of journalism, the public role of the press, and the policies of their own newspaper. On occasion, they may also report and respond to reader complaints. In every case, the goal is to increase public understanding of how and why the press operates as it does.

There has been considerable debate among journalists – and among news executives – about the need for ombudsmen. Supporters argue that the advantages of having a senior staff member respond to readers; the benefits of the message sent that the organization wants to be accountable to those it serves; and the benefits of having a formal mechanism for keeping in touch with reader concerns and interests. Opponents argue that editors need to be confronted in person by readers and that the ombudsman is a barrier.

LOUIS W. HODGES

See also Criticism of Newspapers

Op-Ed Page

Creating space for differing opinions

The origins of both the term "op-ed" and the practice it denotes are unclear. The term simply refers to the page that is opposite the editorial page. The practice is to devote that particular page to articles that invite inquiry, analysis, argument, and expressions of opinion about issues of public importance. Most newspapers place the writings of syndicated columnists on the op-ed page along with occasional articles by informed citizens who are not professional journalists.

The *New York Times* inaugurated its op-ed page on September 21, 1970, explaining, "the health of this democracy has increasingly depended on deeper public understanding of difficult issues. . . . The objective [of the op-ed page] is to afford greater opportunity for exploration of issues and new ideas by writers and thinkers who have no institutional connection with The Times." Other newspapers have accepted the *Times'* logic and followed its lead.

It is helpful to compare op-ed to "hard news" pages and the editorial page. Although actual practice varies from paper to paper and from day to day, the ideal conception of hard news is the reporting of the events of the day in a context that makes them meaningful. Hard news is supposed to be factual, free of opinion and bias, accurate, and balanced. The mood is indicative, not imperative or interrogative.

The editorial page, again ideally, is designed to create a conversation between the newspaper and its readers. While meaningful conversation can exist only when grounded in factual knowledge, it goes beyond fact to values, opinion, argument, and advocacy. Thus, the editorial page typically contains material produced by the newspaper's editors and reader responses, usually in the form of letters to the editor.

The op-ed page is designed to carry on another conversation, one among people knowledgeable about and interested in issues of public importance, such as politics, economics, and social issues such as abortion, education, and health care. Ideally, the purpose is to create what has been called "a marketplace of ideas" available to the community and designed to create community.

While it is not known precisely when the practice of devoting a particular page in the newspaper to that vital function began, the function itself has been performed by newspapers since their birth. John Milton, in *Areopagitica* (1644), wrote about truth grappling with error to enable the people to know and refine the truth. In *On Liberty* (1859), John Stuart Mill showed how democratic societies can exist only where there is opportunity for free and open expression of opinion, especially unpopular opinion. Because no one person or organization knows all of the truth and because those who would rule themselves must know the truth as fully as possible, liberty and variety of expression are absolutely prerequisite for democratic government.

Milton and Mill thus provide the grander human and philosophical framework for the practical function the op-ed page is designed to perform. Its purpose is to provide a daily forum for citizens to make inquiry and express opinions that lead to shared understanding and goals. It is a public or civic purpose that can be achieved only if the public participates in the inquiry.

There has been criticism that, in practice, newspapers build op-ed pages that rely too heavily upon professional columnists and too little upon ordinary citizens. Many critics believe it to be undesirable for citizens to sit back as though they were spectators watching professional columnists in combat. If the op-ed page is to function well, they believe, the public must participate in the inquiry, not just observe others arguing. The modern movement called public journalism or civic journalism grew out of exactly that view. Public journalism may find the op-ed page to be the ideal vehicle for increasing citizen involvement.

LOUIS W. HODGES

See also Criticism of Newspapers; Public Journalism

Open Contract

Used by early advertising agents to help advertisers

For three decades, from 1841 to about 1875, advertising agents competed with each other on the basis of price. Advertisers, in common with other businesses of the day, primarily were concerned about placing their advertising copy in newspapers for the lowest cost possible. Advertisers wrote their own copy and gave it to agents to place. Many advertisers ran campaigns every six months or so, depending upon the seasonal nature of their product, and with each campaign, they solicited bids from agents on the placing of their advertising in newspapers. The lowest bid got the contract. Six months later, however, should the advertiser run another campaign, the agent would have to bid again. In practice, some advertisers stayed with agents they could trust.

Because of the bid system, advertising agents pressured publishers for secret discounts, large commissions, special placement of ads, free reading notices (advertisements written to look like news), and additional insertions for the same price. This alienated publishers. Advertisers, meanwhile, knew that agents got secret discounts for space and that agents substituted one paper for another on a campaign list because the substitute paper, which may have been inferior, paid the agent a larger discount. Publisher and advertiser confidence in the agent had eroded significantly by the 1870s.

Both Francis Wayland Ayer of Philadelphia and George P. Rowell of New York City concluded independently there had to be a better way. Both conceived and implemented the "open contract" in the mid-1870s, but several years passed before either agent could make it a prominent part of his business. Ayer was more successful than the Rowell agency in doing this.

The open contract meant that a contract between advertiser and agent would be signed for a year rather than for the duration of an advertising campaign, and the agent would place copy for all campaigns run during that period. The contract would be open to changes. If, during a campaign, a publisher charged too much for his space, the agent was free to substitute another paper; if a publisher increased circulation, he could earn a spot on the list of ad-

vertising venues. For the first time, the agent made changes in list, placement, or frequency based on what was best for the advertiser.

This simple concept meant that the agent and the advertiser had to agree on several things. First, they had to agree on a commission. The 15 percent agency commission, which was standard in the business for over 110 years, resulted from the open contract. Second, the advertiser trusted the agent to locate the best newspapers for his advertising. Third, the agent revealed his special rates and special commissions and passed them on, in effect, by charging net price plus the agreed upon commission. Fourth, in exchange, the advertiser agreed to keep the special rates secret from competing agents because both Ayer and Rowell continued to submit bids to other advertisers for another quarter century.

These agreements broke down time and again, but they were necessary in forging the advertiser–advertising agency coalition. Advertisers did not convert to the open contract overnight, but Ayer and Rowell proved the value of contracts arrived at openly, with all information on rates, special positions, and other inducements made known to the advertiser. This removed a major conflict of interest between agent and advertiser. The pressure for low rates and special inducements, a major irritant between agent and publisher, was reduced, although publishers first had to learn to hold to their rates.

The dissatisfaction created by previous agency practices provided the motive for change; new market conditions provided the rationale. First, the agents had lost control of information. Rowell had published his *American Newspaper Directory* in 1869; Ayer followed shortly after with *Ayer's Newspaper Directory*. Agents no longer had secret lists to use in securing advertising campaigns. Second, the increasing number of advertising agents depressed profits. Third, experienced advertisers and publishers became as knowledgeable about advertising as many agents. Finally, special agents, or newspaper representatives, appeared. They represented noncompeting newspapers to national advertisers and agencies.

The open contract, with its standard commission, forced the agent to provide services for advertisers. Specialized knowledge of circulation still counted for something, but that knowledge had to relate to the advertiser's products. Agents hired copywriters to write copy for the advertiser and artists to create illustrations. Agencies differentiated among themselves through the services they offered for the standard commissions they received. The full-service agency developed from the successful implementation of the open contract in U.S. advertising.

TED CURTIS SMYTHE

See also Advertising Agencies; Full-Service Advertising Agency

Further Reading
Hower, Ralph M., *The History of an Advertising Agency,* New York: Arno, 1978

Opinion Magazines

Focus on influencing public events, politics, ideas

In the twentieth-century United States, opinion magazines usually took the form of "butcher-paper weeklies" – cheaply printed, scantily illustrated collections of essays, polemics, and interpretive and explanatory articles, often intended to react quickly to the events of the day. Although opinion magazines usually contained at least some non-opinion content – reported stories, fiction, poetry, satire, or, most commonly, reviews and criticism of books, drama, film, and popular culture – they were marked by a narrow focus on public events, politics, and ideas. They should be distinguished from the so-called class magazines, which published opinionated content but were edited for a general readership and with a broad sense of editorial mission; from scholarly reviews; and from alternative publications, which might be similar in content and aspirations but lacked the circulation and respectability to directly affect political, academic, and media leadership.

Influence rather than form or content per se is key to understanding the opinion magazines. An often-repeated anecdote makes the point. The writer Frank Walsh once produced a series on railroads for the Hearst newspapers, with an aggregate circulation of 10,000,000, and an article on the same topic for the *Nation,* whose circulation was

The Nation began its career as an opinion magazine in the nineteenth century.

27,000. "The day the *Nation* went on the Washington newsstands, my telephone started ringing," Walsh reportedly said. "I heard from editors, broadcasters and congressmen." The readership of these magazines might not be large, but it consisted almost entirely of potential opinion leaders and shapers of public policy.

Although opinion and political disputation were part of U.S. magazines from their earliest days, the opinion magazine was a product of the nineteenth century; its parents were the vigorous religious press of the day. The first true opinion magazines were mostly single-issue publications, especially the numerous publications – most of them regional and printed in newspaper formats – devoted to temperance, women's suffrage, and the abolition of slavery. The latter category provides some of the most memorable examples: the *Pennsylvania Freeman,* launched in 1838 and edited by John Greenleaf Whittier; the *National Era,* which serialized Harriet Beecher Stowe's *Uncle Tom's Cabin;* and William Lloyd Garrison's *Liberator* (1837–65).

The classic U.S. opinion magazine – and one of the country's oldest continuously published magazines of any sort – was the *Nation,* founded in 1865 by E.L. Godkin, a 25-year-old Irish immigrant. The young weekly took a liberal perspective; it advocated labor rights, racial equality, democratic principles, and Reconstruction. Its distinguished roster of contributors in its early years included Charles Eliot Norton, James Russell Lowell, Henry and William James, Henry Adams, and Francis Parkman. The *Nation* merged with the *New York Evening Post* in 1881 but broke away in 1918, under the editorship of Oswald Garrison Villard, grandson of Lloyd Garrison, who gave the publication a far more forceful – and controversial – approach.

The Progressive Era was a particularly rich period for the creation of opinion magazines. Magazines of the period included *La Follette's Weekly,* founded by Robert La Follette, the governor of Wisconsin (the magazine published some of Carl Sandburg's early political work and survived into the late 1990s as the *Progressive*); the *Masses,* the embattled magazine of New York's bohemian radicals, unsuccessfully prosecuted under the Espionage Act of 1917; and the *New Republic,* founded just months after the start of World War I under the editorship of Herbert Croly, Walter Lippmann, and Walter Weyl, and one of the most influential of the opinion magazines over most of its history. This period also saw the birth of the *Crisis,* the magazine of the National Association for the Advancement of Colored People, edited by W.E.B. Du Bois. As the century advanced, each successive cause and controversy contributed its magazines, from the Roman Catholic *Commonweal* to William F. Buckley's conservative *National Review* to Charles Peters's neo-Democratic *Washington Monthly,* to the wave of conservative magazines, some of them quite successful, that came to prominence under the administrations of Ronald Reagan and George Bush.

Journals of opinion must evolve or, like the abolitionist magazines, they will die. The history of these magazines is filled with shifts of focus, infusions of new ideas, and occasionally with a paradoxical loss of influence as an idea that once seemed revolutionary becomes a commonplace. Sometimes shifts in editorial approach can be abrupt and extreme, as when editor Norman Podhoretz made the Jewish public-affairs magazine *Commentary* a vehicle first for liberal and then for neoconservative thought. What never seemed to change was the precarious financial situation of virtually all opinion magazines. Some, like *Commentary* in the 1990s, were supported by foundations or organizations; others relied on periodic infusions of philanthropy; almost none could support itself on revenue generated by circulation and advertising sales.

PATRICK J. CLINTON

See also Magazines in the Nineteenth Century; Magazines in the Twentieth Century

P

Pack Journalism

May occur when journalists join together in covering events

"Pack journalism" is a derogatory phrase that describes the tendency of journalists to converge on and pick over a story like a pack of ravenous beasts. Media critics use the phrase to indicate that the media behave more like a marauding mob than like the First Amendment ideal of a diverse group of independent observers. The phrase "pack journalism" suggests that journalists in different media and different locations tend toward conformity of content, ideology, and practice.

Some argue that pack journalism emerges from the legacy of the muckrakers at the turn of the twentieth century, who believed that the primary role of journalists was to act as watchdogs against government corruption. Journalists who autonomously exercised shared professional news values; emphasized factual, fair, objective reporting; and faced constraints of space, staff, and time logically would winnow out for coverage a common body of newsworthy events that focused on the novel, the unusual, the dramatic, the activities of the powerful, and events of conflict or resolution.

Pack journalism, or herd reporting, also occurs because journalists and news media seek safety in numbers. Independent news coverage is costly and risky. Each time a reporter is sent out to investigate a lead, the news organization devotes limited resources to the gamble that something newsworthy will be uncovered in time to meet business deadlines. Those resources also are removed from the coverage of pack news, opening the organization to errors of omission.

Emphasis on organized press conferences, coverage of meetings, and follow-ups to established news stories reduces the risk of time wasted on nonnews-producing leads. It also avoids the chaos of event-driven news gathering.

Consensus reporting is supported by competitive pressure that tends to define as newsworthy anything that is conveyed by a competitor. A system of corporate rewards based less on reward for originality and more on penalty for being scooped further reduces the incentive to engage in independent investigative efforts and diminishes the threat that scoops pose to profits. In addition, the psychological benefits of pack journalism appeal to journalists who fear that peers will judge their independent work critically or that superiors will penalize them for failure to cover stories deemed important by other media.

The individual reporting crusader presents a countervailing tendency, but it is rare that the independent reporter who unearths exclusive information stands alone for long. An initial exclusive report becomes the bait for other journalists to pounce on the lead and develop follow-ups that simultaneously endorse the judgment of the exclusive reporter and ally other media with those news values. As Timothy Crouse noted in his 1972 book on election campaign coverage, the "boys on the bus" tend to operate like "a pack of hounds sicked on a fox."

This image suggests that pack journalism is the natural product of aggressive news people drawn by the sudden appearance of a major figure or dramatic event. Heavy reliance on the same official sources, attention to the same public figures, widespread use of news and wire services, and the reprinting of articles from prestigious news organizations also contribute to pack journalism. The need to be part of the pack produces a tendency to overplay stories once they reach the headlines and to ignore other stories of import. Some media critics suggest that pack journalism's problems of hype and omission generate much of the increased hostility toward media, which further reinforces the distinction between journalists and non-journalists.

But Crouse's work, *The Boys on the Bus*, suggests another fundamental source of that distinction and of pack journalism: the demographics of the newsroom. Despite affirmative action and increased numbers of women and minorities in the newsroom, most media continue to be predominantly white, male, middle-class enclaves.

Hiring practices that have increased demographic diversity in newsrooms actually have been accompanied by decreased political diversity. Editors and elite media set the agenda for the pack and continue to represent and reinforce liberal ideology.

Some journalists assert, however, that what critics call pack journalism is actually the kind of detailed, focused reporting of newsworthy events essential to cause change. Independent studies indicate that media's strongest impact on public opinion results from widespread and lengthy coverage of societal issues.

Critics argue that pack journalism reduces access to

newsworthy information because sources who might be willing to deal with a limited number of journalists are fearful that a media siege will engulf them, focus on insignificant minutiae, and absorb all of their energies. These sources thus refuse to release information that would otherwise be made public.

SUSAN DENTE ROSS

See also Muckraking; Objective Reporting

Further Reading

Ansolabehere, Stephen, Roy Behr, and Shanto Iyengar, *The Media Game: American Politics in the Television Age,* New York: Macmillan, 1993; Toronto, Ontario: Maxwell Macmillan Canada, 1993

Crouse, Timothy, *The Boys on the Bus,* New York: Ballantine, 1973

Hohenberg, John, *A Crisis for the American Press,* New York: Columbia University Press, 1978

Lichter, S. Robert, Stanley Rothman, and Linda S. Lichter, *The Media Elite,* Bethesda, Maryland: Adler and Adler, 1986

Parenti, Michael, *Inventing Reality: The Politics of News Media,* 2nd ed., New York: St. Martin's, 1993

Sabato, Larry, *Feeding Frenzy: How Attack Journalism Has Transformed American Politics,* New York: Free Press, 1991; Toronto, Ontario: Maxwell Macmillan Canada, 1991

Weaver, David, and G. Cleveland Wilhoit, *The American Journalist: A Portrait of U.S. News People and Their Work,* 2nd ed., Bloomington: Indiana University Press, 1991

Paley, William S.

Led CBS development into a powerful network

As head of the Columbia Broadcasting System (CBS), William S. Paley is remembered as both broadcast pioneer and socialite. His parents were Ukrainian Jewish immigrants who built a Chicago cigar store into a multimillion dollar cigar manufacturing company. Upon his graduation from the Wharton Business School at the University of Pennsylvania in 1922, Paley became vice president of the family business, which later experimented successfully with radio advertising. In September 1928, Paley bought controlling interest in a struggling 16-station network called United Independent Broadcasters and its Columbia Broadcasting System (the Columbia Phonograph Company, an early investor, had pulled out the previous year).

As CBS president, Paley creatively negotiated contracts with station affiliates and performers alike. Within six months, the network grew to 49 stations, putting CBS within listening range of almost 90 percent of U.S. homes. Paley realized the importance of quality programming, and during his career he signed top performers such as Will Rogers,

William Paley
(Library of American Broadcasting)

Jack Benny, Kate Smith, George Burns and Gracie Allen, Bing Crosby, Bob Hope, and Frank Sinatra. He also built a world-class news organization around such luminaries as Edward R. Murrow and Walter Cronkite.

During World War II, Paley supervised the Office of War Information in the Mediterranean, eventually serving as deputy chief of the Psychological Warfare Division. Paley became chair of the CBS board in 1946, overseeing its diversification into television and other entertainment ventures. He continued at the helm of CBS until his 1983 retirement, although he returned to the post in 1987 as a result of corporate hostilities.

MARK J. BRAUN

See also Television Networks

Further Reading

Paley, William S., *As It Happened: A Memoir,* Garden City, New York: Doubleday, 1979

Paper, Lewis J., *Empire: William S. Paley and the Making of CBS,* New York: St. Martin's, 1987

Smith, Sally Bedell, *In All His Glory: The Life of William S. Paley, the Legendary Tycoon and His Brilliant Circle,* New York: Simon & Schuster, 1990

Palmer, Volney B.

Early user of "advertising agency" label

Volney B. Palmer used the term "advertising agency" in an advertisement in 1849. He claimed to be the sole representative of 1,300 newspapers, thus allowing merchants to be selective about where they advertised. Palmer also created speculative presentations for prospective advertisers. Of course, advertisers had to pay the total cost for Palmer's services, not just the space rates for each newspaper selected. Palmer received a 25 percent commission from the publisher upon payment.

Both publishers and advertisers were delighted to use his agency. He promoted his services by using endorsements from publishers. By the mid-1850s, with numerous clients considering him a godsend, his agency grew. He opened offices in four major cities. He maintained his office in Philadelphia and hired others to manage the other three, which he visited at various times throughout each year.

In the late 1850s, John E. Joy, W.W. Sharpe, and J.E. Coe became partners. When Palmer retired in either 1862 or 1863, Joy and Coe operated the Philadelphia and the New York offices. Sharpe eventually purchased the latter office. S.R. Niles controlled the Boston office.

Palmer died in 1864 at the age of 65. Perhaps no agent did more for advertising than Palmer. Not only did he help advertisers, he helped newspaper publishers, too. Indeed, he sold the idea of advertising to advertisers and consequently made hundreds of proprietors realize how important a role advertising played in a capitalist society.

EDD APPLEGATE

See also Advertising Agencies; Advertising in the Nineteenth Century

Further Reading

Holland, Donald R., "Volney B. Palmer (1799–1864): The Nation's First Advertising Agency Man," *Journalism Monographs* 44 (1976)

Printers' Ink, *Advertising: Today, Yesterday, Tomorrow; An Omnibus of Advertising*, New York: McGraw-Hill, 1963

Rowsome, Frank, Jr., *They Laughed When I Sat Down; An Informal History of Advertising in Words and Pictures*, New York: Bonanza, 1959

Pamphlets

Communication medium hundreds of years before newspapers

News pamphlets were a mass news medium hundreds of years before newspapers or magazines appeared. In 1508, for example, pamphlets reported the wedding of an English princess to a public eager for the news but unreachable by handwritten correspondence and newsletters.

COMMON SENSE;

ADDRESSED TO THE

INHABITANTS

OF

AMERICA,

On the following interesting

SUBJECTS.

I. Of the Origin and Design of Government in general, with concise Remarks on the English Constitution.

II. Of Monarchy and Hereditary Succession.

III. Thoughts on the present State of American Affairs.

IV. Of the present Ability of America, with some miscellaneous Reflections.

Man knows no Master save creating Heaven,
Or those whom choice and common good ordain.

THOMSON.

PHILADELPHIA;

Printed, and Sold, by R. BELL, in Third-Street.

MDCCLXXVI.

Thomas Paine's "Common Sense" was one of the most popular pamphlets of the Revolutionary period.
(Reproduced from the Collections of the Library of Congress)

Quite rapidly, pamphlets, or newsbooks, became the primary news medium for the masses. They concentrated on sensational news and prominent personalities – subjects that would easily grab the attention of the buying public. Their subject matter was politics, religion, royal weddings, and, more often than not, extraordinary murders and other high crimes. The murder of Sir Thomas Overbury of England, arranged by the countess of Essex and her secret paramour in 1613, resulted in at least 15 pamphlets and broadsides (a single sheet of news on one subject). In fact, until the mid-1800s, pamphlets – unbound, quarto-size paperbacks published for a mass audience and reporting on a single event – continued to be the primary means of disseminating news about sensational crimes and politics even after newspapers had appeared.

Pamphleteers such as Thomas Paine spread the spirit of rebellion during the American Revolution. His pamphlet *Common Sense* was America's first best-seller in 1776, selling 120,000 copies in six months and galvanizing public opinion against Britain.

After the rise of the mass circulation newspapers in the 1830s, pamphlets became less significant as news carriers but did not die out even then. When Ephraim Avery, a minister, stood accused in 1833 of murdering a young Rhode Island woman with whom he had been having an affair, the *Boston Daily Commercial Gazette* issued one pamphlet on the evidence introduced at his trial and two more a few days later to cover the attorneys' closing arguments and the jury's verdict of acquittal. Moreover, these competed for sales with at least five other pamphlets about the trial issued by other publishers.

Nineteenth-century pamphlets were sensationalistic, beckoning readers with lurid drawings, titillating headlines, and florid prose. Hastily prepared and often purposely written to persuade or shock, they frequently distorted the facts. Sometimes defendants charged with murder and other serious crimes issued pamphlets to raise funds for their families or to garner sympathy for themselves.

Among the subjects pamphlets reported were the 1807 treason trial of Aaron Burr, the 1804 trial of editor Harry Croswell for libeling President Jefferson, and the 1892 murder trial of Lizzie Borden. Suffragist Susan B. Anthony, convicted on a charge of illegal voting in 1872, published her own pamphlet that included a summary of her case, a transcript of the trial, an essay condemning the judge, and speeches in support of women's voting rights.

During the twentieth century, pamphlets continued to be an important medium for disseminating radical commentary and muckraking that failed to get coverage in the mainstream media. Muckraker Upton Sinclair published numerous pamphlets from 1920 to 1950 to spread his political views. In addition, labor organizers and protest movements ranging from populist farmer groups to antiwar crusaders relied on pamphlets to rally support.

JAMES AUCOIN

See also American Revolution and the Press; Broadsides; Muckraking

Further Reading
McDade, Thomas M., *The Annals of Murder,* Norman: University of Oklahoma Press, 1961

Panama Invasion

Journalists encountered problems covering 1989 events in Panama

The security of the Panama Canal was a major concern of the United States from its completion in 1914. Although the development of a two-ocean U.S. Navy, advanced transportation modes, and the absence of global war at the end of the twentieth century lessened the importance of the ca-

nal, the United States still considered a continued presence in Panama necessary for maintaining political and economic stability in the Central America–Caribbean region. Under the 1977 treaty with Panama, however, the United States agreed to relinquish control of the canal in 1999 and withdraw its military bases in 2004.

In 1983, Colonel Manuel Antonio Noriega, former Panama National Guard intelligence chief, assumed leadership of the Guard and organized all public security forces into one body known as the Panamanian Defense Forces (PDF), effectively placing him in control of the country. As the nation's "strongman," Noriega worked closely with the U.S. Drug Enforcement Agency, the Department of Defense, the Central Intelligence Agency, and the White House in their programs to control drug trafficking and leftist political influence in Latin America. Noriega personally benefited financially from the drug trade, money laundering activities, and international arms trading. The United States suspended military and economic aid to Panama after revelations of Noriega's aid to the Soviet Union, Cuba, and Nicaragua and discovery of his involvement in the brutal murder of his most vocal critic in 1985. Following an attack on the U.S. embassy by anti-Noriega Panamanians, the Ronald Reagan administration called for Noriega's resignation.

The U.S. government viewed Noriega as a threat to the security of the Panama Canal, to the political stability of the area in the face of leftist influences, and to U.S. attempts to control international drug trafficking. Democratic elections, diplomatic efforts by the Organization of American States, and a coup all failed to oust Noriega.

In mid-December 1989, PDF violence against U.S. armed forces personnel convinced President George Bush of the need to remove Noriega from power. On December 17, the president ordered military intervention in Panama, designating the action Operation Just Cause. At 1 A.M. on December 20, approximately 23,000 U.S. troops began the invasion of Panama with the objectives of protecting U.S. lives, protecting the rights and interests of the United States under the Panama Canal Treaty, restoring democracy in Panama, and apprehending Noriega.

To cover the hostilities in Panama, Secretary of Defense Dick Cheney ordered the activation of the National Press Pool, a group of 16 journalists selected by the media community. The need for a pool of reporters arose from the deliberate military exclusion of the media from the initial hostilities during the 1983 U.S. invasion of Grenada. Responding to vehement protests from the media over denied access to combat sites, Pentagon officials and media representatives formulated guidelines that included ground rules, accreditation of correspondents, and official briefings for the media.

For the media, coverage of Operation Just Cause was a near-total failure. From the outset, the press pool encountered bureaucratic and military obstacles that prevented adequate coverage of the invasion. Fearing security leaks, Cheney did not inform the military officer in charge of military-press affairs in Panama of his decision to use Pentagon-based reporters until it was too late to provide adequate transportation, equipment, communications, and support. Security concerns resulted in the press arriving at

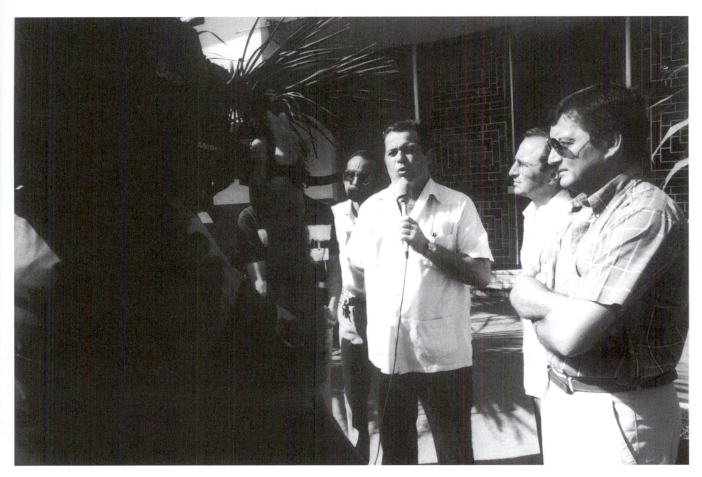

U.S. Army photographers obtain news footage of a Panamanian official making a statement on food distribution during Operation Just Cause.
(Official U.S. Army Photo [Released])

Howard Air Force Base in Panama more than four hours after the invasion began. Inadequate transportation for the pool prevented early coverage of combat, and failure to initially separate the pool into two groups minimized opportunities for stories. Consequently, there was no direct reporting of the fighting around Panama City, the east bank of the canal, or in the city of Colón during the first 48 hours of the invasion.

Military commanders controlled the movement of pool members and prohibited interviews with combat personnel. Officers refused to allow photographs of casualties, wounded personnel, and damaged helicopters, citing security reasons. There were no regular briefings concerning military engagements; therefore, most news stories were of secondary value. Stories that were filed were held up because of inadequate administrative support and insufficient communications equipment. Additional journalists arriving in Panama after the first day of fighting created an added burden on equipment and personnel.

Heightened security concerns of officials and the military thus prevented an accurate presentation of the scale of violence or the level of Panamanian resistance by restricting press movement and obstructing effective coverage of Op-

eration Just Cause. Military denial of access to battle sites resulted in few eyewitness accounts of damages to life and property. As a consequence, casualty estimates ranged from 200 to more than 4,000, including military and civilian deaths. One year after the invasion, an investigation revealed a death toll of approximately 200 to 300.

After the invasion, the press community registered strong objections to the limitations imposed on the media. This resulted in an investigation by Pentagon and media representatives in March 1990. Although it was the only government investigation into the matter, it continued to assess responsibility for each problem encountered in press coverage of U.S. military engagements.

The investigation concluded that increased security needs in a war situation resulted in unnecessary delays in informing the National Press Pool of the planned invasion and in making adequate logistic preparations for media coverage. Secretary of Defense Cheney accepted the blame for decisions that resulted in most of the problems.

The organization of the Pentagon press pool followed guidelines established after the Grenada invasion that sought to allow the media to provide maximum information without endangering U.S. lives or U.S. policy. Military restrictions on access to information rendered the guidelines useless and failed to prevent security leaks, four of which were attributed to the press.

Recommendations from the Pentagon investigation for future military operations requiring press pool coverage stressed the need for government and military cooperation in meeting media needs for prompt assistance, support, and access to information. Other recommendations were designed to facilitate newsgathering and improve relations between the press and the military. The recommendations were tested during the Persian Gulf War in January 1991, and journalists still complained about manipulation of information and limited access to combat sites.

SUE D. TAYLOR

See also Grenada Invasion; Persian Gulf War; Pool Journalism

Further Reading

Boot, William, "Wading Around in the Panama Pool," *Columbia Journalism Review* 28:6 (March 1990), pp. 18–20

Cranberg, Gilbert, "A Flimsy Story and a Compliant Press," *Washington Journalism Review* 12:2 (March 1990), p. 48

Johns, Christina Jacqueline, and P. Ward Johnson, *State Crime, the Media, and the Invasion of Panama*, Westport, Connecticut: Praeger, 1994

Komarow, Steven, "Pooling Around in Panama," *Washington Journalism Review* 12:2 (March 1990), pp. 45 ff

Lord, Arthur A., "Operation *Just Cause* – The Press in the Dark Again," *Nieman Reports* 44:1 (Spring 1990), pp. 7 ff

McConnell, Malcolm, '*Just Cause*': The Real Story of *America's High-Tech Invasion of Panama*, New York: St. Martin's, 1991

Vasquez, Juan, "Panama: Live from the Marriott!," *Washington Journalism Review* 12:2 (March 1990), pp. 44 ff

Watson, Bruce W., and Peter Tsouras, eds., *Operation 'Just Cause': The U.S. Intervention in Panama*, Boulder, Colorado: Westview, 1990

Paperback Books

Modern paperbacks first appeared in 1938

The modern mass market paperback book was originally the brainchild of Robert de Graff, who began Pocket Books in 1938 as a way to publish inexpensive reprint editions of popular books of the day. The standard price for almost two decades from all paperback publishers was just 25 cents. Major competition with Pocket Books (so named because these smaller books could actually fit in one's pocket) came quickly; Avon Books appeared in 1941, Popular Library and Dell Books in 1943, and Bantam Books in 1945.

Paperbacks gained initial popularity with soldiers, who read them during World War II and the Korean conflict. Paperbacks were popular with returning veterans already familiar with the format of the books from copies sent to them while overseas and from reading Armed Service Editions (ASEs) – special paperback editions published by the Council of Books in Wartime, a cooperative of publishers, editors, and the government. More than 130 million ASEs were made available free to troops overseas. Paperbacks also appealed to book buyers who could not afford the expensive hardcover editions that cost three to five dollars each.

In what would later become known as "the paperback revolution," publishers made paperback books available to thousands of nontraditional bookselling outlets across the country at affordable prices. This increased the number of available outlets for paperbacks from the standard 10,000 book stores to more than 100,000 outlets. Millions of people now had access to and purchased the new pocket-size paperbacks. They were a big hit, and for a decade, the market was so strong that publishers could sell almost every copy of every book they printed.

The loftiest ideals of the paperback revolution were best expressed in the motto of the New American Library, which proclaimed, "Good Reading for the Millions." The phrase became an almost unofficial slogan for all Signet Books of that era. The phrase was a marketing interpretation of the more proletarian "Good Books for the Masses," which the high-end progressive publishers of the era (Pocket Books, Penguin, Bantam, Dell, and New American Library with their Signet and Mentor imprints) sincerely tried to follow. These publishers released quality popular fiction, classics, and important current work to create a mix of creative, diverse, and uplifting material.

The intentions of other publishers were not as lofty. Lower-end houses such as Avon, Ace, Popular Library, and Pyramid became known as purveyors of exploitative, cheap, and often sleazy material. Much of it was thought to be trash because of subject matter, title, and cover art, which often depicted lewd and lurid scenes featuring violence or scantily clad women. In truth, many of these books did pander to the lowest common denominator, and in too many cases, good writing was often synonymous with fast typing.

However, many of these paperbacks also dealt with controversial and important topics of the day such as juvenile delinquency, prostitution, homosexual and lesbian situations, interracial love, problems such as racism and discrimination, drugs, beatniks, and much more. Many "Vintage Era" paperbacks (1939–59) dealt with these subjects in varying degrees of accuracy and truthfulness at a time when discussion and knowledge of these topics was severely limited – if not out-and-out taboo. They made a valid contribution to the understanding of these issues. Many more paperbacks from this era, however, were published in a cynical attempt to exploit sensitive topics or to sensationalize those topics in order to make a sale.

In fact, there was so much criticism of some of these publications that in May 1952, the U.S. House of Representatives authorized a probe of paperbacks and other publications for so-called "immoral, obscene or otherwise offensive matter." These hearings attacked various publications, with a particular emphasis on paperbacks and comic books. While the hearings had a devastating effect on the comic book industry, leading to de facto censorship under the Comics Code Authority, paperback publishers were able to weather the storm and continue, albeit with care, with minimal interference.

Ironically, the innovative returns policy that created the mass market and made the paperback revolution possible in the first place by giving the retailer credit on unsold books began to bear bitter fruit in the late 1950s. Unsold books had their covers stripped off by the retailer and sent back to the publisher for credit on future books, while the "guts" of the book were pulped or thrown away. An excessively high rate of return caused a glut on the market, and many paperback publishers went under.

New concepts were introduced into the paperback publishing industry regularly to bolster sales. For instance, early issues of Pocket Books, Bantam Books, and Dell Books were high-quality products with gorgeous laminated covers, which were discontinued because they became too expensive to produce. Dell Books featured "map backs" – a well-drawn and colorful map of where the story in the book took place. They were successful between 1943 and 1953.

Another important concept was the idea of the paperback original, a book published as a paperback for its first printing anywhere. While it was not created by Gold Medal Books, the concept was a mainstay of their publishing line in the 1950s and 1960s. By the 1990s, most genre fiction appeared as paperback originals rather than being reprinted from hardcover first editions.

In the 1960s and 1970s, the instant book made its impact, although it had its origin in 1945 with the paperback published by Pocket Books to memorialize the death of President Franklin D. Roosevelt. In the 1990s the instant book was a staple of the industry and an important concept since news stories and current events could change quickly or have a very short shelf life.

Other marketing gimmicks such as free books, various types of samplers, die-cut covers, embossed and foil covers, holographic covers, and artwork on spines all were used with varying results in the last three decades of the twentieth century to help make a publisher's books stand out from the competition. More than anything else, the paperback publishing story was a distribution story, and distribution was a constant fight for shelf space. Once the book was on the shelf, it had to get noticed by the prospective reader and buyer.

In the early 1950s, a blockbuster mentality was introduced into the paperback publishing industry. In the late 1990s, just as with hardcover publishers, that mentality had a strong grip on the field. The frantic search for the next "big book" or the next million- or 10-million-copy seller caused paperback publishers to neglect new writers, to ignore their backlist (reprints, the bread and butter of publishing), and to gut advertising and promotion budgets for new releases that were not catalog leaders. Since they engaged in little or no advertising except for bestsellers, publishers were hurt by this neglect of their product line.

By the end of the twentieth century, many of the old paperback publishing companies were gone or had been absorbed into corporate conglomerates, but the mass market system of distribution still existed, and paperbacks of all kinds, on all topics, by every type of author still were being published, read, enjoyed, and even collected. The paperback revolution continued.

GARY LOVISI

See also Instant Books; Mass Market Book Publishing

Further Reading

Bonn, Thomas L., *Heavy Traffic and High Culture: New American Library as Literary Gatekeeper in the Paperback Revolution,* Carbondale: Southern Illinois University Press, 1989

_____, *Under Cover: An Illustrated History of American Mass-Market Paperbacks,* New York and Harmondsworth, Middlesex, England: Penguin, 1982

Davis, Kenneth C., *Two-Bit Culture: The Paperbacking of America,* Boston: Houghton Mifflin, 1984

Schreuders, Piet, *Paperbacks, U.S.A.: A Graphic History, 1939–1959,* San Diego, California: Blue Dolphin, 1981; also published as *The Book of Paperbacks: A Visual History of the Paperback,* London: Virgin, 1981

Paramount Communications

Media conglomerate active in movies, television, books

Beginning in 1920, Paramount functioned as one of the major Hollywood studios. Through the 1920s, 1930s, and 1940s, this meant turning out feature films, newsreels, and cartoons. From the 1950s, Paramount, like other major studios, also created (and distributed around the world) television programs.

During the fall of 1993, Viacom took over Paramount, and the studio functioned as part of a diversified media conglomerate that included cable television networks (including MTV, The Movie Channel, and Nickelodeon), television's United Paramount Network, radio and television stations, and a syndication business that owned the rights to such series as *Roseanne, Family Ties, Happy Days, I Love Lucy, Perry Mason,* and *The Twilight Zone.* Viacom's chief executive officer, Sumner Redstone, joined forces with video rental empire Blockbuster and also owned and operated Simon and Schuster, a leading publishing house.

Paramount had a long and distinguished history before 1993. During the 1920s and into the early 1930s, Adolph Zukor headed the company and was responsible for making Paramount a major studio. In 1935, Zukor stepped aside for Barney Balaban, who brought the company to renewed heights of prosperity during the 1940s and early 1950s. Balaban did not react well to the coming of television and in 1966 sold Paramount to Charles Bludhorn's conglomerate Gulf and Western. Bludhorn died in 1983, and his chief assistant, Martin Davis, spun off all conglomerate holdings except the Hollywood studio and publisher Simon and Schuster. Redstone took over from Davis and led Paramount through the 1990s.

DOUGLAS GOMERY

See also Hollywood Studio System

Further Reading

Alexander, Alison, James Owers, and Rod Carveth, *Media Economics: Theory and Practice,* Hillsdale, New Jersey: Lawrence Erlbaum, 1993

Eames, John Douglas, *The Paramount Story,* New York: Crown, 1985; London: Octopus, 1985

Gomery, Douglas, *The Hollywood Studio System,* New York: St. Martin's, 1986; Basingstoke, England: Macmillan, 1986

Participatory Journalism

Creating news and then reporting that news to the public

The term "participatory journalism" refers to a journalism in which individuals consciously act to create news and then report that news, or to report on events in which they have participated. Some examples include Stanley's search for Livingstone; Nellie Bly's travels around the world; the *Chicago Sun-Times*'s operation of the Mirage Bar; and many practices in public, or civic, journalism. These examples are the antithesis of traditional journalism in which reporters separate themselves from news and news sources and write objectively about issues and events.

Feature writers and reporters commonly obtain permission to participate in events and write about them. They drive race cars and cabs, ride on elephants and in hot air balloons, volunteer in shelters and soup kitchens, and go through military, police, and fire training. Journalists also write about covert participation as workers in coal mines, mental institutions, and sweatshops, and as players in various activities at the borders of legality or acceptability. Journalists throughout history also have written about events in which they participated unintentionally: train derailments, airplane crashes, hurricanes, and earthquakes. Journalists also have long made into news any number of personal dramas.

Civic, or public, journalism often requires various levels of participation by journalists and/or news organizations, which have hosted forums on community issues, brought citizens into newsroom meetings, taken the lead on public initiatives, and promoted public discussions and debate. The movement, which strives for a more active citizenry, has been criticized because of its participatory nature, which requires journalists to go outside traditionally defined roles.

The term also has been used to describe many of the "new journalists" and some "literary" or narrative journalists. In the 1960s and 1970s, reporters such as Gay Talese, Tom Wolfe, and Hunter Thompson used literary devices to write news and frequently participated in the events and activities they reported. George Plimpton made a career of writing about his own exploits in the boxing ring, on the football field, and elsewhere. The narrative style employed by some journalists in the 1990s often involved participation or lengthy periods with sources.

Journalists unconsciously participate when they cover any story. Television reporters especially are recognized when they cover events, but the presence of any reporters at meetings, trials, hearings, and other events can subtly and unpredictably alter behavior and outcomes.

The press becomes a conscious and unconscious participant in the news. During the 1800s partisan press, papers promoted political parties and attacked opponents. Press coverage has been an integral part of events from William Randolph Hearst's famous statement, "You furnish the pictures and I'll furnish the war," to the 1990s trials of William Kennedy Smith and O.J. Simpson. Press coverage played a major role in the withdrawals of Gary Hart, Thomas Eagleton, and H. Ross Perot from presidential campaigns and in the resignations of Richard Nixon, John Tower, and Robert Packwood from office.

Other terms similar to "participatory journalism" include "participant-observer" and "advocacy journalism," in which reporters actively participate in the news event or in shaping or slanting news coverage.

ROBERT DARDENNE

See also New Journalism (1960s–1970s); Nixon, Richard M., and the Media; Public Journalism

Further Reading

Charity, Arthur, *Doing Public Journalism,* New York: Guilford, 1995

Rosen, Jay, *Community Connectedness Passwords for Public Journalism: How to Create Journalism that Listens to Citizens and Reinvigorates Public Life,* St. Petersburg, Florida: Poynter Institute for Media Studies, 1993

Wolfe, Tom, *The New Journalism,* New York: Harper & Row, 1973; London: Pan, 1975

Party Press

Close attachment between newspapers and political parties

The party press in U.S. journalism was in its heyday from 1789 to the 1830s. It was marked by a close attachment between newspapers and the parties that made up the U.S. political system. The distinctive characteristic of newspapers was political partisanship.

The era was inaugurated on April 15, 1789, when John Fenno published the first issue of the *Gazette of the United States.* Alexander Hamilton and other leading Federalists supported and subsidized the *Gazette of the United States.* U.S. newspapers before Fenno's had practiced partisan politics, but the *Gazette* was the first founded as an organ of one of the factions comprising the first party system of the United States. It foreshadowed the political and journalistic battles that were to take place for the next generation.

Historians normally divide the party press era into two periods. The first was that of the Federalist-Republican press, beginning in 1789, and the second was that of the Democratic-Whig press, beginning in the early 1820s.

Close associations between editors and politicians marked the party press era. As political leaders recognized the importance of the press, they worked to encourage newspapers to support their cause. Many new papers were started. Some were established directly through the support of politicians, while other papers – those founded with the assistance of parties – were able to continue publication because of partisan aid.

Newspapers were recognized as party spokesmen and as central parts of the political system. Frequently, national, state, or local groups or individuals would provide money for starting a paper by outright contributions of cash or by a mortgage or loan for printing equipment. Sometimes a group would hire a printer for a new paper and name one of its own members editor. In either situation, the papers were established in the expectation that they would support their patrons. Such papers came to be regarded as the organs of these sponsors. Editors of independently established newspapers brought them into the service of a party and also received support from parties, factions, or individual politicians to assist in continuing publication.

Yet, while financial support from politicians was imperative for the success of newspapers, the instances of editors basing their political loyalties on monetary considerations were rare. Most supported parties because of their agreement with the parties' political beliefs.

In general, the purpose of the editors was to present news and views on political action and secondarily to win adherents to the cause. To accomplish these goals, editors and politicians expected the press to perform a number of functions, including promoting political ideals, supporting party principles, defending the party and its politicians, providing a medium for expression of party views, provid-

ing information – always presented as truth from the party viewpoint – influencing public opinion, preaching the party line to the party faithful, attacking opponents, and providing a method of electioneering.

The most prominent Federalist newspapers were Benjamin Russell's *Columbian Centinel* (founded in Boston in 1784), Fenno's *Gazette of the United States* (New York City, 1789), Noah Webster's *American Minerva* (founded in New York City in 1793 through the efforts of a group of 10 leading Federalists, including Hamilton, Rufus King, and John Jay), William Cobbett's *Porcupine's Gazette* (Philadelphia, 1797), and William Coleman's *New York Evening Post* (founded in 1801 by a group of prominent Hamiltonian Federalists after the disastrous 1800 presidential election).

On the Republican side, the preeminent national newspapers were Benjamin Bache's *Aurora* (Philadelphia, 1790), which was continued by William Duane upon Bache's death in 1798; Philip Freneau's *National Gazette* (Philadelphia, 1791); and Samuel Harrison Smith's *National Intelligencer* (Washington, D.C., 1800). Regional newspapers of considerable importance were Thomas and Abijah Adams's *Independent Chronicle* (Boston; the Adams brothers bought it 1788 and waged a vigorous battle against New England Federalism), James Cheetham's *American Citizen* (New York, founded in 1766, before the American Revolution, and converted into a staunch Republican organ when Cheetham was named editor in 1800), and Thomas Ritchie's *Richmond (Virginia) Enquirer* (1804).

Like party spirit, newspaper partisanship intensified during the second party system. When the 1824 election was taken from him, Andrew Jackson turned to newspapers as one of the primary components of his political organization. Using them more effectively during the 1828 election than had any candidate up to that time, he gained widespread popular support in a campaign consumed with abusiveness.

Most important of the Democratic newspapers were those personally associated with Jackson, first Amos Kendall's *Argus of Western America* in Frankfort, Kentucky, then Duff Green's *United States Telegraph* in Washington, and finally Francis P. Blair's *Washington Globe*.

These newspapers promoted Jackson's presidential candidacy and helped him carry out his programs once he gained office. Those three national newspapers were aided by a network of cooperating newspapers stretching across the nation. The *Albany (New York) Argus*, edited by Edwin Croswell, played a central role in the power the Albany Regency exerted in politics in New York and other parts of the nation. Thomas Ritchie of the *Richmond Enquirer* headed the Richmond Junto in Virginia.

Although Jacksonian Democrats used the press more vigorously, Whigs maintained a majority in newspaper numbers. Sensing a critical need for newspaper support, they spent large amounts of money and devoted tireless effort on the establishment and continuation of papers. Along with the eminent National Republican newspapers in Washington – Joseph Gales and William Winston Seaton's *National Intelligencer* and Peter Force's *National Journal* – the party was supported by a network of newspapers stretching through all the states and into virtually every town of any sizable population.

The preeminent Whig papers were Samuel Bowles's *Springfield (Massachusetts) Republican,* James Watson Webb's *New York Courier and Enquirer,* and Thurlow Weed's *Albany Evening Journal.* The *Republican,* founded in 1824 by Samuel Bowles II, was known for the quality of its editorials and was considered the best small-town newspaper in the United States for most of the nineteenth century under the editorship of Bowles, his son, and his grandson. With the *Evening Journal,* founded in 1830, serving as the national spokesman of Whig views, Weed was the party's leading tactical politician. Webb founded the *Courier and Enquirer* in 1827 as a supporter of Jackson but converted to the opposition. It was he who first suggested that the party assume the name "Whig."

Believing that the proper role of the press was to support political causes and parties, editors devoted a large amount of space to political discussions. Because of the editors' intense partisanship, the most striking characteristics of newspaper writing were personal invective and abusive political attacks. That characteristic has caused many historians to berate the party press and is one reason for the damaged reputation that the press suffered with historians until the later twentieth century.

Although the purpose and practices of the party press were definitely partisan, the period did witness the genesis of several devices that became an accepted part of later journalism. These innovations included the first daily newspaper, coverage of the U.S. Congress, the appearance of well-defined editorials, the assignment of the first correspondents to cover the national capital, the emergence of the position of editor, a shift from foreign to domestic news, and the development of the cylinder printing press.

During Jackson's presidency, the press reached its zenith as a partisan voice, and it remained primarily political for years to come. Even with the advent of the popular penny press in the 1830s, most papers continued to operate as partisan organs, but the partisan system was dealt a blow in 1846, when Congress passed legislation requiring the federal government to let bids on printing contracts. That requirement took away the most effective tool that parties and politicians had for financing newspaper supporters. In 1860, the Government Printing Office was established, removing much of public printing from private newspapers and further separating the operations of parties from the press. Still, the ideological relationship between parties and papers remained strong, and a majority of newspapers continued to identify with and work for partisan political goals. It was not until 1884, many journalists and observers believed, when leading Republican papers bolted James G. Blaine in his campaign for the presidency, that newspapers took on a full degree of partisan independence. Still, newspaper editorial allegiance to parties was vigorous as late as World War II.

Despite the growing autonomy of newspapers from political parties in the late 1800s, the period of the party press had witnessed great vigor, and newspapers had played an important role during some of the most critical years of the U.S. political system. While the nature of newspapers in the United States was to change later, the press perhaps never would be any more vital to the political life of the nation than it had been during the age of the party press.

WM. DAVID SLOAN

See also Government Printing and Patronage; Jackson, Andrew, and the Press; Jefferson, Thomas, and the Press; Newspapers in the Nineteenth Century; Penny Press

Further Reading
Baldasty, Gerald J., "The Press and Politics in the Age of Jackson," *Journalism Monographs* 89 (1984)
Knudson, Jerry W., "Political Journalism in the Age of Jefferson," *Journalism History* 1 (1974)
Sloan, W. David, "The Early Party Press: The Newspaper's Role in American Politics, 1788–1812," *Journalism History* 9 (1982)
_____, "The Party Press, 1789–1833," in *The Media in America: A History,* 2nd ed., edited by W. David Sloan, James D. Startt, and James G. Stovall, Scottsdale, Arizona: Publishing Horizons, 1993
Smith, Culver H., *The Press, Politics, and Patronage: The American Government's Use of Newspapers, 1789–1875,* Athens: University of Georgia Press, 1977

To Franklin Bache, Editor of the *Aurora*

Why, in the name of all that is rascally and corrupt, cannot you let me alone? I tell you what, Mr. Bache, you will get nothing by me in a war of words, and so you may as well abandon the contest while you can do it with good grace. I do not wish to fill my paper with personal satire and abuse; but I will not be insulted with impunity; and particularly by you. I have not forgotten the grandson of old Franklin published a paragraph setting forth the justice of cutting my throat. I am getting up in the world and you are going down, for this reason you hate me.

Porcupine's Gazette, March 4, 1797

Stewart, Donald H., *The Opposition Press of the Federalist Period*, Albany: State University of New York Press, 1969

Patent Medicine Advertising

Promoted nostrums that often did more harm than good

Before the days of modern medicine, the nineteenth-century U.S. public found its doctors and druggists mostly ineffective in dealing with most diseases. Instead, the public turned to purported remedies called patent medicines.

Sold initially as quick salves, various concoctions were marketed by pitchmen like John D. Rockefeller's father. By the end of the nineteenth century, the business had grown into an industry valued at $250 million. The products were called patent medicines, proprietary medicines, and nostrums. Generally, patent medicines had copyrighted trademarks, proprietary medicines indicated ownership of the formula, and nostrums were an all-inclusive title. However, the distinctions were seldom made, so the terms were virtually interchangeable.

In 1905, the patent medicine business in a nation of almost 84 million people produced sales estimated variously at between $59 and $90 million. The success of the big business came from heavy advertising in the nation's newspapers and magazines that derived substantial income from the manufacturers. Millions bought the nostrums ignorant of (or ignoring) the fact that some of the syrups contained as much as 80 percent alcohol and many of the tonics used cocaine and morphine.

The nostrums' names gave an indication of their claims – for example, Dr. King's New Discovery for Consumption, Dr. Kline's Great Nerve Restorer, and Radam's Microbe Killer. The claims were far reaching, from eradicating the common cold and dandruff to curing heart ailments and cancer. Patent medicines like Peruna, Liquozone, and Orangeine were enormously popular.

The patent medicine industry was not without its critics, who became more vocal at the turn of the twentieth century. The climate for reform that produced the Progressive movement and the muckraking journalists targeted patent medicines, whose manufacture, sale, and use became considered primarily as a public health problem. Growing support sought passage of pure food and drug legislation that had been languishing in Congress for more than 25 years.

An early leader in the battle against nostrums was Edward Bok, who banned patent medicine advertisements from the *Ladies' Home Journal,* which he edited. Bok, anxious to protect his women readers, sought to warn about the dangers of patent medicines. His efforts were cooled somewhat by a libel action, and the mantle for the main attack on patent medicines passed to *Collier's* magazine and Samuel Hopkins Adams.

As a reporter of medical matters, Adams was certain that some proprietary medicines were being made in 1905 with

Life-and-death drama highlighted patent medicine advertising.

dangerous additives and chemicals. Because most purveyors kept ingredients secret by refusing to disclose them either on the labels or through the patenting process, the task of exposing the false claims of patent medicines seemed enormous. Newspapers, magazines, and journals, all mindful of their heavy advertising income from nostrum makers, were reluctant to support the cause. The federal government, which was more concerned with pure food than drugs, was of little help, restricting its laboratories to analyzing products referred to them by other agencies. Nonetheless, Adams ordered chemical analyses of the contents of patent medicines, gathered fraudulent testimonials, and searched government documents before traveling the country to discuss the medicines and their effects.

The Adams series, "The Great American Fraud," issued a 10-part indictment of patent medicines and the quacks who peddled them. He reported findings that showed death from some preparations and addiction caused by hidden alcoholic and narcotic content in others. He charged the nostrums often masked serious illnesses or caused users to be complacent about their medical condition. Adams called for an aroused public to avoid the patent medicines and for government to take a more active role by requiring patent medicine makers to label the contents of their products. Adams was also critical of the involvement of newspapers and magazines, who accepted an estimated $40 million in advertising. He blasted the press for agreeing to contracts with a "red clause" that voided the contract if labeling legislation passed.

The efforts of Adams, which included working with the politicians pushing pure food and drug legislation, were joined with the call for meat inspection after publication of Upton Sinclair's novel, *The Jungle.* The cry for purity led to passage of the Pure Food and Drug Law in 1906. It included tougher provisions on patent medicines requiring labeling and more restraint on claims.

Although some publications banned nostrum advertising, later court rulings did lessen the impact of the law, and the law did not end patent medicines. Manufacturers continued to advertise them in newspapers, often masquerading their advertising as news stories. What did change, however, was the content of patent medicines, with the most dangerous ingredients eliminated.

SAMUEL V. KENNEDY III

See also Bok, Edward W.; Muckraking

Further Reading

Anderson, Oscar Edward, Jr., *The Health of a Nation; Harvey W. Wiley and the Fight for Pure Food,* Chicago: University of Chicago Press for the University of Cincinnati, 1958

Hechtlinger, Adelaide, comp., *The Great Patent Medicine Era,* New York: Grosset & Dunlap, 1970

Holbrook, Stewart H., *The Golden Age of Quackery,* New York: Macmillan, 1959

Musto, David F., *The American Disease: Origins of Narcotic Control,* New Haven, Connecticut: Yale University Press, 1973

Young, James Harvey, *The Toadstool Millionaires,* Princeton, New Jersey: Princeton University Press, 1961

Payola

Illegal payments designed to gain airplay

Payola, put simply, is the act of providing an incentive, either cash or prize, in return for receiving radio airplay. Despite its being both illegal and unethical, recording companies and promoters have used illicit cash payments to radio disc jockeys (DJs) as a means of promoting artists for decades. In fact, historical evidence indicates that payola dates as far back as Victorian England, when Arthur Sullivan, before joining with William Gilbert, signed over a portion of the royalty payments for one of his songs to a leading baritone of the day. Tin Pan Alley composers played the payola game to get their numbers performed on the vaudeville stage. Frank Sinatra even mentioned the role played by payola in the establishment of his legendary career.

However, most members of the listening public had little reason to be concerned about payola until 1959, when two names already in the national consciousness began making front-page news. Charles Van Doren and Alan Freed became central figures in two of the greatest scandals in the history of broadcasting. Van Doren, a handsome, dashing, intellectual admired by throngs of women, was the most successful contestant ever on the NBC-TV prime-time game show *Twenty-One*. Alan Freed was one of the most popular DJs in the United States and was credited with coining the term "rock and roll" and promoting the genre.

After Van Doren tearfully testified before a congressional committee that the game show *Twenty-One* was fixed by giving contestants answers in advance, investigators turned up evidence implicating musical publishing companies in a scheme to pay the program's producers money to have certain numbers performed during the wildly popular game show. This discovery led to a payola investigation of the music industry in general and of rock and roll radio stations specifically. Critics charged the House investigating committee and the Federal Communications Commission (FCC) with targeting rock and roll stations and artists while ignoring similar practices at stations playing more accepted musical formats.

Alan Freed was fired from his popular radio show at WABC in New York when he refused, on principle, to sign a statement that he had never received funds or gifts in return for playing records. Two days later, Freed stepped down as host from his top-rated television dance show, *Big Beat,* on WNEW-TV. A number of other DJs in major markets across the country also were fired because of involvement in payola. At least three DJs in Detroit, Michigan, were let go after admitting under oath to taking cash payments from record companies. Disc jockeys in Boston and Philadelphia resigned after discussions with station management. Formal charges were brought against six record companies, including RCA Victor. Westinghouse-owned station KYW in Cleveland, Ohio, received so much money from RCA, the record label of Elvis Presley, that the third-floor restroom was fondly called the payola booth.

The FCC demanded from every radio and television station in the country a detailed accounting, under oath, of any programming for which payment or incentive of any kind had been received. President Eisenhower made a public statement and urged government officials to "clean up this mess."

When the House of Representatives Committee on Legislative Oversight opened hearings on payola, Dick Clark of the nationally televised afternoon dance party *American Bandstand* was called to testify. Committee members tried to grill Clark over charges that his music publishing company promoted its own songs on *Bandstand*. Clark failed to yield under pressure, contending that his investments were common business practice and neither illegal nor unethical. Clark maintained his composure throughout the hearings and consistently presented himself as a smooth, yet tenacious, witness. In the end, Clark and the committee parted on relatively friendly terms.

Alan Freed had no such luck. After his congressional testimony, Freed pleaded guilty to a charge of commercial bribery and received a $300 fine and a six-month suspended jail sentence. Later, he was indicted for evading income taxes on his payola earnings. Freed died in 1964, a broken man, at the age of 43. With Freed and several other big name DJs out of the media spotlight, public interest and government investigations waned.

At the end of the twentieth century, the FCC had stringent rules regarding payola for radio or television. Stations were required to disclose any material connection related to products or services promoted on the air. Each payola violation was punishable by a fine of up to $10,000 and up to one year in jail. Yet, rumors of payola persisted. The *New York Daily News,* in November 1995, charged pop star Madonna's recording label, Maverick Records, with using strippers and call girls to influence radio programmers in major markets. Maverick Records executives denied the report.

CORLEY F. DENNISON III

See also Quiz Show Scandals

Further Reading
Passman, Arnold, *The Deejays,* New York: Macmillan, 1971
Shaw, Arnold, *The Rockin' '50s,* New York: Hawthorn, 1974; London: Da Capo, 1987
Szatmary, David, *Rockin' in Time: A Social History of Rock and Roll,* Englewood Cliffs, New Jersey: Prentice-Hall, 1987

Peace/Pacifist Press

Publications designed to promote the cause of peace

Peace has been the central reform movement in U.S. history since the colonial period. Countless citizens have harnessed the press to proselytize for peace. They have recognized, as have, historically, many other advocacy groups from abolitionists to suffragists, the power of the written word to shape public opinion. As the *Advocate of Peace* of the American Peace Society stated in 1838, "Public opinion is our main instrument; and we would cast it in the mould of peace." Some peace advocates, such as members of the historic pacifist churches (the Quakers, the Mennonites, and the Brethren), have been motivated especially by religious convictions, as have members of groups such as the Shakers, the Catholic Worker movement, the Protestant-based ecumenical Fellowship of Reconciliation, and the Jewish Peace Fellowship. Still others have sought peace through nonsectarian affiliations with such organizations as the American Peace Society (founded 1828), the Women's International League for Peace and Freedom (1915), and the Union of Concerned Scientists (1969).

Peace advocacy has inspired innumerable tracts, pamphlets, books, and specialized journalism as a means to sway public opinion. Starting with the first U.S. peace societies, organized in direct response to the Napoleonic wars (the Massachusetts Peace Society and the New York Peace Society in 1815 and the American Peace Society in 1828), peace reformers and radicals have expressed vigorously their conviction that the pen is mightier than the sword. In 1819, the *Friend of Peace* asserted, "It is in the power of the Editors of Newspapers to do much good with little labor and expense. A few well written remarks on the subject of war may occasion thousands to reflect, and eventually save thousands from untimely death by murderous hands."

Exploiting early nineteenth-century advances in printing and transportation technology, many reform organizations of that period such as those seeking the abolition of slavery and temperance, embraced the press as a means to communicate their ideas and recruit new members. They were joined by both religious and nonsectarian peace advocates, who issued thousands of pages of tracts as well as periodicals such as the American Peace Society's *Advocate of Peace,* *Calumet,* and *Harbinger of Peace.* Tracts were an important part of the nineteenth-century peace advocacy

press, but the periodicals issued by peace organizations and other groups held even more significance. As the historian Merle Curti wrote, "the periodicals themselves are the most important printed materials, as they contain the annual reports and many of the sermons and addresses which were also circulated in tract form."

As peace advocacy positions ranged from absolute pacifism to a moderate position legitimizing only "defensive" war, so did viewpoints expressed in the peace advocacy press vary widely. For instance, the American Peace Society maintained a more middle-of-the-road, even conservative, point of view in its periodicals, as did the publications of the Universal Peace Union (founded in 1866), such as the *Bond of Peace,* the *Voice of Peace,* and the *Peacemaker.* The latter three also published special peace education sections for children, containing essays, poems, and stories. An important editor of the *Peacemaker and Court of Arbitration* (the *Peacemaker*'s later title) was Belva Lockwood, the Universal Peace Union's staunch advocate of international arbitration to settle disputes.

Meanwhile, nineteenth-century religious communitarians who embraced peace as one of their tenets often published radical content advocating peace as part of larger plans for society's social and economic transformation. Examples include the Hopedale group, which issued the *Practical Christian* and the *Radical Spiritualist,* and the Oneida Community, which published the *American Socialist, Oneida Circular,* and the *Witness.* Frances Wright, the well-known abolitionist and feminist, served as the utopian New Harmony Community's coeditor and publisher of its *New Harmony Gazette/Free Enquirer.* Another radical view of peace advocacy during the antebellum period was expressed by the abolitionist New England Non-Resistance Society. It issued periodicals such as the *Liberator,* the *Journal of the Times,* and the *Non-Resistant,* which advocated a radical stance of personal nonviolence and nonresistance relative to abolishing slavery.

The Women's Christian Temperance Union, as did many of the other major women's organizations, sponsored a peace department, which prepared written peace advocacy content for insertion in their own periodicals and others (such as the Quaker *Messenger of Peace*). Throughout the nineteenth century, also, the religious publications of the historic peace churches, such as the *Friends' Weekly Intelligencer,* the *Mennonite Quarterly Review,* and the Church of the Brethren *Gospel Messenger,* were a consistent, if less audible, voice for peace advocacy.

In the twentieth century, the peace advocacy press flourished along with the expansion of peace organizations and the development of technology such as desktop publishing. Complex and scattered, this press also expressed a wide range of viewpoints, in keeping with its affiliation with peace, internationalist, and antinuclear organizations including, respectively, *Liberation, International Conciliation,* and the *Bulletin of the Atomic Scientists.* An outstanding early twentieth-century example of peace advocacy expressed in scintillating style was Max Eastman's *Masses* (1911–17), which was suspended by the federal government after it opposed U.S. entry into World War I. Its notable writers included John Reed and Dorothy Day. Another influen-

Messenger of Peace.

Motto: "*Glory to God in the Highest, and on Earth Peace, Good Will to Men.*"

VOL. XII.   SECOND MONTH, 1882.   NO. 2

TABLE OF CONTENTS.

THE Messenger OF Peace

is published monthly by the Secretary of the "Peace Association of Friends in America." It is filled with facts and arguments to prove that war is unchristian, inhuman, and unnecessary. That if men and women of intelligence were as anxious to find a remedy as they are to find an apology for war, the self-imposed scourge of our race would soon be banished from the civilized world. It advocates the brotherhood of mankind, and that *we can not injure another without injuring ourselves.* Terms, Fifty Cents per annum, or copies sent to one address for Two Dollars. Free to ministers of the gospel of all denominations who will read and recommend it to their congregations.

Address   DANIEL HILL,
          New Vienna, Clinton Co., Ohio

WAR'S RECORD.

According to the philosopher Dick, war has destroyed fourteen billions of human beings since man was first placed upon the earth.

Some authors put the number much higher; but, taking Dick's estimate as a basis, the loss of life will be as follows:

2,333,333 annually.
194,444 monthly.
6,481 daily.
270 every hour.
4½ every minute.

Shall the sword devour forever? Not if God's Word is true. Christians, come up to the help of the Lord against the mighty.

Is it Right?"—So long as any person seriously asks this question of himself, in regard to all his acts, the danger of any great departure from the path of rectitude must be small; and we wish that a system of education might make it as common and controlling among our people in after years as now appears to be in youth.

Ode to Peace.

BY WILLIAM TENNENT.

Daughter of God! that sittest on high
Amid the dancers of the sky,
And guidest with thy gentle sway
The planets on their tuneful way;
Sweet Peace! shall ne'er again
The smile of thy most holy face,
From thine eteranl dwelling place
Rejoice the wretched, weary race
Of discord breathing men!

Too long, O gladness-giving Queen!
Thy tarrying in heaven has been;
Too long o'er this fair blooming world
The flag of blood has been unfurled.
Polluting God's pure day;
While, as each maddening people reels
War onward drives his scythed wheels,
And at his horse's bloody heels
Shriek murder and dismay.

Oft have I wept to hear the cry
Of widow wailing bitterly;
To see the parents' silent tear
For children fallen beneath the spear,
And I have felt so sore
The sense of human guilt and woe,
That I, in virtue's passioned glow,
Have cursed (my soul was wounded so)
The shape of man I bore!

Then come from thy serene abode,
Thou gladness-giving child of God!
And cease the world's ensanguined strife,
And reconcile my soul to life;
For much I long to see,
Ere I shall to the grave descen'd,
Thy hand its blessed branch extend,
And to the world's remotest end
Wave Love and Harmony!

Dr. Furnass, of Philadelphia, it is stated, celebrates the Lord's Supper without distributing the elements to the people. The bread and wine are to "stand on the table as sacred symbols, to speak through the eye to the heart, the minister interpreting."

Peace organizations have a long history of publishing their views.

tial twentieth-century periodical was the Women's International League for Peace and Freedom's *Peace and Freedom* (superseding its *Four Lights*).

At the end of the twentieth century, the historic peace churches still published periodicals such as *Brethren Life and Thought, Friends Journal,* and *Mennonite Life.* Dorothy Day's monthly *Catholic Worker,* founded in New York City in 1933, remained a distinctive, influential, lay-produced expression of radical Catholic nonresistant pacifism. Its editors have included Michael Harrington, with writers and illustrators such as Thomas Merton, Daniel Berrigan, Philip Berrigan, Fritz Eichenberg, and Ade Bethune.

Still another variety of peace press was the underground military press, particularly of the Vietnam War era. Examples include the *Ally,* published in Berkeley, California (1968–74), and distributed among U.S. troops in Vietnam, and the *Aboveground,* issued from Colorado Springs, Colorado (August 1969–May 1970), which targeted military personnel stationed at Fort Carson, the Air Force Academy, and elsewhere.

For the most part, the peace press has faced the typical advocacy press fund-raising challenges and often ran in the red. Besides subscription and advertising income, necessary monies frequently came from job printing and donations. Historically, many editors – starting with Noah Worcester, founder of the Massachusetts Peace Society, who edited the American Peace Society's *Friend of Peace* from 1819 to 1828 – worked for free, with the leanest of budgets, propelled by their vision and their readers' largesse. They achieved circulations that ranged from a few thousand (for instance, the *Advocate of Peace,* at 3,000 in 1850) to more than 100,000 (e.g., the *Catholic Worker*). Of course, readership is difficult to gauge because so many periodicals were passed from reader to reader, in some cases exponentially increasing circulation.

NANCY L. ROBERTS

See also Alternative Press; Socialist Press

Further Reading
Brock, Peter, *Pacifism in the United States: From the Colonial Era to the First World War,* Princeton, New Jersey: Princeton University Press, 1968
Chatfield, Charles, *For Peace and Justice: Pacifism in America, 1914–1941,* Knoxville: University of Tennessee Press, 1971
Curti, Merle E., *The American Peace Crusade, 1815–1860,* Durham, North Carolina: Duke University Press, 1929
DeBenedetti, Charles, *The Peace Reform in American History,* Bloomington: Indiana University Press, 1980
Roberts, Nancy L., *American Peace Editors, Writers, and Periodicals: A Dictionary,* New York: Greenwood, 1991
_____, *Dorothy Day and the 'Catholic Worker',* Albany: State University of New York Press, 1984
_____, "'Ten Thousand Tongues' Speaking for Peace: Purposes and Strategies of the Nineteenth-Century Peace Advocacy Press," *Journalism History* 21:1 (Spring 1995), pp. 16–28

Wittner, Lawrence S., *Rebels Against War: The American Peace Movement, 1933–1983,* rev. ed., Philadelphia: Temple University Press, 1984

Penny Press

Made newspapers more easily available to readers

The penny press occupies a pivotal place in standard accounts of the history of U.S. journalism. It is credited with initiating the transition from a partisan press to modern "objective" news-gathering operations and with repositioning the newspaper from an instrument of political persuasion to a consumer-oriented source of practical information of all sorts. In such standard accounts, the penny papers of New York City are highlighted as the agents of change, and their careers are made to stand in for the history of U.S. journalism generally in the period 1830–80. Many aspects of this standard account are debatable.

A definition of penny papers is elusive. Although the first penny papers sold for a penny, successful papers quickly raised their prices – James Gordon Bennett's *Herald* went to two cents in 1836, its second year of publication. Still, these papers remained cheaper than earlier dailies, which sold for six cents. They were also more likely to emphasize daily sales by newsstands and vendors rather than sales by sub-

New York's *The Sun* was the first penny paper in the United States.

scription, although hard evidence on this is rare. They tended to expand circulation, but it is an exaggeration to say that the penny papers were the first mass circulation newspapers – the partisan papers of the Jacksonian era, too, sought expanded circulation by way of appealing to an expanded electorate, and the print media of the evangelical movements of the early nineteenth century also gained mass circulation. In achieving mass circulation, the penny papers are thought to have inaugurated a new level of interest in and dependence on advertising revenue, making them significantly more commercial than earlier newspapers, which were primarily political. They also tended at the outset to proclaim political neutrality, although this stance turned out to be transitory for most. Some scholars draw an association between the market orientation of the penny papers and their political neutrality and argue on this basis that the penny papers invented the objective stance of the journalism of some modern capitalist countries.

These common perceptions of the penny press do not add up to a definition. In addition, some of these perceptions are fanciful. Rather than a firmly defined category, the penny papers that scholars usually refer to are a small but disparate collection of newspapers published in the major eastern cities from the 1830s through the 1850s, specifically New York's *Sun, Herald, Tribune,* and *Times,* along with the *Public Ledger* in Philadelphia and the *Sun* in Baltimore, Maryland.

The New York papers conveniently form a neat narrative of press development. The *Sun* was an artisan's paper, begun by a printer named Benjamin Day; it parlayed reports from the police courts into a loyal readership among the booming city's workers. The succeeding papers moved upscale, with Bennett's *Herald* capitalizing on Wall Street reports (as well as gossip, crime news, and theater reviews) to capture a middle-class readership and Horace Greeley's *Tribune* combining an element of rectitude with an allegiance to the Whiggery. The *Times* completed this cycle by formulating a commitment to accuracy, completeness, and respectability. In the course of this progression from *Sun* to *Times,* the penny press remained ardent in its embrace of the mass market, which stiffened its devotion to news while loosening its ties to a party and luring it gradually away from the lower classes' desires for sensationalist trivialities.

The standard account of the New York penny papers is also a tale of the overthrow of an elite press and the creation of a new one. In fact, the *Sun,* the *Herald,* the *Tribune,* and the *Times* dominated the newspaper scene in New York until the arrival of Joseph Pulitzer and William Randolph Hearst in the 1880s and 1890s. Furthermore, by virtue of their New York preeminence, they also occupied a leading position in the nation as a whole. The leading New York newspapers translated their command of European news into national leadership in news gathering and dissemination, quickly becoming more important than the Washington, D.C., press. Their leadership was reinforced by the creation of national wire services, especially the Associated Press, which allowed the New York papers to sell their news nationwide.

The New York penny papers maintained their position of dominance for so long by investing heavily both in news gathering and in printing technology. They were leaders in investing in telegraph technology, in hiring staffs of professional reporters, in promoting division of labor in the newsroom, in purchasing new printing machinery, and in adopting forms of corporate ownership and control. These innovations allowed them to produce thicker papers with fresher news for more readers at a lower price than their less well-financed competitors.

Not all of the penny papers became members of the new newspaper elite. Most penny papers were poorly financed and short-lived, especially outside the major eastern cities. They rarely moved beyond the realm of the "cheap press" and into the realm of the elite press. Their predecessors were the "workingman's" papers of the 1820s, and their successors were not the modern-day *Times* but a galaxy of marginal papers, ranging from some of the Socialist weeklies of the turn of the century to the latter-day supermarket tabloids. The history of this cheap press is yet to be written.

The consequences of analytically separating the cheap press from the New York penny papers that became the elite press are many. Most obviously, this move challenges the "populist" heritage of the elite press. Central to all accounts of the penny papers is an image of humble origins in rebellion against a well-heeled establishment. Benjamin Day began the *Sun* with limited means, but such was not the case with Greeley's *Tribune* or Henry Raymond's *Times.* The penny press formula may have been the invention of members of the artisan working class, but it was not their property for long.

The modernization of the press, then, should not be seen as the work of the penny press. While the chief modernizers in New York were penny papers, the ingredients of modernization – expanded circulation, market orientation, division of labor, new technology, corporate ownership, and the establishment of property rights in news – were not necessarily linked to a penny press formula, and outside of New York, they were not especially associated with penny papers. The leading modernizers in other cities were generally members of the old political establishment.

Most Atrocious Murder

Our City was disgraced on Sunday by one of the most foul and premeditated murders that ever fell to our lot to record. The following are circumstances as ascertained on the spot . . . he mentioned his jealous suspicions, and expressed a determination to quit her, and demanded his watch and miniature together with some letters. She refused to given them up, and he then drew from beneath his cloak the hatchet and inflicted upon her head three blows, either of which must have proved fatal, as the bone was cleft to the extent of three inches in each place.

Everybody exclaimed "what a horrible affair." News was received from Texas, highly disastrous to the colonists, but the private tragedy of Ellen Jewett almost absorbed all public attention.

New York Herald, April 11, 1836

Likewise, other elements of the standard perception of the penny press do not bear close scrutiny. Most famously, the penny papers (understood either as the elite New York papers or the cheap press) did not inaugurate the modern age of objectivity. Most had a partisan affiliation that was reflected in both news reports and editorials. In fact, marketing strategies dictated party ties in this age of extensive competition in which one market could host up to a score of daily papers. A partisan affiliation attracted more readers than it repelled and made a paper a better advertising organ also. The initial neutrality of papers like Day's *Sun*, which was always more sympathetic to the Democratic party, is better understood as a reactionary response to rabid politics – an invocation of the traditional ideology of impartiality – than as an intimation of modern objectivity. Within a short time, all of the New York penny papers displayed ordinary partisan affiliations.

The reporting style of the penny papers tended to differ from that of conventional papers, although the difference is not easily understood in modern terms. Content analysis has not demonstrated that penny papers were significantly more sensationalist, contrary to conventional wisdom. They did tend to be more terse – both because they deemphasized the extensive reprinting of political speeches and documents that was common in other genres of newspapers at the time and because cheap papers generally had a smaller news hole than others. Penny papers seemed to recognize that their readers had limited time and attention. This terseness makes the penny papers seem more modern than their counterparts.

The conventions of modern objectivity have little to do with the style of the penny papers, whether understood as the cheap press or the elite press. Modern objectivity emphasizes the separation of the reporter's values from the substance of the report and signals that separation through the use of conventions like sourcing (attributing statements, as, for example, "Congressman X claims . . .") and balancing ("But critics from the other side of the aisle . . ."). The news reports in the penny papers were not of this sort. The crime stories were moralistic, the human interest stories were sentimental, and the political news was usually slanted; where the reporter appeared, it was in the guise of an author and not of a value-free expert. The best supportable claim one can make for the penny papers' inventing objectivity would be quite indirect: by promoting the division of labor of the modern newsroom, the elite penny papers helped create the occupational category that would eventually adopt objectivity as its ideology. Such an account of the rise of objectivity reserves due credit for other factors, like the growth of the wire services, the rise of Progressive reform in politics, the professionalization of the social sciences, and the decrease of competition in local markets.

JOHN NERONE

See also Associated Press; Bennett, James Gordon Sr.; Cooperative News Gathering; Greeley, Horace; Hearst, William Randolph; New Journalism (1880s); Objective Reporting; Party Press; Pulitzer, Joseph; Telegraph; Yellow Journalism

Further Reading

Baldasty, Gerald, *The Commercialization of News in the Nineteenth Century,* Madison: University of Wisconsin Press, 1992

Blondheim, Menahem, *News over the Wires: The Telegraph and the Flow of Public Information in America, 1844–1897,* Cambridge, Massachusetts: Harvard University Press, 1994

Nerone, John C., "The Mythology of the Penny Press," *Critical Studies in Mass Communication* 4 (1987)

Schiller, Dan, *Objectivity and the News: The Public and the Rise of Commercial Journalism,* Philadelphia: University of Pennsylvania Press, 1981

Schudson, Michael, *Discovering the News: A Social History of American Newspapers,* New York: Basic, 1978

Pentagon Papers

Battle between press and government over publishing secret report

The Pentagon Papers case has been widely acclaimed as a landmark First Amendment case pitting two of the most well-regarded and highly respected newspapers in the United States against the federal government in a battle over censorship. However, while certainly an endorsement of the principles protected by the First Amendment, the U.S. Supreme Court's 1971 decision in the Pentagon Papers case (*New York Times* v. *United States*) actually did little to further strengthen the defense of news organizations against the threat of prior restraint by the government.

The decision lifted temporary injunctions against the *New York Times* and the *Washington (D.C.) Post*, permitting the newspapers to continue publishing articles based on a classified government document titled "History of U.S. Decision-Making Process on Viet Nam Policy." Certain portions of the document had been leaked to the press, although the government was unsure just how much and which portions. Editors at the *New York Times* had deliberated for several months before deciding what, if anything, to print. On June 13, 1971, the *Times* ran the first in its series of articles; it was able to publish three installments before being served an injunction on June 15. The *Post* began its series on June 18 and promptly was served an injunction as well. The two cases were whisked through their respective jurisdictions until they were brought together for consideration by the high court, which handed down its decision on June 30.

In their defense, the *Times* and the *Post* claimed that the governmental classification system was a sham and the injunction served against them constituted a violation of the First Amendment. The U.S. government argued that the president had the power to censor the press to protect national security, that publication violated federal espionage statutes, and that publication might substantially interfere with the conduct of foreign affairs. When pressed by the

Court, the government was unable to produce convincing examples of excerpts from the document that, if published, would present a direct and immediate threat to national security.

The case resulted in a brief, unsigned majority opinion, six concurring opinions, and three dissenting opinions. The per curiam opinion noted a "heavy presumption" against the constitutional validity of governmental prior restraint and laid a "heavy burden" on the government to justify such measures, echoing Chief Justice Charles Evans Hughes's majority opinion in *Near v. Minnesota* (1931). The Court stopped short of ruling that prior restraint against the media is never justified (a sentiment expressed only by Justices Hugo Lafayette Black and William O. Douglas in their concurring opinions). Rather, it merely held the government had failed to meet its "heavy burden" of justification in this case.

All three dissenting opinions expressed concern that the Court had had neither the information nor the time required to formulate a carefully considered opinion. Because of its unusual circumstances, the case is considered to have set a weak precedent.

ELIZABETH M. KOEHLER

See also Nixon, Richard M., and the Media; Prior Restraint

Further Reading
Griswold, Erwin N., *Ould Fields, New Corne: The Personal Memoirs of a Twentieth Century Lawyer,* St. Paul, Minnesota: West, 1992
Schrag, Peter, *Test of Loyalty: Daniel Ellsberg and the Rituals of Secret Government,* New York: Simon & Schuster, 1974
Sheehan, Neil, et al., *The Pentagon Papers as Published by the 'New York Times',* New York: Quadrangle, 1971
Ungar, Sanford J., *The Papers & the Papers: An Account of the Legal and Political Battle over the Pentagon Papers,* New York: Columbia University Press, 1989

Persian Gulf War

Advanced communications technology dominated news coverage

Contrary to the popular notion that the Vietnam War was the first "television war" in the history of U.S. journalism, this distinction is more appropriately applied to the Persian Gulf conflict of 1990–91 between Iraq and a United Nations (UN) coalition headed by the United States. The Gulf War was the first war covered live on television. It was a war of advanced technology, both on the battlefield and in newsrooms. It was a tightly censored news story that proved that the U.S. military had learned its lessons from the Vietnam War about restricting war zone access for the news media. And, of greatest concern to journalists, the Gulf War showed that a majority of the U.S. public approved of wartime press restrictions.

In the summer of 1990, Iraq quarreled with its oil-ex-

porting neighbors about export quotas and prices. On August 2, Iraq invaded Kuwait with a large force of troops and tanks, ostensibly to keep oil prices high by controlling Kuwait's oil fields. Six days later, Iraqi leader Saddam Hussein formally annexed Kuwait. Fearing the Iraqi spearhead would continue into Saudi Arabia, the United States rushed troops to defend Saudi oil fields. During the next five months of military standoff, U.S. President George Bush fashioned a UN coalition that pitted Iraq against most of the world, including several other Arab states. Saddam vowed retaliatory missile strikes against Israel and reprisals against hostages if the allies invaded Kuwait.

The massive military buildup in the region was matched by a parallel influx of journalists and communication technology into Saudi Arabia and Israel. Citing security and personal safety factors, the U.S. military set up press pools in the combat zone. In the U.S. media, an initial flurry of hard news on the invasion, allied deployment, and Iraqi ill-treatment of Kuwaitis gave way to feature stories on GI life in the harsh desert and hometown support of the troops.

Censorship during the conflict was highly effective and limited where journalists could go rather than what they could report. The U.S. military establishment's limited access strategy to control information was borne of its dissatisfaction with the censorship scheme used during the Vietnam War era, which depended on the press's cooperation. Times had changed. New communication technologies had made field censorship of news stories obsolete. To control the flow of news, journalists would have to be kept out of the theater of operations.

During the invasion of Grenada in 1983, favorable reaction in the United States to a total ban of the press showed military leaders at the Pentagon that the U.S. public would tolerate stricter censorship during wartime. The limited access censorship strategy was codified in the 1984 Sidle Report, a set of guidelines written jointly by military officials, journalism educators, and retired media professionals for wartime censorship that news people could tolerate.

One guideline called for pooling of reporters and photographers – requiring the press to pick its own handful of representatives who would have access to the battle zone and feed stories to all. Of the more than 1,400 news media personnel in the Gulf region during the war, only 192 served in the 24 official press pools. Although they rarely interfered, military supervisors almost always accompanied the pool reporters. Rather than changing stories outright, the military censors controlled unfavorable items by delaying their release until their news value was lost.

Some in-fighting among news pool members was experienced. With so many news organizations covering the war, there was pressure on the reporters to get stories the pool did not have. Some reporters ignored the pool system and went out on their own, including CBS's Bob McKeown and ABC's Forrest Sawyer, but most pool jumpers were detained. While jumping the pool, CBS-TV reporter Bob Simon and his crew got lost in the combat zone, were captured by Iraqi troops, and were held briefly.

After Iraq ignored a UN ultimatum, the United States launched air strikes on military targets in Kuwait and Iraq on January 16, 1991. Dramatic coverage by Cable News

An official press conference during the Persian Gulf War featured Secretary of Defense Richard Cheney, speaking, and Generals Colin Powell and Norman Schwarzkopf, seated center.
(Official U.S. Air Force Photo [Released])

Network (CNN) of the allied bombing of Baghdad – with Peter Arnett, Bernard Shaw, and John Holliman huddling for cover – focused attention on the cable television news service that had struggled for a decade to earn equal footing with ABC, NBC, and CBS. CNN became the "network feed" of choice for independent stations and even a few network affiliates.

Technological innovations such as portable satellite uplinks provided unprecedented access to information about the enemy. CNN's Arnett broadcast live throughout the war from Iraq's capital, Baghdad. A debate raged for months after the war whether Arnett's reports, censored by the Iraqis, were news or propaganda. Arnett countered that reports from the allied side also were censored.

During and after the war, television generally was regarded as the preeminent medium for immediate and compelling coverage of news events and CNN thought of as the preeminent international news organization. Early continuous, commercial-free, real-time coverage by all U.S. television networks gave way to special reports and segments of regular news programs. Military and foreign affairs experts were employed as on-air consultants.

Newspapers and news magazines had to redefine themselves to avoid being preempted by the real-time broadcast media. While producing interpretive and background re-

ports, the writers and editors had to keep in mind what readers already knew from watching television. Circulation gains for all print media covering the war showed that they kept the news fresh. However, print's long-term viability for breaking news was questioned: news sources such as generals and heads of state admitted that they kept up to date by watching CNN.

Correspondents in the gulf used a dizzying variety of electronic technologies to prepare and file stories, including electronic mail, digital photography, facsimile, satellite imaging, laptop computers, and portable telephones. These technologies increased transmission speed, thereby reducing time available for reflection and interpretation. Not to be outdone by the media, the Pentagon dazzled television viewers with its own advanced transmission system, which provided perhaps the definitive images of the war: video pictures beamed continuously by "smart" missiles as they raced toward their targets.

The Pentagon's press officer, Louis A. Williams, planned to open the war to all journalists, but he was overruled, and the press pools were maintained throughout the conflict. Most reporters and photographers grumbled about the pools but complied. Legal challenges to pools and other press restrictions failed for lack of commitment by the large news organizations. Censorship never became a public is-

The presence of CNN's Peter Arnett in Baghdad, Iraq, during the Persian Gulf War was controversial.
(Courtesy CNN)

sue. Opinion polls after the war showed that the U.S. people were satisfied with the news coverage they got.

The allied ground offensive began on February 23, 1991, with a press blackout. Because the allies quickly and decisively defeated Iraqi ground forces, the blackout was lifted in less than a day. When fighting stopped on February 27, U.S. commander General Norman Schwarzkopf gave his now-famous "mother of all press briefings" in which he disclosed that allied strategy included fooling the Iraqis by releasing misinformation to the news media. The military thus succeeded in using and controlling the news media to win both the strategic conflict in the field and the public opinion war back home.

RUSSELL J. COOK

See also Communication Satellite Technology; Grenada Invasion; Pool Journalism; Vietnam War

Further Reading
Cumings, Bruce, *War and Television,* New York and London: Verso, 1992
Dennis, Everette E., et al., *The Media at War: The Press and the Persian Gulf Conflict,* New York: Gannett Foundation, 1991
Kennedy, William V., *The Military and the Media: Why the Press Cannot Be Trusted to Cover a War,* Westport, Connecticut: Praeger, 1993

Personal Attack Rule

FCC regulation designed to protect individual reputations

The personal attack rules of the Federal Communications Commission (FCC) were triggered when the "honesty, character or integrity" of an identified person or group was at-

tacked during a broadcast discussion of a controversial issue of public importance. In the *Red Lion Broadcasting Co. v. FCC* (Fairness Doctrine) case in 1969, the U.S. Supreme Court upheld the personal attack rules as constitutional. Although the FCC subsequently abandoned its general enforcement of the Fairness Doctrine in 1987, two provisions remained in force: the personal attack rules and the Zapple Rule, dealing with access by political parties.

The personal attack rules granted a contingent access right – that is, the right of reply was contingent upon a person's first being attacked personally over the air. The victim of a broadcast personal attack had to be notified by the station within a week, and the station had to provide a script, tape, or accurate summary of the offending remarks. In addition, the station was required to offer a reasonable opportunity for the target of the attack to respond over the air at no charge. The victim had the right to designate a spokesperson or to respond personally, without being questioned or otherwise cross-examined. The rules applied both to station employees and to others using the station, including network broadcasts. Exempt were newscasts, spot news interviews, and news coverage, including commentary or analysis (unlike Section 315 of the Communications Act of 1934, bona fide news documentaries were not exempt). Also exempt were attacks on public figures or foreign groups and attacks made by political candidates or their staffs during the campaign season.

MARK J. BRAUN

See also Broadcast Regulation; "Equal Time" Provision; Fairness Doctrine

Further Reading
Bensman, Marvin R., *Broadcast/Cable Regulation,* Lanham, Maryland: University Press of America, 1990

Photographic Technology

Ability to fix images on a metal plate appeared first in 1839

The story of photography began officially in 1839 when Louis-Jacques-Mandé Daguerre announced the invention of a process that would fix an image on a metal plate, but elements of the process had been known for centuries. The principal precursor, the camera obscura, literally a dark room, had been in use at least since the late Renaissance.

The basic camera obscura was a pinhole camera, in which the light reflecting from an object entered the chamber through a pinhole and projected an image at the other end. As the instrument was refined and made smaller and more portable, a lens was added to focus the image on a plate of ground glass. The addition of a mirror made it possible to set the ground glass level with the top of the box, allowing an artist easily to trace an image that could later be used to guide a painting. However, the image lasted only as long as the light, and efforts were directed toward finding a way to make the image permanent.

Daguerre, whose Diorama exhibition in Paris made exceptionally effective use of light to create three-dimensional effects from flat surfaces, had been experimenting for more than a decade prior to his announcement. In 1829, he joined in a partnership with Joseph-Nicéphore Niepce, another experimenter, who made paper negatives as early as 1816. In 1824, Niépce produced a photograph on a metal plate.

For four years, Daguerre and Niepce carried on their experiments separately and compared results via correspondence. After Niepce died in 1833, Daguerre continued to develop the process until finally, in 1839, he was ready to announce it to the French Académie des Sciences.

Daguerre's process started with a well-polished silver-plated sheet of copper. The sheet was placed over a box containing iodine particles, the fumes from which produced light-sensitive silver iodide upon contact with the silver. The treated plate was put in a light-tight box that was opened for the exposure. Then the plate was removed in semi-darkness and placed over hot mercury, the silver side down. When the mercury fumes condensed on the parts of the plate that had received light, they formed an amalgam with the silver that created a white image. The silver iodide that was not exposed was washed with hyposulfite of soda (sodium thiosulfate) to reduce its sensitivity to light; the plate was rinsed and dried and ready for exhibition.

News of Daguerre's achievement spurred an English scientist, William Henry Fox Talbot, to make public the photographic process he had developed. Exposing paper treated with sodium chloride and silver nitrate to form silver chloride, Talbot first created a negative image. The negative could be displayed or, if transparent paper was used, a positive print could be made from it. Talbot called his invention "photogenic drawing."

Initially, like Daguerre, Talbot had exposed his material for long periods until the image appeared on the paper or plate, but with further experimentation, he discovered that a short exposure time could be used, followed by chemical

A stereopticon camera allowed taking two shots of a scene at the same time for viewing in a nineteenth-century stereoscope.

development of the latent image. This new process, which he announced in 1841 and called the "calotype," had a number of advantages – it was cheaper and faster, processing was easier and chemicals were less toxic, and multiple copies could be made.

Talbot's calotype process was similar to that used today for photographs based on silver salts, but it found little acceptance in the United States, where Daguerre had a head start in the market. The interest in the United States in his daguerreotype, as the resulting photo came to be known, was aided by Samuel F.B. Morse, who was in Paris promoting his telegraph when Daguerre announced his invention. The two men exchanged information, and Morse returned to the United States enthusiastic about the possibilities for the daguerreotype and became one of the first in this country to use the process. Morse set up his own studio and taught others, including Mathew Brady, to make daguerreotypes.

The process was easy to learn, and daguerreotype studios or galleries quickly became a part of U.S. culture. Brady opened studios in New York and Washington, D.C., and a parade of famous people posed for his cameras. Posing for a daguerreotype took patience; initially, exposures were as long as 20 minutes and neck clamps were used to help hold people still. Gradually the exposure time was reduced to about 30 seconds. In 1840, the resulting picture typically was sold for $2, including a case. Often, daguerreotypes were hand-colored.

The daguerreotype remained popular for about a dozen years. In 1851, Englishman Frederick Scott Archer introduced a method employing glass plates on which collodion, a viscous substance, was spread, followed by coatings of potassium iodide and silver nitrate, which produced silver iodide. Because the plates had to be exposed while they were still wet and developed immediately, the term "wet-plate" came into use. Wet-plate photography was the standard for the next three decades. The same method also was applied to thin sheets of iron, creating the tintype. Tintypes were popular because they could be mailed or carried in one's pocket without fear of their breaking.

Development of multiple-lens cameras during this period allowed photographers to take as many as 12 portraits on one wet-plate negative. The print was cut into individual photos that were mounted and used as business or visiting cards – *cartes de visite*. Twin-lens cameras could create stereographs – two images that appeared three-dimensional when viewed through a special device called a stereoscope.

Mathew Brady was one of the most successful U.S. photographers of the mid-nineteenth century. He was 21 when he opened his first daguerreotype studio in 1844, and like most photographers, he switched to wet plates when they became available. In 1860, he photographed presidential candidate Abraham Lincoln when he arrived in New York for a speech at the Cooper Union. Thousands of copies of the photograph were sold, and Lincoln credited them with helping him get elected.

During the Civil War, Brady organized teams of photographers with wagons fitted out as darkrooms to photograph on the battlefields. Although the exposure time required prevented them from photographing action, they recorded more than 7,000 images of the dead and wounded, as well as scenes of military camp life and naval operations. When the photos were exhibited in Brady's studios, they attracted a great deal of attention. After the war, several of Brady's photographers – particularly Timothy O'Sullivan and Alexander Gardner – helped photograph the west as part of survey teams for the government and railroad companies, hauling makeshift developing facilities to remote areas unreachable by their darkroom wagons.

In 1871, thanks to discoveries by an Englishman, Richard L. Maddox, the wet-plate process was replaced by a photographic plate that used gelatin – and, later, sometimes albumin – instead of collodion. The gelatin dried on the plate, which meant that it could be prepared ahead of time and did not have to be developed immediately. Not only did the new materials free photographers from having to stay close to a darkroom, it meant that both plate preparation and development could be done by others, opening new doors for the photographic industry. The new emulsions were more sensitive and permitted shorter exposures; cameras now could be hand-held instead of fixed on a tripod.

Enlargers not only made it possible to make large prints from small negatives, they also invited the reproduction of only part of the negative by editing or cropping – a significant change from the common practice of contact printing the entire negative. Cameras also became smaller, and photography became increasingly popular among amateurs. The growing enthusiasm among amateurs was tempered by the awkwardness, fragility, and expense of glass plates, so inventors sought a better medium on which to expose the image. George Eastman, one of the earliest makers of dry plates in the United States, experimented with paper coated with gelatin; the paper was later replaced with a transparent base of nitrocellulose. In 1888, he introduced the Kodak box camera, which was sold containing a roll of 100 negatives. When a photographer had exposed the entire roll, he sent the camera to the factory, which removed the exposed film, developed and printed it, and put a new roll into the camera. The photo-ready camera cost $25, and owners paid $10 for processing and new film.

Meanwhile, photographers were experimenting with techniques. The first aerial photograph was thought to have been taken in 1858 by a Frenchman, who had problems developing his wet plate because of gas fumes from the balloon in which he was riding. Two years later, James Wallace Black of Boston took the first aerial photo in the United States.

Photographing motion also intrigued photographers. The best-known experiments with motion began in 1873 when former California governor Leland Stanford asked Eadweard Muybridge to help him settle a bet as to whether a galloping horse had all of its feet off the ground at any point. Muybridge had invented one of the first shutters for a camera, eliminating the need to cover and uncover the lens. His initial experiments at Stanford's track were inconclusive, but in 1877, he returned to set up an elaborate arrangement of 12 cameras, each fitted with a shutter with an electromagnetic control. As the horse galloped, it broke strings stretched across the track that triggered the shutters.

The resulting sequence of photos proved that the horse did indeed lift all its feet off the ground at once, although not when observers had expected. The moment came when all legs were folded under the horse, instead of when the legs were spread in the rocking-horse manner. Muybridge's photos led artists like Charles Russell and Frederic Remington to change their portrayals of galloping horses; physician Oliver Wendell Holmes Sr., a photography enthusiast, studied photos of people walking in his efforts to develop artificial limbs for Civil War casualties.

Muybridge's photos were put to another use as well. They were pasted in a strip on a small drum that could be twirled. The resulting image, viewed through a small slit, gave the effect of motion. This device, called a zoetrope, was a forerunner of the kinetoscope and the modern motion picture.

Although simplified by improvements in emulsions and chemicals, film processing continued to be done visually under a dim red light. This meant that film could not be sensitive to red. In the 1880s, after darkroom experimenters established times for different conditions of exposure and development so that processing could be done efficiently in the dark, panchromatic film – an emulsion sensitive to all colors of light – became available. Photographers quickly learned how to use filters to manipulate dark and light.

Printing papers were undergoing similar refinement; gelatin emulsion papers were developed in Germany in 1885. Lenses, shutters, and cameras also were improved in this period, and experiments were under way for color.

Perhaps the photographic development with the greatest impact on U.S. journalism during the late nineteenth century was the halftone. After the invention of photography, photographs frequently formed the basis of illustrations in popular journals, but they were invariably reproduced by means of wood engravings. Although the artists became adept at copying the photos onto the blocks, the images generally lacked the detail and subtlety of the photographs, and efforts continued to develop a better way of reproducing photos.

Talbot's early work provided the basis of photogravure, one method of reproducing photographs. He coated steel plates with gelatin and potassium bichromate. After exposure, the plates were washed, leaving an image in the bare metal that was then etched. In order to texture large dark areas so they would hold ink better, Talbot made his exposure through a fine gauze that created dots on the surface of the plate. A second, better, reproduction method, invented by Walter Bentley Woodbury, produced an image in relief. By forcing a lead block against the relief with a hydraulic press, Woodbury created an intaglio plate that could be filled with ink.

Both processes produced excellent prints that could be framed or hand pasted into books, but they were not suitable for newspaper and magazine work because they could not be used on a page with type. Type was in raised relief, so the photos needed to have their dark sections raised as well to accept ink.

Using the screen method Talbot had pioneered, experimenters made a negative copy of a photograph with a camera fitted with a screen of tiny dots. The negative was then printed on a plate coated with bichromated gelatin. The dots on the negative exposed the gelatin, which did not dissolve

A huge camera with a massive flash attachment was considered progress in the early twentieth century.
(Reproduced from the Collections of the Library of Congress)

when the plate was etched with acid. The varying clusters of dots created the different tones of the photo. The first commercial halftone screens were produced by Max and Louis Levy of Philadelphia and available to newspapers in 1890.

Newspapers were slow to introduce photographs because of readers' and editors' preferences for artists' renderings; some editors thought photos for newspapers were a novelty that would soon wear off. Sunday newspapers, however, quickly accepted the new images, printing them via rotogravure, a variation of photogravure in which the illustrations were put on one press cylinder and the type on another.

By the turn of the century, the camera was an accepted tool of journalism. The single-lens reflex camera allowed a photographer to focus quickly, and improved lenses produced sharper images. The use of flash powder enabled night photography; Jacob A. Riis's photographs of New York tenement districts used such artificial lighting.

In the 1920s, "faster" lenses – that is, lenses that would open wider – made it easier to take "available light" photographs, and at the end of the decade, photographers had access to the Photoflash Lamp, a glass bulb in which flash-powder was ignited by an electrical current. A decade later, flashbulbs were replaced by electronic flashguns, xenon-filled tubes discharged by an electric current, a technology invented in 1938 by Harold E. Edgerton of the Massachusetts Institute of Technology.

Early twentieth-century news photographers commonly used what became known as the press camera. Traditionally of folding-bellows design, the press camera was designed for sheet or roll film. Although it was hand-held, it was hardly inconspicuous, especially when used with flashbulbs, and news photographers grew to prefer the smaller 35-millimeter cameras, the first of which was the Leica, introduced in 1924 by E. Leitz of Germany. Larger-format single-lens reflex cameras, including the Rolleiflex in 1929 and the Hasselblad in 1948, later became available.

The possibility of color photographs also engaged photographic experimenters. In 1861, the British physicist James Clerk Maxwell introduced the notion of additive colors: that is, any color could be obtained by mixing (adding) red, blue, and green light in varying amounts. It was not until 1893, however, that an Irish scientist, John Joly, made a photographic negative with color properties. Joly took his photograph through a screen checkered with microscopic dots of red, green, and blue. When the developed plate was bound to the colored screen, the photograph appeared to have all the hues.

In 1907, the Lumière brothers of France, famous for their role in the development of motion pictures, spread tiny grains of colored starch on a photographic plate that, when properly developed, produced a colored transparency. Their process, called autochrome, was available until 1932.

A different process was based on the principle that objects reflect some colors, and absorb (subtract) others. The technique for separating colors was developed in 1869, and photographers learned to create negatives in magenta, yellow, and cyan and recombine them, ensuring that they were properly lined up, or in "register," into full-color transparencies. In 1935, Eastman Kodak developed Kodachrome, a multiple-layer film using a dye-coupling method that had been invented in 1912. Each layer of emulsion absorbed one color but allowed others to pass through to succeeding layers. The film was first developed to a negative, then, by reversal processing, to a positive. Kodachrome could be processed only by the manufacturer, but Anscochrome (from a competitor, Ansco) and Ektachrome (from Kodak), which could be developed by the photographer, soon entered the market. Kodak introduced Kodacolor for color prints in 1941 and Ektacolor in 1947.

Color motion pictures and magazine photographs quickly became popular, but newspapers still had technological problems to solve. Color printing techniques were similar to the early color transparencies in that separated colors had to be recombined exactly if the photo was not to be blurred. Printing required that paper for a color photograph be run through a press four times, so that each color – cyan, yellow, magenta, and black – could be printed on top of the previous color. Maintaining proper registration was difficult on high-speed newspaper presses until late in the twentieth century.

Photographic processes required that exposed film and paper be handled separately and under special lighting conditions. In the 1930s, Europeans developed a process that produced positives in a single stage. In 1947, Edwin Land, a U.S. inventor, modified the process to create Polaroid material, the processing of which took place within a minute or less inside a camera.

The development of lasers and computers in the second half of the twentieth century had substantial impact on photography. The use of the intense light from lasers to create three-dimensional photographs, or holograms, had limited application in journalism, but as part of the computerization of photography, laser printers were essential.

Initially, photographic prints were electronically scanned into computer-readable digital files that could be manipulated; the invention of digital cameras allowed the printmaking process to be eliminated. Digital cameras store an electronic image that can be transferred directly to a computer for editing. In turn, the computer can electronically send pages of images and text to high-resolution laser printers or directly to printing plate production machines. Digitized images can be manipulated more easily than traditional photographs, opening new creative doors for visual expression.

BARBARA CLOUD

See also Brady, Mathew; Civil War Photography; Documentary Photography; Newspaper Design; Photojournalism in the Nineteenth Century; Photojournalism in the Twentieth Century; Riis, Jacob A.

Further Reading

Eder, Josef Maria, *History of Photography*, translated by Edward Epstean, New York: Dover, 1978

Edgerton, Harold E., and James R. Killian, Jr., *Moments of Vision: The Stroboscopic Revolution in Photography*, Cambridge, Massachusetts: MIT Press, 1979

Gernsheim, Helmut, and Alison Gernsheim, *The History of Photography from the Camera Obscura to the Beginning of the Modern Era*, New York: McGraw-Hill, 1969; London: Thames & Hudson, 1969

Haas, Robert B., *Muybridge: Man in Motion*, Berkeley: University of California Press, 1976

Newhall, Beaumont, *The History of Photography: From 1839 to the Present*, New York: Museum of Modern Art, 1982; London: Secker & Warburg, 1982

_____, *Latent Image: The Discovery of Photography*, Garden City, New York: Doubleday, 1967

Welling, William, *Photography in America: The Formative Years, 1839–1900,* New York: Thomas Y. Crowell, 1978

Photography Awards

At the end of the twentieth century, the profession of news photographer had changed considerably since newspapers first started publishing photographs to accompany stories. Because photographers' work first appeared in newspapers during the period of yellow journalism, the photographer came to be seen as a rough-and-tumble sort of fellow who, with a press card stuck in his hat band, was in a constant battle for the next edition's sensational picture.

By about the middle of the twentieth century, however, the contributions of photojournalists came to be recognized as one of the eight Pulitzer Prize categories in journalism. From 1942, when Milton Brooks of the *Detroit (Michigan) News* was awarded the first Pulitzer Prize for spot news photography, the prestigious award for an outstanding example of news photography was awarded yearly, with the exception of 1946. In 1945, Joe Rosenthal, photographing for the Associated Press, was awarded the Pulitzer for his photograph of the planting of the U.S. flag on Iwo Jima. Between 1942 and 1995, Associated Press photographers were awarded the Pulitzer 13 times, earning far and away the most recognition of the organization. In 1947 and again in 1954, the Pulitzer was awarded to "amateur" photographers. The 1954 award was most remarkable because it honored a woman. In the history of Pulitzer Prizes for spot news photography up to the late 1990s, only one other woman – Carol Guzy – was the award's recipient, once in 1986 and again in 1995. In 1968, the photography award was expanded to include recognition of feature photography.

Newspaper photographers also were honored by the National Press Photographers Association. The association honored outstanding photographers from the 1940s, recognizing the newspaper photographer of the year, the magazine photographer of the year, and the television news photographer of the year, among numerous other categories, ranging from magazine sports action to newspaper feature picture.

ROBIN GALLAGHER

Photography Trade Organizations

With the successful introduction of picture magazines such as *Life* and *Look* in the mid-1930s, the importance of photographic coverage gained significance in the media mix sought by the U.S. public. As professional photographers fought to improve their professional reputations, their employers continued to use photographers not as regular staff members but as speculative freelancers. Competition was fierce, and many photographers practiced less than ethical journalism to get images accepted for publication and payment.

To raise the standards of the profession and gain greater acceptance of their work, two professional photojournalism organizations were formed in the 1940s: the National Press Photographers Association (NPPA) and the American Society of Media (formerly Magazine) Photographers. As World War II ended, many of the best U.S. newspaper photographers recognized the need for a unified voice to represent their profession. In February 1946, photographers met to establish the NPPA.

The new organization immediately began to improve the lot of the working photojournalist through educational programs and national competitions. In the mid-1950s, the NPPA developed its "Flying Short Course" series of workshops. Flying from city to city, a group of master photojournalists would conduct a series of daylong seminars for professionals and students. The informal but educational structure of these sessions served as a model other professional organizations often emulated.

The NPPA also sponsored regional monthly "clip contests" to critique and showcase the best published and broadcast photojournalism and cosponsored the annual Pictures of the Year competition with the University of Missouri School of Journalism. In 1994, more than 30,000 images were entered in this international competition. The organization also took the lead in defending the rights of photographers to have uninhibited access while covering news events and in the development of ethical standards concerning the manipulation of images with the advent of digital picture editing technology.

At about the same time that newspaper photographers were beginning to consider the idea of an organization to improve their professional stature, photographers more closely associated with magazine publication also recognized a need for change. In the mid-twentieth century, most magazines expected photographers to cover events on speculation, making no guarantees about possible use of images submitted. If a photographer's work was accepted for publication, the photographer rarely received a printed credit line, and the publication retained the images for subsequent use, usually without additional compensation to the photographer.

In this environment, a group of leading magazine photographers formed the American Society of Magazine Photographers (ASMP) in 1944. The ASMP developed standards of employment, compensation, and image ownership that eventually guaranteed the photographers contractual security, credit for their published work, and control of when, where, and how their images appeared.

In the late twentieth century, the ASMP served as a clearinghouse of photographic information for the industry, collecting information about photographers' rates, rights, and professional practices. It played a major role in encouraging

Congress to change the Copyright Laws of the United States in 1978. The ASMP changed its name to the American Society of Media Photographers following a referendum of its membership in 1992.

MICHAEL WILLIAMS

Further Reading

Fulton, Marianne, ed., *Eyes of Time: Photojournalism in America,* Boston: Little, Brown, 1988

Kobre, Kenneth, *Photojournalism: The Professionals' Approach,* Somerville, Massachusetts: Curtin & London, 1980

Photography Trade Press

In an effort to combat the viciously competitive atmosphere that colored the news photographer's profession prior to World War II, the National Press Photographers Association founded a monthly magazine in 1946, *National Press Photographer,* and dedicated it to the education of news photographers. Because of the intense competition created by rival New York newspapers earlier in the twentieth century, news photographers were often less than ethical in their efforts to capture the most sensational front-page photograph. Rather than organizing to protest or lobby against existing conditions, the association's founders believed that by educating individual photographers to become responsible professionals, the more egregious problems associated with photographing the news would be resolved. Thus, the association's trade publication was dedicated to the moral, ethical, and educational advancement of news photographers.

The publication, later known as the *News Photographer,* had in the late 1990s about 11,000 subscribers throughout the United States, Canada, Japan, and New Zealand, among other countries. Its articles focused on a number of issues related to news photography, including journalism and the courts, conflict of interest, and privacy issues. Each issue contained award-winning photographs of interest to newspaper, magazine, and television photographers.

The National Press Photographers Association was divided into 11 regions throughout the country. Members of these regional associations also received newsletters regarding the news photography business.

ROBIN GALLAGHER

Photojournalism in the Nineteenth Century

Beginnings of public belief in photography providing an accurate record of events

Long before the introduction of large-format picture magazines in the mid-1930s – even before the 1890s, when the

barons of the yellow press made pictures an intrinsic element of daily newspapers – photographs were used to inform the public about persons, places, and events in the news. From the beginning of photography in 1839, the public believed that photographs were accurate records of whatever happened to be in front of the camera. The use of such apparently irrefutable and truthful documents by the press was inevitable. In one of the medium's first published histories, John Towler equated photography to the invention of the steam engine and magnetic telegraph. "It is one of the great wonders," he wrote, "so far eclipsing the seven vaunted wonders of the world, that these recede into dark nooks, like the wired dolls of an automatic puppet show." Not surprisingly, publishers and editors increasingly anxious to reach a mass audience began looking for ways to use photographs on the pages of their magazines and newspapers.

The first efforts to include photographs on the printed page, however, now seem crude and hopelessly inadequate. For most of the nineteenth century, photographs were painstakingly copied by hand, then transferred to wooden or metal plates as engravings, before being printed with text. As a result, printed pictures based on photographs looked more like artists' drawings or sketches. In order to assure readers that their illustrations were accurate, editors nearly always printed captions attesting to the photographic origin of their images. The picture might look like the work of an ordinary artist, but if the caption read, "From a Photograph," the reader was assured that he or she was looking at the real thing, not a hastily concocted interpretation or the product of someone's vivid imagination.

Frank Leslie, an immigrant from Ipswich, England, was one of the first to fully realize the value of photographs as reportage. Drawing upon his experiences as an artist at the *Illustrated London News* and at T.W. Strong's short-lived *Illustrated American News,* Leslie began publishing his own weekly pictorial in December 1855. *Frank Leslie's Illustrated Weekly* was an immediate success and remained a force in journalism well into the twentieth century. In 1859, Leslie described the importance of press photography in an article on Jeremiah Gurney, a successful photographer in New York City. "The painter's easel is almost abolished," he wrote, "except as a hand maiden to photography." Now

A shantytown shot was the first photograph published in a newspaper.

The War in Virginia—Lieutenant-General Grant in a Council of War at Massaponax Church.—From a Photograph by Gardner.—See Page 264.

Illustrated newspapers often painstakingly copied photographs by hand into line drawings, such as this woodcut depicting a meeting of Union officers in 1864.

(Otto Richter Library/University of Miami)

and in the future, the men "whose actions and deeds fill the world" would be presented to the public with absolute realism. For Leslie, nothing was beyond the capacity of the camera: "Terrible battles, with all their dreadful scenes of carnage and slaughter, are transferred to paper upon the instant, and soon go hurrying over thousands of miles to be viewed by the humble peasant in his peaceful abode."

Fletcher Harper, the youngest of the four brothers who built one of the great publishing dynasties in the United States, followed Leslie's lead. The first issue of *Harper's Weekly* appeared in 1857. For 18 weeks, the magazine was issued with no illustrations at all. Harper, however, soon realized the news value of pictures, especially those based upon photographs, and from May 2, 1857, the magazine printed photographs in every edition. During the Civil War, *Harper's* and *Frank Leslie's Illustrated Newspaper* published countless pictures showing officers and men involved in the war, scenes depicting the awful aftermath of battles, and views of military encampments and fortifications. Mathew Brady, one of the best-known photographers in the country, organized and directed coverage of the Union armies; in 1863, Alexander Gardner left Brady's employ and established a rival photographic unit. Both Brady and Gardner supplied Harper and Leslie with timely views made by staff photographers who dogged the armies looking for telling images. The public became accustomed to seeing history as it was made.

Both during and after the war, photographers augmented their incomes by mass-producing images with broad popular appeal. These were distributed by individual photographers, photo equipment and supply companies, publishers, and newsdealers. Portraits of celebrities and other persons in the news were printed and sold as visiting cards, which were roughly the size of modern business cards. Stereographs, which consisted of two nearly identical views printed on a card measuring approximately $3^1/_2$ by 7 inches, gave the illusion of a third dimension when viewed in a device called a stereoscope. Stereo views were as important to the culture of the Victorian-era United States as televisions and VCRs became in the twentieth century. Their subject matter varied from straightforward depictions of events and places to humorous sequences and travelogues. Visiting cards and stereographs perfectly suited a people enamored of the visual and hungry for information about the world. "It is wonderful what becomes of the countless stereoscopes that are made during a year," enthused the editors of *Anthony's Photographic Bulletin* in 1870. "Pile upon pile, dozen after dozen, gross after gross, have we alone been instrumental in supplying to the still unsatisfied demand." And that was just the premium machines. Cheaper sets by the "hundreds of thousands have been swallowed up in the vortex of popular consumption."

Until late in the century, photographs printed in the press appeared as engravings or woodcuts, for there was no mechanical method of transferring the subtle tones of a photograph onto the printed page. However, in 1878, Frederick Eugene Ives, director of the photographic laboratories at Cornell University, demonstrated a new, if somewhat cumbersome, process of reproducing photographs mechanically. Two years later, the director of graphics at the *New York Daily Graphic,* Stephen Henry Horgan, announced his own halftone process and to prove it, the *Daily Graphic* printed one on March 4, 1880. This was an epochal event in the history of photojournalism, the first successful demonstration of a process for printing photographs mechanically. The halftone assured that photographs used on the printed page looked like photographs, not engravings or woodcuts. Ironically, however, it took another decade and a half for the halftone to be fully accepted by printers and publishers.

Late in the century, the use of photographs by newspapers was encouraged by publishers looking for ways to increase circulation. Joseph Pulitzer and William Randolph Hearst advocated a new kind of journalism, one that reveled in the sensational and visual, and in the process, they institutionalized photojournalism. Despite constant criticism from those who believed that pictures demeaned the intellectual content of newspapers and magazines, Hearst, Pulitzer, and others correctly surmised that their readers still believed in the inherent truthfulness of photographs. Given the strength of that belief, it merely made good sense to publish pictures.

During the brief U.S. war with Spain in 1898, a war that some believed was fomented by strident, jingoistic reporting by Hearst and Pulitzer, photographers were everywhere. Even Hearst made pictures in Cuba. Magazines and newspapers ran special picture pages and photographic supplements designed to take advantage of an enormous outpouring of visual material. Publishers and editors experimented with new ways to use pictures in combinations and began to think about essays and stories told in pictures instead of words. Modern photojournalism had arrived, and the pictorial magazines *Life* and *Look* were still three and a half decades away.

MICHAEL L. CARLEBACH

See also Brady, Mathew; Civil War Photography; Illustrated Newspapers; Photographic Technology; Yellow Journalism

Further Reading

Carlebach, Michael L., *The Origins of Photojournalism in America,* Washington, D.C.: Smithsonian Institution Press, 1992
Sandweiss, Martha, ed., *Photography in Nineteenth-Century America,* New York: Harry N. Abrams, 1991
Welling, William, *Photography in America: The Formative Years, 1839–1900,* New York: Thomas Y. Crowell, 1978

Photojournalism in the Twentieth Century

Photographs quickly became key to a publication's success with its audience

The twentieth century opened with magazines and urban newspapers around the world racing madly for circulation and the advertising dollars circulation drew. With survival at stake, publishers learned quickly that war and photography formed a winning combination.

In New York City, William Randolph Hearst's *Journal* and Joseph Pulitzer's *World* had the resources to keep photographers in the field and to develop a support system and technology to rush the pictures into print. European papers such as the *Times* of London did likewise, as did illustrated magazines such as *Collier's* and the *Illustrated London News.*

The Boer War and the Russo-Japanese War were heavily covered. Photographer James H. "Jimmy" Hare became such a fixture that it was said a war was not official without him. War showed that news photography and circulation grew together; agencies that commissioned pictures for commercial sale, especially as stereographs, were active in wartime. The large market for the latter, right through World War I, indicates an interest in pictures even Hearst and Pulitzer did not completely satisfy.

There were dramatic images at home as well. Widely remembered are Arthur Genthe's picture of San Francisco after the earthquake of 1906 and the ubiquitous Jimmy Hare's picture of a dynamite explosion in New Jersey in 1911. Another is of a Wright brothers flight, taken by a U.S. Coast Guardsman in 1903. Also at home, Lewis Hine, starting in about 1908, followed Jacob Riis in using his camera to crusade for social change. The work of these reformers became milestones, influencing later photographers.

World War I, however, produced less in print than might have been expected. Access to all fronts was tightly restricted, censorship was thorough, and technology was not up to the new types of warfare. There were few published pictures of actual combat. One exception is of an artillery bombardment on the heights of the Meuse. Some of the strongest images came from agency photographers working behind the lines, often in stereo. Most surviving action pictures also are credited to agencies such as Wide World and Underwood and Underwood.

North American newspapers changed little after the war. Numbers rose; style and content remained unsophisticated. Weegee (Arthur Fellig), whose raw images of crime and street life in New York led to a book called *Naked City,* was an icon of this era.

In Europe, however, and in a few North American magazines, photojournalism developed rapidly. Several differences were involved. In Europe and Britain, publications sought regional or national circulation and thus were less parochial. Culture encouraged sophistication. Commercial motives encouraged general topics and multiple-picture packages, and photographers confronted the limitations of early equipment by experimenting with various cameras and formats.

In North America, most newspaper photographers covered local assignments that tended to produce single, often simplistic, images. They had settled early on the Graflex camera, replaced after 1912 by the Speed Graphic. Essentially single-shot cameras, these encouraged an increasingly dated, hit-and-run approach. Equipment-based inertia was compounded by low education level and occupational status.

Europeans, who were never caught in this mentality and were often more educated, embraced change. Martin Munkacsi, Felix Man (Hans Baumann), Kurt Hutton (Kurt Hubschmann), Tim Gidal (Ignatz Gidalewitsch), and others, and later, Alfred Eisenstaedt, Henri Cartier-Bresson, and Robert Capa (Andre Friedmann), developed a candid, interpretive style. Erich Salomon, a lawyer, moved easily in diplomatic circles. The Contax, then the Leica, 35-millimeter–format rollfilm cameras, encouraged this approach. Both (like the Ermanox plate camera) could be used in poor light without flashbulbs.

In Germany, Kurt Safranski and Kurt Korf, in the Ullstein publishing house's *Berliner Illustreirte Zeitung,* explored meanings created by paired or grouped pictures. Stefan Lorant, editor of the *Münchner Illustrierte Presse* (in Munich), experimented with layout growing from the pictures, rather than filling arbitrary designs.

Similar work followed quickly in France with *Vu,* and in England at the *London Illustrated News.* Political publications experimented widely. Art movements, including the Bauhaus, influenced photography and presentation, and there were experiments with color.

Then came Hitler. Lorant was arrested. The Ullstein brothers were Jewish, as were Gidal, Eisenstaedt, and Salomon, and a number of agents, including Simon Guttman of Dephot (Deutsches Photo Dienst), a key figure in developing multiple-picture packages.

Salomon stayed behind and died at Auschwitz. Others fled. Lorant helped found *Picture Post* in England, joined by Man and Hutton. Capa went to the Spanish Civil War. Korf, Safranski, Munkacsi, and Eisenstaedt came to the United States, where they found a magazine industry ready for them.

Korf and Eisenstaedt became involved in *Life.* Munkacsi joined Hearst. Safranski helped found Black Star Picture Agency, developing an almost purely journalistic trade. Its longtime director, Howard Chapnick, influenced two more generations. *Life,* said one of its early picture editors, Wilson Hicks, accorded photographs a place at least equal to that of words. Designers and editors quickly developed from the European model a presentation that consummated the marriage of words and pictures. The term "photojournalism" came of age. *Look,* introduced months later, emphasized features, depending more on the portrait and pictorial traditions; it developed presentations similar to that of *Life* but often more innovative.

Just as *Life* arrived, the historical section of the U.S. Farm Security Administration, under economist Roy Stryker, set out to document the country's agricultural crisis and the agency's depression-fighting work. Among the project's photographers were young Arthur Rothstein, artist Ben Shahn, art documentarian Walker Evans, newspaper photographer Marion Post (Wolcott), social documentarian Dorothea Lange, the indefatigable Russ Lee, clerk John Vachon, journalist Carl Mydans, Austrian émigré Theo Jung, Jack Delano, commercial photographer John Collier, and an unpaid apprentice, a black sleeping-car porter's son, Gordon Parks. Mydans and Parks went on to *Life;* Vachon went to *Look,* where Rothstein became director of photography. Rothstein's *Dust Storm, Cimarron County, Oklahoma,* and Lange's *Migrant Mother* became icons of the period.

World War II, for both photojournalist and reader, was an experience without precedent. Access was immediate, direct, and dangerous. Equipment now allowed work during active combat, and communication allowed publication within days (although censorship remained). Coverage was as intense as the struggle, although material shortages limited publication in Europe and England. The photographer's milieus ranged from homefront industries and training camps to the agony of the front lines. Art photographer Edward Steichen joined the Navy. The Associated Press's Joe Rosenthal took the flag raising on Iwo Jima. Freelancers Robert Capa and W. Eugene Smith showed soldiers as human beings under extreme pressure. *Life*'s Margaret Bourke-White flew in bombers. Carl Mydans was interned in the Philippines before picturing General Douglas MacArthur wading ashore.

In Korea, the pattern was similar, although most work was in 35-millimeter format. During this war, photojournalists discovered Japanese optics by Nikon and Canon. Photographers moved still closer to individual soldiers. David Douglas Duncan, a World War II Marine photographer, followed his old unit, producing haunting images of men pushed to their limit. Michael Rougier showed a single soldier, sitting at a table, stunned by his deliverance from North Korean captivity.

In the postwar period, *Life* developed the multiple-picture package into the clearly defined, often narrative, picture story, a process begun with Margaret Bourke-White's dam builders in the first edition. At first, stories were pieced together by editors. After the war, they came to be pre-visualized, and even, to a degree, scripted, with a clear beginning, middle, and end, structured on the form of a literary short story. Design emphasized the role of each picture and its relation to others. A classic example was Leonard McCombe's "The Private Life of Gwyned Filling," showing the daily life of a young career woman in New York City.

W. Eugene Smith later expanded the genre with "Spanish Village," a story much broader than the "Day in the Life of . . ." approach. Much later, in his book on mercury pollution in Minimata, Japan, Smith explored the still-broader essay form, in which pictures relate through a concept, or concern, rather than through content or narrative.

Two events in this period began to change the structure of magazine photography. One was the American Society of Magazine Photographers' effort to regularize working arrangements, business practices, rates, and especially to define publication rights. A second was the formation of Magnum, a photographers' cooperative, by David "Chim" Seymour, Henri Cartier-Bresson, George Rodger, Robert Capa, and Bill Vandivert.

Magnum photographers initiated their own assignments, and the agency was a pioneer in selling limited rights – that is, pictures were sold for a specified use allowing the photographer additional sales. Later, the speed of self-assignment and the cost-effectiveness of limited-rights sales would form the basis of the major agencies.

Newspaper photography also began to change. In 1945, Joe Costa and Burt Williams helped form the National Press Photographers Association (NPPA), concerned initially with access to courts and with official harassment. But the NPPA also started a magazine, educational seminars, and contests. Multiple and electronic flash, and the use of 35-millimeter equipment, pioneered at the *Milwaukee (Wisconsin) Journal,* the *Denver (Colorado) Post,* and the *Minneapolis (Minnesota) Tribune,* among others, were shown through NPPA activities, as were routine assignments composed for explanatory value and interest.

In Charlotte, North Carolina, photographers applied interchangeable lenses to a pictorial approach. Rich Clarkson and his staff, in Topeka, Kansas, refined these techniques emphasizing meaning. Papers in Louisville, Kentucky, and Wilmington, Delaware, were leaders in expanding this approach. Graduates of university programs, including one started in 1947 by Cliff Edom at the University of Missouri, entered newsrooms in significant numbers.

In the early 1960s, the last Speed Graphics retired, replaced by the 35-millimeter, single-lens reflex Nikon F camera and the lenses it made practical. Gradually, offset printing improved reproduction, encouraging color. North American newspaper photojournalism came of age.

The civil rights movement, the space program, and the war in Vietnam formed a period of transition: for the great North American magazines, the last big stories; for television, a coming of age. During the civil rights movement, photojournalists, including Flip Shulke, Declan Hahn, and Charlie Moore (a southerner still using a Speed Graphic) produced dramatic images daily, adding momentum and drawing recruits.

In Vietnam, access was essentially free. Publication could come within hours. Interest was high, and there was little censorship. Equipment worked well, and the results were stunning. Eddie Adams pictured the summary execution of a prisoner. Nick Ut photographed children in the midst of an accidental napalm attack. At home, John Filo's picture of a young woman screaming over the body of a student killed in Ohio remains a devastating image for viewers not even born when it was taken.

Then it was over. *Look* died in 1971, *Life* a year later. Magazine photojournalism changed radically. News photos at the end of the twentieth century came largely through agencies, mostly French-based, including Gamma, Sipa, Sigma, and Contact Press Images as well as Magnum and Black Star. Photographers became freelances; most work was self-assigned. Even *National Geographic* eventually contracted most work. Major documentary photojournalists, including Eugene Richards and Selbastio Selgado, turned to books. European magazines however, including Germany's *Stern* and France's *Paris Match,* remained major markets.

Several special-interest publications developed photojournalistic reputations, including *Smithsonian* (founded by former *Life* editor Edward K. Thompson). Nevertheless, the locus of news and documentary photojournalism in North America moved to newspapers and television. Even newspapers, however, reduced the quantity of documentary work, emphasizing instead illustration and style. Television also dropped some documentary work.

As the century came to an end, photojournalism was engaged in change potentially as radical as that of the 1930s and 1950s. Digital imaging, at acceptable quality, became common. Such pictures could be computer processed in color, transmitted in a minute or two, and inserted electronically in a page (although film remained common). Digital images, however, were open to invisible manipulation, and published abuses challenged credibility. Digital imaging did relatively conventional things faster and cheaper, but previous changes in technology had ultimately changed the field. Major shifts in style and content would perhaps be as close as the twenty-first century.

JOHN C. PETERSON

See also Black Star Picture Agency; Documentary Photography; Magazine Illustrations; Newspaper Technology; Photographic Technology; Pictorial Magazines; War Photography

Further Reading

Cookman, Claude, *A Voice Is Born: The Founding and Early Years of the National Press Photographers Association Under the Leadership of Joseph Costa,* Durham, North Carolina: National Press Photographers Association, 1985
Edey, Maitland, *Great Photographic Essays from 'Life',* Boston: New York Graphic Society, 1978
Faber, John, *Great News Photos and the Stories Behind Them,* 2nd ed., New York: Dover, 1978
Fulton, Marianne, ed., *Eyes of Time: Photojournalism in America,* Boston: Little, Brown, 1988
Gidal, Tim, *Modern Photojournalism: Origin and Evolution, 1910–1933,* New York: Macmillan, 1973
Hurley, F. Jack, *Portrait of a Decade: Roy Stryker and the Development of Documentary Photography in the Thirties,* New York: Da Capo, 1977
Schuneman, R. Smith, ed., *Photographic Communication: Principles, Problems and Challenges of Photojournalism,* New York: Hastings House, 1972; London: Focal, 1972
Szarkowski, John, ed., *From the Picture Press,* New York: Museum of Modern Art, 1973

Other Photography Entries: Advertising
Photography; Black Star Picture Agency; Brady, Mathew; Cameras in the Courtroom; Civil War Photography; Documentary Photography; Illustrated Newspapers; Magazine Illustrations; Photo Opportunities; Pictorial Magazines; Riis, Jacob A.; Tabloids; War Photography

Photo Opportunities

Events staged primarily to produce pictures for the media

Happenings that the media want to visualize describes a photo opportunity. Some occasions occur naturally because of the substance of the activity to be photographed, for example, athletic contests, disasters, artistic performances, combat. Other events need to be created. Creating such events, "photo opps," is an important publicity tactic.

Since the development of photography in 1839, photos have gained in value to the media. Photojournalism, evolving as the technology of taking, reproducing, and distributing pictures improved, became a news art in its own right around the turn of the twentieth century with the development of halftones, small and portable cameras, and gelatin-based roll film. *Life* magazine, started in 1937 by Henry Luce, increased the importance of photography in the mass media.

Behavioral science research has demonstrated the importance of connecting visuals with stories. More people see photographs in newspapers and magazines than read articles with no visual accompaniment. In addition, people perceive articles with photographs as more important than articles with written words alone. Photos can expand the emotional impact of the basic message, clarify the message, and increase audience interest in the substance of the message.

Television news builds its content around visualization. The publicist, then, seeks to create photo opportunities for clients on the dual assumptions that a "good" picture will catch the eye of the reader or viewer and that a story will more likely be attended to if complemented with a picture.

Happenings that show a limited number of people engaged in spontaneous action that attract human interest constitute the criteria for assessing the quality of photo opportunities.

DAN PYLE MILLAR

See also Media Events

Further Reading

Chapnick, Howard, *Truth Needs No Ally: Inside Photojournalism,* Columbia: University of Missouri Press, 1994
Cutlip, Scott M., Allen H. Center, and Glen M. Broom, *Effective Public Relations,* 7th ed., Englewood Cliffs, New Jersey: Prentice-Hall, 1994; London: Prentice-Hall International, 1994
Yale, David R., *The Publicity Handbook,* Lincolnwood, Illinois: NTC Business, 1995

Pictorial Magazines

Using pictures as a primary attention getter

While conventional journalism history dates the advent of the pictorial magazine to Henry Luce's founding of *Life* in 1936, earlier publishers had experimented with the format. From 1903 to 1917, Alfred Stieglitz's *Camera Work* showcased artistic photography as well as photographs of artwork. During the same time period, the new *National Geographic* became the first magazine to publish a photo-essay (11 pages of photographs of Lhasa, Tibet's "forbidden city," in January 1905) and to include color photography (1913). In 1914, the *New York Times* launched *Mid-Week Pictorial*, a photo-magazine supplement it issued for two decades. During the 1920s, fashion magazines such as *Vogue* and *Harper's Bazaar* thrived largely because of their sophisticated photography, and advertisers, especially carmakers, increasingly used photography in their print ads. Meanwhile, pictorial magazines were flourishing in Germany and Russia.

When the weekly *Life* first appeared on November 19, 1936, all 250,000 newsstand copies sold out in one day. In the magazine's first year, its circulation rose above a million; by the end of its third decade, it peaked at 7 million. During World War II, *Life* published Margaret Bourke-White's photographs of concentration-camp prisoners, Robert Capa's blurry action shot of the June 1944 Normandy invasion, Joe Rosenthal's portrait of the U.S. flagraising at Iwo Jima in February 1945, and Alfred Eisenstaedt's snapshot of sailors celebrating in New York six months later on V-J Day. Other classic *Life* photos were Thomas McAvoy's 1939 portrait of Marian Anderson singing at the Lincoln Memorial, the magazine's exclusive reproduction of frames from the Zapruder film of the 1963 assassination of President John F. Kennedy, and graphic photos of the Vietnam War by Larry Burrows, who was killed in the conflict. The magazine's photographers told ordinary stories as well, such as Gene Smith's 1948 photo essay on the workday of a country doctor and a 1954 chronicle of life in three Mormon towns by Dorothea Lange and Ansel Adams. The last weekly issue of *Life* was dated December 29, 1972. The magazine was revived as a monthly in October 1978, although with a much smaller circulation (1.5 million in 1995).

Look, founded by Gardner ("Mike") Cowles, appeared in February 1937, only three months after the first *Life*, and began as a monthly but went biweekly in its first year. Like its rival, *Look* covered presidents, royalty, celebrities, wars, and lifestyle trends. Its greatest era was the 1960s, when it surpassed *Life*'s circulation of 7 million, thanks to highlights such as Stanley Tretick's informal photos of the Kennedy clan, John Vachon's chronicle of poverty in the United States, and Richard Avedon's now-famous photos of the Beatles. The magazine folded with its October 19, 1971, issue, although it was briefly revived in 1979 (February through August) by French publisher Daniel Filipacchi.

The parallel lives of *Life* and *Look* reflect the phenomena that caused their rise and fall. Their circulations soared in the early 1940s, when the U.S. public wanted photos of the war in Europe, and continued to rise during the affluent, family-oriented 1950s, when readers wanted lifestyle photo features. Together they spawned dozens of imitators with titles such as *Click*, *See*, *Pic*, *Focus*, *Picture*, and *Peek*. Focusing mainly on celebrities, sex, and other sensational subjects (similar to the fare of later tabloid newspapers), most of these periodicals sold fewer than 500,000 copies a month, although the circulations of *Click* and *See* surpassed a million each. Television gave the pictorial magazines stiff competition, but readers did not turn away from *Life* and *Look* until there was a fairly wide variety of color television programming. The magazines were dealt a more significant blow in the late 1960s, when many national advertisers chose television over popular magazines as their primary means of reaching a general interest audience.

The U.S. pictorial magazines that thrived in the middle decades of the twentieth century had several long-term effects on the magazine field. They elevated the status of photographers and designers within the business. Their success led to more frequent use of journalistic and artistic photography by text-driven magazines, from the newsweeklies *Time* and *Newsweek* to lifestyle magazines such as *Esquire*, *Vanity Fair*, and *Rolling Stone*. In the latter publications, photographers including Diane Arbus, Annie Leibovitz, Jill Krementz, and Mary Ellen Mark continued the innovative pictorial traditions begun by the *Life* and *Look* photographers in the 1930s. Finally, travel magazines – a market expanded by the Baby Boomer generation's emphasis on family activities – took their editorial and design cues from pictorial magazines, as did later fan magazines, notably the hugely popular *People*, founded by Time, Inc., in 1974.

CAROLYN KITCH

See also Magazine Illustrations; Magazines in the Twentieth Century; Photojournalism in the Twentieth Century

Further Reading

Abramson, Howard S., *'National Geographic': Behind America's Lens on the World*, New York: Crown, 1987

Janello, Amy, and Brennon Jones, *The American Magazine*, New York: Harry N. Abrams, 1991

Owen, William, *Modern Magazine Design*, New York: Rizzoli, 1991

Rosten, Leo, ed., *The 'Look' Book*, New York: Harry N. Abrams, 1975

Wainwright, Loudon, *The Great American Magazine: An Inside History of 'Life'*, New York: Knopf, 1986

Pinchot, Gifford, and Public Relations

Used public relations to promote U.S. executive branch conservation policy

Gifford Pinchot, forester and Progressive Era politician, was among the first twentieth-century government officials to apply the emerging techniques of public relations to executive branch policy making. As chief of the U.S. Forest Service from 1898 to 1910, Pinchot created what is believed to be the first official federal press bureau. His success at publicizing government conservation of natural resources encouraged other federal experiments in managing the news prior to World War I.

Prior to the late nineteenth century, few federal agencies employed publicists or had regular contact with the press. The Department of Agriculture, the largest disseminator of government information after the Civil War, communicated with its publics primarily through Government Printing Office publications such as the popular *Agriculture Yearbook*, whose preparation and distribution was overseen closely by Congress.

Pinchot, appointed to be chief of the Department of

Agriculture's tiny Division of Forestry in 1898, was, like many progressive reformers, fascinated with the notion of influencing public opinion through the growing mass media of daily newspapers and national magazines. Besides official publications, he assigned his agency's staff to prepare "press bulletins" that might produce what Pinchot regarded as free publicity from editors. Between 1898 and 1910, the agency published 10.8 million copies of advisories, pamphlets, bulletins, and reports promoting Pinchot's vision of scientific forestry and sent them to a mailing list that grew to 750,000 names, including thousands of editors.

Pinchot's publicity activities expanded dramatically after the inauguration of President Theodore Roosevelt in 1901. The two agreed not only on the importance of government conservation of natural resources but also on the need for supportive publicity. Pinchot helped to publicize the 1907–8 White House campaign for conservation, one of the administration's major legacies. Pinchot helped stage the campaign's key publicity events: a presidential cruise down the Mississippi River on a steamboat in 1907 and the White House Conference on Natural Resources in 1908.

Pinchot's successes at publicity were watched closely by other federal officials, including disapproving members of Congress. Beginning in 1906, Pinchot and the Forest Service press bureau were the subject of annual budget attacks and unfriendly amendments to curb their activities. Congressional criticism of agency publicity continued after Pinchot's firing by President William Howard Taft in 1910, after the forester admitted that his staff helped to prepare muckraking stories that attacked a bureaucratic rival, Secretary of Interior Richard Ballinger.

By 1912, however, publicity agents had been hired by dozens of other federal agencies, including the Department of State and the Post Office. In 1913, in a futile attempt to block the spread of executive branch publicity, Congress banned the hiring of any "publicity expert" without congressional approval. The primary effect, however, was to encourage the use of disguised job titles for government publicists.

STEPHEN PONDER

See also Public Relations; Roosevelt, Theodore, and the Press

Further Reading

McGeary, M. Nelson, *Gifford Pinchot: Forester-Politician,* Princeton, New Jersey: Princeton University Press, 1960

Penick, James, Jr., *Progressive Politics and Conservation: The Ballinger-Pinchot Affair,* Chicago: University of Chicago Press, 1968

Pinkett, Harold T., *Gifford Pinchot: Private and Public Forester,* Urbana: University of Illinois Press, 1970

Ponder, Stephen, "Executive Publicity and Congressional Resistance, 1905–1913: Congress and the Roosevelt Administration's PR Men," *Congress and the Presidency* 13 (1986)

_____, "Gifford Pinchot: Press Agent for Forestry," *Journal of Forest History* 31 (1987)

Political Advertising

Media use to promote candidates long-standing; television ads date to 1952

Contemporary political advertising in the United States has its roots in the slogans, pamphlets, and songs of the earliest campaigns, which generated excitement for the candidate's campaign and summarized the nature of the campaign. Using media to advertise a candidate's accomplishments became necessary as early newspapers moved away from blatant partisanship toward neutral reporting of the political environment and as candidates needed to control some of the campaign communication about their candidacy.

The growth of the influence of political advertising in campaigns really began when the first televised broadcasts were used in a presidential campaign. In 1952, both presidential candidates used political ads to relay their messages to the public. Dwight Eisenhower's campaign ads are perhaps remembered more distinctly because their short, to-the-point style foreshadowed future political ads. The ads, dubbed "Eisenhower Answers America," featured a direct question from an "average citizen" and an answer from Eisenhower – speaking into the camera directly to the U.S. public.

After that election, televised political advertising became a part of every presidential campaign. Format and style changed through the next forty years, but presidential campaigns always included a strategy for political advertising.

Advertising plays several key roles in the country's political campaigns, including establishing a candidate's name identification among the public. This function, in the late twentieth century, became more important for candidates in lower-level elections where their names are less familiar. Political advertising also is able to define or redefine a candidate's personal image. If the news media are covering the candidate in an unflattering way, political advertis-

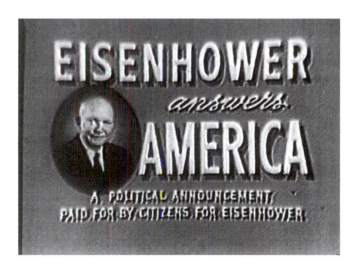

"Eisenhower Answers America," produced in 1952, was the earliest recorded television promotion for a presidential candidate.
(Political Communication Center/University of Oklahoma)

ing can be used to show a different side of the candidate's personality.

Political advertising also can provide a forum for discussion of campaign issues, although most critics argue that issues cannot be discussed sufficiently in the typical 30- or 60-second broadcast ad. Political advertising can, however, allow for the surfacing and recognition of issues not being addressed in mainstream media. Voters sometimes have learned more about issues from political advertising during a campaign than from media coverage. Political advertising also can tie a candidate to specific demographic groups, reinforce voters' decisions to vote for a particular candidate, stimulate participation in a campaign, and attack the opposition.

Political advertising, because it is connected strongly to the context of any political campaign, reflects the political climate and issues current in the election. Ads also allow the candidate to address the changing needs of the campaign. Candidates initially may use ads to give biographical information about themselves and their campaigns. Later, ads may present specific issue positions or provide negative information. Final ads may summarize the candidate's philosophy or reason why he or she is running for office.

Early televised political ads used fairly straight-forward film techniques – showing the candidate going about daily activities or talking directly to the camera. As knowledge about the powers of production components of television were understood more clearly, ads began to use a variety of techniques to get the candidate's message across. Ads featuring a biography of the candidate were used in longer formats (four minutes) in the 1960s, although later presidential candidates featured their biographies in 30- or 60-second formats. All campaigns also have included introspection formats – ads that generally feature the candidate directly addressing the viewing audience about personal policy interests, stands, or philosophies. Other ad formats include testimonials from the average person on the street or from celebrities and political figures; question-and-answer sessions between journalists (i.e., press conferences) or between average citizens and the candidates; and animation, photographs, newspaper headlines, or fast-paced montage.

One highly popular format is the issue-dramatization ad. An issue-dramatization ad borrows techniques from product advertising and features a story or a narrative about some issue. The candidate may never appear in the ad, but the message and demonstration of the issue provide a powerful format, particularly for negative advertising. Like product ads that do not feature the aspects of the product for the audience, issue dramatization political ads set a mood or provide a framework within which the audience is to judge the issue.

Negative advertising is perhaps the most controversial type of political advertising because of the belief that it dominates advertising in national political campaigns and that it does have an impact on voters' attitudes and beliefs. The growth in political action committees or third parties supporting independent negative ads led to growing concern about mudslinging in campaigns by these interest groups.

Because negative advertising has been shown to be effective, all campaigns in the 1990s included plans for a nega-

The "Daisy Girl" political advertisement created an uneasy feeling among viewers and hurt Barry Goldwater's presidential campaign of 1964.
(Museum of Broadcast Communications)

tive advertising strategy. Although negative advertising in presidential campaigns increased from 1952 to the 1970s, the amount of televised negative advertising in presidential campaigns leveled off to about one-third of total ads after the 1980 presidential campaign.

Negative advertising tends to use direct and hard-hitting techniques. Fear appeals are used in negative ads, as are humor and ridicule (making fun of the opponents' shortcomings or irresponsible behavior). Other techniques used include comparing and contrasting the candidates' positions on issues, showing how the opponent has switched position on a variety of issues, and implying that the opponent is guilty of some wrongdoing because of his or her associations with other politicians or interest groups. Because of the concern about the effects of negative advertising, newspapers and broadcast news, in the late 1980s and early 1990s, began to monitor televised political advertising and critique the claims made in the ads. In addition, candidates and their consultants began to broadcast response ads to address the attacks made in the opponents' negative ads.

Political advertising is a staple of all modern elections. It is controversial because it is not regulated by truth in advertising rules and because it uses production techniques that may change a perspective through editing and special effects. Most of a presidential candidate's campaign budget in the late twentieth century was spent on campaign advertising. Political advertising is so much a part of modern elections that most candidates and their consultants work hard to coordinate their advertising strategy with all other forms of campaign communication and potential news coverage.

ANNE JOHNSTON

See also Campaign Financing Reform and the Media

Further Reading
Devlin, L. Patrick, "An Analysis of Presidential Television Commercials, 1952–1984," in *New Perspectives on*

Political Advertising, edited by Lynda Lee Kaid, Dan Nimmo, and Keith R. Sanders, Carbondale: Southern Illinois University Press, 1986

Diamond, Edwin, and Stephen Bates, *The Spot: The Rise of Political Advertising on Television*, 2nd ed., Cambridge, Massachusetts: MIT Press, 1988

Jamieson, Kathleen Hall, "The Evolution of Political Advertising in America," in *New Perspectives on Political Advertising*, edited by Lynda Lee Kaid, Dan Nimmo, and Keith R. Sanders, Carbondale: Southern Illinois University Press, 1986

Kaid, Lynda Lee, "Political Advertising in the 1992 Campaign," in *The 1992 Presidential Campaign: A Communication Perspective*, edited by Robert E. Denton, Jr., Westport, Connecticut: Praeger, 1994

_____, and Anne Johnston, "Negative Versus Positive Television Advertising in U.S. Presidential Campaigns, 1960–1988," *Journal of Communication* 41:3 (Summer 1991), pp. 53–64

Kern, Montague, *30-Second Politics: Political Advertising in the Eighties*, New York: Praeger, 1989

Trent, Judith S., and Robert V. Friedenberg, *Political Campaign Communication: Principles and Practices*, 2nd ed., New York: Praeger, 1991

Pool Journalism

Sharing gathered information with other journalists

Pool journalism had its beginnings in city courthouses during the early part of the twentieth century, when large cities were served by half a dozen or more newspapers. The newspaper reporters assigned to the courts often spent time in a pressroom, where courtroom gossip and court calendars were shared, in spite of fierce circulation competition on the newsstands and streets.

Because often several newsworthy trials would be progressing simultaneously, reporters entered pooling arrangements. The ground rules for these required that each reporter listen to testimony and gather information from the court clerk and other personnel relating to the case he had agreed to cover. All those in the pool then met back at the press room at an agreed-upon time and shared with all the other reporters in the pool the information that had been gathered. From that information, reporters wrote their own stories. It was considered unprofessional to withhold information from others in the pool. Although editors back in the newsroom often viewed the cooperation of their reporters with a pool as a sign of lazy fact gathering, reporters countered that it was impossible to be in two courtrooms listening to testimony at the same time.

Pools have been useful in covering a variety of news stories over the years. Associated Press writer Bob Thomas, for instance, recalled in his obituary of actress Lana Turner that in covering her fourth wedding to millionaire Bob Topping in 1948, he was appointed to be the pool person watching the ceremony inside a Hollywood mansion.

Pool reporting became a necessity when reporting on space launches. The launch site had extremely limited space, and yet the launches often drew representatives from hundreds of news outlets around the world.

When such events must be covered by more reporters than the space can accommodate, pools are set, as are formal and informal rules for participating in such news coverage. Pools involving network television coverage, for example, require that the same raw video be supplied to each participating network or station; each then edits the material to serve its own needs.

Pool coverage is common during election campaigns. Timothy Crouse, in his irreverent insider narrative of the press coverage of the 1972 presidential campaign, explained in a footnote how the pool coverage of the candidates worked. One or two reporters, on a rotating basis, were delegated to stay close to George McGovern or Richard Nixon during motorcades, small dinners, and fund-raising parties. Other press corps members were supplied with photocopies of the pool report, which Crouse characterized as mostly "trivia." Again, pool reporters were not supposed to put in their own stories any information not shared with the others.

Later in the campaign, when the number of political reporters increased so that they filled seven buses, the Nixon staff provided a public address system that piped an audio pool report from the car that directly followed the president. The reporter who narrated became known as the "Z-pooler" because he rode with Press Secretary Ron Ziegler.

An incident in Crouse's book also underlines the reason why members of a press corps assigned to an event should choose among themselves who will represent them as pool reporter or the selection should be made by lot, not by the press aides of the newsmaker. Marty Schram, *Newsday*'s White House correspondent who assisted in the preparation of a series investigating the shady dealings of President Nixon's friend Bebe Rebozo, afterward was excluded repeatedly by Press Secretary Ziegler from pool assignments.

Press complaints about government manipulation of pool arrangements have been most strident as they have related to military action and battle coverage. The Pentagon rules for the establishment of press pools in a combat theater resulted from recommendations of a commission chaired by retired Major General Winant Sidle in 1984 after the invasion of Grenada, when the press had been excluded completely from the invasion.

Just before the ground war phase of Operation Desert Storm, during the Persian Gulf War, began in February 1991, the U.S. Senate Governmental Affairs Committee heard testimony from journalists who objected to miscrediting of copy, delay in transmission of news, and the military pool rules that attempted to control battle information by escorting a few pool reporters and photographers to locations preselected by the officers, who then monitored conversations with the troops. One reporter who testified before the Senate committee referred to the "hostility of some senior officers toward the press." Another described the pool system as "an attempt to control and manipulate information, to sanitize and clean it up, so that the war will sound more like a choir-boys' picnic than the grungy thing that it is."

Pete Williams, assistant secretary of defense for public affairs, defended the pool system, saying,

> There is simply no way for us to open up a rapidly moving front to reporters who roam the battlefield. We believe the pool system does three things: it gets reporters out to see the action, it guarantees that Americans at home get reports from the scene of the action, and it allows the military to accommodate a reasonable number of journalists without overwhelming the units that are fighting the enemy.

The hearing record included reprints of more than 70 newspaper and magazine articles and broadcast reports that protested the media restrictions during the Gulf War. Also included were six Doonesbury cartoon strips from the week of February 25, 1991, that parodied the escorted press pools and the euphemisms from the press briefings.

ANNA R. PADDON

See also Grenada Invasion; Pack Journalism; Persian Gulf War

Further Reading

Carnes, Jeffrey J., "The Department of Defense Media Pool: Making the Media-Military Relationship Work," in *Defense Beat: The Dilemmas of Defense Coverage*, edited by Loren B. Thompson, New York: Lexington, 1991

Crouse, Timothy, *The Boys on the Bus*, New York: Ballantine, 1974

Fialka, John, *Hotel Warriors: Covering the Gulf War*, Washington, D.C.: Woodrow Wilson Center, 1992

United States Congress, Senate Committee on Governmental Affairs, *Pentagon Rules on Media Access to the Persian Gulf War: Hearing Before the Committee on Governmental Affairs, United States Senate, One Hundred Second Congress, First Session, February 20, 1991*, Washington, D.C.: U.S. Government Printing Office, 1991

Post Office and the Media

Long-standing promoter of media distribution

Defining mail classes and setting postage has influenced the operations of the newspaper, magazine, book, and advertising industries from colonial times to the present. Although the U.S. press has long extolled its independence from government, it eagerly sought postal subsidies, which shifted costs from private firms to the public, and it seized on postal regulations as weapons in intra-industry battles.

Capitalizing on their roles as information clearinghous-es, colonial postmasters launched many of the earliest American newspapers. Newspapers circulated through the colonial mails under ad hoc rules until Benjamin Franklin and William Hunter, the British-appointed postmasters general, tried to regularize service in 1758. With the colonists' revolutionary stirrings, the British authorities began censoring the mails and then dismissed Franklin as postmaster general in 1774. Newspaper publisher William Goddard filled the vacuum with a Patriot-controlled "Constitutional Post" that exchanged revolutionary news among the colonies. A year later the Continental Congress adopted Goddard's system as the new nation's official post and appointed Franklin postmaster general.

The United States expressed its first communication policy in postal laws. Despite some reservations about the social effects of a national communication system, there were few serious challenges to the notion that government properly had a role in underwriting the dissemination of public information. The original postal subsidy for newspapers attracted the strong support of both Federalists and Jeffersonian Republicans. The former expected news circulating by post to solidify a strong central government, while the latter hoped that reports of the administration's abuses mailed throughout the nation would topple the opposition. Furthermore, the generation that crafted the first postal policy recognized that the geographically and socially diverse United States would encounter difficulties sustaining national unity.

Consequently, early U.S. postal laws facilitated the widespread circulation of news. From 1792 until 1873, editors were allowed to exchange copies of their newspapers postage-free among one another; this was the most important means of gathering nonlocal news (some editors exchanged hundreds of copies a week) until the telegraph fostered the growth of wire services in the mid-nineteenth century. Congress ended the privilege in 1873. Also, the Post Office occasionally operated express services that sped political and market information to newspapers.

More important in the long run was the nearly flat rate structure for periodicals. A 1792 postal law, modified in 1794, allowed newspapers – regardless of size, weight, or advertising content – to circulate within 100 miles or anywhere in the state of publication for one cent; those mailed outside the state and beyond 100 miles paid 1.5 cents. In sharp contrast, letter postage varied according to distance and the number of sheets; the 1792 law had nine zones, with postage for a single sheet ranging from 6 to 25 cents. With only one short-lived exception, the nearly flat rate structure for periodicals remained intact until 1917.

Despite the persistence of the flat rate for periodicals, congressional debates over postal policy reflected abiding tensions between nationalism and localism. One result, a concession to those who disliked city newspapers circulating in the countryside, was the postage-free delivery of weekly newspapers within the county of publication. Congress eventually modified the in-county privilege, but it remained one of the few preferential rates in effect in the late twentieth century.

The 1870s brought a number of postal reforms. First,

Congress required that publishers pay postage at the office of mailing; previously, postmasters had tried to collect postage from recipients, but half or more of the money due the Post Office went uncollected. Second, magazines, originally assessed higher postage than newspapers, closed the gap in 1863 and were put on equal footing in 1879. The Post Office Act of March 3, 1879, marked the true beginning of modern postal policy, for it created the four mail categories still used in the late twentieth century. The act originated with experienced postal administrators, who sought to reduce advertisers' growing use of the highly subsidized rates for periodicals. To strengthen its hand, the Post Office urged Congress to redefine the primitive second-class mail category so that it would clearly exclude advertising circulars. Postal officials fine-tuned the legislation in consultation with leading newspaper and magazine publishers in a few large cities. Despite differences, newspaper and magazine interests closed ranks with one another and with postal authorities against the so-called illegitimate periodicals, publications designed primarily for advertising purposes.

Congress intended the 1879 act to subsidize informative periodicals in the second class and to relegate advertising matter to the much more expensive third class. Beyond some easily met technical requirements, second-class matter had to disseminate "information of a public character, or [be] devoted to literature, the sciences, arts, or some special industry, and hav[e] a legitimate list of subscribers." The law withheld the privileged rate from "publications designed primarily for advertising purposes, or for free circulation, or for circulation at nominal rates."

Deciding which publications were "designed primarily for advertising purposes" became a nearly impossible task since most periodicals relied heavily on advertising. Difficulties making that distinction, plus the 1885 congressional action halving the second-class rate to one cent a pound, opened the floodgates. "Second Class Matter Fiends," as one official called them, devised ingenious schemes to pass all manner of printed material at the lowest rate. Cheap postage and rural free delivery, which opened the countryside to national publications, abetted an explosion in mass circulation magazines. Advertising-filled periodicals began blanketing the nation; second-class mailings grew 20 times faster than population in the four decades after 1880.

To protect the integrity of the second class, postal officials began scrutinizing publishers who applied for mailing permits. By 1902, publishers had to answer a series of 19 questions before they could mail at the most-favored rate. Publishers had to provide details about ownership, how their other businesses related to the publication, advertising practices, and subscription terms – a rather extensive inquiry by federal officials into the conduct of private enterprises. The 1912 Newspaper Publicity Act wrote some of these key administrative rules into a law that was upheld by the Supreme Court.

Second-class mail reached 1 billion pounds a year in 1913, enough to fill 26,440 railway cars, about double the volume of 10 years earlier. The department estimated that this represented 5 billion newspapers and magazines, or ap-

proximately 50 copies for each man, woman, and child in the country. The 28,707 publications entitled to second-class rates were mailed from 11,091 post offices, with 10 cities accounting for slightly more than half by weight.

Nearly continuous investigations by Congress and commissions after 1900 culminated in a 1917 law that structured second-class rates in the manner still followed at the end of the century. Rates on the advertising portions of periodicals rose as the distance mailed increased; a publication's reading matter, however, paid a flat rate. This creative solution to the long-running second-class rate controversy protected the nationwide dissemination of reading material while charging more to cover the transportation costs of carrying advertising.

With a rate schedule favoring newspapers over other printed matter, some publishers styled books as periodicals. In the 1840s and 1870s, publishers of cheap paper-covered books took advantage of the nebulous definition of "periodicals" to send much of their output through the mail. This practice continued until 1904, when the Supreme Court affirmed the Post Office's authority to restrict such practices. Seizing on an obscure, temporary law in 1938, President Franklin D. Roosevelt finally created a book rate by presidential order. In 1942, Congress added the book rate to the body of postal laws.

Advertising was at the heart of most twentieth-century battles over postal rates. Various segments of the media – notably newspapers, magazines, and direct mail marketers – maneuvered to structure postal rates to gain advantages as channels for advertising. The most heated dispute pitted newspapers against "junk mail," a term the press coined in the early 1950s to disparage a competitor for local retail advertising.

Ironically, the very policies and practices that put the government in the business of distributing publications also positioned the Post Office to become the principal federal censor of printed material in U.S. history. Some censorship was politically motivated, as when Federalist (1790s) and then Jacksonian (1830s–1840s) postmasters meddled with the newspaper mail of their partisan opponents. Southern postmasters destroyed, or allowed mobs to destroy, abolitionist mail sent from the north (1830s–1850s). Various groups interested in enforcing moral codes have used postal laws to limit the availability of erotic material, provocative literature, and even information about birth control. The most concerted postal censorship came before and during World War I, when the Post Office suppressed the supposedly subversive publications of foreign-language groups, Socialists, anarchists, pacifists, and labor unions. The Post Office was used less vigorously to silence radical publications during World War II and the Cold War.

The passage of the Postal Reorganization Act in 1970 altered the postal system's relation to the media. The act removed rate-making control from Congress and vested it in a new quasi-corporate agency, the U.S. Postal Service, and an independent regulatory body, the Postal Rate Commission. The Act tried to rectify the shortcomings of legislative rate making by elevating economic considerations over political lobbying. The act also phased out the below-cost rates enjoyed by the press since 1792 for all except in-county deliveries and the publications of nonprofit organizations.

RICHARD B. KIELBOWICZ

See also Espionage and Sedition Acts; Exchanges; Newspapers in the Eighteenth Century; World War I

Further Reading

Fowler, Dorothy G., *Unmailable: Congress and the Post Office,* Athens: University of Georgia Press, 1977

Fuller, Wayne E., *The American Mail: Enlarger of the Common Life,* Chicago: University of Chicago Press, 1972; London: University of Chicago Press, 1980

Kielbowicz, Richard B., "Mere Merchandise or Vessels of Culture?: Books in the Mail, 1792–1942," *Papers of the Bibliographical Society of America* 82 (1988)

_____, *News in the Mail: The Press, Post Office, and Public Information, 1700–1860s,* New York: Greenwood, 1989

_____, "Origins of the Junk Mail Controversy: A Media Battle over Advertising and Postal Policy," *Journal of Policy History* 5 (1993)

_____, "Origins of the Second-Class Mail Category and the Business of Policymaking, 1863–1879," *Journalism Monographs* 96 (April 1986)

_____, "Postal Subsidies for the Press and the Business of Mass Culture, 1880–1920," *Business History Review* 64 (1990)

Precision Journalism

Using social science research methods to gather and report the news

"Precision journalism" is a term given to the use of social science research methods in the gathering and reporting of news. Thought to have originated in 1971, the term denotes a journalistic approach explored at least as early as the 1930s but rarely practiced until the late 1960s. It was one dimension of the "new journalism" that appeared in many newspapers and magazines during that decade. U.S. journalist and educator Philip Meyer was the principal practitioner, theorist, and crusader associated with precision journalism, although other scholars and journalists, as well as journalism schools, were consistent adherents early on to what was later described as a journalistic movement.

For much of the twentieth century, scientific surveys, field experiments, and content analyses remained the realm of academics. Not to be confused with conventional opinion polls, there were occasional attempts to correlate demographic trends with news developments, and some journalistic outlets, notably the *Minneapolis (Minnesota) Tribune,* did try polling the public at election time. But *Fortune* magazine, with its surveys that began in 1935, was one of the few news organizations to embrace such efforts with a semi-scientific rigor. *Fortune,* a business publication, was more attuned than traditional media to the advanced marketing techniques that were to grow particularly popular during the post–World War II consumer boom.

As the civil rights movement, the Vietnam War, and other developments highlighted and heightened complex social conflicts, some journalists found conventional news sources and reporting practices unsatisfactory. These individuals looked to the kind of careful statistical gauges that *Fortune* had used. New technological tools – especially the computer – along with a growing awareness of social science fueled the curiosity of these journalists.

One of them was Meyer, an editor-reporter in the Knight newspaper group (later Knight-Ridder). Having absorbed the fundamental principles of social science research as a Nieman Fellow at Harvard in 1966–67, Meyer employed precision reporting in the preparation of a landmark 1967 survey for the *Detroit (Michigan) Free Press.* Through deliberate sampling and a painstakingly designed, carefully evaluated process of interviews, he and his colleagues probed the causes of the riots that plagued Detroit that summer. After just three weeks, Meyer's team was able to present an insightful series of articles that helped set a precedent for the systematic use of quantitative measures by journalists.

In 1973, Meyer's book, *Precision Journalism,* was published. Together with a number of articles he wrote and speeches he gave, as well as personal mentoring that he provided, the book helped spread the gospel of the newfound approach. Improvements in the speed and capability of computers provided the critical impetus. By the time Meyer's *The New Precision Journalism* was published in 1991, the methods he advocated had become accepted to the extent that the adjective "precision" was often discarded; many writers and editors simply saw quasi-scientific deliberateness as a given in any thorough investigative report – as an integral part of modern journalism. Concrete data from government and court records could be collected and often easily cross-referenced, and public opinion could be analyzed through sophisticated means. Increasingly, major newspapers, magazines, and television networks – even some local papers and stations – conducted their own polls not just around elections but quite routinely. Pulitzer Prizes were awarded to journalists who used survey research and content analyses to test their hypotheses and reach important conclusions about public issues.

Practices that had preceded Meyer and the term "precision journalism" flourished in the 1980s in step with computers and rapid data transmission. Many journalists who adhered to precision journalism came to call their form of research computer assisted reporting, or CAR.

Meyer, who became a professor at the University of North Carolina at Chapel Hill, remained closely identified with a movement whose other key practitioners have included journalists-turned-pollsters like I.A. "Bud" Lewis of the *Los Angeles Times,* Rich Morin of the *Washington (D.C.) Post,* and James Norman of *USA Today.* Indeed, the latter paper's successful espousal of mass polling and quantitative news was one indication of how dramatically the public's appetite for statistical information had both grown with, and prodded, its supply. More than ever before, consumers of news expected hard numbers – scientifically obtained, thoughtfully interpreted, and reasonably comprehensible. In its true form, precision journalism meets those demands.

EVERETTE E. DENNIS

See also New Journalism (1960s–1970s); Public Opinion Polls

Further Reading

Cranberg, Lawrence, "Plea for Recognition of Scientific Character of Journalism," *Journalism Educator* 44 (Winter 1989)

Demers, David P., and Suzanne Nichols, *Precision Journalism: A Practical Guide,* Newbury Park, California: Sage, 1987

Dennis, Everette E., ed., *The Magic Writing Machine: Student Probes of the New Journalism,* Eugene: University of Oregon School of Journalism, 1971

Hage, George S., et al., *New Strategies for Public Affairs Reporting: Investigation, Interpretation, and Research,* Englewood Cliffs, New Jersey: Prentice-Hall, 1976

Meyer, Philip, *The New Precision Journalism,* Bloomington: Indiana University Press, 1991

_____, *Precision Journalism: A Reporter's Introduction to Social Science Methods,* 2nd ed., Bloomington: Indiana University Press, 1979

Presidential Debates

Regular election debates date from 1976

Although U.S. voters have come to expect a televised presidential debate between at least two candidates during a campaign, there is no guarantee that such an event will take place. Indeed, following the John Kennedy and Richard Nixon debate in 1960, 16 years elapsed without a presidential debate. It was not until 1976, when Gerald Ford and Jimmy Carter debated, that the trend toward regular presidential debates began. After that debate, presidential candidates agreed to such matches in every election to the end of the century. While the U.S. Congress considered several bills that would require that any candidate who accepts federal funds for the financing of his or her campaign agree to debate the other candidates, there was, in the late 1990s, no law that required presidential hopefuls to compete in such a contest.

The model for modern presidential debates was actually senatorial in origin – the 1858 debates between Abraham Lincoln and Stephen A. Douglas in a contest for an Illinois U.S. Senate seat. The two candidates participated in seven three-hour debates in seven congressional districts. Lincoln and Douglas took turns beginning each debate with a one-hour speech. That speech was followed by a 90-minute speech by the opponent. The first speaker was then allowed 30 minutes to rebut his opponent's arguments.

Modern presidential debates are agreed to by the candidates only after considerable negotiation regarding the particulars of the debate's format. Candidates have attempted to control such issues as who would be allowed to ask debate questions, when and where the debates would occur, whether third-party candidates would be included, and whether candidates could use notes and other props. Critics of modern debates say that by the time each political camp has negotiated its conditions, the U.S. public views a debate that is so orchestrated that it provides little concrete information. It fails, in other words, to sufficiently educate the voter about the issues or the candidates on the ballot. Indeed, Casper Weinberger wrote in 1991 that the preceding three presidential debates "were not debates. They were press conferences conducted by reporters acceptable to both sides, complete with packed studio audiences ready to cheer, sneer or otherwise influence the much wider, unseen national audience."

Negotiations over debate format became so problematic that the League of Women Voters, which had sponsored presidential debates in 1976, 1980, and 1984, refused to continue its support for the 1988 debate between George Bush and Michael Dukakis. The league objected to the attempt by the candidates to control which journalists could ask questions of the candidates or even be invited as panelists. The league also objected to the refusal on the part of some candidates to debate presidential contenders from third parties. Sponsorship of the debates fell to the bipartisan Commission on Presidential Debates in 1985.

The role of journalists in these debates is complex. Journalists are interested in many issues involved in the coverage of the debates, all of which are centered on First Amendment guarantees of speech and press. Two of these concerns involve journalist access to the candidates.

In the negotiations over debate format, candidates –

John F. Kennedy, standing left, and Richard M. Nixon square off in the first televised debates between presidential nominees.

(Museum of Broadcast Communications)

who, of course, want to show themselves in the best light – object to showing an audience member reacting to a candidate's comment. Journalists, however, believe that voter reaction to the debate is newsworthy. Such reaction shots were not allowed in the 1976 debate because President Ford's special counsel, Michael Raoul-Duval, objected. Raoul-Duval argued that such a practice would distract the voters' attention from the real election issues.

Journalists also are concerned with the panelist selection practices of the candidates. Reporters object to the control that candidates have over which journalists are given permission to present questions to the candidates. Such authority on the part of the candidates means that the press is restrained in its attempt to provide the public with thorough campaign coverage.

The questions of who should sponsor presidential debates and what format the debates should take remained unanswered at century's end. Those who agitate for congressional action on the subject argued that legislation could demand that debates be educational and informative, rather than calculated to ensure the election of the candidates. They also argued that third-party candidates should be allowed to participate so that voters would be exposed to new ideas and issues.

ROBIN GALLAGHER

See also Kennedy, John F., and the Media; Nixon, Richard M., and the Media

Further Reading
Kraus, Sidney, ed., *The Great Debates: Background, Perspective, Effects,* Bloomington: Indiana University Press, 1962
_____, *Televised Presidential Debates and Public Policy,* Hillsdale, New Jersey: Lawrence Erlbaum, 1988
Reilly, Thomas W., "Lincoln-Douglas Debates of 1858 Forced New Role on the Press," *Journalism Quarterly* 56 (Winter 1979)
Spotts, Susan, "The Presidential Debates Act of 1992," *Harvard Journal on Legislation* 29 (Summer 1992), p. 80
Weinberger, Caspar, "Presidential Debates – A Novel 1858-Type Proposal," *Forbes* 148 (October 14, 1991), p. 35

Presidential News Conferences

Meetings between president and the press a twentiethth-century phenomenon

Although an adversarial relationship between presidents of the United States and journalists has existed since the nation's beginnings, its most public expression, the presidential news conference, was a twentieth-century development. Theodore Roosevelt most often is credited with being its originator. The first press conferences were both informal and tightly regulated monologues. Roosevelt's comments

were off the record, a precedent that would stand for half a century. Reporters thought to be antagonistic toward the administration were barred from the sessions. Presidential news conferences nearly died with Roosevelt's successor, William Howard Taft, who thought they were of little value.

Woodrow Wilson launched formal and regularly scheduled press conferences. Unlike Roosevelt, Wilson welcomed questions from reporters and did not restrict attendance at these sessions. As relations between the president and reporters deteriorated, however, the number of press conferences dwindled to only three in Wilson's second term.

By reviving Wilson's format, President Warren Harding, an ex-newspaperman, is credited with institutionalizing the presidential press conference. "White House spokesman," a term coined to avoid direct attribution to the president, was first used. But, like his predecessor, Harding withdrew as relations with reporters soured – in part owing to reporting on the Teapot Dome scandal. After one year in office, Harding required reporters to submit questions in writing.

Over the next quarter century, there were minor modifications in the structure of the presidential press conference. Franklin Roosevelt dropped the written-question requirement but kept the sessions off the record. He occasionally, however, would distribute statements for direct attribution. Roosevelt was also more accessible than his predecessors, meeting with reporters a record 992 times. Political scientist Blaire Atherton French wrote that Roosevelt "made his press conferences successful occasions for influencing the news, educating the public and reporters, and persuading public opinion."

The end of World War II brought major changes in the conduct of presidential press conferences. As the presidency became a focal point of world power, the number of reporters covering the White House rose sharply. To handle these increased numbers, Harry Truman moved press conferences to the Indian Treaty Room in the Executive Office Building. This necessitated a more formal structure in which reporters, when recognized, stood up and identified themselves. Acknowledging the electronic media's growing influence, Truman occasionally released recorded audio excerpts from his conferences. Dwight Eisenhower permitted delayed broadcast of radio and television recordings and was first to permit direct attribution. John Kennedy took the final step toward the modern press conference by permitting live broadcasts. Eventually, in deference to television, these meetings with reporters were renamed "news conferences."

Although the cumulative effect of these changes was greater access to the president, they also elevated the power and prestige of the White House. Presidents were given a national platform to promote their unfiltered views to the electorate. This proved to be a double-edged sword. For Lyndon Johnson, these sessions highlighted a growing concern over his conduct of the Vietnam War. The resulting credibility gap ultimately led to Johnson's withdrawal from the 1968 presidential race.

Richard Nixon's news conferences were the most confrontational of any president's. As the Watergate scandal widened, his news conferences became an arena for verbal combat. A prime example came March 19, 1974, less than

President Dwight D. Eisenhower's press conferences were major events in the 1950s.
(Courtesy Dwight D. Eisenhower Library)

five months before Nixon's resignation. The White House staged a session in front of an audience of 3,000 people at the National Association of Broadcasters meeting in Houston, Texas. When CBS correspondent Dan Rather was introduced to ask Nixon a question, both applause and boos welled up from the audience. Nixon asked, "Are you running for something?" Rather responded, "No sir, Mr. President. Are you?" Ironically, Gerald Ford said it was the tone of the questioning during his first news conference after Nixon's resignation that convinced him of the need to pardon his predecessor.

After the turbulent Vietnam-Watergate era, the trend was for presidents to reach out to the electorate while bypassing Washington, D.C.–based correspondents. Formal news conferences became less frequent, conducted only when seen to be necessary in advancing a political agenda. Sometimes this strategy backfires, as it did on November 19, 1986, when White House aides had to issue a correction 20 minutes after a news conference designed to blunt criticism of the Iran-contra affair. Ronald Reagan had incorrectly told reporters that an unidentified third country (Israel) had not been involved in unauthorized weapons transfers. Reagan's performance fueled criticism that he was out of touch with his own administration.

DAVID W. GUTH

See also Credibility Gap; Eisenhower, Dwight D., and the Media; Harding, Warren G., and the Press; Johnson, Lyndon B., and the Media; Kennedy, John F., and the Media; Nixon, Richard M., and the Media; Reagan, Ronald, and the Media; Roosevelt, Franklin D., and the Media; Roosevelt, Theodore, and the Press; Truman, Harry S., and the Media; Watergate Scandal; Wilson, Woodrow, and the Press

Further Reading

Cannon, Lou, *President Reagan: The Role of a Lifetime*, New York: Simon & Schuster, 1991; London: Simon & Schuster, 1992

French, Blaire Atherton, *The Presidential Press Conference: Its History and Role in the American Political System*, Washington, D.C.: University Press of America, 1982

Rather, Dan, with Mickey Herskowitz, *The Camera Never Blinks: Adventures of a TV Journalist*, New York: Ballantine, 1977

Smith, Carolyn D., *Presidential Press Conferences: A Critical Approach*, New York: Praeger, 1990

Presidential Press Secretaries

Increasing need to influence public opinion led to creation of position

The creation of the position of presidential press secretary was an indicator of fundamental changes in the relationship between presidents and the news media in the late nineteenth and twentieth centuries. As the president's ability to govern became tied to appealing for public support through the expanding media of mass communications, making news came to depend on the president's interactions with Washington, D.C., news correspondents, especially those assigned specifically to the White House.

In the late nineteenth century, when presidential contacts with the small Washington press corps were infrequent, no separate press secretary existed in the executive mansion. Presidents spoke to the press through official intermediaries, such as party elders in the cabinet or the party leadership in Congress. Or, like President Grover Cleveland, they delegated their personal dealings with journalists to their personal secretaries, then the sole professional staff position.

Interaction between the president and the press corps increased significantly in 1898, however, when William McKinley sought public support for his Spanish-American War policies. As more correspondents called at the president's office seeking information, McKinley's personal secretary, George Cortelyou, was forced to establish regular procedures for briefing the press, responding to inquiries, releasing statements, and creating working space within the executive mansion. Presidential attention to press relations accelerated following the 1901 inauguration of Theodore Roosevelt, for whom appealing to the public through the press was a high priority. Roosevelt invited favored correspondents to meet with him daily and constantly sought publicity. His personal secretaries, first Cortelyou and then William Loeb Jr., spent increasing amounts of time keeping track of an incipient White House press corps and its needs.

By the presidency of Woodrow Wilson, managing press relations had became nearly a full-time job for Wilson's personal secretary, Joseph Tumulty. Tumulty conducted his own daily press briefings and lobbied the correspondents on the president's behalf. Under Warren G. Harding and Calvin Coolidge, the number of budgeted professional positions on the White House staff grew from one to two. The second position, described as a special assistant, was filled by Judson Welliver, a former Washington correspondent who served as unofficial press secretary to both presidents. Welliver helped to prepare the presidents for their regularly scheduled press conferences, which became an established practice in the 1920s. He also helped both presidents to seek publicity through still and newsreel photography and helped Coolidge to experiment extensively with the new medium of radio.

George Akerson, an assistant to President Herbert Hoover, was the first person to hold the official title of press secretary. Hoover had requested congressional authority in 1929 to hire a third professional White House staff member. Despite Akerson's new official status, he and his successor, Theodore Joslin, were unable to reverse Hoover's deteriorating relations with the press corps. The position of press secretary had become a permanent part of the twentieth-century presidency, however, and a growing White House press corps depended on those services.

Under Stephen Early, press secretary to Franklin D. Roosevelt, the position of press secretary grew into a separate office with its own staff. Early became the intermediary between a vigorous president and correspondents who flocked to the White House for his news conferences and broadcasts. Early also tried to centralize an executive branch information policy that included New Deal and wartime executive agencies.

James C. Hagerty, press secretary to Dwight Eisenhower, was the first to speak on the record to the news media as an official spokesman for the president. Eisenhower experimented with the new medium of television but held fewer press conferences than his predecessor, Harry S. Truman, and did not grant personal interviews. Instead, correspondent's inquiries were referred to Hagerty, who spoke on the president's behalf. Hagerty also was the first press secretary whose professional background was primarily in public relations rather than as a news correspondent.

Live televised coverage of presidential news conferences under John F. Kennedy became increasingly a focus of the press secretary's work, as did an increased emphasis on speechmaking. Pierre Salinger held regular meetings with officials from executive departments to gather information for the president's news conferences as well as to try to coordinate executive branch information policy.

By the end of the presidency of Lyndon Johnson, the responsibilities and duties of dealing with the press on a daily basis plus planning a presidential public relations strategy had outgrown the office and the title of press secretary. In 1969, incoming President Richard Nixon established a White House Office of Communications. Although Herbert Klein often was referred to as Nixon's press secretary, he held the additional title of manager of communications, which encompassed managing the president's image in the mass media well beyond Washington and the White House press corps. To Ron Ziegler, a former advertising executive, was delegated the traditional job of traveling with the regular White House press, conducting daily briefings, and answering questions.

President Richard Nixon's press secretary, Ronald Ziegler, ran interference for journalists interested in the Watergate scandal.
(National Archives)

By the inauguration of Jimmy Carter, the president faced 1,700 journalists with White House press credentials and an increasingly adversarial outlook. Partly in response to these demands, Carter's press secretary, Jody Powell, had a staff of two deputy press secretaries, three associate press secretaries, one press assistant, and 11 other professional staff members. Carter, like other presidents after Nixon, created a separate Office of Media Liaison to manage a far more complex relationship with the mass media than had existed 100 years earlier.

STEPHEN PONDER

See also Eisenhower, Dwight D., and the Media; Harding, Warren G., and the Press; Johnson, Lyndon B., and the Media; Kennedy, John F., and the Media; Nixon, Richard M., and the Media; Office of Telecommunications Policy; Presidential News Conferences; Reagan, Ronald, and the Media; Roosevelt, Franklin D., and the Media; Roosevelt, Theodore, and the Press; Spanish-American War; Truman, Harry S., and the Media; Wilson, Woodrow, and the Press

Further Reading

Cornwell, Elmer E., Jr., *Presidential Leadership of Public Opinion,* Bloomington: Indiana University Press, 1965

Edwards, George C., III, *The Public Presidency: The Pursuit of Popular Support,* New York: St. Martin's, 1983

Grossman, Michael Baruch, and Martha Joynt Kumar, *Portraying the President: The White House and the News Media,* Baltimore, Maryland: Johns Hopkins University Press, 1981

Hess, Stephen, *Organizing the Presidency,* rev. ed., Washington, D.C.: Brookings Institution, 1988

Kernell, Samuel, *Going Public: New Strategies of Presidential Leadership,* 2nd ed., Washington, D.C.: CQ, 1993

Maltese, John Anthony, *Spin Control: The White House Office of Communications and the Management of Presidential News,* 2nd ed., Chapel Hill: University of North Carolina Press, 1994

Medved, Michael, *The Shadow Presidents: The Secret History of the Chief Executives and Their Top Aides,* New York: Times, 1979

Tulis, Jeffrey, *The Rhetorical Presidency,* Princeton, New Jersey: Princeton University Press, 1987

Press Agentry

Working to get a client's name before the public

The practice of furnishing a publisher or editor with views, complete stories, or staged events favorable to an interested party by a person not employed by the newspaper defined the functioning of the press agent. The primary purpose was to get the name of the agent's client in the media – to generate publicity. As the media reported the event, the agent's client benefited by the repetition of a name (of a product or service) given credibility by the press. Using the concept of "third party credibility" remained a publicity tactic.

As the news-gathering procedures of the nineteenth century changed from "whatever came in" to publishing what hired reporters witnessed and wrote about, the press agent became a necessary connection between an individual or organization and the newspapers. To counter the potential influence of the resulting publicity, some newspapers headed any story with the label "SXI" if originated by press agents.

Press agentry long has been associated with the entertainment industry, where name recognition was, and remains, important. Buffalo Bill Cody, Annie Oakley, and Daniel Boone all became legends through the efforts of their press agents. P.T. Barnum, perhaps the best example of the stereotypical press agent, supposedly said: "I don't care what you write so long as you spell my name right." He used "advance men," who preceded the circus into a town, armed with press releases and free tickets for newspaper people. Often the press releases exaggerated to the point of being lies, but the advance man's actions filled the seats under the big top.

Barnum used other tactics to attract the press to his show and performers. He shortened the names of stars to suit headline space, as in the cases of Tiny Tim and Jenny Lind. He staged bizarre events such as a legal wedding between the circus characters the fat lady and the thin man. He manufactured stars, like Tiny Tim.

Press agentry has been associated with politics as well. Although the press agent has been operative since the development of the periodical press, John Adams, because of his tactics (stories, speeches, posters, staged events) in promoting the cause of American independence, may be called the father of press agentry in America.

President Andrew Jackson selected Amos Kendall, writer and editor from Kentucky, as his press agent. Kendall became a member Jackson's Kitchen Cabinet, guiding policy and framing the means by which policy would be presented to the nation. Kendall performed all the typical public relations tasks: wrote speeches, position papers, and press releases; conducted opinion polls; and represented the administration to the press. He would distribute press releases to newspapers and magazines before they appeared in the administration's own newspaper as evidence of Jackson's popularity.

The press agent, seeking public attention, has been associated with publicity and publicity tactics. If the media set the agenda of public discussion, then the press agent wants to influence what the press writes and pictures. The dark side of press agentry, then, is its deliberate use of the mass media to manipulate public opinion.

DAN PYLE MILLAR

See also American Revolution and the Press; Barnum, P.T.; Jackson, Andrew, and the Press; Lee, Ivy Ledbetter; Media Events; Public Relations

Further Reading
Bernays, Edward L., *Crystallizing Public Opinion,* New York: Boni and Liveright, 1923

Cutlip, Scott M., Allen H. Center, and Glen M. Broom, *Effective Public Relations,* 7th ed., Englewood Cliffs, New Jersey: Prentice-Hall, 1994; London: Prentice-Hall International, 1994

Grunig, James E., ed., *Excellence in Public Relations and Communication Management,* Hillsdale, New Jersey: Lawrence Erlbaum, 1992

———, and Todd Hunt, *Managing Public Relations,* New York: Holt, Rinehart & Winston, 1984

Lee, Ivy Ledbetter, *Publicity: Some of the Things It Is and Is Not,* New York: Industries, 1925

Miller, John C., *Sam Adams: Pioneer in Propaganda,* Boston: Little, Brown, 1936

Prime-Time Television

Key times for programmers, advertisers to reach audience

Television's prime time is defined as 8 to 11 P.M. (Eastern time) on Monday through Saturday and 7 to 11 P.M. on Sundays. A larger number of viewers tune in for prime-time programming than for any other programming block during the broadcast day. Therefore, networks charge the highest advertising rates and generate the largest profits from shows in prime time. Networks also use prime time to promote programs airing on different evenings.

Stakes are high, and shows that do not generate the desired ratings or demographics quickly are canceled or moved to another time slot. Since shows must attract large audiences, the networks use a series of programming strategies to win and keep viewers. The drop of a rating point or two could mean the loss of millions of dollars in potential revenue.

Four times a year, the four major networks (ABC, CBS, Fox, NBC) participate in a rating period called the "sweeps." Ratings are taken in February, May, July, and November. Generally, November and February are considered the most important sweeps, and the networks roll out their best programming then.

This practice is called "stunting." The best programs are saved for the sweeps periods, or special programming replaces the regular prime-time schedule. In the early 1990s, CBS was in third place in the overall ratings but won the February sweeps by putting together a series of specials recalling the glory days of the network. Remembrances such as *The Best of Ed Sullivan, The Best of M*A*S*H*, and an *All in the Family* reunion won the sweeps and drew criticism from competition.

Prime time has been the jewel of network television since the late 1940s. Even though television has been in existence since its introduction at the 1939 World's Fair, World War II and a cautious approach by the Federal Communications Commission (FCC) hindered television's development. By 1947, network programming was not available to all stations, but the early shows began to attract interest in mostly urban areas. NBC introduced a new show two days after Christmas that featured a cowboy marionette and a cast of characters with names like Buffalo Bob, Clarabell, and Flubberdub: *The Howdy Doody Show* ran for 13 years on NBC and is one of the best-remembered children's shows in television history.

Much of the other early programming consisted simply of what was available. Boxing, professional wrestling, and roller derby filled the airwaves. While Fridays belonged to the fights on NBC, Saturdays belonged to the first major television star in network history – Milton Berle. Berle hosted *Texaco Star Theater* from June 1948 to June 1954. "Uncle Miltie" borrowed heavily from vaudeville, using sight gags and slapstick to delight the ever-increasing television audience.

CBS countered with two shows that enjoyed long runs on prime-time television. *Arthur Godfrey's Talent Scouts* featured unknown entertainers eager for exposure before the growing television audience. Winners were picked by the applause meter, a black box with a moving needle that measured the volume of the studio audience response. *Talent Scouts* and longtime sponsor Lipton Tea had a 10-year run on CBS. Godfrey also hosted a weekly variety show for CBS called *Arthur Godfrey and Friends* for nine years.

Toast of the Town featured host Ed Sullivan with the promise of "a really big shew" for the viewers. Anchored at 8 o'clock on Sunday evening, *The Ed Sullivan Show*, as it would become known, introduced to the U.S. audience some of the leading entertainers of the day. During his more than 20-year run on CBS, Sullivan acquainted the television audience with acts like Dean Martin and Jerry Lewis, Elvis Presley, and the Beatles.

NBC continued to stake its claim on the Saturday comic circuit with the 1949 introduction of the *Admiral Broadway Revue, Your Show of Shows* starring Sid Caesar and Imogene Coca. These two comedians, with Carl Reiner and

a brilliant supporting cast, would make fun of everything from Shakespeare to popular movies and other television shows. In 1953, the name of the show was shortened to simply *Your Show of Shows,* by which it is most remembered. In 1954, the team split up, and neither Caesar nor Coca would ever be as popular again.

By the early 1950s, prime-time television had developed a pattern and a time schedule very similar to that of the programming presented decades later. The sitcom was a network staple. Shows were divided into half-hour and hour blocks, and movies, after some initial hesitancy on the part of the film studios, were featured on certain nights in the 9 o'clock hour. NBC even had extended network hours into late night with the introduction of *The Tonight Show,* starring Steve Allen.

Most network shows were produced live from New York. In 1951, however, a popular radio comedy team began filming a television sitcom on the West Coast. *I Love Lucy,* starring Lucille Ball and Desi Arnaz, would become one of the most watched programs on the planet. Employing sight gags and close-ups of Ball's contorted facial expressions, *I Love Lucy* and the subsequent *Lucille Ball Show* were still seen in syndication in many markets around the world at the end of the century. This show also marked the beginning of a shift of network production emphasis from New York to Hollywood.

Westerns always have had great appeal to American audiences, and early television carried on in this tradition with shows like *The Lone Ranger* and *The Roy Rogers Show.* ABC, in 1955, introduced former baseball player Chuck Conners in the half-hour western *The Rifleman.*

CBS, in the same year, offered *Gunsmoke,* with former football player James Arness as Sheriff Matt Dillon. *Gunsmoke* enjoyed an almost 20-year run on CBS. By the late 1950s, no fewer than a dozen cowboy adventure programs were featured in prime time. NBC continued the tradition of the western into the 1960s with the introduction of *Bonanza.* Tales of the Cartwright clan and the Ponderosa ranch dominated the Sunday night 9 o'clock hour throughout much of the decade.

Network prime-time television had reached its zenith in the 1960s. More than 96 percent of U.S. homes had televisions, and the three networks routinely enjoyed 90 to 95 percent of the total audience share. The 1961 National Association of Broadcasters meeting included an address by the newly elected U.S. president, John F. Kennedy, and newly appointed FCC chief Newton Minnow. Kennedy's speech spoke of the need for a free flow of information, but Minnow directed his remarks at the state of network television. He said that, while television had some great accomplishments, "When television is bad, nothing is worse. . . . I invite you to sit down in front of your television set. . . . I can assure you will observe a vast wasteland." The industry barely had caught its breath when the Dodd Committee took up Senate hearings about excessive violence on television. For the first time, television was being held responsible for what it broadcast, and industry executives chafed under the spotlight.

Following what some historians believe was network television's finest moment, the pooled coverage of the

Kennedy assassination and funeral, network programmers were ready to escape the troubled 1960s. Prime time in the 1960s was filled with adventure, escapism, and silliness. Fred Silverman, at CBS, introduced down-home, cornpone humor with shows like *The Beverly Hillbillies, Green Acres,* and *Petticoat Junction. The Addams Family* on NBC and the rival *The Munsters* on CBS featured creepy but lovable ghouls living in the middle of suburbia. The popularity of the U.S. space program led to alien themes such as *Lost in Space, It's About Time,* and *My Favorite Martian.* Themes such as racial disharmony, controversy about U.S. involvement in Vietnam, or the rising tide of drug abuse noticeably were absent from the prime-time schedule.

Three events of the middle 1970s quietly spelled the end of the Big Three prime-time network era: the rise of the ultrahigh-frequency (UHF) independent station, the creation of domestic communications satellites, and the introduction of the VCR. The advent of the domestic satellites meant that any programmer could buy time to transmit a video signal practically anywhere around the globe. Network executives hardly blinked when a young ad executive, Ted Turner, began offering his newly purchased UHF station to cable operators via satellite. But the creation of WTBS and, in the same year, the launch of HBO by satellite, meant that prime time would never be the same.

At the end of the twentieth century, networks shared the prime-time schedule with hundreds of competing channels. VCRs allowed viewers to buy rented movies or to "time shift" network programming by recording a show and watching it later. This plays havoc with programming and advertising strategies. Audience shares tumbled for the Big Three, from 92 percent in 1976 to 60 percent or lower in the late 1990s. Even so, some traditional network programs could still boast 25 and 30 percent shares in prime time as opposed to a 2 or 3 percent share for the diverse cable networks. This fact alone meant that prime-time network programming was unlikely to disappear any time soon.

CORLEY F. DENNISON III

See also Broadcast Ratings; Cable Networks; Criticism of Broadcasting; Golden Age of Television; Kennedy Assassination and the Media; Television and Violence; Television Networks

Further Reading
Auletta, Ken, *Three Blind Mice: How the TV Networks Lost Their Way,* New York: Random House, 1991
Lackmann, Ronald, *Remember Television,* New York: Putnam's, 1971

Printers' Networks

Associations among colonial printers necessary for economic survival

The economic survival of many early American printers depended on their associations with other printers. These

linkages were the building blocks of informal and loosely structured – yet powerful – trade affiliations, or printing "networks." These were prototypes of the modern corporate media groups.

Most historians view the colonial press from the outside – as remonstrating against authority, deferring to government, or creating a national culture. However, its inner world of economics, alliances, and norms of conduct were hidden carefully from view. Although seldom mentioned, even in private correspondence, the development of the press was shaped by business and organizational factors. The early American press was characterized by interconnections, within which there was a pattern of activity, rather than an agglomeration of isolated, idiosyncratic behavior. These interconnections were the essence of printing networks.

The earliest networks were based on family alliances. The most prominent of the family printing networks was the Green family, which originated with Samuel Green, who operated a press in Cambridge, Massachusetts, as early as 1649. His descendants who carried on the trade were both numerous and prominent in American printing during the seventeenth and eighteenth centuries. As his great-grandson, Timothy Green, recalled, Samuel "had a numerous Family – his sons Samuel, Bartholomew, and Timothy set up the same business in Boston; but my Grandfather who was his youngest Son, removed to New London, in the Year 1714, if I mistake not," extending the geographic reach of the Greens from Massachusetts to Connecticut.

Within the Green clan and other printing families, sons and nephews received printing apprenticeships and journeymen employment and, later, their own shops. They were encouraged to make marriages that would perpetuate the family business. Other notable printing families in colonial America included the Fowles, the Kneelands, the Sowers, and the Bradfords.

However, Benjamin Franklin altered the nature of networks by relying chiefly on nonfamily members. Instead of relatives, Franklin turned to printers, often ones who had worked for him in his Philadelphia shop and whose character and work ethic impressed him. He offered them silent partnerships in large towns that had no printer or that could sustain competition.

Franklin had three motives for creating his own variety of printing network. He sought to encourage the growth of domestic journalism, and he intended the silent partnership arrangement to be a lucrative venture. Most importantly, though, he envisioned the press as the optimal means to disseminate moral instruction to a mass audience and wanted to promote and sponsor printers conveying Franklinesque virtue.

The Franklin network grew to be the largest, most influential, and most geographically extensive of the colonial printing organizations. Composed of Franklin's business partners, trade associates, and a few family members, the network endured from the 1720s to the 1790s, stretched from New England to the West Indies, and comprised more than two dozen printers. As an economic entity and source of mutual support, Franklin's network was integral to the success of many eighteenth-century printers and played a key role in the development of American journalism.

RALPH FRASCA

See also Colonial Press; Franklin, Benjamin

Further Reading

Berger, Sidney E., "Innovation and Diversity Among the Green Family of Printers," *Printing History* 12 (1990)

Frasca, Ralph, "Benjamin Franklin's Printing Network," *American Journalism* 5 (1988)

_____, "From Apprentice to Journeyman to Partner: Benjamin Franklin's Workers and the Growth of the Early American Printing Trade," *Pennsylvania Magazine of History and Biography* 114 (April 1990)

Kiessel, William C., "The Green Family: A Dynasty of Printers," *New England Historical and Genealogical Register* 54 (April 1950)

Prior Restraint

Government actions designed to prohibit the distribution of information

A consistent theme of free press history is that prior restraints on publication are unacceptable. Prior restraints are government actions prohibiting the expression or distribution of information. They take many forms, including court injunctions, licensing, contracts, and taxes that discriminate against the press.

Even before the adoption of the First Amendment in the United States, English jurist William Blackstone wrote that liberty of the press meant "laying no *previous* restraints upon publications, and not in freedom from censure for criminal matter when published." This distinction between prior restraints and subsequent punishments is based on the marketplace of ideas theory – that only when all ideas are permitted to compete for acceptance will the truth emerge. Also, First Amendment theorists argue that prior restraints have a much greater chilling effect on the media than the threat of subsequent punishment.

It is well established that the First Amendment prohibits prior restraints on political speech in the print media in all but the most extreme circumstances. However, prior restraints on nonpolitical communication and on the broadcast media were not uncommon – for example, prior restraints halting advertising that is false or misleading or concerns unlawful activity.

Prior restraints also have been used to halt copyright and trademark violations, and licensing, the prior restraint most loathsome to print journalists, was the cornerstone of government regulation of broadcasting. Some such prior restraints are justified on the grounds that some types of expression were less valuable to society than political speech, others on the grounds that it was easier to determine in advance the truth of statements such as advertising claims than of political speech.

Near v. *Minnesota* (1931) is the U.S. Supreme Court's landmark case on the constitutionality of prior restraints on political speech. The case began when a Minneapolis newspaper publisher violated a Minnesota law that forbade publishing "malicious, scandalous and defamatory" reports unless the publisher could prove they were true and "published with good motives and for justifiable ends." J.M. Near, publisher of the *Saturday Press,* alleged in his newspaper that government officials and others were ignoring local gambling, bootlegging, and racketeering. A state court enjoined further publication of the newspaper. The Supreme Court ruled that this and most other prior restraints violate the First Amendment free-press clause. The Court's majority cited Blackstone and First Amendment author James Madison to support the principle that freedom of the press meant freedom from prior restraints. The Court said that it was the press's duty to ensure that city officials performed their duties properly – which was not a crime warranting punishment. The Court noted that for 150 years there had been almost no attempts to impose prior restraints on the press in the United States. The Court added, however, that prior restraints were justified when publication would jeopardize national security during wartime, when publications were obscene, or when publication would threaten to incite violence or the violent overthrow of the government.

Forty years later, the Supreme Court again heard the government argue for prior restraints on the press. In *New York Times Co.* v. *United States* (1971), known as the Pentagon Papers case, the federal government argued against allowing newspapers to reveal the contents of a secret government report entitled "History of U.S. Decision-Making Process on Viet Nam Policy" that was leaked to the *New York Times,* the *Washington (D.C.) Post,* and other newspapers. The government argued that publication would jeopardize national security by endangering lives and by hindering the peace process and attempts to obtain the release of prisoners of war in Vietnam.

In a brief per curiam opinion, the Supreme Court ruled that the government failed to present sufficient evidence of a serious threat to national security to overcome the Court's presumption that prior restraints were unconstitutional. The Court's decision was fragmented because each justice wrote a separate opinion to expedite the appeal. However, one of the justices explained that the government failed to demonstrate that publication of the Pentagon Papers would "inevitably, directly, and immediately" jeopardize national security. Two others concluded that the Pentagon Papers were merely "embarrassing" to the government. A majority appeared to agree that prior restraints would be allowed only in extraordinary circumstances.

The case that might have satisfied the Supreme Court that a prior restraint was warranted erupted in Madison, Wisconsin, in 1979. The federal government discovered that the magazine *Progressive* was planning to publish directions for the construction of a hydrogen bomb – a secret shared by only a few nations at that time. A U.S. District Court judge issued an injunction barring publication of the article on national security grounds. Applying the legal rules from *Near* and the Pentagon Papers, he said the government proved publication would present an "immediate, direct and irreparable harm" to the nation – that it "could pave the way for thermonuclear annihilation for us all." The court's ruling immediately was appealed, but before a higher court could consider it, the article in question was published by another Wisconsin periodical, rendering the case moot and leaving scholars to speculate about how the Supreme Court might have handled it.

Prior restraints also rarely are allowed on media coverage of judicial proceedings. The U.S. Supreme Court said that trial court judges were to use such prior restraints, often called gag orders, only as a last resort to insure a fair trial. In *Nebraska Press Association* v. *Stuart* (1976), the Court held that a judge presiding over a pretrial hearing in a small-town murder case erred when he imposed a prior restraint on media coverage of the proceeding in order to stifle pretrial publicity concerning the case. The Court said the judge first should have considered other methods of protecting the defendant's right to a fair trial, methods such as a change of venue. The Court proclaimed, "Prior restraints on speech and publication are the most serious and the least tolerable infringement on First Amendment rights." The media continued to be subjected to occasional gag orders, but generally the orders were overturned on appeal.

Cathy Packer

See also First Amendment in the Eighteenth Century; First Amendment in the Twentieth Century; Free Press–Fair Trial Controversy; Pentagon Papers

Further Reading
Friendly, Fred, *Minnesota Rag: The Dramatic Story of the Landmark Supreme Court Case That Gave New Meaning to Freedom of the Press*, New York: Random House, 1981
"The H-bomb Secret: How We Got It – Why We're Telling It," *The Progressive* (November 1979)
Siebert, Fred S., *Freedom of the Press in England, 1476–1776: The Rise and Decline of Government Controls*, Urbana: University of Illinois Press, 1952
Ungar, Sanford J., *The Papers & the Papers: An Account of the Legal and Political Battle over the Pentagon Papers*, New York: Dutton, 1972

Privacy

The right to keep some information from the media

Although the phrase "right to privacy" appears nowhere in the United States Constitution, the U.S. Supreme Court has declared that this right is implied in the First, Third, Fourth, Fifth, and Ninth Amendments and that the Fourteenth Amendment at times applies the other five to the states. The idea that a right to privacy had a basis in law was asserted initially in the United States by Judge Thomas McIntyre Cooley in his first edition (1878) of *A Treatise on the Law of Torts or the Wrongs Which Are Independent of Contract*. He said that tort law included the right of personal immunity, which is the right to be left alone, and the violation of it "is very likely a shock to the nerves" because "the peace and quiet of the individual is disturbed." That it took nearly 100 years for U.S. law to discover this right is not surprising because the notion of privacy includes many antisocial sentiments at odds with the expansionism inherent in a rapidly industrializing nation.

What is thought by many jurists to be the first instance of a judge granting relief in a privacy action occurred in 1890. When a New York actress refused to allow her picture to be taken while wearing the tights she wore onstage, the manager of a Broadway theater hired a photographer to use the newly invented technology of a flashbulb and take her picture surreptitiously during a performance. Afterward, she successfully won an injunction forbidding use of the photograph.

For the most part, though, U.S. trial courts were reluctant at first to recognize a right to privacy because they felt it would open a floodgate of lawsuits that, eventually, would protect all sorts of absurdities, such as insults. In addition, the courts were reluctant to embrace a concept not discussed by the greatest of legal scholars, like Edward Coke, William Blackstone, and James Kent.

Whereas English jurists found the nascent concept of privacy in cases granting relief in civil law on grounds such as implied contract, breach of trust or confidential relationship, defamation of character, and the violation of a property right, U.S. courts preferred to discover an implied right to privacy in the Constitution. In 1890, Samuel D. Warren and Louis D. Brandeis published an article titled "Privacy" in the *Harvard Law Review*. It widely is credited with being the first important attempt to justify the assertion that the law should protect privacy interests from invasions by the mass media.

Although the article had little immediate effect upon the law, it steadily gained influence as courts and legislatures struggled to understand this newly coined and increasingly asserted right. Indeed, the first trial court to address this right rejected it outright in 1902, although a vigorous dissent was filed. The controversy arose when the Rochester Folding Box Company printed, without seeking permission, a picture of a comely young lady along with the words, "The Flour of the Family," on its flour sacks.

Public reaction to *Roberson* v. *Rochester Folding Box Company* was so negative that one of the concurring judges took the unprecedented step of publishing a law review article in defense of the decision. During the New York legislature's very next session, it passed a statute making it a misdemeanor and a tort to use the name, portrait, or picture of any person for advertising purposes without that person's written consent.

Three years later the Supreme Court of Georgia faced nearly the same issue in *Pavesich* v. *New England Life Insurance Company* (1905). In its advertising, New England Life used Pavesich's name, picture, and a spurious testimonial from him. Because the Georgia court did recognize a right to privacy, *Pavesich* became the leading case affirming the existence of the right.

Trial courts vacillated between *Roberson* and *Pavesich* until the 1930s, when the appearance of the first edition of *Restatement of the Law of Torts* turned the tide strongly in favor of recognizing a right to privacy. At first, jurists were preoccupied with the threshold question of whether the right of privacy existed. The undisputed seminal work that analyzed substance was not penned until 1960, when the *California Law Review* published William L. Prosser's essay titled simply "Privacy." Prosser outlined four discrete forms based on the differing interests of the plaintiff: intrusion into a person's solitude; public disclosure of embarrassing private facts about a person's life; publicity that presented a person to the public in a false light; and appropriation of another's name or likeness for benefit. That Prosser's analysis quickly was embraced by trial and appellate courts across the entire nation was made dramatically clear when the second edition of *Restatement of the Law of Torts*, in 1977, embraced the entire four-part schema.

By the late twentieth century, intrusion had been extended to include eavesdropping by wiretapping, microphones, and telephoto lenses, as well as breaching the security of networked computers. Because the interest protected by intrusion was primarily a mental one, it often was thought to be closely allied with the legal notions of trespass, nuisance, and the intentional infliction of mental distress.

The first court of final appeal to deal with what Prosser later called appropriation rejected it. In 1899, the Michigan Supreme Court denied an application by the surviving widow and children of Colonel John Atkinson for an injunction restraining the use of his name on a brand of cigars.

Evidence that appropriation eventually became accepted, however, can be found in the only U.S. Supreme Court decision in this area. In *Zacchini* v. *Scripps-Howard* (1977), the Court said a television station invaded the privacy of a human cannonball by broadcasting for free his entire act. Saying that appropriation was similar to copyright and patent protections, the Court ruled that the First Amendment did not exempt the media from the requirement to pay for using what is in essence a person's identity.

In its first ruling on disclosure, *Time, Inc.* v. *James J. Hill* (1967), the Court asserted that plaintiffs must show that the person who disclosed the private information did so with actual malice. Earlier, the Court had defined actual malice, in a landmark libel case, *New York Times* v. *Sullivan* (1964), as intentionally not telling the truth or recklessly disregarding the truth.

The only other two disclosure cases were elicited when the name of a rape victim was disclosed. In *Cox* v. *Cohn* (1975), the Court said that, since accurate reports of judicial proceedings were public – not private – records, information in them could be disclosed legally. In *Florida Star* v. *B.J.F.* (1989), the Court said that publishing a rape victim's name acquired from a police report also was not necessarily an invasion of privacy, even though there existed a law against doing so. In the first Supreme Court case dealing with false light, *Cantrell* v. *Forest City* (1974), the Court ruled that all plaintiffs must show that the false light in which they were portrayed was created out of actual malice.

In the late 1990s, most privacy interests related to the mass media focused on two areas: freedom from intrusion, especially intrusion by the government, and the quest to achieve a uniquely personal identity.

Douglas S. Campbell

See also Society Reporting

Further Reading

Branscomb, Anne W., *Who Owns Information?: From Privacy to Public Access,* New York: Basic, 1994
Elder, David A., *The Law of Privacy,* Rochester, New York: Lawyers Cooperative, 1991
Nizer, Louis, "The Right of Privacy: A Half Century's Developments," *Michigan Law Review* 39 (1941)
Prosser, William L., "Privacy," *California Law Review* 48 (1960)
Warren, Samuel D., and Louis D. Brandeis, "The Right to Privacy," *Harvard Law Review* 4 (1890)

Professionalism in Journalism

Ongoing debate among journalists about benefits of "profession" versus "trade"

The relationship between journalism and professionalism has been a salient feature of mass media history. Occupations such as medicine, law, and engineering became professions by creating agreed-upon bodies of knowledge acquired through a university education, instituting systems of regulated entry, codifying standards of performance, and developing salaried, rather than wage-earning, bodies of workers. During the nineteenth and twentieth centuries, employees of news organizations debated the advantages and disadvantages of professionalizing their occupation.

The movement to professionalize journalism originated in three broad developments in U.S. history. First, it was a consequence of the division of labor caused by the massive industrialization that occurred throughout U.S. society in the late nineteenth and early twentieth centuries. As editors and publishers became less important in the physical production of the news, they assumed greater significance as managers of businesses. Some journalists, similarly to doctors, lawyers, and engineers, looked to the status and respectability granted to professionals to distinguish themselves from the blue-collar laborers working in the pressroom.

A new scientific positivism that emerged in the late nineteenth century also helped drive the professionalization of journalism. Lawyers, doctors, and members of the social sciences used scientific positivism as a method to achieve the ideal of objectivity, which, they argued, could be obtained only through higher learning and the rational application of knowledge to given situations. The pursuit of objectivity suggested that the professional's role was that of a neutral participant or a mediator. Therefore, journalists pursuing objectivity tried to report the facts about events to the interested public. This new style of reporting contrasted with the self-consciously biased partisan press of an earlier period.

The reforming impulse of the Progressive Era provided the final impetus to professionalization, and it did so in two ways. First, a common characteristic of most professions is their emphasis on serving the public interest. Many journalists came to see their occupation as an opportunity and forum through which they might promote social change. By working for reform, however, publishers and editors also found a way to distance themselves from big business, a frequently criticized group with which they were becoming increasingly identified.

One way in which the combination of these three trends influenced journalism directly was through the creation of journalism schools. The reliance on scientific positivism encouraged journalists to develop an educational program in an attempt to tie the occupation more closely to the social sciences. Joseph Pulitzer, founder of the Columbia University School of Journalism, believed that journalism schools provided students with an education that at once distinguished them from the laboring classes, offered guidance on how to use journalism to the benefit of the public interest, and conferred a degree of detachment and objectivity that could be acquired only through higher education.

While many editors and publishers enjoyed the respectability and power that came with professional status, they often faced strong opposition from other members of news organizations who did not see the professionalization of journalism in such favorable terms. The individuals more concerned with the physical production of the newspaper – such as the typographers and even some reporters – consistently resisted professionalization for financial reasons. Founded in 1933 to represent reporters, the American Newspaper Guild consistently fought professionalization because the acceptance of a salaried pay scale would deny overtime wages to employees who often worked more than 40 hours per week. The American Newspaper Publishers Association countered with the argument that the pursuit of objectivity and journalists' service to the public made them professionals. In 1976, this dispute reached the highest levels of adjudication, with the National Labor Relations Board deciding that journalists were not "professional employees" and therefore were subject to federal wage and hour regulations.

A second area of opposition to professionalization focused on the First Amendment and the freedom of the press. Professionals characteristically employ examinations and licensing to regulate entry into their ranks and use codes of ethics as a means of standardizing performance. They are therefore able to prevent unqualified practitioners from enjoying the benefits and status obtained through membership in the profession. Concerned journalists, however, contended that to deny entry to the occupation of journalism was to deny both an individual's constitutional right to free expression and the freedom of the press itself.

Thus, journalists' opinions of professionalization were often products of their positions within or outside of a news organization. Editors and publishers, at the top end of the industry, sought the benefits of professionalization, while many pressroom workers, reporters, and individuals seeking to enter the field rejected professionalization because it provided fewer rewards for them.

MATTHEW F. JACOBS

See also Business Regulation of the Press; Journalism Education; Newspaper Labor Organizations

Further Reading

Allison, Marianne, "A Literature Review of Approaches to the Professionalism of Journalists," *Journal of Mass Media Ethics* 1 (1986)

Beam, Randal A., "Journalism Professionalism as an Organizational-Level Concept," *Journalism Monographs* 121 (June 1990)

Kaul, Arthur J., "The Proletarian Journalist: A Critique of Professionalism," *Journal of Mass Media Ethics* 1 (1986)

Merrill, John C., "Professionalization: Danger to Press Freedom and Pluralism," *Journal of Mass Media Ethics* 1 (1986)

Salcetti, Marianne, "The Emergence of the Reporter: Mechanization and the Devaluation of Editorial Workers," in *Newsworkers: Toward a History of the Rank and File,* edited by Hanno Hardt and Bonnie Brennen, Minneapolis: University of Minnesota Press, 1995

Schudson, Michael, *Discovering the News: A Social History of American Newspapers,* New York: Basic, 1978

Program-Length Commercials

Infomercials started as a time filler in the 1950s

Program-length commercials (PLCs) first were introduced in the 1950s. Since the medium of television was relatively new at that time, PLCs were used primarily as a filler for airtime. Originally called long-running commercials, some products, such as Vitamix, for example, used available airtime to promote sales. These early program-length commercials were very simple productions in format and generally used a company spokesperson to advertise and demonstrate the product. The spokesperson then would invite viewers to respond to the product by phone or mail.

PLCs evolved to a level of prominence as well as the center of controversy in the 1960s, when they were perceived to be used "as a television-based tool to promote products for children." In a complaint filed with the Federal Communications Commission (FCC) by the Topper Corporation against ABC and Mattel, one of Topper's competitors, Topper complained that the network was broadcasting "a Saturday morning 30-minute children's cartoon series titled *Hot Wheels,* which in reality was a 30-minute commercial for Mattel's miniature racing cars." Topper further argued that Mattel received "commercial promotion for its products beyond the time logged for commercial advertising" and that "the producer designed a format which promotes the product of a major television advertiser of toys; used the trade name of the product as the title of the program, thus identifying the product with the title; used the advertising agent of the toy advertiser to sell the program; and sold the program to a network that broadcasts a substantial amount of advertising for the advertiser." Topper's complaint was just one of many urging the FCC to set some limits on television advertising directed toward children.

By the 1970s, complaints concerning PLCs directed to children's programs continued to soar, and the FCC sought to revise and clarify its policies because it was clear that commercial messages were being integrated with noncommercial messages. The FCC therefore concluded, "the entire program must be considered commercial." However, the FCC "confined application of its program-length commercial policies to programs concerning the sale of goods or services." As a result of the FCC's actions, PLCs were banned for a period during the 1970s and early 1980s. As television became more popular and there was less airtime available for fillers, the FCC rescinded its ban on PLCs in 1984. The government also "lifted restrictions on the duration of TV advertising." Additionally, "the birth of cable television and its tremendous growth to make airtime more abundant and affordable in 30-minute blocks" created a new avenue for the airing of PLCs. The number of PLCs soared from 2,500 a month in 1985 more than 21,000 in 1991. Some of these lengthy ads could produce up to $30 million in revenue annually. During the mid-1980s, the term "program-length commercial" began to disappear and was replaced by the name "infomercial."

DHYANA ZIEGLER

See also Children's Television Programming; Mass Media and Children

Further Reading

Balasubramanian, Siva K., "Beyond Advertising and Publicity: Hybrid Messages and Public Policy Issues," *Journal of Advertising* 23:4 (December 1994), pp. 29–46
Selz, Michael, "Proliferating Get-Rich Shows Scrutinized," *Wall Street Journal* (April 19, 1990)
Wojtas, Gary W., "The Renaissance of the Infomercial," *Direct Marketing* 53 (May 1990)

Propaganda

Systematic effort to shape public opinion

Propaganda is a systematic and deliberate strategy of communication. An all-encompassing definition of propaganda suggesting further delineation may be neither attainable nor appropriate because the term and its connotations are not constant over time or across cultures. Theorists of the late twentieth century proposed that propaganda is a form of communication that systematically and deliberately attempts to promote or injure an individual or group for the purpose of furthering the goals and desires of the propagandist. Furthermore, propaganda is rhetorical, and its influence is not dependent upon an idea but on how the masses perceive the idea, how the propagandist communicates the message, and the ultimate success of the propagandist.

Throughout history, the act of persuasion has influenced individuals and groups. Persuasive discourse influences through intellectual stimulation, not deception, because the individual or group is capable and free to seek out and attend to opposing views and arguments. Although persuasion and propaganda are comparable, the fundamental differences exist in the freedom of the individual and society and the goals and desires of the propagandist. While persuasion is transactional, soliciting voluntary change through intellectual stimulation in an attempt to satisfy the needs of both persuader and persuadee, propaganda is a rhetorical strategy that promotes the desires of the propagandist without regard to the target individual or group. Propagandists deliberately mislead and manipulate audiences through the calculated dissemination of messages that shape audience perceptions. Thus, by shaping perceptions, propaganda can manipulate the cognition and direct the behavior of the audience to support the motives of the propagandist. Furthermore, the true purpose behind the propagandist's willful misrepresentation of the message or intentional exclusion of information remains unknown to the target individual or group.

The term "propaganda" did not become popular until the twentieth century, although its prominent connotations were evident as early as 1622, when the Roman Catholic Church attempted to promote faith through the holy wars, giving the term negative meaning for Protestant countries while Roman Catholic societies celebrated propaganda as positive and faithful. Additional evidence of its use can be traced to the French and American Revolutions. As governments fought for and against independence and sovereignty, the resulting environment became ripe for propaganda.

The influence of propaganda is evident in many civilizations. Governments, organizations, and individuals have employed its use for both positive and negative means. In the United States, the use of propaganda earned condemnation as the "dissemination of biased ideas and opinions" by the totalitarian regimes participating in World War I. Through the mass distribution of newspapers, magazines, and movies, and the prominence of radio and television, propaganda became global. Propagandists were no longer limited to archaic methods of mass communication. Citizens of all societies were gaining exposure to appeals that were more intense and more numerous.

Propaganda seeks to bring about a desired change through manipulation or deception. Propaganda may be based on a lie. It also may be factual but presented in a manner that misleads an individual or group. The purpose of propaganda does not change. However, the process is complex – as evidenced through mass media technology in World War I. Garth S. Jowett and Victoria O'Donnell proposed a model of propaganda based on a social-historical context. To understand the status and potential influence of propaganda, one must first turn to the cultural history of a society. The development of culture occurs in a historical context that includes societal ideologies, myths about that society and others, governmental establishments, economic flow, and specific events.

With the ideology of an "open" media system such as that of the United States and most of the Western world, audiences are free to choose other channels of communication and related messages. Societies that are "closed" do not provide this open exchange of information and thus can create suspicion among their citizens. Furthermore, the closed environment is more resistant to change because the necessity for change becomes obscured or hidden by the propagandist (i.e., the government or institution). In contemporary society, the media control the flow of propaganda to and from the internal structure of a culture.

Within the context of culture operate the complexities of propaganda. Jowett and O'Donnell explicated the complex elements, identifying the institution, propaganda agents, media methods, social networks, and the public as the primary components contributing to the creation and power of propaganda. Propaganda is a rhetorical strategy that is promoted by an institution motivated by structural or financial means to fight or create change, establish a status within the society, and promote its activities. These institutions may remain anonymous to the public by employing the use of propaganda agents to communicate to the masses.

Propaganda agents use the media to promote the messages of an institution. The agents may take the form of powerful leaders or everyday citizens who disseminate messages for the benefit of the institution. The message is homogeneous and appeals to the masses.

The media (television, radio, print, film, and other technologies) are used to send the messages to the target groups. Access to the media is vital to propaganda agents for the purpose of shaping audience perceptions, manipulating their cognitions, and directing their behavior. Because there are multiple sources of media from which the target audience can select and to which it can attend, the homogeneity of the message may be lost.

Social networks include several components that may contribute to the dissemination of propaganda. Opinion leaders may intentionally, as propaganda agents, or unintentionally, as consumers of propaganda, give credence to propaganda by sharing those ideologies with members of their social networks. The distribution and promotion of propaganda through social networks may be facilitated by the media or may be a direct manipulation of the propaganda agents themselves.

The final element of Jowett and O'Donnell's social-historical model of propaganda was the target audience, which may include the general society or a particular subgroup with individual and collective predispositions. Through an understanding of these predispositions, propagandists can better manipulate target audiences.

The model of the process of propaganda through the social-historical context is transactional, identifying the complexities of information dissemination within a society. For example, just as the media may be used by propaganda agents to manipulate and deceive, counterpropaganda may also be communicated to rebut the arguments of the propagandist. The media communicate homogeneous messages to the public that, in turn, influence the social networks, creating an environment for acceptance or rejection.

Through the historical implication of propaganda and the proposed model of the process of propaganda, several generalizations become evident. Propaganda can bring together diverse groups in support of common interests but can divide groups just as easily. It molds perceptions and directs behavior. The homogeneous nature of propaganda makes it appealing to the masses who share a common bond with the propagandist's message. Thus, the use of propaganda does not necessarily result in a negative reaction. Propaganda relies heavily on the development of technology; as new technologies earn prominence in modern society, they, too, will be utilized. Finally, propaganda is not inherently evil. It may be used as a systematic and deliberate attempt to manipulate an audience, but the influence and moral nature can only be evaluated within a given context and by those who are involved in the transaction.

JERRY L. MILLER

See also Broadcast Propaganda; Committee on Public Information; Motion Picture Propaganda; Office of War Information; United States Information Agency; Voice of America

Further Reading

Duncan, Hugh D., *Communication and Social Order*, London: Oxford University Press, 1968; New Brunswick, New Jersey: Transaction, 1985

Jowett, Garth, and Victoria O'Donnell, *Propaganda and Persuasion*, 2nd ed., Newbury Park, California: Sage, 1992

Wasburn, Philo C., *Broadcasting Propaganda: International Radio Broadcasting and the Construction of Political Reality*, Westport, Connecticut: Praeger, 1992

Psychology in Advertising

Efforts to be more directed in advertising appeals

In the 1860s, legendary advertising leader John E. Powers demonstrated some understanding of advertising psychology through the appeals he used. The use of psychology in advertising did not truly come into vogue, however, until 30 years later, when advertisers began to replace techniques such as simple iteration and the jingle with a broader spectrum of forms.

In 1895, advertising publications such as George P. Rowell's *Printer's Ink* began to run articles about the use of psychology in advertising. In 1900, Harlow Gale, a University of Minnesota professor, wrote a pamphlet titled *On the Psychology of Advertising*. In 1901, the advertising publication *Publicity* ran an editorial advising advertising writers to study consumers' imaginations, perceptions, emotions, and instincts.

Walter Dill Scott, a psychology professor at Northwestern University, attended the 1901 annual dinner of the Chicago Agate Club. At that dinner, he met John Lee Mahin, who encouraged him to write more than two dozen articles about psychology and advertising for *Mahin's Magazine*. In 1903, Scott turned these articles into a book titled *The Theory and Practice of Advertising*. At about that same time, he published an article, "The Psychology of Advertising," in the *Atlantic Monthly*. In 1908, Scott published a second book, *The Psychology of Advertising*. Scott argued that "reason why" advertising had been oversold, and he emphasized the importance of emotion in advertising copywriting. He told advertisers to create advertising material that readers could associate with their own experiences or desires and advised them to sell pleasure rather than products.

Scott's writings had far-reaching effects in the advertising community. According to advertising historian Frank Presbrey, the publication of Scott's first book in 1903 represented the real beginning of advertisers' efforts to study appeal as a science and to apply scientifically the principles of psychology to selling. It represented the beginning of a period in which advertisers stopped viewing advertising as information for the rational consumer and began viewing it, instead, as persuasive material targeted to a nonrational public. Advertisers began speaking in psychological terms as well as in printers' terms.

Advertisers conducted many tests of advertising effectiveness based on the psychological school in the first decades of the twentieth century. In 1909, Colgate sponsored a contest in which 60,000 participants viewed two types of advertisements – rational and suggestive – and indicated which they considered most effective. Harry Hollingworth, a psychologist who taught at Columbia University and New York University, conducted advertising copy tests. Other advertising researchers tested subjects' recall of slogans and trademarks.

With the beginning of the 1920s, advertising leaders faced new challenges. As national distribution of goods expanded and the coordination of selling activities became more difficult, it became more important for them to convince clients they could deliver efficient consumer markets. Therefore, advertising leaders became increasingly interested in understanding and controlling the motivational factors that drove human consumption. They asked psychologists for assistance.

John B. Watson, who was hired by the J. Walter Thompson agency in 1920 after leaving the psychology department of Johns Hopkins University, was the most famous behaviorist and the most visible advertising agency psychologist of this era. Watson endorsed a framework of prediction and control that the advertising industry found appealing. He believed that human behavior could be reduced to a set of facts and, therefore, could be channeled. Watson valued ideas rather than products and style rather than substance. Some historians have credited Watson with legitimizing efforts to apply psychology to business.

Throughout the 1920s and 1930s, the United States experienced rapid societal, economic, and technological changes. Advertisers took advantage of these rapid changes by using symbolic messages to appeal to the insecurities and hopes that accompanied them. Also during these decades, psychologists conducted market research. Henry C. Link, who created the "psychological sales barometer" and studied consumer behavior on a large scale, headed the Division of Market and Advertising Research of the Psychological Corporation, an establishment founded by a group of psychologists who hoped to attract businessmen as clients.

After World War II, advertisers began to endorse motivation research – a genre of research that explored the subconscious, nonrational roots of consumer decision making. In the early 1950s, Leo Burnett and Foote, Cone and Belding established motivation research departments. Other large agencies followed suit, despite criticism from psychologists who argued it was impossible to infer hidden motives on a mass level.

The motivational research debate became more heated in 1957, when best-selling author Vince Packard criticized advertising methods in *The Hidden Persuaders*. It continued in the 1970s, when Wilson Bryan Key accused advertisers of subliminal sexual manipulation.

REGINA LOUISE LEWIS

See also Advertising Appeals; Advertising in the Twentieth Century; *Hidden Persuaders, The*

Further Reading

Buckley, Kerry W., "The Selling of a Psychologist: John Broadus Watson and the Application of Behavioral Techniques to Advertising," *Journal of the History of the Behavioral Sciences* 18 (1982)

Kreshel, Peggy J., "John B. Watson at J. Walter Thompson: The Legitimation of 'Science' in Advertising," *Journal of Advertising* 19:2 (1990), pp. 49–59

Strasser, Susan, *Satisfaction Guaranteed: The Making of the American Mass Market,* New York: Pantheon, 1989; London: Smithsonian Institution Press, 1995

Turner, E.S., *The Shocking History of Advertising!,* London: M. Joseph, 1952; New York: Dutton, 1953

Public Access to the Mass Media

Effort to find a way for alternative voices to be heard

The U.S. media often have been slow to respond to new challenges, and in the late 1960s, some U.S. citizens began to feel a distinct disconnection between themselves and their media of information. The civil rights movement and the anti–Vietnam War movement rocked society and left many people believing that because they themselves did not have direct access to the mass media, their stories were not being accurately disseminated.

Out of this discontent came a movement for greater direct access to the media, fueled at least in part by a law review article written by George Washington University Law

School professor Jerome A. Barron. Castigating the press for refusing to share a variety of ideas with the public, Barron wrote that press indifference to new ideas "becomes critical when a comparatively few private hands are in a position to determine not only the content of information but its very availability, when the soap box yields to radio and the political pamphlet to the monopoly newspaper." The mass media, he said, were "using the free speech and press guarantees to avoid opinions instead of acting as a sounding board for their expression."

Because the press refused to deal with controversial ideas, Barron said, new ways of communicating had been developed to "convey unorthodox, unpopular, and new ideas. Sit-ins and demonstrations" showed "the inadequacy of old media as instruments to afford full and effective hearing for all points of view." Barron charged that "jaded and warped standards of the media" meant "that ideas which normally would never be granted a forum are given serious network coverage if they become sufficiently enmeshed in mass demonstration or violence." His goal was

> an interpretation of the first amendment which focuses on the idea that restraining the hand of government is quite useless in assuring free speech if a restraint on access is effectively secured by private groups. A constitutional prohibition against governmental restrictions on expression is effective only if the Constitution ensures an adequate opportunity for discussion.

Although not acting as definitively as Barron would have liked, some newspapers were hearing these complaints. The op-ed page appeared in order to allow some space for opinion that disagreed with that of the publication. Ombudsmen were hired by some newspapers to provide a voice for the readers within corporate discussions. The National News Council began operation in the early 1970s in an effort to deflect public criticism of reporting. The movement toward increased access to the newspaper, however, played itself out in the court system.

The public access movement was dealt a death blow by a unanimous U.S. Supreme Court in *Miami Herald* v. *Tornillo* (1974). The case involved a 1913 Florida statute that required newspapers that criticized a candidate for public office to give that candidate, free on demand, space to answer the charges. Although Chief Justice Warren Burger acknowledged that the conditions under which the press operated in the 1970s were far different from those of the 1790s, when the First Amendment was adopted, he found no reason to interfere in a newspaper's editorial decisions. Despite the difficulty that advocates of unpopular causes had in getting their views put before the public, Burger believed that forcing newspapers to print information would make them even less likely to touch controversial issues.

Much of what the critics wanted from the print media already was required by law or Federal Communications Commission (FCC) policy of broadcast outlets. The personal attack rule, for example, still required licensees to provide individuals attacked on the airwaves with free time to respond to that criticism. The U.S. Supreme Court issued a reminder about that obligation in 1969 in the *Red Lion* v. *FCC* case.

Those still concerned about access to electronic media launched a Fairness Doctrine challenge to an FCC ruling that television networks did not have to sell them time to peddle their ideas over the airwaves. The Democratic National Committee (DNC) and the Business Executives Move for Peace (BEM) wanted to market ideas, and they were willing to pay for the time to do so. The FCC decided that if the DNC and the BEM could prove that the networks had failed to cover opposing ideas to information they were presenting as news, then there might be a Fairness Doctrine case. Until such proof was offered, however, stations did not have to sell time for such purposes.

The U.S. Supreme Court, ruling in *CBS* v. *Democratic National Committee* in 1973, safeguarded the airwaves from a surfeit of ideas. Justice William Brennan wanted to open the airwaves to those who advocated dissident ideas. "The First Amendment embodies," he wrote in dissent, "not only the abstract right to be free from censorship, but also the right of an individual to utilize an appropriate and effective medium for the expression of his views."

The idea of public access to the media disappeared after these U.S. Supreme Court decisions in the late 1960s and early 1970s, but it reappeared thereafter with the burgeoning of cable television systems across the country and with the requirement that certain channels be set aside by the cable franchise operators for the general public's use. Public access television, as it was called, provided the average citizen with access to a wider audience in order to advocate a variety of ideas. Public access television allowed individuals to stop by the cable office and speak their minds. As a result of the spontaneity of such broadcasts, there were no program listings to tell potential viewers of who would speak when. Audiences often were quite limited.

The Internet also provided greater access to a communications medium for the general public. Individuals could and did set up newsgroups, participate in chat rooms, and even launch home pages and "zines" through this new media form. Using the Internet as a means of communicating ideas presented at least two problems. First, a person's audience likely would be only those interested in a particular issue or point of view; finding a broad, general audience was unlikely. Second, to participate in Internet communication, one had to own a computer; this economically based restriction substantially limited both the audience and the participants in this form of communication. Whether either public access television or the Internet were as effective as traditional broadcast channels or newspaper columns in disseminating ideas remained an important question.

MARGARET A. BLANCHARD

See also Fairness Doctrine; Internet; National News Council; Ombudsman; Op-Ed Pages; Personal Attack Rule

Further Reading

Barron, Jerome A., "Access to the Press – A New First Amendment Right," *Harvard Law Review* 80 (1967)
_____, *Freedom of the Press for Whom?*, Bloomington: Indiana University Press, 1973

Friendly, Fred W., *The Good Guys, the Bad Guys, and the First Amendment: Free Speech vs. Fairness in Broadcasting*, New York: Random House, 1976

Public Journalism

Reevaluation of the interaction between journalists and the community

In the late 1980s, growing concerns about the health of two areas of public life converged to produce the public journalism movement. Public journalism – also called civic journalism, citizen-based journalism, or communitarian journalism – sought not just to inform people, as journalists had always done, but to actively engage citizens in creating political agendas and solving community problems.

For many years there had been evidence of what political scientist Robert Putnam called a decline in civic capital – citizens disengaging from political and civic life. For instance, the percentage of eligible voters going to the polls continued to drop from election to election, and community institutions such as service clubs noted sharp declines in membership and support. Democracy's essence, the coming together of citizens to discuss and solve mutual problems and aspirations, seemed to be dissipating. Scholars and other observers noted a wide range of areas in which individualism had replaced community-mindedness. Some critics claimed that the way in which the media covered events – emphasizing problems over solutions, highlighting individuals rather than collective action, focusing on scandal and corruption rather than celebrating success, featuring "experts" dictating solutions – was at least partly responsible for the disengagement of citizens from civic life.

Parallel to the decline in civic capital was a decline in newspaper circulation, jobs in newspapers, and even the number of newspapers published. Since some studies correlated news interest with civic interest, it was argued that there could be self-interest and public good in adopting a new kind of journalism that could reenergize the democratic processes.

Davis W. "Buzz" Merritt, a veteran newspaper editor with the Knight-Ridder group, and Jay Rosen, a journalism professor at New York University, are considered the public journalism movement's founders. Their effort dates to Merritt's dismay at the 1988 presidential elections, when only 50.1 percent of the electorate turned out to vote after a campaign that had been marked by sound bites and campaign performances rather than substantive discussion of important issues. Believing that media coverage was partly to blame for the 1988 campaign, Merritt, editor of the *Wichita (Kansas) Eagle*, revamped his newspaper's coverage of the 1990 Kansas gubernatorial campaigns. In that and subsequent campaigns, Merritt put into practice the basic tenets of public journalism, including: public opinion polling to determine issues most important to citizens; coverage focused on candidates' responses to the citizens' priorities; promoting and engaging citizen discussion of the issues; and diminished coverage of campaign strategy and tactics, in particular playing down "horse-race" polling stories. Other journalists followed Merritt's lead.

The public journalists saw their movement as a new way to conceptualize journalism, but philosophically it could be linked to the communitarian movement, and, journalistically, it had in common features of earlier departures from mainstream journalism, notably muckraking at the beginning of the twentieth century and the New Journalism of the 1960s and 1970s.

In calling for journalists to free themselves from the constraints of objectivity, Rosen echoed the mid-century New Journalism of such writers as Tom Wolfe, and also of some journalists of the muckraking era. New Journalists argued in the 1960s that then-settled craft norms imposed restrictions on journalists, sometimes forcing them into reporting objectively – balancing claim and counterclaim in their stories – rather than reporting truthfully, calling a spade a spade.

What made public journalism unique from previous experiments in journalism was the stress on reconnecting collectivities of citizens with government processes. Behind this notion were the theories of communication and democracy of philosopher Jürgen Habermas and public opinion researcher Daniel Yankelovich and the communitarian ideas of sociologist Amitai Etzioni. The communitarians' challenge to the tradition of individualism and libertarianism in the press stressed interdependence, cooperation, and subordinating individual freedoms for the good of society. For the press, this meant going beyond the watchdog, neutral observer role to enable citizens to complete the process of what Yankelovich called "coming to public judgment." According to Yankelovich, the media's traditional role of informing is just the first step in the process, and to facilitate the process – and remain connected with their audiences – journalists must actively bring about awareness and discussion of core values related to the issues. He drew on the philosophy of Habermas, who stressed the importance to democratic processes of all members of society communicating free of all forms of domination. Habermas's concern was not just overt oppression but subtle forms as well, such as the pervasive use of "experts" to tell people what they must do. True deliberation, according to these theorists, comes only when all stakeholders in an issue have talked things over, understand the various viewpoints, and are willing to accept the consequences of their solutions. The public journalists saw their role as using the power of the press to facilitate that process, from identifying problems, to providing information, to mobilizing citizen communication and action.

FRANK E. FEE JR.

See also Muckraking; New Journalism (1960s–1970s); Public Opinion Polls; Watchdog Concept

Further Reading

Charity, Arthur, *Doing Public Journalism*, New York: Guilford, 1995

Etzioni, Amitai, *The Spirit of Community: Rights, Responsibilities, and the Communitarian Agenda*, New York: Crown, 1993; London: Fontana, 1995

Habermas, Jürgen, *Moral Consciousness and Communicative Action,* translated by Christian Lenhardt and Shierry Weber Nicholsen, Cambridge, Massachusetts: MIT Press, 1990

Merritt, Davis, *Public Journalism and Public Life: Why Telling the News is Not Enough,* Hillsdale, New Jersey: Lawrence Erlbaum, 1995

Putnam, Robert, *Making Democracy Work: Civic Traditions in Modern Italy,* Princeton, New Jersey: Princeton University Press, 1993

Rosen, Jay, *Community Connectedness Passwords for Public Journalism: How to Create Journalism that Listens to Citizens and Reinvigorates Public Life,* St. Petersburg, Florida: Poynter Institute for Media Studies, 1993

_____, *Getting the Connections Right: Public Journalism and the Troubles in the Press,* New York: Twentieth Century Fund, 1996

Yankelovich, Daniel, *Coming to Public Judgment: Making Democracy Work in a Complex World,* Syracuse, New York: Syracuse University Press, 1991

Publick Occurrences, Both Forreign and Domestick

First newspaper in the American colonies victim of prior restraint in 1690

Publick Occurrences, Both Forreign and Domestick, published on September 25, 1690, normally is considered to have been the first newspaper published in what later would become the United States. Although *Publick Occurrences* lasted only one issue, thus not qualifying it as a periodical publication (one of the factors in the definition of a newspaper), its publisher, Benjamin Harris, had intended to issue it as a continuing newspaper.

A recent émigré to Boston who had been energetically involved in the political and religious controversies that surrounded London journalism, Harris published *Publick Occurrences* against the backdrop of England's "Glorious Revolution" and the political chaos in Massachusetts that followed the colony's overthrow of its royal government in 1689. An Anabaptist and opponent of British Tory government, Harris hoped to aid the new Puritan government by providing accurate accounts of military and economic conditions that confronted the colony.

Publick Occurrences contained four pages measuring 7 1/2 by 11 1/2, with one page left blank. In his statement of purpose on page one, Harris emphasized the concern that reports be accurate. He would take, he explained, "what pains he can to obtain a Faithful Relation of all such things; and will particularly make himself beholden to such Persons in Boston whom he knows to have been for their own use the diligent Observers of such matters."

As for providing news, Harris stated that the purpose of *Publick Occurrences* was to furnish "the Countrey . . . once a month (or if any Glut of Occurrences happen, oftener,)

The first newspaper published in the colonies ran for one issue only.

with an Account of such considerable things as have arrived unto our Notice," so that "Memorable Occurrents of Divine Providence may not be neglected or forgotten, as they too often are." In carrying out that plan, Harris filled the pages with reports of such domestic items as Christianized Indians planning a "day of Thanksgiving to God for his Mercy in supplying their extream and pinching Necessities," the abduction of two children by Indians, a recently widowed man hanging himself, the status of a smallpox epidemic that was then on the decline in Boston, and the damages caused by a local fire. He devoted the greatest amount of space to the expedition of a Massachusetts militia against the French and their Indian allies in Canada.

This last report provoked the opposition of the colonial governing council. Only four days after *Publick Occurrences* appeared, the council issued an order forbidding Harris to continue publication. In suppressing the paper, the council invoked the licensing power over printing that the British crown had invested in colonial governments. Some members of the council feared free publishing and its possible consequences, and some objected to some of the newspaper's contents, particularly two stories about barbarous acts committed by the colony's Indian allies against French prisoners and about the French king having seduced his daughter-in-law. One faction within the council also acted because of its opposition to Increase and Cotton Mather, father and son clerics, the latter suspected of having helped Harris prepare some of the paper's content.

WM. DAVID SLOAN

See also Colonial Press; Prior Restraint

Further Reading

Ford, W.C., "Benjamin Harris, Printer and Bookseller," *Massachusetts Historical Society Proceedings* 57 (1923–24)

Kobre, Sidney, "The First American Newspaper: A Product of Environment," *Journalism Quarterly* 17 (1940)

Muddiman, J.G., "Benjamin Harris, the First American Journalist," *Notes and Queries* 163 (1932)

Paltsits, Victor Hugo, "New Light on *Publick Occurrences*," *Annals of the American Academy of Political Science* 5 (1949)

Partington, Wilfred, "The First American Newspaper and the *New England Primer*," *Bookman* 76 (January 1933)

Sloan, W. David, "Chaos, Polemics, and America's First Newspaper," *Journalism Quarterly* 70:3 (Autumn 1993), pp. 666–681

Public Opinion Polls

Straw polls preceded more scientific efforts

Among the earliest public opinion polls to be published were so-called straw polls commonly reported in U.S. newspapers as early as 1824. The July 24, 1824, edition of the *Harrisburg Pennsylvanian,* for example, reported the results of a straw vote in Wilmington, Delaware, taken "without Discrimination of Parties." Andrew Jackson had received 335 votes, the paper reported. John Quincy Adams had placed second with 169 votes. Henry Clay and William Crawford trailed with 19 votes and 9 votes, respectively. Methods for deciding who was included in straw polls varied. In some instances, newspapers published a ballot, which readers were asked to clip, mark, and return. At other times, a straw poll would be taken of people whom some circumstance had brought together. Journalists traveling by rail, for example, commonly conducted straw polls of their fellow passengers. Newspapers of the time considered straw polls newsworthy, whether conducted by a journalist, a political party official, or even a private citizen. Often, the chief consideration was whether the straw poll's results agreed with the partisan leanings of the newspaper's publisher.

Events surrounding the 1936 presidential election, however, discredited straw polls and marked the advent of scientific methods for estimating public opinion. Sixteen years earlier, during the months leading up to the 1920 presidential election, editors of the popular newsmagazine *Literary Digest* had mailed ballots to people whose names and addresses the magazine had gleaned from telephone directories and automobile registration records in six states. Each recipient had been asked to return the ballot after marking it for one of the election's two contenders: Warren Harding or James Cox. After tabulating the ballots returned, the *Digest*'s editors had accurately predicted Harding's victory. Encouraged, the *Digest* had repeated the poll during the 1924, 1928, and 1932 elections, each time successfully predicting the outcome.

As the 1936 election approached, the *Digest*'s editors mailed out some 10 million ballots, the largest number yet. As before, the magazine had culled the names and addresses of ballot recipients from telephone directories and automobile registration records. The 2 million ballots returned indicated that Republican nominee Alf Landon would beat incumbent Franklin D. Roosevelt by a margin of 57 percent to 43 percent. The editors added what would prove a wise disclaimer: "We make no claim to infallibility. We did not coin the phrase 'uncanny accuracy' which has been so freely applied to our Polls. We know only too well the limitations of every straw vote, however enormous the sample gathered, however scientific the method."

Meanwhile, a young man named George H. Gallup predicted that Roosevelt would win with 55.7 percent of the vote. Gallup had arrived at his prediction using a technique with which he had experimented as a doctoral student in marketing research. The technique involved polling a group carefully chosen to match the general population on characteristics thought to be important. Aware that the ongoing depression might prompt the wealthy and the poor to vote differently, Gallup made sure the proportion of wealthy and poor people in his group matched the proportion of wealthy and poor in the general population. Using similar techniques, pollsters Elmo Roper and Archibald Crossley also picked Roosevelt as the winner.

Roosevelt won with 61 percent of the vote. The *Digest*'s sample, it turned out, had vastly underrepresented the poor, who could afford neither telephones nor cars but who most certainly could vote. The *Digest* ceased publication in 1938, although it remains unclear what, if any, role the magazine's 1936 embarrassment played in its demise.

Meanwhile, the new scientific polling method gained prestige as Gallup and other pollsters correctly picked the winners of the 1940 and 1944 elections. The scholarly journal *Public Opinion Quarterly* was founded in 1937, followed by the National Opinion Research Center in 1941. Throughout World War II, pollsters worked on survey research projects for the Research Branch of the U.S. Army and the Office of War Information. In 1947, the American Association for Public Opinion Research was founded. Many journalists remained skeptical of scientific polling and preferred the more familiar and seemingly more direct straw poll method of gauging public opinion, but scientific polling had established itself as a reliable means of measuring public opinion.

As the election of 1948 neared, however, Gallup and his fellow pollsters predicted Governor Thomas Dewey of New York would defeat incumbent Harry Truman. The mistake proved humiliating, both for the pollsters and for the news-

The Literary Digest

NEW YORK   OCTOBER 31, 1936

Topics of the day

LANDON, 1,293,669; ROOSEVELT, 972,897

Final Returns in The Digest's Poll of Ten Million Voters

Well, the great battle of the ballots in the Poll of ten million voters, scattered throughout the forty-eight States of the Union, is now finished, and in the table below we record the figures received up to the hour of going to press.

These figures are exactly as received from more than one in every five voters polled in our country—they are neither weighted, adjusted nor interpreted.

Never before in an experience covering more than a quarter of a century in taking polls have we received so many different varieties of criticism—praise from many; condemnation from many others—and yet it has been just of the same type that has come to us every time a Poll has been taken in all these years.

A telegram from a newspaper in California asks: "Is it true that Mr. Hearst has purchased THE LITERARY DIGEST?" A telephone message only the day before these lines were written: "Has the Repub-lican National Committee purchased THE LITERARY DIGEST?" And all types and vari-eties, including: "Have the Jews purchased THE LITERARY DIGEST?" "Is the Pope of Rome a stockholder of THE LITERARY DIGEST?" And so it goes—all equally ab-surd and amusing. We could add more to this list, and yet all of these questions in recent days are but repetitions of what we have been experiencing all down the years from the very first Poll.

Problem—Now, are the figures in this Poll correct? In answer to this question we will simply refer to a telegram we sent to a young man in Massachusetts the other day in answer to his challenge to us to wager $100,000 on the accuracy of our Poll. We wired him as follows:

"For nearly a quarter century, we have been taking Polls of the voters in the forty-eight States, and especially in Presidential years, and we have always merely mailed the ballots, counted and recorded those returned and let the people of the Nation draw their conclusions as to our accuracy. So far, we have been right in every Poll. Will we be right in the current Poll? That, as Mrs. Roosevelt said concerning the Presi-dent's reelection, is in the 'lap of the gods.'

"We never make any claims before elec-tion but we respectfully refer you to the opinion of one of the most quoted citizens to-day, the Hon. James A. Farley, Chair-man of the Democratic National Commit-tee. This is what Mr. Farley said October 14, 1932:

" 'Any sane person can not escape the implication of such a gigantic sampling of popular opinion as is embraced in THE LIT-ERARY DIGEST straw vote. I consider this conclusive evidence as to the desire of the people of this country for a change in the National Government. THE LITERARY DIGEST poll is an achievement of no little magnitude. It is a Poll fairly and cor-rectly conducted.' "

In studying the table of the voters from

Final Report "Literary Digest" 1936 Presidential Poll

State	Electoral Vote	Landon 1936 Total Vote For State	1932: Rep.	Dem.	Soc.	Others	Did Not Vote	Vote Not Indicated	Roosevelt 1936 Total Vote For State	1932: Rep.	Dem.	Soc.	Others	Did Not Vote	Vote Not Indicated	Lemke 1936 Total Vote For State	1932: Rep.	Dem.	Soc.	Others	Did Not Vote	Vote Not Indicated
Ala.	11	3,060	1,218	1,298	3	3	412	126	10,082	371	8,530	50	1	736	394	68	5	49	4		4	6
Ariz.	3	2,337	1,431	647	18		129	112	1,975	248	1,555	33		70	69	104	22	52	8		10	12
Ark.	9	2,724	1,338	953	7	9	274	143	7,608	228	6,655	16	8	373	328	138	14	98	4	3	9	10
Calif.	22	89,516	65,360	16,200	315	53	3,519	4,069	77,245	15,165	53,520	1,816	13	3,578	3,103	4,977	1,620	2,560	117	25	163	492
Colo.	6	15,949	11,872	2,714	131	12	637	583	10,025	1,747	7,256	284	13	439	286	579	136	333	29	2	26	53
Conn.	8	28,809	22,939	3,376	111	7	1,230	1,146	13,413	2,584	9,113	408	6	788	514	1,489	245	1,006	53	3	70	112
Del.	3	2,918	2,343	328	9		134	104	2,048	503	1,345	34		96	70	35	6	19	3		2	5
Fla.	7	6,087	3,121	2,051	13	5	594	303	8,620	635	6,924	41		614	406	195	37	116	6	2	12	22
Ga.	12	3,948	1,239	1,817	5	11	708	168	12,915	379	10,377	42	9	1,569	539	35	3	23			6	2
Idaho	4	3,653	2,672	698	9	8	103	163	2,611	398	1,989	30	8	89	97	224	69	109	8	11	9	18
Ill.	29	123,297	85,112	25,885	573	69	6,506	5,152	79,035	14,793	54,612	1,542	57	4,790	3,241	6,415	1,172	4,219	169	17	304	534
Ind.	14	42,805	31,913	7,644	134	49	1,290	1,775	26,663	4,513	20,247	302	22	719	860	2,166	476	1,352	64	11	73	190
Iowa	11	31,871	22,823	6,164	135	26	1,272	1,451	18,614	3,190	13,611	258	14	829	712	2,829	560	1,831	86	11	88	253
Kans.	9	35,408	25,315	6,489	147	15	1,466	1,976	20,254	4,182	14,121	257	11	846	837	902	226	482	52	1	43	98
Ky.	11	13,365	8,957	2,939	35	14	793	627	16,592	1,586	13,594	95	6	703	320	732	69	554	24		31	54
La.	10	3,686	1,366	1,742	9	3	384	182	7,902	445	6,401	39		697	320	841	35	667	23	2	55	59
Maine	5	11,742	8,619	1,567	25	35	713	783	5,337	635	3,820	41	1	289	551	418	64	277	3		42	30
Md.	8	17,463	9,754	4,685	110	2	1,479	1,433	18,341	1,891	13,540	328	5	1,366	1,211	614	56	422	22	1	34	79
Mass.	17	87,449	70,567	10,105	330	31	3,213	3,203	25,965	5,141	17,499	744	16	1,635	930	5,415	1,002	3,670	133	3	236	371
Mich.	19	51,478	38,526	8,665	287	22	2,113	1,865	25,686	5,114	17,402	748	26	1,472	924	3,376	680	2,145	128	4	130	289
Minn.	11	30,762	22,386	5,958	109	3	972	1,334	20,733	3,699	14,855	511	22	861	785	5,426	804	3,893	115	14	157	443
Miss.	9	848	269	394	1		137	47	6,080	88	5,396	8	1	298	289	43	5	32	1		2	3
Mo.	15	50,022	33,551	11,149	244	45	2,975	2,058	38,267	4,463	30,608	455	15	1,485	1,241	2,368	322	1,680	73	4	122	167
Mont.	4	4,490	3,336	828	23		139	164	3,562	660	2,517	94	1	151	139	212	57	108	12	1	6	28
Nebr.	7	18,280	12,436	4,241	100	7	685	811	11,770	1,677	9,045	177	2	418	451	862	157	594	31	2	18	60
Nev.	3	1,003	658	272		21	36	37	955	163	716	2		42	32	36	9	22			4	1
N.H.	4	9,207	7,504	1,072	21		253	357	2,737	479	1,984	51	1	114	108	372	84	238	8		18	24
N.J.	16	58,677	45,361	8,625	251	17	2,383	2,040	27,631	5,495	18,642	1,032	14	1,548	900	2,444	441	1,633	89	1	104	175
N.M.	3	1,625	1,003	444	7	1	80	90	1,662	212	1,290	24		70	66	35	5	20	3		4	3
N.Y.	47	162,260	114,574	33,052	805	45	7,125	6,659	139,277	18,241	99,938	4,101	141	10,604	6,252	14,656	2,106	10,414	303	20	670	1,143
N.C.	13	6,113	3,532	1,656	33	5	580	307	16,324	820	13,778	119	6	946	655	389	35	259	20	3	5	4
N. Dak.	4	4,250	2,787	1,157	15		108	182	3,666	694	2,679	30	2	97	164	1,111	192	743	32	5	29	110
Ohio	26	77,896	58,232	13,391	420	66	2,747	3,040	50,778	9,465	35,864	1,315	38	2,454	1,642	8,156	1,580	5,389	249	14	375	549
Okla.	11	14,442	8,393	4,260	29	3	1,050	707	15,075	1,289	12,389	53	2	687	655	217	36	143	10		9	19
Ore.	5	11,747	8,593	2,014	72		521	541	10,951	1,966	7,666	298	7	567	447	655	196	313	46	7	30	63
Pa.	36	119,086	86,433	20,097	543	115	6,461	5,437	81,114	14,502	56,082	1,340	55	5,733	3,402	7,507	1,121	5,089	187	11	467	632
R.I.	4	10,401	8,165	1,269	32	5	511	419	3,489	600	2,470	90		208	121	794	148	545	12	3	31	55
S.C.	8	1,247	216	658	2		300	71	7,105	101	5,943	6	6	701	348	20		20				4
S. Dak.	4	8,483	5,712	2,096	42	14	248	371	4,507	859	3,314	46	5	125	158	770	122	539	20	10	20	59
Tenn.	11	9,883	5,785	2,354	29	31	1,178	506	19,829	1,419	15,510	128	33	1,938	801	100	14	63	2		12	9
Texas	23	15,341	6,302	6,774	43	3	1,559	660	37,501	1,860	31,262	149	5	2,668	1,557	558	58	417	13	1	28	41
Utah	4	4,067	2,906	851	21	1	155	133	5,318	954	3,935	69	8	189	163	119	30	65	8		5	11
Vt.	3	7,241	5,829	822	20	2	239	329	2,458	498	1,756	37		84	83	174	48	90	2		18	16
Va.	11	10,223	5,696	2,848	57	18	1,194	410	16,783	1,121	13,346	141	4	1,517	644	74	17	37	4		8	8
Wash.	8	21,370	14,841	4,800	67	30	806	826	15,300	2,281	11,423	278	53	709	556	683	170	374	28	27	31	53
W. Va.	8	13,660	10,060	2,589	30	15	424	542	10,235	1,278	8,229	52	11	305	360	199	51	119	4	1	11	13
Wis.	12	33,796	22,587	8,495	157	12	1,142	1,403	20,781	3,144	15,578	582	4	799	674	3,642	412	2,517	118	1	110	285
Wyo.	3	2,526	1,830	510	15	1	83	87	1,533	242	1,144	27	1	63	56	78	22	46	1		4	4
State Unknown		7,158	4,763	1,416	35	5	263	676	6,545	924	4,724	97	9	231	560	693	125	406	23	1	35	103
Total	531	1,293,669	920,225	250,059	5,629	825	61,323	55,608	972,897	142,942	714,194	18,420	722	57,310	39,309	83,610	14,845	55,757	2,333	223	3,679	6,773

Results of *The Literary Digest*'s infamous "Landon Wins" poll of 1936
(Davis Library, University of North Carolina at Chapel Hill)

papers that had sponsored them. A review later that year by the Social Science Research Council concluded that the pollsters missed a late surge in support for Truman because they had stopped polling too soon before the election. Other problems included a failure to account for undecided voters and an underrepresentation of Democratic voters in the pollsters' samples.

The mistakes of 1948 prompted improvements in polling techniques that led to greater credibility for pollsters. Dwight Eisenhower monitored poll information during both his candidacy and subsequent administration. Richard Nixon and John F. Kennedy both relied heavily on polls during the 1960 election, as did every presidential candidate thereafter. Major media organizations also set up their own polling operations, starting with CBS news in 1967. According to one study, the number of poll questions asked rose from 6,900 during the 1960s to some 89,000 during the 1980s. Technological improvements helped drive the rise in polling by making polls cheaper, easier, and faster to conduct. With telephones in more than 95 percent of all U.S. households in the late 1990s, pollsters no longer had to send interviewers all over the country to conduct face-to-face interviews. Instead, interviews could be completed more quickly and efficiently over the telephone. Furthermore, development of personal computers and statistical programs designed to run on them enabled pollsters to analyze poll data almost instantly.

Most public opinion polls at the end of the twentieth century were conducted by telephone using a sample of people chosen at random. Straw polls persisted, however. News organizations commonly asked readers or viewers to register their opinion on some issue by calling one or more telephone numbers that the organization published. The results often were reported with a disclaimer indicating that the poll was not conducted scientifically.

KENNETH R. BLAKE

See also Precision Journalism

Further Reading

Babbie, Earl, *The Practice of Social Research*, 6th ed., Belmont, California: Wadsworth, 1992; 7th ed., London: Wadsworth, 1995

Gawiser, Sheldon R., and G. Evans Witt, *A Journalist's Guide to Public Opinion Polls*, Westport, Connecticut: Praeger, 1994

Herbst, Susan, "Election Polling in Historical Perspective," in *Presidential Polls and the News Media*, edited by Paul J. Lavrakas, Michael W. Traugott, and Peter V. Miller, Boulder, Colorado: Westview, 1995

Ladd, Everett Carll, and John Benson, "The Growth of News Polls in American Politics," in *Media Polls in American Politics*, edited by Thomas E. Mann and Gary R. Orren, Washington, D.C.: Brookings Institution, 1992

"Landon, 1,293,669: Roosevelt, 972,897," *Literary Digest* (October 31, 1936)

Moore, David W., *The Superpollsters: How They Measure and Manipulate Public Opinion in America*, New York: Four Walls Eight Windows, 1992

Roll, Charles W., Jr., and Albert H. Cantril, *Polls: Their Use and Misuse in Politics*, New York: Basic, 1972; London: Basic, 1973

Public Relations

Problems associated with industrialization gave rise to new media field

Campaigns to convince people to buy, vote, or think a certain way are undoubtedly as old as civilization, but nineteenth-century industrialization fostered changes that encouraged people to approach such campaigns in new ways. Industrialization brought with it sweeping social and political changes, in addition to the obvious economic ones. One of the strategies people used to deal with these changes was public relations, which became not just an activity but a full-time, paying occupation.

Although industrialization gave many people in the United States consumer goods that they appreciated, its negative by-products included child labor, poor working conditions, and slums in the cities that sprang up around factories across the United States. Journalists, politicians, and social reformers demanded changes, often seeking government regulation of big business. Businesses had become so huge that owners no longer knew their employees or customers by name; by the same token, in big cities, reformers and politicians could no longer reach all their constituencies in face-to-face meetings. Large urban daily newspapers and the national circulation magazines, however, *could* reach large audiences with messages – whether from railroad manager, church official, or government authority. Public relations counselors helped their clients disseminate messages to their public, often through the mass media.

Public relations practitioners drew upon press agentry, advertising, sales promotion, circus publicity, political campaigning, and war propaganda, among other fields, for inspiration. Ivy Lee, generally considered the first public relations counselor (although until about 1919 he described himself as a "publicist"), distinguished his field from these others in several ways. Perhaps most importantly, Lee wanted access to the management of his client's organizations, so he could contribute to communication policy. Lee and George F. Parker formed an agency in 1904, the first of its kind, and they issued a "Declaration of Principles," which promised that Parker and Lee would supply prompt and accurate information to the press and public. They insisted on open sponsorship when providing information to reporters. They also explained that they would not pay for placement of their stories – as many press agents did – arguing that if the information was not of interest, then reporters should simply disregard it.

Lee's representation of the Rockefeller family during the Colorado Fuel and Iron Company strike, which began in 1913, illustrates how public relations could be used to respond to media, public, and employee opposition; it also shows that living up to the high standards proposed in the "Declaration" proved difficult for Lee. During a dispute with the armed guards whom John D. Rockefeller Jr. had hired to subdue the strikers, 20 people (including mine workers, their wives, and children) died. Public outcry forced Rockefeller, who was the mine's principal owner, to take action, and he retained Lee for $1,000 a month. Despite his promise of open sponsorship, Lee did not reveal to the press his relationship with Rockefeller for almost six months. One of his strategies was to write bulletins that Colorado Fuel and Iron issued to prominent individuals and to newspapers; the handouts later were found to include some inaccuracies – Lee had simply accepted his employer's word about the tragedy at the mine. Having violated some of his own principles, Lee found himself tagged with the nickname "Poison Ivy." But he also tried to accomplish some good by recommending that the company establish machinery to address workers' grievances.

Although public relations counseling is associated most closely with big businesses like those run by the Rockefellers, from the beginning, almost every conceivable type of organization experimented with its use. Among the early groups employing persons designated to handle public relations activities were government agencies, churches, and universities. Newspaper correspondents told a congressional committee that many government agencies, ranging from the Departments of Agriculture and State to the Post Office, had press bureaus by 1912. George Parker, who had been a publicist in all three of Grover Cleveland's presidential election campaigns, left Parker and Lee in 1913 to become secretary for press and publicity for the Episcopal Church. The Trinity Church, under attack in the press because it owned some ramshackle tenement buildings in New York City, retained Pendleton Dudley, who had opened an agency there in 1909. In 1916, Robert F. Duncan began work on a fundraising drive for a $10-million teachers' endowment fund for Harvard. Such diversity indicates that public relations counseling advanced rapidly throughout all sectors of U.S. life during the early decades of the twentieth century.

Diversity had its limits in public relations practice, however. Like the leaders of the organizations they represented, virtually all paid public relations counselors were white and male. Moreover, public relations had a class bias; for instance, there were many more practitioners working to put down strikes, like Lee in the Colorado coal strike, than practitioners representing the working class. It did not take long, however, for labor unions to develop public relations offices of their own.

World War I was a watershed in public relations history, although not because of any important innovations in technique. Rather, the unprecedented scale of government propaganda, and the apparent success of that effort, had meaningful consequences for public relations counseling. The wartime Committee on Public Information (CPI), which was the logical culmination of President Woodrow Wilson's policy to consolidate the flow of executive branch information through the White House, was chaired by George Creel, formerly a muckraking journalist. Comprised of photographers, actors, advertising agents, reporters, poets, artists, and teachers, the Creel committee used every available medium and its multimillion-dollar budget to

spread messages about Wilson's plan to "make the world safe for democracy."

The most significant effects of the CPI may have been on the people who worked for Creel rather than the general public. Many of Creel's subordinates pursued careers in public relations after the war: Edward Bernays, William Baldwin, Carl Byoir, and Arthur Page all had successful careers in public relations, the first three in their own New York agencies and Page at American Telephone and Telegraph (AT&T). These men believed that public opinion campaigns could be effective and that the public could be easily influenced. Indeed, many people in the United States thought that propaganda had been an important element in the war; some even claimed that words won the war. World War I solidified the belief among a small but prominent group of practitioners that public relations campaigns could be useful and effective.

The most important CPI alumnus was Edward L. Bernays. A Broadway publicist before the war, Bernays saw a connection between his experiences on the Creel committee and the writings of his famous uncle, psychoanalyst Sigmund Freud. Because Freud argued that people were driven by irrational desires, Bernays believed that the public relations practitioner must tap into the group mind in order to influence or, as he wrote, "crystallize," public opinion. Together with his wife and partner, Doris Fleischman, Bernays built a successful agency that catered to enormous corporations like Procter and Gamble and nonprofit organizations like the Red Cross. Bernays wrote numerous books and taught a college course in public relations, working throughout his lifetime to inform people about the potential benefits of public relations and to change its poor reputation.

Social reform organizations also continued to use public relations tactics to promote their causes. After decades of campaigning, the passage of two constitutional amendments – the Eighteenth Amendment (Prohibition) in 1919 and the Nineteenth Amendment (woman suffrage) in 1920 – indicated that citizens could unite successfully to demand changes in government and society. Although the public relations practitioners (most of whom were women) who worked for these causes were not paid, they had developed sophisticated and successful methods of garnering public attention and support.

The Great Depression, which saw the end of many a business, large or small, was paradoxically a period of expansion for public relations. When big business could not solve the formidable economic problems that plagued the nation, the people of the United States began to seek alternative solutions. Some turned to Communism and Socialism, and many demanded government assistance. President Franklin D. Roosevelt and Congress responded with, among other things, new laws that controlled prices and made it easier for unions to form. Both government intervention and organized labor were anathema to conservative business executives, who believed that only management and owners should make business decisions. They turned to public relations to spread the gospel of free enterprise.

Free enterprise campaigns attempted to persuade the people that they had benefited greatly from private industry and that, therefore, a separation between government and industry should be maintained. The National Association of Manufacturers (NAM) – a conglomeration of many smaller groups, including the Chamber of Commerce – conducted the most prominent of these campaigns during the 1930s. The NAM utilized motion pictures and filmstrips, print and outdoor advertising, direct mail, a speakers' bureau, and a radio program. NAM representatives – and many other business executives, including public relations practitioners – denounced the government, especially Roosevelt, and labor unions whenever the opportunity arose.

Perhaps the master of the use of public relations to maintain the status quo was Arthur Page. Vice president of public relations for AT&T throughout the 1930s and 1940s, Page sought details on his customer's desires about every aspect of telephone service, right down to the placement of notepads in public phone booths. Page was highly lauded because, under his guidance, AT&T listened and responded to its consumers, rather than simply trying to persuade them to accept the company's point of view. The reason for doing so was twofold. Primarily, of course, the company wanted to make a profit. By keeping its customers satisfied, the company also hoped that people would remain content with the status quo of a privately held but government-regulated telephone company, rather than a public utility. Managers, therefore, tried to please consumers by proactively seeking their input into company practices.

Public relations also gained a foothold in the field of political campaigning during the depression. The first public relations agency dedicated to politics, Campaigns, Inc., opened its doors in California in 1933. Founded by a husband-and-wife team, Clem Whitaker and Leone Baxter, Campaigns, Inc., had its first major battle for the 1934 reelection of California governor Frank Merriam. The governor's opponent was Upton Sinclair, a Socialist best known for his exposé of the meatpacking industry, *The Jungle*. Whitaker and Baxter admitted that they did not think Merriam had been a good governor, so rather than seeking reelection on his record, they simply maligned Sinclair. Among their most memorable tactics was a series of cartoons that ran in scores of California newspapers, decrying the "blot of Sinclairism." Each cartoon showed a traditional American scene with a giant blob of ink dashed over it, accompanied by a denigrating quote from Sinclair's writings, including his novels. For instance, one showed a bride and groom outside a church, smeared by the ink blot and a quote that equated marriage and prostitution. Merriam, who had not been especially popular, won the election handily.

Not all public relations campaigns of the depression era were so divisive. Carl Byoir, formerly George Creel's top CPI lieutenant, and one of his oil-industry clients, Henry L. Doherty, were members of the team that built the National Foundation for Infantile Paralysis. Byoir organized a series of local "birthday balls" held on President Roosevelt's birthday. (The president was one of the disease's most famous victims; he had contracted polio at the age of 39.) Despite the economic challenges to fundraising posed by the depression economy, Byoir raised more than $1 million for polio research in 1934 alone, spending money out of his own pocket to get the program started.

Important refinements in the practice of public relations counseling took place during the depression. Two highly respected counselors, Earl Newsom (of Earl Newsom and Associates) and John W. Hill (of Hill and Knowlton), made it regular practice to work closely with the top management of their client organizations. Hill attended virtually every board meeting of the American Iron and Steel Institute for about 40 years; Newsom developed close relationships with such executives as Frank Stanton, president of the CBS television network, and Henry Ford II. This meant that the counselor participated in the formation of a client's policies and could advise management about how an organization's plans might affect or be affected by its relationships with key publics. Edward Bernays also made a substantial contribution to the practice of public relations by developing a set of steps that led to "the engineering of consent," as he titled his 1935 article. Bernays wrote that the public relations counselor must define goals; conduct research on the public; develop a strategy to reach the goals; plan themes, appeals, and tactics; and set a budget. Although many objected to the notion that Bernays thought he could "engineer" public consent, these steps remained important in public relations counseling.

As in World War I, federal public relations activities during World War II concentrated in the executive branch, but the experiences of its participants were markedly different from those on the Creel committee. The Office of War Information (OWI), headed by respected radio commentator Elmer Davis, was charged with providing factual information to the U.S. public about the conduct of the war, developing campaigns to increase participation in programs like bond-buying, and producing materials for overseas audiences, both enemy and ally. This agency concentrated on sober news presentation much more than the CPI had. The OWI also appears to have had a much lesser impact on its workers. It did not spawn a large number of practitioners or agencies as the CPI had; two of the more important postwar counselors, Farley Manning (of Manning, Selvage and Lee) and Harold Burson (of Burson Marsteller), worked as public information officers for the U.S. military, not the OWI. Nor did public relations practitioners leave their wartime positions with the belief that opinion management was simple or easy. On the contrary, World War II studies of propaganda indicated that the effects of mass mediated messages were quite limited.

Despite the growing belief that people were not easily persuaded by mass communication, the post–World War II era was one of unprecedented expansion in public relations. In 1950, there were 19,000 "public relations specialists," according to the U.S. Department of Labor; a decade later, there were 31,000. This growth was, as during the 1930s, driven in many cases by free enterprise campaigns. Although the infusion of government defense funds into the economy had halted the depression, and, therefore, the immediate threat of radicalism, during the 1950s, business leaders continued to promote the free enterprise system at fever pitch. The acceptance of socialism in parts of western

Europe and the rise of the Soviet bloc to the east gave many U.S. executives pause. Fearing such political leanings in the United States, they strove to turn back the tide of government participation in business and economic decision making. Many executives, including public relations counselors like Tommy Ross (of Ivy Lee and T.J. Ross), believed that people turned to Communism or Socialism only because they did not understand the contributions big business had made to the American style of living. Therefore, industrialists like Republic Steel's president, Charles M. White, insisted that their company's advertising and public relations do more than just promote products: they also should promote capitalism. This philosophy opened the door for increased public relations budgets and, therefore, stirred growth in the industry.

The postwar era also saw a drive for public relations professionalization. In 1948, two organizations (the National Association of Accredited Publicity Directors and the American Council on Public Relations) combined to form a national professional organization, the Public Relations Society of America (PRSA). The PRSA developed a system of accreditation, which involved taking an examination to demonstrate expertise in public relations and pledging to uphold the PRSA's Code of Ethics. New professional journals, including *PR News* (1944), *Public Relations Journal* (1945), and *PR Reporter* (1958), also testified to the growing interest in improving the practice and reputation of public relations.

Professionalization also included a push for better public relations education, which developed rapidly after the war. Immediately after World War II, only about two dozen U.S. universities offered instruction on public relations; 40 years later, that number had grown to more than 300, including many that offered graduate degrees. In a trend that can be traced back to Bernays' reliance on his uncle's theories about psychology, public relations educators increasingly drew from other fields of study (including organizational and consumer behavior, rhetoric, and electoral behavior) to develop a better understanding of the most effective ways to communicate with and persuade their diverse audiences. They also recommended greater attention to interpersonal communication than Lee, Bernays, or other pioneers had considered. Educators and practitioners alike displayed an increasing reliance on computers, using them, for example, to target audiences and to analyze survey results that could help them influence opinions and behavior.

By 1990, the number of public relations specialists had risen to more than 160,000. Far more significant was the increasing diversity of public relations practitioners. At the turn of the century there apparently were no full-time, paid public relations counselors who were women. By 1968, about one-quarter of public relations specialists were female, and by 1993, nearly 60 percent were women. Minority participation remained much lower, but it too grew: about 11 percent of public relations practitioners in 1991 were minorities. The career of D. Parke Gibson, an African American practitioner who opened a New York City agency during the 1960s, demonstrates how difficult it was for minorities to move into the mainstream of public relations practice. In Gibson's case, and in many other instances, minority practitioners were forced to work only for minority-owned organizations or were offered accounts that targeted minority audiences only.

KAREN S. MILLER

See also Bernays, Edward L.; Committee on Public Information; *Crystallizing Public Opinion;* Lee, Ivy Ledbetter; Muckraking; Office of War Information; Pinchot, Gifford, and Public Relations; Political Advertising; Professionalism in Journalism

Further Reading

Bernays, Edward L., *Biography of an Idea: Memoirs of Public Relations Counsel Edward L. Bernays,* New York: Simon & Schuster, 1965

Cutlip, Scott M., *The Unseen Power: Public Relations, a History,* Hillsdale, New Jersey: Lawrence Erlbaum, 1994

Lee, Ivy, *Publicity: Some of the Things It Is and Is Not,* New York: Industries, 1925

Olasky, Marvin N., "The Development of Corporate Public Relations, 1850–1930," *Journalism Monographs* 102 (April 1987)

Pimlott, J.A.R., *Public Relations and American Democracy,* Princeton, New Jersey: Princeton University Press, 1951

Ponder, Stephen, "Presidential Publicity and Executive Power: Woodrow Wilson and the Centralizing of Government Information," *American Journalism* 11 (1994)

Raucher, Alan R., "Public Relations in Business: A Business of Public Relations," *Public Relations Review* 16:3 (Fall 1990), pp. 19–26

Tedlow, Richard S., *Keeping the Corporate Image: Public Relations and Business, 1900–1950,* Greenwich, Connecticut: JAI, 1979

Public Relations Awards

In the 1990s, scores of public relations awards were presented each year to public relations practitioners by a variety of organizations, including nonprofit organizations such as the American Heart Association; government agencies at the local, state, and federal levels; journalism schools in universities; and a host of corporations. Perhaps the most widely recognized award, however, was the Silver Anvil, presented annually by the Public Relations Society of America (PRSA).

Established in 1944, the award recognized "outstanding public relations programs of companies, organizations and institutions, and government agencies" and served to "stimulate and encourage improved public relations performance and techniques." Silver Anvil awards were presented in a variety of categories, which expanded over the years following the presentation of the first award. These were: community relations; institutional programs; special events and observances; public service; public affairs; marketing communication: new services; marketing communication:

established services; market communication: new products; market communication: established products; international public relations; emergency public relations; internal communications; special public relations programs; investor relations; and issues management.

The PRSA also presented a Gold Anvil each year. This award recognized a public relations professional who had made outstanding contributions to the field through the practice of public relations. Other PRSA awards included the Bronze Anvil, which honored breakthrough ideas and tactics in publications, audiovisual, writing, and other channels; and the outstanding educator award, presented annually, when merited, to a professor in a college or university who taught public relations and made significant contributions to public relations education.

The International Association of Business Communicators (IABC), a 12,000-member professional association of communication professionals, presented the Gold Quill award annually. The international awards program recognized "superior achievement in the field of organizational communication" in nine divisions – community and government relations, employee communication, media relations, investor and customer relations, marketing communication, crisis communication, benefits communication, multi-audience communication, and management processes.

DULCIE M. STRAUGHAN

Public Relations Trade Organizations

From the early twentieth century, public relations practitioners joined organizations to enhance their professionalism and to project an image of professionalism before the public. Their organizations held meetings, conducted workshops, commissioned studies, sponsored contests, administered accreditation tests, and developed codes of ethics that encouraged honesty and discretion. But, however much these organizations benefited their members, their voluntary nature weakened the effects that they might have had on the practice, and the reputation, of public relations as a whole.

In the late 1990s, the Religious Public Relations Council was the oldest public relations association, having begun in 1929 as a consortium of Protestant publicists. The organization accepted its first Roman Catholic member in 1967 and its first Jew in 1970, so its membership of 500 eventually was ecumenical.

The largest public relations organization was the Public Relations Society of America (PRSA), which was formed when the American Council of Public Relations merged with the National Association of Public Relations Council in 1948. The PRSA absorbed the American Public Relations Association in 1961 and the National Communication Council for Human Services in 1977. The organization, which had more than 15,000 members in the 1990s, published the monthly magazine *Public Relations Journal*.

Next in size to the PRSA was the International Association of Business Communicators (IABC). Formed in 1970 when the American Association of Industrial Editors combined with the International Council of Industrial Editors and Corporate Communicators of Canada, the IABC had more of an internal communications focus. The PRSA, by contrast, emphasized media relations more. Both the IABC and the PRSA facilitated student chapters at universities. IABC had 11,500 members in the 1990s and published the monthly magazine *Communication World*.

Both the PRSA and the IABC accredited qualified practitioners who passed written and oral examinations. Their examinations tested knowledge of public relations practice as well as the association's code of ethics. Because less than half of the members of the PRSA and the IABC were accredited, accreditation was both somewhat prestigious and remunerative.

Public relations practitioners with at least five years of experience could join the International Public Relations Association (IPRA), based in Geneva, Switzerland. From its founding in 1955, the IPRA's purpose was to stimulate international public relations in terms of ethics and skill as well as volume. The IPRA, which had 1,000 members from more than 60 countries in the 1990s, published the quarterly journal *IPRA Review*.

Because a person needs neither a license nor an association membership to practice public relations, it is not surprising that only 1 in 10 public relations practitioners belonged to a trade organization. Those who did belong to one, however, tended to identify themselves more closely with a set of professional values and principles than those who did not belong. In this way, the organizations contributed to professionalism in public relations.

JOHN P. FERRÉ

See also Professionalism in Journalism

Further Reading

Cutlip, Scott M., *The Unseen Power: Public Relations, a History,* Hillsdale, New Jersey: Lawrence Erlbaum, 1994
Dugan, George, Caspar H. Nannes, and R. Marshall Stross, *RPRC: A 50-Year Reflection,* New York: Religious Public Relations Council, 1979
McElreath, Mark P., *Managing Systematic and Ethical Public Relations,* Madison, Wisconsin: Brown & Benchmark, 1993

Public Relations Trade Press

For decades in the twentieth century, the major public relations trade journals were membership publications. *Public Relations Journal* was published monthly by the Public Relations Society of America (PRSA). *Communication World,* successor to the *Journal of Organizational Communication* and *IABC News,* was published from 1983 by the International Association of Business Communicators (IABC). Both of these glossy magazines contained news and discussions about public relations practices, trends, and people.

Changes began in 1994, when the PRSA began publication of *Public Relations Tactics,* a colorful tabloid monthly that concentrated on news and how-tos. In 1995, the PRSA began the *Public Relations Strategist,* a slick, dignified quarterly devoted to discussions of issues and trends that affected senior management and suggested how and why public relations decisions are made – or might be made. By October 1995, *Public Relations Journal,* the PRSA monthly for more than 50 years, was discontinued.

In the April 1996 issue of *Communication World,* the editor announced that the May 1996 issue would be published electronically only. Readers were directed to seek *CW Online* on the IABC's home page on the World Wide Web. Members were encouraged to make the new venture interactive by responding electronically to the contents. The IABC later announced that the August issue also would be on-line only. The future of the traditional printed *Communication World* thereafter would no doubt depend on member acceptance of the electronic version. The PRSA also had a home page for general association information on the World Wide Web.

CAROL REUSS

Other Public Relations Entries:

Agenda Setting; Barnum, P.T.; Bernays, Edward L.; Commercial Speech; Committee on Public Information; Corporate Speech; Crisis Management; *Crystallizing Public Opinion;* Lee, Ivy Ledbetter; Media Events; Office of War Information; Pinchot, Gifford, and Public Relations; Presidential News Conferences; Press Agentry; Puffery; Spin Doctors; Staged News; Trial Balloons

Puffery

Overly exaggerated praise for person, product, or service

Occasionally, a press release, or news story, describing the positive nature of a product, person, or service will be dismissed by the serious journalist as "puffery." The critic means that the story contains unmerited or exaggerated praise for the subject of the piece. The criticism also could describe a darker relationship between a newspaper and the author, suggesting an advertising deal to assure editorial cooperation.

Puffery has its roots in the development of advertising as a basis for the financial support of newspapers and the rise of press agents as sources of publicity. With the phenomenon of the penny press in the early nineteenth century, advertising became the main source of newspaper revenue. As newspapers became dependent upon advertising income, they became susceptible to implicit pressure from the advertiser to be supportive of the product or service being sold.

When advertisers purchased space, they implicitly, sometimes explicitly, expected "free puffs" of information about their products or services to appear in the news or editorial sections of the newspaper. The implied threat was that if the paper did not provide editorial or news space, or both, it would lose the advertising revenue.

For example, in the concluding decade of the nineteenth century, Standard Oil came under attack during the oil pipeline wars. John D. Rockefeller, using an extensive advertising campaign to promote Mica Axle Grease, regularly purchased large ads in every Ohio newspaper. Within a year, most editors had stopped criticizing Standard Oil and Rockefeller. While the editors faced no explicit threat, the potential loss of advertising revenue altered editorial practice by either eliminating negative or increasing positive statements about the axle grease.

Puffs, however, need not have been free: space in the news and editorial sections of newspapers could be purchased, usually for a fee higher than the advertising rates. Space was bought to disseminate corporate promotion disguised as news. Occasionally, these "paid reading notices" were designated by a star or dagger to differentiate their content from the substance of the news stories. Often, no such indication appeared, leaving the reader to believe that the content was gathered and written as regular news.

Standard Oil and Rockefeller again provide an example. Using the Jennings Advertising Agency, articles praising or defending Standard Oil were given to newspapers, and the space paid for, on the condition that the article appear on the news or editorial pages. In fact, the Jennings contract specified the price the agency would pay per line and that the copy would appear without any indication that it was advertising.

The *New York Herald,* one of the first newspapers to ban free puffs, did so in early 1848. However, the practice gained momentum following the Civil War and did not diminish until Congress passed the Bourne Newspaper Publicity Law in 1912. The law required newspapers to label all paid material as advertising. Because puffs, either free or purchased, developed as a practice of the press agent, the term "puffery," unfortunately for the profession, often refers to work of people in public relations.

DAN PYLE MILLAR

See also Muckraking; Penny Press; Public Relations

Further Reading
Adams, Samuel Hopkins, *The Great American Fraud,* Chicago: American Medical Association, 1907
Baldasty, Gerald J., "The Nineteenth-Century Origins of Modern American Journalism," in *Three Hundred Years of the American Newspaper: Essays,* edited by John B. Hench, Worcester, Massachusetts: American Antiquarian Society, 1991
Bernays, Edward L., *Public Relations,* Norman: University of Oklahoma Press, 1952
Kenner, H.J., *The Fight for Truth in Advertising,* New York: Round Table Press, 1936; London: Garland, 1985

Pulitzer, Joseph

Long-lasting influence on U.S. journalism

Most often associated with the development of New Journalism of the 1880s as well as with the yellow press of the late nineteenth century, Joseph Pulitzer had long-lasting influence on U.S. journalism. Arriving in the United States from his Austrian homeland in the waning days of the American Civil War, Pulitzer, not yet speaking English, settled in St. Louis, Missouri, where he became a reporter for the German-language newspaper *Westliche Post.* Thanks to his acumen and his business and political connections, Pulitzer acquired two newspapers that he combined into the *St. Louis Post-Dispatch.* The editorial policies he set in place at the *Post-Dispatch,* emphasizing accuracy, lively writing, and the role of a newspaper as a watchdog on government, became known as New Journalism; using these principles, Pulitzer's newspaper became successful, and other publications copied his approach.

In 1882, Pulitzer purchased the *New York World* and instigated a more sensational version of New Journalism. The *World* became even more sensational when faced with the competition posed by William Randolph Hearst's *New York Journal,* an encounter that climaxed in the sensational yellow journalism approach that characterized both newspapers' coverage of the Spanish-American War.

Because of illness, including failing sight and a nervous sensitivity to sound, Pulitzer supervised his newspaper holdings from his yacht during the last 20 years of his life. During that period, he conducted the protracted negotiations that finally resulted in a $2-million endowment for the graduate School of Journalism at New York's Columbia University.

PATRICIA BRADLEY

See also Hearst, William Randolph; New Journalism (1880s); Yellow Journalism

Further Reading
Bradley, Patricia, "Joseph Pulitzer as an American Hegelian," *American Journalism* 10 (Summer/Fall 1993)

Joseph Pulitzer Sr. in a painting by John Singer Sargent
(David Gulick/Private Collection)

Ireland, Alleyne, *An Adventure with a Genius: Recollections of Joseph Pulitzer,* New York: Dutton, 1920; London: Lovat Dickson, 1938
Seitz, Don C., *Joseph Pulitzer, His Life and Letters,* New York: Simon & Schuster, 1924
Stevens, John D., *Sensationalism and the New York Press,* New York: Columbia University Press, 1991
Swanberg, W.A., *Pulitzer,* New York: Scribner's, 1967

Q

Quiz Show Scandals

*1950s episode eroded trust in influential
new medium*

The quiz show scandals of the 1950s tarnished the image of television's golden era, calling into question the ethics and authenticity of national heroes and undermining the public's faith in the increasingly influential new medium of television. The quiz show scandals tell a tale of money and morality, fame and fortune, truth and trust, decency and deception.

Initially, television quiz shows were not rigged. Program sponsors, however, concerned about ratings and product sales, pressured program producers to make the quiz shows more dramatic, more entertaining. And so the rigging began, subtly at first. For example, contestants might be meant to overhear conversations about topics that would later be included in the quiz show. At first, the contestants were unaware of the rigging, but soon they too became active participants. Before long, contestants were being supplied not only the correct answers but also staging instructions as to how long they should pause before answering the questions, when to mop their brows, and so forth.

The drama of the big-money quiz shows proved to be wildly popular with the viewing audience. During the summer of 1957, five of the 10 top-rated shows were quiz shows, including *$64,000 Question* in the number-one spot. Winning contestants became overnight celebrities and quite wealthy.

Initial reports of the rigging were discounted as the sour grapes of disgruntled contestants. In 1957, Reverend Charles "Stoney" Jackson, who won thousands of dollars on *$64,000 Question* and *$64,000 Challenge,* charged that contestants on *$64,000 Question* were asked questions before the show started, so producers knew which questions they could answer correctly. Further, he said that producers of *$64,000 Challenge* suggested answers to contestants before the program. *Time* magazine never responded to a telegram Jackson sent, and the *New York Times* refused to print his story without more proof, although his story was picked up by syndicated columnist Drew Pearson.

Also in 1957, the *New York Journal-American* refused to print the story of another former quiz show winner, Her-bert Stempel, without further proof. Stempel was supplied questions, answers, and even stage directions in advance by *Twenty-One* producer Daniel Enright.

In the following year, Edward Hilgemeier, a standby contestant on *Dotto,* was in the dressing room before the show when he noticed the champion, Marie Winn, writing in a notebook. Suspicious of the ease with which Winn later answered questions during the show, Hilgemeier looked in the notebook and found the answers. Hilgemeier stole several pages from the notebook and showed them to challenger Yeffe Kimball. Kimball and Hilgemeier confronted the program producers and received thousands of dollars to settle the matter out of court. Not satisfied, Hilgemeier drew up an affidavit that *New York Post* reporter Jack O'Grady gave to the Federal Communications Commission (FCC). The FCC and the CBS network investigated the matter, and CBS and program sponsor Colgate-Palmolive then canceled the program. Hilgemeier, however, also complained to the district attorney of New York County, who launched an investigation into *Dotto* and other quiz shows.

Charles Van Doren, right, "concentrates" before answering a question on the television game show *Twenty-One.*
(UPI/Corbis-Bettmann)

Charles Van Doren, seated right, prepares to answer questions about rigged television quiz shows.
(UPI/Corbis-Bettmann)

After the *Dotto* scandal broke, Stempel's story about the rigging of *Twenty-One* finally was carried by the *New York Journal-American* and the *New York World-Telegram and Sun*. Enright denied the accusations and launched a counterattack to discredit Stempel. Charles Van Doren, the man who defeated Stempel on *Twenty-One,* also denied the accusations.

Van Doren, a Columbia University professor and the long-reigning champion on *Twenty-One,* was undoubtedly the most celebrated of all the personalities involved in the quiz show scandals. Coming from an upstanding family – his father was a Pulitzer-prizewinning poet – Van Doren had a boy-next-door charm that captivated the audience. After defeating Stempel, who was directed to give an incorrect answer so that Van Doren could win, Van Doren became a national celebrity, even appearing on the cover of *Time* magazine and hosting the *Today* show on NBC. It was on the *Today* show that Van Doren first denied Stempel's charges.

Van Doren also denied being involved in any rigging in testimony before a New York grand jury, as did other contestants and program producers. Producers urged the contestants not to tell the truth. Even child actress Patty Duke, a

contestant on *$64,000 Challenge,* was coached to lie in her testimony.

One contestant who did not lie before the grand jury was James Snodgrass, who, in May 1957, mailed himself a series of registered letters with the questions, answers, and directions he had been given prior to appearing on *Twenty-One*. After Snodgrass testified, Albert Freedman, the show producer who supplied Snodgrass with the information but who had previously denied doing so, was indicted on two counts of perjury.

At the conclusion of the grand jury investigation in 1959, Judge Mitchell D. Schweitzer, in an unprecedented decision, sealed the finding from the public. In response to concerns about a possible cover-up, a House of Representatives subcommittee launched its own investigation of the quiz shows. During the congressional hearings, which began in October 1959, many contestants – including, to the public's shock, Charles Van Doren – admitted lying to the grand jury. Van Doren's admission came in November 1959, after he had gone into hiding for a month to avoid testifying at the congressional hearing. Van Doren and 17 other contestants, along with producer Freedman, were convicted of lying under oath to the New York grand jury.

All received suspended sentences. In addition to the action taken against those individuals, the Communications Act was amended to make rigged or deceptive programming punishable by law, and the television networks took control of programming away from program sponsors.

While those involved in the quiz show scandals received little more than a slap on the wrist from the government for their wrongdoing, most lived the rest of their lives in relative obscurity. Most of the quiz show producers were forced out of the television industry. Dan Enright worked for 15 years in Canada, Germany, and Australia before finding employment in the United States again. Charles Van Doren lost his position at Columbia University and remained out of the public eye, save for a brief news item when he collapsed at a Connecticut gas station in September 1995.

Also forever changed was the way in which the U.S. public would view their heroes – and their television sets. In the words of President Dwight D. Eisenhower, the rigging of the quiz shows was a "terrible thing to do to the American people."

JULIA R. FOX

See also Broadcast Regulation; Golden Age of Television; Payola

Further Reading

Anderson, Kent, *Television Fraud: The History and Implications of the Quiz Show Scandals,* Westport, Connecticut: Greenwood, 1978

Karp, Walter, "The Quiz-Show Scandal," *American Heritage* 40:4 (May 1989), pp. 76–88

Stone, Joseph, and Tim Yohn, *Prime Time and Misdemeanors: Investigating the 1950s TV Quiz Scandal: A D.A.'s Account,* New Brunswick, New Jersey: Rutgers University Press, 1992

R

Radio Act of 1912

Early radio regulation enacted by Congress

As radio evolved from point-to-point communication to a mainly broadcast medium in the early twentieth century, Congress sought to organize the airwaves and to ensure that radio served the public. Two of the major concerns were the need for better communication with ships at sea and the growth of interference among experimental stations on land. Congress tried to solve both problems by passing the Radio Act of 1912.

Improving maritime radio had become an international issue, as the *Titanic* sinking and other disasters and near disasters showed. The Radio Act was designed to fulfill U.S. commitments to improve communication at sea. The law detailed how and why radio could be used on ships and regulated the transmission of distress calls.

Those provisions, however, dealt only with point-to-point radio. As far as broadcasting was concerned, the act solved few problems. It gave government broadcasters first priority on the airwaves, and it gave the Department of Commerce the power to set aside broadcast frequencies and to issue licenses – but not to deny them.

The Commerce department declared that all nongovernmental stations would be allowed to use only one frequency, even though many other wavelengths were available. That single frequency soon became too crowded as radio boomed after World War I. Extra frequencies were added, but not enough to keep up with the greater number and power of radio stations. Congress finally passed the Radio Act of 1927 in an effort to correct the problem.

THOMAS LETTS

See also Broadcast Regulation; Radio Act of 1927; Wireless Ship Act of 1910

Further Reading
Douglas, George H., *The Early Days of Radio Broadcasting,* Jefferson, North Carolina: McFarland, 1987
Smith, F. Leslie, *Perspectives on Radio and Television: Telecommunication in the United States,* 3rd ed., New York: Harper & Row, 1990

Radio Act of 1927

Established system of broadcast regulation essentially used today

The Radio Act of 1927 established many broadcast regulations followed today. It resulted from a breakdown of Secretary of Commerce Herbert Hoover's efforts to regulate broadcasting after court decisions stated that Hoover lacked regulatory control under the 1912 Radio Act. Congress finally acted to correct interference from more than 600 stations. Among provisions included in the new bill were establishment of a licensing authority and inclusion of equal opportunity provisions for political candidates. The bill passed February 18, 1927, and President Calvin Coolidge signed it into law five days later.

The act set up the Federal Radio Commission (FRC) and held several key assumptions. The public owned the airwaves, but licenses went to private entities to operate stations in the "public interest, convenience or necessity," better known as PICON. This standard became the yardstick for licensing stations and measuring other rules passed by the commission. The FRC also had discretionary power to select station operators, as there were too many applicants for available frequencies. Not everyone wanting a license could qualify, and the FRC set standards according to the act to choose licensees based on qualifications such as being of "good character," meeting technical standards, and having financial resources to operate a station. Goals for broadcasting included equitable signal distribution to all states so that service would be universal to all U.S. citizens. The act also protected broadcasting as a form of expression covered by the First Amendment. None of these powers to regulate, however, was absolute. FRC decisions could be appealed in the courts. These principles and other provisions related to common carriers (e.g., telephone and telegraph), were reenacted in the Communications Act of 1934.

LOUISE BENJAMIN

See also Broadcast Regulation; Communications Act of 1934; Federal Radio Commission; Hoover, Herbert, and Radio Regulation; Radio Act of 1912

Radio Commentators

Broadcasters' efforts to put news into perspective

The first radio news commentary ever probably was delivered by H.V. Kaltenborn on April 14, 1922, over WVP, a station on Bedloe's Island, New York, operated by the Army Signal Corps. His commentary was on a coal strike. A year later, he began a weekly series.

Commentary on the air built a following after the networks decided to identify the news broadcast by the name of the newsreader. Adding a name to a disembodied but distinctive voice created a personality. By 1927, the newspaper listings identified Kaltenborn, David Lawrence, and Frederick Williams Wile. Within a few years, program titles tacked onto the names told listeners the kind of news and expertise they were getting. Wile discussed the *Political Situation;* George R. Holmes provided the *Washington News;* and Edwin C. Hill offered the *Human Side of the News.*

Definitions of what a commentator was tended to blur because the distinctions between the newscaster and the news analyst and between the news analyst and the news commentator looked clearer on paper than they did when applied to Gabriel Heatter or Kaltenborn or Fulton Lewis Jr. on any particular night. Newscasters simply read accounts of events; analysts tried to put those events into perspective without offering solutions, taking positions, pointing with pride, or viewing with alarm. In theory, the listener should not be able to determine the analyst's politics by what he said. Commentators were known for subtle suggestions about the best course of action and for angry demands that listeners wire their congressman. While editorializing represented the views of the station itself, commentary represented the views of the commentator.

Generally, the more vociferous the commentary, the less influential the commentator. Edward R. Murrow understood this instinctively during the London blitz, and his reputation as a temperate, usually objective analyst served him well when he attacked Senator Joseph McCarthy. The commentator's power lay in the potential; it grew by understatement.

Radio commentators regularly picked over the day's events to find corroboration for their continually voiced beliefs. They filled the same need on radio that columnists did in newspapers, offering a personal voice to explain a world that was daily becoming more depersonalized, complicated, and dangerous. Listeners found it comforting to hear someone who thought as they did, understood their problems and feelings, got the inside scoop, and explained it all so that it made sense.

The number of network news commentators was about 20 when World War II started. By 1947, 600 or more local and national commentators reported the news and analyzed its significance.

A 1938 survey by the Columbia University School of Journalism of 300 national and local radio commentators reported that one in seven was plainly biased, with Boston the worst city for commentator prejudice. Even so, radio commentary showed less partiality than did newspaper editorials or newspaper columnists. Overlooking such zealous partisans as Boake Carter, Lewis, and Cecil Brown, radio commentary was often rather mild. President Franklin D. Roosevelt found in some of these commentators a way to bypass the often hostile and reactionary press lords to seek public support for his programs.

An agreement in 1933 between networks and press associations limited the number of daily newscasts but placed no limit on commentaries providing generalizations and background on the news, and the commentaries could be sponsored. The networks quickly decided to change Walter Winchell, Lowell Thomas, Carter, Kaltenborn, and several others from "news broadcasters" to "commentators." The main reason for the flowering of radio commentary, however, was that people wanted it. The times were out of joint. Commentary feasts on uncertainty; normalcy starves it.

How well educated were the radio commentators? A study of 28 popular commentators showed that 15 were college graduates. Eight claimed to have been explorers and travelers, 12 had been foreign correspondents, one a railroad worker, one a salesman, and one a mapmaker. From the later 1920s to the early 1930s, commentaries usually were offered by knowledgeable, well-traveled men like Thomas, Upton Close, and Kaltenborn. During the 1930s, they were joined by men such as Carter and Lewis, who had strong opinions about – and against – the New Deal, which they talked about night after night. The 1940s saw the popularity of experienced journalists like Murrow and Raymond Gram Swing, as well as commentators who sounded as if they knew much more than they were telling. Winchell and Heatter fell into the latter category.

After war broke out in Europe, the NBC, CBS, and Mutual networks tried to limit the expression of personal opinion, issuing a joint declaration of news policy:

> No news analyst or news broadcaster of any kind is to be allowed to express personal editorial judgment or to select or omit news with the purpose of creating any given effect, and no news analyst . . . is to be allowed to say anything in an effort to influence action or opinion of others one way or the other. . . . His basis for evaluation should, of course, be impersonal, sincere, and honest.

To protect themselves from charges of collusion and antitrust legal action, the networks first cleared the joint declaration with the Federal Communications Commission (FCC), which itself in January 1941 issued the Mayflower Decision opposing editorializing by broadcasters. In 1949, the FCC reversed itself with the Fairness Doctrine, which urged licensees to take editorial stands on public issues.

In 1942, 31 New York commentators organized themselves under Kaltenborn's leadership into a craft guild, the Association of Radio News Analysts (ARNA). Although the name they chose pointed to a willingness to go along with the networks on neutrality, most members opposed the policy. One of the ARNA's first fights was for the right to offer comment in commentaries. The ARNA fought for such causes as Swing's efforts to eliminate the "middle commercial," which interrupted the analysis of events to sell a product. On the other hand, some commentators read their own commercials and did so with enthusiasm. Carter ped-

H.V. Kaltenborn was a leading radio commentator in the 1940s.
(State Historical Society of Wisconsin)

dled Huskies breakfast cereal, and Heatter resonantly switched from the war against Germany to "the great war against gingivitis – gingivitis, that creeps in like a saboteur."

In 1945, *Variety* appraised 30 radio reporters, analysts, and commentators. The paper judged six to be reactionary, five conservative, ten middle-of-the-road, four moderately liberal, none extremely liberal, and five as defying classification.

Radio commentary had grown in the decade of the 1930s from a curiosity to a concatenation of voices with the power to influence political decisions, and by the end of World War II, to a vital, mature force. By 1950, its power had waned.

As television sets pushed radio sets out of the parlors of U.S. homes, the news commentators were pushed out, too. Some, like Eric Sevareid, established themselves as commentators in the new medium, yet there was a sense that an opinion did not have quite the impact when a face was attached to it. Thomas chose not to expand his commentaries to television because he believed that unimpressed viewers would say, "He looks just like Joe Doakes down the street.

. . . Whereas, with radio, a voice from out in space carries with it some of the majesty and authority of the Almighty."

IRVING FANG

See also Fairness Doctrine; Kaltenborn, H.V.; Mayflower Decision; Murrow, Edward R.; Newspaper Columnists

Further Reading

Bliss, Edward, *Now the News: The Story of Broadcast Journalism,* New York: Columbia University Press, 1991

Culbert, David, *News for Everyman: Radio and Foreign Affairs in Thirties America,* Westport, Connecticut: Greenwood, 1976

Fang, Irving E., *Those Radio Commentators!,* Ames: Iowa State University Press, 1977

Hosley, David H., *As Good As Any: Foreign Correspondence on American Radio, 1930–1940,* Westport, Connecticut: Greenwood, 1984

Wecter, Dixon, "Hearing is Believing," *Atlantic Monthly* (July 1945)

Radio Corporation of America

Major player in broadcasting from radio's inception

In the early 1900s, American Marconi was the largest wireless communications company in the United States, controlling almost all U.S. military reports via their British-owned (but U.S.-controlled) facilities. Even though American Marconi had divested itself of many U.S. holdings, President Woodrow Wilson and others were concerned about British control of U.S. communications. This led to a syndicate being formed in 1919 by General Electric (GE) to purchase the British interest in American Marconi, after which GE's American Marconi shares were exchanged for shares in the newly formed Radio Corporation of America (RCA).

Over the next two years, a consolidation took place that brought together all the patents necessary to assemble a complete wireless system, from transmitters to radio receivers. By 1921, GE owned 30 percent of RCA; Westinghouse, 21 percent; American Telephone and Telegraph (AT&T), 10 percent; and United Fruit (Tropical Radio Telegraph), 4 percent. The remaining shares were owned primarily by individuals.

Under the agreement, RCA was to sell the equipment manufactured by GE and Westinghouse and administer the patents pool. GE would manufacture 60 percent of the market and Westinghouse 40 percent. AT&T's Western Electric company would have a monopoly on selling transmitters to outsiders. The main idea was to control every facet of the wireless business. As telephone use increased, AT&T found itself more aligned with others in the telephone industry than with the remaining partners in RCA, who were involved primarily in radio. After a contentious dispute over which company was supposed to do what, AT&T sold its shares in RCA and withdrew from the board.

In January 1926, the National Broadcasting Company (NBC) was formed by RCA, which controlled 50 percent, GE (30 percent), and Westinghouse (20 percent). All the stations owned by the three companies would become a radio network. AT&T's radio station, WEAF in New York, was purchased by NBC. RCA now owned two radio networks: NBC Red (which included WEAF) and NBC Blue. In 1930, RCA became the sole owner of NBC.

An antitrust suit was brought against RCA, GE, Westinghouse, and AT&T by the U.S. Department of Justice in May 1930 because of their cross-licensing agreements. AT&T withdrew from the agreements in 1931. By the end of 1932, a settlement had been arranged: RCA would retain NBC; GE and Westinghouse would withdraw from RCA but would retain their radio stations, which NBC would operate for them. The case was settled out of court, and RCA became an entity unto itself. RCA was forced to sell one of its NBC networks in 1943 when the Supreme Court upheld the Federal Communications Commission's (FCC's) chain broadcasting rules. NBC Blue was sold to Edward J. Noble, manufacturer of Life Savers candy, for $8 million and became the American Broadcasting Company in 1945.

RCA remained a major player in the communications industry by manufacturing radios, televisions, phonographs, and other electronic equipment; owning NBC until 1985, when it was sold to GE (who then sold it to Westwood One in 1987); and manufacturing records and compact discs.

LAURA R. LINDER

See also Radio Networks; Television Networks

Further Reading
Sobel, Robert, *RCA*, New York: Stein and Day, 1986

Radio Entertainment

U.S. listeners quickly found new medium ideal for diversion

Listeners heard the first radio program nearly two decades before what eventually would be termed "broadcasting" began. On December 24, 1906, inventor Reginald Fessenden, experimenting with methods of sending the human voice through the "ether," transmitted a brief but varied program sampling of singing, violin playing, and talking from his makeshift studio in Massachusetts. Startled radio operators who were accustomed to hearing only the dots and dashes of Morse code were Fessenden's only audience.

Fessenden's Christmas Eve transmission ironically set an important precedent for radio programmers once broadcasting to a mass audience got under way in the early 1920s. Music would become a staple of radio from the very beginning. As a matter of fact, listeners to the first U.S. radio station, KDKA in Pittsburgh, Pennsylvania, were treated to plenty of music, much of it produced live in the KDKA studio. By 1922, radio stations also were beginning to air locally produced dramatic programs. As the number of radio stations mushroomed across the United States in the early 1920s, however, the microphone was transported from the studio to remote locations to cover everything from sports events to church services.

Music remained the most popular radio programming throughout the 1920s, however, with classical and popular music holding an equal share in radio listener popularity polls. Orchestra leaders such as Paul Whiteman, Guy Lombardo, and Benny Goodman became famous as a result of their radio appearances. By the end of the 1920s, advertising had established itself in radio to such an extent that advertisers were producing many of their own programs. The result was that many radio orchestra names such as "the Ipana Troubadors" and "the Goodrich Zippers" bore the names of commercial sponsors.

The appearance of radio networks in the mid-1920s pushed radio programming in yet a different direction. Radio listeners in small, out-of-the-way places now could hear big-name entertainers. Network radio ushered in a means by which programs could build a national following as happened with *Amos and Andy*, said to be the most popular show ever to air on radio.

The success of radio networks was assisted by the collapse of vaudeville. Moving from the vaudeville stage to the radio studio were such well-known entertainers as George

A radio drama enacted in an NBC studio featured a sound-effects man and "victims" of a mass murder groaning on the floor.
(Corbis-Bettman)

Burns and Gracie Allen, Jack Benny, Ed Wynn, and Bing Crosby. This pool of talent allowed the creation of the radio variety show, on which a gathering of performers (singers, comedians, actors, etc.) would appear weekly on a program hosted by another popular entertainer. The *Rudy Vallee Show* was the first such program of this kind.

The early 1930s ushered in dozens of radio dramatic series such as *The Shadow, First Nighter,* and *Lux Radio Theater,* as well as popular daytime serials such as *Ma Perkins, Helen Trent,* and *Backstage Wife.* These serials became known as "soap operas" because they were sponsored by soap companies. Amateur talent programs such as *Major Bowe's Original Amateur Hour* and audience participation programs such as *Professor Quiz* were popular radio shows of the 1930s. Juvenile listeners were treated to such hero-laden programs as *Jack Armstrong, The Lone Ranger,* and *Jungle Jim.*

U.S. listeners turned to their radios more and more during the 1930s as a source for news and information. As a result, commentators such as Lowell Thomas and Gabriel Heatter became household names, as did such controversial public figures as Huey Long, who used radio to build a national following for particular political movements. Most notable of all the political uses of radio during the 1930s was President Franklin D. Roosevelt's series of addresses to the nation that came to be known as "fireside chats."

Serious drama also found a place in network radio. Some of the leading stage and screen actors of the day appeared in radio plays either adapted for or written especially for the medium. Playwrights such as Norman Corwin helped elevate the intellectual level of radio's dramatic programming to such a degree that the 1930s and 1940s became known as radio's golden age. The power of radio drama to move listeners was illustrated by the near hysteria that erupted among thousands of listeners to the radio version of H.G. Wells's *The War of the Worlds.* The program, aired on October 30, 1938, and produced by Orson Welles, depicted an invasion of the planet Earth by Martians in such a way that the drama was mistaken for the real thing by many in the audience.

The effort by radio networks to create programs with mass appeal resulted in formulaic programming that by 1935 had evolved into 11 discernible program types. Ranging from most to least numerous in terms of the number of programs comprising each type, the 11 included: drama and comedy; crime, detective and mystery; adventure; musical; quiz, panel, and audience participation; variety; discussion and forum; children's; religious; documentaries; and "human interest."

Threats of war in Europe during the 1930s hastened the development of network radio news organizations. Seasoned reporters such as William L. Shirer, H.V. Kaltenborn, and Edward R. Murrow brought eyewitness accounts of wartime events to listeners. Once the United States itself entered World War II in 1941, radio became the primary means by which the U.S. audience received news of the war's progress.

On the entertainment side, wartime radio programs such as *The Army Hour* and *Stage Door Canteen* were produced especially for stateside listeners as well as military personnel stationed overseas. These programs highlighted the talents of famous entertainers and members of the armed forces alike. Patriotic themes were abundant in programs aimed at adults as well as children. The wartime exploits of lead characters in *Captain Midnight, Terry and the Pirates,* and *Jungle Jim,* for instance, were equaled only by the heroic deeds of *Don Winslow of the Navy* and *Hop Harrigan.*

Dramatic series such as *Counter Spy* and *Alias John Freedom* and frequent documentaries such as *This Is War* and *The Midwest Mobilizes* were added to the repertoire of network radio programming to carry their own unique messages of war mobilization and participation. Writers for a number of popular soap operas interwove wartime situations (for example, characters working in war-related occupations or otherwise coping with wartime conditions) into the standard storylines of their daily programs.

Network radio programming returned to its prewar form in late 1945, but the success networks had enjoyed for more than two decades would be short-lived. Many of the programs that had been popular prior to the war returned along with their stars. And, indeed, radio network program producers scored some of their greatest successes in the early 1950s with such critically acclaimed programs as *Dimension X* and *X Minus One* (on NBC) and *Gunsmoke, Dragnet,* and *Philco Playhouse* (all on CBS). Television, however, was beginning to overwhelm radio as a mass attraction by the late 1940s, and radio network talent, programs, and program production dollars were migrating steadily to the new medium.

Radio was forced by television's competition to develop new and unique approaches to programming. As a result, many nonnetwork affiliated radio stations (called "independents") developed "formula," or "format," programming that consisted of music, news, personality disc jockeys, and heavy station promotion that would appeal strictly to a local audience. The most popular music of the period – rock and roll – actually anchored the first successful radio format called top 40. The top-40 format was carefully crafted to appeal to youth, who were buying most of the records during the period.

More esoteric radio program formats began appearing in the 1960s as a result of FM radio's emergence. Many FM stations at first were co-owned by AM station owners who simulcast the AM station's programming on their FM station. Those owners who programmed FM stations independently often did so using highbrow (generally, classical music), avant garde, underground, or jazz program formats as a way of attracting the few listeners who owned FM receivers and who were particular about the signal quality of what they heard. By the mid-1960s, FM radio began achieving parity with AM radio once the Federal Communications Commission required that co-owned AM and FM stations be programmed separately from one another. Within a few years, FM radio stations were providing program formats quite similar to their AM station counterparts.

Radio programming formats during the 1970s and 1980s evolved into variations of the tried and true. Thus, adult contemporary, easy listening, album-oriented rock, and urban contemporary, to name a few, were aired by a majority of U.S. radio stations, AM and FM alike. The

1980s and 1990s, however, witnessed efforts by radio programmers to reach a narrower and better-defined audience. Formats began appearing that departed from music as their base. As such, the all-news, all-comedy, all-sports, all-business, and, especially, the all-talk formats gained a varying degree of success in finding niche audiences.

RONALD GARAY

See also Commercialization of Broadcasting; Golden Age of Radio; Radio Commentators; Radio Networks; Radio News; Roosevelt, Franklin D., and the Media; "War of the Worlds"

Further Reading

Ditingo, Vincent M., *The Remaking of Radio,* Boston: Focal, 1995

Douglas, George H., *The Early Days of Radio Broadcasting,* Jefferson, North Carolina: McFarland, 1987

Fornatale, Peter, and Joshua E. Mills, *Radio in the Television Age,* Woodstock, New York: Overlook, 1980

Keith, Michael C., and Joseph M. Krause, *The Radio Station,* 3rd ed., Boston: Focal, 1993

MacDonald, J. Fred, *Don't Touch That Dial! Radio Programming in American Life, 1920–1960,* Chicago: Nelson-Hall, 1979

Nye, Russel, *The Unembarrassed Muse: The Popular Arts in America,* New York: Dial, 1970

Willey, George A., "The Soap Operas and the War," *Journal of Broadcasting* 7 (1963)

Radio Networks

*Interconnected system that facilitates
programming distribution*

A broadcasting network distributes programming and advertising to interconnected and independently owned (affiliated) stations for simultaneous broadcast. Radio broadcasting networks developed through four approximate periods: formation (to 1934), dominance (1934–50), decline (1950–85), and satellite-based revival (from 1985).

Several stations experimented with one-time links with other outlets in the early 1920s for special programs (e.g., presidential speeches) or in an attempt to share the rising cost of programs across several stations by reaching smaller market stations with programs from major cities. American Telephone and Telegraph (AT&T) pioneered the use of telephone lines to regularly link stations in 1925–26; its competitors had to use lower-quality telegraph wires. When AT&T sold its radio stations in 1926, the telephone company focused on network interconnection, a role it monopolized for 60 years. The first radio network designed as such was the National Broadcasting Company (NBC), owned by the Radio Corporation of America (RCA). Its four-hour inaugural program aired in November 1926 and was carried by 25 stations. The 1927 Rose Bowl inaugurated a second

NBC network of six stations. The two became known as NBC Red and NBC Blue, respectively, the former always the more popular and carrying more advertising. Regular NBC evening programming began in 1928.

Formation of the Columbia Broadcasting System (CBS) was more complicated and protracted. United Independent Broadcasters was set up early in 1927 as a counter to NBC. The Columbia Phonograph Company took over a few months later, giving the network a new name in time for its inaugural broadcast in September. A year later, the fledgling and money-losing operation was purchased by William S. Paley, vice president of one of the network's early advertisers, the Congress Cigar Company. Paley would run CBS for a half century.

The three networks helped to establish radio as an accepted habit by the early 1930s. Advertising agencies owned and produced most sponsored programs, and network programming began to move into daytime hours. Initial radio audience research – crude "ratings" – was supported partially by the networks beginning in 1929–30.

A fourth network of a very different nature appeared in 1934 when the Mutual Broadcasting System began sharing programs among its four high-powered member stations: WGN in Chicago; WOR in Newark, New Jersey; WLW in Cincinnati, Ohio; and WXYZ in Detroit, Michigan. The latter owned and programmed the popular *The Lone Ranger,* on which the new network expanded. Mutual did not have the centralized ownership pattern of NBC and CBS but was more of a cooperative operation, by 1936 serving mainly small-market stations across the country.

The "golden years" of radio networks lasted for a mere decade and a half and were ended by the rapid rise of television. Supplementing the four national networks were upward of 20 regional network services, 14 of them operating only in a single state. NBC was the largest and by 1935 had affiliation agreements with 14 percent of the nation's stations – a figure that had rose to 25 percent by 1941. CBS affiliated with just under 20 percent of all stations in the late 1930s. Mutual served about the same proportion of stations by 1940, but most were smaller and used lower power, and many had primary affiliations with another network.

Radio appeared too tightly controlled to many of its critics, however, including some in Congress. Network affiliation contracts bound stations to their networks for up to five years, leaving little programming discretion in the hands of local managers. Stations lacking affiliations had little appeal to advertisers because of their generally smaller audiences. Thus, popular big-name programming and advertising largely was controlled by the two NBC networks and CBS, with Mutual lagging behind.

The Federal Communications Commission (FCC) initiated an investigation into what it termed "chain" broadcasting in 1938. After 73 days of testimony and thousands of pages of exhibits, the commission early in 1941 issued its *Report on Chain Broadcasting,* which dictated dramatic changes in how networks interacted with their affiliate stations.

Delayed by court appeals, the rules finally were upheld in a landmark U.S. Supreme Court decision, *NBC* v. *United*

States (1943). With that ruling, NBC was forced to sell one of its networks, and it spun off the weaker Blue chain to Edward J. Noble, a candy manufacturer, who renamed it the American Broadcasting Company (ABC) in 1945.

Network dominance continued as the expansion in number of AM stations was limited by World War II and postwar transition. Whereas 60 percent of all stations had network affiliations before the United States entered World War II, by 1945, 95 percent of all stations were tied to networks. Network radio reached its height of popularity and financial success in the late 1940s. Although it was declining, the network proportion of all radio advertising income was still 35 to 45 percent – and broke $200 million in 1947–49.

Radio network programming permeated the entire schedule of affiliate stations – day and night. Golden age radio programming was nearly all network material. What came to be accepted television genres – such as half-hour situation comedies, daytime soap operas, game and quiz shows, sports play-by-play, and children's programs – all were developed first for network radio, most by the mid-1930s. Radio network newscasts were a primary source of public information. Prime evening hours were given over to programs competing for top Hooperatings. The typical household used radio for more than four hours a day.

More-specialized networks developed to grab part of the rich market. Innovative Texas broadcaster Gordon Mc-Clendon (who would later help pioneer formula top-40 radio) began the Liberty Network in 1948, which had expanded to national status with some 400 affiliates by the early 1950s. His service offered a variety of programs plus news (and cleverly re-created baseball games based on sound effects and narration drawn from wire-service reports of actual game progress). A Continental Network serving FM stations began service in 1947.

But from this peak, network radio declined rapidly in the early 1950s in the face of growing competition from thousands of new radio stations and the growth of commercial television. Far faster than most in the industry expected, advertisers deserted radio for television after 1950, with the result that increasing proportions of network radio time were sustaining (not sponsored) and soon reverted to affiliate stations for local programming. By 1952, less than 60 percent of AM stations on the air were affiliated with a network; by 1960, with more stations, only a third had a network tie.

Faced with decline, the weaker networks gave way. McClendon's Liberty Network collapsed in 1952. ABC was taken over in 1953 and, as with CBS and NBC, devoted more energy to television. The Continental FM network stopped broadcasting in 1954. Mutual changed hands six times in 1956–59 and lost direction as well as affiliates.

Many stations gave up (and new stations seldom sought) network affiliation as it became increasingly clear they could make more money with their own music or "middle-of-the-road" programming. While such programming cost more than "free" network programs, all of a station's hours could now provide revenue; with a network affiliation, the station's best hours were dominated by its network, limiting its revenue potential.

Network programming fast dwindled as its best programs and most popular stars moved to television. Prime-time drama and comedy programming gave way to television first, followed by daytime shows. Radio networks became known as news and special events (and sports) services, having closed down virtually all other programming by the 1960s. In 1955, NBC began *Monitor* as a weekday magazine-style program of news, music, and features. It soon reverted to weekend-only service. NBC, CBS, and Mutual offered short-lived revivals of drama in the 1970s, aiming at both the nostalgia market and those who had never listened to dramatic fare.

In an attempt to tailor network service to local station programming formats (a reversal of the traditional approach), ABC in 1968 broke its single network service into four (later six) different chains, each taking 15 minutes of the hour. One was designated for FM stations (not the first such service – others had been briefly tried in the 1940s), while the other three served differently programmed AM outlets: Contemporary (music stations), Information (talk and news – and the largest and most successful of the four), and Personality (later renamed Entertainment). The change worked. By 1970, about 30 percent of all stations had a tie to ABC. By the mid-1980s, ABC was pulling in about 40 percent of all network radio advertising dollars. CBS and NBC followed suit, although to a lesser degree and not for nearly 20 years. Another type of specialization involved networks aimed at ethnic minorities. Several short-lived networks for African Americans appeared in the 1950s and 1960s. Mutual began one in 1972, and two others – National Black Network in 1973 and Sheridan Broadcasting Network (which acquired the Mutual black network operation) in 1979 – followed. In 1991, these two merged to form the American Urban Radio Network, which offered five audio services to some 300 radio stations.

Throughout these years of decline, network-owned radio stations, all located in major markets, made money. Nothing could hide the fact, however, that radio network service was no longer viable. The definitive sign of the end of traditional radio networks came in 1987, when General Electric sold off the pioneering NBC radio network to Los Angeles–based Westwood One, which had already taken over Mutual in 1985. The NBC radio stations were sold off separately.

By the 1980s, it was becoming harder to define the difference between a radio network and a program syndicator. The company providing twice-a-year radio network ratings information defined a network as "a program service that has continuity of programming; . . . contractual agreements with its affiliates; the capability of an instant feed to all affiliates; and a clearance system to it [that] can determine which affiliates carry which programs." They also offered programs that carried national advertising and paid stations for their time. Syndicators, on the other hand, provided formatted popular music; listeners often assumed that programs on their local station originated there. Stations paid for syndication services that did not usually carry advertising or news. The number of programmers – chiefly syndicators but including networks – expanded from perhaps a dozen in 1980 to about 35 in 1987, and dozens a decade later. The number of distinct formats offered became increasingly specialized ("narrowcasting") in tone.

Using the definition above, only five commercial operations could be termed true networks (although many others used the term) in the mid-1990s: ABC, with eight networks; CBS, with four; American Urban, with four, all aimed at black audiences; Unistar, with five; and Westwood One, with five, including both two NBC and one Mutual service. The last two served more than 1,000 radio stations each (many stations, of course, subscribed to several radio services and might affiliate with one or more networks as well). Several of the listed "sub-networks," in turn, offered multiple channels of music or talk.

Virtually all of these networks used satellite distribution. Just as domestic communications satellites aided distribution of video signals that was more efficient and less expensive than terrestrial links, so, too, did they encourage new audio service. By the late 1980s, there were more than 20 such services, each offering multiple channels of digital music (and some other features). A number of cable television networks marketed audio news and feature services by the late 1980s. Stations could and did pick and choose programs or formats among several service providers, further breaking down the traditional sense of a few recognized national networks with local affiliates.

Similar satellite efficiencies put new life into one of the oldest radio services – educational or noncommercial stations that had lacked any national network until the 1970s. National Public Radio (NPR) had operated as a traditional landline interconnected service for its member stations beginning in 1970. By switching to satellite delivery in 1984 (and showing the way for all other broadcasters), NPR's news, information, and music programming became more widely available. A parallel public radio syndicator, American Public Radio (later Public Radio International), used similar means to provide the programs of Garrison Keillor and others.

CHRISTOPHER H. STERLING

See also African American Media; Broadcast Ratings; Broadcast Regulation; Commercialization of Broadcasting; Golden Age of Radio; Noncommercial Radio; Radio Entertainment; Radio News; Radio Syndication; *Report on Chain Broadcasting;* Television Entertainment

Further Reading

Bergreen, Laurence, *Look Now, Pay Later: The Rise of Network Broadcasting,* Garden City, New York: Doubleday, 1980
Johnson, Frank W., Jr., "A History of the Development of Black Radio Networks in the United States," *Journal of Radio Studies* 2 (1993–94)
Midgley, Ned, *The Advertising and Business Side of Radio,* New York: Prentice-Hall, 1948
Paley, William S., *As It Happened: A Memoir,* Garden City, New York: Doubleday, 1979
Robinson, Thomas Porter, *Radio Networks and the Federal Government,* New York: Columbia University Press, 1943

Radio News

Unfolding events made news vital to radio audiences

Radio news grew up with World War II, according to William S. Paley, president of the Columbia Broadcast System (CBS). During the war, radio newsmen filled the airwaves with the tragedy of conflict. Edward R. Murrow, William L. Shirer, Elmer Davis, H.V. Kaltenborn, Robert Trout, Douglas Edwards, and a new breed of reporters portrayed the news as they saw it unfold. According to Paul White, director of public affairs and special events at CBS, these people did not set out to become radio news reporters. In fact, those first on the European front were sent into the field to organize events for broadcast – public affairs programs such as speeches and choral music. Murrow's original title in Europe was that of Director of Talks and Programs for Europe.

The groundwork for radio news began with events surrounding the Great Depression and industry reactions to those events. Radio had a dramatic effect on the lives of those living through the depression. In the politically charged climate of the New Deal and the debate over the U.S. place in the world, the low cost of radio receivers made radio a powerful source of political information as well as entertainment. As the issues were debated, radio became the platform for ideological discussion. Through the use of radio, President Franklin D. Roosevelt delivered his "fireside chats," and critics Huey P. Long and Father Charles Coughlin responded with their platforms for social justice. During the 1930s, information, news, feature, and commentary programs grew in popularity, but they grew with some resistance from the printed press.

The expression "press-radio war" often is used to describe the struggles of a growing radio news industry of the 1930s. It was not really a war but a two-industry struggle for leadership positions with the media audience. Basically, the newspapers were looking for a way to keep news off the radio because they were afraid of the competition for audience and advertisers. As a result, they pressured the press wire services not to sell their services to the radio networks, and they sought to impose restrictions on radio news itself. The eventual press-radio war restrictions imposed by the print press limited radio news to bulletins. A Press Radio Bureau was organized to supply two five-minute news summaries daily, but these were not to be broadcast until 9:30 in the morning or until after 9:00 in the evening, and news bulletins were limited. As Shirer put it, he and Murrow were busy in Europe putting kids' choirs on the air. During the same time, however, these restrictions were imposed, the number of radio network commentators grew substantially, and both CBS and NBC, although not yet formally in the news business, were working with commentators and their staffs to train them to present the news of the day.

The press-radio war forced the radio networks to nurture in-house news-gathering organizations, which, as the war approached, would be called upon to provide a more comprehensive type of coverage. By September 1938, the Press Radio Bureau ceased to function, but CBS and NBC had already established the foundation for news programming in their commentary and feature programming staffs. As World War II unfolded, the purpose of these fledgling organizations was transformed from commentary and public affairs to news; they were now to provide the first eyewitness news roundups.

Although the press-radio war was nothing more than a public economic struggle between competitive free enterprise systems, it was one of the most important factors in the history of radio news. The networks gambled on the popularity of their growing news commentary programs. These internal organizations grew, and news bureaus were established around the globe. At first, these bureaus arranged events for broadcast, but as the war approached, these outposts were transformed into news-gathering organizations that lasted for years.

The war and the years that followed saw network news programming grow significantly. Network radio news staffs grew as the demand for information increased. At the advent of television, the radio newspeople, many of whom had come to the new media from a print background, made a transition into the new visual medium.

With World War II, the CBS and NBC networks marked the beginning of a new era for broadcast journalism. The foundations of radio and television news were created in the first network news roundups. In the late twentieth century, the emphasis continued to focus on the gathering of information and on-the-spot factual reporting within a format that still resembled those first used in World War II.

Local radio station news, in contrast to network radio news, has always struggled – the only exceptions being today's news and talk formats. Larger stations sometimes were able to dedicate funds for a news wire service (the Associated Press or United Press International), but smaller stations struggled with station staff merely reading the wire copy or the daily newspaper, then moving on to other duties within the station.

The deregulation of radio during the 1970s and 1980s by the Federal Communications Commission (FCC) had a profound effect on radio news. Prior to deregulation, news was one of the programs considered at the time of license renewal. News was a public service to the community at large, and this recognition, along with pressure from the FCC, was enough to encourage many stations to at least maintain a minimal amount of news. Deregulation, however, dramatically altered this pressure, and later studies point to the trend of deemphasizing news and public affairs in favor of a more profitable use of airtime – music. As radio music formats specialized and the marketplace deregulation took hold, any news left in the programming was molded to fit the format – sometimes making it difficult to tell the difference between news and disc-jockey chatter. In the late twentieth century, radio news came in a variety of forms. The traditional news and news patterns moved to the all-news stations; the musical station mixed news with a heavy dose of lifestyle delivery. Radio news and radio music formats were based not on public service but on marketplace demand.

DONALD G. GODFREY

See also Radio Commentators; Radio Networks

Further Reading
Chester, Giraud, "The Press Radio War: 1933–1935," *Public Opinion Quarterly* 13 (Summer 1949)
Fang, Irving E., *Those Radio Commentators!*, Ames: Iowa State University Press, 1977
Godfrey, Donald G., "CBS World News Roundup: Setting the Stage for the Next Half Century," *American Journalism* 7:3 (Summer 1990)
Smith, Robert R., "Origins of Radio Network News Commentary," *Journal of Broadcasting* 9 (Spring 1965)
White, Paul, *News on the Air,* New York: Harcourt, Brace, 1947

Radio Syndication
Preparing programming for distribution to many stations

Syndication – producing programming for sale, lease, trade, or barter to broadcasters – became a factor in radio when the medium was still in its infancy. The idea was hardly new, since newspaper syndicates had been producing and distributing feature articles, comics, and supplementary sections since the 1860s. Shared programming, through either networking or services offered by independent distributors, soon became indispensable for the neophyte radio, as its early-day progenitors began to realize the logistic and financial challenges of maintaining a continuous program schedule.

Electronic transcriptions, a recording process pioneered by Western Electric in the late 1920s, made syndication a growing enterprise, even in the face of the rapid expansion of the radio networks. Transcribed discs made drama, music, and variety programs possible on stations that were unable to obtain affiliation with NBC or CBS. Advertising agencies, major players in the development and production of network programs, also invested in producing transcribed shows as a means of enhancing their clients' opportunities to reach audiences in areas not served by network affiliates. Transcriptions also quickly became a useful tool for nonprofit entities seeking radio exposure. Programs were offered free to stations in exchange for airing the plugs contained within, such as the U.S. Army's popular musical variety program, *Proudly We Hail,* which premiered in 1927.

C.P. MacGregor, who produced *Proudly We Hail,* pioneered the transcription business in 1927, calling his product "advertising records." Historians, however, generally credit Chicago radio actors Charles Correll and Freeman Fisher Gosden with initiating the concept of program syndication. *Amos and Andy,* their popular daily comedy, moved to WMAQ in 1928 with the understanding that the program would be recorded and sold to other stations. The program enjoyed immense success in syndication before it was lured away from WMAQ by the NBC Blue network in 1929.

The late 1920s also gave rise to a rather unusual form of

syndication: informational script services, which were offered free of charge to stations by companies seeking free radio exposure. Several corporations routinely made scripts available to stations, an attractive service in this era predating broadcast news wire services. The most famous of these features was *NewsCasting,* developed by Fred Smith of WLW in Cincinnati, Ohio, in cooperation with *Time* magazine. Daily manuscripts were prepared in *Time*'s news department and airmailed to stations that agreed to clear time for the feature.

Transcribed programs flourished after World War II, as a surge in AM station construction precipitated an increased demand for programming and as broadcasters (including the Federal Communications Commission [FCC]) began to show a more favorable attitude toward airing recordings. Major technological improvements greatly improved the fidelity of transcriptions, and the once-popular idea that the public would never accept recorded programs instead of live performances subsided when entertainer Bing Crosby began to record his weekly show for ABC in 1946. Program syndication thus became a thriving enterprise as entertainers such as Pat O'Brien, Guy Lombardo, and Alan Ladd began to see the advantages of recording programs and selling them to radio stations. Nearly 170 transcription companies sprang up by 1950, and in 1948, the Keystone Broadcasting System became the nation's first "transcription network," providing drama, music, and variety programs for more than 300 small-market, nonnetwork-affiliated stations. Another firm, Ziv, Inc., made syndication a multimillion-dollar industry in 1947, with 24 programs contracted to run on 850 stations. One of Ziv's most popular features, a series of dramatic shows called *Favorite Story,* aired on 223 stations.

Radio's gradual acceptance of music recordings paved the way for the evolution of "disc jockey" formats in the late 1940s. This format was both popular and inexpensive to produce, and as the phonograph record became a mainstay of radio programming, even the networks began to feature such programs. For syndicators, disc jockey formats introduced new opportunities, and it did not take long for them to capitalize on this new trend in programming. Renowned entertainers or major market announcers were contracted to host disc jockey programs – as with bandleader Tommy Dorsey, whose weekly show was first offered to stations in 1948 by syndicator Lewis G. Cowan. Harry S. Goodman Productions offered a similar program that year featuring Duke Ellington. By the mid-1950s, the syndicated disc jockey format became a mainstay of radio syndication. Ziv Productions, for example, featured an hourly program each week with Ginger Rogers, Tony Martin, Peggy Lee, and Dick Powell, who provided timely comments about the music, the artists they featured, and other typical announcer prattle. These programs, interestingly enough, were rarely self-contained; that is, syndicators only provided the announcers' vocal inserts. Stations usually were required to add the records and mix the shows locally. The success of the disc jockey programs positioned syndicators to be on the ground floor of a programming bonanza when automation, the practice of executing radio formats using computers instead of live announcers, became a factor in the early 1960s.

Automation was introduced by the Schafer Electronics Corporation in the mid-1950s as a way to program radio stations more economically. KLIF in Dallas, Texas, using Schafer equipment, became one of the first stations to experiment with automated programming. Automation was a godsend for frugal programming budgets in a time of unprecedented growth on the AM band, as many small markets received their first local radio service. Also, after FCC approval of stereo broadcasting spurred unprecedented development of the FM band in 1961, automation proved to be a thrifty solution to programming this new, yet unproved, venue. Computer-executed programming became even more attractive when a 1967 FCC ruling prohibited "simulcasting" (simultaneously airing the same programming on both stations) on commonly owned AM and FM facilities in cities with a population of over 100,000.

The syndication business flourished as other companies sprang up to meet broadcasters' demands to find prerecorded music formats for their automation systems. As the science of radio programming became more demographically specific in the 1960s and early 1970s, syndicators rushed to provide automated music formats that were more tailored to meet individual broadcasters' needs. For example, instead of providing a single rock music format, a syndicator might offer several renditions in an effort to match more narrowly defined audiences. By the mid-1970s, a time when an estimated one in seven stations in the United States used computer automation, as many as 15 major syndicators, including Bonneville, Century 21, Drake/Chennault, Schulke, William B. Tanner, and TM Productions, were developing and marketing radio music formats.

When satellite program distribution was developed in the late 1970s, format syndication entered a new era. In 1981, two companies, RKO Radio and the Satellite Music Network, announced plans to develop and market music formats and program services delivered via satellite. These centralized formats changed the sound of syndicated radio programming, since satellite distribution allowed for live announcers to introduce the music, eliminating the traditional complaint that automated formats lacked spontaneity and immediacy. Satellite delivery thus made syndicated formats a more viable option for broadcasters, especially in more competitive market situations. By the early 1990s, companies such as Bonneville, BPI, Century 21, and Drake/Chennault provided such services.

STEVEN SMETHERS

See also Feature Syndicates; Radio Entertainment; Readyprint; Television Syndication

Further Reading

Cameron, Jim, and Susan Tyler Eastman, "Network and Syndicated Radio Programming," in *Broadcast/Cable Programming: Strategies and Practices,* 4th ed., edited by Susan Tyler Eastman, Belmont, California: Wadsworth, 1993

Hall, Douglas E., "See Centralized Formats Changing the Face of Radio," *Billboard* (April 11, 1981)

Lichty, Lawrence W., and Malachi C. Topping, comps., *American Broadcasting: A Source Book on the History of Radio and Television,* New York: Hastings House, 1975

MacFarland, David T., *The Development of the Top 40 Radio Format,* New York: Arno, 1973

Routt, Edd, James B. McGrath, and Fredric A. Weiss, *The Radio Format Conundrum,* New York: Hastings House, 1978

Saldan, Elena S., "Music Syndicators Expand Radio Station Offerings," *Television-Radio Age* (September 26, 1977)

"Transcription Boom," *Newsweek* (January 19, 1948)

Radio Technology

Many inventors contributed to development of radio broadcasting

The technology that made radio broadcasting possible cannot be credited to an individual inventor. In the nineteenth century, Samuel Morse's telegraph and Alexander Graham Bell's telephone demonstrated the practicality of using electrical waves for communications purposes. Yet the necessity of hardwired circuits to connect sender with receiver limited the usefulness of both devices. The challenge of overcoming this limitation led other scientists and inventors, notably Guglielmo Marconi, to experiment with freeing the electrical signal from the wires and allowing it to travel in the open air.

The "wireless age" began around the turn of the century when Marconi, an Italian inventor, successfully transmitted messages in Morse code via wireless. Inspired by the theoretical discoveries of James Clerk Maxwell and Heinrich Hertz, Marconi succeeded at first in sending messages over short distances. In 1901, Marconi demonstrated the practicality of wireless by transmitting code across the Atlantic Ocean.

In achieving wireless communication, Marconi employed the transmission technique of amplitude modulation. The electronic dots and dashes of the telegraph key were soon supplanted by the microphone, which converted

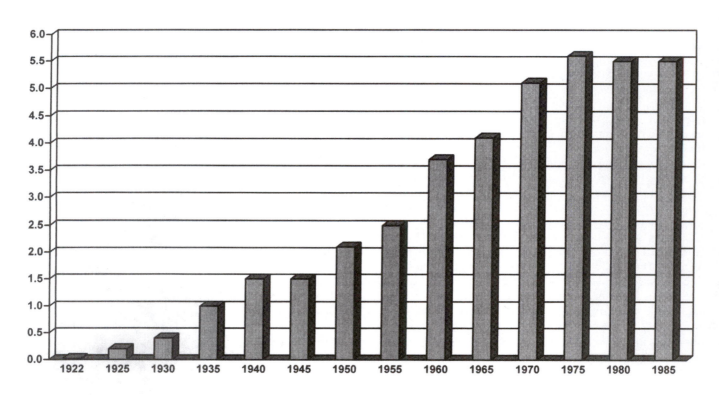

**Radio in the United States
Home Receiver Ownership 1922–1985
(Sets per Household)**

Note: All figures after 1960 include Alaska and Hawaii. There is no increase between 1940 and 1945 due to manufacturing during World War II.

Sources: U.S. Bureau of the Census, *Statistical Abstract of the United States,* 106th ed. (Washington, D.C.: GPO, 1986). U.S. Bureau of the Census, *Historical Statistics of the United States: Colonial Times to 1957* (Washington, D.C.: GPO, 1960). National Association of Broadcasters, *Dimensions of Radio* (Washington, D.C., 1974).

sound energy into electrical impulses and made possible voice communication. By superimposing the electrical impressions of the sound wave onto the transmitter's constant carrier wave, the signal could be made to vary in amplitude, or height, in accordance with the intensity of the sound. Wireless receivers reversed the process, converting the fluctuating electrical impulses into sound energy to be reproduced by headphones and, later, by loudspeakers.

The central component of radio communication was the vacuum tube, which represented essentially a refinement of Edison's incandescent lamp. Vacuum tubes were employed in transmitters to create and modulate radio waves and in receivers to detect and amplify them. Lee De Forest revolutionized the basic two-element (filament and plate) tube in 1906 by adding a third component, the grid, to the design, creating a device he called the audion. Its principle of operation was not clearly understood by the inventor. Nonetheless, the audion dramatically enhanced the sensitivity of receivers with its vast amplification capabilities. Thus, wireless technology was poised for commercial exploitation.

The first practical application of wireless was in maritime communication. The value of linking ship with shore via wireless was underscored when the luxury cruise ship *Titanic* sank in 1912. When distant ships responded to the *Titanic*'s faint distress transmissions, wireless was credited with saving the lives of 700 passengers.

At the outset of World War I, the U.S. government seized control of wireless, authorizing the Navy to administer access to the technology. During this time, Ernst Alexanderson improved the high-frequency alternator, a necessary component of true long-distance communication. Not only did military communication benefit from this refinement, wireless also was credited with advancing diplomatic discussions during the Paris Peace Conference.

The future of wireless shifted direction at the conclusion of the war. A new application of the technology, to become known as broadcasting, emerged. Communications visionaries, including David Sarnoff of the American Marconi telegraph company and Frank Conrad of Westinghouse, foresaw the potential of wireless as a mass communication medium. Westinghouse's KDKA, operating from its manufacturing facility in East Pittsburgh, Pennsylvania, originated radio's first scheduled broadcast on November 2, 1920. Reports of the Harding-Cox presidential election returns were broadcast to hundreds of listeners, many of whom had gathered in churches and meeting halls to collectively witness the event.

The number of station operators grew rapidly during the decade as the novelty of capturing voices and music from the air spread. Crude – but nonetheless operable – radio receivers could be built readily by wrapping a coil of wire around an empty oatmeal box and connecting it to a tuning crystal and a pair of headphones. Listener interest grew rapidly as the number of broadcasting stations increased. Manufacturers responded by introducing increasingly sophisticated receivers.

The Radio Corporation of America (RCA) would assume its role as the pioneer in manufacturing technology during the 1920s. Its 1924 six-tube radio receiver, utilizing Edwin Armstrong's patented superheterodyne circuitry, vastly improved the quality of broadcast reception. Homemade receivers soon gave way to the more elaborate factory-made models, which featured superior reception characteristics and, thanks to amplified loudspeakers, sufficient volume to fill listeners' living rooms.

Radio broadcasting emerged as a social and economic phenomenon during this decade. A sharp rise in the number of broadcasting stations in the mid-1920s resulted in severe airwave congestion and intolerable reception conditions. Congress responded to the problem, imposing order on the fledgling industry by passing the Radio Act of 1927.

The Federal Radio Commission (FRC) was empowered to regulate the technical parameters of station operation by determining the frequencies and transmitter powers that stations utilized. Stations operated on set frequencies, ranging from 540 to 1600 kilocycles, at transmitter powers up to 50 kilowatts. Controlling the frequency and power variables enabled the FRC, by the early 1930s, to authorize the operation of more than 500 stations on the 107 channels. The Federal Communications Commission (FCC) assumed the responsibilities of the FRC following the passage of the Communications Act of 1934.

Atmospheric phenomena assist AM radio waves in traveling much greater distances at night than during daylight hours. During the 1930s, the FCC authorized certain stations, located principally in major cities, to become the sole nighttime operators on 24 specially designated clear-channel frequencies. These powerful clear-channel stations extended relatively interference-free nighttime radio service to listeners in sparsely populated areas of the country.

One liability of AM is its susceptibility to electrical interference, or static. Static is the product both of natural and man-made atmospheric phenomena. In the earliest days of wireless, thunderstorms were the most frequent source of disrupted reception, but the increasing electrification of U.S. homes during the 1930s intensified the problem. Electric motors, present in many of the new labor-saving appliances (refrigerators, washing machines, mixers, and the like), filled the air with interference and provoked intense listener dissatisfaction.

Scientists and engineers labored in vain to remedy the problem by designing more powerful transmitters. Edwin Armstrong adopted a different approach. With the assistance and encouragement of Sarnoff and RCA, Armstrong experimented with an entirely different scheme of signal transmission and reception. In April 1935, RCA dismissed Armstrong from its laboratories and abandoned the project. Sarnoff had decided to lead RCA in the development of a new visual communication medium: television.

Armstrong pressed onward with diligence, channeling thousands of dollars of his personal fortune to cover research expenses. Eventually, the persistent inventor perfected frequency modulation broadcasting, a method virtually impervious to atmospheric interference. Furthermore, FM conveyed sound realistically, in high fidelity. During an early demonstration of FM's capability, astonished engineers heard the sound of water being poured into a glass reproduced with breathtaking clarity – a feat AM transmission could never equal.

Despite its technical promise, FM's commercial exploita-

When a radio set was fit into a handsome cabinet, it moved into the living room and became a center for family entertainment.
(Library of American Broadcasting)

tion began erratically. The FCC shifted FM broadcasting to a different set of channels in 1940 to assist the development of television. In the midst of World War II, the commission imposed a freeze on the issuance of station licenses. Meanwhile, resources necessary in the manufacture of FM receivers were diverted toward the production of war matériel. The most severe setback to FM growth, however, occurred shortly after the war's conclusion. When the FCC reassigned FM frequencies once again (to 88–108 megahertz), 500,000 existing receivers immediately became obsolete.

A period of rampant consumerism followed World War II, and television bolted to the forefront of the electronic communications arena. Radio reeled in the wake as its creative geniuses – those behind the microphones as well in the front office – defected to the new visual medium.

Ever since the rise of networking in the late 1920s, radio had been largely a national medium. A sizable portion of its programming was being delivered by American Telephone and Telegraph long-distance circuits from network studios in the major cities to their affiliates across the country. When radio's classic programming forms (comedies, dramas, and quiz shows) and creative talents migrated to television, those who remained began looking for new ways to attract listeners.

The solution was to reorient the programming philosophy. Many stations capitalized on the public's increasing interest in recorded music by repetitively airing only the best-selling records and interspersing them with banter provided by local announcers. Formula (or top-40) radio emerged, and the disc jockey (DJ) became radio's new star. Most DJs served in the combined capacities of talent and en-

Radio Sets Produced and Households with Radio Sets
1921-1995
(in thousands)

Year	Sets Produced	Households with Radio Sets	Year	Sets Produced	Households with Radio Sets
1921			1961	17,374	50,695
1922	100	60	1962	19,162	51,305
1923	500	400	1963	18,282	52,300
1924	1,500	1,250	1964	19,176	54,000
1925	2,000	2,750	1965	24,119	55,200
1926	1,750	4,500	1966	23,595	57,000
1927	2,350	6,750	1967	21,698	57,500
1928	3,250	8,000	1968	22,566	58,500
1929	4,428	10,250	1969	20,549	60,600
1930	3,789	13,750	1970	16,406	62,000
1931	3,594	16,700	1971		
1932	2,446	18,450	1972		
1933	4,157	19,250	1973		
1934	4,479	20,400	1974		
1935	6,030	21,456	1975		
1936	8,249	22,869	1976		
1937	8,083	24,500	1977		
1938	7,142	26,667	1978		
1939	10,763	27,500	1979		
1940	11,831	28,500	1980		
1941	13,642	29,300	1981		
1942	4,307	30,600	1982		
1943	*	30,800	1983		
1944	*	32,500	1984		
1945	*	33,100	1985		
1946	15,955	33,998	1986		
1947	20,000	35,900	1987		
1948	16,500	37,623	1988		
1949	11,400	39,300	1989		
1950	13,468	40,700	1990		
1951	11,928	41,900	1991		
1952	10,431	42,800	1992		
1953	12,852	44,800	1993		
1954	10,028	45,100	1994		
1955	14,133	45,900	1995		
1956	13,518	46,800			
1957	14,505	47,600			
1958	11,747	48,500			
1959	15,622	49,450			
1960	17.127	50,193			

* Authorization of new radio stations and production of radio receivers for commercial use halted from April 1942 until October 1945.

Notes: In 1970 Census of Housing, only battery-operated radios were enumerated. 1950 is the first year for which figures include Alaska and Hawaii.

Source: U. S. Bureau of the Census, *Historical Statistics of the United States: Colonial Times to 1970* (Washington, D.C.: GPO, 1960).

gineer. In working "combo," the DJ announced the recordings while operating the studio broadcasting equipment.

Technology played an important role in the evolution of formula radio. Large performance studios with their adjoining control rooms gave way to smaller control booths specifically designed to accommodate the DJ. The equipment central to formula radio was the microphone and a pair of turntables (phonographs specially constructed for broadcasting). The DJ operated a control console, mixing the output signals of the various devices for broadcast. Turntables were designed to accommodate the latest innovations in recorded music, the long-play album and the extended-play 45-rpm single.

On the timeline of radio technology, magnetic tape recording is one of the industry's more recent accomplishments. Introduced to broadcasters in the late 1940s, tape recording subsequently revolutionized the production of programming over the next two decades. Prior to this time, the only technology available for prerecording a program for later broadcast (or for archiving a live production) was the electrical transcription. These essentially oversize (16-inch diameter) phonograph records suffered from several limitations. Electrical transcriptions could not be erased and rerecorded, nor could they be edited. In addition, the cutting lathes that produced them were cumbersome and often unpredictable in operation.

Tape recording overcame these disadvantages and more. Perhaps the greatest contribution to the enhancement of formula radio programming was the development of the tape cartridge system. Tape carts, which consist of a continuous-loop reel of tape enclosed within a plastic cassette, freed DJs from the cumbersome tasks of threading and cueing tapes on reproducers. The cart, however, was more than a labor-saving device; its convenience enabled DJs to incorporate increasingly diverse elements into the production of top-40 programming. Carts were ideally suited for reproducing short-duration program matter, including jingles (singing station identifications) and sound effects – two essential elements that helped define the sound of the legendary rock and roll stations of the 1960s.

During this same period, equipment manufacturers perfected automated program-control systems. Automation enabled station operators to record musical selections and station announcements onto tape reels and carts for sequential playback by mechanized or computerized equipment. These devices operated under the supervision of technicians, thus minimizing station operators' reliance upon a costly staff of traditional combo operators. Numerous broadcasters adopted automation as an efficient means for complying with the FCC's 1964 program nonduplication rule, which limited the amount of time most FM stations could simulcast the programming of sister AM stations serving the same community. The satellite dish antenna became a prominent fixture at most stations by the mid-1980s. The capability for delivering high-fidelity, stereo programming to affiliates via satellite revitalized public and commercial radio networks alike.

This technology effectively severed broadcasting's ties to the telephone industry, whose circuits had delivered network programming since the 1920s. Satellite interconnection made possible the formation of new networks specializing in around-the-clock delivery of music-based programming. The downside of this revolution was the fact that a few network DJs displaced scores of local talent from the airwaves. Critics of satellite-delivered programming contended that the loss of the hometown on-air presence compromised one of radio's greatest strengths – its ability to localize programming to the tastes of individual communities.

BRUCE MIMS

See also Broadcast Pioneers; Broadcast Regulation; Communications Act of 1934; De Forest, Lee; Edison, Thomas Alva; Federal Communications Commission; Federal Radio Commission; KDKA; Radio Act of 1927; Radio Corporation of America; Radio Syndication

Further Reading
Archer, Gleason L., *History of Radio to 1926*, New York: Arno, 1971
Lewis, Tom, *Empire of the Air: The Men Who Made Radio*, New York: E. Burlingame, 1991
Sklar, Rick, *Rocking America: An Insider's Story: How the All-Hit Radio Stations Took Over*, New York: St. Martin's, 1984
Sobel, Robert, *RCA*, New York: Stein and Day, 1986

Other Radio Entries: Audience Research for Broadcasting; Blue Book; various Broadcast entries; Commercialization of Broadcasting; Communications Act of 1934; Decency Issues in Electronic Media; "Equal Time" Provision; Fairness Doctrine; Federal Communications Commission; Federal Radio Commission; Golden Age of Radio; Hollywood/Radio Controversy of 1932; Hoover, Herbert, and Radio Regulation; KDKA; Mayflower Decision; Noncommercial Radio; Payola; *Report on Chain Broadcasting*; Voice of America; "War of the Worlds"; Zenith Radio Case

Raymond, Henry J.

A founder of the 'New York Times'

Henry J. Raymond was one of the founders and the first editor of the *New York Times*. Born in Lima, New York, on January 24, 1820, Raymond was an outstanding student who graduated from the University of Vermont. He began his journalism career in 1840 working for Horace Greeley, first at the *New Yorker* magazine and then at the *New York Tribune*. He later served as editorial assistant for James Watson Webb's *Morning Courier* and *New York Enquirer*.

In 1851, Raymond founded the *New York Daily Times* (as it was called until 1857) with George Jones, a former *Tribune* colleague. In contrast to the controversial and sensationalistic New York press of the era, Raymond was determined to make the *Times* moderate and impartial. His insistence on accuracy and fairness established the traits as benchmarks of the paper.

By 1860, the *Times* had become one of New York's leading newspapers, known for its far-ranging coverage of local as well as European news. The *Times* attacked secession, and during the Civil War, it was one of President Abraham Lincoln's most steadfast supporters. Raymond, long active in the Republican party, was elected to the U.S. House of Representatives in 1864. He supported President Andrew Johnson's Reconstruction policies, which eventually led to his ouster from the party's leadership committee.

Under Raymond's leadership, the *Times* crusaded for tariff reduction and against the corrupt Tweed Ring. At about the same time, his frequent spells of illness, caused by stress and overwork, grew worse. He died on June 18, 1869, at the age of 49.

FORD RISLEY

See also Lincoln, Abraham, and the Press

Further Reading

Brown, Francis, *Raymond of the 'Times'*, New York: Norton, 1951

Maverick, Augustus, *Henry J. Raymond and the New York Press*, Hartford, Connecticut: A.S. Hale, 1870

Henry G. Raymond as photographed by Mathew Brady
(Reproduced from the Collections of the Library of Congress)

Readyprint
Mass-distributed material for newspapers

The practice of selling preprinted pages to newspapers dates from the early nineteenth century, when they were first produced in England, but their use increased significantly during the American Civil War, when the number of printers summoned for military service left many small newspapers understaffed. Preprinted pages, commonly known as patent 'sides – the 'sides being either the two outside pages of a sheet or the two inside pages – were adopted around the United States in the latter half of the nineteenth century but were perhaps most popular in the west, where supplies of both labor and paper were irregular. The publisher bought patent 'sides from producers such as Ansel L. Kellogg in Chicago and filled the blank side of the sheet with local news, commentary, and advertising. Kellogg and his imitators profited primarily from the advertising they sold for the preprints, and the newspaper publisher kept production costs low.

Readyprint producers tended to fill their pages with timeless content such as literature, history, and anecdotes. Pages could be customized for each newspaper with long-running local advertising or special features included.

It was estimated that in 1880 the readyprint producers served more than 3,000 of the nation's 8,600 weeklies. Improved communication and technology such as the linotype and stereotyping reduced the benefits of preprinted pages. Instead of buying patent 'sides, a publisher could subscribe to a service to get metal plates pre-cast with stories or drawings that could be affixed in pages at will. National advertisers also used this boilerplate to distribute advertising.

Readyprint often is likened to boilerplate or syndicated material, with which it shared the process of selling to multiple newspapers. However, the fully printed pages did not give editors the flexibility of choice they enjoyed with the other media. As a result, its use was controversial. Editors were criticized for abdicating to others their editorial responsibility for selection of content. Many newspapers were started with the help of readyprint, but publishers commonly shifted to more traditional production if and when they were financially able to do so. Similar complaints were voiced about boilerplate, which continues to have derogatory connotations.

BARBARA CLOUD

See also Feature Syndicates

Further Reading

Harter, Eugene C., *Boilerplating America: The Hidden Newspaper*, Lanham, Maryland: University Press of America, 1991

Watson, Elmo Scott, *History of Auxiliary Newspaper Service in the United States*, Champaign, Illinois: Illini Publishing, 1923

Reagan, Ronald, and the Media

So-called Great Communicator had few problems with the media

President Ronald Reagan was known as "the Great Communicator" for his skillful use of the mass media to generate support for his programs and actions and to build a base of popular appeal matched by few presidents in the twentieth century. He also was known as "the Teflon President" because "nothing would stick to him." Unwilling to take on a popular president, the news media shied away from tough reporting and analysis of trickle-down economics; the quadrupling of the national debt despite Reagan's stated goal of reducing government spending; ethical questions surrounding his attorney general and other appointees; the Strategic Defense Initiative, or "Star Wars," missile defense system; and the broader, more serious issue of the Iran-Contra scandal.

Unquestionably, people in the United States felt good about the country and themselves during the 1980s. Although Reagan's popularity dipped during the 1981–82 recession, the economy had made a recovery by the 1984 election, fueled in large measure by increased defense spending and record budget deficits. Thus, the country was receptive to the Reagan campaign's skillfully crafted "Morning in America" reelection theme that featured flags, morning sunrises, and happy people, in contrast to a Democratic pledge to raise taxes in order to pay for the spending generated by Reagan's defense buildup to combat what his administration termed the Soviet "evil empire."

Several things went right for Reagan as his presidency began. On the day he was inaugurated in 1981, the U.S. hostages who had been held for more than a year in the U.S. embassy in Tehran, Iran, – and whose still-captive status probably had cost Jimmy Carter his presidency – were freed. A few months after that, in a decisive resolution of a labor dispute, Reagan fired striking air traffic controllers. These two incidents enhanced his popularity because he appeared to be in sharp contrast to a series of presidents perceived as failures. Boosting the president's support was his survival of an assassination attempt with a quip and a smile.

Former budget director David Stockman wrote that much of the press during Reagan's first year in office was too intimidated by the president's popularity to make a "grand indictment" of the administration's trickle-down supply-side economic policies. Even White House Assistant Chief of Staff Michael Deaver conceded that, until the Iran-contra affair, Reagan enjoyed the most generous treatment by the press of any president in the post–World War II era. Only after Iran-contra broke in late 1986, when Reagan's popularity dropped 20 points in one month, did he get the sort of grilling from the press that he, like any other president, should have been subjected to all along.

While every administration tries to put the best spin on events, Reagan's extensive public relations apparatus reportedly engaged the services of more than 150 people to control the political agenda and set the terms of public debate. Not surprisingly, Deaver said that whenever he dealt with reporters, his goal was to put the president in a favorable light. To White House Deputy Press Secretary Larry Speakes, his job "was like that of anyone in the public relations business," to tell the press only what his "client," in this case the president of the United States, and the president's top aides, wanted him to say.

There was an undercurrent of antagonism toward the press. "It was Us Against Them," Speakes said of the Washington press corps, as he criticized what he said was a "cult of personality" of reporters who came to create news, not to cover it. As for network correspondents, "they were always complaining about something." He boasted in his book of putting some reporters "out of business" for perceived offenses by not taking their calls and keeping other people in the press office from talking to them. He said he had a "three-time rule" for other reporters: they would have to telephone him three times before he would return their calls. Before presidential news conferences, Speakes said, he told Reagan which reporters he should ignore.

Reagan's political managers believed that even the most controversial ideas could be sold if properly packaged and promoted. Unlike the Nixon administration, which withheld information, the Reagan people gave reporters a "line of the day," provided information, and arranged supporting interviews. The program was known as "manipulation by inundation." Speakes noted that, after a while, reporters stopped bringing their own stories or being investigative. Constant new stories that appealed to the television camera successfully kept reporters from covering ongoing stories with any real depth. Thus, there was little analysis of Reagan's "hands-off" management style that led directly to the Iran-contra affair. Even with Iran-contra – selling arms to Iran in an attempt to free U.S. hostages being held in Lebanon, then diverting the money to support the Nicaraguan contras seeking to overthrow that country's leftist government – the news media did not pursue the story as vigorously as they had Watergate, in part because Congress provided little follow-up and because the public seemed uninterested.

The Reagan people followed a two-pronged media management strategy on a daily basis. They controlled the message by keeping reporters away from a scripted president and captured television's attention by visually attractive photo opportunities that reinforced the "line of the day." Speakes said the Reagan people learned very quickly that when they were presenting a story or trying to get their viewpoint across, they had to think like television producers, with good pictures and a sound bite. Throughout the Reagan years, he said, they not only played to television but based all television judgments strictly on audience size.

The White House skillfully created the impression that Reagan was accessible to reporters, although, as Speakes conceded, Reagan held far fewer full-fledged press conferences than most of his predecessors because "press conferences . . . deteriorated into a game of 'how can I trip him up?' and 'I gotcha.'" Reporters often were reduced to tossing out a question at a photo opportunity, defying "Deaver's rule" against the practice and risking being shut out of photo ops, or trying to shout over the helicopter rotor blades as the Reagans took off for a weekend at Camp David. On one occasion, after successfully eluding corre-

President Ronald Reagan was generally affable when he met with journalists.
(Ronald Reagan Library)

spondents, Speakes told reporters the administration had invented a new game: "Beat the Press." Many major dailies covering the president on a regular basis had no private interviews with Reagan in the first five years of his presidency. Although the *Washington (D.C.) Post* had access, Speakes said the administration always felt the paper's editors "went out of their way to select photos which were as unflattering as possible to President Reagan."

Reagan was kept isolated from reporters, often under the guise of security. Reporters complained of days passing with only distant glimpses of the president at ceremonial events, his staff maintaining a constant vigil to protect him from reporters' questions. Those who resorted to shouted questions often had to be content with one-line answers, often cute quips that deflected serious questions, with no opportunity for follow-up the next day, or the next. His aides cut back on the "mini" news conferences the president held, in part to cut down misstatements and factual errors, although the public seemed forgiving or uncaring. Press conference gaffes often were relegated to the lower paragraphs of a story.

Speakes confirmed that Reagan was prepped for news conferences but said that staff had to be careful, for if the president were confronted with "a blizzard of numbers" at the very last minute, "he might get confused and screw up." Thus, the press office had a rule that "you just didn't clutter him up with a heavy dose of minutiae at the last second." Instead, rehearsal would quit at 3:00 in the afternoon to give the president time to rest and absorb "all he had learned during the preparations."

While the Reagan administration was adept at manipulating the press at home, they were masters when abroad. Their secret was to overwhelm reporters with material that would lead to favorable coverage and attend to their creature comforts. Before each trip, the staff would lay out a communications plan that set out what they wanted said and how it was to be packaged. For example, Reagan's presence at the fortieth anniversary of the D-Day landing at Normandy produced numerous favorable stories and flattering pictures. "We worked very hard to achieve that," Deaver said.

Reagan's "aw-shucks" personality saw him through some scrapes that would have destroyed other politicians. Columnist George Will once said that Reagan was the only person he knew who could "walk into a room, have the ceiling fall in on him, and walk out without a fleck of plaster in his hair." Reagan's administration points out the importance of the traditional "watchdog" function of the press. Whatever happened, whether it was being seduced by Reagan's sunny disposition or acquiescing to the presumption of the president's popularity, the news media did the country a disservice.

W. RICHARD WHITAKER

See also News Management; Nixon, Richard M., and the Media

Further Reading

Armstrong, Scott, "Iran-Contra: Was the Press Any Match for All the President's Men?," *Columbia Journalism Review* 29:1 (May 1990), pp. 27–35

Boot, William, "Iranscam: When the Cheering Stopped," *Columbia Journalism Review* (March/April 1987)

Deaver, Michael, *Behind the Scenes*, New York: Morrow, 1987

Donaldson, Sam, *Hold On, Mr. President*, New York: Random House, 1987

Hertsgaard, Mark, *On Bended Knee: The Press and the Reagan Presidency*, New York: Farrar, Straus and Giroux, 1988

Hoffman, David, "How Reagan Controls His Coverage: At Home the Candidate Packaged and Protected," *Washington Journalism Review* (September 1984)

Matusow, Barbara, "How Reagan Controls His Coverage: Abroad – The White House Writes the Lead," *Washington Journalism Review* (September 1984)

Speakes, Larry, *Speaking Out: The Reagan Presidency from Inside the White House*, New York: Scribner's, 1988

Reconstruction Press in the South

Newspapers suffered many problems, including censorship, in postwar era

During the American Civil War, Southern newspapers suffered greatly from shortages of paper, type, and ink; from lack of transportation and postal services; from enlistment of employees; and from enemy invasions. No accurate census of pre- and postwar Southern newspapers exists, but figures for certain states indicate that from 70 to 90 percent of the South's newspapers were suspended during the war. After the war, some editors were able to revive prewar newspapers, while others started new journals on a shoestring. But even in the postwar years, survival was difficult. In addition to a bad economy and low literacy in the South, newspapers continued to be subject to the threat of military censorship.

In the years immediately following the end of the war, Southern states lived under military occupation while they attempted to reconstruct themselves according to policies established in Washington, D.C. This occupation resulted in more than a dozen editors being arrested and slightly fewer newspapers being suspended for criticizing reconstruction policies and the military presence.

For example, when the *Macon (Georgia) Journal and Messenger* published a humorous editorial against Reconstruction policies, the editor was arrested. When the editor of the *Macon Daily Herald* came to his competitor's defense, he also was arrested and his paper suspended.

Most of the interference with newspapers resulted from criticism of the local military presence. With troops posted in or around every town, it was difficult for editors not to feel, as the *Richmond (Virginia) Whig* did – "cribbed, cabined and confined." After the *Augusta (Georgia) Loyal Georgian*, a weekly black Republican paper, criticized the local military commander, a guard was posted in the pressroom for several days.

By January 1866, all of the Southern states, except Texas, had been reconstructed under policies established by Presidents Abraham Lincoln and Andrew Johnson. But congressional Republicans, dismayed by the failure of Southern states to incorporate blacks into the political and economic life of the South, produced a new congressional plan, the Reconstruction Act of 1867, that once again placed the South under total military control. Under congressional Reconstruction, the military was ordered to oversee the registration of all eligible black and white male voters and supervise the election of state conventions to draft new constitutions.

Editorial reaction to this new Reconstruction plan was caustic. Most Democratic papers campaigned fiercely against voter registration and the constitutional conventions, fearing a government dominated by blacks and Northern carpetbaggers. Moderate Democratic editors promoted voter registration and office seeking, believing that a strong white turnout would dilute the black vote.

Although radical Republicans were the prime movers behind the Reconstruction Act of 1867, the actual day-to-day administration of reconstruction policy rested with moderates. Republican moderates realized that the only salvation for their party in the South was to engage in compromise and reconciliation with Southern whites. A major tool in promoting this new cooperationist attitude was the Republican newspaper.

Republican papers, however, were struggling to survive in the hostile political climate of the South. Most Southerners refused to advertise in or subscribe to Republican newspapers. The Democratic press, on the other hand, had a slightly healthier subscription and advertising base as well as lucrative printing contracts from local, county, and state government agencies. In order to level the playing field and push its own moderate agenda, Congress passed an appropriations law that allowed federal printing contracts to be let to two newspapers in each Southern state.

The South's party press was a natural fallout not only from the politics of Reconstruction but also from the South's weak economy. During this critical period, the party press – whether the rural Democratic sheets or the urban Republican papers – promoted political identity, educated citizens in their political responsibilities, and pressed the party line. Above all, party patronage provided newspapers the economic support that was vital to the restoration of the Southern press after the Civil War.

But the patronage dollar was fickle. Republican newspapers had to toe a moderate line or lose their contracts. For example, the federal printing contract was withdrawn from the *Florida Times* in Jacksonville when it began supporting a group of radicals campaigning across the state in a mule-drawn wagon. In 1868, the *New Orleans (Louisiana) Tribune,* the oldest black newspaper in the South, lost its contract when it went in the opposite political direction and supported a former slave-holder for governor over a former Union officer.

During Reconstruction, more than two dozen black Republican newspapers were published in the South. Black newspapers were an important political tool for moderate Republicans. Republicans soon learned that for the party to remain in power nationally, it had to assure whites that Republicans were not pushing full social, economic, and political incorporation of blacks. Republicans, therefore, used the black press to moderate the local political activity of blacks while also urging blacks to vote the moderate national Republican ticket. Central in the content of these black newspapers were two subtle messages from their white sponsors: if blacks worked hard and stayed out of trouble, the Republican party would ensure them a better life; and blacks should vote the Republican ticket, but they should not become too involved in local politics.

As long as Republicans dominated the South, blacks could be assured of some modicum of progress. By 1870, however, Reconstruction was on the wane, and Republicans were abandoning the South's blacks. Black schools were closed; property qualifications for officeholding were reinstated; segregation was legalized; and the poll tax was inaugurated. When legal means of subordinating the blacks were not enough, violence and intimidation were used.

Reconstruction officially ended in 1877. By then, all of the Republican newspapers had folded, leaving an increasingly profitable Democratic press to dominate the South. This conservative voice practiced a racist rhetoric that was intent on restoring the "white man's South." With only a handful of exceptions, this was the editorial voice that continued to be heard throughout the South for the next 90 years.

DONNA L. DICKERSON

See also Civil War Press (South)

Further Reading
Abbott, Richard, *The Republican Party and the South, 1855–1877: The First Southern Strategy,* Chapel Hill: University of North Carolina Press, 1986
Dickerson, Donna Lee, *The Course of Tolerance: Freedom of the Press in Nineteenth-Century America,* New York: Greenwood, 1990; London: Greenwood, 1991
Foner, Eric, *Reconstruction: America's Unfinished Revolution, 1863–1877,* New York: Harper and Row, 1988
Rabinowitz, Howard N., ed., *Southern Black Leaders of the Reconstruction Era,* Urbana: University of Illinois Press, 1982
Sefton, James, *The United States Army and Reconstruction, 1865–1877,* Baton Rouge: Louisiana State University Press, 1967

Red Scare and the Press

Fear of radicals supported by U.S. newspapers

For two years after World War I, the United States was gripped by its first real "Red Scare." Between 1919 and 1920, U.S. citizens were extremely fearful that the Communist party would launch an attempt to overthrow the U.S. government. Bolstered by the recent Russian Revolution, which brought the Bolsheviks to power, the creation of two Communist parties in the United States, and a torrent of propaganda from the Soviet Union, the United States launched a campaign against dissenters that touched the media in two ways. First, radical journals were targeted for suppression during this period, and, second, members of the mainstream press found themselves essentially endorsing the denial of freedom of the press to their left-wing colleagues.

Communist presses were busy during these years turning out manifestos and diatribes of all kinds. Their talk was fiery, but subsequent action was almost nonexistent. Nonetheless, U.S. senators were concerned about individuals who "have advised the defiance of law and authority, both by the printing and circulation of printed newspapers, books, pamphlets, circulars, stickers, and dodgers, and also by the spoken word." Likewise, they were concerned about those who had "advised and openly advocated the unlawful obstruction of industry and the unlawful and violent destruction of property, in pursuance of a deliberate plan and purpose to destroy existing property rights and to impede and obstruct the conduct of business essential to the prosperity and life of the community."

Such concern led U.S. attorney general A. Mitchell Palmer to act. He ordered federal officials to raid places where he believed alien radicals congregated. Once arrested, hearings were held for most of these aliens, and many of them were ordered deported for their alleged political beliefs – even though not all of those arrested had an interest in communism. The goal was to shut down those who fomented dissent orally or by written word and to remove their most likely followers from the scene.

While the Palmer Raids were ongoing, Congress was considering peacetime sedition legislation, which would have made it a crime to advocate the overthrow or change of the U.S. government in any way, including by written word. Radicals, fearful that they would lose access to the mails, began suggesting that their colleagues carry printed materials to distribute to interested parties. The Red Scare, the Palmer Raids, and the proposed peacetime sedition laws completed the disintegration of the radical press as a force in U.S. society. Although the peacetime sedition acts never did become law, fears that someone might resurrect such proposals remained with radical editors.

Generally, the public supported actions against alleged Communists, and mainstream newspapers were among Palmer's strongest backers. The *New York Times,* for instance, said, "The more of these dangerous anarchists are arrested, the more of them are sent back to Europe, the better for the United States." The *Washington (D.C.) Post* concurred, commenting, "The time has come when foreign enemy propaganda must be prevented from utilizing freedom of speaking and printing in America for the purpose of destroying America itself. The abuse of free speaking and printing must be defined and punished provided." As the *Post* explained, "The right of free speech, printing and assembly in the United States should not include the right to preach bolshevism directly or indirectly."

Not all newspapers supported Palmer's policy. The *St. Louis (Missouri) Post-Dispatch,* for example, noted that "the right and duty of our government to protect itself and to guard our institutions against revolution and unlawful action and propaganda are unquestioned." Palmer's methods, however, were questionable, the *Post-Dispatch* said. "Let us clean up the revolutionists and the propagandists of disorder, lawlessness, and violence. But let us do it in a sane, legal, orderly manner." The *Post-Dispatch* continued, "Free Government cannot be saved by the destruction of the pillars upon which it stands – free speech, free assemblage, and freedom from official oppression in any form."

Opposition to Palmer's tactics grew in many circles, and by 1920, his excesses had led to the dissipation of the Red Scare. No attempt to overthrow the nation had occurred despite his warnings, and the nation was poised to enter the Roaring Twenties and to forget about political problems for a while.

Out of the rubble left by the Red Scare, however, came at least two important developments for freedom of speech and of the press. First, Zechariah Chafee Jr. emerged as a major critic of government actions during this time period. A professor at Harvard Law School, Chafee became the first dominant figure in First Amendment legal scholarship in U.S. history.

The remnants of the Red Scare reached the U.S. Supreme Court as well, where they left a lasting legacy for freedom of speech and of the press. When the justices heard the appeal of Benjamin Gitlow, a New York Socialist who had become a Communist and who had been arrested for violating the state's 1902 criminal anarchy law, few imagined that the case would be long remembered. Gitlow was picked up in a state raid on Communist party headquarters in November 1919; he had been serving as business manager of the party's publication, *Revolutionary Age.* The charges against him were based on the publication of the "Left Wing Manifesto," a document criticizing capitalism and defending the revolutionary ideas of Marx.

Among the points raised in his defense was the notion that the New York state law was unconstitutional because it violated both state and federal constitutional guarantees of freedom of speech and of the press. Although the U.S. Supreme Court upheld Gitlow's conviction for violating the state law, it authorized federal intervention on behalf of civil liberties impaired by state action. Justice Edward Sanford, speaking for seven members of the Court, noted offhandedly, "for present purposes we may and do assume that freedom of speech and of the press – which are protected by the First Amendment from abridgment by Congress – are among the fundamental personal rights and 'liberties' protected by the due process clause of the Fourteenth Amendment from impairment by the States." Known as the legal doctrine of incorporation, this language opened the way for

a new era of civil liberties action by the Court and paved the way for increased protection for speech and press rights in coming years.

MARGARET A. BLANCHARD

Further Reading

Blanchard, Margaret A., *Revolutionary Sparks: Freedom of Expression in Modern America,* New York: Oxford University Press, 1992

Lofton, John, *The Press as Guardian of the First Amendment,* Columbia: University of South Carolina Press, 1980

Murray, Robert K., *Red Scare: A Study of National Hysteria, 1919–1920,* Minneapolis: University of Minnesota Press, 1955

Murphy, Paul L., *The Meaning of Freedom of Speech: First Amendment Freedoms from Wilson to FDR,* Westport, Connecticut: Greenwood, 1972

Preston, William, Jr., *Aliens and Dissenters: Federal Suppression of Radicals, 1903–1933,* Cambridge, Massachusetts: Harvard University Press, 1963

Reeves, Rosser

Practiced "hard-sell" advertising techniques

Rosser Reeves worked for several advertising agencies before joining Ted Bates Advertising in 1940 primarily because he was encouraged to apply his hard-sell style of advertising there. One of Reeves's first major successes for the agency was the Viceroy cigarette campaign, which played up the cigarette's filter. Sales increased, and before 1950, Brown and Williamson Tobacco was spending almost $20 million a year advertising Viceroy.

The agency was hired to produce television commercials for Republican presidential candidate Dwight D. Eisenhower. Reeves created hard-sell commercials that contained little substance about the issues. Nonetheless, the commercials helped Eisenhower win the election.

During the late 1950s, Reeves created an overwhelmingly successful television campaign for the pain reliever Anacin in which he depicted the pain caused by a headache and the subsequent relief as a result of taking an Anacin tablet. The commercial ended with "Anacin gives you fast, fast, fast relief." Sales of the product increased from $17 million to more than $50 million within six months.

His book, *Reality in Advertising,* published in 1961, explained his controversial theories regarding creativity in advertising. In it, Reeves explored the "unique selling proposition," claiming that several selling points about a product could be mentioned in an advertisement but that only one should be emphasized.

The book helped increase the agency's list of clients. In 1965, the year he retired from the agency, he was inducted to the Copywriters Hall of Fame. Active as a consultant for several years, in 1976, he and his son founded Rosser

Reeves, Inc., where he worked for about two years. He died in 1984.

EDD APPLEGATE

See also Unique Selling Proposition

Further Reading

Higgins, Denis, *The Art of Writing Advertising: Conversations with Masters of the Craft*, Lincolnwood, Illinois: NTC Business, 1965

Reeves, Rosser, *Reality in Advertising*, New York: Knopf, 1961

Religious Journalism

Reporting and interpreting events from a religious perspective

Religious journalism, defined as reporting and interpreting events and issues from a particular religious perspective, has been a part of U.S. journalism since the beginning. Because religion was salient to many of the first colonists, early newspapers routinely carried news of religious events and concerns that would be of particular interest in the community.

In some cases, religion shaped editorial content. James Franklin, for example, started his *New England Courant* in 1721 with backing from prominent members of the Anglican Church in Boston, who initially used it to attack the dominant Puritanism. Although most newspapers were not started for religious purposes, and even the *New England Courant* quickly became primarily a business venture, colonial papers often gave a religious slant to the news. Stories interpreting good news as signs of God's pleasure and bad news as signs of divine wrath were quite common.

After the Revolution, religion news and commentary were so popular that historian Frank Luther Mott labeled the years from 1801 through 1833 the "era of religious journalism." During that era, religious newspapers such as the *Boston Recorder* (1816–67) competed on essentially equal terms with secular ones. Both provided extensive coverage of revivals and other religious events, full texts and excerpts from sermons, and other kinds of religious commentary.

By the twentieth century, however, explicitly religious journalism in media intended for a general audience became less common as scientific explanations for natural phenomena began to replace religious interpretations and as economic pressures to appeal to more diverse audiences increased. However, even with a later shift from ideological and personal journalism to more objective reporting, religious journalism never entirely disappeared from the mass media.

Salt Lake City, Utah's, *Deseret News* (founded in 1850) was owned by the Church of Jesus Christ of Latter-day Saints. The *Christian Science Monitor* started publishing in Boston in 1908 following a directive from Mary Baker Eddy, founder of the Church of Christ, Scientist, which later also had broadcast interests. In 1982, the Unification Church bought the *Washington Times*. All generally adhered to professional norms for objective reporting, but evidence of religious influence could be seen in their advertising policies and, to a lesser extent, in story selection and framing.

In other general circulation newspapers, traces of religious perspective lingered in opinion columns and news stories. Cal Thomas, for example, wrote from a conservative Protestant perspective; Roman Catholic influence could sometimes be detected in columns by William F. Buckley, Michael Novak, and George Will.

Since 1912, when the Seventh-day Adventist Church created its publicity bureau to counter criticism of church opposition to Sunday blue laws, every major church and religious organization and many smaller ones established public relations or public information offices to provide information and commentary to the mass media. More subtle influence on media discourse came through prizes such as those given by the Amy Foundation, the Associated Church Press, the Catholic Press Association, and the Religious Public Relations Council to individual journalists and to news media who covered the religious dimension of news in ways the organizations deemed appropriate.

For the most part, however, religious journalism in the late twentieth century occurred in religious media. Such media proliferate and flourish in times of religious ferment or when immigration by members of religious minorities is high and languish at other times.

The first religious magazine, *Christian History*, appeared in Boston in 1743. Like it, most of the early periodicals were short-lived, nondenominational "miscellanies" intended to promote religion and the diffusion of useful knowledge through "edifying" information and entertainment, or to provide appropriate Sabbath reading. The first sectarian publication, the *Arminian*, was started in 1789 to spread teachings of the Methodist Episcopal Church. By 1825, there were almost 200 Christian publications, with every denomination and major religious organization having at least one to publicize its activities and promote its views. Many of them engaged in a journalism of controversy that was fed by splits within established churches and by growing concern over slavery.

Although the earliest religious periodicals were Protestant, Roman Catholics became involved in publishing as early as 1808. Most early Roman Catholic periodicals, such as Boston's *Irish and Catholic Sentinal* (1834–35), defended the faith against Protestantism, provided news from the old country, and interpreted U.S. culture for immigrants. Because many of these publications operated independent of church control and delighted in reporting controversy, in 1899 Pope Leo XIII issued a pastoral letter that led to an era of institutional control that lasted until Vatican II. However, from the 1960s, the Roman Catholic press became an increasingly diverse mixture of official church publications, ones published by church-related organizations, and others that were truly independent of church control.

Official church publications often had larger circulations, but independent magazines tended to be more influential. *Christianity and Crisis* (liberal; founded in 1941), *Christian Century* (moderate, Mainline Protestant; founded

Churches and ministers took to the television screen to deliver their messages, including Robert Schuller's *Hour of Power* at the Crystal Cathedral.
(Museum of Broadcast Communications)

1884), *Christianity Today* (conservative, Evangelical Protestant; founded 1956), *Sojourner's* (socially oriented Evangelical; founded 1971), *America* (Roman Catholic/Jesuit; founded 1909), and *Commonweal* (Catholic/lay-edited; founded 1924) circulated widely among clergy, lay leaders, academics, and policymakers because of their informed commentary on political and social issues. James Dobson's *Focus on the Family* (founded 1982) was also important for its conservative Protestant perspective on lifestyle and family issues.

From the mid-1980s, Dobson's *Focus* programs were among the most widely distributed and popular commentaries on religious radio stations. Their competition came primarily from the Moody Bible Institute's *Christian Per-*

spectives on the News (from 1925) and from Pat Robertson's CBN Radio Network (from 1987).

On television, Robertson's *700 Club* (founded 1963) was the most influential source of news and commentary from a conservative Protestant perspective. From the early 1980s, the apocalyptic interpretations of world events provided by Jack Van Impe and by *Today in Bible Prophecy* also attracted loyal audiences.

Because Christianity has been the dominant religion in the United States, a monthly, the *Jew*, was started as early as 1823 in New York to help combat Christian missionary activity among Jewish immigrants. In general, the Yiddish-language Jewish periodicals have been more political than those published in English. Many of the English-language newsletters, newspapers, and magazines fostered a sense of community and sought to preserve Jewish practices and values by providing promotional and lifestyle material. Of the special-interest publications offering news and commentary on political issues, the *Reconstructionist* (founded 1935) most closely matched the influential Christian publications.

After World War II, the number of publications providing religious journalism from other religious perspectives increased markedly. Among the more than 1,000 religious periodicals, there was probably at least one representing every belief system from atheism to Zen. Most were quite small, but some of those reflecting the Muslim, Buddhist, and Hindu perspectives had circulations at least equal to those of the influential Christian magazines. Like the Roman Catholic and Jewish press before them, many were aimed toward immigrants.

Al-Ittihad (founded 1962) circulated widely among university students; *American-Arab Message* (founded 1950) and *Crescent International* (founded 1972) provided news and commentary for large and more diverse audiences. *Will of Dharma* (founded 1977) was the official organ of the Buddhist Churches of America, while *Western Bodhi* (founded 1963) carried editorials and articles on current events significant to Buddhists. *Hindus Today* (founded 1979) reported news about Hindus worldwide and also promoted Sanathana Dharma.

JUDITH M. BUDDENBAUM

See also Mass Media and Religion

Further Reading

Fackler, Mark, and Charles H. Lippy, eds., *Popular Religious Magazines of the United States,* Westport, Connecticut: Greenwood, 1995

Hubbard, Benjamin J., ed., *Reporting Religion: Facts and Faith,* Sonoma, California: Polebridge, 1990

Marty, Martin E., *The Religious Press in America,* New York: Holt, Rinehart, and Winston, 1963

Schultze, Quentin J., ed., *American Evangelicals and the Mass Media,* Grand Rapids, Michigan: Academie/Zondervan, 1990

Soukup, Paul A., *Christian Communication: A Bibliographical Survey,* New York: Greenwood, 1989

Reporters and Reporting in the Eighteenth Century

Century's news came from variety of non-newspaper sources, not reporters

Reporters in eighteenth-century America did not exist as professional, paid members of a newspaper staff. Instead, American newspapers received information from a number of sources, including ship captains and sailors, private letters, merchants, word of mouth, government decrees and legislation, and information gleaned from other newspapers. Eighteenth-century printers developed the correspon-

dent system, a technique of gathering news from various localities through the use of paid individuals who sent newspapers what printer Benjamin Franklin – who solicited for correspondents in the October 16, 1729, issue of the *Pennsylvania Gazette* – considered to be "every remarkable Accident, Occurrence, &c fit for public Notice." Eighteenth-century newspaper correspondents became the forerunners to paid staff reporters in the nineteenth century.

Newspapers permitted the paid insertion of information by individuals and accepted letters from readers, but rarely did any letter or paid insertion appear with the name of its author. Normally, pen names were used. Printers, too, wrote essays on topics for their newspapers, but these essays also went unsigned.

Eighteenth-century reporting was timely, but timeliness did not carry the same connotation as in later years. Communication in America was dependent upon modes of transportation, the sea being the primary means. Information could move only as fast as ships, which meant that news took from six weeks to six months to reach North America from Europe. News traveling from Boston to Charleston required about three weeks by sea, longer if by the overland mail route, which was completed in 1738. Despite what seem to be excessive amounts of time for news to travel, the reporting of weeks-old events still directly affected individuals receiving it.

News could not be transmitted when ships could not reach port. The winter months were the worst, and printers often reported a "dearth of news" from January to March. This lack of news affected newspapers in the first half of the eighteenth century but was not a serious problem after 1750.

Reporting in eighteenth-century America reflected the concerns of printers and readers. News covered a variety of topics, but citizens of colonial America were very interested in reports about ships and trade, slaves and slave rebellions, and disease outbreaks and medical cures. Graphic descriptions of murders, rapes, and Indian atrocities appeared regularly in the first half of the century.

Printers often began newspapers to promote or refute a cause, as was the case of the *New England Courant* in Boston in 1721. The newspaper, printed by James Franklin, directly attacked the colony's Puritan clergy and its support of smallpox inoculation. Newspapers also were started to provide colonial governments with a means to report legislative mandates and executive decrees.

Even though reporting was sometimes biased, printers almost always declared themselves to be impartial transmitters in the reporting process. Franklin, in his "Apology for Printers" published in the June 10, 1731, issue of the *Pennsylvania Gazette,* explained that printers "are educated in the Belief that, when Men differ in Opinion, both Sides ought equally to have the Advantage of being heard by the Publick. . . . Printers naturally acquire a vast Unconcernedness as to the right or wrong Opinions contain'd in what they print." Forty years, later, Isaiah Thomas claimed the same impartiality in reporting news by adding "Open to All Parties, but Influenced by None" to the nameplate of the *Massachusetts Spy.*

Despite neutrality claims, newspapers in the eighteenth

century became political advocates, a practice that became very evident in the division of newspapers into Patriot and Tory camps during the American Revolution. Political partisanship grew into the distinctive characteristic of newspapers after 1783. Printers and political party members used newspapers to report information they felt would influence public opinion. Impartiality was no longer a purpose of reporting. News became so biased, and the attacks upon the Federalist-run government by opposition Republicans grew so great, that Congress passed the Alien and Sedition Acts in 1798. The acts outlawed printing any news against the government that might be false, scandalous, or malicious.

The focus of reporting changed during the century. Reporting before the 1730s was concerned greatly with European law, trade, finances, and wars. Colonial newspapers were dependent upon English prints to report these events. In the 1730s, colonial printers realized that news from within America was of just as much value to readers. Reporting practices shifted from a European focus to one more colonial in nature. The shift culminated in the reporting of two events in 1739 and 1740 that directly affected all American colonists.

The first was the Anglo-Spanish war known as the War of Jenkins' Ear, which had direct effects upon American shipping and trade in the Caribbean. The second was the preaching tour of George Whitefield, which served as the catalyst for the Great Awakening. The American press's focus upon the two events was universal and represents the first reporting of news that was of intercolonial importance.

Printers during the next 25 years developed a reporting network that used news items, shipping, and the mails to keep colonists apprised of intercolonial activities such as the French and Indian War and the Stamp Act crisis. Papers did not stop reporting European news, but, increasingly, these events were interpreted in light of their effect upon America.

Reporting news that affected all parts of the colonies helped turn newspapers into "official" information organs. Deaths, marriages, births, and other events unique to one locality became official records once they appeared in a newspaper. Printers began to consider news more authoritative if it came from another newspaper rather than from letters, ship captains, or word-of-mouth reports. John and Thomas Fleet, printers of the *Boston Evening-Post,* for example, did not consider news of slave rebellions in Jamaica in 1760 accurate until accounts were published in Jamaican newspapers. Newspapers as authoritative sources diminished during the Revolution because fighting closed or destroyed many papers and halted intercolonial shipping.

Following the Revolution, partisan political reporting stimulated a rise in editorial writing that was often propagandistic, but it still employed the news-gathering network and other reporting methods of the century. The practice of including essays, poetry, and history – used extensively in some papers before the Revolution – increased feature reporting in the last decade of the century.

DAVID A. COPELAND

See also Colonial Press; Exchanges; Franklin, Benjamin; French and Indian War; Newspapers in the Eighteenth Century; Printers' Networks; Stamp Act of 1765

Further Reading

Brigham, Clarence S., *History and Bibliography of American Newspapers, 1690–1820,* Worcester, Massachusetts: American Antiquarian Society, 1947

Brown, Richard D., *Knowledge Is Power: The Diffusion of Information in Early America,* New York and Oxford: Oxford University Press, 1989

Clark, Charles E., *The Public Prints: The Newspaper in Anglo-American Culture, 1665–1740,* New York: Oxford University Press, 1993

Copeland, David A., *Colonial American Newspapers: Character and Content,* Newark: University of Delaware Press, 1997; London: Associated University Presses, 1997

Kobre, Sidney, *The Development of the Colonial Newspaper,* Gloucester, Massachusetts: Peter Smith, 1960

Sloan, W. David, and Julie Hedgepeth Williams, *The Early American Press, 1690–1783,* Westport, Connecticut: Greenwood, 1994

Steele, Ian K., *The English Atlantic, 1675–1740: An Exploration of Communication and Community,* New York: Oxford University Press, 1986

Thomas, Isaiah, *The History of Printing in America,* New York: Weathervane, 1970

Reporters and Reporting in the Nineteenth Century

Modern journalistic practices developed during these years

U.S. journalistic reporting as it became known in modern times developed largely during the nineteenth century. Developments for most of the century conformed to those of a producer-oriented society, but by 1900, they reflected the country's shift toward a consumer society. In general, political essays dominating newspaper content as the century began gave way by mid-century to event-oriented reports, part of what became characterized in modern times as hard news.

The approximately 200 U.S. newspapers in 1800 were aimed at the educated population (primarily white men at the time), but newspapers for other audiences appeared by the 1820s. By the 1880s, the nearly 12,000 periodicals in the United States included African American, anarchist, feminist, and Native American newspapers, which existed to serve particular audiences and to address issues largely absent from mainstream media. By the 1880s, mainstream newspapers employed approximately 300 female reporters, and some editors had begun to emphasize the importance of women as an audience. While different media developed different traditions, common general reporting developments may be traced by breaking the occupation into three areas: identifying the news "story," the elements essential to tell it, and leads to follow for completing it; gathering information to report the story; and constructing the account for the public. By 1900, a focus on hard news, discrimination among newsworthy elements in selection and presentation, and separation of news and opinion, with the latter relegated to editorial pages, approximated some central features of modern reporting practices.

Editors became identifiers of the story, or potential story, and assigned it and the remaining tasks to reporters. By 1900, the construction of news articles for the public included creating leads emphasizing latest developments, foregrounding key elements as "pegs" that signified the news items' importance or appeal, packaging information to entice readers, and manufacturing news (creating events to report) to retain them. Among developments were news values, eyewitness and correspondent accounts, diversification of sources (including the interview and use of multiple sources), attribution, and bylines. Although advances in the first and third areas identified above were notable, news gathering itself developed throughout the century.

Evidence suggests that at least one Boston printer gathered news from passengers and captains when he met ships in the 1780s to collect routinely delivered newspapers. Early American newspaper staffs, however, consisted of only a printer and an assistant or two, and, until the steam-driven press became used widely in the 1830s, the laborious printing process left no time for active news gathering.

Historians emphasize three nineteenth-century phenomena as stimulating developments in U.S. reporting. The first, the War of 1812, brought concerns about timeliness and the practice of pursuing news instead of waiting for news to come to the printing office by way of mail and word of mouth. Second, expansion of newspapers as mass media after 1830 brought additional news values, intensified newsgathering, and shaped reporting as a multifaceted occupation. Third, the challenges of reporting the Civil War entrenched the primacy of hard news over opinion, expanded news gathering methods, and elevated the reporter and reporting.

The twentieth-century meaning of "reporter" as a specific journalistic occupation seems to date from around 1830. Although journalism historian Frank Luther Mott called those who reported on government when Philadelphia was the national capital before 1800 the "first professional reporters" (Joseph Gales, William Duane, James Callender, and James Carey, for example), the word "reporter" seems to have meant one who transcribed congressional proceedings for newspapers. In an 1873 book about U.S. journalism history, author Frederic Hudson, who became managing editor of the New York Herald after editor James Gordon Bennett hired him in 1836, wrote that "reporters were introduced on the Daily Press" only after 1837. In the 1840 census, only 138 of the 16,895 listed in journalistic capacities called themselves reporters. The largest newspaper staffs then might have four reporters, and the number as late as the 1880s might not exceed seven or eight, according to journalism historian Ted Smythe, who wrote of seven reporters at one daily in a city of approximately 100,000.

Changes in the ways news was collected altered tasks associated with creating newspapers and increasingly shaped the occupation of reporter. News-gathering procedures grew from four practices that were routine by 1800: taking items from other papers, culling excerpts from letters, assembling word-of-mouth reports, and taking notes on congressional sessions. Across the century, an aggressive style of reporting on breaking and recent and complex events evolved from mere recording of often very old information chronologically, beginning with the oldest news.

The concepts of timeliness and news gathering received great stimulus from the War of 1812, especially the battle of New Orleans. People in the northeastern United States, expecting a British victory, anxiously waited a month before news came of the U.S. victory. Then, a week later, news of a peace treaty signed seven weeks earlier – two weeks before the battle – revealed that the battle never should have been fought. Printers began using rowboats to meet incoming ships and continued after the war to seek faster means to gather news, relying on the pony express from the late 1820s and then on carrier pigeons and trains by the 1840s. Ultimately, Civil War reporters' reliance on the telegraph established it as an appendage of the news-gathering process. In addition to efforts to speed news to the public, other developments by the 1830s expanded news gathering – and, in the process, the role of reporting. As the growth of the mass press challenged partisan journalism, an interest in facts and nonpolitical news gave impetus to eyewitness reporting, realistic accounts of life in cities and institutions, and traveling to gather nonpolitical news. Eyewitness reporting before the 1830s more often was a by-product of other activities than a deliberate journalistic practice. The only eyewitness report on the American Revolution by a printer, for example, seems to have been Isaiah Thomas's account of the battle of Lexington.

As local and human interest news gained emphasis by the 1830s, certain factors became determinants of newsworthiness as printers and editors, deciding what to print in newspapers, weighed a potential news story's prominence, proximity, timeliness, and human interest. By the turn of the twentieth century, such news values became the basis for the pyramid-style news story lead that emphasized the most newsworthy element first.

Some scholars say that Civil War reporting via the telegraph produced the pyramid lead. Reporters, uncertain how long they would have access for telegraphing a story, developed the habit of transmitting the most important elements first and adding lesser details as access permitted. The pyramid lead ultimately became formulaic, reflecting a set of questions to be answered in news stories. Still called the five W's and H – who, what, when, where, why, how – the formula included that a good lead emphasizes the most newsworthy of those six elements.

Correspondent reporting, established by mid-century, always implied relaying information across a distance and being there where the news happens. With its origins in letter writing, this reporting job developed with the stationing of paid journalists in government seats; ultimately associated with eyewitness reporting, it gained stature as the latter became increasingly valued. The stationing of paid journalists to report from government seats defined correspondent reporting as a routinized job. By 1838, *New York Herald* editor James Gordon Bennett had posted correspondents in six European capitals, in many U.S. cities, and in Texas, Mexico, and Canada. In 1839, he organized a corps of correspondents in Washington, D.C., with Robert Sutton as bureau editor. Increasing value on eyewitness accounts, especially by the end of the Civil War, filled out the concept of correspondent reporting.

The use of sources expanded by the 1860s, with increased emphasis on events and first-person accounts. The use of interviews as sources for news escalated as Civil War reporters gathered information from generals and other officials. After the war, the interview became a fad. These developments, with the need for various sources for reporting such a complex phenomenon as civil war, led to using multiple sources and the practice of probing diverse perspectives for reporting more than one side of issues.

Despite increased pursuit of news, a great amount of newspaper content still came from other newspapers – through the system of editors' exchanges – until the Civil War brought the first organized, systematic news gathering in the field. Hundreds of journalists rode with troops and altered reporting practices as they aggressively pursued news, resisting the first official censorship in the United States and military attitudes against disclosure of facts and conditions of the war. One view is that the Civil War drastically changed reporting forms, while another view is that wartime demands on journalism simply entrenched incipient reporting practices. According to the first view, such modern forms emerged as the summary lead, the use of direct quotations, interviews, and the descriptive techniques found in fiction and poetry. Further, journalistic style changed as writing became more terse, more focused on facts and on the form of the report, more infused with drama, and based on more sources. In accord with the second view, Michael Schudson asserted that before the war a "story" form, filling an entertainment function, developed from the penny press movement, and an "information" form developed from the *New York Times* model, emphasizing facts, minimizing opinion, and aiming at a more educated audience. Both arguments have validity, for, clearly, Civil War journalism fused the two forms identified in the latter argument, and some changes can be traced to the war. It seems likely, for one example, that undercover reporting, which emerged in the 1880s, evolved from reporters working in disguise behind enemy lines.

The period of U.S. journalism after the 1870s is characterized as the "age of the reporter." Historian Richard Hofstadter said that post–Civil War interest in news created demand for bold initiative and good writing and elevated the reporter, whose business was getting news. Between 1870 and 1890, better-educated people were both attracted to and sought by journalism, and reporters' salaries doubled.

Still, reporters in the 1880s worked 14 to 17 hours a day for $10 to $15 per week. Smythe cited one source as saying that New York reporters, the highest paid in the nation, earned $15 to $60 per week between 1880 and 1890. Reporters in most cities were paid far less; one wrote that his starting salary of $4 per week might rise to as high as $15 dollars per week in three years. Smythe said that, in a system

that kept them fearing for their jobs, reporters were hired by verbal order, were paid weekly, worked long hours at a furious pace under extreme pressure with little time off, and had to gather information for 14 to 15 assignments daily, whether or not assignments resulted in published materials.

The last 30 years of the century marked an era of often reckless journalistic conduct and often tasteless, fraudulent newspaper content that culminated in unparalleled sensationalism surrounding the Spanish-American War. Smythe detailed the "space system," which grew out of Civil War journalism and encouraged some forms of irresponsible reporting. This system, widespread by 1880 and continued after 1900, paid reporters a set fee per column – which led to padded copy and accounts in part, no doubt, for much of the flowery writing in late-nineteenth-century newspapers.

Rudiments of the modern model of journalistic responsibility began to develop, but most concepts associated in the twentieth century with responsible journalism were undeveloped in the nineteenth century. Conflict of interest, for example, remained relatively unrecognized as journalists sought and held public office well into the twentieth century. The concept of attribution was undeveloped, and use of bylines, which emerged in the Civil War, was still not routine as late as the 1920s. However, the first known written rules of journalistic conduct date from around 1864, when the *Philadelphia Public Ledger* editor listed 24 rules for employees. Others suggested rules in ensuing decades, setting the stage for the next phase in reporting developments, which, in the twentieth century, emphasized ethics and media responsibility.

HAZEL DICKEN-GARCIA

See also African American Media; Alternative Press; Associated Press; Civil War Press (North); Cooperative News Gathering; Exchanges; Feminist Media; Journalistic Interview; Native American Media; News Concepts; Newspapers in the Nineteenth Century; Penny Press; Telegraph; War of 1812

Further Reading

Dicken-Garcia, Hazel, *Journalistic Standards in Nineteenth-Century America,* Madison: University of Wisconsin Press, 1989

Kielbowicz, Richard, "Newsgathering by Printers' Exchanges Before the Telegraph," *Journalism History* 9 (Summer 1982)

Nilsson, Nils Gunnar, "The Origin of the Interview," *Journalism Quarterly* 48 (Winter 1971)

Rosewater, Victor, *History of Coöperative News-Gathering in the United States,* New York and London: D. Appleton, 1930

Schudson, Michael, "Question Authority: A History of the News Interview in American Journalism, 1860s–1930s," *Media, Culture & Society* 16:4 (October 1994), pp. 565–587

Schwarzlose, Richard A., "Harbor News Association: Formal Origin of the AP," *Journalism Quarterly* 45 (1968)

Smythe, Ted, "The Reporter, 1880–1900. Working

Conditions and Their Influence on the News,"
Journalism History 7 (1980)

Reporters and Reporting in the Twentieth Century

Craft influenced by practitioners, available technology, and community perceptions

Reporting in the 1900s helped shape and was shaped by a multitude of tumultuous events. These included two world wars and other military adventures and woes, from the giddiness of the Spanish-American War at the start of the century to the tragedies of Vietnam and other evidence of limited U.S. influence at the end. The century also witnessed the assassinations of two presidents (William McKinley and John F. Kennedy), the resignation of a third (Richard M. Nixon), and attempts on the lives of four others (Franklin D. Roosevelt, Harry Truman, Gerald Ford, and Ronald Reagan). The United States emerged as a world power. Journalistic introspection and self-criticism increased, yet nevertheless failed to defuse growing public distrust, skepticism, and hostility toward the news media. More than a half century of little technological change was followed by three to four decades of mind-boggling change. Society became increasingly diverse and often fractured, heralding advances in civil rights for wide segments of society, but also laying bare widespread social injustice and divisiveness. First Amendment rights became developed to an extent unique in the world. Fear of Communism affected policymaking at all levels of government and influenced the accompanying news coverage. To even glimpse the scope of reporters and reporting in the twentieth century, one must try to view the century according to categories that include the perceptions of reporters and reporting; the conventions and technology of reporting; and the people of reporting.

Typifying the raucous spirit of reporting in the early years of the century was Ben Hecht, a reporter, playwright, and novelist. Hecht wrote of himself in the early 1900s in *Gaily, Gaily: The Memoirs of a Cub Reporter in Chicago*: "He knew almost nothing. His achievements were nil. He was as void of ambition as an eel is of feathers. He misunderstood himself and the world around him. He thought journalism was some sort of game like stoop-tag."

Such a happy-go-lucky approach can be found at various stages in almost any occupation in which a person understates what he or she brings to the workplace, partly because of the sheer joy of it all. But embracing ignorance, discounting achievements, and denying any ambition plainly were not adequate qualifications for the role of a reporter in a nation that was beginning to emerge as a world power. Journalists, even if they did not all take themselves seriously, were beginning to be taken seriously by others. And certainly, Hecht's views did not reflect the form of journalism that the nation would expect in the depression years of the 1930s and the war years of the 1940s.

Varying journalism practices can be found in almost any

era of a century. For example, while Hecht was extolling the ignorance-is-bliss aspect of his Chicago reporting, muckrakers such as Ida Tarbell, Lincoln Steffens, and Upton Sinclair worked earnestly to expose corporate and political evils. Nevertheless, trends or shifts in emphasis reflect how most journalists perceive their trade, even if there are no bright lines marking the transition from one era to another.

The madcap and jazz journalism practices of the early 1900s had their roots in the yellow journalism of the turn of the century. That era yielded to the sobering impact of the depression years and a need for a concerned, nationalistic press during and after World War II. Such a straightforward, almost subservient, approach to news coverage of public officials was called into question in the mid-1950s. Such journalistic practices probably enhanced – and certainly did not diminish – the credibility of the reckless charges of Communist conspiracies advanced by Senator Joseph McCarthy of Wisconsin. Even then, it was at least a decade after McCarthy's censure by the U.S. Senate in 1954 that reporters came to think of themselves openly and proudly as adversaries of the government, particularly in the conduct of the war in Vietnam.

The Democratic Party's national political convention in Chicago in 1968 qualifies as a watershed event of the twentieth century in terms of how reporters viewed themselves and how they viewed their news coverage of government. In Chicago in August, antiwar demonstrators and police battled in what the public Walker Commission later termed "a police riot." Reporters were among those seriously injured by baton-swinging police as protesters in the glare of television lights chanted "the whole world is watching."

Many reporters were outraged by the manner in which their newspapers – especially those in Chicago – backed away from what the reporters saw as truthful accounts of the "police riot" and took almost pro-government, pro-police stances. Several working-press journalism reviews, in which reporters criticized the work of their own newspapers and wire services, surfaced – most notably in New York with *(MORE)* and in Chicago with the *Chicago Journalism Review.* The *Columbia Journalism Review,* perhaps the best-known of the "establishment" reviews, had been founded at Columbia University's school of journalism in 1961.

Emerging during the 1960s, too, was the concept of a "New Journalism." "New Journalism" was a label for what was called point-of-view reporting, in which the reporter's own interpretation of an event was considered preferable to a traditional account, couched in the canons of objectivity. Such a "new" journalism accomplished less than its adherents claimed. Perhaps it also contributed more than its detractors would admit, inasmuch as newspaper contents became a bit livelier and more readable. The argument for more "involved" reporting certainly points to advances that news coverage helped bring to the civil rights struggles of the 1960s, and it also reflected a growing trend toward interpretative reporting and news analysis that at times – without always telling the reader or viewer – blurred the lines between news reporting and opinion writing.

Reporters' cynicism toward their employers abated in

subsequent years, but cynicism toward government was re-fueled by continuing deception over the war in Vietnam and, of course, by the Watergate scandal. Watergate led to the resignation of President Nixon and to a public and a press perhaps more impressed than ever with the good and with the harm that a vigorous news media can bring to the nation. The Watergate reporting of the *Washington (D.C.) Post* made household names of reporters Bob Woodward and Carl Bernstein.

Discussions of Watergate and press cynicism often con-clude that journalists who hammered away at suspect pub-lic institutions may have cracked some of the foundations of democracy. Small wonder then, at the close of the centu-ry, a new approach to reporting and editing appeared under such terms as "civic," "public" or "communitarian" jour-nalism. In public journalism, the news reporter sought the news angle or the topic that would engage or involve a community in the most positive, responsible fashion. The concept was criticized for its danger of turning news re-porters into community cheerleaders.

The notion that reporters should be objective – devel-oped early in the century and linked with the growth of the wire services – was challenged often in the latter half of the century by the argument that human beings could not be lit-erally objective in assessing any issue worth writing about. Still, readers and viewers were expected to trust news ac-counts, particularly as more and more obviously partisan voices were heard in national debates ranging from A (abortion) to Z (zoology, for animal rights activists).

Beginning during the era of the New Journalism of the 1960s and 1970s and continuing into the era of public jour-nalism was the concept of precision journalism, in which re-porters used the research tools of social science – primarily polling and survey research – to serve the public better. "Precision journalism" – the term popularized by Knight newspaper reporter and University of North Carolina pro-fessor Philip Meyer – could flourish with the new reporting conventions and technology made possible by having com-puters in the newsrooms, one of the major changes in twen-tieth-century reporting.

The major news events of an era certainly shape percep-tions of reporting and reporters. Discerning analysts can document perhaps even more profound and longer-lasting changes when looking at the impact of technology upon an occupation or even more subtle impacts such as – for re-porters – the use of the interview as a way to gather infor-mation or the use of a well-worded lead paragraph to summarize a story.

A reporter from the newspaper newsroom of 1901 would have been right at home in most newspaper news-rooms of the late 1960s or early 1970s. A telephone, a type-writer, and a high-speed rotary press were the tools of the trade for some 70 years. So were the conventional news-gathering practices of attending public meetings and talking with public officials, public figures, and private citizens in the public spotlight.

The most startling change confronting a time-tripping reporter might be that there now were women and some minority group members in the newsroom. For the most part, however, the reporter leaping 70 years would be as much an asset to the new employer as he was to the old.

By the 1980s and the 1990s, print and broadcast news-rooms became computerized. Rather than seeking out sources of information, the reporter was overwhelmed by them. Government databases and the Internet provided lit-erally millions of easily available sources. Yet the audience, by many measures, had less time and less inclination to read, hear, or watch what the reporter had to say. Even if the audience did want the news, in many instances the re-porter had less newspaper space for telling a story and more cramped broadcast time for fitting a story in.

The nature of the story was changed, too, by concerns and market forces that were nonexistent even 30 or 40 years before. On the plus side, the newsroom became sensi-tive to needs for writing for audiences far more complex than those typified by the white adult male for whom most newspapers were written and most broadcasts were aired for much of the twentieth century.

In the last third of the century, consultants changed the design of many newspapers and the formats of many broad-cast stations. Curiously, the changes brought about more uniformity than differences among the news media. The consultants emphasized designs and formats likely to at-tract the most readers and viewers rather than changes to improve the quality of news reporting or to make a news-paper or station distinctive.

Still, in terms of long-term influences, the impact of the technological and marketing changes upon the role of the reporter was uncertain. Plainly, people got news faster: By one estimate, some 68 percent of the U.S. people learned within a half hour on November 22, 1963, that their presi-dent had been shot in Dallas, Texas. And plainly, the news media could reach more people than ever before. The tele-vising of the verdict in the murder trial of O.J. Simpson in October 1995 pushed ratings to one of the highest daytime levels ever, with Nielsen Media Research showing that al-most 50 percent of the nation's 96 million television homes were tuned in. High-speed and saturation reporting took on global aspects in the evolution of the Cable News Network (CNN). Around-the-clock reporting, from almost anywhere to everywhere on Earth, was epitomized in CNN's coverage of the Persian Gulf War in the early 1990s, when news re-ports were filed from Baghdad, Iraq, while Saddam Hus-sein's military was under attack by U.S.-led forces.

Control over the technology and conventions of any pro-fession, trade or craft, however, ultimately is vested in the people of those occupations and vocations and how well they both understand and play their roles. Perhaps the most comprehensive look at reporters toward the end of the twentieth century was in *The American Journalist*, a report of surveys of news reporters by two University of Indiana faculty. The report, by David Weaver and G. Cleveland Wil-hoit, differed from the conventional wisdom that depicted reporters as different from their news audiences in many ways. Weaver and Wilhoit reported that

1.) journalism was becoming more and more a young
    person's profession "at a time when the society [had]

larger proportions of the elderly." Older, skilled workers left the profession;

2.) more women were in the profession. Beginning salaries for men and women were comparable, and women were moving into more management positions. Their presence increased sensitivity to issues involving women and children;

3.) journalists were more centrist politically than was popularly believed; and

4.) journalists held religious beliefs and affiliations that "reflect the larger society almost exactly."

As for specifics, the following persons represent well the men and women who left their marks on reporting in the twentieth century. They are listed in roughly chronological order.

Publishers Joseph Pulitzer and William Randolph Hearst, although they were perhaps best known by the characterization of "yellow journalism," set the tone for reporting styles for most of the century. They also were among the leaders in welcoming women to the corps of newspaper reporters even in the late 1800s and early 1900s. Pulitzer's concept that the highest mission of the newspaper was to render public service reflected the altruism that drew many to become reporters and that was resurrected in the concept of public journalism at the end of the century.

From almost the beginning to the end of the century, the *New York Times* was considered the most respected and most influential newspaper in the nation. Its staff during the 1900s included such talent as managing editor Carr Van Anda and reporters and columnists Harrison Salisbury, Arthur Krock, Tom Wicker, James Reston.

George Seldes, who died in 1995 at the age of 104, spent most of his life as a critic of newspapers and news reporters. He argued that his journalistic colleagues were beholden to corporate and political powers in their work.

Ida B. Wells-Barnett was the first prominent black woman journalist and a vocal civil rights advocate for women and for blacks. Her *Free Speech* newspaper in Memphis, Tennessee, campaigned against lynching at considerable peril to herself, and she continued her campaigns at the *New York Age* and Chicago's *Conservator*.

Ida Tarbell and Lincoln Steffens, recognized as muckrakers, also contributed to the reporting and literature of the century. Tarbell was known for her research and writing on Abraham Lincoln and Steffens for his work on the *New York Evening Post,* his commentary on the Russian Revolution and his autobiography, a centerpiece in the literature of journalism.

Lowell Thomas became one of the first celebrity reporters of the century. He was known internationally for his coverage of *Lawrence in Arabia* (the title of his book) during World War I and then for his radio and television broadcasts and newsreel filmed reports from around the world.

I.F. Stone, an iconoclast reporter and editor of *I.F. Stone's Weekly,* was the mentor and inspiration for reporters who went to the record to document their news stories and unearthed news that all citizens should know. Stone quipped that he loved reading the *Washington Post* because, "You never know where you'll find a front-page story."

Edward R. Murrow became the figurative saint for broadcast journalism in particular and reporting in general. He began a tradition of excellence in broadcast news at CBS radio and then excelled in television with documentaries such as "Harvest of Shame," on migrant farmworkers, and his exposé of the ruthless methods employed by Senator McCarthy's anti-Communist crusade.

Walter Cronkite of CBS and David Brinkley of NBC set standards for network television news programs and marks for longevity in broadcast journalism. Each worked for more than half a century – Brinkley paired with Chet Huntley in the NBC nightly news. Cronkite ranked among the most credible of public figures for much of the latter half of the century.

Merriman Smith of United Press International and Malcom Browne of the Associated Press represent the wire service reporters who provided news reports to newspapers and broadcast stations around the world. Smith was best remembered as a White House correspondent, Browne for his work in Vietnam.

David Broder, reporter and columnist for the *Washington Post,* was among the most respected and the hardest-working of newspaper reporters of the latter half of the century. He was known for his thoughtful reporting and for his fairness in commentary.

Ted Koppel's *Nightline* television program was the flagship of the increasing role of broadcast talk shows and interview programs in setting the nation's political agenda in the last decade or so of the twentieth century.

Almost any general listing of twentieth-century reporters reflects how white males of European descent dominated the nation's news media for most of the century. The picture plainly was changing in the last quarter of the century, however, and newsrooms were expected to diversify in the twenty-first century. Prominent African Americans in reporting circles included Robert C. Maynard of the *Oakland (California) Tribune,* who became the first black person to head a major metropolitan newspaper; Carl T. Rowan, a reporter and columnist for the *Minneapolis (Minnesota) Tribune* and later a syndicated columnist and television commentator; Charlayne Hunter-Gault of the *New York Times* and public television journalism; and William A. Hilliard, one of the first blacks to head one of the mainstream professional news organizations, becoming president of the American Society of Newspaper Editors in 1994.

As late as the 1970s, men made up more than two-thirds of the undergraduate enrollment in the nation's journalism schools. By the 1990s, however, female students had turned the tables, making up about 65 percent of the journalism and mass communication undergraduates. Their female predecessors in reporting included Elizabeth Cochrane Seaman, whose work as "Nellie Bly" for Pulitzer's *World* established her as one of the best-known reporters of the early 1900s; Mary McGrory of the *Washington Star* and *Washington Post;* Meg Greenfield of *Newsweek* and the

Washington Post; Barbara Walters, who made her mark on journalism of the last 30 years of the century with work on NBC's *Today,* as the first female network anchor (at ABC), and with televised interviews that were a television version of *Who's Who;* war correspondent Marguerite Higgins; Marlene Sanders, a vice president and director of documentaries for ABC; and Pauline Frederick of NBC, the first woman to cover a political convention for a network (in 1948) and United Nations correspondent for NBC until 1974.

HERBERT STRENTZ

See also Broadcast Interview Shows; Broadcast Talk Shows; Cold War and the Media; Criticism of Newspapers; Cronkite, Walter; Hearst, William Randolph; *Huntley-Brinkley Report, The;* Interpretative Reporting; Investigative Reporting; Journalism Reviews; Kerner Commission Report; Mass Media and the Antiwar Movement; Media Events; Muckraking; Murrow, Edward R; New Journalism (1960s–1970s); Newspaper Design; Newspapers in the Twentieth Century; Newspaper Technology; Nixon, Richard M., and the Media; Objective Reporting; Persian Gulf War; Precision Journalism; Public Journalism; Pulitzer, Joseph; Seldes, George; Stone, I.F.; Tabloids; Vietnam War; Watergate Scandal; World War II

Further Reading
Belford, Barbara, *Brilliant Bylines: A Biographical Anthology of Notable Newspaperwomen in America,* New York: Columbia University Press, 1986
Leonard, Thomas C., *The Power of the Press: The Birth of American Political Reporting,* New York: Oxford University Press, 1986
Ross, Ishbel, *Ladies of the Press,* New York: Harper & Brothers, 1936
Schudson, Michael, *The Power of News,* Cambridge, Massachusetts: Harvard University Press, 1995; London: Harvard University Press, 1996
Stephens, Mitchell, *A History of News: From the Drum to the Satellite,* New York: Penguin, 1988
Weaver, David H., and G. Cleveland Wilhoit, *The American Journalist: A Portrait of U.S. News People and Their Work,* 2nd ed., Bloomington: Indiana University Press, 1991

Report on Chain Broadcasting

Comments on investigation into possible network monopolies

In 1938, under congressional pressure, the Federal Communications Commission (FCC) began to investigate the monopolistic practices of the radio networks. The result was the *Report on Chain Broadcasting,* issued in 1941. Among the issues that most concerned the FCC were NBC's ownership of two networks (the Red and the Blue), which the

commission saw as anticompetitive, and the contracts between networks and affiliated stations, which basically took away the affiliates' editorial discretion.

Since the FCC did not have the power to regulate the networks, the regulations included in the report were aimed at the affiliated stations. The commission said that the regulations were necessary because it was the station, not the network, that was licensed to serve the public interest.

The regulations did not permit licensees to enter into a contract with any network if such contract prevented a licensee from broadcasting programs from other networks, airing network programs rejected by other licensees, maintaining control over its own programming schedule, rejecting a network program or preempting it and replacing it with another that better served the public interest, and fixing or altering its rates for nonnetwork broadcast time. In addition, licensees could not enter into contracts with organizations that maintained more than one network, and the contracts could not be longer than one year.

In 1943, the U.S. Supreme Court upheld the FCC's power to enforce the chain broadcasting regulations in *NBC* v. *United States.* In that same year, Edward J. Noble bought the NBC Blue Network and formed the American Broadcasting Company.

MILAGROS RIVERA-SANCHEZ

See also Broadcast Regulation; Radio Networks

Further Reading
United States, Federal Communications Commission, *Report on Chain Broadcasting,* Washington, D.C.: Government Printing Office, 1941

Resor, Helen Lansdowne

Pioneer in developing advertising aimed at women

Helen Lansdowne Resor was one of the first women to be successful in national advertising. With her husband, Stanley Resor, she led the J. Walter Thompson Company to world prominence.

Helen Resor was instrumental in the development of national advertising aimed at women, initially through her Crisco campaign and later through her direction of Thompson's Women's Editorial Department, which she founded. This department, run by women primarily for women consumers, provided advertisements for products aimed at women: household and cleaning items, food and beauty products, clothing and accessories.

Resor was also instrumental in the development of the use of sex appeal in advertising through the famous Woodbury's Soap campaign, "A Skin You Love to Touch." Using muted sexuality and what may now appear to be tame physical contact between a man and a woman, these ads created a sensation, and sales of Woodbury's facial soap increased 1,000 percent in eight years. What eventually turned into one of the major controversies in advertising – the portrayal of women as sex objects – was first developed by a woman who most likely saw the recognition of women's sexuality as a step forward in an advertising world that portrayed women primarily as asexual wives and mothers.

Finally, Helen Resor was influential in promoting the hiring of women in the advertising field. In 1920, she was praised in the *Ladies' Home Journal,* which argued that she "not only put manufacturers' products and her own agency on the map; she made a place in advertising geography for women, a place no advertiser or agency ever before had granted them."

JENNIFER SCANLON

See also Advertising Appeals; Advertising in the Twentieth Century; Resor, Stanley B.

Further Reading
Abbott, Harriet, "Doctor? Lawyer? Merchant? Chief? What Shall She Be? Women's New Leadership in Business," *Ladies' Home Journal* (July 1920)
Scanlon, Jennifer, *Inarticulate Longings: The 'Ladies' Home Journal', Gender, and the Promises of Consumer Culture,* New York: Routledge, 1995

Resor, Stanley B.

Built standards of marketing excellence

Lauded as a dominant, legendary force in marketing, and perhaps the greatest advertising executive who ever lived, Stanley Burnet Resor was instrumental in legitimizing advertising as a career. As president of the J. Walter Thompson advertising agency from 1916 to 1955, Resor diffused his own standards of marketing excellence into the advertising industry. These standards included empirically researched, ethical marketing practices.

Following his education at Yale University, Resor began his career in advertising with Procter and Gamble. J. Walter Thompson discovered Resor's talent and earnestness, and the Thompson agency's 1908 expansion to Resor's native Cincinnati, Ohio, provided Resor's first executive leadership opportunity. Eight years later, Thompson retired and sold the agency, then grossing $3 million a year, to Resor and two partners. Over the next 39 years, Resor and his associates dedicated themselves to ad copy based purely upon empirical studies of their clients' products and target populations, thus building the agency into one amassing over $82 million annually. Resor is also credited with the establishment and testing of a new marketing technique, the Consumer Research Panel, in 1939.

Resor's contributions to the advertising industry establish him as a pioneer of modern marketing practices. Beyond fact-based ad campaigns, Resor believed advertisers could produce a "world of peace and understanding" by upholding the highest in ethical standards and showing the public how to satisfy their needs. Resor, a founder of the American Association of Advertising, received the Gold Medal Award for distinguished service in the advertising field in 1949.

KARLA M. LARSON

See also Advertising Appeals; Advertising in the Twentieth Century; Resor, Helen Lansdowne

Further Reading
Jacobs, Laurence W., "Stanley B. Resor: 1879–1962," in *Pioneers in Marketing: A Collection of Twenty-Five Biographies of Men Who Contributed to the Growth of Marketing Through Thought and Action,* edited by John S. Wright and Parks B. Dimsdale, Jr., Atlanta: Georgia State University, 1974
"J. Walter Thompson: The Largest Advertising Agency in the World; Who Runs It, and How It Works," *Fortune* (1947)
Miller, George Laflin, *Copy – The Core of Advertising,* New York: Dover, 1963
Wood, James P., "A Pioneer in Marketing: Stanley Resor," *Journal of Marketing* 6 (1961)

Retail Advertising

Direct advertising placed by advertisers

Retail advertising sprang from two roots: the simple, direct advertising placed by small merchants and advertising placed by large department stores, which appeared with the department store in the mid-nineteenth century. Both of these forms of retail advertising existed at the end of the twentieth century.

The small grocer's ad, often simply a notice that a particular product could be had at a particular location, can be traced back before the American Revolution. Some superlatives, such as "best quality," might be attached to the product, but the real emphasis, in the retailer's mind, was the location of his store. Retailers decided what products would be included and at what price the manufacturer would be compensated.

To trace the history of retail advertising is also to trace the growth of national advertising. The manufacturers' decision in the early part of the nineteenth century to talk directly to their buying public was in part a response to the treatment these manufacturers had received from retailers. Convinced that branding their products and driving consumer demand would topple the retailer autocracy, manufacturers deftly turned the tables in a few short years, leaving retailers complaining that they were little more than manufacturer representatives and creating a class of imperious manufacturer salesmen. Direct sampling campaigns, backed with couponing and consumer trade shows, bankrolled many grocery and general goods stores. Manufacturers sought not only consumers but places to sell their goods while forcing retailers to take their products at their prices.

Consumers had gotten their first tastes of national manufactured goods through catalogs, such as Montgomery Ward and Sears, Roebuck, which arrived on every home's doorstep thanks to the emergence of a more reliable postal system after the Civil War. Encouraged by demand, these catalogers started establishing stores in larger cities and attracted competition from others seeing the advantage in

A nineteenth-century broadside advertises department store retail wares.
(Reproduced from the Collections of the Library of Congress)

carrying a wide variety of products in one location. With competition, retail advertising arose in metropolitan areas and, later, nationally, as chains were built on these initial stores.

These new department stores, their sometimes-related catalog cousins, and the rising chains took advantage of their ability to move more merchandise for less money than their dying predecessors. As *Printer's Ink* argued in a series on chain stores in 1914, the three were related naturally and carried some of the same marketing tactics to consumers.

One area that would differentiate these three would be advertising. Local stores relied primarily on newspapers to ward off the couponing and sampling pressures of national manufacturers. These stores also employed several innovations, such as fixed prices, inventory turns, and departments of similar products, all of which appeared in the chains. As the manufacturers relied on national magazines and later television, local and chain retailers continued well after World War II to prefer newspapers and, later, radio.

As the retail unit evolved so, too, did the advertising used to support it. The retail advertising mix in the late twentieth century included all of the features of retailing's heritage – newspaper, radio and television advertising, cata-

logs, couponing and sampling – and showed signs of branching into new technologies such as infomercials, on-line sales, and interactive television.

THOMAS GOULD

See also Advertising in the Nineteenth Century; Advertising in the Twentieth Century

Further Reading

Haight, William, *Retail Advertising: Management and Technique*, Glenview, Illinois: Scott, Foresman, 1976
Norris, Vincent P., "Advertising History: According to the Textbooks," in *Advertising in Society: Classic and Contemporary Readings on Advertising's Role in Society*, edited by Roxanne Hovland and Gary B. Wilcox, Lincolnwood, Illinois: NTC Business, 1989
Pease, Otis, *The Responsibilities of American Advertising: Private Control and Public Influence, 1920–1940*, New Haven, Connecticut: Yale University Press, 1958
"Sears Talks Newspapers," *Editor & Publisher* (January 15, 1986)
Strasser, Susan, *Satisfaction Guaranteed: The Making of the American Mass Market*, New York: Pantheon, 1989

Riis, Jacob A.

Early documentary photographer

Known as one of the first and foremost muckrakers with a camera, Jacob A. Riis is best remembered for *How the Other Half Lives* (1890), a book that documented through words and pictures the slums of New York. Much of his work from the 10 years he photographed was forgotten for many decades until photographer Alexander Alland Sr. made enlargements in 1947 from Riis's original 4-by-5-inch glass negatives. This effort resulted in an exhibition at the Museum of the City of New York and reproductions in *U.S. Camera 1948*, reviving Riis's legacy as a social reformer.

Born in Denmark, Riis emigrated to the United States in 1870. For three years he lived in poverty before joining a news bureau staff as a reporter. In 1878, he became a reporter for the Associated Press and the *New York Tribune*, assigned to police headquarters on Mulberry Street, which was surrounded by slums and tenements. Seeking graphic illustrations for his articles that exposed life in New York City's tenements, Riis used cumbersome camera equipment, including large glass plates and magnesium flash, to show the human misery and degradation he found inside the slums and police lodging houses.

During his career, Riis published a dozen books, including *The Children of the Poor* and an autobiography. He came to be known at the turn of the twentieth century as the "Emancipator of the Slums." Many of the photographs attributed to Riis actually were taken by two amateur photographers who frequently accompanied him on his ventures into the slums.

C. ZOE SMITH

See also Documentary Photography; Photographic
   Technology; Photojournalism in the Nineteenth Century

Further Reading

Alland, Alexander, Sr., *Jacob A. Riis: Photographer and
   Citizen,* Millerton, New York: Aperture, 1974; London:
   Gordon Fraser, 1975

Doherty, Robert, ed., *The Complete Photographic Work of
   Jacob A. Riis,* New York: Macmillan, 1981; London:
   Collier Macmillan, 1981

Riis, Jacob A., *How the Other Half Lives: Studies Among
   the Tenements of New York,* New York: Dover, 1971;
   London: Constable, 1971

_____, *The Making of an American,* New York:
   Macmillan, 1970; London: Macmillan, 1990

Szasz, Ferenc M., and Ralph F. Bogardus, "The Camera
   and the American Social Conscience: The Documentary
   Photography of Jacob A. Riis," *New York History* 55
   (October 1974)

Ware, Louise, *Jacob A. Riis: Police Reporter, Reformer,
   Useful Citizen,* New York and London: D. Appleton-
   Century, 1938

Roosevelt, Franklin D., and the Media

*President had superior media management
techniques while in office*

Franklin D. Roosevelt, often ranked as one of the great U.S.
presidents, also was reputed to have had among the best, if
not the best, twentieth-century presidential press relations.
His news management, with every kind of mass media
available during his record 12 years in office (1933–45),
may indeed have been the key to his political artistry.

This thirty-second president exerted different kinds of
news management during different kinds of crises. During
the internal domestic crisis of the Great Depression, the
president could be open, tolerating, and even encouraging
varying viewpoints within his administration. His leadership was flexible as he and his officials searched for answers
to the Great Depression. The public was let in on the details, the inside information. Yet, during an external crisis,
World War II, the nation feared for its survival and worried
about possible invasion. The country's information wagons
were drawn in a circle, and the president alone spoke for
the nation and to the world. Roosevelt set up the Offices of
Censorship and War Information to coordinate and control
the war messages.

There are many facets that explain Roosevelt's media
artistry. Foremost, he was a great communicator and as
such understood the mass message process. He considered
himself a journalist and had numerous journalism connections. At the turn of the century when he was a college student, he became editor in chief of the *Harvard Crimson.* He
wrote magazine articles during the 1920s. In both 1940 and
again in 1944, he signed a contact with *Collier's Magazine*

to be a contributing editor when he retired from public office. His wife, Eleanor, had a syndicated daily column, did a
radio series, and wrote many magazine articles. His son-in-
law and his daughter held editorial positions with the *Seattle (Washington) Post-Intelligencer.* A number of his
advisers had been journalists.

Moreover, Roosevelt liked journalists and met with them
formally more than any other president, logging almost
1,000 press conferences. With his twice-a-week meetings
whenever he was in Washington, D.C., he would hold background meetings on what was happening and schooling sessions on the budget and the New Deal programs. Open to
all correspondents, the press conferences gave the president
an excuse to avoid exclusive interviews. As had the presidents prior to 1933 and before televised news conferences,
Roosevelt's meeting stipulations included a "background
rule" of no direct quotes without permission or an "off-the-
record rule" of no references to the president at all. With his
well-known charm and positive nature, he could deflect or
evade questions; with his confidence, he would admit that
he did not know an answer. Yet, as the journalists' most authoritative news source, he could give out the necessary information as well as define the issues and set the news
agenda.

Roosevelt demonstrated information power through media technological artistry. He could go over the heads of
print journalists and their stories by scheduling broadcasts.
He was the consummate broadcaster, speaking clearly and
slowly. His "fireside chats" were memorable because they
were so few in number. During his first eight years in office,
he broadcast 16 fireside chats. Roosevelt's fireside speaking
style made the chats different by being informal and short,
usually less than 30 minutes. The president used the fireside
format to explain his policies or give a general accounting
in such a casual way that it seemed like a personal message.
Washington correspondent Richard Strout remembered,
"You felt he was there talking to you, not to 50 million others, but to you personally."

As with the press conference sessions, what appeared so
informal was highly practiced for content as well as delivery.
Each broadcast went through between three and 10 drafts,
as the president sought the most understandable terms. He
relied on familiar words and well-known homilies, such as
"my friends," and analogies, such as describing the Lend-
Lease program as being like "a neighbor borrowing the hose
to put out the fire." While there were many speech collaborators, the final words were his alone. Roosevelt edited,
studied, reviewed, and rehearsed each address over and over
for clarity, pacing, and emphasis.

Roosevelt also took great care with his pictorial image.
There were to be no exclusive photographs; all photo coverage was to be pooled. His press secretary stipulated the
distance, timing, place, and number of photographers. Roosevelt gave photojournalists something newsworthy to
shoot. His informality and ever-changing facial expressions
sharply contrasted to the stoic and deadpan Herbert
Hoover. He liked the dramatic and the unusual. Both still
and newsreel photographers went on his inspection tours
and his many trips to Hyde Park, New York; Warm Springs,
Georgia; and later the Pacific and Panama Canal.

President Franklin D. Roosevelt communicated well with the public via radio.
(Franklin D. Roosevelt Library)

The biggest image taboo was to depict reminders of the president's lameness. In 1921, Roosevelt had contracted polio, and, while subsequently he made great physical strides, he never again could walk without the aid of crutches, a cane, or assistance. The unwritten photography rule was that he would not be shown in a wheelchair or using crutches. The only exception made was for those photos showing his physical comeback, as when he walked with crutches to a podium in 1924. Rarely, then, were there camera shots depicting his crippled condition. The rule was easily enforced. The press secretary controlled the photo pools. The Secret Service controlled the access and physical proximity to him. Nevertheless, *Life, Look, Fortune,* the *Chicago Tribune,* and the *New York Herald-Tribune* were among those publications that carried such "taboo" pictures.

The subject of Roosevelt's polio-ridden legs was not a secret. Even though the U.S. public saw few pictorial reminders of the president's crippled condition, he was shown in cartoons with a cane. The president himself referred to

his braces or his polio-damaged legs publicly, even in speeches. The image control was not just from the White House but from the U.S. public as well. When there were derogatory graphic references to the president's handicap, people reacted. For example, when *Time* referred to his "shriveled legs" and "hobbled" condition before the first inauguration, indignant letter writers chided the publication. *Time* attempted to answer these critics by stating that they would "contrive to regard Mr. Roosevelt's legs as mentionable – unless a great majority of *Time* readers have commanded otherwise." A great majority did so command, and such references to the president's lameness were seldom found in *Time* or any other publications until 1944, when Roosevelt's health became a campaign issue. Rather, the media over and over emphasized Roosevelt's comeback from infantile paralysis. His constant activity, his own nonchalant air, and carefree remarks about his legs (such as "I've got to run now") countered the image of paralysis.

Roosevelt also carefully controlled the newsreels, the

predecessor to television news. For the camera operators, the rules concerning camera proximity and use of klieg lights were similar to those regarding still photography. For content, the newsreel companies would occasionally film a fireside speech a few days before its delivery so that they could release the speech to the theaters at the time of the actual radio broadcast. For the most part, the newsreels emphasized the president's character and appearances, not the controversial topics of his administrations. Rather, the newsreels projected an image of an energetic, vigorous president working on the nation's problems.

Roosevelt's mass media efforts might not have been so extensive or as painstakingly careful had the newspaper publishers not been his foremost adversaries. During all four of his presidential campaigns, Roosevelt was not supported by a majority of U.S. dailies. Not only were most publishers Republican, but they became infuriated with the National Recovery Act (NRA), which imposed wage, price, and other business controls. The Wagner Labor Relations Act contained many of the same provisions as the unconstitutional NRA, including collective bargaining, which the publishers abhorred.

Roosevelt was assisted by an excellent press secretary, Stephen T. Early. Early oversaw the administration's information system, met with Roosevelt each morning, and held daily press briefings. Together, they established a coordinated press bureaucracy throughout the executive branch. As the first designated press secretary, Early relied upon his previous journalism and newsreel experience to write magazine articles about the White House and the president, schedule radio time for Roosevelt's broadcasts, dribble information to build a large listening audience, keep charts to show the fluctuations in the audience sizes, and oversee the president's photographic images. Early's efforts were public, and he became recognized as the administration's spokesman.

Roosevelt's media operations were credible with the public because he listened to the people and constantly sought a two-way communication system. He not only planned information and controlled its release but also checked his efforts and the public's thoughts. From a Press Intelligence Bureau, which later became part of the White House News Operations, and a more organized publicity system through World War II, to those embryonic public opinion polls, Roosevelt wanted to know what the people were thinking.

Franklin D. Roosevelt's relations with the U.S. news media is a presidential case study of press relations and points to a balance between information access and government controls and between frankness and caution during both domestic and international crises. Roosevelt's World War II censorship and even the Federal Bureau of Investigation wartime investigation of news leaks and unauthorized press disclosures about military losses were mild compared to the excesses during World War I. Unlike the case during the Woodrow Wilson era, journalists and citizens did not go to prison for expressing themselves.

For all of his organization and news management skills, Roosevelt was not always successful. He could not get his programs passed if Congress refused to act or the people were not moved. None of his news management tactics worked to pass his astounding Supreme Court reform proposal: not a trial balloon article that he dictated for journalists months before; not a witty, dramatic press conference; not a startling exclusive interview; not a fireside chat; not even the Democratic National Committee publicity efforts. The people were not convinced.

If one function of the press is to provide enough information on which to judge political leadership, then the U.S. press during the 12 years of the Roosevelt administration fulfilled its obligation. Roosevelt worked very hard to explain his programs and policies. He could send his messages successfully to the public. If there is a second press function, that is to tell not just what is being said or done but also provide an account of what is being thought about what is being done. Roosevelt most actively tried to influence that account, those political opinions. Despite editorial opposition from the majority of newspapers, the electorate voted for Roosevelt affirmatively. By combining his communications skills with his political leadership, Franklin D. Roosevelt left a legacy for subsequent presidents. He demonstrated that a sense of confidence and an optimistic nature during an active presidency could influence the news, especially if the president understood the media technologies and the news process.

BETTY HOUCHIN WINFIELD

See also Motion Picture Newsreels; New Deal and the Media; Office of Censorship; Office of War Information; Presidential News Conferences; Presidential Press Secretaries; World War II

Further Reading
Steele, Richard W., *Propaganda in an Open Society: The Roosevelt Administration and the Media, 1933–1941,* Westport, Connecticut: Greenwood, 1985
White, Graham J., *FDR and the Press,* Chicago: University of Chicago Press, 1979
Winfield, Betty Houchin, "Anna Eleanor Roosevelt Shines a Light on Herself and Women Journalists," *Journalism History* 8:2 (1981)
_____, *FDR and the News Media,* New York: Columbia University Press, 1994
_____, "F.D.R.'s Pictorial Image: Rules and Boundaries," *Journalism History* 5:4 (1978–79)

Roosevelt, Theodore, and the Press

Recognized importance of news in the development of public opinion

Theodore Roosevelt was the first president to recognize the importance of news and its effect on public opinion. During his presidency, from 1901 to 1909, he consolidated the power and authority of the president while manipulating the press to promote himself and his causes, thereby transforming the relationship between the press and the presidency. Roosevelt simultaneously established press relations as a recognized public function of the White House.

After developing techniques for working with the press while he was police commissioner in New York City and governor of New York state, the 42-year-old Roosevelt – the youngest president in history, as of the end of the twentieth century – blasted onto the national scene like a thunderbolt. His first change was to provide reporters with unprecedented access. Soon after entering office, he created space for reporters inside the White House. The pressroom's proximity to the Oval Office made reporters feel that they were working with the president, and perhaps even for him. Roosevelt also aided reporters – and himself – by creating the concept of the "authoritative source." The president was willing to chat informally with reporters and answer any question they asked. His only stipulation was that the reporters attribute sensitive information to anonymous sources. Within weeks of ascending to the presidency, he had succeeded in winning the support of the White House press corps.

Roosevelt related well to reporters. He was a prodigious reader of newspapers as well as of the new 10-cent magazines of the era. In his direct contact with reporters, he was candid and open, adopting a "boy's club" style of press briefing. Twice daily, he invited reporters into his office for 15 minutes of questions and answers. Relaxed and eager to chat, Roosevelt perched on the edge of his huge desk, often with a leg tucked under him, and gave the 50 men in the press corps not only information but also anecdotes, jokes, and legislative gossip. Roosevelt biographer Edmund Morris wrote:

> When required to make a formal statement, he spoke with deliberate precision. The performance was rather like that of an Edison cylinder played at slow speed and maximum volume. Relaxing again, he would confess the truth behind the statement, with such gleeful frankness that the reporters felt flattered to be included in his conspiracy.

Roosevelt's friendliness was not altruistic. He believed reporters would write positive stories about him if he made them feel like part of his team. In other words, Roosevelt manipulated the press with the intent of making the news media an unofficial branch of the government. Reporters remained in the "Paradise Club" as long as they did not write unfavorable stories or attribute sensitive material to him; he made these reporters insiders to an extent never before granted to White House correspondents. Reporters who violated Roosevelt's rules, on the other hand, were pushed into the "Ananias Club" and thereby denied all access to White House news. Roosevelt even tried to use his influence to persuade newspaper publishers to fire reporters who wrote unfavorable stories about him.

The most fundamental of Roosevelt's contributions to the evolution of the press-president relationship was his expansion of the boundaries of presidential news. The traditional definition of White House news as a daily chronicle of official activity was too passive for him. Roosevelt was the first president who understood that, with imagination, he could generate news on demand and dominate the national news.

The image-conscious Republican also recognized that a person in the public eye can increase his or her publicity value through dramatic statements and actions, so Roosevelt staged events and actions to reap publicity – creating the photo opportunities of his day. Overt acts Roosevelt undertook, at least partly as publicity stunts, included descending to the bottom of Long Island Sound in a navy submarine and riding 98 miles on horseback in 17 hours to prove that the commander-in-chief could meet the requirements he had set for senior military officers.

Another important element in Roosevelt's brand of press relations evolved from his awareness that how news is disseminated can influence the quantity and quality of coverage. This astuteness was most clearly demonstrated in his policy of timing the release of announcements to ensure the most desirable treatment in the press. He released bad news on Friday afternoon, thereby guaranteeing the relatively low readership of Saturday papers; he released good news on Sunday, securing prominence in Monday papers because Sunday was a dull news day. Roosevelt also timed news events to deny coverage to his political opponents.

Under Roosevelt, the duties of the White House staff were expanded to include press relations. William Loeb Jr., the president's executive secretary, was given the power and responsibility of a press secretary. Loeb controlled the amount of access reporters had to the White House and established the tradition of presidential aides accepting the blame for actions the president actually had taken.

Another technique Roosevelt used adroitly to ensure coverage was sprinkling his speech with vivid phrasing, choosing words that would look good in the newspaper the next day. Roosevelt carefully considered his words, weighing the precise effect of each one. The list of clever, memorable statements that came from his mouth reads like guidelines for how to be quotable for the press or, in late-twentieth-century terms, how to speak in television sound bites. On foreign policy: "Speak softly and carry a big stick." On the Spanish-American War: "It wasn't much of a war, but it was the best war we had." On his decision to run for reelection: "My hat is in the ring." Roosevelt coined many punchy words and phrases that remained a part of the language long after him, including "square deal" and "lunatic fringe."

From a journalism history point of view, the most important product of Roosevelt's creativity as a wordsmith came in 1906 when he coined the term "muckraker." Although Roosevelt generally championed governmental as well as private-sector reform as part of the Progressive Era, he grew frustrated with what he saw as a tendency of crusading journalists to expose problems without offering solutions. He therefore labeled them "muckrakers," a term suggesting the journalists of the era concentrated too heavily on culling the underbelly of the world for trash.

Roosevelt's success as a press personality coincided with the U.S. newspaper's evolution into a big business. As publishers invested increasingly large sums of capital in newspapers, they felt mounting pressure to build the large circulations that would attract advertisers. Publishers, therefore, responded to their belief that most readers would rather be entertained by personal details about people in the news than read technical details about statecraft. In covering the White House, newspapers eagerly emphasized human-interest material. During the Roosevelt presidency, the personal trivia became a staple of the White House press corps.

Roosevelt recognized that newspapers had changed since the Civil War. The era of powerful publishers such as James Gordon Bennett and Horace Greeley had passed; the era of the news reporter had arrived. Roosevelt said: "In our country, I am inclined to think that almost, if not quite, the most important profession is that of the newspaper man. He wields great influence."

Further, Roosevelt understood that, among the masses of the early 1900s, news stories that appeared on the front page were more effective in molding public opinion than were cerebral editorials. If he could use his personality to influence how reporters wrote about him on page one, it would not matter a great deal what the sages might say about his policies on the editorial page.

In the last year of his second term, however, the *New York World* published accusations that even Roosevelt could not ignore. In 1908, the paper reported that a syndicate of U.S. businessmen had made a quick profit of some $36 million through deals with stocks and bonds related to the company that had constructed the Panama Canal. Among those syndicate members, the paper reported, were the president's brother-in-law as well as the half brother of William Howard Taft, the man Roosevelt had picked to succeed him. Roosevelt then sued the *World* for libel, which prompted the paper to accuse the president of trying to muzzle the press. By early 1909, Joseph Pulitzer and his top editors were indicted for criminally libeling Roosevelt and other government and financial leaders. The final decision in the case by the U.S. Supreme Court in 1911 (*United States v. Press Publishing Co.*) turned on a technicality, but Pulitzer considered the *World* and its editors vindicated.

Theodore Roosevelt, who wrote 38 books during his lifetime, tried his hand at journalism at various points in his life. While in office, he never hesitated to suggest ideas for news articles to the reporters covering him, and he sometimes went so far as to dictate stories to the press corps. After leaving the White House, Roosevelt became a contributing editor for the *Kansas City Star* and wrote monthly columns for *Outlook* and *Metropolitan* magazines.

RODGER STREITMATTER

See also Muckraking; Photo Opportunities; Presidential News Conferences; Presidential Press Secretaries; Trial Balloons

Further Reading
Blum, John Morton, *The Progressive Presidents: Roosevelt, Wilson, Roosevelt, Johnson,* New York: Norton, 1980
Juergens, George, *News from the White House: The Presidential-Press Relationship in the Progressive Era,* Chicago: University of Chicago Press, 1981
McCullough, David G., *Mornings on Horseback,* New York: Simon & Schuster, 1981
Morris, Edmund, *The Rise of Theodore Roosevelt,* New York: Coward, McCann & Geoghegan, 1979; London: Collins, 1979
Pollard, James E., *The Presidents and the Press,* New York: Macmillan, 1947
Streitmatter, Rodger, "Theodore Roosevelt: Public Relations Pioneer," *American Journalism* 7 (1990)

Rowell, George P.

Helped establish a professional role for advertising industry

Coming of age when papers were increasing in size and profit centers, George P. Rowell was a pioneer in establishing a professional role for the burgeoning advertising industry that accompanied the expanding and consuming nineteenth-century economy. From modest beginnings as an errand boy sent out to collect bills from advertisers for the *Boston Post,* Rowell went on to establish an advertising agency with his friend Horace Dodd in 1865. During his first year, Rowell and his partner became "space brokers," purchasing large amounts of space from a list of 100 country newspapers that was sold at economic cost to his clients, a strategy that resulted in an immediate and substantial profit for the new business. Relocating from Boston to New York, Rowell next took the agency's information about newspapers, including circulation figures, and published what had been closely held information in the *George P. Rowell and Company American Newspaper Directory,* published from 1869 until Rowell's death in 1908, when it was absorbed by N.W. Ayer and Son's *American Newspaper Annual.*

Although Rowell was unsuccessful in his 1873 attempt to establish an accrediting organization for advertising agents, the short-lived group was a forerunner of the American Association of Advertising Agencies, founded in 1917. In 1888, he established *Printer's Ink,* the leading trade magazine that represented the interests of the advertising industry for decades. *Printer's Ink* fought for equitable postal rates for advertisers, promoted ethical advertising, and led a national campaign for "truth in advertising" legislation.

PATRICIA BRADLEY

See also Advertising Trade Associations; Advertising Trade Press; *American Newspaper Directory;* Ayer, N.W., & Son

Further Reading
Rowell, George P., *Forty Years an Advertising Agent, 1865–1905,* New York: Printers' Ink, 1906; London: Garland, 1985
Smythe, Ted Curtis, "George Presbury Rowell," in *The Ad Men and Women: A Biographical Dictionary of Advertising,* edited by Edd Applegate, Westport, Connecticut: Greenwood, 1994

S

Sarnoff, David

Radio, television pioneer

As the driving force behind the Radio Corporation of America (RCA) for its first 50 years, David Sarnoff was a pioneer in both radio and television. An immigrant from the village of Uzlian in Minsk, Russia, he worked as a messenger for a telegraph firm while still a teenager, became a competent Morse code radio operator, and eventually was employed by the Marconi Wireless Telegraph Company. When American Marconi became RCA in 1919, Sarnoff was its commercial manager, and as RCA general manager (1921), president (1930), and board chairman (1947), he

David Sarnoff
(Library of American Broadcasting)

oversaw the formation of the National Broadcasting Company and was instrumental in the launch of U.S. television. Sarnoff served as a communications consultant at the rank of brigadier general in World War II and retired from RCA in 1970.

Although Sarnoff was clearly a visionary, his legend was bolstered by two apocryphal tales: that in 1912 he was the lone wireless telegraph operator who worked for 72 hours picking up distress signals from the sinking *Titanic,* and that he wrote a prescient "radio music box" memo in 1915 proposing radio as a "household utility." Later historians discounted both of these stories. Sarnoff's apparent contribution after the *Titanic* disaster simply was to copy the names of survivors transmitted from the rescue liner *Carpathia,* and the "radio music box" memo actually was written five years later than Sarnoff claimed, in 1920, when radio broadcasting was just around the corner. These exaggerations aside, Sarnoff is remembered as a broadcast pioneer of great genius and accomplishment.

MARK J. BRAUN

See also Radio Corporation of America

Further Reading

Benjamin, Louise M., "In Search of the Sarnoff 'Radio Music Box' Memo," *Journal of Broadcasting & Electronic Media* 37:3 (Summer 1993), pp. 325–335
Bilby, Kenneth, *The General: David Sarnoff and the Rise of the Communications Industry,* New York: Harper & Row, 1986
Dreher, Carl, *Sarnoff, an American Success,* New York: Quadrangle/New York Times, 1977
Lyons, Eugene, *David Sarnoff, a Biography,* New York: Harper & Row, 1966

Scientific Advertising

Classic guide for early advertising practitioners

Claude C. Hopkins, one of the most respected copywriters in advertising history, wrote *Scientific Advertising* in 1923 while serving as president of the Lord and Thomas advertising agency. Hopkins intended the 20,000-word book to serve as a textbook for advertising students and a guide for advertising practitioners. It became a classic in the advertising field.

Scientific Advertising reflected Hopkins's "hard-sell" advertising philosophy. Hopkins believed that advertising copy should be direct and rational, and he argued that advertisements could be created based on specific principles and fundamental laws.

Scientific Advertising offered guidelines for all aspects of advertisement development and layout. Hopkins presented mail-order advertising as the ideal advertising model. Hopkins believed that the success of mail-order advertising – which was measurable and controllable in terms of cost and response – solidified the notion that all advertising should be conducted on a scientific basis.

Hopkins recommended that advertisers evaluate their efforts by salespersons' standards. He advocated the use of coupons and samples as inducements for consumer action. He said that solid campaign strategy was critical to successful selling, and he encouraged advertisers to promote unusual aspects of their products as part of that strategy. He emphasized the importance of understanding consumer psychology, and he urged advertising practitioners to monitor advertising campaign manner and tone. He viewed data collection and pretesting as central to campaign planning.

Scientific Advertising made a significant contribution to advertising theory and practice. Although some of Hopkins's arguments have been disproved, many guidelines he provided continued to be taught as fundamentals of effective advertising in the late twentieth century.

REGINA LOUISE LEWIS

See also Advertising Appeals; Advertising in the Twentieth Century; *Madison Avenue, USA;* Psychology in Advertising

Further Reading

Hopkins, Claude C., *My Life in Advertising* [and]
    Scientific Advertising, Chicago: Advertising, 1966
Mayer, Martin, *Madison Avenue, U.S.A.,* New York:
    Harper & Brothers, 1958; London: Bodley Head, 1958

Scripps, E.W.

Builder of early newspaper chains

Edward Willis Scripps, born on June 18, 1854, in Rushville, Illinois, started or acquired 48 newspapers and launched four newspaper chains – Scripps-McRae League of Newspapers, Pacific Coast Penny Papers, Scripps-Kellogg Newspapers (later known as Clover Leaf), and Scripps-Howard – before his death on March 12, 1926. Newspapers constituted only a portion of the Scripps empire. Scripps was instrumental in developing Newspaper Enterprise Association, a syndicated service, in 1902; United Press Associations, in 1907; Science Service, a service created to explain science to the masses, in 1921; United

E.W. Scripps
(Courtesy of The E.W. Scripps Company)

Feature Service, a second syndicated service; and United News Pictures, a newsreel information service, in 1924.

Scripps began his newspaper career in 1873 when he joined his half brother James, owner of the *Detroit (Michigan) News,* as a circulation manager. With some financial backing from James and his brother George, he started the *Cleveland (Ohio) Press* in 1878. The success of the *Press* led him to acquire the *St. Louis (Missouri) Chronicle* in 1880 and the *Cincinnati (Ohio) Post* in 1883. These papers provided the foundation of newspaper chain, and in 1890, Scripps made Milton McRae a partner. Scripps moved to Miramar, California, and between 1892 and 1899, he started or acquired papers in San Diego, Los Angeles, and San Francisco. This new group of papers constituted the second chain, known as Pacific Coast Penny Papers. During this time, he assisted William Kellogg in starting Scripps-Kellogg, a chain of newspapers in Minneapolis, St. Paul, and Duluth, Minnesota; Kansas City, Kansas; and Des Moines, Iowa. In 1922, Scripps consolidated all of his holdings under Scripps-Howard, a new chain headed by his son Robert and Roy Howard.

Politically, Scripps aligned himself with the Progressive movement. He was closely acquainted with conservationist Gifford Pinchot and California governor Hiram Johnson. He backed Woodrow Wilson for president and encouraged his papers to endorse Progressives nationwide. Scripps was instrumental in ushering in the era of chain journalism as well as the creation and expansion of syndicated services.

EDWARD E. ADAMS

See also Feature Syndicates; Newspaper Chains, or Groups; United Press Associations (1907)

Further Reading
Casserly, Jack, *Scripps, the Divided Dynasty,* New York: Donald I. Fine, 1993
Trimble, Vance, *The Astonishing Mr. Scripps: The Turbulent Life of America's Penny Press Lord,* Ames: Iowa State University Press, 1992

Seldes, George

Renowned for critical attacks on press and its leaders

For more than 50 years, George Seldes was a premier media critic in the United States, through his 21 books from the 1920s to the 1980s and a weekly newsletter in the 1940s and 1950s titled *In Fact.* He began his career in 1909 for the *Pittsburgh (Pennsylvania) Leader.* While Seldes spent several decades as a journalist for newspapers in Pittsburgh and Chicago, among others, he is remembered most for critical attacks against a monopolistic press and media owners.

The first challenge came in 1929, a year after he resigned from the *Chicago Tribune,* when Seldes wrote *You Can't Print That! The Truth Behind the News,* detailing stories he said had been suppressed by newspapers. Two of his books in the 1930s made the best-seller lists. They were strong attacks on the newspaper industry, *Freedom of the Press* (1935) and *Lords of the Press* (1938). He wrote and edited books from the 1920s to the 1980s, including *Witness to a Century* (1987). Not all were press attacks. One popular work was a collection called *The Great Quotations.* Still, the title of his 1968 book, *Never Tire of Protesting,* appropriately summarizes his decades of work.

In Fact, a four-page newsletter Seldes published and edited, reached more than 175,000 subscribers at one point. Its purpose was described on the front page as "an antidote for falsehood in the daily press." In the newsletter, Seldes critiqued coverage by New York and national newspapers and wire services.

BRADLEY J. HAMM

See also Criticism of Newspapers; Journalism Reviews

Further Reading
Dennis, Everette E., and Claude-Jean Bertrand, "Seldes at 90: They Don't Give Pulitzers for that Kind of Criticism," *Journalism History* (Autumn/Winter 1980)
Seldes, George, *Never Tire of Protesting,* New York: Lyle Stuart, 1968

_____, *Witness to a Century: Encounters with the Noted, the Notorious, and the Three SOBs,* New York: Ballantine, 1987

Sensationalism

Emphasis on emotional subjects to attract readers

The "ism" surfaced after the Civil War, but criticism of the sensational began before newspapers. The common complaint flourished in the twentieth century. The tabloids of the 1920s eventually gave their stigmatized name to the "tabloid television" shows sharing their excesses.

In 1709, the English essayist Joseph Addison saw that authors of handwritten newsletters "could not furnish out a single paper of news without lighting up a comet in Germany or a fire in Moscow." In 1801, Fisher Ames found printers competing to see "who shall have the most wonders, and the strangest and most horrible crimes."

Early critics of these tendencies denounced the obsession with oddities, earthquakes, and beached whales, while historian Frank Luther Mott listed "crimes, disasters, sex scandals, and monstrosities" as sensational subjects. His successor, Edwin Emery, theorized that "what the critics like to call sensationalism, which is the emphasis on emotion for its own sake," came in waves – 1620, 1833, the 1890s, and 1920 – when newspapers reached out to a new audience. As a pejorative term for excessive journalism, "sensationalism" is associated strongly with the yellow journalism of the 1890s, particularly William Randolph Hearst's banner headline, "Destruction of the War Ship Maine Was the Work of an Enemy," and Joseph Pulitzer's page-one art with bodies flying from the exploding battleship.

The wave of 1833, the dawn of the penny press, was characterized by sensational reportorial detail, not headlines and graphic illustrations. The classic example came from James Gordon Bennett, who romanticized the anatomical curves of a prostitute's corpse. When he added titillating accounts of seductions by clergymen, Bennett set off a "moral war" against his offenses.

Tabloids in the Roaring Twenties, especially the *Mirror* and the *Graphic,* celebrated scandal with doctored photos of wealthy "Daddy" Browning and Peaches, his 15-year-old bride. The *New York Daily News* grew to have the nation's largest daily circulation when it put on the front page the photo of a murderess in the electric chair. The *News* survived into the late 1990s, and the *Mirror* and *Graphic* were reincarnated on the supermarket checkout stands of the 1990s.

If the waves of sensationalism rose higher at times, the sea was never calmed. In the 1730s, Ben Franklin gave readers a servant who "enjoyed my mistress twice" before slaying his master and a soldier who shot his mother "so her brains flew about the room."

After the 1830s, and before the 1880s New Journalism of Pulitzer or the yellow journalism of the 1890s, reporters justified "sickening details" as necessary realism, claiming, "seeing is believing." The 1858 Swill Milk Crusade in

Leslie's Weekly charted bodily evacuations of poisoned children, and Lafcadio Hearn pushed sensory detail ad nauseum in his 1874 Tanyard murder coverage.

"Jerked to Jesus" and "How Babies Are Baked" represent extremes of the era's headlines, and Hearn made dubious history when portraying the Tanyard victim's remains. He described "half-molten flesh, boiled brains and jellied blood," then poked his finger "through the crisp" of the brain and declared it "about the consistency of banana fruit." Little wonder that a leading journalist, Julius Chambers, looked backward from the 1890s and proclaimed the 1870s as "days of Scarlet Journalism . . . compared with which the so-called 'yellow' variety of today is colorless."

Colorful was clearly synonymous with sensational in the 1890s when the "Yellow Kid" cartoon gave the period its conceptual label. In the 1920s, classified ads in *Editor & Publisher* still advertised for an "experienced yellow editor" to produce colorful and sensational news.

Harsher terms than "colorful" often were applied. In 1849, an editorial attacked the penny press for "pandering to whatever is vile and bestial in a corrupted and sensual populace." The struggle to define subjects and treatment, the ingredients of sensationalism, continued over the years, climaxing in a less-than-satisfying effort to measure it empirically.

The idea of pandering, if not the word itself, played a part when definition dwelled on motives or intent. In the simplest equation, Hearst would cause a war to sell papers. The motives of sensationalism traditionally are seen in market-driven economic terms: sensationalism attracts and entertains, gives audiences what they want. As a result, the public does not get what it needs. The Hutchins Commission on the Freedom of the Press argued in the mid-twentieth century that the press was "so occupied with the reporting of sensational events" that it neglected news needed by the community. In the decades following World War II, this warning went unheard by the newspapers with the largest readership in the United States, Great Britain, and Germany – all characterized by photos and headlines featuring sex, crime, celebrity, scandal, and oddities.

A common defense of sensationalism was voiced in 1901 when Lydia Commander argued that it attracted, and thus educated, readers not reached by more erudite journals. Better to raise millions of people, namely new immigrants, an inch than to elevate the few a foot, she explained. Better, the late-twentieth-century version went, to make television news entertaining than lose viewers to sitcoms and sports.

Another defense suggests that the end justifies the means in terms of effects that go beyond education. The ingredients that sell papers and raise ratings also may arouse public opinion to solve real problems. The "sickening" Swill Milk exposures led to new laws.

Jacob Riis, who warred against poverty in the late nineteenth century, admitted, "The old cry of sensation-mongering was raised more than once when I was making my charges." On one occasion, Riis agreed: "I did make a sensation of the campaign. That was the way to put life in it." He put life – rich sensory detail that his targets denounced as sensationalism – into exposures ranging in topic from polluted water to dangerous tenements housing the blind.

Few criticize sensational elements in a Holocaust documentary or in Edward R. Murrow's *Harvest of Shame.* Most will distinguish Truman Capote's *In Cold Blood* from true-crime thrillers that pop into print weeks after celebrity murder. In short, the Bible and Shakespeare offer sensational incident and detail, but context and common sense separate them from the extremes of sensationalism.

WARREN T. FRANCKE

See also Commission on Freedom of the Press; Criticism of Newspapers; Penny Press; Riis, Jacob A.; Tabloids; Yellow Journalism

Further Reading

Dicken-Garcia, Hazel, *Journalistic Standards in Nineteenth-Century America,* Madison: University of Wisconsin Press, 1989
Francke, Warren, "An Argument in Defense of Sensationalism: Probing the Popular and Historiographical Concept," *Journalism History 5* (1978)
Stevens, John D., et al., "Special Issue on Sensationalism," *Journalism History* 12:3–4 (1985)

Shoppers

Advertising-filled, free newspapers

The history of free distribution newspapers, also called shoppers, is somewhat murky, but they probably developed with the population shift to the suburbs coupled with the decline of the inner cities following the Great Depression. As the name implies, these publications are delivered at no cost to every household within a defined geographic area or are offered at no cost on curbside newspaper racks.

Shoppers provide mass or saturation coverage of every potential customer in a defined circulation zone. This makes them especially desirable for merchants who wish to target specific populations. In a very real sense, this makes the shopper a direct competitor for newspaper advertising. In the last decades of the twentieth century, shoppers became financially successful by ensuring that every home in a target circulation zone received the newspaper, particularly in areas where purchase newspapers could ensure only that 30 to 50 percent of the population was a subscriber household. As with all newspapers, however, delivery does not translate into readership.

Free distribution newspaper circulation can be audited, but most of these publications use their own verification service to monitor accurate deliveries. Verification techniques usually include one or more of the following: door-to-door surveys, telephone surveys, and carrier observations. These techniques are necessary because the shoppers' nonpaying customers are much less likely to complain about nondelivery, and the publication will lose its competitive edge if it cannot provide support for its mass circulation claims.

Publishers of shoppers offset their lack of circulation revenue by setting their advertising rates high enough to guarantee profitability. Compared with competing purchase newspapers, shoppers are usually smaller and contain a higher proportion of advertising content.

These publications use the recognizable format of a newspaper, carry display advertising like a newspaper, and may even contain news like a newspaper, but these publications fail to meet the ordinary definition of newspapers because they do not have a paid circulation. Without a paid circulation, the shopper does not qualify as a newspaper under provisions of the law and does not qualify for the coveted second-class privilege of the U.S. Postal Service.

Until late in the twentieth century, shoppers were not permitted to carry legal government notices, but they later became increasingly attractive for legal notices because of their guaranteed saturation coverage. Because legal notices provide substantial revenue, small dailies and weeklies located in county seats fought this move. Regardless of the similarities, shoppers provide a decidedly smaller news hole than purchase newspapers and are really less news vehicles than advertising vehicles, but they remain newspapers as long as they contain some editorial content.

FERRELL ERVIN

Silent Motion Pictures

Movie theaters generally filled by music, sound effects

The first 35 years of motion picture history are referred to as the silent era because no practical means then existed for recording or playing back movie dialogue or other synchronized sounds. Silent films, however, were never truly silent. Musical accompaniment was provided by lone pi-

Proper behavior in motion picture theaters was promoted by on-screen signs.

anists at small theaters, by the house musicians at music halls and vaudeville theaters where many of the earliest films were shown, or by organists playing specially designed pipe organs capable of a wide range of music and sound effects. By the 1920s, a trip to the movies could mean a visit to a "movie palace" – plush theaters famous for their ornate architecture, cadres of uniformed ushers, and accomplished orchestras performing scores written especially for each film. On the screen, the films featured Gloria Swanson, Rudolph Valentino, and other stars of near mythic stature. The cinema had become the world's most popular form of entertainment, a fiercely competitive global industry, and one of the most powerful media for cultural and political expression ever known, all before the advent of talking pictures.

The silent era can be divided into three periods: the primitive (1894–1907), the transitional (1908–17), and the mature (1918–28). Most modern impressions of the silents derive from film images and icons from the latter period, but it was during the primitive and transitional phases that filmmakers worked out many of the fundamental motion picture practices that remain in place to this day.

Audiences were accustomed to being entertained and informed by images projected onto a screen long before the invention of motion pictures. Slide presentations, known as magic lantern shows, had existed since the 1600s. By the late nineteenth century, the advent of photography and perfection of fast-moving slide projection helped inspire the creation of motion pictures. Eadweard Muybridge became an international celebrity on the magic lantern lecture circuit for his "serial photography," a technique that employed multiple still cameras to capture the images of moving animals and people at split-second intervals. In the 1880s, numerous inventors set out to improve on Muybridge by developing a single camera capable of even more rapid photography, as well as a method of playing back the images in continuous motion. This was achieved in 1892 in Thomas Edison's New Jersey laboratory. The inventor of the first motion-picture camera (the Kinetograph) and a peep-show viewing device (the Kinetoscope) was Edison's Scottish-born assistant, W.K.L. Dickson. The first movies were 30-second vignettes of jugglers, weight lifters, dancers, and novelty acts available for arcade-style viewing in U.S. and European cities in 1894.

In France, Auguste and Louis Lumière designed a remarkable alternative to the Edison equipment, and they, more than he, truly made the motion picture a worldwide sensation. Their invention was the Cinématographe, a much lighter camera than Edison's and one that could be converted easily into a projector. In 1895 in Paris, the Lumières held the first public screening of projected motion pictures. Their films were short actualities – scenes of people at the beach, excavators tearing down a wall, trains arriving, and other outdoor activities. The Cinématographe's versatility made it possible for Lumière camera operators to scour the globe for exotic footage. Along the way, they raised money by showing films, fostering interest in motion pictures wherever they traveled.

In 1905, a boom in U.S. movie theater construction coincided with an increase in the sophistication of the movies being made. The earliest films had consisted of a single shot – a lone stationary viewpoint from which to see all the action. Later works, running 10 minutes or more, such as Edwin S. Porter's *The Great Train Robbery* (1903, United States) and Cecil Hepworth's *Rescued by Rover* (1905, United Kingdom), told stories using multiple camera angles, comprehensible chase scenes, and rudimentary crosscutting. The visual "language" of the movies had begun to take shape.

Between 1908 and 1917, motion pictures changed from a diverting and slightly crude form of recreation to a highly formalized and respected aspect of the popular culture. Actors became adept at communicating through pantomime. Dialogue and narrative commentary were provided by artful and often witty intertitles. Without spoken language to translate, the distinction between foreign and domestic films was nil, so U.S. audiences were entertained regularly by imported products. During this period, films grew longer and more lavish in the manner of Italy's biblical spectacle *Quo Vadis?* (1911). New innovations included the serial – a multiple-installment film, often with cliffhanger endings – perfected by French director Louis Feuillade (*Fantomas*, 1913). A number of women directors emerged, most notably Lois Weber of the United States (*Suspense*, 1913). Filmmakers such as Victor Sjostrom of Sweden (*Give Us*

Rudolph Valentino as *The Sheik*
(Wisconsin Center for Film and Theater Research)

This Day, 1913) and Alan Dwan of the United States (*The Half Breed,* 1916) advanced film style through the alternation of close-ups with long shots in smooth continuity to better convey a character's psychological state. Also becoming commonplace were the addition of color tints to black-and-white films, animated cartoons, film adaptations of classic literature and popular plays, and movie reviews for newspapers. Indeed, the cinema of 1917 bore a greater resemblance to that of the late twentieth century than to that of the primitive period.

The most prominent director of the transitional years was D.W. Griffith of the United States. Beginning with the Biograph Company in 1908, Griffith became a master of melodrama who, with cameraman Billy Bitzer and a corps of stage-trained actors, made many of the best-received films of the day. His most discussed work, *The Birth of a Nation* (1915), was an epic depiction of the Civil War and Reconstruction. Praised for its monumental battle scenes and tender personal drama, the film also was condemned for its pointedly racist depiction of African Americans. It sparked riots in numerous U.S. cities, calls for movie censorship in others, and the first admission by a U.S. president (Woodrow Wilson) that he had actually attended (and liked) a movie. The most widely seen film thus far, *The Birth of a Nation* made it plain that this new medium was an art form worthy of serious scrutiny.

By 1917, a major power shift in the film industry had transpired. Until that time, France had been the world's leading exporter of motion pictures, but World War I devastated the French film industry. Consequently, the United States assumed the dominant position in the global film market and never relinquished it. Edison, Biograph, and other largely east coast firms had tried to stabilize and control the exploding U.S. film market by forming a cartel in 1908. Within a few years, however, the public's demand for movies exceeded what Edison and cohorts could supply. Instead, a handful of new west coast studios emerged to make the U.S. film industry the international leader. Run by entrepreneurs with a keener sense of the public's tastes than the eastern cartel, these upstart companies transformed Hollywood, California, from the winter shooting site for New York filmmakers it had been since 1907 into the seat of world film production 10 years later.

The most recognized celebrities in the world by 1920 were Hollywood movie stars Charlie Chaplin, Mary Pickford, and Douglas Fairbanks. Chaplin elevated the art of physical comedy to its most sublime level, and he solidified his stature with critics as well as the general public with his hilarious yet touching film *The Kid* (1921). Pickford, the highest-paid woman in the United States at the time and producer of her own films, was famed for her portrayals of plucky adolescents in such vehicles as *Daddy Long Legs* (1919). Her husband, Fairbanks, was the charismatic star of *The Mark of Zorro* (1920) and numerous other swashbucklers. These were the first years of the systematic marketing of the star as product, and that, along with their haunting silence on the screen, made film actors of the 1920s more luminescent than any movie stars since. Fan magazines and film industry gossip columns thrived. In

Mary Pickford, Douglas Fairbanks, Charlie Chaplin, and D.W. Griffith sign incorporation papers creating United Artists.
(Wisconsin Center for Film and Theater Research)

Hollywood, Grauman's Chinese Theater instigated a major tourist attraction by inviting the screen's top stars to leave their footprints in cement in the theater promenade. Among the public's favorites were the bob-haired Colleen Moore, disguise artist Lon Chaney Sr., cowboy hero William S. Hart, and the thoroughly modern Clara Bow.

The 1920s were a time of great commercial expansion for the Hollywood studios but also a time when some of the most artistic and compelling films were made. Advances in lighting, film stock, and camera mobility enhanced the films of the day. Among the artistic triumphs of the decade were King Vidor's antiwar opus *The Big Parade* (1925), Buster Keaton's masterful comedy *The General* (1927), and Karl Brown's naturalistic drama *Stark Love* (1927). European filmmakers, not wishing to emulate Hollywood's well-made, but still primarily escapist, fare, took pains to develop more intellectual styles. Noteworthy efforts include Sergei Eisenstein's politically charged *Battleship Potemkin* (1925) and Fritz Lang's futuristic *Metropolis* (1927). Yet

Hollywood proved to be a powerful magnet for the world's filmmaking talent, and Lang and scores of other Europeans ultimately were drawn to careers in sunny California.

The studios that dominated Hollywood in those days became so entrenched that many still existed at the end of the century. A merger between Loew's Theatres, Metro Pictures, Goldwyn Studios, and Louis B. Mayer Productions resulted in Metro-Goldwyn-Mayer (MGM), the largest studio in Hollywood, which, under the direction of Irving Thalberg, became known for its grandiose films and bevy of popular stars. Among its productions was *Ben-Hur* (1926), the costliest film of the decade. Universal, Paramount, and Fox also were firmly established studios at the time. However, it was Warner Brothers, a small company best known for a series of films featuring canine star Rin Tin Tin, that would soon bring about the demise of the silent cinema and the most radical shakeup the film industry had ever experienced.

The idea of "talking pictures" was as old as film itself.

Edison and many other inventors had introduced technologies for talking pictures at various times since 1896, but none could ensure good fidelity or sufficient amplification in large theaters. Filmmakers such as Griffith and Chaplin balked at the prospect of sound, fearing the loss of international audiences and the diminishment of what had become a beautiful nonverbal art form. Warner Brothers, however, looking for a way to compete with the larger studios, took a chance on an improved film sound process. Their 1927 film, *The Jazz Singer,* with singing and talking sequences and starring popular recording artist Al Jolson, turned out to be a smash hit. Warner and Fox immediately outfitted all their theaters with sound equipment. The other studios, fearing that "talkies" might be just a fad, decided to continue making silent pictures for another year and then reevaluate.

Hollywood's final year of silent film production resulted in some of the best films of the era. Victor Sjostrom, now working in the United States, directed Lillian Gish in one of the silent screen's greatest performances in *The Wind* (1928). King Vidor's *The Crowd* (1928) and William Wellman's *Beggars of Life* (1928) are among the most striking portrayals of dashed hopes and broken dreams ever filmed. Yet the public preferred any film with talking, however bad, and by 1929, all of Hollywood's studios committed exclusively to sound films. Initially, the sound technology restricted camera movement, creative editing, and outdoor shooting. The early talkies were a step backward, much to the dismay of silent film artists who now saw an era of immense creativity, experimentation, and growth come to a sad end.

BRAD CHISHOLM

See also Animated Motion Pictures; Hollywood Studio System; Motion Picture Serials; Motion Picture Technology; Sound Motion Pictures

Further Reading

Bowser, Eileen, *The Transformation of Cinema, 1907–1915,* Toronto, Ontario: Collier Macmillan Canada, 1990; Berkeley: University of California Press, 1994

Brownlow, Kevin, *The Parade's Gone By,* New York: Knopf, 1968; London: Sphere, 1973

Chisholm, Brad, "Reading Intertitles," *Journal of Popular Film and Television* 15:3 (Fall 1987), pp. 137–142

Everson, William K., *American Silent Film,* New York: Oxford University Press, 1978

Koszarski, Richard, *An Evening's Entertainment: The Age of the Silent Feature Picture, 1915–1928,* Toronto, Ontario: Collier Macmillan Canada, 1990; Berkeley, California, and London: University of California Press, 1994

Musser, Charles, *The Emergence of Cinema: The American Screen to 1907,* Toronto, Ontario: Collier Macmillan Canada, 1990; Berkeley, California, and London: University of California Press, 1994

Pratt, George, *Spellbound in Darkness: A History of the Silent Film,* Greenwich, Connecticut: New York Graphic Society, 1973

Thompson, Kristin, *Exporting Entertainment: America in the World Film Market, 1907–1934,* London: British Film Institute, 1985

Smith Act and the Press

Enacted as prosecution tool against the Communist Party

The Smith Act was a law enacted in 1940 to give federal prosecutors a tool to use against the Communist Party. It prohibited advocating the violent overthrow of the government and organization of or membership in a group that advocated the same. Violators could be imprisoned for up to 20 years or fined, or both.

Sponsored by Representative Howard Smith, a Democrat from Virginia, the Smith Act was used primarily in a series of dramatic trials of U.S. Communists between 1948 and 1956. The Smith Act was used only rarely after the U.S. Supreme Court's decision in *Yates* v. *United States* in 1957, but it remained in effect and was even strengthened somewhat in 1994.

The attitudes of the nation's newspapers regarding the Smith Act and its application have fluctuated. When the measure passed the House of Representatives in 1939, papers in New York protested, while most of the nation's other papers ignored it. The newspapers welcomed Supreme Court decisions in the late 1930s and early 1940s that extended First Amendment protections to Communists and other political minorities; they also, however, enthusiastically supported the government's first major Smith Act prosecution of U.S. Communist leaders when indictments were handed down in 1948 in the case now known as *Dennis* v. *United States.* Most newspapers applauded when the Supreme Court upheld the constitutionality of the Smith Act in *Dennis* in 1951, but most also reacted favorably to the *Yates* decision, which held that the Smith Act did not prohibit advocacy and teaching of forcible overthrow of government as an abstract principle, divorced from any attempt to bring it about. This made it much harder for prosecutors to win convictions under the Smith Act.

The Smith Act also was used as a restraint on the press. Communist newspapers such as the *Daily Worker* and books such as *The Communist Manifesto* were used as evidence against the defendants in most of the trials under the Smith Act. In the *Dennis* trial, for example, prosecutors introduced more than 100 books, newspapers, and other printed items as evidence. This example set the pattern for future prosecutions. After the success of the *Dennis* trial, prosecutors in Smith Act cases came to court "armed with stacks of books and newspapers."

In addition, a portion of the Smith Act specifically prohibited the printing or distribution of any written or printed materials that advocated overthrow of the government by force or violence. The defendants in many of the Smith Act trials were charged with violating that particular section. For example, the indictment in *Yates* charged that in carrying out their conspiracy, the defendants published articles in

Eugene Dennis, general secretary of the Communist Party of the United States, center, is served with a subpoena to appear before the House Un-American Activities Committee. Dennis was a major defendant in early Smith Act action against the party.
(Reproduced from the Collections of the Library of Congress)

the *Daily Worker* and other Communist publications that advocated and taught the necessity of overthrowing the government by force and violence.

The Smith Act had been revised four times by the late 1990s. The original version contained a conspiracy section that was deleted in 1948. The conspiracy section was viewed as unnecessary because a conspiracy to violate the Smith Act could be prosecuted under the general federal conspiracy statute. However, the effect of the change was to put an extra burden on prosecutors. The Smith Act's conspiracy section did not require prosecutors to prove that the defendants took any overt acts to further the conspiracy, while the general conspiracy statute does. Therefore, in 1956, Congress put the conspiracy section back in the Smith Act and increased the maximum fine for its violation from $10,000 to $20,000.

In 1962, Congress amended the Smith Act to overturn a portion of the *Yates* decision, declaring that the term "organize" as used in the act meant to "establish," "found," or "bring into existence." Government attorneys contended that "organize" meant instead a continuing process that in-

cluded recruitment of new members, the forming of new units, and the regrouping of existing units within the Communist party. The Supreme Court reversed the *Yates* convictions on grounds that the prosecutions – begun in 1951 – were brought after the three-year statute of limitations had expired, since the Communist Party, U.S.A., was organized in 1945. The 1962 amendment inserted the federal government's definition of "organizes" and "organize" into the Smith Act.

Congress amended the Smith Act again in 1994 as part of the Violent Crime Control and Law Enforcement Act of 1994, popularly known as the Clinton Crime Bill. That legislation simply removed the $20,000 cap on fines allowed under the Smith Act and seven other federal crimes, in effect allowing federal judges to impose fines of more than $20,000.

THOMAS A. HUGHES

See also Broadcast Blacklisting; Cold War and the Media; Motion Picture Blacklisting

Further Reading

Belknap, Michal R., *Cold War Political Justice: The Smith Act, the Communist Party, and American Civil Liberties,* Westport, Connecticut: Greenwood, 1977

Chang, Hosoon, "The First Amendment During the Cold War: Newspaper Reaction to the Trial of the Communist Party Leaders Under the Smith Act," *Free Speech Yearbook* 31 (1993)

Pember, Don R., "The Smith Act as a Restraint on the Press," *Journalism Monographs* 10 (1969)

Socialist Press

Alternative publications dating from the 1850s

The Socialist press, the publications affiliated with and espousing the ideology of the U.S. Socialist movement, traces its origins to the 1850s and achieved its greatest success in the first two decades of the twentieth century, when the movement was able to achieve broad-based success under the banner of the Socialist Party of America (SPA). The SPA had its peak in 1912, when party membership reached more

"*From the Depths.*"

Controversial illustrations led to problems for the *Appeal to Reason.*

than 100,000 and close to 1 million U.S. citizens voted for SPA leader Eugene Debs for president. The party then had a representative in the U.S. House of Representatives, 79 cities across the country had Socialist mayors, and the number of party-affiliated publications exceeded 320, including 13 dailies and almost 300 weeklies.

Socialism, which favored government intervention on behalf of the working classes, originated in Europe and moved to the United States along with immigrants. The first U.S. newspaper with a Socialist orientation, the antebellum *Republik der Arbeiter,* was published in German, and the first organized Socialist political organization, the Socialist Labor Party (SLP), was founded by German immigrants in 1877. Foreign-language newspapers remained prominent in the Socialist press throughout its history. Of the publications appearing in 1912, eight of the dailies and 36 of the weeklies were in languages other than English. One of the largest Socialist newspapers was the Yiddish-language *Vorwärts* (*The Jewish Daily Forward,* 1897), of New York City, whose circulation was more than 140,000.

Of the English-language dailies, the most prominent were the *New York Evening Call* (1908–23) and the *Milwaukee (Wisconsin) Leader* (1911–42), with circulations of 32,000 and 25,000, respectively. Among the weeklies, the largest and most important was the Kansas-based *Appeal to Reason* (1895–1922). A.J. Wayland, its founder, wanted to give the U.S. Socialist movement an inexpensive, mass-circulation newspaper that relied on advertising and subscriptions for its revenues rather than appeals for financial support from party members. As a result, the *Appeal* was one of the few Socialist papers to turn a profit, and during its peak years before World War I, it circulated close to 750,000 copies.

The paper's policies made the *Appeal* a target for frequent criticism from other Socialist publications. They envisioned the main function of their papers as propagating the ideology of Socialism and attracting, educating, and organizing party members; some, like the *Milwaukee Leader,* also considered it important to counteract "the hateful misrepresentation" of their ideology by the "capitalist press."

The attacks on the *Appeal* show the tendency of Socialist editors to engage in frequent battles with each other, a tendency reinforced by the factious history of U.S. Socialism. Editorial quarrels first flared when the SLP became increasingly dogmatic and narrow in focus after 1890. Even the SPA was plagued by infighting, and it was the struggle between various factions (and their publications) that contributed to the demise of Socialism as a broad-based political movement in the United States. In 1919, disputes split the SPA into three smaller parties, one Socialist and two Communist.

The entry of the United States into World War I proved disastrous for the Socialist press in another way, as the federal government began taking action against antiwar viewpoints. A number of prominent Socialists were jailed, among them Debs, and a provision of the Espionage Act of 1917 gave the postmaster general the right to revoke the second-class mailing privileges of publications whose content interfered with the war effort. Scores of Socialist papers became the victims of this policy, including leading organs like the official party organ, the *American Socialist,* the *Milwaukee Leader,* the *New York Call,* and the *Masses,* a monthly magazine known for the quality of its art, poetry, fiction, and editorials. Like the dailies and weeklies of the Socialist press, the *Masses* espoused the Socialist viewpoint that the war was for the benefit of capitalists only.

Government suppression during and after World War I and strife within the SPA meant the end of the Socialist press as a mass medium with wide popular appeal. Of the few papers that survived after the war, the *Milwaukee Leader* and the *Jewish Daily Forward* both moved away from being primarily party publications. Other publications with a Socialist orientation continued to appear after the 1920s, but their circulations were limited and they were not newspapers in the same sense as their predecessors of the 1900–20 era.

ULF JONAS BJORK

See also Alternative Press; Espionage and Sedition Acts; World War I

Further Reading

Conlin, Joseph R., ed., *The American Radical Press, 1880–1960,* vols. I and II, Westport, Connecticut: Greenwood, 1974

Kessler, Lauren, *The Dissident Press: Alternative Journalism in American History,* Beverly Hills, California: Sage, 1984

Kipnis, Ira, *The American Socialist Movement: 1897–1912,* New York: Monthly Review, 1972

Shore, Elliott, *Talkin' Socialism: J.A. Wayland and the Role of the Press in American Radicalism, 1890–1912,* Lawrence: University Press of Kansas, 1988

_____, Ken Fones-Wolf, and James P. Danky, eds., *The German-American Radical Press: The Shaping of a Left Political Culture, 1850–1940,* Urbana: University of Illinois Press, 1992

Social Responsibility Theory

Suggests how the media should operate in a free society

Social responsibility theory served as a twentieth-century guide for media practice, establishing responsibility as a necessary component of a free press. It is a normative theory: rather than explaining how the media operate, it prescribes how they should operate.

In about 1900, many observers escalated their criticism of the press for its evident responsibility to itself and its own profits rather than to the public. In response, the American Society of Newspaper Editors adopted the Canons of Journalism in 1923, which in part accepted the press's responsibility to the general welfare. The radio, television, and film industries later adopted similar codes.

The adoption of the nonbinding codes did not, however, silence the critics, who saw deeper problems with the me-

dia, especially after the advent of commercial radio in the 1920s. Advances in technology raised costs and limited access to the mass media to fewer people, increasing fears of a lack of media diversity. Publishers and broadcasters could reach huge audiences, which observers feared were susceptible to persuasion from demagogues. In the 1930s, conservative backlash from many publishers against the New Deal's regulatory structure fed criticism of the press as an elite institution out of touch with the public interest.

Social responsibility as a systematic theory evolved from the work of the Commission on Freedom of the Press (the Hutchins Commission). In 1942, Henry R. Luce funded a group of distinguished scholars, headed by Robert M. Hutchins, chancellor of the University of Chicago, assigned to study freedom of the press. The commission deliberated from February 1944 until December 1946. It issued its general report, *A Free and Responsible Press,* in March 1947.

The report argued that if the media (print, broadcast, and film) did not assume greater responsibility, the government (or some outside agency) would eventually force them to do so. The commission recommended that the media provide greater context and meaning to the news, a fair and complete picture of society's constituent groups, and a forum for discussion of important issues, opinions, and values surrounding the news. Commercialization and the influence of advertising were labeled as major threats to press responsibility. These recommendations were not new, but the commission combined them into an overall concept.

Then, in 1956, Theodore Peterson gave social responsibility theory new respectability as the logical successor to libertarian theory in a collection of essays titled *Four Theories of the Press.* Peterson's essay delved into the philosophical basis of social responsibility, and he argued that the libertarian philosophy of laissez-faire could no longer serve democratic society.

Although journalism schools came to teach social responsibility theory by the late twentieth century, there was little empirical evidence that the media had adopted it. Its relevance receded as critics began to rely on more radical and sweeping attacks on the media's political and social relationships and its advertising. Libertarian critics of the theory argued that the concept of social responsibility itself was a threat to the press's freedom. As a reformulation of how a free press should behave, however, the theory provided an ethical standard against which to measure media performance.

ROBERT W. LEWEKE

See also Codes of Ethics; Commission on Freedom of the Press

Further Reading

Altschull, J. Herbert, *Agents of Power: The Role of the News Media in Human Affairs,* New York: Longman, 1984

Blanchard, Margaret A., "The Hutchins Commission: The Press, and the Responsibility Concept," *Journalism Monographs* 49 (1977)

Commission on Freedom of the Press, *A Free and*

Responsible Press, Chicago: University of Chicago Press, 1947

Hocking, William Ernest, *Freedom of the Press: A Framework of Principle,* Chicago: University of Chicago Press, 1947

McIntyre, Jerilyn S., "Repositioning a Landmark: The Hutchins Commission and Freedom of the Press," *Critical Studies in Mass Communication* 4 (1987)

Siebert, Fred S., *Four Theories of the Press,* Urbana: University of Illinois Press, 1963

Udick, Robert, "The Hutchins Paradox: Objectivity Versus Diversity," *Mass Comm Review* 20 (1993)

Society Reporting

Making news of major social events

Society reporting began in 1840 as the brainchild of James Gordon Bennett, owner of the *New York Herald,* who sent reporter William H. Attree to a costume ball in a suit of armor. While the guests at the party were somewhat repulsed by the behavior of the former sports writer, Bennett's readers delighted in the printed report of the event. Prior to the *Herald*'s infiltration of this party, people in the highest so-

Society pages were created to bring women readers to newspapers.

(Perkins Library/Duke University)

cial circles abhorred public notice. Etiquette dictated that a woman's name appeared in print only when she married and when she died. Bennett, however, always an outcast from the old guard, mocked established social mores. After he began publishing reports of major social events, other newspapers followed suit and paid attention to the comings and goings of the important people in local society. For blueblood cities such as New York, Boston, Philadelphia, and Washington, D.C., this meant tracking the parties, debutante balls, and charity events of established families in the *Social Register.* In smaller-circulation areas, newspapers also followed the social events of prominent local celebrities, businesspeople, and politicians.

Although Bennett himself never allowed a woman to report society news, the advent of society reporting during the nineteenth century provided an avenue into newspaper work for many women. Young female assistants who often traveled by bicycle or trolley were sent to party sites in advance to secure the guest list and other major details. Then the society editor, again usually a woman, attended the party as a guest to supply description and color. In fact, during the 1890s in New York, party givers often shaped their entertainment with one eye toward the amount of coverage it could be accorded in the paper. Prancing horses were brought into a banquet hall, while another party featured "blackbird pies."

By the 1930s, society reporting in newspapers usually included a gossip column and more staid reporting of high society. The art of society reporting actually was highly specialized because it required complete familiarity with the history of the important families in a newspaper's circulation area coupled with the ability to be discreet.

Society reporting also included articles on marriages and engagements. Traditionally, wedding and engagement portraits featured only the bride. During the 1970s, however, newspapers gradually began printing photos of the engaged couple and the newlyweds together. While many newspapers printed reports of all the marriages that were submitted to them, some newspapers printed only a select group. Other articles on the society page traditionally focused on high society.

Reports on the activities of the monied gentry, however, gradually gave way to more focused attention on celebrities, which attracted more readers. Gossip columns and glitzy tabloids preferred the divorces, romances, and partygoing of the so-called beautiful people. Newspapers, however, continued to publish photographs and articles on charity events and debutante balls.

AGNES HOOPER GOTTLIEB

See also Women's Pages

Further Reading

Fairchild, John, "Glittering Excess: An Inside Look at Nouvelle Society," *New Woman* 19:11 (November 1989), pp. 72–78

Ross, Ishbel, *Ladies of the Press,* New York: Harper & Brothers, 1936

Sound Bites

Brief quotes used to illuminate, illustrate broadcast news

The sound bite is to television news what a quote is to a newspaper. It evolved from the radio actuality and is a short portion of an interview, speech, or statement edited with video of the story. The use of sound bites in television is one of its most powerful, and abused, tools.

In the early days of television news, sound bites tended to be longer and fewer in number than they were by the 1990s. To air a sound bite using film involved finding the sound bite on the developed roll, splicing it to a leader, and timing it out with the video. The time delay in processing film and finding the bites tended to limit their use.

Although the networks and large stations started using videotape in the mid-1950s, it was the emergence of three-quarter-inch videotape editing and field equipment that led to the dramatic increase in the use of sound bites. Not only were the sound bites easier to edit, the use of a time code on the tape allowed the editor to quickly cue to the start time. For the same reasons, the number of stories using sound bites in each newscast also increased.

Sound bites are common because they allow the viewer to both see and hear the subject or witness, adding an important element to news coverage. The well-chosen sound bite is the emotional punctuation of a television news story. It can illuminate and illustrate the story. It can be used as the dramatic opening to a story, as a bridge from one story segment to the next, or it can conclude the piece. As one experienced news director put it, the sound bite is the "juice" of the story's fruit.

Producers soon found that sound bites bring another dimension to the visual parts of the story. Dramatic video over the voice of the subject adds impact to the pictures. This device is frequently used with longer sound bites to allow the subject to elaborate or underline the key news elements in the story.

Sound bites also establish the pace of a newscast. They break the monotony of hearing only the anchor's voice, if only for a few seconds. Well-established sound bites can give a short story the impact that would be missing in a regular anchor voice-over.

It quickly was discovered that the sound bite should not be used to provide data. This function is better handled by the reporter or by graphics. The information in the story should be given separately from the sound bite, which is then used for emphasis.

Choosing the correct sound bite for a news story developed into an art. Producers and reporters soon discovered that, in most cases, sound bites should be short, in the 10-to-15-second range. While a useful tool, sound bites are criticized for not allowing subjects longer to explain their positions. The most obvious use of this method is in the political arena, where many critics contend that sound bites force candidates to speak in clichés and without substance. Examples are former President George Bush's "read my lips" statement and former President Ronald Reagan's "make my day" comment.

HANEY HOWELL

See also Reagan, Ronald, and the Media

Sound Motion Pictures

Conversion to sound opened new vistas for filmmakers

"Wait-a-minute. . . . Wait-a-minute. . . . You ain't heard nothing yet!" They certainly had not. Movie audiences all over the world were about to have the way they were entertained radically changed. After Al Jolson delivered this brief speech in the 1927 Warner Brothers production *The Jazz Singer,* the movies became "the talkies." While *The Jazz Singer* was not the first movie to use sound, it was the first to capture the imagination of the public, and its huge success at the box office forced the Hollywood studios to convert their production facilities and theaters to sound.

By 1930, the major studios – Metro-Goldwyn-Mayer, Warner Brothers, Universal, Paramount, Fox, Columbia, and RKO – had spent millions on the conversion to sound. Their investment seemed to pay immediate dividends as moviegoers flocked to see and hear flashy gangsters portrayed by Edward G. Robinson in *Little Caesar* (1930) and Paul Muni in *Scarface* (1932). Urbane, fast-paced comedy such as *The Front Page* (1931), powerful antiwar dramas like *All Quiet on the Western Front* (1930), and provocative films that emphasized sex such as *Possessed* (1931), *No Man of Her Own* (1932), and the Mae West smash hit *She Done Him Wrong* (1932) brought a box-office boom.

The lure of sound seemed to make Hollywood immune from the ravages of the Great Depression that were sweeping the country. In 1930, the industry averaged 100 million paid admissions per week and was awash in money. But the view that Hollywood was depression-proof was as illusory as the movies themselves. By 1932, weekly attendance had plummeted to a mere 60 million, and the studios lost more than $50 million. Several studios narrowly avoided bankruptcy as the industry slowly recovered. In 1934, the studios registered a small profit but faced an even greater threat – that of a national boycott by the Roman Catholic Church, which objected to the new frankness in Hollywood sound movies.

The Roman Catholic church played a major role in controlling the content of movies in the United States from 1930 until the ratings system was adopted in 1968. The censorship code was written by a Jesuit priest, Father Daniel Lord from St. Louis, Missouri, and enforced by the Production Code Administration (PCA) of Joseph I. Breen, a rigid lay Catholic from Philadelphia. The code eliminated the ability of Hollywood to interpret morals and manners and the political, social, and ethical issues facing the United States in direct and honest terms.

The industry rapidly adjusted to this rigid self-censorship and made movies that fit within the code that appealed to millions of worldwide fans. The period from roughly 1930 to 1945 was the golden era of studio production. The studios were self-contained sites for the production of movies. They had multiple soundstages that were constantly in use, constituting a veritable factory for movies.

During this golden age, the studios ground out more than 500 movies a year. Each studio had its own style – MGM, for example, was the crown jewel of the industry. Led by studio mogul Louis B. Mayer and production chief Irving Thalberg, until his death in 1936, MGM made lavish musicals and romantic comedies noted for their technical superiority. Hollywood legends such as Clark Gable, Greta Garbo, Joan Crawford, Jeanette MacDonald, William Powell, Spencer Tracy, Katharine Hepburn, Judy Garland, and Mickey Rooney graced the MGM lot. During the 1930s, MGM released such film classics as *Grand Hotel* (1932), *Mutiny on the Bounty* (1935), *Camille* (1937), *The Wizard of Oz* (1939), and David O. Selznick's *Gone with the Wind* (1939).

Warner Brothers, by contrast, made cheaper films that seemed to move directly from newspaper headlines to the screen. Stars like Edward G. Robinson, Bette Davis, Humphrey Bogart, Errol Flynn, and John Garfield dominated Warner films. Typical Warner films were *I Am a Fugitive from a Chain Gang* (1932), *Gold Diggers of 1933* (1933), *The Adventures of Robin Hood* (1938), and *Juarez* (1939).

Paramount, the sophisticated studio, was the largest studio and produced the most variety in its films: sex dramas with stars such as Marlene Dietrich, Mae West, and Carole Lombard; comedies with the Marx Brothers; the "road" films starring Bob Hope, Bing Crosby, and Dorothy Lamour; biblical spectaculars directed by Cecil B. DeMille. During the 1930s, the studio produced such memorable films as the Mae West comedy *She Done Him Wrong* (1932), DeMille spectaculars *Sign of the Cross* (1932) and *Cleopatra* (1934), and Dietrich's *The Scarlet Empress* (1934).

The smaller, "poverty row" studio, Columbia, was identified with the films of Frank Capra. RKO had a troubled history but did manage to produce many first-rate films, including *King Kong* (1933) and the highly popular series of Fred Astaire–Ginger Rogers musicals.

The major studios not only produced films, they also served as distributors and exhibitors. They built huge first-run picture palaces throughout the country and forced local theater owners to "block book," which meant that to play any MGM film, for example, theater owners had to book and guarantee play dates for every MGM film produced that year. Independent and foreign producers were forced to submit films to industry censors for a seal of approval in order to gain access to industry theaters. The result was a tightly controlled vertical monopoly that gave the studios total control over the film industry in the United States. By the end of the decade, the industry was booming, and in 1939, arguably the greatest year in the history of Hollywood, the industry released *Gone with the Wind, Mr. Smith Goes to Washington, Wuthering Heights, Young Mr. Lincoln, Stagecoach, Goodbye Mr. Chips, The Wizard of Oz,* and *Dark Victory*.

When the Japanese bombed Pearl Harbor on December 7, 1941, Hollywood was the most powerful instrument of mass communication in the world. The U.S. film industry released some 80 percent of all films produced in the world, and Hollywood's foreign audience exceeded 80 million paid admissions per week. The federal government immediately recognized the importance of controlling Hollywood as a propaganda weapon. In June 1942, the Office of War Information (OWI), whose goal was to enhance public understanding of the war through the press, radio, and motion pictures, opened an office in Hollywood. OWI director Elmer Davis claimed that the "easiest way to inject a propaganda idea into most people's minds is to let it go in through the medium of an entertainment picture when they do not realize that they are being propagandized."

OWI's Hollywood office wrote a code that asked filmmakers to present the war as a "people's war," to show citizens unified in their support of democracy and their hatred of Fascism, to illustrate the common bonds between the United States and its allies. The OWI requested that producers submit scripts for approval, and most did. Hollywood had two censors during the war – the conservative PCA and the New Deal liberal OWI. For the duration, OWI's views on political issues won out. Combat films such as *Bataan* (1942) and *Sahara* (1943) implied that the armed forces were integrated and that U.S. democracy was color blind. The virtues of the Allies were lauded in *Mrs. Miniver* (1942), starring Greer Garson as the down-to-earth English upper-crust war heroine. *Dragon Seed* (1944) starred Katharine Hepburn as a Chinese freedom fighter, and Warner Brothers' *Mission to Moscow* (1943) told audiences that Stalin was a democrat and the Soviet Union an "evolutionary democracy."

The end of the war marked the high point of Hollywood's power and prestige. In 1945, Will Hays, president of the Motion Picture Producers and Distributors of America since its formation in 1922, retired. He was replaced by Eric Johnston, president of the U.S. Chamber of Commerce. The immediate postwar period saw a continued boom at the box office. The Samuel Goldwyn–William Wyler *Best Years of Our Lives* (1946), a powerful account of the problems of economic and psychological adjustment that soldiers and civilians faced after the war, lured millions to the theaters. In addition to the usual entertainment fare, the movies looked at alcoholism in *The Lost Weekend* (1946) and anti-Semitism in *Crossfire* (1947) and *Gentleman's Agreement* (1947).

The postwar United States, deeply disturbed by the real horror of world war and the fear of nuclear power, was marked by anxiety and cynicism. These feelings were reflected on the screen in a new Hollywood genre – film noir – that used a dark visual style to illustrate violence, corruption, and a sense of hopelessness that faced society. Films like *Detour* (1945) or Orson Welles's *The Lady from Shanghai,* starring Rita Hayworth, attracted small but loyal audiences.

In reality, Johnston had inherited a movie industry at war with itself. Conservatives who formed the Motion Picture Alliance for the Preservation of American Values deeply resented the liberal themes that pervaded World War II movies and carried over into the postwar era. They were de-

David O. Selznick's *Gone with the Wind* **brought a best-selling novel to the screen in 1939.**
(Museum of Broadcast Communications)

termined to purge liberalism from the screen. Liberals were equally determined to use the screen to expose the flaws in U.S. society.

The battle between liberals and conservatives first erupted in a bitter labor dispute between two Hollywood trade unions. Ideology replaced hour and wage concerns when Roy Brewer, head of the International Alliance of Theatrical Stage Employees and Moving Picture Machine Operators, accused a rival union of Communist infiltration.

The charge of Communism erupted on the national scene in November 1947, when the House Un-American Activities Committee (HUAC) and its chairman, J. Parnell Thomas, demanded that a group of Hollywood writers (the "Hollywood 10") answer the question: "Are you now or have you ever been a member of the Communist Party?" The implication was that Communist writers had inserted propaganda into films, especially during World War II. No one mentioned that the industry censorship system prevented any pro-Communist propaganda from seeping into the movies. When the 10 refused to answer, they were sentenced to jail for contempt of Congress. The hearing started one of the most disgraceful periods in U.S. history.

Johnston and industry leaders, at first determined to resist the HUAC purge, quickly caved in and issued the Waldorf Statement, which pledged that the industry would not employ Communists. The era of blacklisting had begun and would last into the 1960s. A second and much larger purge hit the industry in the early 1950s, when HUAC broadened the scope of investigation beyond writers to include actors, directors, and producers. Hundreds of Hollywood personalities were either blacklisted or forced to recant their liberal past by "naming names" of suspected Hollywood "reds." These ideological fights spilled over to the screen and stage. Director Elia Kazan named names before HUAC and then made *On the Waterfront* (1954) to justify his actions. Playwright Arthur Miller refused to give names of his friends and wrote *The Crucible* to justify his actions. Later movies, such as *The Front* (1976), starring Woody Allen, and *Guilty by Suspicion* (1990), starring Robert De Niro, recounted this period of Hollywood history.

The industry was also under economic attack in the immediate postwar era. In 1948, the Justice Department won its long-simmering antimonopoly case against the industry. In what became known as the Paramount Decision, the courts forced Hollywood to break up its vertical monopoly of production, distribution, and exhibition. The studios could no longer produce films, distribute them, and play them in their own theaters. Although it was a major blow, by 1954 the major studios had complied.

The breakup of the studios was a major victory for independent and foreign film producers, who now had increased access to U.S. theaters. Foreign films like Vittorio De Sica's *The Bicycle Thief* (1948), Roberto Rossellini's *Open City* (1946) starring Anna Magnani, and *Germany, Year Zero* (1949) played to small but appreciative audiences. Ironically, it was a foreign film, *The Miracle* (1953), that played a dramatic role in ending film censorship in the United States.

Roberto Rossellini's short film is about a peasant woman who becomes pregnant by a man she claims is St. Joseph.

She is ridiculed by her village and forced to give birth in an isolated church. The film was condemned as sacrilegious and blasphemous by the Catholic Legion of Decency and denied a license by the New York State censorship board. When film importer Joseph Burstyn challenged that ruling, the case went to the U.S. Supreme Court. *Burstyn* v. *Wilson* overturned *Mutual Film Corp.* v. *Ohio,* a 1915 ruling that had left film outside the protection of the First Amendment. In *Burstyn,* the Court ruled that film was a significant medium of the communication of ideas and deserved constitutional protection. The ruling did not immediately end all film censorship, but over the next decade, courts consistently extended First Amendment protection to film.

The early 1950s also marked another radical change in the way U.S. audiences were entertained. They no longer had to depend on the movies; a new medium entered the U.S. market and the U.S. psyche – television. A small piece of furniture containing a 10-inch, black-and-white screen brought moving images to a fascinated audience. The rise of television marked the decline of the movies. In 1945, 90 million people in the United States went to the movies each week. By 1950, only 51 million went; by 1960, attendance was a mere 40 million.

The industry tried to respond with gimmicks to lure fans away from their television sets. Wide-screen spectaculars like the Cinemascope production of *The Robe* (1953), "three-dimensional" productions like the popular *House of Wax* (1953), drive-in theaters, and even Smell-O-Vision attracted large audiences for individual films. They were not, however, a solution to the continuing box-office crisis.

Ever searching for an audience, Hollywood slowly moved away from the highly restrictive censorship code that prevented films from treating adult topics in an adult manner. The decline of government and industry censorship resulted in a new frankness on the U.S. screen. Films such as *Elmer Gantry* (1960), which featured a corrupt minister; *The Defiant Ones* (1958), which dealt with race relations; *The Pawnbroker* (1965); and *The Graduate* (1967), which included nudity, marked a turning point in public acceptance of controversial material on the screen.

As the U.S. audience increasingly accepted this new frankness in their movie entertainment, the old guardians of morality fell by the wayside. In 1966, the Catholic Legion of Decency, which had struck fear in movie producers for three decades, quietly changed to the National Catholic Office for Motion Pictures and no longer demanded that Roman Catholics strictly adhere to their national ratings. More importantly, the industry scrapped its self-censorship system and adopted a ratings system in 1968.

Eric Johnston died in 1966; Jack Valenti replaced him as head of the motion picture association. One of Valenti's first accomplishments was to scrap the 1930 Production Code and replace it with a Rating System in 1968 that told potential consumers the content of individual films. The original ratings were "G," general audience; "M," for mature audiences; "R," restricted, which permitted persons under 16 to be admitted only with an adult; and "X," meaning that no one under 18 would be admitted. Various changes over the years resulted in new categories such as

The first sound motion picture, *The Jazz Singer,* brought long lines to the theaters.
(Springer/Corbis-Bettmann)

PG and PG-13 to indicate material about which parents should be concerned for their children to view, and NC-17, which let filmmakers avoid the connotation of the X rating, which had been adopted by the pornographic film industry. A major criticism of the industry rating system was that it allowed too much violence in its PG and PG-13 ratings.

With the elimination of censorship, Hollywood infused old genres with a heavy dose of sex and violence to wrench fans out of their living rooms. Westerns such as Sam Peckinpah's *The Wild Bunch* (1969) and gangster films like Arthur Penn's *Bonnie and Clyde* (1967) splattered blood across the screen at a dazzling rate. *Midnight Cowboy* (1969) featured homosexuality and drug addiction and an X rating. It was the only X-rated film to win an Academy Award for best picture.

By 1970, the industry had changed radically. The old guard at the studios – Louis B. Mayer of MGM, Harry Cohn of Columbia, and Jack Warner at Warner Brothers –

had all vanished. The New Hollywood was marked by takeovers of international conglomerates. In 1966, Paramount merged with Gulf and Western, whose business portfolio included more than 300 different divisions. Warner Brothers merged several times and finally emerged as Warner Communications, an entertainment powerhouse with interests in music, television, film, and publishing. In 1967, United Artists was taken over by Transamerica, an insurance and financial corporation. In the mid-1980s, media mogul Ted Turner bought the company for its lucrative film and television library and later sold the remaining parts of the company, which emerged as MGM/UA. These corporations no longer fought television – they used it effectively, making television shows and made-for-television-movies, and selling old films to networks and cable companies, which had an insatiable demand for product. The VCR revolution opened a huge market for video rentals and was one of the most popular ways to watch a movie in the 1990s.

The conglomeration of Hollywood led to a new breed of powerful directors who could produce blockbuster hits that made hundreds of millions of dollars for the distributors. Francis Ford Coppola, with the *Godfather* series (beginning in 1972); George Lucas, with *Star Wars* (1977); Steven Spielberg, with *E.T. the Extra-Terrestrial* (1982) and other huge hits; and more specialized directors like Woody Allen and Spike Lee proved that good films would bring fans to the theaters. While the "glass ceiling" for women remained a powerful Hollywood tradition, directors Penny Marshall and Barbara Streisand proved their ability and marketability.

As the industry moved into the 1990s, its goal was to produce megahits like *E.T.*, *Ghostbusters* (1984), or Disney's *The Lion King* (1994). As the average cost of a film moved close to $40 million, the economics of Hollywood drove it toward the blockbuster mentality. Despite its problems, Hollywood emerged from the doldrums of the 1970s as a powerful cultural force and as the most successful U.S. export product. Its movies and television programs dominated world screens of all sizes and were as popular in foreign countries as they were in the United States. The annual glitter of the Academy Awards became the most popular television show in the world. The movies, it seems, are here to stay.

GREGORY D. BLACK

See also Censorship of Motion Pictures; Economics of
  Motion Pictures; Hollywood in World War II;
  Hollywood Studio System; Motion Picture Blacklisting;
  Motion Picture Competition; Motion Picture Ratings;
  Motion Picture Technology; Silent Motion Pictures

Further Reading

Black, Gregory, *Hollywood Censored: Morality Codes,
  Catholics, and the Movies,* New York and Cambridge:
  Cambridge University Press, 1994
Cripps, Thomas, *Slow Fade to Black: The Negro in
  American Film, 1900–1942,* New York: Oxford
  University Press, 1977; Oxford: Oxford University Press,
  1993
Finler, Joel W., *The Hollywood Story,* New York: Crown,
  1988; London: Pyramid, 1989
Gabler, Neal, *An Empire of Their Own: How the Jews
  Invented Hollywood,* New York: Crown, 1988; London:
  W.H. Allen, 1989
Haskell, Molly, *From Reverence to Rape: The Treatment
  of Women in the Movies,* Baltimore, Maryland, and
  Harmondsworth, England: Penguin, 1974
Quart, Leonard, and Albert Auster, *American Film and
  Society Since 1945,* 1st ed., London: Macmillan, 1984;
  2nd ed., New York: Praeger, 1991
Schatz, Thomas, *The Genius of the System: Hollywood
  Filmmaking in the Studio Era,* New York: Pantheon,
  1988; London: Simon & Schuster, 1989
Sklar, Robert, *Movie-Made America: A Cultural History of
  American Movies,* London: Chappell, 1975; rev. ed.,
  New York: Vintage, 1994

Spanish-American War

*Critics claim the press contributed to war fever
that led to hostilities*

The Spanish-American War was one of the most popular wars in U.S. history. Traditional histories of the press during this era have given credence to the idea that the press fanned the warmongering flames of public opinion and thus led the country into the war in 1898. Both big-city dailies and smaller dailies and weeklies were committed supporters of intervention in Cuban affairs. They often used banner headlines apprising the readers of the latest Spanish "crime."

At this time in history, no other institution, including the military and the government, was able to respond to popular demand for national action except the press. When William McKinley became U.S. president, very few political issues were of national import. Most problems were experienced and resolved politically at the local and state level. The military, too, was not in 1898 what it was 100 years later. Oversight of military matters was performed by 10 autonomous bureaus in Washington, D.C. Generals presided over geographic divisions and had little communication with one another. Consequently, the press was the only institution able to respond to the popular will at the national level.

Although newspapers were local in distribution, their influence was not. Members of Congress often referred to or quoted news reports in the leading dailies in debates on the Cuban uprising and the appropriate role of the United States. These congressional remarks were published in the *Congressional Record* and in this way were made available to smaller dailies throughout the land, which often reprinted them.

The press did play a vital role in forming public opinion. Nevertheless, it alone cannot account for the tidal wave of public support for intervention once the battleship U.S.S. *Maine* exploded in the harbor at Havana, Cuba. The Cuban Junta, which also published its own newspaper (*La Patria*), was the propaganda arm of the Cuban revolutionaries. Set up in 1895 by the Constituent Assembly of the revolutionary government, the Junta was headquartered in New York and had field offices in other cities of the United States. Staffed by Cuban-born naturalized citizens sophisticated in the art of persuasion, it raised millions of dollars at the sympathy meetings, public speeches, plays, and fairs it sponsored through the United States. Some historians give it the greatest of credit for persuading the U.S. people to take an interventionist stand.

The U.S. press coverage of the conflict can be divided into two stages: press coverage before intervention and press coverage after the declaration of war. Also, the quality of press coverage, during both stages, must be understood within the context of the times. Journalists then lived in a moral universe that disappeared by the end of World War I. The world in 1895 was thought to be inhabited by the forces of good and evil. The individual was considered a self-sufficient, autonomous unit. Thus, any social problem

The destruction of the U.S.S. *Maine* in the harbor at Havana, Cuba, in 1898 was sensationalized to help build war fever.
(Perkins Library/Duke University)

or wrongdoing was thought to result from the failure of the individual to behave as he or she should.

The center of the moral universe, then, was the individual, whose grit and resolution, whose integrity and honorable dealings with others, were admired and emulated. These ideals can be found in journalists' conduct on the battlefield; they also are embedded in their reports. Professionally, they were as a group committed to accurate reporting of the facts. However, they gave truth of correspondence (factual data on what happened on the battlefield) importance only insofar as it related to truth of significance. Journalists believed that the facts (who, what, when, where, why, and how) could only be properly understood when their underlying moral significance was disclosed.

By 1918, this moral universe had passed away. The significance of this is that later historians began to see the reports of the Spanish-American War as sensational rather than rational, factual accounts of what happened on the battlefield.

Within the context of that world, there were also two types of reporters: professionals, who made their living working for newspapers and magazines, and literary stars. Professionals who gained distinction in their coverage of events were, among others, Sylvester Scovel, George Bronson Rea, and James Creelman. Literary stars included Stephen Crane and Richard Harding Davis. While the public made much of the literary stars, professional reporters were less enamored of them. Most professional reporters thought Scovel was the premier reporter of the war because he had gone everywhere, seen everything, and reported it factually.

The war, however, presented the same problems for all journalists, whether professional or literary star: problems in setting up communications lines, problems in censorship, and problems in military-press relations. In the early days of the Cuban insurrection, the greatest problem facing reporters was passing undetected through Spanish lines of defense. In particular, it was difficult to get through the *trocha,* or the Spanish-held railway system that divided the island into two territories, one dominated by the Spanish, the other by the insurrectionists. Once past the Spanish defense, reporters were faced with dense jungle terrain very difficult to penetrate. Only five reporters managed to locate rebel camps and to set up relay lines, often unreliable, back to points on the shore where dispatch boats picked up news copy and took it back to Florida or to one of the nearby islands having independent telegraph facilities. These almost insurmountable difficulties required personal strength and determination, the very traits that informed their sense of moral rectitude.

Once the United States declared war on Spain, the communication problems faced by reporters were replaced by supply and censorship problems. Reporters working for major dailies could afford to bring their own supplies to Cuba, but others had to rely on the U.S. Commissary. The Commissary was poorly organized, and reporters often were turned away empty-handed because of food shortages. Eventually, the military decided to issue rations to the

press only at the coastal town of Siboney. As a result, reporters who relied on the military for food stationed themselves there, where they wrote stories based on the accounts of wounded soldiers or those who had contracted yellow fever. These stories were criticized by the press itself, as well as the public, for being fabrications rather than factual accounts.

In addition to communications and supply problems, reporters also had to deal with different forms of press censorship. As soon as Cuban insurrectionists launched their revolution, the Spanish imposed censorship on all news and information leaving Cuba. They sought to minimize the importance of the uprising and give the impression that Spain had things well under control. Reporters were fairly resourceful in getting around Spanish censors, often using dispatch boats to evade the Spanish censor.

Once U.S. public opinion against Spain reached fever pitch, the Spanish began to confine reporters to Havana, to forbid them to accompany the Spanish troops, and to arrest and deport those who broke the rules. In April 1898, the United States entered the war. Immediately, censors were set up in all telegraph offices in New York, in the French cable office on the south coast of Cuba, and in the British cable offices in Puerto Rico and Santiago de Cuba. The land lines in Florida were likewise taken over by the military. Censorship was entrusted to the local superintendents who were overseen by officers from the Signal Corps.

Generally, censorship was limited to any news regarding the movement of troops or other military information thought to be essential to successful strategy. Officers read newspapers daily to determine whether censorship rules had been breached. Reporters who broke the rules lost their press credentials. Journalists thought that U.S. military censorship was worse than that of the Spanish, but after covering other wars, many journalists conceded that censorship during the war with Spain was mild in comparison.

Finally, military-press relations posed significant problems for journalists. The military certainly had no policy regarding press relations. Whether journalists got on with the military they were covering was largely a matter of personalities. Some commanders, such as George Dewey or

---

The Heroic Capture of Caney Told by W.R. Hearst

Special Cable Dispatch to the New York Journal – Tonight, as I write, the ambulance trains are bringing in the wounded soldiers from the fierce battle around the island village of Caney. . . . Under the fierce firing of far-heavier artillery forces than it was supposed the Spaniards had, the American infantry and dismounted cavalry have done their work, and done it nobly. I have been at the artillery positions all day to see what our guns could or could not do. There is no question of the skill or courage of American gunners. Their work was as near perfect as gunnery gets to be.

New York Journal, July 4, 1898

Leonard Wood, established good rapport with members of the press. Even within the context of severe naval restrictions, Admiral Dewey was popular with reporters because, when appealed to, he often granted them permission to send reports previously barred by the censors.

On the other hand, the relations between General William R. Shafter and the press were strained. As the leader of the invading armies, Shafter was fighting under impossible conditions. His equipment was outdated and insufficient; the climate in Cuba was decimating his troops; and he had little time or patience with journalists, whom he called "meddlesome scribblers." On one occasion, he resorted to fisticuffs to handle the press. Consequently, he received very poor press.

MARY S. MANDER

See also McKinley, William, and the Press; Yellow Journalism

Further Reading

Brown, Charles Henry, *The Correspondents' War,* New York: Scribner's, 1967

Linderman, Gerald, *The Mirror of War: American Society and the Spanish-American War,* Ann Arbor: University of Michigan Press, 1974

Mander, Mary S., "Pen and Sword: Problems in Reporting the Spanish American War," *Journalism History 9* (1982)

Milton, Joyce, *The Yellow Kids: Foreign Correspondents in the Heyday of Yellow Journalism,* New York: Harper & Row, 1989

Trask, David F., *The War with Spain in 1898,* New York: Macmillan, 1981; London, Collier Macmillan, 1981

Wilkerson, Marcus, *Public Opinion and the Spanish-American War,* Baton Rouge: Louisiana State University Press, 1932

Specialized Business Publications

Designed to provide information to certain businesses, professions

Trade magazines or specialized business publications also are called industrial, technical, business, or professional magazines or papers. Sources of continuing education for executives, managers, and employees, trade magazines provide technical and professional "how-to" knowledge; disseminate news about industry personnel, products, services, equipment, and techniques; interpret industry trends, governmental actions, and public opinion affecting an industry or profession; and, through advertising content, market goods and services of value to an industry or profession. Trade magazines that cover emerging fields in the economy emphasize "how-to" information, and those that cover established fields concentrate on news.

Trade magazines distribute issues to qualified readers through controlled nonpaid circulation, controlled paid circulation, or a combination of paid and nonpaid circulation. As a group, trade magazines and papers in the 1990s had a total paid and nonpaid circulation of approximately 120 million. Trade magazines derive most of their revenue from advertising.

The history of specialized business magazines follows that of the capitalist, industrial, and scientific revolutions, chiefly in Europe and the United States. The *Fugger Newsletter* – developed during the sixteenth century for members of the House of Fugger's financial and commercial organization – was the prototype for the later price-currents that merchants and brokers published for the public, first in The Netherlands, then in England and the American colonies. However, unlike their European predecessors, which failed to develop into commercial papers, the 15 price-currents that appeared in American trading centers during the mid-eighteenth century spawned the modern business and trade press. The *South-Carolina Price-Current* and the Philadelphia *Price-Current,* the first price-currents in what would become the United States, were published in 1774 and 1775, respectively. Price-currents grew in importance until the early years of the nineteenth century, when the *Daily Items for Merchants,* the first daily commercial paper, and the *General Shipping and Commercial List,* the first specialized business title, were published in New York in 1815. The latter continued into the late twentieth century as the *Journal of Commerce.*

The growing dependence of the U.S. economy on infusions of capital throughout the first half of the nineteenth century contributed to further growth of banking and finance journals. Similarly, industrial growth and specialization fostered such trade papers as the *American Railroad Journal* (1832), the *Dry Goods Reporter and Commercial Glance* (1846), the *Hardwareman's Newspaper and American Manufacturer's Circular* (1855), the *American Druggists' Circular and Chemical Gazette* (1857), and the *American Gas-Light Journal* (1859) – all of which survived under revised titles in the late twentieth century.

This expansion of trade periodicals accelerated to meet the needs of, first, a rapidly industrializing economy after the Civil War and, second, a scientifically and technologically sophisticated economy in the twentieth century. The late nineteenth century brought such long-standing titles as *American Grocer* (1868), the *Paper Trade Journal* (1872), the *Engineering News Record* (1874), the *Mining Record* (1880), the *Inland Printer* (1883), the *Lumberman* (1889), the *Sporting Goods Dealer* (1899), and *Motor Age* (1899). The impact of science, technology, knowledge, and services on the twentieth-century economy generated such successful publications as *Chemical Engineering* (1902), *Variety* (1905), *American City and County* (1909), *Aviation Week and Space Technology* (1916), *Chain Store Age Executive* (1925), *Travel Agent* (1930), *Restaurants and Institutions* (1937), *Datamation* (1955), *Ocean Industry* (1966), *Genetic Engineering News* (1981), and *Environmental Protection* (1990).

In 1994, *Business Publications Advertising Source* included 4,455 trade magazines and businesspapers, only 1,709 of which were audited by the Business Publications

Audit of Circulation or the Audit Bureau of Circulations. The categories with the greatest number of titles reflected the economic importance of science and technology: there were 651 medical and surgical, 224 computer, 175 local and regional business, 134 educational, 107 national business, 103 engineering and construction, 89 science research and development, 81 electronic engineering, 81 advertising and marketing, and 74 automotive products magazines. In 1993, the 10 trade magazines boasting the highest revenues were all computer titles.

Most early trade magazines were published by experts and enthusiasts from the fields they covered. Employment of trained journalists and specialists in publishing, marketing, or advertising came as the magazines grew into corporate entities. As these magazines matured, combined, and repositioned, companies emerged – McGraw-Hill, Harcourt Brace, Chilton, Gralla, Advanstar, Crain, Penton, Cahners – that published several magazines and sought profitable titles to purchase. This expansion of multiple-magazine publishers accelerated during the 1960s as profits continued to climb. Cahners, a subsidiary of Reed Elsevier, in the late 1990s published about 90 magazines; Harcourt Brace and Advanstar, about 60 each; Miller Freeman, about 50; and Penton, Raven, Chilton, Argus Business and Chilton, between 40 and 50. Mergers and acquisitions brought about the control of numerous U.S. trade magazine publishers by such major European companies as VNU and Reed Elsevier.

JOSEPH P. BERNT

See also Magazines in the Nineteenth Century; Magazines in the Twentieth Century

Further Reading
Elfenbein, Julien, *Business Journalism, Its Function and Future,* rev. ed., London: Harper & Brothers, 1947; also published as *Business Journalism,* 2nd rev. ed., New York: Harper & Brothers, 1960
Endres, Kathleen L., "Business Press Journalists: Who They Are, What They Do, and How They View Their Craft," *Gallatin Review* 8 (1988–89)
_____, ed., *Historical Guides to the World's Periodicals and Newspapers: Trade, Industrial, and Professional Periodicals of the United States,* Westport, Connecticut: Greenwood, 1994
_____, "Ownership and Employment in Specialized Business Press," *Journalism Quarterly* 65:4 (Winter 1988), pp. 996–998
Fisher, William, ed., *Historical Guides to the World's Periodicals and Newspapers: Business Journals of the United States,* New York: Greenwood, 1991
Forsyth, David P., *The Business Press in America: 1750–1865,* Philadelphia: Chilton, 1964
Grunwald, Edgar A., *The Business Press Editor,* New York: New York University Press, 1988
Gussow, Don, *The New Business Journalism: An Insider's Look at the Workings of America's Business Press,* San Diego, California: Harcourt Brace Jovanovich, 1984

Spin Doctors

Place events in most positive light for employer

The first reported use of the term "spin doctors" occurred in 1984, and by the late 1990s, it had already found its way into at least one dictionary. *Merriam Webster's Collegiate Dictionary, Tenth Edition,* defined a spin doctor as "a person (as a political aide) responsible for ensuring that others interpret an event from a particular point of view." However, the concept of "spin" control was not new and had been practiced at least since the time of Woodrow Wilson.

The term "spin doctor" particularly is associated with political campaigns, although it also came to be seen more broadly as a general approach to public relations. The underlying notion is a conceptual enhancement or reversal of perspective from which to view any event. The spin metaphor derives from an event being turned around, turned aside, or turned back to place it in the best possible light according to the views of the spinner. "Spinning a story involves twisting it to one's advantage, using surrogates, press releases, radio actualities, and other friendly sources," wrote John Anthony Maltese. Successful spin often involves persuading the media that a particular spin to a story is the correct one.

The most frequently used spin doctors in the late 1990s were political consultants, media handlers, and political party officials. All could generally be relied upon by the media to provide a perspective on any political event that favored the candidate or party they were supporting. In some cases, the media turned to actual "doctors," or academicians. These experts, although not always on the campaign payroll, also could direct commentary in one direction or another.

Spin doctors are associated especially with political campaigns and politics at the presidential level. During the 1988 campaign, it was reported that in the Iowa caucuses, each campaign had a designated spin doctor responsible for mingling with the media and putting the best possible face on disastrous events. The Michael Dukakis campaign reportedly paid one spin doctor an enviable salary to "sit, swizzle and spin" from sunset to closing time in the bar of a downtown Des Moines hotel.

The 1992 campaign offered a classic example of spin in the case of ultimately successful presidential candidate Bill Clinton. The Clinton campaign was shaken relatively early on by allegations of his having had an extramarital affair with Gennifer Flowers, having smoked marijuana (but, he said, he did not inhale), and having evaded the draft during the Vietnam War. When he then finished an undistinguished third in the New York primary, he was portrayed by his campaign handlers as a scrappy "Comeback Kid," and a moral victory was proclaimed, evidently on the theory that he did not finish last, thereby exceeding any reasonable expectations. This approach of portraying the glass as not half empty but as half full exemplifies the theory of spin. The "doctor" part no doubt derives from the employment of professionals by the campaigns to administer the spin, rather than depending on the amateurish efforts of the untrained patient-candidate.

LYNDA LEE KAID

Further Reading

Kopkind, Andrew, "Gimme Some Spin," *The Nation* 246:7 (February 20, 1988), pp. 220–221

Maltese, John Anthony, *Spin Control: The White House Office of Communications and the Management of Presidential News,* 2nd ed., Chapel Hill: University of North Carolina Press, 1994

Sumpter, R., and J.W. Tankard, "The Spin Doctor: An Alternative Model of Public Relations," *Public Relations Review* 20:1 (1994)

Sports Journalism

Longtime staple for U.S. publications

Sports reporting has grown from an occasional and anecdotal feature of the daily press to arguably the most recognized and popular element of modern mass media. The flourishing of sports talk radio and all-sports television networks, along with the circulation stimulus of sports reporting in the daily and weekly print media, disguises the marginal attention given to sports and leisure during the first half of the national existence of the United States.

As early as the first decade of the eighteenth century, newspapers in colonial New England reported on bowling and billiards. Fowling and bullbaiting also were reported in colonies clinging to Massachusetts and Chesapeake Bay. It was in the middle and southern colonies, where horse racing developed as a means of stock selection, that a substantial readership developed for racing news.

Puritan leaders deplored "that cursed and senseless party spirit" shown in sport, and following the American Revolution, people relied more on the *Weekly Dispatch,* published in London, for systematic reporting on the turf, ring, and cricket fields. The *American Farmer* and the *American Turf Register and Sporting Magazine,* published by John Stuart Skinner between 1819 and 1829, were the first indigenous publications to tap the widening enthusiasm for horse racing.

The leading sporting journal of the middle third of the nineteenth century was *Spirit of the Times,* launched by William Trotter Porter in New York in 1831. Porter's ceaseless promotion of horse and foot racing, rowing, yachting, angling, and cricket included coverage of baseball in the decade before the Civil War. It was Porter who presumably labeled baseball the "national game" and developed box scores and personality profiles, or what he called "dope" stories, to build fan interest. Antebellum baseball was a gentleman's game, primarily played by social clubs in eastern cities. Like prizefighting and horse racing, it got its greatest coverage not from newspapers but magazine editors like Porter, Frank Forester of the *American Monthly Magazine,* George Wilkes and Richard Kyle Fox of the *National Police Gazette,* and Frank Queen and Henry Chadwick of the *New York Clipper.*

James Gordon Bennett of the *New York Herald* saw the commercial possibilities of sports by the 1840s and assigned eight reporters and published four extras after a famous horse race in the middle of the decade. Bennett used pony express riders to beat the competition in reporting fight news, including the dispatch of boats in New York harbor to receive first word of the 37-round draw fought outside London in April 1860 between the United States' John C. Heenan and British champion Tom Sayers. Horace Greeley charged boxing was only worthy of "grog shops and brothels" but still sent *New York Tribune* reporters to the big fights. So did Henry Raymond of the *New York Times.* Charles A. Dana, the editor of the *New York Sun,* was a ringside reporter when John L. Sullivan fought Charlie Mitchell at the old Madison Square Garden in 1883.

That was the year in which Joseph Pulitzer bought the *New York World,* where he soon organized the first sports department. Twelve years later, at the *New York Journal,* William Randolph Hearst developed the first sports section. Both publishers recognized the circulation possibilities of the cycling craze of the 1890s and of college football. Football had been systematically celebrated by Caspar Whitney, the editor of *Harper's Weekly,* which featured Walter Camp's All-America teams. The *World* and the *Journal* projected onto amateur athletics and its heroes the qualities of rugged individualism threatened by the closing of the frontier. Professionalizing sports like baseball were touted for their team play and pastoral association at a time of rapid industrialization and urbanization. The *Sporting News,* published in St. Louis, Missouri, lobbied successfully for an expanded major league and helped to establish the American League in 1900, headed by former baseball writer Ban Johnson.

Humor and exaggeration characterized sports-page storytelling at the turn of the century. Charles Seymour, Finley Peter Dunne, and Harry Palmer in Chicago; Sam Crane and Charles Dryden in New York; Tim Murnane in Boston; Al and Charlie Spink in St. Louis, Missouri; Joe Gruber in Pittsburgh, Pennsylvania; and Ren Mulford in Cincinnati, Ohio, became the most widely read journalists of their day. Their whimsical and ubiquitous coverage of baseball, boxing, football, racing, and golf put specialty publications like the *New York Clipper* and the *National Police Gazette* on the ropes or out of business.

The voice of the modern sports reporter reached its mature development during the Jazz Age. Two competing schools of storytelling – "gee whiz" and "aw, nuts," also known as the boost and the knock – dominated a golden age for sports writers, who commanded impressive salaries and national reputations. Grantland Rice, Ring Lardner, Damon Runyon, Heywood Broun, Westbrook Pegler, Paul Gallico, Irvin Cobb, John Kieran, Robert Edgren, W.O. McGeehan, Hype Igoe, and Otto Floto were the bylines that stimulated circulation while pushing journalism into a bitter debate over professionalism. Many leading editors deplored the 50 percent surge in space given to sports since

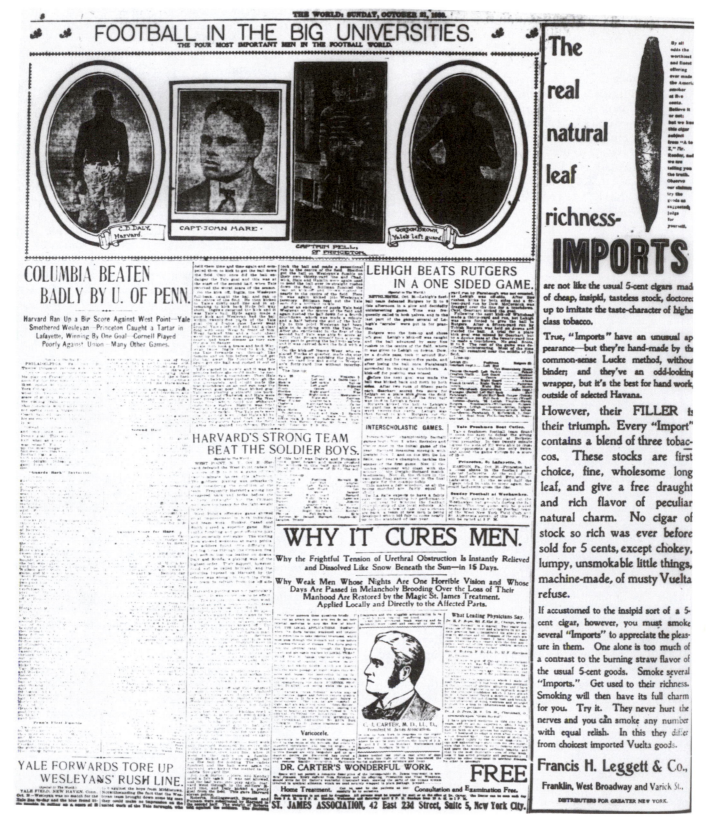

College sporting events were reported heavily in early sports pages.
(Perkins Library/Duke University)

the turn of the century, not only because of its excesses but because of the increasing independence of the sports page. Three-quarters of all sports stories bypassed the copy editor, leading to charges that circulation managers and not veteran editors were in charge of the nation's newspapers.

During the interwar era and in the years after, sports accounted for an average of between 15 and 20 percent of a newspaper's news hole and 40 percent of its local news coverage, with the percentage approaching 50 percent in many major dailies. Jazz Age circulation managers voted heavyweight champion Jack Dempsey the number-one circulation getter of his generation. Future editors would say the same about Joe Louis and Muhammed Ali. Americans gathered in record numbers to hear and read about the Jazz Age's Jack Dempsey–Gene Tunney title fights and, even in the 1990s, two-thirds of all readers surveyed said they wished their newspapers had more sports. The Super Bowl and the Olympics remained the most read about and watched events by mass culture.

Mass media and leisure industries like sport became intimately linked. Each relied on the other's capacities of self-promotion to attract a wide following. That following was distinctly middle class. Blue-collar sports like bowling and stock-car racing received scant attention in print dailies, with noncompetitive sports like hunting and fishing receiving even less.

Football, baseball, and basketball remained the mass media's favorite sports, with hockey, golf, and tennis next in order of space and coverage enthusiasm. The reason was economic. Sports represented one-third of network weekend programming, with one-quarter of baseball's revenues, one-third of basketball's, and nearly half of pro football's revenues coming from broadcasting contracts. By 1972, a television commercial during a pro football game could command $200,000 a minute. A generation later, one network signed a multibillion-dollar contract to televise pro football.

On the eve of the twenty-first century, the major U.S. television networks produced more than 1,500 hours of sports programming annually, 15 percent of their total schedules. Sportscasts represented two of every three of the 25 highest rated broadcasts of all time. To this had to be added radio's half million annual hours of sports broadcasts and the one-third of all newspaper readers who said that the sports page was the primary reason they buy a newspaper.

BRUCE EVENSEN

Further Reading

Betts, John Rickards, "Sporting Journalism in Nineteenth-Century America," *American Quarterly* 5 (Spring 1953)

Evensen, Bruce J., "Jazz Age Journalism's Battle over Professionalism, Circulation, and the Sports Page," *Journal of Sport History* 30 (Winter 1993)

Francis, Roy G., "The Sportswriter," in *Motivations in Play, Games and Sports,* edited by Ralph Slovenko and James A. Knight, Springfield, Illinois: Charles C. Thomas, 1967

Gallico, Paul, *Farewell to Sport,* New York: Knopf, 1938; London: Simon & Schuster, 1988

Class Moment for a Classic Pitcher

WASHINGTON, Oct. 10 – Destiny, waiting for the final curtain, stepped from the wings today and handed the king his crown. In the most dramatic moment of baseball's sixty years of history, the wall-eyed goddess known as Fate, after waiting eighteen years, led Walter Johnson to the pot of shining gold that waits at the rainbow's end. For it was Johnson, the old Johnson, brought back from other years with his blazing fast ball singing across the plate for the last four rounds, that stopped the Giant attack. Washington won just at the edge of darkness, and it was Johnson's great right arm that turned the trick.

New York Tribune, October 10, 1924

Mandell, Richard D., *Sport: A Cultural History,* New York: Columbia University Press, 1984

Noverr, Douglas A., and Lawrence E. Ziewacz, *The Games They Played: Sports in American History, 1865–1980,* Chicago: Nelson-Hall, 1983

Nugent, William Henry, "The Sports Section," *American Mercury* (March 1929)

Stevens John, "The Rise of the Sports Page," *Gannett Center Journal* 1 (1987)

Staged News

Effort to control manner of news presentation

Staged news generally falls into two categories: events that are created by people seeking media attention and news coverage and the dramatization of news events by the media, primarily television, for visual impact. Staged news also is used by people who want to control access to and the presentation of information.

Staged news, or "pseudo-events," as they were labeled by historian Daniel Boorstin in his 1961 book *The Image,* are commonly staged by public relations people attempting to draw news media coverage of activities that otherwise would go unnoticed. Ground breakings, ribbon cuttings, and grand openings are common examples. In politics, candidates and government officials use the press conference or the staged announcement event in an attempt to ensure favorable coverage of their activities.

During the 1950s and 1960s, social movements such as the civil rights movement and the opposition to the war in Vietnam began to hold staged news events such as rallies, parades, and demonstrations to attract coverage by the news media. These events became especially successful with the development of television, where visual images became a necessity of covering the news. This trend toward the importance of video coverage led to the adoption of staged events such as demonstrations and parades by a wide variety of individuals and organizations as they fought for the attention of the news media. Providing the media with a photo opportunity can go a long way in determining whether the staged event will appear on the nightly news.

This staged news played an important role in much of the social and political activity of the second half of the twentieth century. By creating news events that drew the attention of the media, particularly television, social activists such as Martin Luther King Jr. were able to establish a national base for their reform movements. As the number of individuals and organizations using staged events to attract media attention increased, the size and scope of the events increased. In an effort to guarantee attention, organizations resorted to the use of celebrities, larger-scale demonstrations and marches, and, sometimes, violence to attract coverage.

With the evolution of television news and the rise in importance of visual images to accompany stories, staged news took on a second form, the creation of visuals by news-gathering organizations for impact. In the early 1990s, a series of controversial uses of video by the three major TV news networks – NBC, CBS, and ABC – brought the issue into focus. NBC received criticism from inside and outside the media for exaggerating the consequence visually in a story about hazardous gas tanks on General Motors pickup trucks. ABC was criticized for a shadowy dramatization that implied that it was actual footage of an accused spy passing U.S. military secrets to foreign agents, and CBS drew fire for using old footage of Soviet fighter planes in a story about Soviet activity in Afghanistan and implying that they were part of the current incident. With development of computerized editing and enhancement techniques, it might be possible in the future to create totally fictitious video coverage of a "news" event or to create a totally fictitious event itself.

DAVID CASSADY

See also Image, The; Media Events; Photo Opportunities

Further Reading
Boorstin, Daniel, *The Image, or, What Happened to the American Dream*, London: Weidenfeld and Nicolson, 1961; also published as *The Image: A Guide to Pseudo-Events in America*, New York: Harper & Row, 1964
English, John, "American Television – What Is Truth?," *Economist* (October 14, 1989)
_____, "The Show That Backfired," *IPI Report* 42:4 (April 1993), pp. 6–7
_____, "Spy Tape Verdict: ABC Blew It," *Washington Journalism Review* 11 (1989)

Stamp Act of 1765

Spurred newspapers to lead opposition to British tax

The Stamp Act of 1765 was the first direct tax ever levied by the British Parliament on the American colonies. Designed to raise funds to help with the upkeep of troops sta-

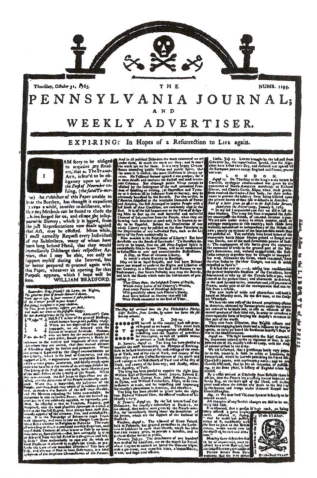

The imposition of the Stamp Act in 1765 led to serious complaints from newspapers.

tioned in the colonies, it placed a tax on newspapers, almanacs, pamphlets, and broadsides, as well as on legal documents, licenses, and gaming devices.

Opposition to the Stamp Act did much to unite the colonies. Decrying "taxation without representation," the colonies asserted that their right to govern their own internal affairs had always been recognized by the Crown.

The Sons of Liberty were formed in the summer of 1765 throughout the colonies to organize opposition to the Stamp Act. These groups sometimes resorted to violence to force stamp agents to resign their posts and merchants to cancel orders for British goods. Before the effective date of the Stamp Act on November 1, 1765, all stamp agents in the colonies had resigned.

Colonial newspaper editors generally opposed the Stamp Act and helped to foment resistance to the tax in their communities. Many editors became actively involved in the Sons of Liberty, setting the stage for their political involvement in promoting revolution in the 1770s.

Leading merchants of New York, Boston, and Philadelphia agreed to ban the purchase of European goods until the Stamp Act was repealed, which led to a decline in British exports to America. British merchants requested Parliament to repeal the act, and it was repealed on March 18,

1766. Colonial newspaper editors claimed much of the credit for achieving repeal.

ELSIE HEBERT

See also American Revolution and the Press; Colonial Press

Further Reading

Morgan, Edmund S., and Helen M. Morgan, *The Stamp Act Crisis: Prologue to Revolution*, new rev. ed., New York: Collier, 1963; London: Collier, 1970

Schlesinger, Arthur M., *Prelude to Independence: The Newspaper War on Britain, 1764–1776*, New York: Vintage, 1965

Standing Committee of Correspondents

Regulates journalists' access to congressional press galleries

Standing committees of correspondents elected by fellow reporters and broadcasters scrutinize applications for admission to the congressional press galleries and issue credentials to those who meet the U.S. House of Representatives and Senate rules. Such accreditation offers journalists working space in the press galleries of the Senate and House, badges to enter closed areas of the Capitol, and

Congressional press galleries are a long-standing tradition in both houses of Congress.
(Davis Library, University of North Carolina at Chapel Hill)

access to press conferences and other media events. The committees also issue press passes for the national party conventions.

When the Senate first established a gallery for reporters in 1841, the vice president and, later, the Senate Rules Committee determined admissions; the speaker of the House governed access to the House press gallery established in 1857. The politicians tended to admit all reporters who applied. During the 1870s, revelations that some reporters had used the press gallery to engage in lobbying caused prominent members of the press corps to propose that reporters themselves police the galleries through a Standing Committee of Correspondents. The first Standing Committee was elected in 1879, and the House soon after adopted a five-point set of rules that the committee had prepared. The Senate adopted similar rules in 1884. These rules prohibited lobbying and required that correspondents receive the largest share of their income from reporting and file their stories by telegraph to daily newspapers.

The new rules eliminated lobbyists as well as many government clerks who moonlighted as correspondents. Lobbying remained prohibited at the end of the twentieth century, so even such respectable journals as *Consumer Reports* were barred because their parent organizations lobbied Congress. The rules later forbade anyone engaged in paid publicity or promotional work. Perhaps unintentionally, the rules also closed the press galleries to female reporters, who were generally assigned to file society reports by letter rather than pay telegraph tolls. Women had sat in the press galleries prior to 1880, but the rules limited their return until the 1940s. Similarly, because the black press consisted of weekly papers, no black reporter received accreditation to the press galleries between 1879 and 1947.

The Standing Committee of Correspondents supervised both the Senate and House press galleries, whose membership consisted entirely of newspaper reporters. When new media emerged in the twentieth century, the committee resisted changing the rules to admit them. Radio news broadcasters could gain accreditation only if they also reported for daily newspapers. In 1939, the radio correspondents persuaded Congress to establish a separate radio gallery, which after 1947 became the Radio and Television Gallery. Congress also established galleries for the periodical press (magazines and newsletters) and for press photographers, with separate rules for each gallery. Each gallery elected its own Standing Committee of Correspondents.

Elections to the two-year terms on the committees are held on an alternating basis each January, and journalists campaign to win election, shaking hands, and making pledges. Committee members then elect a chairperson and secretary. The names of the members of each of the standing committees, the rules of the press galleries, and the membership of the galleries are published annually in the *Congressional Directory*.

DONALD A. RITCHIE

Further Reading

Hess, Stephen, *Live from Capitol Hill! Studies of Congress and the Media*, Washington, D.C.: Brookings Institution, 1991

Marbut, F.B., *News from the Capital: The Story of Washington Reporting*, Carbondale: Southern Illinois University Press, 1971

Ritchie, Donald A., *Press Gallery: Congress and the Washington Correspondents*, Cambridge, Massachusetts: Harvard University Press, 1991

Stanton, Frank N.

Helped develop CBS prominence in news arena

Born in Muskegon, Michigan, and raised in Dayton, Ohio, Frank N. Stanton graduated from Ohio Wesleyan University with a degree in psychology. As a doctoral student at Ohio State University, he invented a device to measure radio audiences. Upon completion of his doctorate in 1935, he joined CBS, where he worked with Paul Lazarsfeld to develop a program analyzer to gauge audience reaction.

Within a decade, Stanton became a CBS vice president in charge of eight departments. Shortly afterward, he was named company president. He handled policy matters and served as consultant to various boards during the World War II years. A careful and dedicated manager, he was responsible for handling operational matters, fine-tuning and carrying out the policies of CBS chairman William S. Paley.

Frank Stanton
(Library of American Broadcasting)

Frequently called upon to respond to challenges made by the Federal Communications Commission, Stanton emerged as respected spokesperson.

As president of CBS, Stanton took a special interest in news and documentaries. His efforts to have Congress suspend the "Equal Time" rule of the Communications Act in 1960 permitted the televised Kennedy-Nixon debates to take place. A decade later, he stood up to the threat of a congressional contempt citation on First Amendment grounds by refusing to provide materials related to preparation of the *CBS Reports* documentary, "The Selling of the Pentagon." His successful defense of this program preceded his retirement by one year.

MICHAEL D. MURRAY

See also Paley, William S.; Presidential Debates; Television Networks

Further Reading

Boyer, Peter J., *Who Killed CBS?*, New York: Random House, 1988

Paper, Lewis J., *Empire: William S. Paley and the Making of CBS*, New York: St. Martin's, 1987

Smith, Sally Bedell, *In All His Glory: The Life of William S. Paley, the Legendary Tycoon and His Brilliant Circle*, New York: Simon & Schuster, 1990

Stone, I.F.

Investigative journalist and editor

The labels "gadfly" and "radical," although fitting, obscure the level of professionalism and political impact attained by investigative journalist and editor Isidor Feinstein "Izzy" Stone. Rather than cultivate sources at the center of power, Stone relished the role of outsider looking in, combing through public documents to challenge the government's version of the truth. *I.F. Stone's Weekly*, published from his Washington, D.C., home between 1953 and 1971, flourished during the Vietnam War, when Stone's influence reached its peak.

Stone was born in Philadelphia in 1907 to Russian-Jewish immigrants. He dropped out of the University of Pennsylvania to devote himself full time to the journalism interests he had pursued since his early teens, going on to write for the *Philadelphia Record* and *New York Post* and prominent left-liberal journals such as the *Nation*. Stone launched his antiestablishment newsletter during a dark period marked by the closing of the radical newspaper for which he worked, widespread negative reaction to his book *The Hidden History of the Korean War*, and the effects of McCarthyism.

Stone could be faulted personally for his egotism and politically for giving more latitude to leftist regimes than to rightist ones, but his financially successful newsletter's crusade against U.S. policies in Southeast Asia influenced establishment journalism and helped set the agenda for the

New Left of the 1960s. Although frail health forced him to stop publishing the weekly, he had won acclaim as a best-selling author and folk hero by the time of his death in 1989.

JONATHAN Y. HILL

Further Reading

Cochran, David, "I.F. Stone and the New Left: Protesting U.S. Policy in Vietnam," *The Historian* 53:3 (Spring 1991), pp. 505–520

Cottrell, Robert C., *Izzy: A Biography of I.F. Stone*, New Brunswick, New Jersey: Rutgers University Press, 1992

Patner, Andrew, *I.F. Stone: A Portrait*, New York: Anchor, 1990

Stone, I.F., *The Haunted Fifties*, New York: Random House, 1963; London: Merlin, 1964

_____, *The Trial of Socrates*, Boston: Little, Brown, 1988; London: Cape, 1988

Suffrage Press

Publications helped promote "votes for women" cause

Newspapers produced by women's rights activists played a key role in creating and sustaining the woman suffrage movement during the seven decades before 1920, when women won the vote. In the 1850s, women's rights activists began publishing their own periodicals because the mainstream press ignored or disparaged their calls for reforms. Between 1870 and 1890, more than 30 suffrage papers from New England to Oregon nurtured the sense of identity, unity, and commitment that transformed woman suffrage from a radical demand by outspoken individuals into a nationwide social movement.

The suffrage press forged this community by fulfilling several functions: It politically educated and socialized women. It refined arguments for suffrage while refuting arguments against suffrage. It informed women of suffrage conventions and related news that reinforced their sense of purpose and progress. It engaged women in activism by soliciting signatures for suffrage petitions. It recruited converts and sustained followers by offering role models for "new women" willing to test the boundaries of the domestic sphere. It forged a sense of history by publishing articles about women's contributions, emphasizing that suffragists themselves were making history. It gave suffragists a forum to articulate goals and counter hostility in the mainstream press.

The first newspaper created specifically to champion suffrage was the *Revolution,* published by Susan Anthony and Elizabeth Cady Stanton beginning in 1868. It succeeded several more genteel women's newspapers that included suffrage in their agenda, beginning with the temperance paper the *Lily* (1849–56) and others that disappeared during the Civil War. *Revolution's* daring fare – including articles on prostitution and illegitimacy – appalled more conservative

Susan B. Anthony's *The Revolution* set a militant tone for the suffragist press.
(Davis Library, University of North Carolina at Chapel Hill)

suffragists, who drove it out of business in 1870 with the *Woman's Journal.*

The *Journal* continued as the most influential of more than a dozen major suffrage publications in the twentieth century. The voice of the National American Woman Suffrage Association, its 50,000 subscribers in 1917 outnumbered by 10 times those of its closest competitor.

The *Journal's* pages exemplified characteristics of suffrage journals, which largely served white, middle-class readers. Besides editorials and suffrage news, it covered other women's issues such as working women, child welfare, and unfair marriage laws and published columns on women's accomplishments, biographical sketches of heroines, fiction, poetry, cartoons, and book reviews.

In contrast, the other national twentieth-century suffrage publication, the *Suffragist* (1913–21), limited itself to the single issue of obtaining a federal suffrage amendment. The National Woman's Party (NWP) tabloid defied the federal government with its combative coverage of jailed NWP protesters who had picketed the White House.

Other notable suffrage publications included the *Wom-*

an's Era, launched in 1895 in Boston by African American suffrage leader Josephine St. Pierre Ruffin; the *Woman's Exponent* (1872–1914), which argued in Utah for polygamy and woman suffrage; the *Woman's Tribune* (1883–1909), a Nebraskan enterprise that moved to Washington, D.C., to better cover and convert Congress; the *San Francisco Pioneer* (1869–73), the west's first suffrage newspaper; and the *Woman Voter* (1911–17), which chronicled bold new campaign techniques introduced by the Women's Political Union in New York City.

LINDA LUMSDEN

See also Alternative Media; Feminist Media

Further Reading

Bennion, Sherilyn Cox, "The *New Northwest* and *Woman's Exponent*: Early Voices for Suffrage," *Journalism Quarterly* 54 (1977)

_____, "Woman Suffrage Papers of the West, 1869–1914," *American Journalism* 3 (1986)

Lumsden, Linda, "Suffragist," in *Women's Periodicals of the United States: Volume 2: Reform and Reaction,* edited by Kathleen Endres, Westport, Connecticut: Greenwood, 1997

Masel-Walters, Lynne, "A Burning Cloud by Day: The History and Content of the *Woman's Journal*," *Journalism History* 3 (1976–77)

_____, "Their Rights and Nothing More: A History of *The Revolution,* 1868–70," *Journalism Quarterly* 53 (1976)

_____, "To Hustle with the Rowdies: The Organization and Functions of the American Woman Suffrage Press," *Journal of American Culture* 3 (Spring 1980)

Solomon, Martha, ed., *A Voice of Their Own: The Woman Suffrage Press, 1840–1910,* Tuscaloosa: University of Alabama Press, 1991

Steiner, Linda, "Finding Community in Nineteenth Century Suffrage Periodicals," *American Journalism* 1 (1983)

T

Tabloids

Smaller-size papers have sensationalistic heritage

Tabloids are half-size newspapers that developed in the United States beginning in the 1920s as sensational newsmongers and prospered into the 1990s as entertainment weekly magazines often sold in supermarkets. A tabloid-size publication need not be sensational (the *Christian Science Monitor* and Long Island *Newsday* were tabloids, for example), but the term "tabloid journalism" refers to the more garish displays with large headlines, many photographs, and simplistic stories of crime, sex, and celebrity gossip. In the 1990s, the term even came to apply to so-called tabloid television shows such as *A Current Affair* and *Inside Edition,* which presented similar topics in a sensational manner.

Although the concept of sensationalism has been traced to the beginning of human society, printed predecessors of the tabloids may be the broadsides and news books of the seventeenth century, filled with murders, natural disasters, unusual births, and other bizarre tales. In the United States, the tabloids were an extension of sensational journalism begun in the 1830s with the penny press, which appealed to a mass audience by focusing on human interest and crime stories told with a sensational slant. The New Journalism and the sensational yellow journalism of the 1880s and 1890s, practiced especially by the newspapers of Joseph Pulitzer and William Randolph Hearst, further set the journalistic stage for the tabloids, relying on violence and human interest stories to help boost circulation into the hundreds of thousands.

The factors favoring the growth of the sensational papers of the late nineteenth century were also in place for the success of the tabloids in the early twentieth century. Newspapers had developed the mechanical means to produce and distribute thousands and even millions of copies per day. News accounts became more condensed, written in inverted pyramid style. Headlines grew larger so that hurried readers quickly could glean the news. New forms of amusement competed with the daily newspaper for readers' time, forcing papers to become more entertaining, with more photographs, features, columns, fiction, comic strips, and special departments such as sports, society, and the stage. The growth of large department stores spawned advertising revenue for newspapers. Production costs soared with the price of newsprint, and publishers searched for higher circulation.

The successful British tabloids of the early twentieth century presented the solution, even though Pulitzer and Hearst – the most likely press lords to do so – were reluctant to bring the tabloid to the United States. By 1909, the *Daily Mirror* of Alfred Harmsworth (Lord Northcliffe) was selling a million copies a day in Britain and on the Continent. Soon, imitators sprang up in London. Harmsworth told Joseph Patterson, publisher of the *Chicago Tribune,* that if he did not start a tabloid in the United States, Harmsworth would.

The *Illustrated Daily News* – published by Patterson and his cousin Robert R. McCormick – rolled off the press for the first time on June 26, 1919, as a morning tabloid for two cents a copy. The first issue featured a half-page photo story on the prince of Wales, who was scheduled to visit the United States; the paper's own beauty contest; a detective series; and short personality stories. The editorial promised that the *News* was the readers' paper, that it would print only interesting stories and the best features, and that it would never jump a story. Although circulation was modest at first, within two years, the *Daily News* ("Illustrated" was quickly dropped) had a circulation of 400,000 – the largest in New York – and by 1938, its daily circulation was 1,750,000, and its Sunday edition had a circulation of 3,250,000.

Daily News readers received more than tales of the bizarre. They received a condensed, simplified, and entertaining version of the news; the feature-filled pages with large headlines, photographs, and other illustrations had room only for a brief summary of the day's news. Readers, however, received extensive coverage and sensationalized treatment of such events as Rudolph Valentino's death ("VALENTINO POISONED Broadway Hears Doctors Deny"), Charles Lindbergh's solo Atlantic flight, and murderer Ruth Snyder's death in the electric chair. Readers bought a million extra copies of that edition, with its retouched photo of Snyder as the electric current raged through her body. A *News* photographer had snapped the infamous picture with a hidden camera attached to his leg. The *News* reported gossip about the rich and famous, oddities, sex, crime, and sex and crime ("QUADRANGLE OF LOVE SHRINKS TO TRIANGLE"). Although aware that tabloids appealed to the masses, Patterson sought a middle ground for the *News* – definitely not highbrow, but not too lowbrow either. In 1924, Hearst started New York's second tabloid, the *Daily Mirror,* proclaiming it to be the voice of the people and promising "90 percent entertainment, 10 percent information – and the information without boring you." The *Mirror* gave even less space to serious news and more to crime and sport. Circulation grew to 600,000 in 1937 with the help of celebrity columnists such as Walter Winchell, but it failed to become a very profitable enterprise and finally closed in 1963.

The *New York Evening Graphic,* introduced in 1924 by Bernarr Macfadden, was called "the new black plague" and "the worst form of debauchery to which a daily newspaper has ever been subjected" by critics. Unlike the *Daily News* and *Daily Mirror,* the *Graphic* carried no standard news, specializing in crime stories, pictures of scantily clothed women, and stories of the weird and bizarre. The *Graphic* developed the "composograph," a staged photo of "real life" scenes. One showed Valentino on the operating table, the attending doctor and nurses looking remarkably like certain *Graphic* staffers. The *Graphic*'s circulation grew to 350,000 by 1929, but it failed to receive advertising support in the more sober 1930s and folded in 1932. However, it planted the seed for the supermarket tabloids of the latter half of the century.

Tabloids flourished in other cities, and by 1937, 49 tabloids were being published with a combined circulation of 3,525,000. Among them were the *Chicago Times,* the *Boston Record,* the *Philadelphia News,* the *New Orleans (Louisiana) Tribune,* the *Los Angeles Daily News,* the *Washington (D.C.) News,* and later, the *Chicago Sun-Times,* the *New York Post,* and *Newsday,* on Long Island. Tabloids became more respectable in the 1930s with the more somber times. Advertisers found the *Daily News* even more appealing with its coverage of more serious national and foreign news after 1930, although it still featured gossipy stories. It even won a Pulitzer Prize in 1936 for a series on syphilis.

The national tabloids, found often in supermarkets in the 1980s and 1990s, sprang from many of the elements of the 1920s tabloids. The *National Enquirer,* founded in 1926 as a broadsheet, was purchased in 1952 by Generoso Pope, who turned a 7,000-circulation tabloid into perhaps the most successful tabloid of all time. By 1968, its circulation of 1 million thrived on stories of murders, accidents, mysteries, bizarre tales, and celebrity gossip. Pope made the paper a weekly that did not cover fast-breaking news, and he targeted supermarkets and drugstores for sales. In the 1970s, the *Enquirer* went through a "clean" decade, dropping much of the gore and featuring unusual human-interest stories, pop psychology, and flattering celebrity stories.

The *Star,* launched in color in 1974 by Australian tabloid king Rupert Murdoch, emphasized a circus layout and steamy prose. Later, the *Star* focused on more celebrity coverage, battling for readers with the *Enquirer* in television commercials ("Enquiring Minds Want to Know"). By 1990, the Pope group bought the *Star* for $400 million. Murdoch introduced in 1980 the *World Weekly World News,* which brought even more bizarre happenings – UFO sightings, two-headed aliens – to U.S. grocery lines. Globe Communications, beginning in 1954, built a tabloid collection, including the *National Examiner,* the *Globe,* and the *Sun.*

Unlike the daily news tabloids, the national weekly tabloids made no pretense of covering the news. Much of the content related to miracle diets, pseudoscience, miraculous births, the occult, sex scandals, and celebrity gossip. Readers followed talk show host Oprah Winfrey's yo-yo weight fluctuations, read the scandalous inside poop on the rape trial of William Kennedy Smith and the murder trial of O.J. Simpson, and learned the intimate details of the private lives of presidential candidate Gary Hart and President Bill Clinton.

At the end of the twentieth century, supermarket tabloids were considered trashy, sensational, and sleazy. Libraries ignored them, but many millions of people did not. Some scholars who studied the tabloids concluded that they continued the tradition begun in the 1920s of giving readers a way to deal with the complexities of life by simplifying it, ordering it, and making sense of it with dramatic stories. Tabloid readers are often people with little real power who are made to feel empowered, in control, by knowing the "untold story" about a celebrity's romance or a government official's indiscretion, about the tales of sin and woe that have befallen famous people and, to a lesser extent, common people who have been more unfortunate than the readers. The tabloids were designed to quicken the pulse of people locked in humdrum lives, at the same time reassuring them that the world remained fairly constant from day to day and week to week.

The *New York Evening Graphic* was noted for its "composographs" in which staff members and others reenacted newsworthy scenes such as this hanging.
(Davis Library, University of North Carolina at Chapel Hill)

ELIZABETH LYNNE FLOCKE

See also New Journalism (1880s); Penny Press; Sensationalism; Yellow Journalism

Further Reading
Bessie, Simon Michael, *Jazz Journalism: The Story of the Tabloid Newspapers*, New York: Dutton, 1938
Bird, S. Elizabeth, *For Enquiring Minds: A Cultural Study of Supermarket Tabloids*, Knoxville: University of Tennessee Press, 1992
Chapman, John, *Tell It to Sweeney: The Informal History of the 'New York Daily News'*, Garden City, New York: Doubleday, 1961
Murphy, James E., "Tabloids as an Urban Response," in *Mass Media Between the Wars: Perceptions of Cultural Tension, 1918–1941*, edited by Catherine L. Covert and John D. Stevens, Syracuse, New York: Syracuse University Press, 1984
Stevens, John D., *Sensationalism and the New York Press*, New York: Columbia University Press, 1991

Technology

Media developments claim worldwide heritage

Communication is central to human development. Many societies have contributed developments that coalesced into the mass media of the late twentieth century – television, radio, cable, newspapers, magazines, commercial films, and other words or images that could be distributed by computer satellite hookup.

The Chinese contributed playing cards, the Phoenicians and Egyptians developed language and writing materials, and the Romans posted regular information during the days of the empire. In the 1440s, a German printer, Johannes Gutenberg, put together a printing press using metal printing blocks. Soon, printing spread throughout much of western Europe. England's William Caxton printed books by 1477.

The printing press, one of the most revolutionary inventions in human history, democratized information by making books and other printed products available to people of all social and economic ranks. For centuries, books were handwritten, treasured, and kept in cloistered places, such as monasteries. Printing allowed a single set of type to create many impressions. By the 1620s, a few printers were producing cheap news sheets, called corantos, for sale, and by 1665, a British printer produced a regularly published newspaper, the *Oxford Gazette*.

Printing influenced history. Books showed that communication technology can alter culture in ways no one can anticipate. Historian Elizabeth Eisenstein found that books led to pressures for standardization in style and a decline in the use of mnemonic aids, based on rhyme and cadence, to commit information from manuscripts to memory. This might, perhaps, have been anticipated.

Less anticipated was that the very process of standardization made individuals stand out from norms and even gave rise to a cult of personality far more than could have been supported in a manuscript age. Expansion of the book market resulted in books for particular audiences – for example, women's and children's books. Students could learn far more from books than they could from listening to teachers who read from ancient manuscripts and copying it down. Whereas rare manuscript books brought people together to hear them read, printed books eventually separated people into private mental compartments. Freed from having to copy earlier detailed observations, scientists found far more time to observe the heavens, the oceans, and Earth, including the humans that populated it.

There were social implications. When writers staked out positions in print, it was hard to retreat, generating battles with books. Cheap paper resulted in more personal correspondence, more printed sermons, copybooks, notebooks, and – eventually – newspapers and magazines. With the earliest printing, patterns emerged that often were replicated with newspapers, magazines, film, radio, and television.

In colonial America, newspapers proved important engines of propaganda as patriots such as Sam Adams and Isaiah Thomas used words to incite followers. Pamphlets, such as the one containing Thomas Paine's stirring "These are the Times that Try Men's Souls," often reached sales of 100,000 or more. Meanwhile, almanacs lay on farmers' shelves for fireside reading for decades, filled with literary stories, calendar information about planting, or political essays. The words of leading ministers, such as Massachusetts's Jonathan Edwards, could reach far beyond the pulpit in pamphlet form.

The significance of developments is not always evident to those in the period. Historian Arthur Schlesinger credited newspapers as a major revolutionary force in the eighteenth century, writing that revolutions are in the hearts and minds, rather than on the battlefield. Political scientist Richard Merritt found that the press reflected a sense of growing national community from 1735 to 1775, as newspapers became far more likely to use words of local reference, such as "governor," than of foreign reference, such as "king."

Presses operated by a steam engine were developed in the early nineteenth century in England. In the United States, Robert Hoe and his son Richard began production of improved cylinder steam presses. The steam press allowed newspapers to escape the limits of human strength, a development so important that it might be considered a shift in kind rather than degree. In the same period, cheap methods were found to produce wood-based paper, which displaced paper made with cloth or fibers in popular publications such as newspapers and inexpensive books. Because newspapers could reach so many, printers needed to make the content lively and diverse. Penny newspapers established regular patterns of gathering news, called "beats," and employed easy and quick methods of gathering news, such as the interview technique.

Samuel Morse perfected the telegraph and in 1844 transmitted this message between Baltimore, Maryland, and Washington, D.C.: "What Hath God Wrought?" Soon, merchants used the telegraph to learn about prices and engage in trade far beyond the local communities. Telegraph lines followed railroads west to help control rail traffic. As early as 1846, seven New York newspapers formed the co-operative Associated Press to share costs of gathering and distributing information. Newspapers began to publish from a common source, beginning a trend of content similarity that still held true at the end of the twentieth century.

The telegraph had unanticipated consequences. News came faster and from farther away. In the 1820s, only one of five stories in daily newspapers were about events that had happened within the past three days. In the 1850s, three of every five news stories were about events within the previous three days. The telegraph encouraged writers to keep messages lean because extra words were expensive, and the telegraph line might be disrupted during long messages.

Telegraph stories were short, factual, and shorn of context. The telegraph decontextualized information from its political setting. Historian Dwight Teeter argued that the historical high point of newspaper coverage came in pre-telegraph days, when political stories were put into a political context, sometimes with adjectives. Editors thought it was a duty to put political stories into a context in which the good side could be distinguished from the bad one. Telegraph news did not often take sides.

The telegraph's influence on news generated different historical views. One view is that the telegraph was an important part of the evolving journalistic goal of objectivity. Wire service customers reflected different political parties and presumably did not want their stories written with a slant different from their own. Another historical view is that of sociologist Michael Schudson, who argued that the development of journalistic objectivity was not associated with the telegraph or other technical developments but rather with the emergence in the twentieth century of science with its idea of objective observation. To Schudson, journalism is driven by ideas; to some other scholars, journalism is driven by economics.

Each technological development changed journalism in ways that could not always be anticipated. By the 1870s, the typewriter had developed sufficiently for newsrooms to take on a noisy tone that lasted until the quieter modern computer era. The same decade saw use of the telephone and the appearance of the rewrite journalist, who took information by phone and seldom visited news sites. Journalists conducted phone interviews. By 1879, camera images could be translated crudely onto a newspaper page, thereby ending the well-established role of sketch artists, who had illustrated Civil War battles. In 1886, Ottmar Mergenthaler, a German, introduced his Linotype – a machine that could cast metal type line by line. Back shop production time was cut by approximately half.

In the 1890s, experiments with moving images attracted attention. In 1903, many saw the 12-minute film *The Great Train Robbery*. In 1915, *The Birth of a Nation*, D.W. Griffith's film about southern race relations, caused riots in some cities. Where newspapers and magazines started with elites – upper income and educated individuals who could read – film started on the other end of the social spectrum and evolved toward the middle class. By the 1920s, the final years of silent film, about 40 million people went to movies each week. The first sound experiment, a segment

THE RISE & FALL OF AMERICAN MASS MEDIA

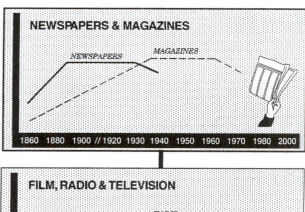

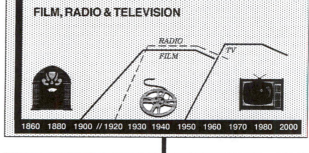

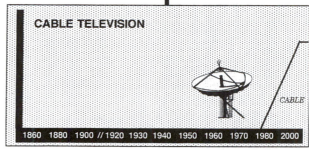

Figure 1
(Graphic by Bradley Hamm)

in *The Jazz Singer* in 1927, was so successful that all films carried sound by 1934, and many were in color. Silent film died, showing how one technology can displace or transform another.

By the 1920s, disk recordings enabled people to hear segments of famous concert singers, such as opera tenor Enrico Caruso. Commercial radio in the same decade allowed listeners to hear Caruso in concert. David Sarnoff founded the National Broadcasting Company (NBC) in 1926, and William Paley was the pioneer behind the Columbia Broadcasting System (CBS) in 1927. By the time President Franklin Roosevelt used radio for a series of "fireside chats" after his 1933 inauguration, during the early days of the Great Depression, radio had permeated U.S. politics. Political party power began to decline as political leaders learned to use the media to speak directly to large audiences. That decline continued throughout the century.

Radio and film demonstrated the power to reach millions and to shape emotions. In the 1930s, these technological developments could be used to uplift the masses in times of trouble, as with Roosevelt's chats or with a powerful message from Prime Minister Winston Churchill, who encouraged British citizens to stay the course during the dark days of World War II by saying in tribute to British airmen, "never have so many owed so much to so few."

Few developments can parallel the influence of television. It was known in the 1920s that pictures, like sound, could be sent by airwaves, but World War II delayed the development of television, a medium that interested people at the World's Fair in New York in 1939. By 1948, there were 108 stations, then the Federal Communications Commission stopped issuing licenses for about four years until some technical issues could be resolved. Soon, commercial television took off. By the end of the 1950s, there were approximately 510 commercial television stations, most of which were affiliated with three networks, NBC and CBS, both from radio, and the new American Broadcasting Company (ABC), created in 1945.

In the 1950s, audiences grew as television spread. Popular programs such as *I Love Lucy,* with actress Lucille Ball, drew close to 70 percent of prime-time viewers. Soon other media felt the effects. Network radio went into decline as prime-time audiences and advertisers jumped to television. Radio experimented, shifting more to the higher-quality sound of FM, while AM stations experimented with various programs and eventually became a major medium for "talk" radio. By the 1990s, nearly everyone heard radio at some point each day, especially in cars, and the power of some radio talk show hosts, such as political conservative Rush Limbaugh, had reached great levels with segments of the audience.

Magazines felt the impact of television. Magazines about movie stars in the 1950s were hard hit in terms of declining circulation. Other long-standing magazines, such as *Collier's* (started in 1888) and the *Saturday Evening Post* (1821), retained audiences but lost advertisers. Some magazines succeeded. Magazine innovator Henry Luce, cofounder of *Time* in 1923, started *Sports Illustrated* in 1954 and achieved success, perhaps because television increased interest in sports. Other major magazines failed. Luce's experiment with a magazine based heavily on photographs, *Life,* begun in 1936, died in 1972 (although it was revived later as a monthly), while a competitor, *Look,* founded in 1937, closed in 1971. *Collier's* died in 1956; the *Saturday Evening Post* died in the late 1960s, although it was revived as both a quarterly and monthly publication.

Films began a decline even before television diffused widely. More people went to see films in 1946–47, the postwar years just before television exploded into nearly all homes. Like all media confronted with competition for audience or advertising revenues, films fought back. In the 1950s, Hollywood produced films such as *The Ten Commandments,* directed by Cecil B. DeMille, that captured a big-screen drama impossible for television. Films such as the 1954 *On the Waterfront,* with Marlon Brando and Rod Steiger, explored themes that, then, were taboo on television, where most programs were either happy-ending stories or predictably dramatic detective or western programs. In the 1950s, drive-in theaters made it easy to put the kids in pajamas, put them in the car, and take them to the movies. Theaters developed huge screens, and some film makers experimented with three-dimensional action. Yet none of

this kept people going to see films. Attendance, with ups and downs, dropped steadily from the late 1940s to the late 1990s, although increases in admissions prices cushioned the economic effects of declining audiences.

In July 1962, the United States hoisted *Telstar,* its first successful commercial satellite, a development that, along with the transistor, revolutionized communication transmission. As satellites began to fill the appropriate spots in the skies, the economics of information transfer changed. With the telegraph, telephone, and ocean cable, it was more difficult and, therefore, more expensive to send messages over long distances. With satellites, distance became nearly irrelevant because the cost of sending a telephone message is about the same whether the distance traveled was 6 miles, 600 miles, or 6,000 miles.

Transistors replaced vacuum tubes in radios and televisions, and receivers could be made small and inexpensive. Whereas family members once huddled around a single radio or television receiver, individuals came to use personal receivers in their own rooms or cars. An explosion of FM radio stations provided much choice of music, while AM radio provided a wide range of public service and talk programs. Via satellites, cable television provided the same wide choices on television receivers. Innovator Ted Turner was a pioneer in using cable to send news (on the cable channels CNN and Headline News) and entertainment programs (on TBS and TNT). The direction of communication technology is always toward enlargement of choice.

Newspaper innovator Al Neuharth of the Gannett Newspaper Group founded a national newspaper, *USA Today,* in 1982. Using satellites to send ready-to-print pages to printing shops around the nation, *USA Today* soon reached much of the nation (and other countries as well). Technology could be used to help older media adjust to changes in audience and advertiser tastes.

There is a limit on how much news, entertainment, and advertising information audiences want, just as there is a limit to how much food one can eat in a given day. Charles E. Scripps of the Scripps-Howard newspaper group concluded in the late 1950s that media audiences and advertisers together accounted for about 5 percent of the gross national product. That figure held steady for about 50 years, in contrast with expenditures for health care, which exploded during the last two decades of the century, from about 5 percent to around 14 percent of the gross national product. The health care field was growing, while the traditional mass media were not.

The logical conclusion is this: If expenditures for mass media are relatively fixed, a new medium takes away from an older medium, as magazines took audiences and advertisers from newspapers. Television took audiences from film, and both audiences and advertising from radio. The mass media have natural life cycles, from birth and youth through adulthood to declining age. Figure 1 sketches one argument for several media.

Characteristic of the media in Figure 1 is that each mass medium achieved high circulation and that there were relatively few mass media. Daily newspapers achieved their highest point of audience approval and use in the 1920s and 1930s, when individuals read an average of about one and a half newspapers per day. In the late 1990s, only about one half of the population read a daily newspaper. The highest number of dailies published in the nation was before World War I, when there were about 2,600. Late in the twentieth century, there were about 1,600. The number of daily newspapers declined an average of one per month in about the last 70 years of the century. Afternoon daily newspapers played an important part in U.S. history and were themselves becoming history. Film drew the most people in the late 1940s, a period when network radio also gleaned most of the prime-time audience. Commercial television began an audience decline in the early 1980s, partly as a result of competition from cable television. For years NBC, CBS, and ABC dominated television, but their slice of the prime-time audience in the 1990s was less than two-thirds what it was in the 1950s. Cable television reached about 60 percent of U.S. homes in the late 1990s and was thought by some to have reached the limit of its audience unless cable operators could provide a diversity of services that could not be delivered through small-dish home satellite receivers.

The mass media were most powerful during the period 1930–80, years in which daily newspapers held their own in circulation and also in which film, radio, and television achieved their highest period of audience usage in attendance or prime-time usage. In this period, those at the top of political, economic, and social structures were more likely to be able to control the types of information that flowed down the triangle because there were few mass media, relatively speaking, and also a limited number of news sources.

In Germany, Adolf Hitler and his Nazi party showed the chilling power of the state to influence masses of people once the messages were limited and controlled at the top and the competition of alternative messages at the bottom was cut off. In those days, telephones and telegraphs were available to ordinary citizens, but these instruments are relatively easily controlled. The mass media fit democracies such as the United States and England well, but the mass media clearly fit totalitarian states as well. The eras of the dictatorship of Germany's Hitler and the Soviet Union's Joseph Stalin – the most powerful and destructive dictatorships of modern times – fit completely with the era of mass media, 1930 to 1980. When new media undermine old media, they undermine the symbiotic relationship between social structures and social information.

In the post 1930–80 mass media era, governing large mass states was considered to be more challenging. Leaders could no longer be assured of the attention of large, accepting audiences. Never before had so many ordinary citizens had access to so many communication opportunities for other points of view. Further, technologies such as electronic mail allowed alliances around interests that ranged from the environment to pornography.

One 1993 book, *The Virtual Community*, described how some people, in effect, traded the place in which they actually lived for a distant, electronically connected virtual community. The spread of communication technology provided leaders with new opportunities to listen, just as it provided opportunities for citizens to speak.

DONALD L. SHAW, BRADLEY J. HAMM

See also Magazine Technology; Motion Picture Technology; Newspaper Technology; Photographic Technology; Radio Technology; Television Technology

Further Reading
Eisenstein, Elizabeth, *The Printing Press as an Agent of Change: Communications and Cultural Transformations in Early Modern Europe,* New York and Cambridge: Cambridge University Press, 1979
Innis, Harold Adams, *Empire and Communications,* Oxford: Clarendon, 1971; Toronto, Ontario: University of Toronto Press, 1972; Buffalo, New York: University of Toronto Press, 1975
McCombs, Maxwell E., "Mass Media in the Marketplace," *Journalism Monographs* 24 (1972)
Merritt, Richard, *Symbols of American Community, 1735–1775,* New Haven, Connecticut: Yale University Press, 1966
Rheingold, Howard, *The Virtual Community: Homesteading on the Electronic Frontier,* Reading, Massachusetts: Addison-Wesley, 1993
Schlesinger, Arthur M., *Prelude to Independence: The Newspaper War on Britain, 1764–1776,* New York: Knopf, 1958
Schudson, Michael, *Discovering the News: A Social History of American Newspapers,* New York: Basic, 1978
Shaw, Donald L., "News Bias and the Telegraph: A Study of Historical Change," *Journalism Quarterly* 44 (1967)

Telegraph

A revolutionary force in U.S. society

When inventor Samuel F.B. Morse relayed a tidbit of news to a Baltimore, Maryland, newspaper while testing the telegraph on May 24, 1844, few of his contemporaries likely realized how Morse's apparatus would revolutionize society. The telegraph was to become a vital communication link for commerce and industry and a major force in shaping the nation's burgeoning mass media system. Most notably, telegraphy would be a preferred form of communication for over a century.

Telegraph companies sprang up almost immediately as investors hungrily eyed the medium's potential. One enterprise, founded in 1851 as the New York and Mississippi Valley Printing Telegraph Company, dedicated itself to establishing nationwide service. In 1856, after changing its name to Western Union, the company acquired smaller systems to mold a more effective unified network of cables, which finally culminated with the completion of a line that linked the west coast with the rest of the nation in 1861. Western Union became a communications monolith, enjoying a virtual monopoly in the telegraph business. Only one firm, the Postal Telegraphy Company, founded in 1881 by inventor Elisha Gray, provided any degree of competition with Western Union in the telegraphic messaging business.

Telegraph offices were indispensable in the nineteenth-century United States.
(Reproduced from the Collections of the Library of Congress)

But Postal, which was not affiliated with the U.S. Post Office, never achieved more than 17 percent of the market. (The company was finally absorbed by Western Union in 1943.)

Telegraphy became the lifeblood of domestic and overseas news dissemination. In 1849, a consortium of New York newspaper publishers financed a system for collecting international news from European vessels arriving in New York and, in turn, forwarding the information to subscribing newspapers via telegraph. The Harbor News Association was the forerunner of the Associated Press, a name adopted in the 1860s, when an expanding nationwide network of telegraph cables enabled newspapers in all regions to share news dispatches. The telegraph continued to be the link between newspapers and the Associated Press, United Press, and the International News Service until the advent of the teletype in the 1930s.

Western Union maintained a Commercial News Division (CND) in Chicago that specialized in furnishing subscribers with up-to-the-minute commodity news and sports reports. Information could be received on tickers (machines that printed information directly on paper tape), through direct messages (that is, providing requested information via telegram), or over a special circuit installed in the subscriber's place of business, which required a telegrapher to receive and translate the information. The service was offered to a variety of clients, including newspapers, brokers, boards of trade, and advertising agencies. Baseball and football stadiums depended on the CND's sports ticker service to provide scores from other games in progress around the nation. An additional service called Paragraph One provided play-by-play accounts from baseball and football games and other sports events, which were sold on a subscription basis to newspapers and, oddly enough, radio stations, who used Western Union accounts as the basis of studio-produced dramatizations of baseball games, otherwise known as re-creations.

Qualified telegraph operators were in great demand in this era. Young men and women trained in sending and receiving Morse code found almost immediate employment

---

The Annihilation of Space

MAGNETIC TELEGRAM – The new invention is complete from Baltimore to Washington. The wire, perfectly secured against the weather by a covering of rope yarn and tar, is conducted on the top of posts about twenty feet high and one hundred yards apart. The nominations of the convention this day (Democratic national) are to be conveyed to Washington by this telegraph, where they will arrive in a few seconds. . . . At half past 11 A.M. the question being asked, what was the news at Washington, the answer was almost instantaneously returned: "Van Buren Stock is rising." This is indeed the annihilation of space!

New York Sun, May 27, 1844

Western Union Telegraph Company – Summary of Telegraph Offices, Miles of Wire, and Messages Handled: 1866–1895
(in thousands, except for telegraph offices)

Year	Offices	Miles of Wire	Messages	Year	Offices	Miles of Wire	Messages
1866	2,250	76		1881	10,737	327	32,500
1867	2,565	85	5,879	1882	12,068	374	38,842
1868	3,219	98	6,405	1883	12,917	433	41,181
1869	3,607	105	7,935	1884	13,761	451	42,076
1870	3,972	112	9,158	1885	14,184	462	42,097
1871	4,606	121	10,646	1886	15,142	490	43,290
1872	5,237	137	12,444	1887	15,658	525	47,395
1873	5,740	154	14,457	1888	17,241	616	51,464
1874	6,188	176	16,329	1889	18,470	648	54,108
1875	6,565	179	17,154	1890	19,382	679	55,879
1876	7,072	184	18,730	1891	20,098	716	59,148
1877	7,500	194	21,159	1892	20,700	739	62,387
1878	8,014	206	23,919	1893	21,078	769	66,592
1879	8,534	212	25,007	1894	21,166	791	58,632
1880	9,077	234	29,216	1895	21,360	803	58,307

Source: U.S. Bureau of the Census, *Historical Statistics of the United States: Colonial Times to 1957* (Washington, D.C.: GPO, 1960).

with telegraph companies, railroads, or various industries with a vital need for instantaneous information. It was not unusual for stockbrokers to employ a staff of telegraph operators to send and receive commodity information. Newspapers employed press telegraphers (called brass pounders) to receive incoming news accounts from press services and reporters.

Technology gradually eroded the dominance of the telegraph as the preferred tool of communication in the United States. The teletype, which was a more efficient way of sending messages, news, and other information, was phased in throughout the 1930s and 1940s; consequently, thousands of Morse telegraphers lost their jobs. Most of the nation had dependable telephone service by the 1950s, which meant that Western Union eventually would be forced to leave the message-handling business. The company valiantly fought to exist by expanding into other types of communication services. In April 1990, however, Western Union was dissolved, and a new company, Western Union Businesses Group, continued to offer money transfers, airline reservations, and check-cashing services.

STEVEN SMETHERS

See also Associated Press; Cooperative News Gathering

Further Reading

Coe, Lewis B., "Telegraph Companies Have Come to the End of the Line," *Antique Week* (August 14, 1989)
Smethers, J. Steven, and Lee B. Jolliffe, "The Partnership of Telegraphy and Radio in 'Re-creating' Events for Broadcast," *Journal of Radio Studies* 1 (1991)

Television and Violence

Debate of medium's influence spans television's history

During the time that television has been a part of the U.S. cultural landscape, perhaps no single aspect of commercial broadcasting has generated as much public concern, scientific interest, and political debate as the issue of violent programming content. Fears over the possible effects of exposure to its often-violent content have guided literally thousands of studies of television messages, inspired numerous attempts to regulate broadcast content, and led television violence to become one of the most complex and controversial media-related social issues of the second half of the twentieth century.

Formal research on mass media "effects" began well before the initial introduction of television into the United States. As early as the 1920s, social scientists attempted to determine if a correlation existed between exposure to specific mass media messages and subsequent effects on attitudes and patterns of behavior.

The Payne Fund Studies (1929), part of the first large-scale series of scientific media effects research, sought to examine the effects of viewing motion picture images on adolescent and child audience attitudes and behavior. Researchers speculated that young audiences potentially were being "corrupted" by inappropriate or antisocial themes prevalent in movies of the era. The preliminary findings of the studies appeared to support this hypothesis, suggesting that exposure to particular film images did, in fact, influence some younger viewers in certain ways.

A succession of other studies also provided early support for the notion of possible effects associated with exposure to mass media. Research on reactions to Orson Welles's "War of the Worlds" radio broadcast (1938), on voter attitudes in Erie County, Ohio, following a mass-mediated political campaign (1940), on persuasive films used to educate U.S. soldiers during World War II (1942), and on the effects of reading comic books on juvenile delinquency (early 1950s) all concluded that exposure to media messages can influence attitudes, perceptions, and behaviors of some audience members under certain conditions.

The results of many of these early media effects studies were later reviewed by the scientific community because of questionable interpretations of data and methodological flaws. Nevertheless, they made important initial contributions toward understanding the possible link between media exposure and subsequent attitudinal and behavioral effects. By the time television began to grow as a commercial entity in the late 1940s and early 1950s, researchers already were suggesting that previous effects findings with other media also would apply to television.

From its inception, television was considered a rather violent medium, as a multitude of early successful programs contained graphic depictions of violence. Media research had yet to explore the specific effects of viewing violence, and the new medium was besieged immediately by public and political criticism over its reliance on violent imagery as a major narrative content element. These violent portrayals also coincided with increases during the early 1950s in domestic youth crime and delinquency. Political leaders were quick to accuse television of contributing to the rising juvenile crime rate, and by 1952, Tennessee senator Estes Kefauver had convened hearings to address the possible connection between television and societal violence.

Behavioral scientists Paul Lazersfeld and Eleanor Macoby, who had conducted previous research on radio and film effects, used the hearings to call for research in the area of the effects of television violence. Citing previous findings with other media to implicate television in affecting behaviors, they reached conclusions that added fuel to the growing debate over the issue of regulating broadcasting to protect impressionable viewers from its content and helped to inspire several future generations of television violence studies.

At the time of the inaugural congressional television hearings, preliminary research findings seemed likely to spark legislative action on the issue of television violence. However, federal officials soon discovered that any effort to establish restrictive content-based regulation of commercial television would be met with strong resistance from the television industry.

In 1952, industry leaders had established a "television code" as a means of self-regulation, assuring regulators that the code's guidelines would compel broadcasters to create higher-quality programming. Although the code eventually proved to be ineffective and virtually unenforceable, the promise of self-regulation allowed the industry to fend off proposed government-imposed content restrictions.

The practice of self-regulation also was supplemented later by other preemptive measures, including promises to conduct further research on media effects, vigorous campaigns to discredit research findings that linked television violence to societal violence, and constitutional arguments to defend against government "censorship" of programming content. Together with self-imposed regulations, the combination of promises, challenges, and First Amendment posturing created a difficult barrier for federal legislators to overcome in their ongoing efforts to compel the industry to improve broadcast content.

In the 1960s, societal violence escalated amid a violent television landscape, and researchers identified more concrete links between exposure to violent media and violent behavior. Wilbur Schramm, Lyle, and Parker completed a landmark three year study of television's effects on children in 1961. The researchers observed television viewing habits and subsequent behavior patterns and found indications that *some* television may be harmful to *some* children, under *some* conditions.

In 1963, Albert Bandura at Stanford University examined the effects of viewing aggressive behavior in media portrayals on a group of nursery school children. In his "Bobo doll" experiment, Bandura found that some young children exposed to media portrayals of aggressive behavior were more likely to imitate the aggressive acts when the acts were rewarded and the children were already in a previously frustrated state. Bandura referred to the reactions as behavior "modeling" or "social learning," in support of his theory that media portrayals of violence and aggression could lead to real-life violence through imitation.

Shortly after Bandura's study, Leonard Berkowitz (1964) explored exposure to media violence among college students at the University of Wisconsin. Students were exposed to a film sequence of a brutal beating and then were asked to administer an electronic shock to a human subject each time the subject gave an inaccurate answer to a test question. Berkowitz found that when those administering the shocks were told that the televised beating was "justified," they were more likely to increase the voltage of the shock they believed they were delivering to the subjects. Berkowitz concluded that violent media depictions provide "aggressive cues," which under certain circumstances may "prime" some audience members to emulate the acts. He used his findings to advance the "neo-association" theory, which posited that certain media portrayals may trigger short-term similar reactions among some viewers. Although the Bandura and Berkowitz studies measured behavior only in experimental settings, both clearly indicated that media violence contributed to increased aggressiveness or hostility among some participants in two different age groups.

The increasing evidence of a correlation between media violence and societal violence, coupled with an extended period of domestic social unrest, led to action in the late 1960s. Following the assassinations of Martin Luther King Jr. and Robert Kennedy in 1968, President Lyndon Johnson formed the National Commission on the Causes and Prevention of Violence. As part of the 15 volume study on violence and society, the commission examined available research on media violence and in 1969 concluded that violence was predominant on television and that media violence should be of concern – especially with regard to children.

This report was followed by additional hearings attended by Surgeon General J. Stewart. Stewart declared television violence a public health issue and approved $1 million in funds for continued research by the National Institute of Mental Health (NIMH). This ultimately led to the creation of the Surgeon General's Scientific Advisory Committee on Television and Social Behavior. The Advisory Committee examined the issue of television violence from a public health perspective and concluded in a five-volume 1972 report that television violence may influence some children in varying ways, may lead to aggressive behavior in certain children, and may be considered harmful to young viewers.

The growing body of research and political attention to the issue of television violence in the late 1960s and early 1970s led to renewed demands for regulation of broadcast content. Legislators strongly urged television industry leaders to address the violence issue in order to avert government intervention. Once again, the industry promised increased self-regulation and enacted the Family Viewing Policy (1974) to encourage broadcasters to air more family-oriented programming. This move allowed the industry to continue to hold legislators at bay, although, in the long run, the voluntary nature of the policy left it unenforceable and led to its abolition in the early 1980s.

Along with ongoing research on the behavioral effects of viewing television violence, the increased public and political attention to the television violence issue during the late 1960s spawned the additional area of violence effects research. As part of the federally funded research exploring media violence effects, George Gerbner at the University of Pennsylvania began to explore the notion that television violence may also increase feelings of fear among some viewers.

Gerbner began a systematic content analysis of U.S. television programming in 1967 to measure television violence levels and assess yearly trends in violent program content. By the mid-1970s, Gerbner began to theorize that television violence may not only lead to aggression, it may also "cultivate" certain feelings about the outside world. Gerbner conducted a series of "cultivation analyses" that correlated perceptions of social reality with amount of television viewing. He found that heavier viewers of television perceived the outside world to be closely related to the television world and that heavy viewers believed the world to be a much more violent and hostile place than lighter viewers. Gerbner dubbed this finding the "mean world effect." He also found that other consistent themes ubiquitous on U.S. television may influence perceptions of heavier-viewing audience members. Gerbner labeled this effect "mainstreaming."

Other research in the 1970s also helped to generate new theories of television-related effects. Drabman and Thomas (1974) pioneered efforts to explore the possibility that exposure to media violence could desensitize viewers and leave them less responsive to real-world violence and the plight of victims of actual violence. Zillmann and Tannenbaum (1975) advanced the theory of "arousal and excitation transfer" and suggested that media depictions of aggression may leave audience members momentarily in a heightened state of physical arousal that could provoke or contribute to aggressive behaviors. Pingree, Collins, and others (1973–86) added that media effects appear to be mitigated through a variety of individual variables, leading to differing reactions for different audience members based on their individual experiences and resulting perceptions.

The theories and findings encountered criticism. Some scholars argued that the research results were achieved in artificial situations and therefore could not be extrapolated to predict real-world behavior. Some critics raised additional questions regarding the validity of the approaches adopted and interpretations of relevant data, and others maintained that television violence did not contribute to violent behavior. Several researchers, led by Seymour Feshbach (1971), even suggested that exposure to media violence may have a cathartic effect on some viewers, reducing the need to act violently or aggressively.

One of the stronger arguments against earlier findings was that they did not account for the fact that those predisposed to violent behavior may simply gravitate toward more violent programming. Eron, Lefkowitz, and Huesman (1972, 1986), Singer and Singer (1980), and Milavsky (1982) examined long-term patterns of television viewing and subsequent violent behavior among large groups of children and found indications that exposure to media violence may, in fact, be a precursor to violent behavior for some subjects. Several of these studies were also cross-cultural in nature, indicating that the effects of viewing media violence may be universal.

As the 1980s began, television violence research continued to expand as scientists explored a variety of new perspectives on the effects of exposure to media. But despite ever-increasing scientific interest in, and understanding of, the television violence issue, political interest in the issue decreased steadily with the start of the Ronald Reagan administration and its policy of deregulation. Several proposed regulatory policies that would have either limited objectionable programming or mandated increases in children's television offerings were struck down for being overly restrictive. These decisions, condemned by some legislators, ultimately gave the television industry increased latitude in determining what types of programming were suitable for airing.

Although the political tide had turned against violence effects advocates during the 1980s, evidence on the impact of exposure to television violence continued to mount. Nearly 10 years after the original Surgeon General's report, a follow-up report released by the NIMH (1982) concluded that violence was ubiquitous on U.S. television, that viewing this violence may contribute to aggressive behavior in some viewers, and that viewing violence may have other, more wide-ranging effects.

In addition to the NIMH report, several large-scale studies explored the sociological impact of television's introduction into selected communities within the United States and abroad. In 1982, Karen Hennigan at Northwestern University examined crime-rate fluctuations in selected U.S. cities before and after the introduction of television. The investigation revealed that particular types of crime showed significant increases in selected cities after television was introduced. Hennigan concluded that the results likely were due to feelings of deprivation left by television portrayals of wealth and material possessions and possibly were due to social learning of violent behavior depicted in programming.

The Hennigan study was followed by two other societal-level investigations – one conducted by Tannis Williams in Canada and another by Brandon Centerwall in the United States, Canada, and South Africa. In the Williams study, researchers analyzed the comparative behavior patterns of children in three Canadian towns, finding that aggressive behavior increased significantly among some children within two years after the introduction of television. Centerwall analyzed homicide rates in the three countries during a 30-year period before and after the introduction of television, finding that homicide rates increased dramatically in all three countries approximately 15 years after television became readily available. He concluded that this increase probably represented the time it took for one generation of television viewers to become young adults.

Also during the 1980s, Donnerstein, Malamouth, and others (1980–84) examined the effects of exposure to violent pornographic images on male audience members and found that the portrayals appeared to increase insensitivity toward females who had been victims of physical assaults. Cantor, Hoffner, Sparks, and others (1984–87) studied fear reactions to media depictions among children and found that in all age groups, children may be affected emotionally by violent images and characterizations.

The issue of television violence effects returned to the top of the political agenda in the early 1990s, as steady increases in juvenile violence raised public concern and inspired renewed calls for legislative action. In 1993, the Surgeon General's Committee stated that the "causal" link between television violence and violent behavior warranted immediate action. Shortly thereafter, Congress threatened that government intervention was justified and would be initiated if the broadcasting industry did not do more to address the violence issue. The television industry quickly reacted, agreeing to launch an extensive antiviolence programming campaign and to fund several studies of television content.

Not satisfied that the industry's response would lead to any significant improvements, political leaders also pushed to enact new regulatory policies designed to combat the proliferation of violent programming without infringing on the First Amendment rights of broadcasters. After several previous failed attempts to enact an effective children's television act during the 1980s, renewed efforts in the 1990s culminated in an agreement that called for increases in educational programming oriented toward younger audiences. Additionally, a "V-chip" policy designed to allow parents to block out excessively violent or objectionable television programming was approved by Congress and signed into law by President Bill Clinton in 1996.

GREGORY MAKRIS

See also Broadcast Ratings; Decency Issues in Electronic Media

Further Reading

Baker, Robert K., David L. Lange, and Sandra Ball-Rokeach, *Mass Media and Violence: A Report to the National Commission on the Causes and Prevention of Violence,* Washington, D.C.: U.S. Government Printing Office, 1969
Bryant, Jennings, and Dolf Zillmann, *Media Effects: Advances in Theory and Research,* Hillsdale, New Jersey: Lawrence Erlbaum, 1994
_____, eds., *Perspectives on Media Effects,* Hillsdale, New Jersey: Lawrence Erlbaum, 1986
Centerwall, Brandon S., "Television and Violence: The Scale of the Problem and Where to Go from Here," *Journal of the American Medical Association* 267:22 (June 10, 1992), pp. 3059–3063
Comstock, George A., *The Evolution of American Television,* Newbury Park, California: Sage, 1989
Comstock, G., and V.C. Strasburger, "Media Violence Q & A," *Adolescent Medicine: State of the Art Reviews* 4:3 (1003)
Gerbner, George, and L. Gross, "Living with Television: The Violence Profile," *Journal of Communication* 26 (1976)
Lowery, Shearon, and Melvin DeFleur, *Milestones in Mass Communication Research: Media Effects,* New York: Longman, 1988
U.S. Surgeon General's Scientific Advisory Committee on Television and Social Behavior, *Television and Growing Up: The Impact of Televised Violence,* Washington, D.C.: U.S. Government Printing Office, 1972

Television Entertainment

Radio show formats provided early television program models

Television was introduced to the U.S. public by the Radio Corporation of America (RCA) at the New York World's Fair on April 30, 1939. At that time, there were no more than 200 television sets in the New York area. The next day, television sets went on sale in New York department stores, but very few people bought them because they were too expensive and because the television program schedule was so meager, offering only about two hours of programs daily, consisting mainly of sports and vaudeville-type shows.

World War II delayed the growth of television from 1942 until 1945. When the government lifted the ban on new television licenses in 1945, nine television stations were on the air in New York, Los Angeles, Chicago, Philadelphia, and Schenectady, New York, but fewer than 7,000 television sets were in operation. The television networks were eager to begin developing programs, but production proceeded slowly. Sports programs, primarily boxing and wrestling, dominated the schedule.

In those early days of commercial television, many programs were copies of early radio shows with the video added. By 1950, several programs were transplanted to television from radio, including the quiz shows *Truth or Consequences* (1950–51), *Quiz Kids* (1948–52), and *Stop*

Early television shows were broadcast live into the homes of viewers.
(Museum of Broadcast Communications)

the Music (1949–52), and the comedy programs *The Ed Wynn Show* (1949–50), *The Aldrich Family* (1949–53), *The Goldbergs* (1949–54), *The Life of Riley* (1949–51, 1953–58), *Beulah* (1950–53), and *The Burns and Allen Show* (1950–58). Some shows were successful in the transition; most were not.

The 1948–49 season marked the first full prime-time program schedule for the networks. Two very different vaudeville-style shows set the tone for television entertainment for the next few years. The first, *Texaco Star Theatre*, starred Milton Berle, a former radio comedian who found his niche in television doing slapstick vaudeville routines and dressing in drag. This program would top the ratings for the next four years and inspire other comedy-variety shows, including *Your Show of Shows* with Sid Caesar and Imogene Coca (1950–54); *Cavalcade of Stars* (1950–52), which was hosted by various popular comedians; and *The Jackie Gleason Show* (1952–55; 1966–70). The situation comedy *The Honeymooners* (1955–56) began as a skit on *Cavalcade of Stars* when it was hosted by Gleason.

The second influential show, *Toast of the Town*, was hosted by Ed Sullivan, a New York newspaper columnist who had a knack for finding and promoting talented entertainers. On his show, Sullivan introduced Elvis Presley, the Beatles, the comedy team of Dean Martin and Jerry Lewis, and other performers who would become successful in show business. Later, the title of the program was changed to the *Ed Sullivan Show*, which lasted for 23 years (1948–71).

All of these programs were performed live, as were most on early television, with the exception of a few independently filmed programs, such as *The Lone Ranger* or *Hopalong Cassidy*. The major film studios would have nothing to do with television until the mid-1950s, and videotape recording was not invented until the late 1950s. There was a certain excitement and challenge in doing a live television comedy-variety show or a dramatic program that was performed much like a vaudeville or a theatrical performance on stage, but with a close-up camera. Many popular film and television actors and actresses, directors, and writers got their start on live television during the golden age of television drama (1948–58) in anthology series such as *Kraft Television Theatre* (1947–58), *Philco Television Playhouse* (later *Philco-Goodyear Playhouse;* 1948–57), *Westinghouse Studio One* (1948–58), *Armstrong Circle Theater* (1950–63), *U.S. Steel Hour* (1953–63), and *The Hallmark Hall of Fame* (1952–55).

These dramatic anthology series all were produced in New York, which had a tradition of live theater. By the end of the 1950s, television had moved to Hollywood, and few programs were produced live. The exodus began to occur early in the decade when such series as *I Love Lucy* (1951–57) and *Dragnet* (1952–58, 1967–70) were produced on film by independent companies. Lucille Ball and Desi Arnez bought a small studio in Hollywood, which they named Desilu, and began producing the *I Love Lucy* show in front of a live audience. For six years, the show was regularly the top-rated show on television. Its nearest competition was *Dragnet*, produced by and starring Jack Webb as Sergeant Joe Friday of the Los Angeles Police Department. This was the first program that portrayed the police officer as a dedicated public servant whose job was sometimes dangerous but often routine and boring. *Dragnet* became the archetype of the police procedural genre for many years.

The first major film studio to make inroads into television was Disney. In 1954, Disney studios produced *Disneyland* for ABC. Hosted by Walt Disney until his death in 1966, *Disneyland* was not only an advertisement for the recently established "Magic Kingdom" in Anaheim, California, but was also entertaining and educational, presenting fictional stories along with cartoons and nature films. Through the years, until the 1980s, the program was known by various titles including *Walt Disney Presents*, *Walt Disney's Wonderful World of Color*, *The Wonderful World of Disney*, and *Disney's Wonderful World*. It was resurrected in the late 1990s as *The Wonderful World of Disney*.

Warner Brothers was the next major studio to begin producing programs for television, with *Warner Brothers Presents* (1955), a program of three alternating series, based on the successful Warner movies *Kings Row*, *Casablanca*, and *Cheyenne*. By the following season, *Cheyenne* (1955–63) was the only series remaining. That same season of 1955–56 saw the arrival of *The Life and Legend of Wyatt Earp* (1955–61) and *Gunsmoke* (1955–75), the longest-running western on television. Within three years, the western became the most popular genre on television, with seven of the top 10 shows including *Cheyenne*; *Gunsmoke*; *Have Gun, Will Travel* (1957–63); *Maverick* (1957–62); *The Rifleman* (1958–63); *Sugarfoot* (1957–60); and *Wagon Train* (1957–65). A total of 32 western series were made in Hollywood in 1959, including *Bonanza* (1959–73), the most popular of the "family"-type westerns. The era of the television western ended when *Gunsmoke* left the air in 1975.

Another popular genre in the late 1950s was the quiz show. Although quiz and game shows had always been popular with the viewers, the big-money giveaways significantly increased the ratings for the networks. *The $64,000 Question*, based on the 1940s radio giveaway show *The $64 Question*, was the first to go on the air in 1955. Contestants selected categories of questions, and for each correct answer they could choose to keep the money they had won or go on to the next level. When contestants reached the $8,000 level, they were required to enter an isolation booth, supposedly to prevent audience members from giving away the answers. The success of the show encouraged producers and sponsors to develop new concepts for big-money game shows. Very shortly, several others appeared including *Twenty-One*, *The Big Surprise*, *Tic-Tac-Dough*, *Dotto*, and *Dough-Re-Me*. The producers of *The $64,000 Question* countered with *The $64,000 Challenge*, on which winning contestants on the first show could double their money on the second.

By 1958, the ratings of these big-money shows began to fall off amid allegations that they were fixed, which was denied by the sponsors, producers, and most of the contestants. Hearings were held on the matter by a New York grand jury, the Federal Communications Commission, and a U.S. congressional committee. Eventually, witnesses revealed that the correct answers routinely were given to the

Jack Paar, left, entangled in a fishnet, amused sidekick Hugh Downs and television audiences in the late 1950s.
(UPI/Corbis-Bettmann)

contestants to enhance the entertainment value of the program. The networks canceled all of the big-money game shows, and television westerns reaped the benefits.

During the 1960s, television anthologies had all but disappeared, but filmed television dramatic series became increasingly popular. Some of the more highly rated programs included *Naked City* (1958–63), *The Untouchables* (1959–63), *Route 66* (1960–64), *The Defenders* (1961–65), and *The Fugitive* (1963–67). Police and detective dramas continued in popularity through the years. *Mannix* (1967–75), *Cannon* (1971–76), *Barnaby Jones* (1973–80), with Buddy

Ebsen, and *The Rockford Files* (1974–80), with James Garner, were long-running private-eye series. Police procedurals followed the lead of *Dragnet* with such programs as *Adam-12* (1968–75), *The Streets of San Francisco* (1972–77), and *Kojak* (1973–77). In 1981, *Hill Street Blues* (1981–87) replaced *Dragnet* as the neo-archetypal form of police drama combining the serial (soap opera) with the police procedural. The female version of police work was shown in *Cagney and Lacey* (1982–89).

By the early 1960s, CBS was the ratings leader, and NBC was looking for ways to improve its audience figures. NBC made a deal with Twentieth Century-Fox to show feature movies on television and added *Saturday Night at the Movies* to its programming lineup. ABC soon followed, and feature movies had become popular television fare for prime-time audiences by the end of the decade.

However, the mainstay of network programming was always situation and domestic comedy. The problem was in finding the right personalities, settings, and style for the comedy shows. The "zany" style of *I Love Lucy* was evident in *You'll Never Get Rich* (1955–59), with Phil Silvers; *The Many Loves of Dobie Gillis* (1959–62), with Dwayne Hickman and Bob Denver; *McHale's Navy* (1962–65), with Tim Conway; *Gilligan's Island* (1964–66), with Bob Denver; *Gomer Pyle, USMC* (1964–68), with Jim Nabors; and *Laverne and Shirley* (1976–80), with Penny Marshall and Cindy Williams. Through the years, programmers tried several different types of situation comedy – including young single girls (e.g., *Laverne and Shirley*); single parents (e.g., *Bachelor Father* [1957–62]; *My Three Sons* [1959–65]; *The Courtship of Eddie's Father* [1969–72]; and *Alice* [1976–80]); military settings (e.g., *McHale's Navy*); police comedy (e.g., *Car 54, Where Are You?* [1961–63] and *Barney Miller* [1975–80]); and magical gimmicks (e.g., *Mr. Ed*, the talking horse [1961–66]; *My Favorite Martian* [1963–65]; *Bewitched* [1964–72]; *I Dream of Jeannie* [1965–69], and *Mork and Mindy* [1978–82]).

The rustic or rube type of situation comedy was extremely popular in the 1960s, particularly *The Beverly Hillbillies* (1962–71), *Petticoat Junction* (1963–70), and *Green Acres* (1965–71). In an attempt to change its image, CBS dropped all of its rustic comedy in 1971 for more "relevant" programming appealing to younger viewers. During the 1970–71 season, the network presented two comedy programs that would change the course of future network programming. *The Mary Tyler Moore Show* (1970–77) began as a rather traditional situation comedy about a 30-year-old single woman working as a news producer in a small television station in Minneapolis, Minnesota. *All in the Family* (1971–79), featuring Carroll O'Connor as Archie Bunker, the "lovable bigot," on the other hand, exploded onto television screens by promptly destroying the image of the happy nuclear family living in middle-class America proposed by *The Adventures of Ozzie and Harriet* (1952–66), *Father Knows Best* (1954–62), and *Leave It To Beaver* (1957–63). With the ratings success of *All in the Family*, *The Mary Tyler Moore Show* began to treat life issues with more openness and creativity. Together, these shows significantly changed the ground rules for what constituted permissible television content by offering a more realistic portrayal of characters and settings.

The success of these shows also opened the door for the irreverent humor of *M*A*S*H* (1972–83) and ethnic comedy on television. Between 1972 and 1977, several comedies involving ethnic minorities debuted on television, including *Sanford and Son* (1972–77), *Chico and the Man* (1974–78), *Good Times* (1974–78), and *The Jeffersons* (1975–82).

While the 1970s was the decade for change in television entertainment, the Ronald Reagan years of the 1980s signaled a movement back to a more traditional and conservative programming. In this decade, the serial format found its way into prime-time programming and changed the look of traditional genres. *Dallas* (1978–91), *Knots Landing* (1978–89), *Falcon Crest* (1978–89), and *Dynasty* (1981–91) were high-budget soap operas, but *Hill Street Blues*; *St. Elsewhere* (1982–88), a hospital drama; and *LA Law* (1987–93) used the serial form to develop and show complex, believable characters, who confronted realistic problems in realistic settings. By this time, almost any serious issue could be portrayed on television including divorce, AIDS, homosexuality, and sex itself. Television entertainment continued to change with the development and expansion of cable networks, which could take more liberties than the networks in presenting specialized and controversial programs.

PHILIP J. LANE

See also Golden Age of Radio; Golden Age of Television; Quiz Show Scandals; Radio Entertainment

Further Reading

Castleman, Harry, and Walter J. Podrazik, *Watching TV: Four Decades of American Television*, New York: McGraw-Hill, 1982

Marc, David, and Robert J. Thompson, *Prime Time, Prime Movers: From 'I Love Lucy' to 'LA Law' – America's Greatest TV Shows and the People Who Created Them*, Boston: Little, Brown, 1992

O'Connor, John E., ed., *American History, American Television: Interpreting the Video Past*, New York: Frederick Ungar, 1983

Television Networks

Television networks primarily carried over from radio

Traditional over-the-air television networks provide programming to their affiliates. They make money by selling time during these programs. Affiliates may be paid a token amount to carry their programs. Network affiliates also gain financially from the agreement because they receive profits from commercial minutes in prime-time programming allocated in each hour for local sponsors. In large cities, or markets, networks often own their affiliates (these are termed "owned and operated"), which are very profitable for the networks. Although the audience for the Big Three networks (ABC, NBC, and CBS) was declining in the late 1990s owing to the many alternatives that were available, the Big Three still drew about two-thirds of all viewers.

The basic television network arrangement came from radio broadcasting (as did the original networks), but many credit CBS chairman William Paley for creating the system. The first network program was presented by NBC, which televised President Franklin D. Roosevelt's opening of the New York World's Fair on April 30, 1939, on station W2XBS. CBS, NBC, ABC, and the financially troubled Du-

Television in the United States
Home Receiver Ownership 1946-1985
Percentage of Households with Television

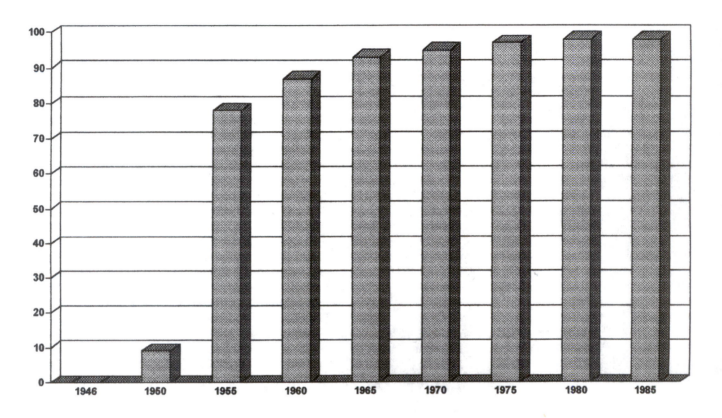

Source: U.S. Bureau of the Census, *Statistical Abstract of the United States,* 106th ed. (Washington, D.C.: GPO, 1986).

mont networks (all of which had their origins in radio) began presenting sporadic noncommercial programming.

In the late 1930s, television networks raided radio and one other for talent. For instance, CBS hired NBC radio's Al Jolson and Eddie Cantor. The Dumont radio network's *The Original Amateur Hour* moved to television. Milton Berle made the medium transition so successfully that he became known as "Mr. Television." The NBC network was the first to put the talent into a regular program schedule of ten hours a week.

In February 1940, the Federal Communications Commission (FCC) agreed to partial commercialization of the networks. The commission allowed networks to run commercials to recoup the costs of the shows alone (not operating expenses). But after the Radio Corporation of American (RCA, NBC's parent company) announced that it would link New York City and Philadelphia with a series of television relay stations and filed applications for stations in Philadelphia, Washington, D.C., and Chicago, the FCC suspended its ruling. In 1941, the FCC allowed commercial television to begin. When WNBT charged Bulova Watches $9 for an ad it ran, it became clear that television networks would be supported by advertising.

By 1945, seven stations programmed regularly: NBC's WNBT, CBS's WCBW, and Dumont's WABD in New York City; General Electric's WRGB in Schenectady, New York; Philco's WPTZ in Philadelphia; WBKB in Chicago; and W6XAO in Los Angeles. Even though these stations broadcast on a reliable schedule, that schedule rarely filled more than two hours daily.

In 1948, the FCC imposed a freeze on television stations to allow it to catch up with the huge demand for new frequencies. The almost four-year freeze hurt both the Dumont and ABC networks because it was difficult for them to catch up to NBC and CBS, both of which already had affiliates in many cities. During these years, networks in general became a strong force in television broadcasting. By 1949, 90 of the 98 radio stations in operation were affiliated with networks, and the networks attracted most of the advertising dollars flowing to television. By the end of 1949, network shows garnered half of the advertising dollars.

In 1949, Bell System (a subsidiary of American Telephone and Telegraph) linked the major U.S. cities with cables and radio relays. Now broadcasts could be seen from Boston to St. Louis, Missouri. The catch was that the four networks – CBS, NBC, ABC, and Dumont – had to share one cable. The first broadcast on the system in January 1949 featured a 15-minute sampling from the programming of each network. The networks also began experimenting with new formats. One very popular format of the times was the big money quiz show. A scandal over the authenticity of a CBS quiz show – *The $64,000 Question* – led to a congressional hearing, which had a substantial impact on the image of network television. In reaction, networks assumed more active control over program development as opposed to giving the control to producers and sponsors.

The early 1950s often are called the golden age of television programming. The airwaves were dominated by comedy and variety shows. The NBC network led the first half of the 1950s with talent including Bob Hope, Milton Berle, and Groucho Marx. CBS introduced filmed situation comedies such as *I Love Lucy.* ABC launched *The Adventures of Ozzie and Harriet* in 1952. Next, the drama and action formats began to take center stage, including *The Kraft Theatre* and *The Adventures of Superman.* The networks also

began daytime programming with serialized weekday soap operas adapted from radio. Other genres developed in the 1950s included children's shows such as *Captain Kangaroo* and westerns such as *Gunsmoke.*

By the late 1950s, Hollywood had taken over much of television program production. Independents such as Bing Crosby Productions and Quinn Martin Productions joined motion picture companies like MGM, MCA/Universal, Twentieth Century-Fox, and Paramount to provide series for the networks. The 1950s also set a pattern for network affiliation with stiff competition between NBC and CBS. ABC was struggling to survive in terms of affiliates and financial stability. In 1951, ABC merged with United Paramount Theaters in an attempt to obtain the vital capital it needed to survive. By 1954, 40 of the 354 stations operating in the United States were ABC affiliates, 164 were NBC affiliates, and 113 were CBS affiliates.

In the 1960s, network documentaries gained attention, but the most popular format seemed to be a new type of

Television Sets Produced and Households with Television Sets 1946–1970 (in thousands)

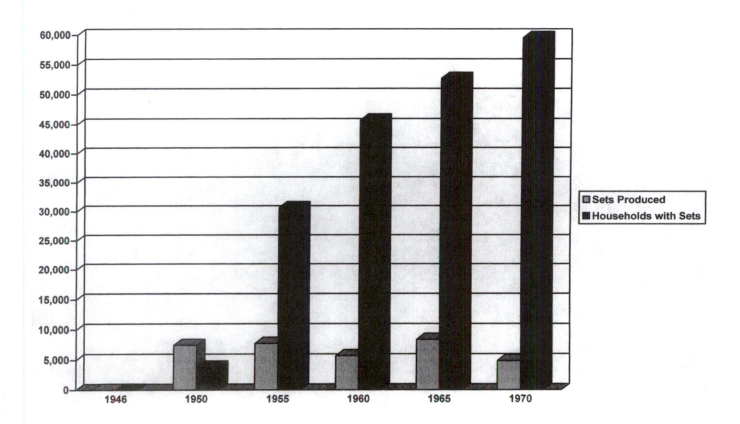

Note: 1959 denotes the first year for which figures include Alaska and Hawaii.

Source: U.S. Bureau of the Census, *Historical Statistics of the United States: Colonial Times to 1970* (Washington, D.C.: GPO, 1960).

comedy typified by *The Beverly Hillbillies* and *The Andy Griffith Show*. During the same time, a new type of network surfaced. Educational television stations exchanged taped programs. The arrangement, known as the "bicycle tape network," evolved into National Educational Television. In 1967, in the wake of the Carnegie Commission report on noncommercial broadcasting, Congress passed the Public Broadcasting Act, which established the Public Broadcasting Service (PBS). While it was a step forward, PBS was never given the power to be a centralized network programming service or the long-term government funding to assure stable growth. Despite these restraints, PBS produced award-winning programs such as *Masterpiece Theatre* and *Sesame Street*.

As commercial network programming gained in popularity, the FCC worried that networks were dominating local television broadcasting, and so in 1971, commissioners handed down the Prime Time Access Rule. The ruling stopped networks from buying cable franchises, and it also regulated network programming. The new rule allowed networks to produce their own shows, but it kept them from syndicating the shows they produced. The most important part of the ruling restricted networks from supplying more than three hours of prime-time television programming per evening, excluding news, public affairs, and children's shows. Thus, local stations were required to avoid running network programming from 7:30 to 8 P.M., Eastern time. The intent of the rule was to encourage local stations to present more locally originated shows dealing with community issues. Many local stations, however, turned to low-cost syndicated shows to fill the programming hole instead. The ruling did help the financially ailing ABC network because it reduced the stress on it to present more hours of programming. In 1975, the U.S. Department of Justice limited the number of hours a network could fill with its own productions.

Network programming evolved into an institution intimately intertwined with movie production facilities and other external programming outlets. For the most part, networks came to provide financial backing to independent production companies. Even with skyrocketing program costs, however, producers rarely made the networks pay the entire bill. Instead, they charged the networks for the licensing right to run each new show twice. The producing company then had the right to sell the "property" to another company, which syndicated the show and resold it directly to stations or cable outlets. If the show was a hit during its original broadcast, it became a very lucrative deal for the company that owned the original rights.

In the 1970s, the networks added new formats such as evening soaps (e.g., *Dallas* and *Falcon Crest*) and increased production of news programming. The three traditional commercial networks faced new competition. Cable companies expanded their programming, and the number of independent television stations increased. Finally, many people added VCRs to their households. The increased competition for the audience could be seen in network program ratings. By the late 1980s, the three major networks' share of the audience declined from an earlier high of 90 percent to less than 70 percent.

In the 1980s, networks had to deal with financial uncertainties brought on by a new trend – buyouts. Big companies made headlines with multimillion-dollar deals to buy the networks or attempt to take them over. In 1985, Capital Cities acquired ABC. A year later, General Electric reacquired NBC by buying its parent company, RCA. CBS fended off two hostile takeover attempts (one by Turner Broadcasting). In general, as the networks were absorbed into the big corporations that bought them, they were forced to operate closer to a bottom-line mentality. This philosophy translated into massive layoffs. The impact was felt by all three networks and affiliates as network employees sought employment lower down in the broadcast structure.

In 1987, another player joined the network ranks – the Fox Television network – founded by Australian-born Rupert Murdoch. Murdoch purchased stations from the Metromedia company and acquired the 20th Century Fox TV studio to produce programs for these stations. The network's first effort was an unsuccessful late-night talk show featuring Joan Rivers. The network then developed two very popular series – *Married With Children* and *The Simpsons*.

In January 1995, two other over-the-air networks joined the competition – United Paramount Network (UPN) and Warner Brothers (WB), both operating on limited schedules. These networks drew affiliates from the ranks of independent stations in markets where the other networks were already taken.

The addition of UPN, WB, and Fox to the traditional network list resulted in more choices for local stations seeking a network affiliation. Further, as multibroadcast station owners (MSOs) bought more television stations, they often cut deals to affiliate with a particular station. For example, the New World Communications station group agreed to switch 12 of its stations' affiliations to Fox, and the CBS network lost eight affiliate stations in the process. Local stations in markets where affiliations were in flux faced the difficult task of trying to promote a new program lineup to the public and their advertisers – sometimes with little advance notice. This made it hard for the local stations to maintain the strong ratings essential for their financial well-being.

Meanwhile, ratings remained a constant concern at the network as well. In October 1995, during the first six weeks of the new prime-time season, the Nielsen ratings for all four networks were down. The 1995 combined ratings for ABC, CBS, NBC, and Fox were 40.6 percent, down from the 1994 rating of 43.2 percent. CBS was hit the hardest by the drop. Despite the arrival of new networks and competition from other sources, however, the four biggest networks still maintained a share of the audience that was appealing to advertisers. In 1994, networks saw their biggest ad revenue figures since 1990, with the combined broadcast/cable-related revenue for the four companies – Capital Cities/ABC, CBS, NBC, and Fox – totaling more than $14.6 billion. Capital Cities/ABC was the top-performing company, with more than $1.1 billion in broadcast operating profit, while CBS profits were down by 27 percent from 1993.

One final trend of importance at the end of the twentieth century was likely to be the continuation of the merger and buyout mania that began in the 1980s. The rush to secure control of network properties became frantic in 1995. Disney Companies purchased ABC in August 1995 for $18.5 billion. In the same month, Westinghouse bid $5.4 billion for CBS; CBS merged with Westinghouse in November 1995. The trend of centralization of media ownership was likely to continue. The 1996 Telecommunications Act cleared the way for more ownership interplay between broadcast companies, telephone companies, the computer industry, and cable companies. The impact of this newly passed law on networks remained to be seen.

PAMELA K. DOYLE

See also Broadcast Documentaries; Broadcast Ratings; Broadcast Regulation; Golden Age of Television; Noncommercial Television; Paley, William S.; Prime-Time Television; Radio Corporation of America; Radio Networks; Television Entertainment; Television Syndication

Further Reading

Barnouw, Erik, *Tube of Plenty: The Evolution of American Television*, rev. ed., New York and Oxford: Oxford University Press, 1982

Bergreen, Laurence, *Look Now, Pay Later: The Rise of Network Broadcasting*, Garden City, New York: Doubleday, 1980

Brooks, Tim, and Earle Marsh, *The Complete Directory to Prime Time Network TV Shows, 1946–Present*, 3rd ed., New York: Ballantine, 1985

Dominick, Joseph R., Barry L. Sherman, and Gary A. Copeland, *Broadcasting/Cable and Beyond: An Introduction to Modern Electronic Media*, 2nd ed., New York: McGraw-Hill, 1993

MacDonald, J. Fred, *One Nation Under Television: The Rise and Decline of Network TV*, New York: Pantheon, 1990

Mazzocco, Dennis, *Networks of Power: Corporate TV's Threat to Democracy*, Boston: South End, 1994

Udelson, Joseph H., *The Great Television Race: A History of the American Television Industry, 1925–1941*, Tuscaloosa: University of Alabama Press, 1982

Television News

Conveying news through sounds and pictures

The term "television news" broadly refers to almost any type of information conveyed through the television medium. Special events coverage, documentaries, public affairs programs, political debates, interview programs, and talk shows can fall under the umbrella of television news. By the 1990s, television included "on-demand" services, such as videotext, that could be accessed in homes and offices with computers. Nevertheless, when people spoke of television news, they most often referred to the regularly scheduled news reports called "newscasts." Major broadcast networks, some cable networks, and most local television stations centered their journalistic activities on these reports.

In some ways, the newscast was analogous to the newspaper. Newscasts were seen daily and drew from journalists who worked in newsrooms. Television newscasts differed from newspapers in key respects, however. First, television news could be prepared and received simultaneously, and thus it emphasized immediacy. Second, only television could deliver both pictures and sound. Television stressed its uniqueness in providing the sights and sounds of the news. There was a third difference: while many newspapers went out of business and left monopolies in several locales, a competitive system endured and flourished in television news. News wars, which vanished in newspapers, remained a way of life for television journalists. Immediacy, pictures and sound, and direct competition instilled in television a journalistic tradition distinct from print.

Actually, there were three television news traditions. The oldest grew from the original broadcast networks, CBS and NBC. This network tradition emphasized "hard" news stories, frequently from foreign locations, in newscasts delivered by single, authoritative newscasters. Later, and eventually more widely seen, was the local tradition. Local television news sought a mixture of hard and soft news, embraced sports and weather as news, and featured teams of newscasters who were not news oracles but rather "friends" of the audience. Later still was the all-news tradition, which advanced in cable television, notably through services provided by the Cable News Network (CNN). Partially a synthesis of network and local styles, the all-news tradition was distinguished by its complete abandonment of adjacent entertainment programming. News was provided 24 hours per day.

Fundamentals of the network tradition were established before commercial television in the United States had officially begun. The first regularly scheduled newscasts were two 15-minute reports delivered by Richard Hubbell on

John Cameron Swayze's *Camel News Caravan* was one of the first television news broadcasts.
(Corbis-Bettmann)

CBS's experimental television station, WCBW in New York, beginning in the spring of 1941. In them, Hubbell sat behind a desk and read wire service dispatches aloud into a single television camera. Practically all of the content in this newscast was international in orientation and related to World War II. WCBW and several other stations were formally licensed by the Federal Communications Commission (FCC) in July 1941, although the first newscast was suspended in early 1942. The United States had by then entered the war, and CBS had to sacrifice lights and other studio equipment to the war effort. Nevertheless, CBS and NBC, which started in television with a New York station called WNBT, continued to broadcast newsreels and War Department films in 10- and 15-minute nightly reports. The NBC version evolved into a postwar program called *Newsreel Theatre,* the forerunner of a sponsored program called *Camel Newsreel Theatre.* (Camel was a brand of cigarettes.) Hosted by John Cameron Swayze, *Camel Newsreel Theatre* in February 1948 was transmitted to a four-station chain of NBC stations and thus became the first network newscast. It later was renamed *Camel News Caravan.* CBS followed in August 1948 by assigning a radio correspondent named Douglas Edwards to what became the *CBS Evening News.*

CBS and NBC quickly sought to employ television's picture and sound capabilities. Radio bureaus in foreign capitals were outfitted with film cameras so that events there could be seen. When film coverage was not possible, the networks had artists draw pictures of events, and sometimes animate them, to simulate what had happened. Immediacy often was achieved by necessity. Live shots, usually from fixed locations in New York and Washington, D.C., were common in the 1950s because film was slow and networks frequently had no other way to get their material on the air.

Because the constraints in nightly news reporting were numerous, the networks concentrated on documentary productions. Documentaries were less immediate but were considered more substantive than newscasts. They also pioneered techniques for integrating pictures into news reporting. Edward R. Murrow of CBS became known as the father of broadcast journalism because of his radio reports from Europe during World War II and also because of the television documentaries he prepared in the 1950s. Between 1951 and 1958, Murrow hosted a documentary series called *See It Now.* A *See It Now* investigation of Senator Joseph McCarthy in March 1954 helped turn public opinion against McCarthy's witch hunt of alleged subversives in government. Murrow's 1960 *Harvest of Shame,* which exposed the plight of migrant workers, remains one of the most-studied television documentaries ever produced. Documentaries, however, had small followings and could not effectively compete for viewers against entertainment programs, which dominated network schedules. Documentaries faded from network television, and after the 1950s, they were seen principally on public television.

While less sophisticated than documentaries, network newscasts in the 1950s drew considerable audiences. Even though the newscasts were only 15 minutes in length, they appeared in prime time and at an early stage competed with each other for ratings points, much in the way newspapers in

earlier years had vied for the largest circulation. A revealing development occurred in 1956, when Swayze's ratings declined and NBC fired him. NBC then installed Chet Huntley, who delivered part of NBC's news from New York, and David Brinkley, who delivered the rest from Washington, D.C. When NBC's news ratings soared, CBS then removed Edwards and in 1962 replaced him with Walter Cronkite. These events demonstrated the influence of direct competition in shaping the conveyance of television news.

The networks took a major stride in 1963, when the CBS and NBC broadcasts were expanded to a half hour. Occurring just weeks before President John F. Kennedy's assassination that November, these expansions set the stage for television journalism's so-called finest hour, the continuous coverage of the assassination and its aftermath during a four-day period when all commercial interruptions were eliminated. It largely was through network broadcasts that the U.S. audience witnessed other notable events in the 1960s, including the Vietnam War, the civil rights movement, the assassinations of Martin Luther King and Robert Kennedy, student protests, and space exploration. The networks' coverage of the *Apollo 11* moon landing on July 20, 1969, remained the most widely viewed program of any type ever seen on U.S. television, according to the Nielsen rating company.

The 1960s and 1970s marked the heyday of the network tradition. In 1970, Huntley retired from NBC, which soon returned to a lone newscaster, John Chancellor. In the same year, the third network, ABC, installed Harry Reasoner. For most of the next 25 years, ABC, CBS, and NBC featured single newscasters who personified not only their news divisions but, to many in the United States, the news itself. ABC's attempt in 1976 to team a female newscaster, Barbara Walters, with Reasoner was short-lived. In that same year, *U.S. News and World Report* referred to Cronkite as "the most trusted man in America."

This period also marked the beginning of two extremely successful prime-time network news series. At CBS, Murrow's *See It Now* series evolved into another called *CBS Reports,* which in 1968 seeded a third series, called *60 Minutes.* A weekly, hourlong magazine known for its investigative reporters, who initially included Mike Wallace and Morley Safer, *60 Minutes* commanded ratings that regularly exceeded those of the most popular entertainment programs. In 1978, ABC introduced a similar prime-time series called *20/20,* which also became a network news fixture because of its popularity.

All this time, however, network news had labored under a handicap. The strength of the networks was determined by each chain's 200 individual local affiliates, which were not owned by the networks and under no obligation to carry network news programming. As late as the mid-1960s, the *CBS Evening News* could not be seen in major cities such as Atlanta, Georgia, and Cincinnati, Ohio. Only two-thirds of ABC's affiliates cleared that network's newscast when it expanded to a half hour in 1968. Eventually, virtually all affiliates did carry evening newscasts. In 1980, in a venture that spun from special late-night reports relating to the Iran hostage crisis, a program called *Nightline,* with Ted Koppel was cleared by most ABC outlets. However, repeat-

Broadcast cameras covered Martin Luther King Jr.'s march on Washington, D.C., in August 1963.
(Reproduced from the Collections of the Library of Congress)

ed attempts by the networks to expand their main newscasts to an hour or longer were flatly rejected by affiliates. The main reason was the public's attraction to the local stations' own newscasts, some of which ran for two or three hours. Beginning in the 1970s, these local newscasts started to generate larger ratings than the network programs.

Local broadcasters took leave of the network tradition for a number of reasons. For one, they were uneasy about clearing newscasts produced in New York and Washington because these newscasts were not subject to local editorial control. Local newspapers, on the other hand, always had been able to edit and interpret material received from national media centers. In local television, suspicions were evidenced in the 1970s, when several affiliates threatened to remove network newscasts because they thought the networks were biased in their coverage of the Vietnam War. Symbolic of these concerns was a 1971 CBS documentary called *The Selling of the Pentagon,* which accused the government of deception in prolonging the war. More prominently, local broadcasters felt they were slaves of the networks because of the many hours of network entertainment programs they were compelled to carry. News was a means for a local station to profit from the entertainment shows and still assert its own local identity. Westinghouse, which would own local stations in the major markets of Philadelphia; San Francisco; Boston; Pittsburgh, Pennsylvania; and Baltimore, Maryland, was particularly active in blunting the networks' influence and in developing its local news as a means of doing so.

The local news tradition began with diversions from the networks' once-rigid 15-minute newscast formats. Following shortly behind a Sacramento, California, station called KCRA, but two years before the networks had even a half-hour newscast, KNXT in Los Angeles initiated an hourlong newscast in 1961. Known as *The Big News,* its considerable length enabled the assimilation of weather and sports segments. Further, reporters for the first time made regular and extended appearances, and they had time during the broadcast to interact with the main newscaster. This newscaster, a figure named Jerry Dunphy, coordinated on camera the many local newscast components, much as network newscasters had coordinated coverage during political conventions and in that role had been known as anchors. Beginning with Dunphy, the term "anchor" came to refer to all who hosted television newscasts.

Soon after *The Big News* began in Los Angeles, significant departures from the network tradition appeared at two Cleveland, Ohio, stations. In 1963, WJW established the first coanchor format, in which two newscasters, Doug Adair and Joel Daly, sat side by side during broadcasts and fostered a personal dialogue while delivering the news. Meanwhile, under news director Al Primo, Westinghouse station KYW stressed on-the-scene coverage with numerous field reporters and extensive visualization, in a format it called *Eyewitness News.* Following a Justice Department decree, KYW in 1965 was moved from Cleveland to Philadelphia, where *Eyewitness News* was perfected by Primo.

Local stations owned by ABC, finally, were most responsible for advancing nearly a total break from the networks'

style of newscasting. Chicago's WBKB, later WLS, hired Daly from the Cleveland station and in 1968 paired him with a former CBS figure named Fahey Flynn, who had left CBS in protest because the network did not consider his bow tie to be suitable for a serious newscaster. WLS manager Richard O'Leary encouraged Flynn and Daly to project their personalities, in what the trade publication *Variety* termed "happy talk." Almost simultaneously, ABC hired Primo from Philadelphia and had him initiate *Eyewitness News* at WABC in New York. A synthesis of the personality projection seen in Chicago with the team-oriented reporting system seen in New York produced the *Eyewitness* concept that hundreds of local television stations would emulate in the 1970s. The impetus was five- and six-fold ratings increases by WLS and WABC. Ratings in New York, where NBC-owned WNBC fought *Eyewitness News* with network correspondents as anchors and registered an unprecedented zero rating in 1974, signaled a weakness in the network tradition.

Local stations owned by CBS also had been affected by the popularity of *Eyewitness News.* In challenging, CBS scored a significant technological breakthrough in 1973 by unveiling the first efficient electronic field cameras, in an engineering partnership with the Ikegami Tsushinki company of Japan. "Electronic news gathering," or ENG, as CBS termed it, permitted convenient live coverage and spelled the demise of film as a news-gathering medium. The capabilities of ENG were illustrated dramatically in May 1974, when CBS-owned KNXT televised a shoot-out between Los Angeles police and a terrorist group called the Symbionese Liberation Army.

Instrumental in the proliferation of ENG and the *Eyewitness* concept were firms called news consultants. The first consulting firm was the Detroit-based McHugh and Hoffman, which began in 1962. Eventually the largest firms were Frank Magid Associates, based in Marion, Iowa, and Audience, Research and Development, based in Dallas, Texas, which began journalistic consulting in the 1970s. Consultants recommended acceptance of friendly anchors and appealing news stories in hundreds of newsrooms. Their major contributions, however, were systematic, empirical studies of audiences. This research showed, for example, that in the 1970s viewers wanted to see more women as news anchors. Women had been allowed only an insignificant role in television news prior to this time. Local television news was the first component of the news media to accept professional audience research nearly universally, and this was highly consequential to the rest of the news media. Critics complained that journalists should not give the public what it wants. However, the use of consultants and their research would expand into other news media.

The heyday of the local tradition began in the mid-1970s and continued through the 1990s. During this period, it was estimated that nearly half the adult population tuned in to at least one local newscast each day. Local stations depended on two or three half-hour newscasts for 50 percent or more of their profits. Still, both network and local news were buffeted by the growth of cable television and alternative television media in the 1980s. Satellites greatly reduced the cost of television distribution and invited scores of new cable services, which narrowcasted to a specialized audience. All-news services represented some of the first attempts at narrowcasting.

While the all-news tradition was diverse and ranged from talk-show channels to the cable service C-SPAN, which televised special events from beginning to end, its model became CNN, begun by Ted Turner in 1980. CNN was created as an on-demand service that provided some type of news at any time of the day. Still, like local news, CNN's service was divided into newscasts and featured multiple anchors, sports and weather segments, and extensive on-scene, live reporting. A companion service, CNN Headline News, relied on single anchors much as networks had. Noteworthy was the satellite delivery system CNN required. This not only made CNN available to viewers all over the world but also enabled continuous coverage of breaking events without regard to the geographic limitations that previously had impeded television journalism's development. CNN's reporting of the Persian Gulf War in 1991 was hailed as a milestone in television news. Moreover, during this crisis and others, diplomats at home and abroad followed a news agenda set by CNN.

As the 1990s began, separate network, local, and all-news traditions structured almost all television news seen in the United States. Polling data, as they had for 30 years, showed television news to be the most-used and most-believed source of information for a vast majority of people in the United States. Networks remained the dominant source of national and international news for the millions of viewers without cable. Prime-time network magazine broadcasts such as *60 Minutes* and *20/20* weekly drew tens of millions of viewers. The 1990s found the networks effectively adding more magazine programs to offset declines in the newscast ratings. Local news, with a larger nightly audience base than the networks and not threatened by the global spectaculars of CNN as the networks were, thrived in the 1990s. The all-news concept, having demonstrated its acceptance and impact, was expected to spawn more sophisticated on-demand news systems.

While newer technology led to newer traditions, it was doubtful that television news ever would stray from its unique ability to cover events immediately, with pictures and sound. Further, a historical promise of commercial competition was likely to indefinitely influence the content of the news, how much was available, and who produced and delivered it.

CRAIG ALLEN

See also Broadcast Documentaries; Broadcast Interview Shows; Broadcast Newsmagazines; Broadcast Talk Shows; Cable News; Motion Picture Newsreels; Presidential Debates; Radio News

Further Reading

Bliss, Edward, *Now the News: The Story of Broadcast Journalism,* New York: Columbia University Press, 1991
Dary, David, *TV News Handbook,* Blue Ridge Summit, Pennsylvania: Tab, 1971
Friendly, Fred, *Due to Circumstances Beyond Our Control . . . ,* New York: Random House, 1967; London: MacGibbon & Kee, 1967
Jacobs, Jerry, *Changing Channels: Issues and Realities in Television News,* Mountain View, California: Mayfield, 1990
Matusow, Barbara, *The Evening Stars: The Making of the Network News Anchor,* Boston: Houghton Mifflin, 1983
Powers, Ron, *The Newscasters,* New York: St. Martin's, 1977
Robinson, John P., and Mark R. Levy, *The Main Source: Learning from Television News,* Beverly Hills, California: Sage, 1986
Westin, Av, *Newswatch: How TV Decides the News,* New York: Simon & Schuster, 1982

Television Program Ratings

Effort to stave off federally mandated program controls

In 1997, the major television networks began rating all entertainment programs in response to pressure from Congress to do something about sex and violence on television. The ratings system, used in conjunction with the federally mandated "V-chip" technology, enabled parents to block programs with specified ratings from their television sets. The ratings scheme included entertainment news programs and talk shows, although news programs were exempt. Producers and distributors rated their own programs, and these ratings were subject to review by a panel of industry executives and child advocacy groups. A ratings icon appeared in the upper left corner of the picture frame for the first 15 seconds of the program. If the program was longer than one hour, the icon reappeared at the beginning of the second hour.

The Telecommunications Act of 1996 mandated that new television sets sold in the United States come equipped with a V-chip, an electronic device allowing viewers to block programs based on an encoded rating. Massachusetts Democratic representative Ed Markey, a proponent of television ratings, authored the V-chip provision. The act also urged the television industry to implement its own ratings system within a year of the law's passage or submit to a system devised by the Federal Communications Commission (FCC). Television network executives formed a ratings group headed by Jack Valenti, president of the Motion Picture Association of America (the organization responsible for rating feature films). This group created an age-based ratings system that went into effect in January 1997. It rated programs on a six-tier scheme, ranging from TV-Y and TV-Y7 for children's programs to TV-G, TV-PG, TV-14, and TV-MA for general audience programs. According to the rating group's explanation of its categories, a TV-Y program was considered suitable for all children. A TV-Y7 program was designed for children seven and older and might contain "mild physical or comedic violence" that could frighten younger children. A TV-G program had "little or no" violence or sex and was intended for general audiences. A TV-PG program had some violence or sexual content that might be unsuitable for young children. A TV-14 program included material unsuitable for children under 14. Finally, a TV-MA program was described as for "mature audiences only" and was possibly unsuitable for children under 17.

The age-based system met with intense criticism from Congress and advocacy groups including the American Psychiatric Association and the Parent-Teacher Association because of its failure to provide content information. In July 1997, after several months of contentious negotiations, the ratings group unveiled a revamped system that included content warnings. The new system, effective October 1, 1997, provided the following content ratings in addition to the six age-based ratings: fantasy violence (FV), violence (V), sexual situations (S), coarse or indecent language (L), and suggestive dialogue (D). The FV rating, used with the TV-Y7 age rating, indicated that a program had "intense or combative" fantasy violence. The other content ratings were used with the TV-PG, TV-14, and TV-MA categories. The amount and intensity of the specified content depended upon the age category. For example, a program rated TV-PG and V contained "moderate violence," while a program rated TV-MA and V contained "graphic violence." All the major networks except NBC agreed to implement the new system. NBC refused to air the content-based ratings, calling them a violation of its free speech rights, and announced that it would continue to use only the age-based categories.

The television industry historically has relied on its standards and practices departments to practice self-regulation of program content. These departments have been guided by several factors, including a desire not to offend advertisers, affiliated stations, the audience, and the FCC. The National Association of Broadcasters adopted a code for television in 1952 that included guidelines for program content. Adherence to the code, however, was strictly voluntary. Cutbacks in the standards and practices departments in the 1990s, combined with changing public tastes and the airing of uncensored films on cable, led to relaxed network restrictions on sex and violence. Shows such as *Seinfeld* and *NYPD Blue* pushed the limits in terms of suggestive dialogue, sexual themes, and even nudity on prime-time broadcast television. Public concern about sex and violence on television, although a perennial issue since the beginning of the medium, peaked in the mid-1990s and contributed to the passage of the Telecommunications Act of 1996.

The television ratings system met with mixed reactions. Advocates of the system called it an empowerment tool for parents, while critics called it censorship. Others were dubious about the system's effectiveness in protecting children from television violence and sex. A study by Joanne Cantor and other researchers at the University of Wisconsin suggested that programs carrying content warnings might actually attract certain children, particularly adolescent boys. Other critics agreed that the system did too little to stem the tide of television sex and violence. Senator Joseph Lieberman, a Democrat from Connecticut, for example, supported legislation to establish a "safe harbor" period in the broadcast schedule, which would require family programming in prime time (8 P.M.–10 P.M.) and restrict programs with sex and violence to later time slots. Industry executives worried that V or S ratings would cost them advertising, although advertisers downplayed its impact, saying that they would continue to preview programs for themselves. Although these issues were far from resolved in the late 1990s, proponents of the television ratings system urged viewers to give the system a chance.

DOLORES FLAMIANO

See also Broadcast Regulation; Mass Media and Self-Regulation; Television and Violence

Further Reading
Albiniak, Paige, "Ratings Get Revamped," *Broadcasting & Cable* 127:29 (July 14, 1997), pp. 4–10
Barnouw, Erik, *Tube of Plenty: The Evolution of American Television,* rev. ed., Oxford: Oxford University Press, 1982; 2nd rev. ed., New York: Oxford University Press, 1990
Blum, Richard A., and Richard D. Lindheim, *Primetime: Network Television Programming,* Boston: Focal, 1987
Cantor, Joanne, and Kristen Harrison, "Ratings and Advisories for Television Programming: University of Wisconsin, Madison Study," in *National Television Violence Study,* vol. 1., Thousand Oaks, California, and London: Sage, 1997
Dominick, Joseph R., Barry L. Sherman, and Gary A. Copeland, *Broadcasting/Cable and Beyond: An Introduction to Modern Electronic Media,* 3rd ed., New York: McGraw-Hill, 1996

Television Syndication
Helps provide sufficient programming to fill broadcast hours

Securing programming to fill local program schedules during television's formative years was a rather challenging task. A majority of the nation's fledgling stations (except for those in the densely situated cities of the northeast) were unable to receive live network transmissions, since American Telephone and Telegraph's coaxial cable lines did not extend west of the Mississippi River until 1950. A majority of network affiliates west of Kansas City were not connected until 1951, and some stations in the southwest were forced to wait for live service until the summer of 1952. During this time, the networks could only serve their nonconnected affiliates by providing kinescope recordings of their popular programs.

Thus, broadcasters were forced to find alternative program sources to fill their schedules until live network service arrived, a rather formidable task in an era when planning and producing television programs was virtually an unknown craft. Although local stations produced a respectable amount of local programming, it was impossible for most broadcasters to generate enough of their own shows to adequately expand program lineups. Additionally, once affiliates achieved interconnection, they still could not rely on their networks to provide around-the-clock service. Initially, the NBC, CBS, ABC, and Dumont networks could not financially justify scheduling programs for all parts of the day. The networks attempted only to accommodate evening viewing, and even then, prime-time schedules before 1955 had occasional "dark" periods when no programs were scheduled, leaving the airtime to be filled by the stations.

Consequently, local television's initial audiences viewed hours of test patterns during periods unoccupied by local and network shows. Another option was available, however, almost from television's earliest days – syndicated programming, a concept developed during radio's formative years that had become a well-established business by the time television arrived. Some syndicators, who shrewdly eyed television as a medium for lucrative new opportunities, were already poised to market filmed features to television stations. Frederick W. Ziv, who had been immensely successful in radio program syndication, for example, quickly moved into television. Ziv's first syndication offerings consisted of nothing more than old theater film packages, cartoons, and features. But by 1952, Ziv, Inc., was in the position to offer films that had been produced especially for television. *The Cisco Kid,* starring Duncan Renaldo, was a Ziv original, as well as *Boston Blackie,* which featured Kent Taylor in the leading role. Ziv also developed original dramas, such as *The Unexpected,* which was a prime-time success in many markets, and a weekly anthology series, *Story Theatre,* featuring acclaimed Hollywood stars in television adaptations of literature classics.

Television also was becoming a worldwide phenomenon in the early 1950s, showing remarkable growth in European countries and well as South America and Japan. Foreign broadcasting represented a potentially profitable future for the syndication business, and new companies in New York and Hollywood such as Screen Gems (Columbia Pictures's short-film production company), Hal Roach Productions, and the MCA talent agency's Revue Studios soon began plans for overseas distribution.

Perhaps the most famous syndicator of this era was Desilu, founded by actors Lucille Ball and Desi Arnaz. The couple filmed their popular *I Love Lucy* series in Hollywood because their careers were based there and they had a family. Consequently, all episodes of the series were filmed and sent to New York – at that time, the center of television production – for broadcast. This gave Lucy and Desi the unique opportunity to market the reruns. *Lucy* thus became the first of hundreds of popular network series to go into syndication as other producers followed suit, and Desilu soon became one of Hollywood's leading distributors when other Desilu programs also went into syndication. Reruns soon dominated much of local television's nonnetwork schedule, and by the mid-1950s, the syndication business was firmly established as a major factor in television programming.

The syndicated programming market enjoyed remarkable growth in the 1970s and 1980s, spurred by some important changes in the television industry. First, due to escalating production costs (which, for an average series, tripled between 1965 and 1975) and network executives balking at the notion of paying increased licensing fees to compensate the producers' spiraling expenses, syndication became the only way to make a series profitable. Producers thus began a business practice that still continues: breaking even financially – or, more likely, losing money – on network program sales with the later expectation of earning a profit through syndication.

The Prime Time Access Rule of the Federal Communications Commission (FCC), adopted in 1971, was another factor contributing to the flourishing syndication business. Under this ruling, networks were forced to relinquish an hour of prime time to their affiliates each evening, which allowed stations to glean more revenue by scheduling either locally produced programs or syndicated shows. The ruling created an urgent demand for syndicated features, especially original material, since stations in the nation's 50 largest markets were prohibited from airing off-network programs. However, broadcasters in cities below the "top 50" market designation and independent channels still were allowed to carry network reruns; in 1995, the FCC voted to repeal the Prime Time Access Rule.

Another bonanza for distributors was the budding independent television industry. Independent (or nonnetwork-affiliated) stations signed on in massive numbers in the 1980s (a 400 percent growth rate between 1980 and 1989) as enterprising broadcasters bravely went about the once-formidable task of competing with the more established network affiliates. Without an obligation to clear network programs, independent channels were free to counterprogram the local network affiliates with both "first-run" (programs developed especially for syndication) and off-network series.

The syndication market boomed as satellite technology spawned the growth of independent superstations, such as WTBS in Atlanta, Georgia, and WGN in Chicago, and cable television networks, beginning with pay-cable enterprises in 1978 and basic cable networks in the early 1980s. Pay-cable channels created a new market for feature films and original productions, while the basic services like the USA Network, Nickelodeon, and Lifetime needed both original and off-network material. Consequently, existing distributors and new companies launched efforts to cash in on the demand for programming. By the early 1990s, there were more than 100 syndication firms in the United States, although a handful of companies handled a majority of the domestic market: Columbia Pictures Television, Fox, King World Productions, MCA-TV, Paramount Domestic Television, Turner Program Sales, Viacom, and Warner Brothers.

STEVEN SMETHERS

See also Cable Networks; Prime-Time Television; Television Entertainment; Television Networks

Further Reading

Andrews, Bart, *The 'I Love Lucy' Book,* Garden City, New York: Doubleday: 1985

Brooks, Tim, and Earle Marsh, *The Complete Directory to Prime Time Network TV Shows, 1946–Present,* New York: Ballantine, 1979

Von Soosten, John, "Domestic Syndication," in *Broadcast/Cable Programming: Strategies and Practices,* 4th ed., edited by Susan Tyler Eastman, Belmont, California: Wadsworth, 1993

Television Technology

Development of television dated to 1873

The development of television, the transmission of pictures in motion with accompanying sound over great distances, was dependent on an understanding of the physics of light energy and radio waves, persistence of vision, and radio and motion picture technology. It was a history of finding more efficient ways of converting light energy into electrical energy; the seemingly simultaneous transmission of that signal with ever-increasing quality at greater distances; and the ability to control or manipulate that signal in increasingly complex ways, using the methods of the time, starting with mechanical devices, then fully electronic from analog to digital.

Although discoveries were incremental, most scholars place television's start in 1873, when English telegraph engineer Joseph May and May's supervisor, Willoughby Smith, discovered that selenium produced an electric current in direct response to the amount of light falling on it. George R. Carey of the United States in 1877 proposed a way to copy the human eye by setting up rows of selenium cells wired individually to send the elements of a picture as electrical signals from each cell simultaneously to a bank of lamps that lit in response to the electricity. In 1880, English scientists Ayrton and Perry attempted the experiment, resulting in a mosaic similar to many animated advertising billboards seen in the 1990s. Although this would be the basis of future television cameras, they were actually still frames and very impractical.

Engineers continued to rely on mechanical systems, taking into account the ways in which the human eye and brain worked. In 1884, Paul G. Nipkow, a Russian-German scientist, patented the scanning disc, a thin metal disc perforated with small holes in a spiral pattern allowing for the scanning of an image by way of synchronized rotating discs between the object and the source of light and the viewer. The scanning method is reliant on persistence of vision, first proposed by Peter Mark Roget in 1824, as a human phenomenon: the retina retains an image for a brief instant; if there are more than 10 complete still images displayed within one second, there will be the illusion of continuous movement.

Using the mechanical scanning system, both John Logie Baird in 1924 in Great Britain and Charles Francis Jenkins in 1925 in the United States demonstrated very crude, but recognizable, silhouette television images. Eventually replaced by the electronic system, the mechanical system was the basis for initial experiments in color transmission and was used for transmitting color images from the moon to Earth in 1969.

In 1908, A.A. Campbell Swinton of England suggested a completely electronic system of television that relied on the electronic reading of a storage and discharge surface. This surface was initially within a vacuum tube, and 50 years later, on a solid-state transistor chip. In 1907, Boris Rosing in Russia received a faint television signal adding photocells to a cathode-ray oscilloscope.

A student of Rosing's in Russia, Vladimir K. Zworykin, came to the United States in 1919 and joined the Westinghouse research team in 1920. Zworykin developed the iconoscope tube, a storage-type camera tube patented in 1923 and demonstrated publicly in 1928. The iconoscope camera incorporated a photosensitive mosaic tube that continued to store energy until the scanning beam struck it again. Because the iconoscope allowed for greater sensitivity at lower light levels than anything had previously, live images could be picked up in studios without lighting that was too uncomfortable for actors.

Concurrently, Philo T. Farnsworth of the United States was developing an electronic image dissector tube that allowed the photoelectric current to be measured one point at a time; the output signal was directly proportional to the amount of light falling on the cathode. It was an instantaneous, or nonstorage-type, tube that would be useful for scanning motion picture film but required too much light for practical use in live situations.

By combining Zworykin's iconoscope and Farnsworth's image dissector, Radio Corporation of America (RCA) laboratories, joined by Westinghouse and General Electric engineers, continued to work for better picture definition and more flexibility. The RCA laboratories produced pictures of 60 lines in 1930, 120 lines in 1931, 343 lines in 1935, and 441 lines in 1939. They developed the image iconoscope camera and then the orthicon tube, both described by Zworykin and others in 1939. RCA laboratories introduced interlaced scanning, scanning first the odd lines then the even lines to reduce flicker. In 1941, the National Television System Committee, composed of industry engineers, set the standards for television transmission that would remain virtually the same for more than 50 years: the pictures would consist of 525 lines, 30 frames per second, or 60 fields per second, each scan covering only 262 1/2 lines, on channels 6 megahertz (MHz) wide.

The inventors always were seeking to reproduce color images, starting with the mechanical/electronic cameras. Bell Laboratories demonstrated color in July 1929. Reflected light was scanned by three banks of photocells that were filtered to receive one of the primary colors: red, blue, or green, using the additive principle. Three separate transmission channels carried the color signals to the receiving point. CBS continued development on this partially mechanical field sequential color television system that won Federal Communications Commission (FCC) approval in 1950. When the FCC insisted that the color system had to be compatible with the black-and-white standards set in 1941, RCA developed such a color system, which was approved by the FCC in 1953.

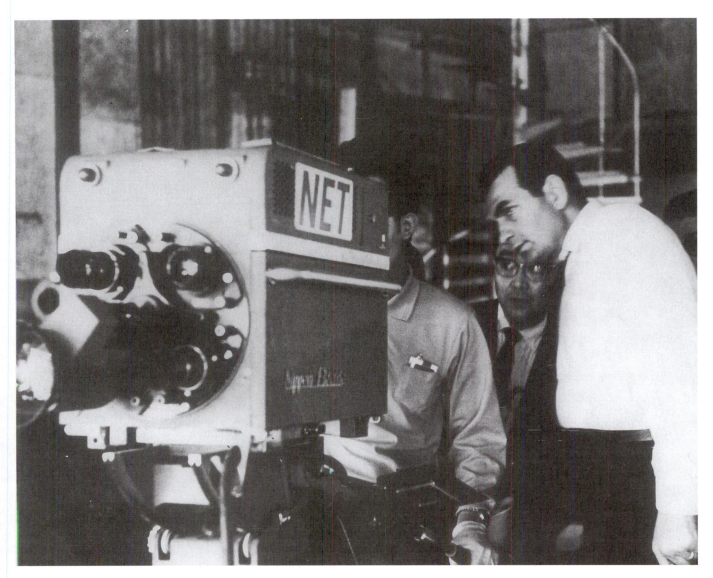

Large cameras were commonplace in the early years of television.
(National Public Broadcasting Archives)

In 1950, RCA developed the much smaller vidicon tube with a photoconductive target, which was useful for film transmission but, because of poor light sensitivity, was not useful for live productions. In 1963, Phillips introduced a similarly small camera called the Plumbicon; with its lead-oxide target, it was as sensitive as the black-and-white industry standard, the image orthicon. Then, in the 1970s, the transistor started to replace the vacuum tube. In 1979, Sony introduced the charge-coupled device (CCD) cameras, cameras made with solid-state, light-sensitive chips containing a large number of silicon-sensing devices called pixels. The CCD cameras allowed for even greater flexibility because they could be smaller and lighter than those with tubes.

For most of television's history, the camera-control units sent the amplified audio and video signals separately to the transmitter, where the video signal was amplitude-modulated and the audio signal was frequency-modulated. The two were joined together and propagated from an antenna radi-

ating from 30 to 65 miles, depending on channel placement, power, and geographic factors, according to standards set in 1941 by the FCC, which allocated 6 MHz of the bandwidth for each television channel. Although the placement of these channels would change by 1952, their width remained the same.

The standards were set for a system of community stations producing their own programming, but the industry sought interconnection among stations from the very start. Early experimenters relied on high-grade telephone wire and, later, coaxial cable for transmission over substantial distances.

In 1947, the first microwave relay system was inaugurated between New York and Boston. Many stations relied on microwaves for receiving their network signals and, after the development of portable cameras and recorders, for live remotes in the late 1970s. By 1951, there was coast-to-coast transmission, and by 1962, live transatlantic transmission

Repairing broadcast equipment took a variety of instruments.
(Reproduced from the Collections of the Library of Congress)

by the communications satellite *Telstar I*. Coaxial cable, microwave relay, and communications satellites also would serve as transmission devices for cable television, which started as a rebroadcasting system in 1949. Cable television eventually became a powerful alternative to over-the-air broadcasting when the pay-cable service Home Box Office started its satellite network services in 1975.

There was always an interest in recording the moving pictures for storage, time-delay transmission, and manipulation. Attempts started with John Logie Baird's 1927 phonoscope – a phonograph that could record his 30-line pictures, R.T. Friebus's 1929 U.S. patent for recording video on a disc, and Lee De Forest's 1931 etching of an electrical discharge on 35-millimeter film coated with pure metallic silver. The first commercially successful attempts were with film in 1948, but the disadvantages of film led to the search for electronic recording.

On November 11, 1951, the Electronic Division of Bing Crosby Enterprises demonstrated videotape recording in black-and-white with 12 recording heads. Although the res-

olution was poor, it did prove that television could be recorded on magnetic tape. Ampex demonstrated a videotape recorder with greater picture resolution in 1956. Known as the quadraplex system, it had four heads on a drum revolving at 14,400 revolutions per minute, scanning the 2-inch tape, moving at 15 inches per second in an up-and-down or transverse pattern. In 1957, RCA unveiled the first color recording machine, and improvements continued to make video a viable production alternative to film.

During the 1960s and 1970s, companies made smaller and more practicable video recorders. Helical scanning tape recorders with one or two heads recording the signal onto the tape on a slant allowed for slow-motion playback and still frames. In 1971, Sony, with the cooperation of Victor Company of Japan (JVC) and Matsushita Electric (Panasonic), developed the U-Matic tape recorder, using the helical scanning principle on 3/4-inch videotape and recording a composite signal, with the color and luminance together. In 1975, Sony introduced the Betamax format, and in 1976, Matsushita introduced VHS, marketed through JVC. VHS won the battle for the home market, but until the introduction of digital time-base correction in 1973, the helical scanning system was not useful to the broadcast industry.

For even greater production flexibility, RCA demonstrated a 1/2-inch camera/recorder combination in 1980 using an M-format, and Sony demonstrated a Betacam format. Both used the component system, which recorded a stronger signal than the composite recording process, reducing signal deterioration. More analog component video recorders came out in various sizes. Sony came out with a component digital videotape recorder in 1989, while Ampex displayed a digital composite recording system.

It was always necessary for television broadcasting to be able to switch between sources, whether it be within or between productions, and to manipulate the image. For image selection, the early video cameras used standard 35-millimeter lenses on lens-turrets, offering four different focal-length lenses. In 1947, the Zoomar lens was introduced to change the field of view rapidly from a full wide-angle view to a tight shot.

To help ease switching among sources, particularly during the busy time of station breaks, stations devised presetting systems first by mechanical switches, mechanical-latching relays, punch cards, and beam-switching tube memory elements. In 1960, CBS station KNXT in Hollywood, California, was the first station to install computer-controlled automatic switching for all switching events. The computer was used subsequently for the business side of broadcasting and then program production.

Switching between cameras within production, later identified as video mix effects, was handled by the electronic wizardry of individuals at each station or production house. In 1957, NBC first used the effect of chroma-keying, combining two video images electronically into one image, such as a city backdrop for a reporter. By the 1970s, switcher manufacturers routinely incorporated multiple-channel video mixing effects often controlled by computers. More sophisticated production techniques were available with the introduction of the digital framestore synchronizer in 1974.

By 1958, the first mechanical tape editing process was introduced, but it was very difficult to do without picture breakup. In 1960, both Ampex and RCA developed a means of locking videotape machines to an external sync source. This meant that videotape could be used as a switchable source for production, adding some precision to the editing process. To allow for more reliable editing and retrieval, the Electronic Engineering Company in 1967 developed a time-code system giving each video frame a unique eight-digit address. On a prototype basis in 1970, CBS and Memorex developed the CMX computerized video editing system, and by the 1990s, nonlinear editing systems were in use.

By 1995, television stations were becoming entirely digital facilities. With the understanding that digital compression of the signal would allow for more efficient use of the spectrum, an industry committee, the Advanced Television Systems Committee, in 1995 recommended to the FCC standards for a totally digital television system.

Margot Hardenbergh

The remote control caused great excitement in the late 1950s when it was introduced.
(Museum of Broadcast Communications)

Further Reading

Abramson, Albert, *The History of Television, 1880 to 1941,* Jefferson, North Carolina: McFarland, 1987

Bray, John, *The Communications Miracle: The Telecommunication Pioneers from Morse to the Information Superhighway,* New York: Plenum, 1995

Inglis, Andrew F., *Behind the Tube: A History of Broadcasting Technology and Business,* Boston: Focal, 1990

Krupnick, Michael A., *The Electric Image: Examining Basic TV Technology,* White Plains, New York: Knowledge Industry, 1990

O'Brien, Richard S., and Robert B. Monroe, with contributions by Charles E. Anderson and Steven C. Runyon, "101 Years of Television Technology," *SMPTE Journal* 100:8 (August 1991)

Ritchie, Michael, *Please Stand By: A Prehistory of Television,* Woodstock, New York: Overlook, 1994

Other Television Entries: Army-McCarthy Hearings; Audience Research for Broadcasting; various Broadcast entries; Cameras in the Courtroom; Communications Act of 1934; Decency Issues in Electronic

Media; Docudramas; Federal Communications Commission; Golden Age of Television; Noncommercial Television; Prime-Time Television; Program-Length Commercials; Quiz Show Scandals; Vietnam War

Textbook Publishing

Early, important aspect of book publishing industry

Although it is a rich and important aspect of U.S. culture, textbook publishing remains historically unexplored for the most part. Even its origins are difficult to define, since the distinction between schoolbooks and textbooks in colonial times is often hard to define. While the *New England Primer* often is cited as the first schoolbook, it also was much read by children at home and so is regarded as perhaps the first children's book. Most early schoolbooks originated in England; in colonial America, they were produced by local printers who also distributed them in their villages; consequently, there was no uniformity. After the American Revolution, however, U.S. texts began to come into their own. One of the first and most celebrated was Noah Webster's *Blue-Back Speller,* printed in Hartford, Connecticut, in 1793, which was still in print in 1952. Other subjects were slow to develop. Before 1829, there were fewer than a dozen textbooks in American history.

Textbooks had a similarly slow physical development through the eighteenth century and much of the nineteenth. Early textbooks often were paperbacks, although Latin and Greek grammars often were bound in leather. Books for the upper grades commonly used rag paper. Early textbooks had only one thing in common, however – their long titles.

Educational publishing, as thought of in the late twentieth century, did not truly exist until the early part of the nineteenth century. Until 1865, the only major changes were in binding and distribution, the latter of which produced textbook publishing's first real problem. Companies hired agents to sell books directly to the schools, causing cutthroat competition that became a broad pattern of corruption. This system was flourishing by 1850, postponing any hope of a common price structure.

One book outsold by far all the others handled by the agents, then and for many decades afterward. It was McGuffey's *Readers,* the work of William Holmes McGuffey, who began issuing them in 1833. No book in U.S. publishing history has sold more copies – at least 105,000,000; it was still in print in the late twentieth century as a curiosity. After the Civil War, the history of textbook publishing, until modern times, is a record of continuing plans by responsible publishers to bring some order into their specialty, especially to reform its ethics. This occurred in the face of efforts by less scrupulous houses to exploit the constantly growing demand for textbooks that began after the Civil War and continued to increase rapidly decade after decade. In this atmosphere, the agency system thrived. By 1868, a publisher might have as many as 300 agents in the field, and corruption was rampant.

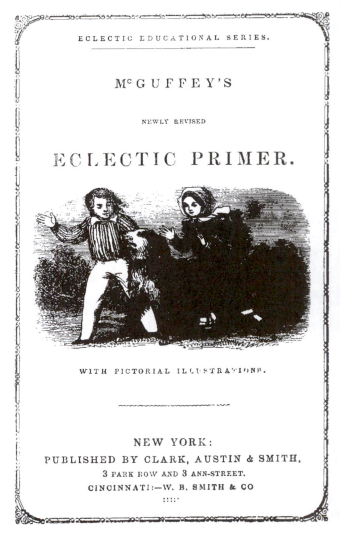

McGuffey's Primer was a popular textbook for children.
(Davis Library, University of North Carolina at Chapel Hill)

Attempting reform, several leading publishers organized a Board of Trade in 1870 designed to stabilize prices and sales practices, but it lasted only eight years. Expansion had another face, however. Physical production of books was improving rapidly, particularly in the use of pictures. The situation, however, was complicated further when some states began making and distributing their own books in an effort to control prices.

By 1890, clearly only a major effort by publishers would bring about some kind of order, and in that year, the attempt was made by four publishers – D. Appleton and Company; A.S. Barnes; Ivison, Blakeman and Company; and Van Antwerp, Bragg and Company – who formed the American Book Company. Attacked by others in the trade as a monopoly since these were the four major textbook houses, the new firm, whose members kept their individual identities, nevertheless brought enough pressure to bring about needed reforms.

After the turn of the twentieth century, expansion in the textbook business was rapid. By 1906, there were about 80 textbook houses in operation, and by 1910, textbooks had become a $12 million-a-year industry. By that time, most of the earlier problems had been mitigated, if not solved. One, however, remained and would become much more serious in the new century: censorship. Almost entirely ideological, censorship came from many sources. While the sciences generally escaped, except for biology, history created the most controversy. Publishers were faced with the problem of telling the story of the United States in ways that would offend no one, a virtually impossible task. Two versions of the same textbook resulted for north and south, and violent controversies erupted in the Chicago schools and elsewhere over teaching the American Revolution. Censorship battles in history and biology still were being fought at the end of the century.

By 1930, textbooks had became a $50,000,000-a-year business, and more than 64 million books were being distributed annually. The end of World War II brought another sharp increase owing to the impact of the GI Bill and the baby boom. In the 1970s, textbook publishing began to change because of the technological revolution.

JOHN TEBBEL

See also Censorship of Books

Thomas, Isaiah
Published the first history of U.S. journalism

A prominent eighteenth-century printer, publisher, journalism historian, and antiquarian, Isaiah Thomas began his career as a printer's apprentice in Boston when he was six. First recognized as a colonial leader when he began publishing the fiery, revolutionary *Massachusetts Spy* in 1770, Thomas moved his newspaper to Worcester, his new permanent headquarters when British troops occupied Boston in 1775.

After the American Revolution, Thomas withdrew from political activities and concentrated on his printing and publishing enterprises. When he turned his printing ventures over to his son in 1802, he had built one of the largest printing businesses in the country, was joint owner of several newspapers, and had published at least 900 volumes of educational, religious, and literary books. One of the wealthiest men in the country, he then could concentrate on his other philanthropic interests.

Using his collection of colonial and revolutionary American newspapers, by 1810, he had published the first journalism history, *The History of Printing in America*, which remained the standard reference of eighteenth-century printers and publishers. In it, he listed the printers by states, their publications, the size of their printing shops, and the related functions of typecasting and papermaking.

Thomas proposed the founding of a society "for the collection and the preservation of the antiquities of our country" to the Massachusetts legislature. He became the first president of the American Antiquarian Society at its founding in 1812.

PERRY J. ASHLEY

Further Reading

Hynes, Terry, "Isaiah Thomas," in *Dictionary of Literary Biography: American Newspaper Journalists, 1690–1872*, vol. 43, edited by Perry J. Ashley, Detroit, Michigan: Gale, 1985

Marble, Annie Russell, *From 'Prentice to Patron: The Life of Isaiah Thomas*, New York and London: D. Appleton-Century, 1935

Shipton, Clifford K., *Isaiah Thomas: Printer, Patriot and Philanthropist*, Rochester, New York: Leo Hart, 1948

Time Warner
Media conglomerate covers range of field

The vast media conglomerate Time Warner was created in 1989 with the merger of a major Hollywood studio and music company, Warner Communications, and a leading publisher, Time, Inc. One of the world's largest media companies at the end of the twentieth century, Time Warner owned a stake in many businesses. Its Warner Brothers studio produced a vast array of television programs and motion pictures. Its cable television division counted millions of subscribers in the United States and owned and operated leading networks such as Home Box Office and Cinemax. Each year, Time Warner also sold millions of music cassettes and CDs, videos, magazines, and books. Structurally, Time Warner was organized into four divisions: film and television entertainment, music, publishing, and cable television, in order of their revenue generation.

The leading force behind the merger was Warner Communications chief executive officer (CEO), Steven J. Ross. The merger was advertised as a combination of equals, and, at first, Ross and J. Richard Monro of Time, Inc., were listed as co-CEOs. But this "sharing of power" proved short-lived; within a year Ross stood alone atop the Time Warner media colossus. Ross, however, died in December 1992. The actual day-to-day running of Time Warner during the 1990s then fell to Ross's protégé, Gerald M. Levin.

Both Warner and Time had long and distinguished histories. Warner began as a studio in 1924 and pioneered sound motion pictures and Hollywood-produced television series. During the 1920s, Henry Luce began *Time* and innovated a string of world-famous magazines including *Fortune* and *Sports Illustrated*.

In 1996, Time Warner purchased Turner Broadcasting System for $6.7 billion, creating the world's largest media conglomerate. Ted Turner brought cable networks, movies, and professional sports teams to the Time Warner mix.

DOUGLAS GOMERY

Further Reading

Alexander, Alison, James Owers, and Rod Carveth, eds., *Media Economics: Theory and Practice*, Hillsdale, New Jersey: Lawrence Erlbaum, 1993

Bruck, Connie, *Master of the Game: Steve Ross and the Creation of Time Warner*, New York: Simon & Schuster, 1994

Trade Book Publishing

Volumes intended for general public consumption

To book publishers, "trade" publishing means the books on their list intended for the general public, as distinct from textbooks, scientific and technical books, religious books, or other specialized lines. The distinction, however, becomes blurred when a trade list also may include specialized but still general books such as those related to self-help or New Age. Religious books, like textbooks, are a separate enterprise in many cases, although these titles also can be included in a general list. To the ultimate reading public, trade books are simply fiction and nonfiction.

In the colonial period, there were no such distinctions. Printers were the publishers, and they issued whatever came to hand. By the end of the eighteenth century, however, a young Irishman, Mathew Carey, had organized the first modern publishing house in Philadelphia, and the stage was set for the kind of publishing known since then.

Between 1830 and 1852, the entire structure of modern publishing, including trade books, was created in an explosion of entrepreneurship. John Wiley and Sons was the first of these family-owned businesses to arrive on the scene, and it remained until the late twentieth century as the last of these establishments. The other publishing families who founded their firms in this period were equally long-lived, keeping their original identities until the major changes that were brought about by mergers beginning in the 1970s.

The names of these family houses became familiar landmarks on the publishing scene: Harper Brothers, D. Appleton and Sons, A.S. Barnes, G.P. Putnam and Sons, Dodd, Mead, Charles Scribner's Sons, D. Van Nostrand, and E.P. Dutton and Company, which was the last to be founded, in 1852. All of these houses published both general and specialized books, but their trade divisions gradually became separate parts of their enterprises, with such specialized divisions as textbooks functioning separately within the general structure. It was a pattern that persisted to the end of the twentieth century. General fiction and nonfiction are what most of the public sees, although other divisions are usually larger and more profitable. Trade books appear on the best-seller lists; others are the largest income producers.

Until late in the twentieth century, trade book departments were usually the least profitable of a multidepartmental publishing house. Their products were subject to unpredictable public taste and the ability of editors to secure profitable titles and authors. Through the nineteenth century and well into the twentieth, some old-line publishers were content to issue some trade books they knew would not make money, or were unlikely to do so, simply "for the good of the house," as one of them put it, meaning that good books deserved to be published whether there was a discernible market for them or not. This philosophy had nearly vanished by the 1920s, with only a few exceptions, and by the end of the century, with marketing forces in virtual complete control of publishing decisions, it had disappeared.

One thing that remained unchanged was the organization of a trade department. At its head was the editor in chief, responsible to the firm's executives, who in turn might report to conglomerate managers. Associate editors were the next rung down the ladder, followed by assistant editors, and other editorial trainees under various names. Until the latter part of the twentieth century, copy editors supplemented the staff, but these departments began to break up in the 1970s, and their work was farmed out to freelances.

In earlier days, publishers were flooded with unsolicited manuscripts – in larger houses, a thousand or more in a week – and they were at least looked at by lower-echelon editors. By the late twentieth century, most of the larger houses did not read unsolicited material and did not return it. Manuscripts normally came through agents or an editor's personal contacts.

Once in house, most manuscripts are read by more than one editor, and at periodic meetings of the editorial staff, they are discussed in terms of acceptance or rejection. Earlier, these meetings consisted only of editorial staff, but then advertising, promotion, and publicity departments were represented, as marketing became a primary concern. Acceptance practices vary among houses. Often, the editor who brings a trade book to the house and finds it accepted does the contract negotiating. In other houses, this is done by the editor in chief or some other executive. In many houses, the acquiring editor follows a book through the entire publishing process from acceptance to finished book; in others, the work is divided. Similarly, some editors work closely with an author, suggesting changes in the manuscript, while others are simply acquirers. In the old era, editors and authors worked closely together, and there are legendary stories of these collaborations, such as the work of Maxwell Perkins at Scribner's and Edward Aswell at Harper's with Thomas Wolfe. In the structure of trade publishing in the late twentieth century, these alliances virtually had disappeared in the larger houses. Editors moved frequently from one house to another or were preoccupied with major writers on their list, leaving others neglected; consequently, editor-author relationships were no longer studies in loyalty, for the most part.

Trade books themselves fall into rather loosely defined categories. At the top, although not necessarily in a commercial sense, is so-called serious fiction, meaning novels by writers with literary intentions. Again, in earlier days, houses were measured by the number and quality of these books. They carry on the literary tradition of trade publishing. The bulk of latter-day fiction lists consists of commercial books – that is, those designed to reach the broadest possible market and make the best-seller lists. There are also subcategories, such as romance novels, which became a genre in themselves in the late twentieth century, along with the detective novel and the so-called suspense novel. Trade fiction tends to follow patterns, as with, for example, family novels or coming-of-age novels.

Nonfiction trade books cover a much wider range and also tend to follow changing tastes as far as the number of titles produced annually is concerned. Biography and memoirs, for example, rise and fall with changing tastes. Humor is a perennial category, changing from one generation to the next. Books about sports were popular, but by the

1990s, the largest single category was books by or about celebrities, part of a national cultural phenomenon. Self-help, how-to, gardening, and similar specialized interests relevant to broad segments of the general market became quite popular.

Sales figures are publisher's secrets, for the most part, but commercial fiction easily topped all the others in the late-twentieth-century United States. Some authors sold millions of copies. Sales of 10,000 copies for any trade book was considered a minimum figure, generally speaking, for a book to be considered successful. Bookstore sales were only part of the income earned by trade books in modern publishing. Additional possible income came from paperback rights, book clubs, motion picture and television sales, and such multimedia possibilities as audio books and CD-ROMs.

JOHN TEBBEL

See also Book Publishing in the Eighteenth Century; Book Publishing in the Nineteenth Century; Book Publishing in the Twentieth Century; Economics of Book Publishing

Transatlantic Cable

Linked the United States and England in 1866

The transatlantic telegraph cable, which linked the United States with England, began successful operation in 1866. When Cyrus W. Field first proposed his idea of a transatlantic, submarine telegraph cable in 1854, communication between the two countries took at least six days by steamship. Gaining support of the British and the U.S. governments, Field and his Atlantic Telegraph Company set out to stretch a cable across the 1,600 miles of ocean between Ireland and Newfoundland, Canada, the two closest points, which would then be connected to overland wires.

After leaving Ireland on July 17, 1858, the cable expedition reached Newfoundland on August 5. The symbolic linkage of the Old World with the New was greeted with great fanfare in the United States. For the first time, virtually instantaneous communication to Europe was possible. But the cable suddenly fell silent after only four weeks. The last official message, received on September 1, 1858, congratulated Field on his success. Since the cable had never been opened for public use, it quickly was labeled a hoax by the media.

In 1862, Field once again tried to obtain financing for the project. Scientific developments in the intervening years had improved the technology, and after a total of four failed expeditions, the Atlantic cable finally was laid successfully on July 27, 1866. The opening of the cable meant that newspapers no longer had to rely on steamships for their overseas information, and it facilitated the exchange of news between the Associated Press and European press agencies.

KARLA K. GOWER

See also Associated Press; Cooperative News Gathering; Telegraph

Further Reading

Briggs, Charles, F., *The Story of the Telegraph, and a History of the Great Atlantic Cable,* New York: Rudd & Carleton, 1858

Carter, Samuel, III, *Cyrus Field: Man of Two Worlds,* New York: Putnam's, 1968

Field, Henry M., *The Story of the Atlantic Telegraph,* New York: Scribner's, 1892; London: Gay and Bird, 1893

Transradio Press Service

News service for independent radio stations

Arising in 1934 amid a bitter struggle between daily newspapers and radio broadcasters for control of news dispatches used by broadcasters, Transradio Press Service provided an innovative news service for independent radio stations for 17 years. During the 1920s, radio grew from zero to 618 U.S. stations, and 100 daily newspapers suspended publication. Although dailies owned nearly 90 stations in 1930, most newspaper publishers feared that radio would take their advertising revenues.

After radio's stunningly successful coverage of the 1932 presidential election, Associated Press (AP) newspapers in the spring of 1933 ordered the AP to deliver news bulletins only to AP papers' stations and to charge them a fee. Within weeks, United Press (UP) and International News Services (INS), bowing to newspaper clients' pressure, quit delivering news dispatches to broadcasters.

Retaliating, NBC and CBS opened news departments in late 1933, forcing a secret Biltmore Hotel meeting at which wire-service, network radio, and newspaper representatives agreed to set up the Press-Radio Bureau on March 1, 1934. They agreed that the wires would supply brief newscasts to networks and their station affiliates in exchange for stoppage of network news gathering. Because this "Biltmore plan" affected only the networks and their affiliates, more than 400 independent radio stations remained outside of the agreement.

The Biltmore agreement prompted Herbert S. Moore to begin planning Transradio Press Service for launching in March 1934. Moore, a former UP reporter then working for CBS news, was driven by two forces in creating Transradio. Independent radio stations offered promising business prospects, and he was outraged by what he saw as newspapers' secretiveness and selfishness in the Biltmore plan.

Transradio opened its wire late on February 28, 1934, with 20 radio clients from Boston to Los Angeles, delivering a 10,000-word teletyped daily news report that consisted of four 15-minute newscasts and news bulletins in between. By August 1934, Transradio was delivering a daily 30,000-word teletype report to 50 subscribers and introducing a shortwave service that delivered a shorter, cheaper news report for 75 smaller stations.

By the end of 1934, Transradio had 150 clients and 10 domestic bureaus and received foreign news from Havas in France and Reuters in England. Moore charged clients whatever the market would bear – in the first year, from $5 to $1,500 per week for stations broadcasting unsponsored news. If the newscasts contained advertisements, Transradio increased its weekly fee by at least 50 percent. At its height, in 1937, Transradio had 230 radio clients, including some newspapers, and in 1938, Transradio's teletype service delivered a 40,000-word, 20-hour-per-day news report, gathered in 34 foreign and domestic bureaus.

Although it was an early success in radio news gathering, Transradio was joined by UP and INS in 1935 and by AP in 1941, all attracted by the revenue in the radio news field. On December 1, 1951, Transradio Press Service, its client list down to 50 and a victim of wire service competition, suspended operation.

RICHARD A. SCHWARZLOSE

See also Associated Press; International News Service; Radio News; United Press Associations (1907)

Further Reading
Chester, Giraud, "The Press-Radio War: 1933–1935," *Public Opinion Quarterly* 13 (1949)
Moore, Herbert, & Associates, *"More News – After This . . . ,"* *The Untold Story of Transradio Press,* Warrenton, Virginia: Sun Dial, 1983
Moore, Herbert, "The News War in the Air," *Journalism Quarterly* 12 (1935)
White, Paul W., *News on the Air,* New York: Harcourt, Brace, 1947

Trial Balloons
Testing public opinion before making a policy commitment

A trial balloon is a technique used by politicians, government officials, political candidates, and policymakers to test public opinion before making a final commitment on a controversial issue. The technique relies on testing public reaction to a certain action prior to finalizing the action. It involves making information public through leaks to the media, waiting a short time, then measuring the reaction of the media and the public by monitoring the media and surveying public opinion.

One of the most common uses of trial balloons is by political figures deciding if they should run for public office. Because of the tremendous cost involved in conducting a major campaign, many would-be candidates "allow" rumors of their possible candidacy to be floated in public. They base their decision to run on whether there is adequate positive reaction by potential voters and, perhaps more importantly, potential financial contributors, to indicate a good chance of success.

Another common use of trial balloons is by government officials attempting to gauge public reaction to possible policy changes before the changes are finalized. Again, information is leaked, generally by officials within the government or organization, to the media that a specific change is being considered. Public reaction is monitored. Favorable reaction may lead to the formalization of the new policy, or if the negative reaction is strong enough, the considered action may be abandoned. Adverse public opinion also may lead to a revision of the policy or to the development of a better way of presenting the policy to the public.

Trial balloons generally are made public through anonymous sources and not connected directly with the key officials involved to prevent strong negative reaction from having a negative effect on the officials. The news media play a strong role in the use of trial balloons. They provide access to the public for the balloonists, and the publication of anonymous rumors and suggestions by the news media gives them credibility as significant public issues.

DAVID CASSADY

See also Roosevelt, Theodore, and the Press

Truman, Harry S., and the Media
President made friends with working press members who covered him

Harry S. Truman was thrust into the U.S. presidency at a fateful moment in national experience. A largely unknown figure from Missouri, Truman had been vice president for less than three months when President Franklin D. Roosevelt died on April 12, 1945. The country was still at war with Germany and Japan, and crucial decisions lay immediately ahead: whether to deploy the awesome new atomic bomb against Japan, how to define the U.S. role in the embryonic United Nations, and whether to commit resources to contain Soviet expansionism into eastern Europe and to rebuild postwar Germany and Japan.

Historians tend to agree that Truman stood tall throughout his years of crisis, that he faced the awesome issues of his presidency with courage and conviction. His blunt and often combative personality won him much respect – and many enemies.

More than a few of these enemies were in the nation's press, then largely controlled by pro-Republican owners. Powerful publishers and columnists opposed Truman's liberal-minded "Fair Deal" domestic political agenda. Truman's often-pugnacious defense of his policies and angry denunciation of his opponents raised questions as to whether he lacked the dignity and stature expected of the presidency. Truman brought many of his troubles upon himself. Fondly remembering favorable publicity he got early in his administration for rapid-fire and direct answers to reporters' questions, Truman continued to shoot from the hip at press conferences, often with embarrassing results. This, added to his stubborn insistence on unvarnished, harsh language, materially reduced his effectiveness.

President Harry S. Truman liked reporters to accompany him on the presidential yacht.
(Harry S. Truman Library)

But if Truman was despised by some publishers and columnists, he nevertheless enjoyed highly favorable relations with the working press. Unlike some of his predecessors in the Oval Office, Truman was personally comfortable with reporters and photographers. He liked and respected them, played poker and drank bourbon with them, granted interviews and answered their questions – two press conferences a week during much of his presidency.

Indeed, it is likely that Truman's most remarkable political victory – his election to a full term, against overwhelming odds, in 1948 – was achieved not in spite of the press but because of it. While editorial pages overwhelmingly endorsed Truman's Republican opponent, Thomas E. Dewey, the news columns of the daily press – with a considerably wider readership – faithfully and accurately described the success Truman was having with crowds and his "give 'em hell" strategy. If the voters made up their minds on the ba-

sis of facts, as Truman himself alleged, then the press was his friend, not his enemy, in his uphill election campaign. "It is a personal satisfaction to me that nearly all of our columnists," Truman's press secretary, Charles G. Ross, wrote to a friend in England, "including Walter Winchell, Walter Lippmann and the Alsops [Joseph and Stewart] took a terrible beating over the election."

Ross, who had grown up with Truman in Independence, Missouri, before becoming a Pulitzer Prize-winning reporter and distinguished editor of the *St. Louis (Missouri) Post-Dispatch*, had responded to an urgent summons from the White House within days after Truman's accession. Far more than a press secretary, Ross served as a close friend and confidant to the president. Ross's personality was such that it helped create an atmosphere of civility throughout the inner offices of the White House, and this was a contribution of the first importance – a contribution that became even more evident by its absence after Ross's death in 1950. Ross was succeeded as press secretary by Joseph Short, who had been a reporter for the *Baltimore (Maryland) Sun*. Like Charlie Ross, Joe Short would suffer a heart attack and die in office. Knowing the grinding demands he had placed on his press secretaries, Truman took both men's deaths hard and felt personally responsible. "I feel as if I killed them," he said. Succeeding Short was Roger Tubby, who had been his assistant.

Unconcerned with his own image and by nature opposed to spin doctors and other such cosmetic techniques so central to modern-day politics, Truman unintentionally made life difficult for his press secretaries and for the journalists covering the White House during this presidency, the last one in which the then new medium of television was not a major factor. His feisty and often ill-considered remarks during press conferences could cause acute embarrassment and, on at least one occasion, a grave international incident. During the early days of the Korean War, careless responses to reporters' questions led the press – and much of the international community – to believe mistakenly that Truman actively was considering use of the atomic bomb against the invading North Koreans, a move that, if taken, threatened the world with nuclear holocaust.

Truman was his own man; he said and did what he wanted, often without giving much thought to the impact his actions might have. Occasionally, he would not even inform the press office of changes in his plans, with the awkward result that the press secretary would be caught telling reporters the president was going to do one thing while he demonstrably was doing something else. Nor was Truman interested in "managing" the news for maximum political advantage. One example of this occurred in June 1947, when Truman ordered release of several other important news stories on the same day that Secretary of State George Marshall was announcing his monumental European Relief Project (the Marshall Plan) in a major address at Harvard. The upshot was that Marshall was clearly, if unwittingly, upstaged by, of all people, the White House press office.

But if these and other shortcomings detracted from Truman's effectiveness with the press and general public, the working journalists who covered the White House nevertheless admired the president and respected him. His blunt, outspoken manner was recognized and even applauded for the integrity it represented. As one *New York Times* correspondent at the White House wrote, "Harry Truman worked less to ingratiate himself with people but succeeded at it better than any public figure I have ever known. . . . He did it, I think, because he was so utterly honest with and about himself, so free of what we call . . . 'put on.'" His beleaguered press secretaries, who idolized their boss even as they worked brutally hard for him, never tried to "sell" Truman to the press. Like much of the rest of the country, White House journalists appreciated Harry Truman as a straightforward, unpretentious man of the people who sustained a common touch throughout extraordinarily uncommon times.

RONALD T. FARRAR

See also Korean War; Presidential News Conferences; Presidential Press Secretaries

Further Reading

Farrar, Ronald T., *Reluctant Servant: The Story of Charles G. Ross*, Columbia: University of Missouri Press, 1969
Ferrell, Robert H., *Harry S. Truman and the Modern American Presidency*, Boston: Little, Brown, 1983
McCullough, David, *Truman*, New York: Simon & Schuster, 1992
Phillips, Cabell, *The Truman Presidency: The History of a Triumphant Succession*, New York: Macmillan, 1966

Truth in Advertising Movement

Effort to build trust in the practice of advertising

In the early twentieth century, in an effort to professionalize the practice of advertising, magazine publishers, manufacturers, and advertising agencies promoted what they called Truth in Advertising. The Associated Advertising Clubs of America (AACA) adopted the slogan at its first meeting in 1904, and both informal and legislative attempts to regulate the uses and abuses of persuasion quickly followed.

False promises, gross exaggerations, and misleading testimonials already had led to a public distrust of advertising by the late nineteenth century. Patent medicines, which promised life-giving results but often contained alcohol, opiates, or other drugs, served as a symbol of the disreputable industry preying upon uneducated consumers. Cyrus Curtis, publisher of the *Ladies' Home Journal*, dropped all patent advertising from his magazine in the 1890s. *Journal* editor Edward Bok later printed an advertisement for Lydia Pinkham's patent medicine that included a picture of Mrs. Pinkham endorsing her product; next to this, Bok placed a photograph of Lydia Pinkham's grave – she had actually died several years earlier. Advertisers hardly could ignore the implication that the Pinkham ad and others like it represented the general direction of the industry. Recognizing the need to work with rather than against publishers and editors like Curtis and Bok, advertising agencies began a campaign of self-regulation.

The federal government also became involved in regulation with the passage of the 1906 Food and Drug Act, which required patent medicines to disclose the presence of alcohol, barbiturates, and several other drugs in their products. Nevertheless, advertisers had a long way to go to convince the public, and the nascent consumer rights movement, of their ethics. "Advertising has a thousand principles, one purpose, and no morals," wrote Samuel Hopkins Adams in *Collier's* magazine in 1909, in an article that would plague advertisers and prompt them to further attempt to legitimize their work.

Only two years after Adams's article, at the AACA national conference in 1911, the Truth in Advertising "fires burst into brilliant flames," according to movement leader H.J. Kenner. Following this convention, local and national groups called vigilance committees formed to prevent the use of false and fraudulent advertising.

During the same year, John I. Romer, editor of the advertising trade journal *Printer's Ink,* hired a lawyer to draft a model state statute that could be used to prosecute the purveyors of false advertising. The resulting 153-word sentence declared deception through advertising to be a misdemeanor. Many states adopted the statute in whole or in part; unfortunately, however, many changed the language to read that a manufacturer or advertiser had to have "knowingly" provided false information. It was difficult to prove that a certain advertiser crossed the arguably thin line between ethical and unethical claims; it was even more difficult to prove that they had knowingly done so with an intent to deceive. Nevertheless, by 1921, 23 states had passed some form of the *Printer's Ink* statute, and a few advertisers had faced prosecution.

The climate was right for legislative action around false advertising. Although the *Printer's Ink* statute did not result in tremendous numbers of convictions on the basis of false advertising, it did have another result: the development, out of the National Vigilance Committee, of Better Business Bureaus. The bureaus, which sought to curb unethical advertising and selling practices, applied the *Printer's Ink* statute to enforce the regulation of advertising, even in states that had not adopted the model state statute. The independently supported Better Business Bureaus, funded by all types of businesses, could investigate claims against advertisers without exposing the source of the complaints. By 1921, 29 cities had Better Business Bureaus headed by full-time workers, and in 1925, the National Better Business Bureau was formed.

The Truth in Advertising movement received further national support in 1914 with the establishment of the Federal Trade Commission (FTC), which prosecuted unfair methods of competition in commerce. The FTC's first chairperson, Joseph E. Davies, speaking at the 1915 AACA convention in Chicago, called for cooperation between the government and advertisers. The FTC followed up later that year by granting the AACA permission to bring to court interstate cases not covered by weak state statutes.

As a Progressive Era reform, the Truth in Advertising movement represents more than the efforts of an industry to become more professional and responsible. It also provides a case history of internal regulation meant to solidify a growing corporate structure and bypass externally imposed regulations. Corporate advertising interests, by the second decade of the twentieth century, saw their money in national, not local, advertising; as a consequence, most of the investigations of the Better Business Bureaus focused on the abuses of local rather than national advertising campaigns. The Better Business Bureaus had few confrontations with big business, and the movement as a whole did little to define "truth" in advertising. "'Puffing' is one thing; lying another," *Printer's Ink* declared in 1916, but few explored the distinction in any detail. As Daniel Pope argued, "those who discouraged lying were often those who hoped to perfect the more sophisticated means of persuasion."

The movement also enabled advertising men to maintain the ethnic identity of the industry as one driven by white Protestant men. Associating their Protestant identity with clean advertising messages, advertisers promoted an ethnocentric vision of "truth" and closed their doors to diversity in employment.

The advertising industry of the early twentieth century clearly saw advantages in self-regulation, and the Truth in Advertising movement represents its effort to legitimate its work. It also may, as Jackson Lears argued, represent advertisers' attempt to reassure themselves as much as their audience, to declare their "disinterested involvement in the new public space defined by the corporation." And while it may provide a few success stories for reducing abuses in advertising, it did little to regulate the industry as a whole. In fact, in its effort to legitimize the development of national, corporate advertising, the Truth in Advertising movement may have helped define half-truths and quarter-truths as truths.

JENNIFER SCANLON

See also Advertising in the Twentieth Century; Better Business Bureau; Federal Trade Commission; Food and Drug Administration; Muckraking; Patent Medicine Advertising

Further Reading

Lears, T.J. Jackson, *Fables of Abundance: A Cultural History of Advertising in America,* New York: Basic, 1994

Pope, Daniel A., *The Making of Modern Advertising,* New York: Basic, 1983

Turner, Ted

Major player in cable television world

Robert Edward Turner III, best known as Ted Turner, was one of the world's most powerful players in the broadcasting, cable, and film industries in the late twentieth century. To sports enthusiasts, Ted Turner was recognized as "Captain Courageous," the underdog who in 1977 became a sailing hero when he won the world championship yachting trophy.

Born in Cincinnati, Ohio, Turner was a 1950s Brown University dropout. After his father's suicide in 1963, he took his father's outdoor billboard advertising business and used it as the base for building a personal fortune of more than $3 billion. His successful rise in the broadcasting industry began in 1970, when he purchased a single independent station, Channel 17, in Atlanta, Georgia. From that transaction, his global empire, with its headquarters in Atlanta, grew to include the Turner Broadcasting System superstation, Cable News Network, Headline News, Turner Network Television, Cartoon Network, the Turner Classic Movies network, Castle Rock Entertainment, New Line Cinema, Hanna-Barbera Cartoons, the Atlanta Braves and Atlanta Hawks sports teams, Cable News Network Center, and World Championship Wrestling.

A media maverick whose broadcasting reputation was

built on mergers and negotiations, the Turner Broadcasting chairman continued to seek ways to expand his media acquisitions empire. In 1996, Turner merged his holdings with Time Warner, taking the position of vice chairman of the new conglomerate.

The media mogul, who received a 1989 special degree from Boston University, was married to actress Jane Fonda. He had five children from previous marriages.

TERESA JO STYLES

See also Time Warner

Further Reading
Bibb, Porter, *It Ain't as Easy as It Looks: Ted Turner's Amazing Story,* New York: Crown, 1993; London: Virgin, 1994
Whittemore, Hank, *CNN, The Inside Story,* Boston: Little, Brown, 1990
Williams, Christian, *Lead, Follow or Get Out of the Way: The Story of Ted Turner,* New York: Times, 1981

U

Underground Press

Radical and countercultural papers for a decade of dissent

The underground press consisted of hundreds of radical and countercultural papers that were influential from 1964 to 1973. While important papers were published elsewhere, most notably in England and Australia, the United States was the hotbed of the form. Underground papers arose in nearly every U.S. city, as well as at hundreds of colleges and high schools.

Underground papers reflected and fueled the radical challenge that took place during the 1960s. Primarily community-based (differentiating them from sectarian journals of both the Communist or Socialist left and the far right), they also chronicled changing times within "the Movement": papers covered Vietnam and race; feminism and gay liberation; sex, drugs, and rock music; environmentalism; prison reform; and, both at home and overseas, GI rights and rebellion.

In the process, the papers challenged mainstream corporate journalism. Using cheap offset technology, they published colorful sheets with unfettered content that included dispatches from a radical news service, the Liberation News Service. Ownership became increasingly collective, and members of the Underground Press Syndicate shared material without copyright restriction.

Underground papers could be under-researched, uncritical, or shrill, and had difficulty critiquing causes that were coming under increasing attack. But they gave the lie to false government reports while espousing alternate ways to live. Their creators and practitioners often were amateur in terms of journalistic technique, in their love for the work, and in their inability to differentiate it from the rest of life.

Historically, the underground press traced its roots to the American Revolution broadsides of Thomas Paine, the nineteenth-century abolitionist and suffrage presses, and the leftist and artistic outpouring of the World War I era. This lineage, however, ignores such important pop-culture progenitors as beat poetry, the community-based (Greenwich) *Village Voice* that began in the mid-1950s, the absurdities of *Mad,* and Paul Krassner's iconoclastic early-1960s *Realist.*

A quintet of underground papers led the way. The *L.A. Free Press* came first, in 1964; Art Kunkin, an alumnus of left publications, was moved by a potpourri of coffeehouses and folk music clubs popping up around town. The paper's launch coincided with a Renaissance Pleasure Faire, but its reporting during the Watts riot went beyond pacification or patronization to explore black discontent.

Soon, the *Berkeley (California) Barb* was linking the experience of southern Freedom Riders with the infantile treatment students found within the multiversity – while raging against the U.S. role in Vietnam. The *Paper* of East Lansing, Michigan, proved that college towns had antiwar as well as pep rallies.

The two other papers of this first wave took a more counterculture tack. New York's nonlinear *East Village Other* described "the intergalactic world brain," presaging connections forged by the Internet of a generation later. In San Francisco's Haight-Ashbury, the *Oracle*'s tripped-out graphics and apocalyptic poetry aspired to be LSD in ink.

Papers proliferated: a dozen by 1967, 500 by 1969, along with more than 1,000 in schools across the country. They supported a network of coffee houses and communes in a language that sounded silly or scary to outsiders but authentic to core readers. They organized demonstrations, opposed rampant consumerism, and contested mainstream police-are-always-right coverage.

Until the late 1960s, there was much truth to the one-liner that "Marx and Lennon" referred to Groucho and John rather than Karl and Vladimir, but the continuation of the Vietnam War led many underground writers to connect with the struggles of anticolonial governments. Papers increasingly reported on, and praised, Third World movements from Vietnam to Palestine. Coverage could romanticize; then again, while established publications excoriated Nelson Mandela as a South African terrorist, underground papers embraced his cause.

Vietnam, racism, alienation, alternate visions, and the thrashing of demonstrators at the 1968 Democratic National Convention pushed the papers to merge political and counterculture ideas in the name of "revolution" – even as polls showed most people in the United States disliking radicals and hippies more than the war they increasingly questioned. As the underground press promulgated revolt, however, the axiom that "the personal is political" caused a revolution within the revolution. Feminists rebelled against being second-class citizens inside their own movement: in

The underground press was primarily a 1960s phenomenon.

tisers; FM rock stations, rock magazines, and newer, softer, more traditionally journalistic "alternative papers" soon drew them away. By 1973, as U.S. troops left Vietnam, the Underground Press Syndicate – embodiment of a waning press – became the Alternative Press Syndicate.

The underground press had many warts, but its disproportionate influence helped to end a war and topple two warrior presidents. It expanded professional journalism's tightly justified margins (and later influenced a new wave of cultural broadsides and eclectic "zines"). Finally, it offered dissidents a place to speak aloud to each other, away from a mass culture that continued to commodify journalism.

ABE PECK

See also Abolitionist Press; Alternative Press; Broadsides; Feminist Media; Socialist Press; Suffrage Press

Further Reading

Albert, Judith Clavir, and Stewart Edward Albert, eds., *The Sixties Papers: Documents of a Rebellious Decade,* New York: Praeger, 1984

Armstrong, David, *A Trumpet to Arms: Alternative Media in America,* Los Angeles: J.P. Tarcher, 1981

Gitlin, Todd, *The Whole World Is Watching: Mass Media in the Making and Unmaking of the New Left,* Berkeley: University of California Press, 1980

Glessing, Robert J., *The Underground Press in America,* Bloomington: Indiana University Press, 1970

Leamer, Laurence, *The Paper Revolutionaries: The Rise of the Underground Press,* New York: Simon & Schuster, 1972

Mungo, Raymond, *Famous Long Ago: My Life and Hard Times with Liberation News Service,* Boston: Beacon, 1970

Peck, Abe, *Uncovering the Sixties: The Life and Times of the Underground Press,* New York: Citadel, 1991

Rips, Geoffrey, *The Campaign Against the Underground Press,* San Francisco: City Lights, 1981

1969, women seized New York's *Rat* after an issue of underground comics let male libido "all hang out." Staffs reconfigured: editors, many of them white, male, and straight, gave way to multi-gender, more integrated collectives.

The total assault became a crucible. Even as napalm dropped in Vietnam and Black Panthers went on trial, the Federal Bureau of Investigation's COINTELPRO campaign disrupted operations, local "red squads" and other police arrested staff and vendors, and ultraright groups shot up offices. Within the counterculture, the ideology of "free" led some street sellers to abscond with the papers' cut of 25- or 35-cent cover prices. And staffs of a press once characterized by anticensorship argued in print over whether the police ever could be right, whether revolutionaries were ever wrong, and whether writing or drawing well was "bourgeois" while people were dying. Liberation News Service split into pro–Third World and back-to-the-land factions. Exhausted, or even appalled, writers and editors exited before being censured for insufficient zeal, before committing acts they had once (or still) opposed.

As the most fiery radicals moved from "Peace Now" to "Armed Love," many papers hectored readers and denounced record company and local "hip capitalist" adver-

Unique Selling Proposition

Effort to endow each product with distinctive characteristics

The unique selling proposition, or USP, is an advertising theory conceived in the 1940s by Rosser Reeves, who served as chairman of the board of Ted Bates and Company. The theory proved especially useful in the post–World War II marketplace, when parity products became increasingly common. Consumers were confronted by several different brands with similar features, making it difficult to discern any benefit one product might have over another in the same category. Brand names and packaging were indeed different, but many products performed the same basic task. Often the only realized difference in consumers' minds between many of these goods was the image created by the advertising.

The goal of the USP is to provide consumers with an advertising message containing a benefit of the product that no other competitor offers. The USP intends to remain focused on the one point of difference, whether it be a characteristic inherent in the design of that particular brand or one created by the advertising, that will cause that brand to stand out as superior in the consumers' minds. Reeves defined the USP by dividing it into three parts:

1.) Each advertisement must make a proposition to the consumer – not just words, not just product puffery, not just show-window advertising. Each advertisement must say to each reader: "Buy *this* product, and you get *this specific benefit*."
2.) The proposition must be one that the competition either cannot, or does not, offer. It must be unique – either a uniqueness of the brand or a claim not otherwise made in that particular field of advertising.
3.) The proposition must be so strong that it can move the mass millions (i.e., pull over new customers to the product).

The unique aspect of a USP alone, however, is not the sole theoretical base for a successful advertisement, for, as Reeves was careful to point out, a unique proposition can be created that does not sell the product. It is important to remain focused on what motivates the consumer to purchase. If the proposition is of no importance to the target audience, it will not result in a sale. The proposition must be both unique and relevant.

It is easy to expect that the proposal about the product will be contained in the headline or body copy of the ad. The USP is not necessarily always presented solely in a verbal structure. It might be the end result of a combination of advertising elements, including words, pictures, and sound effects or music.

The USP is a theory that appears deceptively simple. In reality, it requires an advertisement to work on many different levels. It demands the advertising communication be unique as a result of the product claim and a result of the artistry that must be present to make the message a memorable one. It requires not only the communication of product information but also the act of salesmanship in the message in order to persuade the consumer to purchase a particular brand. Moreover, it is not enough to simply make a proposal to the target audience; the offer must be one that piques the consumer's interest and must explain how the product will make a difference in his or her life.

Reeves utilized the USP theory for many of the clients on the Ted Bates agency's roster. "M&Ms Melt in Your Mouth, Not in Your Hands," and "Double Your Pleasure, Double Your Fun" are two of the USPs made famous by Reeves.

ARLO OVIATT

See also Advertising Appeals; Reeves, Rosser

Further Reading
Reeves, Rosser, *Reality in Advertising,* New York: Knopf, 1961

United Press (1882)
Strong opponent to dominance of Associated Press

Of the four post–Civil War news-gathering agencies that arose to deliver news reports to newspapers outside of the Associated Press's (AP's) membership, the most powerful was the United Press (UP), which operated between 1882 and 1897 and nearly caused AP's downfall in 1892. After the Civil War, AP members, many of which were old and powerful dailies, protected themselves by prohibiting their local competitors from receiving AP news reports. Needing national and foreign news, these non-AP papers relied on a series of mediocre news services before the UP appeared.

Growing dissatisfaction with the news report of the National Associated Press (NAP) led to the creation by NAP papers of the UP as a New York State stock company in June 1882. Beginning operation with 100 subscribers, after two years the UP had 166 subscribers (compared with the AP's 425 members the previous year).

When Walter P. Phillips became the UP's general manager on October 1, 1883, the wire gained a leader who could challenge the AP's dominance. Phillips, who between 1875 and mid-1882 had advanced in the AP's Washington, D.C., bureau from telegrapher to bureau chief, was a master at finding economical telegraphic routes outside of the AP–Western Union alliance and, as a seasoned newsman, quickly brought the UP's news report up to AP standards.

The UP's principal financial benefactors were Charles H. Taylor of the *Boston Globe* and James W. Scott (and later John R. Walsh) of the *Chicago Herald,* who were denied AP memberships. They poured large sums of money into the UP to make its news report competitive with the AP's.

Within three years of its inauguration, the UP was strong enough to entice the AP's management into secret stock trusts and collusive agreements. During the mid-1880s, unruly New England AP papers seeking lower rates threatened each wire with jumping to its rival; many eventually ended up in the UP, convincing both wires' managers that covert cooperation was safer than competition.

In 1885 and 1887, UP officers pooled a large amount of UP stock and sold half of it to members of the AP's executive committee, secretly binding the two wires together. At a 4 percent annual dividend and with redemption of earlier stock issues, some AP committee members received a six-year income of $6,500. Meanwhile, Phillips and the AP's general manager, William Henry Smith, signed several secret agreements to avoid competing for newspapers and to share each other's news dispatches.

When they discovered this collusion in 1892, midwestern AP editors broke up the trust, reorganized the AP as a national wire, and went to war with the UP, both wires fighting nationally for the allegiance of all U.S. dailies. In the realignment after the trust, the UP's new benefactors were the *Sun,* the *Herald,* and the *Tribune* in New York City, each paying large amounts to finance the UP's war effort. In 1895, the AP had 396 members and the UP had 338 clients, but as newspapers defected to the AP at an increasingly faster pace in 1896 and 1897, the UP was forced to shut down on April 7, 1897. The AP emerged with 637 members.

RICHARD A. SCHWARZLOSE

See also Associated Press; Cooperative News Gathering; United Press Associations (1907); United Press International

Further Reading
Schwarzlose, Richard A., *The Nation's Newsbrokers: Vol. 2, The Rush to Institution: From 1865 to 1920,* Evanston, Illinois: Northwestern University Press, 1990

United Press Associations (1907)

E.W. Scripps started strongest competitor to the Associated Press

Before its merger with Hearst's International News Service (INS) in 1958, the United Press Associations (UP) for 60 years offered a wide variety of news and feature services for newspapers and broadcast outlets in the United States and abroad and served as the news wire of the Scripps-Howard news conglomerate. The UP was one of six international wire services and the only serious domestic news competitor for the Associated Press (AP).

When an earlier United Press (founded in 1882) was discovered to be colluding secretly with AP leaders in the delivery of news dispatches to their newspapers, midwestern publishers reorganized the AP, went to war with the UP, and forced the latter out of business in 1897. The loss of the UP left without wire service reports those newspaper publishers who were blocked from AP news by local AP competitors.

One publisher left without an AP report was E.W. Scripps, who in 1897 owned five dailies, had a large piece of another daily, and was establishing a chain of dailies on the Pacific coast. Able to get AP membership for some but not all of his papers, Scripps believed that the AP's members would never allow AP news to be delivered to some of the newspapers that Scripps intended to create in the future.

Because 70 percent of U.S. dailies were outside of the AP for one reason or another in 1897, Scripps formed a national wire service, creating Scripps-McRae Press Association in the midwest and Scripps News Association in the west, and allying with the independent Publishers' Press Association in the east. Serving 150 papers in their first year, this coalition of wires exchanged news and jointly served a national news report. By 1907, the coalition had 369 subscribers, and although the AP had 800 members that year, the coalition's totals were growing six times faster than the AP's.

Rumors that Publishers' Press dispatches were untrustworthy and that the wire was deeply in debt prompted Scripps to purchase the wire and merge it with his own wires on July 15, 1907. This created the United Press Associations, a New York State stock corporation and a subsidiary of the Scripps newspaper chain. Scripps's new wire was called the United Press and had John Vandercook as its first president. He was followed in 1912 by young, brash, and ambitious Roy Howard.

Howard brought energy and self-respect to the UP, constantly visiting UP bureaus, vigorously promoting the wire everywhere, and constantly upgrading the report. The UP's news report in 1912 consisted of 10,000 to 12,000 words per day. Howard demanded colorful and readable copy, interviews, and news features in addition to trying to beat the AP on breaking news.

World War I coverage gave the UP an opportunity to expand its own international reporting and its list of clients at the expense of the AP, which was limited by international cartel arrangements with Reuters. A news service designed for evening newspapers, the UP and its clients benefited from the time difference between the European battlefield and the United States.

In 1920, when Howard left the UP for other Scripps duties, the UP had 780 clients (compared with the AP's 1,258), a growth during Howard's eight years of nearly 60 percent (compared with the AP's growth of 45 percent). William W. Hawkins succeeded Howard for three years, and from 1923 to 1935, Karl A. Bickel was president. Under Bickel, the UP gained a reputation as a rapid-fire, risk-taking, underpaid, rowdy bunch of reporters who were hard to scoop and who wrote bright, engaging news copy. He also spearheaded the UP's opening of service for radio stations. When Bickel took office, the UP had 867 clients in 36 countries, and when he left, the UP had 1,360 clients in 49 countries.

Hugh Baillie became UP president in 1935, and when he retired in 1955, the UP served 4,515 clients in about 80 countries (compared with AP's 7,000 news outlets in 68 countries). A skilled and dramatic writer who occasionally left his presidential office to help cover major news, Baillie sought and rewarded reporters (or Unipressers, as they called themselves) who wrote with flair and feeling.

By the time Frank H. Bartholomew became UP president in 1955, the UP and the INS were slowly but steadily losing clients to the AP as a result of a 1945 Supreme Court decision that opened AP membership to all who could afford its service. Dating from the 1920s, discussions of a merger between the UP and the INS came to fruition on May 24, 1958, when the UP absorbed the INS, forming United Press International.

RICHARD A. SCHWARZLOSE

See also Associated Press; Cooperative News Gathering; United Press (1882); United Press International

Further Reading
Baillie, Hugh, *High Tension,* New York: Harper, 1959; London: Werner Laurie, 1959
Bartholomew, Frank H., *Bart: Memoirs of Frank H. Bartholomew – President, United Press, 1955–58,*

United Press International, 1958–62, Sonoma,
California: Vine Brook, 1983

Bickel, Karl A., *New Empires: The Newspaper and the
Radio,* Philadelphia: Lippincott, 1930

Morris, Joe Alex, *Deadline Every Minute: The Story of the
United Press,* Garden City, New York: Doubleday, 1957

Schwarzlose, Richard A., *The Nation's Newsbrokers: Vol.
2, The Rush to Institution: From 1865 to 1920,*
Evanston, Illinois: Northwestern University Press, 1990

United Press International

Formed by merger of key Associated Press rivals

In the 1950s, Scripps newspapers' United Press (UP) and the Hearst newspapers' International News Services (INS) were slowly but steadily losing clients to the Associated Press (AP) as a result of a 1945 Supreme Court antitrust decision that opened AP membership to all who could afford its service. Dating from the 1920s, discussions aimed at merging the UP and the INS came to fruition on May 24, 1958, when the UP absorbed the INS, forming United Press International (UPI), one of six international wires in the 1990s.

In 1958, the UP had 5,063 clients and the INS reported having 3,000 clients, but after the merger, in which some clients dropped at least one wire service, the emerging UPI, a subsidiary of E.W. Scripps newspaper company, entered the field with 5,600 print and broadcast clients around the world, as compared with the AP's 7,275 U.S. members and foreign subscribers. UPI's news department, representing the best from UP and INS staffs, offered a lively and bright news report of aggressive spot news reporting and interpretation that challenged and, on most occasions, matched the AP's dependable and accurate, if stodgy, news reporting. But as more news voices crowded into the news marketplace after the 1950s, and as the costs of computerizing news handling and delivery soared in the 1970s, two national news wires clearly could not survive the competition.

From 1958 until the late 1960s, UPI and the AP had roughly comparable circumstances in terms of worldwide outlets and staffs, technology, and their respective reputations as news reporting organizations. Financially, however, the AP had the edge, its annual budget running about 15 percent larger than UPI's; the AP relied more on lucrative newspaper contracts, and UPI depended on cheaper broadcast contracts.

As broadcast news reporting reduced newspapers' opportunity to capitalize on scoops and extra editions and as the growth of daily circulation slowed to a halt, newspapers reduced the number of news wires they received, replacing them with supplemental news and feature syndicates. In 1948, 31 percent of daily newspapers took more than one news wire, a figure that went down to 25 percent in 1962, 18 percent in 1980, and 6 percent in 1990.

UPI gradually became known as the second wire in the United States in the 1970s, and as it passed from owner to owner in the 1980s, UPI's share of the U.S. daily newspaper market eventually plummeted. UPI served 54 percent of U.S. dailies in 1966, 37 percent in 1985, and only 16 percent in 1990. (In those same years, the AP served 68 percent, 73 percent, and 87 percent of dailies, respectively.)

Like its UP and INS forerunners, UPI, although a profit-making subsidiary of a newspaper company between 1958 and 1982, seldom made an annual profit, needing either the revenues of feature subsidiaries or subsidies from its parent newspaper company to break even. As long as Scripps newspapers were profitable, UPI survived.

The 1970s, however, brought sweeping computerization of news handling, which was costly for both wires and all newspapers. UPI posted a $5 million deficit in 1978, and Scripps, finding it increasingly difficult to pay UPI's bills, proposed the creation of a partnership among newspaper leaders to sustain UPI. When industry response proved insufficient, Scripps announced in 1980 that it was selling UPI.

Two years later, Media News Corporation, a consortium headed by Douglas Ruhe and William Geissler formed to purchase the wire, acquired UPI and $12 million in cash and forgiven debt for $1. Inexperienced in the news business, Media News officers filed for bankruptcy protection in April 1985.

Mexican publisher and businessman Mario Vázquez-Raña purchased UPI in bankruptcy court for $40 million in 1986 and spent $12 million upgrading the wire's technology. Fearing Vázquez's political influence on UPI's news reports, clients began leaving UPI, forcing Vázquez to relinquish control of UPI to Infotechnology in 1988.

UPI filed for bankruptcy again in August 1991, after the wire's employees took a 35 percent pay cut to help save UPI. The Saudi-financed Middle East Broadcasting Centre, which provided a news and entertainment service in English and Arabic for the Middle East, North Africa, and Europe, purchased UPI for $3.95 million in June 1992.

In the mid-1990s, UPI announced plans to reorganize its services to emphasize the needs of broadcasters, government and business clients, and international, rather than U.S., markets. UPI had lost much ground. UPI's global client total had fallen from 5,600 in 1958 to 2,000 in 1992, and its employee total had fallen from 1,840 in 1984 to 500 in 1992.

RICHARD A. SCHWARZLOSE

See also Associated Press; Cooperative News Gathering; United Press (1882); United Press Associations (1907)

Further Reading

Bartholomew, Frank H., *Bart: Memoirs of Frank H.
Bartholomew – President, United Press, 1955–58,
United Press International, 1958–62,* Sonoma,
California: Vine Brook, 1983

Gordon, Gregory, and Ronald Cohen, *Down to the Wire:
UPI's Fight for Survival,* New York: McGraw-Hill, 1990

Schwarzlose, Richard A., "The Associated Press and
United Press International," in *The Future of News:
Television–Newspapers–Wire Services–Newsmagazines,*
edited by Philip S. Cook, Douglas Gomery, and

Lawrence W. Lichty, Baltimore, Maryland: Johns Hopkins University Press, 1992

United States Information Agency

Spreads information about the United States throughout the world

President Dwight D. Eisenhower authorized creation of the U.S. Information Agency (USIA) in 1953, following a campaign promise to introduce greater efficiency in government. Several departments, chiefly the Department of State, had carried out overseas information activities with little coordination and some waste. Eisenhower also saw merit in bringing public opinion overseas to facilitate understanding and acceptance of U.S. policies. Secretary of State John Foster Dulles had little interest in public opinion and was content to be rid of media operations such as the Voice of America. However, the Department of State maintained

control over "people to people" exchange programs until 1978, when they became part of the USIA.

The USIA's basic mission over the years remained constant: to explain U.S. governmental policy and objectives to the rest of the world, usually meaning the "opinion elite" (government and military officials, religious leaders, teachers and students, etc.); to counteract foreign information activities directed against the United States; and to familiarize the rest of the world with U.S. culture and society so as to increase understanding and acceptance of U.S. policy. Its director also could act as informal presidential advisor on public diplomacy, but that was rare; some presidents did not even invite directors to sit as observers, much less as participants, on the National Security Council. Several USIA directors had media experience; Edward R. Murrow and Carl Rowan were renowned journalists. Regardless, few had the strong presidential support that would provide political clout with Congress or influence over foreign policy.

The USIA carried out its missions through several Washington, D.C.–based operations: a press bureau, with its own wireless file service and periodicals; a broadcasting bureau,

USIA offices abroad house a variety of information about the United States.
(National Archives)

with radio (Voice of America and Radio Martí), television (Worldnet), and motion picture services; exchanges of persons through the Fulbright Program and other programs; exhibits and cultural performances; and book translations. Several services – libraries, binational centers, publication of magazines and periodicals – operated through U.S. Information Service (USIS) posts, which functioned as the USIA's overseas offices in almost every nation where the United States had diplomatic relations. Much of the USIA's material appeared in foreign languages, although English predominated in much of its output. It offered English lessons through the binational centers and broadcast programs; certain radio programs and printed materials were in simplified English, chiefly for language learners.

As of 1995, the USIA cost roughly $1.35 billion a year – modest, compared with defense appropriations, but large enough to attract congressional budget-cutters, some of whom proposed the economy measure of re-merging the USIA with the State department in the 1995 session. The Agency has grown very little over the years, despite having USIS posts in nearly three times as many nations as it did in 1953 and despite the proliferation of communications technologies. The USIA's output also provoked congressional attention. Supporters and critics of governmental foreign policy alike might denounce its uncritical or overcritical coverage of the administration's foreign policy initiatives or its too frequent or infrequent presentation of U.S. social problems.

The USIA has been called "the place where journalism and diplomacy meet." That sums up much of its dilemma. Its messages had to come across as truthful and balanced if they were to gain credibility with a sometimes skeptical world public, and its journalistic staff strove for credibility and balance. But pressure from Congress, the Department of State, and the president might cause the USIA to concentrate heavily, and perhaps selectively, on some foreign policy events, while paying little attention to others. Vietnam dominated the USIA's output in the late 1960s, but the State department forbade the agency to cover the U.S. evacuation of Saigon in 1975. Its coverage of life in the United States angered some southern congressional members for its overemphasis on civil rights protests in the 1950s and 1960s. The White House attempted to alter the agency's carefully balanced coverage of Watergate. The USIA's influence on U.S. public opinion was not at issue: with very few exceptions, the congressional act establishing the agency enjoined it from distributing its material within the United States.

Surveys conducted by the agency on its effectiveness generally showed quite high levels of credibility. When its audiences saw it as less credible, it was usually because they felt that the U.S. government would not be truthful when the truth would harm its interests. They saw the USIA as part of the U.S. government, however hard its staff worked to maintain some degree of independence. Congress considered many proposals to reorganize the USIA over the years, but, at the end of the twentieth century, all of them had failed.

DONALD R. BROWNE

See also Broadcast Propaganda; Propaganda

Further Reading
Bogart, Leo, *Premises for Propaganda: The United States Information Agency's Operating Assumptions in the Cold War,* New York: Free Press, 1976
Dizard, Wilson P., *The Strategy of Truth: The Story of the U.S. Information Service,* Washington, D.C.: Public Affairs Press, 1961
Elder, Robert E., *The Information Machine: The United States Information Agency and American Foreign Policy,* Syracuse, New York: Syracuse University Press, 1968
Green, Fitzhugh, *American Propaganda Abroad,* New York: Hippocrene, 1988
Hansen, Allen C., *USIA: Public Diplomacy in the Computer Age,* 2nd ed., New York: Praeger, 1989
Henderson, John W., *The United States Information Agency,* New York: Praeger, 1969
Rubin, Ronald I., *The Objectives of the U.S. Information Agency: Controversies and Analysis,* New York: Praeger, 1968
Sorensen, Thomas C., *The Word War: The Story of American Propaganda,* New York: Harper & Row, 1968

University Presses

Provide major outlet for scholarly publications

University presses are publishing houses attached to universities through a variety of arrangements, reflecting greater or lesser involvement by the institution's administration and faculty. Editorial and publication decisions typically are made with the approval of a supervisory editorial board composed of university faculty and sometimes administration. Historically, they have been the major source of scholarly publications, both periodicals and books, venturing in the later twentieth century into trade and other types of publishing as well. Because scholarly publishing is rarely profitable, they are customarily subsidized by university support of overhead or operating costs. Additional funding from agency and government grants has become increasingly necessary.

The history of university presses in the United States spans the history of publishing in the United States, but university presses in their modern form appeared with the rise of the U.S. university system following the Civil War. Although there were only about 80 U.S. university presses in the 1990s, together with 20 other scholarly presses they produced 18 percent of the titles published in 1992, representing 10 percent of total book sales.

In contrast to the British model of the university press (typified by the "Oxbridge" model of the Oxford and Cambridge University presses) designed to produce fine editions of established authors and works, U.S. university publishing reflects the influence of the German and French model of education and publishing. In such a system, the scholarly output of academic efforts carried on in research-oriented institutions is disseminated by a university-based publishing system – particularly necessary in the absence of publication by commercial publishers.

The first printing press in the American colonies was acquired by Harvard College in 1639, when its first president, Henry Dunster, married the widow of the man who had brought the press to Massachusetts. Its earliest publications included the *Bay Psalm Book* and the *Indian Bible,* among the first books printed in America. However, the print shop was not a formal publishing house, and in any case, it shortly became a private business separate from Harvard. Between the American Revolution and the Civil War, similar presses appeared and disappeared in association with the early colleges, functioning primarily as print shops for their own institutions as well as others in their communities; in some instances, they served as workshops for student printers and journalists.

The first U.S. university press in its modern form was arguably that founded with Cornell University in 1869. Although Cornell's press was the first to carry the formal imprint as a university press, it closed in 1884, not to reopen until 1930. The founding of the Johns Hopkins press in 1876 under Daniel Coit Gilman is cited as the beginning of the first continuously operating university press and, according to some, the establishment of the U.S. model of university publishing. Indeed, Gilman is reputed to have been the originator of the "publish or perish" ethos in U.S. higher education, and Hopkins's earliest publication was a periodical, the *American Journal of Mathematics.*

In the era up to World War I, several universities, and with them several attendant university presses, were founded, including University of Pennsylvania, Notre Dame, Sewanee, Howard, Chicago, Columbia, Northwestern, North Carolina, Stanford, Princeton, University of California, Harvard, and Yale, among others. Many, like the University of Chicago's press, were established as part of the new university's structure. Others, like Princeton's and Harvard's, were built through the efforts of interested individual faculty or alumni.

The rise of technology, research, and education in the United States saw a proliferation of university presses in the decades of the two world wars and the Great Depression, particularly at state universities, religious universities, and private universities in the south, midwest, and far west. The need to distinguish printing from publishing became increasingly evident with the establishment of university presses as formal academic publishing houses. The benefit of university involvement in editorial decisions often was undermined by the economic and administrative demands of printing. Most university presses eventually abandoned printing activities in favor of subcontracting to private print shops. The role of the editorial board in accepting scholarly writing for publication became the characteristic strength of a university press, having at stake the prestige and sometimes even the tenure of its authors – who were more and more frequently scholars from other universities.

Scholarly publishing benefited from the educational boom following World War II, sparked in part by the influx of returning soldiers going to college on the GI Bill and fueled by Cold War–era demands for rapid development in technology. University presses increased their market share during the 1950s and 1960s, but the economic situation saw serious deterioration in the 1970s as universities faced substantial cutbacks. The financial crunch had become a constant fact of life by the 1980s, under pressure from diminished support from parent universities and changes in the market for scholarly publishing. Many presses responded by expanding their involvement in publishing serious trade books and books of regional interest such as poetry and cookbooks.

The advent of electronic word-processing and publishing meant both challenge and opportunity. While the production of books can be facilitated with electronic editing, some presses adopted the new and rapidly changing technologies more easily than others. Moreover, unpredictable standardization in editing and publishing technologies presented further problems. Electronic publishing seems to lend itself to scholarly periodicals, notably those in the sciences, which become outdated rapidly and are extremely expensive to produce on paper. However, putting periodicals on-line changes the critical role of the university press editorial board and staff.

The value of the university imprint traditionally has been rooted in the authority and knowledge underlying its editorial policies and judgment. At the same time, the mission of the university, and by extension its press, was declared by Daniel Coit Gilman to be "to advance knowledge, and to diffuse it not merely among those who can attend the daily lectures . . . but far and wide." The historical tension between the two concerns, gatekeeping and dissemination, promised to become the defining struggle for university presses in the twenty-first century.

PRISCILLA COIT MURPHY

See also Book Publishing in the Eighteenth Century; Book Publishing in the Nineteenth Century; Book Publishing in the Twentieth Century

Further Reading

Geiser, Elizabeth A., ed., *The Business of Book Publishing: Papers by Practitioners,* Boulder, Colorado: Westview, 1985

Jeanneret, Marsh, *God and Mammon: Universities as Publishers,* Urbana: University of Illinois Press, 1989; Toronto, Ontario: Macmillan of Canada, 1989

Kerr, Chester, *A Report on American University Presses,* Washington, D.C.: Association of American University Presses, 1949

Parsons, Paul, *Getting Published: The Acquisition Process at University Presses,* Knoxville: University of Tennessee Press, 1989

Tebbel, John, *A History of Book Publishing in the United States: Volume II: The Expansion of an Industry, 1865–1919,* New York: Bowker, 1975

_____, *A History of Book Publishing in the United States: Volume III: The Golden Age Between Two Wars, 1920–1940,* New York: Bowker, 1978

_____, *A History of Book Publishing in the United States: Volume IV: The Great Change, 1940–1980,* New York: Bowker, 1981

USA Today

Innovative newspaper founded in 1981

From its founding on September 15, 1981, *USA Today* caused as much debate and discussion as any media venture in U.S. journalism history. Published by the 90-newspaper group Gannett Company, *USA Today* was the creation of Allen H. Neuharth, who saw it as a national publication that could halt the decline of newspaper readership through innovations in writing, typography, and the use of extensive statistics, color, and graphics. From its earliest issues, the four-section paper was praised for its revolutionary approach to news presentation and criticized as "Al Neuharth's Technicolor Baby," "fast-food news," "McPaper," "mediocre," "fluff," and "cartoon journalism."

In addition to its colorful, organized appearance, *USA Today* also was noted for its full-page weather map and a sports section, often described as one of the best in the nation for its comprehensive coverage and statistics. The paper had a distinctive editorial page that provided an opposing viewpoint under its own house piece and columns that reflected the wide diversity of its readers. It also provided brief nuggets of news from every state and placed heavy emphasis on coverage of television.

Journalism educator George Albert Gladney said it was no coincidence that *USA Today* was invented soon after the rise of television's "news doctors." Gannett consciously borrowed from television news. Neuharth conceded that planners "blatantly stole what we thought would work from other segments of the media." Neuharth said that the paper also stole the best talent from Gannett's nationwide chain in a plan called the "Loaner Program."

An early analysis of *USA Today* by Robert Logan identified three controversial innovations because they clashed with traditional journalism: overformatting, or layout dictated not by traditional news values but by inflexible design considerations; reliance on market research aimed at what readers want (entertainment) rather than what they need, such as information; and lighter news that would lead away from investigatory or in-depth reporting. Although touted as a national newspaper, critic Ben Bagdikian saw *USA Today* more as a five-day-per-week magazine that did not pretend to be a primary carrier of serious news.

In 1992, *USA Today* stimulated a major ethical controversy when one of its sports writers confirmed that tennis champion Arthur Ashe had contracted the AIDS virus. Before the article was scheduled to appear, Ashe called a news conference to announce that he suffered from AIDS and to criticize the media for intruding into private lives. Ironically, *USA Today* had decided against going with the story.

According to a 1992 study of 230 of the nation's largest newspapers, the newspaper industry still had a long way to go before all U.S. dailies looked and acted like *USA Today*. Smaller, group-owned papers showed more tendency to adopt *USA Today* characteristics, while big "elite" papers and independents resisted adopting "McPaper" traits.

Results from another study by John K. Hartman suggested that taking *USA Today*'s approach represented the best known hope in the newspaper industry for reversing the decline in young adult readers and the best known way for rival editors to protect against encroachment by *USA Today*.

ALF PRATTE

See also Audience Research for Newspapers; Neuharth, Al

Further Reading
Gladney, George Albert, "The McPaper Revolution? *USA Today*-Style Innovation at Large U.S. Dailies," *Newspaper Research Journal* 13:1–2 (Winter 1992), pp. 54–71

Hartman, John K., "*USA Today* and Young-Adult Readers: Can a New-Style Newspaper Win Them Back?," *Newspaper Research Journal* 8 (1987)

Logan, Robert A., "*USA Today*'s Innovations and Their Impact on Journalism Ethics," *Journal of Mass Media Ethics* 1 (1986)

Neuharth, Allen, *Confessions of an S.O.B.*, New York: Doubleday, 1989

Prichard, Peter, *The Making of McPaper: The Inside Story of 'USA Today'*, Kansas City, Missouri: Andrews, McMeel & Parker, 1987

V

Vietnam War
War changed the role of the press in U.S. affairs

The Vietnam War was a long, costly, and divisive struggle in which wartime censorship of the U.S. press was redefined, the press's impact on public opinion moved from secondary to primary concern in conduct of war, and the press's role to oppose political establishment was cemented in the minds of the U.S. public. Advocates credited the press with revealing failed military strategy and tactics and expediting the U.S. withdrawal from an untenable position in southeast Asia. Critics charged the press with playing into the hands of the enemy by creating a "second front" of growing antiwar sentiment within the United States that made defeat inevitable. After the war, North Vietnamese leaders acknowledged the second-front thesis. Their massive Tet Offensive of 1968 was waged not to win military objectives but to discourage the U.S. public and thus became the turning point in the war. The U.S. military's well-learned lessons about controlling access to information about the Vietnam War were brought to bear two decades later in its effective control of the world press during the Persian Gulf conflict.

The Vietnamese expected independence after liberation during World War II, but the French, with U.S. financial backing, returned in 1946 to reassume their prewar colonial control of the Asian nation. The colonialists were opposed by Vietnam's national hero, Ho Chi Minh, and his guerrilla army, the Viet Minh, which had resisted the Japanese and which now turned to the Communist bloc for support. After nine frustrating years and a humiliating military defeat at Dienbienphu, the French pulled out. The 1954 Geneva agreements ended hostilities, partitioned Vietnam at the 17th parallel, and scheduled reunification through national elections in 1956. However, the South's chief of state, Premier Ngo Dinh Diem, refused to sign the accord and appealed to the United States for assistance to fight the Communists. Diem proved an increasingly oppressive ruler. His opposition in the South, the National Liberation Front, formed a guerrilla force known as the Vietcong and prepared for civil war.

During the administrations of Dwight D. Eisenhower and John F. Kennedy, U.S. involvement was limited to provision of military equipment and advisers for South Vietnam's army. The number of U.S. military advisers grew from less than 1,000 in 1960 to more than 16,300 in 1963. Buddhist uprisings in Saigon and Hue and increasing unrest in rural areas led to overthrow of the Diem regime in 1963. The U.S. military secretly helped the coup. During the political chaos that followed, the United States increased its commitment of combat troops and national resources.

President Lyndon Johnson believed if South Vietnam fell to communism, neighboring states soon would follow. In 1964, he manipulated a naval skirmish with North Vietnamese forces to convince Congress to endorse the Tonkin Gulf Resolution, which authorized expanded U.S. commitment. By the end of the year, the U.S. force stood at about 200,000 troops and eventually exceeded 500,000. Large-scale bombing of the North began in February 1965.

The U.S. purpose in Vietnam was called into question by a television news story in August 1965. CBS correspondent Morley Safer filed film showing U.S. Marines shooting up and torching the village of Cam Ne. The shocking pictures shook millions of loyal U.S. citizens who believed that their sons were in Vietnam to stop aggression. Now their sons looked like the aggressors.

U.S. field commander William Westmoreland accused the networks of using graphic portrayals of violence to undermine public support for the war. Actually, the networks were sensitive to controversy and generally avoided violence, which was considered unsuitable for broadcast. Safer's so-called "Zippo lighter" story was the exception rather than the rule. Fewer than one quarter of television reports on the war before 1968 showed actual combat. Fewer still were critical of U.S. policy, although not because the government censored news.

U.S. military planners decided against compulsory censorship in the Vietnam War because they felt enforcement was impossible. Civilian circulation in the war zone simply could not be controlled. Instead, the Pentagon asked journalists for voluntary cooperation, which on the whole it got. Between August 1964 and December 1968, less than 1 percent of journalists breached the Pentagon's voluntary guidelines. In June 1971, the Pentagon dropped the word "censorship" and instituted the Wartime Information Security Program (WISP) for control of wartime news. By the end of the decade, WISP was phased out because new communication technologies made field censorship obsolete.

Before 1968, most U.S. news media were "hawkish," or supportive of government policy in South Vietnam. Brief-

A Buddhist monk sets himself afire in Saigon, South Vietnam, in 1963 to protest the government's policies against his faith.
(UPI/Corbis-Bettmann)

ings held every afternoon at the U.S. Embassy in Saigon, nicknamed the "five o'clock follies" by the press corps, showed that the enemy was losing a war of attrition to the superior technology of the United States. For each U.S. or South Vietnamese casualty, many enemy killed and wounded were recorded.

Some field correspondents, such as David Halberstam of the *New York Times,* Neil Sheehan of United Press International, Malcolm Browne and Peter Arnett of the Associated Press, and Charlie Mohr of *Time,* had their own news sources that raised doubts about U.S. strategy. They reported military defeats, government corruption, and fewer enemy casualties. Their discouraging dispatches were downplayed or ignored altogether by their editors because they contradicted the experts at the White House and the Pentagon.

The first public debate about whether a war of attrition could be won came in the U.S. Senate Foreign Relations Committee hearings of 1966. The televised hearings were headed by Senator William Fulbright of Arkansas, who had lost confidence in the president's war policies after pushing

Johnson's Tonkin Gulf Resolution through the Senate two years earlier. After U.S. senators challenged the president on national television, criticism of the war policy became conceivable, even respectable.

Late in 1966, the senior editor-correspondent of the *New York Times,* Harrison Salisbury, began filing stories from North Vietnam's capital, Hanoi. Salisbury's detailed accounts with pictures showed missed bomb targets, civilian casualties, and untouched war industries, which belied Defense Secretary Robert McNamara's assertions that pinpoint bombing was wearing down the North. Critics loyal to the government charged Salisbury and the *Times* with aiding the enemy, and his Pulitzer Prize was retracted. Nevertheless, the Pentagon's credibility was further eroded.

Hanoi's strategy to neutralize superior U.S. technology had been to hit and run in rural areas under cover of darkness. But, after months of infiltrating the South with troops and supplies via the Ho Chi Minh Trail through neighboring Cambodia, the rebels were strong enough to attack openly and in daylight. During the Tet holiday of January 1968, the enemy simultaneously struck U.S. strongholds in cities and outposts all over the South. The U.S. Embassy in Saigon was overrun and held briefly by the Vietcong. The city of Hue was held for 25 days. The U.S. command admitted that it had been caught off guard.

Although U.S. commanders claimed tactical victory, the audacity of the North laid bare for even the most loyal news editors in the United States the credibility gap between Washington, D.C.'s, claim of winning a war of attrition and what really was happening. The editors no longer could ignore their correspondents' fears of failed U.S. strategy in Vietnam. Tet revealed to the U.S. public the stamina and determination of the Communist insurgents.

CBS television news anchor Walter Cronkite had led the approving consensus, but Tet changed his mind. He returned from a tour of the action convinced that investing more U.S. troops in the struggle would be futile. Risking his reputation for journalistic objectivity, he decided to broadcast a personal editorial. He said that Washington must start thinking about getting out of the war. Cronkite's public turn of faith devastated President Lyndon Johnson, who felt he had lost public support. On March 31, 1968, Johnson stunned the nation by calling for peace negotiations and withdrawing his candidacy for reelection.

One magazine issue probably contributed to antiwar feeling in the United States more than any other print publication: the June 27, 1969, issue of *Life* magazine, featuring the photographs of 242 U.S. troops killed the previous week. The pictures of the dead told all and needed no adornment by text. Their plainness lent to the issue an air of a high school yearbook, which added to the dead soldiers' innocence. The pictures laid bare the inequities of the war. Most of the dead were black, poor, rural, or blue-collar; many upper-class and college-bound youths had draft deferments.

Having promised an end to the war, the new president, Richard Nixon, announced in November 1969 a plan to withdraw U.S. ground forces gradually. Another phase of Nixon's plan was kept secret: to bomb the enemy into submitting to peace negotiations. To close the Ho Chi Minh Trail, the Pentagon had begun regular B-52 raids of Cambodia the previous March. In 1971, the bombing spread to neighboring Laos. The bombing campaign was kept secret and was not revealed to the U.S. public until congressional probes in 1973.

The secret bombing did not stop enemy infiltration from the North. On April 30, 1970, President Nixon announced a ground invasion of neutral Cambodia to wipe out North Vietnamese strongholds. Nixon's expansion of operations shocked and angered the people of the United States, who thought the war was winding down. Demonstrations on many college campuses became violent as students clashed with local authorities, and a few demonstrators at Jackson State and Kent State Universities were killed. Surreal scenes of khaki-clad National Guard troops facing angry students suggested that the Asian war had spread to the United States.

The Nixon administration accused the press of bias. Vice President Spiro Agnew gave a series of speeches that virtually accused journalists of treason and abandonment of U.S. troops in the field. The White House included several prominent journalists in its secret "enemies list" of political opponents. Agnew's attacks were the public part of a secret White House campaign of domestic intelligence activities, including illegal wiretaps and burglaries, to undermine detractors and conceal the Cambodian bombing.

In June 1971, the White House's worst fears were realized in release of the *Pentagon Papers,* a 47-volume classified report on conduct of the Vietnam War. The government tried to block newspaper publication on grounds of national security, but the U.S. Supreme Court decided that the essentially historical document did not warrant prior restraint. Nixon authorized the creation of a surveillance team to plug leaks of classified information and sabotage political opponents. Nixon won a landslide victory in the 1972 presidential election, but he was forced to resign in disgrace two years later when the press uncovered illegal White House activities in the so-called Watergate scandal.

In January 1973, Nixon and Secretary of State Henry Kissinger proclaimed "peace with honor" in formal agreements signed in Paris by all warring parties. The United States would retire from the conflict, leaving the defense of South Vietnam to its own army. In March, Hanoi began releasing U.S. prisoners of war. Efforts to find U.S. soldiers who were listed as missing in action lasted two decades.

The South Vietnamese army was demoralized by U.S. withdrawal and yielded to a major assault by the Communists in January 1975. Saigon surrendered on April 30, 1975, as the last civilian evacuees departed by helicopter from the roof of the U.S. Embassy. The 30-year struggle for

A U.S. Army officer sets aflame a hut used to train Vietcong guerrillas.
(UPI/Corbis-Bettmann)

national reunification by Ho Chi Minh's followers was over. From 1961 to 1975, more than 50,000 U.S. troops died in combat and several hundreds of thousands were wounded. U.S. news correspondents also suffered casualties. The war's cost of life for Vietnam, Cambodia, and Laos was in the millions.

By exposing the war's costs and injustices, the press in the United States had helped end it. Yet most U.S. journalists were as late as other U.S. citizens in recognizing the war's futility. Reporters lacked historical perspective and were overwhelmed by the war's complexity. Particularly in the Diem years, editors were reticent to believe their own correspondents' dispatches instead of official government sources. The press establishment's failure was exposed in the My Lai story of October 1969, which told of Vietnamese civilians massacred by U.S. soldiers. The story was overlooked for months until released through a little-known news service by Seymour Hersh, who won the 1970 Pulitzer Prize for international reporting.

RUSSELL J. COOK

See also Agnew, Spiro T., and the Media; Credibility Gap; Johnson, Lyndon B., and the Media; Mass Media and the Antiwar Movement; Mass Media and the Military; Nixon, Richard, and the Media; Pentagon Papers; Persian Gulf War; War Photography; Watergate Scandal

Further Reading

Browne, Donald, "The Voice of America: Policies and Problems," *Journalism Monographs* 43 (1976)

Cumings, Bruce, *War and Television,* New York and London: Verso, 1992

Dennis, Everette E., et al., *The Media at War: The Press and the Persian Gulf Conflict,* New York: Gannett Foundation, 1991

Fall, Bernard, *The Two Viet-Nams: A Political and Military Analysis,* 2nd rev. ed., New York: Praeger, 1967; London: Pall Mall, 1967

Halberstam, David, *The Making of a Quagmire,* New York: Random House, 1965; London: Bodley Head, 1965

Hallin, Daniel, *The "Uncensored War": The Media and Vietnam,* New York: Oxford University Press, 1986

Violence Against Journalists

Critics of journalists' work take frustration out physically

Thousands of journalists have been injured and hundreds killed. Many of the victims have been war correspondents, exposed to the same dangers as the soldiers they covered. Other journalists, however, have been attacked in the United States by critics of their work.

Especially during the 1800s, it was common for citizens upset by a story to attack the journalist responsible for it. Thus, at least 43 journalists had been killed in the United States by the end of the twentieth century, hundreds injured, and thousands involved in brawls of one kind or another.

The violence started during the American Revolution. Before then, editors emphasized facts, often simply reprinting stories from other papers. During the revolutionary era, editors began to report and take sides on more controversial issues, and readers, angered by their stories, sometimes canceled their subscriptions and withdrew their advertisements. Angrier critics might hang an editor in effigy. If that failed, they might beat, horsewhip, or tar-and-feather the editor, destroy the press, then escort the editor out of town.

Some critics used their fists. Others used a stick, cane, knife, sword, pistol, or shotgun. Especially in the south and the west, editors also became involved in duels, and at least eight died in them. Regardless of the consequences, few of the people involved in the duels and other violence were ever arrested. Fewer were convicted.

To protect themselves, some journalists kept a pistol in their desk and took it out at the start of work every day. A few editors hired bodyguards. Others fortified their offices.

The violence occurred everywhere in the United States and usually involved men. Journalists were most likely to fight two other groups of men: politicians and the editors of rival journals. Then, as today, journalists frequently criticized politicians, and politicians hated the attacks.

The violence involved many of journalism's most famous editors: James Gordon Bennett was mailed a bomb, Horace Greeley was beaten on a street, and Joseph Pulitzer shot a political rival. In 1882, Pulitzer's chief assistant at the *St. Louis (Missouri) Post-Dispatch* shot and killed a lawyer angered by the paper's criticisms.

Some cities were more violent than others. Work at the *Vicksburg (Mississippi) Sentinel* was especially dangerous. Four or five of the paper's editors were killed, one was drowned, and another was imprisoned. Violence was also common in Denver, Colorado; New Orleans, Louisiana; and San Francisco. Similarly, some groups of editors were more likely than others to be attacked, especially abolitionist editors in the North before the Civil War, and black editors in the South after the war.

Five of journalism's most famous victims include the following:

1.) William Lloyd Garrison, editor of the *Liberator,* opposed slavery vehemently and was attacked by a mob in Boston.
2.) Elijah Lovejoy, an editor and Presbyterian minister, opposed alcohol, tobacco, Catholicism, and slavery. Lovejoy's presses were destroyed repeatedly, and when a new one arrived, it was taken to a warehouse. A mob gathered outside the warehouse on the night of November 7, 1837, threatening to set the entire building afire. In the struggle that followed, Lovejoy was shot and killed.
3.) and 4.) Frederick G. Bonfils and Harry Tammen, publishers of the *Denver Post,* were attacked in their office by a lawyer. Bonfils was critically wounded and Tammen shot in the left shoulder.
5.) James King, editor of the *Evening Bulletin* in San Francisco, was shot and killed by a politician whom he had criticized.

The violence seemed to subside during the early- and

mid-1900s. Why? As newspapers were acquired by chains, more professional managers replaced journalism's once colorful (and powerful) editor/owners. Also, hundreds of dailies ceased publication, leaving only one in most cities. As dailies died, so did the fierce competition between them. Reporters also changed. Most of them in the 1990s were now college graduates with middle-class backgrounds and values; few still carried guns. Moreover, some people upset by a story often preferred to sue a paper for libel.

About 20 journalists were killed in the United States during the twentieth century. Many of the victims in the later part of the century were Haitian, Cuban, and Vietnamese immigrants who worked for foreign-language media. Because of the continuing violence (and threats of more violence), newspapers everywhere increased their security. Typically, they hired guards to provide 24-hour security and began monitoring visitors, inspecting packages, and more.

War correspondents also continued to die. About 58,000 U.S. military personnel died in Vietnam. Forty-five correspondents also died, and 18 were still missing at the end of the century. Another 27 correspondents were killed in just the first 18 months of fighting in the former Yugoslavia. The casualty rate there was unusually high because combat zones were open to the press.

Several organizations monitored developments threatening the free flow of information throughout the world. In 1992, the Overseas Press Club called the previous 10 years an "open season" on journalists, with unprecedented violence directed against them. The club calculated that, from 1982 to 1991, 341 journalists were killed, 131 were kidnapped or disappeared, 1,938 were arrested, and 363 were expelled. A second study found that 273 journalists died in accidents, were murdered, or died from other causes on the job from 1982 through 1989. Latin America was especially dangerous, with high numbers of deaths in Colombia, Peru, El Salvador, and Mexico.

In a single year – 1994, one of the worst on record – 72 reporters, photographers, and editors were slain, many the deliberate targets of political assassination. Typically, no one was immediately arrested or tried for the crimes.

FRED FEDLER

See also Abolitionist Press; Party Press; Penny Press; Yellow Journalism

Further Reading
Myers, John Myers, *Print in a Wild Land,* Garden City, New York: Doubleday, 1967
Nerone, John C., *Violence Against the Press: Policing the Public Sphere in U.S. History,* New York: Oxford University Press, 1994
Simon, Paul, *Freedom's Champion: Elijah Lovejoy,* Carbondale: Southern Illinois University Press, 1994
Sussman, Leonard R., "Dying (and Being Killed) on the Job: A Case Study of World Journalists, 1982–1989," *Journalism Quarterly* 68:1–2 (Spring 1991), pp. 195–199
Wilmer, Lambert A., *Our Press Gang, or, A Complete Exposition of the Corruptions and Crimes of the American Newspapers,* Philadelphia, J.T. Lloyd, 1859; London: S. Low, 1859

Voice of America
Official U.S. international broadcasting service

The U.S. government created the Voice of America (VOA) as its official international broadcasting service in 1942, then placed it under the Office of War Information. By the war's end, the VOA broadcast in more than 30 languages. Congress nearly abolished it in 1946, but anti-Western broadcasting from the Soviet Union and its allies rescued it, and it soon surpassed its wartime dimensions. It operated through the Department of State from 1945 to 1953, then came under the newly created U.S. Information Agency, its home into the late 1990s. It had transmitter sites in 11 countries, was on the Internet, and broadcast in nearly 50 languages – chiefly English, with several hours daily each for Arabic, French, Mandarin, Russian, and Spanish.

The VOA often faced congressional criticism from members who regarded government-operated broadcasting as the voice of the administration, who resented the VOA for carrying programs critical of foreign governments or of U.S. foreign policies they supported, or who felt that private industry would do its job better and less expensively. (Private industry was uninterested.) The VOA's charter obligated it to present "accurate, objective, and comprehensive" news, a "balanced and comprehensive projection of significant American thought and institutions," and "the policies of the United States." Accordingly, it offered a variety of programming – mainly news and other informational formats but also music and other cultural material. Rare among international broadcasters, it carried editorials presenting U.S. government policy. Many of the VOA staff wished to see it more independent of government control, like the British Broadcasting Corporation's World Service, but Congress disagreed. Surveys showed it to be both credible and popular.

DONALD R. BROWNE

See also Broadcast Propaganda; Propaganda; United States Information Agency

Further Reading
Alexandre, Laurien, *The Voice of America: From Detente to the Reagan Doctrine,* Norwood, New Jersey: Ablex, 1988
Browne, Donald R., "The Voice of America: Policies and Problems," *Journalism Monographs* 43 (1976)
Fitzgerald, Merni Ingrassia, *The Voice of America,* New York: Dodd, Mead, 1987
Pirsein, Robert W., *The Voice of America: A History of the International Broadcasting Activities of the United States Government, 1940–1962,* New York: Arno, 1979
Shulman, Holly C., *The Voice of America: Propaganda and Democracy, 1941–1945,* Madison: University of Wisconsin Press, 1990

W

Wall Street Journal

Leading financial newspaper

Several news agencies were working New York's Wall Street financial district in the 1800s, collecting information and distributing it to financial offices. Two agency reporters named Charles H. Dow and Edward D. Jones began a rival news service, Dow Jones and Company, in 1882.

The reporters' financial bulletin service was named the *Customers' Afternoon Letter,* and then, in 1889, the *Wall Street Journal.* The paper was successful largely because its information was faster and more reliable than its rivals.

Dow kept an index of 12 leading stocks, later expanding the number to 20, as an attempt to represent the performance of the stock market. That index, which included 30 stocks in the late 1990s, was called the Dow Jones Industrial Averages and was still an important daily indicator of the market's performance.

In 1902, Clarence Walker Barron bought Dow Jones and Company and the *Wall Street Journal.* He also started a weekly magazine for investors, called *Barron's,* in 1921. Early on, the paper was written primarily for those in financial markets, but that changed in the 1940s under the leadership of Barney Kilgore. Seeking a wider circulation, stories were written more clearly for a broader audience across the country. It remained a national newspaper, successful because of its reach and its quality writing.

Scandals appeared during the Barron days, when some columnists' opinions on movements of the stock market were "for sale." Another major scandal occurred in 1982 when a columnist sold information about his forthcoming column, "Heard on the Street," to a stockbroker.

Dean Nelson

War Advertising Council

Advertisers joined to promote the war effort

As the United States moved out of the Great Depression in the late 1930s, advertising executives, rightly or wrongly, felt that their livelihood was being targeted for elimination.

As Sidney R. Bernstein, editor of *Advertising Age,* wrote in 1941, advertising as a profession had been "smarting under the endless stream of restrictions and anti-advertising statements by bureaucrats and advocates of serious social change."

Against this backdrop, members of the Association of National Advertisers and the American Association of Advertising Agencies met just three weeks before the United States entered World War II to discuss what could be done to turn the tide. Bernstein recounted that James Webb Young, one of advertising's most celebrated copywriters, suggested that advertising would have to show that it could be a force for good. "A greater use of advertising for social, political and philanthropic purposes will help remove the distaste for advertising which now exists among many influential people." Furthermore, Young argued, if advertising helped social institutions such as government, schools, and churches, then criticism of the profession would shift from the general to specific advertisements that could be found objectionable without cries for outright bans. If critics could use advertising to further their own ends, Young reasoned, then advertising would be insulated from significant government intrusion.

Within three months after the Japanese attack on Pearl Harbor, the Advertising Council (later renamed the War Advertising Council) had been formed, with Young and Rubicam chairman Chester LaRoche as its first chairman. Unlike the Committee for Public Information, its counterpart in World War I, the War Advertising Council (WAC) was run independent of government.

With little merchandise to sell during the war, advertisers turned to WAC campaigns as an effective means of showing support for the war effort and keeping their corporate logos in the public's eye. Some famous campaigns were developed during the war, as the council responded to the government's need to encourage the public to be careful about discussing troop movements ("A Slip of the Lip Will Sink a Ship") and begged the public's patience when such movements resulted in delays ("The Kid in Upper Four"). These ads and others reinforced to the U.S. public the need for food rationing, price controls, conservation, and the purchase of War Bonds, allowing the average citizen to be a part of the war effort in many ways.

It should be noted that advertising agencies across the country were producing ads independent of the WAC,

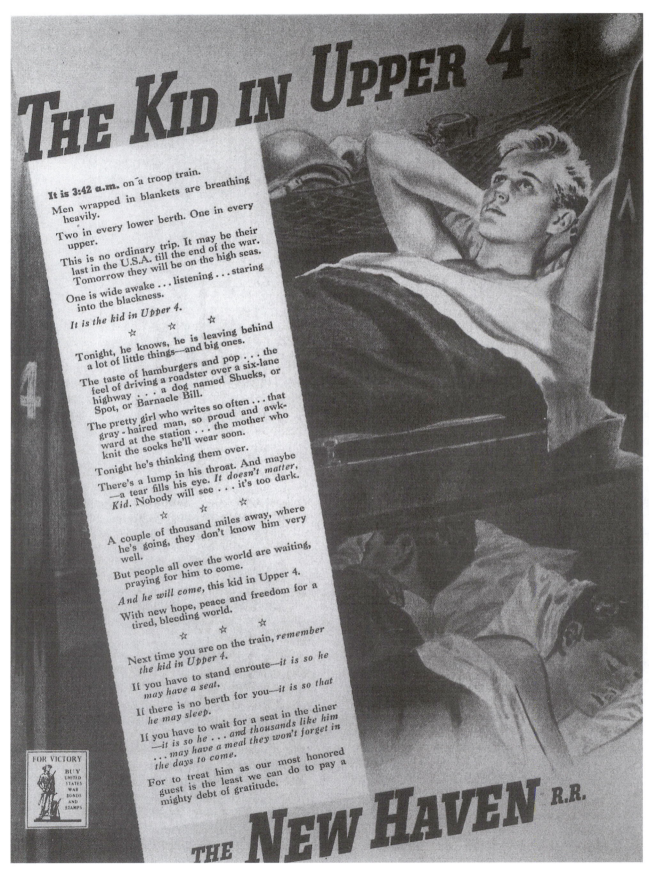

One of the most popular public service ads produced during World War II
(Courtesy of The Advertising Council, Inc.)

working with local publishers, usually newspapers. As *Advertising Age* pointed out several times in the summer of 1942, advertising agencies and their clients were anxious to be seen as supporting the war effort.

Yet the council had been seen as so successful – it had placed an estimated $1 billion in advertising – that following the war, there was widespread support for the organization to continue its efforts in such areas as driving safety ("The Life You Save May Be Your Own"), forest fire prevention (Smokey Bear), and support of a humanitarian campaign to assist postwar Europe through CARE and the American Red Cross.

THOMAS GOULD

See also Advertising Council; Committee on Public Information

Further Reading

Berger, Warren, "Ad Council: A Grand Idea That Worked," *Advertising Age* (November 11, 1991)

Bernstein, Sidney, "A Crucial Meeting on the Eve of War," *Advertising Age* (November 11, 1941)

Young, James Webb, *The Diary of an Ad Man*, Chicago: Advertising, 1944

War Correspondents

Journalists who follow wars face some similar problems

The profession of war correspondent has had at least some problems remain consistent over the years: food and shelter; a line of communication to one's news organization; transport to the front lines and elsewhere; the prospect of being wounded, killed, or captured; dealing with or evading censorship; determining the "big picture" of a battle or war without being smothered and misled by official sources; deciding where one's loyalties lie; maintaining an independent position on matters both military and political; and convincing editors back home that the correspondents have a better view of the war than the editors do. This list of war reporting variables points to the difficulties that emerge when foreign correspondence – the reporting of political events around the globe – turns into war correspondence. The political elements remain in war news, but the focus shifts to combat; the stakes are elevated from discussion and dialogue to death and destruction. The reporting of war becomes a professional obsession, and the messenger is a frequent target for military leaders, politicians, and the news consumer.

U.S. journalism reported wars almost from the dawn of newspaper and magazine publishing on the North American continent, but the emergence of a U.S. tradition of war reporting is most accurately dated from the Mexican War (1846–47). George Wilkins Kendall of the *New Orleans (Louisiana) Picayune* and others produced a steady flow of dispatches from a U.S. expeditionary force deep in Mexico, overcoming problems of distance and communication with

their persistence and enterprise. Their work predates that of William Howard Russell of the *Times* of London, usually acknowledged as the father of war correspondence as a special function of journalism. His independent reporting of British miscues and mismanagement in the Crimean War (1854–56) led to early news management in official London but earned him the respect of soldiers and citizens alike for his forthrightness in writing about what he saw and knew.

Robert Furneaux labeled the period 1854–1914 the "golden age of war correspondence." War raged intermittently around the globe, and those who reported those wars became a special breed of journalist providing essential links to the battlefield. Visual journalism rose in status with the printed word, as both photographers and artists rushed to the combat areas to exercise their talents.

The people of both the North and the South were ill-prepared either to fight the Civil War or to cover it as news, but they adapted quickly. Five hundred journalists, few of whom knew anything about war fighting, flooded Washington, D.C., at the outset, and the army of reporters on the Northern side stayed near that level throughout the four deadly years. The *New York Herald,* for instance, put at least 40 reporters in the field, at a cost of $500,000 in 1860 currency. Northern journalists made use of the telegraph net, largely controlled by the government, or evaded censorship by a variety of means. While reporters on the Confederate side were less likely to challenge censorship or criticize the war, Northern generals often complained that their battle plans showed up in Union newspapers and wound their way back to Confederate camps.

The Civil War expanded the visual aspects of news, a precursor to the rush to cover late-twentieth-century warfare with live television. Photographers' wagons brought

Ernie Pyle at work in Anzio, Italy, in 1944
(Courtesy of the Scripps Howard Foundation)

the cumbersome wet-plate equipment to the wars. Stark exhibits of pictures of the dead in battlefield repose gave the public a somber, realistic view of war. Artists' sketches filled such publications as *Harper's Weekly* and *Frank Leslie's Illustrated Newspaper*, although such artwork was sometimes less than faithful to reality.

The Indian Wars (1866–91) found the U.S. Army executing a federal policy of corralling Native American tribes on reservations; their near annihilation was a dismal side effect. Although it was difficult, tedious campaigning, at least 20 accredited correspondents rode with units during the war on the plains. Oliver Knight described the status of these reporters as a privileged one in which military secrecy was seldom a problem, the reporters shared spartan conditions and dangers with soldiers, and the government needed all the news it could get from the campaigns, criticism and all. Much of the reporting, Knight argued, was superior to the sometimes formulaic writing in the modern press.

The zenith of the war correspondent, in terms of glamour and freewheeling freedom, came in the series of short wars at the turn of the century. The Boer War, the Russo-Japanese War, and the Spanish-American War took reporters to faraway places, and, with luck, close to the action. While there is no evidence to support the myth that William Randolph Hearst was responsible for the latter conflict, he led the press corps in zeal and spared no expense to report the action.

World War I saw imposition of severe restrictions on all journalists – some for supportable military goals, others simply to protect against political and public challenge and embarrassment. With heavy restrictions imposed, much war writing was propagandistic, although many journalists wrote forthright, readable, honest, and comprehensive stories.

By the eve of World War II, radio, telegraph, and telephone links girdled the globe, changing communication at all levels. Radio reporters and commentators brought battles live to U.S. living rooms. Photos and prolific illustrations filled newspapers and magazines. With world freedom at stake, Allied journalists submitted – not always without protest – to censorship. There is little evidence on the whole, however, that the people of the United States were not given a fair idea of how the war was going, what dangers their family members faced around the world, or criticism of both the military and political course of the war.

The emergence of television and limited war both changed the face of post–World War II war correspondence. Jets moved "resources" – reporters and equipment – to war areas in hours. Satellites made instantaneous transmission of words and pictures a common practice. The military security problem was heightened by these facts of modern communication, and reporters were less likely to serve as conduits for official government versions of foreign policy decisions, including waging war. The long anguish of the Vietnam War led some to blame the press for a military failure, but the reporting from the early days of that war included ample evidence of the difficulty of winning such a war and the frailty of the South Vietnamese government.

Limited war, with its predictable division over aims and goals; instant and easy satellite communication; and rapid worldwide transportation all changed the role of war correspondents and the way they work in the age of information. Those who practice the trade are just as committed to aggressive and truthful reporting as their predecessors; the luster of the job, however dangerous and controversial, still remains.

WALLACE B. EBERHARD

See also Civil War Photography; Civil War Press (North); Foreign Correspondents; Indian Wars; Korean War; Mexican War; Spanish-American War; Telegraph; Vietnam War; War Photography; World War I; World War II

Further Reading

Bullard, Frederic Lauriston, *Famous War Correspondents,* Boston: Little, Brown, 1914; London: Pitman, 1914

Desmond, Robert W., *Tides of War: World News Reporting, 1940–1945,* Iowa City: University of Iowa Press, 1984

Furneaux, Rupert, *News of War: Stories and Adventures of the Great War Correspondents,* London: M. Parrish, 1964

Hodgson, Pat, *The War Illustrators,* New York: Macmillan, 1977; London: Osprey, 1977

Knight, Oliver, *Following the Indian Wars: The Story of the Newspaper Correspondents Among the Indian Campaigners,* Norman: University of Oklahoma Press, 1960

Knightley, Phillip, *The First Casualty: From the Crimea to Vietnam: The War Correspondent as Hero, Propagandist, and Myth Maker,* New York: Harcourt Brace Jovanovich, 1975; London: Quartet, 1982

Mathews, Joseph J., *Reporting the Wars,* Minneapolis: University of Minnesota Press, 1957

Pedelty, Mark, *War Stories: The Culture of Foreign Correspondents,* New York: Routledge, 1995

Warner Communications

Began as a family-owned movie studio

Warner Communications blossomed from a small family-owned film studio appropriately named for the brothers who ran it. Although there were four Warner brothers – Sam, Albert, Harry, and Jack – who were in love with show business in general and film in particular, Harry and Jack Warner formed the foundation of the Warner Brothers film studio.

The first hit for the brothers was a propaganda film, *My Four Years in Germany,* which opened in New York in March 1918. Warner Brothers entered into an agreement in 1925 with Western Electric to sell a sound process for film called Vitaphone. This led to the first "talkie." The sound era of film was ushered in on October 6, 1927, with Warner's *The Jazz Singer,* starring Al Jolson.

For 20 years from the 1940s until the 1960s, Warner

Brothers was the dominant studio in the area of animation. Outpacing even Walt Disney, Warner created lasting cartoon characters such as Bugs Bunny, Porky Pig, and Daffy Duck.

Warner Brothers was purchased by Seven Arts in 1966 and a few years later by a parking lot conglomerate called the Kinney Company. This company then changed its name to Warner Communications. That company merged in 1989 with Time Inc., creating the country's largest media company. Holdings of the new company, called Time Warner, are spread over cable, broadcast, film, and publishing industries. In the 1990s, some of these included Warner Books, Home Box Office, and magazines such as *Time, People,* and *Sports Illustrated.* In 1996, Time Warner and Turner Broadcasting System combined, bringing Turner's additional film and television studies as well as several cable networks – including TBS, TNT, and CNN – and two sports teams to the parent company.

ANTHONY HATCHER

Further Reading

Auletta, Ken, *Three Blind Mice: How the TV Networks Lost Their Way,* New York: Random House, 1991

Clurman, Richard M., *To the End of Time: The Seduction and Conquest of a Media Empire,* New York: Simon & Schuster, 1992

Gabler, Neal, *An Empire of Their Own: How the Jews Invented Hollywood,* New York: Crown, 1988; London: W.H. Allen, 1989

Higham, Charles, *Warner Brothers,* New York: Scribner's, 1975

Maltin, Leonard, *Of Mice and Magic: A History of American Animated Cartoons,* New York: McGraw-Hill, 1980

War of 1812

Unpopular war led to newspaper disagreements about fighting it

The War of 1812 often has been called one of the United States' most unpopular wars because of the questionable motives leading to its start. For Republicans, the war was the only salvation for the nation. Without war, the country would continue to cower to the British, and the Republicans would be disgraced to the point of losing their dominance in Washington, D.C. For Federalists, the war was an immoral war perpetrated by Republicans against the economic interests of the country.

When the Peace of Amiens between France and Great Britain was broken in May 1803, U.S. ships were seized, sailors were impressed into the British navy, blockades were imposed, and U.S. commerce was disrupted by both the British and the French. In retaliation, the Republican-dominated Congress voted for the Embargo Act that prohibited U.S. trade with Britain and France and halted all sailings.

Federalists – a party dominated by northeastern mer-

chants, shipping firms, and large landowners – launched a bitter and successful campaign against the Embargo Act. Leading the campaign were Federalist newspapers, particularly the more prosperous mercantile and shipping newspapers in Boston, Philadelphia, and New York. These newspapers, always the first to carry stories of British victories in Europe, warned that the United States could never win a war against Britain's mighty naval force. When President James Madison asked the governors to call up their volunteer militias, Federalist editors counseled men to think carefully before answering the call.

As the war spirit grew, however, it became evident to some Republicans that the Federalists' antiwar attitude had to be silenced. For example, the governor of Massachusetts asked his legislature to investigate the mounting problem of sedition in the state's Federalist newspapers. However, before the legislature could take action, the governor was defeated by a Federalist, who called off all investigations into the libel problem.

Despite the concern about possible seditious writings, little if any official action was taken, leaving Federalist newspapers free to continue their opposition to Republican foreign policy. This was a significant achievement, considering that 14 years earlier the offenses of an opposition political faction had resulted in the Alien and Sedition Acts. Yet, in 1812, when the country did go to war, and when the dominant political party was opposed by a strong minority party, lawmakers refused to counter opposition with legislation. Once the war began, however, the citizens did not share that tolerance.

When the first U.S. surrender occurred at Detroit, Michigan, in August 1812, Federalists sharpened their attacks. But the citizenry fought back, literally. In Baltimore, Maryland, the *Federal Republican* was mobbed twice, leaving one dead and 11 seriously injured. The *American Patriot* of Savannah, Georgia, was forced to close when a mob attacked the editor, and a mob assaulted the editor of the *Norristown (Pennsylvania) Herald.* In 1813, the office of the Elizabethtown *(New Jersey) Essex Patriot* was burned to the ground. Public opinion became the censor, and freedom of the press and of expression disappeared.

While Federalist newspapers were condemning the war, Republican newspapers were relating heroic stories about the exploits of military heroes. Most of the information came by way of dispatches from the front, letters from the War Department, and newspapers closer to the action. Newspapers had no system of war correspondents, and newspapers that were published near military camps recounted battles almost as if they were social affairs, with much description but little detail. Hence, what the public read of the war was mostly positive and congratulatory. Because of the lack of any organized effort by the newspapers to cover the war, the military found no need to institute censorship systems.

After Andrew Jackson's arrival in New Orleans, Louisiana, in December 1814, he placed the city and surrounding areas under martial law. In January, Jackson soundly defeated the British in the battle of New Orleans, three weeks after the Treaty of Ghent was signed. Jackson did not lift martial law until March, however, and he warned newspapers not to print anything about the treaty unless he approved the stories. He even had one prominent legislator arrested and several officials banished from New Orleans for criticizing his heavy-handedness after the treaty had been signed. Later Jackson wrote that "unlimited liberty of speech is incompatible with the conduct of a camp and that of the press is more dangerous when it is made the vehicle of conveying intelligence to the enemy or exciting to mutiny." The question of how much the constitutionally guaranteed civil liberties must yield during unstable times and during wartime continues to be a major point of contention between the watchdogs of the press and the military.

DONNA L. DICKERSON

See also Alien and Sedition Acts of 1798

Further Reading
Dickerson, Donna Lee, *The Course of Tolerance: Freedom of the Press in Nineteenth-Century America*, New York: Greenwood, 1990; London: Greenwood, 1991
Gilje, Paul, "The Baltimore Riots of 1812 and the Breakdown of the Anglo-American Mob Tradition," *Journal of Social History* 13 (1980)
Hofstadter, Richard, *The Idea of a Party System: The Rise of Legitimate Opposition in the United States, 1780–1840,* Berkeley: University of California Press, 1969
Lofton, John, *The Press as Guardian of the First Amendment,* Columbia: University of South Carolina Press, 1980

"War of the Worlds"

Broadcast showed how much some listeners believed radio

The CBS broadcast on Halloween Eve, 1938, by Orson Welles and his Mercury Company of the H.G. Wells science fiction classic *The War of the Worlds* created widespread panic across the United States, demonstrated the power of radio in a war-wary era, and launched Welles's career. The realism of the broadcast forced thousands from their homes in New York and New Jersey, site of the supposed Martian invasion, and briefly tied up the nation's emergency and newspaper offices with calls from distraught listeners certain that the nation had come under enemy attack.

The script, written by Howard Koch, seized upon news flashes in telling the story of a modern-day Armageddon. Listeners who tuned in late missed the announcement that they were only hearing a radio drama. In the panic that followed, many reported "seeing" the flames of battle and personal attacks by Martian madmen. Hospitals treated victims for shock. The hysterical demanded that their cities be immediately blacked out to avoid annihilation. Some gathered in groups to pray. Others threatened suicide.

Editorial writers later charged that radio was preying upon the fears of its listeners and demanded that the Feder-

al Communications Commission investigate. At the time, Welles told reporters he was "bewildered" by the broadcast's impact. In later years, he admitted "War of the Worlds" was a forceful and troubling reminder that in 1938 hearing was believing and that "people believed what they heard on the radio." This truth makes "War of the Worlds" a case study in the power of mass communication to move audiences.

BRUCE EVENSEN

War Photography

Technology limited earliest pictures to those of bodies only

War photography began with Roger Fenton, who reached the Crimean War front in April 1855 and returned to London three months later with 300 glass-plate negatives, none of which showed combat action. Long exposures imposed by the slow chemicals and lenses of mid–nineteenth-century photography made action photos impossible.

Fenton, like many who followed him, complained that requests for portraits interfered with his work, but to refuse meant that he would get no help in moving his darkroom van from one location to the next. Once, a shell blew the roof off his van. The climate was so hot that developing fluid burned his hands. Always, there was the need to prepare wet collodion plates in total darkness inside the crowded van just before they were exposed.

Fenton, James Robertson – who in 1857 photographed the fall of Sebastopol during the Bengal-Sepoy rebellion in India – and Civil War photographers led by Mathew Brady from 1861 to 1865, had to document the aftermath of battle. This showed more than the daguerreotype portraits of soldiers during the Mexican War, 1846–48, but a public accustomed to dashing scenes of battle painted by artists found war photos dull at first, until the impact of faithful documentary by the unblinking camera sank in. Despite equipment limitations, Brady and 300 other Union-accredited photographers during the Civil War showed the effects of combat that emphasized the human element, rather than panoramas of smoke-filled battlegrounds populated by saber-wielding icons.

At the outbreak of the war, the editor of the *American Journal of Photography* wrote that battle scenes were "fine subjects" for any artist but that photographers would be safe, since they would "have to be beyond the smell of gunpowder or their chemicals would not work." He quickly was proven wrong.

Brady and his assistants, called Brady's Photographic Corps, were the first to take the field. They were driven by Brady's own sense of history and aided considerably by his intimate acquaintance with government leaders, who helped him and his skilled cameramen enter combat zones and document, in more than 7,000 photos, the fullest coverage of war up until that time. Nearly killed at the first battle of Bull Run, Brady and his crew escaped. The first battle scenes produced by their cameras caused a sensation, and they soon returned to action.

The fairly new medium of photography captured a new wartime tool: observation balloons used to spot enemy movements and to direct artillery fire. Battlefields and trenches strewn with dead and wounded, artillery, ships, railroads, field hospitals, gutted buildings, and soldiers drawn stiffly to parade-ground attention – all were captured by Brady and his assistants.

Many of the latter chafed at Brady's insistence on copyrighting in his name all the photos taken, including those photos made with their own equipment on their own time. Alexander Gardner, who had been in charge of Brady's Washington, D.C., gallery, broke with him and formed his own photographic corps in 1863, taking with him some of Brady's most skilled photographers, including Timothy O'-Sullivan, later famed for his photographic documentation of the west.

Technical advances made things easier for photographers of the Spanish-American War, who could use dry glass plates coated with gelatin bromide in their cameras. Early roll film, combined with faster lenses, permitted handheld photography in bright light. Most startling of all were motion pictures showing troops in action, albeit mostly posturing.

World War I saw continued improvements in equipment and materials that some argue were not matched by photographers using them. A photo of a dead German machine gunner is described as aesthetically no better than Gardner's photo of a slain Southern sharpshooter slumped against a stone wall at Gettysburg. Others contend that, as frozen by the lens, the dead grow deader, that there is no reason to expect one battlefield casualty to look any different from another, regardless of when the picture was taken or with what equipment. More than just a record, a photograph confronts the viewer with unchanging reality, the opportunity to verify.

This was applied professionally in World War I trench warfare. Edward Steichen, peacetime painter and soft-focus photographer, was put in charge of aerial reconnaissance photography during the second battle of the Marne. He was so impressed with the beauty of straight photographs requiring maximum detail, brilliance, and contrast that he repudiated his previous work style and began mastering pure photographic techniques. Steichen later led in developing photography's own aesthetic, independent of traditional art forms.

Between world wars came the development of 35-millimeter cameras like the Leica and Contax that used inexpensive, motion picture film. Coupled with more light-sensitive lenses, these cameras revolutionized action photography and encouraged photographers to expand one photo into a story when appropriate, dealing in film frames as writers handle paragraphs. Even so, the single photo encapsulating history often remains most memorable.

Two examples stand out. Alfred Eisenstaedt covered the Ethiopian War in 1935 with a Leica. His photo of a dead, barefoot Ethiopian soldier, calves wrapped in World War I–era puttees, emphasized the plight of a primitive nation attempting to defend itself with spears against Mussolini's bombers and machine guns. It aroused early opposition to Fascism. A newsreel photo of a Chinese baby, crying helplessly in the bombed wreckage of Shanghai in 1937, signaled the beginning of total war against civilian populations.

Robert Capa's career started with the Spanish Civil War in 1936 and ended when he was killed by a land mine in French Vietnam, his fifth war, in 1954. He embodied the professional that, in the century since Roger Fenton, had become the photojournalist, one whose vision illuminated humankind's struggle to understand, and survive, forces beyond individual control.

World War II was photographed by stars like Capa, Eisenstaedt, Margaret Bourke-White, Steichen, Eliot Elisofon, W. Eugene Smith, and many anonymous servicemen and women. They parachuted, or waded ashore, or rode and marched into combat beside armed troops and sustained proportional or higher casualties. By emphasizing the human element, perhaps the expression on a single infantryman's face, they recorded a world struggle in a universally understood dimension.

The Korean War continued this approach. Photographers increasingly showed an aversion to war, entirely natural for anyone who has seen enough bodies on a battlefield, whether at Gettysburg or Anzio or Inchon. This showed in their work and became even more marked during the Vietnam conflict.

There, with few battle lines clearly defined, photographers learned to survive by being resourceful and analytical. This was best exemplified by Horst Faas, twice wounded, who survived eight years of Vietnam combat photography. In the absence of a formal declaration of war, the lack of military censorship allowed journalists free coverage of war's brutality by either side: the execution of a bound Vietcong captive in Saigon, a naked child running and screaming with terror after being burned accidentally with napalm by her own country's air force, atrocities committed by the Vietcong on Vietnamese villagers allied with the United States.

U.S. Marines, who had been fired on in a village area, retaliated by burning the village after the enemy had slipped away. A CBS television report, "The Burning of the Village of Cam Ne," showed an atrocity committed by U.S. troops. The network was criticized for making the troops look bad, but the U.S. public had to confront – through the unblinking eye of the camera – the inhumanity generally wreaked in war.

ROBERT H. LAWRENCE

See also Brady, Mathew; Civil War Photography; Photographic Technology; Photojournalism in the Nineteenth Century; Photojournalism in the Twentieth Century; Vietnam War

Further Reading

Capa, Robert, *Images of War*, New York: Grossman, 1964; London: Paul Hamlyn, 1964

The Great Themes, New York: Time-Life, 1970

Meijer, Emile, and Joop Swart, eds., *The Photographic Memory*, London: Quiller, 1988

Newhall, Beaumont, *The History of Photography: From 1839 to the Present Day*, rev. ed., New York: Museum of Modern Art, 1964; London: Secker & Warburg, 1972
Photojournalism, rev. ed., Alexandria, Virginia: Time-Life, 1983

Washington, George, and the Press

First president encountered problems with journalists

Throughout his public career, George Washington had interactions with the press. As a Virginia planter, he used local newspapers to advertise for horses and runaway slaves. As commander in chief of the Continental Army during the American Revolution, he feared that the media gave too much military information to the British. As president, he perceived the importance of the press in keeping the people informed, but he also became increasingly upset over media attacks aimed at him personally. After leaving public office in 1797, he continued to read newspapers in an effort to keep informed about national and international events.

During the American Revolution, Washington continually perceived the usefulness of newspapers as sources of information and as morale builders. He tried to control reports about the activities of the Continental Army in order to deny information to the British while, at the same time, working to gain copies of Loyalist papers (particularly from New York City) in hopes of finding out details of the movements of the British army. He encouraged people to save rags for making paper so that newspapers would continue to be published, thus providing reports about the war to their readers. Washington's greatest support for the newspapers, however, came about because of the media's role as a wartime morale booster. The most famous example of this type of encouragement came when General Washington assembled the troops to publicly hear a reading of the first of Thomas Paine's "Crisis" essays, published in the *Pennsylvania Packet* in December 1776.

As president during the early years of the new nation, Washington perceived the press as an essential mechanism for keeping good citizens informed and involved. In his annual address to Congress in 1793, Washington declared:

> There is no resource so firm for the Government of the United States, as the affections of the people guided by an enlightened policy; and to this primary good, nothing can conduce more, than a faithful representation of public proceedings, diffused, without restraint, throughout the United States.

For Washington, the newspapers provided the means for achieving this goal.

Washington's belief in the important role of the media in a republic continued throughout his public career, for he perceived "infinite benefits resulting from a free press." However, the rise of political parties in the 1790s produced partisan newspapers that impugned the opposition in strong, derogatory language. Washington mourned such press behavior:

> It is to be lamented that the Editors of the different Gazettes in the Union, do not more generally, and more correctly (instead of stuffing their papers with scurrility, and nonsensical declamation, which few would read if they were apprised of the contents) publish the debates in Congress on all great national questions, and this with no uncommon pains, everyone of them might do. The principles upon which the difference of opinion arises, as well as the decisions would then come fully before the public, and afford the best data for its judgment.

Even Washington himself, the "Hero of the Revolution," did not escape newspaper attacks. Washington refused to respond publicly to these verbal assaults, but he considered them "outrages on common decency" that were "meant to impede the measures of . . . Government" and "to destroy the confidence, which it is necessary for the people to place . . . in their public servants."

Particularly upsetting to Washington were personal comments in Benjamin Franklin Bache's *Aurora*. Washington concluded that the papers referred to him "in such exaggerated and indecent terms as could scarcely be applied to a Nero, to a notorious defaulter, or even to a common pick pocket." For Washington, such attacks were incomprehensible and served no useful purpose in the public arena. He feared the results of a press with no restraints: "In a word if the government and the Officers of it are to be the constant theme for News-paper abuse, and this too without condescending to investigate the motives or the facts, it will be impossible, I conceive, for any man living to manage the helm, or to keep the machine together."

Washington escaped the public eye in 1797 by retiring from office. His reputation recovered from the press attacks of his presidency following his death in 1799, but his struggles with, and his concerns about, the press during his public career reflected the ongoing tension between government officials and the press that has been a part of American politics ever since.

CAROL SUE HUMPHREY

See also American Revolution and the Press; Party Press

Further Reading

Smelser, Marshall, "George Washington and the Alien and Sedition Acts," *American Historical Review* 59 (1954)
Ward, Harry M., "George Washington and the Media," *Media History Digest* 7 (1987)

Washington Post

The *Washington Post,* the largest newspaper in Washington, D.C., in the late twentieth century, was considered one of the leading newspapers of the world due mainly to its intensive coverage of the U.S. political scene and access to highly placed sources. Its stature went up dramatically in the decades after it played a pivotal role in exposing the Watergate crisis that led to the resignation of President Richard M. Nixon in 1974.

In the late 1990s, about 50 percent of Washington households subscribed to the *Post* each morning – 66 percent on Sunday – giving it the highest market penetration rate of any U.S. metropolitan newspaper and a virtual monopoly of the newspaper field in the capital. As of 1994, daily circulation was 830,081, down slightly from 832,332 in 1993, while Sunday circulation held steady at 1,152,441 compared with 1,152,272 the previous year. A weekly national edition had a circulation of 110,000. The *Post* attained clear preeminence in Washington in 1981 when its afternoon rival, The *Washington Evening Star,* ceased publication.

Founded in 1877 as a Democratic newspaper, the *Post,* known in the 1990s for its liberal editorial policy, was purchased at a bankruptcy sale in 1933 by Eugene and Agnes E. Meyer, parents of Katharine Graham, who became the chair of the executive committee of the Washington Post Company board. Graham turned the family-owned company into a public corporation after assuming control of the newspaper in 1963 following the suicide of her husband, Philip Graham, the company president. She brought in Benjamin Bradlee, widely credited with improving the newspaper's quality, to run the newspaper and broke a strike against pressmen in 1975. Her son, Donald Graham, succeeded his mother as chair of the board and chief executive officer.

The newspaper became the cornerstone of a diversified media empire that included the newsmagazine *Newsweek;* six television stations; cable television systems; newsprint manufacturing and distribution operations; a chain of weekly community newspapers, mainly free distribution, in the Maryland suburbs; the *Herald,* a newspaper in Everett, Washington; and ownership interests in the Los Angeles Times–Washington Post News Service, the *International Herald Tribune,* and Cowles Media Company as well as the Stanley Kaplan Educational Center, which prepared students to take standardized tests. In 1995, it launched an ambitious on-line information service to provide computer access to the newspaper's contents and archives and to enable subscribers to interact with the newspaper and each other.

In the late 1990s, the newspaper maintained 29 foreign, 5 national, and 11 metropolitan news bureaus. Some critics said that its lively, aggressive coverage, including spicy social gossip, lessened after Bradlee's retirement in 1991. Over the years, the *Post* won at least 30 Pulitzer Prizes, with 29 going to individual staff members and one to the newspaper itself for public service in the Watergate affair. In 1981, it was forced to return a Pulitzer Prize awarded to a reporter who had made up a story about an eight-year-old heroin addict in Washington's inner city. African Americans led a 13-week protest against the newspaper in 1986 on the grounds that its redesigned Sunday magazine portrayed them as criminals. Bradlee subsequently apologized.

Maurine H. Beasley

See also Watergate Scandal

Further Reading
Bray, Howard, *The Pillars of the 'Post': The Making of a News Empire in Washington,* New York: Norton, 1980
Felsenthal, Carol, *Power, Privilege and the 'Post': The Katharine Graham Story,* New York: Putnam's, 1993
Roberts, Chalmers M., *The 'Washington Post': The First 100 Years,* Boston: Houghton Mifflin, 1977

Watchdog Concept

News media keeping an eye on government officials

The idea that the news media serve the public as a check on the operation of their government commonly is referred to as the "watchdog concept." The U.S. population is enormous and its government units numerous. Because no individual citizen has either the time or the resources alone to be sure that the government is operating effectively and justly, journalists must perform that task. Under the watchdog concept, therefore, the news media act as agents of the citizenry, keeping a watchful eye on the government, watchdogs guarding the house of the republic itself.

The exact origin of the watchdog concept is unknown, although one scholar suggested that it grew out of free-press case law of the nineteenth century. Clearly, the concept is rooted in democratic press theory and is championed today by those who argue that the public has a "right to know." The existence of such a right is hotly debated in the literature and is usually said to be implied by the First Amendment to the U.S. Constitution, which prohibits Congress from creating laws that abridge free speech or press. In protecting the individual's right to speak and publish, in other words, the framers of the Constitution intended to ensure full participation in the democratic process, enabling citizens themselves to serve as a check on their own governance. Conceived as a watchdog, then, the news media perform a role that is of central importance in the democratic process.

However, some First Amendment scholars have argued that such a role may carry with it unwanted responsibilities. They have suggested that portraying the news media as public servants may entitle citizens to access to the pages of newspapers or may justify mandating that the media cover certain issues. In fact, the public servant model has been employed as partial justification for the regulation of the broadcasting industry.

Discussion of the news media as watchdog has been widespread among those in the industry and has found its way into journalism textbooks and the journalism trade press. Attorneys and judges have used the watchdog concept in free-press litigation to argue for special institutional protections for the news media, such as protection from newsroom searches (*Zurcher* v. *Stanford Daily,* 1980) or immunity from being forced to testify and reveal confidential news sources (*Branzburg* v. *Hayes,* 1979). Such attempts were rejected by the U.S. Supreme Court, which decided that the First Amendment applies to all citizens equally – that the First Amendment rights of journalists are no greater than those of all other citizens. Even so, reinterpretation of U.S. Supreme Court decisions by lower courts has extended some amount of privilege to journalists.

ELIZABETH M. KOEHLER

See also First Amendment in the Twentieth Century; First Amendment Theory; Journalists' Privilege

Further Reading

Bailyn, Bernard, *The Ideological Origins of the American Revolution,* Cambridge, Massachusetts: Belknap Press of Harvard University Press, 1967

Baldasty, Gerald J., and Roger A. Simpson, "Deceptive 'Right to Know': How Pessimism Rewrote the First Amendment," *Washington Law Review* 56 (July 1981), pp. 365–395

Blasi, Vincent, "The Checking Value in First Amendment Theory," *American Bar Foundation Research Journal* 3 (1977)

Chafee, Zechariah, Jr., *Free Speech in the United States,* Cambridge, Massachusetts: Harvard University Press, 1942

Gleason, Timothy W., *The Watchdog Concept: The Press and the Courts in Nineteenth-Century America,* Ames: Iowa State University Press, 1990

Levy, Leonard Williams, *Emergence of a Free Press,* New York and Oxford: Oxford University Press, 1985

Van Alstyne, William W., *Interpretations of the First Amendment,* Durham, North Carolina: Duke University Press, 1984

Watergate Scandal

Crisis that led to resignation of President Richard M. Nixon

The expression "Watergate" refers to the political scandal that forced Richard Nixon to resign the presidency. Washington, D.C., police arrested five burglars who had just broken into the Democratic National Committee (DNC) headquarters at the Watergate apartment and office complex on June 17, 1972, and Nixon resigned on August 9, 1974. Between those two dates was the progressive revelation of illegal campaign practices, of "dirty tricks," of presidential abuses of power in the use of illegal wiretapping, of Internal Revenue Service pressure, of other harassment of alleged political enemies, and of president-directed obstruction of justice to conceal from federal investigators these and other acts. The Watergate scandal preoccupied President Nixon, his closest aides, and, ultimately, Congress, the courts, the press, and the public. The Watergate crisis precipitated several showdowns between the executive and the legislature and the executive and the judiciary and is regarded as one of the more important constitutional crises in U.S. history.

The press took a hand in revealing the misdeeds of the Nixon administration, and the role of the press became an issue itself in the unfolding of the crisis. At first, journalists did not take the DNC break-in seriously. It seemed at most a campaign tactic too stupidly risky to have been authorized by any significant figure in the Republican campaign hierarchy. But the *Washington Post* pursued the story and linked the burglars to the Nixon re-election campaign (the Committee to Re-elect the President, or CREEP, as it became known) and tied dubious CREEP activities to White House staff members.

Still, between the burglary and the 1972 presidential election in November, most journalists and most citizens did not take Watergate seriously. Of 433 Washington correspondents, at most 15 worked full-time on Watergate during this period. The *Washington Post*'s Watergate coverage went out on the *Post* news wire, but few papers picked it up. The White House attacked the *Post* directly by public denunciation and private threat – this seemed one more act in a long-standing war between Richard Nixon and the "liberal news media." Even at the *Post* itself, the national staff was dismissive, and White House correspondents discouraged the two young journalists who were carrying the story, metro desk reporters Bob Woodward and Carl Bernstein, from pursuing it further. The story at first, *Washington Post* publisher Katharine Graham later recalled, "was small and sort of a farce.... It just looked sort of lunatic and not very consequential."

That changed in March 1973, when James McCord, one of the Watergate burglars, notified John Sirica, the federal judge in charge of the case, that the burglars had perjured themselves under pressure. By April, there were credible allegations that President Nixon's two closest advisers, chief of staff H.R. Haldeman and domestic affairs adviser John Ehrlichman, were implicated in this Watergate cover-up along with the president's counsel, John Dean. All three resigned along with Attorney General Richard Kleindienst, who was replaced by Elliot Richardson.

Over the next year, one stunning development followed another. The Senate held riveting, televised hearings in the summer of 1973, highlighted by Dean's astonishingly detailed account of White House meetings with the president at which strategies for covering up Watergate had been discussed. Dean's accusations were ridiculed by White House spokesmen until a second bombshell hit: it came out that conversations in the president's Oval Office were all tape-recorded. This meant that the evidence to verify Dean's damning accusations existed.

For months, a legal battle ensued between the White House and Archibald Cox, the special Watergate prosecutor appointed by Attorney General Richardson, each side seeking control over the White House tapes. The president argued that "executive privilege" required that he not turn over the tapes to the prosecutor. Cox did not back off. Finally, in October 1973, Nixon ordered Richardson to fire Cox. Richardson resigned rather than carry out the order; William Ruckelshaus, second in command at the Justice Department, also refused to carry out the order and was fired. Solicitor General Robert Bork then carried out the president's directive and sealed off the offices of the special prosecutor. The "Saturday night massacre," as it became known, prompted the House of Representatives to initiate

Senator Sam Ervin, standing left, presides over a televised investigation into the Watergate scandal.
(National Archives)

impeachment proceedings against the president. Meanwhile, when Texas lawyer Leon Jaworski was appointed the new special prosecutor, he did not relent in efforts to obtain the tapes.

Everything came to a head in July as the House Judiciary Committee voted largely along party lines to support three articles of impeachment; the Supreme Court voted 8–0 that the president was obligated by law to turn over the tape recordings of all subpoenaed conversations, and the president's lawyers revealed one tape recording from June 23, 1972, just six days after the burglary. This so-called "smoking gun" tape convinced even Nixon's staunchest defenders that he was guilty of obstructing justice.

The *Washington Post* was awarded a Pulitzer Prize for its Watergate coverage. Being out in front on the Watergate story helped establish the *Post*'s national reputation as a serious and aggressive newspaper and a rival to the *New York Times*. When Woodward and Bernstein published their dra-

matic account of the early coverage of the scandal, *All the President's Men,* months before Nixon resigned, the book became a runaway best-seller, and Woodward and Bernstein became national celebrities.

The book and, a year later, the stunning film version pictured Watergate as an epic struggle between young journalists unencumbered by political conviction and seeking only to do their job and a vindictive White House guilty as could be. The Republican version of this, promoted by President Nixon and his allies, depicted a noble president besieged by a hostile liberal press. Both versions exaggerated media power, critic Edward Jay Epstein insisted in *Commentary* in July 1974. It was not the press, he argued, that uncovered Watergate. Woodward and Bernstein's book systematically ignored or minimized the role of the Federal Bureau of Investigation (FBI), federal prosecutors, the Watergate grand jury, and the Congress in coming up with pieces of the puzzle – and similarly minimized how much their own investigation was based on leaks from the proceedings of these other investigators. It ignored the roles of Democratic presidential candidate George McGovern and the civil suits of Common Cause and the Democratic National Committee in keeping Watergate in the public eye and forcing critical disclosures.

It became a common view to picture Nixon driven from office by a hostile press. But most of the press was very slow and very reluctant to take up the story, and the White House constructed this picture itself as a defensive maneuver to displace onto the unbeloved press the responsibility for an investigation in fact carried on more directly by the FBI, the grand jury, Judge Sirica himself, and the Congress.

Even so, as time went by, the press cherished the view of its central role in Watergate as much as anyone. Leonard Downie, one of Woodward and Bernstein's editors and later *Washington Post* executive editor, insisted on the important lesson of Watergate for journalism:

It was hard. It was not glamorous at the time. Later it was glamorous with movies and movie premieres at the Kennedy Center . . . but at the time it was dirty. People weren't sleeping, people weren't showering, Bernstein's desk was a mess, he and Woodward were fighting all the time . . . we were all under such great pressure, it was difficult to figure out what was going on because everybody was against us, because people were whispering to Katharine Graham that they'll ruin her newspaper, and that's still what it's about, you know, initiative and bravery and enterprise. That's what makes a difference.

Watergate became the apotheosis and justification for investigative reporting. It became the central mythological moment in modern U.S. journalism. Still, its impact can be exaggerated. Contrary to a popular belief, Watergate did not initiative a wave of interest in journalism; journalism and communication majors already were shooting upward before Watergate, doubling at the undergraduate level between 1967 and 1972. But Watergate reporting did contribute significantly to the emergence of journalists as public celebrities. It did provide a capstone to the wave of investigative reporting that the Vietnam War and the movements of the 1960s had inspired.

If there was a Watergate myth, there was also a reaction against it. The film *All the President's Men*, which glorified aggressive shoe-leather journalism, was followed a few years later by *Absence of Malice* (1981), which condemned overaggressive journalists whose zealousness in following a story damages innocent lives and reputations. Editors and publishers began worrying out loud even before Nixon's resignation about the dangers of "overkill" in investigative journalism. Nonetheless, a new monument to muckraking existed, thanks to Watergate, and serves still as an inspiration and focal point in the media.

MICHAEL SCHUDSON

See also Agnew, Spiro T., and the Media; Investigative Reporting; Nixon, Richard M., and the Media; *Washington Post*

Further Reading
Bagdikian, Ben, "The Fruits of Agnewism," *Columbia Journalism Review* 11 (January/February 1973)
Epstein, Edward Jay, "Did the Press Uncover Watergate?," in *Between Fact and Fiction: The Problem of Journalism*, edited by Edward Jay Epstein, New York: Vintage, 1975
Lang, Gladys Engel, and Kurt Lang, *The Battle for Public Opinion: The President, the Press, and the Polls During Watergate*, New York: Columbia University Press, 1983
Schudson, Michael, *Watergate in American Memory: How We Remember, Forget, and Reconstruct the Past*, New York: Basic, 1992

Wells-Barnett, Ida B.

Journalist who campaigned to right social wrongs

If Ida B. Wells-Barnett had written for leading white newspapers during the early part of the twentieth century, she would have ranked among the most respected of the muckraking journalists. But Wells-Barnett began her career in the 1880s, and as such, she is remembered as a tough-minded African American woman who, although deeply involved in the post–Civil War struggle for Negro rights, never compromised her journalistic standards.

Her career began in earnest in 1887, when an article she had written for the *Living Way* was received favorably. The story detailed her lawsuit against a railroad company for having refused her a seat in the first-class section of a railroad car even though she had purchased a first-class ticket. The account was picked up by several black papers; subsequently, black editors throughout the country asked her to submit articles. Later, as part owner of the *Memphis (Tennessee) Free Speech*, an African American weekly, she wrote strong editorials about the deaths of three black Memphis businessmen who were lynched after opening a black grocery store in a town monopolized by white grocers. The editorials encouraged blacks to leave Memphis, which many of them did. The exodus hurt the white grocers' business. Ultimately, white mobs destroyed the *Memphis Free Speech* office, forcing Wells-Barnett to move to New York, where she became part owner and writer for the black weekly *New York Age*.

In her coverage of social injustice, she touched upon the sensitive issue of rape. She attempted to expose as a lie the idea that black males sought to rape white women, suggesting that the white men perpetuating the myth might consider that public opinion ultimately would turn against them. An overemphasis on black men as rapists would be damaging to the moral reputation of white women, she wrote. Wells-Barnett did not, however, reserve her criticism for whites only. She wrote that among black educators there were many whose mental and moral defects made them unsuitable as teachers of black children.

In addition to serving as editor of the *Memphis Free Speech* and *Chicago Conservator*, columnist for the *New York Age*, foreign correspondent for the *Chicago Inter-*

Ocean, Wells-Barnett wrote four books on black civil rights issues. Their topics ranged from the injustices of lynch laws to the refusal to include blacks in the World's Columbian Exposition in 1893.

ROBIN GALLAGHER

See also African American Media

Westinghouse
Important in development of radio broadcasting

An electrical equipment manufacturer established in Pittsburgh, Pennsylvania, in 1886, Westinghouse was an important broadcaster from the inception of radio broadcasting. Seeking to retain and expand its radio equipment business after World War I military work, a company official decided to put a radio station on the air to attract listeners – and thus buyers of receivers. Based on experimental wireless work of company engineer Frank Conrad, pioneer radio station KDKA first aired November 2, 1920, from East Pittsburgh. It is usually cited as the oldest station in the country. Westinghouse added other stations over the years, including stations in Boston, Philadelphia, Chicago, Los Angeles, New York, and Fort Wayne, Indiana.

The company entered television with its March 1944 application to the Federal Communications Commission (FCC) to build stations in Boston, Philadelphia, and Pittsburgh. Nervous about costs and the new medium's appeal to viewers and advertisers, Westinghouse pursued only the Boston station, placing WBZ-TV on the air in June 1948. Westinghouse later purchased stations in other major markets, including stations in Philadelphia, San Francisco, Pittsburgh, and Baltimore, Maryland.

Westinghouse Broadcasting Corp. was renamed Group W in mid-1963. Always a wholly owned subsidiary of the manufacturing giant, Group W often fought network dominance of the industry. Concerned about network compensation of affiliates, Group W helped bring about the FCC's third investigation into network operations in the late 1970s. Westinghouse expanded its role in broadcasting when it purchased the CBS radio and television networks for $4.5 billion in 1995.

CHRISTOPHER H. STERLING

See also Broadcast Pioneers; Conrad, Frank; KDKA; Television Networks

Wheeler-Lea Amendments
Focus on false and misleading advertising

The Federal Trade Commission (FTC) was empowered to regulate false and misleading advertising with its inception in 1914. Although the commission did develop and bring cases during its infancy, the agency's powers to regulate advertising were quite constrained until the passage of the Wheeler-Lea Amendments in 1938.

During the 1930s, both the FTC and the Food and Drug Administration sought expanded powers. Despite intense lobbying against such legislation from business interests, both agencies won amendments to their basic charters.

The new wording said, "unfair methods of competition in commerce and unfair or deceptive acts or practices in commerce are hereby declared unlawful." The new legislation deleted a requirement that competitors be harmed and said that the FTC no longer had to prove that the ad had deceived people – only that it had a tendency or capacity to deceive. The 1938 amendments expanded the product areas over which the FTC had jurisdiction and allowed the commission to request preliminary injunctions in some product areas in which continued advertising would be dangerous to health.

The Wheeler-Lea Amendments put some real teeth in the FTC and allowed it to become a watchdog of consumer interests in relation to false and deceptive advertising. Although the commission's powers further expanded over time, the Wheeler-Lea Amendments were still the basis of prosecution of deceptive advertising in interstate commerce at the end of the twentieth century.

ERIC J. ZANOT

See also Federal Trade Commission; Food and Drug Administration

Further Reading
Fueroghne, Dean K., *Law and Advertising: Current Legal Issues for Agencies, Advertisers, and Attorneys,* Chicago: Copy Workshop, 1995
McCall, James R., *Statutory Supplement to Cases, Notes, and Materials on Consumer Protection,* St. Paul, Minnesota: West, 1977
Preston, Ivan, *The Great American Blow-Up: Puffery in Advertising and Selling,* Madison: University of Wisconsin Press, 1975
Stern, Louis W., and Thomas L. Eovaldi, *Legal Aspects of Marketing Strategy: Antitrust and Consumer Protection Issues,* Englewood Cliffs, New Jersey, and London: Prentice-Hall, 1984
Wagner, Susan, *The Federal Trade Commission,* New York: Praeger, 1971

White, William Allen
Influential small-town newspaper editor

Born in a small Kansas town, where the business community was all-important, editor William Allen White espoused business values, a Judeo-Christian ethic, and Republicanism in the editorial pages of the *Emporia Gazette,* which he purchased in 1895 for $3,000. His eloquent editorials earned him the title "Sage of Emporia."

White first gained national prominence with an August 1896 editorial, "What's the Matter with Kansas?," in which he chastised radical Populist farmers who were challenging the dominant business interests that controlled the politics of the state. He supported social values such as suffrage, prohibition, and equal opportunity.

White gained a national reputation as a spokesman for the grass-roots Republican midwest. His friends included prominent political figures such as Theodore Roosevelt. A loyal, but progressive, Republican, White supported the party ticket until 1912 when Roosevelt ran as the candidate of the Progressive movement; after Roosevelt's defeat, White rejoined the Republican mainstream. White became a popular magazine writer and wrote several novels and nonfiction books.

On July 27, 1922, White again achieved national fame with a local editorial, "To an Anxious Friend." The editorial dealt with efforts to prevent demonstrations of support for striking railroad men. Arguing for the importance of free expression, White wrote: "This nation will survive . . . if only men can speak in whatever way given them to utter what their hearts hold – by voice, by posted card, by letter, or by press. Reason has never failed men. Only force and repression have made the wrecks in the world." The following year he received the Pulitzer Prize for his eloquent plea.

JEAN FOLKERTS

Further Reading
Folkerts, Jean, "William Allen White: Editor and Businessman During the Reform Years, 1895–1916," *Kansas History* 7:2 (1984)
_____, "William Allen White's Anti-Populist Rhetoric as an Agenda-Setting Technique," *Journalism Quarterly* 60:1 (1983)
Griffith, Sally Foreman, *Home Town News: William Allen White and the 'Emporia Gazette'*, New York: Oxford University Press, 1989
Johnson, Walter, *William Allen White's America*, New York: Henry Holt, 1947
White, William Allen, *The Autobiography of William Allen White*, New York: Macmillan, 1946

White House Correspondents' Association

Organization works to improve working conditions of reporters

The White House Correspondents' Association was founded in 1914 and by 1996 had a membership of approximately 600 newspaper, magazine, and broadcast journalists. Officially, the association existed to negotiate with White House staff over working conditions for the White House press corps. In practice, however, the association was known primarily for its annual dinner, which featured a lighthearted address by the president of the United States and a star-studded audience of politicians, journalists, and show business celebrities. As famed United Press International (UPI) White House correspondent Helen Thomas described it in a 1995 interview, "The whole raison d'être of the association was to have one dinner a year with the president of the United States as the guest of honor." The association also honored several journalists each year with awards announced at the annual dinner.

For most of its history, the association was run in a private club atmosphere. Seats on its governing board were awarded by invitation only. Once a member was selected for the board, the member – for decades, almost always a man – would move through the ranks and eventually become president. Board meetings were held in private; the rank and file were shut out. Women were allowed to be members but were not allowed at the annual dinner until President John F. Kennedy threatened not to attend unless women members were admitted.

That atmosphere began to change in the late 1980s. Board seats became elected positions in 1988, and board meetings were opened to the rank and file in 1989.

THOMAS A. HUGHES

See also National Press Club; Standing Committee of Correspondents

Further Reading
Garneau, George, "Democracy Among the White House Press Corps," *Editor & Publisher* 122:25 (June 24, 1989), p. 16
Gersh, Debra, "White House Correspondents Group Shifting Direction," *Editor & Publisher* 123:34 (August 25, 1990), p. 15
"Roasted and Toasted in D.C.," *The New Yorker* 71 (May 15, 1995), pp. 33–34
"Uncovering the White House: Journalist Helen Thomas Talks About Presidents Past and Present," *The San Francisco Chronicle* (January 29, 1995)

Wilson, Woodrow, and the Press

Valued press coverage but had problems with journalists during his presidency

Throughout his political career, Woodrow Wilson had faith in public opinion. This led him to value publicity and the role the press played in political life. Wilson began to interact with the press early in his political career. The press coverage he received as a scholar, popular lecturer, and university president gave him national prominence. He enjoyed friendly press relations when he ran for governor of New Jersey and later when he served in that office from 1910 to 1912. Journalists played major roles in Wilson's campaign for the presidency in 1912. The strength of press support he received in that campaign came as no accident.

As president, Wilson tried to nurture good relations with the press. Those relations fall into three periods, beginning with the years 1912–17. During this period, Wilson enacted one of the most successful legislative reform programs in the history of the country, and he faced some major international crises regarding Mexico and, in particular, the world war that began in Europe in the summer of 1914. Despite his recognition of the importance of the press, a number of problems emerged to hamper his relations with journalists during these years. Wilson was a president who guarded his privacy while reporters wished to penetrate it. His natural reserve and sense of propriety made him seem aloof to many reporters. He had little respect for the human interest stories in newspapers that the reporters were so anxious to write. Although he had considerable respect for the more serious Washington, D.C., correspondents and for various other accomplished journalists, he considered many reporters brash and ill informed and held them, as well as the popular press in general, in low esteem.

Nevertheless, Wilson endeavored to build solid relations with the press. He appointed Joseph Tumulty his secretary; part of the secretary's duties in those days, when there was no position of press secretary, was to oversee press relations. Tumulty would serve as his personal secretary during the eight years Wilson was president. Wilson's belief in "pitiless publicity" for all official matters could not have been implemented without Tumulty. Reporters found him friendly and attentive to their needs. They appreciated him and the friendly atmosphere of their meetings with him created by his lively Irish personality. Tumulty and his staff also tried to keep the president informed about public opinion as reflected in the press. They clipped items representing a wide sampling of the press and arranged them by topic for Wilson to study daily. Tumulty also urged the president to hold regular press conferences.

Preceding presidents Theodore Roosevelt and William Howard Taft had held various sorts of meetings with the press. It was Wilson, however, who introduced regular presidential press conferences. These twice weekly (later, weekly) conferences were opened to all accredited correspondents, and they lasted until May 1915, when Wilson discontinued them as war drew nearer. Historians usually point out that

President Woodrow Wilson preferred addressing Congress to talking with journalists.
(National Archives)

these conferences failed to work well for the president. They claim he was too guarded, too intellectual, and too inclined to match his wits against those of the reporters. Wilson made careful preparations for the conferences, and he allowed his irritation to show when the triviality of some of the reporters' questions annoyed him. Regardless, some historians came to believe that a more balanced view of these conferences was in order.

Wilson was an excellent orator, and he used his public speaking ability as a means to reach the public. He was the first president since John Adams to speak before Congress, and he ventured out from Washington to deliver speeches on a number of important occasions. His speeches made news, received wide press coverage, and connected Wilson and the public through the press.

The second period of Wilson's press relations corresponds to the years of U.S. participation in World War I (1917–18). Although his press conferences had been discontinued by then, his need for publicity was greater, for the country had entered a total war that necessitated the mobilization of opinion as well as of arms. Consequently, Wilson experimented with another innovation involving publicity and the press. He created the Committee on Public Information (CPI) and named the progressive journalist George Creel to head it.

The CPI was probably the greatest effort in publicity and propaganda in U.S. history. Creel brought many journalists into its ranks. The CPI created a vast national network for distributing news and publicity and supervised the U.S. propaganda operation both at home and abroad. Creel was responsible, too, for the censorship of news during the war. Instead of a strict censorship law, which he opposed, he introduced a system of voluntary censorship that allowed the press to censor itself in accordance with distributed guidelines.

For the most part, the system of voluntary censorship worked well. Wilson, however, believed that there had to be something beyond moral obligation to protect the nation from publication of matter harmful to war effort. Congress responded with the Espionage Act (1917), the Trading with the Enemy Act (1917), and the Sedition Act (1918). Wilson, the widely recognized liberal, found himself forced by the demands of modern war to create a system of statutory censorship. The laws were used mostly against the radical and German American press, and some journalists claimed that they infringed on the First Amendment rights of the press.

The last discernible period of Wilson's press relations encompassed the year 1919. It focused first on the peace negotiations in Paris and then on Wilson's efforts to have the treaty, including the League of Nations, ratified by the Senate. While he was in Paris, Wilson fought against censorship and for as much openness in the proceedings as possible, and he created a press bureau for the correspondents directed by the well-liked journalist Ray Stannard Baker. Wilson provided the means to help the correspondents defray some of their expenses, and he had his advisers, Colonel Edward M. House in particular, meet with the journalists frequently. Nevertheless, many correspondents claimed that there was too much secrecy at the conference and that Wilson did not make himself available to them.

Some of the frustrations of the press at Paris were carried over to the debate about the treaty at home. By that time, many Republican papers had launched a serious attack on the treaty. They were joined by leading liberal journals like the *New Republic,* whose editors believed that Wilson had compromised too much at Paris. Press lords William R. Hearst and Frank A. Munsey, old opponents of Wilson, were adamant in their opposition to "Wilson's" treaty. Despite his failing health, Wilson tried once again to appeal to the public, this time by means of a speaking tour. Journalists traveled with him, and every speaking stop became a local and national news event. This time, his effort to mobilize public opinion would fail. Ill and exhausted after a speech at Pueblo, Colorado, he suffered a complete physical collapse and was rushed back to Washington on the verge of death. The years of his effective presidency ended as they began, with an effort to move the public and the press to support programs he believed were vital for the public good.

JAMES D. STARTT

See also Committee on Public Information; Espionage and Sedition Acts; Presidential News Conferences; Presidential Press Secretaries; Roosevelt, Theodore, and the Press; World War I

Further Reading

Bloomfield, Douglas M., "Joe Tumulty and the Press," *Journalism Quarterly* 42 (1965)
Cornwell, Elmer E., Jr., "The Press Conferences of Woodrow Wilson," *Journalism Quarterly* 39 (1962)
Daniels, Josephus, *The Wilson Era: Years of Peace, 1910–1917,* Chapel Hill: University of North Carolina Press, 1944
Howard, Vincent W., "Woodrow Wilson, the Press, and Presidential Leadership: Another Look at the Passage of the Underwood Tariff, 1913," *Centennial Review* 24 (1980)
Juergens, George, *News from the White House: The Presidential-Press Relationship in the Progressive Era,* Chicago: University of Chicago Press, 1981
Ponder, Stephen, "Presidential Publicity and Executive Power: Woodrow Wilson and the Centralizing of Government Information," *American Journalism* 11 (1994)

Wireless Ship Act of 1910

Early legislation requiring shipboard radio equipment

In 1903, the government of imperial Germany called the first international convention on radio. This Berlin Conference stemmed partly from the refusal of the Marconi Company to relay signals from a yacht belonging to a German prince on a visit to North America. The nations attending –

except for the United Kingdom and Italy – issued a protocol calling for all wireless systems to communicate under all conditions with all other wireless systems, with the requirement that each country would have to pass enabling laws.

In 1906, another conference proposed communication without regard for the type of equipment used, and the international distress call was changed from CQD (which meant "calling all stations, disaster") to SOS (which did not stand for anything, although it was sometimes believed to mean "Save Our Ship").

Congress initially refused to ratify the agreements, feeling that these rules would stifle the development of radio and place it under international rather than national control. When another conference to be held in London in 1912 quietly withdrew an invitation to the United States, Congress passed its first radio law – the Wireless Ship Act of 1910. This act required oceangoing vessels with 50 or more passengers traveling between ports 200 or more miles apart to carry radio apparatus capable of reaching 100 miles, day or night, and an operator to run it.

In 1912, the London Conference agreed, among other items and partially as a result of the *Titanic* disaster that year, that two operators be available on most vessels. The United States amended the 1910 Wireless Ship Act to provide similar protections.

MARVIN R. BENSMAN

Women in Journalism

Roles in male-dominated field changed over the years

Women have played important roles in U.S. journalism from colonial to contemporary times, but they have had to fight for acceptance in a male-dominated field. While a few women inherited newspapers and ran them successfully, many women in journalism battled their way up the professional ladder, struggling to prove that they could report and edit the news in terms of male-oriented professional norms. A third group established its own periodicals to push for changes to improve the status of women as well as to promote other causes.

Newspapers in the United States began as family enterprises in the colonial period, when labor was in short supply. Wives and other family members assisted male printers in the operation of print shops that turned out a variety of materials, including newspapers. Some 30 women became known as printers, publishers, and compositors, and several succeeded their husbands and male relatives as printer-publishers of newspapers that told the story of the Revolutionary period. The best-known, Mary Katherine Goddard of Baltimore, Maryland, published the *Maryland Journal* and was the first official printer of the Declaration of Independence with the names of the signers attached.

In the nineteenth century, both white and minority women turned to journalism for two main purposes. One was to advocate reform, particularly the abolition of slavery and the advancement of women's rights, by establishing their own newspapers and contributing to like-minded publications. The other was to earn income by writing columns, travel letters, and other literary fare for general circulation newspapers and magazines as well as religious and women's periodicals.

Those who tried to compete directly with male journalists found their options limited. Following the American Civil War, for example, a group of women achieved short-lived success as correspondents, writing feature articles and columns on the political and social scene in Washington, D.C., for major newspapers. After male journalists limited admission to the U.S. Capitol press galleries to full-time correspondents in 1879, most of these women, who were considered "special writers," were cut off from news sources and relegated to reporting society gossip. Some women journalists of the era used male pseudonyms in keeping with the Victorian idea that women's lives should be confined to the private, not public, sphere of activity, but others dared to write under their own by-lines.

Before the turn of the twentieth century, many newspapers established women's pages to encourage women to patronize the growing number of department stores that were local advertisers. Women's pages offered opportunities for women to be employed on newspapers, but they occupied offices segregated from male reporters, were paid less than men, and had little status. The content of women's pages, such as fashion, beauty tips, cooking, child rearing, advice to the lovelorn, and social news, reinforced stereotypical roles for women.

Yet women's pages did contain news of women's clubs. This helped bolster interest in middle-class women's organizations and may have aided the suffrage movement. Among activities featured were those of newspaperwomen themselves, who banded together from the 1880s on to seek social and professional camaraderie in the face of exclusion from male press clubs that did not end until the 1970s.

Occasionally, token women who performed extraordinary feats in reporting or writing were employed on the general news staffs of newspapers in the yellow journalism era at the turn of the twentieth century. These rare individuals were known as "sob sisters" and "stunt girls." By exploiting emotions thought to exemplify women's nature, sob sisters specialized in sentimental accounts of lurid events.

Going up in balloons and down in diving bells, stunt girls carried out sensational adventures to titillate newspapers readers. The most famous, Nellie Bly, whose real name was Elizabeth Cochrane, dashed around the world in 72 days in 1889 as a reporter for Joseph Pulitzer's *New York World* to beat author Jules Verne's fictional record of an 80-day trip. Some assignments carried out by stunt girls, such as posing as working girls in factories and reporting on poor conditions there, verged on the investigative journalism of the muckraking movement, which attempted to reform injustices by exposing them.

Women's role in investigative journalism, however, was broader than the scope given to stunt girls. Ida M. Tarbell, the best-known female muckraker, meticulously documented the unfair business practices of the Standard Oil Compa-

Elizabeth Cochrane, who wrote under the pseudonym Nellie Bly, traveled around the world in 72 days, beating the fictional record set in Jules Verne's novel *Around the World in Eighty Days.*

ny in a series of articles published in *McClure's Magazine* in 1902. Another crusader, Ida Wells-Barnett, spoke up against lynching in her African American newspaper, the *Memphis (Tennessee) Free Speech,* in 1892. Although her newspaper office was destroyed as a result, she continued to gather facts on lynching and to campaign against it.

Spurred in part by the need for newspapers to cover the suffrage movement that culminated in women receiving the vote in 1920, the number of women employed full-time in journalism grew from 4,000 in 1910 to about 12,000 by 1930. Yet, few women were seen as competent enough to break into the male preserve of "hard" news, which included politics, government, criminal justice and related areas. Those who did still lacked the stature of male journalists

and were referred to as "front page girls" during the heyday of tabloid journalism in the 1920s.

Women obtained degrees in journalism as soon as the first journalism schools opened their doors before World War I, but they had difficulty obtaining jobs except on women's pages and as writers of feature stories, the "soft" news. To promote the employment of women journalists, Eleanor Roosevelt, who wrote a daily newspaper column herself in a diary format, held White House press conferences for women only during her years as first lady from 1933 to 1945. In spite of discrimination, however, some exceptional individuals like Anne O'Hare McCormick attained distinction. The first woman journalist to win a Pulitzer Prize, McCormick received the award in 1937 for foreign correspondence for the *New York Times.*

Both World War I and World War II opened doors for women journalists who replaced men serving with the armed forces. Although discouraged by the government and military, women also fought to be accepted as war correspondents. Some 125 women attained accreditation as World War II correspondents, with Margaret Bourke-White, an acclaimed photojournalist for *Life* magazine, the most notable. Nevertheless, after peace came, most women found themselves back on the women's pages or out of jobs.

One who tenaciously continued to prove herself equal or superior to male reporters was Marguerite Higgins of the *New York Herald-Tribune,* the first women to be awarded a Pulitzer Prize for war correspondence. She was honored for coverage of the Korean War after she resisted an order to leave Korea because the Army claimed it lacked facilities for women at the front. Higgins later was one of 267 female U.S. correspondents accredited to cover the Vietnam War in the 1960s and 1970s.

In radio, women journalists faced discrimination for decades following the advent of commercial broadcasting in the 1920s. Women's voices were considered to lack authority and to be unsuitable for newscasts, even though stations hired women during World War II. The well-modulated voice of Pauline Frederick was not deemed good enough to get her a network job in radio when the war ended, although she did freelance assignments covering women. Her opportunity finally arrived in the new medium of television. After conducting live interviews with candidates' wives at political conventions, Frederick was hired by ABC in 1948, becoming the first newswoman to hold a network staff position in television.

Overt prejudice against female journalists in hiring and promotion did not end until the civil rights and women's movements of the 1960s and 1970s, when passage of federal legislation outlawed discrimination. These movements also had some impact on news coverage, with proponents insisting that women, like minorities, should be depicted more positively. Although the women's movement received some initial publicity on women's pages, feminist complaints about their sex-segregated contents resulted in their transformation into "lifestyle" sections in the late 1960s and 1970s. Women reporters moved into areas formerly barred to them, such as government, police, business and sports news, broadening news content somewhat to include more stories about women. Newspapers also reacted to feminism by hiring columnists like Ellen Goodman of the *Boston Globe,* who won a 1980 Pulitzer Prize for commentary, to voice a feminist perspective.

Much news of the women's movement, however, was spread by alternative feminist publications. These grew from one newsletter in 1968 to more than 560 periodicals five years later, including the mass circulation magazine *Ms.* Written by women who often did not have formal training in journalism, these publications provided material on women's health and other issues not normally offered in the mass media.

Many of the gains of women in mainstream journalism came only after legal battles for equality. Sex discrimination complaints and suits, often ended after years of litigation with settlements calling for more opportunities for women, were brought in the 1970s against numerous news organizations and broadcasters. These included the *New York Times,* the Associated Press, NBC, and the *Washington Post.* The complaint against the *Washington Post,* ironically, targeted a corporation headed by a woman. Katharine Graham took control of the *Post* company after the suicide of her husband in 1963 and built it into a leading news organization.

Help for women in broadcasting came from a Federal Communications Commission ruling in 1971 that required women, like minorities, be given equal opportunities in hiring. Barbara Walters, an acclaimed interviewer but not a journalist, became a symbolic figure of success for women when she received a $1-million contract from ABC in 1976 to coanchor the network's nightly newscast and do other programs. The first woman network news coanchor, Walters was removed from the position in 1977 after the newscast ratings failed to improve.

Connie Chung, the only other woman to coanchor a nightly newscast, lost her job on CBS in 1995 due to low ratings and friction with her male counterpart. As of the late 1990s, no other woman had attained the position of anchor on a nightly network newscast. Women journalists in television, more than men, continued to be judged on their looks and appearance, factors highlighted in the case of Christine Craft, who lost a suit against a Kansas City television station after losing an anchor job there in 1981 on grounds of her age, appearance, and lack of deference to men.

In the 1990s, the influence of women in journalism did not seem to match their presence in the field. Despite efforts to achieve diversity in hiring, the proportion of women rose only from 33.8 percent in 1982 to 34 percent in 1992 out of a total journalistic workforce of about 122,000, according to an Indiana University study of journalists in print and broadcasting. This finding raised speculation that women were leaving the field more quickly than men. A survey by the National Federation of Press Women showed that about 8.7 percent of the nation's newspaper publishers were women in 1992, as were 19.4 percent of executive editors, representing an average yearly growth rate of only about 1 per cent over a 16-year span.

Minority women, in particular, tended to be in the lower echelons. No effort was made to recruit minorities until the Kerner Commission Report, written after outbreaks of racial violence in U.S. cities in 1967, criticized the mass media for ignoring blacks. After that, affirmative action efforts did occur, but progress was slow. In 1992, minority women made up 7 percent of the newspaper workforce. In television, a 1991 report estimated that 3.2 percent of news directors were minority women. A statistical profile of newsrooms analyzed in a 1991 Ohio University study showed that 67 percent of women journalists overall were reporters or copy editors, relatively low-level positions in terms of decision-making, but that "three-quarters of African-American women, 97 percent of Latino women and 78 percent of Asian-American women [were] reporters or copy editors, compared to 57 percent of white men."

With newspapers losing women readers at a faster rate than men readers, efforts in the late 1990s wre being made to bring back women's pages staffed by both men and

Television journalist Christine Craft lost her job on grounds of her age, appearance, and lack of deference to men.

(Museum of Broadcast Communications)

women. Some media companies, particularly Gannett Company, publishers of *USA Today,* took definite steps to promote women. Yet women still had a long way to go before gaining parity with men.

MAURINE H. BEASLEY

See also African American Media; Feminist Media; Frederick, Pauline; Kerner Commission Report; Magazines for Women; Muckraking; Society Reporting; Standing Committee of Correspondents; Suffrage Press; Wells-Barnett, Ida B.; Women's Pages

Further Reading

Beasley, Maurine H., and Sheila J. Gibbons, *Taking Their Place: A Documentary History of Women and Journalism,* Washington, D.C.: American University Press, 1993

Hosley, David H., and Gayle K. Yamada, *Hard News: Women in Broadcast Journalism,* New York: Greenwood, 1987

Marzolf, Marion, *Up from the Footnote: A History of Women Journalists,* New York: Hastings House, 1977

Mills, Kay, *A Place in the News: From the Women's Pages to the Front Page,* New York: Columbia University Press, 1990

Robertson, Nan, *The Girls in the Balcony: Women, Men, and the 'New York Times',* New York: Random House, 1992

Sanders, Marlene, and Marcia Rock, *Waiting for Prime Time: The Women of Television News,* Urbana: University of Illinois Press, 1988

Streitmatter, Rodger, *Raising Her Voice: African-American Women Journalists Who Changed History,* Lexington: University Press of Kentucky, 1994

Weaver, David, and G. Cleveland Wilhoit, *The American Journalist in the 1990s,* Arlington, Virginia: Freedom Forum, 1992

Women's Pages

Special sections designed to appeal to women's interests

Designed to cater to the reading interests of women, special sections called women's pages existed in U.S. newspapers from the 1880s to the 1970s. The rise of women's pages in the press resulted from rapid social changes in the late nineteenth century. Both sexes left home in the Revolutionary era to enter the growing public school system. Consequently, women, achieving the same high rate of literacy as men, became a significant factor in circulation.

Women also emerged as significant subjects of news in this period because of their increasing participation in the public sphere. More importantly, the industrialization of U.S. society transformed women's primary economic role from that of home workers to that of consumers. Many goods formerly produced by women for home use were now manufactured through mass production and sold at department stores and chain stores, which relied on advertising to build a citywide clientele. In this system of capital industrialism, women became supervisors of the increasing consumption of their families. Because of their role as primary purchasing agents of consumer goods, women became the target of advertisers, whose patronage provided a crucial source of revenues to newspapers.

One of the first publishers to respond to these social changes was Joseph Pulitzer, who popularized women's pages in daily newspapers as a means to attract advertisers by creating a concentrated female readership in a separate section. In 1886, his *New York World* started to carry columns devoted to women. By 1891, a page for women had become a steady feature in his Sunday *World.* After 1894, the "For and About Women" section was a daily feature in the *World.* In developing a special news forum for women, Pulitzer had to negotiate the conflict between the progressive trend toward the emancipation of women and the conservatism of the majority of his working-class readership. He compromised by giving attention to women's concerns with an emphasis on their domestic life. Echoing the Victorian idea that women belonged at home, the women's page of the *World* featured fashion, etiquette, recipes, beauty tips, club activities, social gatherings, and so forth. Columns and articles about notable women supplemented these features to acknowledge women's growing interests and accomplishments outside the domestic sphere without alienating the more traditional readers.

The innovations of Pulitzer became the convention of a feminine genre in the newspaper as the pages evolved in the twentieth century. Service features such as announcements of weddings and engagements, news about women's clubs, society news, advice columns, food and fashion coverage, tips on beauty and homemaking, and expert advice on child care constituted the backbone of the pages. According to the underlying editorial principle, all news for and about women, regardless of its social significance, was clustered in the back pages of the newspaper instead of being integrated into appropriate sections. Moreover, women's pages, created not so much for women as for advertisers, remained captive throughout their history to a salient commercial nature that undercut their journalistic integrity. Lamenting the lack of autonomy in the women's department, journalist Genevieve Jackson Boughner advised women's editors in 1926 to "face the 'brute' fact that the women's page is a bid for the advertiser's patronage." Similarly, columnist Nicholas von Hoffman noted five decades later that "the advertising director of the city's largest department store has more power on the paper than its women's page editor has." Despite their importance to the finances of newspapers, women's pages were marginalized as "the stepchild of the profession," and their staff, mostly women, suffered from low pay and low status in the newsroom.

The tension between feminism and conservatism that characterized Pulitzer's approach also remained inherent in the evolution of the pages. Against the backdrop of a constant emphasis on women's roles as wives and mothers, the pages changed in parallel to the ebb and flow of women's history in U.S. society. During World War I, the pages reported on the war effort of women, especially female workers who moved into traditionally male-dominated industries. News on the suffrage movement also found its way into the women's pages. After women won the right to vote, many newspapers stopped labeling their women's pages as sections exclusively for women.

The severe manpower shortage in World War II created unprecedented employment opportunities for U.S. women. Women's pages in the war years covered the phenomenon of "Rosie the Riveter," showcasing the accomplishments of women who took on men's jobs in columns such as the "Women in War" of the *San Francisco Chronicle* and "Women in War Work" of the *Chicago Tribune*. The pages also chronicled the influence of wartime changes such as rationing, relocation, and the conflict between war work and child care on family life. Influenced by the back-to-home movement after the war, women's pages again played up the importance of domesticity in women's lives. Through the 1950s and the early 1960s, the pages addressed women mainly as housewives and mothers despite the fact that more women than ever before were working.

The women's movement in the 1960s raised concerns with media images of women, leading to evaluation of women's pages. Considered dull, trivial, and out of touch with women's lives, the pages were criticized for perpetuating the sexist stereotype of women as homebound housewives. Critics maintained that the segregation of all news about women marginalized and trivialized their concerns. Instead of adhering to the women's angle, a general interest section – known in some papers as "Style," "Day," or "Scene" – was promoted to inform both women and men about important issues such as social trends, family life, child care, consumer affairs, and so forth.

The demise of women's pages was hailed as a "flight from fluff." After two decades of hiatus, however, the pages were showing signs of revival. Prompted by the steady decline in female readership, some newspapers, most notably the *Chicago Tribune,* were resurrecting the idea of a separate section for women.

MEI-LING YANG

See also Feminist Media; Society Reporting

Further Reading

Cox, James, "Newspapers Court Women," *USA Today* (November 24, 1992)

"Flight from Fluff," *Time* (March 20, 1972)

Guenin, Zena, "Women's Pages in American Newspapers: Missing Out on Contemporary Content," *Journalism Quarterly* 52 (1975)

Israel, Betsy, "Pages of Their Own," *New York Times* (October 3, 1993)

Miller, Susan, "Changes in Women's/Lifestyle Sections," *Journalism Quarterly* 53 (1976)

Van Gelder, Lindsy, "Women's Pages: You Can't Make News Out of a Silk Purse," *Ms.* (November 1974)

Von Hoffman, Nicholas, "Women's Pages: An Irreverent View," *Columbia Journalism Review* 10 (July/August 1971)

Yang, Mei-ling, "Women's Pages or People's Pages: The Production of News for Women in the *Washington Post*

in the 1950s," *Journalism & Mass Communication Quarterly* 73:2 (Summer 1996), pp. 364–378

World War I

Media well positioned to cover the battlefield

When World War I began on July 28, 1914, the U.S. media were in a better position to cover and report a foreign war than at any previous time. Popular newspapers and magazines, emphasis on news, and foreign correspondence all had expanded in the years before the war. Film journalism also was assuming a place alongside the printed media, thus enlarging the media's outreach. Nevertheless, the totality and unprecedented scope of the war presented a great challenge for the media.

Although the United States did not enter the war until 1917, the press employed all its resources in reporting it from the start. Some correspondents managed to reach the front in western Europe at first, but soon censorship and restrictions on movement were imposed to control their reporting. Nevertheless, a number of U.S. newspapers, such as the *New York Times* and the *Chicago Daily News,* had correspondents in place in the major European capitals before the outbreak of the war, and along with the additional war correspondents who now arrived, they strained every effort to fight press restrictions and to report as much war news as possible.

Public interest in the conflict was spontaneous and intense. Titanic losses suffered on the European battlefields underscored the fact that this was an event of enormous proportion and significance. U.S. public opinion favored the Allied cause, and when the press, showing less scrutiny than was warranted, reported news of alleged brutalities committed by German soldiers in Belgium and northern France, that sentiment became more pronounced.

In the end, however, events brought a halt to U.S. neutrality. The sinking of the *Lusitania* in 1915 with the loss of more than 1,000 passengers, including 124 from the United States, and the German announcement of its intention to

---

Reporting on the Use of Poison Gas in World War I

BOULOGNE, April 25 – The gaseous vapor which the Germans used against the French divisions near Ypres last Thursday, contrary to the rules of the Hague Convention, introduces a new element into warfare. The attack of last Thursday evening was preceded by the rising of a cloud of vapor, greenish gray and iridescent. That vapor settled to the ground like a swamp mist and drifted toward the French trenches on a brisk wind. Its effect on the French was violent nausea and faintness, followed by an utter collapse. It is believed that the Germans, who charged in behind the vapor, met no resistance at all, the French at their front being virtually paralyzed.

New York Tribune, April 27, 1915

launch unrestricted submarine warfare against neutral as well as belligerent shipping in European war zones shocked U.S. opinion. Then on March 1, 1917, reports of the intercepted "Zimmerman Note," one of the great news stories of the twentieth century, were spread across the U.S. press. The note invited Mexico to ally itself with Germany should the United States and Germany go to war, and it outraged the people of the United States. Shortly thereafter, on April 2, 1917, when President Woodrow Wilson asked Congress to declare war on Germany, the press and the public were behind him.

Now an even larger wave of correspondents converged on Europe from the United States. News services expanded their European staffs, and special correspondents provided readers at home with news from all the Allied countries. With the arrival of the American Expeditionary Force (AEF), provision was made for a press headquarters for war correspondents. About 50 correspondents were accredited to the AEF at any one time. In their ranks were Floyd Gibbons, Wythe Williams, Paul Scott Mowrer, Peggy Hull, and others who would gain notable places in journalism history. Other correspondents reported the war from across Europe, and some even found their way to east Asia. Everywhere they fought against restrictions and censorship imposed upon them and worked to make the U.S. public the best informed in the world about the war. Within the limits of what was possible, they succeeded in that task.

Reporting from Russia and the eastern front was less successful. Only a few U.S. correspondents were in Russia when the war began, and their movements were restricted, as was the news they received from official handouts. Most of the news of the eastern front came from correspondents working behind German lines during the years of U.S. neutrality. With the start of the Russian Revolution in March 1917 and the entry of the United States into the war a month later, Russian news acquired a mounting significance. Several U.S. correspondents managed to perform creditable service in Russia as the Revolution unfolded. Among them were Isaac Don Levine, Rheta Childe Dorr, and the brilliant, if partisan, young radical reporter, John Reed. His eyewitness account of the Bolshevik phase of the Revolution, *Ten Days that Shook the World* (1919), became a classic account of that traumatic event. Mainly, however, U.S. understanding of events occurring in Russia remained poor. Russian news had never been easy to procure, and conditions for the correspondents worsened with the Revolution. News sources dried up, and censorship, along with the threat of arrest, made the correspondents' work almost impossible.

The U.S. government also imposed a milder yet irritating control of news. At first, the Wilson administration introduced a system of voluntary censorship, but in order to guard against comment or news considered harmful to the national interest, Congress passed a series of laws (the Espionage Act, the Trading with the Enemy Act, and the Sedition Act). Radical and German-language papers were the chief targets of their enforcement. Nevertheless, most of the press remained enthusiastic in its support of the war effort.

It is, in fact, difficult to overestimate the support the mainstream media gave to the war effort. In general they re-

Journalists check their gas masks in France during World War I.
(National Archives)

ported, analyzed, idealized, and, too often, sensationalized the participation of the United States in the war. They portrayed it as a democratic crusade in defense of liberty and against the autocracy of the Hohenzollerns. The media focused on Germany, by far the most powerful of the Central Powers, and portrayed it as the antithesis of democracy. Germany became an "outlaw nation" accused of the savagery of the "Hun." Indeed, Hunish rhetoric stereotyped Germans, and their leaders in particular, as twentieth-century barbarians. Such enthusiasm and exaggeration made life difficult for German Americans and fanned an emotional disregard of their rights as U.S. citizens. Moreover, the media discovered that spies had infested the country. They were "everywhere," claimed the *New York Tribune*. The media, indeed, attacked all opponents of the war. "Pacifism is Prussianism," declared the *New York World*. Critics of the nation at war were not to be tolerated.

Less enthusiasm for the war effort could be expected from at least several parts of the press. Both the German American press and the black press had reason to be critical of U.S. intervention in the conflict. Ever since 1914, the German American press had claimed that U.S. neutrality was far from neutral and that President Wilson showed partiality toward the British. Once the United States entered the war, the fate of German American papers became precarious. They became targets for the nation's superpatriots, in whose judgment they were highly suspect, and in some cases, they were victimized by mob violence. In October 1917, Congress passed a law requiring all German-language publications to submit translations of all war-related matter in their papers to local postmasters until the government became convinced of their loyalty. When their loyalty was established, permits exempting them from continued translations could be issued. Translation of war-related matter was costly, and the power the government had in deciding whether or not to issue permits was considerable. Consequently, dozens of papers were forced to suspend publication. Others lost their second-class mailing privileges. Most, however, backed the war effort and agreed with the *New Yorker Staatszeitung* when it editorialized after the declaration of war that now there was "but one duty – American."

The black press also could be a problem for the government. Because of the many failings of democracy at home and the many inequalities African Americans endured, the black press had good reason to be critical of the U.S. effort to conduct an international crusade for democracy. Yet in June 1918, 31 black editors gathered at a conference in Washington, D.C. One document produced by the conference was an "Address to the Committee on Public Information," in which the editors promised to do all they could to promote "self-sacrificing participation in the war" among African Americans. Shortly afterwards, W.E.B. DuBois, the radical black editor of the *Crisis*, published his famous, if controversial, editorial, "Close Ranks," advising African Americans to make common cause with their "white fellow citizens" in the war against Germany. The majority of the black press followed these leads, but the government had to employ intimidation and even the threat of legal action against some black papers to stifle their criticism.

Considering the extent of the press's involvement in the war as well as the sense of urgency and duty that shaped the political atmosphere owing to the pressures of total war, it is no wonder that its performance during the war defies simple generalization. Despite the many restrictions that authorities and circumstances imposed on its operation, the press excelled in providing news to an anxious public. It also supplied illuminating background information in abundance. In mobilizing public opinion in support of the war and in sustaining national morale, its services were indispensable. By its exaggerated rhetoric and crude stereotyping, however, the press sometimes encouraged the wave of intolerant hysteria that surfaced in the country during the war. Moreover, any inquiry into the subject of World War I and the media produces questions about the role that journalists should fill during times of war, about when they cross the line separating journalism and propaganda, and about how far governments should go in restricting media operations to guard national security.

JAMES D. STARTT

See also African American Media; Committee on Public Information; Espionage and Sedition Acts; Ethnic Press; Mass Media and the Military; Socialist Press; War Correspondents; War Photography

Further Reading

Campbell, Craig W., *Reel America and World War I: A Comprehensive Filmography and History of Motion Pictures in the United States, 1914–1920,* Jefferson, North Carolina: McFarland, 1985

Creel, George, *How We Advertised America,* New York and London: Harper and Brothers, 1920

Desmond, Robert W., *Windows on the World: The Information Process in a Changing Society, 1900–1920,* Iowa City: University of Iowa Press, 1980

Ellis, Mark, "'Closing Ranks' and 'Seeking Honors': W.E.B. Du Bois in World War I," *Journal of American History* 79:1 (June 1992), pp. 96–124

Knightley, Phillip, *The First Casualty: From the Crimea to Vietnam: The War Correspondent as Hero, Propagandist, and Myth Maker,* New York: Harcourt Brace Jovanovich, 1975; London: Quartet, 1982

Kornweibel, Theodore, Jr., "'The Most Dangerous of all Negro Journals': Federal Efforts to Suppress the *Chicago Defender* During World War I," *American Journalism* 11 (1994)

Mock, James R., *Censorship, 1917,* Princeton, New Jersey: Princeton University Press, 1941; London: H. Milford, Oxford University Press, 1941

Read, James Morgan, *Atrocity Propaganda, 1914–1919,* New Haven, Connecticut: Yale University Press, 1941; London: H. Milford, Oxford University Press, 1941

Vaughn, Stephen, *Holding Fast the Inner Lines: Democracy, Nationalism, and the Committee on Public Information,* Chapel Hill: University of North Carolina Press, 1980

World War II

Few press-government problems in this war

World War II was notable among twentieth-century wars in which the United States participated because there were few problems between the press and the government. While military censors approved war correspondents' copy from abroad, the government depended upon reporters in the United States to exercise voluntary censorship, and the press cooperated willingly. As a result, the government took action against far fewer publications than it had in World War I.

When the United States entered the war in December 1941, the federal Espionage Act of 1917 immediately went into effect. It limited freedom of expression during wartime by making it unlawful to do the following: make false statements that interfered with the military; attempt to cause "insubordination, disloyalty, mutiny, or refusal of duty" in the military; or obstruct the military recruiting or enlistment services. In addition, the act allowed the postmaster general to declare any printed material unmailable that might violate the law, which could lead to the loss of a publication's second-class mailing permit.

Journalists interview military sources at the battlefront during World War II.
(National Archives)

During World War I, the government declared unmailable or revoked the second-class mailing permits of about 100 newspapers and periodicals. In World War II, however, despite massive, generally secret investigations of newspapers and magazine by a number of federal agencies, only six radical publications had their second-class permits revoked by the Post Office, and two of those were restored before the war ended. Furthermore, only 33 persons had Espionage Act convictions sustained during the war for speech and publication violations, compared to 1,055 in World War I.

The few Espionage Act convictions in World War II, as well as the low number of second-class postal permits that were rescinded, can be attributed to several factors. One was the press's overall supportive tone, which was largely attributable to abhorrence of the Japanese surprise attack at Pearl Harbor. Another was the presence of Francis Biddle as attorney general. He believed strongly in the First Amendment and felt that there should be no sedition laws. As a result, the Justice Department took to court only a handful of journalists from small, radical publications, and it generally refused to support the Post Office in its desire to take away a large number of second-class mailing permits. J. Edgar Hoover, director of the Federal Bureau of Investigation, also wanted to bring a number of Espionage Act indictments against the press, particularly against black publications, but the Justice Department refused to sanction most of them.

On one occasion, the government sought an Espionage Act indictment against a mainstream newspaper. In August 1942, the Justice Department went to a grand jury about a *Chicago Tribune* article on the battle of Midway. Stanley Johnston's story described the Japanese fleet, thus revealing indirectly that the enemy's naval code had been broken by the U.S. Navy, which was a military secret. The grand jury refused to indict the *Tribune*, however, because the secretary of the Navy, fearing that the testimony would leak to the Japanese, would not allow government lawyers to reveal what harm had been done by the story.

Other than the Espionage Act, the domestic press had few wartime restraints. In December 1941, President Franklin D. Roosevelt created a new agency, the Office of Censorship. "All Americans abhor censorship, just as they abhor war," Roosevelt said in a press conference. "But the experience of this and of all other nations has demonstrated that some degree of censorship is essential in wartime, and we are at war. The important thing now is that such forms of censorship as are necessary shall be administered effectively and in harmony with the best interests of our free institutions." The president named Byron Price, executive editor of the Associated Press, as the agency's director.

Price immediately promised the press that there would be only "voluntary" domestic censorship, and a code of wartime practices was put out in booklet form by the Office of Censorship in January 1942. Price summed up the code's content, which suggested what could be run, in one sentence: "A maximum of accomplishment will be attained if editors will ask themselves with respect to any given detail, 'Is this information I would like to have if I were the enemy?' and then act accordingly." Price's agency helped keep secret several important stories, including the Allied plans for the invasion of North Africa in November 1942, the time and place of the D-Day landings in France in June 1944, and the development of the atomic bomb.

The press cooperated willingly, frequently contacting the Office of Censorship, which was open for inquiries 24 hours a day, every day of the year, to inquire whether stories violated the code. While few deliberate violations occurred, although the press sometimes complained that certain stories could not be run, it overwhelmingly supported the vol-

---

This . . . Is London

I'm standing again tonight on a rooftop looking out over London, feeling rather large and lonesome. In the course of the last fifteen or twenty minutes there's been considerable action up there, but at the moment there's an ominous silence hanging over London. But at the same time a silence that has a great deal of dignity. Just straightaway in front of me the searchlights are working. I can see one or two bursts of antiaircraft fire far in the distance. Just on the roof across the way I can see a man wearing a tin hat, a pair of powerful night glasses to his eyes, scanning the sky. Again, looking in the opposite direction, there is a building with two windows gone. Out of one window there waves something that looks like a white bed sheet, a window curtain swinging free in this night breeze. It looks as though it were being shaken by a ghost. There are a great many ghosts around these buildings in London. . . .

Edward R. Murrow
CBS, September 22, 1940

untary censorship and appreciated the way that Price ran the agency. Further evidence of the press's acceptance of diminished wartime rights were occasional blunt comments by journalists that the government should shut down radical, Fascist publications. "Why can't a democracy be strong and tough enough to squelch the little minority which is out to destroy it?" famed broadcaster and author William Shirer asked in the *Atlantic Monthly* in May 1942. "Is there anything undemocratic about being strong and tough?"

When stories originated overseas, however, the censorship was not voluntary. Military censors had to approve both written and broadcast copy, but few major problems developed. The government also paid close attention to photographs. Until September 1943, the government withheld all pictures that showed dead U.S. soldiers because it feared that they would make those at home want to stop the war. Then, in September 1943, the first such photographs were released to the public to motivate the country's people to continue to seek a final victory. At the same time, the government further deployed public relations tactics by refusing to allow any photographs to be run during the war that were deemed "horrific" or showed mentally ill soldiers.

A final form of censorship was invoked against publications mailed outside of the United States. On occasion, the government deleted what was considered unacceptable copy in publications before they were sent, causing complaints from the press; at other times, entire publications were destroyed. In these cases, the press had no recourse but to accept what occurred because the government stood firmly behind its censorship decisions.

While there were a number of well-known war correspondents, including Ernest Hemingway, Bill Mauldin, Margaret Bourke-White, and Shirer, two were particularly famous. Ernie Pyle, a columnist for the Scripps-Howard newspaper chain, became noted for writing about common soldiers, particularly on the front lines in Europe. After winning a Pulitzer Prize in 1944 for his wartime correspondence, he was killed by a sniper's bullet on the Pacific island of Ie Shima on April 18, 1945. Edward R. Murrow of CBS earned fame as the foremost front-line radio broadcaster,

beginning with his accounts of the British air blitz by the Germans. Later, he did notable broadcasts of an Allied bombing run over Germany and the horrors he encountered as one of the first war correspondents to reach the German concentration camp of Buchenwald. He survived the war to become one of television's earliest news stars in the 1950s.

When the war ended in August 1945, the Espionage Act as well as the voluntary code of wartime practices were no longer applicable. However, both the Army and the White House asked Price to consider requesting that the press continue withholding information about the atomic bomb. He refused. "I believe that if you were in my position you would agree with the decision to abolish Censorship," he wrote a man in Houston in mid-August. "I have seen so many incidents in which Censorship did harm that I was determined I would do what I could to get rid of it as soon as the harm began to overbalance the military benefit."

The press clearly appreciated what Price had accomplished. At the war's end, Washington journalists presented him with a scroll that concluded, "In less capable hands a voluntary censorship would have failed."

PATRICK S. WASHBURN

See also Office of Censorship; War Correspondents; War Photography

Further Reading:
Biddle, Francis, *In Brief Authority*, Garden City, New York: Doubleday, 1962
Roeder, George H., *The Censored War: American Visual Experience During World War Two*, New Haven, Connecticut: Yale University Press, 1993
Voss, Frederick, *Reporting the War: The Journalistic Coverage of World War II*, Washington, D.C.: Smithsonian Institution, 1994
Washburn, Patrick S., "The Office of Censorship's Attempt to Control Press Coverage of the Atomic Bomb During World War II," *Journalism Monographs* 120 (1990)
_____, *A Question of Sedition: The Federal Government's Investigation of the Black Press During World War II*, New York: Oxford University Press, 1986

Y

Yellow Journalism

Sensational stories and large, garish headlines typified period

Yellow journalism took the prototype of the modern newspaper typified by the *St. Louis (Missouri) Post-Dispatch* and the *New York World* of Joseph Pulitzer, dipped it into a vat of colored ink, and threw it with screaming headlines half an inch or more tall into the faces of big-city newspaper readers. In general, readers lapped it up, pushing the circulations of some of the leading newspapers to heights they never before had achieved.

In the latter 1890s, the yellow journals were brash and bold, telling their sensational stories of sex, sin, and scandal with big headlines and garish illustrations. They crusaded against corrupt politicians and greedy businessmen. They entertained their largely immigrant audience with colored comics and Sunday supplements. And they never failed to boast of their own achievements, whether they were solving a murder that had stumped the police, exposing a shady franchise proposal between the city and a natural gas company, or raising the funds to assemble the Statue of Liberty in New York Harbor.

The sensationalism, self-promotion, and crusades were hardly new. But in the last two decades of the nineteenth century, advances in printing technology produced high-speed presses that could print editions of more than 50 pages in colored ink; typesetting machines that could make multicolumn headlines in large type; and photoengraving processes that could print large, complicated illustrations and halftone photographs. Thus, the yellow journals looked new, even though much of what they purveyed consisted of old techniques dressed up in gaudier trappings.

Yellow journalism was gestated in the womb of Pulitzer's "new journalism." Pulitzer made sensational reporting, stunts, crusades, a progressive editorial policy, and self-promotion the hallmarks of the *Post-Dispatch* and the *World*. Watching the successful Hungarian immigrant from the sidelines was the wealthy William Randolph Hearst, a former college student who had worked for the *World* as a cub reporter before taking over his father's newspaper in San Francisco. As editor of the *Examiner,* Hearst adopted Pulitzer's techniques and practiced them on an even grander scale, fueled by the millions available from his family's silver and copper fortunes. When Hearst bought the *New York Journal* and moved to New York to compete with Pulitzer head-to-head, yellow journalism was ready to be born.

Hearst operated out of an office in the *World* building, and he talked with his checkbook. The brash young Californian knew that the way to have an excellent newspaper was to hire an excellent staff, and he devised a plan to get the best people while hurting Pulitzer at the same time. Shortly after arriving in New York in 1895, Hearst started secret negotiations with staff members of the *World*'s Sunday edition, and in a short time, he had hired most of them to work on the *Journal*.

The astounded Pulitzer hired them back, but Hearst's bank account was too full, and most of Pulitzer's staff made a permanent move. Among them was Richard F. Outcault, an artist who drew a popular comic panel called "Hogan's Alley." It featured a goofy-looking youth who wore a yellow nightshirt, and soon the character was dubbed the Yellow Kid. In replacing his staff, Pulitzer hired George B. Luks, another artist who soon was drawing his own version of "Hogan's Alley" and the Yellow Kid. The character caught on, and Pulitzer and Hearst used its popularity to promote their newspapers by splashing the Kid's image on billboards all over town. Some critics of the Pulitzer and Hearst style of journalism thought the Kid, with his garishly colored nightshirt and vacant expression, aptly captured this gaudy, admittedly entertaining, but somewhat shallow approach to newspapering. They called it yellow journalism, a phrase that came to refer to any kind of sensationalistic reporting.

The style, which spread to a number of other dailies inside and outside of New York, reached its zenith during the Cuban revolution of 1895 and the ensuing Spanish-American War. Fueled by a strong propaganda effort by revolutionary sympathizers in Florida and New York, the yellow journals so sensationally covered the Spanish attempts to control the colonists that many people in the United States thought that the U.S. government should intervene.

Many newspapers dispatched reporters and illustrators to Cuba, who sent back sensational and sometimes inflated accounts of Spanish "atrocities" allegedly perpetrated by the Spanish commander. At one point, Hearst's illustrator, the artist Frederic Remington, who had been sent to Cuba with reporter Richard Harding Davis, cabled Hearst that things were so quiet that he and Davis wanted to come home. Hearst, according to the published account of another of his war correspondents, cabled back: "Please remain. You furnish the pictures and I'll furnish the war."

The war was not long in coming. The U.S. battleship *Maine* exploded in Havana harbor on February 15, 1898, with the loss of 266 sailors. Pulitzer responded with a graphic illustration that covered about half of the front page depicting the catastrophe, and Hearst, in a banner headline, indirectly accused Spain of being responsible and offered a $50,000 reward for any information that would lead to "the Detection of the Perpetrator of the Maine Outrage!"

The incident was the final spark that ignited the flames of war. The four-month conflict that followed was covered more thoroughly than any previous war in U.S. history. Reporters and illustrators traveled with and sometimes fought beside U.S. troops, sailed with the fleet to the Spanish Philippines, and roamed the staging areas on the Gulf coast of the United States. The cream of U.S. journalism and literature, including the novelist Stephen Crane, went to Cuba to cover the war. Even Hearst outfitted a yacht for war duty and covered some of the action.

The war pushed newspaper circulation to unheard-of heights of more than a million for some of the big-city newspapers, although that did not translate into profits for most. Some of the circulation gains were fueled by the production of expensive extra editions, sometimes as many as 40 a day. Combined with a drop in advertising revenue and the cost of keeping correspondents in the field, most of the newspapers lost money. Hearst, with his family fortune, could afford it, but Pulitzer felt the drain.

With the end of the war, most of the yellow journals tried to maintain their high circulations by continuing their old practices. But Pulitzer, perhaps influenced by the success of the more conservative *New York Times* under the leadership of Adolph Ochs, toned down the *World*. The assassination of President William McKinley brought an outraged reaction against Hearst, who had attacked the president so strongly that many considered Hearst at least partly responsible for the shooting. Both factors contributed to the decline of yellow journalism, which eventually died out after the first decade of the twentieth century.

Many criticize the yellow journalists for using sensationalism to increase circulation. Journalists had turned to sensationalism before, however, and would do so again with the jazz journalism of the 1920s and the "trash television" of the 1980s and 1990s. Yellow journalism also had its positive side, emphasizing the use of color, graphics, and photographs that continued to improve the appearance of the newspaper in the United States, and introducing the comics section and the Sunday supplement that continue to entertain readers throughout the country.

MICHAEL BUCHHOLZ

See also Hearst, William Randolph; New Journalism (1880s); Newspaper Technology; *New York Times*; Ochs, Adolph Simon; Pulitzer, Joseph; Spanish-American War

Further Reading

Kobre, Sidney, *The Yellow Press and Gilded Age Journalism,* Tallahassee: Florida State University Press, 1964

Milton, Joyce, *The Yellow Kids: Foreign Correspondents in the Heyday of Yellow Journalism,* New York: Harper & Row, 1989

Z

Zenger, John Peter

Milestone in early free press history

The trial of John Peter Zenger in 1735 for seditious libel in New York City is a landmark event in the history of freedom of the press. A poorly educated German immigrant who had little understanding of what was published in the newspaper, Zenger was a printer working for James Alexander, the managing editor and chief editorial writer of the *New-York Weekly Journal*. In 1733–34, Alexander published a series of essays announcing that he would pursue his political opponents with the "lash of satire." One essay referred to New York's governor, William Cosby, as a "rogue."

Cosby responded by ordering the *Weekly Journal* to be burned. Zenger was arrested and imprisoned for nine months awaiting trial. On the day of trial, August 4, 1735, Andrew Hamilton of Philadelphia rose from the audience and introduced himself as Zenger's attorney. He admitted that Zenger had printed the libels and insisted that Zenger had the right to print the truth. The judge stopped Alexander, insisting that truth could not be admitted into evidence to justify a libel. Alexander, however, daringly played to the jury over the head of the judge, arguing that the facts alleged in the complaint were "notoriously known to be true."

Hamilton's concluding remarks urged the jury to consider the cause of this "poor printer" as the "cause of liberty":

> Every man who prefers freedom to a life of slavery will bless and honor you as men who have baffled the attempt of tyranny; and by an impartial and uncorrupt verdict, have laid a noble foundation for securing to ourselves, our posterity, and our neighbors that to which nature and the laws of our country have given us a right – the liberty – both of exposing and opposing arbitrary power . . . by speaking and writing truth.

After withdrawing for a short time, the jury returned a verdict of not guilty, "upon which there were three huzzas in the hall, which was crowded with people," it was reported. The Zenger trial stands for more than the idea that evidence of truth ought to be admitted in a defamation trial in order to justify libel or slander. The trial also vindicates a basic democratic principle – that a jury may determine for itself the law that ought to apply in a particular case.

RICHARD SCHEIDENHELM

See also Colonial Press; Libel; Newspapers in the Eighteenth Century

Further Reading

Katz, Stanley Nider, ed., *A Brief Narrative of the Case and Trial of John Peter Zenger, Printer of the 'New York Weekly Journal'*, 2nd ed., Cambridge, Massachusetts: Belknap Press of Harvard University Press, 1972

Levy, Leonard Williams, *Emergence of a Free Press*, New York and Oxford: Oxford University Press, 1985

Zenith Radio Case

Decision helped prompt federal regulation

Eugene F. McDonald, the president of the Zenith Radio Corporation, in 1924 requested a license from the Department of Commerce, under the provisions of the Radio Act of 1912, for a station in Chicago. He promised that the Zenith station would only operate between the hours of 10:00 and 12:00 on Thursday nights, as that was the only frequency and time available in Chicago. Zenith's license was confirmed on September 3, 1925.

McDonald soon demanded more time on the air and threatened legal action on the grounds that the Radio Act of 1912 did not give the Department of Commerce authority to deny broadcast licenses or restrict hours of operation or frequency. The Department of Commerce then determined that WJAZ had been broadcasting in violation of the voluntary restrictions placed on the WJAZ license on 910 kilohertz, which was reserved for seven Canadian stations. Because of treaty agreement and protest by the Canadian government, the use of this wavelength by the Zenith Radio Corporation required the Department of Commerce to take action.

The Department of Commerce asked the Justice Department to file suit against Zenith. On April 16, 1926, Federal Judge Wilkerson ruled that Congress had not granted the Department of Commerce power to prescribe regulations to control frequency, power, or hours of operation of radio stations. The Zenith case and other stations that moved frequencies and increased their power without governmental approval convinced Congress to pass the Radio Act of 1927.

MARVIN R. BENSMAN

See also Hoover, Herbert, and Radio Regulation

Further Reading

Bensman, Marvin R., "Regulation of Broadcasting by the Department of Commerce, 1921–1927," in *American Broadcasting: A Source Book on the History of Radio and Television*, compiled by Lawrence W. Lichty and Malachi C. Topping, New York: Hastings House, 1975

_____, "The Zenith-WJAZ Case and the Chaos of 1926–1927," *Journal of Broadcasting* 14 (1970)

Zworykin, Vladimir

Did pioneering work on television

Modern television technology can trace some of its roots to Russia, where Vladimir Zworykin gained his inspiration to convert television from a mechanical to an electronic medium. Zworykin studied under physicist Boris Rosing, who developed a crude electronic picture tube in 1907. Zworykin was swept up in Rosing's enthusiasm and, after serving in the Russian Army Signal Corps during World War I, emigrated to the United States and became one of broadcasting's great pioneers.

Zworykin researched for Westinghouse and the Radio Corporation of America (RCA), two of the leaders in broadcasting's development in the United States. He started in 1920 with Westinghouse, where he invented an all-electronic camera, the iconoscope, in 1923. Six years later, Zworykin came up with the kinescope, an electronic picture tube that improved on Rosing's 1907 invention. Zworykin had built a fully electronic television system, yet Westinghouse, wanting to capitalize on radio's boom, showed little interest.

The following year, Zworykin was transferred to RCA when that firm took over Westinghouse's research program. RCA's new president, David Sarnoff, promised to back Zworykin. The kinescope was soon demonstrated.

With RCA's support, Zworykin spent the 1930s on his crowning achievement, the image orthicon camera tube, which was much more light-sensitive than the iconoscope

Vladimir Zworykin was a pioneer in the development of television.

(Library of American Broadcasting)

and could be used in normal daylight. RCA introduced it in June 1939, and television was ready at last to take its place in U.S. life. Zworykin worked independently of the era's other great television inventor, Philo Farnsworth, who found private financial support and formed his own company.

THOMAS LETTS

See also Broadcast Pioneers; Farnsworth, Philo Taylor; Television Technology

Further Reading

Floherty, John J., *Television Story*, rev. ed., Philadelphia: Lippincott, 1957

Willis, Edgar E., and Henry B. Aldridge, *Television, Cable, and Radio: A Communications Approach*, Englewood Cliffs, New Jersey: Prentice-Hall, 1992

NOTES ON CONTRIBUTORS

ABEL, Trudi. Scholar-in-residence, History Department, Duke University, Durham, North Carolina.

ABRAHAMSON, David. Associate professor of journalism, Medill School of Journalism, Northwestern University, Evanston, Illinois. Author, *The American Magazine: Research Perspectives and Prospects* (1995); *Magazine-made America: The Cultural Transformation of the Postwar Periodical* (1996).

ADAMS, Edward E. Assistant professor, Department of Communications, Drama, and Journalism, Angelo State University, San Angelo, Texas. Articles in *Journalism & Mass Communication Quarterly, Journalism & Mass Communication Educator, Journalism History, American Journalism, Journal of the West, Southern Historian, Web Journal of Mass Communication Research, Southwestern Mass Communication Journal, Dictionary of Literary Biography, Encyclopedia of Popular Culture,* and *Dictionary of American Biography.*

ALLEN, Craig. Associate professor, Walter Cronkite School of Journalism and Telecommunication, Arizona State University, Tempe. Author, *Eisenhower and the Mass Media: Peace, Prosperity, and Prime-Time TV* (1993). Articles in *Journal of Broadcasting & Electronic Media* and *Journalism Quarterly.*

AMANA, Harry. Associate professor, School of Journalism and Mass Communication, University of North Carolina, Chapel Hill. Articles in *Africa News, CLIO, Dictionary of Literary Biography.*

APPLEGATE, Edd. Associate professor of advertising, School of Journalism, Middle Tennessee State University, Murfreesboro. Author, *Literary Journalism: A Biographical Dictionary of Writers and Editors* (1996); *Print and Broadcast Journalism: A Critical Examination* (1996); *Journalistic Advocates and Muckrakers: Three Centuries of Crusading Writers* (1997); *Personalities and Products: A Historical Perspective on Advertising in America* (1998). Co-author, *Advertising: Concepts, Strategies, and Issues* (1993). Editor, *The Ad Men and Women: A Biographical Dictionary* (1994). Co-editor, *British Reform Writers, 1789–1832* (1996).

ASHLEY, Perry J. Distinguished Professor Emeritus, University of South Carolina, Columbia. Editor, *American Newspaper Journalists 1873–1900* (1983), *1901–1925* (1984), *1926–1950* (1984), *1860–1872* (1985), *1950–1990* (1993).

ATWOOD, Roy Alden. Director, School of Communication, University of Idaho, Moscow.

AUCOIN, James. Assistant professor, Communications Department, University of South Alabama, Mobile. Article in *Journal of Mass Media Ethics.*

AUSTIN, Bruce A. Research consultant, Rochester Institute of Technology, Rochester, New York. Author, *The Film Audience: An International Bibliography of Research with Annotations and an Essay* (1983); *Immediate Seating: A Look at Movie Audiences* (1989); *The American Arts and Crafts Movement in Western New York, 1900–1920* (1992). Article in *Psychological Reports.*

AVERY, Donald R. Professor and chairman, Communication Department, East Connecticut State University, and former president, American Journalism Historians Association.

BALDASTY, Gerald J. Faculty, Communications and Women Studies Program, University of Washington, Seattle. Author, *The Commercialization of News in the Nineteenth Century* (1992). Articles in *Journalism History.*

BALLOTTI, R. John, Jr. Assistant professor of communication, Quincy University, Quincy, Illinois.

BASS, S.M.W. Associate professor of journalism and head of the magazine sequence, William Allen White School of Journalism and Mass Communication, University of Kansas, Lawrence. Author, *For the Trees: An Illustrated History of the Ozark St. Francis National Forests, 1908–1978.* Articles in *The Trade Press in the United States, Literary Journalism: A Research Guide to a Developing Genre* (ed. Thomas B. Connery), *Journalism History,* and *Dictionary of Literary Biography.*

BAUGHMAN, James L. Professor of journalism and mass communication, University of Wisconsin, Madison. Author, *Television's Guardians: The FCC and the Politics of Programming, 1958–1967* (1985); *Henry R. Luce and the Rise of the American News Media* (1987); *The Republic of Mass Culture: Journalism, Filmmaking, and Broadcasting in America Since 1941* (1992, 1997). Article in *Reviews in American History.*

BEASLEY, Maurine. Professor of journalism, University of Maryland, College Park, and former president, American Journalism Historians Association and Association for Education in Journalism and Mass Communication. Author, *The First Women Washington Correspondents* (1976); *Eleanor Roosevelt and the Media: A Public Quest for Self-Fulfillment* (1987). Co-author, *Women in Media: A Documentary Source Book* (1977); *Voices of Change: Southern Pulitzer Winners* (1979); *The New Majority: A Look at What the Preponderance of Women in Journalism Education Means to the Schools and to the Professions* (1988); *Taking Their Place: A Documentary History of Women and Journalism* (1993). Editor, *The White House Press Conferences of Eleanor Roosevelt* (1983). Co-editor, *One Third of a Nation: Lorena Hickok Reports on the Great Depression* (1981). Articles in *Newspaper Research Journal, Journalism History, American Journalism.*

BEKKEN, Jon. Assistant professor, Suffolk University, Boston, Massachusetts. Articles in *Journalism History, Journalism & Mass Communication Quarterly,* and *Newsworkers: Towards a History of the Rank and File* (eds. Bonnie Brennan and Hanno Hardt). Articles in *Journalism History*.

BELLAMY, Robert V., Jr. Associate professor, Media Studies, Duquesne University, Pittsburgh, Pennsylvania. Co-author, *Television and the Remote Control: Grazing on a Vast Wasteland* (1996). Co-editor, *The Remote Control in the New Age of Television* (1993).

BENJAMIN, Louise. Associate director of the George Foster Peabody Awards and assistant professor, Henry W. Brady College of Journalism and Mass Communication, University of Georgia, Athens. Articles in *Free Speech Yearbook* and *Journal of Broadcasting & Electronic Media*.

BENSMAN, Marvin R. Professor of electronic media, Department of Communication, University of Memphis, Memphis, Tennessee. Author, *Broadcast Regulation: Selected Cases and Decisions* (1983, 1985); *Broadcast/Cable Regulation* (1990).

BERNT, Joseph P. Associate professor of journalism, Scripps School of Journalism, Ohio University, Athens.

BERTRAND, Claude-Jean. Professor Emeritus, L'Institut Français de Presse Université de Paris. Author, *Les Mass Media Aux États-Unis* (1974); *Les Conseils de Press dans le Monde* (1977). Articles in *Public Relations Review* and *Media Studies Journal*.

BETTIG, Ronald V. Assistant professor, College of Communications, Pennsylvania State University, University Park. Author, *Copyrighting Culture: The Political Economy of Intellectual Property* (1996). Article in *Critical Studies in Mass Communication*.

BJORK, Ulf Jonas. Associate professor, School of Journalism, Indiana University, Indianapolis. Articles in *Journalism History*; *Journalism & Mass Communication Educator*; *Historical Journal of Film, Radio, and Television*; and the *Gazette*.

BLACK, Gregory D. Professor, Communication Studies, University of Missouri, Kansas City. Author, *Hollywood Censored: Morality Codes, Catholics, and the Movies* (1994); *The Catholics Crusade Against the Movies, 1940–1975* (1997). Co-author, *Hollywood Goes to War: How Politics, Profits, and Propaganda Shaped World War II Movies* (1987, 1990). Article in *Literature-Film Quarterly*.

BLAKE, Kenneth R. Assistant Professor, College of Mass Communication, Middle Tennessee State University, Murfreesboro.

BLANCHARD, Margaret, A. William Rand Kenan Jr. Professor of journalism and mass communication, University of North Carolina, Chapel Hill, former president, American Journalism Historians Association; associate editor, *Journalism & Mass Communication Quarterly*. Author, *The Hutchins Commission: The Press and the Responsibili-*

ty Concept (1977); *Exporting the First Amendment: The Press-Government Crusade of 1945–1952* (1986); *Revolutionary Sparks: Freedom of Expression in Modern America* (1992).

BLOOM, Stephen G. Associate professor of journalism and mass communication, University of Iowa, Iowa City. Articles in *American Journalism Review*, *The American Editor*, and *The Bulletin of the American Society of Newspaper Editors*.

BONN, Thomas L. Librarian, Cortland Memorial Library, State University of New York, Cortland. Author, *Paperback Primer: A Guide for Collectors* (1981); *Under Cover: An Illustrated History of American Mass-Market Paperbacks* (1982); *Heavy Traffic and High Culture: New American Library as Literary Gatekeeper in the Paperback Revolution* (1989).

BOW, James. Formerly associated with the Department of Journalism, Central Michigan State, Mt. Pleasant.

BRADLEY, Patricia. Associate professor, School of Communications and Theater, Temple University, Philadelphia, Pennsylvania. Articles in *Journalism & Mass Communication Quarterly* and *Journalism History*.

BRAUN, Mark J. Associate professor and chairman, Department of Communication Studies, Gustavus Adolphus College, St. Peter, Minnesota. Author, *AM Stereo and the FCC: Case Study of a Marketplace Shibboleth* (1994). Article in *Journal of Broadcasting & Electronic Media*.

BRENNAN, Bonnie. Assistant professor, School of Mass Communications, Virginia Commonwealth University, Richmond. Articles in *The Journal of Research into New Media Technologies*, *Journal of the European Institute for Communication and Culture*, *American Journalism*, *Studies in Popular Culture*, and *Journal of American History*.

BROOKS, Dwight E. Assistant professor, Department of Telecommunications at the Radio-TV Center, Indiana University, Bloomington.

BROWN, James A. Associate professor of telecommunication and film, University of Alabama, Tuscaloosa. Author, *Television "Critical Viewing Skills" Education: A Survey and Evaluation of Major Media Literacy Projects in the United States and Selected Countries*. Co-author of *Radio-Television-Cable Management*, *Broadcast Management: Radio-Television*. Articles in *Journal of Communication*, *Journal of Broadcasting and Electronic Media*, *Journal of Broadcasting*, *Encyclopedia of Television*, and *New Catholic Encyclopedia*.

BROWN, Pamela A. Professor of journalism and communications, Rider University, Lawrenceville, New Jersey, and former president, American Journalism Historians Association.

BROWNE, Donald R. Professor and chairman, Department of Speech-Communication, University of Minnesota, Minneapolis. Author, *The Voice of America: Policies and Problems* (1976); *International Radio Broadcasting: The Limits of the Limitless Medium* (1982); *Comparing Broadcast Systems: The Experiences of Six Industrialized Nations* (1989); *Electronic Media and Indigenous Peoples: A Voice of Our Own?* (1996). Co-author, *Television/Radio News and Minorities* (1994). Article in *Journal of Broadcasting & Electronic Media*.

BRYSKI, Bruce G. Associate professor of speech and media studies, State University of New York, Buffalo State College, Buffalo. Co-editor, *Experiences in Speech*. Articles in *Journal of Applied Communication Research* and *Journal of Human Communication*.

BUCHHOLZ, Michael. Associate professor of journalism, Communication Department, Indiana State University, Terre Haute. Articles in *The Quill, Journalism Quarterly, The Media in America: A History* (eds. Wm. David Sloan and James G. Stovall) and *Dictionary of Literary Biography*.

BUDDENBAUM, Judith M. Professor, Department of Journalism and Technical Communication, Colorado State University, Boulder. Co-editor, *Religion and Mass Media: Audiences and Adaptations* (1996).

CAMPBELL, Douglas S. Chairman, Department of Journalism and Mass Communication, Lock Haven University, Lock Haven, Pennsylvania. Author, *The Supreme Court and the Mass Media: Selected Cases, Summaries, and Analyses* (1990); *Free Press v. Fair Trial: Supreme Court Decisions Since 1807* (1994).

CARISTI, Dom. Electronic media studies coordinator, Department of Journalism and Mass Communication, Iowa State University, Ames. Author, *Expanding Free Expression in the Marketplace: Broadcasting and the Public Forum* (1992). Articles in *Journal of Broadcasting & Electronic Media* and *Journalism History*.

CARLEBACH, Michael L. Associate professor, School of Communication, University of Miami, Coral Gables, Florida. Author, *The Origins of Photojournalism in America* (1992); *Farm Security Administration Photographs of Florida* (1993); *American Photojournalism Comes of Age* (1997).

CASSADY, David. Associate professor and chairperson, Media Arts Department, Pacific University, Forest Grove, Oregon.

CASWELL, Lucy Shelton. Professor, Ohio State University, and curator, Ohio State University Cartoon Research Library, Columbus. Co-author, *Billy Ireland* (1980). Editor, *Guide to Sources in American Journalism History* (1989).

CAUDILL, Edward. Professor, School of Journalism, University of Tennessee, Knoxville. Author, *Darwinism in the Press: The Evolution of an Idea* (1989); *Darwinian Myths: The Legends and Misuses of a Theory* (1997). Articles in *Journalism History* and *Journal of the History of Ideas*.

CHANCE, Jean C. Associate professor, College of Journalism and Communications, University of Florida, Gainesville. Articles in *Journalism & Mass Communication Quarterly* and *Newspaper Research Journal*.

CHARISSE, Marc. Assistant professor of communications, Jacksonville University, Jacksonville, Florida.

CHISHOLM, Brad. Associate professor, Department of Theatre and Film Studies, St. Cloud State University, St. Cloud, Minnesota. Articles in *Critical Studies in Mass Communication, Journal of Political Cinema, The Journal of Popular Film and Television*.

CHORBA, Frank J. Professor of mass media studies, Washburn University, Topeka, Kansas, and founding editor, *Journal of Radio Studies*.

CLINTON, Patrick J. Assistant professor, Medill School of Journalism, Northwestern University, Evanston, Illinois. Author, *Guide to Writing for the Business Press* (1997).

CLOUD, Barbara. Professor of communication, Hank Greenspun School of Communication, University of Nevada, Las Vegas; former president, American Journalism Historians Association; and editor, *Journalism History*. Author, *The Business of Newspapers on the Western Frontier* (1992).

CONNERY, Thomas B. Professor, Department of Journalism and Mass Communication, University of St. Thomas, St. Paul, Minnesota, and former president, American Journalism Historians Association. Editor, *A Sourcebook of American Literary Journalism: Representative Writers in an Emerging Genre* (1992).

COOK, Russell J. Associate professor of communication, Bethany College, Bethany, West Virginia. Articles in *Journalism History*.

COPELAND, David A. Assistant professor, Department of Mass Communication, Emory & Henry College, Emory, Virginia. Author, *Colonial American Newspapers: Character and Content* (1997).

CRAIG, R. Stephen. Professor and chairman, Department of Radio, Television, and Film, University of North Texas, Denton. Editor, *Men, Masculinity, and the Media* (1992).

CSAPÓ-SWEET, Rita M. Assistant professor of communication and fellow, Center for International Studies, University of Missouri, St. Louis.

DANIEL, Douglass K. Assistant professor, A.Q. Miller School of Journalism and Mass Communications, Kansas State University, Manhattan. Author, *Lou Grant: The Mak-*

ing of TV's Top Newspaper Drama (1996). Article in *News Photographer*.

DARDENNE, Robert. Associate professor of mass communications, Journalism Studies Program, University of South Florida, St. Petersburg. Co-author, *The Conversation of Journalism: Communication, Community, and News* (1994). Articles in *Journal of Mass Media Ethics* and *Journalism Educator*.

DAVIS, Charles N. Assistant professor of journalism, Center for Communication Arts, Southern Methodist University, Dallas, Texas. Articles in *The Quill*, *Newspaper Research Journal*, *Journal of Broadcasting & Electronic Media*, and *Communications and the Law*.

DE MOTT, John. Professor Emeritus of journalism, University of Memphis, Memphis, Tennessee. Co-editor, *The Journalist's Prayer Book: Prayers by Prominent Writers, Editors, and Newsmen* (1972).

DENNIS, Everette E. Distinguished Professor, Fordham Graduate School of Business, New York, New York; President, American Academy in Berlin, Berlin, Germany.

DENNISON, Corley F., III. Associate professor, Page Pitt School of Journalism and Mass Communications, Marshall University, Huntington, West Virginia. Articles in *The Journal of Radio Studies*, *Signals*, *Via Satellite*, and *The Encyclopedia of Popular Culture*.

DESANTO, Barbara J. Assistant professor of public relations, School of Journalism and Broadcasting, Oklahoma State University, Stillwater. Article in *Journalism & Mass Communications Educator*.

DICKEN-GARCIA, Hazel. Professor, School of Journalism and Mass Communication, University of Minnesota, Minneapolis. Author, *Journalistic Standards in Nineteenth-Century America* (1989); *To Western Woods: The Breckinridge Family Moves to Kentucky in 1793* (1991). Co-author, *Communication History* (1980).

DICKERSON, Donna L. Professor, Department of Mass Communications, University of South Florida, Tampa. Author, *A Typestick of Texas History* (1971); *Florida Media Law* (1982, 1991); *The Course of Tolerance: Freedom of the Press in Nineteenth-Century America* (1990). Co-author, *College Student Press Law* (1979).

DOMINICK, Joseph R. Professor, Department of Journalism, University of Georgia, Athens. Author, *The Dynamics of Mass Communication* (1983, 1987, 1990, 1993, 1994, 1996). Co-author, *Mass Media Research: An Introduction* (1983, 1987, 1991, 1994, 1997); *Broadcasting/Cable and Beyond: An Introduction* (1990, 1993, 1996). Co-editor, *Broadcasting Research Methods* (1985). Article in *Journal of Communication*.

DONATELLO, Michael C. Manager of market research, Newspaper Association of America, Reston, Virginia, and doctoral candidate, School of Journalism and Mass Communication, University of North Carolina, Chapel Hill.

DOYLE, Pamela K. Assistant professor of telecommunication and film, College of Communication, University of Alabama, Tuscaloosa. Freelance producer, *Living on Earth*, Voice of American Radio Services and CNN Radio.

EBERHARD, Wallace B. Professor of journalism, Henry W. Grady School of Journalism and Mass Communication, University of Georgia, Athens, and editor, *American Journalism*. Articles in *Journalism Quarterly*, *Journalism History*, *Military Review*, and *Newspaper Research Journal*.

EDGERTON, Gary R. Professor and chairman, Communication and Theatre Arts Department, Old Dominion University, Virginia Beach, Virginia, president, American Culture Association, and senior associate editor, *Journal of Popular Film and Television*. Author, *American Film Exhibition and an Analysis of the Motion Picture Industry's Market Structure, 1963–1980* (1983). Editor, *Film and the Arts in Symbiosis: A Resource Guide* (1988). Co-editor, *In the Eye of the Beholder: Critical Perspectives in Popular Film and Television* (1997). Articles in *Journal of Popular Culture*, *Journal of Popular Film and Television*, *Journal of American Culture*, and *Television Quarterly*.

EMERY, Michael. (Deceased) Author, *On the Front Lines: Following America's Foreign Correspondents Across the Twentieth Century* (1995). Co-author, *Readings in Mass Communication: Concepts and Issues in the Mass Media* (1972, 1974, 1977, 1980, 1983, 1986, 1989); *The Press and America: An Interpretive History of the Mass Media* (1978, 1984, 1988, 1992, 1996). Co-editor, *America's Front Page News, 1960–1970* (1970).

ENDRES, Fred F. Professor, School of Journalism and Mass Communication, Kent State University, Kent, Ohio. Articles in *Journalism & Mass Communication Educator*, *Journalism Educator*, *Journalism Quarterly*, *Newspaper Research Journal*, and *Journalism History*.

ENDRES, Kathleen L. Professor, School of Communication, University of Akron, Akron, Ohio. Editor, *Trade, Industrial, and Professional Periodicals of the United States* (1994). Co-editor, *Women's Periodicals in the United States: Consumer Magazines* (1995), *Social and Political Issues* (1996). Article in *Journalism & Mass Communication Quarterly*.

ERVIN, Ferrell. Professor and chairman, Department of Mass Communication, Southeast Missouri State University, Cape Girardeau.

EVENSEN, Bruce. Associate professor, Department of Communication, DePaul University, Chicago, Illinois. Articles in *Gazette: The International Journal for Mass Communication Studies*, *Journalism Quarterly*, *Journal of Sports History*, *Pennsylvania History*, *Journal of Newspaper and Periodical History*, *Journalism History*, and *American Journalism*.

EVERETT, George. Professor Emeritus of journalism, University of Tennessee, Knoxville.

FANG, Irving. Professor, School of Journalism and Mass Communication, University of Minnesota, Minneapolis. Author, *Television News: Writing, Editing, Filming, Broadcasting* (1968); *Television News* (1972); *Television/Radio News Workbook* (1974); *Those Radio Commentators!* (1977); *Television News, Radio News* (1980, 1985); *The Computer Story* (1988); *Pictures* (1993); *Writing Style Differences in Newspaper, Radio, and Television News* (1991); *A History of Mass Communication: Six Information Revolutions* (1997).

FARRAR, Ronald T. Reynolds-Faunt Memorial Professor of journalism, University of South Carolina, Columbia. Author, *Reluctant Servant: The Story of Charles G. Ross* (1969); *Mass Media and the National Experience: Essays in Communications History* (1971); *College 101* (1984, 1988); *Mass Communication: An Introduction to the Field* (1988, 1995, 1996). Co-author, *The Ultimate College Survival Guide* (1995); *Advertising and Public Relations Law* (1997).

FEDLER, Fred. Professor, School of Communication, University of Central Florida, Orlando. Author, *Reporting for the Print Media* (1973, 1979, 1984, 1989, 1993); *An Introduction to the Mass Media* (1978); *Media Hoaxes* (1989). Co-author, *Reporting for the Media* (1997). Article in *Journalism & Mass Communication Educator*.

FEE, Frank E., Jr. Knight Professor of editing, E.W. Scripps School of Journalism, Ohio University, Miami.

FERRÉ, John P. Associate professor, Department of Communication, University of Louisville, Louisville, Kentucky. Author, *Merrill Guide to the Research Paper* (1983); *A Social Gospel for Millions: The Religious Bestsellers of Charles Sheldon, Charles Gordon, and Harold Bell Wright* (1988). Co-author, *Rhetorical Patterns: An Anthology of Contemporary Essays* (1981); *Public Relations and Ethics: A Bibliography* (1991); *Good News: Social Ethics and the Press* (1993). Editor, *Channels of Belief: Religion and American Commercial Television* (1990).

FIELDING, Raymond. Dean, School of Motion Picture, Television and Recording Arts, Florida State University, Tallahassee. Author, *The Technique of Special Effects Cinematography* (1965, 1972, 1985); *A Technological History of Motion Pictures and Television* (1967); *The American Newsreel, 1911–1967* (1972); *The March of Time, 1935–1951* (1978).

FITZPATRICK, Kathy R. Assistant professor, Center for Communication Arts, Southern Methodist University, and head, Public Relations Department, Southern Methodist University, Dallas, Texas. Co-author, *Public Relations Ethics* (1995); *Journalism Ethics* (1997). Editor, *Guide for Cruising Maryland Waters* (1984). Articles in *Public Relations Review*, *Public Relations Quarterly*, and *Journal of Mass Media Ethics*.

FLAMIANO, Dolores. Doctoral student, School of Journalism and Mass Communication, University of North Carolina, Chapel Hill.

FLOCKE, Elizabeth Lynne. Associate professor, Newhouse School of Public Communication, Syracuse University, Syracuse, New York.

FOLKERTS, Jean. Professor and director, School of Media and Public Affairs, The George Washington University, Washington, D.C., and editor, *Journalism & Mass Communication Quarterly*. Co-author, *Media In Your Life* and *Voices of a Nation*. Articles on the agrarian and small town press of the nineteenth century.

FOX, Julia R. Instructor of journalism, Department of Communication, Northern Illinois University, DeKalb.

FRANCKE, Warren T. Professor of communication, University of Nebraska, Omaha. Articles in *Journalism Quarterly, Journalism History, American Journalism,* and *Dictionary of Literary Biography*.

FRASCA, Ralph. Associate professor of journalism, School of Communication, Hofstra University, Hempstead, New York. Author, *The Rise and Fall of the Saturday Globe* (1992).

FREEMAN, John. (Deceased) Author, *Keep the Media Free: The Text of a Speech* (1976). Articles in *News Photographer*.

GALLAGHER, Robin. Doctoral student, School of Journalism and Mass Communication, University of North Carolina, Chapel Hill.

GARAY, Ronald. Professor and associate dean, Undergraduate Studies and Administration, Manship School of Mass Communication, Louisiana State University, Baton Rouge. Author, *Congressional Television: A Legislative History* (1984); *Cable Television: A Reference Guide to Information* (1988); *Gordon McLendon: The Maverick of Radio* (1992).

GLEASON, Timothy W. Associate professor and acting dean, School of Journalism and Communication, University of Oregon, Eugene. Author, *The Watchdog Concept: The Press and the Courts in Nineteenth-Century America* (1990). Co-author, *Social Research in Communication and Law* (1990). Articles in *News Photographer, Journalism History,* and *American Journalism*.

GOBLE, Corban. Associate professor, Department of Journalism, Western Kentucky University, Bowling Green.

GODFREY, Donald G. Professor, Walter Cronkite School of Journalism and Telecommunication, Arizona State University, Tempe. Author, *Reruns on File: A Guide to Electronic Media Archives* (1992). Co-editor, *The Diaries of Charles Ora Card: The Canadian Years, 1886–1903*

(1993); *Television in America: Local Station History from Across the Nation* (1997); *Historical Dictionary of American Radio* (1998). Article in *Journalism History*.

GOMERY, Douglas. Professor, College of Journalism, University of Maryland, Chevy Chase. Author, *The Hollywood Studio System* (1986); *Movie History: A Survey* (1991); *Shared Pleasures: A History of Movie Presentation in the United States* (1992). Co-author, *Film History: Theory and Practice* (1985, 1993); *The Art of Moving Shadows* (1989). Editor, *High Sierra* (1979); *The Will Hays Papers* (1986). Co-editor, *American Media: The Wilson Quarterly Reader* (1989); *The Future of News: Television-Newspapers-Wire Services-Newsmagazines* (1992). Articles in *American Journalism Review, The American Enterprise, Historical Journal of Film, Radio, and Television, Current*, and *The Wilson Quarterly*.

GORDON, David. Adjunct professor, School of Journalism, Northeastern University, Boston, Massachusetts.

GOTTLIEB, Agnes Hooper. Associate professor and director of women's studies, Seton Hall University, South Orange, New Jersey. Article in *Journalism History*.

GOULD, Lewis L. Eugene C. Barker Centennial Professor of American history, University of Texas, Austin. Author, *Wyoming: A Political History, 1868–1896* (1968); *Progressives and Prohibitionists: Texas Democrats in the Wilson Era* (1973, 1992); *Reform and Regulation: American Politics, 1900–1916* (1978); *The Presidency of William McKinley* (1980); *The Spanish-American War and President McKinley* (1982); *Reform and Regulation: American Politics from Roosevelt to Wilson* (1986); *Lady Bird Johnson and the Environment* (1988); *The Presidency of Theodore Roosevelt* (1991); *Wyoming: From Territory to Statehood* (1989); *1968: The Election that Changed America* (1993). Co-author, *Photojournalist: The Career of Jimmy Hare* (1977); *William McKinley: A Bibliography* (1988); *Texas, Her Texas: The Life and Times of Frances Goff* (1997). Editor, *The Progressive Era* (1974); *American First Ladies: Their Lives and Their Legacy* (1996). Co-editor, *The Black Experience in America: Selected Essays* (1970); *The Presidents* (1992). Articles in *The Quill*.

GOULD, Thomas. Assistant professor, Mount Vernon College, George Washington University, and doctoral student, School of Journalism and Mass Communication, University of North Carolina, Chapel Hill.

GOWER, Karla K. Doctoral student, School of Journalism and Mass Communication, University of North Carolina, Chapel Hill. Articles in *American Journalism, Free Speech Yearbook, Journalism & Mass Communication Quarterly*, and *Southwestern Mass Communication Journal*.

GREEN, Norma Fay. Director, Graduate Journalism Program, Journalism Department, Columbia College, Chicago, Illinois.

GUTH, David W. Associate professor, William Allen White School of Journalism and Mass Communications, University of Kansas, Lawrence. Articles in *Public Relations Review, American Journalism, Communication World*, and *Kansas Bar Association*.

GUTJAHR, Paul. Assistant professor of English and American studies, Department of English, Indiana University, Bloomington. Author, *An American Bible: A History of THE Book in the United States, 1777–1880*. Articles in *Mosaic, Approaches to Teaching Uncle Tom's Cabin* (eds. Elizabeth Ammons and Susan Belasco Smith), and *Cultural Studies, Rhetoric, and Composition Theory* (eds. Karen Fitts and Alan W. France).

HAMM, Bradley J. Assistant professor of journalism and communications, Elon College, Elon, North Carolina.

HANSON, Christopher. Doctoral student, School of Journalism and Mass Communication, University of North Carolina, Chapel Hill. Articles in *Columbia Journalism Review*. Former writer, "Capital Letter" in *Columbia Journalism Review*.

HARDENBERGH, Margot. Assistant professor, Communication and the Arts Division, Marist College, Poughkeepsie, New York. Articles in *Television in America: Local Station History from Across the Nation, Women in Communication: A Biographical Sourcebook, ERIC, Journal of the New Haven Colony Historical Society*, and *Mass Communication Review*.

HATCHER, Anthony. Assistant professor, Mount Olive College, Mount Olive, North Carolina, and doctoral student, School of Journalism and Mass Communication, University of North Carolina, Chapel Hill, North Carolina.

HEBERT, Elsie. Professor, Department of Journalism and Mass Communication, Louisiana State University, Baton Rouge.

HEMLINGER, T.J. Assistant professor, University of Scranton, Scranton, Pennsylvania.

HILL, Jonathan Y. Doctoral student, School of Journalism and Mass Communication, University of North Carolina, Chapel Hill.

HIMEBAUGH, Glenn A. Professor of journalism, College of Mass Communication, Middle Tennessee State University, Murfreesboro. Author, *The History of Publishing in Tennessee*. Articles in *Tennessee Encyclopedia of History and Culture, Biographical Dictionary of American Journalism* (ed. Joseph P. McKerns), *American Journalism, Journalism Educator, Editor & Publisher*, and *West Tennessee Historical Society Papers*.

HIXSON, Richard F. Professor, Department of Journalism and Mass Media, Rutgers University, New Brunswick, New Jersey. Author, *Introduction to Journalism: College Level*

(1966); *The Press in Revolutionary New Jersey* (1975); *Privacy in a Public Society* (1987); *Mass Media and the Constitution: An Encyclopedia of Supreme Court Decisions* (1989); *Pornography and the Justices: The Supreme Court and the Intractable Obscenity Problem* (1996). Editor, *Mass Media: A Casebook* (1973).

HLAVACH, Laura E. Assistant Professor, Southern Methodist University, Dallas, Texas.

HODGES, Louis W. Fletcher Otey Thomas Professor of the Bible, Department of Society and the Professions, Washington and Lee University, Lexington, Virginia. Co-author, *The Christian and His Decisions: An Introduction to Christian Ethics* (1969). Articles in *Journal of Mass Media Ethics*.

HODGSON, Jack. Assistant professor, School of Journalism, Oklahoma State University, Stillwater. Articles in *Encyclopedia of Television News*, *The Journal of Central Asian Media Studies*, *Encyclopedia of United States Popular Culture*, and *RTNDA Communicator*.

HOLSTEAD, Carol E. Associate professor of magazine studies, William Allen White School of Journalism and Mass Communications, University of Kansas, Lawrence. Article in *Folio: The Magazine for Magazine Management*.

HOWARD, Herbert H. Professor of broadcasting and associate dean for graduate studies and research, College of Communications, The University of Tennessee, Knoxville. Author, *Multiple Ownership in Television Broadcasting: Historical Development and Selected Case Studies* (1979); *Group and Cross-Media Ownership of Television Stations*. Co-author, *Broadcast Advertising: A Comprehensive Working Textbook* (1978, 1984, 1991); *Radio and TV Programming* (1983); *Radio, TV, and Cable Programming* (1994). Article in *Journalism & Mass Communication Quarterly*.

HOWELL, Haney. Associate professor, Department of Mass Communication, Winthrop University, Rock Hill, South Carolina. Author, *Roadrunners: Combat Journalists in Cambodia* (1989). Co-editor, *Raising Hell: Straight Talk with Investigative Journalists* (1997).

HUFF, Kelly W.A. Associate professor of mass communication, Savannah State University, Savannah, Georgia. Articles in *Journalism Quarterly, Feedback, Journal of Radio Studies, Disasters*, and *Popular Music and Society*.

HUGHES, Thomas. Doctoral student, School of Journalism and Mass Communication, University of North Carolina, Chapel Hill. Articles in *Communications and the Law, Communication Law and Policy, American Journalism*, and *Perspectives on Mass Communications History* (ed. Wm. David Sloan).

HUMPHREY, Carol Sue. Associate professor of history, Oklahoma Baptist University, Shawnee. Author, *This Popular Engine: New England Newspapers During the Ameri-*

can Revolution, 1775–1789 (1992); *The Press of the Young Republic, 1783–1833* (1996).

HUNTZICKER, William E. Freelance writer and lecturer, Department of Journalism and Mass Communication, University of Minnesota, Minneapolis.

HUTTON, Frankie. Associate professor, Department of Mass Media, Hampton University, Hampton, Virginia. Author, *The Early Black Press in America, 1827 to 1860*. Co-editor, *Outsiders in 19th-Century Press History: Multicultural Perspectives* (1995).

JACOBS, Matthew F. Graduate student, Department of History, University of North Carolina, Chapel Hill.

JETER, James Phillip. Professor, Division of Journalism, Florida A&M, Tallahassee. Co-author, *International Afro Mass Media: A Reference Guide* (1996).

JOHNSON, Thomas J. Associate professor, School of Journalism, Southern Illinois University, Carbondale. Author, *The Rehabilitation of Richard Nixon: The Media's Effect on Collective Memory*; co-editor of *Engaging the Public: How the Government and the Media Can Reinvigorate American Democracy*. Articles in *Journalism & Mass Communication Quarterly, Political Communication, Mass Communication Review, Journal of Media Economics and Communication*.

JOHNSTON, Anne. Associate professor, School of Journalism and Mass Communication, University of North Carolina, Chapel Hill. Co-author, *Political Campaign Communication: A Bibliography and Guide to the Literature, 1973–1982* (1985). Articles in *Journalism Quarterly* and *Political Communication*.

JONES, Clifford A. Lecturer, Legal Studies, College of Business Administration, University of Oklahoma, Norman.

JUNG, Donald J. Assistant professor, Department of Communication, University of Missouri, St. Louis. Author, *Implications of Deregulation on the Public Administration of the Federal Communications Commission, 1981–1987: An Annotated Bibliography* (1989); and *The Federal Communications Commission, the Broadcast Industry, and the Fairness Doctrine, 1981–1987* (1996).

KAID, Lynda Lee. George Lynn Cross Research Professor of communication and director of the Political Communication Center, University of Oklahoma, Norman. Co-author, *Political Campaign Communication: A Bibliography and Guide to the Literature* (1974), *1973–1982* (1985). Co-editor, *New Perspectives on Political Advertising* (1986); *Mediated Politics in Two Cultures: Presidential Campaigning in the United States and France* (1991); *Political Advertising in Western Democracies: Parties and Candidates on Television* (1995). Articles in *American Behavioral Scientist, Journalism & Mass Communication Quarterly*, and *Political Communication*.

KENNEDY, Samuel V., III. Chairman, Newspaper Department, S.I. Newhouse School of Public Communications, Syracuse University, Syracuse, New York. Articles in *American National Biography, Hamilton Alumni Review,* and *Biographical Dictionary of American Journalism.*

KESSLER, Lauren. Professor and director of the graduate program in creative non-fiction, School of Journalism and Communication, University of Oregon, Eugene. Author, *The Dissident Press: Alternative Journalism in American History* (1984). Co-author, *When Words Collide: A Journalist's Guide to Grammar and Style* (1984, 1988, 1992, 1996); *Uncovering the News: A Journalist's Search for Information* (1987); *Mastering the Message: Media Writing with Substance and Style* (1989); *The Search: Information Gathering for the Mass Media* (1992). Articles in *Writer's Digest* and *Journalism History.*

KIELBOWICZ, Richard B. Associate professor, School of Communications, University of Washington, Seattle. Author, *Origins of the Second-Class Mail Category and the Business of Policymaking, 1863–1879* (1986); *News in the Mail: The Press, Post Office, and Public Information, 1700–1860s* (1989). Articles in *Civil War History* and *Social Science Quarterly.*

KILMER, Paulette D. Assistant professor, Communication Department, University of Toledo, Toledo, Ohio. Author, *The Fear of Sinking: The America Success Formula in the Gilded Age.*

KINDEM, Gorham A. Professor, Communication Studies, University of North Carolina, Chapel Hill. Author, *Toward a Semiotic Theory of Visual Communication in the Cinema* (1980); *The Moving Image: Production Principles and Practices* (1987); *The Live Television Generation of Hollywood Film Directors: Interviews with Seven Directors* (1994). Co-author, *Introduction to Media Production: From Analog to Digital* (1997). Editor, *The American Movie Industry: The Business of Motion Pictures* (1982).

KITCH, Carolyn. Assistant professor, Medill School of Journalism, Northwestern University, Evanston, Illinois, and former articles editor for *McCall's* and *Good Housekeeping.* Article in *Reader's Digest.*

KNUDSON, Jerry W. Professor Emeritus, School of Communications and Theater, Temple University, Philadelphia, Pennsylvania. Author, *The Press and the Bolivian National Revolution* (1973); *Herbert L. Matthews and the Cuban Story* (1978); *Bolivia, Press, and Revolution, 1932–1964* (1986). Articles in *Journalism & Mass Communication Quarterly* and *Journalism History.*

KOEHLER, Elizabeth M. Doctoral student, School of Journalism and Mass Communication, University of North Carolina, Chapel Hill.

KORWAR, Arati R. Assistant professor, Manship School of Mass Communication, Louisiana State University, Baton Rouge. Author, *War of Words: Speech Codes at Public Colleges and Universities* (1994). Article in *Journalism & Mass Communication Monographs.*

KRESHEL, Peggy J. Associate professor, Henry W. Grady School of Journalism and Mass Communication, University of Georgia, Athens. Articles in *Journal of Communication Inquiry, Journal of Current Issues and Research in Advertising, Public Relations Review, Journal of Advertising.*

LANE, Philip J. Professor, Mass Communication and Journalism, California State University, Fresno.

LANIER, Gene D. Professor, Department of Library Studies and Educational Technology, East Carolina University, Greenville, North Carolina. Distinguished Professor at East Carolina University in the School of Education. Frequent speaker on intellectual freedom and censorship. Awards from the American Library Association, the *Playboy Foundation,* University of Illinois, University of North Carolina at Chapel Hill, Social Issues Resources Series, North Carolina Library Association, People for the American Way, and the North Carolina Press Association.

LARSON, Karla M. Doctoral candidate in Communication at the University of Oklahoma. Articles in *Journal of Broadcasting and Electronic Media* and *Journal of Communication.*

LAWRENCE, Robert H. Professor Emeritus, University of New Mexico, Albuquerque.

LAWSON, Linda. Associate dean of research and graduate studies, School of Journalism, Indiana University, Bloomington. Author, *Truth in Publishing: Federal Regulation of the Press' Business Practices, 1880–1920* (1993). Article in *Journalism Quarterly.*

LETTS, Thomas. Doctoral student, School of Journalism and Mass Communication, University of North Carolina, Chapel Hill.

LEWEKE, Robert W. Doctoral student, School of Journalism and Mass Communication, University of North Carolina, Chapel Hill.

LEWIS, Charles W. Associate professor of mass communication, Mankato State University, Mankato, Minnesota. Articles in *St. Louis Journalism Review* and *Journalism & Mass Communications Quarterly.*

LEWIS, Regina Louise. Assistant professor, Department of Advertising and Public Relations, University of Alabama, Tuscaloosa.

LICHTY, Lawrence W. Professor of radio/television/film, Northwestern University, Evanston, Illinois. Author, *A Study of the Careers and Qualifications of Members of the Federal Radio Commission and the Federal Communications Commission, 1927–1961* (1961). Co-author, *Rating*

Analysis: Theory and Practice (1991). Co-editor, *American Broadcasting: A Source Book on the History of Radio and Television* (1975); *American Media: The Wilson Quarterly Reader* (1989); *The Future of News: Television-Newspapers-Wire Services-Newsmagazines* (1992).

LIEBOVICH, Louis W. Professor, Department of Journalism and Media Studies, University of Illinois, Urbana. Author, *The Press and the Origins of the Cold War, 1944–1947* (1988); *Bylines in Despair: Herbert Hoover, the Great Depression, and the U.S. News Media* (1994); *The Press and the Modern Presidency: Myths and Mindsets from Kennedy to Clinton* (1998).

LIMBURG, Val E. Associate professor, Edward R. Murrow School of Communication, Washington State University, Pullman. Author, *Mass Media Literacy: An Introduction to Mass Communications* (1988); *Electronic Media Ethics* (1994).

LINDER, Laura R. Assistant professor, Broadcasting/Cinema and Theatre Department, University of North Carolina at Greensboro.

LINDLEY, William R. Researcher and writer on journalism and mass communication topics, newspaper experience in Oregon, Washington, Idaho, and Utah, and former instructor, University of Puget Sound and Idaho State University. Author, *20th Century American Newspapers in Content and Production* (1993). Article in *Journal of the West*.

LISBY, Greg. Associate professor, Department of Communication, Georgia State University, Atlanta. Articles in *Communication and the Law, Journalism Monographs, Georgia Historical Quarterly,* and *Journal of Communication Inquiry.*

LIST, Karen K. Professor of journalism, University of Massachusetts, Amherst. Articles in *The Significance of Media in American History, To Improve the Academy, Journalism History, Journalism Quarterly, Journal of Mass Media Ethics.* Winner, 1995 Covert Award for the best article published in journalism history.

LIVINGSTON, Steven. Associate professor of political communication and international affairs, School of Media and Public Affairs, George Washington University, Washington, D.C. Author, *The Terrorism Spectacle* (1994). Articles in *Political Communication.*

LOVISI, Gary. Freelance writer, founder of Gryphon Publications, and editor and publisher of *Hardboiled* and *Paperback Parade.* Author, *Sherlock Holmes and the Loss of the British Bark Sophy Anderson* (1992); *The Nemesis in the Claws of the Falcon* (1994); *Minesweeper* (1995). Co-author, *The Woman in the Dugout: The Story of the Brooklyn Kings* (1992). Editor, *Dashiell Hammett and Raymond Chandler: A Checklist and Bibliography of Their Paperback Appearances* (1994).

LUMSDEN, Linda. Assistant professor, Journalism Department, Western Kentucky University, Bowling Green. Author, *Rampant Women: Suffragists and the Right of Assembly* (1997). Articles in *Journalism & Mass Communication Quarterly.*

MAKRIS, Gregory. Doctoral student, School of Journalism and Mass Communication, University of North Carolina, Chapel Hill. Article in *Journal of Communication Inquiry.*

MANDER, Mary S. Associate Professor, College of Communications, Media Studies Program, Pennsylvania State University, University Park. Editor, *Communication in Transition* (1983) and *Perspectives on Media and Social Conflict* (1998). Articles in *Journalism History, Journal of Broadcasting, Antioch Review, Communication Research, European Journal of Communication, American Journalism,* and *Communication.*

MANSFIELD-RICHARDSON, Virginia. Associate professor of communication, College of Communication, Pennsylvania State University, University Park, and former reporter for *The Washington Post.* Articles in *News Coverage of U.S. Racial Minorities, 1934–1994, Media Ethics, Developing Values in Mass Communication* (ed. Michael J. Bugeja), *The Best of Style Plus,* and *Statistics: An Inferential Approach.*

MARLER, Charles H. Professor of journalism and mass communication, Abilene Christian University, Abilene, Texas. Editor, *Lone Star Christmas: Seasonal Editorials of Frank Grimes* (1989).

MAYEUX, Peter E. Harold A. and Ethel Bash Soderlund Professor of broadcasting, College of Journalism and Mass Communications, University of Nebraska, Lincoln. Author, *Writing for the Broadcast Media* (1985); *Broadcast News: Writing and Reporting* (1991, 1995, 1996); *Writing for the Electronic Media* (1994).

McINTYRE, Jerilyn S. Professor of communication and vice president for academic affairs, University of Utah, Salt Lake City. Co-author, *Self, Symbols, and Society: An Introduction to Mass Communication* (1984). Article in *Journal of the West.*

McKERNS, Joseph P. Associate professor of journalism, School of Journalism and Communication, Ohio State University, Columbus. Author, *News Media and Public Policy: An Annotated Bibliography* (1985). Editor, *Bibliographical Dictionary of American Journalism* (1989). Articles in *Journalism History, Journalism Quarterly, Critical Studies in Mass Communication, American Studies International, Journalism Monographs.*

MEESKE, Milan D. Director, Nicholson School of Communication, University of Central Florida, Orlando. Co-author, *Copywriting for the Electronic Media: A Practical Guide* (1987, 1992, 1998); *Electronic Media and Govern-*

ment: The Regulation of Wireless and Wired Mass Communication in the United States (1995).

MILLAR, Dan Pyle. Professor, Department of Communication, Indiana State University, Terre Haute, and senior consultant, Institute for Crisis Management, Louisville, Kentucky. Author, *Introduction to Small Group Discussion* (1986). Co-author, *Messages and Myths: Understanding Interpersonal Communication* (1976).

MILLER, Jerry L. Associate professor, Journalism Department, Franklin College, Franklin, Indiana. Article in *Communications Studies*.

MILLER, Karen S. Assistant professor, Grady College of Journalism and Mass Communication, University of Georgia, Athens. Articles in *Public Relations Review, Journalism Monographs, Business History Review*.

MIMS, Bruce. Assistant professor of mass communication, Southeast Missouri State University, Cape Girardeau.

MULCRONE, Mick. Assistant professor of communication studies, University of Portland, Portland, Oregon. Articles in *Journalism History* and *The Great Famine and the Irish Diaspora in America*.

MURPHY, Priscilla Coit. Doctoral candidate, School of Journalism and Mass Communication, University of North Carolina, Chapel Hill.

MURPHY, Sharon M. Provost, Bradley University, Peoria, Illinois. Author, *Other Voices: Black, Chicano, and American Indian Press* (1974). Co-author, *Let My People Know: American Indian Journalism, 1828–1978* (1981); *Great Women of the Press* (1983). Co-editor, *International Perspectives on News* (1982).

MURRAY, Michael D. Professor and chairman, Department of Communication, University of Missouri, St. Louis, and former president, American Journalism Historians Association. Author, *The Political Performers: CBS Broadcasts in the Public Interest.* Co-editor, *Teaching Mass Communication: A Guide to Better Instruction; Television in America: Local Station History from Across the Nation.* Articles in *St. Louis Journalism Review, Journalism History,* and *Journalism & Mass Communication Quarterly.*

NELSON, Dean. Professor, Journalism Department, Point Loma Nazarene College, San Diego, California. Author, *Small Medium, Large Impact: The Miracle of World Mission Radio* (1993). Articles in *Christianity Today, World Press Review,* and *The Quill.*

NERONE, John. Associate professor, University of Illinois, Urbana. Author, *Press and Popular Culture in the Early Republic – Cincinnati, 1793–1848* (1989); *Violence Against the Press: Policing the Public Sphere in U.S. History* (1994). Editor, *Last Rights: Revisiting Four Theories of the Press* (1995). Articles in *Media Studies Journal* and *Journal of Communication.*

NEUZIL, Mark. Assistant professor, Department of Journalism and Mass Communication, Environmental Studies Program, University of St. Thomas, St. Paul, Minnesota. Co-author, *Mass Media and Environmental Conflict: America's Green Crusades* (1996). Articles in *Nieman Reports, Journalism & Mass Communication Quarterly, Journalism Quarterly,* and *Newspaper Research Journal.*

NORD, David Paul. Professor, School of Journalism, Indiana University, Bloomington. Author, *A Guide to Old Wade House Historical Site* (1978); *Newspapers and New Politics: Midwestern Municipal Reform, 1890–1900* (1981).

NYBERG, Amy Kiste. Assistant professor, Department of Communication, Seton Hall University, South Orange, New Jersey. Author, *Seal of Approval: The History of the Comics Code* (1998).

OGLES, Robert M. Associate professor, Department of Communication, Purdue University, West Lafayette, Indiana. Author, with H.H. Howard, *Radio: The Electronic Revolution of Mass Communication.*

OVIATT, Arlo. Assistant professor, William Allen White School of Journalism and Mass Communication, University of Kansas, Lawrence.

PACKER, Cathy. Associate professor, School of Journalism and Mass Communication, University of North Carolina, Chapel Hill. Author, *Freedom of Expression in the American Military: A Communication Modeling Analysis* (1989). Articles in *Journalism & Mass Communication Quarterly.*

PADDON, Anna R. Visiting associate professor, Department of Journalism, National Chenchi University, Taipei, Taiwan. Former instructor of journalism, Southern Illinois University, Carbondale, Illinois; Benedict College, Columbia, South Carolina; and University of Tennessee, Knoxville, Tennessee. Article in *Newspaper Research Journal.*

PAYNE, Darwin. Professor of journalism, Center for Communication Arts, Southern Methodist University, Dallas, Texas, and former president, American Journalism Historians Association. Author, *The Man of Only Yesterday: Frederick Lewis Allen, Former Editor of Harper's Magazine* (1975); *The Press Corps and the Kennedy Assassination* (1970); *Dallas, an Illustrated History* (1982); *Owen Wister, Chronicler of the West, Gentleman of the East* (1985); *Big D: Triumphs and Troubles of an American Supercity in the 20th Century* (1994); *Texas Chronicles: The Heritage and Enterprise of the Lone Star State* (1994).

PECK, Abe. Chairman, Magazine Program, Medill School of Journalism, Northwestern University, Evanston, Illinois.

Author, *Uncovering the Sixties: The Life and Times of the Underground Press.*

PETERSON, John C. Professor of photojournalism emeritus, Loyalist College, Belleville, Ontario.

PLASTER, Sarah Wright. Doctoral student, Mass Communication Research, E.W. Scripps School of Journalism, Ohio University, Miami.

PONDER, Stephen. Associate professor, School of Journalism and Communication, University of Oregon, Eugene. Articles in *Journalism & Mass Communication Quarterly*, *Mass Comm Review*, *Presidential Studies Quarterly*, and *Journalism History.*

PRATTE, Alf. Professor of communications, Brigham Young University, Provo, Utah, and former president, American Journalism Historians Association. Specialist, opinion writing and media history. Writer and teacher, schools and newspapers in Canada, Utah, and Pennsylvania. Author, *Gods Within the Machine: A History of the American Society of Newspaper Editors, 1923–1993* (1995).

REDDICK, Randy. Director and editor, FACSNET, and senior vice president, Foundation for American Communications, Los Angeles, California. Co-author, *The Online Journalist: Using the Internet and Other Electronic Resources* (1995, 1997); *The Online Student: Making the Grade of the Internet* (1996); *Saunders Internet Guide for Astronomy* (1996); *Saunders Internet Guide for Earth Science* (1996).

REED, Barbara Straus. Associate professor, Information and Library Studies, School of Communication, Rutgers University, New Brunswick, New Jersey. Co-editor, *Outsiders in 19th-Century Press History: Multicultural Perspectives* (1995). Articles in *Journalism Educator, American Journalism*, and *Journalism History.*

REILLY, Tom. Professor of journalism, California State University, Northridge, and founding editor, *Journalism History*. Articles in *Journalism Quarterly* and *Journalism History.*

REUSS, Carol. Professor Emeritus, School of Journalism and Mass Communication, University of North Carolina, Chapel Hill. Co-editor, *Inside Organizational Communication* (1981, 1985); *Impact of Mass Media: Current Issues* (1985, 1988); *Controversies in Media Ethics* (1996).

RHODES, Jane. Assistant professor, Department of Ethnic Studies, University of California at San Diego, La Jolla, California. Articles in *Federal Communications Law Journal*, *Critical Studies in Mass Communication, Women Making Meaning: New Feminist Directions in Communication* (ed. Lana Rakow), and *Journalism History.*

RILEY, Sam G. Professor, Communication Studies, Virginia Tech, Roanoke. Author, *Magazines of the American South* (1986); *Index to Southern Periodicals* (1986); *Bibliographical Dictionary of American Newspaper Columnists* (1995). Co-author, *Index to City and Regional Magazines of the United States* (1989). Editor, *American Magazine Journalists, 1741–1850* (1988), *1850–1900* (1989), *1900–1960* (1990, 1994); *Corporate Magazines of the United States* (1992); *Consumer Magazines of the British Isles* (1993); *The Best of the Rest: Non-Syndicated Newspaper Columnists Select their Best Work* (1993). Co-editor, *Regional Interest Magazines of the United States* (1991). Article in *Journalism & Mass Communication Educator.*

RISLEY, Ford. Assistant professor, College of Communications, Pennsylvania State University, University Park.

RITCHIE, Donald A. Associate historian, United States Senate Historical Office, Washington, D.C. Author, *James M. Landis, Dean of the Regulators* (1980); *The Senate* (1988); *The U.S. Constitution* (1989); *Press Gallery: Congress and the Washington Correspondents* (1991); *The Young Oxford Companion to the Congress of the United States* (1993); *Doing Oral History* (1995); *Journalists* (1997); *A History of the United States Senate Republican Policy Committee, 1947–1997* (1997). Co-author, *Heritage of Freedom* (1986); *American History and National Security* (1989); *History of a Free Nation* (1992, 1996). Article in *Media Studies Journal.*

RIVERA-SANCHEZ, Milagros. Assistant professor, College of Journalism and Communications, University of Florida, Gainesville. Articles in *Federal Communications Law Journal, Communications and the Law, Journalism & Mass Communication Monographs*, and *Journalism History.*

ROBBS, Brett. Associate professor, School of Journalism and Mass Communication, University of Colorado, Boulder. Articles in *Journalism & Mass Communication Educator, Advertising Educator*, and *Advertising Age.*

ROBERTS, Nancy L. Professor of journalism history, School of Journalism and Mass Communication, University of Minnesota, Minneapolis. Author, *Dorothy Day and the Catholic Worker* (1984); *American Peace Writers, Editors, and Periodicals: A Dictionary* (1991). Co-author, *The Press and America: An Interpretive History of the Mass Media* (1996). Co-editor, *American Catholic Pacifism: The Influence of Dorothy Day and the Catholic Worker Movement* (1996).

ROCHE, Bruce. Associate Professor Emeritus of advertising and public relations, University of Alabama, Tuscaloosa.

RODRIGUEZ, América. Professor, Departments of Radio, Television, Film, and Journalism, University of Texas, Austin. Author, *Race, Class and Language in the Making of U.S. Latino News.* Articles in *Critical Studies in Mass Communication, Communication Review*, and *Quarterly Journal of Film and Video.*

ROSE, Patricia B. Chairwoman and associate professor, Department of Advertising and Public Relations, School of Journalism and Mass Communication, Florida International University, Miami. Articles in *International Academy of Business Disciplines Yearbook, Journal of Continuing Higher Education, Journal of Marketing for Higher Education, Journal of Macromarketing, Journalism Educator,* and *Public Relations Quarterly.*

ROSS, Susan Dente. Assistant professor of journalism and communication, Edward R. Murrow School of Communication, Washington State University, Pullman. Articles in *Newspaper Research Journal* and *Rutgers Computer Technology Law Journal.*

RUSSELL, Dennis E. Assistant professor of journalism, Walter Cronkite School of Journalism and Telecommunication, Arizona State University, Tempe. Article in *Communications and the Law.*

RUTENBECK, Jeffrey. Associate professor, School of Communication, University of Denver, Denver, Colorado. Articles in *Journal of Communication Inquiry, American Journalism,* and *Journalism & Mass Communications Quarterly.*

SCANLON, Jennifer. Associate professor and director, Women's Studies, State University of New York, Plattsburgh. Author, *Inarticulate Longings: The Ladies' Home Journal, Gender, and the Promises of Consumer Culture.* Co-author, *American Women Historians, 1700s–1990s.* Articles in *Feminist Teacher* and *NWSA Journal.*

SCHEIDENHELM, Richard. Department of History, Colorado State University, Boulder.

SCHUDSON, Michael. Professor, Department of Communication, and adjunct professor of sociology, University of California at San Diego, La Jolla, California. Author, *Discovering the News: A Social History of American Newspapers* (1978); *Advertising, the Uneasy Persuasion: Its Dubious Impact on American Society* (1984); *What Time Means in a News Story* (1986); *Origins of the Ideal of Objectivity in the Professions: Studies in the History of American Journalism and American Law, 1830–1940* (1990); *Watergate in American Memory* (1992); *The Power of News* (1995). Co-editor, *Reading the News: A Pantheon Guide to Popular Culture* (1986); *Rethinking Popular Culture: Contemporary Perspectives in Cultural Studies* (1991). Articles in *Media, Culture & Society, Columbia Journalism Review, Media Studies Journal, American Heritage, The American Prospect, Journalism & Mass Communication Quarterly,* and *International Social Science Journal.*

SCHWARZLOSE, Richard A. Professor of journalism, Medill School of Journalism, Northwestern University, Evanston, Illinois. Author, *The American Wire Services: A Study of Their Development as a Social Institution* (1979); *Newspapers, a Reference Guide* (1987); *The Nation's Newsbrokers* (1990).

SEMONCHE, Barbara P. Librarian, School of Journalism and Mass Communication, University of North Carolina, Chapel Hill. Editor, *News Media Libraries: A Management Handbook* (1993).

SHAVER, Mary Alice. Professor, School of Journalism and Mass Communication, University of North Carolina, Chapel Hill. Author, *Make the Sale!: How to Sell Media with Marketing* (1995). Articles in *Journalism & Mass Communication Quarterly, Newspaper Research Journal,* and *Journalism Quarterly.*

SHAW, Donald L. Kenan Professor of journalism, School of Journalism and Mass Communication, University of North Carolina, Chapel Hill; former editor of *Journalism & Mass Communication Quarterly.* Co-author, *Handbook of Reporting Methods* (1976); *The Emergence of American Political Issues: The Agenda-Setting Function of the Press* (1977); *Advanced Reporting: Beyond News Events* (1986). Editor, *Decision Points in Mass Communication Research: Survey, Content Analysis, Historical, and Experimental Methods* (1967). Co-editor, *Foreign News and the New World Information Order* (1984); *Communication and Democracy: Exploring the Intellectual Frontiers in Agenda-Setting Theory* (1997).

SHIDLER, Jon A. Assistant professor of Advertising, School of Journalism, Southern Illinois University, Carbondale.

SIMON, Todd F. Chair, School of Journalism, Kansas State University, Manhattan. Co-author, *The Economics and Regulation of United States Newspapers* (1993).

SLOAN, Wm. David. Professor, Department of Journalism, University of Alabama, Tuscaloosa, and former editor, *American Journalism.* Author, *Pulitzer Prize Editorials: America's Best Editorial Writing, 1917–1979* (1980), *1917–1993* (1994); *American Journalism History: An Annotated Bibliography* (1989); *Perspectives on Mass Communication History* (1991). Co-author, *Historical Methods in Mass Communication* (1989); *Great Editorials* (1991, 1997); *The Great Reporters* (1992); *The Early American Press, 1690–1783* (1994). Editor, *Makers of the Media Mind: Journalism Educators and Their Ideas* (1990). Co-editor, *The Best of Pulitzer Prize News Writing* (1986); *The Media in America: A History* (1989, 1993); *The Significance of the Media in American History* (1994); *The History of American Journalism* (1994); *Masterpieces of Reporting* (1997).

SMETHERS, Steven. Assistant professor, School of Journalism and Broadcasting, Oklahoma State University, Stillwater.

SMITH, C. Zoe. Associate professor of Journalism, University of Missouri, Columbia. Articles in *Journalism & Mass Communication Educator* and *News Photographer.*

SMITH, Carol. Assistant professor of management/communication, and coordinator, Managerial and Professional

Communication Program, School of Business Administration, Fort Lewis College, Durango, Colorado. Articles in *AORN Journal* and *Journalism Monographs*.

SMITH, F. Leslie. Chairman, Department of Telecommunication, University of Florida, Gainesville. Author, *Perspectives on Radio and Television: An Introduction to Broadcasting in the United States* (1979, 1985, 1990). Co-author, *Electronic Media and Government: The Regulation of Wireless and Wired Mass Communication in the United States* (1995). Article in *Journalism Quarterly*.

SMITH, Kim A. Professor, Department of Journalism and Mass Communication, Iowa State University, Ames. Articles in *Journalism Quarterly, Communication Research, Newspaper Research Journal,* and *Journalism Monograph*.

SMITH, Penny Pence. Adjunct faculty and marketing consultant, School of Dramatic Art, University of North Carolina, Chapel Hill. Author, *Marketing – Plain and Simple, Under a Maui Sun,* and *The Essential Guide to Maui*. Articles in *Public Relations Quarterly* and *Diagnostic Imaging*.

SMYTHE, Ted Curtis. Professor Emeritus, California State University, Fullerton. Co-author, *Readings in Mass Communication: Concepts and Issues in the Mass Media* (1972, 1974, 1977, 1980, 1983, 1986, 1989).

STARTT, James D. Professor, Department of History, Valparaiso University, Valparaiso, Indiana. Author, *Journalism's Unofficial Ambassador: A Biography of Edward Price Bell, 1869–1943* (1979); *Journalists for Empire: The Imperial Debate in the Edwardian Stately Press, 1903–1913* (1991); *New Americans* (1994). Co-author, *Historical Methods in Mass Communication* (1989). Co-editor, *The Media in America: A History* (1989); *The Significance of the Media in American History* (1994); *The Media in America: A History* (1993); *The History of American Journalism* (1994).

STEPHENS, Lowndes F. Professor, College of Journalism and Mass Communications, University of South Carolina, Columbia. Articles in *Journalism Quarterly, Journal of Consumer Research, Journal of Retailing, Armed Forces & Society, Public Relations Review, Journal of Advertising Research,* and *Journalism Educator*.

STEPP, Carl Sessions. Associate professor, College of Journalism, University of Maryland, College Park, and senior editor, *American Journalism Review*. Author, *Editing for Today's Newsroom: New Perspectives for a Changing Profession* (1989). Articles in *American Journalism Review*.

STERLING, Christopher H. Professor of media and public affairs and telecommunication, Colombian School of Arts and Sciences, George Washington University, Washington, D.C. Author, *The Media Sourcebook: Comparative Reviews and Listings of Textbooks in Mass Communications* (1974); *Broadcasting Trends* (1984); *Electronic Media: A Guide to Trends in Broadcasting and Newer Technologies,*

1920–1983 (1984). Co-author, *The Mass Media: Aspen Institute Guide to Communication Industry Trends* (1978); *Stay Tuned: A Concise History of American Broadcasting* (1978, 1990); *Broadcasting in America: A Survey of Television, Radio, and New Technologies* (1982); *Broadcasting in America: A Survey of Electronic Media* (1987, 1990, 1991, 1994, 1996); *Telecommunications Research Resources* (1995). Editor, *International Telecommunications and Information Policy* (1984). Articles in *Telecommunications Policy* and *Journal of Broadcasting & Electronic Media*.

STRAUGHAN, Dulcie M. Associate professor, School of Journalism and Mass Communication, University of North Carolina, Chapel Hill. Articles in *Journalism & Mass Communication Quarterly, Corporate Communications: Theory and Practice, Teaching PR,* and *The International Journal for Mass Communication Studies*.

STREITMATTER, Rodger. Professor, School of Communication, American University, Washington, D.C. Author, *Raising Her Voice: African-American Women Journalists Who Changed History* (1994); *Unspeakable: The Rise of the Gay and Lesbian Press in America* (1995); *Mightier than the Sword: How the News Media Have Shaped American History* (1997). Articles in *Journalism & Mass Communication Quarterly, American Journalism,* and *Journalism History*.

STRENTZ, Herbert. Professor and director of graduate studies, School of Journalism and Mass Communication, Drake University, Des Moines, Iowa. Author, *News Reporters and News Sources: What Happens Before the Story is Written* (1978); *News Reporters and News Sources: Accomplices in Shaping and Misshaping the News* (1989). Co-author, *The Critical Factor: Criticism of the News Media in Journalism Education* (1974).

STYLES, Teresa Jo. Assistant professor of mass communication, North Carolina Agricultural and Technical State University, Greensboro.

SUMNER, David E. Associate professor and head of the magazine sequence, Department of Journalism, Ball State University, Muncie, Indiana. Author of *Graduate Programs in Journalism and Mass Communication* and *The Episcopal Church's History 1945–1985*. Articles in *Journalism Quarterly, American History Illustrated, Howard Journal of Communication, Tennessee Historical Quarterly,* and *Tennessee Encyclopedia of History and Culture*.

SWEENEY, Michael S. Assistant professor, Communication Department, Utah State University, Logan.

TAYLOR, Sue D. Doctoral student, School of Journalism and Mass Communication, University of North Carolina, Chapel Hill.

TEBBEL, John. Media historian, and former chairman, Department of Journalism, New York University, New York. Author, *Open Letter to Newspaper Readers* (1968); *An*

American Dynasty: The Story of the McCormicks, Medills, and Pattersons (1968); *The American Magazine: A Compact History* (1969); *The Compact History of the American Newspaper* (1969); *A History of Book Publishing in the United States* (1972–1981); *The Media in America* (1974); *Between Covers: The Rise and Transformation of Book Publishing in America* (1987). Co-author, *The Press and the Presidency: From George Washington to Ronald Reagan* (1985); *The Magazine in America, 1741–1990* (1991).

TEETER, Dwight L., Jr. Dean and professor, College of Communications, University of Tennessee, Knoxville, and former president, Association for Education in Journalism and Mass Communication. Co-author, *Law of Mass Communications: Freedom and Control of Print and Broadcast Media* (1969, 1973, 1978, 1982, 1986, 1989, 1992, 1995); *Voices of a Nation: A History of Media in the United States* (1989, 1994, 1998).

THEOHARIS, Athan G. Professor of history, Marquette University, Milwaukee, Wisconsin. Author, *The Yalta Myths: An Issue in U.S. Politics, 1945–1955* (1970); *Seeds of Repression: Harry S. Truman and the Origins of McCarthyism* (1971); *Spying on Americans: Political Surveillance from Hoover to the Huston Plan* (1978); *The FBI: An Annotated Bibliography* (1994); *J. Edgar Hoover, Sex, and Crime: An Historical Antidote* (1995). Co-author, *The United States in the Twentieth Century* (1978); *Imperial Democracy: The United States Since 1945* (1988); *The Boss: J. Edgar Hoover and the Great American Inquisition* (1988).

TRAHAN, Joseph V., III. Assistant professor, Department of Communication, University of Tennessee, Chattanooga.

TRAVIS, Trish. Visiting assistant professor, Department of English, Trinity College, Hartford, Connecticut.

TREISE, Debbie. Assistant professor, Department of Advertising, University of Florida, Gainesville. Articles in *Health Marketing Quarterly, Journalism Educator,* and *Journal of Advertising.*

VARGAS, Lucila. Assistant professor, School of Journalism and Mass Communication, University of North Carolina, Chapel Hill. Author, *Social Uses and Radio Practices: The Use of Participatory Radio by Ethnic Minorities in Mexico.* Articles in *FEM* and *The Americas Review.*

VAUGHN, Stephen. Professor of history of communication, University of Wisconsin, Madison, and associate editor, *Dictionary of American History.* Author, *Holding Fast the Inner Lines: Democracy, Nationalism, and the Committee on Public Information* (1980); *Ronald Reagan in Hollywood: Movies and Politics* (1994).

WADSWORTH, Sarah. Doctoral candidate, Department of English, University of Minnesota, Saint Paul.

WALDEN, Ruth. Professor, School of Journalism and Mass Communication, University of North Carolina, Chapel Hill.

Author, *Mass Communication Law in North Carolina.* Articles in *Journalism & Mass Communication Monographs, Journalism Educator, Journalism & Mass Communication Quarterly, Hastings Journal of Communication and Entertainment Law,* COMM/ENT.

WALSH, Kay. Associate professor, Communication and Theatre Arts, Frostburg State University, Frostburg, Maryland.

WALSH-CHILDERS, Kim. Associate professor, Journalism Department, College of Journalism and Communication, University of Florida, Gainesville. Articles in *Journalism & Mass Communication Quarterly* and *Newspaper Research Journal.*

WASHBURN, Patrick S. Professor and assistant director, E.W. Scripps School of Journalism, Ohio University, Miami. Author, *A Question of Sedition: The Federal Government's Investigation of the Black Press During World War II* (1986). Articles in *Journalism Quarterly, Journalism History.*

WASKO, Janet. Professor, School of Journalism and Communication, University of Oregon, Eugene. Author, *Movies and Money: Financing the American Film Industry* (1982); *Hollywood in the Information Age: Beyond the Silver Screen* (1995).

WATSON, John C. Doctoral student, School of Journalism and Mass Communication, University of North Carolina, Chapel Hill.

WHITAKER, W. Richard. Associate professor, Communication Department, Buffalo State College, Buffalo, New York. Co-author, *MediaWriting: Print, Broadcasting and Film.* Articles in *Journalism History, Middle East Review, Northwest Ohio Quarterly, The Curator, U.S. Navy Medicine,* and *Navel Reservist News.*

WILLIAMS, Julie K. Hedgepeth. Instructor of journalism and mass communication, Samford University, Birmingham, Alabama. Co-author, *The Early American Press, 1690–1783* (1994).

WILLIAMS, Michael. Associate professor, Journalism and Mass Communication, University of North Carolina, Chapel Hill.

WINFIELD, Betty Houchin. Professor, School of Journalism, University of Missouri, Columbia. Author, *FDR and the News Media* (1990, 1994). Articles in *Media Studies Journal, Journalism Quarterly,* and *Journalism History.*

WINSHIP, Michael. Professor, Department of English, University of Texas, Austin. Author, *Television* (1988, 1989); *Hermann Ernst Ludewig: America's Forgotten Bibliographer* (1986); *Ticknor and Fields: The Business of Literary Publishing in the United States of the Nineteenth Century* (1992); *American Literary Publishing in the Mid-Nineteenth Century: The Business of Ticknor and Fields* (1995).

Co-author, *Epitome of Bibliography of American Literature* (1995); *Bibliography of American Literature: A Selective Index* (1995).

YANCY, Thomas L. Associate professor of electronic media, Morehead State University, Morehead, Kentucky.

YANG, Mei-ling. Doctoral candidate, School of Journalism and Mass Communication, University of North Carolina, Chapel Hill. Article in *Journalism & Mass Communication Quarterly.*

YOUNG, Mark E. University of Texas, Austin.

ZANOT, Eric J. Associate professor, College of Journalism, University of Maryland, College Park. Articles in *Journal of Advertising, American Journalism, International Journal of Advertising, Journalism Quarterly, Journal of Marketing Education, Business Journal,* and *Journalism Monograph.*

ZIEGLER, Dhyana. Professor, Department of Broadcasting, University of Tennessee, Knoxville. Articles in *Broadcasting and Electronic Media, Journal of Radio Studies, Journal of Black Studies, Journalism Quarterly, FEEDBACK Journal, Thought and Action: The NEA Higher Education Journal,* and *Journal of Studies in Technical Careers.*

INDEX

Listings are arranged in alphabetical order. Page numbers in **bold** indicate entries on the subject.
Page numbers in *italics* indicate illustrations.